HUMAN RIGHTS WITH A HUMAN TOUCH
LIBER AMICORUM PAUL LEMMENS

HUMAN RIGHTS WITH A HUMAN TOUCH

Liber Amicorum Paul Lemmens

Koen LEMMENS
Stephan PARMENTIER
Louise REYNTJENS
(eds.)

intersentia
Cambridge – Antwerp – Chicago

Intersentia Ltd
8 Wellington Mews | Wellington Street
Cambridge | CB1 1HW | United Kingdom
Tel.: +44 1223 736 170 | Fax: +44 1223 736 169
Email: mail@intersentia.co.uk
www.intersentia.com | www.intersentia.co.uk

Distribution for the UK and Ireland:
NBN International
Airport Business Centre, 10 Thornbury Road
Plymouth, PL6 7 PP
United Kingdom
Tel.: +44 1752 202 301 | Fax: +44 1752 202 331
Email: orders@nbninternational.com

Distribution for Europe and all other countries:
Intersentia Publishing nv
Groenstraat 31
2640 Mortsel
Belgium
Tel.: +32 3 680 15 50 | Fax: +32 3 658 71 21
Email: mail@intersentia.be

Distribution for the USA and Canada:
Independent Publishers Group
Order Department
814 North Franklin Street
Chicago, IL60610
USA
Tel.: +1 800 888 4741 (toll free) | Fax: +1312 337 5985
Email: orders@ipgbook.com

Human Rights with a Human Touch. Liber Amicorum Paul Lemmens
© Koen Lemmens, Stephan Parmentier and Louise Reyntjens (eds.)

Cover artwork: © Benoît van Innis, *Olijvennet.*
Photograph of Paul Lemmens: © Jogchum Vrielink

ISBN 978-1-78068-874-9
ISBN 978-1-78068-873-2 (PDF)
D/2019/7849/90
NUR 828

British Library Cataloguing in Publication Data. A catalogue record for this book is available from the British Library.

PREFACE

Compiling a liber amicorum is always a difficult exercise. Not only because it is not easy to choose the authors from amongst the many friends of the one being celebrated, but also because it is often difficult to align the theme and style of the contributions offered. While one friend enjoys collecting amusing, but not always very relevant memories for the reader, the other exhausts himself/herself in an extensive legal-technical argument. While one contributes to a classical and sometimes segmented theme, the other writes a contribution on a niche topic from an already niche area.

This tribute avoids the classic pitfalls and contains contributions that are focused on human rights, in all their diversity, but with a strong emphasis on the European Convention on Human Rights. The aim of the book is to meet the highest academic standards, as Paul Lemmens has always embodied them. The well-renowned group of international authors already guarantees that quality.

But this volume is also, primarily a *Festschrift*, with each contribution having a clear link to Paul Lemmens. Many authors make this link explicit, while others do this more implicitly, by dealing with a theme that they know Paul takes to heart. It is obvious that the contributors express their great appreciation for Paul Lemmens.

The image of Paul as known and appreciated by his friends and colleagues emerges from the collected contributions: that of an excellent and knowledgeable lawyer, but especially that of a warm and committed person. Few people may know that Judge and Professor Lemmens is a big fan of the American rock star Bruce Springsteen. The title of this book is grafefully derived from one of his albums, *Human Touch*. Indeed, there is no better way to describe Paul's relationship with human rights than "Human Rights with a Human Touch".

The editors

CONTENTS

CURRICULUM VITAE

Paul LEMMENS

° 29 June 1954
Married (Anne Dewaele), three children (Martine & Marcelo, Eric, Vincent),
two grandchildren (Lisandro, Malena)

Address

Leuven Centre for Public Law
Tiensestraat 41
3000 Leuven
Tel. +32 16–32.51.17
E-mail: paul.lemmens@kuleuven.be

Education

Licentiate (now master) in law (University of Antwerp, 1971–74; KU Leuven,
1974–76)
Master of laws (Northwestern University, Chicago, 1978)
Doctor in law (KU Leuven, 1987)

Main professional occupations

- 1976–84: member of the Brussels Bar; part-time assistant KU Leuven (public
  law, later civil procedure).
- 1984–87: *auditeur* in the Raad van State [Council of State]; part-time assistant
  KU Leuven (civil procedure).
- 1987–94: full-time professor KU Leuven (civil procedure and human rights);
  member of the Brussels Bar.
- 1994–2012: judge in the Council of State (alternating advisory section and
  contentious section); part-time professor KU Leuven (civil procedure, until
  1995); administrative procedure (1995–97), constitutional law (1997–2007),
  human rights (entire period)).
- since 2012: judge in the European Court of Human Rights (Strasbourg); part-
  time professor KU Leuven (human rights).

Promoter of nine defended PhD theses and one ongoing PhD project; co-promoter of six defended PhD theses.

Other academic activities

- President, Interuniversitair Centrum Mensenrechten [(Flemish) Inter-University Centre for Human Rights], 1992–2003.
- Member, Commissie Rechtswetenschap [Commission for Legal Science], Fonds voor Wetenschappelijk Onderzoek [(Flemish) Research Foundation], 1996–2005.
- Member of the Council of Directors and lecturer, European Master Programme in Human Rights and Democratisation (Venice), 1997–2012. Since then: occasionally lecturer in the programme.
- Visiting professor, Northwestern University School of Law, Chicago, 1999.
- Expert for Belgium in FRALEX (Group of Legal Experts), EU Fundamental Rights Agency, 2007–10.
- "Chargé d'enseignement vacataire", Université de Strasbourg, since 2013.

Other activities and functions

- Member, Raadgevende Commissie [Consultative Commission], later Commissie voor de bescherming van de persoonlijke levenssfeer [Commission for the Protection of Private Life], 1987–97.
- Member, Wervingscollege voor de magistraten [Recruitment College for Members of the Judiciary], 1992–94.
- Member, Board of Administrators of the Centrum voor gelijkheid van kansen en voor racismebestrijding [Centre for Equal Opportunities and Opposition to Racism], 1993–94.
- Member, Nationale Commissie voor de Rechten van het Kind [National Commission for the Rights of the Child], 2007–12.
- Member, "Human Rights Advisory Panel", United Nations Mission in Kosovo, 2007–12.

LIST OF PUBLICATIONS

1. BOOKS

a. Author or co-author

- & Walter VAN NOTEN: *Openbaarheid van bestuur in België*, Preadvies, Vereniging voor de vergelijkende studie van het recht van België en Nederland, Zwolle, 1981.
- & Stefaan RAES: *Arresten en documenten gerechtelijk recht*, Leuven, 1988, 1ste uitg., 435 pp.; 1992, 2nd ed., 344 pp.
- *Geschillen over burgerlijke rechten en verplichtingen. Over het toepassingsgebied van de artikelen 6, lid 1, van het Europees Verdrag over de rechten van de mens en 14, lid 1, van het Internationaal Verdrag inzake burgerrechten en politieke rechten*, Publikaties Interuniversitair Centrum voor Staatsrecht – Proefschriften en verhandelingen, XIII, Antwerpen, 1989, XX + 316 pp.
- & David D'HOOGHE: *Het recht van verdediging in tuchtzaken*, Antwerpen, 1989, VI + 56 pp.
- *Herziening van het Gerechtelijk Wetboek, Wet en parlementaire voorbereiding*, Gent, 1993, IX + 149 pp.
- *Vrijheid van meningsuiting. Een grondrecht ingebed in plichten en verantwoordelijkheden*, Preadvies, Vereniging voor de vergelijkende studie van het recht van België en Nederland, Deventer, 2005, IV + 103 pp.

b. Editor

- *Gelijkheid en non-discriminatie. Egalité et non-discrimination*, Antwerpen, 1991 (& A. ALEN, editor).
- *De opleiding en de werving van magistraten*, Publ. Inst. Ger. R., vol. 3, Gent 1993 (editor).
- *Vertrouwen in het gerecht. Confiance dans la justice*, Interuniversitair Centrum Gerechtelijk Recht, Antwerpen, 1995 (& M. STORME, editor).
- *Themiscahier, Staatsrecht*, nr. 18, Brugge, 2003 (& A. ALEN, editor).
- *De betekenis van de mensenrechten voor het personen- en familierecht*, Antwerpen, 2003 (& P. SENAEVE, editor).

- *Protocol No. 14 and the Reform of the European Court of Human Rights*, Antwerpen, 2005 (& W. VANDENHOLE, editor).
- *Uitdagingen door en voor het EVRM*, Mechelen, 2005 (editor).
- *Out of the Ashes. Reparation for Victims of Gross and Systematic Human Rights Violations*, Antwerpen, 2005 (& K. DE FEYTER, S. PARMENTIER and M. BOSSUYT, editors).
- *Themiscahier, Staatsrecht*, nr. 36, Brugge, 2006 (& A. ALEN, editor).
- *The Framework Convention for the Protection of National Minorities: a Useful Pan-European Instrument?*, Antwerpen, 2008 (& A. VERSTICHEL, A. ALEN and B. DE WITTE, editors).
- *Themiscahier, Staatsrecht*, nr. 54, Brugge, 2009 (& A. ALEN, editor).

2. ARTICLES

a. Articles in journals and contributions in edited collections

- "De raadplegingen van de Koning bij het begin van een regeringscrisis", *Jura Falconis*, 1976–77, 407–426.
- & Anne DEWAELE: "De grondrechten in de Europese Gemeenschappen, en de gemeenschappelijke verklaring van het Europese Parlement, de Raad en de Commissie van 5 april 1977", *Jura Falconis*, 1977–78, 307–318.
- & Anne DEWAELE: "Rechtsstudies in de Verenigde Staten", *Interuniversitair Studententijdschrift*, 1979, 238–242.
- "Het geheim karakter van tuchtprocedures", *Rechtskundig Weekblad*, 1979–80, 1665–1682.
- "Gemeenschapsrecht en Duitse grondrechten, vijf jaar na het "Solange-Beschluss"", *Sociaal-Economische Wetgeving*, 1980, 619–628.
- "Het recht op behandeling van een "burgerlijke" zaak binnen een redelijke termijn", in *Tien jaar gerechtelijk wetboek, Interuniversitair Studententijdschrift*, vol. 1, Antwerpen, 1981, 150–151.
- "De voorlopige hechtenis van militairen", *Rechtskundig Weekblad*, 1982–83, 1107–1116.
- "De vakbondspremie in de overheidssector", *Tijdschrift voor Bestuurswetenschappen en Publiekrecht*, 1983, 3–10.
- "The Independence of the Judiciary in Belgium", in *Effectiveness of Judicial Protection and the Constitutional Order, Belgian Reports at the IInd International Congress of Procedural Law* (M. STORME, ed.), *Bibliotheek van gerechtelijk recht*, XI, Deventer, 1983, 49–82.
- "Het optreden van verenigingen in rechte ter verdediging van collectieve belangen", *Rechtskundig Weekblad*, 1983–84, 2001–2026.
- "De uitvoeringsimmuniteit van publiekrechtelijke rechtspersonen in strijd met de rechten van de mens?", *Tijdschrift voor Bestuurswetenschappen en Publiekrecht*, 1984, 163–168.

- "Het recht op een eenvoudig en snel proces", in *De vereenvoudiging en versnelling van het burgerlijk proces* (H. GEINGER, ed.), Antwerpen, 1984, 1–13.
- "Mensenrechten in de Kerk: kanttekeningen door een burgerlijk jurist", in *Het nieuwe kerkelijk recht. Analyse van de Codex iuris canonici 1983* (R. TORFS, ed.), Leuven, 1985, 167–172.
- "Het strafproces en het Europees Verdrag over de rechten van de mens", in *Strafrecht voor rechtspractici* (L. DUPONT and F. HUTSEBAUT, eds.), *Publ. Inst. Strafrecht*, nr. 1, Leuven, 1985, 163–197.
- "Het beroep op de rechter in sportzaken", in *Sport en recht* (A. DE BECKER, ed.), Antwerpen, 1986, 83–119.
- "Verbod voor een magistraat om, na regeling van de zaak in kort geding, ten gronde te beslissen?", in *Expertise, Interuniversitair Studententijdschrift*, vol. 8, Antwerpen, 1987, 149–153.
- "De Raad van State en de internationale verdragen over de rechten van de mens", *Tijdschrift voor Bestuurswetenschappen en Publiekrecht*, 1987, 367–386.
- "De rechtspleging voor de Europese Commissie en het Europees Hof voor de Rechten van de Mens", in *Actuele problemen van strafrecht, XIVde Postuniversitaire Cyclus Willy Delva, 1987–1988* (A. DE NAUW, J. D'HAENENS and M. STORME, eds.), *Interuniversitaire Reeks Criminologie en Strafwetenschappen*, dl. 15, Antwerpen, 1988, 313–383.
- "De invloed van het Europees Verdrag over de rechten van de mens op bepaalde aspecten van de strafprocedure in België", *Rechtskundig Weekblad*, 1988–89, 793–808; err., 1072.
- "Uitputting interne rechtsmiddelen en rechtsbescherming", *Nederlands Juristenblad*, 1989, 267–268.
- "Het recht op eerbiediging van het privé-leven", in *Privacy in de administratiefrechtelijke praktijk* (LIGA VOOR MENSENRECHTEN, ed.), Gent, 1989, 9–27.
- "Le contentieux administratif: fondements et développements", in *Le citoyen face à l'administration. Commissions et juridictions administratives: quels droits de défense?*, Liège, 1990, 19–62.
- "Van blaam tot consilium abeundi. Het disciplinair statuut van de student", *Jura Falconis*, 1989–90, 575–591.
- "Over de eentaligheid van akten van rechtspleging. Pleidooi voor een functionele interpretatie van de Taalwet Gerechtszaken", in *"Houd voet bij stuk", Xenia iuris historiae G. van Dievoet oblata*, Leuven, 1990, 511–521.
- & Liesbeth VAN SCHOUBROECK, "Kiesrecht van vreemdelingen als een fundamenteel recht", *Rechtskundig Weekblad*, 1990–91, 1145–1158; err., 1418.
- "Het verbod van onderwerping van een persoon aan een lichamelijk of geestesonderzoek", *Liber amicorum Prof. em. E. Krings*, Brussels, 1991, 659–669.

- "Un point de vue d'avocat", in *Le recours des particuliers devant le juge constitutionnel* (F. DELPÉRÉE, ed.), Paris-Brussels, 1991, 57–62.
- *Commentaar Gerechtelijk Recht*, losbladig, art. 705 Ger.W., Antwerpen, (1991) (dagvaarding van de Belgische Staat).
- "Gelijkheid en non-discriminatie in het internationale recht: synthese", in *Gelijkheid en non-discriminatie – Egalité et non-discrimination* (A. ALEN and P. LEMMENS, eds.), Antwerpen, 1991, 85–91.
- "De kerkelijke overheid in de greep van de wereldlijke rechter?", in *Rechtsbescherming in de kerk* (H. WARNINK, ed.), Leuven, 1991, 69–86.
- & Joost VERLINDEN, "Toegang tot de rechter in milieuzaken", in *Rechtspraktijk en milieubescherming. Eerste Antwerps Juristencongres* (CENTRUM VOOR BEROEPSVERVOLMAKING IN DE RECHTEN, ed.), Antwerpen, 1991, 223–264.
- & Ann-Sofie MAERTENS, "Toestaan van betalingsfaciliteiten inzake consumentenkrediet", *Jura Falconis*, 1991–92, 4–109 to 4–136.
- "Independence and responsibility of members of the bar", in *Rôle et organisation de magistrats et avocats dans les sociétés contemporaines. IXème Congrès mondial de droit judiciaire* (M. STORME, ed.), Antwerpen, 1992, 127–144; translation (Czech): "Nezávislost a odopvědnost advokátu v Belgii", *Bulletin Advokacie*, 1995, vol. 8, pp. 92–102.
- "Rechterlijke organisatie", in *Het vernieuwd gerechtelijk recht. Eerste commentaar bij de Wet van 3 augustus 1992 tot wijziging van het Gerechtelijk Wetboek* (INTERUNIVERSITAIR CENTRUM VOOR GERECHTELIJK RECHT, ed.), Antwerpen, 1992, 49–70; translation: "L'organisation judiciaire", in *Le droit judiciaire rénové. Premier commentaire de la loi du 3 août 1992 modifiant le Code judiciaire* (CENTRE INTERUNIVERSITAIRE DE DROIT JUDICIAIRE, ed.), Brussels, 1992, 47–67.
- "Effects of the ECHR on certain areas of civil law", *All-European Human Rights Yearbook*, 1992, 213–233; translation: "Les effets de la CEDH dans certains domaines du droit civil", *Revue universelle des droits de l'homme*, 1992, 447–455.
- "Informatique et protection de la vie privée: la loi du 8 décembre 1992", in Y. POULLET *et al.*, *Droit de l'informatique: enjeux-nouvelles responsabilités*, Brussels, 1993, 407–444.
- "Synthese", in *De opleiding en de werving van magistraten* (P. LEMMENS, ed.), *Publ. Inst. Ger. R.*, vol. 3, Gent, 1993, 91–97.
- "De verwerking van persoonsgegevens door politiediensten en de eerbiediging van de persoonlijke levenssfeer", *Liber Amicorum Jules D'Haenens*, Gent, 1993, 205–218.
- "What can legal policy expect from the sociology of law?", *Sociology of law, social problems and legal policy in Europe* (J. VAN HOUTTE and F. VAN LOON, eds.), Leuven, 1993, 95–99.

- & Liesbeth VAN SCHOUBROECK, "De verslagen van de Belgische regering voor het Comité voor de rechten van de mens", *De betekenis van het Internationaal Verdrag inzake Burgerrechten en Politieke Rechten voor de interne rechtsorde* (INTERUNIVERSITAIR CENTRUM MENSENRECHTEN, ed.), Antwerpen, 1993, 23–37.
- "De opleiding en werving van magistraten: de nieuwe procedure definitief van start", *Vlaams Jurist Vandaag*, 1993, no. 4, pp. 25–27.
- & Jean-Marie POUPART (+) and Ann-Sofie MAERTENS, *Commentaar gerechtelijk recht*, losbladig, artt. 1050–1072*bis* Ger.W., Antwerpen, 1994 (hoger beroep.)
- "De procedure zoals in kort geding betreffende de bescherming van de persoonlijke levenssfeer", in *Le développement des procédures "comme en référé". De ontwikkeling van de procedures "zoals in kort geding"* (J. VAN COMPERNOLLE and M. STORME, eds.), Antwerpen, 1994, 175–183.
- "Het recht op eerbiediging van de persoonlijke levenssfeer, in het algemeen en ten opzichte van de verwerking van persoonsgegevens in het bijzonder", *Om deze redenen. Liber Amicorum Armand Vandeplas*, Gent, 1994, 313–326.
- "Mensenrechten en Europese veiligheid: een selectief overzicht van het optreden van CSCE", *Jaarboek Mensenrechten*, 1993, 438–445.
- "Toezichtsmechanismen ter bescherming van de persoonlijke levenssfeer", in COMMISSIE VOOR DE BESCHERMING VAN DE PERSOONLIJKE LEVENSSFEER, *Welke commissie voor welke persoonlijke levenssfeer? Quelle Commission pour quelle Vie Privée?*, s.l., s.d. (1994), 101–126; also in *Persoonsgegevens en privacybescherming* (J. DUMORTIER and F. ROBBEN, eds.), Brugge, 1995, 177–213.
- "Mijmeringen bij een emeritaat", *Vlaams Jurist Vandaag*, 1995, no. 6, pp. 2–3.
- "Artikel 6 E.V.R.M., in het licht van de algemene rechtsbeginselen die het huldigt en van de doelstellingen die eraan ten grondslag liggen", *De norm achter de regel. Hommage aan Marcel Storme*, Antwerpen, 1995, 161–180.
- "Het tuchtrecht van de gerechtsdeurwaarders – Le droit disciplinaire des huissiers de justice", *De Gerechtsdeurwaarder – L'Huissier de Justice*, 1996, 57–89.
- "Quelques réflexions au sujet des garanties procédurales en matière pénale", *La justice pénale et l'Europe. Travaux des XVes journées d'études juridiques Jean Dabin* (F. TULKENS and H.D. BOSLY, dir.), Brussels, 1996, 201–208.
- "Onderzoek naar mensenrechten: synthese van de resultaten en conclusies", *NJCM Bulletin*, 1997, 65–69.
- "Opdrachten aan de Koning voor de omzetting van internationale handelingen in de interne wetgeving", *Liber Amicorum Prof. Dr. G. Baeteman*, Deurne, 1997, 565–584.

- "The Gaygusuz decision situated in the case law of the European Court of Human Rights", *Social security, non-discrimination and property* (S. VAN DEN BOGAERT, red.), Antwerpen, 1997, 25–33.
- "De ethische dimensie van de rechten van de mens", *Heeft de traditie van de mensenrechten toekomst?* (J. DE TAVERNIER and D. POLLEFEYT, eds.), Leuven, 1998, 201–204.
- "New religious movements and the law in Belgium", *New religious movements and the law in the European Union* (EUROPEAN CONSORTIUM FOR CHURCH-STATE RESEARCH, ed.), Milano, 1999, 87–104.
- "De programmawet van 12 augustus 2000 en de rol van de Senaat in het wetgevingsproces", *Tijdschrift voor Wetgeving*, 2000, I, 191–194.
- "The Relation between the Charter of Fundamental Rights of the European Union and the European Convention on Human Rights – Substantive Aspects", *Maastricht Journal of European and Comparative Law*, 2001, 49–67.
- & Wouter VANDENHOLE, "De heropening van de strafprocedure na een veroordelend arrest van het Europees Hof voor de Rechten van de Mens", *Tijdschrift voor Strafrecht*, 2001, 49–74.
- "Honderd jaar mensenrechten": enkele ontwikkelingen op het internationale niveau", *Nieuwsbrief Liga Mensenrechten*, juni 2001, pp. 2–6.
- "Rechten van de mens in een klimaat van terrorisme", *Schokgolven* (B. PATTYN and J. WOUTERS, eds.), Leuven, 2002, 137–146 and 194.
- "De amicus curiae en het Europees Verdrag over de rechten van de mens", *Amice curiae, quo vadis? Het openbaar ministerie in privaatrechtelijke, administratieve en sociale zaken* (P. VAN ORSHOVEN and M. STORME, eds.), Antwerpen, 2002, 19–38.
- "Afsluitende beschouwingen", *Strafrechtelijke vervolging van ernstige schendingen van mensenrechten* (S. GUTWIRTH, S. SMIS *et al.*, eds.), Antwerpen, 2002, 181–188.
- "De waarborgen van een eerlijk proces in een cassatieprocedure", *Liber Amicorum Lucien Simont*, Brussels, 2002, 149–165.
- "S.O.S. voor het Europees Hof voor de Rechten van de Mens (en voor het individueel klachtrecht?)", *Themiscahier, Staatsrecht*, no. 18 (A. ALEN and P. LEMMENS, eds.), Brugge, 2003, 79–98.
- "De betekenis voor het personen- en familierecht van de VN-verdragen inzake de burgerlijke en politieke rechten, inzake de economische, sociale en culturele rechten, en inzake de rechten van de vrouw", *De betekenis van de mensenrechten voor het personen- en familierecht* (P. SENAEVE and P. LEMMENS, eds.), Antwerpen, 2003, 171–201.
- "Respecting human rights in the fight against terrorism", in *Legal instruments in the fight against international terrorism. A transatlantic dialogue* (C. FIJNAUT, J. WOUTERS and F. NAERT, eds.), Leiden, 2004, 223–249.
- & Pietro SARDARO, "Restitution", in *Encyclopaedia of Genocide and Crimes Against Humanity* (D. SHELTON, ed.), Detroit, 2004, 910–913.

- "(The) right to life and prohibition of torture as basic values in democratic societies in Europe", in *Vukovar '91. International echoes and significance* (J. JURČEVIĆ, D. ŽIVIĆ and B. ESIH, eds.), Zagreb, 2004, 33–44 (https://www.pilar.hr/wp-content/images/stories/dokumenti/zbornici/24_en/z_24_en _033.pdf) (access 30.8.19); translation: "Pravo na život i zabrana mučenja kao osnovne vrijednosti demokratskih društava u Europi", in *Vukovar '91: Međunarodni odjeci i značaj* (J. JURČEVIĆ, D. ŽIVIĆ and B. ESIH, eds.), Zagreb, 2004, 31–41 (https://www.pilar.hr/wp-content/images/stories/ dokumenti/zbornici/24_hr/z_24_hr_031.pdf) (access 30.8.19).
- "Single-judge Formations, Committees, Chambers and Grand Chamber", in *Protocol No. 14 and the Reform of the European Court of Human Rights* (P. LEMMENS and W. VANDENHOLE, eds.), Antwerpen, 2005, 31–43.
- "Het 14de Protocol bij het E.V.R.M.: het Europees Hof tegen zijn ondergang behoed?", in *Uitdagingen door en voor het EVRM* (P. LEMMENS, ed.), Mechelen, 2005, 103–143.
- "Death penalty, life sentence and long-term sentences: inhuman punishments?", in *Strafrecht als roeping. Liber amicorum Lieven Dupont*, Leuven, 2005, 467–486.
- "Enkele aspecten van de "doctrine" van het Europees Hof voor de Rechten van de Mens", *Themiscahier, Staatsrecht*, nr. 36 (A. ALEN and P. LEMMENS, eds.), Brugge, 2006, 71–100.
- "Het 7ᵉ Protocol bij het Europees Verdrag over de rechten van de mens: een "discreet" verdrag?", *Vigilantibus Ius Scriptum. Feestbundel voor Hugo Vandenberghe*, Brugge, 2007, 167–184.
- "Contrôle préventif de constitutionnalité par la Cour constitutionnelle de la République Démocratique du Congo", *Premiers scrutins et contrôle de constitutionnalité en RDC: la mise en œuvre d'une constitution "régionaliste", Fédéralisme Régionalisme*, vol. 7, 2007, no. 1. (http://popups.ulg.ac.be/ federalisme/document.php?id=558) (access 30.8.19)
- "Recente ontwikkelingen in verband met het EVRM en andere mensenrechtenverdragen", *Recht in beweging. 15ᵈᵉ VRG-Alumnidag* (2008), Antwerpen, 2008, 491–518.
- "De rechten van het kind als grondrechten in de Belgische rechtsorde", *Kinderrechten in België* (W. VANDENHOLE, ed.), Antwerpen, 2008, 37–58.
- "Guidance by supreme courts to lower courts on the requirements of the European Convention on Human Rights", *The role of Supreme Courts in the domestic implementation of the European Convention on Human Rights. Proceedings of the Regional Conference, Belgrade, 20–21 September 2007*, Council of Europe, 2008, 36–51 (https://rm.coe.int/0900001680695a94) (access 30.8.19); translation: "Guider les juridictions inférieures sur les exigences de la Convention européenne des droits de l'homme", *Le rôle des Cours suprêmes dans la mise en œuvre de la Convention européenne des droits de l'homme au niveau*

interne. Actes de la Conférence régionale, Belgrade, 20–21 septembre 2007, Conseil de l'Europe, 2008, 39–54 (https://rm.coe.int/09000016806f14cb) (access 30.8.19).

- & Ludovic HENNEBEL, Arnaud van WAEYENBERGE and Evelien VANDEVEN, "Belgium: a reference instrument, but without binding force", *60 years of the Universal Declaration of Human Rights in Europe* (V. JAICHAND and M. SUKSI, eds.), Antwerpen, 2009, 7–18.

- "Bescherming tegen discriminatie", *Staatsrecht, Themiscahier*, no. 54 (A. ALEN and P. LEMMENS, eds.), Brugge, 2009, 79–102.

- "Een eerlijk proces, ook in kort geding", *Voorafname op vriendschap. Vrienden schrijven voor Dirk Lindemans bij zijn 60ᵉ verjaardag*, Brugge, 2010, 245–262.

- "De motivering van rechterlijke beslissingen als element van het eerlijk proces", *Liber amicorum Ludovic De Gryse*, Gent, 2010, 575–584.

- & Nathalie VAN LEUVEN, "Do legal persons enjoy a right to respect for their private life, their home and their correspondence?", *Over grenzen. Liber amicorum Herman Cousy*, Antwerpen, 2011, 983–1001.

- "Enkele beschouwingen bij de zogenaamde "volle rechtsmacht" van de rechter bij de toetsing van administratieve sancties", *Liber amicorum Marc Boes*, Brugge, 2011, 393–410.

- & Koen LEMMENS, "De herziening of heropening van de strafprocedure: een passend middel tot herstel van een schending van fundamentele rechten?", *Het strafrecht bedreven. Liber Amicorum Alain De Nauw*, Brugge, 2011, 571–590.

- & Nathalie VAN LEUVEN, "Les destinataires des droits constitutionnels", *Les droits constitutionnels en Belgique*" (M. VERDUSSEN and N. BONBLED, dir.), Brussels, 2011, vol. 1, 111–146.

- & Guan SCHAIKO, "Democracy in Europe, from a human rights perspective", *Liber Amicorum René Foqué*, Brussels, 2012, 391–407.

- "The right to a fair trial and its multiple manifestations. Article 6(1) ECHR", *Shaping Rights in the ECHR. The Role of the European Court of Human Rights in Determining the Scope of Human Rights* (E. BREMS and J. GERARDS, eds.), Cambridge, 2013, 294–314.

- "Conclusions", *Les droits de l'homme. Une réalité quotidienne*, (D.FRIES, coord.), Limal, 2014, 223–232.

- & Guan SCHAIKO and Koen LEMMENS, "Belgium", in *Implementation of the European Convention on Human Rights and of the judgments of the ECtHR in national case law* (J. GERARDS and J. FLEUREN, eds.), Cambridge, 2014, 95–143.

- "The contribution of the European Court of Human Rights to the rule of law", *The Contribution of International and Supranational Courts to the Rule of Law* (G. DE BAERE and J. WOUTERS, eds.), Cheltenham, 2015, 225–241.

- "Reply to the statement by Mr Jean Marc Sauvé", *Subsidiarity: a two-sided coin? Dialogue between judges*, Strasbourg, 2015, 33–41 (https://www.echr.coe.int/Documents/Dialogue_2015_ENG.pdf) (access 30.8.19); "Réponse à l'exposé de Monsieur Jean Marc Sauvé", *Subsidiarité: une médaille à deux faces? Dialogue entre juges*, Strasbourg, 2015, 33–41 (https://www.echr.coe. int/Documents/Dialogue_2015_FRA.pdf) (access 30.8.19).

- "Visie van het Europees Hof voor de Rechten van de Mens op het Grondwettelijk Hof", *Grondwettelijk Hof 1985-2015 – Cour constitutionnelle 1985-2015* (A. ALEN, J. SPREUTELS, L. LAVRYSEN, P. NIHOUL, E. PEREMANS, B. RENAULD, J. THEUNIS and W. VERRIJDT, eds.), Brugge, 2016, 155–162.
- "Het recht op een eerlijk proces volgens artikel 6 van het Europees Verdrag over de rechten van de mens", *Efficiënt procederen voor een goede rechtsbedeling. XLIste postuniversitaire cyclus Willy Delva, 2014-2015*, (P. TAELMAN, ed.), Mechelen, 2016, 753–800.
- "Conclusions", *Human Rights as a Basis for Reevaluating and Reconstructing the Law* (A. HOC, S. WATTIER and G. WILLEMS, eds.), Brussels, 2016, 535–545.
- "De deskundige, het bestuur, de rechter en het recht van de partijen op een eerlijk proces", *Nederlands Juristenblad*, 2017, 574–580.
- & Ine DECONINCK, "International child abduction and the assessment of the best interests of the child, in the light of the Hague Convention and the European Convention on Human Rights", *Liber amicorum Patrick Senaeve*, Mechelen, 2017, 639–662.
- "Zien, denken en oplossen", *Brieven aan jonge juristen* (S. DE REY and B. TILLEMAN, eds.), Veurne, 2018, 142–146.
- "Money Laundering and Confiscation of the Proceeds from Crime from the Point of View of the European Convention on Human Rights", *Libertés, (l) égalité, humanité. Mélanges offerts à Jean Spreutels*, Brussels, 2018, 925–942.
- & Marie COURTOY, "Le Code judiciaire et la Convention européenne des droits de l'homme: interactions autour des principes d'un procès équitable et des droits de la défense", *Le Code judiciaire a 50 ans. Et après?- 50 jaar Gerechtelijk Wetboek. Wat nu?*, Brussels, 2018, 61–76.
- "The European Convention on Human Rights as an Instrument of European Public Order, Based on Common Values", *Les droits humains comparés. À la recherché de l'universalité des droits humains*, Paris, 2019, 11–28.
- "'Disputes over rights' within the meaning of Article 6 §1 of the European Convention on Human Rights, in the context of administrative litigation: back to the future?", *Liber Amicorum Guido Raimondi*, Tilburg, 2019, 429–447.

b. Case notes

- "De veiligheidsgordel en het recht op eerbiediging van het privé-leven", noot onder Cass. 11 april 1979, *Rechtskundig Weekblad*, 1979–80, 837–846.
- "Verplicht medisch onderzoek, beperking van vrije keuze van arts en eerbiediging van het privé-leven", noot onder Cass. 23 juni 1980, *Rechtskundig Weekblad*, 1980–81, 448–451.

- "Le contrôle de la "légalité" d'une privation de liberté, au sens de l'article 5, §4 de la Convention européenne des droits de l'homme", noot onder Cass. 14 februari 1980, *Journal des Tribunaux*, 1980, 596–597.
- "De vordering tot bindendverklaring van een reeds gewezen vonnis", noot onder Kort ged. Kh. Brussel, 12 maart 1981, *Rechtskundig Weekblad*, 1981–82, 2624–2626.
- "De actiemogelijkheden van degene die beweert door een misdrijf benadeeld te zijn", noot onder Cass. 7 september 1982, *Rechtskundig Weekblad*, 1982–83, 935–938.
- "De ondertekening van het afschrift van een exploot door de gerechtsdeurwaarder", noot onder Cass. 14 juni 1982, *Rechtskundig Weekblad*, 1982–83, 991–994.
- "De aanstelling van een sekwester in kort geding", noot onder Kort ged. Kh. Brussel, 8 december 1981, *Rechtskundig Weekblad*, 1982–83, 1146–1149.
- "Homosexualiteit, privé-leven en discriminatieverbod", noot onder Cass. 7 december 1982, *Rechtskundig Weekblad*, 1982–83, 1912–1913.
- "Tuberculosepreventie en het recht op eerbiediging van het privé-leven", noot onder Cass. 8 september 1982, *Vlaams Tijdschrift voor Gezondheidsrecht*, 1983, 144–145.
- "De ambtshalve aanvulling van rechtsgronden en de eerbiediging van de rechten van de verdediging", noot onder Cass. 22 oktober 1982, *Rechtskundig Weekblad*, 1982–83, 2188–2191.
- "Artikel 751 van het Gerechtelijk Wetboek en de motiveringsverplichting", noot onder Cass. 21 mei 1981, *Rechtskundig Weekblad*, 1982–83, 2245–2250.
- Noot onder R.v.St., 4 maart 1982, Canoot, nr. 22.094, *Rechtskundig Weekblad*, 1982–83, 2625 (voordelen aan gesyndikeerden).
- "Het einde van de betwisting rond de openbaarheid van tuchtzaken", noot onder Cass. 14 april 1983, *Rechtskundig Weekblad*, 1983–84, 86–87.
- Noot onder Gent, 8 september 1983, *Rechtskundig Weekblad*, 1983–84, 1986 (onpartijdigheid van de rechter).
- "De voorlopige regeling van de toestand der partijen door de rechter ten gronde, na een behandeling ter inleidende zitting", noot onder Rb. Antwerpen, 24 mei 1984, *Rechtskundig Weekblad*, 1984–85, 2011–2016.
- "De redelijke termijn in strafzaken", noot onder Antwerpen, 19 december 1984, *Rechtskundig Weekblad*, 1985–86, 325.
- "Contestations sur des droits et obligations de caractère civil", noot onder Comité Rechten v.d. Mens, 8 april 1986, Y.L./Canada, *Administration Publique (Trimestriel)*, 1987, 93.
- "De bijstand van een advocaat in een procedure voor een bestuurlijk orgaan", noot onder Kort ged. Rb. Kortrijk, 18 juni 1987, *Rechtskundig Weekblad*, 1987–88, 406–407.

- "De bewijslast inzake prijsvergelijkingen en het vermoeden van onschuld", noot onder Voorz. Kh. Brussel, 31 augustus 1989, *Jaarboek Handelspraktijken*, 1989, 32–37.
- "De eerbiediging van de godsdienstige en filosofische overtuigingen van de ouders van schoolgaande kinderen", noot onder R.v.St., 10 juli 1990, V., nr. 35.442, *Rechtskundig Weekblad*, 1990–91, 571.
- "Over de toepassing van beginselen van behoorlijk tuchtrecht", noot onder Kort ged. Rb. Antwerpen, 12 april 1990, *Tijdschrift voor Onderwijsrecht en Onderwijsbeleid*, 1990–91, 47.
- "Het onderzoek van de ogenschijnlijke rechten van de partijen door de rechter in kort geding en het toezicht door het Hof van Cassatie", noot onder Cass. 22 februari 1991, *Tijdschrift voor Belgisch Handelsrecht*, 1991, 675–684.
- "De moeizame tenuitvoerlegging van het arrest Marckx in de Belgische rechtsorde", noot onder E.H.R.M., 29 november 1991, Vermeire t. België, *NJCM Bulletin*, 1992, 677–683.
- "De niet-verschijning van de verweerder inzake schriftonderzoek", noot onder Brussel, 9 december 1991, *Proces & Bewijs*, 1993, 46–47.
- "Loyauteit en oprechtheid in tuchtzaken", noot onder Cass., 18 februari 1994, *Jaarboek Mensenrechten 1994*, Antwerpen, 1995, 319.
- "Toetsing van de wettigheid van een vrijheidsberoving met het oog op uitlevering", noot onder Cass., 1 juni 1994, *Jaarboek Mensenrechten 1994*, Antwerpen, 1995, 327–328.
- "De redelijke termijn en de verplichting tot het stellen van een prejudiciële vraag", noot onder Cass., 23 november 1994, *Jaarboek Mensenrechten 1994*, Antwerpen, 1995, 335–336.
- "Ontvankelijkheid van de voorziening in cassatie door een veroordeelde wiens onmiddellijke aanhouding is bevolen", noot onder Cass., 11 april 1995, *Jaarboek Mensenrechten 1995–1996*, Antwerpen, 1997, 412–415.
- Noot onder Gent, 20 maart 1996, *Rechtskundig Weekblad*, 1996–97, 1260–1261 (verplichte medische behandeling).
- Noot onder E.H.R.M., 16 september 1996, Gaygusuz, *Tijdschrift Rechtsdocumentatie en -informatie*, 1997, 92 (vertaling: *Information & Documentation juridiques*, 1997, 79) (niet-discriminatie vreemdelingen inzake sociale zekerheid).
- "Het vreemdelingencontentieux: noch burgerlijk, noch strafrechtelijk", noot onder E.H.R.M., 5 oktober 2000, Maaouia / Frankrijk, *Jaarboek Mensenrechten*, 2000–2001, 206–214.

c. Chronicle "Human Rights"

- "De zaak Buchholz en het recht op behandeling van een zaak binnen een redelijke termijn", *Rechtskundig Weekblad*, 1981–82, 53–54.
- "Verbod van publiciteit in een vrij beroep", *Rechtskundig Weekblad*, 1981–82, 1245.

- "Homoseksualiteit en het recht op eerbiediging van het privé-leven (zaak Dudgeon t/ Verenigd Koninkrijk)", *Rechtskundig Weekblad*, 1981–82, 1579–1581.
- "De onpartijdigheid van de voorzitter van het Hof van Assisen", *Rechtskundig Weekblad*, 1981–82, 1699–1701.
- "Het "closed shop"-systeem en de vrijheid van vakvereniging (zaak Young, James & Webster)", *Rechtskundig Weekblad*, 1981–82, 1701–1703.
- "De internering van geesteszieken", *Rechtskundig Weekblad*, 1981–82, 1908–1911.
- "Lijfstraffen op school (zaak Campbell en Cosans)", *Rechtskundig Weekblad*, 1982–83, 53–56.
- "De vindingrijkheid van het Oostenrijkse "Oberster Gerichtshof" (zaak Adolf)", *Rechtskundig Weekblad*, 1982–83, 55–58.
- "De economische delicten en de duur van het strafproces (arrest Eckle)", *Rechtskundig Weekblad*, 1982–83, 1019–1020.
- "De terbeschikkingstelling van de regering van recidivisten en gewoontemisdadigers (arrest Van Droogenbroeck)", *Rechtskundig Weekblad*, 1982–83, 1072–1077.
- "De zaak Jespers: geen "onbillijk proces"", *Rechtskundig Weekblad*, 1982–83, 1948–1950.
- "Onteigeningen en stedenbouwkundige voorschriften", *Rechtskundig Weekblad*, 1982–83, 2025–2031.
- "De zaak Piersack en de onpartijdigheid van de rechter", *Rechtskundig Weekblad*, 1982–83, 2295–2296.
- "De afschaffing van de doodstraf", *Rechtskundig Weekblad*, 1982–83, 2425.
- "Het honorarium van de advocaat in een procedure in verband met de rechten van de mens", *Rechtskundig Weekblad*, 1982–83, 2644–2645.
- "De "redelijke termijn" in strafzaken: arresten Foti e.a. en Corigliano", *Rechtskundig Weekblad*, 1982–83, 2837–2838.
- "Een nieuwe tuchtzaak voor het Europees Hof", *Rechtskundig Weekblad*, 1983–84, 119–120.
- "Censuur op de correspondentie van gedetineerden", *Rechtskundig Weekblad*, 1983–84, 197–199.
- "Het verval van de strafvordering en het vermoeden van onschuld", *Rechtskundig Weekblad*, 1983–84, 404–405.
- "De kosteloze bijstand van een advocaat in een cassatieprocedure", *Rechtskundig Weekblad*, 1983–84, 532–534.
- "De overbelasting van een administratief rechtscollege en de duur van de rechtspleging", *Rechtskundig Weekblad*, 1983–84, 819–821.
- "Vergoeding voor advocaten-stagiairs: geen hulp uit Straatsburg...", *Rechtskundig Weekblad*, 1983–84, 2637–2640.

- "Openbaarheid en cassatieprocedure", *Rechtskundig Weekblad*, 1983–84, 2717–2719.
- "De administratieve sanctie en het recht van verdediging in strafzaken", *Rechtskundig Weekblad*, 1984–85, 419–422.
- "De voorlopige hechtenis van militairen in Nederland", *Rechtskundig Weekblad*, 1984–85, 1101–1107.
- "Gedetineerden, tuchtprocedures in de gevangenis en juridische bijstand", *Rechtskundig Weekblad*, 1984–85, 1171–1174.
- "Het afluisteren van telefoongesprekken en het registreren van uitgaande en binnenkomende oproepen", *Rechtskundig Weekblad*, 1984–85, 1735–1739.
- "De onderzoeksrechter als vonnisrechter in de correctionele rechtbank", *Rechtskundig Weekblad*, 1984–85, 2418–2423.
- "Vrijheid van meningsuiting in een vrij beroep", *Rechtskundig Weekblad*, 1985–86, 131–134.
- "Het Hof van Straatsburg als wetgever in strafzaken", *Rechtskundig Weekblad*, 1985–86, 265–267.
- "Immigratiebeleid, gezinsleven en discriminatieverbod", *Rechtskundig Weekblad*, 1985–86, 1650–1656.
- Bespreking van E.H.R.M., 26 augustus 1997, Balmer-Schafroth, *Rechtskundig Weekblad*, 1998–99, 509–510 (recht van omwonenden om een bezwaar i.v.m. een kerncentrale in te dienen).
- Bespreking van E.H.R.M., 2 september 1997, Spuri e.a./Italië, *Rechtskundig Weekblad*, 1998–99, 513–514 (toepasselijkheid van het recht op een eerlijk proces op geschillen inzake het statuut van ambtenaren).
- Bespreking van E.H.R.M., 9 juni 1998, Teixeira de Castro, *Rechtskundig Weekblad*, 2000–01, 281–282 (recht op een eerlijk proces en politionele uitlokking van een misdrijf).
- Bespreking van E.H.R.M., 23 september 1998, Malige, *Rechtskundig Weekblad*, 2000–01, 676 (recht op toegang tot rechter na intrekking rijbewijs).
- Bespreking van E.H.R.M., 25 oktober 1998, Aït-Mouhoub, *Rechtskundig Weekblad*, 2000–01, 678–679 (consignatie door burgerlijke partij).
- Bespreking van E.H.R.M., 18 februari 1999, Waite en Kennedy, en Beer en Regan, *Rechtskundig Weekblad*, 2000–01, 1035–1036 (jurisdictionele immuniteit van internationale instellingen).
- Bespreking van E.H.R.M., 28 oktober 1999, Zielinski en Pradal, en Gonzalez en anderen, *Rechtskundig Weekblad*, 2001–02, 1005–1006 (inmenging van de wetgever in hangende gedingen).
- Bespreking van E.H.R.M., 8 december 1999, Pellegrin, *Rechtskundig Weekblad*, 2001–02, 1114–1116 (toepasselijkheid van het recht op een eerlijk proces op geschillen m.b.t. de rechten van personen in overheidsdienst).
- Bespreking van E.H.R.M., 1 februari 2000, Mazurek, *Rechtskundig Weekblad*, 2002–03, 232–233 (erfrechtelijke discriminatie van natuurlijke kinderen).

- Bespreking van E.H.R.M., 22 juni 2000, Coëme, *Rechtskundig Weekblad*, 2002–03, 395–397 (eerlijke behandeling van een strafzaak ten laste van een oud-minister).
- Bespreking van E.H.RM., 29 maart 2001, D.N. / Zwitserland, *Rechtskundig Weekblad*, 2002–03, 997–998 (onpartijdigheid van een rechter-rapporteur).
- Bespreking van E.H.R.M., 12 juli 2001, Ferrazzini / Italië, *Rechtskundig Weekblad*, 2002–03, 1518–1519 (niet-toepasselijkheid van de waarborgen van een eerlijk proces op fiscale procedures).
- Bespreking van E.H.R.M., 11 juli 2002, Göç / Turkije, *Rechtskundig Weekblad*, 2003–04, 1196–1197 (openbaarheid van de terechtzitting en het antwoord op de conclusie van het openbaar ministerie).
- Bespreking van E.H.R.M., 26 juli 2002, Meftah / Frankrijk, *Rechtskundig Weekblad*, 2003–04, 1197–1198 (pleitmonopolie van de advocaten bij het Hof van Cassatie en antwoord op de conclusie van het openbaar ministerie).
- Bespreking van E.H.R.M., 6 mei 2003, Kleyn / Nederland, *Rechtskundig Weekblad*, 2004–05, 354–355 (cumulatie van adviserende en rechtsprekende functies door de Raad van State).
- Bespreking van E.H.R.M., 16 december 2003, Cooper / Verenigd Koninkrijk en Grieves / Verenigd Koninkrijk, *Rechtskundig Weekblad*, 2004–05, 1237–1238 (onafhankelijkheid van militaire rechtscolleges).
- Bespreking van E.H.R.M., 12 februari 2004, Perez / Frankrijk, *Rechtskundig Weekblad*, 2005–06, 156–157 (burgerlijkepartijstelling).
- Bespreking van E.H.R.M., 22 juni 2004, Broniowki / Polen, *Rechtskundig Weekblad*, 2005–06, 1154–1156 (uitvoering van een pilootarrest van het Europees Hof).
- Bespreking van E.H.R.M., 17 december 2004, Cumpănă en Mazăre / Roemenië, *Rechtskundig Weekblad*, 2006–07, 116–118 (veroordeling van journalisten wegens eerroof en belediging).
- Bespreking van E.H.R.M., 13 januari 2005, Capeau / België, *Rechtskundig Weekblad*, 2006–07, 697–698 (vermoeden van onschuld en vergoeding voor onwerkzame voorlopige hechtenis).
- Bespreking van E.H.R.M., 2 juni 2005, Claes e.a. / België, *Rechtskundig Weekblad*, 2007–08, 250–251 (strafprocedure tegen oud-ministers).
- Bespreking van E.H.R.M., 2 juni 2005, Cottin / België, *Rechtskundig Weekblad*, 2007–08, 1088–1089 (tegenspraak bij deskundigenonderzoek in strafzaken).
- Bespreking van E.H.R.M., 19 oktober 2005, Roche / Verenigd Koninkrijk, *Rechtskundig Weekblad*, 2007–08, 1091–1093 (immuniteit overheid ten aanzien van bepaalde aansprakelijkheidsvorderingen).
- Bespreking van E.H.R.M., 12 april 2006, Stec / Verenigd Koninkrijk, *Rechtskundig Weekblad*, 2008–09, 1061–1063 (gelijke behandeling van mannen en vrouwen inzake pensioenleeftijd).
- Bespreking van E.H.R.M., 23 november 2006, Jussila / Finland, *Rechtskundig Weekblad*, 2009–10, 123–124 (beroep tegen fiscale boete).

3. NATIONAL REPORTS (FRALEX) FOR THE EU FUNDAMENTAL RIGHTS AGENCY (2008–2010)

- & Ben HEYLEN, Evelien VANDEVEN and Jogchum VRIELINK, *Legal Study on Homophobia and Discrimination on Grounds of Sexual Orientation, Report on Belgium*, March 2008.
- & Frank VERBRUGGEN, Ken VAN HOOGENBEMT and Tim VAN HOOGENBEMT, *Thematic Study on Child Trafficking – Belgium*, September 2008 (http://fra.europa.eu/fraWebsite/attachments/Child-trafficking-09-country-be.pdf) (access 30.8.19).
- *Thematic Legal Study on National Human Rights Institutions and Human Rights Organisations – Belgium*, October 2008.
- & Pierre SCHMITT, *Thematic Legal Study on Assessment of Data Protection Measures and Relevant Institutions – Belgium*, March 2009.
- & Pierre SCHMITT, *Thematic Legal Study on Impact of the Race Equality Directive – Belgium*, May 2009.
- & Michael MERRIGAN and Pierre SCHMITT, *Thematic Legal Study on Assessment of Access to Justice in Civil Cases in Belgium*, December 2009 (http://fra.europa.eu/fraWebsite/attachments/access-to-justice-2011-country-BE.pdf) (access 30.8.19).
- & Katrien HANOULLE and Frank VERBRUGGEN, *Thematic Legal Study on Mental Health and Fundamental Rights – Belgium*, December 2009 (http://fra.europa.eu/sites/default/files/fra_uploads/2138-mental-health-study-2009-BE.pdf) (access 30.8.19).
- & Jogchum VRIELINK, *Legal Study on Homophobia and Discrimination on Grounds of Sexual Orientation and Gender Identity – Belgium*, update, April 2010 (http://fra.europa.eu/fraWebsite/attachments/LGBT-2010_thematic-study_BE.pdf) (access 30.8.19).

4. OTHER ACADEMIC REPORTS

- *The Impact of Article 6, §1, of the European Convention on Human Rights on the proceedings before the Belgian Council of State*, report for the Conference of the Association of the Councils of State and Supreme Administrative Jurisdictions of the European Union, 2000 (http://193.191.217.21/colloquia/2000/belgium.pdf) (access 30.8.19).
- "The main features of judicial control of administrative action in the light of the case-law of the European Court on Human Rights", *The possibility and scope of the judicial control of administrative decisions. First Conference of the Presidents of Supreme Administrative Courts in Europe*, Strasbourg, 7–8 October 2002, 15–26; translation: "Les principales caractéristiques du contrôle juridictionnel des décisions administratives à la lumière de la jurisprudence de la Cour européenne des droits de l'homme", *La possibilité et*

la portée d'un contrôle juridictionnel des décisions administratives. Première Conférence des Présidents des Juridictions Administratives Suprêmes en Europe, Strasbourg, 7–8 octobre 2002, 15–27.
- & Jogchum VRIELINK, Stephan PARMENTIER and the LERU WORKING GROUP ON HUMAN RIGHTS, *Academic Freedom as a Fundamental Right*, League of European Research Universities (LERU) Advice Paper, No. 6, December 2010 (https://www.leru.org/files/Academic-Freedom-as-a-Fundamental-Right-Full-paper.pdf) (access 30.8.19).

5. ANNOTATED CODES OF LAW

- & André MAST (+) and Alfons VANDER STICHELE (+), *Wetboek Publiek Recht*, losbladige en geannoteerde uitg., Mechelen (11 boekdelen).
- & Ann EYLENBOSCH, *Wetboek Milieurecht*, losbladige en geannoteerde uitg., Mechelen (8 boekdelen).

6. MASTER THESIS AND PHD THESIS

- *Ex Parte Communications Between Persons Outside an Administrative Agency and Persons Within the Agency*, LL.M. thesis, Northwestern University School of Law, Chicago, U.S.A., 1978.
- *"Geschillen over burgerlijke rechten en verplichtingen." Het toepassingsgebied van de artikelen 6, lid 1, van het Europees Verdrag over de rechten van de mens en 14, lid 1, van het Internationaal Verdrag inzake burgerrechten en politieke rechten*, doctoraatsthesis, K.U. Leuven, 1987.

7. OTHER

- & André MIROIR: *Vrijheid van meningsuiting – Bibliografie van Belgische rechtsleer*, Interuniversitair Centrum voor Staatsrecht, 1977.
- & André BRUYNEEL: *English translation/summary of the most important Belgian legal provisions in the field of banking and securities regulation*, 1980.
- & Stefaan RAES, Véronique WORTELAERS and Joost VERLINDEN: *Gerechtelijk privaatrecht*, Leuven, 1991, 1ste uitg., 300 pp.; 1994, 2de uitg., 309 pp; 1995, 3de uitg., 333 pp.
- "Le droit à un procès équitable", in *La transformation de la "Prokuratura" en instance compatible avec les principes démocratiques de la justice et la Convention européenne des droits de l'homme*, doc. Conseil de l'Europe THEMIS2 CR(97)1, 1997, 39 pp.
- & Wouter VANDENHOLE: *De gevolgen binnen de Belgische rechtsorde, op strafrechtelijk gebied, van arresten van het Europees Hof voor de Rechten van de Mens waarbij een schending wordt vastgesteld*, Preadvies Vereniging voor de vergelijkende studie van het recht van België en Nederland, 1998, 40 pp.

- "Recente ontwikkelingen van rechten van de mens", *Verslagboek 7ᵈᵉ VRG-Alumnidag*, (Leuven), 2000, 177–184.
- "Right to life, right to die ...and human rights", World Conference of the World Federation of Right to Die Societies, Brussels, September 2002, 7 pp.
- "Conflits d'attribution entre les juridictions de l'ordre judiciaire et les juridictions de l'ordre administratif", *Le Potentiel* (Kinshasa), 16 February 2007.

8. BOOK REVIEWS

- H.J. van EIKEMA HOMMES, Encyclopedie der rechtswetenschap. Methode der encyclopedie en Hoofdlijnen van de geschiedenis der rechts- en staatsfilosofie (Zwolle, 1975), in *Tijdschrift voor Privaatrecht*, 1977, 381–383.
- A.M. BOS, De voorgeschiedenis van de grondrechten. Van Magna Charta tot Déclaration des droits de l'homme et du citoyen (Deventer, 1976), in *Rechtskundig Weekblad*, 1977–78, 142–143.
- S. ERCMAN, European Environmental Law. Legal and Economic Appraisal (Bern, 1977), in *Tijdschrift voor Bestuurswetenschappen en Publiekrecht*, 1979, 359.
- E.A. ALKEMA, Studies over Europese grondrechten. De invloed van de Europese Conventie op het Nederlandse recht (Deventer, 1978), in *Sociaal-Economische Wetgeving*, 1979, 542–543.
- Procesrecht vandaag, M. STORME (ed.), Bibliotheek van gerechtelijk recht, VII (Antwerpen, 1980), in *Rechtskundig Weekblad*, 1980–81, 2085–2086.
- J. LAENENS, De bevoegdheidsovereenkomsten naar Belgisch recht, Bibliotheek van gerechtelijk recht, X (Antwerpen, 1981), in *Sociaal-Economische Wetgeving*, 1983, 278–279.
- J. KROPHOLLER, Europäisches Zivilprozessrecht: Kommentar zum EuGVÜ, Schriftenreihe Recht der internationalen Wirtschaft, Bd. 22 (Heidelberg, 1983), in *Sociaal-Economische Wetgeving*, 1983, 592.
- J.J.M. van der VEN, Mensenrechten in rechtsvergelijking. Een onderzoek binnen het raam van de Internationale Arbeidsorganisatie, Geschriften van de Nederlandse Vereniging voor Rechtsvergelijking, no. 35 (Deventer, 1984), in *Rechtskundig Weekblad*, 1984–85, 2716–2717.
- Tuchtrecht en Fair Play (Nederlandse Vereniging voor Procesrecht, ed.) (Zwolle, 1984), in *Rechtskundig Weekblad*, 1984–85, 3003–3004.
- Les sciences humaines et les droits de l'homme (R. BRUYER, ed.) (Brussels, 1984), in *Rechtskundig Weekblad*, 1984–85, 3004.
- P. PEETERS, Minderjarigen en hun recht op vrijheid en op toegang tot de rechter, Werken en Studies Interuniv. Centrum voor Staatsrecht (Antwerpen, 1984), in *Tijdschrift voor Privaatrecht*, 1985, 1020–1023.

- J. DE MEYER, Toepassing van het Europees Verdrag voor de rechten van de mens in België, en E.A. ALKEMA, Toepassing van de Europese Conventie voor de rechten van de mens in Nederland, Preadviezen voor de Vereniging voor de vergelijkende studie van het recht van België en Nederland (Zwolle, 1985), in *Rechtskundig Weekblad*, 1985–86, 1452.
- J.A. WINTER, De Europese Gemeenschap, ontwikkelingssamenwerking en de rechten van de mens. Enige beschouwingen rond de Derde Conventie van Lomé (Zwolle, 1985), in *Rechtskundig Weekblad*, 1986–87, 1245–1246.
- J.C.G. van AGGELEN, Le rôle des organisations internationales dans la protection du droit à la vie (Brussels, 1986), in *Rechtskundig Weekblad*, 1987–88, 269.
- Rechten van de Mens in mundiaal en Europees perspectief, Ars Aequi Libri – Rechten van de Mens, vol. 1 (Nijmegen, 1986, 3de uitg.), in *Rechtskundig Weekblad*, 1987–88, 269–270.
- G.P. KLEIJN en M. KROES, Mensenrechten in de Nederlandse rechtspraktijk (Zwolle, 1986) in *Tijdschrift voor Bestuurswetenschappen en Publiekrecht*, 1988, 168.
- P. LAMBERT, La Convention européenne des droits de l'homme dans la jurisprudence belge (Brussels, 1987), in *Tijdschrift voor Privaatrecht*, 1988, 1063–1064.
- J. VAN DEN BROECK, De rechten van de mens omstreeks 1789 in de Oostenrijkse Nederlanden Antwerpen, 1986), in *Tijdschrift voor Privaatrecht*, 1988, 1067–1069.
- B.W.N. de WAARD, Beginselen van behoorlijke rechtspleging, met name in het administratief procesrecht (Zwolle, 1987), in *Tijdschrift voor Bestuurswetenschappen en Publiekrecht*, 1989, 135.
- A.F.M. BRENNINKMEIJER, De toegang tot de rechter. Een onderzoek naar de betekenis van onafhankelijke rechtspraak in een democratische rechtsstaat (Zwolle, 1987), in *Tijdschrift voor Bestuurswetenschappen en Publiekrecht*, 1989, 201–202.
- L. GOFFIN, Convention européenne des droits de l'homme, in Formulaire analytique de procédure, Fascicules A-K-1 en A-K-2, losbl. (Paris, 1988), in *Rechtskundig Weekblad*, 1989–90, 29.
- R. ERGEC, Les droits de l'homme à l'épreuve des circonstances exceptionnelles. Etude sur l'article 15 de la Convention européenne des droits de l'homme, Coll. dr. int., vol. 19 (Brussels, 1987), in *Rechtskundig Weekblad*, 1989–90, 270–271.
- M.C. BURKENS, Algemene leerstukken van grondrechten naar Nederlands constitutioneel recht, Handboeken staats- en bestuursrecht, II (Zwolle, 1989), in *Tijdschrift voor Bestuurswetenschappen en Publiekrecht*, 1990, 533–534.
- M. BOES, Administratieve sancties en art. 6 EVRM in België, en A.W.M. BIJLOOS, Administratieve boeten en art. 6 EVRM in Nederland,

Preadviezen voor de Vereniging voor de vergelijkende studie van het recht van België en Nederland (Zwolle, 1989), in *Rechtskundig Weekblad*, 1990–91, 1416–1417.

- Lelio Basso International Foundation for the Rights and Liberation of Peoples (ed.), Theory and practice of liberation at the end of the XXth century (Brussels, 1988), *Rechtskundig Weekblad*, 1990–91, 1417.
- G.J.M. VAN WISSEN, Grondrechten, Studiepockets staats- en bestuursrecht, no. 12 (Zwolle, 1989), *Tijdschrift voor Bestuurswetenschappen en Publiekrecht*, 1991, 496.

9. REPORTS AND OPINIONS IN COURTS AND FOR PUBLIC AUTHORITIES

a. Published reports as auditor in the Council of State

- Verslag voor R.v.St., 5 juni 1986, Janssens, nr. 26.611, *Tijdschrift voor Aannemingsrecht*, 1991, 229–234 (inrichting van ontwerp-gewestplannen en gewestplannen).
- Verslag voor R.v.St., 12 juni 1986, Koninklijke Federatie der Zelfstandige Landmeters-Experts, nr. 26.640, *Rechtskundig Weekblad*, 1986–87, 653–664 (bindende kracht omzendbrief).
- Verslag voor R.v.St., 13 oktober 1987, Kamer van de Raadgevende Ingenieurs van België, nr. 28.581, *Tijdschrift voor Aannemingsrecht*, 1988, 341–353 (reglement van beroepsplichten architecten).
- Verslag voor R.v.St., 26 april 1990, Vancoillie, nr. 34.816, *Rechtskundig Weekblad*, 1990–91, 1056–1060 (benoeming hoofdgriffier).
- Verslag en advies voor R.v.St., 31 oktober 1991, De Moor, nr. 38.014, *Rechtskundig Weekblad*, 1991–92, 638–650 (mogelijkheid van beroep tegen handeling van Orde van advocaten).

b. Opinions for Parliament

- & Arne VANDAELE, advies over de herziening van titel II van de Grondwet, om nieuwe bepalingen in te voegen die de bescherming van de rechten van het kind op morele, lichamelijke, geestelijke en seksuele integriteit verzekeren, *Parl. St.*, Senaat, 1999–2000, no. 2–21/4, pp. 59–69.
- Advies over de herziening van titel II van de Grondwet, om een nieuw artikel in te voegen betreffende het recht op gelijkheid van vrouwen en mannen, *Parl. St.*, Senaat, 2000–01, no. 2–465/4, pp. 19–43.
- & Wouter VANDENHOLE, advies over een wetsvoorstel tot wijziging van het Wetboek van strafvordering, wat de herziening van de veroordeling in strafzaken betreft, en tot wijziging van het Gerechtelijk Wetboek, wat de

herroeping van het gewijsde betreft, *Parl. St.*, Kamer, 2001–02, no. 50-1083/8, pp. 6–20 en 92–93.

-   Advies over de invoeging van een artikel in de Grondwet, met het oog op de afschaffing van de doodstraf, *Parl. St.*, Kamer, 2003–04, no. 51-226/6, pp. 33–40.
-   & Fiona ANG, adviezen over de herziening van artikel 22*bis* van de Grondwet, teneinde een lid toe te voegen betreffende de bescherming van aanvullende rechten van het kind, *Parl. St.*, Senaat, 2004–05, no. 3-265/3, pp. 33–44, 55–58, 59–61, en 70–72 (voetnoten).

c. Opinions for the "European Commission for Democracy through Law" ("Venice Commission")

-   & Stephan GASS, *Expert opinion on the Law of Ukraine No. 2453-VI on the Judiciary and the Status of Judges*, 2010 (DGHL(2010)18) (www.venice.coe.int/files/DGHL(2010)018-e.doc) (access 30.8.19).
-   & Stephan GASS, *Expert opinion on the draft Law of Ukraine amending the Law on the Judiciary and the Status of Judges*, 2011 (DGHL(2011)14).

INTRODUCTION

In Search of a Human Rights Lens for Modern Times

Stephan PARMENTIER
Professor of Criminology and Human Rights, KU Leuven

Koen LEMMENS
Professor of Human Rights, KU Leuven

Louise REYNTJENS
Ph.D. Researcher in Human Rights, KU Leuven

HUMAN RIGHTS ARE CELEBRATED ALL OVER THE WORLD

In the past year, and particularly since the fall of 2018, human rights have been figuring high on several national and international agendas, for a variety of reasons.

First of all, a long list of events has taken place around the world to celebrate the achievements of human rights in the last decades. In December 2018, the Universal Declaration of Human Rights (UDHR) turned 70. The product of years of intense discussions and negotiations with representatives from all corners of the globe, it was accepted on 10 December 1948 by the General Assembly of the United Nations convening in Paris, to become the "international Magna Carta for all men everywhere", in the words of Eleanor Roosevelt.[1] While the UDHR is widely celebrated every year, 1948 also witnessed the adoption of two other important human rights instruments that have attracted far less attention ever since. One is the American Declaration of the Rights and Duties of Man, adopted in Bogotá six months prior to the UDHR, in May 1948, by the newly established Organisation of American States. Interestingly, it contains a catalogue of both rights and duties, since the Preamble states that "rights and duties are interrelated

---

[1]   Https://www.humanrights.com/voices-for-human-rights/eleanor-roosevelt.html.

in every social and political activity of man". And just the day before 10 December 1948, the same UN General Assembly adopted the Convention for the Prevention and Punishment of the Crime of Genocide, the first legally binding human rights instrument related to this "crime of crimes", in the words of Winston Churchill.

Although the UDHR is a non-binding instrument in strictly legal terms, its direct and long-lasting influence on the production of additional human rights norms and standards in the context of the United Nations cannot be overestimated.[2] In the following two decades since 1948, the two basic UN conventions (on civil and political rights, and on economic, social and cultural rights) were elaborated and became binding upon the dozens of state parties ratifying them. And mostly since the late 1970s several additional conventions were drafted for the protection of specific categories of people (women, migrants, disappeared) and against specific practices (torture). A variety of procedures – reporting, complaint, investigative – ensures that human rights are being closely monitored in a variety of settings, and blatant transgressions are being denounced. The most successful universal human treaty is without any doubt the International Convention on the Rights of the Child, adopted just two weeks after the fall of the Berlin Wall, in November 1989, and quickly securing nearly universal ratification (with the notable exception until today of the United States of America). Since 1993, the High Commissioner for Human Rights coordinates the extensive human rights framework, and the related activities, of the United Nations.

Parallel to these worldwide celebrations of the last months, also regional organisations found reasons to engage in human rights celebrations. In May 2019, the Council of Europe celebrated its establishment seven decades earlier, as one of the leading regional organisations for human rights, democracy, and the rule of law.[3] Originally an organisation of mostly Western European states, it played a major role in the integration of the Central and Eastern European member states after the end of the cold war. And May 2020 will see the 70th anniversary of the European Convention of Human Rights, the first binding regional human rights treaty for all member states of the Council of Europe, particularly through the important work of the current permanent European Court of Human Rights. Its counterparts in other continents are much younger, the Inter-American Court of Human Rights being established in 1978 and the African Court of Human and Peoples' Rights in 2004. Despite their limited existence and practice, also their case-law has come to exert a profound influence on the legal orders of the state parties.

Besides incorporating international human rights norms and standards in their domestic legal orders, many countries have also expanded the scope of human

[2]   Https://www.ohchr.org/EN/pages/home.aspx.
[3]   Https://www.coe.int/en/web/portal.

rights. These days, nearly 80 countries from across the globe have set up national human rights institutions that both sensitise about human rights in society and monitor human rights compliance by state and non-state actors. Interesting enough, Belgium was one of the last countries in Europe to set up an overarching National Human Rights Institution, in April 2019, although several institutions already for some time looked into specific areas of fundamental rights (like discrimination, gender equality, poverty, privacy, etc.).

Perhaps the strongest indicator of the importance of human rights lies with non-state actors, who have embraced the human rights discourse, the procedures and institutions, both at national and international levels. Whether small action groups or large international non-governmental organisations, whether working with professionals or volunteers, many NGOs focus on human rights from a legal, political, social, cultural and religious point of view. In recent years, also the business sector is slowly but gradually exploring the field of human rights, most often under the heading of 'corporate social responsibility'. This is not to forget the crucial role of educational institutions, like schools, universities and other places of learning, where human rights belong to the standard curriculum since many years.

The rapid proliferation of human rights in the last decades form a strong illustration of the famous statement by American scholar Louis Henkin already back in 1990 – 30 years ago – that "human rights are the paradigm of our time". In his view, the norms, standards and practices that are grounded in human rights have replaced their counterparts based on religion, socialism and other grand paradigms of modernity.[4] This unprecedented breakthrough of international human rights spans Paul's personal life. He belongs to the generation that witnessed these important evolutions from the first row.

HUMAN RIGHTS ARE CHALLENGED ON VARIOUS GROUNDS

The above overview should not lead to the conclusion that human rights are undisputed, neither in their globality nor in their specific forms, quite on the contrary. The following examples illustrate that human rights are also challenged from various sides and perspectives.

Some critiques come from 'within' the field of human rights, and are often voiced by persons and organisations with a critical human rights orientation themselves. International courts are sometimes criticized for being too

---

[4]   L. Henkin, *The Age of Rights*, New York, Columbia University Press, 1990.

'internationalist' and leaving too little freedom to the state parties that have ratified the international treaties. E.g. the European Court of Human Rights is sometimes said to be too directive towards state parties and leaving too little space for the national 'margin of appreciation', while at the same time the Court is also accused of referring too easily to this margin in order not to seriously question some state parties' practices.[5] In other cases, the Inter-American Court of Human Rights is under scrutiny for being too 'activist' against the state parties on behalf of the victims of human rights violations, particularly in its judgments on victim reparations. Furthermore, an increasing number of critical questions is being asked about the quasi-exclusive focus on the aspect of 'rights', without an equally strong emphasis on the aspect of 'duties' of individuals and groups.[6] In such conception, rights and duties are deemed two sides of the same coin and inextricably linked in modern-day societies. Others criticize human rights for having become "a professional business" for too many persons and organisations, policy-makers, activists, and academics.[7] As a result, they argue, the highly abstract reasoning and technical language create an ever larger gap between professionals and common people.

Another set of critiques has its origins outside of the regular human rights circles, and relate to broad societal developments that may curtail the traditional application of human rights, and also block any further expansion. In the aftermath of the substantial migration flows into Europe of 2015, some think that large groups of migrants (including refugees) should not enjoy the same level of protection as other citizens, with a view to safeguard the social and political structures of the host societies. Others argue that certain categories of suspects and convicts of 'heinous crimes' – like terrorism and sexual delinquency – should not benefit from the same procedural and substantive rights as suspects and convicts of more 'ordinary' crimes. Even further, the worldwide fight against terrorism sometimes requires that rights be limited in scope, space or time, e.g. the right to fair trial, the right to free movement, etc. Likewise, new technologies in communication and artificial intelligence, can be seen as all-encompassing and therefore allowed to invade the privacy of citizens. In these situations, human rights standards and procedures become subjected to the need for security. Other situations relate to cultural and religious diversity, and even 'superdiversity', in

---

5   P. Popelier, S. Lambrecht and K. Lemmens, *Criticism of the European Court of Human Rights. Shifting the Convention System: Counter-Dynamics at the National and EU Level*, Cambridge/ Antwerp, Intersentia Publishers, 2016.

6   S. Parmentier, H. Werdmölder and M. Merrigan, *Between Rights and Responsibilities: A Fundamental Debate*, Cambridge/Antwerp, Intersentia Publishers, 2016.

7   J. Froestad and C. Shearing, The Zwelethemba Model: Practicing Human Rights Through Dispute Resolution, in S. Parmentier and E. Weitekamp (eds), *Crime and Human Rights*, Series in Sociology of Crime, Law and Deviance, vol. 9, Amsterdam/Oxford, Elsevier/JAI Press, 2007, p. 193–214.

modern societies, which may result in the belief that all attitudes and practices are equal, even those that may limit the rights and freedoms of certain groups. This argument is grounded in the cultural relativist critiques on human rights. Finally, also discourses of globalization and economic development may create tensions for human rights, particularly when economic and social rights are under pressure from the strong commercial actors that operate on a worldwide scale.

In her recent and again seminal book on human rights, Kathryn Sikkink discusses two fundamental critiques on human rights that seem to encompass the above criticisms, particularly in the United States.[8] The first relates to the legitimacy of human rights law, institutions and movements, in the sense of being "desirable, appropriate, and authentic". Human rights critics have cast serious doubts about each of these aspects. Some portray them as 'foreign' or 'western', others as 'liberal' or 'capitalist'. Some, like Kennedy fights the 'over-virtuous' nature of human rights and the idolatry of its followers. Others, like Hopgood (*The Endtimes of Human Rights*), argue that they are irrelevant outside of the specialized circles in middle-class enclaves like Geneva, London, and New York. The second critique addresses the effectiveness of human rights law, institutions and movements, and questions "whether human rights work produces positive change in the world". Critics like Posner (*The Twilight of Human Rights Law*) argue that governments commit themselves to new laws and regulations but allow human rights violations to persist, even to increase, in practice. Moyn for his part (*Not Enough. Human Rights in an Unequal World*) stated multiple times that human rights cannot survive unless they start focusing on the broader agenda of social and economic justice, to overcome the fundamentalism of the market and the global economy. And certain human rights activists around the world start doubting about the effects of human rights on the ground. According to Sikkink, both types of critiques can be voiced by a variety of actors, including governments with a poor human rights record, the general public, academics from various viewpoints, and also human rights activists. She counter-argues that the critics remain very ambiguous – explicitly or implicitly – about their points of reference, namely "compared to what" human rights would lack legitimacy and/or effectiveness. In her view, the point of reference lies in the Senian 'optimum approach', namely to study the best alternatives in the realm of the possible, not in the realm of the ideal. As a result, her highly sophisticated quest, based on a candid social science epistemology, to study legitimacy and effectiveness issues creates very convincing insights into the current state of human rights today. She concludes that there is "evidence for hope" that human rights can "work", provided the field can be taken to the next level of scientific scrutiny and policy, which requires a novel and interdisciplinary approach.

---

8   K. Sikkink, *Evidence for Hope. Making Human Rights Work in the 21st Century*, Princeton, Princeton University Press, 2017, particularly p. 3–21.

A BOOK BY FRIENDS AND DISCIPLES OF PAUL LEMMENS

The above overview clearly illustrates that human rights have acquired a very central place in many debates and policy fields, national and international, as well as in the legal systems of states and international organisations. At the very heart lies the idea that human beings all belong to humanity and share a fundamental 'human dignity'[9], which implies that all should be treated in a human way and in the presence of a 'human touch'.

These values in particular underpin the philosophy and conduct of the person of Paul Lemmens, to whom this volume is dedicated. In the past two years, many colleagues, disciples and friends of his expressed their keen interest and great enthusiasm to contribute to this book and pay tribute to the life and work of Paul Lemmens on the occasion of his retirement as a professor of human rights law from the University of Leuven. All contributions have the objective to contribute to a scientific debate, and have thus undergone a thorough peer review by the editors before being accepted for publication.

It would be overly ambitious to try to address all aspects of human rights raised above, related to the major themes of legitimacy and effectiveness, through both time and space. No single volume could even hope to come close to this. The editors of this book had a more modest objective in mind, namely to sketch some important debates around human rights in Europe, partly inspired by and with ramifications to other parts of the world. In this way, these debates reflect the multiple personality of Paul Lemmens, who was and still is strongly rooted in European academia and practice, but has always possessed a very open mind for other parts of the world, mostly in the Americas and Africa. His rich experience constituted the basic source of inspiration for the editors to subdivide this volume into four parts, followed by an epilogue.

I.   THE PERSON OF PAUL LEMMENS

In the first part, the person of Paul Lemmens, his vision of human rights and his work as a scholar, an attorney, and a judge, are central. The first two pieces take the angle of the concurring and dissenting opinions of Judge Lemmens at the European Court of Human Rights (ECtHR). From the analysis by Doug Cassel of several major cases of the ECtHR, Judge Lemmens emerges as a very meticulous lawyer and a very balanced judge. The same assessment results from

---

[9]   See the contribution by Frédéric Vanneste in this volume.

the second discussion of some separate opinions by Judge Lemmens, carried out by Wouter Vandenhole through the lens of the notions of vulnerability and autonomy. Then follows a lengthy piece on the life and work of Thomas More, a lawyer, politician and scholar in 16th century England, whose 'Utopia' might be seen as a quest for the sources of human rights. Ludovic De Gryse argues that both More and Lemmens emerge as 'men for all seasons' and constitute, each in their own right, sources of trust and inspiration for many colleagues and friends. The first part concludes with the account by Egbert Myjer and Peter Kempees on the origins and developments of human rights in Europe and the world. Their specific format, in the form of a story told to the grandchildren of Paul Lemmens, adds a very personal touch to the analysis.

II. HUMAN RIGHTS IN THE WORLD: FROM THE NATIONAL TO THE GLOBAL

The second part is devoted to the grand narrative of human rights in various parts of the world, and at various levels. A wide number of authors, from Belgium and abroad, focus on the interrelationships between the domestic systems of human rights protection and the international ones. Jean Spreutels en Sylviane Vélu start this part by providing an overview of the legal analysis and the case-law of the Belgian Constitutional Court in cases of terrorism, which constitutes a global challenge. André Alen and Willem Verrijdt study the prerequisites for a judicial dialogue between the European Court of Human Rights on the one hand, and the Belgian Constitutional Court on the other hand, as a form of conflict resolution in a context of constitutional pluralism. Sébastien Van Drooghenbroeck addresses the protection of human rights, and the prevention of human rights violations, at the national level by looking at the supervisory functions of the Belgian Council of State over the legislative power, as sources of inspiration for the European Court of Human Rights. Marc Bossuyt exposes the case of Father Ryan, an Irish asylum seeker to Belgium in 1988, to argue that the protection of human rights is also a task for independent administrative authorities like the Commissioner General for Refugees. In his ('tongue-in-cheek') piece for Paul Lemmens, Koen Lemmens gives an overview of the case-law of the European Court of Human Rights in relation to the right to a name, and the impact on Belgian legislation of the last years. Siofra O'Leary in her contribution provides a comparative view about the strategies and instruments for the surveillance of the masses in Europe through the case-law of the ECtHR and the European Court of Justice (ECJ). The bodies of human rights case-law of the same courts are compared by Eva Brems and Jogchum Vrielink, in their chapter focusing on the wearing of religious symbols or dress in specific contexts. Another topic of comparison between the two courts lies in the troublesome issue of child abduction against the general values of child welfare and protection, as Koen Lenaerts amply explains. Manfred Nowak from his side focuses on another aspect of private and family life, namely the right to same-sex marriages, through the case-law of several international courts as compared to that of national courts. Marek Nowicki, Christine Chinkin and Françoise Tulkens present the Human Rights Advisory Panel of the United Nations Interim Administration in Kosovo (UNMIK), specifically in the case of polluted water wells as a form of human rights violation. Jan Wouters and Evelien Wauters sketch the origins and the main characteristics of the United Nations Compact on Migration, a non-binding agreement that provoked the fall of the Belgian central government in December 2018, less than six months before federal and regional elections were to be held. Finally, Joaquin González Ibáñez provides us with an overview of the divergent approaches between the United States and Europe when it comes to the fight against terrorism, with a specific focus on the place of human rights and the values that underpin them.

III. HUMAN RIGHTS IN THE COUNCIL OF EUROPE AND THE EUROPEAN CONVENTION ON HUMAN RIGHTS

The third part of this book focuses specifically on human rights in the work of the Council of Europe, and its 'jewel in the crown', the European Convention on Human Rights (ECHR). Its starts with two more general pieces. Andrew Drzemczewski highlights the reasons for and the specificities of the absence – for many years – of Russian parliamentarians in the Parliamentary Assembly of the Council of Europe. Mark Villiger gives a detailed overview of the Research Division of the ECtHR and its relevance and impact on the Court's case-law. Françoise Elens-Passos brings to life a largely unknown aspect of the ECtHR's procedure, namely the amicable settlements that are quite often concluded between the applicant(s) and the state(s). Several contributions then focus on the famous Article 6 of the ECHR, which has constituted a central piece of Paul Lemmens's scholarly interest, as well as a prominent feature of his work as an attorney and a judge. Georges Ravarani tackles the traditional core problem in the extensive case-law of the ECtHR on how to interpret the notion of 'civil rights' as contained in Article 6 of the ECHR, and he proposes a 'magic formula'. Dean Spielmann in his part analyses the provisions of 'fair trial', and its counterpart the 'denial of justice', as these notions emerge through the case-law of the ECtHR. Robert Spano deals with another interesting aspect of Article 6, namely the level at which the ECtHR exercises its supervisory function over domestic courts in their interpretations of domestic procedural rules. In this part of the book, also other Convention articles and issues come to the fore. Egidijus Kūris discusses the less known Article 18 and the case-law of the ECtHR in relation to the restrictions of human rights allowed under the ECHR, from the perspective of counteracting the 'hidden agenda' of national governments. Janneke Gerards addresses one core element of the Europe-wide protection of human rights, namely how to ensure a level of uniformity of human rights protection in Europe through the case-law of the ECtHR. Isabelle Niedlispacher deals with the same topic, but from another angle, namely to understand the interpretation of the ECtHR in relation to the margin of appreciation of the national authorities. The contribution by Jenny Goldschmidt focuses on the relationship between two different human rights regimes, as she looks at the implementation of the United Nations Convention on the Rights of Persons with Disabilities (CRPD) in the case-law of the ECtHR. This part is concluded by Charline Daelman with a chapter on the potential existence of a judicial dialogue between the ECtHR and international investment law and arbitration, and the characteristics of such relationship.

IV. HUMAN RIGHTS AND SOCIETAL TRANSFORMATIONS

In the fourth and final part, a number of contributions discuss the relationship between human rights and the wider society, and particularly some highly important recent societal transformations. Jos Silvis analyses the viewpoints of the ECtHR, as grounded in the ECHR, when it comes to the very concept of terrorism in today's world. Nathalie Van Leuven addresses the rapidly changing right of privacy in modern-day societies through the lens of both Belgian legislation and the case-law of the ECtHR. Michaël Merrigan highlights a topic that received little attention thus far, namely the place of duties and responsibilities under the ECHR, and examines its link with the rise of illiberal democracies. Gerhard van der Schyff and Stefan Sottiaux take the recent discussions about the ritual slaughter of animals in Belgium as their starting point for an analysis about fundamental rights in the multi-level governance structure of the country. The complex concept of human dignity is central to the contribution of Frédéric Vanneste, who analyses both its philosophical and legal dimensions from a concrete – not an abstract – point of view. And last, but certainly not least, Marie-Claire Foblets and Jan Velaers write about the responsibility – from a human rights perspective – for religious diversity in Europe as a complementary arrangement that requires the cooperation among courts, parliaments and society.

EPILOGUE

This book brings together a rich collection of essays and reflections about many different aspects of human rights, from perspectives as diverse as law, politics and society. Yet, it is concluded on a non-scientific note, through an epilogue by Anne Dewaele, the spouse of Paul Lemmens for many decades. Under the general title of creating an 'ensemble' with Paul as a husband, a family man, a friend, a colleague, and a rich human being, she adds a very personal, and truly unique, dimension to this volume. Even more, without her professionalism, her enthusiasm, her care, her artistic mind and her warm personality, this volume would have looked very differently. The editors extend their eternal gratitude to Anne for this wonderful and exceptional collaboration.

Part I

The Person of Paul Lemmens:
'A Man for All Seasons'

JUDGE PAUL LEMMENS'S APPROACH TO JUDGING ON THE EUROPEAN COURT OF HUMAN RIGHTS

Douglass CASSEL
Emeritus Professor, Notre Dame Law School
Counsel, King & Spalding, New York

What kind of judge is Paul Lemmens on the European Court of Human Rights? How does he see his role? How does he carry it out?

I must disclose at the outset that I am not an entirely impartial observer (though in the analysis which follows I try to be objective). I have known Judge Lemmens for two decades as a friend and sometimes as an academic colleague. I have found him to be a consistently careful, thoughtful, meticulous, scrupulously fair-minded jurist. However, I have not had occasion until now to review his performance as a judge on the European Court of Human Rights, which he joined in September 2012. I am grateful for this opportunity.

I. A NON-SCIENTIFIC SAMPLE

To assess Judge Lemmens's record on the Court definitively, one would ideally undertake a thorough analysis of all his published opinions. That may indeed be an agenda for further research. Lacking time for such an ambitious project, I have glimpsed only an unscientific sample of 25 of his separate opinions in important and controverted cases. Just over half – thirteen – are solely his own dissenting or concurring opinions. In the other twelve he joined or was joined by other judges in separate dissents (or in one case a concurring opinion). In all 25 cases, whether dissenting or concurring, and whether in sole or joint opinions, Judge Lemmens was sufficiently motivated to express or join in expressing ideas contrary or supplementary to those of the majority opinion. Through this lens we can view at least a measure of his individuality as a judge on the European Court.

The sample is not scientific. My selection focused on cases that span his years on the court, cover a range of issues, address issues that were novel or controverted among the judges, or were of public interest as reflected in the news media or in the blogosphere. The sample includes cases from 2013 (his first full year on the Court) through 2018 (his most recent full year). Moreover, all 25 cases are important, controversial, or both. Eleven were Grand Chamber judgments, and four more were Chamber judgments later reviewed by the Grand Chamber. Grand Chamber cases are important by definition. Parties may refer a case to the Grand Chamber, the European Court's largest adjudicating body with 17 judges[1], only if it "raises a serious question affecting the interpretation or application of the Convention or the Protocols thereto, or a serious issue of general importance."[2] Very few cases pass this test. In 2017, for example, of more than one thousand judgments rendered by the European Court, only 19 were delivered by the Grand Chamber.[3]

The remaining ten judgments in the sample were rendered solely by seven-judge Chambers. Many were commented upon in the media and the blogosphere. And, whether Grand Chamber or Chamber judgments, all 25 cases were, by definition, debatable or controversial enough to divide the Court.

The 25 cases cover a range of rights and subject matters (even if not a statistically representative sample of the caseload of the Court).[4] They include cases on the rights of journalists (3 cases), deportations and expulsions on various grounds (4 cases), family matters (5 cases), environmental health (2 cases), criminal law and judicial procedure (4 cases), torture or ill treatment (2 cases), dismissal from employment (1 case), rights of disabled persons (1 case), and damages as a form of reparation (3 cases).

The 25 cases were not bunched in a handful of countries. They were distributed among 15 of the 47 member States of the Council of Europe[5] (although they do not include several European States with the most judgments in recent years).[6]

---

[1] European Convention on Human Rights (hereafter "Convention"), Article 26.1.

[2] Convention, Article 43.2. Article 30 establishes similar criteria for referrals by Chambers to the Grand Chamber.

[3] European Court of Human Rights, *Annual Report 2017*, p 155. The figures shown in the annual reports are comparable for all the years since Judge Lemmens joined the Court in 2012.

[4] The European Court reported that, of 1068 total judgments in 2017, 207 involved the right to fair trial, 182 involved inhuman and degrading treatment (often at issue in cases of deportations and expulsions), 80 involved rights to privacy and family life, 44 involved freedom of expression, 13 involved issues of torture, and one involved the right to education. *Annual Report 2017*, p 173.

[5] As shown in text below, they included Belgium (3 cases), Czech Republic, Denmark, Finland (2 cases), France, Hungary, Iceland, Italy (3 cases), Latvia, Moldova (2 cases), Spain (2 cases), Sweden, Switzerland (3 cases), Turkey (2 cases), and the United Kingdom. On the other hand, it should be noted that nine of the 25 cases concerned only three countries, each with three cases: Belgium, Italy and Switzerland. (As the Belgian judge, Judge Lemmens generally sits on all Grand Chamber cases against Belgium. Convention, art 26.4.).

[6] In 2017, four of the top five adjudged States, unintentionally not included in the sample, were Russia (305 cases), Ukraine (87 cases), Romania (69 cases) and Bulgaria (39 cases). In

II. CAPSULE SUMMARIES OF THE 25 CASES

This Part briefly summarizes the 25 cases, grouped by category and chronologically within categories. Although many may fall in more than one category, each case is listed only once for the sake of brevity.

The goal is not to engage in a substantive review of jurisprudence, or to applaud or critique decisions, but simply to seek insight into Judge Lemmens's approach to his role as a judge on the Court. Inferences gleaned from the sample are presented in Part III. Even the capsule summaries reveal factual complexity and legal difficulty, as might be expected from cases that divide the Court. The sample, then, is one where we may see Judge Lemmens at work in some of his most challenging cases.

A. RIGHTS OF JOURNALISTS

- *Haldimann v Switzerland*[7], Chamber Judgment in 2015. Journalists were criminally convicted and modestly fined for use of a hidden camera in an interview with an insurance broker, as part of their exposé of poor advice by brokers. The majority found a violation of freedom of expression (Article 10).[8] Judge Lemmens, the sole dissenter, argued that the law violated by the journalists was a generally applicable law protecting private conversations and that, in view of the "margin of appreciation,"[9] their criminal conviction was not disproportionate.
- *Pentikainen v Finland*[10], Grand Chamber Judgment in 2015. A journalist was arrested at a demonstration and subsequently convicted of the crime of contumacy toward the police, but no punishment was imposed. The majority

---

the sample, Turkey (116 cases), Italy (31 cases) and Hungary (24 cases) were among the most frequently adjudged countries. None of the other 12 countries in the sample had more than 16 judgments in 2017. *Annual Report 2017*, pp 172–73.

7   App no 21830/09, Judgment of 24 February 2015.
8   All references herein to "articles" are to articles of the Convention or, when so indicated, of its Protocols.
9   The "margin of appreciation" refers to the degree of deference given by the European Court to judgments by national authorities about permissible restrictions on rights under the European Convention on Human Rights. The "width" of the margin varies – i.e., it allows for more or less deference to judgments by national authorities – depending on such factors as the nature of the right at issue, whether there is a "European consensus," and whether the Court must balance private and public rights or competing Convention rights. See, e.g., *Handyside v UK*, App No 5493/72, Judgment of 7 December 1976, pars 48–49; *Dudgeon v. The United Kingdom*, App no 7525/76, Judgment of 22 October 1981, pars 52, 56, 59–61; *S.H. and Others v Austria*, App no 57813/00, Judgment of 3 November 2011 (Grand Chamber), par 94. For Judge Lemmens's views on the margin of appreciation, see Part III.F below.
10 App no 11882/10, Judgment of 20 October 2015.

found no violation of the Convention. Judge Lemmens and two other judges joined in a dissent authored by Judge Spano, which found a violation of freedom of expression (Article 10.2).

– *Einarsson v Iceland*[11], Chamber Judgment in 2017. In an exchange of invective, an outspoken journalist was the subject of an Instagram bearing his image with the caption, "Fuck you rapist bastard." Treating these words as a value judgment, rather than a statement of fact, the national courts declined to hold their author liable for defamation of the journalist. The European Court majority found a violation of the right to respect for the journalist's private life (Article 8). Judge Lemmens, the sole dissenter, argued that the national court, in treating the statement as a value judgment, acted within its margin of appreciation and achieved a fair balance between the privacy rights of the journalist and the expressive rights of the author.

B. DEPORTATIONS AND EXPULSIONS

– *F.G. v Sweden*[12], Chamber Judgment in 2014. Sweden proposed to deport a Muslim convert to Christianity to Iran, where such conversion is punishable by death and Christians are persecuted. A four-judge Chamber majority found no violations of the right to life (Article 2) or the rights to be free of inhuman or degrading treatment (Article 3). Judge Lemmens was among three judges in a Joint Dissenting Opinion, arguing that there had not been a serious assessment of the risk to the applicant if he were to be deported, and that the argument that Iran was not aware of his religious conversion was "dangerous." The case was referred to the Grand Chamber, which in 2016 unanimously ruled that deporting the applicant to Iran without an assessment of the consequences of his conversion would constitute a violation of Articles 2 and 3.[13]

– *Tatar v Switzerland*[14], Chamber Judgment in 2015. Switzerland proposed to deport a Turkish citizen suffering from severe schizophrenia, and who had murdered his wife, to Turkey. The majority found no real risk of inhuman treatment in Turkey, and hence no violation of Article 3, because proper treatment was available in Turkey. Judge Lemmens, the lone dissenter, argued that the applicant was so ill that it was "somewhat probable" that he would not obtain treatment on his own, and there was no indication that anyone in Turkey would assure that he obtained treatment.

– *V.M. v Belgium*[15], Grand Chamber Judgment in 2016. A Roma family from Serbia who sought asylum in Belgium alleged that they had not been given

---

[11]   App no 24703/15, Judgment of 7 November 2017.
[12]   App no 43611/11, Judgment of 16 January 2014.
[13]   App no 43611/11, Judgment of 23 March 2016.
[14]   App no 65692/12, Judgment of 14 April 2015.
[15]   App no 60125/11, Judgment of 27 November 2016.

accommodations in Belgium and had to return to Serbia, where one of their daughters died and the family suffered persecution. While the case was pending before the Grand Chamber, their attorney lost contact with them and the majority therefore struck the case off the list. Judge Lemmens and two other judges joined the dissent by Judge Ranzoni, arguing that the Grand Chamber should nonetheless have ruled on the case in order to clarify the situations when asylum seekers should be considered especially vulnerable, thus requiring greater attention by the State, and also to clarify the remedies that should be made available to them. In the earlier Chamber decision[16], Judge Lemmens had joined the majority in finding inhuman treatment and a lack of adequate remedies for the family in Belgium (violations of Article 3 and Article 13 in connection with Article 3).

– *Paposhvili v Belgium*[17], Grand Chamber Judgment in 2016. Belgium proposed to deport an armed robber suffering from cancer to his native Georgia. (The applicant died while his case was before the Grand Chamber, but his family continued the case.) The Grand Chamber ruled unanimously that applicant's deportation without an assessment of treatment availability in Georgia and of the impact of deportation on his health would have violated his right to be free of inhuman treatment (Article 3) and respect for his family life (Article 8). Judge Lemmens issued a concurring opinion in which he explained that he had changed his vote from the earlier Chamber decision[18], because the Grand Chamber opinion effected an evolution in the European Court's jurisprudence, which "may be seen as the Court's response to the concerns" of Belgian courts, namely that deportations of seriously ill persons pose a risk of inhuman or degrading "if no appropriate treatment exists in the receiving country."

C. FAMILY MATTERS

– *Raw v France*[19], Chamber Judgment in 2013. Despite their obligations under the Hague Convention on the Civil Aspects of International Child Abduction, French authorities did not do all they could have to bring about the return of children of a French father to their English mother. The children had protested vociferously that they wished to remain with their father. The Chamber majority found a violation of respect for family life (Article 8). Judge Lemmens, the lone dissenter, argued that French authorities, in the difficult circumstances they faced, acted within their margin of appreciation.

---

[16] App no 60125/11, Judgment of 7 July 2015.
[17] App no 41738/10, Judgment of 13 December 2016.
[18] App no 41738/10, Judgment of 17 April 2014.
[19] App no 10131/11, Judgment of 7 March 2013.

- *Hamalainen v Finland*[20], Grand Chamber Judgment in 2014. When a transsexual husband had a sex change operation, Finnish authorities refused to register her as a woman, eligible to transform her marriage into a same-sex registered partnership, because her spouse had not consented. (Both spouses had religious objections to dissolving their marriage.) The majority found no right to same-sex marriage and hence no violation of family rights under Article 8 or the right to marry under Article 12. Judge Lemmens joined two other judges in dissent, arguing that there was a violation of Article 8 and that the majority, having found no violation of Article 8, should have considered whether Article 12 protects the right, not only to marry, but also to remain married, as well as whether there was discrimination on the basis of gender identity under Article 14.

- *Dubska v Czech Republic*[21], Chamber Judgment in 2014. Czech law allows home births but prohibits midwives from attending at home births. The majority found no violation of the right to private life under Article 8. Judge Lemmens, the lone dissenter, argued that the public health argument was overstated and that the law seemed to reflect a "power struggle between doctors and midwives." The case was later reviewed by the Grand Chamber, which ruled by a 12–5 vote in 2016 that there was no violation.[22]

- *Paradiso v Italy*[23], Grand Chamber Judgment in 2017. An Italian couple had a child through a surrogate mother in Russia. On their return to Italy, it was discovered that the husband was not the biological father. They were prosecuted for violating adoption laws, and the child was taken from them and placed with an adoptive family. The majority found no violation of the right to family life under Article 8, because the child and the couple did not constitute a "family." Judge Lemmens was one of five dissenters arguing in a joint opinion that *de facto* families can be families, and that " 'family life' is essentially a question of fact depending upon the real existence in practice of close personal ties."

- *R.L. v Denmark*[24], Chamber Judgment in 2017. National courts refused to reopen paternity proceedings, even though a deceived husband proved not to be the biological father of the children of a married couple. The national courts noted that he continued to treat the children as his own for some years, and that finding the real father might not be possible. By five votes to two, the Chamber majority found that the national courts acted within their margin of appreciation, and there was no violation of privacy and family rights under Article 8. In a separate concurring opinion, Judge Lemmens expressed his "considerable hesitation" because of "troubling elements."

---

20 App no 37359/09, Judgment of 16 July 2014.
21 App nos 28859/11 and 28473/12, Judgment of 11 December 2014.
22 App nos 28859/11 and 28473/12, Judgment of 15 November 2016.
23 App no 25358/12, Judgment of 24 January 2017.
24 App no 52629/11, Judgment of 7 March 2017.

Had he been a national judge, he "might very well" have reopened paternity, but as a European judge he recognized that different views are "reasonably possible."

D.   ENVIRONMENTAL HEALTH

- *Otgon v Moldova*[25], Chamber Judgment in 2016. Applicant and her daughter fell ill after drinking tap water and were hospitalized for about two weeks. Moldovan courts awarded them damages, but "considerably below the minimum" awarded by the European court in similar cases against Moldova. The majority found a violation of the right to private life under Article 8. Judge Lemmens was the sole dissenter. Except for the period of hospitalization, he saw no effect on applicant's private life. The case had thus been improperly "upgraded" from an ordinary torts case to an Article 8 case.
- *Bursa v Turkey*[26], Chamber Judgment in 2018. The Chamber found a violation of fair trial rights under Article 6.1, because of the failure to enforce judicial rulings setting aside an administrative authorization to build a starch factory on farmland. In a concurring and dissenting opinion, Judge Lemmens agreed, but added that the Court should also have examined the impact of the factory on the right to life under Article 2 and the rights to private and family life under Article 8.

E.   CRIMINAL LAW AND JUDICIAL PROCEDURE

- *Avotins v Latvia*[27], Grand Chamber Judgment in 2016. In view of the mutual recognition provisions of the Brussels I Regulation of the European Union, the majority found no violation of the right to fair trial under Article 6, when a Latvian court enforced a Cypriot court judgment against the applicant. Judge Lemmens and one other judge joined in a concurring opinion reaching the same result, but under a different reading of the application of the EU regulation.
- *Pascari v Moldova*[28], Chamber Judgment in 2016. The majority found a violation of the right to fair trial under Article 6.1 where the national court, in a case against another defendant in which applicant was not a party, ruled that applicant was responsible for a traffic violation. A police official then declared the applicant responsible, but imposed no sanction because

---

[25]   App no 22743/07, Judgment of 25 October 2016.
[26]   App no 25680/05, Judgment of 19 June 2018.
[27]   App no 17502/07, Judgment of 23 May 2016.
[28]   App no 25555/10, Judgment of 30 August 2016.

prosecution was now time-barred. Judge Lemmens joined in a dissent with two other judges, arguing that, because the applicant had not been tried, there could be no violation of his right to a fair trial. Although there might have been an issue as to whether the national court violated his presumption of innocence, applicant had not raised that claim.

- *Ibrahim v UK*[29], Grand Chamber Judgment in 2016. After unsuccessful attempts to bomb London subways and a bus, two weeks after an earlier terrorist attack that left 52 people dead and hundreds injured, three Somali nationals were convicted of conspiracy to murder, and a British citizen of Somali origin was convicted of assisting one of the bombers and failing to disclose information after the event. The three Somalis claimed a violation of the right to fair trial under Article 6, because their access to a lawyer during interrogation by police had been delayed, and the statements they gave without legal counsel were admitted into evidence at trial. The Grand Chamber found no violation because the trial viewed in its entirety was fair. However, a majority ruled that the failure to caution and provide a lawyer to the British citizen, once it became clear that he was not only a witness but also a suspect, irretrievably prejudiced the overall fairness of his trial. In a joint dissent with regard to the British citizen, six judges including Judge Lemmens argued that there were compelling reasons of public safety to delay his cautioning and access to a lawyer. They stressed that he had never challenged the truth of his statement. In their view the majority had failed to "identify the appropriate relationship between the fundamental procedural right to a fair trial of persons charged with involvement in terrorist-type offences and the right to life and bodily security of the persons affected …"[30]

- *G.I.E.M. v Italy*[31], Grand Chamber Judgment in 2018. Land was confiscated because of allegedly unlawful site development, even though the developers had not been convicted of a crime. The Grand Chamber unanimously found a violation of their right to property under Article 1 of Protocol 1 to the Convention and, by 15–2, a violation of Article 7 of the Convention (no punishment without law) because a criminal sanction was imposed without a criminal conviction. Judge Lemmens joined one other judge in a separate opinion, concurring in the violation of the right to property, but dissenting on the violation of Article 7, because the purpose of the confiscation was not punishment, but restoration of the ordinary purpose of the land and reparation. In their view the majority decision undermined environmental protection in Italy.

---

[29] App nos 50541/08 et al, Judgment of 13 September 2016.

[30] Judge Lemmens also issued a separate, partly dissenting opinion, in which he clarified that, because he found no violation of the rights of the British citizen, he also voted against awarding him costs and expenses.

[31] App nos 1828/06 et al, Judgment of 28 June 2018.

F. TORTURE OR ILL TREATMENT

- *Bouyid v Belgium*[32], Grand Chamber Judgment in 2015. On two occasions, exasperated police officers slapped young men across the face while they were in custody. A 14–3 majority of the Grand Chamber ruled that the slaps amounted to "degrading" treatment in violation of Article 3. Judge Lemmens joined two other judges in a dissent on this issue, arguing that there are instances of violations of human dignity that do not meet the "minimum level of severity" required to rise to the level of "degrading."
- *Nait-Liman v Switzerland*, Chamber Judgment in 2016[33], Grand Chamber Judgment in 2018.[34] By a vote of 4–3, a Chamber found that Switzerland did not violate applicant's right of access to a court under Article 6, by not permitting him to bring in Swiss courts a civil suit for damages for torture against the former Minister of the Interior of Tunisia. The former Minister had been in Switzerland for medical treatment but apparently left the country by the time suit was brought. In a lone concurring opinion, Judge Lemmens argued that neither the text of the UN Convention against Torture, nor the jurisprudence of the UN Committee against Torture, requires a State to grant victims the right to obtain reparation for torture before its courts, unless the claimant resided in the State at the time of the torture, or the perpetrator resides in the State when suit is brought. Later the Grand Chamber, by a vote of 15–2, found no violation of the right of access to a court, noting that although the UN Committee against Torture encouraged universal civil jurisdiction for torture, it did not require States to provide such jurisdiction.

G. DISMISSAL FROM EMPLOYMENT

- *Fernández Martínez v Spain*[35], Grand Chamber Judgment in 2014. A married priest who taught Catholic religion and ethics in a Spanish State-run school was not renewed in his position, after publicly disagreeing with church teaching on celibacy and advocating lay election of priests and bishops. A bare majority of the Grand Chamber held that Spain acted within its margin of appreciation in declining to renew his employment contract, and that Spain did not violate his right to private life under Article 8. Judge Lemmens joined seven other judges in dissent. Even if the priest could not be renewed as a religious teacher, they argued that he could have been considered for another teaching position. Moreover, the consequences of his non-renewal

---

[32] App no 23380/09, Judgment of 28 September 2015.
[33] App No 51357/07, Judgment of 21 June 2016.
[34] App no 51357/07, Judgment of 15 March 2018.
[35] App no 56030/07, Judgment of 12 June 2014.

were harsh, since he had to live on unemployment benefits until he eventually found a "not so attractive job" in a museum.

H.   DISABILITY RIGHTS

- *Enver Sahin v Turkey*[36], Chamber Judgment in 2018. A majority found that Turkey's refusal to make adequate accommodations for a paraplegic university student violated his right under Article 14 not to be discriminated against, in connection with his right to education under Article 2 of Protocol 1 to the European Convention. Judge Lemmens, the sole dissenter, argued that the issue was not accommodation but access, that there must be a fair balance between rights of access and community interests – in this case the cost of modifying the architecture of an existing building – and that Turkey was entitled to allow the university more time to make its buildings accessible.

I.   DAMAGES

- *Del Río Prada v Spain*[37], Grand Chamber Judgment in 2013. Changes in Spanish legislation had the effect of retroactively extending the length of a prison term for a convicted terrorist. The Grand Chamber held unanimously that her continued detention violated her right to liberty under Article 5 of the Convention, and that she should be released from detention "at the earliest possible date." It also ruled by 15–2 that Spain violated her rights under Article 7 (no punishment without law). By a vote of 10–7, it also awarded her non-pecuniary damages of 30,000 euros. Together with four other judges, Judge Lemmens observed that she had been convicted of terrorist offenses including numerous murders, and that she therefore should not be awarded non-pecuniary or moral damages.
- *Laszlo Magyar v Hungary*[38], Chamber Judgment in 2014. After prolonged proceedings, a man was convicted of three murders as well as assaults and burglaries of elderly persons and sentenced to life imprisonment without possibility of parole. The Chamber unanimously found that his sentence amounted to inhuman or degrading treatment under Article 3, and that his excessively lengthy criminal proceeding violated his right to trial within a reasonable time under Article 6. The majority awarded him 2000 euros in non-pecuniary damages. Judge Lemmens, the lone dissenter, did not consider

---

[36]   App no 23065/12, Judgment of 30 January 2018.
[37]   App no 42750/09, Judgment of 21 October 2013.
[38]   App no 73593/10, Judgment of 20 May 2014.

an award of non-pecuniary damages appropriate in light of applicant's convictions for "many serious offences."

- *Khlaifia v Italy*[39], Chamber Judgment in 2016. A Chamber held that Tunisian immigrants detained at Lampedusa during the Arab spring, and then repatriated, suffered violations of their rights to liberty under Article 5, to be free of inhuman or degrading treatment under Article 3, to a remedy under Article 13, and not to be collectively expelled under Article 4 of Protocol 4 to the European Convention. The majority awarded each of the three applicants 10,000 euros in non-pecuniary damages. Judge Lemmens, the lone partial dissenter, argued that this amount was excessive in light of the "actual situation of the victims" in Tunisia, where the cost of living (as he documented) is far lower than in Italy. The Grand Chamber later upheld only the findings of violations of the rights to liberty and to a remedy, and reduced the non-pecuniary damages award to 2,500 euros for each applicant.[40]

III. WHAT KIND OF EUROPEAN COURT JUDGE IS PAUL LEMMENS?

This sample of 25 important and controverted cases suggests noteworthy characteristics of Paul Lemmens as a judge on the European Court. Among them are the following:

A. JUDGING EACH CASE ON THE FACTS AND THE LAW

Judge Lemmens appears not to decide cases dogmatically by issue or category or based on what is "politically correct." He focuses instead on the factual and legal particularities of each case.

At the most general level, this is consistent with the fact that, of the 22 cases where his separate opinion addressed the merits (the other three opinions were on damages), his views on the contested issues were about evenly divided between arguing for or against violations of the Convention: he found violations in ten cases[41], and no violations in twelve cases.[42]

---

[39]   App no 16483/12, Judgment of 1 September 2015.

[40]   App no 16483/12, Judgment of 15 December 2016.

[41]   *Pentikainen, F.G., Tatar, V.M., Paposhvili, Hamalainen, Dubska, Paradiso, Bursa* and *Fernández Martínez*. In *V.M.* he voted for a violation in the Chamber decision and opposed the Grand Chamber's decision to strike the case from the list.

[42]   *Haldimann, Einarsson, Raw, R.L., Otgon, Avotins, Pascari, Ibrahim, G.I.E.M., Bouyid, Nait-Liman* and *Enver Sahin*.

Some categories of cases also appear to support this assessment. Judge Lemmens cares about the environment. He made this clear in *Bursa*[43], by calling for evaluation of whether placing a starch factory on farmland jeopardized the rights to life and private and family life, and in *G.I.E.M.*[44], by criticizing the majority for weakening environmental protection in Italy. But in *Otgon*[45], he did not consider that contaminated tap water, which led to a hospitalization for two weeks, rose to the level of a violation of the right to private life. Litigants contemplating environmental cases before Judge Lemmens would do well to study the factual and legal particularities of their cases.

The same is true for litigation over rights of journalists. In *Haldimann*[46] Judge Lemmens found no violation when journalists were prosecuted for use of a hidden camera in order to expose shoddy practices, and in *Einarsson*[47] he found no violation where a journalist was labeled a "rapist bastard" but could not sue for defamation. Yet in *Pentikainen*[48] he found a violation where a journalist was arrested at a demonstration and convicted, but no punishment was imposed. Judge Lemmens's views in free press cases, too, turn on the particularities of each case.

His focus on particularities also seems to immunize him from the perils of political correctness: he voted against a disabled person in *Enver Sahin*[49], against a finding of degrading police conduct in *Bouyid*[50], and an environmental claim in *Otgon*.[51]

On the other hand, one can take these levels of generality only so far. Judge Lemmens voted for violations in all four of the deportation and expulsion cases[52], and against violations in all four of the cases focused on criminal law and judicial procedure.[53]

On closer inspection, however, no tendentiousness on his part emerges in these cases. The four deportation and expulsion cases illustrate the point. In *F.G.*[54], his dissent from the Chamber judgment, in which he argued that deporting a Christian convert to Iran was dangerous, was later vindicated by a unanimous

---

43 Note 26 above.
44 Note 31 above.
45 Note 25 above.
46 Note 7 above.
47 Note 11 above.
48 Note 10 above.
49 Note 36 above.
50 Note 32 above.
51 Note 25 above.
52 *F.G.*, *Tatar*, *V.M.*, and *Paposhvili*.
53 *Avotins*, *Pascari*, *Ibrahim*, and *G.I.E.M.*
54 Note 12 above.

judgment of the Grand Chamber. Likewise in *Paposhvili*[55], he concurred in a unanimous judgment of the Grand Chamber. In *V.M.*[56], he joined other judges in dissenting only from the Grand Chamber majority's decision to strike the case off the list, after counsel lost touch with the applicant. Although he was the sole dissenter from a Chamber judgment in *Tatar*[57], his opinion was well-reasoned, and in any event one case does not a tendency make.

Nor do his opinions in the four cases on criminal law and judicial procedure display any troublesome tendency. These cases dealt with markedly diverse issues, and Judge Lemmens was not alone in dissenting in any of them.

The lesson is that assessments of his judicial opinions, like the opinions themselves, must be done carefully, case by case. While this brief space does not allow for detailed assessments, the following sections consider his assessments of facts, his sense of equity, his resistance to overreaching on rights, his embrace of the concept of "fair balance" to decide cases, and his respect as a European judge for national authorities, but without granting them *carte blanche*.

B.   FACTS

Judge Lemmens pays attention to factual detail and insists on realism. Although the following excerpt, from their opinion arguing for a violation of freedom of the press in *Pentikainen*, was written by Judge Spano and only joined by Judge Lemmens, it is a good example of the attention to detail prized by Judge Lemmens:

> "... [I]t is worth recalling the pertinent facts ... *Firstly*, ... applicant took no direct or active part in the demonstration. He was apprehended for not obeying police orders to disperse when the police decided to engage with the last remaining participants in the cordoned-off area, and not for rioting or other violent behaviour. *Secondly*, ... applicant was not readily identifiable as a journalist prior to his apprehension. *Thirdly*, ... applicant identified himself to the apprehending officer. When the police officer asked for his identification, the applicant presented his press card."[58]

Judge Lemmens also insists on realism in assessing facts. In *Tatar*, his sole dissent objected to the majority's "very theoretical assessment" that a

---

[55]   Note 17 above.
[56]   Note 15 above.
[57]   Note 12 above.
[58]   Note 10 above, Dissenting Opinion of Judge Spano, Joined by Judges Spielmann, Lemmens and Dedov, par 11.

murderous schizophrenic would somehow seek out treatment on his own if expelled to Turkey.[59] In *Dubska*, his sole dissent viewed the public health argument against midwives attending home births as overstated, and more likely reflecting a power struggle between doctors and midwives.[60] In *Paradiso*, he joined dissenters in wondering whether domestic courts were not "excessively formal" in declaring a child borne of a surrogate mother and unknown father to be "abandoned," when the child had lived with the contractual parents for eight months from the day he was born and would have remained with them if not removed by the State.[61] In *Ibrahim*, he joined a dissent arguing that the majority's demand that police immediately caution a suspected aider of terrorism and provide him a lawyer, in the midst of a terrorism crisis, was "somewhat divorced from reality" and asked of States "something approaching perfection."[62] And in *Bouyid*, he joined a dissent calling the majority's treatment of isolated incidents of police slaps of two insolent young men in custody a "clear underestimation of the various difficulties that may be encountered in real-life situations," and an "overly theoretical approach" which "risks being completely at odds with reality."[63]

C. EQUITY

Judge Lemmens also displays a strong sense of equity. His sole dissent in *Tatar* objected to the applicant's expulsion to Turkey on "compelling humanitarian grounds." In *Fernández Martínez*, where a priest's contract to teach Catholic religion was not renewed, Judge Lemmens joined other dissenters in arguing that the Spanish Ministry failed to take any alternative measure to adapt its decision

> "to the applicant's situation and the seriousness of the interference with his private and family life. As a result of the Ministry's decision, the applicant was obliged, with little notice, to give up the professional activity he had carried on for several years. He had to live on unemployment benefit and later found an apparently not so attractive job in a museum."[64]

---

59   Note 14 above, Partly Dissenting Opinion of Judge Lemmens, par 4.
60   Note 21 above, Dissenting Opinion of Judge Lemmens, par 3.
61   Note 23 above, Joint Dissenting Opinion of Judges Lazarova Trajkovska, Bianku, Laffranque, Lemmens and Grozev, par 8.
62   Note 29 above, Joint Partly Dissenting Opinion of Judges Hajiyev, Yudkidska, Lemmens, Mahoney, Silvis and O'Leary, par 16.
63   Note 32 above, Joint partly dissenting opinion of Judges De Gaetano, Lemmens and Mahoney, par 8.
64   Note 35 above, Joint Dissenting Opinion of Judges Spielmann, Sajo, Karakas, Lemmens, Jaderblom, Vehabovic, Dedov and Saiz Arnaiz, par 35.

D. NOT OVERREACHING

Regional human rights judges succumb at times to a tendency to overreach on the scope of rights. Apparent injustices may seem to demand a response, even if the regional treaty does not supply one. Sympathy motivates; judges are human. Many judges on human rights courts have, or acquire, a vocation for advancing human rights.

While understandable, this tendency can undermine both the institution (the regional court) and its project (the treaty and its interpretation). Overreaching on rights (and in controversial matters, applying the treaty even without overreaching) may lead to a loss of public confidence, as well as State refusals or delays to comply with the court's judgments[65], and even threats to withdraw from the treaty and court, whether on principle or for reasons of political opportunism.[66]

The three cases discussed in this section show Judge Lemmens resisting the temptation to overreach with regard to ill treatment under Article 3, environmental infringements of private life under Article 8, and fair trial rights under Article 6. (A fourth such case, where he found no violation of the rights of disabled persons to education, is discussed in the section that follows on the "fair balance" test.)

1.   Degrading treatment

In *Bouyid,* Judge Lemmens joined two other judges in recognizing that

> "police officers who needlessly strike an individual under their control are committing a breach of professional ethics. Moreover, in a democratic society it is only to be expected that such an act should also constitute a tort and a criminal offence. We wish to emphasise that a slap by a police officer is unacceptable."[67]

"However," they added, "it is not for the Court to issue opinions on the basis of professional ethics or domestic law."[68] They were unable to find that the slaps in this case "attained the minimum level of severity to be classified as 'degrading treatment' under Article 3."[69]

---

[65]   For example, Britain took 12 years to comply, and then only partially, with the judgment of the Grand Chamber of the European Court in *Hirst v UK (No. 2)*, App No 74025/01, Judgment of 6 October 2005, which held that certain categories of convicted criminals had the right to vote. Owen Bowcott, *Council of Europe accepts UK compromise on prisoner voting rights*, The Guardian, December 7, 2017.

[66]   See, e.g., Theresa May 'will campaign to leave the European Convention on Human Rights in 2020 election', The Independent, December 30, 2016.

[67]   Note 32 above, Joint partly dissenting opinion of Judges De Gaetano, Lemmens and Mahoney, par 3.

[68]   Ibid.

[69]   Id. par 6.

They appreciated the "laudable aim" of the majority "to display zero tolerance towards police officers who resort to physical force that has not been made strictly necessary by the conduct of the person with whom they are dealing."[70]

Nonetheless, they protested that "we should avoid trivialising findings of a violation of Article 3. The situation complained of in the present case is far less serious than the treatment inflicted by law-enforcement officers in many other cases that the Court has unfortunately had to deal with."[71]

2. Environmental health

In *Otgon,* Judge Lemmens, the sole dissenter, declined to find that contaminated tap water that led to a hospitalization for two weeks amounted to a violation of private life in the circumstances of the case. Explaining that, "in my opinion, not every damage that relates to the environment attracts the applicability of Article 8 …," he elaborated that in this case

> "there has been only one incident, and it has not been demonstrated that the illness has affected the applicant in the quality of her private life, except for the period spent in the hospital … While I do not question that the applicant has been seriously ill, I do not see the effects on her private life."[72]

He regretted that, "thanks to a very generous interpretation of the notion of private life, this case has been 'upgraded' from an ordinary torts case to a case raising an issue under Article 8."[73]

More generally, he concluded, cases must be decided on the basis of law, not sympathy: "While I have sympathy for the applicant, from a purely legal point of view I would have preferred a more restrained approach to the scope of application of Article 8."[74]

3. Fair trial

In *Ibrahim,* where the Grand Chamber majority found a violation of fair trial because the cautioning and access to counsel of a suspected aider of terrorism was delayed, Judge Lemmens joined a dissent arguing that individual procedural rights must be viewed in "appropriate relationship" with community rights:

---

[70] Id. par 9.
[71] Id. par 7.
[72] Note 25 above, Dissenting Opinion of Judge Lemmens, par 3.
[73] Id. par 4.
[74] Ibid.

> "Contracting States and then this Court are required to identify the appropriate relationship between the fundamental procedural right to a fair trial of persons charged with involvement in terrorist-type offences and the right to life and bodily security of the persons affected by the alleged criminal conduct."[75]

In seeking that appropriate relationship in the context of terrorist attacks, the dissenters opined that

> "there is a risk of "failing to see the wood for the trees" if the analysis is excessively concentrated on the imperatives of criminal procedure to the detriment of wider considerations of the modern State's obligation to ensure practical and effective human rights protection to everyone within its jurisdiction."[76]

To be clear, this does not license authorities to repress the "very essence" of individual rights:

> "Human rights protection in a democracy entails that, even when the authorities are confronted with indiscriminate attacks on innocent people going about the ordinary business of living their lives, the legitimate aim of securing the right to life and bodily security of the public cannot justify recourse to unfair and unjust means of repression. ... [P]ublic-interest concerns, including the fight against terrorism, cannot justify measures which extinguish the very essence of a suspect's or an accused person's defence rights."[77]

However, a "parallel consideration," they added, "is that neither can the imperatives of criminal procedure extirpate the legitimacy of the public interest at stake, based as it is on the core Convention rights to life and to bodily safety of other individuals."[78]

E.   THE "FAIR BALANCE" TEST

One tool that Judge Lemmens often uses to resist the temptation to overreach is the concept of "fair balance." In the European Court's 2015 annual seminar, he explained that a "fair balance" is "not necessarily the 'best' balance for the individual concerned."[79] He cited *Hatton v UK*, where the Grand Chamber

---

[75]   Note 29 above, Joint Partly Dissenting Opinion of Judges Hajiyev, Yudkidska, Lemmens, Mahoney, Silvis and O'Leary, par 2.

[76]   Id. par 36.

[77]   Ibid.

[78]   Ibid.

[79]   *Dialogue between judges*, Proceedings of the Seminar, 31 January 2015, "Subsidiarity: a two-sided coin?", Paul Lemmens, *Reply to the Statement by Jean Marc Sauvé*, p 36 note 04, accessible at https://www.echr.coe.int/Documents/Dialogue_2015_ENG.pdf%23page=22 (last consulted 22 January 2019).

overruled a Chamber judgment. The Chamber had held "that States (were) required to minimise, as far as possible, the interference with (Article 8) rights, by trying to find alternative solutions and by generally seeking to achieve their aims in the least onerous way as regards human rights."[80] This "least onerous alternative" approach, Judge Lemmens observed, "was overruled by the Grand Chamber, which was satisfied that the State had not failed to strike a 'fair balance' between the rights of the individuals involved and the conflicting interests of others and of the community as a whole."[81]

In *Hatton* the Grand Chamber ruled that night flights did not violate the right to private life of persons living near London's Heathrow airport. The Court explained that whether the "right balance" had been struck between privacy rights and "other conflicting community interests depends on the relative weight given to each of them."[82] On the one hand, relatively few people had suffered sleep disturbances, their property values were not adversely affected, and they could move if need be. On the other hand, Heathrow airport was important to the English economy, and the government had taken noise-reducing measures, engaged in public consultations and studies, and monitored the situation on an ongoing basis.[83] In these circumstances, the government had not exceeded its margin of appreciation in striking a "fair balance."[84]

Although *Hatton* dealt with privacy rights under Article 8, Judge Lemmens sees the principle of "fair balance" as undergirding the entire Convention system. In *Enver Sahin*, involving the right of a disabled person to access to education, he stated broadly that "fair balance between individual rights and general interests ... characterizes this Convention in its entirety."[85] Indeed, he appears to view "fair balance" as a guiding precept for human rights in general: "The protection of human rights is based on the search for a fair balance between the fundamental rights of the individuals and the interests of the society in which they live."[86]

The "fair balance" concept provides a strong antidote to the tendency to overreach on rights. As Judge Lemmens explained in a 2015 book chapter, the European Court often examines whether domestic authorities

---

[80] *Hatton v UK*, App No 36022/97, Judgment of 2 October 2001, par 97.

[81] *Hatton v UK*, App No 36022/97, Judgment of 8 July 2003, par 129.

[82] Id. par 125.

[83] Id. pars 125–28.

[84] Id. par 129.

[85] Author's unofficial English translation from Judge Lemmens's opinion, published in French, which stated that the European Convention "ne peut pas être interprétée comme imposant une obligation "inconditionnelle" d'assurer l'accessibilité, sans avoir égard au juste équilibre entre droits individuels et intérêts généraux, qui caractérise l'ensemble de cette convention." Note 36 above, Opinion Dissidente de Juge Lemmens, par 4.

[86] *Dialogue between judges*, note 79 above, p 41.

> "struck a fair balance between the human rights of the applicant, on the one hand, and rights of others or the general interest, on the other hand ... Given the potential weight of the opposing rights and interests, it should not come as a surprise that violations of human rights are in fact not easily found."[87]

Like other judicial balancing tests, however, the "fair balance" test is inherently subjective and vulnerable to potential abuse. Reviewing the growing use of balancing tests in U.S. jurisprudence a generation ago, one scholar noted their advantages, but also signaled their risks:

> "Serious questions can also be raised about whether the [balancing] test endangers those fundamental liberties it is called upon to interpret, ... Its most serious flaws, however, are jurisprudential. The test fails to ensure that like cases will be treated alike, and it gives inadequate guidance about what future actions are permitted to the citizenry."[88]

This scholar concluded that "continued use of the test is ill-advised."[89] Other scholars have criticized the balancing test in U.S. jurisprudence as requiring a court to "measur[e] the unmeasurable ... [and] compare the incomparable."[90] One went on to "question the ability of courts to identify the myriad of interests – individual, group, and governmental – at stake in many constitutional cases, and the appropriate measurement of those interests."[91]

Nonetheless, although the U.S. Supreme Court has cut back on its use in some areas[92], the balancing test "remains ubiquitous in [U.S.] federal constitutional analysis."[93]

This is not the place for a full evaluation of balancing tests in general, or of the "fair balance" test in particular. Except for rights deemed absolute – such as the prohibition of torture – use of some form of balancing test is often unavoidable in human rights adjudication. For example, Article 8.2 of the European Convention prohibits public authorities from interfering with the right of private and family

---

[87]   P. Lemmens, *The contribution of the European Court of Human Rights to the rule of law*, in The Contribution of International and Supranational Courts to the Rule of Law (Geert De Baere and Jan Wouters, eds, Edward Elgar Publishing, 2015), p 225, at p 227.

[88]   P.M. McFadden, *The Balancing Test*, 29 Boston College Law Review 585, 588 (1988).

[89]   Ibid.

[90]   T.A. Aleinikoff, *Constitutional Law in the Age of Balancing*, 96 Yale Law Journal 943, 972 (1987) (alterations in original) (quoting Laurent B. Frantz, *Is the First Amendment Law? – A Reply to Professor Mendelson*, 51 California Law Review 729, 748 (1963)).

[91]   T.A. Balmer and K. Thomas, *In the Balance: Thoughts on Balancing and Alternative Approaches in State Constitutional Interpretation*, 76 Albany Law Review 2027, 2036–37 (2013), summarizing Aleinikoff, note 89 above, at 974–79.

[92]   Balmer and Thomas, note 91 above, pp 2029 note 8 and 2036.

[93]   Id. p 2029.

life, except where in accordance with the law and "necessary in a democratic society in the interests of national security, public safety or the economic well-being of the country, for the prevention of disorder or crime, for the protection of health or morals, or for the protection of the rights and freedoms of others." Whether this provision is applied under the European Court's longstanding formula of requiring a State to show that it used "proportionate" means to achieve a "pressing social need" to protect one of these legitimate aims[94], or whether the same analysis is labeled as a "fair balance" test, the Court cannot escape the need to weigh the individual's rights to private and family life against society's legitimate interests.

Similarly, in the *Ibrahim* case discussed above, where the police failed to caution and provide counsel to a terrorism suspect, the dissent joined by Judge Lemmens criticized the majority for missing the "appropriate relationship" between the individual's fair trial rights and the rights of society.[95] The dissent might have reached the same result, on the same reasoning, by using instead the phrase "fair balance." Although the words may differ, the weighing of interests is the same.

Even so, critiques of the balancing test in other contexts counsel against uncritical use of a "fair balance" test. Judges should be aware of its shortcomings and guard against them by striving for as much objectivity and clarity as they can muster when they deploy it. While a degree of subjectivity can never be eliminated, it is significant that Judge Lemmens's separate opinions articulate in some detail, both the opposing interests he balances, and the reasons why the balance tips for or against finding a violation of Convention rights.

In the cases discussed below, Judge Lemmens applied the "fair balance" concept to find no violation in a case involving the rights of disabled persons to education under Article 2 of Protocol 1 to the Convention. On the other hand, he applied "fair balance" to find violations of the family rights of a transsexual and of parents whose child was birthed by a surrogate mother. Where "a particularly important facet of an individual's existence or identity is at stake,"[96] and countervailing community interests are in his view less than compelling, the "fair balance" concept leads him (and others) to find violations of Convention rights.

1. Rights of disabled persons to education

In *Enver Sahin*, Judge Lemmens was the lone dissenter from the Chamber majority's ruling that Turkey discriminated in failing to make reasonable

---

94 E.g., *Handyside v UK*, App No 5493/72, Judgment of 7 December 1976, pars 48, 49.
95 Note 29 above, Joint Partly Dissenting Opinion of Judges Hajiyev, Yudkidska, Lemmens, Mahoney, Silvis and O'Leary, par 2.
96 *Hamalainen*, note 20 above, Joint Dissenting Opinion of Judges Sajó, Keller and Lemmens, par 5.

accommodation to enable a paraplegic student to attend classes in classroom buildings not designed for accessibility. He grounded his position in the broad principle that the Convention "cannot be interpreted as imposing an 'unconditional' obligation to assure accessibility, without regard to a fair balance between individual rights and general interests, which characterizes this Convention in its entirety."[97]

In weighing the "fair balance," it mattered to Judge Lemmens that making the university buildings accessible would be costly[98], and that applicant requested accessibility within six months, even though Turkish law, reflecting general interests, allowed the university at least seven years to make its buildings accessible.[99] In these circumstances Judge Lemmens found no violation.

2. Family rights of a transsexual

In *Hamalainen*, the Grand Chamber found no violation of the right to family life where Finland refused to recognize a transsexual as a woman while still married to her wife. The dissent joined by Judge Lemmens weighed the interests. On the one hand, the applicant had a vital privacy interest

> "in being granted a female identification number because otherwise she will be required to identify herself as transgender – and thus reveal an aspect of her personality belonging to her most intimate sphere – every time the discrepancy between her gender presentation and her identity card has to be explained."[100]

As for society's interests, the only two relevant grounds under Article 8 were the rights and freedoms of others, which would "in no way" be affected by her request, and "certain moral concerns" which did "not provide sufficient justification" to deny her request.[101] Although "the public interest in keeping the institution of marriage free of same-sex couples" was legitimate, it was not weighty in her case because "the institution of marriage would not be endangered by a small number of couples who may wish to remain married in a situation such as that of the applicant."[102]

---

97 Author's unofficial English translation from Judge Lemmens's opinion, published in French, which stated that the European Convention "ne peut pas être interprétée comme imposant une obligation "inconditionnelle" d'assurer l'accessibilité, sans avoir égard au juste équilibre entre droits individuels et intérêts généraux, qui caractérise l'ensemble de cette convention." Note 32 above, Opinion Dissidente de Juge Lemmens, par 4.

98 See id., pars 8 and 9.

99 Id. par 7.

100 Note 20 above, Joint Dissenting Opinion of Judges Sajó, Keller and Lemmens, par 8.

101 Id. pars 9–11.

102 Id. par 12.

Even while acknowledging that "the State has a certain margin of appreciation regarding whether a fair balance was struck," the dissenters "nevertheless [found] that the Government have not shown that the danger to morals is substantial enough to warrant the interference in issue."[103]

3. Surrogate births

In some cases, the "fair balance" is struck in favor of a violation of Convention rights, not because an applicant's rights were weighed in the balance by national authorities and found wanting, but because they were not weighed at all. In such cases, the "fair balance" test is not a substantive criterion but a procedural requirement which, if omitted, may demonstrate a violation.

This may have been the view of Judge Lemmens in a joint dissent with four other judges in *Paradiso*. The Grand Chamber majority found no violation of the right to family life where Italy removed from a married couple a child birthed in Russia by a surrogate mother using an unknown father's semen. The dissenters argued that Italian courts had simply failed to weigh the interests of either the child or the parents: "At no point did the courts ask themselves whether it would have been in the child's interest to remain with the persons who had assumed the role of his parents. The removal was based on purely legal grounds." Likewise, Italian courts "did not address the impact which the immediate and irreversible separation from the child would have on the applicants." This "serious shortcoming" could not be justified on the ground that applicants' conduct "was illegal and their relationship with the child precarious." The mere fact that the domestic courts "did not find it necessary to discuss the impact on the applicants of the removal of a child who was the specific subject of their parental project" demonstrated that they "were not really seeking to strike a fair balance between the applicants' interests and any opposing interests, whatever these might have been."[104]

F. RESPECT FOR NATIONAL AUTHORITIES

An aspect of Judge Lemmens's approach to judging that emerges most clearly from the sample of cases is his profound respect as a regional court judge for the legitimate decisions of national courts and authorities, and his keen understanding that the European Court plays only a subsidiary role in ensuring that national authorities act within their margin of appreciation in striking a

---

[103] Id. par 13.
[104] Note 23 above, Joint Dissenting Opinion of Judges Lazarova Trajkovska, Bianku, Laffranque, Lemmens and Grozev, par 12.

"fair balance" between individual rights and the rights and interests of others and society.[105]

In other words, the "fair balance" test allows a range of possible decisions by national authorities. The European Court does not generally insist on a particular solution[106], but recognizes that States have a "margin of appreciation" in balancing Convention rights and legitimate societal interests. The scope of the margin of appreciation is variable, depending on the nature of the right and the aim of any restriction on the right, among other factors.[107] In any event the margin of appreciation is not "unlimited," but "goes hand in hand with a European supervision."[108] However, only where national authorities exceed their margin of appreciation should the regional court exercise its supervisory power to declare a violation. Judge Lemmens characterizes the primary role of national courts and the subsidiary role of the regional court as a "shared responsibility" for the protection of human rights.[109]

There has been voluminous debate over the margin of appreciation and the European Court's limited but nonetheless important subsidiary role.[110] Rather than enter that broader debate, this section focuses on how the sample of cases and Judge Lemmens's published remarks show his conception of the margin of appreciation; his respect for national laws and their proper interpretation; his respect for national judicial assessments of evidence, facts, and the meaning of words; and his views on whether national courts must mechanically follow the case law of the European Court.

1. Margin of appreciation

While Judge Lemmens finds the "existence as such of a margin of appreciation self-evident," the doctrine has become so complicated that he argues that the "almost holy notion of the margin of appreciation could be demystified." In his

---

[105]   Lemmens, note 87 above, p 231.

[106]   It does so on occasion where a single remedy is essential. For example, in cases where a person is wrongly deprived of liberty, the European Court ordinarily rules that they must be released, as in *Del Río Prada v Spain*, note 37 above.

[107]   *Dudgeon v UK*, App No 7525/76, Judgment of 22 October 1981, par 52. Other factors may include, for example, whether the alleged violation was of a positive or negative State duty and whether there is a European consensus. *Hamalainen*, note 20 above, par 67.

[108]   *Handyside v UK*, App No 5493/72, Judgment of 7 December 1976, par 49.

[109]   *Dialogue between judges*, Proceedings of the Seminar, 31 January 2015, "Subsidiarity: a two-sided coin?" (hereafter "*Dialogue*"), Paul Lemmens, *Reply to the Statement by Jean Marc Sauvé*, p 36 note 04, accessible at https://www.echr.coe.int/Documents/Dialogue_2015_ENG. pdf%23page=22 (last consulted 22 January 2019).

[110]   Even among the European Court judges themselves, including Judge Lemmens, see, e.g., *Dialogue*, note 109 above.

opinion, perhaps for the sake of clarity, it would be "better to shift the attention to the principle of proportionality and its implications."[111]

In applying the margin of appreciation, Judge Lemmens seems to strive for simplicity: In *Haldimann*, he was content to find that Swiss authorities, in prosecuting journalists for the use of hidden cameras, acted within their margin of appreciation because the Federal Court did not appear to be "arbitrary or manifestly unreasonable" in its assessment.[112]

He has also criticized the excessive emphasis sometimes given by the Court, in defining the width of the margin of appreciation, to whether there exists a European consensus on the right at issue. In *Hamalainen*, he joined a dissent noting "past criticism of the consensus approach, which has been considered a potential instrument of retrogression and of allowing the 'lowest common denominator' among the member States to prevail." Deference to European consensus "must have its limits." Lack of consensus could not "widen the State's narrowed margin of appreciation" in a case affecting intimate personal rights of a transsexual. Consensus must not require a common approach "in a super-majority of States." Trends may also be considered, and the "legal recognition of the rights of transsexual and intersex persons is being steadily strengthened worldwide."[113]

2.　National laws

Judge Lemmens respects national laws even when he may disagree with them. In *Paradiso*, even while asserting surrogate rights, he and his fellow dissenters clarified, "We do not intend to express any opinion on the prohibition of surrogacy arrangements under Italian law. It is for the Italian legislature to state the Italian policy on this matter." Their dissent relied instead on the fact that the surrogate birth for an Italian couple took place in Russia, where the law allows surrogate births, and "Italian law does not have extraterritorial effects."[114]

Not only should European judges respect the policy decisions embodied in national law (unless the law itself violates the Convention), they should also respect national interpretations of national law. In their concurring opinion in *Avotins*, Judge Lemmens and his fellow judge avowed, "It is in principle not for the Court to interpret domestic law."[115] In G.I.E.M. he and another judge

---

111　*Dialogue,* note 109 above, p 37.
112　Note 7 above, Dissenting Opinion of Judge Lemmens, par 5.
113　Note 20 above, Joint Dissenting Opinion of Judges Sajó, Keller and Lemmens, par 5.
114　Note 23 above, Joint Dissenting Opinion of Judges Lazarova Trajkovska, Bianku, Laffranque, Lemmens and Grozev, par 11.
115　Note 27 above, Joint Concurring Opinion of Judges Lemmens and Briede, par 3.

cited case law establishing that the European Court "can only depart from the domestic courts' interpretation of domestic law when that interpretation is arbitrary or manifestly unreasonable."[116]

National laws entitled to respect include those regulating judicial proceedings. In *Avotins*, Judge Lemmens and another judge took issue with the majority view that the Supreme Court of Latvia should have examined the issue of burden of proof in Cyprus. They pointed out that "[t]he Supreme Court proceedings, including those relating to the burden of proof and the reasoning of its judgments, are regulated by Latvian law. It was for the Supreme Court to deal with the applicant's argument according to the rules of domestic law."[117]

National legal systems are entitled not only to respect but also to understanding. In *Ibrahim*, Judge Lemmens and fellow dissenters disputed the majority's criticism that the directions given by an English judge "left the jury with excessive discretion." They answered, "This criticism seems to be at odds with the role of the jury in common-law criminal-justice systems ... It is not the Court's task to standardise the legal systems in Europe by imposing any given model of jury trial or given degree of involvement of citizens in the administration of justice."[118]

3. National judicial assessments[119]

In *Einarsson*, where the national courts ruled that a particular labeling of a journalist as a "rapist bastard" was in context a value judgment, not a statement of fact, Judge Lemmens, the lone dissenter, reminded the majority that it is "not the Court's task to substitute its own assessment of the facts for that of the domestic courts and, as a general rule, it is for those courts to assess the evidence before them." Moreover, "An assessment of the meaning of a given word, read in its context, is typically one for which the domestic judge is better placed than the European Court."[120]

---

[116] Note 31 above, Joint Partly Dissenting, Partly Concurring Opinion of Judges Spano and Lemmens, par 16.

[117] Ibid.

[118] Note 29 above, Joint Partly Dissenting Opinion of Judges Hajiyev, Yudkidska, Lemmens, Mahoney, Silvis and O'Leary, par 34.

[119] Although decided too recently to be included in the sample analyzed here, see also *Astradsson v Iceland*, App no 26374/18, Judgment of 12 March 2019, Joint Dissenting Opinion of Judges Lemmens and Gritco. The two dissenters objected that the five-member majority disregarded the principle of subsidiarity, BY substituting their judgment for that of the Supreme Court of Iceland with regard to the gravity of A breach OF certain DOMESTIC rules FOR the appointment of judges of the Court of Appeal. *Id.* par 8.

[120] Note 11 above, Dissenting Opinion of Judge Lemmens, par 4.

4. National Court acceptance of European Court case law

Commenting in 2015 on the "controversial" question of the extent to which domestic courts are bound to follow the case law of the European Court[121], Judge Lemmens made two points clear. First, States (including their judicial branches) must execute European Court judgments against them.[122] Second, once the Grand Chamber has "clearly decided an issue," it should be considered "settled" by all European national courts.[123]

"Exceptionally" in other situations, however, Judge Lemmens allowed room for judicial dialogue between the European Court and national courts, including refusals by national courts to follow European case law, provided the refusal is "for good reasons."[124] He gave the example of the use of hearsay testimony in British courts.[125] A European Court Chamber decided that using hearsay testimony violated the right of the accused to a fair trial.[126] The UK Supreme Court then, in another case, "explicitly disagreed with the Chamber's reasoning, arguing that the latter had underestimated certain procedural guarantees existing in English law."[127] On rehearing of the first case, the Grand Chamber "took into account the opinion of the Supreme Court, adapted its own case-law, and came to the conclusion that there had been no violation of the right to a fair trial."[128]

Judge Lemmens believes this example of judicial dialogue can be and has been usefully followed in other situations where the European Court has perhaps not fully understood a national law or practice. In 2016 in *Paposhvili*, he noted with apparent satisfaction that the Grand Chamber decision "may be seen as the Court's response to the concerns" of Belgian courts which, dissatisfied with earlier European Court jurisprudence, relied on domestic law to bar deportations of ill persons "where there is a risk of inhuman or degrading treatment if no appropriate treatment exists in the receiving country."[129] In 2018, partly dissenting with one other judge in *G.I.E.M.*, he regretted that the majority

> "miss the opportunity to engage in a meaningful dialogue with the Italian Constitutional Court and to correct the [European] Court's case-law. Instead,

---

121 *Dialogue*, note 109 above, p 39.
122 Id. p 40.
123 Id. p 41.
124 Ibid.
125 Id. p 42.
126 *Al-Khawaja and Tahery v. the United Kingdom*, App Nos 26766/05 and 22228/06, Judgment of 20 January 2009.
127 *R. v. Horncastle and Others*, [2009] UKSC 14, judgment of 9 December 2009.
128 *Dialogue*, note 109 above, p 42, citing *Al-Khawaja and Tahery v. the United Kingdom* [Grand Chamber], App Nos 26766/05 and 22228/06, Judgment of 15 December 2011.
129 Note 17 above, Concurring Opinion of Judge Lemmens, par 5.

they continue to force upon the domestic authorities an interpretation of domestic law which ignores its essential features and to submit the domestic system of environmental protection to Convention requirements that seriously weaken its effectiveness."[130]

CONCLUSION

This summary review of an unscientific sample of 25 important and controversial cases, in which Judge Paul Lemmens authored or joined in a separate opinion, suggests that becoming a judge of the European Court of Human Rights has not gone to his head. His published opinions bespeak a judge who is consistently careful, thoughtful, meticulous, and scrupulously fair-minded. Moreover, he has a clear sense of both the limits and the importance of the regional Court's subsidiary role in protecting human rights in Europe. He is a realist, not only in assessing facts in cases, but also in understanding the European Court's vulnerable institutional setting: he well understands that the Court is "somewhat dependent" on the support of the 47 member States of the Council of Europe, and that: "Such support is not self-evident, given the fact that it is precisely these same States that can be held responsible by the Court for violations of human rights."[131]

I offer these positive assessments, not to suggest that I agree with his views in all the cases discussed here (I do not). His seemingly uncritical embrace of the "fair balance" test, and his perhaps overstated view of its centrality in human rights jurisprudence, give me pause. On the other hand, I applaud his call to "demystify" and simplify the currently convoluted and confusing role of the "margin of appreciation" in the Court's jurisprudence. And most important, I have no doubt that litigants who desire a fair hearing before the European Court can count on Judge Lemmens to pay close attention to the legal and factual intricacies of their cases, and to strive to render a fair, well-informed, persuasively argued, transparent and respectful resolution. In the context of an honest, independent and impartial adjudication before an international tribunal, Who could ask for more?

---

[130] Note 31 above, Joint Partly Dissenting, Partly Concurring Opinion of Judges Spano and Lemmens, par 1.
[131] Lemmens, note 87 above, p. 228.

OF PRINCIPLES AND VALUES

An Explorative Reading of Separate Opinions of Judge Paul Lemmens

Wouter VANDENHOLE
Chair in Human Rights
Law and Development Research Group, University of Antwerp

INTRODUCTION

This contribution deals with the principles and values that have informed Judge Paul Lemmens's stance in separate opinions.

The initial idea for this contribution was to analyse how the meta-legal concepts of vulnerability and autonomy impact on Judge Lemmens's views. These concepts have often informed the European Court of Human Rights' understanding of the right to life, the prohibition of torture, and the right to private life, among others.[1] This exercise proved unfeasible. On the one hand, the concepts of vulnerability and autonomy only feature with some prominence in less than a handful of cases. Even in these cases, they do not seem the primary or exclusive factor informing Judge Lemmens's stance.[2] On the other hand, while reading the separate opinions, I realised that the reasoning drawn upon in separate opinions was more diverse than the mere invocation of the meta-legal concepts of vulnerability and autonomy: often, only a mix of principles and values seems to be able to explain the position taken.

Therefore, the approach taken in this contribution is to look into a selection of judgments in which Article 8 ECHR or Article 3 ECHR is at stake. No comprehensive or exhaustive treatment is envisaged, nor is an encyclopaedic account provided. The chapter's findings are inevitably rather eclectic,

---

[1]   See, e.g., ECtHR (GC) 28 September 2015, *Bouyid and Bouyid v. Belgium*; ECtHR (GC) 5 June 2015, *Lambert and others v. France*.
[2]   See, e.g., ECtHR (GC) 28 September 2015, *Bouyid and Bouyid v. Belgium*.

explorative and hypothetical.[3] Nonetheless, the chapter provides some new and fresh hypotheses that may be tested in follow-up research. Methodologically, the reason for focusing on separate opinions is that these can be seen as the vehicles "par excellence" for discovering the particular views of a particular judge. Of course, judgments more generally may reveal the views held by judges too, but since they are typically adopted by a body of seven or seventeen judges, they reveal less the individual position held by a particular judge.

One finding is that a particular principled view on the institutional role of the European Court of Human Rights (ECtHR) and its relationship with States Parties to the ECHR, rather than a moral value framework, is often invoked by Judge Lemmens to justify his position in a separate opinion. The next section will outline the elements of that view on the Court and its relationship with States. The third section dissects some separate opinions from a principles and values perspective.

I. THE ROLE OF THE STRASBOURG COURT

There is a longstanding debate on the specific role of the Strasbourg Court in human rights protection, as reflected more recently in High Level Conferences and institutional reforms.[4] Amending Protocols have been adopted and a process of reform is being undertaken. Amending Protocol No. 15 introduces a reference to subsidiarity and the margin of appreciation.[5]

Judge Lemmens seems to emphasise Strasbourgian restraint in human rights supervision. He recalls the limits of the supervisory powers of the ECtHR, emphasises that the Strasbourg Court is not a court of fourth instance, and shows deference to the margin of appreciation of national courts. E.g., in his concurring opinion in *Putistin v. Ukraine*, he acknowledges that the Strasbourg Court is not a court of fourth instance.[6] In his concurring opinion in *R.L. v. Denmark*, he explicitly invokes "the limits of the supervisory power" of the Court in situations where different views on an issue are reasonably possible. In a nutshell and in well-rehearsed wording, these limits to the Strasbourg Court's supervisory powers mean that the "Court's task is not to take the place of the

---

3   Follow-up research, including interviews with Judge Paul Lemmens and other section judges would help to corroborate or debunk some of the preliminary findings of this chapter.

4   See, inter alia, https://www.coe.int/en/web/human-rights-intergovernmental-cooperation/ echr-system (31 July 2018); https://www.echr.coe.int/Pages/home.aspx?p=basictexts/reform &c= (31 July 2018). See also P. Popelier, S. Lambrecht and K. Lemmens (eds.), *Criticism of the European Court of Human Rights. Shifting the Convention System: Counter-Dynamics at the National and EU Level*, Cambridge, Intersentia, 2016.

5   As of 31 July 2018, 43 out of the 47 States Parties had ratified the Protocol.

6   ECtHR 21 November 2013, *Putistin v. Ukraine*, concurring opinion of Judge Lemmens, §2.

national courts, which have, *inter alia*, the benefit of direct contact with the interested parties, but rather to review whether the decisions the courts have taken pursuant to their power of appreciation are compatible with the provisions of the Convention relied on (references omitted)."[7] In a footnote, Judge Lemmens sheds further light on his reading of the not-a-fourth-instance-court principle, in which he clearly chooses for less deference than the majority in that judgement:

> "This does not mean that 'when domestic authorities carefully assess the best interests of the child, the Court should not, in principle, contradict their findings, in particular if they are made by an independent court in judicial proceedings' (see paragraph 47 of the judgment, [...]). Such a standard of review would result in too much deference by the Court to the domestic courts. I prefer to adhere to the standard according to which, 'where the balancing exercise has been undertaken by the national authorities in conformity with the criteria laid down in the Court's case-law, the Court would require strong reasons to substitute its view for that of the domestic courts'" [references omitted].[8]

In other words, there is no blind deference to national courts, but only to the extent that the Court's criteria have been observed.[9] Judge Lemmens tends to take a principled, procedural stance on how decisive this qualified deference to national courts is in concrete cases. Even if he disagrees with the substantive outcome, he feels that the not-a-fourth-instance-court principle must prevail:

> "That is why in the end, without any enthusiasm at all, I felt compelled to conclude that, having due regard to the margin of appreciation enjoyed by the domestic courts and the reasons given by the High Court [footnote omitted], the latter had struck a fair balance between the various interests involved."[10]

A second, more strategic-pragmatic approach, is to refer to developments in the country concerned. Judge Lemmens seems to adopt this approach only in cases in which his home country, Belgium, is involved, in the sensitive area of migration (control) policies. In his concurring opinion to *S.J. v. Belgium*, while not challenging the principles outlined by the Grand Chamber in a similar case on expulsion of a seriously ill irregular migrant (the *N. v. UK* case), he suggested

---

7 ECtHR 7 March 2017, *R.L. v. Denmark*, concurring opinion of Judge Lemmens, §3.

8 Ibid., footnote 2. This is the standard that the Grand Chamber applies in Article 10 cases, see also section III.D. below.

9 In another case later in 2017, on the assessment of the meaning of a given word used in a given context, a more unqualified approach to the subsidiary nature of the Strasbourg Court's role was taken by Judge Lemmens: since there was no cogent reason to depart from the national court's assessment, that assessment was found to be in conformity with the Convention (ECtHR 7 November 2017, *Egill Einarsson v. Iceland*, dissenting opinion of Judge Lemmens, §§4 and 6).

10 ECtHR 7 March 2017, *R.L. v. Denmark*, concurring opinion of Judge Lemmens, §3.

that the State could well go beyond the Convention requirements. In the case at hand, he suggested a creative interpretation of the Belgian Aliens Act:

> "I observe that under Belgian law an alien may be given leave to remain in the Kingdom in 'exceptional circumstances' (section 9*bis* of the Aliens Act). It is left to the competent authorities to assess whether such circumstances exist. I am conscious of the fact that the term 'exceptional circumstances' refers to circumstances which preclude the alien's temporary return to his or her country of origin in order to complete the necessary formalities with a view to lodging an application for leave to remain. I am also aware that 'the factors relied on in the context of a request for leave to remain on the basis of section 9*ter*' 'cannot be regarded as exceptional circumstances' (section 9*bis*, paragraph 2, sub-paragraph 4, of the Aliens Act). Nevertheless, I wonder whether section 9*bis* does not allow the Belgian authorities – in the exercise of their discretionary powers of course – to attribute to the humanitarian considerations referred to in the present judgment the importance they deserve, above and beyond the requirements of the Convention."

In his concurring opinion to the *Paposhvili v. Belgium* case, he points out how the consistently less restrictive approach by domestic courts (in this case, by the Belgian Aliens Appeal Board) has impacted on the ECtHR's understanding of the requirements of Article 3 ECHR with regard to the expulsion of seriously ill irregular migrants[11]:

> "I would like to take this opportunity to draw attention to the fact that the present judgment is not unrelated to developments occurring within Belgium. [...] The Aliens Appeals Board was able to draw the Court's attention to the issue raised by its case-law. The present judgment may be seen as the Court's response to the concerns expressed by the Aliens Appeals Board."[12]

In other words, an approach that takes jurisprudential developments before domestic courts seriously may result in higher levels of human rights protection, if domestic courts are willing to go beyond Strasbourg minimum standards.

Judge Lemmens's overall Strasbourgian restraint approach also seems to have implications for admissibility and applicability questions. Over the years, he has taken a more restrictive position than the majority on the admissibility of certain complaints, and on the scope of application of Article 8 ECHR in particular. E.g., he has argued that an individual cannot claim to be a victim of a violation if the complaint only relates to the intention of authorities that have had no concrete effects. In casu, a university rector had proposed to assign a

---

[11]　This reference to developments in domestic courts' jurisprudence must be read in tandem with the clear discontent within the Strasbourg Court on the approach outlined in *N. v. UK*.

[12]　ECtHR (GC) 13 December 2016, *Paposhvili v. Belgium*, concurring opinion of Judge Lemmens, §5.

personal assistant to a physically disabled student. The student argued that being assisted by a third person would have made him dependent on that person and would have deprived him of his intimacy, which would have amounted in his view to a discriminatory violation of the right to respect for private life. Judge Lemmens submitted that the complaint about a violation of Article 8 ECHR should have been declared inadmissible, since the proposed personal assistant had never been assigned, and had been refused by the complainant.[13] Likewise, in a terrorism case, Judge Lemmens argued that the complaint based on Article 8 ECHR should have been declared inadmissible. Police officers had threatened to search the applicant's apartment in order to obtain two items (a drill and a gas gun), but had not done so in the end because he had handed over the two items. In Judge Lemmens's view, there were not "sufficiently convincing elements to conclude that the police officers entered the applicants' apartment or that they interfered in any other way with the inviolability of their home".[14]

Likewise, Judge Lemmens has sometimes argued in favour of a more restrictive approach to the scope of application of Article 8 ECHR, in particular where the right to respect for private life is invoked as a proxy for the right to health. However, his reasoning in these cases was no so much with reference to certain principles or views on the role of the Strasbourg Court, but more in substantive legal terms. E.g., in a case of the temporary pollution of drinking water and the health effects on the applicant, he submitted that there should be repercussions on the affected person's private life in order to make Article 8 applicable:

> "thanks to a very generous interpretation of the notion of private life, this case has been "upgraded" from an ordinary torts case to a case raising an issue under Article 8"; "from a purely legal point of view I would have preferred a more restrained approach to the scope of application of Article 8".[15]

Similarly, in a case where the parents of a new-born baby complained that their second baby had disappeared, Judge Lemmens doubted that there had been an interference with the physical integrity of the young mother. She had been diagnosed as being pregnant of twins, but gave birth to only one child. Since the diagnostic error had not affected the health of the mother, judge Lemmens believed that a diagnostic error should not be equated with an interference with the physical integrity.[16]

---

[13] ECtHR 30 January 2018, *Enver Sahin v. Turkey*, dissenting opinion of Judge Lemmens, §14. A referral request to the Grand Chamber was rejected on 2 July 2018.

[14] ECtHR 15 November 2012, *Koval and others v. Ukraine*, partly dissenting opinion of Judge Lemmens.

[15] ECtHR 25 October 2016, *Otgon v. Moldova*, dissenting opinion of Judge Lemmens, §4.

[16] ECtHR 10 April 2018, *Eryiğit v. Turkey*, concurring opinion of Judge Lemmens, §4. Since the parents complained (also) about the disappearance of the second child, the issue could be brought under the right to respect for family life (§5).

Judge Lemmens does not always advocate a restrictive approach to the scope of application of Article 8 ECHR. In his view, video-surveillance of lecturers as a measure of control by the dean falls within the scope of application of Article 8 ECHR, since a teacher may have an expectation of privacy, also outside his or her home or private premises: "at least in an academic environment, where both the teaching and the learning activities are covered by academic freedom, the said expectation of privacy can be considered a 'reasonable' one."[17] With regard to family life too, he has pleaded for not limiting the scope of application to biological or legal ties, but to include *de facto* family life, regardless of its legal status: "For us it is important that the cohabitation started from the very day the child was born, lasted until the child was removed from the applicants, and would have continued indefinitely if the authorities had not intervened to bring it to an end."[18]

In sum, deference to national courts provided that they apply the European Court of Human Rights' criteria, seems a major guiding principle in Judge Lemmens's separate opinions. Whereas that deference has often led to the finding that no violation had occurred, occasionally it may also result in a further development of the Strasbourg Court's case-law and to higher levels of human rights protection. Strasbourgian restraint more generally has not only guided Judge Lemmens's decisions on the merits, but also admissibility decisions. The impact of that principle on scope of application decisions in the context of Article 8 ECHR is less unequivocal.

II. TOPIC AREAS

In what follows, some substantive issues on which Judge Lemmens has taken a separate opinion, are highlighted. To the extent that this is rendered explicit in the reasoning, I examine which principles and values have guided Judge Lemmens in his separate opinions on these topics.

A. GENDER RE-ASSIGNMENT

Since the *Christine Goodwin*-case, the Strasbourg Court's case-law on gender re-assignment recognition has been well established. Article 8 ECHR requires States to recognise the new gender identity after gender re-assignment.

---

[17] ECtHR 28 November 2017, *Antović and Mirković v. Montenegro*, joint concurring opinion of Judges Vučinić and Lemmens §§3–4.

[18] ECtHR (GC) 24 January 2017, *Paradiso and Campanelli v. Italy*, joint dissenting opinion of Judges Lazarova Trajkovska, Bianku, Laffranque, Lemmens and Grozev, §4.

The *Hämäläinen* case dealt with a new dimension. The male to female transgender person Hämäläinen could be granted a female identification number under Finish law, but only if she was prepared to accept that her civil marriage ended, for same-sex marriage was not allowed in Finland.[19] For the majority of the grand chamber, having to make a choice between gender re-assignment recognition or marriage was not problematic. A minority of three judges, among which Judge Lemmens, dissented. In their view,

> "[t]he applicant has an interest in being granted a female identification number because otherwise she will be required to identify herself as transgender – and thus reveal an aspect of her personality belonging to her most intimate sphere – every time the discrepancy between her gender presentation and her identity card has to be explained. We believe that this amounts to more than a regrettable "inconvenience" (see paragraph 87 of the judgment). [...] A conflict between social reality and law arises which places the transsexual in an anomalous position, in which he or she may experience feelings of vulnerability, humiliation and anxiety (see *Christine Goodwin*, cited above, §77)."[20]

Therefore, the minority thought that it was "highly problematic to pit two human rights – in this case, the right to recognition of one's gender identity and the right to maintain one's civil status – against each other".[21]: "the applicant is forced to choose between the continuation of her marriage, which falls under 'family life' for the purposes of Article 8, and the legal recognition of her acquired gender identity, which falls under 'private life' for the purposes of Article 8 (see paragraphs 57–61 of the judgment)." In the minority's view, "she will suffer an interference with her rights under Article 8 no matter which of these 'options' she chooses."[22] Therefore, the gender reassignment undergone by one spouse cannot be considered "to be a compelling reason justifying the dissolution of a marriage where both spouses expressly wish to continue in their pre-existing marital relationship."[23] Although not explicitly stated, the meta-legal value of autonomy seems to have guided the minority's view. As submitted in the *Christine Goodwin*-case,

> "Under Article 8 of the Convention in particular, where the notion of personal autonomy is an important principle underlying the interpretation of its guarantees, protection is given to the personal sphere of each individual, including the right to

---

19 For an analysis, see M. D'Amico and C. Nardocci, "LGBT rights and the way forward: the evolution of the case law of the ECtHR in relation to transgender individuals' identity", 17 *ERA Forum* 2016, 191–202.

20 ECtHR (GC) 16 July 2014, *Hämäläinen v. Finland*, joint dissenting opinion of Judges Sajó, Keller and Lemmens, §8.

21 Ibid., §6.

22 Ibid., §8.

23 Ibid., §16.

establish details of their identity as individual human beings [references omitted]. In the twenty first century the right of transsexuals to personal development and to physical and moral security in the full sense enjoyed by others in society cannot be regarded as a matter of controversy requiring the lapse of time to cast clearer light on the issues involved."[24]

Yet a different aspect of gender identity recognition under Article 8 ECHR was at stake in *Y.Y. v. Turkey*. Under Turkish law, a permanent inability to procreate was a prior condition for gender reassignment surgery. Whereas Judge Lemmens agreed with the majority that a permanent inability to procreate as a prior condition for gender reassignment surgery was incompatible with Article 8 ECHR, he reserved his position – perhaps somewhat surprisingly in light of his position in the *Hämäläinen* case – like the majority, on a permanent inability to procreate as a precondition for legal recognition of gender reassignment.[25] The reason invoked was mainly procedural: "the Court was right not to rule on the condition in question in this broader context. Not just because that issue was not submitted to it, but also because there is insufficient evidence in the file to enable it to rule in full knowledge of the facts." Meanwhile, the Court has ruled in a case against France that the requirement to demonstrate an irreversible change in appearance is in violation of Article 8 ECHR. Although a matter of uncertainty due to vague wording, the Court held that this requirement "made recognition of the gender identity of transgender persons conditional on sterilisation surgery or on treatment which, on account of its nature and intensity, entailed a very high probability of sterility."[26] It then summarised the situation as follows:

> "Making the recognition of transgender persons' gender identity conditional on sterilisation surgery or treatment – or surgery or treatment very likely to result in sterilisation – which they do not wish to undergo therefore amounts to making the full exercise of their right to respect for their private life under Article 8 of the Convention conditional on their relinquishing full exercise of their right to respect for their physical integrity as protected by that provision and also by Article 3 of the Convention."[27]
> "[L]aw [...] presented transgender persons not wishing to undergo full gender reassignment with an impossible dilemma. Either they underwent sterilisation surgery or treatment – or surgery or treatment very likely to result in sterilisation – against their wishes, thereby relinquishing full exercise of their right to respect for their physical integrity, which forms part of the right to respect for private life under Article 8 of the Convention; or they waived recognition of their gender identity and hence full exercise of that same right."

---

24 ECtHR (GC) 11 July 2002, *Christine Goodwin v. United Kingdom*, §90.
25 ECtHR 10 March 2015, *Y.Y. v. Turkey*, concurring opinion of Judges Lemmens and Kūris, §3.
26 ECtHR 6 April 2017, *A.P., Garçon and Nicot v. France*, §120.
27 Ibid., §131.

Judge Lemmens sat not on the bench in this case, so it is impossible to tell what his position would have been. Nonetheless, analytically, the situation is not dissimilar to that in Hämäläinen, whereby two rights are pitted against each other, and where the meta-legal value of autonomy takes centre-stage. On the other hand, Judge Lemmens might also have been with Judge Ranzoni on this issue. The latter questioned whether it was appropriate to assume that States had only a narrow margin of appreciation, since he failed to see a European consensus on the issue. He pleaded instead for a cautious approach[28], and Judge Lemmens might have preferred a similar deferential approach.

B.   BEST INTERESTS OF THE CHILD

The Strasbourg Court increasingly pays attention to children's rights in its case-law, and the best interests of the child is often used as a proxy for children's rights.[29] It has identified two limbs to the best interests of the child: one, ties with the family must be maintained. Family ties can only be severed by the State in very exceptional circumstances; everything must be done to preserve personal relations and to rebuild the family. Second, the child's development in a sound environment must be ensured. Therefore, no measures are allowed that harm the child's health and development.[30]

In a grand chamber judgment on the removal of a young child following an illegal surrogacy, Judge Lemmens was part of the dissenting minority. The majority held that the removal of the child by the authorities had not violated the applicants' right to respect for private life. They mainly relied on the state of abandonment of the child, and on the illegal conduct of the applicants.[31]

The minority takes as a starting point for its analysis the child's best interests as defined in the *Neulinger and Shuruk*-case. In light of this understanding of the best interests of the child, and given the recognition of de facto family life as being protected under Article 8 ECHR, the minority is of the opinion that the domestic courts' finding that the child was in a state of "abandonment" was excessively formal:

> "[...] we cannot but express our surprise as to the finding that the child, who was cared for by a couple that fully assumed the role of parents, was declared to be in a

---

28   Ibid., dissenting opinion of Judge Ranzoni, §§18–19.
29   See W. Vandenhole and G. Erdem Türkelli, "The Best Interests of the Child" in J. Todres and S. King (eds.), *The Oxford Handbook of Children Rights Law*, Oxford, Oxford University Press, forthcoming.
30   ECtHR (GC) 6 July 2010, *Sheulinger and Nuruk v. Switzerland*, §136.
31   ECtHR (GC) 24 January 2017, *Paradiso and Campanelli v. Italy*, §§199 and 204.

state of 'abandonment'. If the only reason for such a finding was that the applicants were not, legally speaking, the parents, then we wonder whether the domestic courts' reasoning is not excessively formal, in a manner that is incompatible with the requirements stemming from Article 8 of the Convention in such cases."[32]

The best interests of the child and the protection of de facto family life seem to have been overshadowed by the illegal surrogacy at the origin of the child's birth and of the family life. Whereas the minority does not want to take position on the prohibition of surrogacy per se, it makes clear that the illegality of the surrogacy arrangement should not impact on the subsequent placement into care decision:

"[w]here a couple has managed to enter into a surrogacy agreement abroad and to obtain from a mother living abroad a baby, which subsequently is brought legally into Italy, it is the factual situation in Italy stemming from these earlier events in another country that should guide the relevant Italian authorities in their reaction to that situation. In this respect, we have some difficulty with the majority's view that the legislature's reasons for prohibiting surrogacy arrangements are of relevance in respect of measures taken to discourage Italian citizens from having recourse abroad to practices which are forbidden on Italian territory (see paragraph 203 of the judgment). In our opinion, the relevance of these reasons becomes less clear when a situation has been created abroad which, as such, cannot have violated Italian law. In this respect, it is also important to note that the situation created by the applicants in Russia was initially recognised and formalised by the Italian authorities through the consulate in Moscow."[33]

In sum, in the minority's view, the majority attaches too much weight "to the need to put an end to an illegal situation (in view of the laws on inter-country child adoption and on the use of assisted reproductive technology [...] and the need to discourage Italian citizens from having recourse abroad to practices which are forbidden in Italy [...]." On the other hand,

"[w]ith respect to the interest of the child, [...] [a]t no point did the courts ask themselves whether it would have been in the child's interest to remain with the persons who had assumed the role of his parents. The removal was based on purely legal grounds. Facts came into play only to assess whether the consequences of the removal, once decided, would not be too harsh for the child. We consider that in these circumstances it cannot be said that the domestic courts sufficiently addressed the impact that the removal would have on the child's well-being. This is a serious omission, given that any such measure should take the best interest of the child into account [...]".[34]

---

[32]   Ibid., joint dissenting opinion of Judges Lazarova Trajkovska, Bianku, Laffranque, Lemmens and Grozev, §8.

[33]   Ibid., §11.

[34]   Ibid., §12.

Finally, with regard to the interests of the parents, the minority feels "that their interest in continuing to develop their relationship with a child whose parents they wished to be [...] has not been sufficiently taken into account".[35] Likewise, "the impact which the immediate and irreversible separation from the child would have on the applicants" had not been properly addressed.[36] In sum, the group of dissenters, among which Judge Lemmens, advocates a less formalistic and legalistic approach than the domestic court, and prefers a real balancing of interests based on the facts of the case, and in which the best interests of the child are paramount. The reasoning seems consistent with Judge Lemmens's view that deference to domestic courts is due in so far as domestic courts have duly assessed the situation in line with the Court's criteria. In this case, the domestic court failed to balance the interests at stake, including the best interests of the child, and hence violated the ECHR.

In the *R.L. case*, another dimension of the best interests of the child as read into Article 8 ECHR was at stake. The domestic courts had refused to reopen the paternity proceedings, as a consequence of which the former presumed father was "locked in a father-child relationship which he had accepted without being informed of the true situation".[37] Both the mother and the presumed father had applied for the reopening of paternity proceedings. In his concurring opinion, Judge Lemmens raised the question what the best interests of children in the long run were[38], and emphasised the importance of the biological reality. He argued that the latter "is an important guiding principle. In this respect I would like to refer to the Court's case-law to the effect that a situation in which a legal presumption is allowed to prevail over biological reality might not be compatible, even having regard to the margin of appreciation left to the State, with the obligation to secure effective 'respect' for private and family life [references omitted]".[39] Two dissenting judges took the issue one step further: they commented that domestic legislation "failed to give due regard to the right of children to know their own origin" and that the reasoning of the majority judges of the domestic court did not demonstrate that it "paid any attention to the right of children to express their views freely or that it carried out a sufficiently detailed analysis of the various interests at stake, especially of the best interests of the children involved".[40] In the dissenting judges' view, in weighing the interests of the child, the putative father and the general interest, "the best interests of the child should be given priority. This is especially important in such sensitive cases as the present one, where the discovery of the

---

[35]   Ibid., §12.
[36]   Ibid., §13.
[37]   ECtHR 7 March 2017, *R.L. and others v. Denmark*, concurring opinion of Judge Lemmens, §1.
[38]   Ibid., §1.
[39]   Ibid., §2.
[40]   Ibid., §6.

truth concerning the identity of a child's parents [reference omitted] is highly relevant for his or her personal development".[41]

In a case on contact rights of one of the parents, a tight majority of four judges found a violation of Article 8 ECHR. The majority read a strong obligation in Article 8 ECHR to "identify the causes of the children's resistance towards their mother, and to address them accordingly".[42] The minority of three, among which Judge Lemmens, refused to read "such a strict obligation into the Convention".[43] They believe that it is "within the authorities' discretion to consider that it was at no point in the children's best interests to *force* them, through a therapy or otherwise, to adopt a different attitude towards their mother".[44]

In sum, the best interests of the child must be given due attention and appropriate weight in balancing interests as part of the proportionality test. Often, a less deferential stance towards the domestic judge is taken in cases where the best interests of the child are at stake. Nonetheless, Judge Lemmens has stopped short of reading strict positive obligations based on the best interests of the child into Article 8 ECHR.

C. HOME: THE RIGHT OF LEGAL PERSONS TO THE PROTECTION OF THEIR "HOME"

Judge Lemmens has also adopted a separate opinion in some cases on the right to respect for the home. When the home of a legal entity is at stake, "the possibilities of interference are on the face of it greater than in a case concerning a natural person [references omitted]. I consider that it is only with due regard to this aspect of the case that we can conclude that the exceptions to Article 8 §2 are to be interpreted narrowly and that the need for them must be convincingly established".[45] This suggests that whereas Judge Lemmens does not oppose to extend the protection of Article 8 ECHR to legal persons, he believes that restrictions should be allowed to be applied more leniently. A clear reasoning in terms of principles and values was not provided.

In a case on the legality of secret measures in the context of counter-terrorist operations, Judge Lemmens, together with others, implicitly argued that not the conformity of the Suppression of Terrorism Act itself, but rather a specific

---

41 Ibid., §8.
42 ECtHR 14 March 2017, *K.B. v. Croatia*, §144.
43 Ibid., joint separate opinion of Judges Karakaş, Lemmens and Ravarani, §3.
44 Ibid., §5.
45 ECtHR 18 April 2013, *Saint-Paul Luxembourg S.A. v. Luxemburg*, concurring opinion of Judge Lemmens, §2.

operation undertaken within the framework of that Act, had to be examined. Likewise, he did not necessarily think that a written order is always needed in the context of a counter-terrorist operation:

> "[W]e agree with the majority that the fact that no individual decision authorising the operation has been produced is problematic. We are not persuaded that a written order is always needed in the context of a counter-terrorist operation. However, where no such order is produced, the Government should at least submit other documents relating to the operation which make sufficiently clear the reasons for which the operation was ordered at that precise moment and how the operational limits were defined. Without an order or other documents, the Court is unable to conclude, for instance, that recourse to the extraordinary powers under the Act was justified by ascertainable facts, or that the incursion into the applicants' house was justified by the existence of an imminent danger to human life or health. [...] We therefore conclude, like the majority, that the interference was not "in accordance with the law", but we do so on a somewhat narrower basis."[46]

The latter case seems to suggest that Judge Lemmens is prepared to apply Article 8 ECHR in a more lenient way in the context of counterterrorism operations. This may be seen as yet another dimension of the deference to be shown to States, although that rationale was not made explicit and the principle of Strasbourgian restraint was not invoked.

It is not possible to draw any strong general conclusions on Judge Lemmens's stance on Article 8 ECHR in separate opinions. But clearly, Strasbourgian restraint and deference to domestic courts are not the only decisive elements in his assessment of alleged violations. More substantive considerations seems to play a role as well, in particular the value of autonomy and the need to properly balance interests while due weight is being given to the best interests of the child.

D. PROTECTION OF PRIVATE LIFE AND FREEDOM OF EXPRESSION OF THE PRESS

Judge Lemmens has written a separate opinion in a couple of cases on freedom of expression in which the protection of private life was also at stake. Technically, the analysis takes place under Article 10 ECHR in that type of cases, and the question is whether and to what extent protection of private life allows for limitations to the freedom of expression, in particular of the press.[47] Two of

---

[46]   ECtHR 18 July 2013, *Taziyeva v. Russia*, concurring opinion of Judge Lemmens and Judge Dedov.

[47]   In Judge Lemmens's own words, the "'classic' conflict between the rights and freedoms of an organ of the press, which relies on the protection of Article 10 of the Convention, and those of a person who was the subject of a report and who relies on the protection of Article 8 of

these cases raised new questions of interpretation and application, and were after the Chamber had given its judgment accepted for referral to the Grand Chamber.

There is established case-law on the necessity to interfere with the freedom of expression of the press in order to protect private life. The following criteria must be applied to assess whether the freedom of expression outweighs the protection of private life: whether the publication makes a "contribution to a debate of public interest, the degree of notoriety of the person affected, the subject of the news report, the prior conduct of the person concerned, the content, form and consequences of the publication, and, where appropriate, the circumstances in which the photographs were taken. Where it examines an application lodged under Article 10, the Court will also examine the way in which the information was obtained and its veracity, and the gravity of the penalty imposed on the journalists or publishers [...]."[48]

In a case on the disclosure by the press of records of interviews and the letters sent by the accused to the investigating judge, Judge Lemmens together with two other judges disagreed with the majority that there had been a violation of Article 10 ECHR. In their view, the case was of more general importance for determining the burden and standard of proof in cases of disclosure of confidential information by the press.[49] Key to them was the question whether the press article had been capable of contributing to public debate on the subject in question, and they concluded it had only done so to a limited extent, since most of the information it contained had already been made public by the authorities. As to the question of the burden of proof, the minority "consider[ed] that the respondent Government cannot be expected to provide proof that the disclosure of confidential information caused actual and tangible harm to the interests protected. Such a requirement would deprive the secrecy of judicial investigations of much of its meaning. In our view it would be more appropriate to determine whether the article at issue was, at the time of publication, capable of causing damage to the interests protected."[50] The minority judges looked both into the content of the information in question and the potential threat posed by its publication. They concluded that the content might have had a negative impact on the accused's right to be presumed innocent and the proper conduct of the criminal proceedings at both the investigation and the trial stages, and that publishing information of a personal nature clearly amounted to interference in the concerned person's private life.[51] Moreover, "the 'sensational' presentation

---

the Convention." ECtHR 12 June 2014, *Couderc and Hachette Filipacchi Associés v. France*, separate opinion of Judges Villiger, Zupančič and Lemmens, §2.

48   ECtHR (GC) 10 November 2015, *Couderc and Hachette Filipacchi Associés v. France*, §93.

49   ECtHR 1 July 2014, *A.B. v. Switzerland*, joint dissenting opinion of Judges Karakaş, Keller and Lemmens, §1.

50   Ibid., §3.

51   Ibid., §3.

of the article in question considerably detracted from the importance of its contribution to the public debate [which is] afforded special protection by Article 10 of the Convention [cross-reference omitted]."[52] They therefore agreed with the domestic courts that Article 10 ECHR had not been violated.

The minority position, including that of Judge Lemmens, seems strongly informed by the principle of deference to the domestic courts:

> "In conclusion, we note that the domestic courts weighed the rights and interests at issue against each other, including the applicant's right to freedom of expression. The courts have a certain margin of appreciation in assessing whether interference with the exercise of the right to freedom of expression is necessary in a democratic society, and thus in weighing the rights and interests at stake against each other. Where this balancing exercise has been undertaken by the national authorities in conformity with the criteria laid down in the Court's case-law, the Court would require strong reasons to substitute its view for that of the domestic courts."[53]

Referring to the margin of appreciation enjoyed by the domestic courts, the minority judges concluded that Article 10 ECHR had not been violated. Important to note is that deference is only due where the balancing exercise with other rights and interests has been undertaken "in conformity with the criteria laid down in the Court's case-law".

In the subsequent Grand Chamber judgment on the case, no violation of Article 10 ECHR was found, in line with Judge Lemmens's (and others') dissenting opinion to the chamber judgement. The reasoning referred to the margin of appreciation of States and the fact that the balancing exercise had been properly conducted.[54]

In another case on the freedom of the press in relation to the protection of private life of the reigning Prince of Monaco, the margin of appreciation enjoyed by domestic courts again informed Judge Lemmens's and other dissenting judges's assessment of the case:

> "In conclusion, having regard to the margin of appreciation enjoyed by the national courts when balancing competing interests, we are of the view that these courts could legitimately have considered in the present case that the interference in the applicants' right to freedom of expression corresponded to a pressing social need. In addition, the reasons given by them are in our opinion relevant and seem sufficient to determine that there was a reasonable relationship of proportionality between, on the

---

52   Ibid., §4.
53   Ibid., §6.
54   ECtHR (GC) 29 March 2016, *Bédat v. Switzerland*, §82.

one hand, the restriction on that right in respect of the applicants, and, on the other, the protection of the Prince's right to respect for his private life."[55]

In a subsequent judgment, the Grand Chamber held that the domestic courts had not given "due consideration to the principles and criteria as laid down by the Court's case-law for balancing the right to respect for private life and the right to freedom of expression"[56], and hence unanimously found a violation of Article 10 ECHR. The disagreement between the dissenting judges to the chamber judgement and the Grand Chamber basically concerned the correct application of the principles by the domestic courts, not any matter of interpretation of principle. The Grand Chamber judgment confirms that deference to domestic courts is only justified if the latter apply the principles emerging from the Court's case-law in a systematic way, which the Grand Chamber felt had not been done in the case under review.

Only rarely has Judge Lemmens dissented because he found a violation had occurred, while the majority did not reach that conclusion. In the *Seferi Yilmaz* case, the majority did not think that Article 8 ECHR had been violated by publishing in a newspaper documents that had been prepared by police officers in the context of a criminal procedure. Judge Lemmens disagreed:

"Le fait que des documents aient été rédigés par des policiers, dans le cadre d'une procédure pénale contre d'autres personnes, ne permet pas à mon avis de dire qu'un journal peut tout simplement s'appuyer sur ces documents sans avoir à émettre des réserves. Une prudence s'impose en tout cas quand il s'agit de documents basés sur des dénonciations anonymes ou sur des conversations portant à première vue sur des sujets anodins.

J'ai des doutes concernant le respect de l'éthique journalistique par un journal qui publie des informations d'une nature telle qu'elles créeront l'impression que la personne concernée est impliquée dans des faits aussi graves que des actes de terrorisme, sans émettre la moindre réserve au sujet de la véracité de ces informations.

À mon avis, cet aspect n'a pas reçu tout le poids qu'il méritait dans les appréciations par les juridictions compétentes. C'est pour cette raison que je suis d'avis que, en ce qui concerne ces deux articles également, l'État a manqué à son obligation positive de protéger le droit à la vie privée du requérant."[57]

Again, this dissenting opinion does not reflect a different view on a matter of principle, but rather on how the principle of deference to domestic courts is applied.

---

55   ECtHR 12 June 2014, *Couderc and Hachette Filipacchi Associés v. France*, joint dissenting opinion of Judges Villiger, Zupančič and Lemmens, §8.

56   ECtHR (GC) 10 November 2015, *Couderc and Hachette Filipacchi Associés v. France*, §153.

57   ECtHR 13 February 2018, *Seferi Yilmaz v. Turkey*, dissenting opinion of Judge Lemmens, §3.

Taken together, Judge Lemmens's dissenting opinions seem to suggest that in weighing Article 8 against Article 10 ECHR, he is inclined to a stronger protection of private life, although it is nowhere stated as such. Explicit reference is only made to deference to the domestic court provided it observes the Court's criteria.

E.   EXPULSION OF VERY ILL MIGRANTS

The compatibility of expulsions of very ill irregular migrants with Article 3 ECHR has sparked quite some controversy outside and within the Court.[58] In the 2008 *N. v. UK* case, the Grand Chamber in a majority judgement consolidated earlier case-law on the issue, to the effect that "very exceptional cases where the humanitarian considerations are [...] compelling" were required for the minimum threshold of severity to be reached.[59] Typically, a threefold set of criteria needed to be reached cumulatively, as stipulated in the *D. v. the United Kingdom* case: "the very exceptional circumstances were that the applicant was critically ill and appeared to be close to death, could not be guaranteed any nursing or medical care in his country of origin and had no family there willing or able to care for him or provide him with even a basic level of food, shelter or social support."[60]

In *S.J. v. Belgium*, Judge Lemmens in his concurring opinion argued that he felt compelled to follow the Grand Chamber principles as established in the *N. v. UK* case, but he made clear that the minimum threshold of severity was very high. However, he stopped short from submitting that the threshold was too high. So while he believed that there were strong humanitarian reasons present in the case, in his view they were not strong enough to reach the Article 3 minimum threshold of severity and to prevent expulsion. In this instance, he seemed to value the institutional hierarchy more (it is up to the Grand Chamber to set and possibly review principles) than his own values and substantive principles.

In the chamber judgment in the *Paposhvili v. Belgium* case, the Court unanimously applied the *N. v. UK* criteria to Paposhvili, who suffered amongst others from chronic lymphocytic leukaemia, a fatal and incurable disease, but whose life was not in imminent danger (§120). It held that "[h]aving regard to the high threshold of severity required under Article 3 of the Convention, particularly in cases which do not engage the direct responsibility of the

---

[58]   See inter alia E. Webster, "Medical-related expulsion and interpretation of article 3 of the European Convention on Human Rights", 6 *Inter-American and European Human Rights Journal* 2013, 36–53.

[59]   ECtHR (GC) 23 May 2008, *N. v. The United Kingdom*, §43.

[60]   Ibid., §42.

Contracting State concerned, the Court is of the view that the present case is not characterised by compelling humanitarian considerations weighing against the applicant's expulsion."[61] Judge Lemmens sat on the bench. The case was subsequently referred to the Grand Chamber, of which Judge Lemmens was also part. The Grand Chamber came to another assessment of the case, by extending the category of very exceptional cases to seriously ill people who face a real risk of an irreversible decline in their state of health or a significant reduction in life expectancy. It concluded from the recapitulation of the case-law that aliens who were seriously ill, but whose condition was less critical than being close to death, had been excluded from the benefit of Article 3 ECHR. It felt a need for clarifying its approach[62], and argued that the "other very exceptional cases"

> "which may raise an issue under Article 3 should be understood to refer to situations involving the removal of a seriously ill person in which substantial grounds have been shown for believing that he or she, although not at imminent risk of dying, would face a real risk, on account of the absence of appropriate treatment in the receiving country or the lack of access to such treatment, of being exposed to a serious, rapid and irreversible decline in his or her state of health resulting in intense suffering or to a significant reduction in life expectancy. The Court points out that these situations correspond to a high threshold for the application of Article 3 of the Convention in cases concerning the removal of aliens suffering from serious illness."[63]

This means that the returning state "must verify on a case-by-case basis whether the care generally available in the receiving State is sufficient and appropriate in practice for the treatment of the applicant's illness so as to prevent him or her being exposed to treatment contrary to Article 3 [cross-reference omitted]"[64] as well as "consider the extent to which the individual in question will actually have access to this care and these facilities in the receiving State."[65] Finally, where "serious doubts persist regarding the impact of removal on the persons concerned – on account of the general situation in the receiving country and/ or their individual situation – the returning State must obtain individual and sufficient assurances from the receiving State, as a precondition for removal, that appropriate treatment will be available and accessible to the persons concerned so that they do not find themselves in a situation contrary to Article 3 [cross-reference omitted]."[66]

Since Judge Lemmens had voted as a member of the chamber that there was no violation, but in the Grand Chamber judgment voted with the majority that there

---

[61]   ECtHR (GC) 17 April 2014, *Paposhvili v. Belgium*, §124.
[62]   Ibid., §§181–182.
[63]   Ibid., §183.
[64]   Ibid., §189.
[65]   Ibid., §190.
[66]   Ibid., §191.

was a violation, he felt a need to explain his change of position in a concurring opinion. In essence, he acknowledged that respect for the authority of the Grand Chamber, rather than a principled position, guided his approach in the chamber judgment: "During the Chamber's examination of the case I took the view that we should follow the strict interpretation of Article 3 of the Convention applied by the Court since the Grand Chamber judgment in *N. v. the United Kingdom*."[67] Since the Grand Chamber had subsequently found that a gap in protection under Article 3 ECHR existed for seriously ill people, he argued to "have no difficulty finding, like my colleagues in the Grand Chamber, that such a gap exists, and in clarifying our case-law in order to fill that gap while at the same time maintaining a high threshold for the application of Article 3 of the Convention (see, in particular, paragraph 183 of the present judgment)."[68] Likewise, he agreed with the procedural approach adopted, whereby it is primarily up to the authorities of the returning state to examine the removal's compatibility with Article 3 ECHR.

In sum, in cases on an absolute right like Article 3 ECHR in the politically sensitive area of migration, it is not deference to domestic courts, but rather deference to the Grand Chamber that has guided Judge Lemmens in his separate opinions.

F. PHYSICAL VIOLENCE BY LAW ENFORCEMENT OFFICERS

In another Grand Chamber judgment, in the case of *Bouyid and Bouyid v. Belgium*, unlike the majority, Judge Lemmens and two other judges could not find a violation of the substantive aspect of Article 3 ECHR. The brothers Bouyid had been slapped in the face by a police officer at a police station. The majority found the slaps in contravention with Article 3 ECHR. Judge Lemmens dissented with that characterisation, arguing that by "suggesting that any interference with human dignity resulting from the use of force by the policy will necessarily breach Article 3", the majority had "departed from the well-established case-law to the effect that where recourse to physical force diminishes human dignity, it will 'in principle' constitute a violation of Article 3."[69] In particular, the minority judges submitted that "an unrealistic standard [had been introduced] by rendering meaningless the requirement of a minimum level of severity for acts of violence by law-enforcement officers".[70]

---

[67] Ibid., concurring opinion Judge Lemmens, §2.
[68] Ibid., §3.
[69] ECtHR (GC) 28 September 2015, *Bouyid and Bouyid v. Belgium*, joint partly dissenting opinion of Judges De Gaetano, Lemmens and Mahoney, §5.
[70] Ibid., §7.

Judge Lemmens's dissent in this case is clearly informed by substantive disagreement with the majority, although there is also a more formal argument, i.e. that the majority have departed from the well-established case-law. The latter is not necessarily problematic: the Grand Chamber can of course depart from established case-law, but it should not do so implicitly: one would therefore have expected the standard phrase used on such occasions ("While the Court is not formally bound to follow its previous judgments, it is in the interests of legal certainty, foreseeability and equality before the law that it should not depart, without good reason, from precedents laid down in previous cases.").[71] The real criticism seems to be of a substantive nature, i.e. that there is no longer a requirement of a minimum level of severity maintained for violence committed by police officers. Interestingly, a prohibition of violence without a minimum threshold of severity reflects the standard with regard to violence against children in the Convention on the Rights of the Child (Article 19) and the Revised European Social Charter (Article 17). One possible reading of the majority judgment is therefore that it implicitly aligns the interpretation of Article 3 ECHR in the context of violence against children by law enforcement officers with the children's rights instruments and provisions. The minority seems to reject such a reading:

> "The victim's vulnerability is a factor that may be taken into account in assessing the seriousness of an interference with human dignity. The majority refer in this connection, admittedly as a secondary consideration, to the fact that the first applicant was a minor at the material time (see paragraphs 109–110 of the judgment). We consider that the Court does not have enough information to treat the first applicant's age as a truly relevant factor in the present case. This was not his first confrontation with the police. Moreover, he was a member of a family who had had difficult relations with the police for years and who had lodged several criminal complaints against police officers. Referring simply to the first applicant's age as a basis for concluding that he was a vulnerable person towards whom the police officers should have shown 'greater vigilance and self-control' (see paragraph 110 of the judgment) is in our view an overly theoretical approach. The conclusion reached on this point risks being completely at odds with reality."[72]

This paragraph raises many important and interesting issues from a children's rights perspective, in particular whether young age and vulnerability coincide. These questions are, however, beyond the scope of this chapter. Suffice it to say here that Judge Lemmens cannot be said to be per definition against a reading of the ECHR in line with a thematic or specialised treaty, as his dissenting opinion in the *Enver Şahin* case illustrates, for example. In the latter case, which concerned the Convention on the Rights of Persons with Disabilities

---

71   ECtHR (GC) 11 July 2002, *Christine Goodwin v. The United Kingdom*, §74.
72   ECtHR (GC) 28 September 2015, *Bouyid and Bouyid v. Belgium*, joint partly dissenting opinion of Judges De Gaetano, Lemmens and Mahoney, §8.

(CRPD), he argued that as much as possible, the ECHR must be interpreted against the background of the CRPD provisions, which show the existence of an international consensus on the rights of persons with disabilities.[73] On the other hand, he seems not to be willing to defer *automatically* to more specialised norms, such as the prohibition of any form of violence against children, as the *Bouyid* case shows.

CONCLUSION

This contribution set out to explore the principles and values underlying Judge Lemmens's separate opinions in Article 8 and Article 3 ECHR cases. A particular principled view on the institutional role of the ECtHR and its relationship with States Parties to the ECHR, rather than a moral value framework, is often invoked by Judge Lemmens to justify the stance he takes in a separate opinion. In case where the protection of private life or the home is at stake, he tends to show Strasbourgian deference to domestic courts, to the extent that they fully abide by the Court's criteria, even if he disagrees with the substantive outcome. Whereas such a principled stance on qualified deference to national courts can be justified on procedural and strategic grounds, it may be hard to explain to those who expect the Strasbourg court to show leadership in matters of substantive justice. However, Strasbourgian restraint and deference to domestic courts are not the only decisive elements in Judge Lemmens's assessment of alleged violations. More substantive considerations seems to play a role as well, in particular the value of autonomy and the need to properly balance interests while due weight is being given to the best interests of the child.

In cases on an absolute right like Article 3 ECHR in the politically sensitive area of migration, deference to established case-law of the Grand Chamber can be seen. More substantive considerations and meta-legal values do seem to play a role as well, but Judge Lemmens is much less explicit in that regard. In order to pierce that procedural veil, and also to help corroborate or debunk some of the preliminary findings of this chapter, more empirical follow-up research, in particular interviews with Judge Lemmens and other section judges is needed. That research may shed more light on the importance of meta-legal values in Judge Lemmens's assessment of alleged human rights violations. More generally, more empirical work and more research on separate opinions[74] would enrich our understanding of the case-law of the Strasbourg Court.

---

[73]   ECtHR 30 January 2018, *Enver Şahin v. Turkey*, dissenting opinion of Judge Lemmens, §4.
[74]   For a rare study of separate opinions, see F.J. Bruinsma, "The Room at the Top: Separate Opinions in the Grand Chambers of the ECHR (1998–2006)", *Recht der werkelijkheid* 2007, 7–24.

A MAN FOR ALL SEASONS

Ludovic DE GRYSE

Avocat à la Cour de Cassation honoraire – Ancien bâtonnier
Professeur honoraire à l'université d'Anvers (UFSIA)

Conformément au sens premier d'un «liber amicorum», ma présence parmi les auteurs est due à l'amitié qui me lie à Paul et Anne.

J'ai eu le privilège de travailler avec Paul au barreau et d'avoir pu compter sur son précieux concours dans les dossiers de cassation.

Invoquant l'excuse de l'âge et l'absence, depuis quelque temps, d'activité professionnelle, je fus autorisé à consacrer ma contribution à un sujet non juridique, remontant à cinq siècles.

Ainsi j'offre à Paul et Anne une modeste évocation de Thomas More (1477 (1478)–1535) et de son *Utopia* (1515–1516).

I. « A FIGURE OF WORLD HISTORY »

Dans une biographie de référence, recommandée par P. Turner comme un livre qui «practically reads itself», R.W. Chambers attribue à Socrate et à Thomas More le qualificatif de «figures of world history»: «In the case of Socrates, this is recognized, but we are still» (1935–1938) «too near to see the full greatness of More». Selon l'auteur, «More is a hero of whom the whole of England is proud». Il ajoute toutefois que «strangely enough, this has not been to the advantage of his reputation».[1]

Dans son édition du 17 janvier 1982, le *Sunday Times* de Londres publiait un article sous le titre «A welcome nuncio" qui saluait la normalisation – «it was high time» – des relations diplomatiques entre le Vatican et l'Angleterre. Le journal rappelle qu'en 1935, au moment de la canonisation à Rome de Thomas More et de John Fisher, décapités sur ordre du roi Henry VIII en 1535, le Foreign Office fit savoir au Saint Siège «to have nothing to do with the affair». Le *Sunday Times* se montrait indigné par «(…) such a display of bigotry and sheer lack of feeling for christendom». Et de conclure: «Thomas More after all has a fair chance to be considered the greatest Englishman of all time».

---

[1] R.W. Chambers, *Thomas More, The Bedford Historical Series*, 1938 (1ère éd. 1935), éd. 1945, p. 351; P. Turner, *Thomas More – Utopia, translated with an introduction*, Penguin Classics, 1965 (1979), p. 16.

Ayant recours à une tout autre source d'information, Elisabeth-Marie Ganne[2] évoque le témoignage «d'un fils d'une longue lignée de pasteurs luthériens», le philosophe Emmanuel Kant (1724–1804) qui, «bien qu'antagoniste du concept éthique de la loi naturelle universelle préconisée par Thomas More (…) a loué en lui un exemple «qui mène de la simple approbation à l'admiration, de l'admiration à l'émerveillement, et en fin de compte inspire la plus grande vénération et un désir de l'imiter».

Le 31 octobre 2000, cette «admiration» allant jusqu'à la «vénération», aboutit à la proclamation officielle, par le Pape Jean-Paul II, à la demande d'un nombre considérable de responsables politiques, de «saint» Thomas More, comme «Patron des responsables de gouvernement et des hommes politiques».[3]

II. PORTRAIT DE MORE : « A MAN FOR ALL SEASONS »

Thomas More est entré dans l'histoire comme «A man for all seasons».

L'expression est surtout connue grâce au titre de la pièce de théâtre écrite par Robert Bolt en 1969[4]. La pièce connut un grand succès aussi bien dans sa version originale en anglais que dans la traduction en plusieurs autres langues. Dans la version française, l'expression devint: «L'homme qui fait face à toutes les circonstances». Plus tard le film correspondant portait le titre «un homme pour l'éternité».

Ainsi, l'idée qui s'est forgée de Thomas More s'exprime dans une appellation dénotant des qualités qui dépassent un cadre déterminé de temps et de lieu.

Le professeur André Prévost fait remarquer que l'expression «A man for all seasons» remonte à Erasme qui, dans la préface à son Eloge de la Folie («Encomium Moriai»), s'adresse à son jeune ami, Thomas More, à qui il dédie son livre, par la phrase suivante[5]:

> «cum omnibus omnium horarum hominem agere et potes et gaudes».

---

2   Thomas More – L'homme complet de la Renaissance, éditions historiques, Nouvelle Cité, 2012, p. 141–142.
3   Texte de la lettre apostolique en forme de «Motu proprio» du 23 octobre 2000, publié par E-M Ganne, livre précité, p. 266–273.
4   R. Bolt, A man for all seasons, London, Heineman Education Books, 1969.
5   A. Prévost, L'Utopie de Thomas More, Présentation – texte original – apparat critique – exégèse – traduction et notes, préface par Maurice Schumann de l'Académie française, éd. Mame, Paris 1978, CLXI, p. 191, note 3, réf. à l'Encomium Moriai d'Erasme.

Prévost précise que cette idée fut traduite par Robert Whittington en l'expression « A man for all seasons ».

Remontant dans le temps, Chambers résume l'historique comme suit :

> « The magnificent encomium of Erasmus set a fashion in public testimonials. Robert Whittington, in the following year, having occasion to write a book on Latin prose composition, selected certain current topics for translation. Here is what he tells of More :
> "More is a man of an angel's wit and singular learning. I know not his fellow. For where is the man of that gentleness, lowliness and affability ? And, as time requireth, a man of marvellous mirth and pastimes and sometime of as sad gravity. A man for all seasons." »[6]

De la présentation par Whittington il semble résulter que l'épithète « a man for all seasons » doive surtout s'expliquer par la phrase « (...) as time requireth, a man of marvellous mirth and pastimes, and sometime of as sad gravity » : des sentiments de joie intense alternant avec des moments d'un profond sérieux, voire de tristesse, les uns souvent imbriqués dans les autres, ce qui rend le personnage complexe et fascinant. Erasme se rendait bien compte du caractère complexe de son ami humaniste, son cadet de douze ans, sans doute une des rares personnes qui ait trouvé grâce à ses yeux critiques : « (...) it is not every man who can catch the complete More « (...) « His face is a mirror of the nature, reflecting the kindness and a hearty friendliness that holds him of ready banter ». Et le grand humaniste s'étend sur les qualités de More : « The great disdain in which he holds tyranny and his lively interest in equality made court life and intimacy with princes distasteful to him for a time » (...) ; « To find the perfect model of friendship one need look no further than More (...) ; the most downcast moods and the most irritating situations, even whole gatherings, are not proof against the infectious sweetness of More's disposition ».

Et enfin, un dernier trait de ce portrait de More, peint par Erasme pour son distingué ami-humaniste Ulrich von Hutten[7] : « There is no wiser counselor for grave matters nor is there an easier companion in pleasant conversation. More provides discreet handling of delicate situations offering mutually satisfactory solutions. And the man cannot be bribed. What a boon for the world if only Mores were installed as magistrates ».

---

6   R.W. Chambers, *o.c.*, p. 177 se référant à Robert Whittington, *Vulgaria*, 1520, ed. White, E.E.T.S., p. 64.

7   Le texte complet de la lettre à von Hutten, dans la traduction en anglais, est reproduit dans *UTOPIA and Other Essential Writings of Thomas More*, selected and edited by James J. Greene and John P. Dolan, 1967, A meridian classic, New American Library, New York and Ontario, 1984, p. 286–294 ; la traduction en français est reproduite dans *La Correspondance d'Erasme*, par M.A. Nauwelaerts et autres, Institut pour l'étude de la Renaissance et de l'humanisme, MCMLXX, Presses académiques européennes, S.C. Bruxelles, Vol. IV, p. 19–29.

Propos sincères d'un grand ami, certes, mais néanmoins d'un ami ayant gardé son esprit très critique, qui n'appréciait pas trop la formation et la carrière juridiques de More et encore moins son entrée définitive au service du roi : il le considérait comme « perdu » pour la bonne cause des humanistes. Et Erasme, prudent diplomate, prit ses distances, au sens propre et figuré, à l'égard de More et des positions prises par ce dernier dans le conflit avec le roi. « Il aurait mieux fait de ne pas s'occuper de ces questions dangereuses et d'abandonner l'affaire théologique aux théologiens. »[8]

L'historien néerlandais Huizinga croit avoir aperçu chez Erasme une certaine réserve à l'égard de son ami, ce qui n'enlevait sans doute rien à sa grande et sincère peine lorsqu'il apprit l'exécution de More.

Terminons le portrait de Thomas More par « More's virtues », telles qu'épinglées par l'humaniste espagnol Juan Luis Vives[9] :

> « The keenness of his intelligence, the breadth of his learning, his eloquence, his forsight, his moderation, his integrity and his 'suavitas', the sweetness of his temper ».

Comme on le voit, l'épithète "A man for all seasons" appliquée à Thomas More, a une longue histoire et couvre un ensemble de qualités. Elle évoque également la diversité de ses activités et centres d'intérêt. Dans une conférence, faite à Anvers le 14 octobre 1978[10], Jean Mertens de Wilmars souligna que (en traduction) : « En lui (Thomas More) vivaient aussi bien un juriste, un homme d'état, qu'un humaniste : à juste titre, on l'a appelé "A man for all seasons" ».

La même idée se trouve exprimée et développée par Marie-Claire Phélippeau[11] : « Chez Thomas More sont réunies quatre fibres essentielles. En lui cohabitent l'homme de loi, l'homme de lettres, l'homme d'Etat et l'homme de Dieu ». Et l'auteure ajoute que Thomas More est encore un « homme d'humour ». Il ne faut pas oublier cette qualité qui revêt plus qu'une valeur anecdotique.

III. SOURCIER DES DROITS DE L'HOMME ?

« Sans doute trouvera-t-on des points de rattachement entre More et les droits de l'homme », avais-je laissé entendre lors de la présentation de mon sujet. Il me fut

---

8   Extrait d'une lettre d' Erasme, cité par J. Huizinga, Erasmus, A.D. Donker, Rotterdam, 6ème éd., 1978, p. 206.
9   R.W. Chambers, *o.c.*, p. 177, se référant à Augustine, *De civitate Dei*, per J.L. Vivem, Basel, 1522, p. 41.
10   J. Mertens de Wilmars, "Thomas Morus, Vijf eeuwen Utopie", *R.W.*, 1978, n° 16, col. 1009–1024 (1012).
11   *Thomas More*, éd. Gallimard, 2016, p. 9.

d'autant plus agréable de trouver dans le livre cité d'E.-M. Ganne, un chapitre XII, le dernier chapitre, portant le titre énigmatique «Le sourcier» (sans point d'interrogation) (p. 247–257). L'auteure y suit le «regard paisible du sourcier des droits de l'homme» (p. 249) du haut du socle de sa statue dans une ruelle située dans la partie de Lincoln's Inn (à Londres), vers des horizons lointains jalonnés par la Déclaration d'Indépendance des Etats-Unis, la Déclaration des droits de l'homme de 1789 et la Déclaration universelle des Droits de l'Homme de 1948. Et selon E.-M. Ganne, «c'est à croire que dans leurs bagages, les émigrés (anglais) avaient également trouvé place chacun pour son exemplaire de l'Utopie de Thomas More» (p. 251).

Si j'ai bien compris l'auteure, Thomas More pourrait être considéré comme le «sourcier» des droits de l'homme, celui qui a été capable de découvrir les sources cachées de ces droits fondamentaux.

Peut-on dans l'enthousiasme pour la personnalité de Thomas More, lui attribuer l'épithète de «Sourcier des droits de l'homme»?

Analysant les valeurs de la «cité utopienne», la professeure S. Goyard-Fabre, insiste quant à elle, sur le fait qu'il s'agit véritablement d'une «communauté civile». «Il n'est pas question que se glissent en elle les prérogatives ou les revendications de l'individu. La personnalité des Utopiens n'est pas pour autant niée; mais nul n'est fondé à réclamer cette espèce de droits que l'évolution juridique de la Modernité définira comme «droits de l'homme» ou «droits subjectifs». Revenant aux idées de More lui-même, S. Goyard-Fabre rappelle que «dès le début du XVIème siècle, (il) a entrevu les dangers de l'individualisme pour la gouverne des cités. La vie communautaire de son Utopie est une «déclaration de guerre» au principe individualiste qui commence à poindre dans la politique moderne»[12].

Si ces deux opinions peuvent surprendre par des accents apparemment divergents, elles ne paraissent cependant pas contradictoires. L'optique est différente: d'une part l'influence d'idées chères à Thomas More, telles que le respect de la liberté de la conscience personnelle, d'autre part le monde strictement «utopien» gouverné par l'esprit de communauté et le bien-être de tous, fondé sur des vertus raisonnables dérivées du droit naturel.

Qu'il suffise pour l'instant de souligner la nature complexe du «man for all seasons» dont les idées restaient, même pour ses proches et ses amis, difficiles sinon impossibles à comprendre. La compréhension devient d'autant plus difficile

---

[12]   S. Goyard-Fabre, *L'Utopie (…)*, présentation et notes, précédant la traduction par M. Delcourt, GF Flammarion, 1987, p. 42.

pour ceux qui se trouvent à des centaines d'années de distance dans le temps, dans un tout autre contexte. L'homme d'aujourd'hui qui s'aventure à apprécier ou à juger Thomas More, se gardera de toute conclusion qui risque d'être trop inspirée par des idées devenues actuellement fondamentales et évidentes.

Je préfère maintenir un point d'interrogation après l'épithète «sourcier des droits de l'homme», laissant le champ libre à la perspicacité d'un chercheur ou d'une chercheuse pour approfondir la question et aboutir à une conclusion motivée.

IV. LA VIE DE THOMAS MORE : DIVERSITÉ D'ACTIVITÉS

Avant d'aborder *L'Utopie*, il parait utile de rappeler quelques jalons de la vie de More (1477 (1478)–1535).

Son parcours est marqué par une ascension fulgurante, dès son enfance et sa jeunesse, grâce à ses talents et à l'appui de son père magistrat, aidé par John Morton, cardinal archevêque et chancelier d'Angleterre, chez qui il put passer deux ans comme «page». Après des études à Oxford et une formation de juriste, More s'épanouit comme brillant juriste, professeur de droit et avocat renommé. En 1499, il rencontre pour la première fois Erasme: l'amitié entre ces deux hommes, fort différents à plusieurs égards, sera intense et durable jusqu' à un certain point. A l'âge de 27 ans, More devient député au Parlement où il doit surtout défendre les intérêts des merciers, membres de la grande corporation de Londres, spécialisés dans le commerce de la laine. Comme jeune député, il fait déjà preuve d'indépendance d'esprit en s'opposant aux exigences financières du roi de l'époque, Henry VII, qui ne lui pardonnera pas le manque de docilité. More montra en plus de grands talents d'arbitre et devint un magistrat très respecté. Tout en s'adonnant à ses tâches professionnelles, il prit, entre 1499 et 1503, pension au prieuré de la Chartreuse de Londres. Ce séjour exerça une influence capitale et durable dans la vie de Thomas More qui s'affirma comme un «homme de Dieu»[13].

Le nouveau roi, Henry VIII, le charge de plusieurs missions diplomatiques, en Flandres, à Bruges, Calais, Amiens et Cambrai. Nommé sous-shérif de Londres, il se trouve confronté à la révolte du Ier mai 1517, «evil May day», contre les «étrangers» séjournant et travaillant à Londres. Cet événement a été relaté dans une pièce de théâtre, écrite vers 1595; le discours de More exhortant les

---

[13] A. Prévost, *o.c.*, XIII-XV.

manifestants au calme, aurait été écrit par William Shakespeare[14]. Anobli, Sir Thomas More entra au conseil privé du roi, devint Maître des requêtes, sous-trésorier du royaume, «Speaker» du House of commons et Chancelier du Duché de Lancaster. La carrière de More fut couronnée par sa nomination, le 25 octobre 1529, comme Lord Chancellor d'Angleterre, après le roi la fonction civile la plus importante du royaume. En cette qualité, il présidait également la Star Chamber, haute cour de justice fonctionnant à la fois comme cour d'appel et comme juridiction statuant sur les recours directs introduits par des gens modestes ou indigents. En 1532, More résigne sa fonction de chancelier, officiellement pour «raisons de santé», en réalité, en raison du conflit surgi avec le roi au sujet du (re) mariage de ce dernier qui souhaitait obtenir le divorce, voire l'annulation de son premier mariage, depuis 18 ans, avec Catherine d'Aragon, pour s'unir à Anne Boleyn qui sera, en l'absence de More, couronnée nouvelle reine d'Angleterre. Un conflit plus profond, au sujet de la suprématie exigée par le roi sur l'Eglise d'Angleterre, que More refuse de reconnaître, mène finalement ce «héros de la conscience» à l'échafaud. Par mesure de grâce, il ne subit pas l'horrible peine d'écartèlement («death by disembouweling») infligée aux condamnés pour «haute trahison» mais il sera décapité (le 6 juillet 1535). Apprenant la «mesure de grâce», More aurait murmuré: «God forbid that the King should use any more mercy into any of my friends»[15]. Ses dernières paroles sur l'échafaud, qui paraissent authentiques, sont qu'il mourait «the King's good servant, but God's first». Le 19 mai 1935, après quatre cents ans, Thomas More fut canonisé par l'Eglise catholique comme «saint–martyr». La tête de More, ce qui en restait, fut «sauvée» par sa fille Margaret, avant qu'elle ne fût jetée dans la Tamise après avoir été exposée sur un pic au pont de Londres. Elle se trouve actuellement enterrée près des os de sa fille Margaret, épouse de William Roper, à St. Dunstan's Church, Canterbury. La réalité de ce fait a été établie lors des fouilles effectuées en 1978. Les visiteurs peuvent y lire et méditer la sobre inscription suivante qui me fut rapportée par ma fille Laetitia:

> «Beneath this floor is the vault of the Roper family in which is interred the head of Sir Thomas More of illustrious memory sometime Lord Chancellor of England who was beheaded on Tower Hill, 6th July 1535.
> Ecclesia Anglicana libera».

Ce bref aperçu montre la diversité des activités et la complexité de la vie de More. Pour être complet, il faudrait évidemment s'étendre sur sa vie privée au sein de sa famille, entouré de sa femme Jane Colt et de ses quatre enfants, Margaret (Meg), Elisabeth, Cécile et John, d'une fille adoptive et hôte gracieux de nombreux

---

[14]   A. Munday – Henry Chettle et autres dont William Shakespeare, *The booke of Sir Thomas More*, 1595, traduit en néerlandais par J. Kuijper, introduction par W. Van Tongeren, éd. Atheneum- Polak & Van Gennep, Amsterdam, 2016.

[15]   R.W. Chambers, *o.c.*, p. 343, se référant à Stapleton XX, p. 352, XVIII, 340.

amis humanistes anglais et étrangers. En 1511, sa femme décède et, six semaines plus tard, il épouse Alice Middleton, veuve d'un marchand londonien, qu'il appelait une « jolly Master-woman »[16]. Il est connu que More prenait très à cœur la formation et l'éducation des membres de sa famille. Surtout sa fille (préférée) Meg (Margaret) faisait preuve d'une intelligence exceptionnelle; elle écrivait couramment en latin avec une perfection telle qu'elle égalait son père et même Erasme qui ne tarissait pas d'éloges à son sujet. Elle se mit à écrire elle-même un texte destiné à la publication, que son père empêcha, craignant que le succès ne lui monte à la tête[17].

L'énumération des principaux jalons de la vie ou de la « carrière » de More ne découvre pas grand-chose sur l'objet précis de ses diverses activités comme juriste, avocat, juge, humaniste, diplomate, haut fonctionnaire, conseiller du roi et homme d'Etat. Afin de mieux comprendre ce que couvrent ses diverses fonctions et la personnalité du « man for all seasons », il faut se tourner vers ses écrits dont la plupart ont été sauvés et préservés grâce aux membres de sa famille. En plus, les nombreux témoignages de ses contemporains peuvent nous éclairer. Enfin, parmi la multitude de biographies et études, un choix si possible judicieux s'impose.

Le grand défi, pour comprendre la personnalité de Thomas More, est d'essayer de se mettre dans « le monde de More ». Dans un discours fait lors de la commémoration de More, le 6 juillet 2017, M. Worgan rappelle que

> « What mortals had to fear wasn't death, it was damnation. What really mattered was your immortal soul. Unless we understand and remember the vital fact of that belief, we cannot get anywhere near to understand Thomas More's world »[18].

V.   LES ÉCRITS DE MORE

Les écrits de More sont nombreux et de nature très diverse.

Chambers souligne que « the most important guide to the man who would write a life of More is to be found in the letters written to and by him, in Latin or in English ». Leur nombre est estimé à environ deux cents. Ces lettres comportent

---

[16]   P. Ackroyd, *The Life of Thomas More*, Vintage, 1999, p. 138.

[17]   Sur les rapports entre More et sa fille Margaret, voy. le livre émouvant de John Guy, *A daughter's love, Thomas and Margaret More*, Fourth Estate, London, 2008.

[18]   Rev. M. Worgan, *The Polarity of Thomas More as Saint and Sinner*, shortened version of the Address at the Annual Commemoration Service on July 6, 2017, Fellowship of St. Thomas More, 2018; la brochure contenant ce texte m'a été ramenée par ma fille Laetitia d'une visite à St. Dunstan's Church, Canterbury.

entre autres douze lettres en anglais et une en latin, écrites par More à ses amis lorsqu'il se trouvait, pendant quinze mois, prisonnier dans la Tour de Londres. Elles revêtent une valeur particulière « because they were evidently written with no idea that they would be printed, or read save amongst a very small band of friends ».[19]

En plus des lettres, More s'est adonné à tous les genres possibles d'écrits : poèmes, traductions, études biographiques et historiques, « short stories », pièces de théâtre, épigrammes, traités de philosophie et de religion, sans oublier des pamphlets. La plupart de ces écrits ont été préservés grâce à sa fille Margaret et à son neveu William Rastell.

More écrivait couramment en latin et en anglais, dans un style adapté au public spécifique auquel il s'adressait. Chambers fait remarquer que, dans ses controverses avec Luther, « More showed his extraordinary power of calling bad names in good Latin »[20]. Selon E.-M. Ganne, More aurait même parfaitement maîtrisé le français.

On ne peut oublier que Thomas More a fait grand usage de l'invention « nouvelle » de l'imprimerie. Le premier livre imprimé en Angleterre date du 18 novembre 1477, soit l'année de naissance de More. L'imprimerie devint l'instrument qui rendait possible la Renaissance et qui allait permettre la Réforme[21]. Grâce à l'imprimerie de son beau- frère, John Rastell et du fils de ce dernier, William Rastell, More avait un imprimeur à sa disposition ce qui lui permettait de répondre sur-le- champ aux pamphlets de ses opposants.

Dans ce qui suit, je propose de me concentrer sur *L'Utopie*, œuvre sans doute la plus connue de More, susceptible d'encore séduire et de faire réfléchir le lecteur d'aujourd'hui.

VI. L'UTOPIE (« UTOPIA »)

A. LES TERMES « UTOPIE », « UTOPIQUE », « UTOPISTE » : HÉRITAGE DANS LES LANGUES MODERNES

Même ceux qui n'ont pas de connaissance particulière de l'auteur ni des idées contenues dans ses œuvres écrites, se voient régulièrement confrontés aux mots « utopie », « utopique » ou « utopiste ». Ainsi ils diront ou ils entendent dire de quelqu'un qu'il défend des idées courageuses mais un peu ou entièrement

---

19   R.W. Chambers, *o.c.*, p. 19–20.
20   *Id.*, *o.c.*, p. 105.
21   A. Prévost, *Thomas More et la crise de la pensée européenne*, éd. Mame, 1969, p. 31.

« utopiques », qu'on n'a guère de temps à perdre avec des « utopies » ou, dans un sens plus positif, « heureusement que certaines idées soient propagées même si, à l'heure actuelle, elles paraissent encore (un peu) « utopiques », au moins témoignent-elles d'une « vision (à long terme) ».

Voilà un héritage linguistique incontestable de *L'Utopie* de More, œuvre écrite en 1515–1516 et dont la première édition date de 1516. Le terme « utopie », emprunté à cette « île du bonheur » fictive se retrouve dans toutes les langues modernes, évoquant une idée visionnaire, idyllique mais chimérique, irréaliste ou impraticable. L'introduction dans les langues courantes modernes, d'un nom propre figurant dans une œuvre littéraire d'il y a cinq siècles, paraît assez unique.

Les auteurs d'une publication originale, réalisée par l'Université Catholique de Louvain (Louvain-la-Neuve), pour commémorer la parution à Louvain en 1516 de la première édition de *L'Utopie*[22], établissent un pont entre l'Utopie et les « utopies ». Dans sa préface, le professeur Philippe Van Parijs plaide pour une « ouverture à l'utopie » : « Par-delà l'Utopie avec un U majuscule, il s'agit de mettre en avant une multitude d'utopies avec un u minuscule, une multitude d'idées modestes mais audacieuses qui ne sont réalisées nulle part et peuvent sembler irréalisables mais n'en méritent pas moins de nourrir nos espoirs. Il s'agit d'affirmer la légitimité et l' importance d'une pensée utopique déniaisée (…) qui n'accepte pas pour autant de capituler face à la pesanteur du réel ». Le même auteur a élaboré une intéressante « utopie » dans son récent ouvrage *Belgium, une utopie pour notre temps* (Académie royale de Belgique, 2018).

B. LES ÉDITIONS ORIGINALES EN LATIN – LEUR SUCCÈS

La copie autographe d' « Utopia » n'a pas été retrouvée. La première édition en latin fut réalisée en 1516 sur les presses de Dirk (Thierry) Martens à Louvain (Leuven), ville que More visita brièvement en 1508 et où, depuis 1425 est établie l'université, « Alma Mater » du destinataire de ce *Liber Amicorum* et centre de ses activités professorales.

L'objectivité commande de signaler que cette première édition de *L'Utopie* portait apparemment « les stigmates de l'improvisation », que More en souffrait et qu'il soupira même que « ce livre n'aurait pas dû quitter son île » et « lui avait échappé avant qu'il n'eût été vraiment travaillé »[23].

---

[22] *Chemins d'Utopie, Thomas More à Louvain*, 1516–2016, sous la direction de P.A. Deproost, Ch.H. Nyns et Chr. Vielle, Presses Univ. de Louvain, 2015.

[23] A. Prévost, *o.c.*, CXCIII–CXCIV, p. 223–224, se référant à une lettre de More à Bonvisi (Rogers, ep. 34, p. 88, II-6) ainsi qu'à une lettre à Warham (Rogers, ep. 31, p. 87, II, 35–36).

Une deuxième édition fut entreprise et vit le jour à Paris en 1517. Erasme, qui suivait de près les travaux de préparation et d'impression, ne put que constater la mauvaise qualité du travail: « J'ai vu enfin l'Utopie imprimée à Paris: elle est pleine de fautes »[24].

Des améliorations nécessaires et des embellissements furent apportés au texte ainsi qu'un assemblage judicieux de divers documents notamment des lettres d'amis humanistes étroitement associés à l'entreprise – Erasme, Pieter Gilles (« Petrus Aegidius » d'Anvers), Busleiden –, des poèmes de Gérard de Nimègue et de Cornelius Schrijver et des « accessoires » tels qu'une carte géographique de l'île d'Utopie, une initiation à la langue des Utopiens, tous ces documents enveloppant les deux pièces maîtresses, les livres I et II constituant *L'Utopie*. Le résultat se trouve dans les éditions de Bâle de mars et de novembre 1518, cette dernière édition étant considérée comme l'édition la plus complète et définitive.

Après l'édition de Bâle de novembre 1518, il y eut encore quatre autres éditions, notamment en 1519 à Florence, à Venise, à Vienne et, à nouveau à Bâle en 1520.

L'Utopie a donc connu, dans son texte original en latin, huit éditions en quatre ans. Le succès de l'œuvre amena Froben, l'imprimeur de Bâle, à s'exclamer que « les talents de More sont reconnus non seulement chez les Anglais mais dans le monde entier ». Prévost souligne que d'ailleurs, déjà au début de l'année 1517, « L'Utopie est devenue l'une des œuvres que tout humaniste se doit avoir lue ». Les amis de More, Erasme en tête, se démenaient pour faire connaître L'Utopie dans la société européenne de l'époque. Même Martin Luther, dans une lettre adressée au prieur d'Erfurt, Joh. Lang, soupire: « J'ai soif de l'Utopie de More »[25].

Un tel succès d'un livre écrit en latin, ne cesse d'étonner devant le rôle prépondérant et universel du latin dans le monde occidental du 16ème siècle.

C. LES TRADUCTIONS

P.A. Deproost, un des auteurs du livre cité *Les chemins d'Utopie*,[26] rappelle que Thomas More répugnait à ce que son livre fût traduit dans les langues vernaculaires: « dans son esprit, Utopia devait rester un discours seulement accessible à des humanistes éclairés qui en maîtrisaient la langue et le langage ». Il ajoute: « Pour le meilleur et pour le pire, il ne fut donc pas suivi ». Compte tenu de la connaissance du latin assez relative dans le chef des lecteurs potentiels de

---

24   *Id., o.c.*, p. 231.
25   *Id., o.c.*, CSX, p. 240; XCIV, p. 224 et CCII, p. 232, note 1.
26   P.A. Deproost, Introduction, Entrer en Utopie, dans *Chemins d'Utopie* (...), p. 25.

ma génération, a fortiori, parmi ceux des générations futures, c'est sans doute « pour le meilleur » que More n'a pas été suivi dans sa répugnance de voir son œuvre traduite.

André Prévost a réussi à présenter, en 1978, une édition magistrale de *L'Utopie*, bilingue, latin-français, fondée sur l'édition originale et complète de Bâle (novembre 1518) (voy. *supra* note 5)). Je me suis sagement, en pleine confiance, laissé guider par le professeur Prévost, dans sa traduction, ses nombreuses notes et savants commentaires. Les références à *L'Utopie* se rapportent à l'ouvrage de Prévost. Si j'ai parfois omis de préciser la référence exacte à un passage de ce livre, cet oubli doit être considéré comme couvert par une référence générale. Je me permets d'ajouter que cette belle édition est, pour ainsi dire, tombée sur mon bureau à Damme, offerte par ma belle-fille, Delphine Misonne. Avec sa perspicacité professionnelle de « chercheuse », elle avait déniché ce magnifique exemplaire doré chez un des nombreux libraires de Damme. L'exemplaire est signé par l'auteur-traducteur et dédicacé à un monsieur dont je tairai le nom. Les conséquences de cette heureuse trouvaille n'égalent évidemment en rien ce que Chambers[27] raconte au sujet d'un « ex-Cabinet minister (…) who dates his political career from the accidental purchase of a copy of Utopia at a second-hand bookstall ». Si l'ouvrage de Prévost est un peu encombrant pour servir de livre de chevet, on peut toujours avoir recours à la traduction également en français par Marie Delcourt, recommandée d'ailleurs par André Prévost. Cette traduction, présentée et annotée par la professeure Simone Goyart-Fabre, a été publiée dans un format de livre de poche[28]. Les néerlandophones pourront en plus se servir, ne fût-ce que pour comparer, d'une traduction par P. Silverentand[29] ou d'une autre traduction par Marie H. van der Zeyde.[30]

Il existe plusieurs traductions de *L'Utopie* en anglais dont une, déjà citée, par le professeur Paul Turner de l'université d'Oxford, publiée dans les « Penguin Classics »[31]. Turner raconte que plusieurs de ses amis, lorsqu'ils apprirent qu'il s'était mis à traduire Utopia de Thomas More, « have looked faintly puzzled and asked : 'Into what ?' ». Ainsi, « educated people », a fortiori les autres, « are often unaware that the book was written in Latin ». En fait, la première traduction en anglais, de Ralph Robinson, ne date que de 1551, soit 16 ans après la mort de l'auteur et après les traductions en allemand (1524), en italien (1548) et en français (1550) alors que la première édition originale en latin datait de 1516.

---

27 R.W. Chambers, *o.c.*, p. 125.
28 Ed. Flammarion, Paris, 1987, *La Renaissance du livre*, Ière éd., 1966.
29 Athenaeum-Polak & Van Gennep, Amsterdam, éd. 2008, 2010, 2014, 2017.
30 Thomas More, *Utopia*, Salamander Klassiek, Athenaeum-Polak & Van Gennep, Amsterdam, 2007.
31 Thomas More, translated with an introduction by Paul Turner, Penguin Classics, 1965, p. 22.

Le choix de la traduction pour la compréhension de *L'Utopie* est important. Apparemment, il existe dans diverses langues des traductions peu fiables, soit que le traducteur ou la traductrice n'ait pas travaillé sur un texte latin correct, soit qu'il (elle) ait pris trop de libertés, souvent dans l'espoir de rendre *L'Utopie* plus « intelligible » au lecteur moderne, alors que le texte de More n'a guère besoin d'être « modernisé » pour être compris.

D. GENÈSE ET COMPOSITION DE *L'UTOPIE*

Revenons à ce « libellus vere aureus, nec minus salutaris quam festivus » : « un vrai livre d'or, non moins salutaire qu'agréable » (« as entertaining as it is instructive »), présentant « la meilleure forme de communauté politique et la nouvelle île d'Utopie »[32]. C'est en ces termes que le livre est annoncé aux lecteurs. Il est précisé qu'il est l'œuvre du « très célèbre et très éloquent Thomas More, citoyen et shérif de l'illustre cité de Londres ».

L'Utopie se compose de deux livres avec la particularité que le second a été écrit en premier lieu (en 1515) pendant le séjour de More en Flandre, à l'occasion d'une mission diplomatique à Bruges. Cette mission devait résoudre, à tout le moins aplanir, des conflits d'ordre politique et économique surgis entre le roi Henry VIII et le Prince Charles de Castille, le futur empereur Charles Quint.

Les négociations traînaient et furent interrompues pendant plusieurs mois ce qui laissait le temps à More de rendre visite à un ami d'Erasme, à Anvers, Pieter Gilles, humaniste et secrétaire de la ville. Apparemment, ils ont, ensemble avec d'autres amis, échangé des idées sur un monde « idyllique » que More allait mettre sur papier. Ce « second » livre contient une description détaillée de l'île, appelée Utopia : sa géographie, son histoire, les villes, le gouvernement, les métiers, la vie sociale, les familles, les mœurs – le mariage, le divorce, même l'euthanasie... –, la guerre, les principes fondamentaux gouvernant la société, la ou les religion(s).

Le livre « premier » fut écrit par More à son retour à Londres en 1516 grâce à l'insistance d'Erasme. Les spécialistes font remarquer que ce livre « premier » ne possède pas les qualités littéraires du second livre et qu'il souffre de la hâte et de l'improvisation dans la finition. Quoi qu'il en soit, il est très important dans la mesure où il contient une vigoureuse critique de la situation économique et sociale dans l'Angleterre sous Henry VII, le prédécesseur d'Henry VIII, avec qui More, en tant que jeune parlementaire, avait eu quelques sérieux débours. Ce livre « premier » s'étend également sur l'extrême sévérité, voire la barbarie du

---

[32] A. Prévost, *o.c.*, p. 309 et 311 ; P. Turner, *o.c.*, p. 7.

régime des sanctions en matière pénale (la peine de mort infligée aux voleurs peu importe la gravité ou les motifs des faits), sur le rôle des conseillers du roi, sur l'influence néfaste de l'argent et sur les abus de la propriété privée.

Le personnage central, le narrateur, qui, en 1515, aurait été présenté à More par Pieter Gilles sur le parvis de l'église Notre-Dame d'Anvers, est un marin portugais ayant navigué sur toutes les mers et visité des pays lointains, doté d'un esprit critique et philosophe par surcroît. More lui a donné le nom de Raphaël Hythlodaeus, c.à.d. pour les lecteurs humanistes qui connaissaient également le grec: «celui qui répand des histoires insensées» ou «du babillage». Prévost qualifie Hythlodée d «expert en balivernes»[33]. Dans la traduction de P. Turner, ce personnage devient Raphaël «Nonsenso» et le traducteur en néerlandais a opté pour «Rafaelo Babellario».

Le nom du narrateur à lui seul semble donc indiquer qu'il ne faut pas trop prendre au sérieux certains de ses propos, à moins que ce soit là une astuce de More pour masquer ses propres idées. Ce personnage bizarre raconte l'histoire de ses voyages. De temps en temps, Gilles et More l'interrompent et font connaître leur propre avis. Autre personnage important qui surgit dans le livre premier où Hythlodée raconte son passage en Angleterre, est John Morton, archevêque de Canterbury, Cardinal et Grand Chancelier d'Angleterre sous plusieurs rois dont le dernier fut Henry VII. Si l'apparition de ce personnage est fictive dans *L'Utopie*, John Morton était une personne réelle bien connue de More et vénérée par lui depuis sa jeunesse. C'est l'occasion de rendre tribut à Morton dont, par la bouche d'Hythlodée More loue les qualités: «un homme qui s'imposait moins par son autorité que par ses qualités de jugement et sa valeur morale (…). Sa parole était à la fois élégante et persuasive, sa connaissance du Droit très étendue, son intelligence exceptionnelle, sa mémoire prodigieusement fidèle. L'étude et l'exercice avaient encore développé ses éminentes qualités naturelles. Le roi faisait le plus grand cas de ses avis et (…) l'Etat, visiblement reposait en grande partie sur lui» (Ut. I, 35)[34]. N'est-ce pas le portrait de Thomas More lui-même tel qu'il aurait aimé le laisser à la postérité et tel qu'en effet plusieurs de ses contemporains l'ont peint?

Les commentateurs de *L'Utopie* soulignent que cet ouvrage doit être considéré comme le deuxième volet d'un diptyque, dont le premier est constitué par *l'Eloge de la Folie* (1508–1509) («*Encomium Moriae*») d'Erasme, terminé dans la demeure de More et dédié par son auteur à son ami. Comme l'écrit Erasme dans une lettre d'introduction à son «Eloge»: «j'ai pensé d'abord à ton propre

---

[33]   A. Prévost, *o.c.*, notes complémentaires, p. 27–28.
[34]   La référence se rapporte à *L'Utopie*, livre I et le numéro de la page, indiqué en haut, à droite de la traduction par Prévost; la même méthode de référence est adoptée tout au long de cet article.

nom de 'Morus', lequel est aussi voisin de celui de la 'Folie' ('Moria') (en grec) que ta personne est éloignée d'elle»[35]. Selon Prévost, «spontanément, l'idée germe dans l'esprit des deux amis, que l'Eloge de la Folie, ne peut être que le premier volet d'un diptyque»: après l'Eloge de la «Folie», l'Eloge de la «Sagesse», sagesse qu'on ne trouve «nulle part» («Nusquama nostra» – «notre Nulle part») comme les deux amis appelaient l'ouvrage en gestation. Ce n'est qu'en septembre-octobre 1516 que More «inventa» le titre U-topia, soit la traduction en grec (ou-topos) de «Nusquama», «nulle part». Ce nom connaîtra d'ailleurs encore une évolution. Prévost relève que dans le sizain qui occupe une page entière des éditions de 1518 et précède la carte d'Utopie, More appelle son île: «EU-Topie, l'île du Bonheur»[36].

C'est apparemment Erasme qui a donné l'idée d'un livre où serait décrit le pays idyllique qui remplacerait le «monde des fous», sujet de son «Eloge de la Folie». Cette idée semble avoir surgi dès 1509 et aurait mûri pendant des années, pour enfin prendre une forme précise au cours des conversations que More a eues avec Pieter Gilles et d'autres amis humanistes lors de l'interruption salutaire de sa mission diplomatique en Flandre durant les premiers mois de 1515. Il s'agit donc d'une œuvre pas du tout née de l'inspiration d'un moment ni écrite d'un seul jet mais d'un livre dont la gestation a pris plusieurs années[37].

E.   SENS – MESSAGE DE *L'UTOPIE*

Reste la question la plus difficile. Quel est le sens à attribuer à *L'Utopie*? Comment faut-il comprendre et interpréter son contenu? Cette œuvre de 1515–1516, garde- t-elle quelque valeur pour le lecteur du 21ème siècle? Voilà plusieurs questions liées entre elles.

Je ne compte pas m'immiscer dans la «guerre des interprétations» qui a certainement rempli plus de pages, dans toutes les langues, que le «libellus vere aureus» lui- même. Comme on peut sans doute le dire de certains autres «classiques», «few books have been more misunderstood than 'Utopia'» et «a good deal has been read into Utopia which is not really to be found there»[38]. Parmi les positions extrêmes, il y a celle qui ne voit dans *L'Utopie* que le fruit d'une fantaisie de son auteur, destiné à distraire ses amis humanistes. Selon Chesterton, *L'Utopie* n'exprime que «the idle fantasies and hypotheses which More had thrown out in the day-dreams of his youth, to be the laws

---

[35]   Erasme, *Eloge de la Folie*, éd. P. de Nolhac, p. 3, cité par A. Prévost, *o.c.*, XXXVI, p. 66.
[36]   A. Prévost, *o.c.*, LI, p. 81.
[37]   A. Prevost, *Thomas More et la crise de la pensée européenne*, éd. Mame, 1969, p. 78–79.
[38]   R.W. Chambers, *o.c.*, p. 125.

of fairy land».[39] L'autre position extrême considère *L'Utopie* comme un livre doctrinaire, idéologique reflétant exactement la philosophie de More et dont tous les propos doivent être pris à la lettre et être considérés comme constituant le programme détaillé d'une société «nouvelle», même, selon certains, comme annonçant une société communiste «avant la lettre»[40]. Non tenté par ces positions extrêmes, je préfère m'en tenir à la «mise en garde» des «historiens de More» rappelée par E.M. Ganne, «contre les multiples tentatives tendant à lire dans l'ouvrage quelque profession de foi, de doctrines religieuses ou autres à attribuer au pied de la lettre à l'auteur»[41]. La même auteure ajoute que «More ne fut jamais un doctrinaire à ranger parmi les dissertateurs professionnels. Simple prudence, il a délibérément prêté à son Utopie cette touche d'un humour piquant qu'il partage avec son modèle, le cher Platon». Cet humour se trouve déjà exprimé dans des lettres fictives qui précèdent ou accompagnent le texte proprement dit des deux livres composant *L'Utopie*. Ainsi, dans une lettre (fictive) de More à son ami Pieter Gilles, More estime qu'il faut d'urgence éclaircir la location de l'île d'Utopie. Il avoue éprouver quelque «honte à ne pas savoir dans quelle mer se trouve une île sur laquelle je rapporte tant de détails». Cette omission devient encore «plus ennuyeuse du fait que «plusieurs personnes, mais surtout un homme profondément pieux, théologien de profession voudraient s'y rendre, le «théologien» en question souhaitant même, poussé par «une sainte ambition» se faire nommer évêque des Utopiens»[42]. Comme on le voit, l'humour se double ici d'ironie, chère à More.

La difficulté reste à distinguer les idées de More des histoires, paradoxes et même outrances qui, selon Ganne, constituent la nécessaire enveloppe parabolique qui lui sert habilement à brouiller des pistes passablement aventureuses»[43].

André Prévost résume parfaitement les difficultés d'interprétation et leur raison:

«L'Utopie, naturellement, subit la loi de tous les chefs-d'œuvre riches de la multiplicité des aspects sous lesquels on peut les considérer. Les lecteurs en apprécient tantôt un point, tantôt un autre et, sans observer cette tolérance, en honneur dans la «République Heureuse», ils en excluent d'un jugement rapide tout ce qu'ils n'y ont

---

[39]   G.K. Chesterton, *The English Way*, p. 213, cité par A. Prévost, *Thomas More et la crise (…)*, p. 77, note 2.

[40]   E.a. la poétesse néerlandaise Henriette Roland Holst – Vander Schalk, *Thomas More, een treurspel in verzen*, 5ème éd., W.L & J. Brusse's Uitgeversmaatschappij, 1941, p. 105–106.

[41]   E.M. Ganne, *Thomas More, L'homme complet de la Renaissance*, p. 83.

[42]   Lettre (fictive) de Thomas More à P. Gilles, reproduite dans l'édition citée, traduite par Prévost, Préface, 20–21, p. 349–350.

[43]   E.M. Ganne, *o.c.*, p. 83.

point vu. De là les opinions contradictoires qui font de More, soit un fantaisiste, soit un réformateur avant la lettre, un libéral, un déiste, voire un communiste »[44].

Les juristes en particulier savent que pour comprendre un texte, rien ne vaut sa lecture attentive, suivie d'une deuxième lecture qui incitera le lecteur à réfléchir au contenu en tenant compte du contexte dans lequel il faut le situer et comprendre. Comme Chambers le rappelle : « We must never think of More as writing Utopia for 19th century radicals or 20th century socialists. Even he could not do that ». Le même auteur conclut : « More's contemporaries agree in describing Utopia as « a warning against the evils which beset states. These evils are all forms of self-willed, individualist violence ; the national ambition which disregards the rights of the rest of Christendom (…) ; commercial greed (…) ; violence in matter of religion (…) ».

Il faut prendre garde à ne pas interpréter l'histoire ou un épisode du passé, a fortiori lorsqu'il s'agit d'un passé de cinq siècles, avec nos yeux et à la lumière de nos opinions d'aujourd'hui : « The first step to our appreciation of Utopia is to understand how it must have struck a scholar in the early 16th century »[45]. Dès sa parution en latin, *L'Utopie* fut un événement et un succès considérable parmi ceux que nous appelons les « humanistes » c.à.d. « disciples of a 'new learning' which they believed could direct European society towards a golden age of harmony and progress ».[46] Cinq siècles après cette parution, nous faisons bien de (re)prendre en main ce « manifeste de l'humanisme » (Prévost) et de le (re)lire et de méditer son contenu. En effet, si More a réussi à faire réfléchir les lecteurs, « il n'avait pas d'autre ambition que celle-là »[47].

Dans un passage du premier livre de *L'Utopie*, More, par la bouche du narrateur, stigmatise les peines excessives allant jusqu' à la peine de mort, appliquées aux voleurs et il soutient qu'il serait bien préférable de pourvoir aux moyens d'existence de chacun, afin que personne ne soit confronté à la si cruelle nécessité de voler d'abord, de périr ensuite. Commentant ce passage, madame Françoise Tulkens, professeure émérite à l'université catholique de Louvain, ancienne vice-présidente de la Cour européenne des droits de l'homme, avoue avoir « rarement vu un texte aussi fort sur le terreau des injustices sociales où bien souvent la délinquance plonge ses racines ». Elle conclut son commentaire par ce qui doit être considéré comme une exhortation à (re)lire *L'Utopie* : « Aujourd'hui, en 2015, l'Utopie nous ouvre les yeux, nous force à regarder et engager notre responsabilité »[48].

---

[44]   A. Prévost, *Thomas More et la crise* (…), p. 77.
[45]   R.W. Chambers, *o.c.*, p. 125 et 387.
[46]   Derek Wilson, *England in the Age of Thomas More*, 1978, p. 2.
[47]   A. Prévost, *T. More et la crise* (…), p. 77 et 82.
[48]   « Une justice spécieuse » dans *Chemins d'Utopie, Thomas More à Louvain* (…), Presses univ. Louvain, 2015, p. 67–68.

Comme le souligne M.C. Phélippeau au sujet du passage de *L'Utopie* concernant « la guerre », « More, une fois de plus, ne donne pas de solutions magistrales, mais s'amuse à secouer les consciences »[49].

Pour clôturer ce chapitre sur le sens de *L'Utopie*, on ne peut mieux faire que de revenir aux critères établis dans la présentation de l'œuvre, figurant à sa page-titre, et qui se résument en deux mots : « (nec minus) salutaris (quam) festivus » (« non moins 'salutaire' qu'agréable »), ou, dans la traduction en anglais de Turner : « as entertaining as it is instructive ». En lisant *L'Utopie*, il importe de ne pas oublier un de ces deux aspects.

F. LES MANCHETTES (NOTES MARGINALES)

Je ne résiste pas à dire un mot des brèves notes ou mentions figurant « en marge » de plusieurs pages de *L'Utopie*.

André Prévost nous éclaire sur l'origine et la signification de ce procédé, à première vue bizarre :

> « Les premiers lecteurs Gilles, Erasme, Budé et les autres ont si bien compris que l'Utopie les 'interpellait' qu'ils ont semé dans les marges du manuscrit et enrichi au cours des premières éditions ces notes marginales qui expriment leurs réactions. Certaines de ces manchettes sont didactiques mais d'autres chargées d'émerveillement et d'admiration, sont des apostrophes au lecteur (…). Ces notes introduisent dans l'œuvre une nouvelle dimension dramatique, une connivence avec un autre personnage ce qui développe la distance esthétique recherchée ».[50]

Exceptionnellement, More lui-même a tenu à mentionner en marge, le nom d'une personne qui lui était particulièrement proche ou chère. Ainsi se voient attribuer ce signe d'amitié : Cuthbert Tunstall (Cuthbertus Tunstallus) et Pieter Gilles (Petrus Aegidius), deux amis dont More fait expressément l'éloge dans *L'Utopie* (Ut. I, 25–26).

Voici quelques perles de ces manchettes (chaque fois suivies de l'indication de la page appropriée dans l'édition de Bâle et sa traduction par Prévost) :
- Des lois trop peu conformes à la justice (Ut. I 35)
- L'Etat bien organisé déteste les tyrans (Ut. II 78)
- Sens admirable de l'équité chez ce peuple (Ut. II 119)
- La modestie prend des risques mais non sans précautions (Ut II 121)

---

49 M.C. Phélippeau, *Thomas More*, Gallimard, 2016, p. 154.
50 A. Prévost, *o.c.*, CXXV, p. 155, note 2.

- C'est en louant les bienfaits de la religion qu'on lui attire des adeptes (Ut. II 143))
- Que partout la liberté soit respectée afin que rien ne soit fait par contrainte (Ut. II 90)
- O République sainte que même les chrétiens devraient imiter. La République n'est rien d'autre qu'une sorte de grande famille (Ut. II 94)
- Les oisifs doivent être exclus de la République (Ut. II 80)
- Pas même les magistrats ne s'abstiennent de travailler (Ut. II 83)
- Les avocats, une foule de gens inutiles – « Advocatorum inutilis turba »

Si le procédé des « notes marginales » peut être conseillé aux lecteurs de ce texte, c'est évidemment à condition qu'ils l'appliquent aux livres de leur propre bibliothèque et que le contenu soit pertinent afin d'éviter qu'un lecteur suivant secoue la tête en murmurant : « pauvre, il n'a rien compris ».

G. LE ROI ET L'UTOPIE

Une question qui surgit naturellement est celle de l'impact de *L'Utopie* sur les rapports entre More et son roi, Henry VIII. Cette question est liée à une question préalable : le roi, a-t-il eu connaissance de cette œuvre de More ?

Je n'ai pas trouvé de réponse claire et motivée à ces deux questions.

En ce qui concerne la question de savoir si le roi avait eu connaissance de *L'Utopie*, la professeure S. Goyard-Fabre estime, d'une façon prudente et sans étayer son opinion, que Henry VIII « ne semble pas avoir connu le livre de More »[51]. En revanche, M. Rousset, dans un article publié dans *Le Monde* du 29 juillet 2017 (p. 5), sous le titre « la mère de toutes les chimères », se limite, après une analyse de *L'Utopie*, à formuler la question plutôt rhétorique : « Est-il possible que Henry VIII n'en ait pas eu connaissance ? ». Les considérations consacrées à la question par E.M. Ganne, sont plus circonstanciées mais pas pour autant plus convaincantes. Elle situe *L'Utopie* dans le cadre des sollicitations royales pour faire entrer More au Conseil et au service du Roi. Elle aborde la question dans un élan littéraire qui engendre une réplique fictive de More :

> « (...) notre compère (Thomas More) aussi droit et scrupuleux que matois semble avoir finalement répliqué en substance aux avances royales : « Commencez par lire mon Utopie, Sire. On en reparlera ensuite et vous me direz si je conviens toujours ».

---

[51] Présentation de la traduction de *l'Utopie* par Marie Delcourt, éd. GF Flammarion, 1987, p. 26.

La même auteure précise que « ce qui ne pourra échapper au roi, c'est le sens très aigu de l'ordre social que relève More, très particulièrement dans le livre I de l'ouvrage »[52].

Même si ces propos semblent plutôt relever d'une envolée littéraire, ils reposent quand même sur l'idée que le roi avait – évidemment? – connaissance de *L'Utopie* et que l'intention de son auteur était que le roi lise le livre et s'inspire de son contenu. Un commentateur néerlandais estime même, sans toutefois apporter d'arguments, que « tout indique que More a écrit son Utopie dans l'espoir d'encourager Henry VIII à devenir un meilleur roi que son père »[53].

Il existe certes de sérieux arguments en faveur de la connaissance par le roi, de *L'Utopie* de More : Henry VIII était un homme cultivé, proche du cercle des « humanistes », apparemment fin latiniste : « He was a proficient linguist, an excellent musician and a student of theology who had developped a fine Latin style » et « soon after entering court, More described his master as a courteous and benevolent monarch who increased daily in both erudition and 'virtus' »[54]. Le roi estimait et admirait sans doute More qui, à l'époque de son Utopie (1516), jouissait déjà d'une solide réputation et faisait de plus en plus l'objet de pression de la part du roi pour remplir des fonctions importantes et, finalement, pour entrer dans le cercle de ses hommes de confiance qui devaient le conseiller et l'assister. Tous ces éléments et, en plus, l'énorme succès national et international de *L'Utopie* semblent justifier la conclusion que le roi a très probablement eu connaissance de cette œuvre, déjà peu après sa parution.

L'autre question reste toutefois pertinente. Si le roi a connu et a sans doute lu *L'Utopie*, quel en a été l'impact sur ses rapports avec More, entré au Conseil privé du roi en octobre 1517 alors que la parution de la première édition de *L'Utopie* date de 1516.

Lorsque les rapports entre les deux protagonistes sont devenus conflictuels, *L'Utopie*, l'œuvre la plus connue de More, n'a-t-elle pas été utilisée contre lui? Il ne faut en effet pas oublier que ce livre contient des critiques acerbes contre le système social, économique et judiciaire dans l'Angleterre sous Henry VII. More s'en prend avec ironie, voire sarcasme, à la noblesse, aux grands propriétaires terriens et aux conseillers du roi qui ne pensent qu'à favoriser la guerre au lieu d'inciter le roi à instaurer et maintenir la paix dans son royaume.

---

52   E.M. Ganne, *o.c.*, p. 74 et 77.
53   Traduit du néerlandais, Marja Brouwers, « Nawoord », *Utopia*, traduction en néerlandais par Paul Silverentand, Atheneum-Polak & Van Gennep, Amsterdam, 2014, p. 167 ; p. 175 de l'édition de 2016.
54   P. Ackroyd, *The Life of Thomas More*, Vintage, 1998, p. 191–192 avec référence à *The Correspondence of Sir Thomas More*, III, E.F. Royers (ed.), Princeton University Press, 1947.

Le lecteur reste intrigué par le fait que *L'Utopie* ou certains aspects de son contenu n'aient apparemment jamais été invoqués à charge de Thomas More alors que ce dernier faisait l'objet de nombreux reproches plutôt futiles et sans fondement sérieux.

L'argument que *L'Utopie* ne méritait pas qu'on s'en serve contre More parce qu'elle ne serait perçue que comme pure fantaisie ne paraît guère convaincant. Le succès de l'œuvre dans le milieu européen des humanistes et les réactions montrent que *L'Utopie* était, sur beaucoup de points, prise au sérieux et dépassait le caractère anecdotique, parfois humoristique dont More avait habilement enveloppé le message.

N'est-il pas plus plausible que le roi et son bras droit, Thomas Cromwell, se soient délibérément abstenus d'utiliser *L'Utopie* «à charge» de Thomas More?

N'ont-ils pas préféré ne pas se servir de cette «arme», en raison de la grande renommée de l'œuvre, de sa complexité et du talent de son auteur qui, écrivain et avocat accompli, aurait certainement présenté une réponse valable à tout argument tiré de son œuvre et n'aurait pas manqué d'utiliser le contenu de *L'Utopie* contre ceux qui essaieraient de s'en servir contre lui?

More avait d'ailleurs pris certaines précautions, pas toutes convaincantes, il est vrai, pour échapper à la censure et aux reproches qui pourraient lui être adressés. Ainsi, les sévères critiques exprimées contre les princes qui ne pensaient qu'à faire la guerre, étaient, dans le récit, le roi de France et le roi Henry VII, prédécesseur d'Henry VIII. Les injustices les plus flagrantes ainsi que les abus dans l'exploitation agricole, se situaient également sous le règne d'Henry VII. D'autre part, ces critiques étaient, comme il a été dit, mises dans la bouche d'un narrateur original, le marin portugais Hythlodée, soit «l'expert en balivernes» ou «dispenser of nonsense». More lui-même n'a d'ailleurs pas hésité à prendre personnellement ses distances par rapport à certaines opinions exprimées par le narrateur: ainsi, par exemple, en ce qui concerne la prétendue inutilité et l'aversion que ce dernier exprimait sur la mission de «conseiller du roi» (Ut. I, 62) et quant à la communauté absolue des biens (Ut. I, 67). A la fin du livre second (Ut. II, 161), More résume ses propres idées comme suit:

> «Dès que Raphaël eut achevé son récit, un bon nombre de questions se présentèrent à mon esprit: il y avait dans les mœurs et les lois de ce peuple, des pratiques qui m'apparaissaient complètement absurdes, non seulement leur façon de conduire la guerre, leurs cultes et leur religion et plusieurs autres de leurs institutions, mais surtout, ce qui constitue le fondement suprême de toutes leurs institutions, la vie commune et la communauté des moyens d'existence sans aucun échange de monnaie" (Ut. II, 161).

Et More conclut:

> «(…) autant il m'est impossible d'accorder mon assentiment à toutes les paroles de cet homme, bien qu'elles fussent l'expression incontestable de l'érudition la plus riche et en même temps de la plus vaste expérience des choses humaines, autant il m'est facile d'avouer que, dans la République des Utopiens, il existe un très grand nombre de dispositions que je souhaiterais voir en nos Cités: dans ma pensée, il serait plus vrai de le souhaiter que de l'espérer» (Ut. II, 162).

A boire et à manger donc dans *L'Utopie* suivant More lui-même. Cela aurait pu donner lieu à un débat passionnant, qui ne s'est pas produit parce qu'apparemment ses persécuteurs n'avaient pas intérêt à le susciter.

Dans ce qui suit, je propose d'aborder certains aspects du livre «non moins salutaire qu'agréable» en essayant d'établir quelque lien avec la vie et les opinions de l'auteur.

H. LA JUSTICE – LES LOIS – LES TRAITÉS – L'ÉQUITÉ – LES ACTEURS : LES JUGES – LES AVOCATS – LES JURISTES

1. *Pour une meilleure justice: rôle du juge – exemple de More*

Hythlodée affirme que «le salut ou la ruine de la communauté politique dépendent de la conduite de ceux qui exercent l'autorité et la justice» et que "dès que ces deux maux, partialité et cupidité interviennent dans le jugement, c'en est fait sur-le-champ, de toute la justice, le nerf le plus puissant de l'Etat» (Ut. II, 126–127).

C'est comme si on entendait More, lui qui durant toute sa vie s'est personnellement engagé pour une meilleure justice, impartiale, à l'abri de toute forme de corruption.

Comme Lord Chancellor d'Angleterre, il apportait, selon Prévost (*o.c.*, p. 204), toute son attention à rendre une justice équitable, rapide, insensible aux pressions de la parenté ou de l'intérêt. Il défendait le principe de la séparation des pouvoirs entre la politique et le spirituel. «More had a reputation for quick and fair decisions; it seems that no one promoted London justice more effectively and, in addition, More often remitted the fees which litigants were generally obliged to pay. As a result he was held in the highest affection by the

City».[55] More mit toute son intelligence et la rapidité de son esprit au service des fonctions judiciaires qu'il exerçait. Comme le souligne Chambers: «(...) he now applied to the legal business of Chancery that peculiarly rapid mind which in earlier days had enabled him to grasp the meaning of a Greek sentence with a quickness which astonished his humanist colleagues». Et le même biographe ne résiste pas à remémorer l'«heure de gloire» du juge More: «his day of triumph (...) when, having taken his seat and settled a case, he called for the next, and was told that there was no man or matter to be heard. This, we are told, he caused to be enrolled in the public acts of the Court». «Two generations later, it remained a marvel. It is strange to them that know there have been causes there depending some dozen years»[56].

Et la réputation de More comme juge efficace donna même lieu à quelques vers dont le jeu de mots n'a de sens qu'en anglais:

> «When More some time has Chancellor been,
> No more suits did remain.
> The like will never more be seen
> Till More be there again».

Une justice efficace était également le souci des Utopiens.

> «Les Tranibores délibèrent des affaires publiques et règlent sans tarder les rares conflits qui pourraient s'élever entre particuliers» (Ut. II, 78).

Et le texte de la «manchette» accompagnant cette pratique de régler les conflits «sans tarder», prend la forme d'un précepte pour le bon fonctionnement de la justice qui n'a rien perdu de son actualité:

> «Trancher au plus vite les controverses: ne pas les prolonger indéfiniment de propos délibéré comme on le fait aujourd'hui».

2. Les Lois

Chez les Utopiens, «les lois sont très peu nombreuses»: «elles suffisent à des gens qui ont de telles institutions. (Les Utopiens) reprochent avant tout aux autres peuples d'utiliser une quantité infinie de volumes de lois et commentaires et, malgré cela de n'en avoir jamais assez. C'est, disent-ils, une très grave iniquité que d'obliger des hommes à respecter des lois trop nombreuses pour qu'on puisse les lire ou trop obscures pour qu'elles puissent être comprises par le premier

---

55 P. Ackroyd, *o.c.*, p. 135 et note 32, référence à Erasme, *Epistolae*, Vol. 4, 20.
56 R.W. Chambers, *o.c.*, p. 274, avec référence à Ro. Ba., *Life of Sir Thomas More; Ecclesiastical Biography*, II, p. 80.

venu» (Ut. II, 125). Ce qui porte atteinte au bon fonctionnement de la justice dans d'autres pays, c'est précisément «l'accumulation invraisemblable des lois» et «leur caractère extrêmement compliqué» (Ut. II, 126). Et lorsque Hythlodée réfléchit «aux institutions si sages et si saintes des Utopiens», il souligne que «avec si peu de lois ils administrent si aisément leurs affaires tandis que dans d'autres nations, on transforme sans cesse les lois sans jamais réussir à établir un ordre satisfaisant» (Ut. I, 65). Une des raisons majeures du succès de l'organisation chez les Utopiens est que chez eux «la vertu a du prix» (*l.c.*). Voilà une des idées maîtresses de *L'Utopie* et de son auteur dans sa vie personnelle: la suprématie de la «vertu morale» que tout homme et toute société doivent cultiver à tout prix.

Les Utopiens estiment en plus que les lois doivent être compréhensibles pour tous: «chez eux, tout le monde est expert en droit» (Ut. II, 126). «Car, (…) d'une part, les lois sont très peu nombreuses et, d' autre part, plus l'interprétation proposée en est simple, plus (les Utopiens) la considèrent comme conforme à la justice. Ils estiment en effet que la seule raison pour laquelle toutes les lois sont promulguées est de permettre à chacun d'être par elles averti de son devoir. Or, si l'interprétation du droit exige trop de subtilité, très peu de gens seront avertis de leur devoir; au contraire, si c'est le sens le plus simple et le plus courant qui s'impose, la loi est claire pour tout le monde» (Ut. II, 126). Les Utopiens estiment qu'il faut respecter non seulement les contrats («pacta») établis entre particuliers mais aussi «les lois de Droit public qui assurent la répartition des biens (…)» (Ut. II, 105).

Ces observations sur la législation n'ont rien perdu de leur valeur. Loin de vouloir les reléguer au monde irréaliste de la fantaisie, elles méritent qu'on en retire tout ce qui reste valable.

3.   Les traités

En revanche, les «traités» ou les pactes entre peuples ou nations, ne trouvent pas grâce aux yeux des Utopiens et ils n'en concluent pas (Ut. II, 127–128). L'expérience leur a montré que les princes d'autres nations et la justice qu'ils prétendent pratiquer, font preuve d'une «insigne mauvaise foi à respecter les traités». Hythlodée ajoute, non sans une pointe d'ironie à la More, «que les Utopiens changeraient peut-être d'avis s'ils vivaient par ici» (Ut. II, 128 et note 6).

Sans doute que Thomas More, grand expert de la négociation et de la conclusion de traités, partageait au fond les sentiments des Utopiens: il ne faut pas trop compter sur la bonne foi des princes de ce monde qui ne pensent qu'à leurs intérêts matériels et à l'accroissement de leurs territoires. N'empêche que More se dépensait sans relâche à utiliser l'instrument des traités qui, au moins, devaient permettre d'éviter pour quelque temps de nouvelles guerres ou de rétablir des liens économiques jugés salutaires. Il est significatif que son épitaphe qu'il a rédigée lui- même, mentionne expressément parmi «les hauts faits» de sa carrière que

> «he served as royal ambassador at different times and in a variety of places, the last of which was at Cambrai (1529) as an associate and colleague of Cuthbert Tunstall, (...). There he witnessed as ambassador, to his great joy, the renewal of a peace treaty between the supreme monarchs of Christendom and also the restoration of a long-desired world peace»[57].

N'oublions d'ailleurs pas que L'Utopie a pris forme grâce aux contacts avec des amis humanistes, lors d'une interruption salutaire de la mission diplomatique en Flandre qui aboutit finalement à un accord signé le 24 janvier 1516 entre l'Angleterre et Charles de Castille (Ut. I, 25, et la note 2).

4. L'équité

Un autre point, sans doute moins connu, où More exerçait son autorité et son influence, fut sa réaction contre les excès dans l'application du «common law». More essayait de tempérer les décisions jugées parfois trop rigides des «common law judges». En sa qualité de président de la Chancery Court, plutôt que d'avoir recours aux «injunctions staying the execution» des décisions jugées contraires à l'équité, More entrait en discussion avec les «common law judges» et s'efforçait de les convaincre de mitiger la rigueur de la loi. Les conflits entre l'application rigoureuse de la loi («common law») et le principe de l'«equity», donnaient lieu à des situations délicates qui apparemment n'étaient pas toujours résolues d'une façon satisfaisante[58].

La voie pratiquée par More en faveur de l'equity est difficile à comprendre pour un juriste d'aujourd'hui tout comme elle le fut d'ailleurs pour les «common law judges» de l'époque.

Le souci d'équité surgit également dans L'Utopie lorsque Hythlodée critique la rigueur et le caractère disproportionné des sanctions pénales en vigueur en Angleterre où aussi bien les grands criminels–assassins que de simples voleurs risquaient la même peine capitale. Cette peine en cas de vol, est, selon l'observateur critique, «une suprême injustice» et «contraire au Droit» («non licet») (Ut. I, 44–45 et Prévost, note 1). Dans la mesure où cette peine

---

[57] Texte reproduit dans *Thomas More – Utopia and other writings*, selected and edited by J.J. Greene and J.P. Dolan, p. 285.
[58] R.W. Chambers, *o.c.*, p. 271–273.

est appliquée à des faits sans lien de ressemblance, elle est contraire à l'équité («aequitas»). Prévost rappelle que l'«équité», vertu prônée par les humanistes, est le sentiment supérieur de la justice «tendant à appliquer la loi dans son esprit plus que dans sa lettre» (Ut. I, 44 note 7).

Françoise Tulkens souligne «l'immense actualité» du passage de *L'Utopie* sur la peine et sa forme ultime, la peine de mort, appliquée en flagrante méconnaissance de la nécessaire proportionnalité des sanctions par rapport à la gravité des infractions[59].

5.   *Un monde sans avocats*

Une des plus féroces critiques dans *L'Utopie* vise les avocats et, par extension, les «juristes» en général. On a dit de More qu'il aimait en effet davantage la justice que les juristes.

Cette critique se trouve, sans ambages, résumée dans la manchette en marge du passage relatif aux membres de cette profession: «Advocatorum inutilis turba» – «Les avocats, une foule de gens inutiles» (Ut. II, 125 et les notes complémentaires, 126).

Voici ce que les Utopiens pensent des avocats et comment et pourquoi ils préfèrent s'en passer:

> «Les avocats, ces hommes qui font appel à la ruse pour plaider un procès et usent de fourberie pour discuter des lois, sont absolument exclus chez eux» (Ut. II, 125).

Leur intervention devant les tribunaux n'est nullement requise: les plaignants se défendent eux-mêmes; c'est à eux d'expliquer au juge ce qu'ils auraient raconté à un avocat. On évite ainsi bien des complications et la vérité est plus facilement mise en lumière, puisque celui qui la rapporte n'a pas appris de son avocat de feindre» ; «Le juge apprécie dès lors avec compétence les détails de l'affaire et donne raison aux gens simples en dépit des roueries des chicaniers» (Ut. II, 125–126).

Le portrait tracé des «juristes» en général, n'est guère moins critique. Ainsi, Hythlodée observe que:

> «Pendant mon discours, notre juriste avait pris ses dispositions pour répondre et avait décidé de le faire à la manière habituelle des chicaneurs, plus enclins à répéter

---

59   F. Tulkens, «Une leçon de criminologie avant la lettre», dans P.-A. Deproost, Ch.-H. Nyns, Ph. Van Parijs, Chr. Vielle (Éd.), *Chemins d'Utopie. Thomas More à Louvain*, p. 55.

les arguments qu'à les réfuter : ils mettent une bonne part de leur honneur dans leur 'mémoire'» (Ut. I, 43).

Comment expliquer cette critique et ce jugement sévère de la part de quelqu'un qu'on pourrait qualifier de juriste ou d'avocat « par excellence » : « He was a judge and a lawyer to his fingertips[60] ». Dans sa biographie, Peter Ackroyd analyse, à la suite d'Erasme et d'autres auteurs, les qualités de More, pour conclure « that he made the perfect advocate ». En effet, il réunissait en sa personne « the makings of a perfect lawyer – skilful yet detached, cautious as well as theatrical, persuasive and practical in equal measure » : More mettait ses qualités en œuvre pour créer une pratique « eminently succesful ; as well as being involved in most major cases, he also engaged in the general law business of the day »[61].

Dans une lettre écrite en octobre 1516 à Pieter Gilles, More invoque ses activités professionnelles débordantes pour excuser le retard de près d'un an, mis à terminer L'Utopie :

« Tandis que, continuellement engagé dans des affaires judiciaires, tantôt je plaide, tantôt j'écoute, tantôt j'arbitre un différend, tantôt je prononce un jugement (...) »[62] ; et le 14 janvier 1517, il avoue à Erasme : « Je n'ai pas le temps d'écrire, ni le goût de penser, tant m'accablent la presse des affaires, le 'pétrin' du métier d'avocat ».

Son gendre, William Roper, remarque que « there was at that time in none of the princes courtes of the Laws of the realm, any matter of importans in controversie wherein he was not with one part of Councell »[63].

Sa clientèle d'avocat était apparemment très variée : il ne défendait pas uniquement des gens modestes ou indigents mais il était aussi le conseil attitré de puissants marchands de Londres, notamment de la corporation des « merciers » (« the guild of the Mercers ») dont il devait défendre les intérêts même à l'étranger (e.a. à Bruges et à Anvers). Une affaire importante qui se trouve relatée dans les annales judiciaires de l'époque est celle où, en 1516, More défendait devant la Star Chamber les intérêts commerciaux du pape Léon X dont un des navires avait dû s'abriter pour la tempête dans le port de Southampton où il fit l'objet d'une saisie de la part de l'Etat anglais (le roi)[64]. More gagna le

---

60 Lord Hailsman, *Thomas More through many eyes*, ed. Chelsea Old Church, London-Oxford, 1978, p. 10, cité par J. Mertens de Wilmars, « Thomas Morus, Vijf eeuwen utopie », *R.W.,* 1978–79, 1009 (1013, note 23).
61 P. Ackroyd, *o.c.,* p. 117, citant Erasme, *Epistolae*, Vol. I, 422 ; *id., o.c.,* p. 52 et 148.
62 A. Prévost, *o.c.,* p. 345–346, (19) et note 1.
63 W. Roper, ed. Hitchcock, 9, cité par P. Ackroyd, *o.c.,* p. 135.
64 P. Ackroyd, *o.c.,* p. 180–181.

procès. Bon signe d'indépendance de l'avocat More qui osait, dans l'exercice de sa profession, s'opposer au roi. Ce dernier, impressionné par la compétence de son «adversaire», augmenta la pression pour le faire entrer dans son Conseil privé, ce que More fit en 1517.

Comme avocat, More avait d'ailleurs la réputation de conseiller à ses clients de régler leurs différends, dans la mesure du possible, à l'amiable, en dehors du tribunal. Si cela s'avérait impossible, il prenait la peine de leur indiquer la voie judiciaire la moins onéreuse[65].

More était sans doute le premier avocat du royaume d'Angleterre. Dans son épitaphe il souligne l'exercice de cette profession:

> «several years as an advocate in the law courts».

Pourquoi alors l'exclusion de cette profession dans la société d'Utopie? Après avoir souligné qu'il s'agit bien d'une des «plus féroces» critiques contenues dans l'Utopie, Prévost essaie d'en mitiger un peu l'impact en relevant que cette exclusion des avocats ne s'appliquait pas aux relations commerciales et financières[66]. Quoi qu'il en soit, les commentateurs restent perplexes. E.-M. Ganne attribue cette «exclusion» des avocats à un goût de More pour «multiplier les paradoxes et même outrances, (…) pour préserver, sous les fatras de costumes de charades, la nécessaire enveloppe parabolique qui lui sert habilement à brouiller des pistes passablement aventureuses». En effet, «qui diable prendrait au sérieux, venant de la plume du plus éminent plaideur du royaume, la cocasse absence de tout homme de loi au beau pays de l'Utopie, où les chicaneurs se voient tenus de disputer en personne leurs différends devant les juges?». Ainsi, cette critique des avocats et leur exclusion dans la société utopienne, devraient plutôt être considérées comme «une boutade, une caricature, auxquelles se prête un quotidien que More connaît par cœur»[67].

Dans sa carrière de juge et d'avocat, Thomas More a sans doute, dans l'Angleterre de son temps, connu beaucoup de juristes et d'avocats qui ne répondaient pas aux exigences de compétence et d'éthique professionnelles qu'il s'imposait à lui-même. Il en a rencontré qui incarnaient les vices décrits dans *L'Utopie*. Il pouvait penser que ces juristes ne présentaient aucune «plus-value» dans le monde «idéal» de «l'île du bonheur» où la société était fondée sur la raison, l'ordre, la discipline, la poursuite du bien commun, où les lois étaient claires et peu nombreuses, susceptibles d'être comprises par tous et où, surtout en raison

---

[65]   J. Mertens de Wilmars, *o.c.*, 1014, se référant à W. Roper; E.M. Ganne, *o.c.*, p. 24.
[66]   A. Prévost, *o.c.*, *Ut.* II, notes complémentaires, p. 128 (4).
[67]   *Thomas More, L'homme complet (…)*, p. 83–84.

de l'absence de propriété privée et de monnaie et grâce à une gouvernance rigoureuse veillant exclusivement au bien commun, les conflits étaient rares (Ut. II, 78) et se prêtaient à un règlement rapide par le juge qui entendait directement les justiciables concernés. Dans un tel monde idéal, l'intervention d'un avocat pour chaque partie était considérée comme ' inutile.

Rien ne permet toutefois de conclure que l'auteur, l'avocat le plus renommé du pays, plaidait également pour une telle absence d'avocats dans le monde réel qui était le sien.

Et les avocats d'aujourd'hui, dans nos pays «civilisés», auront tendance à croire qu'ils ne présentent pas, au moins la grande majorité d'entre eux, les vices décrits dans *L'Utopie* et que leur intervention reste une garantie nécessaire du bon fonctionnement de la justice et de l'Etat de droit.

En tout cas, voilà un beau sujet de dissertation à proposer aux candidats avocats/magistrats: «Advocatorum inutilis turba» – «Qu'en pensez-vous? Motivez votre réponse».

I.   CONSEILLER DU ROI

Entre Hythlodée, Pieter Gilles et Thomas More surgit une discussion animée au sujet de la fonction de «conseiller du roi».

Hythlodée ne croit pas à l'utilité de ce rôle. Lorsque Gilles lui fait remarquer que «servir» le roi ne signifie pas «s'asservir» au roi, Hythlodée répond: «servir! ce mot n'a qu'une syllabe de moins qu'asservir» (Ut. I, 32). Thomas More intervient alors dans la discussion pour convaincre le narrateur de mettre ses talents au service d'un prince ou d'un roi: «(…) Vous agiriez d'une manière vraiment digne d'un esprit aussi généreux et aussi profondément ami de la sagesse que le vôtre, si vous acceptiez de mettre vos dons et votre activité, même au prix de quelques sacrifices personnels, au service des affaires publiques» (Ut. I, 33). «Or, vous ne pouvez jamais réaliser cet idéal plus efficacement qu'en faisant partie du conseil de quelque grand prince auquel vous inspireriez (…) des mesures conformes au droit et à la morale» (Ut. I, 33).

Plus loin dans la discussion, Hythlodée fait valoir que «chez les princes, il n'y a pas de place pour la philosophie» Ut. I, 61). «Oui, c'est bien vrai», répond More, «il n'y a pas de place pour cette scolastique qui prétendrait que n'importe quelle solution est applicable n'importe où. Mais il existe une autre philosophie, même instruite de la vie en société: elle connaît son théâtre et elle s'y accommode; dans la pièce, elle accepte le rôle qui lui revient et le joue avec beaucoup d'élégance et de grâce. C'est cette philosophie-là que vous devriez cultiver (Ut. I, 61–62) Et More applique cette philosophie au rôle à jouer dans les «affaires de l'Etat» et aux «délibérations des princes».

> «Si vous ne pouvez supprimer radicalement les idées fausses ni porter remède aux abus consacrés par l'usage comme vous jugez devoir le faire en votre âme et conscience, ce n'est pas une raison pour délaisser les intérêts de l'Etat, pas plus qu'on ne doit abandonner un navire en pleine tempête sous prétexte qu'on est impuissant à maîtriser le vent. Il ne faut donc pas chercher à faire pénétrer dans l'esprit de personnes imbues d'opinions toutes différentes des idées inattendues et déconcertantes qui, on le sait, ne sauraient peser bien lourd. Mieux vaut prendre une voie moins directe: dans la mesure du possible, traiter de tout avec habileté et, si vos efforts ne peuvent transformer le mal en bien, qu'ils servent au moins à atténuer le mal. De fait, puisqu'il est impossible que tout aille bien sans que tous ne soient bons, je ne m'attends pas à voir cet idéal réalisé avant de nombreuses années» (Ut. I, 62).

Prévost souligne le caractère essentiel de ce texte qui traduit les idées personnelles de More (Ut I, 62, notes 3 et 5, note complémentaire, 62 (4)): "Ce paragraphe qui propose 'une voie moins directe' est essentiel; il définit les règles de conduite que suivra More lorsqu'il s'engagera au service du roi; il lui faudra à la fois, sauvegarder les exigences de sa conscience, qui ne cessera pas de protester contre les abus, et accepter les ambiguïtés et les servitudes de la politique, art du possible. A la voie directe, More substitue la voie indirecte, tout aussi exigeante que la méthode directe mais pragmatique et apparemment plus efficace. Il arrive cependant, et More en fera l'expérience (…), que les 'principes' et la conscience fassent entendre à la 'politique' un non catégorique».

Cet échange de vues fictif mais essentiel pour comprendre la philosophie politique de More date de 1516, année où, de retour à Londres, et sous la pression de ses amis, il rédigea et finit enfin le premier livre de *L'Utopie*; en octobre 1517, More entra au Conseil privé du roi, dès lors, 'au service' du roi. Ainsi il fut amené à mettre ses principes, énoncés avec conviction dans *L'Utopie*, en pratique et cela, jusqu'au bout, jusqu'au moment où il dut conclure que la politique compromissoire n'était plus possible parce qu'inconciliable avec les impératifs de sa conscience. Au moment où More fit connaître dans *L'Utopie* ses opinions au sujet d'une vie comme conseiller au service du roi, loin d'être une question théorique ou hypothétique, cela constituait pour lui une question existentielle qui le préoccupait personnellement. Ce sont des passages de *L'Utopie* dont le contenu correspond étroitement à la vie et aux idées de More.

J. LIBERTÉ DE RELIGION – LA TOLÉRANCE ET SES LIMITES

Les Utopiens mettent au nombre de leurs institutions les plus anciennes celle qui prescrit de ne faire grief à personne de sa religion (Ut. II, 143). Il faut se garder de tout sentiment de supériorité et d'agressivité à l'égard de ceux qui ne partagent pas sa conviction religieuse. Ainsi quelqu'un qui ne cessait pas ses harangues contre ceux qui ne partageaient pas sa conviction religieuse et qui faisait preuve de «plus de zèle que de prudence» «fut accusé non pas d'outrage à la religion mais d'excitation au tumulte dans le peuple: il passa en jugement, fut condamné et puni d'exil» (Ut. II, 143).

Ce principe de la liberté de religion remontait déjà à Utopus, le fondateur de la République d'Utopie: «dès sa victoire, il décréta que chacun serait libre de pratiquer la religion qui lui plaisait»; si on pouvait «s'efforcer de gagner les autres à la sienne», il fallait le faire «en exposant paisiblement, avec modération, ses raisons de croire, sans s'acharner à détruire les autres sectes si les moyens de persuasion se révélaient impuissants à faire naître la conviction, sans recourir à la violence, ni se permettre aucune insulte: celui qui montrerait, en cette matière, un zèle insolent serait puni d'exil ou de servitude» (Ut. II, 143). La liberté et la diversité des religions impliquent que chaque Utopien est libre de reconnaître et d'adorer un être suprême de son choix: le soleil, la lune, un astre errant, un homme qui a brillé autrefois par ses vertus ou par sa gloire, ou, ce fut le cas de la grande majorité des Utopiens, une divinité unique, inconnaissable, éternelle, infinie, diffuse à travers tout cet univers (...) que les Utopiens nomment «l'Etre-qui-engendre», «parens» en latin, celui qui donne la vie, le géniteur suprême, la source de tout ce qui existe, appelé dans la langue des Utopiens, Mythra (Ut. II, 141 note 2).

Le principe de la diversité et de la liberté des opinions religieuses fut érigé comme un des piliers de la société utopienne, à une époque où le monde réel ne connaissait pas (encore) le dialogue entre les religions ou les opinions religieuses.

La «tolérance religieuse», telle qu'elle est prônée dans la société utopienne, connaissait d'ailleurs ses limites, également tracées par le fondateur d'Utopia.

Utopus promulgua en effet «une loi sévère et inviolable pour interdire que nul ne dérogeât à la dignité humaine jusqu'à penser que l'âme meurt avec le corps ou que le caprice préside aux destinées du monde, en l'absence de toute Providence». Voilà les deux dogmes fondamentaux qui forment les limites de la tolérance: d'une part, la croyance obligée à un au-delà où l'âme continue à vivre après la mort et connaîtra les récompenses d'une vie vertueuse ou des châtiments sanctionnant le vice ; d'autre part l'obligation de reconnaître le rôle essentiel de la Providence dans la marche du monde (Ut. II, 144). Quelqu'un qui refuse de reconnaître ces deux principes fondamentaux, n'est plus compté au nombre des hommes « puisqu'il a ravalé la sublime nature de son âme à la vile condition du corps de la bête » : à une telle personne, on ne donne plus sa place parmi les citoyens (Ut. II, 144) ; il est « l'objet du mépris que l'on affiche à une nature molle et sans élévation. Pour le reste, (les Utopiens) ne lui infligent aucune peine corporelle, persuadés qu'il n'est pas au pouvoir de l'homme de croire ce qui lui plaît » (Ut. II, 145). Le sens de cette dernière phrase n'est pas évident. Prévost, dans une note en bas de page, établit un lien avec l'opinion énoncée par More à la fin de sa vie en 1535, lorsqu'il dit :

> « Je ne vois personne qui puisse légitimement commander à un autre homme de changer d'opinion ou qui puisse le forcer à le faire, l'obligeant ainsi à faire passer sa conscience d'un côté à l'autre » (Ut. II, 145, note 1 et notes complémentaires, p. 128 (4)).

Le respect de la diversité des opinions religieuses se montre également dans les prières rituelles qui constituent des moments forts de la vie des Utopiens et dont les paroles ont été composées de manière à pouvoir être récitées en même temps par tous et à s'appliquer à chacun en particulier : « Après avoir loué et remercié Dieu notamment pour la religion qui, espère-t-il, est la plus vraie », l'Utopien ajoute, tout modestement, que « si jamais, sur ce sujet, il était dans l'erreur ou, si une religion meilleure avait reçu de Dieu une approbation plus grande encore, il supplie sa bonté de la lui faire connaître : il est prêt à suivre, quelle qu'elle soit, la voie dans laquelle Il le conduirait » (Ut. II, 155).

Comment Thomas More qui proclame ainsi dans son « Utopie » la reconnaissance et le respect de la diversité des opinions religieuses et qui trouva la mort comme victime de l'intolérance de son roi, mettait-il lui-même en pratique les principes de tolérance et de respect de la diversité d'opinions ?

Les avis sur cette question restent partagés.

Il est certain que More, à la demande expresse du roi, a joué un rôle prépondérant dans la défense de la foi catholique contre les « hérétiques », les protestants luthériens. La façon dont More s'exprimait dans ses écrits et pamphlets contre Luther, Tyndale et leurs fidèles et les efforts qu'il déployait concrètement sur le terrain, notamment par des descentes à domicile et des saisies pour empêcher l'entrée et la distribution en Angleterre d'écrits « suspects », semblent difficilement conciliables avec la modération et la tolérance prêchées dans *L'Utopie*. More lui-même n'a jamais caché sa virulente opposition aux théories propagées par Luther et les réformateurs. Dans son épitaphe, il se vante d'avoir été «admolester of» – «unpleasant to» – «thieves, murders and heretics»[68]. Ainsi, les «hérétiques» sont, avec les assassins et les voleurs, mis dans la même catégorie des personnes pouvant ou devant craindre les foudres de More.

Indépendamment des instructions du roi qui, en tant que «Defensor Fidei» était à l'époque encore vigoureusement opposé aux «réformateurs» et à leurs idées, le comportement de Thomas More s'expliquait sans doute par une crainte existentielle de la division de la chrétienté en Europe. Celle-ci était confrontée aux menaces venant de l'étranger: les Turcs devant les portes de Vienne, les émeutes et guerres en Allemagne, le sac de Rome en 1527 par Charles Quint et ses troupes de mercenaires et protestants allemands. Ce n'était certes pas l'époque où les tenants de plusieurs tendances religieuses allaient se mettre autour de la table, en reconnaissant humblement les mérites des thèses opposées. En 2000, la plus haute autorité de l'Eglise catholique, le pape Jean-Paul II, considéra que Thomas More, dans son action contre les «hérétiques», «fut tributaire de la culture de son temps»[69]. Si «la culture du temps» n'est pas toujours une excuse valable, il faut néanmoins tenir compte du contexte historique pour comprendre le comportement de Thomas More et se garder de le juger d'une façon péremptoire à la lumière des idées et principes «modernes» de «liberté d'opinion» et de «tolérance».

En Angleterre, particulièrement dans le monde anglican, il y a toujours eu une vision fort critique de Thomas More à qui on reproche la «persécution» des réformateurs et des atrocités qui auraient été commises sur ses ordres ou, à tout le moins couvertes par son silence. Le débat s'est trouvé réanimé à l'occasion de l'émission à la BBC en 2014 d'une version télévisée du roman historique *Wolf Hall*, écrit par Hilary Mantel qui réhabilite Thomas Cromwell aux dépens de Thomas More, présenté comme un fanatique religieux obsédé par la persécution des protestants sans défense[70]; Cette émission télévisée donna lieu à de vives réactions dans les médias. Un commentateur a fait remarquer que l'auteur de *Wolf Hall*, Hilary Mantell, a, lors de ses «Reith lectures» pris soin d'expliquer que comme les deux personnages principaux de son livre, Thomas Cromwell et Anne Boleyn, furent les ennemis déclarés de Thomas More, ce dernier ne pouvait, de leur point de vue, qu'être présenté sous un angle négatif[71].

---

[68] Thomas More, *Utopia and other essential writings (...)*, p. 285; R.W. Chambers, *o.c.*, p. 286.
[69] Lettre apostolique reproduite par E.M. Ganne, *o.c.*, p. 266 (272).
[70] A ce sujet, voy. BBC-History Magazine, Janvier 2015, *The Cromwell enigma*, p. 47–50.
[71] Rev. Maurice Worgan, *The Polarity of Thomas More as Saint and Sinner*, Address at the annual Commemoration Service, July 6th, 2017, Fellowship of St. Thomas More, 2018, n° 57, p. 17. Dans un livre récent, *Thomas Cromwell: A Life*, Diarmaid MacCulloch présente un 'Thomas Cromwell', jugé plus conforme à la réalité historique que le portrait tracé par Mantel, voy. la recension dans *The Economist*, October 2018, 75.

Eamon Duffy, professeur d'histoire de «Christianity» à l'université de Cambridge, a résumé la question dans un article, publié fin janvier 2015, sous le titre «More or less»[72]. Sa conclusion est que More «was neither blood-soaked nor a hypocrite, but he was a man of his time, not of ours (…). (…) More's world was not our world. By the standards of his age, he was a compassionate and just man. (…) like most of his contemporaries, he believed that heresy was a kind of spiritual murder. He viewed the preaching of heresy as we do the peddling of hard drugs, a moral cancer that ruined lives, corrupted the young, dissolved the bonds of truth and morality, and undermined the fabric of Christian society. He was horrified by the religious wars tearing Europe apart in the 1520s, shattering the vision of Christian harmony that he and Erasmus had promoted in their writings. Like Erasmus, More blamed those wars on Luther and his fellows, and he feared that the spread of Protestantism would wreak the same havoc in England. He believed he had a duty to persuade, coax and if necessary, coerce heretics to abandon their beliefs, or at least to stay silent about them».

Chambers, lui non plus, ne conteste pas la virulence des réactions de More contre les «hérésies». L'analyse documentée des accusations portées contre More, plus particulièrement le fait d'avoir commis des cruautés, voire d'avoir ordonné la mise à mort sur le bûcher d'hérétiques récalcitrants, conduit toutefois ce biographe à la conclusion que ces accusations ne sont ni prouvées ni fondées. Il est, selon Chambers, significatif que ces accusations n'ont pas été portées contre More du temps de son vivant au cours du procès qui a conduit à sa condamnation à mort : «After More's execution, a wave of protest against his death passed over Europe; (…) there is evidence that the Government tried to counter this by inventing, and circulating in Germany, stories of More's 'cruelty' to heretics».

Chambers conclut que «More's hatred of heresy has its root, not in religious bigotry, but in the fear of sedition, tumult and civil war, characteristic of Sixteenth- Century statesmen» et que «the charge against More of inconsistency rests upon refusing to notice the distinction between liberty to hold an opinion and liberty to preach that opinion; between a man being in More's phrase 'a heretic alone by himself' and being «a seditious heretic».[73]

Cela ne rejoint-il pas ce qui est dit dans L'Utopie au sujet de celui qui ne cesse de s'attaquer publiquement à ceux qui ne partagent pas sa conviction religieuse et qui fut accusé et condamné à l'exil, non pas pour outrage à la religion mais pour «excitation au tumulte dans le peuple» (Ut. II, 143)? En d'autres mots, aussi bien dans L'Utopie que dans l'attitude de More à l'égard des «réformateurs», ce

---

[72] *The Tablet*, 31 janvier 2015, p. 4.
[73] R.W. Chambers, *o.c.*, p. 274–282 : «The Chancellor and the heretics».

qu'il considérait comme inadmissible était un comportement «séditieux» qui «exciterait au tumulte dans le peuple». Un tel comportement était jugé contraire aux valeurs essentielles prônées par More, notamment, le respect de l'ordre et de l'autorité, l'horreur de tout ce qui risquait de créer le désordre et la division dans le monde chrétien. Chambers estime dès lors que Thomas More, dans la position prise à l'encontre des luthériens ne se mettait guère en contradiction avec le respect de la diversité des religions, prêché et pratiqué par les Utopiens : «(…) Utopia would have tolerated no reformer in religion if 'reformer' implies persistent censure of the unreformed»; «(…) the same feeling for European solidarity which runs through Utopia runs also through More's treatises against the Reformers»[74].

Comme une biographe le souligne: «Cette rigueur morale de Thomas More (…) ne s'explique jamais seule mais dans une compréhension globale de l'homme de Dieu. More ne demande pas qu'on le suive en cultivant des vertus héroïques, il prêche la morale la plus droite parce qu'il a une foi inébranlable dans la récompense future dans l' au-delà». «Son intolérance à l'hérésie est à la mesure de sa peur de la damnation éternelle». L'on pourrait ajouter que, dans son action contre les luthériens, More se sentait responsable du bien-être spirituel et durable de la chrétienté qu'il estimait devoir à tout prix servir et défendre contre ce qu'il considérait comme les forces destructrices. M.C. Phélippeau rappelle à cet égard, «que la tolérance est une vertu qui n'est apparue comme telle que dans le siècle qui suivait celui de More» tandis qu'au XVIème siècle, tolérance «c'est accepter le mal, c'est travailler avec Satan».[75]

K.   L'ÎLE D'UTOPIE : PARADIS TERRESTRE ?

La société utopienne présente sans doute des aspects estimés positifs: e.a. la distribution gratuite de produits alimentaires et de biens à tous, selon les besoins de chacun, la mise en place d'excellents soins de santé, l'organisation d'une formation professionnelle et d'activités culturelles, le respect de diverses opinions religieuses, l' absence d'exploitation et d'abus de pouvoir, les autorités (élues) ne visant que le bien commun et la réalisation d'une société harmonieuse, fondée sur une organisation rationnelle et équitable.

Je doute néanmoins que l'île d'Utopie puisse attirer les lecteurs de ce Liber Amicorum comme un «paradis terrestre».

---

[74]   R.W. Chambers, *o.c.*, p. 265.
[75]   M.C. Phélippeau, *Thomas More*, éd. Gallimard, 2016, p. 206.

Tout y était réglementé en détail, la méconnaissance des règles se trouvant sévèrement sanctionnée : ainsi, à titre d'exemple, celui qui s'aventure hors de sa ville sans permis de voyage ou «sauf-conduit», est considéré comme «fugitif», passable d'un châtiment sévère, la récidive pouvant entraîner la peine de «servitude» (Ut. II, 93). Le système utopien connaît même la peine de mort dans plusieurs cas, notamment pour récidive d'adultère (Ut. II, 123); les condamnés à la servitude ou aux travaux forcés pour crime majeur qui se rebellent ou regimbent, sont mis à mort «comme des bêtes sauvages et indomptées, des êtres que ni la prison, ni les chaînes n'ont réussi à maîtriser» (Ut. II, 123).

La société utopienne est loin de pratiquer l'égalité entre hommes et femmes, l'épouse devant une obéissance totale à son mari qui la «corrige» en cas de fautes commises (Ut. II, 123) que, les jours de fête, avant de se rendre au temple, elle lui confesse à genoux (Ut. II, 153), l'inverse n'étant pas prévu.

Une règle d'or en Utopie, à respecter par tous, est la nécessaire absence totale d'oisiveté : «en aucun endroit et à aucun moment, il n'est permis d'être oisif : sans cesse exposé aux yeux de tous, chacun se trouve dans la nécessité de se livrer au labeur coutumier, soit à des loisirs qui n'aient rien d'amoral» (Ut. II, 94). Et l'ami-humaniste a ajouté la note marginale : «O République sainte que même les chrétiens devraient imiter !».

Certains commentateurs, impressionnés par ces caractéristiques de la vie en Utopie, plus particulièrement par le «contrôle social» et par toutes les restrictions et obligations, imposées aux Utopiens, ont souligné «the lack of personal liberty» ou «privacy» en Utopie. Selon Paul Turner, «George Orwell's 'Nineteen Eighty-Four' with its telescreens in every room, and its slogan 'Big Brother is watching you' is merely a logical development from the situation in Utopia». Le même auteur rappelle toutefois que l'Angleterre du temps où *L'Utopie* était conçue et écrite, était marquée par de graves injustices sociales et par la cruauté des sanctions pénales en sorte que l'austérité et la réglementation régissant la vie en Utopie, étaient sans doute perçues comme un prix modeste à payer pour échapper à l'injustice. Et en ce qui concerne la «personal liberty», Turner souligne qu' «in Tudor England, there was no freedom of speech; there was not even freedom of thought». «More himself was executed not for anything he had said or done, but for private opinions which he had resolutely kept to himself (…). More's very silence was a political crime »[76].

En dépit des éléments positifs, il paraît difficile de présenter la société utopienne comme une société «idéale», voulue par More. N'oublions pas que *L'Utopie* donne l'image d'une société fictive. Tout en «reconnaissant» ses qualités, More

---

[76]   P. Turner, *Thomas More, Utopia*, Penguin classics (1965), 1979, p. 13–15.

insiste que beaucoup reste à faire, surtout sur le plan de l'éducation morale des citoyens, ce qui, selon lui, exige également l'important apport de la religion. C'est cet appel à la réforme morale qui constitue le fond de la pensée de More et de ses amis-humanistes. Comme le résume Prévost, en établissant le lien entre *L'Utopie* et les idées fondamentales de More : « Sans cette réforme morale, les institutions les mieux conçues seraient vaines. Beaucoup de lecteurs (de *L'Utopie*) ne l'ont pas vu. Sous l'affabulation de L'Utopie, l'éthique transparaît » (Ut. I, 67, note 1)).

VII. THOMAS MORE : HÉROS DE LA CONSCIENCE

De ce que More a dit et écrit et des biographies qui lui ont été consacrées, résulte l'importance du rôle de la « conscience » personnelle. Lors de son procès – la négation d'un procès équitable –, More a présenté son « plea of liberty of conscience" ou « plea for the liberty of silence ». Ses paroles ont été notées par plusieurs personnes présentes. L'authenticité de la transcription de ces paroles ne paraît pas faire de doute. Le passage clé de cette plaidoirie est libellé comme suit :

> "Ye must understand that in things touching conscience, every true and good subject is more bound to have respect to his said conscience and to his soul than to any other thing in all the world beside; namely, when his conscience is in such sort as mine is, that is to say, when the person giveth no occasion of slander, of tumult and sedition against his prince, as it is with me; for I assure you that I have not hitherto to this hour disclosed and opened my conscience and mind to any person living in all the world".

Le terme « conscience » se retrouve à quatre reprises dans ce passage. Et le texte original, en français, de la « News-Letter » qui, après l'exécution de More, fut envoyée à Paris, frappe par la clarté des termes suivants qui énoncent les (seules) limites auxquelles More soumet sa « liberté de conscience » :

> « pourvu que telle conscience, comme est la mienne, n'engendre scandale ou sédition à son Seigneur : vous assurant que ma conscience ne s'est pas découverte à personne vivante ».

Chambers[77], qui cite ce texte ainsi que le texte anglais, ajoute : « There is no doubt as to the authenticity of this : the same statement occurs a dozen times in More 's letters ». Ces paroles de More qui affirment la liberté de la conscience moyennant le respect de l'autorité et de l'ordre social – « no slander, tumult or sedition against the Prince » – font nécessairement penser aux principes gouvernant

---

[77]   R.W. Chambers, *o.c.*, p. 334, note 1, p. 336–337 et p. 367, note 3.

la vie en société utopienne: liberté d'opinion en matière religieuse et liberté d'expression pour autant qu'il n'y ait pas d'excitation au tumulte (Ut. II, 143).

Ceux qui ont étudié la correspondance échangée entre Thomas More et sa fille Margaret et entre cette dernière et Alice Alington, fille de Dame Alice, la seconde épouse de More, nous apprennent que le mot « conscience » revient constamment dans les explications données par More, soit aux commissaires du roi, chargés de lui extorquer le serment d'allégeance, soit lors de la conversation qu'il a eue avec sa fille et dont celle-ci a fait le récit à Alice Alington.

Les juges de More étaient irrités par l'invocation constante des impératifs de sa conscience pour refuser le serment. Imploré par Alice Alington de ne pas retirer son soutien à Thomas More, Sir Thomas Audley, le successeur de More comme Lord Chancellor, lui répond: «Je souhaiterais voir votre père moins scrupuleux sur le chapitre de sa conscience[78]. Plusieurs biographes anglais relatent le même épisode: «He (Lord Audley) said he would do as much for More as for his own father (…) but he marvelled that More was so obstinate in his own conceit »[79].

More ne prêchait nullement la révolution contre le roi. Au contraire, il se gardait bien de commettre un acte ou de prononcer une parole mettant en cause la personne du roi. Chaque fois que, lors des interrogatoires, les commissaires du roi ou les juges lui demandaient de donner les motifs de son refus de prêter le serment, il invoquait les problèmes de conscience insurmontables. A la fin, il n'offrait plus que son silence aux questions. Comme le dit un de ses biographes: «he entered silence, or, rather silence entered him ». La voie du silence n'était d'ailleurs pas sans valeur juridique. More, avocat accompli, croyait que son seul silence ne suffirait jamais à le condamner, certainement pas, à le condamner à mort. Il se trompait sur la valeur de son silence face à ceux qui voulaient à tout prix, sa mort comme exemple. Ce n'est qu'à la fin de son procès, plus précisément lorsque le verdict de «guilty» avait été rendu et que le président de la cour, Lord Audley, allait entamer le prononcé du jugement, que More eut l'audace de l'interrompre et de lui rappeler les droits de tout accusé:

> «My Lord, when I was toward the law, the manner in such case was to ask the prisoner, before judgment, why judgment should not be given against him».

Recevant la parole, More estima enfin le moment venu d'expliquer les motifs de conscience qui le forçaient à refuser le serment par lequel il aurait reconnu la suprématie du roi sur l'Eglise d'Angleterre:

---

[78]   E.M. Ganne, *o.c.*, p. 222.
[79]   R.W. Chambers, *o.c.*, p. 308; P. Ackroyd, *o.c.*, p. 367.

«Seeing that I see you are determined to condemn me (God knoweth how) I will, now in discharge of my conscience speak my mind plainly and freely touching my indictment and your statute withal»[80].

More explique que sa conscience ne lui permet pas de reconnaître une demande fondée sur une loi du Parlement «directly repugnant to the laws of God and his holy church». A l'appui de cette thèse, il invoque l'immunité et l'autonomie de l'Eglise, reconnue par la *Magna Carta* de 1215, par le serment que le roi lui-même avait prêté lors de son couronnement et par la «continuity of English Christianity». Ainsi, More plaçait le conflit sur le terrain connu – pensons à l'Antigone de Sophocle – entre une loi humaine et un ordre moral ou religieux, estimé supérieur. More s'en explique longuement «for the discharge of my conscience».

La fin était inévitable: «More died for the right of the individual conscience against the State»[81]. Comme le souligne E.M. Ganne: «Dans la mémoire du peuple anglais, c'est bien ce mot 'conscience' qui perdurera dans toute évocation»[82].

Au cours des siècles et jusqu'à ce jour, le titre de «héros de la conscience» a été reconnu[83] à un homme qui n'a toutefois pas pu réaliser les grandes idées qui lui étaient les plus chères, à savoir, la paix universelle entre les «christian princes», l'uniformité dans la religion et une solution acceptable du «King's marriage»[84].

Indépendamment du dilemme de conscience qui a entraîné sa mort, Thomas More nous a laissé un message exprimé dans les termes simples et profonds de sa réponse à Cromwell qui lui reprochait de donner le mauvais exemple à d'autres qui se trouveraient ainsi confortés dans leur résistance aux exigences du Roi. Dans une note manuscrite adressée à sa fille Margaret, More relate en détail cet entretien qui contient notamment le passage suivant dans lequel «he expressed his indignation in some of the most forceful terms he had ever used in the Tower»:

«I do nobody no harm, I say no harm, I think none harm, but wish everybody good. And, if this be not enough to keep a man alive, in good faith I long not to live».

---

80   R.W. Chambers, *o.c.*, p. 340.
81   R.W. Chambers, *o.c.*, p. 400; Lord Hailsham, *Thomas More, Through many eyes*, Oxford, 1978, cité par J. Mertens de Wilmars, «Thomas Morus, Vijf eeuwen later», *R.W.*, 1978–79, 1009–1024 (1023).
82   E.M. Ganne, *o.c.*, p. 222–223.
83   Cardinal Etchegaray, discours prononcé en 2000 à l'occasion du Jubilé des responsables des affaires publiques, E.M. Ganne, *o.c.*, p. 274–276.
84   R.W. Chambers, *o.c.*, "The failure of More", p. 385–389.

Selon le commentateur, « This touched even Cromwell, who closed the interview by saying 'full gently' that no advantage should be taken of anything More has spoken »[85]. Même Cromwell était touché par ces paroles. Elles continuent à présenter au lecteur d'aujourd'hui, le précepte d'un honnête homme, « héros de la conscience » qui, par sa personne, ses actes, ses écrits, continue à nous inviter à réfléchir à l'essentiel.

CONCLUSION

Revenons au destinataire de ce *Liber Amicorum*.

Au cours de sa carrière, Paul a réussi à maîtriser une diversité d'activités grâce à une intelligence et une force de travail prodigieuses. L'équilibre et l'harmonie, il les doit sans doute également à la présence à ses côtés, d'Anne, elle-même excellente juriste, versée dans les subtilités de la technique de cassation.

Les propos de Paul ne sont souvent pas dénués d'humour et il pratique l'art de relativiser s'il y a lieu.

> « (…) as time requireth, a man of marvellous mirth and pastimes, and sometime of as sad gravity" : "A man for all seasons". »

Et dans un avenir lointain, le dédicataire de ce livre aura peut-être envie de meubler ses loisirs en consacrant, moyennant l'accord préalable d'Anne, une partie de son temps, à une étude approfondie des rapports entre Thomas More et les Droits de l'Homme : même si elle ne sera pas écrite en latin, tous les humanistes s'arracheront le fruit de ses pensées.

---

[85]   Idem, *o.c.*, p. 324 ; P. Ackroyd, *o.c.*, p. 375.

HUMAN RIGHTS, NATIONALIST POPULISM AND THE PROMISE TO LEAVE NO-ONE BEHIND

The Story of Human Rights, Told to Paul Lemmens's Grandchildren

HUMAN RIGHTS, NATIONALIST POPULISM AND THE PROMISE TO LEAVE NO-ONE BEHIND

The Story of Human Rights, Told to Paul Lemmens's Grandchildren

Egbert MYJER
Former Judge, elected in respect of The Netherlands,
European Court of Human Rights

Peter KEMPEES
Head of Division, Registry of the European Court of Human Rights

Dear Lisandro and Malena,

It will probably be a long time before you read this story.

It may well be that by then everything will be digital and it will be very old-fashioned to read a story in a book. I have no way of knowing. As I write this, it is 2019: it will be quite some time before you can read this for yourselves. It may be even longer before you actually enjoy reading this, if you ever do.

Together with Peter Kempees I am writing about matters that normally interest people who are already grown up. Peter is someone I worked with in Strasbourg, a grown-up who knows a lot about human rights and like me is passionate about them, and so I have asked him to help me with this story.

It may be that by the time you read this, much of what we have written about the most recent developments of our own time has been overtaken by later events. Such things cannot always be foretold. In any case: I enjoy writing this for you now. Here is one awkward thing though: we have to write this in English because we have been told that all the bits of this book have to be in English or French. That is so that other people can read them too. Still, by the time you want to read this, you will be able to read English and French. Of that I am sure. In any case I am certain your mother Tine or your father Marcelo will agree to help you.

This story is about human rights. Your bompa Paul has had a great deal to do with those. He studied them when he was writing his thesis – a thesis is a book you write to show other people how clever you are – and later, as a professor in Leuven, taught them to students. He kept busy with them when he was a member of the Belgian Council of State and most of all when he was a judge in the European Court of Human Rights. I have had the pleasure of doing human rights work with him from time to time. Sometimes that was because we went together to teach human rights in Leuven or in Venice; if in Venice, which is a beautiful old city in Italy, your oma Anne always came with us. For seven weeks, from 12 September 2012 until 31 October 2012, we worked closely alongside one another because we were at that time both of us judges in the European Court of Human Rights.

I think your bompa Paul is a star of human rights. He knows lots of things about them and takes them very seriously. He can say very serious things about them, like for example: "The quality of legislation, administration and the judiciary in Europe would be much reduced if the big stick of Strasbourg did not exist." Even so, sometimes we can have a good laugh together.

Peter and I would like to tell you about human rights. We are writing this specially for you and so we will not use long and complicated learned sentences. It will be more like a story. If you write in that way, using simple language that people can understand, you can sometimes explain very difficult things. Or you can more easily see the most important part of a problem, which helps you to find a solution. It is however a less learned way of going about it – or as your bompa Paul might say, using a learned word, a less academic way. For that reason there will be no footnotes.[1]

What we want to tell you about is where these human rights come from and why they are so important. Also, why it is so important that we protect these human rights, both nationally (that means: within our countries) and internationally (in all of our countries). We will be telling you a little of what we see happening today, in the year 2019: how in some countries people are starting once again to take a narrow, self-centred view of human rights, chanting slogans that suggest that human rights apply only to themselves. We will try to explain why this worries us. We will try to show that simplifying things can be good but has its dangers too.

---

[1]   Except this one. This is a footnote. Footnotes are sentences at the bottom of a page. Writers may use them to tell you where they got their clever ideas. Sometimes writers use them to impress other people with the number of learned books they have read and how learned they themselves are. And sometimes writers use them to explain something, as we do here.

It is our profound belief that human rights should apply to everyone everywhere. Fortunately, your parents think the same way, as do your grandparents. Certainly your bompa Paul does, who is such a star of human rights.

Now read on.

Best wishes from Egbert Myjer (his wife Marja sends her love).

HOW WERE HUMAN RIGHTS CREATED? PROTECTION IN NATIONAL CONSTITUTIONS

Everything was different in the old days. So were human rights. The books written about their history would fill a whole library. We cannot hope to summarise that history, not even a little bit. We will therefore put on our seven-league boots and stride through it.

It may be simplest to say that for a long time Western countries were ruled by only one person, or a small group of persons, and their word was law. There were the "people in power" – for example kings and queens, nobles, clergy and in some cases a few wealthy commoners – and everybody else: the common people. Ordinary commoners had little or no influence. In so far as commoners were listened to at all, they were almost always men: officially at least, nobody cared what women had to say. There were even people who had no rights at all: those who were kept as slaves. There was great inequality and lack of freedom. Often there were wars with neighbouring countries, or even within countries, with all the misery that they caused. That was because people were expected to fight for their king or their lord; and even those who did not themselves fight might expect to find themselves surrounded by a battle.

Take, for example, the country from which your father Marcelo comes: Argentina. That country was ruled for a long time by people from Spain. The native people had no say at all. Only in 1816 did Argentina become independent. Even then most of its inhabitants had little say in anything. Worse still, there were bloody civil wars over the following decades.

Or take Belgium, the country in which your mother Tine was born: for centuries that part of the world was a part of the Habsburg Empire, until 1795 when it was taken over by France. For a few brief years it was part of the Kingdom of the Netherlands. Belgium only became an independent kingdom in 1830. (Some people in the Netherlands would say that Belgium only became independent much later, in 1839, but that is not important now.)

The first Constitution of Belgium came into existence in 1831, shortly after independence. It included a special chapter with the title "*Des Belges et leurs droits*". This chapter was very modern for its time: it set out rights for all Belgian citizens to enjoy. For example, all Belgian citizens were equal before the law. A citizen could not be deprived of his or her freedom in any way except by order of a judge. The right to property and the privacy of correspondence were inviolable. All citizens were entitled to state their opinion and follow the religion of their choice. But of course, at that time the Belgian Constitution existed only in French.

Belgium was not the first country to write human rights into its constitution. That idea had first appeared some sixty years earlier. It was a time when ordinary people were no longer willing to accept that they had no influence over their own lives. Colonies abroad started to claim independence from mother countries in Europe; in Europe itself, people rose against royal and noble families who had ruled since time immemorial.

In 1776, the North American colonies of England adopted their *Declaration of Independence*, which said that all men were created equal. Well, perhaps not quite all … it took another ninety years, and a bloody civil war, before all American slaves were free.

In France, the *Déclaration des droits de l'homme et du citoyen* was proclaimed in 1789. In the years that followed, the common people took over power, deposing the old ruling families and even cutting their heads off. The French *Déclaration* became part of the French Constitution of 1793. This Constitution also included a sentence about what, in those days of *liberté, égalité et fraternité*, was considered the basic meaning of equality (Article 3):

> Tous les hommes sont égaux par la nature et devant la loi.

and of liberty (Article 6):

> La liberté est le pouvoir qui appartient à l'homme de faire tout ce qui ne nuit pas aux droits d'autrui: elle a pour principe la nature; pour règle la justice; pour sauvegarde la loi; sa limite morale est dans cette maxime: *Ne fais pas à un autre ce que tu ne veux pas qu'il te soit fait.*

Note the bit in italics. It is another way to phrase an ancient rule, already to be found in the Bible (Matthew 7:12):

> Therefore all things whatsoever ye would that men should do to you: do ye even so to them …

There is one thing to note about these old texts: the "equality of all men" and *droits de l'homme* did not mean equal rights for men and women. True, in English as in French, the word "man"/*homme* means not only "male person" but also "human being" as you know. But in those early days, women did not enjoy the same rights as their husbands and brothers; and to enjoy full rights, even a male citizen had to pay a certain amount of money in taxes. Much worse, slavery continued to exist, in some countries for many more decades.

Even so, in the nineteenth century many European countries adopted constitutions including basic rights. At least some male citizens could elect the representatives of the people or stand for election themselves; the right to rule no longer belonged only to certain families. There were also, in more and more countries, rights everyone could enjoy, for example the right to express one's opinion.

Change was slow, more so in some countries than in others. For example, in the Netherlands, women were allowed to vote in 1920. The Netherlands was the eighth country to grant women that right (the first had been New Zealand, in 1893). In Belgium, women had to wait longer still. Although permitted to vote in local elections from 1919, they were only given the same voting rights as men in 1948. In some parts of Switzerland, women were not given full voting rights until 1991.

We must pull on our seven-league boots and make another leap through history at this point.

THE TWENTIETH-CENTURY BACKLASH AGAINST HUMAN RIGHTS

Between 1914 and 1918 the Great War, later called the First World War, ravaged Europe. Hundreds of thousands of young men lost their lives fighting other young men. Some of the worst battles were fought in Flanders; to this day, a century later, unexploded artillery shells and even the remains of soldiers are found there. Other terrible things happened besides battles: in what was then the Ottoman Empire, between one million and one million and a half Armenian civilians – men, women and children – died in what has become known in recent years as the Armenian genocide.

When the war was over, new forms of government emerged in Europe. In Russia, the Communists came to power after a revolution and a civil war. They transformed Russia into a new state, the Soviet Union, which vested power in the industrial working class. In Italy the Fascists took over and established totalitarian rule, in which individual citizens were expected to think of themselves as subordinates of the *Duce* or leader.

In the 1930s, in the Soviet Union, there was first a deliberate campaign by the Communist regime to starve independent farmers to death. Millions died. A few years later, in a second campaign known as the "Great Terror" or the "Great Purge", hundreds of thousands more were sent to prison camps or shot by firing squads after unfair trials.

At around the same time, in Spain, a vicious civil war led to the overthrow of an elected government by a dictatorship that was to last for four decades. No one knows how many died.

Still, the best remembered horror of this time remains the measures taken by the government of Nazi Germany and, later, Nazis in occupied countries against Jewish people. This began after the Nazis won a victory in the German elections. Suddenly there was a political majority that had the power to decide, just like that, that their fellow citizens of Jewish descent no longer had any rights. Things went from bad to worse, to the point where special camps were built for no other purpose than to put Jews – and members of other minorities, such as Roma and Sinti – to death. By this time another great war had broken out, the Second World War, in which all the rights and freedoms conceived and nurtured by previous generations were trampled underfoot by the inhuman Nazi jackboot. Countless millions died, perhaps two-thirds of them civilians – murdered deliberately, caught up in the fighting or starved of life's basic needs.

All the glorious human rights guarantees enshrined in national constitutions and laws had failed to prevent this from happening. These were crimes so horrendous that new names had to be invented for them – crimes against peace, war crimes, crimes against humanity and genocide.

The world said: never again.

AFTER THE SECOND WORLD WAR: THE INTERNATIONAL HUMAN RIGHTS MOVEMENT

After the horrors of the Second World War (1939–1945) it was clear to anyone that you could lay down all sorts of things in *national* laws and constitutions but that national arrangements were not enough. There was still the danger that a majority of the population would forget their duties towards minorities and commit the most inhuman crimes against them.

Since the nineteenth century and the early years of the twentieth, rules had been developed to limit the worst inhumanities of warfare – the Hague Regulations (agreed in The Hague, just across the border in the Netherlands) and the Geneva

Conventions (agreed in Geneva in Switzerland). All countries agreed after the Second World War that these needed to be brought up to date, and they were, but equally most of the countries affected by that war agreed that that would not be enough.

In the years after the war, the worst of the war criminals were arrested and brought to trial before war crimes tribunals. This was meant to be a warning to future generations that those who committed crimes against peace, war crimes, crimes against humanity and genocide should not expect to get away with them.

But even as this was happening, Communists – supported by the Soviet Union – were overthrowing democratic governments in Central and Eastern Europe. In the Soviet Union itself the regime resumed its repressive hold on power.

The international human rights movement had its early beginnings already during the Second World War. On 6 January 1941 the president of the United States, Franklin D. Roosevelt, gave a great speech in which he proposed four freedoms that people everywhere in the world should enjoy. These four freedoms were freedom of speech, freedom of worship, freedom from want and freedom from fear. Later during the war the Allies – the countries fighting Nazi Germany – adopted these freedoms as war aims.

President Roosevelt did not live to see the war won: he died a few weeks before its end.

THE PREAMBLE TO THE CHARTER OF THE UNITED NATIONS

After the war, new organisations were set up to try to prevent new wars from breaking out. The most important of these was the United Nations Organization, or UN for short. In the Preamble to the Charter of the UN – a kind of introduction to the document that created the UN, which explains what the document is for – we find a short but very clear explanation of what is intended. It seems very solemn, and so it is, but it is so important that we include all of it here:

WE THE PEOPLES OF THE UNITED NATIONS DETERMINED

- to save succeeding generations from the scourge of war, which twice in our lifetime has brought untold sorrow to mankind, and
- to reaffirm faith in fundamental human rights, in the dignity and worth of the human person, in the equal rights of men and women and of nations large and small, and

- to establish conditions under which justice and respect for the obligations arising from treaties and other sources of international law can be maintained, and
- to promote social progress and better standards of life in larger freedom,

AND FOR THESE ENDS

- to practice tolerance and live together in peace with one another as good neighbours, and
- to unite our strength to maintain international peace and security, and
- to ensure, by the acceptance of principles and the institution of methods, that armed force shall not be used, save in the common interest, and
- to employ international machinery for the promotion of the economic and social advancement of all peoples,

HAVE RESOLVED TO COMBINE OUR EFFORTS TO ACCOMPLISH THESE AIMS

Our respective Governments, through representatives assembled in the city of San Francisco, who have exhibited their full powers found to be in good and due form, have agreed to the present Charter of the United Nations and do hereby establish an international organization to be known as the United Nations.

Take a closer look at those words, "to reaffirm faith in fundamental human rights, in the dignity and worth of the human person, in the equal rights of men and women and of nations large and small". You can see immediately the difference from the earlier texts. The basic idea is no longer "do as you would be done by": it is the basic dignity and worth of every human person.

This basic idea reappears in the preambles of many later documents, including first and foremost the Universal Declaration of Human Rights which we will now introduce to you.

THE UNIVERSAL DECLARATION OF HUMAN RIGHTS

In the spring of 1947 another new organisation, the United Nations Educational, Scientific and Cultural Organisation (now better known as UNESCO), called together a group of experts to think about what human rights should really be all about. This committee, which was called the "Committee on the Philosophical Principles of the Rights of Man", consulted thinkers from all over the world. On 31 July 1947 they published an important document, with the grand title "The Grounds of an International Declaration of Human Rights". This document said that the most basic right everyone had was the right to live; in order to live, to enjoy health care and to work for a living (or to be supported if one could not work); and to own property for one's personal use and the use of one's family. It also said that everyone should be entitled to develop themselves through education, to participate in society and to have a fair share in progress.

This document was given to a new committee set up within the UN itself to work out the details. This committee included President Roosevelt's widow, Eleanor Roosevelt. The document this committee came up with was adopted by the General Assembly of the United Nations – the meeting of the representatives of the countries taking part – on 10 December 1948. This became the Universal Declaration of Human Rights.

It too had a preamble, of which we will quote the beginning:

- Whereas recognition of the inherent dignity and of the equal and inalienable rights of all members of the human family is the foundation of freedom, justice and peace in the world,
- Whereas disregard and contempt for human rights have resulted in barbarous acts which have outraged the conscience of mankind, and the advent of a world in which human beings shall enjoy freedom of speech and belief and freedom from fear and want has been proclaimed as the highest aspiration of the common people,
- Whereas it is essential, if man is not to be compelled to have recourse, as a last resort, to rebellion against tyranny and oppression, that human rights should be protected by the rule of law, …

You will note the mention, in the first paragraph, of the basic dignity and worth of every human person as the basic value for all that follows. In the second paragraph the Four Freedoms defined by President Roosevelt reappear.

The Universal Declaration itself sets out the rights that should, as a minimum, be enjoyed by all men and women in the world. Here is a brief summary of them:

Article 1: All human beings are born free and with equal rights.
Article 2: Human rights apply to everyone, everywhere in the world, and without discrimination.
Article 3: Everyone has the right to life, freedom and safety.
Article 4: No one shall be a slave.
Article 5: No one shall be tortured and no one shall suffer cruel treatment or punishment.
Article 6: Everyone everywhere has the right to be recognised as a person before the law.
Article 7: The law is the same for everyone and gives everyone the same protection.
Article 8: If your human rights are violated, the courts must protect them.

Article 9: You may not be arrested, imprisoned or thrown out of the country without good reason.

Article 10: If you have to go to court to protect your rights, or if you are accused of a crime, you have the right to be heard in a fair and public hearing by an independent and impartial judge.

Article 11: If you are accused of a crime, you shall be considered to be innocent unless and until the opposite is proved. You may not be punished for something that is not a crime.

Article 12: The law must protect your privacy, family, home and correspondence and your honour and reputation.

Article 13: You may go where you like within your own country. You may also go abroad and come back.

Article 14: If your human rights are threatened in your own country, you may flee to another country.

Article 15: You have the right to a nationality. You may also change your nationality.

Article 16: If you are an adult man or woman, you may marry whoever will have you and found a family with that person. Men and women are each other's equals in this respect.

Article 17: You may own property.

Article 18: You may follow the religion of your choice or, if you prefer, no religion at all.

Article 19: You may receive information. You may also form your own opinions and express them.

Article 20: You may, if you wish, join an association or set one up yourself.

Article 21: Everyone has the right to vote and to stand for election. Everyone should have an equal chance to work in government service. The government must reflect the will of the people as expressed in elections.

Article 22: You have the right to enjoy the economic, social and cultural rights offered in your country.

Article 23: You have the right to work for your living, for a fair wage and under fair conditions.

Article 24: You have the right to rest and free time.

Article 25: You have the right to a reasonable standard of living. Mothers and children are entitled to special protection.

Article 26: You have the right to proper education so that you can at least earn a decent living, and to a fair chance to receive higher education if you are clever enough.

Article 27: You have the right to enjoy art and culture and to benefit from scientific progress.

Article 28: All countries must see to it that everyone can enjoy these rights.

But there are duties as well as rights:

Article 29: You must be a good citizen and recognise everyone else's rights too; and

Article 30: You may not use your rights to destroy the rights of other people.

If you have been paying attention, you will have noticed that you enjoy some of these rights automatically – simply being a human is enough. This applies to all the rights that protect you against abuse of the power of the government: those are to be found in Articles 1 to 21. There are other rights, those set out in Articles 22 to 27, that require the government to take action so that you can actually enjoy them. And of course, as pointed out in Articles 29 and 30, you must do your bit. That is only fair.

HUMAN RIGHTS TREATIES

The Universal Declaration of Human Rights was a wonderful catalogue of rights, beautifully expressed and solemnly stated, but what if a government violated them nevertheless? Where could you turn for protection then?

More was needed. A Declaration is a bit like telling your boyfriend or girlfriend that you love them. You mean it, of course you do, but just telling them so does not tie you together forever. But if you decide to make use of your rights under Article 16 of the Declaration and get married, and say so at your wedding, then you are bound. For better, for worse, for richer, for poorer, in sickness and in health.

There you have the difference between a Declaration and a Treaty. A Treaty is a formal agreement between countries, one that creates rights and duties between them; not just a list of good intentions, like your New Year resolutions.

That is why the countries that were members of the United Nations found it difficult to agree on a Treaty. In fact, they could not even agree to put all the rights in a single Treaty: in the end, there were two of them. The first covered the rights you enjoy automatically – and here, exceptionally, we use a learned expression: these are the "classical" human rights, or "civil and political" rights. The second covered the remaining rights, those that need the government to organise ways for you to enjoy them: for these, the learned expression is "economic, social and cultural rights". Predictably, the first treaty was called the International Covenant on Civil and Political Rights; the second, the International Covenant on Economic, Social and Cultural Rights". It took many years for the texts to be finished: this was only achieved in 1966. And it took a further ten years, until 1976, until the first countries actually agreed to be bound by them.

Within the United Nations, other human treaties were prepared, elaborating on some of the rights set out in the Universal Declaration in greater detail. These included the International Convention on the Elimination of All Forms of Racial

Discrimination (1965); the Convention on the Elimination of Discrimination against Women (1979); the Convention against Torture and Other Cruel, Inhumane or Degrading Treatment or Punishment (1984); the Convention on the Rights of the Child (1989); the International Convention on the Protection of the Rights of Migrant Workers and Members of Their Families (1990); the International Convention for the Protection of All Persons from Enforced Disappearance (2006); and the Convention on the Rights of Persons with Disabilities (2006). We mention them because they deserve to be mentioned.

This is not the place to dwell on all these United Nations human rights treaties, important though they are. We must, once again, put on our seven-league boots and move on. We are nearly at the point where your bompa Paul becomes part of the story.

THE COUNCIL OF EUROPE

On 19 September 1946 Winston Churchill, who had been the British prime minister during the Second World War, gave a speech at the University of Zürich in Switzerland in which he called for "a kind of United States of Europe". That turned out to be an idea whose time had not yet come, but Europeans did agree that closer cooperation between like-minded countries would be a good thing. After a conference held in The Hague in May 1948 in which some of the basic ideas were hammered out, the Council of Europe was created on 5 May 1949.

The name "Council of Europe" may seem a bit over-ambitious, at this point, for an organisation consisting only of the United Kingdom, France, Italy, Ireland, Belgium, Luxembourg and the Netherlands and the three Scandinavian countries, Denmark, Norway and Sweden. However, they were soon joined by Greece and Turkey (9 August 1949), followed by Iceland (9 March 1950) and the Federal Republic of Germany (or Western Germany, as it was also called at the time, the part of post-war Germany that was occupied by France, the United Kingdom and the United States; 13 July 1950). The countries of Eastern Europe did not join; they had by this time turned to Communism under the influence of their big neighbour, the Soviet Union. Some countries, like Switzerland and Austria, chose to stay outside for the time being because they wanted to be neutral. Spain and Portugal were not welcome to join as long as they were still ruled by dictators; they were to remain dictatorships for another twenty-five years.

The Council of Europe has its seat in Strasbourg. But that you surely know already.

There is much that we would like to tell you about the Council of Europe, but that will have to wait until another time perhaps. For now it is enough to say that the Council of Europe exists to promote Democracy, Human Rights and the Rule of Law. Democracy is a word in Greek that means "rule by the people"; it implies that the people decide how they are governed. "Rule of law" is an important, but complicated idea: it means that the government itself is bound by laws and can be held to them by independent and impartial judges. It is a pity that we cannot go any further into these two ideas, but we need to delve deeper into the third: Human Rights. Nevertheless, all three are important: if one of them is under threat, then all three are. It cannot be that you can take away one of them and hope that the other two will be all right.

The first big project within the Council of Europe was the creation of the European Convention on Human Rights. Compared to how the United Nations got on, this went very quickly: the Convention took less than a year to draft. On 4 November 1950 all the countries taking part were ready to agree on a text.

We will cite the Preamble of this Convention too. Here it is:

> The Governments signatory hereto, being members of the Council of Europe,
> Considering the Universal Declaration of Human Rights proclaimed by the General Assembly of the United Nations on 10th December 1948;
> Considering that this Declaration aims at securing the universal and effective recognition and observance of the Rights therein declared;
> Considering that the aim of the Council of Europe is the achievement of greater unity between its members and that one of the methods by which that aim is to be pursued is the maintenance and further realisation of Human Rights and Fundamental Freedoms;
> Reaffirming their profound belief in those fundamental freedoms which are the foundation of justice and peace in the world and are best maintained on the one hand by an effective political democracy and on the other by a common understanding and observance of the Human Rights upon which they depend;
> Being resolved, as the governments of European countries which are like-minded and have a common heritage of political traditions, ideals, freedom and the rule of law, to take the first
> steps for the collective enforcement of certain of the rights stated in the Universal Declaration,
> Have agreed as follows:
> (follows the text of the Articles of the Convention).

You will see that it refers to the Universal Declaration of Human Rights. You will also notice the link between democracy and human rights. And most of all, you will notice that the idea was to carry on where the Universal Declaration left off. By making the solemn undertaking to be bound to the Convention, they had transformed the pious intentions of the Universal Declaration into promises to which they could be held.

But the countries of the Council of Europe went even further than that. They decided that if anyone thought that even the highest courts of the land had got it wrong and misapplied the Convention, they could complain to a new international complaints body – the European Commission of Human Rights. If that Commission thought that there might be something in the complaint, the case might be brought before the European Court of Human Rights. All that was to be found in the Convention too. And if that Court decided that the country concerned had not kept its promises written in the Convention, then that country had to make it up to the victim – and even, if need be, alter its own laws so that the same thing could not happen again.

In practice, all the other countries of the Council of Europe would also sit up and take notice if the Court found a country at fault: they would then make sure, in their own way, that the same thing could not happen to them. After all, it would never do for the other countries of the Council of Europe to be caught making a mistake already made by someone else.

Since 1998 there is no longer a European Commission of Human Rights, only a European Court of Human Rights. There is one judge in that Court for every one of the member countries of the Council of Europe, usually someone who is very clever and very experienced. This is where your bompa Paul enters the story: he has been the judge elected in respect of Belgium since 2012.

As we mentioned: there were, in the beginning, only ten countries taking part, but before long others followed suit. Austria, Cyprus, Switzerland and Malta joined in the 1950s and 60s; Spain and Portugal joined in the 1970s, after their dictators were gone; and more. After the "fall of the Berlin Wall" and in its wake the collapse of the Communist dictatorships in Central and Eastern Europe and the end of the Cold War, many newly-democratic Central and Eastern European countries joined too. As we write, the Council of Europe has forty-seven members, all of them parties to the European Convention on Human Rights: (deep breath) Albania, Andorra, Armenia, Austria, Azerbaijan, Belgium, Bosnia and Herzegovina, Bulgaria, Croatia, Cyprus, the Czech Republic, Denmark, Estonia, Finland, France, Georgia, Germany, Greece, Hungary, Iceland, Ireland, Italy, Latvia, Liechtenstein, Lithuania, Luxembourg, Macedonia (or "North Macedonia", to give it its official name), Malta, Moldova, Monaco, Montenegro, the Netherlands, Norway, Poland, Portugal, Romania, Russia, San Marino, Serbia, Slovakia, Slovenia, Spain, Sweden, Switzerland, Turkey, Ukraine and the United Kingdom (phew). That is all of Europe except for Belarus, Vatican City and (if you like) Kosovo.

Complaints were brought almost from the moment the Convention entered into force. Over the years, the vast majority of them have been "declared inadmissible". That is an expression lawyers use to say that there is something wrong with the complaint, so that it cannot be examined: for example, the complaint may be out of time, or it should have been presented to the national judges first but wasn't, or it is about a right not guaranteed by the Convention, or it clearly has nothing to do with what the Convention was intended for. Still, people will try their luck and you cannot blame them for that, can you? But as it is, only a minute percentage of complaints is "declared admissible" and examined in depth.

Between 1959 – the year in which the Court considered its first case – and this year, 2019, the Court has examined complaints in depth in no fewer than 21,651 cases. Those are, as you will have understood by now, cases declared admissible. When the Court does so, it is said to "give judgment", as the expression is: the Court's pronouncements in such cases are called "judgments". Of the 21,651 cases there were 18,187 in which the Court found that the country concerned had got it wrong, that is, had failed to live up to its solemn promise to abide by the Convention. Some of those judgments were about very serious matters: it turned out that people had been killed or tortured, perhaps, or kept as modern slaves in kitchens or on strawberry farms, or had been kept prisoners in situations where the law did not so permit, or had been given unfair trials, perhaps because they were not allowed to question witnesses, or had been discriminated against because they were women or belonged to some minority or other, or had been punished for expressing their own opinions, or had been prevented from following a minority religion, or had their land taken away from them without proper payment, or … You name it, the chances are that the Court has had to consider it.

Before you say: surely none of those cases can have concerned Belgium or the Netherlands, think again. The Court has given 252 judgments against Belgium up until 2019. In 175 of those judgments the Court has found fault with Belgium. For the Netherlands, the figures are: 164 judgments, of which 92 in which the Court has found that the Netherlands got it wrong. Do not for one moment think that that means that Belgium does worse than the Netherlands: it is also possible that Belgian people, and Belgian lawyers, are perhaps quicker to complain to the Court. Or more likely perhaps, Belgian lawyers may have had better education in human rights and how to vindicate them. If that is the correct explanation, then it is – in large part – thanks to your bompa Paul.

Countries do not like being rapped on the knuckles for failing to live up to their solemn promises. Once or twice countries have signalled that they considered the Court's judgment in a particular case silly. But they have almost always ended up doing what they had promised: they have paid the damages ordered by the Court, they have changed their national laws if necessary. There have been times when the governments of the forty-seven countries met to discuss how to move forward: the question was whether the Court was perhaps too strict in its views. Between 2010 and 2018 they met in beautiful places like Interlaken (Switzerland), İzmir (Turkey), Brighton (United Kingdom), Brussels (that's right) and Copenhagen (Denmark). Each time they declared in clear ringing tones that they considered the Convention very important and that they were happy for the Convention to be there, that they would do their level best to see that those pesky human rights were respected in their countries and that they would do as the Court told them. But they also said that they would like the Court to remember that they were forty-seven different countries and that each country needed a little breathing space to find its own solutions to its own problems. Actually that was something they really did not need to say: the Court itself had always said so too.

We think we should just mention a few other things that were done within the Council of Europe, without discussing them in detail. The first is the adoption of the European Social Charter, a treaty to protect economic and social rights with a complaints procedure of its own. The other is the adoption of the Convention for the Prevention of Torture and Inhuman or Degrading Treatment or Punishment, which has a Committee that keeps an eye on prisons, police stations, psychiatric hospitals and other places where people may be kept locked up. And finally, there is the appointment of the Human Rights Commissioner, who has a mandate of her own to make sure human rights standards are maintained.

THE EUROPEAN UNION

In a separate development, other European organisations were set up after the Second World War so that the countries of Europe could work together peacefully for their common prosperity: the European Coal and Steel Community, the European Economic Community and the European Atomic Energy Community. In 1993 the three were merged into a single, admirable, organisation: the European Union. The European Union is run on a day-to-day basis by two bodies called the Council and the Commission, which are watched over by the European Parliament and the European Court of Justice. You may already have seen, or even visited, the office buildings of the Council and the Commission in Brussels (and if not, you surely will); and you will probably one day visit the European Parliament in Strasbourg and the European Court of Justice in Luxembourg.

In 2000 the European Parliament, the Council and the Commission solemnly proclaimed the Charter of fundamental rights of the European Union. This Charter is addressed to the European Union itself, not to the countries of which it is made up; and it respects the human rights and fundamental freedoms recognised in the Convention – the rights and freedoms guarded by the European Court of Human Rights, in which your bompa Paul is a judge.

OUTSIDE EUROPE

Outside Europe also, regional treaties for protecting human rights have been agreed. We must mention the African Charter on Human and Peoples' Rights, which was adopted in 1981 and now covers the entire continent of Africa. Another is the American Convention on Human Rights of 1969, to which Argentina became a party in 1984. Both provide for a Commission and a Court to monitor compliance, much like the European Convention until 1998. Curiously, however, the United States of America, which has done so much to for the cause of human rights over the centuries (perhaps more than any other country), has not joined the American Convention on Human Rights – which means that the United States is beginning to fall behind. The United States is one of a diminishing number of countries that still carry out the death penalty, and one of very few that maintain a prison in a foreign country to keep people locked up for years without ever bringing them before a judge.

We will now put on our seven-league boots one more time, for a final leap through history.

TROUBLE BREWING IN EUROPE: TERRORIST ATTACKS, REFUGEES AND MIGRANTS, THE RISE OF NATIONALIST POPULISM

A feeling of optimism reigned throughout Europe after the "fall of the Berlin wall" in 1989 and the collapse of the Communist dictatorships. Freedom would prevail. Europe would be united. A new era of peace and prosperity had arrived.

Or so we thought. In 1992 a series of wars broke out in the former Yugoslavia that altogether were to last three and a half years, take hundreds of thousands of lives, displace millions from their homes and result in the creation of six new states – seven if you count Kosovo (your bompa Paul does we know, but some people don't). Many of the displaced had to find a new home elsewhere in the region or in other countries.

In the 1990s a new form of terrorism emerged. An Islamist fundamentalist organisation called al-Qaeda, founded by a Saudi Arabian multi-millionaire called Osama Bin Laden, took to launching attacks on mainly American targets. These included hotels, embassies, warships, and famously the World Trade Centre in New York and the Pentagon Building in Washington D.C. The latter attacks, carried out on 11 September 2001 using four hijacked airliners, killed approximately three thousand people. Their effects were enormous.

Throughout the Western world, divisions emerged between majority indigenous populations and Muslim immigrant populations – precisely as the attackers had intended. Some people began to mistrust traditional Muslims; then all Muslims; then all immigrants. This mistrust grew with every subsequent terrorist attack – and as you may know, there were two in Brussels in 2016.

Towards the end of September 2001 President George W. Bush of the United States declared a "war on terror". This led to acts by the United States and its allies, including many European countries, in which – it has to be said – human rights were not always respected as they should have been.

In other parts of the world, such as Somalia, Sudan, Eritrea, Afghanistan and Iraq, fighting had been going on sometimes for decades. Popular uprisings in countries like Libya and Syria were at first welcomed in Europe as the dawn of a new democratic age, much as had been seen in Eastern Europe, but in Syria especially the situation soon degenerated into the bloodiest war this century so far. Refugees from all these places started to make their way to Europe in search of safety and a new life. They sought freedom from fear.

Added to that, large numbers of migrants started to arrive mainly from Africa. These were people who found it difficult to make a decent living in their own countries and hoped to find greater prosperity in Europe. They sought freedom from want.

For many in Europe these flows of refugees and migrants became a worry. Many were afraid that all these people would need to be housed and fed at the expense of the local taxpayer. Others feared losing their jobs to immigrants willing to work for lower wages. Others still were worried that the character of their villages or neighbourhoods might change as a result of the inflow of strangers with foreign habits. Was it really necessary for these strangers to build Islamic houses of prayer? Why should women cover themselves in black from head to foot, and why should even intelligent and educated women have to wear Islamic headscarves when hardly anyone did before? Why should these foreigners not assimilate and adopt local customs and traditions? This suspicious and, on occasion, even discriminatory attitude had its effect on immigrant communities, some of which had been around for generations: it led them to feel unwelcome and unsafe in their turn. Some separated themselves from the wider community;

others became radical Islamists themselves. And of course, reports of new Islamist terrorist attacks, wherever these might have taken place, did nothing to help matters: for those who were already scared, they merely confirmed that you could not be careful enough.

Worse, an economic crisis broke out that caused great unemployment in some countries and destroyed the savings of many. Many feared for their livelihoods.

These fears were played on by nationalist populist movements and political parties. They promised voters that if they were given enough votes, they could see to it that borders would be closed to refugees and migrants. They, as patriots, would take care of their own. It was hard luck for the refugees whose very lives might be in danger; but that was a problem for them to solve in their countries of origin. In some European countries nationalist populist politicians managed to gain a large following, and in a few they even secured parliamentary majorities.

But is it not precisely the main feature of a democracy that the majority of the people should decide?

It seems so simple but it is not. The answer is, yes, but provided that the rule of law and human rights also be protected – including, if a democracy is to be worthy of the name, the human rights of minorities. As we pointed out above, the three belong together.

In Hungary and Poland the parliamentary majority has caused much damage to the rule of law. There is an expression for that in the English language; "rule of law backsliding". The Hungarian prime minister has even called his country an "illiberal democracy". The parliamentary majority has pushed through laws that directly attacked the independence of the courts. Judges in the highest courts who by rights still had years to serve were dismissed by new legislation; the selection of their replacements was carefully monitored by the government. Groups and institutions that might otherwise be expected to serve as "public watchdogs", such as the national ombudsman, the press and some NGOs (non-governmental organisations to you) were subjected to new controls. An entire university was driven out of Hungary for harbouring critical intellectuals – actually, critical intellectuals are the whole point of a university – and its founder was declared an enemy of the state. European organisations including the Council of Europe, and both European courts – the European Court of Human Rights and Court of Justice of the European Communities – have made it clear that they are very uncomfortable about developments such as these. The governments of Hungary and Poland have taken no notice: they continue to look to their majorities for support. As to the destruction of the rule of law: what of that? What does the majority care for the critical opinions of "so-called" judges, "fake news" media and "elitist" intellectuals? What is more, they have ensured that some of these laws can be changed only with great difficulty, requiring a qualified majority far greater than one half of the parliament plus one vote.

In other parts of Europe there have been other worrisome developments. In 2014 Russia took control of Crimea, hitherto an autonomous republic within its neighbour Ukraine. This led other countries to deploy sanctions against Russia. Relations between Russia and the rest of Europe plunged to new depths. The suspicion that has been expressed by some governments that Russia is responsible for the destruction of a civilian airliner, Malaysian Airlines MH17, on 17 July 2014 over Eastern Ukraine – which Russia denies – has done nothing to improve matters.

In Turkey, a failed coup d'état in July 2016 prompted the Turkish government to declare a state of emergency that was allowed to continue for two years. There too measures have been taken that reduced the checks on the government offered by the courts, the press, intellectuals and non-governmental organisations.

These are very worrying developments. You will forgive us a difficult expression but we must use it here: *the erosion of the democratic state governed by the rule of law in Europe.* It is a direct attack on what great minds tried to secure in the years following the Second World War, namely the recognition of the inherent dignity and the equal and inalienable rights of *all* members of the human community as the foundation of freedom, justice and peace in the world. We emphasise the little word "all" to indicate that this is not just about the majority. This is about human dignity, not only for the native population, but for all human beings, including those who have had to flee their homes and their countries because their lives and those of their children were no longer safe there.

To understand the point, it can do no harm to look back at the lessons of history. Picture Jewish Europeans during the Second World War. Many were forced to go into hiding. Some who were fortunate enough to make their escape made great contributions to their new adoptive countries, even becoming household names; but what if they had not been aided and accepted elsewhere?

Closer to your own time: what if you were *not* a member of the majority population of your country and were discriminated and cast out, how would *you* feel? What if another war breaks out in Europe – and why should it not? Europe's history is a long list of them. What if some terrible environmental disaster happens – a famine caused by a drought perhaps, why should that be unthinkable? Already the summer of 2018 is the driest on record. Would *you* not hope to be welcomed in another, more fortunate part of the world?

That does not mean that you should dismiss the fears of a majority out of hand. They too have a right to freedom from fear and freedom from want. Of course it is infuriating to find that you have been pushed down the waiting list for social housing because the needs of a refugee family are found to be more urgent than yours. Of course it is upsetting to notice that a neighbourhood where one may have grown up changes all of a sudden as new people come in from outside. It must be possible to achieve great things simply by listening to each other, explaining, listening again and explaining again. Looking after number one, as the saying is, cannot be the answer.

Just to put things into perspective: it has happened many times before in human history that large groups have settled elsewhere in the world. Things have usually worked out all right in the end. There may even be people you know who have foreign ancestry.

SO WHAT NEXT? DO SUSTAINABLE DEVELOPMENT GOALS PROVIDE A SOLUTION?

Can the European Court of Human Rights not halt these unfortunate developments?

Again, you may well ask. The answer, however, will probably have to be no. The Court decides whether the countries that are parties to the European Convention on Human Rights have kept their solemn promises to respect the rights guaranteed by that Convention within their jurisdiction. That it does almost exclusively by accepting individual complaints. As it happens, there are piles of complaints against Turkey, for example, about the measures taken against individual judges, journalists and intellectuals. But most of these complaints cannot even be considered until they have been dealt with at the national level by the Turkish courts. There are things the Court can do, but it too is limited by rules and procedures.

Halting the erosion of the democratic state governed by the rule of law calls for determined political action.

It will need the other countries of the Council of Europe (and where appropriate, the European Union) to take their responsibility and demonstrate in word and deed that certain developments are incompatible with the three interconnected concepts: democracy, human rights and the rule of law.

But is there nothing more positive to be said?

Here our answer is a resounding yes. Much has improved in Europe over the past decades. On the whole the countries that are parties to the Convention take the judgments of the Court very seriously. Especially if the complaints concerned are not particularly politically sensitive.

For example, it is no longer possible for a country to lock up a prisoner and throw away the key. Even the worst criminals, those serving life sentences, now have the right to have their sentences reviewed after a time – even though that may be a very long time – and hope to be set free if there is no longer any need for them to be in prison. All prisoners, even those serving life sentences, should be allowed to keep in touch with the outside world, especially their families. Migrants and refugees rescued at sea may not be taken back to the countries they sailed from without first being given a chance to argue that those countries are dangerous for them; and even illegal migrants may not be kept and used as slaves.

Another positive development: there is an attempt afoot within the United Nations to work towards a better world in a different way. Here we refer to the Sustainable Development Goals adopted by the General Assembly of the United Nations on 25 September 2015. These are goals that all countries aim to reach by 2030.

Like the Universal Declaration on Human Rights of 1948, this is a declaration – a statement of what countries hope to achieve, not a formal agreement. But this one was adopted by all countries without even a vote, and it is so recent that no one can back out of it. Best of all: it aims to realise the human rights of all people.

Again, the Preamble is important enough to quote:

> This Agenda is a plan of action for people, planet and prosperity. It also seeks to strengthen universal peace in larger freedom. We recognize that eradicating poverty in all its forms and dimensions, including extreme poverty, is the greatest global challenge and an indispensable requirement for sustainable development.
>
> All countries and all stakeholders, acting in collaborative partnership, will implement this plan. We are resolved to free the human race from the tyranny of poverty and want and to heal and secure our planet. We are determined to take the bold and transformative steps which are urgently needed to shift the world on to a sustainable and resilient path. As we embark on this collective journey, we pledge that no one will be left behind.
>
> The 17 Sustainable Development Goals and 169 targets which we are announcing today demonstrate the scale and ambition of this new universal Agenda.
>
> They seek to build on the Millennium Development Goals and complete what they did not achieve. They seek to realize the human rights of all and to achieve gender equality and the empowerment of all women and girls.

They are integrated and indivisible and balance the three dimensions of sustainable development: the economic, social and environmental.

The Goals and targets will stimulate action over the next 15 years in areas of critical importance for humanity and the planet.

And here are the goals:

Goal 1. End poverty in all its forms everywhere

Goal 2. End hunger, achieve food security and improved nutrition and promote sustainable agriculture

Goal 3. Ensure healthy lives and promote well-being for all at all ages

Goal 4. Ensure inclusive and equitable quality education and promote lifelong learning opportunities for all

Goal 5. Achieve gender equality and empower all women and girls

Goal 6. Ensure availability and sustainable management of water and sanitation for all

Goal 7 Ensure access to affordable, reliable, sustainable and modern energy for all

Goal 8. Promote sustained, inclusive and sustainable economic growth, full and productive employment and decent work for all

Goal 9. Build resilient infrastructure, promote inclusive and sustainable industrialization and foster innovation

Goal 10. Reduce inequality within and among countries

Goal 11. Make cities and human settlements inclusive, safe, resilient and sustainable

Goal 12. Ensure sustainable consumption and production patterns

Goal 13. Take urgent action to combat climate change and its impacts (Acknowledging that the United Nations Framework Convention on Climate Change is the primary international, intergovernmental forum for negotiating the global response to climate change.)

Goal 14. Conserve and sustainably use the oceans, seas and marine resources for sustainable development

Goal 15. Protect, restore and promote sustainable use of terrestrial ecosystems, sustainably manage forests, combat desertification, and halt and reverse land degradation and halt biodiversity loss

Goal 16. Promote peaceful and inclusive societies for sustainable development, provide access to justice for all and build effective, accountable and inclusive institutions at all levels

Goal 17. Strengthen the means of implementation and revitalize the Global Partnership for Sustainable Development

Each of these goals is subdivided into sub-goals, called targets – 169 of them in all. It might seem at first sight that human rights have only a small role to play in this document, but if you take the trouble to study the Preamble and the separate targets, you will soon find that they are replete with freedom, equality, brotherhood and sisterhood and giving everyone their fair share. And even if it were not so: these Sustainable Development Goals do not replace human rights. All countries remain bound by their solemn promises to respect those rights.

Actually, the Sustainable Development Goals tie into the UNESCO document "The Grounds of an International Declaration of Human Rights", of 31 July 1947 in that they set out, with the knowledge of our time, what is needed for everyone to live as a human being. This brings us full circle, with an additional solemn promise contained in the Preamble:

"we pledge that no one will be left behind".

We can think of no better thing to say. It is a pledge worthy of your bompa Paul, and already for that reason worth repeating as often as possible.

You will be young adults in 2030. That will be your job.

Part II

Human Rights in the World: From National to Global

LA LUTTE CONTRE LE TERRORISME DANS LA JURISPRUDENCE DE LA COUR CONSTITUTIONNELLE DE BELGIQUE

Jean Spreutels
Président honoraire de la Cour constitutionnelle de Belgique
Professeur ordinaire honoraire de l'Université libre de Bruxelles

Sylviane Velu
Conseiller honoraire à la Cour de cassation de Belgique

INTRODUCTION

La mission essentielle d'une Cour constitutionnelle est le maintien de l'Etat de droit démocratique. Face aux défis majeurs posés à notre société par le phénomène du terrorisme, les Etats ont adopté des législations destinées à prévenir et à réprimer ce fléau. Les juridictions nationales et les cours européennes sont ainsi amenées à contrôler ces lois au regard des droits fondamentaux. À cette occasion, il leur appartient de rechercher un équilibre, souvent délicat, entre les droits des individus et les intérêts de la société démocratique[1], dont fait partie la sécurité nationale.[2]

La Belgique a adapté sa législation en la matière, souvent en application de ses obligations internationales, mais elle n'a ni décrété l'état d'urgence, qui d'ailleurs n'appartient pas à son ordre constitutionnel[3], ni fait application de l'article 15 de

---

[1]   Voy., pour un exemple récent : CEDH, 13 septembre 2018, *Big Brother Watch and others c. Royaume-Uni*, § 357 : «Consequently, while the Court does not doubt that related communications data is an essential tool for the intelligence services in the fight against terrorism and serious crime, it does not consider that the authorities have struck a fair balance between the competing public and private interests by exempting it in its entirety from the safeguards applicable to the searching and examining of content».

[2]   CEDH, 26 mars 1987, *Leander c. Suède*, § 49.

[3]   Voy. G. Van Haegenborgh en W. Verrijdt, «De noodtoestand in het Belgische publiekrecht», in VVSRBN (éd.), *Preadviezen 2016*, Den Haag, Boom juridische uitgevers, 2016, pp. 11-85.

la Convention européenne des droits de l'homme, qui permet de déroger, dans des conditions strictes, aux obligations prévues par celle-ci.

L'importance de cette question n'a pas échappé au dédicataire de ce *Liber Amicorum*, toujours attentif aux nombreux aspects de la protection des droits de l'homme.[4]

Dans le cadre de notre modeste contribution, il ne s'agit pas d'étudier l'ensemble de la problématique de la lutte contre le terrorisme et des droits fondamentaux[5], mais d'analyser comment la Cour constitutionnelle de Belgique[6] a contrôlé la compatibilité avec ces droits des dispositions législatives en ce domaine qui ont été soumises à son contrôle. Nous nous limiterons aux législations spécifiques à cette lutte[7], qui ont donné lieu aux arrêts n° 73/2005 du 20 avril 2005[8], n° 125/2005 du 13 juillet 2005[9], n° 145/2011 du 22 septembre 2011[10], n° 9/2015 du 28 janvier 2015[11], n° 8/2018 du 18 janvier 2018[12], n° 31/2018 du 15 mars 2018[13] et n° 44/2019 du 14 mars 2019.[14]

---

[4]   P. Lemmens, «Respecting Human Rights in the Fight against Terrorism», in C. Fijnaut, J. Wouters et F. Naert (éd.), *Legal intruments in the Fight against International Terrorism. A Transatlantic Dialogue*, Leiden/Boston, Martinus Nijhoff, 2004, pp. 223-249; «Rechten van de mens in een klimaat van terrorisme», in B. Pattyn et J. Wouters (éd.), *Schokgolven. Terrorisme en fundamentalisme*, Louvain, Davidsfonds, 2002, pp. 137-146.

[5]   Voy. notam. J. Velaers, «La lutte contre le terrorisme et les droits de l'homme : développements récents en Belgique», in P. D'Argent, D. Renders et M. Verdussen (coord.), *Les visages de l'Etat, Liber Amicorum Yves LEJEUNE*, Bruxelles, Bruylant, 2017, pp. 775-792.

[6]   Ci-après : la Cour. Ses arrêts figurent sur son site www.const-court.be.

[7]   La Cour a contrôlé d'autres dispositions législatives qui peuvent être appliquées en matière de terrorisme, mais qui visent autant celui-ci que d'autres formes graves de criminalité. Voy., par exemple : arrêts n° 105/2007 (méthodes particulières de recherche), n° 89/2014 (organisation criminelle), n° 16/2018 (déchéance de nationalité), n° 96/2018 (conservation des données des communications électroniques), n° 174/2018 (méthodes particulières de recherche concernant Internet et les communications électroniques) ou n° 41/2019 (recueil de données par les services de renseignement et de sécurité).

[8]   Recours en annulation de l'article 379 de la loi-programme du 22 décembre 2003 (article 10,6°, du Titre préliminaire du Code de procédure pénale).

[9]   Recours en annulation de la loi du 19 décembre 2003 relative aux infractions terroristes (articles 137 et 138 du Code pénal, 6,1°*ter*, et 10*ter* du Titre préliminaire du Code de procédure pénale et 90*ter*, § 2, du Code d'instruction criminelle).

[10]   Recours en annulation de la loi du 4 février 2010 relative aux méthodes de recueil des données par les services de renseignement et de sécurité (article 3, 15°, de la loi organique des services de renseignement et de sécurité).

[11]   Recours en annulation de la loi du 18 février 2013 modifiant le livre II, titre Ier*ter* du Code pénal (articles 140*bis*, 140*ter*, 140*quater* et 140*quinquies* du Code pénal).

[12]   Recours en annulation de l'article 2 de la loi du 20 juillet 2015 visant à renforcer la lutte contre le terrorisme (article 140*sexies* du Code pénal).

[13]   Recours en annulation de la loi du 3 août 2016 portant des dispositions diverses en matière de lutte contre le terrorisme (III) (articles 140*bis* du Code pénal et 16, § 2, de la loi du 20 juillet 1990 relative à la détention préventive).

[14]   Recours en annulation de la loi du 17 mai 2017 modifiant le Code d'instruction criminelle en vue de promouvoir la lutte contre le terrorisme. Cet arrêt ayant été rendu après la rédaction de

Les droits fondamentaux au regard desquels la Cour a statué dans ces arrêts sont le principe de légalité en matière pénale, les libertés d'expression, de réunion et d'association, la liberté individuelle ou le droit à la libre circulation des personnes[15], le droit au respect de la vie privée, le principe d'égalité et de non-discrimination, ainsi que l'obligation de *standstill* contenue à l'article 23 de la Constitution.

I. PRINCIPE DE LÉGALITÉ EN MATIÈRE PÉNALE

La plupart des recours en annulation formés contre les lois anti-terroristes en Belgique se fondent sur la violation du principe de légalité en matière pénale. Ce principe revêt de nombreux aspects[16], dont seuls deux ont été invoqués par les parties requérantes : l'exigence de précision de la loi pénale et l'interdiction de la rétroactivité de celle-ci.

Dans ces affaires, les moyens sont pris de la violation des articles 12 et 14 de la Constitution, lus ou non en combinaison avec l'article 7 de la Convention européenne des droits de l'homme, avec l'article 15 du Pacte international relatif aux droits civils et politiques et, le cas échéant, avec l'article 49, § 1, de la Charte des droits fondamentaux de l'Union européenne.

A. PRÉCISION DE LA LOI PÉNALE

En règle, la Cour[17] énonce tout d'abord que le principe de légalité en matière pénale procède notamment « de l'idée que la loi pénale doit être formulée en des termes qui permettent à chacun de savoir, au moment où il adopte un comportement, si celui-ci est ou non punissable. Il exige que le législateur indique, en des termes suffisamment précis, clairs et offrant la sécurité juridique, quels faits sont sanctionnés, afin, d'une part, que celui qui adopte un comportement puisse évaluer préalablement, de manière satisfaisante, quelle sera la conséquence pénale de ce comportement et afin, d'autre part, que ne soit pas laissé au juge un trop grand pouvoir d'appréciation ». Elle ajoute que « toutefois,

---

la présente étude mais avant la correction des épreuves, nous n'avons pas pu le commenter de manière aussi détaillée que les autres arrêts analysés.

15   L'article 12, alinéa 1er, de la Constitution garantit la liberté individuelle. Cet article a pu servir de fondement au droit à la libre circulation au sens le plus large (A. Bailleux, « Le droit à la libre circulation des personnes », in M. Verdussen et N. Bonbled (dir.), *Les droits constitutionnels en Belgique*, vol. 2, Bruxelles, Bruylant, 2011, p. 1150.

16   Voy. J. Theunis, « Le droit à la légalité des incriminations et des peines », in M. Verdussen et N. Bonbled (dir.), *op. cit.*, pp. 763-788.

17   Voy. par exemple l'arrêt n° 125/2005, B.6.2.

le principe de légalité en matière pénale n'empêche pas que la loi attribue un pouvoir d'appréciation au juge. Il faut en effet tenir compte du caractère de généralité des lois, de la diversité et de la variabilité des situations, ainsi que des matières auxquelles elles s'appliquent et de l'évolution des comportements qu'elles répriment». Elle expose ensuite la jurisprudence de la Cour européenne des droits de l'homme à cet égard.[18] Elle en déduit que ce n'est qu'en examinant une disposition pénale spécifique qu'il est possible, en tenant compte en particulier des éléments propres aux infractions qu'elle entend réprimer, de déterminer si les termes généraux utilisés par le législateur sont à ce point vagues qu'ils méconnaîtraient le principe de légalité en matière pénale.

1. Définition de l'infraction terroriste

Dans un recours en annulation notamment de l'article 3 de la loi du 19 décembre 2003 relative aux infractions terroristes[19], les parties requérantes soutenaient que cette disposition viole le principe de légalité parce que l'infraction terroriste serait définie trop largement ou de manière imprécise. Elles critiquaient en particulier le caractère indéterminé des termes utilisés dans l'article 137, § 1er, du Code pénal[20], inséré par cet article 3, termes suivant lesquels constitue une infraction terroriste l'infraction qui, «de par sa nature ou son contexte, peut porter gravement atteinte à un pays ou à une organisation internationale». Elles considéraient encore que l'élément intentionnel, le dol spécial requis, est, lui aussi, insuffisamment défini. La formulation de cette intention serait à plusieurs égards incertaine.[21]

Quant aux termes «contexte» dans lequel l'infraction terroriste est commise et «nature» de celle-ci, la Cour constate que la disposition attaquée s'inspire du texte de la décision-cadre du Conseil de l'Union européenne du 13 juin 2002 relative à la lutte contre le terrorisme. Elle cite la déclaration de la ministre de la Justice au cours des travaux préparatoires de la loi du 19 décembre 2003, selon laquelle le mot «contexte» «permet de prendre en compte non seulement la nature de l'infraction, mais aussi ses conséquences sur l'organisation et la

---

18   CEDH, 15 novembre 1996, *Cantoni c. France*, §§ 29, 31 et 35, 25 mai 1993, *Kokkinakis c. Grèce*, §§ 40 et 52, et 22 novembre 1995, *S.W. c. Royaume-Uni*, § 36, cités par l'arrêt n° 125/2005, B.6.3.

19   Arrêt n° 125/2005.

20   Selon cette disposition, «constitue une infraction terroriste, l'infraction prévue aux §§ 2 et 3 qui, de par sa nature ou son contexte, peut porter gravement atteinte à un pays ou à une organisation internationale et est commise intentionnellement dans le but d'intimider gravement une population ou de contraindre indûment des pouvoirs publics ou une organisation internationale à accomplir ou à s'abstenir d'accomplir un acte, ou de gravement déstabiliser ou détruire les structures fondamentales politiques, constitutionnelles, économiques ou sociales d'un pays ou d'une organisation internationale».

21   B.4-B.7.4.

gestion d'un pays» et qu' «il appartiendra aux cours et tribunaux d'apprécier au cas par cas si, par le contexte dans lequel l'infraction est commise, celle-ci porte gravement atteinte à un pays ou à une organisation internationale ».[22]

La Cour admet que la définition de l'élément intentionnel de l'infraction pourrait dans certains cas donner lieu à des difficultés d'interprétation. Toutefois, il ressort des termes «gravement», «indûment» ou «détruire» que les faits doivent manifester «une intention de porter substantiellement atteinte aux éléments visés, ce qui circonscrit de manière suffisante les éléments constitutifs de l'infraction».[23] En outre, «il ne peut être fait grief à un texte de portée générale de ne pas donner une définition plus précise de l'intention exigée pour un ensemble d'infractions susceptibles d'être réprimées comme infractions terroristes. Le juge, comme il lui appartient de le faire lorsqu'il doit mesurer la gravité de faits qui lui sont soumis, devra apprécier cette intention non pas en fonction de conceptions subjectives qui rendraient imprévisible l'application de la disposition en cause mais en considération des éléments objectifs constitutifs de chaque infraction, en tenant compte des circonstances propres à chaque affaire. De même, il appartient au juge d'apprécier le dol spécial requis».[24]

La Cour conclut que, «même s'il laisse au juge un large pouvoir d'appréciation, l'article 3 de la loi du 19 décembre 2003 ne lui confère pas un pouvoir autonome d'incrimination qui empiéterait sur les compétences du législateur».

2. Diffusion d'un message préconisant la commission d'infractions terroristes

La Cour a aussi été invitée à statuer sur la compatibilité de l'article 140*bis* du Code pénal[25], inséré par la loi du 18 février 2013 modifiant le livre II, titre Ier*ter* du Code pénal, avec le principe de légalité en matière pénale, en ce que cette

---

[22]   *Doc. parl.*, Chambre, 2003-2004, DOC 51-0258/004, p. 14.

[23]   « Il en est de même du terme 'massives' qui qualifie, à l'article 137, § 3, 1°, du Code pénal, inséré par le même article 3, la destruction ou la dégradation d'une infrastructure, d'un système de transport, d'une propriété publique ou privée, et du terme 'considérables' qui qualifie l'intensité des pertes économiques que ces actes entraîneraient. Ces termes ne permettent pas aux juges chargés de les interpréter de considérer comme infractions terroristes des actes dont les effets ne seraient pas manifestement importants».

[24]   «Quant aux pouvoirs excessifs qui seraient, selon les parties requérantes, attribués, en raison de l'indétermination des termes utilisés, aux services de police, la Cour observe que les missions de la police s'exercent, en matière pénale, sous le contrôle des cours et tribunaux».

[25]   Qui dispose : «Sans préjudice de l'application de l'article 140, toute personne qui diffuse ou met à la disposition du public de toute autre manière un message, avec l'intention d'inciter à la commission d'une des infractions visées à l'article 137, à l'exception de celle visée à l'article 137, § 3, 6°, sera punie de la réclusion de cinq ans à dix ans et d'une amende de cent euros à cinq mille euros, lorsqu'un tel comportement, qu'il préconise directement ou non la commission d'infractions terroristes, crée le risque qu'une ou plusieurs de ces infractions puissent être commises».

disposition législative tend à punir l'«incitation indirecte» ou la «provocation indirecte» à commettre une infraction terroriste et utilise le mot «risque».[26]

La Cour constate que l'article 140*bis* tend à assurer l'exécution de l'obligation formulée par l'article 3, § 1, a), de la décision-cadre 2002/475/JAI du Conseil de l'Union européenne du 13 juin 2002 «relative à la lutte contre le terrorisme», tel qu'il a été inséré par l'article 1er, 1), de la décision-cadre 2008/919/JAI du 28 novembre 2008 «modifiant la décision-cadre 2002/475/JAI relative à la lutte contre le terrorisme», et que les termes de l'article 140*bis* sont identiques à ceux de cet article 3, § 1, a). Le considérant 14 précédant la décision-cadre 2008/919/JAI indique que l'infraction qu'elle prévoit est une infraction intentionnelle. L'exigence de ce dol spécial est également prise en compte par le législateur.[27] Il s'agit de «l'intention d'inciter à la commission d'une des infractions visées à l'article 137, à l'exception de celle visée à l'article 137, § 3, 6°».

Se référant à la jurisprudence de la Cour de cassation[28], la Cour indique que «lorsqu'un terme n'est pas défini par le législateur, il y a lieu de lui donner son sens usuel, sauf lorsqu'il apparaît que le législateur a voulu s'en écarter, ce qui n'est pas le cas en l'espèce».

Partant du sens commun du mot «inciter», qui «signifie pousser quelqu'un à faire quelque chose (en néerlandais : aanzetten)», la Cour estime qu'il ne suffit pas que le message diffusé ou mis à la disposition du public préconise directement ou non la commission d'infractions terroristes et crée le risque qu'une ou plusieurs de ces infractions puissent être commises. Il faut encore qu'il soit prouvé que la personne qui diffuse le message ou le met à la disposition du public ait eu pour intention de pousser autrui à commettre une infraction terroriste». Elle rappelle, comme dans son arrêt n° 125/2005 précité, qu'il appartient au juge d'apprécier cette intention non pas en fonction de conceptions subjectives qui rendraient imprévisible l'application de la disposition attaquée mais en considération des éléments objectifs constitutifs de l'infraction, en tenant compte des circonstances propres à chaque affaire.

De même, «'préconiser' signifie recommander vivement (en néerlandais : aansturen). En incriminant le comportement qui préconise directement ou non la commission d'infractions terroristes, la disposition attaquée permet à la personne qui diffuse le message ou le met à la disposition du public de savoir qu'elle se met en infraction, que ce message dise clairement (préconisation

---

[26]   Arrêt n° 9/2015, B.9-B.20.
[27]   *Doc. parl.*, Chambre, 2012-2013, DOC 53-2502/001, p. 13.
[28]   Cass., 27 avril 1999, *Pas.*, 1999, I, n° 242.

directe) ou non (préconisation indirecte) que des infractions terroristes doivent être commises, ce qu'il appartient au juge d'apprécier en fonction de tous les éléments de la cause». En outre, «un 'risque' signifie un danger prévisible (en néerlandais : risico)».[29]

Enfin, la Cour rappelle «le souci constant du législateur de ne pas porter atteinte, en incriminant les infractions, à l'exercice des libertés fondamentales, raison pour laquelle les articles 139, alinéa 2, et 141*ter* ont été insérés dans le Code pénal» et souligne que le juge doit tenir compte de cette volonté du législateur dans son appréciation des éléments constitutifs de l'infraction.[30]

L'article 140*bis* a ensuite été modifié par l'article 2 de la loi du 3 août 2016 portant des dispositions diverses en matière de lutte contre le terrorisme (III)[31], pour préciser que l'incitation à la commission d'infractions terroristes peut être directe ou indirecte. Cette disposition a été jugée conforme aux exigences du principe de légalité parce que son libellé permet à la personne qui diffuse le message ou le met à la disposition du public de savoir qu'elle se met en infraction, que ce message dise clairement (préconisation directe) ou non (préconisation indirecte) que des infractions terroristes doivent être commises.[32]

---

29   La Cour ajoute : «Il appartient au juge d'exercer à cet égard le pouvoir d'appréciation évoqué en B.17.1 et d'examiner si ce risque se fonde sur des 'indices sérieux' en tenant compte de l'identité de la personne qui diffuse le message ou le met à la disposition du public, de son destinataire, de sa nature et du contexte dans lequel il est formulé (*Doc. parl*, Chambre, 2012-2013, DOC 53-2502/001, pp. 12-13)».

30   L'article 139, alinéa 2, du Code pénal, inséré par l'article 5 de la loi précitée du 19 décembre 2003, interdit de considérer comme un groupe terroriste «une organisation dont l'objet réel est exclusivement d'ordre politique, syndical, philanthropique, philosophique ou religieux ou qui poursuit exclusivement tout autre but légitime». Aux termes de l'article 141*ter* du Code pénal, aucune disposition du titre Ier*ter* du livre II de ce Code ne peut être «interprétée comme visant à réduire ou à entraver des droits ou libertés fondamentaux tels que le droit de grève, la liberté de réunion, d'association ou d'expression, y compris le droit de fonder avec d'autres des syndicats et de s'y affilier pour la défense de ses intérêts, et le droit de manifester qui s'y rattache, et tels que consacrés notamment par les articles 8 à 11 de la Convention européenne de sauvegarde des droits de l'homme et des libertés fondamentales».

31   Qui dispose : «A l'article 140*bis* du Code pénal, inséré par la loi du 18 février 2013, les modifications suivantes sont apportées :
     1° les mots ' directement ou indirectement ' sont insérés entre les mots ' avec l'intention d'inciter ' et les mots ' à la commission ' ;
     2° les premiers mots ' à l'article 137 ' sont remplacés par les mots ' aux articles 137 ou 140*sexies* ' ;
     3° les mots ' lorsqu'un tel comportement, qu'il préconise directement ou non la commission d'infractions terroristes, crée le risque qu'une ou plusieurs de ces infractions puissent être commises ' sont abrogés».

32   Arrêt n° 31/2018, B.10-B.15.

3. Recrutement pour commettre une infraction terroriste

La Cour a également statué sur la compatibilité, avec le principe de légalité en matière pénale, de l'article 140*ter* du Code pénal[33], inséré par l'article 5 de la loi du 18 février 2013, d'une part, en ce que les éléments constitutifs de l'infraction instaurée par la disposition législative attaquée ne pourraient être établis et, d'autre part, en ce que cette disposition rendrait imprévisible le niveau de la peine à appliquer au cas de recrutement au profit d'une troupe étrangère prévu par l'article 1er de la loi du 1er août 1979 concernant les services dans une armée ou une troupe étrangère se trouvant sur le territoire d'un Etat étranger.[34]

Après avoir cité les textes des instruments internationaux auxquels la loi attaquée donne suite et les travaux préparatoires de celle-ci, la Cour juge que les termes de l'article 140*ter*, qui sont suffisamment précis, ne permettent pas la condamnation de toute personne approchant une autre avec un discours considéré par l'autorité poursuivante comme illégitime, radical ou extrême. En outre, «ni le fait qu'il puisse, dans certaines circonstances, être malaisé pour l'autorité poursuivante de rapporter la preuve de l'un ou l'autre élément constitutif de l'infraction instaurée par ce texte, ni le fait que le comportement visé par ce dernier puisse être réprimé sur la base d'autres dispositions du Code pénal ne rendent l'article 140*ter* du Code pénal incompatible avec le principe de la légalité pénale».

Tant l'article 1er de la loi du 1er août 1979, remplacé par l'article 2 de la loi du 22 avril 2003 «de mise en conformité du droit belge avec la Convention internationale contre le recrutement, l'utilisation, le financement et l'instruction de mercenaires, adoptée à New York le 4 décembre 1989», que l'article 140*ter* du Code pénal attaqué autorisent la poursuite d'un individu qui recrute une autre personne au profit d'une troupe étrangère, mais les circonstances qui permettent cette poursuite sont différentes : «le recrutement visé par l'article 140*ter* du Code pénal a pour but la commission d'une infraction terroriste au sens de l'article 137, § 1er, du Code pénal, alors que le recrutement visé par l'article 1er de la loi du 1er août 1979 peut poursuivre d'autres objectifs». Enfin, en vertu de l'article 65 du Code pénal, «lorsqu'un même fait constitue plusieurs infractions […], la peine la plus forte sera seule prononcée». Dès lors, la Cour a jugé qu'une personne qui recrute une autre personne au profit d'une troupe étrangère dans des circonstances visées à la fois par l'article 1er de la loi du 1er août 1979 et par l'article 140*ter* du Code pénal est en mesure de savoir qu'elle est passible de la peine de réclusion prévue par cette dernière disposition.[35]

---

[33]   Qui dispose : «Sans préjudice de l'application de l'article 140, toute personne qui recrute une autre personne pour commettre l'une des infractions visées à l'article 137 ou à l'article 140, à l'exception de celle visée à l'article 137, § 3, 6°, sera punie de la réclusion de cinq ans à dix ans et d'une amende de cent euros à cinq mille euros».

[34]   Arrêt n° 9/2015.

[35]   B.27-B.33.

4.   *Instructions ou formation données en vue de commettre une infraction
       terroriste*

En ce qui concerne l'article 140*quater* du Code pénal[36], inséré par la même loi du 18 février 2013, la Cour décide qu'il est compatible avec l'exigence de précision, découlant du principe de légalité en matière pénale. Les parties requérantes soutenaient que les termes utilisés par cette disposition législative pour définir tant l'élément matériel que l'élément moral de l'infraction ne sont suffisamment clairs et précis.[37]

Après avoir analysé les dispositions internationales auxquelles cet article tend à donner suite et les travaux préparatoires de celui-ci, la Cour constate qu'il ne vise que les instructions ou la formation relatives à des «méthodes et techniques spécifiques», c'est-à-dire des méthodes et des techniques qui sont propres à la commission d'infractions terroristes : «Le commentaire de cette disposition législative indique certes que celle-ci vise non seulement les 'instructions pour des méthodes et techniques propres à être utilisées à des fins terroristes', mais aussi 'd'autres méthodes ou techniques'. Toutefois, en se référant à la fabrication ou à l'utilisation d'explosifs, d'armes à feu ou d'autres armes ou de substances nocives ou dangereuses ou d'autres méthodes et techniques spécifiques en vue de commettre les infractions qu'il vise, le législateur a adopté des termes qui sont suffisamment précis et clairs pour permettre à chacun de savoir quel est le comportement passible de la peine prévue. L'imprécision éventuelle des termes qui auraient été utilisés lors de l'élaboration d'une loi et qui, en l'espèce, conduiraient à considérer que le législateur entendait également viser des méthodes et techniques qui ne sont pas propres à la commission d'infractions terroristes, ne saurait en tout cas prévaloir sur les termes clairs que cette loi utilise».

Quant à l'élément moral de l'infraction, le texte de l'article 140*quater* du Code pénal vise les instructions ou la formation données «en vue de commettre l'une des infractions» terroristes auxquelles il est renvoyé. La Cour juge que la disposition attaquée respecte l'exigence de précision, sous réserve qu'elle soit interprétée dans le sens indiqué par la Cour. En effet, la décision-cadre à laquelle cet article donne suite se réfère à des actes intentionnels. Selon la Cour, «rien n'indique que le législateur aurait entendu s'écarter de cette prescription, le commentaire précité de l'article 140*quater* du Code pénal indiquant au contraire que la formation visée peut avoir pour but non seulement de 'commettre' une

---

[36]   Qui dispose : «Sans préjudice de l'application de l'article 140, toute personne qui donne des instructions ou une formation pour la fabrication ou l'utilisation d'explosifs, d'armes à feu ou d'autres armes ou de substances nocives ou dangereuses, ou pour d'autres méthodes et techniques spécifiques en vue de commettre l'une des infractions visées à l'article 137, à l'exception de celle visée à l'article 137, § 3, 6°, sera punie de la réclusion de cinq ans à dix ans et d'une amende de cent euros à cinq mille euros».

[37]   Arrêt n° 9/2015, B.39-B.42.

infraction terroriste mais aussi de 'contribuer à la commission d'une infraction terroriste'. Il indique aussi que l'infraction créée par cette disposition législative n'existe 'que lorsque le formateur sait que la formation est dispensée avec l'intention de commettre l'une des infractions'».[38]

5. *Instructions reçues ou formation suivie en vue de commettre une infraction terroriste*

L'article 140*quinquies* du Code pénal[39], inséré par la même loi du 18 février 2013, a également été soumis au contrôle de la Cour. Il est, en effet, indissociablement lié à l'article 140*quater* précité. Or, l'élément matériel de l'infraction incriminée par l'article 140*quinquies* du Code pénal est, entre autres, défini par une référence aux instructions et à la formation «visées à l'article 140*quater*» du Code pénal. Comme l'a Cour l'a déjà jugé, l'élément matériel de cette infraction a été défini dans des termes suffisamment clairs et précis.[40]

6. *Fait de quitter le territoire national ou d'entrer sur celui-ci en vue de la commission d'une infraction terroriste*

L'article 140*sexies* du Code pénal[41], inséré par l'article 2 de la loi du 20 juillet 2015 visant à renforcer la lutte contre le terrorisme, a fait l'objet d'un même contrôle de constitutionnalité.[42] Il lui était reproché qu'il ne donnerait pas au juge de critère permettant d'apprécier l'existence de l'intention qu'il requiert, ne préciserait pas le moment à partir duquel l'infraction créée est consommée, exigerait une intention de commettre d'autres infractions intentionnelles et autoriserait la répression de comportements déjà punissables en tant que tentative de commettre d'autres infractions terroristes.

Selon la Cour, «la circonstance que la disposition attaquée ne mentionne pas les éléments sur la base desquels le juge peut établir l'existence de l'élément

---

38 Même arrêt, B.48-B.50.
39 Qui dispose : «Sans préjudice de l'application de l'article 140, toute personne qui, en Belgique ou à l'étranger, se fait donner des instructions ou suit une formation visées à l'article 140*quater*, en vue de commettre l'une des infractions visées à l'article 137, à l'exception de celle visée à l'article 137, § 3, 6°, sera punie de la réclusion de cinq ans à dix ans et d'une amende de cent euros à cinq mille euros».
40 Arrêt n° 9/2015.
41 Qui dispose : «Sans préjudice de l'application de l'article 140, sera punie de la réclusion de cinq ans à dix ans et d'une amende de cent euros à cinq mille euros :
1° toute personne qui quitte le territoire national en vue de la commission, en Belgique ou à l'étranger, d'une infraction visée aux articles 137, 140 à 140*quinquies* et 141, à l'exception de l'infraction visée à l'article 137, § 3, 6° ;
2° toute personne qui entre sur le territoire national en vue de la commission, en Belgique ou à l'étranger, d'une infraction visée aux articles 137, 140 à 140*quinquies* et 141, à l'exception de l'infraction visée à l'article 137, § 3, 6°».
42 Arrêt n° 8/2018, B.9.1-B.10.

---

intentionnel de l'infraction créée par cette disposition ne suffit pas pour considérer que celle-ci empêche la personne qui quitte le territoire national ou qui entre sur celui-ci d'évaluer, préalablement et de manière satisfaisante, quelle sera la conséquence pénale de son comportement. Cette personne peut raisonnablement déterminer, à partir du texte des articles auxquels renvoie la disposition attaquée, si elle a l'intention de commettre une ou plusieurs des infractions qu'ils définissent ».

Il s'agit d'un crime, dont la tentative est donc punissable.[43] Le législateur a ainsi visé tant l'action de quitter le territoire national ou d'entrer sur ce territoire que son commencement d'exécution, lorsque les conditions de la tentative sont réunies.[44] Il a donc prévu, en des termes suffisamment précis, clairs et offrant la sécurité juridique, quels faits sont sanctionnés, sans laisser au juge un trop grand pouvoir d'appréciation.

L'application de l'article 140*sexies* suppose que soit rapportée la preuve qu'une personne quitte le territoire ou y entre avec l'intention d'adopter un comportement déterminé, lui-même motivé par l'intention plus précise requise par les dispositions auxquelles l'article 140*sexies* renvoie. La Cour constate que la circonstance qu'il puisse être malaisé pour l'autorité poursuivante de rapporter la preuve de ces deux intentions ne suffit pas à rendre l'article 140*sexies* du Code pénal incompatible avec le principe de légalité en matière pénale.

Pour la Cour, il résulte de ce qui précède que la disposition attaquée ne porte pas atteinte à ce principe.

7. *Obligation d'information imposée aux membres du personnel des institutions sociales*

La loi du 17 mai 2017 modifiant le Code d'instruction criminelle en vue de promouvoir la lutte contre le terrorisme insère notamment dans le Code d'instruction criminelle un article 46*bis*/1, § 3, qui dispose qu' « en application de l'exception visée à l'article 458 du Code pénal et par dérogation à des dispositions contraires, les membres du personnel des institutions de sécurité sociale (…) qui, de par leur profession, prennent connaissance d'une ou de plusieurs informations pouvant constituer des indices sérieux d'une infraction terroriste visée au livre II, titre Ier*ter*, du Code pénal en font la déclaration (au procureur du Roi) conformément à l'article 29 (du Code d'instruction criminelle) ». Par son arrêt n° 44/2019, la Cour annule la disposition attaquée qu'elle juge contraire à l'exigence de précision de la loi pénale découlant du principe de légalité. Elle estime en effet qu'« il ne peut pas être attendu d'un membre du personnel d'une

---

[43]   Article 52 du Code pénal.
[44]   Article 51 du Code pénal.

institution de sécurité sociale, qui n'a ni la compétence, ni les moyens nécessaires pour ce faire, de s'assurer qu'il existe chez un tiers (l') élément intentionnel de commettre une infraction terroriste. En conséquence, ce membre du personnel ne peut pas suffisamment prévoir s'il commet une infraction pénale en dévoilant, à propos de ce tiers, des informations couvertes par le secret professionnel ». Dès lors, « en faisant référence à des ' informations pouvant constituer des indices sérieux d'une infraction terroriste visée au livre II, titre I^{er}ter, du Code pénal', l'article 46bis/1, § 3, du Code d'instruction criminelle est formulé en des termes trop vagues, qui sont source d'insécurité juridique ».[45]

B.   NON-RÉTROACTIVITÉ DE LA LOI PÉNALE

Une loi du 13 mars 2003 a inséré un article 10, 6°, dans la loi du 17 avril 1878 contenant le Titre préliminaire du Code de procédure pénale, qui étend la compétence *ratione loci* des juridictions belges aux infractions visées à l'article 2 de la Convention européenne pour la répression du terrorisme du 27 janvier 1977, qui ont été commises sur le territoire d'un Etat partie à cette convention par un étranger et dont les auteurs présumés se trouvent sur le territoire belge.[46] L'article 3 de la loi du 13 mars 2003 dispose que l'article 2 ne s'applique qu'aux faits commis après l'entrée en vigueur de cette loi.

L'article 379 de la loi-programme du 22 décembre 2003, en abrogeant l'article 3 de la loi du 13 mars 2003, permet aux juridictions belges de se déclarer compétentes pour des faits qui auraient été commis avant l'entrée en vigueur de la loi du 13 mars 2003.

---

[45]   B.15 de cet arrêt. Il s'agit de l'obligation active d'information. En revanche la Cour a jugé que l'obligation passive d'information imposée par cette même loi (article 46bis/1, §§ 1er et 2, du Code d'instruction criminelle), selon laquelle les institutions de sécurité sociale doivent communiquer sans délai les renseignements administratifs que le procureur du Roi leur demande, lorsque celui-ci juge cette communication nécessaire dans le cadre de la recherche des infractions terroristes visées au livre II, titre I^{er}ter, du Code pénal, est rédigée en des termes suffisamment clairs, compte tenu du caractère général et abstrait de la loi pénale (B.11-B.14).

[46]   L'article 2 de la Convention européenne pour la répression du terrorisme vise les actes graves de violence autres que ceux qui sont visés à l'article 1er de ladite Convention et qui sont dirigés contre la vie, l'intégrité corporelle ou la liberté des personnes, ou contre des biens lorsqu'à cette occasion, un danger collectif pour des personnes a été créé. Il en va de même pour la tentative de commettre l'un de ces faits ou la participation à une telle infraction en tant que co-auteur ou complice. Il est par ailleurs exigé que le Gouvernement belge ait rejeté une demande d'extradition en vertu de l'exception d'extradition pour les infractions politiques (article 2 de la Convention), en vertu de la clause de non-discrimination (article 5 de la Convention), au motif de l'existence de la peine capitale dans l'Etat qui a demandé l'extradition (article 11 de la Convention européenne d'extradition) ou à cause de la dureté particulière de l'extradition pour la personne concernée.

Saisie d'un recours en annulation de cet article 379, la Cour a dû déterminer si la loi du 13 mars 2003 est ou non une loi pénale à laquelle s'applique le principe de non-rétroactivité.[47] Elle a jugé que, si cette loi ne crée pas de nouvelles incriminations, étant donné que tous les faits visés à l'article 2 de la Convention précitée étaient déjà en soi punissables en droit pénal belge, elle étend la compétence extraterritoriale des juridictions belges et donne une base légale à une poursuite et à une sanction en Belgique. Par conséquent, il s'agit d'une disposition de droit pénal matériel.

Se référant expressément à la jurisprudence de la Cour européenne des droits de l'homme, la Cour énonce que l'article 7 de la Convention européenne des droits de l'homme consacre le principe de légalité en matière pénale et interdit en particulier l'application rétroactive de la loi pénale lorsqu'elle joue en défaveur de l'intéressé.[48] Il est ainsi requis qu'au moment où le prévenu a accompli l'acte qui donne lieu aux poursuites et à la condamnation, une disposition législative existât qui rendait cet acte punissable.[49] La Cour constate qu'au moment où la requérante aurait commis les faits dont elle était soupçonnée, il n'existait pas en Belgique de base légale pour qu'elle pût y être poursuivie et jugée pour ces faits. Elle a donc annulé l'article 379 de la loi-programme du 22 décembre 2003.

II. LIBERTÉS D'EXPRESSION, DE RÉUNION ET D'ASSOCIATION

A. DIFFUSION D'UN MESSAGE PRÉCONISANT LA COMMISSION D'INFRACTIONS TERRORISTES

L'article 140bis du Code pénal, inséré par la loi du 18 février 2013 précitée et qui, comme il a été exposé plus haut, a été jugé compatible par la Cour avec le principe de légalité en matière pénale, a été contrôlé, par le même arrêt[50], au regard de la liberté d'expression et de la liberté d'association.[51]

Se référant à la jurisprudence de la Cour européenne des droits de l'homme[52], la Cour constate que la liberté d'expression, garantie par l'article 10 de la

---

47   Arrêt n° 73/2005, B.4-B.8.3.
48   CEDH, 25 mai 1993, *Kokkinakis c. Grèce*, § 52, 22 juin 2000, *Coëme et autres c. Belgique*, § 145.
49   Arrêt *Coëme et autres* précité, § 145.
50   Arrêt n° 9/2015, B.21-B.26.
51   Les moyens étaient pris de la violation des articles 19, 25 et 27 de la Constitution, lus isolément ou en combinaison avec les articles 10 et 11 de la Convention européenne des droits de l'homme, avec les articles 19 et 22 du Pacte international relatif aux droits civils et politiques et avec les articles 11 et 12 de la Charte des droits fondamentaux de l'Union européenne.
52   CEDH, 30 juin 2009, *Herri Batasuna et Barasuna c. Espagne*, § 74 ; grande chambre, 12 août 2011, *Palomo Sánchez et autres c. Espagne*, § 52 ; 25 septembre 2012, *Trade Union of the Police*

Convention européenne des droits de l'homme, est l'un des objectifs de la liberté d'association reconnue par l'article 11 de cette convention.[53] La liberté d'expression constituant l'un des fondements essentiels d'une société démocratique, les exceptions à la liberté d'expression doivent s'interpréter strictement. Il doit être démontré que les restrictions sont nécessaires dans une société démocratique, qu'elles répondent à un besoin social impérieux et qu'elles demeurent proportionnées aux buts légitimes poursuivis. L'article 140*bis* du Code pénal érige en infraction la diffusion de certains messages ou toute autre manière de les mettre à la disposition du public. Cette disposition constitue dès lors une limitation de l'exercice du droit à la liberté d'expression.

En s'appuyant, à nouveau, sur la jurisprudence de la Cour européenne qu'elle cite, ainsi que sur les travaux préparatoires de la disposition attaquée, la Cour relève que, dans une société démocratique, il est nécessaire de protéger les valeurs et les principes qui fondent la Convention européenne des droits de l'homme contre les personnes ou les organisations qui tentent de saper ces valeurs et principes en incitant à commettre des violences et par conséquent à commettre des actes terroristes.[54] Lorsqu'une opinion exprimée justifie que soient commis des actes terroristes afin d'atteindre les objectifs de l'auteur de cette opinion, l'autorité nationale peut imposer des restrictions à la liberté d'expression.[55]

La Cour relève que «le législateur a, à cet égard, considéré que cette possibilité n'allait pas jusqu'à permettre que l'incrimination de l'incitation publique à commettre des actes terroristes puisse aboutir à la répression d'actes n'ayant aucun rapport avec le terrorisme, répression 'risquant de porter atteinte à la liberté d'expression'[56]». À nouveau, la Cour insiste sur le fait que cette préoccupation a été traduite dans les articles 139, alinéa 2, et 141*ter* précités du Code pénal. En outre, «le juge doit prendre en compte l'identité de la personne qui diffuse le message ou le met à la disposition du public, le destinataire, la nature du message et le contexte dans lequel il est formulé. Le juge qui doit apprécier ce message ne peut sanctionner la personne qui le diffuse ou le met de toute autre manière à la disposition du public que lorsque cette personne agit avec un dol spécial consistant à inciter à commettre des infractions terroristes. Dès lors, même si un large pouvoir d'appréciation est laissé au juge, celui-ci ne peut en aucun cas prononcer une condamnation qui emporterait une atteinte injustifiée à la liberté d'expression».

---

[53] *in the Slovak Republic and Others v. Slovakia*, § 51 ; 18 juin 2013, *Gün et autres c. Turquie*, § 76 ; 8 juillet 2014, *Nedim Sener c. Turquie*, § 112.
Dans la suite de sa motivation, la Cour se limite à la seule liberté d'expression.
[54] CEDH, 23 septembre 2004, *Feriduin c. Turquie*, § 27 ; 8 juillet 1999, *Sürek c. Turquie*, § 63 ; 19 décembre 2006, *Falakaoglu et Saygili c. Turquie*, § 28.
[55] CEDH, 8 juillet 2014, *Nedim Sener c. Turquie*, § 116.
[56] *Doc. parl.*, Chambre, 2012-2013, DOC 53-2502/001, p. 12.

L'article 140*bis* du Code pénal a plus tard été modifié par l'article 2 de la loi du 3 août 2016 portant des dispositions diverses en matière de lutte contre le terrorisme (III). Le législateur a supprimé l'exigence selon laquelle la diffusion de certains messages ou toute autre manière de les mettre à la disposition du public avec l'intention d'inciter à la commission d'une infraction terroriste devait impliquer un risque qu'une ou plusieurs infractions terroristes puissent être commises. On a vu que cette référence au risque, qui figure dans le droit de l'Union européenne, a été jugée conforme au principe de légalité en matière pénale par l'arrêt n° 9/2015, qui se référait à cet égard au pouvoir d'appréciation du juge. Il est assez piquant de constater que cette référence au risque a été supprimée par la loi du 3 août 2016 afin de simplifier la preuve de l'incitation au terrorisme, parce que la portée de cette exigence n'était, selon le législateur lui-même, pas claire !

La constitutionnalité de l'article 140*bis* ainsi amendé a été soumise à la Cour, les parties requérantes soutenant que cette disposition violait la liberté d'expression et le droit d'association.[57] Après avoir constaté, sur la base d'un examen de la jurisprudence de la Cour européenne des droits de l'homme, que la disposition attaquée limite l'exercice de la liberté d'expression, la Cour cite les motifs de son arrêt n° 9/2015 par lequel elle a jugé que l'article 140*bis* originaire du Code pénal, par ailleurs compatible avec le principe de légalité, n'emportait pas d'atteinte injustifiée à la liberté d'expression. Elle indique qu'il ressort des travaux préparatoires de cet article que l'exigence d'un risque a été considérée comme une garantie contre la répression d'actes sans rapport avec le terrorisme et qu'il ressort des travaux préparatoires de la disposition modificative que la suppression de cette exigence vise à simplifier la preuve de l'incitation au terrorisme, parce que la portée de cette exigence ne serait pas claire. Elle ajoute que «la nécessité de simplifier l'administration de la preuve ne justifie pas qu'une personne puisse être condamnée à un emprisonnement de cinq à dix ans et à une amende de cent à cinq mille euros pour incitation au terrorisme, même s'il n'existe pas d'indices sérieux qu'il existe un risque qu'une infraction terroriste puisse être commise». Elle juge dès lors que la disposition attaquée n'est pas nécessaire dans une société démocratique et limite la liberté d'expression de manière disproportionnée, soulignant que le droit européen en la matière exige bien un tel risque.[58]

---

57   Arrêt n° 31/2018, B.4-B.8.
58   Article 3 de la décision-cadre 2002/475/JAI du Conseil du 13 juin 2002 relative à la lutte contre le terrorisme, modifiée par la décision-cadre 2008/919/JAI du Conseil du 28 novembre 2008 et article 5 de la directive 2017/541/UE du Parlement européen et du Conseil du 15 mars 2017 «relative à la lutte contre le terrorisme et remplaçant la décision-cadre 2002/475/JAI du Conseil et modifiant la décision 2005/671/JAI du Conseil» (à laquelle les Etats membres doivent se conformer au plus tard le 8 septembre 2018).

B. RECRUTEMENT ET INSTRUCTIONS OU FORMATION EN VUE DE COMMETTRE UNE INFRACTION TERRORISTE

La Cour a également dû décider si les articles 140*ter* et 140*quater* précités du Code pénal sont compatibles avec, d'une part, les articles 19 et 25 de la Constitution, lus en combinaison avec l'article 10 de la Convention européenne des droits de l'homme, avec l'article 19 du Pacte international relatif aux droits civils et politiques et avec l'article 11 de la Charte des droits fondamentaux de l'Union européenne, et avec, d'autre part, l'article 27 de la Constitution, lu en combinaison avec l'article 11 de la Convention européenne des droits de l'homme, avec l'article 22 du Pacte international relatif aux droits civils et politiques et avec l'article 12 de la Charte des droits fondamentaux de l'Union européenne, en ce que les dispositions attaquées ne seraient ni prévues par la loi, ni nécessaires dans une société démocratique.[59, 60]

La Cour juge que les dispositions attaquées sont compatibles avec la Constitution. En effet, l'article 140*ter* du Code pénal prévoit la poursuite de toute personne qui recrute une autre personne, soit pour commettre une infraction terroriste visée par cet article, soit pour participer à une activité d'un groupe terroriste ou diriger celui-ci, mais ne permet pas la condamnation de toute personne approchant une autre avec un discours considéré par l'autorité poursuivante comme illégitime, radical ou extrême. Dans la mesure où il autorise la poursuite de toute personne qui recrute une autre personne pour participer à une activité d'un groupe terroriste ou diriger celui-ci, l'article 140*ter* du Code pénal pourrait certes être compris comme restreignant l'exercice de la liberté d'association. Cette restriction est toutefois jugée nécessaire, dans une société démocratique, à la sauvegarde de la sécurité nationale, à la sûreté publique, à la défense de l'ordre, à la prévention du crime et à la protection des droits et libertés d'autrui.

Quant à l'article 140*quater* précité du Code pénal, il permet la poursuite de toute personne qui donne les instructions ou la formation décrites par cette disposition. Le seul fait pour une personne d'approcher une autre avec un discours considéré comme illégitime, radical ou extrême par l'autorité poursuivante n'est pas non plus incriminé par cette disposition. Si l'article 140*quater* pouvait être compris comme restreignant l'exercice du droit à la liberté d'association, la Cour juge de même que cette restriction est nécessaire, dans une société démocratique, à la sauvegarde de la sécurité nationale, à la sûreté publique, à la défense de l'ordre, à la prévention

---

[59]   Arrêt n° 9/2015, B.34-B.38 et B.43-B.47.
[60]   La Cour arrive à la même conclusion en ce qui concerne la compatibilité de l'article 140*quinquies* du Code pénal avec la liberté d'expression et avec la liberté d'association.

du crime, ou à la protection des droits et libertés d'autrui. Par ailleurs, la Cour constate que les articles 140*ter* et 140*quater* du Code pénal ne constituent pas une restriction à la liberté d'expression, de sorte qu'il n'y a pas lieu de les contrôler au regard de l'article 10.2 de la Convention européenne des droits de l'homme.

III. LIBERTÉ INDIVIDUELLE

A. FAIT DE QUITTER LE TERRITOIRE NATIONAL OU D'ENTRER SUR CELUI-CI EN VUE DE LA COMMISSION D'UNE INFRACTION TERRORISTE

L'article 140*sexies* précité du Code pénal a également été attaqué en ce qu'il violerait les dispositions qui «garantissent la libre circulation des personnes».[61] La Cour a jugé que tel n'est pas la cas parce qu'il constitue une norme visant à lutter contre le terrorisme et à répondre aux obligations résultant d'une résolution du Conseil de sécurité des Nations Unies qui prévoit que les Etats membres prennent les mesures adéquates pour empêcher la circulation des terroristes.[62]

B. INDICATION DE RAISONS SÉRIEUSES DANS LE MANDAT D'ARRÊT

Enfin, l'article 16, § 1er, alinéa 4, de la loi du 20 juillet 1990 relative à la détention préventive prévoit que si le maximum de la peine applicable ne dépasse pas quinze ans de réclusion, le mandat ne peut être décerné que s'il existe de sérieuses raisons de craindre que l'inculpé, s'il était laissé en liberté, commette de nouveaux crimes ou délits, se soustraie à l'action de la justice, tente de faire disparaître des preuves ou entre en collusion avec des tiers. Cette disposition a été modifiée par l'article 6 de la loi précitée du 3 août 2016 portant des dispositions diverses en matière de terrorisme (III) afin de ne plus subordonner la délivrance d'un mandat d'arrêt aux raisons que cette disposition prévoit lorsqu'il s'agit d'infractions terroristes pour lesquelles le maximum de la peine

---

[61]   Il s'agit de l'article 12, alinéa 1er, de la Constitution, lu ou non en combinaison avec l'article 2.2 du Quatrième Protocole à la Convention européenne des droits de l'homme et avec l'article 3.2 du Traité sur l'Union européenne, les articles 20.2, a) et 21 du Traité sur le fonctionnement de l'Union européenne, l'article 45 de la Charte des droits fondamentaux de l'Union européenne et l'article 27 de la directive 2004/38/CE du Parlement européen et du Conseil du 29 avril 2004 «relative au droit des citoyens de l'Union et des membres de leurs familles de circuler et de séjourner librement sur le territoire des Etats membres, modifiant le règlement (CEE) n° 1612/68 et abrogeant les directives 64/221/CEE, 68/360/CEE, 72/194/CEE, 73/148/CEE, 75/34/CEE, 75/35/CEE, 90/364/CEE, 90/365/CEE et 93/96/CEE».

[62]   Arrêt n° 8/2018, B.12-B.13.4.

applicable dépasse cinq ans d'emprisonnement et que la détention préventive se révèle absolument nécessaire pour la sécurité publique.[63]

Le moyen est pris de la violation par l'article 6 de la loi du 3 août 2016, des articles 11 et 12 de la Constitution, combinés ou non avec l'article 5 de la Convention européenne des droits de l'homme, «en ce que la disposition attaquée limiterait de manière illicite la liberté d'appréciation du juge relativement à la détention préventive pour une catégorie d'infractions, à savoir les infractions dites terroristes, sans que cette distinction repose sur un critère objectif, pertinent et clair».

Les travaux préparatoires ont justifié la mesure attaquée en considérant notamment que «l'impact énorme du terrorisme sur la société dans son ensemble renforce toutefois par rapport aux autres infractions la nécessité de permettre des mesures de protection de la société dans le cadre de la procédure pénale et avant la phase de la condamnation et de l'exécution de la peine».[64]

La Cour rappelle qu'eu égard à l'importance fondamentale de l'*habeas corpus*, toutes les limitations de la liberté individuelle doivent être interprétées de manière restrictive et leur constitutionnalité doit être traitée avec la plus grande circonspection. Mais, comme l'a indiqué la Cour européenne des droits de l'homme qu'elle cite, «par leur gravité particulière et par la réaction du public à leur accomplissement, certaines infractions peuvent susciter un trouble social de nature à justifier la détention préventive, si celle-ci est expressément motivée par une menace concrète et actuelle pour l'ordre public».[65] La Cour procède à un contrôle de proportionnalité de la mesure attaquée en se référant, cette fois, à l'avis de la section de législation du Conseil d'Etat qui a observé que la disposition attaquée ne porte pas atteinte aux autres conditions de fond et de procédure dans lesquelles la détention préventive peut être ordonnée par le juge d'instruction.[66] De surcroît, la disposition attaquée laisse entière la condition selon laquelle la détention préventive doit être absolument nécessaire pour la sécurité publique.

La Cour juge dès lors que le législateur n'a pas porté une atteinte disproportionnée à la liberté individuelle.

---

63   Arrêt n° 31/2018, B.10-B.20.

64   *Doc. parl.*, Chambre, 2015-2016, DOC 54-1951/001, p. 12. Il y est aussi précisé que «la modification proposée n'a pas pour effet de permettre la détention préventive dès qu'il y a des indices sérieux de culpabilité d'une infraction terroriste. La présomption d'innocence fait que la détention préventive doit rester une mesure dérogatoire. Il faudra toujours prouver que la détention préventive s'impose dans le cas d'espèce pour protéger la sécurité publique».

65   CEDH, 16 juillet 2009, *Prencipe c. Monaco*, §§ 79-81.

66   *Doc. parl.*, Chambre, 2015-2016, DOC 54-1951/001, p. 16.

IV. DROIT AU RESPECT DE LA VIE PRIVÉE

Par son arrêt n° 145/2011[67], la Cour déclare non fondé un moyen pris de la violation de l'exigence d'accessibilité et de prévisibilité de la loi découlant des article 22 de la Constitution et 8 de la Convention européenne des droits de l'homme, garantissant le droit au respect de la vie privée, par l'article 3 de la loi du 4 février 2010 relative aux méthodes de recueil des données par les services de renseignement et de sécurité, qui a inséré un article 3,15°, dans la loi du 30 novembre 1998 organique des services de renseignement et de sécurité. Cet article 3,15°, définit le «processus de radicalisation» comme étant «un processus influençant un individu ou un groupe d'individu de telle sorte que cet individu ou ce groupe d'individus soit mentalement préparé ou disposé à commettre des actes terroristes».

Citant la jurisprudence de la Cour européenne des droits de l'homme[68], la Cour rappelle que l'article 8.2 de la Convention n'admet d'ingérence dans l'exercice du droit au respect de la vie privée «que pour des raisons de sécurité nationale, à condition que cette ingérence soit prévue par une loi et que cette loi soit accessible à l'intéressé et précise. Ces exigences d'accessibilité et de prévisibilité de la loi visent à éviter tout arbitraire de la part de l'autorité publique. La loi est précise si les termes dont elle use permettent au citoyen d'estimer sans ambiguïté les conséquences qui peuvent découler de son application». Elle précise que «la Cour européenne des droits de l'homme admet que le niveau de précision de la loi puisse être moindre dans le domaine de la sécurité nationale que dans les autres domaines».[69]

La Cour relève que le «processus de radicalisation» n'est pas incriminé et que cette notion ne se situe pas dans le cadre d'une instruction pénale mais est en rapport avec la nature et la finalité propres d'une enquête de renseignement.

L'emploi de la notion de «processus de radicalisation», combinée avec celle de «terrorisme»[70], renvoie ainsi à la phase qui précède la commission d'actes terroristes. «En particulier, le processus de radicalisation vise un processus préparatoire de manipulation ou d'influence faisant apparaître des risques sécuritaires». La Cour a donc jugé que «l'article 3, 15°, de la loi du 30 novembre

---

[67] B.93-B.97. Ces motifs s'inscrivent dans un arrêt qui n'est pas examiné ici pour le surplus, dès lors qu'il traite de manière générale des méthodes de recueil des données par les services de renseignement et non spécifiquement des actes liés au terrorisme.

[68] CEDH, 29 juin 2006, *Weber et Saravia c. Allemagne*, § 95.

[69] La Cour ne cite pas d'arrêt de la Cour européenne. Voy. CEDH, 26 mars 1987, *Leander c. Suède*, § 51 ; J. Velu et R. Ergec, *Convention européenne des droits de l'homme, R.P.D.B.*, 2e éd. par R. Ergec, Bruxelles, Bruylant, 2014, p. 189, n° 194.

[70] Contenue aux articles 18/9, § 1er, et 8, 1°, b), de la loi précitée du 30 novembre 1998. Ce dernier article définit le terrorisme comme étant «le recours à la violence à l'encontre de personnes ou d'intérêts matériels, pour des motifs idéologiques ou politiques, dans le but d'atteindre ses objectifs par la terreur, l'intimidation ou les menaces».

1998 indique clairement qu'il s'agit d'un processus consistant à influencer l'intéressé de telle manière qu'il soit préparé ou disposé à commettre des actes terroristes. L'habilitation à utiliser les méthodes exceptionnelles de renseignement dans le cadre d'une menace grave relative à une activité du processus de radicalisation s'inscrit donc dans l'action préventive contre le terrorisme». Elle en a déduit que la disposition attaquée ne porte pas atteinte au principe de légalité consacré par l'article 22 de la Constitution.

V. PRINCIPE D'ÉGALITÉ ET NON-DISCRIMINATION

Dans un moyen dirigé contre certaines dispositions de la loi du 19 décembre 2003 relative aux infractions terroristes, les parties requérantes estiment que celles-ci génèrent des différences de traitement au détriment des personnes soupçonnées d'avoir commis les infractions visées au paragraphe 2 de l'article 137 du Code pénal introduit par l'article 3 de la loi attaquée.[71] Ces différences de traitement se manifesteraient au cours de l'enquête préliminaire, en raison des méthodes particulières de recherche que les infractions terroristes autorisent, dans la phase de jugement, parce que des témoignages anonymes peuvent servir de preuves à part entière et, enfin, en raison des sanctions infligées qui sont toujours aggravées pour les infractions terroristes.

La Cour formule les limites de son contrôle. Il ne lui appartient pas «d'apprécier s'il est opportun, compte tenu des obligations internationales de la Belgique, d'aggraver les peines et d'étendre dès lors le champ d'application de la détention préventive et, partant, de restreindre le champ d'application de la transaction et celui de la correctionnalisation», ainsi que d'étendre les méthodes particulières d'enquête aux auteurs soupçonnés d'infractions terroristes, «vu la nécessité de combattre efficacement les actes de terrorisme». Selon les travaux préparatoires de la loi attaquée, «le législateur a voulu punir sévèrement des infractions qu'il estimait particulièrement graves, tout en étant conscient que le juge devait pouvoir apprécier le degré de gravité dans chaque cas». Ici encore la Cour souligne à cet égard le souci constant que le législateur a poursuivi qu'il ne soit pas porté atteinte, en incriminant les infractions terroristes, à l'exercice des libertés fondamentales, raison pour laquelle les articles 139, alinéa 2, et 141ter ont été insérés dans le Code pénal. Elle tire enfin argument du fait que «le législateur n'a pas souhaité transposer en droit belge le principe du recours aux repentis, pourtant préconisé dans la décision-cadre comme une mesure utile pour déjouer des attentats en préparation ou pour démonter des filières. Il a, en effet, été objecté que le recours à cette mesure 'se heurte à des objections d'ordre

---

[71]   Arrêt n° 125/2005, B.9-B.11.4.

éthique, puisque le principe même de cette méthode est d'offrir une récompense aux auteurs d'une infraction' ».

Une dernière discrimination était dénoncée : l'extension de la compétence territoriale du juge belge aux infractions terroristes lorsqu'elles sont commises contre un ressortissant ou une institution belge ou contre une institution de l'Union européenne ou un organisme créé conformément au Traité instituant la Communauté européenne ou au Traité sur l'Union européenne qui a son siège en Belgique. Soulignant la nécessité de prendre en compte l'activité de réseaux opérant au niveau international, l'absence de frontières dans l'Union européenne et le droit de circulation des personnes, la Cour décide que «le législateur a pu, sans violer les articles 10 et 11 de la Constitution, mettre en œuvre la décision-cadre en choisissant comme critère de rattachement de la compétence du juge belge celui de la personnalité passive. Le choix de ce critère est d'autant plus justifié que la Belgique est le siège de nombreuses institutions de l'Union européenne qui peuvent être la cible d'actes de terrorisme incriminés par la loi entreprise».

VI. OBLIGATION DE *STANDSTILL*

L'article 23 de la Constitution contient, en ce qui concerne les droits à la sécurité sociale et à l'aide sociale, une obligation de standstill qui interdit au législateur compétent de réduire significativement le niveau de protection offert par la législation en vigueur, sans qu'existent pour ce faire des motifs liés à l'intérêt général. L'arrêt n° 44/2019 rejette le moyen pris de la violation de cet article. Les parties requérantes soutenaient « que la disposition attaquée altère le lien de confiance entre les institutions de sécurité sociale et les bénéficiaires des aides qu'elles procurent, ce qui entraînerait une recrudescence du phénomène du 'non-recours', c'est-à-dire des cas dans lesquels les bénéficiaires de l'aide ou de la sécurité sociale renoncent à faire valoir leurs droits, alors qu'ils remplissent les conditions pour pouvoir y prétendre. Pour la Cour, « si phénomène de 'non-recours' il y a, et s'il résulte de ce phénomène un recul dans l'effectivité des droits à l'aide sociale et à la sécurité sociale, force est de constater que ce recul ne résulte pas de la disposition attaquée. En effet, l'article 46*bis*/1, §§ 1er et 2, du Code d'instruction criminelle, qui prévoit une obligation d'information passive, ne contient pas de disposition qui réduise, a fortiori de manière significative, le niveau de protection des personnes qui ont recours à la sécurité sociale ou à l'aide sociale ».[72]

---

[72] B.31-B.32.2. Voy. *supra*, I, A, 7°.

CONCLUSION

Le contentieux lié au terrorisme est particulièrement difficile car, ainsi que les développements qui précèdent le confirment, il charge chacun des plateaux de la balance de la justice, de droits et de libertés si fondamentaux que leur pesée en est extrêmement délicate.[73]

Sur l'un de ces plateaux, l'interdiction de la torture et des traitements ou peines inhumains ou dégradants ou, comme dans les arrêts que nous avons analysés, le principe de légalité en matière pénale, qui implique la précision et la non-rétroactivité de la loi, les libertés d'expression, de réunion et d'association, la liberté individuelle, le droit au respect de la vie privée, le principe d'égalité et de non-discrimination ou l'obligation de *standstill* en matière de sécurité sociale ou d'aide sociale, dont peuvent notamment se prévaloir les suspects et les prévenus d'infractions liées au terrorisme.

Sur l'autre plateau, pour ne citer qu'eux, le droit à la vie et à l'intégrité physique, la liberté individuelle, les libertés de réunion, d'association et d'expression, le droit à la propriété des victimes de pareils actes, le droit mais aussi le devoir de tout Etat d'assurer la sécurité des personnes[74] et la sauvegarde de ses structures politiques, constitutionnelles, économiques et sociales, qui sont menacées frontalement par le terrorisme.

Cette pesée, Paul Lemmens la connaît bien, lui qui la pratique très régulièrement avec toute la minutie et la conscience qui sont les siennes.

Dans la recherche de cet équilibre, il n'appartient pas à la Cour constitutionnelle de se substituer au législateur. Ainsi, comme elle l'a rappelé, il ne lui revient pas d'apprécier s'il est opportun d'accroître la sévérité de la répression à l'égard des auteurs d'infractions terroristes.

Dans les sept arrêts analysés, la Cour a néanmoins annulé deux dispositions législatives, violant, l'une, le principe de non-rétroactivité d'une disposition du droit pénal matériel défavorable au prévenu, et l'autre, la liberté d'expression en raison de l'absence de nécessité et du caractère disproportionné de la limitation

---

[73] Comme l'ont écrit J. Velu et R. Ergec, «la pondération des intérêts en présence qu'implique la nécessité de la mesure peut soulever un conflit entre différents droits garantis par la Convention. Se pose alors la délicate question de savoir lequel des deux doit être limité pour assurer le libre exercice de l'autre. (…) La Convention n'établissant pas de hiérarchie entre les deux droits qu'elle garantit, la jurisprudence aborde ces questions *in concreto*» (op. cit., p. 190, n° 194).

[74] P. Lemmens, «Respecting Human Rights in the Fight against Terrorism», *op. cit.*, p. 225, citant CEDH, 28 octobre 1998, *Osman c. Royaume-Uni*, § 115.

apportée par la mesure concernée à ce droit fondamental. Elle a réaffirmé à cet égard que, cette liberté constituant l'un des fondements essentiels d'une société démocratique, les exceptions qui lui sont apportées doivent s'apprécier strictement. En outre, toujours à propos de la liberté d'expression, elle a rejeté un recours sous réserve que l'élément intentionnel de l'infraction soit interprété de la manière indiquée par la Cour.

Elle a souligné également qu'eu égard à l'importance fondamentale de l'*habeas corpus*, les limitations à la liberté individuelle doivent être interprétées de manière restrictive et leur constitutionnalité doit être traitée avec la plus grande circonspection.

Elle a par ailleurs écarté certaines justifications avancées par le législateur, comme la nécessité de simplifier une preuve incombant à la partie poursuivante.

Seule une disposition a été annulée parce qu'elle n'était pas formulée d'une manière suffisamment précise. Il est vrai que, parfois, la Cour a admis que la définition de l'infraction pourrait dans certains cas donner lieu à des difficultés d'interprétation, qu'il peut être malaisé pour la partie poursuivante de rapporter la preuve de l'intention requise ou que le législateur n'a pas mentionné les éléments sur la base desquels le juge peut établir l'existence d'un élément intentionnel. Mais, en règle générale, la Cour a conclu à la précision suffisante de la loi en se référant à la clarté de ses termes (qui doivent prévaloir sur l'ambiguïté éventuelle de certains passages des travaux préparatoires), à leur sens commun ou aux travaux préparatoires lorsque ceux-ci sont univoques.

Elle a, bien entendu, eu égard au fait que les dispositions législatives attaquées devant elle n'étaient que la mise en œuvre de décisions-cadres du Conseil de l'Union européenne ou d'autres dispositions internationales liant la Belgique.

Dans plusieurs arrêts, elle a également pris en compte le souci du législateur de ne pas porter atteinte, en incriminant les infractions terroristes, à l'exercice des libertés fondamentales, rappelant que ce souci a justifié notamment l'insertion des articles 139, alinéa 2, et 141*ter* dans le Code pénal, cités à la note 30 *supra*.

Les termes de la loi étant ainsi éclairés, la Cour s'en remet alors au large pouvoir d'appréciation laissé par la loi au juge, auquel il appartient de statuer au cas par cas, en prenant en considération concrètement les données particulières de la cause qui lui est soumise, sans pour autant qu'il soit conféré au juge un pouvoir d'incrimination ou qu'il lui soit permis de porter une atteinte injustifiée à un droit ou à une liberté. Elle rejoint sur ce point Paul Lemmens, selon qui le juge remplit un rôle important comme bastion contre une ingérence excessive dans les droits fondamentaux.[75]

A l'instar de la Cour européenne des droits de l'homme, elle se prononce en prenant en compte expressément le contexte des infractions, lequel, ainsi qu'il ressort des travaux préparatoires qu'elle cite, a été déterminant dans l'adoption de nombre des dispositions législatives soumises à sa censure. Elle souligne qu'il est nécessaire de combattre les actes de terrorisme et qu'en raison de leur impact énorme sur la société dans son ensemble, ceux-ci justifient l'adoption de mesures de protection de la société renforcées par rapport aux autres infractions et répondant au caractère international des réseaux terroristes. Comme la Cour européenne, elle constate en particulier que, par leur gravité particulière et par la réaction du public à leur accomplissement, ils peuvent susciter un trouble social de nature à justifier la détention préventive si celle-ci est expressément motivée par une menace concrète et actuelle pour l'ordre public, voire même que le niveau de précision de la loi qu'exige le droit au respect de la vie privée puisse être moindre dans le domaine de la sécurité nationale que dans les autres domaines.[76]

On l'a constaté, dans la plupart des arrêts rendus en la matière, la Cour se réfère expressément à la jurisprudence de la Cour européenne des droits de l'homme. Elle rappelle que «lorsqu'une disposition conventionnelle liant la Belgique a une portée analogue à celle d'une des dispositions constitutionnelles dont le contrôle relève de la compétence de la Cour et dont la violation est alléguée, les garanties consacrées par cette disposition conventionnelle constituent un ensemble indissociable avec les garanties inscrites dans les dispositions constitutionnelles concernées».[77, 78]

La Cour met ainsi en œuvre le principe de subsidiarité, suivant lequel le respect de la Convention européenne des droits de l'homme incombe d'abord au juge national, la Cour européenne n'intervenant qu'en cas de défaillance du juge interne.

---

[75] P. Lemmens, *op. cit.*, p. 249.

[76] Dans l'arrêt n° 44/2019, en rejetant un moyen pris de la violation du droit au respect de la vie privée, la Cour a précisé que l'objectif poursuivi par le législateur de lutter contre le terrorisme « correspond incontestablement à un besoin social impérieux » (B.22).

[77] Arrêt n° 31/2018, B.18.3.

[78] Voy. notam. A. Alen, J. Spreutels, E. Peremans et W. Verrijdt, «Grondwettelijk Hof en het internationaal en Europees recht», *T.B.P.* 2014, pp. 619-652 et «Cour constitutionnelle de Belgique», in R. Huppmann et R. Schnabl (éd.), *La coopération entre les Cours constitutionnelles en Europe. Situation actuelle et perspectives*, Vienne, Verlag Österreich, 2014, vol. 1, pp. 293-347. Pour Guy Canivet, la Cour constitutionnelle de Belgique prend ainsi part, de manière constante et raisonnée, «à la construction interactive d'une conception européenne des droits fondamentaux» («Convergences et divergences des jurisprudences de la Cour constitutionnelle belge et du Conseil constitutionnel français. L'hypothèse d'une fraternité gémellaire», in A. Alen, J. Spreutels e.a., *Grondwettelijk Hof 1985-2015 – Cour constitutionnelle 1985-2015*, Bruges/Bruxelles, La Charte, 2016, p. 99).

A ce propos, Paul Lemmens a souligné que «la protection des droits de l'homme repose sur la recherche d'un équilibre entre les droits fondamentaux des individus et les intérêts de la société dans laquelle ils vivent. Les juridictions nationales et la Cour européenne doivent s'aider mutuellement à trouver les bonnes solutions. S'il appartient à la Cour européenne de fixer les normes minimales, il incombe aux juridictions nationales d'appliquer ces normes dans leur ordre juridique comme faisant partie du cadre légal applicable. La réussite de tout le système réside dans le degré de coopération existant entre les deux types de juridiction».[79]

Selon Paul Lemmens, la Cour constitutionnelle de Belgique remplit bien ainsi le rôle qui lui est imparti en tant que juridiction nationale au sein du système de la Convention : «Het integreert de minimumstandaarden van het EVRM binnen de Belgische constitutionele orde en vervult aldus een brugfunctie tussen de rechtsorde van het EVRM en de Belgische rechtsorde».[80] Pour lui, il ne fait aucun doute que la Cour est un «allié fort» de la Cour européenne face aux grands défis que rencontre la défense des droits de l'homme dans le monde actuel.

Il va sans dire qu'il est, à l'inverse, très précieux pour la Cour de pouvoir se revendiquer de l'autorité des arrêts de la Cour européenne dans les décisions difficiles qu'elle est amenée à rendre et de savoir que celles-ci sont ainsi l'expression non seulement de sa propre opinion mais aussi de celle de nombre de juges partageant avec elle une commune conception des exigences d'un Etat de droit démocratique.

---

[79] P. Lemmens, «Réponse à l'exposé de M. Jean-Marc Sauvé», in *Subsidiarité : une médaille à deux faces ?, Dialogue des juges, Actes du séminaire du 30 janvier 2015*, Cour européenne des droits de l'homme, Strasbourg, 2015, p. 41, https ://www.echr.coe.int/Documents/Dialogue_2015_FRA.pdf (1er octobre 2018). Nous voudrions ici exprimer notre gratitude à l'égard de Paul et Anne Lemmens qui, en marge de la rentrée judiciaire de la Cour européenne, réunissent chaque année, d'une manière amicale et conviviale, les membres des hautes juridictions belges participant à cet événement, ce qui est toujours l'occasion de fructueux échanges.

[80] P. Lemmens, «Visie van het Europees Hof voor de Rechten van de Mens op het Grondwettelijk Hof», in A. Alen, J. Spreutels e.a., *Grondwettelijk Hof 1985-2015 – Cour constitutionnelle 1985-2015*, p. 162. De son côté, après avoir récemment rappelé qu'«à l'ère de la subsidiarité et du renforcement de nos liens avec les juges internes, en appliquant la Convention européenne des droits de l'homme, une Cour constitutionnelle est bien dans son rôle», M. Guido Raimondi, président de la Cour européenne des droits de l'homme, a insisté sur l'importance à cet égard du Réseau des cours supérieures, mis en place en octobre 2015, qui facilite les contacts entre la Cour européenne et les plus hautes juridictions nationales. (G. Raimondi, *Allocation d'ouverture*, Audience solennelle de rentrée de la Cour européenne des droits de l'homme, Strasbourg, 26 janvier 2018, https ://www.echr.coe.int/Documents/Speech_20180126_Raimondi_JY_FRA.pdf (1er octobre 2018).

THE DIALOGUE BETWEEN THE EUROPEAN COURT OF HUMAN RIGHTS AND DOMESTIC CONSTITUTIONAL COURTS

The Belgian Example

Prof. em. dr. André ALEN
President of the Belgian Constitutional Court
Professor emeritus at the KU Leuven

Willem VERRIJDT
Law clerk in the Belgian Constitutional Court
Lector at the KU Leuven

Paul Lemmens has always combined his academic work at the KU Leuven with legal practice, as an attorney-at-law, as an auditor in and as a member of the Council of State, and as the Belgian judge in the European Court of Human Rights (ECtHR). In each of these capacities, he has always been held in very high esteem, both because of his brilliant legal skills and because of his kind and modest personality. Having had the pleasure to work with him at the Leuven Centre of Public Law, we can definitely confirm this reputation.

One of his typical characteristics is his willingness to engage in dialogues with students, colleagues and legal practitioners alike, taking into account their counterarguments and criticisms. His role then typically consists of nuancing absolute statements and offering new perspectives on the topic at hand. It therefore seems appropriate to honour Paul Lemmens with a contribution on the dialogue between 'his' ECtHR and 'our' Belgian Constitutional Court (BCC), containing both an academic analysis and a practical overview.[1]

---

[1]   During a conference in 2015, Paul Lemmens proudly recalled that he is familiar with the BCC, having pleaded several human rights related cases before the Court of Arbitration, which was the BCC's name before 8 May 2007 (P. Lemmens, "Visie van het Europees Hof voor de Rechten van de Mens op het Grondwettelijk Hof", in A. Alen a.o. (eds.), *Grondwettelijk Hof 1985–2015 – Cour constitutionnelle 1985–2015*, Bruges, la Charte, 2016, 155).

We recently wrote that the dialogue between constitutional courts and the European Court of Justice (ECJ) is not a perfect one, because of how the ECJ applies the principles of primacy, full effect and uniform application of EU law.[2] The aim of the current contribution is to show that the dialogue between the ECtHR and the constitutional courts is not hindered by such principles, that the BCC is well equipped for taking part in a dialogue with the ECtHR and that a strong dialogue between both courts already exists.

I. JUDICIAL DIALOGUE WITH THE ECtHR

A. THE IMPORTANCE OF JUDICIAL DIALOGUE IN A SETTING OF CONSTITUTIONAL PLURALISM

1. Constitutional pluralism and conflict potential

The concept of 'constitutional pluralism' describes the reality of present day constitutionalism, especially in the European Union and in the Council of Europe. In many European countries, legislative and executive norms are reviewed against the human rights catalogues of four legal orders: the national Constitution, the Charter of Fundamental Rights of the European Union, the European Convention on Human Rights (the Convention) and international law. Insofar as the simultaneous application of constitutional norms of distinct legal orders leads to conflicting claims, none of these legal orders is hierarchically superior over the other.[3] Moreover, such conflicting constitutional claims usually being equally legitimate, conflicts cannot be set aside by picking the most legitimate one.[4]

Constitutional pluralism is not a normative concept itself, but it has normative consequences when combined with the principle of legal certainty. This principle requires all legal actors to minimise the potential of conflict and to resolve existing conflicts, by acknowledging, accommodating and integrating all claims by these legal orders, without installing a formal hierarchy between them.[5]

---

[2]   A. Alen and W. Verrijdt, "L'influence de la Cour constitutionnelle belge sur la Cour européenne des Droits de l'Homme et sur la Cour de Justice de l'Union européenne", in I. Ziemele (ed.), *The Role of Constitutional Courts in the Globalised World of the 21st Century. Proceedings of the 2018 Conference of the Constitutional Court of the Republic of Latvia*, Riga, Constitutional Court of the Republic of Latvia, 2019, 132-139.

[3]   N. Walker, "The Idea of Constitutional Pluralism", *Modern Law Review* 2002, 337.

[4]   F. Mayer and M. Wendel, "Multilevel Constitutionalism and Constitutional Pluralism" in M. Avbelj and J. Komarek (eds.), *Constitutional Pluralism in the European Union and beyond*, Oxford, Hart Publishing, 2012, 130.

[5]   M. Poiares Maduro, "Three claims of constitutional pluralism" in M. Avbelj and J. Komarek (eds.), *Constitutional Pluralism in the European Union and beyond*, Oxford, Hart Publishing, 2012, 71-72.

In such a setting, conflicts between constitutional norms from distinct legal orders must be avoided, and, when they occur, they must be resolved. On the other hand, such conflicts must not only be seen as harmful: at the same time, they are the opportunities to further clarify the relation between the national, European and international legal orders.

2. Judicial dialogue as a mechanism of conflict resolution

This difficult task usually falls on the shoulders of the domestic constitutional courts and of the two European courts. Their job is to safeguard the interpretation and the effectiveness of their own constitutions, while taking into account constitutional claims from the other legal orders. When doing so, they cannot confine themselves to the legitimacy of their own legal order and their own constitution, but they are bound to take into account the legitimate stakes of the other legal orders, by paying respect to the reasoning of their respective 'constitutional courts'. In turn, the interpretative solutions they reach, must be taken into account by these other courts as well. In recent years, this judicial activity has often been analysed in the framework of 'judicial dialogue'[6], which is a normative concept following from the aforementioned pluralist reality.[7]

In the absence of political solutions, judicial dialogue is the only available tool for clarifying the relation between all constitutional texts and the only realistic option for reaching balanced solutions to existing and potential conflicts. Through judicial dialogue, the domestic and European constitutional courts must try to avoid a type of legal uncertainty that would catch the judicial and administrative judges between a rock and a hard place, as they should not be put in a position where they are bound to respect conflicting constitutional norms. Therefore, by engaging in judicial dialogues, these courts fulfil their core task of guiding all judges in the application of constitutional norms and values.[8]

---

[6]   The notion of 'dialogue' as a constitutional value was first developed in the US doctrine on the 'countermajoritan difficulty'. In Europe, it's first use was confined to the relation between the ECJ and national judges. Its use in the relation between the ECtHR and domestic judges is of a more recent date (L. Glas, "Dialogue in the European Convention on Human Rights System: inspiration, added-value and means", *EJHR* 2015, 250–252).

[7]   E.g. M. Claes, P. Popelier, M. De Visser and C. Van de Heyning, *Constitutional Conversations in Europe – Actors, Topics and Procedures*, Antwerp, Intersentia, 2012; L. Garlicki, "Cooperation of Courts: The role of supranational jurisdictions in Europe", *I-Con* 2008, 509–530; L. Glas, *o.c.*, 258–260; A. Torres Pérez, *Conflicts of Rights in the European Union. A Theory of Supranational Adjudication*, New York, Oxford University Press, 2009; A. Vosskuhle, "Multilevel Cooperation of the European Constitutional Courts – Der Europäische Verfassungsgerichtsverbund", *EuConst* 2010, 175–198.

[8]   E. Bribosia, "Le dilemme du juge national face à des obligations contradictoires en matière de protection des droits fondamentaux issus de deux ordres européens", in M. Dony and E. Bribosia (eds.), *L'avenir du système juridictionnel de l'Union européenne*, Brussels, ULB, 2002, 265–272.

Hierarchical approaches may also bring legal certainty, but the systematic prevalence of only one set of constitutional claims over all others is very unlikely to lead to the best outcome for any given case.[9] It is often impossible to determine for every single divergence between the ECtHR, the ECJ and/or the domestic constitutional courts, which court's interpretation is the 'correct' one. Most of the time, all divergent interpretations do make sense, taking into account the arguments used and the context in which every court operates. It is impossible to check these divergent interpretations against an objective truth, using the analytical methods known in positive sciences. As human rights are a social construction, the correctness of a normative judgment cannot be explained along the lines of a corresponding theory of truth.[10] Or put in other words: constitutionalism is not a single set of truths, but an ongoing debate about the meaning of the rule of law in a democratic political order.[11]

In such a context, the meaning of human rights is not a scientific discovery to be realised through a process of individual reasoning.[12] But on the other hand, rejecting objectivism does not automatically lead to embracing subjectivism, i.e. the view that the interpretation of human rights cannot be constrained and that interpreters are free in their activity.[13] The task of a human rights judge is thus not an easy one, as he can neither apply mathematical standards, nor limitless creativity. Maintaining his legitimacy towards the democratically elected legislators or towards Member States thus becomes a daunting task, the success of which depends on the choice of his interpretative methods.

In this setting, judicial dialogue does not only play a role in avoiding legal uncertainty, but it also amounts to a new foundation of judicial legitimacy in a pluralist legal order.[14] This is especially the case for dialogues between domestic and supranational human rights judges, who are forced, in an ongoing dialectic process, to reach the best-reasoned interpretation of human rights, reflecting both the supranational stakes at hand and the national identities.[15] Interpretative outcomes based on participation also allow more participants to

---

9   It would, moreover, be a denial of the aforementioned pluralist reality, because it would jeopardize the effectiveness of all other constitutions involved (L. Glas, *o.c.*, 251; see also M. Cartabia, "Europe and Rights: Taking Dialogue Seriously", *EuConst* 2009, 23).

10   J. Habermas, *Between Facts and Norms*, MIT Press 1998, 226.

11   P.W. Kahn, "Interpretation and Authority in State Constitutionalism", *Harvard Law Review* 1993, 1147–1148.

12   A. Torres Pérez, *o.c.*, 109.

13   O. Fiss, "Conventionalism", *Southern California Law Review* 1985, 183–184.

14   E.g. A. Torres Pérez, *o.c.*, 110–117. At the same time, judicial dialogue is itself legitimised by the need to balance the legitimate stakes of *'inclusive sovereignty'* with the effectiveness of international human rights conventions, as interpreted by international judges (H. Dumont and I. Hachez, "Repenser la souveraineté à la lumière du droit international des droits de l'homme", *RBDC* 2017, 320 and 337–354).

15   A. Torres Pérez, *o.c.*, 113–114.

offer their input, which even further strengthens judicial legitimacy, provided
that the reasoning style adopted by the dialoguing constitutional courts shows
that they are willing to take that input into account.[16] Moreover, if the resulting
interpretation is regarded by all as a shared outcome, it is more likely to be
widely accepted, which, in turn, fosters legal certainty.[17] In addition, a successful
judicial dialogue pays respect both to the agenda of building a shared identity
and to the reality of the framework of constitutional pluralism.[18]

B.   PREREQUISITES FOR A SUCCESSFUL JUDICIAL DIALOGUE

The judicial dialogue will never operate in an ideal speech situation, which would
require all relevant courts to meet at a certain place and debate for an unlimited
amount of time until consensus is reached. But the absence of ideal circumstances
should not lead to abandoning the ideal of dialogue. Judicial dialogues will
necessarily require multiple consecutive steps, as they develop on a case-by-
case basis.[19] Nevertheless, judicial dialogue can only thrive when the conditions
are favourable. TORRES PÉREZ has identified six such prerequisites, based on
HABERMAS' work on communicative rationality.[20] Hereinafter, we will argue that
these prerequisites are met in the dialogue between the ECtHR and the BCC.

1.   Differing viewpoints

A difference of opinion does not preclude dialogue. Quite the opposite, it is
the necessary fuel for starting it.[21] Differences of opinion between courts may
arise from their distinct institutional perspective.[22] In the relation between the

---

[16]   A. Torres Pérez, o.c., 114–116; J. Weiler, "Epilogue: The Judicial Après Nice", in G. de Búrca
and J. Weiler (eds.), The European Court of Justice, Oxford, OUP, 2001, 225.

[17]   J. Habermas, Moral Consciousness and Communicative Action, MIT Press, 1990, 67.

[18]   A. Torres Pérez, o.c., 116–117.

[19]   A. Torres Pérez, o.c., 111.

[20]   J. Habermas, Between Facts and Norms, MIT Press 1998, 107–110. Torres Pérez applies these
six prerequisites to the relation between the ECJ and the national constitutional courts
(o.c., 118–130). See, for a slightly different account, distinguishing between prerequisites,
facilitators and instruments, applied to the relation between the ECJ and the national courts
L. Glas, o.c., 260–265.

[21]   R. Cover and A. Aleinikoff, "Dialectical Federalism: Habeas Corpus and the Court", Yale Law
Journal 1977, 1049–1050; L. Friedman, "The Constitutional Value of Dialogue and the New
Judicial Federalism", Hastings Constitutional Law Quarterly 2000, 114; L. Glas, o.c., 266; C.
Kilpatrick, "Community or Communities of Courts in European Integration? Sex Equality
Dialogues between UK Courts and the ECJ", ELJ 1998, 129; A. Torres Pérez, o.c., 118.

[22]   R.B. Ahdieh, "Between Dialogue and Decree: International Review of National Courts",
NYU Law Review 2004, 2095–2096. This is certainly true for differences of opinion between
national constitutional courts and the ECJ, because the EU is a supranational organization
created with the goal of establishing a common market (G.F. Mancini and D.T. Keeling,

ECtHR and the BCC, their respective judicial roles entail significant institutional differences. The BCC is involved in a *contentieux objectif*, in which it examines *in abstracto* whether a legislative provision violates the human rights laid down in the Constitution, while the ECtHR examines *in concreto* whether the application of the law in the petitioner's case amounts to a human rights violation.[23] This may lead to differing viewpoints, as a legislative provision's potential of violating human rights is not always clear from its text, but is often only revealed in its application. It is also possible that a piece of legislation only violates human rights in specific circumstances, while the BCC has only examined an unproblematic part of its scope.

Differing viewpoints may also arise from the constitutional court's stressing a Member State's national identity, which had, until then, not fully been taken into account by the ECtHR.[24] Or they may arise from a supreme court's finding that the Strasbourg jurisprudence in a certain matter is difficult to apply in a Member State with an entirely different legal system.[25] The tension between the ECtHR's judgments imposing uniform standards and the diversity of legal systems in 47 Member States inherently holds some conflict potential, but at the same time, judicial dialogue is a legitimate technique for informing the ECtHR about such problems. As the ECtHR often explains, it suffers from a 'knowledge gap' *viz.* domestic courts concerning the law's context and application in the specific context of each Member State[26], and this may lead to unfit solutions. If domestic courts share that specific knowledge in somewhat critically formulated

---

"Democracy and the European Court of Justice", *Modern Law Review* 1995, 186; J. Weiler, "Eurocracy and Distrust: Some Questions Concerning the Role of the European Court of Justice in the Protection of Fundamental Rights within the Legal Order of the European Communities", *Washington Law Review* 1986, 1118–1119).

[23] According to the ECtHR, its task is not to review domestic law *in abstracto*, but to determine whether the manner in which it was applied to or has affected the applicant, has violated the Convention (ECtHR 6 September 1978, *Klass v. Germany*). Or as Paul Lemmens puts it: "If we are to take subsidiarity seriously, it is, in my opinion, the decisions of the courts, in particular those of the court of appeal and the Court of Cassation, which should be the starting point of this Court's review" (dissenting opinion in ECtHR 30 May 2013, *Nataliya Mikhaylenko v. Ukraine*).

[24] E.g. ECtHR (GC) 18 March 2011, *Lautsi v. Italy*, in which the Grand Chamber reversed the Chamber judgment, which had ruled that the presence of crucifixes in classrooms violated the freedom of religion of non-catholics, after the Italian Constitutional Court had pointed out that the Chamber had not sufficiently taken into account the importance of the catholic religion in the Italian society.

[25] E.g. ECtHR (GC) 15 December 2011, *Al-Khawaja and Tahery v. United Kingdom*, in which the Court modified its jurisprudence on hearsay evidence after the UK Supreme Court had explained that the British legal system has other techniques of examining the admissibility of evidence and of judging the overall fairness of criminal proceedings.

[26] The Court usually formulates this knowledge gap as follows: '*By reason of their direct and continuous contact with the vital forces of their countries, the State authorities are, in principle, in a better position than the international judge*' (e.g. ECtHR 7 December 1976, *Handyside v. United Kingdom*, §48; ECtHR (GC) 3 March 2011, *S.H. v. Austria*, §94).

judgments, the ECtHR can take this new information into account in later cases, which may lead it to amend its point of view.[27]

Even in the absence of such situations, the interpretation of human rights is a matter *par excellence* for differing opinions, because they are open norms, the precise scope and content of which are constantly being refined.[28] When the ECtHR, using its established interpretative techniques, offers an evolutive interpretation with far-reaching consequences for national legal orders, constitutional courts confronted with the difficulties it poses, may then feel the need to challenge the ECtHR's position or to take a more nuanced stance.

In sum, a potential for differing viewpoints between the BCC and the ECtHR exists. Until present, however, the BCC has never openly challenged the ECtHR's jurisprudence (see *infra* n. 156). On the contrary, as will be set out below, it rather shapes its interpretation of the Belgian Constitution to the model of the ECtHR's interpretation of the Convention.

2.   Common ground of understanding

Whereas differing viewpoints are needed to start a dialogue, the differences may not go as far as an absence of collective understandings and experiences providing both courts with the required communication tools for an intelligible dialogue.[29] This does not mean that jurisdictions entering into a dialogue should start using each other's language: it is perfectly possible to keep using the own terminology and style of reasoning, as long as sufficient space is left to accommodate the constitutional claims from other legal orders.[30] The language used must nevertheless be understandable, as a useful dialogue can only take place if the parties exchange sufficient and sufficiently clear information, reasoning and, if necessary, criticism.[31]

This common ground of understanding is definitely present in the relation between the BCC and the ECtHR, which are both judicial bodies sharing a certain legal, historical, cultural and philosophical background, and both safeguard constitutional texts guaranteeing rather similar human rights. Differences between these texts can often be dealt with by applying the principle of the most extensive human rights protection laid down in Article 53

---

[27]   L. Glas, *o.c.*, 256–258.
[28]   Moreover, the ECtHR was never intended to be the sole and exclusive interpreter of the Convention rights (H. Dumont and I. Hachez, *o.c.*, 349; L. Hennebel and H. Tigroudja, *Traité international des droits de l'homme*, Paris, LGDJ, 2016, 626–628).
[29]   A. Torres Pérez, *o.c.*, 121.
[30]   M. Poiares Maduro, *o.c.*, 73 and 82.
[31]   L. Glas, *o.c.*, 267.

of the Convention. Furthermore, the BCC even goes to great lengths to speak the ECtHR's language, using two techniques allowing it to apply the ECtHR's jurisprudence in its own constitutional review.[32]

The first technique is based on the principle of equality and non-discrimination, guaranteed by the Articles 10 and 11 of the Constitution. According to the BCC, these provisions *'have a general scope, forbidding all discriminations, regardless their origin: the constitutional rules on equality and non-discrimination apply to all rights and all liberties granted to the Belgians, including those laid down in international conventions binding Belgium'*.[33] Although the Constitution only stipulates the BCC's competence to review the compliance of legislative provisions with the human rights guaranteed by the Constitution and with the rules on the division of powers between the federal and the federated levels, the BCC uses the aforementioned reasoning as a go-between allowing it to indirectly review legislative provisions against rights and liberties laid down in other constitutional provisions[34], in unwritten principles of law[35] and in international and European law.[36] When the BCC combines the Articles 10 and 11 of the Constitution with a provision of the Convention, it applies the ECtHR's jurisprudence, e.g. its criteria for restricting human rights.[37]

The second technique is based on the BCC's competence, granted by the special majority Act of 9 March 2003, for reviewing the compliance of legislation with the human rights provisions enshrined in the Articles 8–32, 170, 172 and 191 of the Constitution. Many of these constitutional rights have a counterpart in the Convention. According to the BCC, such *'analogous human rights provisions'* form an *'inextricable unity'*, implying that it must *'take into account'* the analogous Convention provisions when interpreting the Constitution.[38] But the BCC does much more than merely 'take into account' the Convention.

---

[32] See A. Alen, J. Spreutels, E. Peremans and W. Verrijdt, "Cour constitutionnelle de Belgique", in R. Huppman and R. Schnabl (eds.), *La coopération entre les Cours constitutionnelles en Europe. Situation actuelle et perspectives*, Vienna, Verlag Österreich, 2015, 295–303.

[33] E.g. CC no. 23/89, 13 October 1989; CC no. 62/93, 15 July 1993.

[34] E.g. CC no. 14/97, 25 March 1997; CC no. 122/98, 3 December 1998.

[35] Many of these principles are also protected under the ECtHR's caselaw. E.g. CC no. 49/96, 12 July 1996 (the principle of legal certainty); CC no. 46/2000, 3 May 2000 (the professional secrecy of attorneys-at-law); CC no. 43/2001, 29 March 2001 (the personal character of a criminal punishment); CC no. 81/2007, 7 June 2007 (the proportionality of a criminal punishment).

[36] E.g. CC no. 18/90, 2 May 1990; CC. no. 105/2000, 25 October 2000. More recent examples are discussed below.

[37] E.g. CC no. 45/96, 12 July 1996; CC no. 124/2000, 29 November 2000.

[38] E.g. CC no. 136/2004, 22 July 2004; CC no. 189/2005, 14 December 2005; CC no. 195/2009, 3 December 2009; CC no. 23/2011, 10 February 2011. See on this "analogy doctrine" G. Rosoux, *Vers une dématérialisation des droits fondamentaux?*, Brussels, Bruylant, 2015, 135–183; M. Bossuyt and W. Verrijdt, "The Full Effect of EU Law and of Constitutional Review in Belgium and France after the *Melki* Judgment", *EuConst* 2011, 356–360.

Whenever it applies its analogy doctrine, it cites and applies all relevant ECtHR jurisprudence, thus updating the Belgian human rights catalogue, largely unchanged since 1831, with the evolutive interpretations offered by the Strasbourg Court. In doing so, it also maximises human rights protection: whenever a human right is guaranteed by both the Constitution and the Convention, the legislator may only limit it if he satisfies both the formal restriction criteria in the Constitution[39] and the Convention system's material restriction criteria.[40]

The legal doctrine agrees that, when the BCC uses these two techniques, the constitutional provisions serve to ground the Court's competence, allowing it to apply the indirect reference norms such as the Convention.[41] This is also true if the BCC uses the first go-between, because it rules that all human rights violations discriminate between those whose human rights have been violated and those whose human rights have not been violated.[42]

In sum, it is easy to argue that the BCC and the ECtHR possess a common ground of understanding, because the Constitutional Court effectively uses the ECtHR's jurisprudence as a minimum standard for its own review.

3. Lack of complete authority over each other

An inter-systemic judicial dialogue requires that none of the participants can claim total sovereignty.[43] Each court should be able to exercise some pressure on the other, without being able to impose its will. Such a setting leads to stronger incentives for co-operation and for finding common understanding. On the other hand, this prerequisite does not amount to a requirement of strict equality

---

[39] Limiting a constitutional right usually requires an Act of Parliament, and the limitations may usually only amount to 'regulatory measures' and 'repressive measures', but not to 'preventive measures' requiring a prior authorization or consent (G. Schaiko, P. Lemmens and K. Lemmens, "Belgium", in J. Gerards and J. Fleuren (eds.), *Implementation of the European Convention on Human Rights and the Judgments of the ECtHR in national case law*, Antwerp, Intersentia, 2014, 97).

[40] I.e. a legal basis, a legitimate aim and the necessity in a democratic society.

[41] R. Ergec, "La Cour constitutionnelle belge et le droit européen", in A. De Walsche and L. Lévy (eds.), *Mélanges en hommage à Georges Vandersanden. Promenades au sein du droit européen*, Brussels, Bruylant, 2008, 172; P. Martens, "L'influence de la jurisprudence de la Cour européenne des droits de l'homme sur la Cour constitutionnelle", *CDPK* 2010, 351; P. Vanden Heede and G. Goedertier, "De doorwerking van het internationaal recht in de Belgische rechtsorde", in J. Wouters en D. Van Eeckhoutte (eds.), *Doorwerking van het internationaal recht in de Belgische rechtsorde*, Antwerp, Intersentia, 2006, 243; M. Verdussen, *Justice constitutionnelle*, Brussels, Larcier, 2012, 129.

[42] E.g. CC no. 29/2010, 18 March 2010.

[43] R. Ahdieh, *o.c.*, 2088–2095; R. Cover and A. Aleinikoff, *o.c.*, 1048; A. Torres Pérez, *o.c.*, 123–125.

between the dialoguing partners: differences in strength and level are possible, as long as they don't lead to total subordination.[44]

The BCC and the ECtHR are not in a hierarchical position, as none of them can quash the other's judgments. They belong to different judicial structures within different legal systems.[45] Moreover, the ECtHR's judgments lacking executory force, the Strasbourg Court needs the cooperation of domestic judges for their implementation.[46] The ECtHR thus has strong reasons to engage in dialogues with domestic courts. The principle of subsidiarity, which is a cornerstone of the Convention system, also indicates that the relation between the ECtHR and the Member State courts is not a hierarchical one, but one of shared responsibility[47], which, in turn, only increases the necessity of cooperation.[48] As we have already described elsewhere, the BCC does not apply a hierarchical approach to the relation between the Constitution, EU law and the Convention, but rather uses a pluralist perspective.[49]

4. Mutual recognition and respect

Mutual recognition is essential for a dialogue which is at the same time mutually intelligible, potentially critical and free of *a priori* privileged status for any vision.[50] Participants must therefore acknowledge each other as part of a common enterprise, in which all participants' viewpoints need to be treated with equal respect. This recognition must pertain to both the other court's authority and legitimacy, and to the possibility that it has good reasons to differ on how human rights should be interpreted and applied.[51]

This mutual recognition is clearly present in the relation between the BCC and the ECtHR, as they both often refer to each other's jurisprudence (see *infra* n. 85 and 204). Their common enterprise consists of upholding the rule of law, and

---

[44] H. Dumont and I. Hachez, *o.c.*, 350.

[45] Comp., for the relation between constitutional courts and the ECJ, A. Torres Pérez, *o.c.*, 124.

[46] H. Dumont and I. Hachez, *o.c.*, 351; L. Glas, *o.c.*, 255; E. Lambert Abdelgawad, *The Execution of Judgments of the European Court of Human Rights*, Strasbourg, CoE Publishing, 2008, 10–12.

[47] See J. Gerards, "The European Court of Human Rights and the national courts: giving shape to the notion of shared responsibility", in J. Gerards and J. Fleuren (eds.), *Implementation of the European Convention on Human Rights and the Judgments of the ECtHR in national case law*, Antwerp, Intersentia, 2014, 32–34.

[48] L. Glas, *o.c.*, 255–256 and 267–268.

[49] A. Alen and W. Verrijdt, "La relation entre la Constitution belge et le droit international et européen", in I. Riassetto, L. Heuschling and G. Ravarani (eds.), *Liber amicorum Rusen Ergec*, Pasicrisie Luxembourgeoise, 2017, 31–54.

[50] F. Michelman, "Traces of self-government", *Harvard Law Review* 1986, 30–32; A. Torres Pérez, *o.c.*, 125–126.

[51] L. Glas, *o.c.*, 265–266.

they acknowledge each other as courts using a language based on reasoned interpretation, logical deduction and systemic and temporal coherence.[52]

Mutual recognition can only be further increased by engaging in intelligible and fair judicial dialogues, as such a pattern builds trust and confidence among the participants, leading to a greater receptivity of alternative perspectives offered by the other.[53] At the same time, mutual recognition means that the situation of conflict should be exceptional, and that constitutional courts should as a general rule apply the Strasbourg jurisprudence, and only enter into a critical dialogue in the rare cases in which they have strong reasons to call a specific line of jurisprudence into question.[54] Moreover, if the situation of conflict would become the rule, the common ground of understanding between the courts would also be jeopardized, the main victim being the principle of legal certainty, which should rather be served than damaged by judicial dialogue.[55] As will be illustrated below, the dialogue between the ECtHR and the BCC is already very significant, but it almost always leads to adopting and approving each other's solutions, and only very rarely becomes critical.

5.   Equal opportunity to participate

A dialogue can only play its legitimating role when all participants have the opportunity to share their arguments. Dialoguing courts must be able to forward their own interpretations and to challenge the interpretations of others. No claim should be free of criticism.[56]

---

[52]   See J. Weiler, "A quiet revolution. The European Court of Justice and its Interlocutors", *Comparative Political Studies* 1994, 521, who calls this the shared 'Legalese' language.

[53]   R. Ahdieh, *o.c.*, 2100; N. Bratza, "The Relationship between the UK Courts and Strasbourg", *EHRLR* 2011, 510; A. Torres Pérez, *o.c.*, 126.

[54]   H. Dumont and I. Hachez, *o.c.*, 349. Even then, resistance against an ECtHR judgment must be driven by the ambition to engage into a judicial dialogue, and it must take place in an environment of loyalty towards international obligations and institutions (J. Andriantsimbazovina, "Unité et divergences de jurisprudences constitutionnelles et supranationales: respect du droit, irrégularité, dialogue. L'exemple des rapports du Conseil constitutionnel et de la Cour européenne des droits de l'homme" in X. Magnon a.o. (ed.), *L'office du juge constitutionnel face aux exigences supranationales*, Brussels, Bruylant, 2015, 74; F. Sudre, *Droit européen et international des droits de l'homme*, Paris, P.U.F., 2015, 403).

[55]   The link between judicial dialogue and legal certainty was also made by the Venice Commission, in its opinion of 11–12 March 2016, CDL-AD(2016)005 on the Russian Act which allows its constitutional court to refuse the application of an ECtHR judgment. In that opinion, the Venice Commission stated that the objective of a judicial dialogue consists in coordinating the Convention's interpretation and application for the sake of future cases.

[56]   R. Alexy, *A Theory of Legal Argumentation. The Theory of Rational Discourse as Theory of Legal Justification*, Clarendon Press, 1989, 120; A. Torres Pérez, *o.c.*, 126.

In the relation between domestic judges and the ECtHR, a preliminary reference procedure was absent until very recently. This lack of direct dialogue was detrimental to the domestic courts' opportunity to enter into a dialogue with the ECtHR, but even then dialogue was not impossible. A constitutional court which disagrees with an interpretation by the ECtHR, is free to voice any criticism in its own judgments. Although it cannot always be ascertained whether the ECtHR will become aware of this criticism, the aforementioned *Lautsi* and *Al-Khawaja* cases have proven that even such indirect dialogue may lead to satisfying results. Meanwhile, the ECtHR has set up a *'Superior Courts Network'* in October 2015, which aims at improving the exchange of information between the ECtHR and the highest domestic courts. Currently, 79 highest courts from 36 Member States participate in this network, including the BCC and the Belgian Council of State.[57] Each member court has to appoint a 'focal point' among its staff, who may post Convention related material on the Network's secure website, allowing them to disseminate critical judgments to the relevant audience. Lastly, at the occasion of the opening of each judicial year, the ECtHR organizes a conference titled *'Dialogue between judges'*, to which some 300 judges in the highest courts of the Member States participate.

The recent entry into force of Protocol no. 16 has opened new opportunities for starting a dialogue. Its entry into force on 1 August 2018 only concerns the 10 Member States which have already ratified it[58], but the Belgian ratification is currently being prepared. This Protocol allows the highest courts of all participating Member States to refer a case to the ECtHR for a non-binding advisory opinion on Convention related matters. This procedure can be used for expressing counterarguments regarding standing ECtHR case law.

The ECtHR itself also has ample opportunity to participate in the dialogue. Given the requirement to exhaust domestic remedies laid down in Article 35 of the Convention, most of its judgments already respond to a decision by one of the highest domestic courts, allowing it to duly take into account and to criticise that national point of view.[59] When a case is dealt with by both a Chamber and the Grand Chamber, the Court can take into account domestic jurisprudence reacting against the Chamber judgment, as it did in the aforementioned *Lautsi* and *Al-Khawaja* cases. And the advisory opinions procedure does not only allow the domestic courts to dialogue, but always involves the ECtHR's participation.

---

[57]   *Https://www.echr.coe.int/Pages/home.aspx?p=court/network&c=*, last checked on 4 July 2019.

[58]   These Member States are Albania, Armenia, Estonia, Finland, France, Georgia, Lithuania, San Marino, Slovenia and the Ukraine. Meanwhile, Andorra, Greece and the Netherlands have also ratified it.

[59]   L. Glas, *o.c.*, 271–272.

Nevertheless, the opportunity for judicial dialogue always depends on the availability of relevant pending cases, as judicial bodies cannot initiate judicial proceedings of their own motion.[60] Therefore, judicial dialogue will often depend on the cases being submitted to the constitutional courts and to the ECtHR, or as DUMONT and HACHEZ put it, '*un heureux hazard de calendrier*'.[61] But this inevitable characteristic of judicial activity does not threaten the judicial dialogue's viability. First, this very same characteristic implies that domestic and supranational courts will only need to start a dialogue when dealing with a relevant case. Second, dialogue does not require that an argument is called into question soon after it is made: constitutional courts may also challenge older and well-settled lines of ECtHR jurisprudence. Indeed, the very nature of dialogue holds that the current state of consensus has no claim on eternity, but can change due to new arguments and due to changes in society. And third, the requirement to exhaust domestic remedies increases the likelihood that human rights questions will be dealt with both by constitutional courts and by the ECtHR, triggering a dialogue between them.

6. Continuity over time

The prerequisite of continuity is closely linked to the prerequisite of equal opportunity to participate. Courts engaging in a dialogue are not able to gather and argue until a consensus is reached, but they have to await new opportunities to challenge arguments forwarded by other courts. None of both parties should therefore be able to end a dialogue with a binding decision which can never be called into question again.[62] Moreover, factual developments and the imperfections inherent in legal discourse lead to a continuous challenge of the status quo. Therefore, judicial dialogue does not end all conflict, but manages it over time in a process of constant mutual accommodation.[63] Furthermore, it may take a series of critical judgments coming from different domestic courts for a supranational court to develop a good understanding of sensitivities and of national knowledge.[64]

The dialogue between constitutional courts and the ECtHR is an ongoing one. When the ECtHR condemns a Member State for having violated a human right, even though the constitutional court had not found a violation in the same case,

---

[60]   A. Torres Pérez, *o.c.*, 127.
[61]   H. Dumont and I. Hachez, *o.c.*, 348. See also L. Glas, *o.c.*, 275–276. Dumont and Hachez therefore suggest that the Article 43 of the Convention be amended in order to allow a Member State to submit a case decided by a Chamber to the Grand Chamber, even outside the normal three months delay, if one of its highest judicial bodies criticises that Chamber judgment.
[62]   A. Torres Pérez, *o.c.*, 129–130.
[63]   A. Torres Pérez, *o.c.*, 111.
[64]   L. Glas, *o.c.*, 266.

this constitutional court will usually start applying the new Strasbourg case law, but in rare cases, it can also challenge it in later judgments, which might convince the ECtHR, as the aforementioned *Lautsi* case shows. The Strasbourg case law can also be challenged by other judges from the same Member State or by judges from other Member States. Since the entry into force of Protocol no. 16, some constitutional courts may also opt for a direct dialogue through the advisory opinion procedure.

C.   DIALOGUE AND STRATEGY

A successful judicial dialogue tackles some of the main problems posed by the reality of constitutional pluralism in Europe. It allows the 'constitutional courts' of distinct legal orders to accommodate each other's claims and visions, in an ongoing participative debate aiming at managing tension, resolving conflict, reaching ever better-reasoned outcomes and enhancing legal certainty. This idealistic account should, however, not ignore the possibility that courts entering a dialogue may have strategic goals and pursue their own agenda, such as institutional power, independence, influence and authority, rather than aiming for the best-reasoned outcome.[65] But this does not mean that judicial dialogue loses its legitimising potential: even when purely legal and argumentative goals coincide with strategic goals, the topic of the dialogue between human rights judges still relates to the interpretation of human rights, and its operation still consists of an exchange of arguments in order to find the best-reasoned outcome.[66] Moreover, the obligation imposed on all judicial bodies to give reasons for their judgments strongly limits the possibility to exclusively pursue other agendas than finding the best legal argument to decide a case.[67] Finally, a judge pursuing strategic goals is not equal to a judge pursuing selfish goals: a constitutional court's strategic use of judicial dialogue may well be driven by the legitimate ambition to find a better balance between the effectiveness of international human rights conventions, as interpreted and applied by supranational courts, and the *'inclusive sovereignty'* of a Member State.[68] It would not be correct to see such a judicial behaviour as merely strategic, as it is linked to some of the most fundamental legal concepts. In this context, constitutional courts' arguments may well consist of demanding more leeway to reconcile the Convention standards with national particularities, thus referring to legal concepts such as the subsidiarity principle and the margin of appreciation doctrine.

---

65   K. Alter, *Establishing the Supremacy of European Law. The Making of an International Rule of Law in Europe,* Oxford University Press 2001, 38–45.
66   A. Torres Pérez, *o.c.,* 132.
67   M. Cappelletti, *The Judicial Process in Comparative Perspective*, Clarendon Press 1989, 133.
68   H. Dumont and I. Hachez, *o.c.,* 320 and 337–354.

In any event, a dialogue which meets the aforementioned prerequisites, leads to an exchange of arguments concerning the interpretation of human rights, and results to solutions based on persuasiveness rather than on coercion.[69] It also channels tension towards balanced decision-making before it can become a lasting conflict, avoiding a situation of distrust incompatible with the duties of judges in a pluralist framework.

The remainder of this contribution aims at showing that the operationalisation of the aforementioned principles in the ongoing dialogue between the ECtHR and the BCC leads to satisfactory results. We will do so by consecutively discussing the two directions of the dialogue, i.e. from Brussels to Strasbourg and vice-versa, addressing procedural questions and giving examples of both courts' caselaw.

II. THE BELGIAN CONSTITUTIONAL COURT SPEAKING

The BCC's position in the dialogue with the ECtHR mainly consists of implementing the Strasbourg Court's case law, whereas reasoned counterarguments and criticisms are very scarce.[70] It may seem odd that a Court which has only been granted the competence to review the compliance of legislative provisions with the constitutional rights and with the rules on the division of powers between the federal and the federated levels[71], can make such ample use of an international treaty. The Convention itself does not hold such a

---

[69]   L. Glas, *o.c.*, 259.

[70]   See also A. Alen, K. Muylle and W. Verrijdt, "De verhouding tussen het Grondwettelijk Hof en het Europees Hof voor de Rechten van de Mens", in A. Alen and J. Theunis (eds.), *Leuvense Staatsrechtelijke Standpunten 3. De Europese dimensie in het Belgische publiekrecht*, Bruges, die Keure, 2012, 3–45; A. Alen, J. Spreutels, E. Peremans and W. Verrijdt, *o.c.*, 619–652; L. Lavrysen and J. Theunis, "The Belgian Constitutional Court: A Satellite of the ECtHR?", in A. Alen, V. Joosten, R. Leysen and W. Verrijdt (eds.), *Liberae Cogitationes. Liber amicorum Marc Bossuyt*, Antwerp, Intersentia, 2013, 331–354; P. Martens, *o.c.*, 350–358; P. Popelier, "Belgium. The supremacy dilemma: The Belgian Constitutional Court caught between the European Court of Human Rights and the European Court of Justice", in P. Popelier, C. Van de Heyning and P. Van Nuffel (eds.), *Human rights protection in the European legal order: The interaction between the European and the national courts*, Antwerp, Intersentia, 2011, 149–171; G. Schaiko, P. Lemmens and K. Lemmens, *o.c.*, 122–127; P. Vanden Heede and G. Goedertier, "De doorwerking van het internationaal recht in de rechtspraak van het Arbitragehof", in J. Wouters and D. Van Eeckhoutte (eds.), *Doorwerking van internationaal recht in de Belgische rechtsorde. Recente ontwikkelingen in een rechtstakoverschrijdend perspectief*, Antwerp, Intersentia, 2006, 239–294.

[71]   See Article 142 of the Belgian Constitution and the Articles 1 and 26, §1, of the Special Majority Act of 6 January 1989 on the Constitutional Court.

requirement.[72] The explanation lies in the go-between techniques developed by the BCC, allowing it to indirectly review legislative Acts against international treaties (see *supra* n. 32). The analogy doctrine 'institutionalizes' this technique of interpreting constitutional rights[73], implying that the application of a constitutional right automatically entails the application of its Convention counterpart and the relevant ECtHR jurisprudence. The Convention rights lacking a constitutional counterpart can just as easily be used, as the Articles 10 and 11 of the Constitution constitute a general go-between (see *infra* n. 92).

This raises the question whether the BCC should only apply the ECtHR's judgments against Belgium, or also its judgments against other Member States.[74] In the first case, it would have to disregard the vast majority of ECtHR case law, the number of cases against Belgium being rather limited. Article 46 of the Convention limits the judgments' binding effect to the parties to the case. But the ECtHR's role is not confined to deciding cases: it must also elucidate and develop the meaning of the rights protected by the Convention.[75] It has indeed developed abstract and general definitions applicable in broad categories of cases[76], and it is not likely to depart from its own case law without good reasons.[77] Although these interpretations are not formally binding, Member States who fail to adopt them risk being condemned themselves. Moreover, the viability of the Convention system requires the avoidance of repetitive cases and the ECtHR's ability to set minimum standards.[78] Therefore, the ECtHR's judgments are said to have *res interpretata* authority[79] or '*autorité de chose interprétée*'.[80] The ECtHR has even adopted a formulation borrowed from the ECJ, requiring all domestic courts to ensure the 'full effect of the Convention standards, as interpreted by the Court'.[81] Hence, domestic courts should in principle apply the ECtHR case law, which they may only contradict very exceptionally, if they have solid reasons to do so, and in the spirit of starting a genuine and loyal judicial dialogue.[82]

---

[72] E.g. ECtHR 21 February 1986, *James a.o. v. United Kingdom*; J. Gerards and J. Fleuren, *o.c.*, 24–25.

[73] G. Schaiko, P. Lemmens and K. Lemmens, *o.c.*, 119.

[74] See G. Ress, "The Effect of Decisions and Judgments of the European Court of Human Rights in the Domestic Legal Order", *Texas International Law Journal* 2005, 359–374.

[75] ECtHR 18 January 1978, *Ireland v. United Kingdom*, §154.

[76] J. Gerards and J. Fleuren, *o.c.*, 2.

[77] ECtHR 26 June 2012, *Herrmann v. Germany*, §78.

[78] J. Gerards and J. Fleuren, *o.c.*, 23.

[79] ECtHR 9 June 2009, *Opuz v. Turkey*; ECtHR 7 January 2010, *Rantsev v. Cyprus and Russia*; J. Gerards and J. Fleuren, *o.c.*, 21–23.

[80] H. Dumont and I. Hachez, *o.c.*, 348; J. Velu, "Considérations sur quelques aspects de la coopération entre la Cour européenne des droits de l'homme et les juridictions nationales", in P. Mahoney a.o. (eds.), *Protecting Human Rights: The European Perspective*, Köln, Carl Heymanns Verlag, 2000, 1521.

[81] ECtHR (GC) 7 February 2013, *Fabris v. France*.

[82] H. Dumont and I. Hachez, *o.c.*, 348.

When applying the Convention, the BCC clearly adopts this *res interpretata* logic, as it refers to judgments against Belgium and against other Member States alike. This approach differs from the one taken by the Council of State and Court of cassation, which also implement the ECtHR's interpretations, but rather tend to limit their references to judgments against Belgium.[83] The following analysis provides an overview of statistics, examples and criticisms, aiming to elucidate and explain the full extent of the BCC's position in its judicial dialogue with the ECtHR.

A. STATISTICS

A look at the sheer number of references already reveals the importance of the ECtHR's case law for the BCC's jurisprudence. Statistics between 2009 and 2013 have already been published.[84] An overview of the figures from 2014 to 2018 is given in the following table.

Year	Judgments	Convention	Case law ECtHR
2014	191	55 (28,8%)	41 (21,5%)
2015	180	75 (41,7%)	55 (30,6%)
2016	170	55 (32,4%)	43 (25,3%)
2017	151	44 (29,1%)	35 (23,2%)
2018	183	62 (33,8%)	45 (24,6%)

In the course of the last five years, the BCC has applied the Convention in 33,2% of its judgements and cited or quoted the ECtHR's case law in 25% of them.[85] In addition, some lines of the BCC's jurisprudence are clearly inspired by the ECtHR's case law, although the standing formulations used by the BCC do not explicitly refer to it.[86]

---

[83] G. Schaiko, P. Lemmens and K. Lemmens, *o.c.*, 125–127.

[84] P. Popelier, "Judicial Conversations in Multilevel Constitutionalism", in M. Claes, M. De Visser, P. Popelier and C. Van de Heyning (eds.), *Constitutional Conversations in Europe*, Cambridge, Intersentia, 2012, 81 and 85 (in 2009 and 2010, the Convention was applied in 32% of the cases before the BCC, and the ECtHR's jurisprudence was mentioned in 30,6% of its cases); A. Alen, J. Spreutels, E. Peremans and W. Verrijdt, *o.c.*, 625 (the BCC referred to the Convention in 49 of its 201 judgments in 2011 (24,4%), in 38 of its 166 judgments in 2012 (23,6%), and in 35 of its 183 judgments in 2013 (19,1%)).

[85] These figures do not include cases in which the petitioners or the referring judge used the Convention, but which were declared inadmissible. They do include admissible cases in which the BCC concluded that the Convention right referred to does not apply to the case at hand.

[86] E.g. concerning the *lex certa* principle (CC no. 47/2015, 30 April 2015; CC no. 61/2015, 21 May 2015; CC no. 8/2018, 18 January 2018; CC no. 26/2018, 1 March 2018), retroactive legislation (CC no. 48/2016, 24 March 2016) and interpretative legislation (CC nos. 22/2017 and 23/2017, 16 February 2017). See L. Lavrysen and J. Theunis, *o.c.*, 334–338.

The BCC often refers to more than one ECtHR judgment a time. For example, in its case concerning the financing of political parties, it mentioned 18 distinct Strasbourg Court judgments, while it had already mentioned 17 other judgments in its interlocutory judgment concerning the parties' motion to have some of the BCC's judges recused.[87]

B. LOOKING BEYOND THE CONSTITUTIONAL FRAMEWORK

Both go-betweens between the Constitution and the Convention (see *supra* n. 32) allow the BCC to apply the Convention outside the scope of the rights enshrined in the Belgian Constitution. The analogy doctrine applies both in case of full analogy between the constitutional right and the Convention right[88] and in case of partial analogy between them. In case of partial analogy, interpreting a constitutional right by analysing the corresponding Convention right broadens its scope and its substantive protection. For example, Article 16 of the Constitution, which only contains a right to full compensation in case of expropriation, has been declared to be analogous to Article 1 of the First Additional Protocol by the BCC, also insofar as the latter applies to other measures regulating the use of property.[89] Likewise, Article 13 of the Constitution, which only explicitly confers a right to access to the judge provided for by the law, is analogous to the full range of substantive rights in Article 6 of the Convention, because access to a judge would be meaningless if he would not meet the due process standards.[90] Finally, whereas the Articles 12 and 14 of the Constitution only require that the essential elements of an incrimination and of a punishment be determined by an Act of Parliament, their combination with Article 7 of the Convention and Article 15 of the International Covenant on

---

[87] CC no. 195/2009, 3 December 2009; CC no. 157/2009, 13 October 2009, see P. Martens, *o.c.*, 351.

[88] E.g. Article 22 of the Constitution and Article 8 of the Convention. When Article 22 was laid down in the Constitution in 1994, the *travaux préparatoires* explicitly stated that it should receive a scope and interpretation identical to Article 8 of the Convention (*Parl. Doc.* Senate 1991–1992, no. 100–4/5, p. 6; *Parl. Doc.* House of Representatives 1992–1993, no. 997/5, p. 2). Hence, the BCC also applies Article 22 of the Constitution to cases concerning environmental pollution and airplane nuisance (CC no. 50/2003, 30 April 2003). See for additional examples L. Lavrysen and J. Theunis, *o.c.*, 338–343.

[89] CC no. 32/2010, 30 March 2010; CC no. 132/2015, 1 October 2015; see A. Alen, "Het eigendomsrecht in de rechtspraak van het Grondwettelijk Hof. Over de samenlezing van de relevante grondwets- en verdragsbepalingen", in D. D'Hooghe, K. Deketelaere and A.M. Draye (eds.), *Liber amicorum Marc Boes*, Bruges, die Keure, 2011, 263–281; A. Alen and W. Verrijdt, "Recente evoluties inzake de bescherming van het eigendomsrecht in de rechtspraak van het Grondwettelijk Hof", in M. Boes, J. Ghysels, D. Lindemans and R. Palmans (eds.), *Vijftig jaar bescherming van het eigendomsrecht. Liber amicorum Martin Denys*, Antwerp, Intersentia, 2012, 5–7.

[90] CC no. 195/2009, 3 December 2009; CC no. 148/2017, 21 December 2017. This reasoning is the inverse of what the ECtHR did in its *Golder* judgment of 21 January 1975.

Civil and Political Rights extends their scope to the *lex certa* principle and the principle of non-retroactivity.[91]

The Articles 10 and 11 of the Constitution's use as a general go-between allows the BCC to apply Convention rights lacking a constitutional counterpart. For example, the absence of a prohibition on inhuman or degrading treatment in the Constitution did not preclude the Court from annulling legislative provisions imposing a systematic 'nude body search' of all prisoners after every visit, the BCC judging that its indiscriminate application violated the Articles 10 and 11 of the Constitution *juncto* Article 3 of the Convention.[92]

When applying the Articles 10 and 11 of the Constitution, the BCC even refers to ECtHR judgments when the Convention is not involved. In some cases, such references contribute to defining the stakes concerned. For example, when adjudicating an unequal treatment between minors and adults who have successfully challenged the presumption of fatherhood, only the minors being able to change their name to the name of their biological father, the BCC invoked the ECtHR's jurisprudence explaining that hindrances to the possibility to carry the biological father's name constitute a limitation to Article 8 of the Convention.[93] And when dealing with an unequal treatment between tenants of a house and tenants of a shop concerning the statutory limitation of their actions against the landlord, the Court referred to the ECtHR's case law in order to describe the stakes of all landlords and tenants concerned.[94]

References to ECtHR case law without mentioning the Convention also occur in arguments justifying an unequal treatment. For example, the BCC referred to the *Stec* judgment when accepting that a legislative reform only gradually resolves an existing discrimination.[95] Likewise, when the legislator decreased some delays for appealing to first instance judgments in criminal cases, the BCC referred to ECtHR case law taking into account the clear and unambiguous

---

[91] CC no. 92/2005, 11 May 2005.
[92] CC no. 20/2014, 29 January 2014, referring to, a.o., ECtHR 12 June 2007, *Frérot v. France* and ECtHR 31 October 2013, *S.J. v. France*.
[93] CC no. 50/2017, 27 April 2017, referring to ECtHR 25 November 1994, *Stjerna v. Finland*.
[94] CC no. 78/2017, 15 June 2017. The tenant of a shop's stake of maintaining his place of business is protected under Article 1 of the First Additional Protocol (ECtHR (GC) 25 March 1999, *Iatridis v. Greece*); the tenant of a house's stake is protected by Article 8 (ECtHR (GC) 8 March 2006, *Blečić v. Croatia*) and the landlord's stake of being protected against abuses by his tenants is protected by Article 6 and by Article 1 of the First Additional Protocol (ECtHR 27 May 2004, *Connors v. United Kingdom*; ECtHR (GC) 8 July 2004, *Vo v. France*). The ambition to reconcile these conflicting stakes gives the legislator a significant leeway, which was *in casu* not overstepped.
[95] E.g. CC no. 104/2015, 16 July 2015, referring to ECtHR (GC) 12 April 2006, *Stec a.o. v. United Kingdom*.

formulation of such a decrease and its being compensated by the simplification of other procedural requirements.[96]

Obviously, references to ECtHR case law without mentioning the Convention also occur in arguments supporting the statement of a violation of the Articles 10 and 11 of the Constitution. For example, the BCC declared a legislative provision which did not contain time limits for the tax authorities' right to tax an undeclared estate unconstitutional, referring to the ECtHR's case law on the need for fixed terms and clear statutes of limitation in tax matters.[97] In a case concerning an unequal treatment in the admissibility of an adoption, the Court took into account that, both according to Article 22*bis* of the Constitution and according to the ECtHR's case law, the child's best interest must always prevail.[98] And in a case concerning tax fraud, the BCC stated that the obligation to pay the entire sum of a tax fine before being able to appeal against it, is unconstitutional if the alleged tax offender's financial situation does not allow him to make such a payment; here, the Court could rely on an ECtHR judgment condemning Belgium in a similar case.[99]

C. IDENTICAL OR SIMILAR LEGAL CONCEPTS

The aforementioned go-between techniques do not only allow the BCC to apply the scope of the human rights guaranteed by the Convention, but also to adopt the interpretations laid down in the ECtHR's case law. A full overview would not be possible in the scope of the current contribution.[100] It is, however, interesting to note that the BCC applies several legal concepts developed by the ECtHR.

1.   Equality and proportionality

The principle of equality and non-discrimination is still the BCC's core business.[101] The criteria for applying this constitutional principle are derived from

---

96 E.g. CC no. 155/2015, 29 October 2015, referring to ECtHR (dec.) 21 November 2000, *Comité des quartiers Mouffetard et bords de Seine a.o. v. France*; ECtHR 23 October 2007, *Beauseigneur v. France*.

97 CC no. 149/2015, 22 October 2015, referring to ECtHR 3 March 2015, *Dimitrovi v. Bulgaria* and ECtHR 6 November 2008, *Kokkinis v. Greece*.

98 CC no. 11/2018, 1 February 2018, referring to ECtHR 5 November 2002, *Yousef v. Netherlands*; ECtHR 6 July 2010, *Neulinger and Shuruk v. Switzerland*; ECtHR 22 March 2012, *Ahrens v. Germany*.

99 E.g. CC no. 44/2016, 17 March 2016, referring to ECtHR 25 September 2007, *Loncke v. Belgium*.

100 Many examples are developed in L. Lavrysen and J. Theunis, *o.c.*, 331–354.

101 In 2017, the Articles 10 and 11 of the Constitution were applied in 128 of the Court's 151 judgments, either as a self-standing framework of reference or as a go-between for applying international treaties, unwritten principles of law or the constitutional provisions not

the ECtHR's famous *Belgian Linguistic case*[102]: the BCC distinguishes between a 'difference in treatment' and a 'discrimination', and it applies the same threefold test for examining whether a difference in treatment is justified.[103] Since 1994, the BCC applies a similar test to an equal treatment of categories of persons who find themselves in distinct positions for the purposes of the legislative provision under scrutiny.[104] The ECtHR has later adopted the same jurisprudence.[105]

In general, proportionality review is at the heart of the ECtHR's human rights review, and the same holds true for the BCC. When applying its analogy doctrine, the BCC takes into account Article 53 of the Convention, thus requiring limitations to human rights to meet both the formal criteria in the Constitution and the substantive criteria in the ECtHR's case law. Therefore, the enjoyment of a human right guaranteed both by the Constitution and by the Convention may only be limited if four conditions are met: (1) the limitation is prescribed by an accessible and clear legislative provision; (2) it responds to a pressing social need; (3) its aims are legitimate; and (4) its consequences are proportionate to that aim.[106]

2. *Margin of appreciation*

In its human rights review, the BCC often refers to the ECtHR's margin of appreciation doctrine[107], acknowledging the legislator's significant leeway in

---

belonging to its direct reference provisions. In 2018, they were applied in 144 of its 183 judgments.

[102]   ECtHR 23 July 1968, *Belgian Linguistic case*.

[103]   A. Alen and D. Haljan (eds.), *Belgium*, in: *International Encyclopaedia of Laws: Constitutional Law*, edited by A. Alen and D. Haljan, Alphen aan den Rijn, Kluwer Law International, 2013, nos. 231 and 412; L. Lavrysen and J. Theunis, *o.c.*, 332–334. According to the BCC's established caselaw, 'the Constitutional principles of equality and non-discrimination do not rule out that a difference in treatment may be instituted between different categories of persons, provided that such difference in treatment is based on objective criteria and that it is reasonably justified. The existence of such a justification must be assessed in the light of the purpose and the effects of the challenged measure and the nature of the principles applicable to the case. The principle of equality and non-discrimination is violated if there is no reasonable relationship of proportionality between the means employed and the aim sought to be realized'.

[104]   CC no. 1/94, 13 January 1994.

[105]   ECtHR 6 April 2000, *Thlimmenos v. Greece*.

[106]   CC no. 115/2004, 30 June 2004; CC no. 202/2004, 21 December 2004; CC no. 151/2006, 18 October 2006; CC no. 170/2008, 27 November 2008; CC no. 29/2010, 18 March 2010; see the examples in G. Schaiko, P. Lemmens and K. Lemmens, *o.c.*, 136–137. For example, the BCC mentioned Article 53 of the Convention when explaining that its Article 8 cannot be construed to limit the requirement of a formal legislative provision when limiting the right to respect for private and family life in Article 22 of the Constitution: CC no. 131/2005, 19 July 2005.

[107]   Belgium has ratified Protocol no. 15 to the Convention, which adds a reference to the margin of appreciation doctrine to the Convention's preamble, on 4 April 2018.

adopting a socio-economic policy[108], in taxation[109] and in other matters relating to the use of property.[110] In certain circumstances, the margin is reduced, for example if a limitation of the use of property may lead to the loss of a family's housing.[111]

Whereas the concept used is identical, its reason differs. The ECtHR grants a margin of appreciation to all organs of a Member State, including national judicial bodies[112], because an international court inherently suffers from a knowledge gap (see *supra* n. 26). When the BCC uses the same doctrine, it grants a margin of appreciation to the legislator, and the reasons rather relate to issues such as the democratic legitimacy and the separation of powers.[113] The knowledge gap being absent, the domestic constitutional courts are in a position to afford a smaller margin of appreciation than the ECtHR.

Especially when the ECtHR attaches its margin of appreciation to the lack of consensus among the Member States, the BCC can disregard it, thus offering a more extensive protection. For example, in its *Ahrens* judgment, the ECtHR nuanced its jurisprudence concerning the best interest of the child, explaining that this is only one of the factors to be taken into account, and deferring the balancing between all relevant principles to the Member States.[114] The BCC took note of this deference, but nevertheless maintained its strict jurisprudence based on Article 22*bis*, paragraph 4 of the Constitution, disapproving all legislative hindrances to the search for the biological truth, such as the inadmissibility of the action for rejecting the presumption of fatherhood when the child has been living together with his official father.[115]

3. Autonomous interpretation as a minimum standard

Applying the ECtHR case law also allows the BCC to use the autonomous interpretation given by the Strasbourg Court to the Convention concepts. Hence, the scope of Article 6 of the Convention being determined by the concepts 'civil rights and obligations' and 'criminal charge', the Belgian reading

---

[108]   E.g. CC no. 173/2008, 3 December 2008; CC no. 104/2015, 16 July 2015, referring to ECtHR (GC) 12 April 2006, *Stec a.o. v. United Kingdom*.

[109]   CC no. 54/2015, 7 May 2015; CC no. 114/2015, 17 September 2015; CC no. 46/2017, 27 April 2017, referring to ECtHR 31 January 2006, *Dukmedjian v. France*; ECtHR 16 March 2010, *Di Belmonte v. Italy*. Nevertheless, a succession tax amounting to more than 80% of the inheritance exceeds that margin of appreciation (CC no. 107/2005, 22 June 2005).

[110]   CC no. 79/2016, 25 May 2016, referring to ECtHR 2 July 2013, *R.Sz. v. Hungary*.

[111]   CC no. 24/2015, 5 March 2015, referring to ECtHR 13 May 2008, *McCann v. United Kingdom*.

[112]   ECtHR (GC) 19 February 2009, *A. a.o. v. United Kingdom*; J. Gerards and J. Fleuren, *o.c.*, 31–32.

[113]   G. Schaiko, P. Lemmens and K. Lemmens, *o.c.*, 135–136.

[114]   ECtHR 22 March 2012, *Ahrens v. Germany*, par. 69–70 and 89.

[115]   CC no. 29/2013, 7 March 2013.

---

of these concepts cannot be used for determining the scope of Article 6 of the
Convention. Therefore, access to a judge must be guaranteed for company
managers who are obliged to pay the social security fees evaded by their
company.[116] Article 6 of the Convention also applies to administrative fines
imposed by the city council for minor offences, but not to a temporary ban from
visiting certain places imposed by the mayor to these offenders, as the latter is
not a criminal punishment, but a measure intended to maintain order.[117]

But even when Article 6 of the Convention does not apply, the material rights
laid down in Article 6 of the Convention are still applicable as unwritten principles
of law, the enjoyment of which must be guaranteed without discrimination.
Therefore, the BCC can usually abstain from examining whether or not Article 6
is applicable, because it can apply the due process standards, as interpreted by the
ECtHR, both within and outside its scope.[118] The ECtHR's interpretation of the
scope of Article 6 is thus a minimum standard, extended by the BCC to virtually
all court proceedings. This reasoning also allowed the BCC to decide that the
limitations in the scope of Article 6 of the Convention, such as its non-applicability,
prior to *Vilho Eskelinen*[119], to proceedings concerning civil servants, do not amount
to a discrimination, because Article 53 of the Convention allows all Belgian courts
to apply all due process rights to proceedings concerning civil servants.[120]

Triggered by the ECtHR's autonomous interpretation in its *Ruiz-Matéos*
judgment[121], the BCC also applies Article 6 of the Convention to its own
procedure. In 1987, it had decided that Article 6 of the Convention did not apply
to proceedings related to the recusal of its judges, because the BCC only deals
with abstract questions about legislative provisions, without taking into account
the facts of the case before the referring judge.[122] But in 1994, it overruled that
position, explaining that, 'according to the ECtHR, Article 6 of the Convention
may be applicable to a constitutional court'.[123] In that case, it turned down the
recusal of a judge who had, in his prior position as an MP, approved the legislative
provisions under scrutiny, referring to the *Padovani* judgment, in which the
ECtHR had explained that the petitioner's fear of partiality is not decisive, but
that it must be ascertained whether this fear is objectively justified.[124]

---

[116] CC no. 79/2014, 8 May 2014, referring to ECtHR 9 December 1994, *Schouten and Meldrum v. Netherlands*.

[117] CC no. 44/2015, 23 April 2015.

[118] E.g., in a case concerning the access of aliens to the Belgian territory, CC no. 49/2015, 30 April 2015.

[119] ECtHR (GC) 19 April 2007, *Vilho Eskelinen v. Finland*.

[120] CC no. 33/94, 26 April 1994.

[121] ECtHR 23 June 1993, *Ruiz-Matéos v. Spain*.

[122] CC no. 32, 29 January 1987.

[123] CC no. 35/94, 10 May 1994.

[124] ECtHR 23 February 1993, *Padovani v. Italy*. According to the BCC, this MP had confined
himself to voting with the majority, as did all MP's belonging to his political party. Such a
small contribution does not suffice to justify the petitioner's fear of impartiality.

The BCC has even used the ECtHR's autonomous interpretations outside the scope of the Convention. For example, when deciding cases about the *non bis in idem principle*, it immediately started interpreting this right by referring to the Grand Chamber's *Sergey Zolotukhin* judgment[125], even though the Seventh Protocol only entered into force in Belgium on 1 July 2012.

4. Positive obligations

Like the ECtHR, the BCC also reads positive obligations in the Convention, and therefore also in the Belgian Constitution, because such obligations are essential for an effective human rights protection.[126] Most applications relate to Article 8 of the Convention, especially in adoption[127] and other affiliation[128] proceedings, this provision requiring the Member States to ensure the possibility of establishing and developing family ties.[129]

The same principle was applied in a case concerning minors residing on Belgian soil illegally, together with their parents. The legislator had provided for a right to material aid for these alien minors if their parents were unable to sustain them, stipulating that this material aid had to be offered inside a federal centre. According to the BCC, however, the legislator had thus failed to live up to his positive obligation following from Article 22 of the Constitution and Article 8 of the Convention, because he had not at the same time allowed the parents to accompany these minors in the federal centre, thus causing the separation of families. It therefore annulled the legislative provision under scrutiny, albeit 'only insofar as it does not guarantee that the parents are also sheltered in the centre where their child receives material help', giving the legislator eight months to make the necessary legislative amendments.[130]

Outside family law, Article 22 of the Constitution and Article 8 of the Convention also require the authorities to take sufficient measures in order to protect people living near an airport from excessive airplane noise, although they enjoy a significant margin of appreciation to balance all individual and societal interests involved.[131]

---

[125] ECtHR (GC) 10 February 2009, *Sergey Zolotukhin v. Russia*. E.g. CC no. 91/2010, 29 July 2010; CC no. 28/2012, 1 March 2012.

[126] CC no. 131/2017, 23 November 2017, referring to ECtHR (GC) 3 October 2014, *Jeunesse v. Netherlands*.

[127] CC no. 93/2012, 12 July 2012; CC no. 94/2015, 25 June 2015; CC no. 131/2017, 23 November 2017; CC no. 3/2018, 18 January 2018.

[128] CC no. 122/2011, 7 July 2011; CC no. 127/2014, 19 September 2014; CC no. 38/2015, 19 March 2015; CC no. 126/2015, 24 September 2015.

[129] The BCC refers, *inter alia*, to ECtHR 4 October 2012, *Harroudj v. France* and ECtHR 16 December 2014, *Chbihi Loudoudi a.o. v. Belgium*.

[130] CC no. 131/2005, 19 July 2005.

[131] CC no. 50/2003, 30 April 2003, referring to ECtHR 2 October 2001, *Hatton v. United Kingdom*.

D. PROCEDURAL TECHNIQUES

The BCC's attachment to the ECtHR's case law goes further than merely copying its interpretations. The following examples show the BCC's procedural creativity in order to ensure that its case law meets the ECtHR standards.

The first example, mentioned by Paul MARTENS, concerns the BCC's agenda management in order to await an expected ECtHR judgment.[132] In 2005, the BCC adjudicated a preliminary reference about a Flemish Act which temporarily disenfranchised the right to vote and to stand for election for anyone convicted to a prison sentence of four months or higher. The BCC held a public hearing on 22 June 2005, but then postponed the case's treatment until the ECtHR's Grand Chamber had rendered its *Hirst* judgment.[133] Subsequently, it referred to that judgment when deciding that this disenfranchisement violated the Articles 10 and 11 of the Constitution insofar as it automatically applied to all convicts, without a judge examining *in concreto* whether the loss of voting right was justified and how long the measure should last.[134]

The second example concerns a re-hearing in a pending case and a reversal of established case law on the very severe sanctions applicable in case of customs fraud, after a new development in the ECtHR's jurisprudence. The legislative provision under scrutiny obliged the criminal judge to impose a fine amounting to exactly ten times the unpaid customs duties, depriving him of any appreciation to mitigate it considering the facts of the case. In earlier judgments, the BCC had found this severe sanction and the lack of proportionality review to be constitutional, given the legislator's aim to tackle the large-scale fraud in cross-border transportation.[135] In 2006, a criminal judge disagreeing with the BCC's previous findings renewed the dialogue, submitting an identical preliminary reference. Oral hearings in that case were held on 11 January 2007. On that very same day, the ECtHR pronounced its *Mamidakis* judgment, in which it established that an incompressible fine amounting to ten times the unpaid customs duties violates Article 1 of the First Additional Protocol.[136] Following that judgment, the BCC held new oral hearings, specifically concerning the consequences of the *Mamidakis* judgment. Subsequently, it overruled its earlier case law, taking into account the fact that such severe administrative fines may amount to a violation of Article 1 of the First Additional Protocol, and mentioning the *Mamidakis* judgment. It concluded that, the relevant legislative

---

[132] P. Martens, *o.c.*, 352.
[133] ECtHR (GC) 6 October 2005, *Hirst (no. 2) v. United Kingdom*.
[134] CC no. 187/2005, 14 December 2005.
[135] CC no. 16/2001, 14 February 2001; CC no. 60/2002, 28 March 2002.
[136] ECtHR 11 January 2007, *Mamidakis v. Greece*.

provision's not empowering the judge to avoid a violation of the protection of property, also amounts to a violation of Article 6 of the Convention.[137]

The third example concerns a preliminary reference to the ECJ in order to ensure the full effect of the human rights guaranteed by the Convention. In order to effectively fight terrorism and organized crime, the Belgian legislator obliges telecommunications operators to keep records of all communications' metadata, such as the users' identity and location and the communication's duration. But the ECJ's recent case law on the right to respect for private life forbids such indiscriminate data retention, only allowing targeted retention for predetermined locations or groups.[138] According to the Belgian legislator and intelligence services, however, such a selective data retention could not work, as only an indiscriminate retention allows revealing unknown threats to public safety. The BCC sustained this point of view and therefore submitted new preliminary references to the ECJ, suggesting it to mitigate its jurisprudence. One of the BCC's key arguments for doing so mentions the positive obligations in the Articles 3 and 8 of the Convention, requiring the Member States to take measures in order to guarantee the physical and moral integrity of minors and other vulnerable persons.[139] Furthermore, the BCC notes that taking into account the importance of national security, the ECtHR has granted the national legislators a large margin of appreciation in the field of massive data retention, and that it has meanwhile approved the very same Swedish legislation which was disqualified by the ECJ in its *Tele2* judgment.[140]

This last example shows the difficulty of operating in a framework of constitutional pluralism. The ECJ's interpretation of a human right may well enter into conflict with its interpretation by the ECtHR, causing legal uncertainty for Member State institutions and citizens. In order to address this problem, the BCC chose the path of judicial dialogue. Currently, it can only enter into a direct dialogue with the ECJ. When Belgium will have ratified Protocol no. 16, it will be able to simultaneously address the same questions to the ECtHR.

---

[137] CC no. 81/2007, 7 June 2007. See J. Theunis, "Grondwettelijk Hof of Grondrechtenhof? De evenredigheid van de straf als casus", in A. Alen and J. Van Nieuwenhove (eds.), *Leuvense Staatsrechtelijke Standpunten 1*, Bruges, die Keure, 2008, 173–196. Following that judgment, the legislator amended that legislative provision by Act of 21 December 2009: the fine now amounts to five to ten times the unpaid customs duties.

[138] ECJ 21 December 2016, *Tele2 Sverige AB v. Post-och telestyrelsen*, C-203/15 and *Secretary of State for the Home Department v. Tom Watson a.o.*, C-698/15.

[139] CC no. 96/2018, 19 July 2018, B.22, referring to ECtHR 2 December 2008, *K.U. v. Finland*.

[140] CC no. 96/2018, 19 July 2018, B.6.8, referring to ECtHR (GC) 4 December 2015, *Roman Zakharov v. Russia* and ECtHR 19 June 2018, *Centrum för Rättvisa v. Sweden*.

E.   THE BOUNDARIES OF A *CONTENTIEUX OBJECTIF*

As was mentioned above (see *supra* n. 23), one of the main differences between
the ECtHR and the BCC is the latter's competence being confined to a
contentieux objectif, adjudicating the constitutionality of legislation instead of
factual elements. Hence, the BCC does not always possess sufficient remedial
powers in order to set a violation of the Convention straight.

Its judgment on the Belgian legislation on internment is indicative for
these boundaries of a *contentieux objectif*. After several previous condemning
judgments, the ECtHR adopted a pilot judgment against Belgium, pointing out
a structural problem consisting of a lack of capacity in specialized institutions
in which detained persons can receive adequate care.[141] When the BCC
subsequently adjudicated a case concerning the legislation on internment, it
extensively quoted the pilot judgment, but it nevertheless had to dismiss several
of the petitioners' arguments, because they did not relate to the legal framework,
while only the judicial judge may examine the factual problems caused by the
lack of specialized institutions. It did nevertheless recall that all competent
authorities must organise the system in such a way that all detained persons are
offered adequate care in a specialized institution.[142]

The BCC's abstract review also implies that its judgments cannot avoid all later
violations, which are usually of a more factual nature. For example, the *Singh*
case concerned the full jurisdiction of the *Conseil du contentieux des étrangers*
(CCE, an administrative tribunal) when reviewing the decisions taken by the
Commissariat général aux réfugiés et aux apatrides (CGRA, an administration)
refusing to grant asylum because the petitioner fails to prove that he is at risk
of treatment contrary to Article 3 of the Convention when being sent back to
his country of origin. According to the BCC, the CCE must, in such cases, take
into account new elements invoked by the petitioner proving the reality of the
risk of ill-treatment, even though they had not been submitted to the CGRA.[143]
In the *Singh* case, the petitioner had submitted new documents before the CCE,
which the ECtHR qualified as 'significant, important and credible'. Nevertheless,
the CCE had refused to examine them, stating that they are easily falsifiable. It
had thus left the only relevant question, i.e. whether the applicant was at risk
of ill-treatment, open and it had not taken any steps to examine whether these
documents were actually falsified.[144]

This gap between the BCC's *contentieux objectif* and the ECtHR's factual
approach does not preclude dialogue, because of the solid common ground of

---

[141]   ECtHR 6 September 2016, *W.D. v. Belgium*.
[142]   CC no. 80/2018, 28 June 2018.
[143]   CC no. 148/2008, 30 October 2008.
[144]   ECtHR 2 October 2012, *Singh a.o v. Belgium*.

understanding between both courts (see *supra* n. 29). Moreover, the BCC often bridges this gap by combining its *in abstracto* review with recalling the judicial judge's task. It often decides that the legal framework under scrutiny only passes constitutional muster insofar as all persons subjected to the measure concerned have access to a judge possessing full jurisdiction to investigate all matters of law and of fact and to make a proportionality assessment. For example, the BCC has accepted that in cases involving terrorism and organized crime, the prosecution may store parts of the case file in a secret file inaccessible to the defence, provided that an independent and impartial judge may examine the entire case file, including the reasons for using a secret case file and its proportionate use.[145] Any limitation to the judge's competences in this regard entails the legislation's unconstitutionality.[146] Likewise, the powers conferred to the intelligence services to keep secret records of certain persons were declared constitutional insofar as these records are examined by a judge possessing full jurisdiction.[147] And in a case concerning hindrances to the peaceful enjoyment of real estate possessions because of the limitations following from a heritage conservation measure, the BCC validated the Flemish Act concerned while stressing that the judicial judge must assume jurisdiction to grant financial compensation for excessive limitations to the peaceful enjoyment of property.[148]

Such a reserve of interpretation mentioned in the judgment's operative part is binding, because it must be considered to be a *conditio sine qua non* for the legislative provision's constitutionality.[149] This technique of referring the *in concreto* human rights review to the judicial judge allows the BCC to respect the constitutional boundaries of its role as a *contentieux objectif* judge, while at the same time respecting the human rights standards laid down in the ECtHR's jurisprudence. It also illustrates that the BCC is only one part of a complete system of rights protection.

F. DIALOGUE OR MONOLOGUE?

The question rises whether the BCC's position can be called a dialogue with the ECtHR or rather constitutes a monologue. First of all, the next chapter of this contribution will show that the ECtHR does take part in the dialogue. Second, several of the aforementioned cases prove that the BCC amends its case law after new developments in the ECtHR's jurisprudence (see *supra* n. 123 and 137).

---

[145] CC no. 105/2007, 19 July 2007.
[146] CC no. 202/2004, 21 December 2004.
[147] CC no. 145/2011, 22 September 2011.
[148] CC no. 132/2015, 1 October 2015.
[149] CC no. 52/2006, 19 April 2006; see G. Rosoux, "Les réserves d'interprétation dans la jurisprudence de la Cour d'arbitrage: une alternative à l'annulation", *RBDC* 2001, 385–406.

Third, the BCC particularly takes into account the judgments condemning Belgium, whether or not it had been involved in the case leading to the ECtHR's condemning judgment. It had been involved in the *Pressos Compania Naviera* case, which concerned the retroactive exclusion of the Belgian State of all liability for the damage caused by pilot services. The BCC rejected this case, deciding that Article 1 of the First Additional Protocol did not apply, because it only protects acquired property.[150] The petitioners subsequently applied to the ECtHR, which extended this provision's scope to financial claims representing a legitimate expectation and condemned Belgium for having retroactively barred the legitimate claim the ship-owners had against the Belgian State.[151] The BCC modified its case law in the same direction[152], although it sometimes avoids answering the difficult question about this provision's applicability by simply stating that, regardless whether it applies, the legislator has not surpassed his wide margin of appreciation in this field.[153]

By contrast, the BCC was not involved in the cases in which Belgium was condemned for excessive formalism in limitations to the access to the Council of State and the Court of Cassation.[154] Nevertheless, it refers to these judgments ever since, in all cases involving measures limiting the access to court.[155]

The BCC's approach must therefore be considered to be a part of a judicial dialogue. Until present, this dialogue consists of accepting and applying all ECtHR case law, without voicing any criticism in this regard.

The only matter in which the BCC showed some hesitation to follow the ECtHR's vision concerned the applicability of Article 1 of the First Additional Protocol to social security benefits.[156] In 2004, the BCC had to decide a case involving a distinction between Belgians and aliens regarding allowances for disabled persons. The BCC did mention the ECtHR's *Koua Poirrez* judgment, which states that only very weighty reasons can justify a distinction based on nationality in this regard[157], but it distinguished the case at hand stating that the aliens concerned could still apply for an allowance under the general scheme of social

---

150   CC no. 36/90, 22 November 1990.
151   ECtHR 20 November 1995, *Pressos Compania Naviera SA a.o. v. Belgium*.
152   CC no. 134/2016, 20 October 2016; CC no. 101/2018, 19 July 2018.
153   CC no. 151/2003, 26 November 2003; see P. Martens, *o.c.*, 353.
154   ECtHR 24 February 2009, *L'Erablière v. Belgium*; ECtHR 29 March 2011, *RTBF v. Belgium*.
155   E.g. CC no. 109/2010, 30 September 2010; CC no. 44/2013, 28 March 2013; CC no. 4/2014, 16 January 2014; CC no. 167/2014, 13 November 2014; CC nos. 151/2015 and 155/2015, 29 October 2015; CC no. 13/2016, 27 January 2016; CC no. 35/2017, 16 March 2017; CC no. 119/2017, 12 October 2017; CC no. 2/2018, 18 January 2018; CC no. 92/2018, 19 July 2018.
156   P. Martens, *o.c.*, 355–356.
157   ECtHR 30 September 2003, *Koua Poirrez v. France*.

assistance.[158] Several judicial judges disagreed with this reasoning and referred new cases to the BCC for a preliminary reference. In the end, the BCC partially yielded to this criticism, accepting that aliens legally residing on Belgian soil and registered in the 'population register' had established a sufficiently strong connection with Belgium to be granted an allowance for disabled persons to the same extent as Belgian citizens. But it did maintain that aliens legally staying in Belgium and registered in the 'aliens register', and therefore not establishing the same connection with Belgium, could still be excepted from the same type of social security benefits.[159]

Apart from this one matter, the BCC's position in the dialogue with the ECtHR has never turned critical or reluctant. By contrast, the BCC has already voiced some objections concerning certain aspects of the ECJ's jurisprudence.[160] But the explanation of this difference may well lie in the fact that the ECtHR's case law has so far never threatened delicate constitutional arrangements, nor the effectiveness of constitutional review.[161] In the relation with a supranational judge exclusively competent for human rights review, such a situation is less likely to occur than in the relation with a supranational judge operating in a far broader perspective. Moreover, in the relation with the ECtHR, applying Article 53 of the Convention will usually allow accommodating divergent constitutional claims. Nevertheless, the theoretical possibility of a conflict between a Convention right and a rather institutional constitutional provision still exists. The 'letters of credential' cases show some potential in this regard: according to Article 48 of the Constitution, unamended since 1831, only the newly elected MP's are competent to decide whether they meet the conditions of eligibility, to the exclusion of all judicial review. The ECtHR, however, has explained that such an absence of judicial review violates Article 13 of the Convention and Article 3 of the First Additional Protocol.[162] Several similar cases against Belgium are currently pending before the ECtHR.[163] Cases revealing such a conflict must be awaited in order to see how the BCC will deal with such a situation.

---

[158]   CC no. 92/2004, 19 May 2004.

[159]   CC no. 153/2007, 12 December 2007.

[160]   CC no. 89/2011, 31 May 2011; CC no. 96/2018, 19 July 2018. See A. Alen and W. Verrijdt, "L'influence...", l.c., 132-135.

[161]   P. Popelier, "Belgium: faithful, obedient, and just a little bit irritated", in P. Popelier, S. Lambrecht and K. Lemmens (eds.), Criticism of the European Court of Human Rights. Shifting the Convention System: Counter-Dynamics at the National and EU Level, Antwerp, Intersentia, 2016, 123–124.

[162]   ECtHR 2 March 2010, Grosaru v. Romania.

[163]   Case no. 58302/10, G.K. v. Belgium; case no. 77940/14, Verzin v. Belgium; case no. 310/15, Mugemangango v. Belgium; case no. 18918/15, Van De Cauter v. Belgium. These cases have been communicated to the Belgian government on 27 November 2017. The Court has not addressed this issue in its G.K. judgment of 21 May 2019, but it has referred the Mugemangango case, which focuses on that issue, to the Grand Chamber by decision of 19 June 2019.

G. CRITICISMS

Most authors welcome the BCC's aforementioned approach towards the Convention, which it also applies to EU law and to general international law. Nevertheless, two interesting criticisms have been voiced in case notes.

1. Analogy and distinguishing

The first one relates to the BCC's application of ECtHR judgments to clearly distinguishable situations, the author criticizing a BCC judgment applying the ECtHR's *TV Vest* judgment.[164] Both judgments found a violation of the freedom of opinion because of an absolute and permanent ban on TV commercials for political parties. The author claims that, as the ECtHR's reasoning took into account the petitioner's being a small political party which could not reach the general public in any other way, the BCC should not have applied it in an action for annulment introduced by mighty media groups pursuing their financial profit.[165]

This criticism is interesting, because it alludes to the boundaries of analogy reasoning. The BCC's applying ECtHR case law to distinct situations has two reasons. First, the aforementioned *res interpretata* effect of ECtHR judgments (see *supra* n. 79) implies that the BCC will often have to apply case law which originated in a legal system well different from the Belgian one. Second, the difference between the ECtHR's factual review and the BCC's *contentieux objectif* (see *supra* n. 23) implies that the legislation scrutinized by the BCC usually applies to a wider variety of situations than the sole set of facts examined by the ECtHR.

In most cases, the BCC can easily deal with such differences. For example, the aforementioned technique of confining itself to an *in abstracto* review, while deferring the *in concreto* review to the judicial and administrative judge (see *supra* n. 145) may be used in order to deal with the difference in scope. Moreover, as the BCC's review is an abstract one, the importance of the facts of the case should not be exaggerated. One should especially be careful not to confuse the substance of a human rights argument with the case's admissibility. As soon as the petitioner before the BCC proves that he is directly and adversely affected by a legislative provision, the case is admissible, and he is then free to use all

---

164 CC no. 161/2010, 22 December 2010; ECtHR 11 December 2008, *TV Vest AS and Rogaland Pensjonistparti v. Norway*.

165 P. Docquir, "Accès à la tribune médiatique par la voie publicitaire: l'annulation de l'interdiction de la publicité politique dans les médias audiovisuels n'était pourtant pas nécessaire", *JLMB* 2011, 505.

possible arguments relating to its constitutionality. This was overlooked by the author voicing the aforementioned criticism.

Nevertheless, this criticism does indicate that the BCC should always consider whether and how the ECtHR itself would apply the case law mentioned on the piece of legislation at hand.[166]

2. Blind compliance

A second criticism was voiced by a family law professor.[167] He criticizes the BCC's jurisprudence declaring certain aspects of the new legislation on affiliation unconstitutional[168], although that legislation's 2006 reform had itself aimed at conforming it to the BCC's earlier jurisprudence. Using the analogy between the Articles 22 and 22*bis* of the Constitution and Article 8 of the Convention, and referring to the ECtHR's case law[169], the BCC concluded that several hindrances, still present in the new legislative provisions, to the possibility to establish an affiliation based on the biological truth, violate the primacy of the interest of the child.[170] The author argues that the BCC should not 'blindly comply' with ECtHR jurisprudence which is itself subject to severe criticism in the legal doctrine.

This is an interesting argument, because it indicates that the BCC's current position towards the ECtHR is not a full-grown judicial dialogue yet, as it lacks criticism and counterarguments, but rather consists of an ambition to fully implement the human rights standards set by the Strasbourg Court. This criticism was, moreover, expressed before the ECtHR nuanced its strict case law in its aforementioned *Ahrens* judgment (see *supra* n. 114). The BCC applied the leeway offered by the ECtHR by maintaining the severity in its jurisprudence, still disqualifying all hurdles to the search for the biological truth. This should be seen as an application of Article 53 of the Convention, taking into account that Article 22*bis*, paragraph 4 of the Constitution offers a higher standard of human rights protection than Article 8 of the Convention, because it imposes that the interest of the child must always be the primordial concern in all decisions relating to it. The aforementioned author indeed did not note that this constitutional provision was only inserted on 22 December 2008, and thus

---

[166] See for an example where the BCC distinguished between the facts of the ECtHR case and the legislation at hand CC no. 117/2015, 17 September 2015.

[167] P. Senaeve, "Kan er inzake afstamming nog zinvol wetgevend werk verricht worden?" *T.Fam.* 2011, 171.

[168] E.g. CC no. 96/2011, 31 May 2011; CC no. 122/2011, 7 July 2011. See also CC no. 18/2016, 3 February 2016.

[169] E.g. ECtHR 27 October 1994, *Kroon e.a. v. Netherlands*; ECtHR 12 January 2006, *Mizzi v. Malta*; ECtHR 6 July 2010, *Backlund v. Finland*.

[170] The primacy of the interest of the child in all decisions concerning it has been anchored in Article 22*bis* of the Constitution since 22 December 2008.

post-dated the 2006 reform of affiliation law. The BCC therefore had to apply this severe provision in all its cases concerning aspects of this new affiliation law from 2009 onwards.

H. EXPLANATION

After these criticisms, and taking into account the BCC's rather unique position among the European constitutional courts, the aforementioned approach calls for an explanation. It probably has to do with the fact that the BCC's dialogue with the ECtHR has significant advantages for all actors involved.

1. The European Court of Human Rights

The ECtHR benefits from the BCC's behaviour, both in terms of legitimacy and in terms of docket control. The frequent use made of the Convention by the BCC indeed enhances the legitimacy of the ECtHR, because the statement of a human rights violation by a national court reduces the existing perception that the ECtHR interferes in national policy.[171]

As far as the ECtHR's caseload is concerned, the BCC's *contentieux objectif* comes with strong remedial powers. If it annuls a legislative provision because of a human rights violation, this provision is deemed never to have existed. All Executive acts and all judicial decisions based on it can be retroactively retracted.[172] This *erga omnes* effect of an annulment avoids or redresses several violations in specific cases, without the victims having to turn to the ECtHR. If the BCC finds a human rights violation in a judgment answering a preliminary reference, neither the referring judge nor any other judge adjudicating the same case may apply the legislative provision disqualified by the BCC.[173] Likewise, any judge deciding similar cases is to ignore that legislative provision.[174] Moreover, the BCC's judgment reopens the 6 month delay to initiate an action for annulment against that legislative provision.[175] This 'enhanced *inter partes* effect' leads to the same benefits for the ECtHR's caseload. The domestic judges' ability to redress human rights violations within the national legal order is indeed one of the key

---

[171]   J. Gerards and J. Fleuren, "Comparative analysis", in J. Gerards and J. Fleuren, *o.c.*, 372, who submit that the strong criticism towards the ECtHR in the UK and the Netherlands has to do with the absence of constitutional review in these countries.

[172]   Articles 8–18 of the Special Majority Act of 6 January 1989 on the Constitutional Court.

[173]   Article 28 of the Special Majority Act of 6 January 1989 on the Constitutional Court.

[174]   Article 26, §2, paragraph 2, 2°, of the Special Majority Act of 6 January 1989 on the Constitutional Court.

[175]   Article 4, paragraph 2, of the Special Majority Act of 6 January 1989 on the Constitutional Court.

requirements for the long term viability of the Convention system, and the BCC's handling of the Convention shows that it takes this responsibility seriously.

The ECtHR could further strengthen the BCC's position in this regard through Article 35.1 of the Convention, requiring the alleged human rights victim to exhaust a procedure before the BCC, insofar as the alleged human rights violation has a legislative basis.[176]

As Paul Lemmens has explained, the six month deadline for petitioning for the annulment of legislative provisions[177] usually means that the action for annulment was an unavailable remedy for future victims, who could not foresee that this legislative provision would ever be applied to them.[178] Such victims cannot be blamed for not having exhausted the action for annulment. If however, the applicant should have known, in the course of the six month deadline, that the relevant legislative provision would be applied to him and that this application would enter into conflict with his human rights, the action for annulment must be considered as an available domestic remedy. The ECtHR has adopted this point of view in a case concerning a legislative ban on advertising for telephone lines with an erotic content, which was alleged, by a frequent user, to violate Article 10 of the Convention. The ECtHR declared the case inadmissible because the applicant had failed to submit an action for annulment before the BCC in due delay, thus depriving the Belgian courts of the opportunity to redress the alleged violation.[179] In other cases, however, the ECtHR dismissed similar exceptions by the Belgian government, applying its jurisprudence that the applicant who has availed himself of a remedy capable of redressing directly the situation complained of, is not bound to have recourse to other available remedies.[180]

As far as preliminary references are concerned, the victim status does not pose a problem, because they always arise in specific cases pending before a judge. In Belgium, all judicial and administrative judges are obliged to refer a question on

---

[176] M. Verdussen, "La Cour européenne des droits de l'homme et l'épuisement préalable du recours interne au juge constitutionnel", in *Liber amicorum M.-A. Eissen*, Brussels, Bruylant, 1994, 443; W. Verrijdt, "The Belgian Constitutional Court as a domestic remedy for ECHR violations", in A. Alen, V. Joosten, R. Leysen and W. Verrijdt (eds.), *Liberae Cogitationes. Liber amicorum Marc Bossuyt*, Antwerp, Intersentia, 2013, 901. See also, a bit more hesitant concerning preliminary references, G. Rosoux, *Vers une dématérialisation des droits fondamentaux?*, Brussels, Bruylant, 2015, 360–389.

[177] Article 3, §1, of the Special Majority Act of 6 January 1989 on the Constitutional Court.

[178] P. Lemmens, "S.O.S. voor het Europees Hof voor de Rechten van de Mens (en voor het individueel klachtrecht)", in A. Alen and P. Lemmens (eds.), *Themis Staatsrecht*, Bruges, die Keure, 2003, 90–91.

[179] ECtHR (dec.) 6 April 2004, *S.B. v. Belgium*.

[180] ECtHR (dec.) 6 May 2004, *Avci v. Belgium*; ECtHR (dec.) 10 November 2005, *EEG-Slachthuis Verbist Izegem v. Belgium*.

the constitutionality of a legislative provision suggested by one of the parties to the
BCC.[181] This obligation also exists if the alleged human rights violation concerns
both a constitutional right and an analogous Convention right: in such cases, the
judicial or administrative judge must first refer the case to the BCC, which will
take into account the ECtHR's relevant case law, and is only allowed to conduct
his own conventionality review after receiving the BCC's answer.[182] According to
the ECtHR's case law, the refusal, by a judge, to ask for a preliminary judgment
by a constitutional court despite a legal obligation to do so, violates Article 6 of
the Convention.[183] Nevertheless, the ECtHR does not consider the preliminary
reference procedure to be an available remedy to be exhausted before applying
to the Strasbourg Court, because it is initiated by a judge, and not directly by the
applicant.[184] This position seems to be too lenient, because the judge's decision to
refuse submitting a preliminary reference is to be distinguished from the parties'
possibility to suggest it. Suggesting a preliminary reference does not require
a lot of effort, because it can be developed in the written submissions or in the
oral hearings before any judge. The ECtHR should, in its examination of the
exhaustion of domestic remedies, take into account whether the applicant raising
a human rights issue before a judicial or administrative judge has suggested that
judge to refer the case to the BCC.

The ECtHR should become stricter in applying Article 35.1 of the Convention
to the BCC. This would not only be beneficial for its own docket control, but it
would also, in cases where the alleged human rights violation has a legislative
basis, institutionalize the prior involvement of a domestic judge specialized
in human rights review. That prior involvement would tighten the ECtHR's
knowledge gap (see *supra* n. 26), it would be consistent with its subsidiary role,
and it would enhance the judicial dialogue with the BCC, because the ECtHR
would possess a BCC judgment in most cases against Belgium.[185]

2. The Constitutional Court

The BCC's approach to the dialogue with the ECtHR does not only benefit
the ECtHR, but also the BCC itself. First, it allows the BCC to update the
constitutional rights catalogue, which largely dates back to 1831, by linking it

---

[181] Article 26, §2, of the Special Majority Act of 6 January 1989 on the Constitutional Court,
provided the exceptions to that obligation mentioned in Article 26, §§2 and 3 of the same
Special Majority Act.

[182] Article 26, §4, of the Special Majority Act of 6 January 1989 on the Constitutional Court,
provided the exceptions to that obligation listed there.

[183] ECtHR 22 June 2000, *Coëme a.o. v. Belgium*; ECtHR 15 July 2003, *Ernst a.o. v. Belgium*;
ECtHR 10 April 2012, *Vergauwen v. Belgium*; ECtHR 21 July 2015, *Schipani v. Italy*.

[184] ECtHR 19 December 1989, *Brozicek v. Italy*; ECtHR 26 February 1993, *Padovani v. Italy*;
ECtHR (GC) 17 September 2009, *Scoppola (no. 2) v. Italy*.

[185] W. Verrijdt, "The Belgian Constitutional Court as a domestic remedy...", *l.c.*, 900–902.

to the present day interpretation of human rights conventions, thus increasing the scope of its review competences. Nevertheless, it should be kept in mind, as VERDUSSEN rightly states, that this strategy may not lead to abandoning the specificities of constitutional rights protection insofar as the Constitution still offers a higher standard of human rights protection than the Convention.[186]

Second, engaging into a dialogue with other judicial bodies shows an understanding of the specificities of constitutional pluralism and therefore enhances the legitimacy of the judicial body concerned (see *supra* n. 14). The BCC's frequent references to ECtHR or ECJ jurisprudence do not diminish the legitimacy of its constitutional review, but rather prove that the BCC is willing to take into account all relevant sources, stakes and arguments.

Third, the BCC's handling of the Convention and of EU law builds trust in the relation with the ECtHR and the ECJ, strengthening the common ground of understanding necessary for the judicial dialogue to thrive (see *supra* n. 29). This existing trust is crucial in the rare occasions in which this dialogue must turn critical, i.e. when a piece of ECtHR or ECJ jurisprudence conflicts with the Belgian Constitution and the BCC starts a dialogue with the ECJ or the ECtHR in order to ask for more leeway in order to resolve that conflict.

3.   *The parties*

The BCC's approach also benefits the parties. The BCC's frequent use of the Convention and of EU law saves them the procedural steps, the time and the costs involved in turning to supranational infringement procedures. It also gives them a direct access to EU law review and Convention review of legislation, while they often do not possess a direct access to the ECJ or the ECtHR in this regard.

This is especially true for the so-called 'repeat players', i.e. organisations which frequently use judicial proceedings as a means to achieve their long-term goals.[187] Before the BCC, the bar associations, human rights organisations and several other non-profit organisations systematically challenge legislation which goes against the social goal they pursue or harms the category of persons they usually

---

[186]   M. Verdussen, *Justice constitutionnelle*, Brussels, Bruylant, 2012, 134–135.
[187]   The distinction between repeat-players and one-shotters was first made by M. Galanter, "Why the 'Haves' come out ahead: speculations on the limits of legal change", *Law and Society Review* 1974 (9), 97–98. According to him, one-shotters only rarely turn to courts, and they only pursue their interest in that specific case, whereas repeat-players, usually organisations with extensive financial resources, frequently start court procedures, even if their stake in that specific case is not very big, in order to pursue their long-term interest of provoking legal change.

defend. Such non-profit organisations have an easy access to the BCC, which has set the bar for accepting their standing rather low. Practice shows that these organisations, which usually file voluminous actions for annulment, are very agile in raising arguments of conventionality, invoking ECtHR case law to their benefit.

4.   The legal order

Most importantly, the legal order as a whole also benefits from the BCC's approach. By ensuring that the constitutional rights meet the minimum standards following from the Convention and by frequently referring to the ECtHR's case law, the BCC presents the resulting interpretation of constitutional rights as a shared outcome, which is more likely to be widely accepted (see *supra* n. 17). Thus, the BCC tackles one of the most important dangers present in the pluralist legal order, i.e. the legal uncertainty following from contradictory obligations imposed by the highest national and supranational judges' case law, placing the judicial and administrative judges between a rock and a hard place (see *supra* n. 8).

Legal certainty is further improved because the BCC's 'rank and authority', as the ECtHR puts it[188], allows it to disseminate the ECtHR's case law among other Belgian judges. The BCC's ambition to offer a coherent human rights jurisprudence and to improve legal certainty also explains why it even refers to ECtHR case law even when the Convention does not apply (see *supra* n. 93, 118 and 125).

Finally, the BCC's approach should also lead to reducing the risk of Belgium being condemned by the ECtHR. The domestic statement of a human rights violation is to be preferred over a condemnation by a supranational court, the international visibility of which would be detrimental to Belgium's reputation.

III. THE EUROPEAN COURT OF HUMAN RIGHTS SPEAKING

Several interpretative techniques and reasoning styles adopted by the ECtHR facilitate its judicial dialogue with national judges. For example, its systematic stressing the subsidiarity principle and the margin of appreciation doctrine sends the message to domestic courts that they have the power to decide human rights cases themselves and that the ECtHR gives them the leeway to

---

[188]   ECtHR 20 November 1995, *Pressos Compania Naviera v. Belgium*; ECtHR (dec.) 10 November 2005, *EEG-Slachthuis Verbist Izegem v. Belgium*.

do so. Indeed, the ECtHR often explains that 'where the balancing exercise has been undertaken by the national authorities in conformity with the criteria laid down in the Court's case-law, the Court would require strong reasons to substitute its view for that of the domestic courts'.[189] It thus motivates domestic judges to apply the Convention standards and to quote and apply the ECtHR's interpretations, strengthening the common ground of understanding and reducing the conflict potential. Furthermore, the margin of appreciation doctrine absorbs both the cultural differences between the Northern and Southern Member States and the political differences between the Eastern and Western Member States[190], and it lowers the tensions in sensitive ethical issues.[191]

The Court's consensus interpretation, in which it examines how human rights and other legal principles are applied by judges in a vast majority of Member States, is sufficiently lenient to accommodate diversity, while making the ECtHR less vulnerable for criticism. Such a reasoning enhances dialogue, as it requires the ECtHR to listen to the arguments used by all high judicial bodies in the Member States.[192]

The tension potential is further reduced by the ECtHR's procedural approach, which shifts the focus from the substantive reasons provided by the respondent State to the quality and transparency of the national procedure and judicial remedies. Whereas the substance of a human right may be controversial and therefore lead to tensions with domestic judges, examining the procedures leads to a rather value-neutral way of reasoning.[193] In turn, this approach motivates domestic courts to apply these procedures, which facilitates further dialogue.

Remedial discretion is also instrumental in enhancing dialogue. The ECtHR's judgments being merely declaratory, their execution depends on the Member States and their courts. They are free in the use of the tools in order to remedy the violation, as long as they do remedy it. Reopening domestic cases or amending

---

[189] ECtHR (GC) 10 May 2001, *Z. a.o. v. United Kingdom*, §101; ECtHR (GC) 19 October 2005, *Roche a.o. v. United Kingdom*, §120; ECtHR 19 February 2009, *A. a.o. v. United Kingdom*, §174; ECtHR (GC) 7 February 2012, *Von Hannover v. Germany (no. 2)*, §107. See S. Lambrecht, "The attitude of four supreme courts towards the European Court of Human Rights: Strasbourg has spoken...", in S. Besson and A. Ziegler (eds.), *Le juge et le droit international et européen – The Judge in International and European Law*, Zurich, Schulthess, 2013, 304–305.

[190] W. Sadurski, "Accession's Democracy Dividend: The Impact of the EU Enlargement upon Democracy in the New Member States of Central and Eastern Europe", *ELJ* 2004, 374.

[191] L. Glas, *o.c.*, 267–268.

[192] *Ibid.*, 269.

[193] *Ibid.*, 270.

domestic case law are themselves part of a direct dialogue.[194] Moreover, whenever the ECtHR gets involved in the execution of its judgments[195], it can take a further step to keep the dialogue going.[196] This potential is, however, limited, because the execution of judgments is a task for the Committee of Ministers, and the Court only gets involved insofar as the execution process gives rise to new violations of the Convention.[197]

On the other hand, one of the ECtHR's most important interpretative techniques rather constitutes a source of tensions with domestic judges. The ECtHR's evolutive and dynamic interpretation extends the Court's field of action to political issues involving the environment and social security, and its development of positive obligations requires the Member States to take specific action. Although such techniques have, initially, strongly contributed to the Court's success, they currently make it vulnerable for criticism.[198] But it should be kept in mind that the existence of differing viewpoints is itself a necessary requirement for starting a dialogue (see *supra* n. 21).

The aforementioned techniques allow the ECtHR to play a role confined to it by the High Contracting Parties in the Brighton Declaration, i.e. to engage in open dialogues with the highest courts of the States Parties 'as a means of developing an enhanced understanding of their respective roles in carrying out their shared responsibility for applying the Convention'.[199]

In the following lines, we examine how the ECtHR adjudicates cases against Belgium in which the BCC had already been involved.

A. THE BCC THROUGH THE EYES OF THE ECtHR

Judges SAJÓ and TSOTSORIA have qualified the Belgian Constitution 'the first lasting document of European constitutionalism'.[200] And as Paul Lemmens describes[201], the ECtHR has also been asked to qualify the BCC.

---

194   *Ibid.*, 271.
195   See W. Verrijdt, "De rol van het Grondwettelijk Hof in de uitvoering van veroordelende arresten van het EHRM", in W. Pas, P. Peeters and W. Verrijdt (eds.), *Liber discipulorum André Alen*, Bruges, die Keure, 2015, 513–516.
196   L. Glas, *o.c.*, 274.
197   ECtHR (GC) 5 February 2015, *Bochan v. Ukraine*; ECtHR 6 September 2018, *Kontalexis v. Greece*.
198   J. Gerards and J. Fleuren, *o.c.*, 3–4.
199   High Level Conference on the Future of the European Court of Human Rights, 19–20 April 2012, Brighton Declaration, §12, c), i).
200   ECtHR (GC) 16 June 2015, *Delfi AS v. Estonia*, dissenting opinion judges Sajó and Tsotsoria, §3.
201   P. Lemmens, "Visie…", *l.c.*, 155.

In the *Vergauwen* case, the Flemish legislator had himself granted some building permits following an exceptional procedure specifically enacted for the enlargement of the port of Antwerp, thus depriving the Council of State of its normal jurisdiction in this matter. The BCC thus becoming the sole competent court for reviewing these building permits, the petitioners complained that they were deprived of their access to an independent and impartial court possessing full jurisdiction. The ECtHR dismissed the complaints, pointing out that the BCC is a tribunal meeting the full jurisdiction standards enshrined in Article 6 of the Convention. Furthermore, the BCC gives ample reasons for its decisions, including for its decision *in casu* not to send a case to the ECJ for a preliminary reference.[202] Even when it examines a case *in globo*, without separately answering all arguments advanced by the parties, it shows that it has examined the case to its full extent. Furthermore, the fact that half of the BCC's bench consists of former MP's does not jeopardize its impartiality, not even in politically sensitive cases.[203]

B.   THE BCC'S CASE LAW UNDER EUROPEAN SCRUTINY

The ECtHR's judgments against Belgium are increasingly mentioning the BCC's case law[204], but not all mentions are of equal importance. Often, they consist of mere references, without any visible implication for the ECtHR's adjudication of the case at hand.[205] For example, in the *Bamouhammad* case, the ECtHR condemned Belgium because of an inhuman and degrading treatment consisting of a dangerous prisoner's frequent relocation, which included nude body searches.[206] In that judgment (§89), it referred to a BCC judgment annulling a legislative provision extending the possibilities of nude body search[207], although that legislative provision post-dated the facts of the case.

In other cases, the BCC is only mentioned when the ECtHR examines whether the petitioner has exhausted domestic remedies.[208] And in one case the ECtHR

---

[202]   The BCC had thoroughly examined the special procedure and the building permits following from it: CC no. 94/2003, 2 July 2003; CC no. 151/2003, 26 November 2003; CC no. 56/2006, 19 April 2006.

[203]   ECtHR (dec.) 10 April 2012, *Vergauwen a.o. v. Belgium*, §§82–83, 91, 103 and 105.

[204]   See also A. Alen and W. Verrijdt, "L'influence…", *l.c.*, 143-157.

[205]   E.g. ECtHR (dec.) 6 September 1994, *Laboratoire médical Saint-Pierre et Marie-France Leclerq v. Belgium*; ECtHR 30 January 2003, *Göcke a.o. v. Belgium*; ECtHR 20 September 2011, *Ullens de Schooten and Rezabek v. Belgium*; ECtHR (dec.) 20 March 2012, *Boelens a.o. v. Belgium*; ECtHR 27 February 2014, *S.J. v. Belgium*; ECtHR 7 July 2015, *V.M. a.o. v. Belgium*; ECtHR (GC) 13 December 2016, *Paposhvili v. Belgium*; ECtHR 17 January 2017, *Habran and Dalem v. Belgium*; ECtHR 23 May 2017, *Van Wesenbeeck v. Belgium*.

[206]   ECtHR 17 November 2015, *Bamouhammad v. Belgium*.

[207]   CC no. 20/2014, 29 January 2014.

[208]   E.g. ECmHR 2 September 1996, *Aerts v. Belgium*; ECtHR 22 June 2000, *Coëme v. Belgium*; ECtHR 15 July 2003, *Ernst v. Belgium*; ECtHR 13 October 2005, *GERFA v. Belgium*.

concluded that the involvement of the BCC had rendered the case complex, concluding that the reasonable delay had not been surpassed.[209]

But in other cases, the BCC's case law mentioned by the ECtHR did have a more important influence, and concerning these cases, Paul Lemmens concludes that the BCC has an excellent track record in Strasbourg.[210] We will illustrate that point with some examples.

1. The BCC's case law approved in cases against Belgium

If the BCC does not state a human rights violation, the ECtHR usually adheres to that conclusion, often even declaring the case manifestly ill-founded in a decision of non-admissibility.[211] This statement is probably linked to the BCC's techniques of indirect review against the Convention, including its ample use of ECtHR case law when interpreting the Belgian Constitution (see *supra* n. 32 and 85), and to the ECtHR's taking a more deferential approach if a national judge has already conducted a thorough proportionality review (see *supra* n. 189). One might indeed expect that an increasing common ground of understanding leads to a decreasing likeliness that both courts reach different outcomes.

2. The BCC's case law approved in cases against other Member States

As Paul Lemmens describes[212], the BCC's case law has also been influential in cases against other Member States. The *Michaud* case concerned French legislation obliging attorneys-at-law to report all possible money laundering activities undertaken by their clients to the competent judicial authorities. The BCC had approved similar Belgian legislation, albeit imposing a very restrictive interpretation, requiring that attorneys-at-law cannot be obliged to file such reports if they discover money laundering activities in the normal line of their work, i.e. when giving legal opinions or representing their clients in court.[213] The BCC thus tried to reconcile the legitimate aim of fighting against money

---

209 ECtHR (dec.) 9 December 2004, *Stevens*.

210 P. Lemmens, "Visie…", *l.c.*, 158.

211 E.g. ECmHR (dec.) 14 January 1998, *nv Remo Milieubeheer v. Belgium* (following CC no. 51/95, concerning expropriation cases being adjudicated by the justices of the peace instead of the Council of State); ECtHR (dec.) 10 November 2005, *EEG-Slachthuis Verbist v. Belgium* (following CC no. 17/2000 approving a retroactive legislative provision); ECtHR (dec.) 8 January 2008, *Epstein v. Belgium* (following CC no. 149/2004 concerning war victims); ECtHR (dec.) 14 February 2012, *Gallez and Verhaegen v. Belgium* (following CC no. 64/2008 concerning a retroactive legislative provision); ECtHR (dec.) 11 September 2012, *Optim and Industerre v. Belgium* (following CC no. 177/2005 concerning a retroactive legislative provision).

212 P. Lemmens, "Visie…", *l.c.*, 160.

213 CC no. 10/2008, 23 January 2008.

laundering with the imperatives of professional secrecy and the attorney-client privilege. The ECtHR subsequently approved the French legislation, but only because it was formulated in such a way that it adequately dealt with the same concerns.[214]

The ECtHR also mentioned the BCC's case law in its famous *S.A.S.* judgment, concerning the French burqa ban.[215] The Belgian federal legislator had punished the wearing of clothing entirely or substantially covering the face by an administrative fine between 120 and 200 euros or a term of imprisonment between one and seven days. The BCC accepted that this legislative provision pursued three legitimate aims: public safety, the equality between men and women and 'a certain vision on living together in society'. It also stated that these aims are protected under Article 9.2 of the Convention. The legislative provision under scrutiny was, moreover, proportionate to that aim. First, identity checks by police officers would become impossible if one could hide his or her identity by covering the face. Second, the proper functioning of the public sphere in a democratic society requires every participant's face to be visible. And third, the legislator may decide that a democratic society must protect women from undue pressure by their family members or their community to hide their faces when entering the public sphere. Although wearing a burqa might also correspond to a deliberate religious choice made without external pressure, a democratic society may oppose to its manifestation in the public sphere, as such a religious obligation only downsizes women's abilities to take part in normal societal life. Furthermore, the fundamental character of the democratic principles involved justifies the use of criminal punishment. The BCC did, nevertheless, impose a restrictive interpretation: the wearing of a burqa within a place of worship may never be subjected to criminal punishment.[216]

In its *S.A.S.* judgment, the ECtHR amply quoted the BCC's judgment, but although it eventually adopted the same solution, it did not agree with all statements made by the BCC. It rejected the public safety argument, stating that such an important limitation to women's religious rights can only be justified by a clear and present danger. The only legitimate aim accepted by the ECtHR involves the 'vision on living together in society', as an element of the protection of the rights and liberties of others: the face playing an essential role in all social interaction, the State may oppose to practices jeopardizing the possibility of establishing interpersonal relations. The ECtHR also accepts that the measure

---

[214] ECtHR 6 December 2012, *Michaud v. France*. Paul Lemmens ("Visie...", *l.c.*, 161, footnote 30) points out that the analogy between the BCC's and the ECtHR's reasonings might be explained by the involvement of the French-speaking bar association of Brussels, which was one of the petitioners before the BCC, and which also intervened in the *Michaud* case.

[215] ECtHR (GC) 1 July 2014, *S.A.S. v. France*.

[216] CC no. 145/2012, 6 December 2012.

under scrutiny is proportionate to that aim, granting the respondent government a large margin of appreciation, and stating that French law does not forbid the wearing of all religious clothing in the public sphere and that it is not based on religious motifs.[217]

This judgment illustrates that judicial dialogue can be reciprocal. The BCC had cited several ECtHR judgments involving several Member States in its own decision, which was in turn used by the ECtHR in a case involving another Member State.

Three years later, the ECtHR also had to examine burqa bans by Belgian local authorities. Referring to the 'living together in society' argument and to the knowledge-gap, and again quoting the BCC's judgment, it granted the Belgian authorities a large margin of appreciation. Conducting an abstract review of the local regulations at hand, without addressing the petitioners' case *in concreto*, it concluded that this margin of appreciation had not been surpassed.[218]

3. Only four violations, concerning only three subject matters

Until present, the ECtHR has only found a violation in four cases, concerning three subject matters, after the BCC's concluding to a non-violation. One of them, the *Pressos Compania Naviera* case, has already been mentioned (see *supra* n. 150).

Two other judgments relate to criminal convictions *in absentia*. In its former version, Article 187 of the Code of Criminal Procedure did not require the authorities notifying the person convicted *in absentia* about his conviction to mention the procedures and terms of limitation for requesting a new court hearing in his presence. The BCC had decided that this lack of information did not violate the Articles 10 and 11 of the Constitution *juncto* Article 6 of the Convention. The referring judge had compared the legislative provision at hand with administrative law, which requires all unilateral administrative acts to mention all appeal procedures and their terms of limitation. The BCC, however, could not examine the merits of that case, because it decided that criminal and administrative procedure are too different to be compared.[219] The ECtHR did mention that judgment in two cases against Belgium, in which it concluded to the violation of Article 6 ECtHR, explaining that persons convicted *in absentia* must be notified about the delay for requesting a new court hearing.[220] It is not unlikely

---

217 ECtHR (GC) 1 July 2014, *S.A.S. v. France*. The ECtHR's use of the BCC's judgment might be explained by the Belgian Government's intervention in the *S.A.S.* case.

218 ECtHR 11 July 2017, *Belkacemi and Oussar v. Belgium*; ECtHR 11 July 2017, *Dakir v. Belgium*.

219 CC no. 210/2004, 21 December 2004.

220 ECtHR 29 June 2010, *Hakimi v. Belgium*; ECtHR 1 March 2011, *Faniel v. Belgium*.

that the BCC would have come to the same conclusion if it would have had the opportunity to examine the merits of the case, but *in casu* it was hindered by the fact that Article 6 of the Convention is only an indirect reference provision, which could, at that time, only be invoked through the prism of the principle of equality and non-discrimination laid down in the Articles 10 and 11 of the Constitution.[221]

The *Lachiri* case is another example in which the BCC was unable to answer a preliminary reference to the merits in a case similar to a later case before the ECtHR. Article 759 of the Code of Civil Procedure stipulates that parties in a courtroom may not wear any headgear. In the case examined by the BCC in 2008, the defendant in a criminal case insisted on wearing a cap, claiming that he felt ill and that it was cold in the courtroom. That judge referred the case to the BCC, asking whether Article 759 of the Code of Civil Procedure violates the freedom of religion. The BCC declared the case inadmissible, because the case at hand did not involve religious reasons, which meant that the BCC's answer to the preliminary reference could not contribute to the solution of the case before the referring judge.[222] In a later case examined by the ECtHR in 2018, the petitioner, a witness in a criminal trial, was ordered to leave the courtroom because she refused, invoking religious reasons, to take of her headscarf. Without mentioning the BCC's prior judgment, the ECtHR condemned Belgium because removing a civilian not representing the State from a public building, although she did not behave in a disorderly way, constituted a disproportionate limitation to her freedom of religion.[223] That condemning judgment might have been avoided if Article 759 of the Code of Civil Procedure had been submitted to the BCC in a case which did involve religious reasons.

4. The Europeanisation of domestic judicial dialogue

The ECtHR has often been called upon to adjudicate cases revealing a divergent jurisprudence between the BCC and one of the two other highest judicial bodies, the Court of Cassation and the Council of State. In these cases, the ECtHR has always endorsed the BCC's approach.

The earliest example is the *Vermeire* case. After the *Marckx* judgment[224], most Belgian judges applied Article 8 of the Convention in order to eliminate all discriminations between children born in and out of wedlock which were at that time still present in the legislation in the fields of affiliation, succession and adoption. The Court of

---

[221] Meanwhile, the BCC has accepted that the full extent of Article 6 of the Convention is analogous to the right of access to a judge enshrined in Article 13 of the Constitution, thus avoiding such complications (CC no. 195/2009, 3 December 2009).

[222] CC no. 8/2008, 17 January 2008.

[223] ECtHR 18 September 2018, *Lachiri v. Belgium*.

[224] ECtHR 13 June 1979, *Marckx v. Belgium*.

Cassation, however, ruled that Article 8 of the Convention was only self-executing insofar as it forbids the authorities to violate the right to respect for family life, but not insofar as it obliges them to take action in order to guarantee family life, that obligation lacking precision, as the authorities remain free to choose how they fulfil it.[225] It therefore refused to apply the legislation postdating the *Marckx* judgment to the estate of persons deceased between that judgment and that legislative amendment. The BCC disagreed, stressing that Article 8 of the Convention is always self-executing, and that children born in and out of wedlock had to be treated equally from the *Marckx* judgment onwards, even in the absence of legislation repairing the violation found by the ECtHR.[226] The ECtHR referred to that judgment in the *Vermeire* case, explaining that 'an overall revision of the legislation, with the aim of carrying out a thoroughgoing and consistent amendment of the whole of the law on affiliation and inheritance on intestacy, was not necessary at all as an essential preliminary to compliance with the Convention as interpreted by the Court in the *Marckx* case'.[227] The Court of Cassation subsequently adapted its case law in order to comply with both courts' interpretation.[228]

The *Silvester's Horeca Service* case concerned the access to a judge in case of an administrative fine. According to the Court of Cassation, the judge lacks competence to examine the fine's proportionality, to mitigate it or to replace it by a conditional fine.[229] According to the BCC, the judge's review competence should equal the administration's: if the administration may mitigate the fine or inflict a merely conditional fine, then so may the judge.[230] The ECtHR has endorsed the latter point of view, noting that the BCC had already remedied the violation of Article 6 of the Convention, but that this jurisprudence came too late for the petitioner.[231]

The *Cottin* case concerned the possibility to contradict reports filed by judicial experts in criminal cases. The Court of Cassation ruled that no legislative provision allowed such reports to be submitted to contradictory debate.[232] The BCC, however, found a violation of the principle of equality and non-discrimination because expert opinions in civil cases were open for contradictory debate, whereas expert opinions in criminal cases were not.[233] In the *Cottin* case, the ECtHR explained that reports filed by judicial experts must always be open

---

[225]   Cass. 3 October 1983, *Arr.Cass.* 1983–1984, 110; Cass. 10 May 1985, *Pas.* 1985, I, 1122.
[226]   CC no. 18/91, 4 July 1991.
[227]   ECtHR 29 November 1991, *Vermeire v. Belgium*, §26.
[228]   Cass. 15 May 1992, *RW* 1992–1993, 325; Cass. 21 October 1993, *JLMB* 1995, 180.
[229]   Cass. 5 February 1999, *Arr.Cass.* 1999, 142.
[230]   CC no. 96/2002, 12 June 2002.
[231]   ECtHR 4 March 2004, *Silvester's Horeca Service v. Belgium*.
[232]   Cass. 24 November 1998, *Pas.* 1998, I, 490.
[233]   CC no. 24/97, 30 April 1997.

for contradictory debate if they can influence the outcome of the case and if they concern a technical matter falling outside the judge's normal knowledge.[234]

The *Loncke* case concerned the obligation to pay the entire sum of a VAT fine inflicted by the administration as a requirement for launching an admissible judicial appeal against it. According to the BCC, that obligation violates the right of access to a judge if the fine is so high that the person concerned cannot make the payment; in such cases, the administration must renounce to that requirement and allow the tax payer to appeal anyway.[235] The Court of Cassation has acknowledged that case law, but at the same time it validated a judgment deciding that the tax payer concerned had not proven that he was unable to pay the VAT fine. It added that VAT fines are not 'criminal' in the meaning of Article 6 of the Convention.[236] The tax payer subsequently petitioned before the ECtHR, which stated that a tax fine amounting to the double of the unpaid taxes is criminal in nature. Moreover, he had sufficiently proven that an independent dealer of second-hand cars is unable to pay a fine of 3,77 million euros before challenging it in court. Both the administration and the domestic judges being aware of that disproportion but failing to take it into account, the ECtHR concluded to the violation of Article 6.1 of the Convention.[237]

The *RTBF* case involved the freedom of opinion. The BCC had established that, the Constitution offering a wider human rights protection than the Convention, 'preventive measures', i.e. forbidding the publication or broadcasting of an opinion before it has been made public, is inadmissible: criminal offences or other faults committed while expressing an opinion, such as slander and libel, can only be sanctioned *a posteriori*.[238] The Court of Cassation, however, did validate a judicial interim measure against the French-speaking public broadcasting company, consisting of the preventive ban on broadcasting a documentary about a doctor's malpractices.[239] According to the ECtHR, this divergent jurisprudence itself shows that the impugned measure did not have a sufficiently clear legal basis in Belgian law, and that Article 10 of the Convention was violated.[240]

The most recent example is the *Ronald Vermeulen* case, concerning the requirement that the petitioner before the Council of State does not only possess a legitimate interest in the case's outcome when initiating it, but also that this interest persists throughout the procedure. According to the Constitutional Court, that requirement

---

[234]   ECtHR 2 June 2005, *Cottin v. Belgium*.
[235]   CC no. 73/92, 18 November 1992; CC no. 75/95, 9 November 1995.
[236]   Cass. 3 January 2003, *Pas.* 2003, I, 26.
[237]   ECtHR 25 September 2007, *Loncke v. Belgium*.
[238]   CC no. 157/2004, 6 October 2004.
[239]   Cass. 2 June 2006, *AM* 2006, 355.
[240]   ECtHR 29 March 2011, *RTBF v. Belgium*.

violates the Articles 10 and 11 of the Constitution if it means that cases are declared inadmissible when the long duration of Council of State procedures are the main cause of the disappearance of the petitioner's interest. The Council of State should also take into account all aspects of the petitioner's interest, including if he intends to use its judgment in a subsequent tort case before a civil judge.[241] Moreover, referring to the ECtHR's case law, the BCC has warned the Council of State that it should not apply the legitimate interest requirement in an excessively formalistic manner.[242] Ronald Vermeulen was a civil servant challenging the result of a comparative exam for the promotion to a higher rank in his department's hierarchy because the decision was ill-reasoned. When the Council of State rendered its judgment, the pool of civil servants having passed the exam had already expired. Hence, any promotion of a civil servant in his department could only take place after a new comparative exam. The Council of State therefore declared his petition inadmissible because of the disappearance of the petitioner's interest, even though he intended to use the Council of State's judgment in a later tort case.[243] The ECtHR accepted that this admissibility criterion pursues a legitimate aim, i.e. avoiding that Executive decisions are called into question spuriously, leading to the paralysis of the judicial review system. But at the same time, it noted that *in casu* the Council of State was the only judicial body competent to annul the decision challenged by the petitioner, that he had met all procedural requirements when filing his petition, and that the auditor before the Council of State had concluded that the petition was well-founded. When the petition was filed, the pool was still valid. Yet, the Council of State never examined the true cause of the disappearance of the petitioner's interest, nor its own role therein. It had therefore applied the admissibility criterion in an overly formalistic manner.[244]

These cases indicate that the legal uncertainty following from a divergent jurisprudence between the highest domestic courts is itself an important trigger for the ECtHR to conclude to a violation, endorsing the line of domestic case law offering the highest standard of protection. But it also shows that petitioners may involve the ECtHR as an arbiter in a domestic judicial dialogue.

CONCLUSION

Judicial dialogue is being called the new 'buzzword' of constitutional law[245], but it is much more than that. Given the open texture of human rights, judges will often disagree about how they should be interpreted and applied. Legal certainty

---

[241] CC no. 117/99, 10 November 1999.
[242] CC no. 109/2010, 30 September 2010.
[243] Council of State 5 July 2005, *Ronald Vermeulen*, no. 147.284.
[244] ECtHR 17 July 2018, *Ronald Vermeulen v. Belgium*.
[245] L. Glas, *o.c.*, 248 and 275.

is not served by the persistence of such a disagreement. As hierarchical approaches of the relation between domestic and European judges are more and more being rejected, dialogue becomes all the more relevant for dealing with such disagreements. At the same time, 'in law, as in politics, disagreement can be a productive and creative force, revealing error, showing gaps, moving discussion and results in good directions'.[246] If the prerequisites for a judicial dialogue are met, its operation can solve disagreements, obliging all judges involved to give strong reasons for their judgments, and leading to a better-reasoned outcome. This does not necessarily mean a uniform outcome: sometimes, the best outcome consists of the supranational court deferring the interpretative decision to the national level.[247]

The aim of the present contribution in honour of Paul Lemmens was to show that, in the relation between the ECtHR and the BCC, these prerequisites are fulfilled and that an intensive dialogue does take place. The BCC has adopted interpretative techniques allowing it to involve the ECtHR's case law in its interpretation of analogous constitutional provisions, and it systematically refers to that case law in its own judgments. The solutions it reaches are, in turn, usually endorsed by the ECtHR.

The current dialogue between the BCC and the ECtHR is not a critical one, as both courts usually agree with each other's solutions. If, occasionally, the dialogue would become critical, that would not be a sign of its deterioration, but rather of its maturity, as an intelligible disagreement requires mutual respect and an open mind.

Such a disagreement can currently only be voiced through an indirect dialogue, because Belgium has not yet ratified Protocol no. 16. Hence, if the ECtHR disagrees with the BCC's criticism, it might have to condemn Belgium for the BCC's point of view. Therefore, we are in favour of a swift ratification of this 'protocol of dialogue' by Belgium, provided that it does not alter the current division of competences between the highest Belgian courts, as set out in Article 26, §4, of the Special Majority Act of 6 January 1989 on the Constitutional Court. It would allow the BCC to address new questions of interpretation to the ECtHR, and it would be a safer method for voicing criticisms. In any event, it would be unwise for Belgium to remain absent from this procedure, now that it has entered into force.[248]

---

[246] C. Sunstein, *Legal Reasoning and Political Conflict*, OUP 1996, 58.

[247] A. Torres Pérez, *o.c.*, 112.

[248] M. Cartabia, *o.c.*, 39; L. Glas, *o.c.*, 276: 'When only a minority of domestic courts is able to engage in dialogue by way of this instrument, the possibility materializes that the minority imposes its views on a majority of inactive courts'.

LES AVIS DU CONSEIL D'ÉTAT DANS LE RAISONNEMENT DE LA COUR EUROPÉENNE DES DROITS DE L'HOMME

Sébastien Van Drooghenbroeck
Professeur à l'Université Saint-Louis – Bruxelles
Assesseur à la Section de législation du Conseil d'État de Belgique

Dans la foulée des textes du même acabit qu'il l'ont précédée[1], la récente Déclaration de Copenhague[2] (avril 2018) «appelle les Etats Parties à continuer de renforcer la mise en œuvre de la Convention (européenne des droits de l'Homme) au niveau national (...) en particulier (...) en veillant, en y impliquant les parlements nationaux selon des modalités appropriées, à ce que les politiques et la législation soient pleinement conformes à la Convention, notamment en vérifiant, de manière systématique et à un stade précoce du processus, la compatibilité des projets de loi et de la pratique administrative à la lumière de la jurisprudence de la Cour».

Bien que celle-ci ne s'y trouve pas expressément formulée, on ne peut manquer d'apercevoir, entre les lignes de cette Déclaration, l'affirmation du caractère

---

[1]   Selon la Déclaration de Brighton : «En conséquence, la Conférence : c) exprime en particulier la détermination des Etats parties à veiller à la mise en œuvre effective de la Convention au niveau national, en prenant les mesures spécifiques suivantes, s'il y a lieu : [...] ii) mettre en œuvre des mesures concrètes pour faire en sorte que les politiques et législations respectent pleinement la Convention, y compris en fournissant aux parlements nationaux des informations sur la compatibilité avec la Convention des projets de loi de base proposés par le gouvernement» (A. 9. c.ii.). Voy. aussi la «Déclaration de Bruxelles» du 27 mars 2015 clôturant la Conférence de haut niveau sur *La mise en œuvre de la Convention européenne des droits de l'Homme, une responsabilité partagée*, point B. 1, d) : «prendre les mesures appropriées pour améliorer la vérification de la compatibilité des projets de loi, des législations existantes et des pratiques administratives internes avec la Convention, à la lumière de la jurisprudence de la Cour» Voy. enfin le Rapport du Comité Directeur des Droits de l'Homme sur l'avenir à plus long terme du système de la Convention européenne des droits de l'Homme, 11 décembre 2015, CDDH (2015)R84, spéc. pp. 24 à 26.

[2]   Adoptée par la Conférence de haut niveau réunie à Copenhague les 12 et 13 avril 2018 à l'initiative de la présidence danoise du Comité des Ministres du Conseil de l'Europe, consultable sur https://rm.coe.int/declaration-de-copenhague/16807b915b.

positif de la mission consultative que certains États membres du Conseil de l'Europe assignent, dans le cadre de la «fabrique» de leur droit national, à leurs Conseils d'État respectifs.[3] Etrange retournement : voici en effet que cette mission est mise à l'honneur comme alliée objective du rôle assumé par la Cour européenne des droits de l'Homme, alors qu'il y a une grosse vingtaine d'années, cette dernière avait répandu autour d'elle un parfum de souffre, en laissant entendre que la réunion de cette mission consultative et d'une mission contentieuse entre les mêmes mains pouvait en soi poser un problème structurel d'impartialité au regard de l'article 6 de la Convention...[4]

Le bénéfice escompté de l'intervention consultative des Conseils d'État se situe, dans l'optique de la Déclaration de Copenhague et des textes qui lui sont apparentés, au niveau de la *prévention*. En allumant le feu rouge ou le feu orange face à des normes qui pourraient receler quelque vice d'inconventionnalité, et en suggérant les corrections aptes à purger ces vices, le Conseil d'État désamorce une ou plusieurs – voire des centaines – de requêtes en puissance, et permet ainsi de faire l'économie complète de la mobilisation de l'instance strasbourgeoise.

L'observation de la jurisprudence de la Cour européenne de ces dernières années montre cependant l'existence d'autres formes d'interactions entre, d'une part, l'intervention consultative d'un Conseil d'État national, et, d'autre part, le contrôle de conventionnalité exercé par ladite Cour.

Ces interactions sont au demeurant de plus en plus nombreuses et spectaculaires. La présence d'anciens conseillers d'État au sein des délibérés strasbourgeois y serait-elle étrangère ? Le dédicataire des présents *Mélanges* aura sans doute sa petite idée sur la question...

---

[3] Voy. d'ailleurs l'Annexe à la Recommandation Rec(2004)5 du 11 mai 2004 du Comité des Ministres aux Etats membres sur la vérification de la compatibilité des projets de loi, des lois en vigueur et des pratiques administratives avec les normes fixées par la Convention européenne des Droits de l'Homme : «Des consultations pour s'assurer de la compatibilité avec les normes en matière de droits de l'homme sont envisagées à divers stades du processus législatif. Dans certains domaines, la consultation est facultative. Dans d'autres, en particulier si le projet de loi est susceptible d'affecter des droits fondamentaux, la consultation sera obligatoire, prévue par la loi, auprès d'une instance déterminée, par exemple le Conseil d'Etat dans certains Etats membres. Lorsque le gouvernement n'a pas procédé à une consultation obligatoire, l'acte pris sera frappé d'une irrégularité formelle. Si après consultation il décide de ne pas tenir compte de l'avis reçu, il assume les conséquences juridiques ou politiques qui peuvent découler d'une telle décision».

[4] On vise évidemment l'arrêt *Procola c. Luxembourg* (Cour eur. D.H., arrêt *Procola c. Luxembourg* du 27 septembre 1995), à tout le moins dans les interprétations les plus radicales qui lui ont été données. Ces interprétations, cependant, n'ont pas fait l'unanimité (voy. en effet, l'Annexe 1 au Rapport annuel 1995-1996 du Conseil d'État de Belgique, pp. 133 et suiv, et réf. citées, disponible sur www.raadvst-consetat.be).

Schématiquement, deux types d'interaction peuvent être aperçus. Dans une première série d'hypothèses, et sur un plan substantiel, la Cour européenne des droits de l'Homme s'inspirera de l'un ou l'autre avis d'un Conseil d'État pour interpréter la Convention elle-même (I). Dans une seconde série d'hypothèses, et cette fois-ci dans un registre procédural, la Cour prendra argument de l'intervention du Conseil d'État et des échos explicites donnés à celle-ci dans la procédure parlementaire, pour justifier la marge d'appréciation concédée à l'État dans telle ou telle affaire (II). Loin s'en faut cependant que les lignes jurisprudentielles ainsi ouvertes ne présentent pas quelque sinuosité : la méthodologie suivie accuse, sur l'un ou l'autre point, un certain manque de transparence.

I. LES AVIS DES CONSEILS D'ÉTAT COMME SOURCES D'INSPIRATION POUR L'INTERPRÉTATION DE LA CONVENTION EUROPÉENNE DES DROITS DE L'HOMME

« La Cour n'a jamais considéré les dispositions de la Convention comme l'unique cadre de référence dans l'interprétation des droits et libertés qu'elle contient (…) ; elle s'est toujours référée au caractère 'vivant' de la Convention à interpréter à la lumière des conditions de vie actuelles et (…) elle a tenu compte de l'évolution des normes de droit national et international dans son interprétation des dispositions de la Convention ».

Ces *dicta*, empruntés à l'arrêt de principe *Demir et Baykara c. Turquie* du 12 novembre 2008[5], sont bien connus. Les illustrations qu'ils reçoivent dans le raisonnement strasbourgeois sont aussi nombreuses que remarquables.[6]

Les « sources externes » mobilisées par la Cour pour « enrichir » son interprétation conventionnelle, sont d'origine et d'essence les plus diverses.[7] Pour ne reprendre qu'un exemple, l'arrêt *Magyar Helsinki Bizottsag* du 8 novembre 2016 concrétise les conceptions actuelles relatives au droit d'accès aux documents détenus par l'autorité en se référant, non seulement à la pratique des autres Etats parties à la Convention, mais aussi au Pacte international relatif aux droits civils et politiques et à la jurisprudence du Comité de Genève portant interprétation de celui-ci,

---

[5]   Cour eur. D.H. (GC), arrêt *Demir & Baykara* du 12 novembre 2008, §§ 67 et 68.

[6]   Pour une analyse (critique) récente, voy. A. Rachovitsa, « The Principle of Systemic Integration in Human Rights Law », (66) *International and Comparative Law Quarterly*, 2017, n° 3, pp. 555 à 588.

[7]   Voy., pour une synthèse récente, D. Staes, *When the European Court of Human Rights refers to External Instruments. Mapping and Justifications*, thèse de doctorat, Université libre de Bruxelles et Université Saint-Louis – Bruxelles, juin 2017.

à la Déclaration universelle des droits de l'Homme, aux travaux du Rapporteur des Nations Unies sur la promotion et la protection du droit à la liberté d'opinion et d'expression, à la Charte des droits fondamentaux de l'Union européenne et à la législation européenne dérivée relative au droit d'accès aux documents administratifs, à une Recommandation du Comité des Ministres du Conseil de l'Europe et à une convention spécialisée issue de cette organisation internationale, à la jurisprudence de la Cour interaméricaine des droits de l'Homme et, *last but not least*, à la Déclaration de principes sur la liberté d'expression en Afrique adoptée par la Commission africaine des droits de l'homme et des peuples en 2002. Et la Cour de conclure cet inventaire en affirmant qu'il «ressort donc clairement des considérations exposées ci-dessus que depuis l'adoption de la Convention, le droit interne de l'écrasante majorité des États membres du Conseil de l'Europe ainsi que les instruments internationaux pertinents ont effectivement évolué au point qu'il se dégage un large consensus, en Europe et au-delà, quant à la nécessité de reconnaître un droit individuel d'accès aux informations détenues par l'État afin d'aider le public à se forger une opinion sur les questions d'intérêt général».[8]

Il y aurait beaucoup à dire sur les «métissages juridiques» ainsi réalisés et la méthode – effective ou souhaitée – au travers de laquelle la Cour européenne des droits de l'Homme les réalise ou devrait les réaliser.[9]

Notre propos sera cependant plus modeste, et consistera uniquement à mettre en lumière que la très grande flexibilité dont la Cour fait montre dans la sélection des sources externes pareillement susceptibles de guider son interprétation conventionnelle, l'a conduite sans difficulté à y intégrer la «jurisprudence» consultative de certains Conseils d'État européens.

Une illustration significative peut être trouvée, en la matière, dans l'arrêt *S.A.S. c. France* du 1er juillet 2014.[10] De larges échos y sont effet donnés, non seulement au Rapport du Conseil d'État français du 25 mars 2010 portant «*Etude relative aux possibilités juridiques d'interdiction du port du voile intégral*»[11], mais aussi à quatre avis du Conseil d'État des Pays-Bas dédiés à la même question.[12]

Les références ainsi faites ne sont pas, loin s'en faut, purement cosmétiques ou anecdotiques. C'est en effet en s'appuyant explicitement sur l'*Etude* précitée que l'arrêt *S.A.S* énonce, en son § 119, que

---

8   Cour eur. D.H., arrêt *Magyar Helsinki Bizottsag c. Hongrie* du 8 novembre 2016, § 148.
9   Voy. e.a. S. Van Drooghenbroeck, «Le *Soft Law* et la Cour européenne des droits de l'Homme», *Soft Law et droits fondamentaux*, sous la dir. de M. Ailincai, Paris, Pedone, 2017, pp. 185 à 205.
10 Cour eur. D.H., GC, arrêt *S.A.S c. France* du 1er juillet 2014.
11 Cour eur. D.H., GC, arrêt *S.A.S c. France* du 1er juillet 2014, §§ 20 à 23.
12 Cour eur. D.H., GC, arrêt *S.A.S c. France* du 1er juillet 2014, §§ 49 à 52.

«un État partie ne saurait invoquer l'égalité des sexes pour interdire une pratique que des femmes – telle la requérante – revendiquent dans le cadre de l'exercice des droits que consacrent ces dispositions, sauf à admettre que l'on puisse à ce titre prétendre protéger des individus contre l'exercice de leurs propres droits et libertés fondamentaux. *Elle observe d'ailleurs que, dans son rapport d'étude du 25 mars 2010, le Conseil d'État est parvenu à une conclusion similaire*».[13]

Ce disant, la Cour faisait tout sauf enfoncer une porte ouverte. Les opinions issues du Palais Royal, convoquées en soutien de ce *dictum*, s'en trouvent par là-même lestées d'une autorité, d'un «poids» argumentatif de toute première importance. Faut-il en effet le rappeler ? En déniant ainsi toute pertinence à l'argument paternaliste fondé sur l'égalité des sexes, l'arrêt *S.A.S c. France* introduisit une inflexion certaine dans la jurisprudence antérieure de la Cour[14], et ruina l'un des motifs sur base desquels le législateur belge[15] – avec la bénédiction expresse de la Cour constitutionnelle[16] – avait cru pouvoir fonder sa loi du 1er juin 2011 'visant à interdire le port de tout vêtement cachant totalement ou de manière principale le visage'…

Pour perceptible qu'il soit, le «poids» que le raisonnement de la Cour prête pareillement à la jurisprudence consultative d'un Conseil d'État ne se laisse pas facilement mesurer, et, *a fortiori*, prédire.

---

[13]   Notre accent.

[14]   Voy. en effet S. Ouald Chaib and L. Peroni, («Missed Opportunity to Do Full Justice to Women Wearing a Face Veil», publié sur https ://strasbourgobservers.com) qui soulignent la distance prise par la Cour, dans l'arrêt *S.A.S*, par rapport aux précédents *Dalhab c. Suisse* et *Leyla Sahin c. Turquie.* La position retenue par la Cour dans l'arrêt *S.A.S.* n'est évidemment pas sans évoquer la critique qui avait été celle de Mme la Juge Françoise Tulkens dans son opinion dissidente jointe à l'arrêt de Grande Chambre rendu le 10 novembre 2005 dans l'affaire *Leyla Sahin c. Turquie* : «A cet égard, je vois mal comment le principe d'égalité entre les sexes peut justifier l'interdiction faite à une femme d'adopter un comportement auquel, sans que la preuve contraire ait été apportée, elle consent librement. Par ailleurs, l'égalité et la non-discrimination sont des droits subjectifs qui ne peuvent être soustraits à la maîtrise de ceux et de celles qui sont appelés à en bénéficier. Une telle forme de «paternalisme» s'inscrit à contre-courant de la jurisprudence de la Cour qui a construit, sur le fondement de l'article 8, un véritable droit à l'autonomie personnelle (…)».

[15]   Voy. X. Delgrange, «Quand la Burqa passe à l'Ouest, la Belgique perd-t-elle le Nord ?», *Quand la burqa passe à l'ouest. Enjeux éthiques, politiques et juridiques*, sous la dir. de D. Koussens, Presses universitaires de Rennes, Coll. «Science des religions», Rennes, 2013, pp. 209 et suiv.

[16]   C., n°145/2012, 6 décembre 2012 ; *Administration Publique*, 2013, liv. 2, 167, note G. Ninane ; *Journal des Tribunaux*, 2013, liv. 6515, p. 234, note L.-L Christians, S. Minette et S. Wattier ; *Jurisprudence de Liège, Mons et Bruxelles*, 2013, liv. 11, p. 628, note G. Ninane ; *Nieuwe Juridische Weekblad*, 2013, liv. 274,p. 20, note C. Conings. V. ég. J. Vrielink, «De Grondwet aan het gezicht onttrokken. Het Grondwettelijk Hof en het 'boerkaverbod'», *Tijdschrift voor Bestuurswetenschappen en Publiekrecht*, 2013, pp. 250-260. Voy. en effet le pt. B.23 de l'arrêt : «Même lorsque le port du voile intégral résulte d'un choix délibéré dans le chef de la femme, l'égalité des sexes, que le législateur considère à juste titre comme une valeur fondamentale de la société démocratique, justifie que l'État puisse s'opposer, dans la sphère publique, à la manifestation d'une conviction religieuse par un comportement non conciliable avec ce principe d'égalité entre l'homme et la femme».

Le lecteur ingénu de l'arrêt *S.A.S.* pourrait en effet y déceler une forme de «deux poids – une mesure». S'il s'avère réellement que la jurisprudence nationale consultative peut avoir une telle «autorité» dans le raisonnement de la Cour de Strasbourg – ce que tendrait à démontrer le § 119 précité de l'arrêt *S.A.S.* –, alors pourquoi diable les quatre avis négatifs donnés par le Conseil d'État des Pays-Bas quant à la possibilité d'interdire la Burqa, bien que cités par la Cour[17], n'ont-ils pas quant à eux pesé plus lourd dans le verdict finalement atteint par cet arrêt ? N'y a-t-il pas là une forme de *cherry picking* ?

Au vrai, la question dépasse largement la seule problématique de la prise en compte, par la Cour, de la jurisprudence «consultative» des Conseils d'État nationaux. Que l'on songe par exemple aux «géométries variables» qui caractérisent l'arrêt *Mursic c. Croatie* du 20 octobre 2016 quant au «poids» qu'il entend conférer aux standards élaborés par la Comité pour la Prévention de la Torture (CPT). En l'occurrence, la Cour avait estimé que, lorsqu'elle est appelée à statuer sur la compatibilité avec l'article 3 de situations de surpopulation carcérale, elle n'est pas liée de manière déterminante par les normes relatives à la surface minimale à allouer aux détenus, telles que définies par le CPT. Aux fins de justifier sa position, la Cour soulignait la différence entre sa propre mission et le rôle dévolu au CPT. Selon l'arrêt du 20 octobre 2016,

> «La principale raison de la réticence de la Cour à considérer les normes du CPT en matière d'espace disponible comme déterminantes pour sa conclusion sur le terrain de l'article 3 tient à ce que dans le cadre de son appréciation au regard de cette disposition, elle doit tenir compte de toutes les circonstances pertinentes de la cause, tandis que les autres organes internationaux tels que le CPT élaborent des normes générales en la matière à des fins de prévention des mauvais traitements (...). De même, les normes nationales relatives à l'espace personnel varient grandement et constituent des exigences générales en matière d'hébergement adéquat dans un système pénitentiaire donné (...).
>
> De plus, la Cour joue un rôle conceptuellement différent de celui confié au CPT, ce que celui-ci a lui-même reconnu. Le CPT n'a pas pour tâche de dire si des faits donnés sont constitutifs de peines ou de traitements inhumains ou dégradants au sens de l'article 3 (...). Il agit principalement en amont dans un but de prévention, démarche qui tend par sa nature même vers un degré de protection plus élevé que celui qu'applique la Cour lorsqu'elle statue sur les conditions de détention d'un requérant (...). Le CPT joue un rôle préventif tandis que la Cour est chargée de l'application judiciaire à des cas individuels de l'interdiction absolue de la torture et des traitements inhumains ou dégradants posée à l'article 3 de la Convention (...). La Cour tient néanmoins à souligner qu'elle demeure attentive aux normes élaborées par le CPT et que, nonobstant cette différence de fonctions, elle examine soigneusement les cas où les conditions de détention ne respectent pas la norme de 4 m² fixée par lui (...)»[18]

---

[17]   Cour eur. D.H. (GC), arrêt *S.A.S c. France* du 1er juillet 2014, §§ 49 à 52.
[18]   Cour eur. D.H. (GC), arrêt du 20 octobre 2016, *Mursic c. Croatie*, §§ 112-113.

Le poids du *soft law* du CPT se voyait ainsi minoré, tout en n'étant pas totalement ignoré. L'arrêt *Mursic* clôturait en effet son raisonnement comme suit :

> «La Cour tient à souligner l'importance du rôle préventif du CPT, qui contrôle les conditions de détention et élabore des normes à cet égard. Elle rappelle que lorsqu'elle statue sur les conditions de détention d'un requérant, elle demeure attentive à ces normes et à leur respect par les États contractants»[19]

Le raisonnement ainsi tenu, et la position sur laquelle il déboucha, se heurtèrent à des nombreuses critiques, au sein de la Cour et à l'extérieur de celle-ci.[20] S'exprimant en marge de l'arrêt, les juges Sajo, Lopez Guerra et Wojtyczek firent entre autres valoir que ce dernier n'était pas des plus cohérents dans la manière dont il «pondérait» l'impact du *soft law* produit par le CPT pour l'interprétation de l'article 3 de la Convention. Alors que certains standards du Comité se trouvaient en effet «minorés» par l'arrêt – ceux qui concernaient, en l'occurrence, l'espace minimal à réserver à chaque détenu –, d'autres standards développés par le même Comité sur des thèmes adjacents étaient quant à eux silencieusement «acceptés tels quels» et convertis en *hard law* par le relais de l'article 3 de la Convention. «Une telle différence de traitement», estimaient les juges précités, «appellerait une explication».[21]

Mutatis mutandis, une même «explication» peut être attendue de la Cour lorsqu'elle décide de prêter des «poids» variables aux positions issues de la jurisprudence consultative de tel ou tel Conseil d'État. Il n'est évidemment pas question d'exiger par principe un traitement mécanique et uniforme sur le mode du «tout ou rien» juridique. Une telle binarité est radicalement étrangère à la logique gradualiste – le «plus ou moins» – qui conduit la Cour européenne des droits de l'Homme, depuis l'arrêt *Demir et Baykara* précité, à enrichir son interprétation conventionnelle de références à des «sources externes».[22] «C'est à la Cour qu'il appartient de décider des instruments et rapports internationaux qu'elle juge dignes d'attention ainsi que du poids qu'elle entend leur accorder» : ce *dictum* bien connu de l'arrêt *Tanase*[23] peut sans difficulté être étendu à toutes les «sources externes» mobilisées par la Cour et, notamment aux jurisprudences consultatives nationales qui, çà et là, commencent à faire leur apparition dans le raisonnement strasbourgeois. Sur le plan de l'heuristique juridique, la logique

---

19   *Ibid.*, § 141.
20   Voy. F. Tulkens, «Cellule collective et espace personnel – Un arrêt en trompe-l'œil», *Rev. Trim. Dr. Homme,* 2017, pp. 989 et suiv.
21   Opinion en partie dissidente aux juges Sajo, Lopez Guerra et Wojtyczek, p. 6.
22   Voy. F. Tulkens, F. Krenc et S. Van Drooghenbroeck, «Le *soft law* et la Cour européenne des droits de l'Homme. Questions de légitimité et de méthode», *Les sources du droit revisitées,* t. 1, *Normes internationales et constitutionnelles,* sous la dir. de I. Hachez et *al.*, Anthémis-Université Saint-Louis- Bruxelles, 2012, p. 413.
23   Cour eur. D.H., arrêt *Tanase c. Moldova* du 27 avril 2010, § 176.

ainsi décrite investit la Cour d'une grande liberté. Cette liberté va cependant de paire avec une importante responsabilité. Le juge international qui se borne à appliquer les normes de son instrument-source n'a pas à justifier le *pourquoi* de cette application ; le caractère intrinsèquement obligatoire de ces normes tient lieu de justification suffisante. Cette dispense de justification n'est par contre plus systématiquement acceptable dans le champ heuristique nettement plus vaste où se meuvent aujourd'hui les interprétations strasbourgeoises.

II. LES AVIS DU CONSEIL D'ÉTAT ET LA PROCÉDURALISATION DES DROITS SUBSTANTIELS GARANTIS PAR LA CONVENTION EUROPÉENNE DES DROITS DE L'HOMME

Une attention doctrinale massive a été consacrée, depuis quelques années, au phénomène dit de «procéduralisation» des droits substantiels garantis par la Convention européenne des droits de l'Homme.[24]

Cette procéduralisation est protéiforme, et, de ce fait même, particulièrement périlleuse à définir d'un seul trait. En toute grosse approximation, on dira qu'elle consiste à tirer d'entre les lignes des dispositions conventionnelles garantissant des droits substantiels, une série d'impératifs procéduraux dont le respect conditionne la licéité des restrictions aux droits qu'elles consacrent ou des abstentions qui, sous leur visa, sont reprochées à l'État. Dans la perspective du mouvement procédural, c'est moins le fond des décisions qui importe, que la manière dont on a décidé, ou permis que la décision soit contestée *ex post*.

L'une des multiples manifestations de ce mouvement de procéduralisation consiste en l'examen, par la Cour européenne des droits de l'Homme, de la

---

[24] Voy. e. a., parmi les travaux les plus récents, N. Le Bonniec, *La procéduralisation des droits substantiels par la Cour européenne des droits de l'Homme. Réflexions sur le contrôle juridictionnel des droits garantis par la Convention européenne des droits de l'Homme*, Bruxelles, Larcier, 2017 ; E. Brems et J. Gerards (dir.), *Procedural Review in European Fundamental Rights Cases*, Cambridge University Press, 2017 ; O.M. Arnardóttir, «The «procedural turn» under the European Convention on Human Rights and presumptions of Convention compliance», *International Journal of Constitutional Law*, 2017, p. 9-35 ; P. Popelier et C. van de Heyning, «Subsidiarity Post-Brighton : Procedural Rationality as Answer ?», *Leiden Journal of International Law* 2017, p. 5-23 ; L.M. Huijbers et J.H. Gerards, «Procedurele toetsing», in : R. Ortlep e.a. (red.), *De rechter onder vuur*, Oisterwijk, Wolf Legal Publishers, 2016, p. 191-122 ; L.M. Huijbers, «The European Court of Human Rights' procedural approach in the age of subsidiarity», *Cambridge International Law Journal* (6) 2017, pp. 177-2011 ; M. Saul, «The European Court of Human Rights' Margin of Appreciation and the Processes of National Parliaments», (2015) *Human Rights Law Review*, 745-774.

qualité du processus parlementaire qui a conduit à l'adoption de telle ou telle législation qui, en son principe même ou dans son application concrète, se trouve querellée devant elle.[25]

Un exemple remarquable de cette déclinaison «parlementaire» du mouvement procédural est fourni par l'arrêt *Hirst (n°2) c. Le Royaume-Uni*, à propos de la suspension automatique du droit de vote des personnes détenues suite à une condamnation pénale. En soutien de la condamnation finalement intervenue sous le visa de l'article 3 du premier protocole additionnel, la Cour énonça en effet que :

> «rien ne montre que le Parlement ait jamais cherché à peser les divers intérêts en présence ou à apprécier la proportionnalité d'une interdiction totale de voter visant les détenus condamnés. La question a certes été examinée par la conférence multipartite de députés qui s'est tenue en 1968 sur la loi électorale et qui a recommandé à l'unanimité de ne pas autoriser un détenu condamné à voter. Il est également vrai que le groupe de travail qui a préconisé d'amender la loi pour permettre aux détenus non condamnés de voter a pris note de l'avis exprimé par les gouvernements successifs selon lequel les détenus condamnés avaient perdu l'autorité morale nécessaire pour voter, et n'a donc pas recommandé de modification de la législation pour ces derniers. Peut-être peut-on considérer qu'en se prononçant comme il l'a fait, c'est-à-dire en exemptant les détenus non condamnés de la restriction au droit de vote, le Parlement a implicitement reconnu la nécessité de maintenir cette restriction pour les détenus condamnés. Cependant, on ne saurait dire que les députés ont tenu un débat de fond sur le point de savoir s'il se justifiait toujours, à la lumière de la politique pénale moderne et des normes en vigueur en matière de droits de l'homme, d'appliquer une telle restriction générale au droit de vote des détenus».[26]

Le *dictum* s'était attiré une virulente critique de la part des juges Wildhaber, Costa, Jebens, Kovler et Lorenzen. A leur estime en effet, «ce n'est pas à la Cour qu'il appartient de dire au législateur national comment il doit faire son travail».[27]

---

[25] Voy. p. ex. Cour eur. D.H., arrêt *Bayev et autres c. Russie* du 20 juin 2017, § 63 «la Cour rappelle que, pour déterminer la proportionnalité d'une mesure générale, elle doit commencer par étudier les choix législatifs à l'origine de cette mesure, en tenant compte de la qualité de l'examen parlementaire et judiciaire de la nécessité de cette mesure ainsi que du risque d'abus que peut emporter l'assouplissement d'une mesure générale». Voy. aussi Cour eur. D.H., arrêt *A.-M V. c. Finlande* du 23 mars 2017, § 82 ; Cour eur. D.H., arrêt *Orlovskaya Iskra c. Russie* du 21 février 2017, § 126.

[26] Cour eur. D.H. (GC), arrêt *Hirst c. Royaume-Uni (n° 2)* du 6 octobre 2005, § 79.

[27] Opinion dissidente commune jointe à l'arrêt *Hirst c. Royaume-Uni (n° 2)* par les juges des juges Wildhaber, Costa, Jebens, Kovler et Lorenzen. Voy. aussi E. Dubout, «La procéduralisation des droits», *Le principe de subsidiarité au sens du droit de la Convention européenne des droits de l'Homme*, sous la dir. de F. Sudre, Anthemis, Louvain-La-Neuve, 2014, p. 297.

Dans l'arrêt *Animal Defenders International c. Royaume-Uni*, sur lequel il sera revenu dans une autre contribution des présents *Mélanges*[28], la Cour affirma qu'elle attachait un «poids considérable aux contrôles exigeants et pertinents auxquels les organes parlementaires et judiciaires ont soumis le régime réglementaire complexe encadrant la diffusion à la radio et/ou à la télévision de messages politiques au Royaume-Uni (…)».[29] Entre autres considérations, l'arrêt souligne ce qui suit :

«Alors que l'interdiction fait partie intégrante du paysage de la télédiffusion au Royaume-Uni depuis les années 1950, la Commission Neill en a expressément réexaminé et confirmé la nécessité dans son rapport de 1998. Un Livre blanc maintenant cette interdiction fut donc publié (…). A tous les stades ultérieurs de l'examen prélégislatif, l'impact de cet arrêt sur la compatibilité de l'interdiction avec la Convention a été examiné de manière approfondie. En 2002, à l'issue de la consultation sur le Livre blanc, un projet de loi a été publié avec une note explicative détaillée étudiant les implications de l'arrêt *VgT*. Tous les organes spécialisés consultés ultérieurement sur ce projet de loi (la Commission mixte des droits de l'homme, la Commission mixte sur le projet de loi, la Commission indépendante sur la télévision et la Commission électorale) se sont (…), déclarés favorables au maintien de l'interdiction et ont estimé que, même analysée à la lumière de l'arrêt *VgT*, celle-ci représentait une mesure générale proportionnée. Le Gouvernement, par l'intermédiaire du DCMS, a joué un rôle important dans ce débat, expliquant fréquemment et en détail les raisons qui justifiaient de maintenir l'interdiction et de la considérer comme proportionnée, allant même jusqu'à rendre public l'avis juridique qu'il avait sollicité sur la question (…). La loi de 2003, qui reprenait l'interdiction, a ensuite été adoptée sans aucune voix contre. Le maintien de l'interdiction est donc l'aboutissement d'un examen exceptionnel, effectué par les organes parlementaires, de tous les aspects culturels, politiques et juridiques de cette mesure, qui s'inscrivait dans le cadre plus large de la réglementation de la liberté d'expression sur des sujets d'intérêt public à la radio et à la télévision au Royaume-Uni. Au cours de cet examen, tous les organes consultés ont estimé que l'interdiction litigieuse constituait une restriction nécessaire des droits garantis par l'article 10».[30]

Un autre exemple significatif[31] – et qui donna pour sa part lieu à un peu moins de controverses au sein de la Cour –, est fourni par l'arrêt *Parrillo c. Italie* rendu

---

[28] Voy. en effet la contribution du Professeur Patricia Popelier.
[29] Cour eur. D.H. (GC), arrêt *Animal Defenders International c. Royaume-Uni* du 22 avril 2013, § 116.
[30] *Ibid.*, § 114.
[31] Voy. encore, e. a., outre les références citées ponctuellement ci-après, Cour eur. D.H., arrêt *S.H c. Autriche* du 3 novembre 2011, § 117-118 ; Cour eur. D.H., arrêt *Satakunnan Markikinaporssi Oy et Satamedia Oy c. Finlande* du 27 juin 2017, §§ 192-193 ; Cour eur. D.H., arrêt *James et autres c. Royaume-Uni* du 21 février 1986, § 48 ; Cour eur. D.H., arrêt *Evans c. Royaume-Uni* du 10 avril 2007, § 86 ; Cour eur. D.H., arrêt *Shindler c. Royaume-Uni* du 7 mai 2013, § 117, Cour eur. D.H., arrêt *Dickson c. Royaume-Uni* du 4 décembre 2007, §§ 78 à 84 ; Cour eur. D.H., arrêt *Alajos Kiss c. Royaume-Uni*, du 20 mai 2010, § 41 ; Cour eur. D.H., arrêt *Maurice c. France* du 6 octobre 2005, § 121.

en Grande Chambre le 27 août 2015.[32] La question qui se posait en l'espèce était celle de la compatibilité avec l'article 8 de la Convention (droit au respect de la vie privée) de l'interdiction légale faite à la requérante de faire don, à des fins de recherche scientifique, de ses embryons issus d'une fécondation *in vitro*. La Cour répondit en l'occurrence de manière affirmative. En soutien de cette conclusion, elle fit valoir que

> «lors du processus d'élaboration de la loi litigieuse, le législateur avait déjà tenu
> compte des différents intérêts ici en cause, notamment celui de l'État à protéger
> l'embryon et celui des personnes concernées à exercer leur droit à l'autodétermination
> individuelle sous la forme d'un don de leurs embryons à la recherche».[33]

L'argument était lui-même étayé, entre autres, par le constat que le débat parlementaire dont était issu l'interdiction litigieuse, avait été «enrichi par les contributions de médecins, spécialistes et associations engagées dans le domaine de la procréation médicalement assistée et que les discussions les plus vives ont porté en général sur la sphère des libertés individuelles, opposant les partisans d'une conception laïque de l'État aux tenants d'une approche confessionnelle de celui-ci».[34]

Que tirer de ces premiers exemples ? On ne discutera pas ici des mérites et démérites des conclusions de fond *in fine* atteintes dans les trois affaires précitées, ainsi que dans celles qui, au registre de la procéduralisation, leur sont comparables. Notre accent portera uniquement sur la pertinence même de la démarche qui consiste, pour la Cour, à s'intéresser à la «qualité» du débat parlementaire dont les *outputs* sont querellés devant elle. Il convient sur ce terrain de distinguer soigneusement les questions.

A notre estime, et sur un plan tout à fait fondamental, cet examen par la Cour n'a rien d'illégitime ; c'est tout au contraire son absence qui serait absurde.

On peut ici rappeler une évidence, mise en lumière par le juge S.K Martens en marge du vieil arrêt *Markt Intern Verlag GmBH et Klaus Beerman*[35] : il n'y a

---

32   Cour eur. D.H. (GC°, arrêt *Parillo c. Italie* du 27 août 2015 ; Cour eur. D.H., arrêt *National
      Union of Rail, Maritime and Transport Workers (RMT) c. Royaume-Uni* du 8 avril 2014 ; Cour
      eur. D.H., arrêt *Anchugov et Gladkov c. Russie* du 4 juillet 2013, § 108-109 ; Cour eur. D.H.,
      arrêt *Dubska et Krejzova c. République Tchèque* du 11 décembre 2014.
33   *Ibid.*, § 188.
34   *Ibid.*, § 185.
35   Opinion dissidente de M. le Juge Martens, approuvée par M. le juge Macdonald, jointe
      à Cour eur. D.H., arrêt *Markt Intern Verlag GmBH et Klaus Beermann c. Allemagne* du
      20 novembre 1989 : «Il découle à mes yeux de ces considérations que la Cour aurait dû
      estimer qu'en l'espèce elle avait à juger une affaire dans laquelle l'appréciation des autorités
      nationales était atteinte d'un vice fondamental, et que par là elle aurait elle-même à apprécier
      si l'ingérence était nécessaire dans une société démocratique. En effet, dans une telle situation

pas lieu de réserver une marge d'appréciation aux autorités nationales lorsqu'il apparaît que, dans le processus décisionnel qu'elles ont suivi, elles n'ont en réalité pas fourni le moindre exercice d'appréciation sur la question en litige, ou qu'elles se sont livrées à son propos à une appréciation fondamentalement viciée et/ou lacunaire, par exemple en estimant à tort que le droit ou la liberté dont la restriction était en jeu, n'était pas applicable. Affirmer que les autorités nationales sont «mieux placées» que la Cour pour répondre à une question qu'elles ne se sont pas posée, ou qu'elles se sont mal posée, est un non-sens total. Le véritable respect de la légitimité du débat parlementaire et de celles et ceux qui y prennent part, impliquerait tout au contraire que, par une condamnation, la Cour incite à la tenue d'un nouveau débat parlementaire, cette fois-ci autour des bonnes questions, quitte à voir celui-ci déboucher sur une autre issue que celle du débat manqué, bâclé ou biaisé qui a eu lieu à l'origine.

La question n'est donc pas celle de la légitimité de principe de cette prise en compte de la qualité du débat parlementaire, mais bien celle de l'identification des paramètres qui la guideront et de la sévérité du contrôle juridictionnel qui la mettra en œuvre : y a-t-il en effet une manière «check-list», précise, transparente et uniformément applicable, des conditions de possibilité d'un débat parlementaire «de qualité», mené «en profondeur», pour paraphraser le *dictum* de l'arrêt *Hirst (n°2)* ? Ici survient la difficulté, sous-jacente à l'opinion dissidente précitée des juges Wildhaber, Costa, Jebens, Kovler et Lorenzen, et remarquablement analysée par plusieurs contributions du récent ouvrage *Procedural Review in European Fundamental Rights Cases*[36] dirigé par Eva Brems et Janneke Gerards.

Selon nous, la condition de possibilité minimale d'un débat de qualité est – dans la ligne de ce que nous écrivions ci-dessus – que toutes les questions «conventionnelles» que soulève la problématique aient été mises sur le tapis parlementaire à un moment ou à un autre, et de préférence à l'entame de celui-ci.

C'est en ce sens que l'on peut comprendre la recommandation formulée par le Comité Directeur des droits de l'Homme (ci-après CDDH) dans son *Rapport sur l'avenir à plus long terme du système de la Convention européenne des droits de l'Homme* du 11 décembre 2015[37] :

---

la marge d'appréciation ne joue aucun rôle, parce qu'elle ne saurait justifier des appréciations incompatibles avec les libertés garanties par la Convention».

[36]   J. Gerards et E. Brems (dir), *Procedural Review in European Fundamental Rights Cases*, Cambridge University Press, 2017. Voy. surtout les contributions de J. Gerards (p. 131), E Brems (pp. 35-37) et A. Nussberger (p. 169). Voy. eg. A. Kavannagh, «Proportionality and Parliamentary Debates : Exploring Some Forbidden Territory», *Oxford Journal of Legal Studies*, Volume 34, Issue 3, 2014, pp. 443-479.

[37]   CDDH (2015)R84, Addendum 1, p. 26.

«Il convient de souligner tout particulièrement l'importance du contrôle de la conformité des projets de loi aux normes de la Convention (…), même si le CDDH reconnaît qu'il s'agit là d'une responsabilité partagée au niveau national entre les instances gouvernementales et les parlements. Les instances gouvernementales devraient vérifier de manière systématique la compatibilité des projets de loi avec les normes de la Convention à un stade précoce de leur élaboration, y compris au moyen de consultations, si nécessaire, avant qu'une politique ne soit inscrite dans le marbre. La pratique consistant à expliquer dans l'exposé des motifs d'un projet de loi pourquoi celui-ci est jugé compatible avec les obligations découlant des normes relatives aux droits de l'homme s'est révélée très utile à la tenue d'un débat parlementaire éclairé. Il convient également d'encourager un examen attentif des normes de la Convention à la lumière de la jurisprudence de la Cour, qui accorde une importance considérable à la qualité du processus législatif et à une motivation des choix politiques s'appuyant sur l'examen des questions en jeu sous l'angle des principes de la Convention».

Dans cette démarche de «mise à plat» de l'ensemble des questions de conventionnalité soulevées par la législation en devenir, les Conseils d'État nationaux peuvent évidemment jouer un rôle de premier plan. En effet, et quoiqu'il soient intrinsèquement non contraignants, leurs conclusions, questions et avertissements appellent minimalement un positionnement explicite de la part du Gouvernement et du Parlement, positionnement explicite en l'absence duquel le débat parlementaire pourrait *ex post* être qualifié de «superficiel» par la Cour européenne des droits de l'Homme. *Comply or explain,* dirait-on dans le registre de la gouvernance d'entreprises. Le Conseil d'État inventoriera, par exemple, l'ensemble des intérêts conventionnellement protégés, soulignera la nécessité de ménager un juste équilibre entre ceux-ci, ou encore, dans le registre le plus orthodoxe de l'exigence de proportionnalité[38], invitera le législateur à rechercher des alternatives moins restrictives aux mesures qu'il envisage *hic et nunc.* Ce faisant, il contribuera, sous un angle procédural, à la tenue d'un «débat de qualité».

Une contribution de ce type peut être aperçue dans les avis n⁰ˢ 59.484/3 et 59.485/3 donnés le 29 juin 2016 par le Conseil d'État de Belgique à propos de propositions de décret visant à interdire, de manière pure et simple, l'abattage d'animaux sans étourdissement préalable.[39] A l'estime de la Rue de la Science, pareille interdiction absolue méconnaissait notamment l'article 9

---

[38] Pour une discussion relative à la question de savoir si, et avec quelle intensité, le choix de l'alternative la moins restrictive est inclus dans l'exigence de proportionnalité, on consultera l'opinion concordante jointe par le dédicataire des présents mélanges à l'arrêt *Gulbahar Ozer et Yusuf Ozer c. Turquie* du 29 mai 2018. Voy. ég. L. Larvrysen, «On sledgehammers and nutcrackers : recent developments in the Court's less restrictive means doctrine», publié sur https://strasbourgobservers.com.

[39] *Doc. Vl.* Parlement, 2014-2015, n°111/2. Sur la problématique de l'abattage rituel, voy., dans le présent ouvrage, la contribution de MM. Sottiaux et Van der Schyff.

de la Convention européenne des droits de l'Homme, faute de réaliser le juste équilibre des intérêts en présence. Les avis ajoutent cependant, dans une visée « thérapeutique », que des mesures alternatives sont concevables qui, tout en poursuivant l'objectif de réalisation du bien-être animal, représenteraient une limitation admissible à la liberté de religion du fait qu'elles n'iraient pas jusqu'à impliquer l'interdiction totale d'abattage sans étourdissement. Et le Conseil d'État d'ajouter que pareilles mesures (traduction libre)

> « gagnent à être élaborées dans le dialogue, lequel suppose lui-même que chacune des deux parties se montre ouverte aux alternatives. Dans cette optique, l'audition qui a été organisée sur ce point par le Parlement flamand est une première étape, mais des démarches supplémentaires semblent être envisageables. Il appartiendra ultimement au législateur décrétal de déterminer un équilibre entre, d'une part, le respect dû à la liberté de religion et, d'autre part, l'objectif de réduction de la souffrance animale, et ce, compte dûment tenu de la protection conventionnelle et constitutionnelle des droits fondamentaux ». [40]

Côté strasbourgeois, l'arrêt *Garib c. Pays-Bas*[41] illustre de manière assez significative la reconnaissance du rôle que les avis d'un Conseil d'État peuvent avoir dans l'approfondissement du débat parlementaire. [42]

Le droit de choisir librement sa résidence garanti par l'article 2 du Protocole n°4 additionnel à la Convention peut, en vertu du quatrième paragraphe de cette disposition, « dans certaines zones déterminées, faire l'objet de restrictions qui, prévues par la loi, sont justifiées par l'intérêt public dans une société démocratique ».

L'affaire *Garib c. Pays-Bas* concernait précisément un refus d'autorisation de résidence. La requérante souhaitait quitter le logement qu'elle occupait dans un quartier situé au sud de Rotterdam (Tarwewijk) pour emménager avec sa famille dans un autre immeuble, plus grand et plus adapté, situé dans le même quartier. Contrainte de solliciter une autorisation de résidence (*huisvestingsvergunning*) en vertu de dispositions nouvellement édictées en vue de favoriser la mixité

---

40 *Ibid.*, p. 16 : « Naast deze reeds in beide voorstellen van decreet vervatte maatregel zijn ook andere maatregelen denkbaar – bijvoorbeeld inzake de toegepaste slachtmethoden en de controle erop – die het dierenleed kunnen terugdringen, zonder de godsdienstvrijheid te miskennen. Dergelijke maatregelen kunnen het best worden uitgewerkt in dialoog, waarbij van beide kanten een openheid voor alternatieven vereist is. De hoorzitting die het Vlaams Parlement in dat verband heeft georganiseerd (.), is daarvoor beslist een eerste stap, maar verdere demarches lijken wel mogelijk te zijn. Uiteindelijk zal het aan de decreetgever toekomen om het evenwicht te bepalen tussen de eerbied voor de vrijheid van godsdienst enerzijds en het streven om het dierenleed terug te dringen, anderzijds, daarbij rekening houdend met de grondwettelijke en verdragsrechtelijke bescherming van de grondrechten ».

41 Cour eur. D.H. (GC), arrêt du 6 novembre 2017.

42 Voy. L. Huijbers, « Procedurele toetsing, het EHRM en rechtseenheid en diversiteit », *Ars Aequi*, 2018, pp. 77.

dans certains quartiers défavorisés (*Wet bijzondere maatregelen grootstedelijke problematiek*), la requérante n'avait pu obtenir cette autorisation. Ce refus s'inscrivait dans une politique urbaine des autorités néerlandaises visant à imposer des conditions liées aux revenus afin d'inciter des ménages percevant des revenus autres qu'issus de la sécurité sociale à s'installer dans des quartiers où la paupérisation grandissante est propice à l'installation de «ghettos».

Dans son arrêt du 6 novembre 2017, la Grande Chambre annonce d'emblée que le contrôle par elle exercé comportera un volet procédural[43] : «Il (lui) incombe», affirme-t-elle, «d'examiner attentivement les arguments dont le législateur a tenu compte pour parvenir aux solutions qu'il a retenues et de rechercher si un juste équilibre a été ménagé entre les intérêts de l'État et ceux des individus directement touchés par les solutions en question». Se livrant alors *in concreto* à l'examen annoncé, la Cour énonce entre autres que :

> «Il ressort de l'historique de la loi sur les mesures spéciales pour les agglomérations urbaines que le Conseil d'État a examiné de façon approfondie le projet de loi, que le gouvernement a répondu aux préoccupations de ce dernier (…), et que le Parlement lui-même était soucieux de limiter les effets négatifs éventuels de ce texte».[44]

En l'occurrence, le Conseil d'État des Pays-Bas, dans son avis n°W04.576/1 du 2 février 2005[45], avait attiré l'attention de l'auteur du projet sur divers points. Y figurait, entre autres, la question de la compatibilité de ce projet avec les traités relatifs aux droits de l'homme, et notamment le Pacte international relatif aux droits civils et politiques et le Protocole n° 4 à la Convention. A cet égard, le Conseil d'État soulignait la nécessité d'offrir une justification distincte pour chacune des dispositions en cause, et non un raisonnement global supposément valable pour l'une et l'autre. Par ailleurs, le Conseil d'État mettait en lumière que la distinction implicite fondée sur les revenus, caractéristique du dispositif en projet, était susceptible de conduire à des distinctions indirectes fondées sur des considérations de race, de couleur ou d'origine nationale ou ethnique.

L'exposé des motifs révisé du projet de loi[46] s'était efforcé d'apporter une réponse aux préoccupations et objections du Conseil d'État. Entre autres considérations, il avançait que les mesures en question étaient justifiées au regard de l'article 12

---

[43] § 138 de l'arrêt. L'arrêt de chambre intervenu dans l'affaire (23 février 2016) énonçait pour sa part que (§ 113) : «Pour déterminer la proportionnalité d'une mesure générale, la Cour doit commencer par étudier les choix législatifs à l'origine de la mesure. La qualité de l'examen parlementaire et judiciaire de la nécessité de la mesure réalisé au niveau national revêt une importance particulière à cet égard, y compris pour ce qui est de l'application de la marge d'appréciation pertinente».

[44] L'arrêt de Chambre (23 février 2016) ajoutait, au § 126 : «Il est naturel que, au cours du processus législatif, les projets de loi fassent l'objet de critiques».

[45] *Kamerstukken*, 2004-2005, n° 30091/5.

[46] *Kamerstukken*, 2004-2005, n° 30091/3.

§ 3 du Pacte international relatif aux droits civils et politiques et de l'article 2 § 3 du Protocole n° 4 à la Convention. Le Gouvernement reconnaissait que l'on ne pouvait *a priori* exclure que des membres de catégories minoritaires puissent pâtir indirectement du dispositif en projet[47], mais il s'était efforcé de démontrer l'objectif poursuivi était légitime, que les moyens choisis pour y parvenir étaient appropriés, qu'il n'existait pas d'alternatives moins restrictives aux mesures envisagées, et que le principe de proportionnalité était respecté.

On aperçoit ici, de manière relativement claire, comment l'intervention consultative d'un Conseil d'État peut aboutir à enrichir et à approfondir un débat législatif, et le bénéfice que l'État concerné pourra en tirer ultérieurement, lorsque la Cour européenne des droits de l'Homme exercera à son tour un contrôle de conventionalité de la législation concernée.[48] Contrôle qui, en l'occurrence, se solda par une réponse positive. Prenant en considération, sous un angle général, les garanties offertes par le dispositif néerlandais (exigence d'une offre de logement suffisante pour les personnes ne réunissant pas les conditions donnant droit à une autorisation de résidence ; limitation du dispositif à certains quartiers et pour un certain temps ; obligation pour le ministre compétent de rendre compte au Parlement de l'efficacité des mesures adoptées ; possibilité de solliciter une dérogation en cas d' «iniquité majeure » ; possibilité de solliciter un contrôle juridictionnel d'un refus d'autorisation), la Cour a tout d'abord considéré qu'«elle ne saurait conclure que les décisions de politique publique prises par les autorités nationales n'ont pas correctement pris en compte les droits et intérêts des personnes se trouvant dans la situation de la requérante ».[49] S'attachant ensuite à la situation personnelle de la requérante, la Cour a estimé, en substance, que la requérante n'avait pas fourni suffisamment d'éléments permettant de considérer que son intérêt particulier devait, en l'occurrence, primer sur l'intérêt général. Ainsi, «une préférence individuelle non définie pour laquelle aucune justification n'est avancée ne saurait l'emporter sur une décision des autorités publiques, car cela aurait pour effet de réduire à néant la marge d'appréciation de l'Etat ».[50] Or, celle-ci est, depuis l'arrêt *James c. Royaume-Uni*[51], traditionnellement étendue quant à la conduite de politiques publiques.

---

[47] *Ibid.* : « Indirect onderscheid op een van de voornoemde gronden kan echter niet op voorhand volledig worden uitgesloten ».

[48] Contrôle de conventionnalité qui, en l'espèce, ne trouva pas à s'exercer au regard du principe d'égalité (§§ 95 à 102), ce qui est fort regrettable.

[49] *Ibid.*, § 156.

[50] *Ibid.*, § 166.

[51] Cour eur. D.H., arrêt *James et autres c. Royaume-Uni* du 21 février 1986.

Le verdict de l'arrêt *Garib c. Pays-Bas* a fait l'objet de nombreuses critiques, au sein de la Cour[52] et à l'extérieur de celle-ci.[53] Tant par leur existence que par leur contenu, ces critiques rappellent une vérité essentielle : la qualité du processus décisionnel suivi accroît sans doute la probabilité d'atteindre une « bonne réponse » sur le fond, mais ne l'assure cependant pas de manière nécessaire.[54] Les exigences procédurales que l'on tire d'entre les lignes des dispositions substantielles de la Convention sont un *complément, un supplément* aux exigences de fond dont elles sont naturellement porteuses, et non un *substitut* à celles-ci.[55] En mettant l'accent sur les premières, la Cour européenne des droits de l'Homme ne doit pas se montrer oublieuse des secondes, et du contrôle qu'elle a pour mission d'exercer à leur égard. Dans un arrêt ancien[56] – et trop souvent perdu de vue[57] –, cette Cour avait en substance affirmé que la prise en compte de sa propre jurisprudence par le juge national n'était pas une garantie absolue de la conventionalité des décisions de ce dernier. Ce *caveat* nous semble parfaitement pouvoir être extrapolé à l'ensemble des facettes du mouvement de procéduralisation : ce n'est pas parce que l'on parle abondamment de la Convention européenne des droits de l'Homme et de la jurisprudence de la Cour éponyme l'occasion de l'adoption d'une loi, que la conformité de cette loi aux exigences conventionnelles est, *ipso jure*, acquise. Il revient à la Cour, en dernière analyse, d'éprouver la rectitude des

---

[52] Voy. l'opinion dissidente commune aux juges Tsotsoria et De Gaetano ; l'opinion dissidente du juge Pinto de Albuquerque, à laquelle se rallie le juge Vehabović ; l'opinion dissidente du juge Kuris

[53] Voy. V. David et S. Ganty, « Strasbourg fails to protect the rights of people living in or at risk of poverty : the disappointing Grand Chamber judgment in Garib v the Netherlands », publié sur https://strasbourgobservers.com/.

[54] Voy. A. Nussberger, « Procedural Review by the ECHR : view from the Court », *Procedural Review…, op. cit.*, p. 167.

[55] Voy. F. Tulkens, « Conclusions Générales », in Sudre, Frédéric (ed.), *Le principe de la subsidiarité au sens du droit de la Convention européenne des droits de l'Homme* (Anthemis 2014), p. 406 : « le danger de la procéduralisation est que le contrôle de la Cour s'épuise dans le constat qu'il est satisfait aux impératifs procéduraux et ne comporte plus d'aspect substantiel. La procéduralisation risque alors d'être un alibi d'un contrôle sur le fond et pourrait faire le jeu de ceux qui veulent alléger la surveillance de la Cour sur les décisions étatiques. »

[56] Cour eur. D.H., arrêt *Zielinski et Pradal & Gonzales et autres c. France* du 28 octobre 1999, § 52 (arguments du gouvernement) et 59 (réponse de la Cour).

[57] Comp. en effet avec Cour eur. D.H., arrêt *Ndidi c. Royaume-Uni* du 24 septembre 2017, § 76 : « The requirement for « European supervision » does not mean that in determining whether an impugned measure struck a fair balance between the relevant interests, it is necessarily the Court's task to conduct the Article 8 proportionality assessment afresh. On the contrary, in Article 8 cases the Court has generally understood the margin of appreciation to mean that, where the independent and impartial domestic courts have carefully examined the facts, applying the relevant human rights standards consistently with the Convention and its case-law, and adequately balanced the applicant's personal interests against the more general public interest in the case, it is not for it to substitute its own assessment of the merits (including, in particular, its own assessment of the factual details of proportionality) for that of the competent national authorities. The only exception to this is where there are shown to be strong reasons for doing so (…) ».

choix posés. S'agissant spécifiquement des processus de décision législative, l'hypertrophie de la démarche procédurale et l'excessive attention portée à la qualité et à la profondeur du débat parlementaire présentent de surcroît deux risques spécifiques, distincts mais étroitement liés : le déploiement d'un contrôle purement abstrait indifférent aux injustices criantes que provoque l'application des lois concernées au cas individuel – tel est l'un des reproches majeurs que l'on peut adresser à l'arrêt *Garib* –, et l'oubli, par la Cour, de la logique « contre-majoritaire » des droits conventionnels et de son propre rôle de rempart des minorités vulnérables face aux majorités démocratiques.[58] S'exprimant en marge de l'arrêt *Belcacemi et Oussar*[59], les juges Spano et Karakas énoncent à raison que « l'histoire a amplement démontré que les sociétés démocratiques portent en elles le risque que des sentiments majoritaristes, qui se traduisent par la suite en textes législatifs, germent sur le terreau d'idées et de valeurs qui menacent les droits fondamentaux. Les catégories isolées et vulnérables n'ont alors plus que le recours de s'adresser aux tribunaux. Et ces tribunaux, qu'ils soient nationaux ou internationaux, à l'instar de la Cour, ont le devoir de rechercher et de détecter, dans la mesure du possible, si l'imposition de mesures qui ont pourtant été largement entérinées par la sphère législative est motivée par une hostilité ou une intolérance à l'égard d'une idée, d'une opinion, ou d'une confession religieuse en particulier ».

L'approche procédurale doit donc être cantonnée à une juste mesure. L'évocation de l'affaire *Belcacemi* et *Oussar* nous permet par ailleurs de mettre en exergue un second écueil de cette approche, et, par là-même, un second point d'attention à l'intention de la Cour : l'insuffisante transparence, les géométries variables inexpliquées[60] qui, une fois encore, génèrent le soupçon d'un *cherry picking*.

Dans l'arrêt précité, la Cour devait en effet se prononcer sur la compatibilité, avec l'article 9 de la Convention, lu isolément ou en combinaison avec l'article 14 du même instrument, de la loi belge du 1er juin 2011 'interdisant le port de tout vêtement cachant totalement ou de manière principale le visage'. L'arrêt, daté du 11 juillet 2017, résolut cette question de manière affirmative. A l'appui de cette conclusion, il fit valoir, entre autres considérations, que « le processus décisionnel ayant débouché sur l'interdiction en cause a duré plusieurs années et a été marqué par un large débat au sein de la Chambre des représentants ainsi que par un examen circonstancié et complet de l'ensemble des intérêts en jeu par la Cour constitutionnelle ».[61] L'affirmation, que l'on

---

[58]   Voy. A. Nussberger, « Procedural… », *op. cit.*, p. 167.

[59]   Cour eur. D.H., arrêt *Belcacemi et Oussar c. Belgique* du 11 juillet 2017.

[60]   Voy. ég. l'opinion dissidente du juge Pinto de Albuquerque, auquel se joint le juge Sajo, en marge de l'arrêt *Correia de Matos c. Portugal* du 4 avril 2018, pts 37 et suiv.

[61]   *Ibid.*, § 54.

retrouve également – à titre d'*obiter dictum* cette fois-ci – dans l'arrêt *Dakir c. La Belgique,* laisse relativement songeur.[62] Ainsi que le fit observer le Centre des droits de l'Homme de l'Université de Gand, tiers-intervenant en l'affaire *Dakir*[63], le processus d'adoption de la loi précitée du 1er juin 2011, tout «long» qu'il ait été, ne fut pas vraiment caractérisé par sa profondeur et le souci de ses protagonistes de documenter leur dossier, en fait et en droit...[64] Les demandes d'audition des représentants du milieu associatif, très critique à l'égard de la loi en devenir, furent systématiquement repoussées.[65] Les députés ne jugèrent pas non plus utile d'entendre les femmes portant un voile intégral. *Last but not least,* la Chambre des représentants refusa à plusieurs reprises de consulter, pour avis, la Section de législation du Conseil d'État. Un député, le plus sérieusement du monde, justifia ce refus en affirmant qu'il ne «souhait(ait) en aucun cas s'engager dans un débat qui consiste à vérifier si l'interdiction du port de la *burqa* ou d'autres vêtements du genre viole le droit international ou le droit européen, auquel cas ceux qui sont en faveur de la *burqa* pourraient gagner ce combat». «Ce débat», ajoutait-il, «serait, de surcroît, superflu, eu égard à la jurisprudence et la doctrine relatives à cette matière».[66] Quelle jurisprudence ? Les avis du Conseil d'État des Pays-Bas, qui, rappelons-le, affirmaient l'inadmissibilité d'une interdiction du port du voile intégral (voy. *supra*) ? Le Rapport du Conseil d'État de France qui, rappelons-le également, récusait toute pertinence à l'argument fondé sur l'égalité entre hommes et femmes pour soutenir une telle interdiction (voy. *supra*) ? On peine vraiment à qualifier pareil discussion parlementaire de «profonde», au sens au sens de l'arrêt *Hirst (n° 2)* ... La conclusion en sens contraire de la Cour, qui pourtant s'était vue mettre sous les yeux tous les éléments d'appréciation utiles de la part du Centre des droits de l'Homme de l'Université de Gand, est donc pour le moins surprenante.

* * *

Quiconque a délibéré avec Paul Lemmens, à la Rue de la Science ou au Palais des droits de l'Homme, connait son perfectionnisme, que servent une connaissance absolument sans faille des questions qu'il aborde et une grande ténacité dans la poursuite du débat d'idées. Ce fut un privilège de profiter de

---

[62] Pour rappel, le législateur et la Cour constitutionnelle belge avaient complètement fait fausse route en estimant que le principe de l'égalité entre hommes et femmes pouvait étayer l'interdiction du port du voile intégral.

[63] Le texte intégral de la note du tiers-intervenant peut être consulté à l'adresse suivante : http ://www.hrc.ugent.be/wp-content/uploads/2015/11/Dakir_hrc.pdf.

[64] Pour une analyse en profondeur des travaux parlementaires, Voy. X. Delgrange, «Quand la Burqa passe à l'Ouest, la Belgique perd-t-elle le Nord ?», *op. cit.*, pp. 200 et suiv.

[65] *Ibid.* p. 202.

[66] Voy. *Doc parl Chambre*, Doc 52 – 2289/5, p. 21 et 22.

cette connaissance et de prendre part à quelques-uns de ces débats, d'abord au cours de mes travaux doctoraux, et ensuite, durant mes premiers mois en Section de législation. Qu'il trouve dans les lignes qui précèdent l'expression de ma plus grande gratitude.

FATHER RYAN, AN IRISH ASYLUM SEEKER IN BELGIUM (1988)

Marc Bossuyt

Honorary Commissioner General for Refugees and Stateless Persons
Emeritus Professor of International Law, University of Antwerp
Emeritus President of the Constitutional Court

In 1988, the asylum request of Patrick Ryan was denied because he alleged persecution by the British Government without being a British citizen. Despite a positive opinion of the Court of Appeal of Brussels on the British extradition request, the Belgian Government decided to return him to the country of his nationality (Ireland) as was recommended in the opinion of the Commissioner General for Refugees and Stateless Persons.

Because the case of Father Patrick Ryan is now more than 30 years old, I dare to write about it, despite my strong involvement in that case, as I was at that time Commissioner General for Refugees and Stateless Persons (1987–1997). I do it in honour of my colleague and good friend Paul Lemmens, Judge at the European Court of Human Rights. I have the pleasure to know Paul since my first year (1973/1974) at the University of Antwerp where he was then a student. I know that he has always taken a keen interest in legal issues concerning refugees and asylum seekers. Rather than writing another critical review of the case law in that field of his Court, I preferred to deal with a case that was one of the most sensitive of the nearly 100,000 I had to deal with as Commissioner General. For me it shows, that – even in highly sensitive cases – a specialised and independent administrative authority does not necessarily protect asylum seekers any less than judicial bodies.

I.   THE ARREST OF PATRICK RYAN

The Irish citizen Patrick Ryan, born on 26 June 1930 in Tipperary (Ireland), was active as a catholic priest in the Irish Republic (from 1954 on) and in Great-Britain between 1965 and 1968. He then returned to the Irish Republic to collect money for African countries. In 1969, he was present in Derry as a spectator at a protest march against the British presence in Northern Ireland. He witnessed the killing by the British of a clergy man who tried to give assistance to wounded persons. That day, 12 persons were killed. From then on, Ryan acted against the British presence in Ulster by collecting money to support Irish activists. Suspected to be a member of the Provisional Irish Army and the Irish Republican Army, he went to Italy in 1976. In the 70's, he travelled to many European countries, and in particular to France and Spain, bearing his real Irish passport. For leaving from or returning to Italy, he used a false Irish passport. In 1977, he was arrested in Switzerland on the pretext of a minor motoring offence and after two weeks expelled to Madrid.

On 28 June 1988, he left by bus Benidorm for Brussels. He had bought his ticket in Brussels five months earlier during a short stay. When he was arrested on 30 June 1988 by the communal police of Uccle (Brussels Region) acting on a tip-off, he was in the possession of an Irish identity card which had expired six years before and a false British identity card under a different name. Among his belongings, the police discovered manuals for explosives, 52 watches, 5 memo parks (parking meter mechanical timers) and 14 dowels and receivers. According to Ryan, those "switches" served to count the minutes in order not to be surprised by parking meters. On 1 July 1988, an arrest warrant was delivered on the account of forgery of documents, the use of false documents and violations of the law of 28 May 1956 concerning explosives. On 6 September 1988, the examining judge delivered a provisional arrest warrant based on a communication by the British authorities that an extradition request was forthcoming. The next day Ryan applied for asylum in Belgium.

II. THE INTERFERENCES BETWEEN THE ASYLUM AND THE EXTRADITION PROCEDURES

On 15 September 1988, a new arrest warrant was delivered for conspiracy to form a gang with the aim of committing crimes. An official extradition request was notified by the Embassy of the United Kingdom on 20 October 1988:

> « A divers jours, entre le 1er février 1986 et le 1er juillet 1988, dans la juridiction de la Cour criminelle centrale pour l'Angleterre et le pays de Galles, avoir conspiré avec d'autres personnes inconnues, dans le but d'occasionner à l'aide de matières explosives des explosions de nature à mettre la vie d'autrui en danger ou à causer de sérieux dommages à des propriétés situées dans le Royaume-Uni ».

Ryan was suspected of conspiracy to murder by using explosives, having in his possession without a legitimate purpose explosive substances (switches – memo park, etc.) intended to put lives and goods in danger in the United Kingdom.

That same day, the Aliens Office decided to refuse his stay in Belgium as an asylum seeker in application of Article 52 of the Aliens Law of 15 December 1980. He was considered to be a risk for the public order and the national security, not to rely on any of the criteria which could justify an asylum application, to have stayed during more than three months in different other European countries (such as Italy, France and Spain) and to have left the latter country without any well-founded fear for persecution in the meaning of Article 1 (A) of the Geneva Convention relating to the Status of Refugees. Moreover, more than eight days had elapsed between his entry of the country and the submission of his asylum application. Finally, he had tried to misled the Belgian authorities by confused and incomplete statements in respect of his multiple activities and travels.

While detained in the prison of St-Gilles, Ryan appeared on 3 November 1988 before a Chamber of the Court of Appeal of Brussels which had to express an opinion on the extradition request. In those proceedings, Ryan referred to Article 6 of the Belgian Extradition Law of 1 October 1833 which requires Belgian treaties to stipulate that "[T]he foreigner shall not be prosecuted or punished for any political offence prior to extradition, nor for any act connected with such an offense". Belgium has uphold that principle in Article 7 of the Extradition Treaty of 29 October 1901 concluded between Belgium and the United Kingdom and in its reservation to the European Convention of 27 January 1977 on the Suppression of Terrorism. According to Ryan, the United Kingdom had requested his extradition with the sole intention to prosecute and punish him on the basis of his political, ideological, national or religious conviction. He referred also to various publications in the British press which labelled him as a dangerous terrorist. He considered that such accusations would hamper a fair trial as required by Article 6 of the European Convention on Human Rights.

III. HIS ASYLUM PROCEDURE

On 28 October 1988, Ryan had lodged to the Minister of Justice an urgent request of re-examination of the decision to refuse his stay in Belgium. Such a request required a (non-binding) opinion of the Commissioner General for Refugees and Stateless Persons, a newly established independent administrative authority. That authority replaced the Representative of the UN High Commissioner for Refugees in the examination of asylum applications submitted after 31 January 1988. In his opinion of 14 November 1988 (*Belgian Review of International Law*, 1991–1, pp. 200–202) on Ryan's request of urgent re-examination of the decision to refuse his stay in Belgium, the Commissioner General examined the various grounds invoked by the Aliens Office to justify its refusal.

Since his asylum application was not submitted later than three months after the cause for his refugee declaration (the extradition request) originated, the argument that he had stayed more than three months in one or more other countries could not validly be invoked to refuse his access to the refugee determination procedure. Neither was he too late when he submitted his asylum application the day after the extradition request was notified to him, as he could not be expected to submit it before his fear for extradition could arise. The possession of a false passport was not considered sufficient in itself to constitute a risk for the public order and the national security of Belgium. However, since the responsibility for public order and national security belongs to the competence of the Minister of Justice and the applicant was suspected to be an active member of the Irish Republican Army, the Commissioner General considered that the Minister had not gone beyond his discretionary competence in that matter.

In view of the pending extradition request and the insecurity surrounding his access to the refugee determination procedure, his confused and incomplete statements in respect of his multiple activities and travels should not necessarily be considered to be intended to mislead the Belgian authorities. Since the applicant invoked his religion, his nationality, his membership of a particular social group and his political opinion, it was not possible to conclude at this stage of the procedure that his application was manifestly foreign to the criteria mentioned in the Geneva Convention. However, he did not apply for asylum on the basis of a well-founded fear of being persecuted by the State of which he was a national (the Irish Republic) and there was *a priori* no reason to assume that his national authorities would not lend him their protection. The Commissioner General referred to the UNHCR *Handbook on procedures and criteria for determining refugee status* (1979) which states that

> "an applicant's well-founded fear of persecution must be in relation to the country of his nationality. As long as he has no fear in relation to the country of his nationality, he can be expected to avail himself of that country's protection. He is not in need of international protection and is therefore not a refugee".

For those reasons, the Commissioner General gave an unfavourable opinion as to the stay of the applicant in Belgium as an asylum seeker. But, as far as his expulsion of Belgium was concerned, the Commissioner General expressed the opinion that, since Ryan had stated to fear for persecution in the United Kingdom – on grounds of his religion, his nationality, his membership of a particular social group and his political opinion – due to his activities against the policy of that country in Northern Ireland, he should be returned to the country of which he had the nationality, namely the Irish Republic. Those authorities were considered to be in a better position than those of Belgium to evaluate whether that fear was well-founded.

IV. HIS EXTRADITION PROCEDURE

The Chamber of the Court of Appeals of Brussels expressed to the Minister of Justice on 17 November 1988 a positive opinion in respect of the British extradition request. The Chamber considered that the facts referred to by the British Government could amount to the formation of a gang to commit crimes as provided for in the Articles 323 and 324 of the Criminal Code. Such a crime is also envisaged in Article 1, 1°, of the Extradition Treaty of 29 October 1901 concluded between Belgium and the United Kingdom. The Chamber considered that, while this formation of a gang took place outside the territory of the United Kingdom, the criminal organisation exteriorised activities on British territory. Since Ryan did participate in activities of such a criminal organisation and one of the constitutive elements of that crime took place in the United Kingdom, the whole crime was supposed to have taken place on British territory.

Referring to Article 6 of the Extradition Law of 1 October 1874, the Chamber did not consider that the United Kingdom had requested the extradition of Ryan solely with the intention to prosecute and punish him on the basis of his political, ideological, national and religious opinions. It did not consider the facts as constituting a political crime because

«l'exposé des faits ainsi qu'à la lumière de la qualification pénale retenue, ne relève pas d'un crime ou délit qui par leur nature possèdent nécessairement la qualité d'infraction politique, en raison de la circonstance qu'ils visent par définition les institutions ou l'ordre politique et ce en excluant l'atteinte à d'autres intérêts particuliers ou privés».

According to the Chamber, it was neither a "fact connected with a political crime". That Ryan had political motives to commit those facts does not qualify them as a "mixed political crime", because they did not constitute a direct attack on the British political institutions or the public order in Great Britain.

The Chamber also referred to the European Convention on the Suppression of Terrorism which considers that a number of offences shall not be regarded as a political offence, as an offence connected with a political offence or as an offence inspired by political motives. In conformity with Article 13 of that Convention, Belgium, however, had reserved the right to refuse extradition in respect of any offence mentioned in Article 1 which it considers to be a political offence, an offence connected with a political offence or an offence inspired by political motives, provided that it undertakes to take into due consideration, when evaluating the character of the offence, any particularly serious aspects of the offence. The facts imputed to Ryan are envisaged in Article 1, (e) and (f), of the Convention on which the reservation is applicable:

"(e) an offence involving the use of a bomb, grenade, rocket, automatic firearm or letter or parcel bomb if this use endangers persons;

(f) an attempt to commit any of the foregoing offences or participation as an accomplice of a person who commits or attempts to commit such an offence".

However, according to Article 13 of that Convention, the reservation may not be applied when that offence

(a) "created a collective danger to the life, physical integrity or liberty of persons"; or

(b) "affected persons foreign to the motives behind it"; or

(c) when "cruel or vicious means have been used in the commission of the offence".

In view of the foregoing, the Chamber concluded that:

« Attendu qu'il n'apparaît pas à la cour, chambre des mises en accusation, dans le cas d'espèce et dans les limites de sa mission, qu'en raison des dispositions de cette Convention et des réserves exprimées par la Belgique, que l'extradition ne pourrait être accordée ».

The Chamber considered that possessing electrical material destined to commit an attack was an offence of a particularly serious character. The Chamber did not consider that Ryan's position would be unfavourably influenced in case of his extradition to the United Kingdom. Considering that all conditions prescribed by the law of 15 March 1874 and by the Extradition Treaty between Belgium and the United Kingdom were fulfilled, the Chamber expressed a positive opinion on the extradition of Ryan to the United Kingdom.

V. HIS RETURN TO IRELAND

Nevertheless, on 25 November 1988, the Minister of Justice decided not to extradite Ryan and, late that same Friday, Ryan, who was in his third week of a hunger strike, was returned by military plane to the country of his nationality (Ireland). The decision was strongly criticised in the United Kingdom:

"Why the decisions have to go the Belgian cabinet; when decisions are reached in the political forms, the reasoning is likely to be political ..." (*The Times*, 29 November 1988).

Indeed, while it was formally a decision of the Minister of Justice, M. Wathelet, the decision was taken that same day in the Council of Ministers. In his Memoirs, Prime Minister W. Martens (*De Mémoires: Luctor et emergo,* Tielt, Lannoo, 2006, p. 793) stated that the decision was taken after a "short but intense deliberation". According to the Minister of Foreign Relations, L. Tindemans

(*Een Politiek Testament: Mijn plaats in de tijd. Dagboek van een minister*, Tielt, Lannoo, 2009, p. 546), the vice-prime-ministers Ph. Moureau and H. Schiltz were the greatest opponents of the extradition. He himself favoured the extradition but he was not authorized to inform the British before the military plane landed in Ireland. When learning about the decision, the British Minister of Foreign Affairs, Sir Geoffrey Howe, abruptly put his phone down.

On early Saturday 26 November 1988, the Commissioner of the Metropolitan Police of Dublin received four extradition request concerning Ryan. The grounds on which those four requests were based were the same as in the request addressed to Belgium. There was a lot of speculation in the media that the Irish Attorney General would reject those requests by lack of sufficient proof. The *Irish Sunday* of 27 November 1988 referred even to "a Government source". Yet before the Attorney General had the opportunity to examine the file, the *Sunday Press* of the same day wrote: "AG to block British bid on Father Ryan. The indications in Dublin last night were that the Irish Attorney General will refuse the request".

In the Belgian House of Representatives on 29 November 1988, MP Jean Gol criticized the decision "not to extradite to the United Kingdom a person accused of terrorism in that country" by stating that it went contrary to the policy pursued hereto in matters of European cooperation to combat terrorism in the framework of the European legal space.

At the European Council in Rhodes during the weekend of 2 and 3 December 1988, the British Prime Minister M. Thatcher had hard words for the Belgian and Irish Governments accusing them of cowardice. This led to a debate in the Irish Parliament on 6 December 1988. Irish MP's wondered whether in such a climate Ryan could expect a fair trial in the United Kingdom when the British Prime Minister could not mention his name without labelling him as a terrorist. An Irish MP said:

> "In prevailing circumstances it is very difficult to allow people to be extradited to Britain since they still occupy part of our national territory. In those circumstances I have a difficulty in that extraditing people to the North or Britain recognizes the right of the British to be in Ireland and to impose their will and laws on our country, flouting our aspirations and the constitutional position of the State".

British MP's were also critical of Prime Minister Thatcher's statements concerning Ryan:

> "What she did was cheered to the echo by those who wish to see relations between the Irish Government and the British Government at their worst possible level because they know that that would damage the fight against terrorism".

Ms Thatcher replied that extradition between the United Kingdom and Ireland did not function properly and that this should be emphasized.

The Irish Extradition Law requiring from the Attorney General

> "to direct that a warrant for the extradition of a person from the State shall not be endorsed unless, having considered such information as he deems appropriate, he is of the opinion that there is a clear intention to prosecute that person, founded on the existence of sufficient evidence",

he found, on the separate ground of whether there was sufficient evidence to warrant a prosecution, that there was. But

> "he found it unnecessary to reach a conclusion on the other two cases because on no charge could Patrick Ryan get a fair trial".

The Attorney General based his decision on articles in the British press and on statements by British MP's and members of the British Government, including the Prime Minister. According to the Attorney General, it was not possible to apply the Irish Extradition Law in a manner that would not prejudice Ryan's constitutional rights, such as the right to a fair trial. It was considered necessary to protect him against a "creation of prejudice or animosity in the minds of potential jurors".

In her Memoirs, Ms M. Thatcher (*The Downing Street years*, New York, HarperCollins, 1993, pp. 413–414) stated that the case showed how little the British "could seriously hope for from the Irish". She could also not understand that the Belgian Government disregarded the positive opinion of the Brussels Court of Appeal and put Ryan on a military plane to Ireland:

> "Presumably this political decision was prompted by fear of terrorist retaliation [...] The [Belgian] Cabinet decided to ignore the court's opinion and to fly Ryan to Ireland, only telling us afterwards. [...] At the European Council in Rhodes, I told to the Irish Attorney General Mr Haughey and to the Belgian Prime Minister Mr Martens "how appalled I was. I was particularly angry with M. Martens. [...] I was unconvinced and unmoved by M. Martens's explanations. [...]But [...] it would take more than this to provide them with a spine. And Patrick Ryan is still at large."

In October 1989, the Director of Public Prosecutions in Ireland announced that he had decided not to initiate proceedings against Ryan. In 1989, Ryan was a candidate for the European Parliament in the Munster constituency as an independent with Sinn Fein support. He failed to be elected despite the more than 30,000 votes he obtained. In 1993, he was tried in Ireland's Special Criminal Court on charges of receiving stolen goods but was found not guilty.

CONCLUSION

Patrick Ryan had travelled all over Europe during years before he was arrested in Belgium at the request of the British authorities. His activities were to be seen in the context of the Anglo-Irish relations. As an Irish national not persecuted by the Irish Government, he was not in need of international protection, because he could rely on his national authorities for the protection of his rights. If the United Kingdom authorities would succeed in establishing solid proof of his responsibility in terrorist activities, Ireland would have no choice but extraditing him to the United Kingdom. However, the extradition request was very vague and lacked convincing proof of such activities. Nevertheless, the Belgian judicial authorities did express a favourable opinion on the British request for extradition to the United Kingdom. In the absence of persecution of Ryan by his national authorities, the Commissioner General for Refugees and Stateless Persons did not recognize him as a refugee. However, the Commissioner General did not want that his decision to reject Ryan's asylum application would be used as a basis to extradite him to the United Kingdom. That is why the Commissioner General expressed the opinion that Ryan should be sent to Ireland rather than to the United Kingdom. This suggestion was the basis for the decision of the Council of Minister, after a heated debate, to expel him to Ireland. By arresting him, Belgium had cooperated with the British authorities in fighting terrorism. However, to take the decision to extradite him or not to the United Kingdom, the Irish authorities were in a better position than the Belgian. The Belgian decision was not motivated by fear of terrorist retaliation but by a fair repartition between the responsibilities of their own and those of the country of Ryan's nationality in full respect of its international obligations as well towards the United Kingdom as towards the individual rights of the person concerned.

TO PAUL FROM KOEN: THE RIGHT TO A NAME AND THE EUROPEAN CONVENTION ON HUMAN RIGHTS

Koen LEMMENS

Associate Professor of Human Rights law, KU Leuven

> *"Mijn moeder is mijn naam vergeten.*
> *Mijn kind weet nog niet hoe ik heet.*
> *Hoe moet ik mij geborgen weten?*
>
> *Noem mij, bevestig mijn bestaan,*
> *Laat mijn naam zijn als een keten.*
> *Noem mij, noem mij, spreek mij aan,*
> *o, noem mij bij mijn diepste naam.*
>
> *Voor wie ik liefheb, wil ik heten."*
> Neeltje Maria Min

INTRODUCTION

When I had the pleasure back in 2010 to join Leuven University to teach human rights, Paul Lemmens was the head of the human rights department. Obviously, colleagues were gently making fun of the two professors Lemmens and students were keen on ironically insinuating nepotism. Paul and I, however, are no relatives and we did not even find the remotest indication of family ties. It doesn't matter: ever since, the running gag in the Law Faculty is that we are the "Lemmens Institute".[1] In Leuven, that is the name of a famous school of music, founded in 1879. Its first director was Jacques-Nicolas Lemmens, an organist and music pedagogue. The school was later renamed after its first director.[2]

---

[1]   Former dean Professor Van Orshoven was probably the first to have launched it.
[2]   http://www.luca-arts.be/historiek-0 and https://nl.wikipedia.org/wiki/Jacques-Nicolas_Lemmens (both accessed on 14 November 2018). Today, it is known as "Leuven School of Arts – Campus Lemmens". I was surprised to find out that there is hardly any literature on Jacques Nicolas

Paul Lemmens has not been working extensively on the impact of human rights in traditional private law issues[3] and I am not an expert either. Yet, this *Festschrift* offers the perfect occasion, not only to stress that we are indeed not relatives, but first and foremost to analyse how the European Convention on Human Rights deals with questions related to something both as trivial and fundamental as a name. Admittedly, there are more urgent human rights problems. Nevertheless, it is worth exploring the topic, since it illustrates human rights issues of a new kind. Where in the past human rights, in their vertical dimension, were used to protect individuals against arbitrary interference by public authorities and later, through the mechanism of *Drittwirkung*, against fellow citizens, a new kind of conflicts can be underscored. Although I have not yet a comprehensive understanding of what is really happening[4], I am struck by a new kind of cases in which not so much the behaviour of fellow citizens is questioned, nor the all too intrusive or arbitrary interventions of public authorities, but where human rights are used against social and cultural norms, irrespective of them being mere social rules or incorporated in legislation.

One such an example are the rules on names. Obviously, there is a very technical part of the rules on names, which has little or even nothing to do with the social context as such. However, the underlying choices (patrilineal or matrilineal name giving) do clearly reflect social and cultural choices.[5] Moreover, in countries such as Belgium, there was until recently very little legislation on the topic. Verschelden states that the very basis of the applicable rules dates back to the French Revolution and that the issue was further regulated by customary rules[6] and case-law.[7] The link with social practices is therefore undeniable.

In this contribution, I first want to start with some reflections on the significance of a name for an individual, seen from a legal perspective, with a focus on Belgian law. Here, human rights and family law interact. Then, I will move on to an analysis of the ECtHR's case-law in the field. Finally, I will turn back

---

Lemmens (or, in the Flemish version: Jaak Nikolaas Lemmens) available in the KU Leuven library catalogue. A master paper has been written on his work: H. Helsen, *Jaak Nikolaas Lemmens (1823-1881) en de kerkmuzikale hervorming in België*, master paper KU Leuven (Faculty of Arts), 2000.

3   However, see the PhD he supervised: N. Van Leuven, *Contracten en mensenrechten. Een mensenrechtelijke lezing van het contractenrecht*, Antwerpen, Intersentia, 2009 (commercial edition).

4   For philosophers such as Jean-Claude Michéa, this phenomenon would be probably be an illustration of the "atomisation du monde", as F. Engels put it. J.-Cl. Michéa, *Le loup dans la bergerie*, Climats, *s.l.*, 2018, p. 35.

5   P. Malaurie and L. Aynès, *Droit des personnes*, Issy-les-Moulineaux, LGDJ, 2017, p. 53; W. Pintens, *Naam* in *Algemene Practische Rechtsverzameling*, Gent, E. Story-Scientia, 1981, p. 3.

6   J. Carbonnier stresses that the "customary rule" was rooted in a patriarchal conception of the family. Quoted in: W. Pintens, *Naam* in *Algemeen Practische rechtsverzameling*, Gent, E. Story-Scientia, 1981, p. 20.

7   G. Verschelden, *Handboek Belgisch Personen- en Familierecht*, Brugge, die Keure, 2016, p. 160.

to Belgian law and assess to what extent the new legislation is in line with the Strasbourg case-law. The subject matter is vast, I will therefore concentrate on the issue of the attribution of the surname, in cases were both maternal and paternal affiliation is established.[8]

I.   WHAT'S IN A NAME?

In the simplest words, the Belgian jurist Dekkers described the name as the "word that identifies a person in order to distinguish him from all other people in society".[9]

It is truism to observe that a name has a multiple purposes. On the hand, the name is a fundamental attribute of a person's personal identity.[10] In Western Europe, the first name is a way of distinguishing members of the same family from each other.[11] On the other hand, the name is also a way of identifying an individual within the social group. The surname is indeed a tool for distinguishing families within society.[12] In doing so, the surname also underlines the fact that someone is part of a family.[13] It exposes thus, to some extent, (some) family ties.[14]

Underneath, we can already discern two main functions of a name.[15] First, a name is a tool of identification of a person as a member of a family (mainly the

---

[8]   A comprehensive overview of the name with respect to other situations of affiliation can be found in J.-L. Renchon, "Le nom de famille" in N. Massager and J. Sosson (eds.), *Cour constitutionnelle et droit familial*, Limal, Anthemis, 2015, pp. 9–24 and A- C. Van Gysel, *La famille*, Limal, Anthemis, 2015, pp. 157–180.

[9]   R. Dekkers (bijgewerkt door A. Wylleman, E. Dirix and G. Baeteman), *Handboek Burgerlijk recht*, deel I, Antwerpen, Intersentia, 2009, p. 67 (translation is mine); See as well: W. Pintens, *Naam* in *Algemene Practische Rechtsverzameling*, Gent, E. Story-Scientia, 1981, p. 1; H. De Page, *Traité élémentaire de droit civil* I, Brussels, Bruylant, 1961, p. 401.

[10]   F. Terré and D. Fenouillet, *Droit civil. Les personnes, la famille, les incapacités*, Paris, Dalloz, 2005, p. 153.

[11]   R. Dekkers (bijgewerkt door A. Wylleman, E. Dirix and G. Baeteman), *Handboek Burgerlijk recht*, deel I, Antwerpen, Intersentia, 2009, p. 68.

[12]   *Ibid.*

[13]   O.N. Retea, "Attribution of Last Name to a Child. National and European Aspects", *Conf. Int'l Dr.*, 2015, p. 15.

[14]   As Paul and Koen Lemmens know: by wearing the name Lemmens, they expose their belonging to a family called "Lemmens", but, clearly, this does not mean that there cannot exist various families having the same name, without being related to one another.

[15]   F. de Varennes and E. Kuzborska, "Human Rights and a Person's Name: Legal Trends and Challenges", *Human Rights Quarterly*, 2015, p. 983: they describe the evolution of the function of the name as "from Identification to Identity". Pintens highlights that other interests may be pursued. Thus, nationalistic feelings may be promoted by only allowing traditional, "domestic", names. In some cases, names may also serve to indicate a persons' sex. W. Pintens, *Naam* in *Algemene Practische Rechtsverzameling*, Gent, E. Story-Scientia, 1981,

last name). But, second, it also is an important element for a person's identity (mainly the first name?). The name combines both societal and personal aspects. As Malaurie and Aynes put it:

> "Apparaît ainsi dans son nom le double visage de la personne humaine. Son patronyme, devenu le nom de famille, traduit son appartenance à une famille; son prénom l'individualise."[16]

It doesn't come as a surprise, therefore that the legal system intervenes to regulate the name, as one of the aspects of the personal status, since the name is both of interest to the individual and to society.[17] In this respect it is interesting to note how close traditional private law and public law interrelate in this field.[18]

This double function of the name, identification and individualization[19], are reflected in the somewhat ambiguous observation that wearing a name is both a right and an obligation.[20] Under Belgian law, for instance, persons have a subjective personality right to a name.[21] Under human rights law, it can even be ascertained that there is a trend towards the recognition of the human right to a name. Indeed, as scholars[22] as well as the European Court of Human Rights[23] observe, international human rights treaties are growingly paying explicitly attention to the "right to a name".[24] This right puts the accent on autonomy.[25]

[ ] pp. 3-4. J. Fierens gives even more reasons. J. Fierens, "« Où t'es, papa où t'es ? » ou comment la Cour européenne des droits de l'homme choisit d'ignorer la fonction fondamentale", *Rev. trim. d.h.*, 2015, p. 710.

[16] P. Malaurie and L. Aynès, *Droit des personnes,* Issy-les-Moulineaux, LGDJ, 2017, p. 54.

[17] F. Terré and D. Fenouillet, *Droit civil. Les personnes, la famille, les incapacités,* Paris, Dalloz, 2005, p. 133.

[18] *Ibid.*; A.-S. Versweyvelt, *De naam. Analyse van rechtspraak van het EVRM en het Grondwettelijk Hof,* Antwerpen, Intersentia, 2014, p. 29.

[19] A.-S. Versweyvelt, *De naam. Analyse van rechtspraak van het EVRM en het Grondwettelijk Hof,* Antwerpen, Intersentia, 2014, p. 1. F. Swennen, *Het personen- en familierecht,* Antwerpen, Intersentia, 2017, p. 93.

[20] F. Swennen, *Het personen- en familierecht,* Antwerpen, Intersentia, 2017, p. 93.

[21] F. Swennen, *Het personen- en familierecht,* Antwerpen, Intersentia, 2017, p. 100.

[22] F. de Varennes and E. Kuzborska, "Human Rights and a Person's Name: Legal Trends and Challenges", *Human Rights Quarterly,* 2015, p. 981 et seq.; F. Swennen, *Het personen- en familierecht,* Antwerpen, Intersentia, 2017, p. 100; A.-S. Versweyvelt, *De naam. Analyse van rechtspraak van het EVRM en het Grondwettelijk Hof,* Antwerpen, Intersentia, 2014, p. 23 et seq.

[23] ECtHR, *Burghartz v. Switzerland,* 22 February 1994, § 24; see further point II of this contribution; A.-S. Versweyvelt, *De naam. Analyse van rechtspraak van het EVRM en het Grondwettelijk Hof,* Antwerpen, Intersentia, 2014, p. 12.

[24] See e.g.: Article 24 International Covenant on Civil and Political Rights; Article 7 Convention on the Rights of the Child; Article 18 American Convention on Human Rights, Article 6 African Charter on the Rights and Welfare of the Child.

[25] In this sens: I. Boone, "Van vadersnaam naar dubbele naam" in I. Boone, J. Put, F. Swennen and G. Verschelden (eds.), *Liber amicorum Patrick Senaeve,* Mechelen, Wolters Kluwer, 2017, p. 82.

Yet, there is also an obligation to wear a name.[26] This is the clear consequence of the need to be identifiable in society. In any event, it should be clear to anyone that giving a name is not just a pure private act whereby parents give a name to their new-born child. It is also a socially embedded practice, which has been subject to regulatory practices.[27] From this perspective, we understand why in French law – and sometimes echoed in Belgian law[28] – the name is considered an *"institution de police civile"*[29], although others may cast doubts on this statement.[30]

In this article, I will focus on the surname, which in Belgian law could be rightly called patronym. Indeed, traditionally, children whose maternal and paternal affiliation were both established, were only given the father's name.[31] This was, literally, an ancient rule, as it origins date back to Roman Law.[32] Only in 1987, a systematic legal framework pertaining to the attribution of surnames was adopted.[33] Although some scholars, such as Pintens[34], already advocated as early as 1981 a parental right to choose, the focus was still on patrilineal attribution.[35]

In 2014, Belgian legislation changed. It was clear, indeed, that the legislation in force would have serious problems to meet the requirements set forth in the meantime by the European Court of Human Rights.[36] Under title IV, I will describe the new Belgian legislation, but at this point, I first need to describe how the ECHR deals with the name.

---

[26] F. Swennen, *Het personen- en familierecht*, Antwerpen, Intersentia, 2017, p. 93.

[27] For a typology of models of how states interfere in this field, see F. de Varennes and E. Kuzborska, "Human Rights and a Person's Name: Legal Trends and Challenges", *Human Rights Quarterly*, 2015, p. 980.

[28] W. Pintens, *Naam* in *Algemene Practische Rechtsverzameling*, Gent, E. Story-Scientia, 1981, p. 116.

[29] F. Terré and D. Fenouillet, *Droit civil. Les personnes, la famille, les incapacités*, Paris, Dalloz, 2005, p. 172.

[30] Malaurie and Aynès indicate that this idea was developed by Planiol, but they argue that this qualification is not anymore tenable. It would be anathema to the increased autonomy given to citizens and the greater instability of names. P. Malaurie and L. Aynès, *Droit des personnes*, Issy-les-Moulineaux, LGDJ, 2017, p. 71; P. Jestaz, "À propos du nom patronymique: diagnostic et pronostic", *RTDciv* 1989, p. 269.

[31] I. Boone, "Van vadersnaam naar dubbele naam" in I. Boone, J. Put, F. Swennen and G. Verschelden (eds.), *Liber amicorum Patrick Senaeve*, Mechelen, Wolters Kluwer, 2017, p. 77.

[32] A-C. Van Gysel, *La famille*, Limal, Anthemis, 2018, 161 et les références aux digestes.

[33] *Ibid.*, p. 162.

[34] W. Pintens, *Naam* in *Algemene Practische Rechtsverzameling*, Gent, E. Story-Scientia, 1981, p. 23.

[35] I. Boone, "Van vadersnaam naar dubbele naam" in I. Boone, J. Put, F. Swennen and G. Verschelden (eds.), *Liber amicorum Patrick Senaeve*, Mechelen, Wolters Kluwer, 2017, p. 77.

[36] I. Boone, "Van vadersnaam naar dubbele naam" in I. Boone, J. Put, F. Swennen and G. Verschelden (eds.), *Liber amicorum Patrick Senaeve*, Mechelen, Wolters Kluwer, 2017, p. 81.

II. THE NAME IN THE ECHR

It has already been said that the European Convention on Human Rights does not explicitly mention the right to a name. However, this does not mean of course that issues related to the name haven't been submitted to the Court. Under the Convention, two articles seem to particularly fit to address issues concerning the name. The first one is Article 8 protecting the right to private and family life. The second is Article 14, which deals with equality and anti-discrimination.[37] It should be borne in mind though that this article has no independent existence, and can only be invoked to the extent that a difference in treatment complained of is related to the rights and freedoms protected by the Convention.[38] As a consequence, the pivotal article in this area is doubtlessly Article 8.

In early decisions, the Strasbourg organs were unwilling to deal with issues related to names.[39] Thus, in a Swiss case on the use of a patronymic name in elections, the European Commission of Human Rights left the question as to the applicability of Article 8 open. It further found that the obligation placed on members of the same family to bear the same name, be it the name of the husband, was not discriminatory given the need to be easily identifiable by third parties.[40] On other occasions, the Commission was more outspoken and decided even that Article 8 simply did not apply.[41]

It is generally considered that the *Burghartz case* is a landmark in the domain of names and the ECHR.[42] The Court acknowledged that although a right to a name is not explicitly included in Article 8, it does not imply that Article 8 cannot apply:

> "As a means of personal identification and of linking to a family, a person's name none the less concerns his or her private and family life. The fact that society and the State have an interest in regulating the use of names does not exclude this, since

---

[37] F. de Varennes and E. Kuzborska, "Human Rights and a Person's Name: Legal Trends and Challenges", *Human Rights Quarterly*, 2015, p. 986 et seq.; A.-S. Versweyvelt, *De naam. Analyse van rechtspraak van het EVRM en het Grondwettelijk Hof*, Antwerpen, Intersentia, 2014, p. 11 et seq.

[38] J. Gerards, "Prohibition of Discrimination" in P. Van Dijk, F. Van Hoof, A. Van Rijn and L. Zwaak (eds.), *Theory and Practice of the European Convention on Human Rights*, Cambridge, Intersentia, 2018, p. 999.

[39] This part of the article is based on A.-S. Versweyvelt, *De naam. Analyse van rechtspraak van het EVRM en het Grondwettelijk Hof*, Antwerpen, Intersentia, 2014, p. 12 et seq.

[40] Eur. Commission Human Rights, *Lucie Hagmann-Hüsler v. Switzerland*, appl. no. 8042/77, 15 December 1977.

[41] Eur. Commission Human Rights, *David Lant v. United Kingdom*, appl. no. 11046/84, 10 December 1985.

[42] A.-S. Versweyvelt, *De naam. Analyse van rechtspraak van het EVRM en het Grondwettelijk Hof*, Antwerpen, Intersentia, 2014, p. 12.

these public-law aspects are compatible with private life conceived of as including, to a certain degree, the right to establish and develop relationships with other human beings, in professional or business contexts as in others."[43]

Article 8 therefore applies to issues related to the name.

Since *Burgerhartz*, the Strasbourg Court has had many occasions to fine-tune its case-law.[44] For the purpose of this contribution, the case of *Bijleveld* is important.[45] Here, the Court was asked whether the refusal by the Dutch authorities to change the applicants' daughter's surname from the father's one to the mother's, constituted a violation of Article 8 and Article 14 of the Convention. The sons of the applicant would still bear the names of the father.

The Court addressed the question first from the perspective of negative obligations stemming from Article 8. It was not convinced that in this case there was an interference. However, it decided to analyse the question from a different perspective, that of the positive obligations. Were the Dutch authorities under the duty to accept the change? The Court observed that this is a matter of striking a fair balance between the interests of the individual and those of the "community as a whole".[46] Moreover the Court stressed that in this field, the State enjoys a wide margin of appreciation: it is essentially up to the State to decide which policy is most appropriate in the field of changing surnames. In this specific case, the parents sought a solution that was not compatible with the old Dutch rules (patrilinial name), nor with the new rules, which allowed parents the choice between the name of the father and the name of the mother. Indeed, the applicant wanted her daughter to bear her name, whereas her sons would bear the name of the father. The applicant's interest in having her surname continued did not outweigh the State's interest in preserving legal stability.[47]

The Court went further and also assessed whether Article 14 had been violated. Here, the Court essentially observed that indeed the (new) Dutch rules made it possible for a couple to pass the mother's surname to their offspring, on the

---

[43]   ECtHR, *Burghartz v. Switzerland*, 22 February 1994, § 24.

[44]   However, as Jacques Fierens rightfully recalls, the case-law of the Court concerned issues related to the use of surnames of spouses. Together with Fierens, I have serious doubts as to the applicability of that case-law to parent-child relations. See: J. Fierens, "« Où t'es, papa où t'es ? » ou comment la Cour européenne des droits de l'homme choisit d'ignorer la fonction fondamentale du patronyme", *Revue trimestrielle des droits de l'homme*, 2015, p. 708.

[45]   Eur. Commission Human Rights, *Catharina Bijleveld v. Netherlands*, appl. no. 42973/98, 27 April 2000.

[46]   Eur. Commission Human Rights, *Catharina Bijleveld v. Netherlands*, appl. no. 42973/98, 27 April 2000, § 3.

[47]   Eur. Commission Human Rights, *Catharina Bijleveld v. Netherlands*, appl. no. 42973/98, 27 April 2000, § 3.

condition that there was an agreement between the parents. The "default" position however remained that the children would bear the father's surname. The Court acknowledged that this was a difference in treatment between the female and the male parent, but in light of the social aim pursued, i.e. the fact that all children of the same family bear the same surname, the distinction was considered to be proportionate.[48]

One can see this case as a mile stone in the field. Although the Court ultimately finds that there is no violation of the Convention, it clearly indicates as well that the systematic preference to pass the father's name constitutes a difference in treatment. In light of the specific circumstances of the case, it was still of the opinion that the difference was justified and did not amount therefore to discrimination.[49] Yet is was crystal clear that, precisely because of the fact that gender equality had become a major concern in our societies – as the Court pointed out – changes in the Court's position may have to be expected.

In the more recent case of *Cusan and Fazzo*[50] the Court then made an important *aggiornamento*. In this case an Italian couple complained of the impossibility, under Italian law, to pass the mother's name to their new-born daughter. The Court first observed that the question was protected under Article 8, but then immediately moved on to analyse it from the perspective of Article 14. Here, the Court found that there was indeed a difference in treatment between both parents, as it had already confirmed in *Bijleveld*. Yet, the question is whether this difference in treatment was (still) justified.

The Court now finds that there is a problem. According to the Court, that the fact that, under Italian law, there was no possibility for the parents to depart from the general rule, constituted a violation of Article 14 combined with Article 8. However, the reasons the Court puts forward are not all very convincingly construed.

Let me first start with the argument that may have had an important impact on the Court's finding. The Strasbourg judges highlighted that both the Italian Constitutional Court and the Supreme Court had indicated that the rule of automatic attribution of the father's name was part of a patriarchal idea of the family at odds with international law and with the Italian Constitution. Though it was argued that only the Italian legislature would be entitled to intervene.[51]

---

[48] Eur. Commission Human Rights, *Catharina Bijleveld v. Netherlands*, appl. no. 42973/98, 27 April 2000, § 4.

[49] Eur. Commission Human Rights, *Catharina Bijleveld v. Netherlands*, appl. no. 42973/98, 27 April 2000, § 4.

[50] ECtHR, *Cusan and Fazzo v. Italy*, 7 January 2014.

[51] ECtHR, *Cusan and Fazzo v. Italy*, 7 January 2014, § 17 with reference to the internal case-law (Corte Costituzionale, 16 February 2006, no. 61).

Moreover, it appears that the rule of the automatic attribution of the father's surname did not have a clear legal basis but was the result of a rule that was anchored in Italian social and historic consciousness.[52] In view of these facts – although the Court does not mention the customary nature of the rule in its analysis of the merits – it may not come as a surprise that the Strasbourg judges found a violation of the Convention. That is, the Court expresses the view that the rule of automatic transmission of the husband's surname in case of "legitimate" children may be necessary from a practical point of view and does not necessarily violate the Convention, but that the impossibility to derogate from it is exaggeratedly rigid and constitutes a discrimination towards women.[53]

I must admit that I find that argument puzzling, for two reasons. First, I fail to see how the Court can both admit that a rule that does not necessarily violate the Convention and yet is exaggeratedly rigid and therefore violates the Convention. The consequence of the Court's dictum is clearly that the automatic preference for the father's surname in case of children born in wedlock is a violation of the Convention. It will only be acceptable if, upon registration of the child with the civil administration, exceptions can be made. This means, obviously, that the transmission is not automatic, but conditional and in any event subject to a decision at each registration: only if the parents do not derogate from the rule, and therefore implicitly decide to agree to its application, it will be applied. If they want to derogate from it, they should have the legal possibility to do so. The Court thus operates a strategic shift: whereas before its judgement, the rules on the transmission of the surname seemed to be of public order, in that considerations of public policy overrode private parties' interests, it now submits these public policy considerations to a (possible) veto of the parents. Thence, the private interests are given a more important weight.[54] This is not to say, of course, that even in a system where automatic transmission is preferred, exceptions to the rule cannot be foreseen. But in such a hypothesis, one could argue that (1) these exceptions are defined by law, so expressing a public interest and (2) that conceivably the possibility to have the name changed could still be submitted to an approval by the authorities.[55]

---

52 ECtHR, *Cusan and Fazzo v. Italy*, 7 January 2014, § 13. Along the same lines: L. Tullio, "The Child's Surname in the Light of Italian Constitutional Legality", *Italian Law Journal*, 2017, p. 225.

53 ECtHR, *Cusan and Fazzo v. Italy*, 7 January 2014, § 67.

54 I. Boone, "Van vadersnaam naar dubbele naam" in I. Boone, J. Put, F. Swennen and G. Verschelden (eds.), *Liber amicorum Patrick Senaeve*, Mechelen, Wolters Kluwer, 2017, p. 82, for whom it is a matter of the "growing importance of autonomy".

55 In Belgium, however, the right to change a family name has become a subjective right further to the changes introduced by the Act of 18 June 2018 "portant dispositions diverses en matière de droit civil et des dispositions en vue de promouvoir des formes alternatives de résolution des litiges", *Mon. b.*, 2 July 2018.
See: I. Boone, "Naamsverandering van gunst naar recht", *RW*, 2018-2019, p. 82.

The second point is, as others have highlighted as well[56], that the Court did not come up with a profound analysis of the difference in treatment at stake. Why, in fact, is it that "practical reasons" may justify the default preference for the father's name? Which reasons are at stake and, given that the rule dates back to Roman law, can we still say that they are valid in today's society? Furthermore, the Court does not say anything about the way it conceives the derogation. Admittedly, it would be primarily a task for the legislator to establish a precise policy in this respect, yet the Court could have foreseen at least some self-evident questions. For instance, one may wonder to what extent the derogation of the default patriarchal standard requires the fathers' consent. It this is the case, obviously, the father is placed in a stronger position than the mother. The general rule would then be: the child bears the name of the father unless the father agrees that the name of the mother be used. Decidedly, this position is more even than the previous situation, but one may wonder whether the still "uneven" position of the mother is acceptable pursuant to Convention's standards.[57]

The Court has avoided to give more information about this. In part, this is quite understandable: the Court's function is in the first place to decide specific cases. Nevertheless, in doing so, it will have to interpret the Convention and, as such, it does not have to shy away from clarifying the Convention. In the words of the Courts:

> "The Court's judgments in fact serve not only to decide those cases brought before the Court but, more generally, to elucidate, safeguard and develop the rules instituted by the Convention, thereby contributing to the observance by the States of the engagements undertaken by them as Contracting Parties".[58]

A more profound analysis under Article 14 would have been very welcome indeed, as the Belgian experience shows.

III. THE NEW BELGIAN LAW

Before the 2014 reform, Belgium appeared to be, together with Italy, one of the few European states where the automatic transmission of the father's surname

---

[56]   C. Draghici, *The Legitimacy of Family Rights in Strasbourg Case Law 'Living Instrument' or Extinguished Sovereignty?*, Oxford, Hart, 2017, p. 261.

[57]   *Ibid.*

[58]   ECHR, *Ireland v. United Kingdom*, 18 January 1978, § 154; see J. Gerards and J. Fleuren, "Introduction" in J. Gerards and J. Fleuren (eds.), *Implementation of the European Convention on Human Rights and of the judgements in national case-law*", Cambridge, Intersentia, 2014, pp. 1–2.

was the default option.[59] In this respect, the old Article 335 § 1 of the Civil Code
was similar to the Italian rule.

Not surprisingly, especially given the fact that many European states had already
softened the strict application of the transmission of the *patronymicum*, lawyers
in Belgium had also advocated a change in the legal rules.[60] One of the experts in
the field of family law even argued that Article 335 § 1 of the Civil Code was the
most despicable article of Belgian federal law.[61]

In this respect, it must be recalled that the Belgian Constitutional Court had
delivered some question begging judgements. Still in 2002, the Constitutional
Court rejected a complaint about the discriminatory nature of the provision. The
Court observed that the contested rule was the legal translation of a longstanding
cultural norm. The rule pursued two clear social goals: on the one hand, it strives
to create a simple mechanism of determining surnames; on the other, it aims
to keep surnames to a certain degree invariable.[62] The Court acknowledged
that the choice in favour of the patronymicum was based on an old patriarchal
conception of the family and that other rules, more in line with actual ideas,
could aim at securing the legitimate social concerns. Yet, this consideration was
not sufficient in itself to find a violation of the constitutional non-discrimination
provision.[63] The reason for that, according to the Constitutional Court, was that
the right to transmit a surname is not a fundamental right, which implies that
the legislature benefits from a wide margin of manoeuvre.[64] This affirmation,
repeated in 2004, was perhaps confusing.[65] The role of the Constitutional Court
is, amongst others, to review legislation against the protection of fundamental
rights. So in many cases the legal rules under review will not constitute
fundamental rights. Yet, that point is not relevant: what matters is that they
respect fundamental rights. In this case, the Constitutional Court did not have
to reflect upon the nature of the rights in Article 335 § 1. It only had to assess
whether they respected the non-discrimination provision and the protection
of private and family-life. Since the Strasbourg Court had considered that the
transmission of family names is covered by Article 8 ECHR, one could have
expected the Constitutional Court at least to have assessed these rules in light

---

[59] I. Boone, "Van vadersnaam naar dubbele naam" in I. Boone, J. Put, F. Swennen and G.
      Verschelden (eds.), *Liber amicorum Patrick Senaeve*, Mechelen, Wolters Kluwer, 2017, p. 81.

[60] I. Boone, "Van vadersnaam naar dubbele naam" in I. Boone, J. Put, F. Swennen and G.
      Verschelden (eds.), *Liber amicorum Patrick Senaeve*, Mechelen, Wolters Kluwer, 2017,
      pp. 77-78.

[61] G. Verschelden, "Wat is het meest verwerpelijke wetsartikel", *Juristenkrant*, 29 September
      2010, p. 3.

[62] Constitutional Court, case no. 161/2002, 6 November 2002, B.3.

[63] Constitutional Court, case no. 161/2002, 6 November 2002, B.6.

[64] Constitutional Court, case no. 161/2002, 6 November 2002, B.7.

[65] Constitutional Court, case no. 82/2004, 12 May 2004, B.4.2.

of the relevant constitutional right of private and family life. This is all the more interpellant since hardly two months later, the Constitutional Court held that when a constitutional provision is referred to and a norm of international law that is binding upon Belgium has an analogous meaning, the safeguards and guarantees of that international provision are to be considered part of the constitutional protection.[66] It is not unreasonably to state that, at least in 2004, the Constitutional Court could have more thoroughly included Articles 8 and 14 ECHR in its reasoning.

In a later case, in 2016, the Constitutional Court recalled that transmitting a surname is not a fundamental right, but significantly added that this wide leeway is nevertheless restricted by the non-discrimination provision read together with the protection of private and family-life.[67] It occurs to me that this is the correct reasoning.

Be it as it may, the Constitutional Court in its 2002 judgement indicated that the preference for the fathers' name was not any longer uncontested and in any event far from being unproblematic.

The scholarly debate, the Constitutional Court's case-law and the *Cusan and Fazzo* judgment indicated unequivocally that the legislature could not just leave things untouched. In 2014, a new law was passed to profoundly modify Article 335 § 1 of the Civil Code.[68]

Whenever both the maternal and paternal affiliation was established, the child can be given the name of the father, the mother or a composed name. In this case the parents can choose whether the father's name will follow the mother's name or the other way round. In any event, the composed name may only be composed of one name for each parent.

The problem concerned the situation in which the parents could not agree on the name. The 2014 reform proposed that in this case, the father's surname would be automatically transmitted. In other words, the father would be given a veto-right. This was generally seen as the weak point in the new legislation: if a reform is supposed to foster gender equality, then it is of course question begging that it precisely confirms the position of the man.[69] (In fact, one could even say that it worsened the situation. Indeed, before the modification of the law, the system may have been patriarchal, but it was institutionalized patriarchy, giving no

---

[66]   Constitutional Court, case no. 136/2004, 22 July 2004, B.5.3 and B.5.4.
[67]   Constitutional Court, case nr. 2/2016, 14 January 2016, B.7.1.
[68]   Loi du 8 mai 2014 modifiant le Code civil en vue d'instaurer l'égalité de l'homme et de la femme dans le mode de transmission du nom à l'enfant et à l'adopté, *Mon. b.*, 26 May 2014.
[69]   G. Verschelden, *Handboek Belgisch Personen-en Familierecht*, Brugge, die Keure, 2016, p. 165.

particular say to the individual father. The 2014 reform did confer individual veto-rights to the father.[70])

A constitutional complaint has been filed against the reform (and a preliminary ruling was requested). The Constitutional Court found that the proposed solution did violate the non-discrimination principle, in that it made a distinction between the father and the mother without any strong justification. Nor tradition, nor the will to gradually make further progress are, in the eyes of the Court, sufficiently strong reasons to justify such a distinction. Therefore, the system put in place to deal with cases of disagreement violated the Constitution.[71]

The legislature had to intervene another time, in order to respond to the objections of the Constitutional Court. The law of 25 December 2016 modified Article 335 § 1. It inserted a new rule of conflict. As of 1 January 2017, children will bear the names of their mother and father in alphabetical order, if both parents cannot agree on the child's surname. Should any of the parents have a double-name, (s)he can choose which part of the name will be transmitted. If no choice is made in this respect, alphabetical order will prevail again: that part of the name that comes first alphabetically, will be transmitted.

As it stands, there seems to be little doubt that this legislation is in line with the European Convention on Human Rights. The issue of non-discrimination as identified in *Cusan and Fazzo* do not exist any longer in Belgian Law.

IV. CRITICAL CONSIDERATIONS

One can understand that I am happy to be a Lemmens, especially within the context of this volume. All jokes aside, I have no strong feelings about this new reform. Some scholars clearly did: Verschelden was very critical of the old system[72], whereas Senaeve – at least initially – appeared to have doubts on the new system.[73] As I mentioned in the introduction, I am not an expert in family law, and it would therefore be inappropriate to voice criticism in one way or another. Nevertheless, I would want to put three considerations to the table. They may shed another light at the discussion and bring human rights at the forefront of the debate.

---

[70]   I. Boone, "Van vadersnaam naar dubbele naam" in I. Boone, J. Put, F. Swennen and G. Verschelden (eds.), *Liber amicorum Patrick Senaeve*, Mechelen, Wolters Kluwer, 2017, p. 85.

[71]   Constitutional Court, case no. 2/2016, 14 January 2016, B. 8.7. As to the case with the preliminary ruling: Constitutional Court, case no. 162/2016, 14 December 2016.

[72]   See quote in note 61.

[73]   P. Senaeve, "Naar een vrijheid in keuze van de familienaam?", *Tijdschrift voor Familierecht*, 2014, pp. 30–33.

My first question pertains to the transmission of the surname as a human rights issue. I understand that the legal framework on surnames can affect human rights of individuals, for instance in case of people belonging to national minorities or indigenous peoples, as Varennes and Kuzborska have indicated.[74] But I am less convinced that this is necessarily true for the mere *transmission* of those surnames. In this respect, I understand what the Belgian Constitutional Court tried to explain when it said that the right to transmit a surname to a child is not a fundamental right.

The approach to surnames now clearly is inspired by the idea of personal autonomy and identity. Personal, or in this case, the parents' choice is made the cornerstone of the system. However, I am not convinced that individuals should have a say on all aspects of their identity. I admit that this is not a fashionable view and runs counter to the evolution of family law and rules on personal status. For instance, in the Netherlands a 69-year old man tries to officially change his age. If you can change your sex in official documents, why not your age, he wonders.[75] Eccentric as the claim may be, professor Swennen[76], an expert in family law, tweeted that the discussion was interesting, precisely because it invites us to reflect on the limits of personal autonomy, now that it has been recognized in the fields of sex and names. To avoid any misunderstanding, I am not saying that professor Swennen is in favour of the argument. As an expert in the field, he precisely advised the Belgian legislator not to create a system of choice, but to establish a rule according to which a child would always bear a double name composed of the mothers surname followed by the father's one. Swennen was clearly against the possibility of a system of choice, not the least because the right to a name, is a child's right, not that of the parents.[77]

Be it as it may, I observe that in the political discussion moderate attention has been paid to the argument that a surname constitutes a bond between previous generations and future generations. In this view, a person does not "own" his surname but it is rather given to him in custody, and passed on to the

---

[74] F. de Varennes and E. Kuzborska, "Human Rights and a Person's Name: Legal Trends and Challenges", *Human Rights Quarterly*, 2015, p. 994 et seq.

[75] https://www.volkskrant.nl/nieuws-achtergrond/ratelband-haalt-internationale-media-met-zijn-rechtszaak-om-geboortedatum-te-veranderen-ik-lijd-onder-mijn-leeftijd-~b78f70b5/ consulted on 30 November 2018. The complaint was dismissed, but the applicant considered appealing against it. https://www.rtlnieuws.nl/nieuws/artikel/4505306/emile-ratelband-wil-hoger-beroep-ik-zie-allerlei-gaten-de-uitspraak consulted on 11 January 2019.

[76] https://twitter.com/frederikswennen/status/1060499842613555202 consulted on 30 November 2018.

[77] Chambre des Représentants, Projet de loi modifiant le Code civil en vue d'instaurer l'égalité de l'homme et de la femme dans le mode de transmission du nom à l'enfant et à l'adopté, Avis fait au nom du comité d'avis pour l'émancipation sociale, 14 February 2014, Doc 53 3145/002, p. 9.

next generations.[78] Toon Vandevelde could not be more clear *"Men* kiest *zijn naam niet, men* krijgt *hem."*[79] How this transmission is operated (according to patriarchal, matriarchal or mixed-lines) is then not so important: it reflects a social choice, that goes in any event beyond the autonomy of the single individual. Yet, what is important in this interpretation, is that an individual living in a society does not fully master his or her identification. Identity is the result of an interplay between personal choices and social norms.[80] Personally, I do not think that identity equals self-identification. I would have loved, in this debate, a more profound reflection on the position of an individual within a genealogic line[81] and within society and to what extent this position conditions the scope of personal autonomy. The present case offers a good illustration for a debate on the evolution of human rights and their entanglement with social norms.

The second observation concerns the choice for, or rather against, the specific mode of transmission. In the literature and the case-law, it is an almost uncontested fact that the idea of patriarchal transmission is related to patriarchy. The argument goes that we are not living in the Roman era anymore and that the times of the *pater familias* have gone. Of course, it would be hard and ridiculous to deny all this. Luckily so, I would add. However, the argument may be – and I say this with hesitation – a form of *"cum hoc ergo propter hoc"* fallacy. Is it sufficient to say that a rule saw the light in a patriarchal society for it to be indeed patriarchal? The question is not without importance since some authors, but relatively few[82], have referred to psychoanalysts, for whom the rule of the transmission of the fathers name has another meaning.[83] This is exactly the point Fierens makes when he writes that the preference for a patrilineal transmission is not only a matter of patriarchy.[84] The saying, *"la mère donne la vie, le père donne le nom"*[85] summarizes

---

[78] Arguably this idea is akin to the notion of stewardship. The luxury brand of Swiss watches *Patek Philippe* has this brilliant slogan "You never actually own a Patek Philippe. You merely look after it for the next generations". Would it be different for a surname?

[79] "You don't choose your name, you receive it". T. Vandevelde, "What's in a name? Over de gevaren van keuzevrijheid inzake naamgeving", *Ethische Perspectieven*, 2006, p. 7. Emphasis in the original text.

[80] See, e.g., P. Verhaege, *Identiteit*, Amsterdam, De Bezige Bij, 2012, p. 21.

[81] Fierens refers to Claude Lévi-Strauss: "Le patronyme appartient aux enfants de plein droit; on peut dire que dans nos sociétés, c'est un classificateur de lignée" (C. Lévi-Strauss, La pensée sauvage, p. 256) in J. Fierens, "« Où t'es, papa où t'es ? » ou comment la Cour européenne des droits de l'homme choisit d'ignorer la fonction fondamentale", *Rev.trim. d.h.*, 2015, p. 711.

[82] Renchon and Fierens did in the contributions I referred to.

[83] For instance Jacques Lacan, referred to by J. Fierens, "« Où t'es, papa où t'es ? » ou comment la Cour européenne des droits de l'homme choisit d'ignorer la fonction fondamentale", *Rev. trim. d.h.*, 2015, p. 711-712.

[84] J. Fierens, "« Où t'es, papa où t'es? » ou comment la Cour européenne des droits de l'homme choisit d'ignorer la fonction fondamentale", *Rev.trim. d.h.*, 2015, p. 708.

[85] T. Vandevelde attributes it to Lacan. T. Vandevelde, "What's in a name? Over de gevaren van keuzevrijheid inzake naamgeving", *Ethische Perspectieven*, 2006, p. 3.

this point quite well. In fact, by giving the child the name of the father, a third person is introduced in the visceral relation between mother and child.[86]

In the parliamentary debate, the point has been made by parliamentarians of the extreme-right party Vlaams Belang.[87] The reaction by the then Minister of Justice was in this respect deceiving: she indicated that the idea expressed by the saying corresponded to a bygone society.[88] However, this answer misses the point: if, what has to be proven, the *patronymicum* is the expression of a deep anthropologic and human reality, the mere fact that our society has changed in that it treats women more equally than in earlier times is of little interest. What would have to be demonstrated is that in a more equal society, the deeper human realties have changed as well in such a way that the rule of patrilineal name inheritance are no longer appropriate. The French legal sociologist Irène Théry highlighted a shift of meaning: the patrilineal name does not illustrate the authority of the father anymore, but it rather constitutes a cultural asymmetry in response to a biological asymmetry.[89]

There is a final point, I want to raise. Leaving aside discussions of a more anthropological nature, one can wonder whether from a technical point of view, the anti-discrimination argument has been properly constructed. The first step in every anti-discrimination case is to indicate the two comparators, that have to be comparable. In others words, are the two terms in the comparison in fact and *de iure* comparable? This is doubtlessly so in cases of adoption, where a child is adopted by a couple, without having any privileged bond with either of the partners. However, in the hypotheses of pregnancy, the mother finds herself in a different situation than the father of the child, who has not yet developed any particular bond with the child. This is an objective fact. I do not know to what extent this fact is sufficiently relevant to cast doubts on the comparability

---

[86] T. Vandevelde, "What's in a name? Over de gevaren van keuzevrijheid inzake naamgeving", *Ethische Perspectieven*, 2006, p. 4.

[87] Chambre des Représentants, Projet de Loi modifiant le code civil en vue d'instaurer l'égalité de l'homme et de la femme dans le mode de transmission du nom à l'enfant et à l'adopté (y compris 3 propositions de loi jointes), Rapport fait au nom de la Commission de la Justice, 17 March 2014, Doc. 53 3145/004, p. 7 http://www.dekamer.be/FLWB/PDF/53/3145/53K3145004.pdf; Sénat de Belgique, Projet de loi modifiant le Code civil en vue d'instaurer l'égalité de l'homme et de la femme dans le mode de transmission du nom à l'enfant et à l'adopté, Rapport fait au nom de la Commission de la Justice, 23 avril 2014, 5 – 2785/3, pp. 15-17. https://www.senate.be/www/?MIval=/publications/viewPub html&COLL=S&LEG=5&NR=2 785&VOLGNR=3&LANG=nl

[88] Chambre des Représentants, Projet de Loi modifiant le code civil en vue d'instaurer l'égalité de l'homme et de la femme dans le mode de transmission du nom à l'enfant et à l'adopté (y compris 3 propositions de loi jointes), Rapport fait au nom de la Commission de la Justice, 17 March 2014, Doc. 53 3145/004, p. 13.

[89] Quoted in: A. Chemin, "La loi du genre", *Le monde*, 23 May 2013, https://www.lemonde.fr/societe/article/2013/05/23/au-nom-du-pere_3416401_3224.html, consulted on 3 December 2018.

of the two situations, but I am struck by the fact that the Strasbourg Court has hardly paid any attention to question of the comparability of the situations, what it should have been done under anti-discrimination or equality law. In reality, only in paragraph § 63 of the Cusan and Fazzo judgment it states that there is a comparability. However, this statement is rather apodictic and could have expanded more on the reasons why exactly there is such a comparability.

This last argument is in a way the legal translation of the previous argument. It is what Fierens rightly pointed out: what is at stake is not the difference between the male and the female sex, but the difference between paternity and maternity.[90] Regrettably, the discussion has not been focused on these concepts but, on the contrary, was entirely concentrated on sex-discrimination. A more nuanced approach to the discussion may have led to a richer debate. But again, this is not to say that such a debate would have automatically resulted, or should have resulted, in an approval of the status quo.

CONCLUSION

At this point, I can only draw some general conclusions.

First, undeniably the judgment in the *Cusan and Fazzo* case has had an important influence on the new Belgian legislation on the transmission of surnames. The reasoning in the Strasbourg case is mirrored in the (political) debate on the newly adopted Belgian legislation.[91]

What is striking is how easily the idea is accepted that the name can be a matter of choice and personal autonomy. Yet, the privatization of the bond between generations is far from being a trivial decision. One does not choose its affiliation nor family, why would choosing a surname then be self-evident? As Pierre Legendre said: "*Aucun individu ne peut se fonder lui-même*".[92] Théry warns us and observes that naming is no longer the result of the application of societal rules, but rather the result of the rules of the core family ("*la loi*

---

[90] J. Fierens, "« Où t'es, papa où t'es? » ou comment la Cour européenne des droits de l'homme choisit d'ignorer la fonction fondamentale", *Rev.trim. d.h.*, 2015, pp. 708 and 713.

[91] See also: J. Fierens, "« Où t'es, papa où t'es? » ou comment la Cour européenne des droits de l'homme choisit d'ignorer la fonction fondamentale", *Rev.trim. d.h.*, 2015, p. 714.

[92] Quoted in P. Jestaz, "À propos du nom patronymique : diagnostic et pronostic», *RTDciv*, 1989, p. 276. I must add, however, that Jestaz himself is in favour of a much greater autonomy. Admittedly, the personal choice here is not made by the person who receives the name, but by those transmitting the name. The underlying question, however, remains valid: should the "transmitters" enjoy autonomy here, or is this an issue to be left solely to strict social and/or legal norms only?

familiale interne").[93] She interprets this as a form of individualism against the individual.[94]

The European Convention on Human Rights was certainly not created as a libertarian Convention[95] or a Convention that aimed to profoundly change society. According to historian Marco Duranti, the Convention was highly influenced by conservative thinkers and politicians, many of whom wanted to protect the existing social model against left-wing policies of the post-war governments.[96]

Second, it is equally remarkable how little attention after all has been paid to considerations of a more psychological, psycho-analytical and anthropological nature. Patrilineal transmission of surnames has been presented as a remnant of patriarchal societies. Doubtlessly this is true, but the question is whether arguments of psychological and psycho-analytical nature – not only voiced by conservatives but also by people from the left – cannot be advanced to explain patrilineal affiliation. This is not to say, as I previously already made clear, that these arguments necessarily are convincing or hold true. Yet, in the seminal *Cusan and Fazzo* case they simply have not been debated. Arguably, this may be because the parties in that case did not bring them up.[97] However, the Court could have analysed the question from a broader perspective.

In this regard, and even if the argument goes beyond the scope of this modest contribution, I would argue that the Court – in general – badly needs *amicus curiae* support in the extra-legal field. Doubtlessly, the judges can perfectly deal with questions that arise under Article 6. Judges are experts in fair trial. But when it comes to issues with important ethical dimensions (under Articles 2 and 8 ECHR, think about topics as abortion, euthanasia, medically assisted procreation, etc.) or, as the case may be, cultural, anthropological and psychological dimensions, judges may need help to have a broader understanding of the rights and interests at stake as well as of the state of the arte in a specific domain. The Convention and the Rules of Court do foresee the possibility of third party intervention.[98] But, as far as I can see – and without having done any quantitative research on the issue – *amicus curiae* interventions are often NGO's and academic groups with a strong focus on human rights.[99] The quality

---

93   I. Théry, "Le nom, entre préséance et préférence", *Esprit*, 2002, p. 112.

94   *Ibid.*, p. 111 ("l'individualisme se retourne contre l'individu").

95   R. McCrea, "The Ban on the Veil and European Law", *Human Rights Law Review*, 2013, p. 86.

96   M. Duranti, *The Conservative Human Rights Revolution*, Oxford, OUP, 2017.

97   J. Fierens, "« Où t'es, papa où t'es ? » ou comment la Cour européenne des droits de l'homme choisit d'ignorer la fonction fondamentale", *Rev.trim. d.h.*, 2015, p. 712.

98   Article 36 ECHR, Rule 44 of the Rules of Court.

99   On these interventions, see: N. Bürli, *Third-Party Interventions before the European Court of Human Rights. Amicus Curiae, Member-State and Third-Party Interventions*, Cambridge, Intersentia, 2017.

of the Court's case law would gain from interventions from experts in non-legal fields. It would be an interesting challenge to think about the integration of this kind of knowledge in the procedure. Perhaps, not all judges will be very happy with such non-legal specialist intervention, for they may not feel the need for it or they may fear that it will delay proceedings. But I believe that the idea is worth the discussion.

LA SURVEILLANCE DE MASSE ET LA CONVENTION EUROPÉENNE DES DROITS DE L'HOMME

Síofra O'Leary[*]

Juge à la Cour européenne des droits de l'homme
Professeur au Collège d'Europe, Bruges

INTRODUCTION

Il n'est pas inhabituel, dans des affaires devant la Cour européenne des droits de l'homme (CourEDH), y compris dans celles provenant de la Belgique, de voir des points d'interconnexion, parfois forts, parfois plus faibles, entre la Convention européenne des droits de l'homme (CEDH) et le droit de l'Union européenne (UE). Des exemples assez fréquents peuvent être retrouvés dans des affaires relatives, par exemple, à l'immigration et l'asile[1] ou à l'exécution de mandats d'arrêt européen.[2] Un autre domaine où cette interaction devient de plus en plus marquée est celui de la surveillance de masse, où les deux juridictions européennes sont appelées à examiner des questions relatives au droit au respect de la vie privée et, dans ce contexte, de la protection des données personnelles.[3] Il s'agit d'un

---

[*] Les opinions exprimées dans cet article sont purement personnelles.
[1] Voir *M.S.S. c. Belgique et Grèce* [GC], no. 30696/09, 21 janvier 2011 ; *V.M. c. Belgique* [GC], no. 60125/11, 17 novembre 2016, ou *Thimothawes c. Belgique*, no. 390611, 4 avril 2017 (système commun d'asile et la directive 2008/115/CE du Parlement européen et du Conseil du 16 décembre 2008 relative aux normes et procédures communes applicables dans les États membres au retour des ressortissants de pays tiers en séjour irrégulier (JO L 348/98).
[2] Voir, par exemple, *Paci c. Belgique*, no. 45597/09, §§ 69-73, 17 avril 2018 ou *Pirozzi c. Belgique*, no. 21055/11, 17 avril 2018.
[3] Voir, en ce qui concerne la CJUE : *Satakunnan Markkinapörssi et Satamedia*, C-73/07, EU:C:2008:727; *Volker und Markus Schecke et Eifert*, C-92/09 et C-93/09, EU:C:2010:662; *Digital Rights Ireland e.a.*, C-293/12 et C-594/12, EU:C:2014:238; *IPI*, C-473/12, EU:C:2013:715; *Schrems*, C-362/14, EU:C:2015:650 (*Schrems I*) ; *Tele2 Sverige et Watson e.a.*, C-203/15 et C-698/15, EU:C:2016:970; *Avis 1/15*, EU:C:2016:572. En ce qui concerne la CourEDH, voir, entre autres : *Klass et autres c. Allemagne*, 6 septembre 1978, série A no 28 ; *S. et Marper c. Royaume-Uni* [GC], nos. 30562/04 et 30566/04, CEDH 2008 ; *Roman Zakharov c. Russie* [GC], no. 47143/06, CEDH 2015 ; *Liberty et autres c. Royaume-Uni*, no. 58243/00, 1ᵉʳ juillet 2008 ; *Kennedy c. Royaume-Uni*, no. 26839/05, 18 mai 2010 ; *Szabó et Vissy c. Hongrie*, no. 37138/14, 12 janvier 2016 ; *Centrum för rättvisa c. Suède*, no. 35252/08, 19 juin 2018, §§ 112-113 et §§ 179-181 (demande de renvoi à la Grande Chambre acceptée le 4 février 2019), et *Big*

sujet qui fait l'objet d'une jurisprudence strasbourgeoise bien établie et d'une jurisprudence de la CJUE en pleine évolution et d'actualité à cause, entre autres, des révélations concernant la collecte et le transfert des données personnelles par les autorités des États-Unis faites par Edward Snowden ou[4], plus récemment, celles relatives à l'accès à et l'utilisation massive de données des membres de Facebook dans le cadre de campagnes électorales, américaine et autres. Du point de vue juridique, la surveillance de masse soulève des questions complexes, souvent très techniques et, pour les États membres tant de l'UE que du Conseil de l'Europe, très sensibles.

Après un bref exposé de la jurisprudence de la CourEDH relative à la surveillance de masse (II), cet article examinera la jurisprudence pertinente des deux juridictions européennes autour de trois axes. Il s'agira d'analyser en premier lieu l'articulation entre les droits à la vie privée et à la protection des données personnelles, consacrés respectivement par l'article 8 de la Convention et les articles 7 et 8 de la Charte européenne des droits fondamentaux (Charte) (III). L'examen portera ensuite sur la méthodologie suivie par les deux Cours dans ce domaine, avec un accent mis sur les similarités et certaines divergences qu'on peut déceler dans leurs jurisprudences respectives (IV). Il est enfin proposé de réfléchir au contexte actuel dans lequel ces affaires de surveillance de masse s'inscrivent, avec une référence au contentieux plus large relatif à la sécurité nationale, au terrorisme et à la criminalité grave (V). La CJUE a été traditionnellement très peu confrontée à des questions juridiques liées au terrorisme et à la criminalité, que celle-ci soit grave ou non. Sa jurisprudence récente sur la protection des données a été focalisée, toutefois, sur des ingérences résultant des mesures et systèmes mis en place notamment pour prévenir des actes terroristes et agir face à la criminalité grave.[5] En revanche, la Cour de Strasbourg a développé son contentieux relatif

---

Brother Watch et autres c. Royaume-Uni, nos. 58170/13, 62322/14 and 24960/15, 13 septembre 2018 (demande de renvoi à la Grande Chambre acceptée également le 4 février 2019). Deux autres affaires sont pendantes – *Association confraternelle de la presse judiciaire c. France et 11 autres* (requête n°s 49526/15, 49615/15, 49616/15, 49617/15, 49618/15, 49619/15, 49620/15, 49621/15, 55058/15, 55061/15, 59602/15 et 59621/15) ou *Breyer c. Allemagne*, n° 50001/12. Voir la fiche thématique *Surveillance de masse* (http://www.echr.coe.int/Documents/FS_Mass_ surveillance_ENG.pdf) et le rapport préparé par la Division de recherche de la CourEDH, *Sécurité nationale et jurisprudence de la Cour européenne des droits de l'homme*, 2013 (http ://www.echr.coe.int/Documents/Research_report_national_security_FRA.pdf). Voir également, pour un examen de la jurisprudence des deux juridictions européennes dans ce domaine S. O'Leary, «Balancing rights in a digital age» (2018) 59 *Irish Jurist* 59-91.

4   Ces révélations constituaient l'arrière-fond de la procédure entamée en Irlande par Max Schrems, aboutissant dans l'arrêt de la CJUE dans *Schrems I*, précité, §§ 28-30. Une affaire *Schrems II* a été décidée en 2018 – C-498/16 EU:C:2018:37 – et une affaire *Schrems III* est récemment arrivé à la CJUE suite à un renvoi préjudiciel le 11 avril 2018 par un juge de la High Court (Irlande) dans *Data Protection Commissioner c. Facebook*.

5   On pourrait, certes, citer la jurisprudence du tribunal de l'UE et de la CJUE relative aux mesures restrictives dans le contexte de la PESC – voir, par exemple, *Kadi c. Conseil de l'UE*, C-402/05 P et C-415/05 P, EU:C:2008:461. Les droits fondamentaux en cause dans de telles

au terrorisme et à la criminalité au cours de plusieurs décennies et en répondant à des questions juridiques très variées se posant en relation avec différents articles de la Convention, notamment les articles 2, 3, 5, 6 et 7, de même que l'article 8.

I. BREF EXPOSÉ DES ARRÊTS PHARES DE LA CourEDH DANS CE DOMAINE

Il n'est pas possible, dans le cadre restreint de cette contribution, d'examiner en détail les différents arrêts de la Cour de Strasbourg relative à la surveillance de masse. On se limitera à un bref exposé de trois affaires – anciennes et plus récentes – et des principes généraux y appliqués.

Dans *Klass*, des avocats dénonçaient la législation allemande qui permettait aux autorités de surveiller leur correspondance et leurs communications téléphoniques sans qu'elles aient l'obligation de les informer ultérieurement des mesures prises contre eux. La Cour a conclu que la législation créait par sa simple existence, pour tous ceux auxquels on pourrait l'appliquer, une menace de surveillance entravant forcément la liberté de communication. Elle constituait par là une ingérence dans l'exercice du droit à la vie privée.[6] Toutefois, en évaluant l'étendue de la sauvegarde offerte par l'article 8, la Cour a constaté que les sociétés démocratiques se trouvaient menacées par des formes très complexes d'espionnage et par le terrorisme, de sorte que l'État devait être capable, pour combattre efficacement ces menaces, de surveiller en secret les éléments subversifs opérant sur son territoire.[7] Le pouvoir de surveiller en secret les citoyens était jugé, *devant une situation exceptionnelle*, nécessaire à la sécurité nationale, à la défense de l'ordre et à la prévention des infractions. Quant au choix des modalités d'un tel système, le législateur national jouissait d'«un certain pouvoir discrétionnaire», la Cour précisant qu'elle n'avait pas qualité pour substituer à l'appréciation des autorités nationales une autre appréciation à ce que pourrait être la meilleure politique en ce domaine.[8] La latitude des États membres n'était bien sûr pas illimitée compte tenu «du danger, inhérent à pareille loi, de saper, voire de détruire, la démocratie au motif de la défendre». La Cour devait se convaincre de l'existence de garanties adéquates et suffisantes contre les abus ; ce qui était le cas dans l'affaire Klass, où elle a conclu à une non-violation de l'article 8.[9]

---

affaires sont principalement le droit au respect de la propriété, le droit d'être entendu et le droit à un contrôle effectif. Il s'agit, toutefois, d'un domaine de compétence relativement récent de l'UE et d'une ligne jurisprudentielle très particulière.

6   *Klass*, précité, § 41.
7   Ibid., § 48.
8   Ibid., § 49.
9   Ibid., §§ 50, 59-60. L'appréciation du caractère adéquat et suffisant des mesures prises pour prévenir des abus revêt elle-même un caractère relatif : «elle dépend de toutes les

Nous sommes devenus très familiers de la méthodologie et du langage de la Cour utilisés dans l'affaire *Klass*. Pourtant, il faut souligner que l'affaire concernait une surveillance qui ne se limitait pas à des données relatives au trafic et de localisation – comme c'était le cas de la législation européenne et nationale en cause dans les affaires *Digital Rights* et *Tele2*[10] – mais concernait également sinon surtout le contenu des communications interceptées.[11] Il peut paraître étrange de faire référence à un arrêt qui date de presque 40 ans, les moyens technologiques à la disposition des autorités étatiques depuis le prononcé dudit arrêt étant en effet devenus incomparablement plus étendus et sophistiqués. Il semble toutefois indispensable, pour la discussion de la protection des données personnelles, de bien retracer les origines de la jurisprudence de la Cour de Strasbourg dans ce domaine. Il semble également utile, pour une analyse de la mise en balance des intérêts exigée par les deux juridictions européennes, de réfléchir à la façon dont nos prédécesseurs ont traité des intérêts concurrents en jeu.

À la différence de l'affaire *Klass*, dans les affaires *S. et Marper*, la Cour conclut à une violation de l'article 8. Prononcé 20 ans après *Klass*, cet arrêt apporte une contribution importante à la jurisprudence de Strasbourg dans le domaine de la protection des données personnelles, soulignée par le fait que l'arrêt *Marper* est souvent cité par la CJUE dans sa jurisprudence récente dans ce domaine, qui s'y réfère en effet explicitement dans son arrêt *Digital Rights* et indirectement dans les arrêts *Schrems* et *Tele-2*. Les enseignements y contenus semblent avoir joué un rôle primordial lorsque la Cour de Luxembourg a restreint de manière importante la marge d'appréciation dont jouissent tant le législateur de l'UE que le législateur national.[12] Il est toutefois nécessaire de souligner que, du point de vue de l'article 8 et la jurisprudence de la Cour de Strasbourg, l'arrêt *Marper* ne constitue pas une affaire de surveillance de masse proprement dite. Dans cette affaire britannique, ce qui était en cause, c'étaient notamment les empreintes digitales et les échantillons d'ADN prélevés sur des personnes soupçonnées d'avoir commis des infractions pénales. Ces données pouvaient être conservées sans limite de temps, même lorsque la procédure pénale se concluait par

---

circonstances de la cause, par exemple, la nature, l'étendue et la durée des mesures éventuelles, les raisons requises pour les ordonner, les autorités compétentes pour les permettre, exécuter et contrôler, le type de recours fourni par le droit interne». Voir également *S. et Marper*, précité, § 67.

[10] Voir *Digital Rights Ireland Ltd*, précité, §§ 16 et 39. Étaient en cause, dans ces affaires, le nom et l'adresse de l'abonné ou de l'utilisateur inscrit, le numéro de téléphone de l'appelant et le numéro de l'appelé ainsi qu'une adresse IP pour les services Internet.

[11] Au § 99 de l'arrêt *Tele2*, précité, en s'appuyant sur les conclusions de son avocat général, la CJUE relève que «ces données fournissent les moyens d'établir, [...], le profil des personnes concernées, information tout aussi sensible, au regard du droit au respect de la vie privée, que le contenu même des communications».

[12] Voir *Digital Rights*, précité, §§ 47, 54-55 ; *Schrems*, précité, § 78, et *Tele2*, précité, § 93-96.

l'acquittement de l'accusé ou par un non-lieu. Vu leur caractère éminemment personnel, la nature et la quantité des informations personnelles contenues dans les échantillons cellulaires et le fait que les profils ADN fournissent un moyen de découvrir les relations génétiques et de tirer des conclusions quant à l'origine ethnique, la conservation de ces données s'analysait en soi en une atteinte au droit au respect de la vie privée.[13]

Dans l'arrêt *Marper*, la Cour n'a pas d'abord tranché la «légalité» de l'ingérence dans le sens bien établi de l'accessibilité et de la qualité de la loi. Elle a préféré aborder cette question dans le cadre de l'examen de la proportionnalité. Ce chevauchement entre légalité et proportionnalité apparaît dans certains arrêts de Strasbourg et avec force dans l'affaire *Digital Rights* où l'avocat général Cruz Villalón et la CJUE ont suivi deux chemins distincts pour aboutir au même résultat d'invalidation de la directive en cause.[14] Quant à la question de savoir si la conservation des données était nécessaire, la CourEDH a d'abord reconnu une «certaine marge d'appréciation» dont jouissent les autorités nationales, pour la restreindre par la suite, s'agissant de données particulièrement intrusives et contenant le patrimoine génétique de la personne concernée.[15] Elle a ensuite relevé que la protection offerte par l'article 8:

> «[S]erait affaiblie de manière inacceptable si l'usage des techniques scientifiques modernes dans le système de la justice pénale était autorisé à n'importe quel prix et *sans une mise en balance attentive des avantages pouvant résulter d'un large recours à ces techniques*, d'une part, et des intérêts essentiels s'attachant à la protection de la vie privée, d'autre part».[16]

Selon la CourEDH dans l'arrêt *Marper*, le caractère général et indifférencié du pouvoir de conservation, tel qu'il avait été appliqué aux requérants, y compris un mineur, sans limite dans le temps et avec peu de possibilités d'effacement malgré l'acquittement, ne traduisait pas un juste équilibre entre les intérêts publics et

---

[13] Voir *S. et Marper*, précité, §§ 72-73. La Cour a reconnu que la conservation des empreintes digitales, en revanche, a un impact moins grand sur la vie privée mais a conclu que la conservation de ces éléments ne saurait passer pour une mesure neutre ou banale et pouvait en soi donner lieu à des préoccupations importantes concernant le respect de la vie privée. Voir *S. et Marper*, §§ 84-85. Comme dans l'arrêt *Klass*, la Cour, au § 71 de l'arrêt *S. et Marper*, a pris note des innovations dans le domaine des technologies de l'information (et de la génétique) et a conclu qu'elle ne pouvait écarter la possibilité que les aspects de la vie privée se rattachant aux informations génétiques fassent à l'avenir l'objet d'atteinte par des voies nouvelles, qu'elle ne pouvait pas prévoir à l'époque de son jugement avec précision.

[14] Directive 2006/24/CE du Parlement européen et du Conseil, du 15 mars 2006, sur la conservation de données générées ou traitées dans le cadre de la fourniture de services de communications électroniques accessibles au public ou de réseaux publics de communications, et modifiant la directive 2002/58/CE (JO L105/54).

[15] Voir *S. et Marper*, précité, §§ 102-103 et 120-125.

[16] *Ibid.*, § 112.

privés concurrents en jeu. L'État défendeur avait donc outrepassé toute marge d'appréciation acceptable en la matière.[17]

En 2018, dans l'affaire *Big Brother Watch*, une des cinq chambres de la Cour a été confrontée à un système de surveillance électronique mis en œuvre par les autorités britanniques qui permettaient l'interception massive de communications et le partage de renseignements avec des États étrangers.[18] Dans ce contexte nouveau, la Cour a fait un tour d'horizon de sa jurisprudence relative à l'interception – l'interception ciblée mais, surtout, l'interception massive – de communications afin de dégager les principes clés sur la manière de concilier le recours à de telles mesures de surveillance et la protection de la vie privée et des données personnelles.[19] La chambre a rappelé qu'une législation habilitant l'interception massive de communications doit, au minimum, indiquer les exigences suivantes : la nature des infractions susceptibles de donner lieu à un mandat d'interception ; la définition des catégories de personnes susceptibles de voir intercepter leurs communications ; la limite à la durée de l'interception ; la procédure à suivre pour l'examen, l'utilisation et la conservation des données recueillies ; les précautions à prendre pour la communication des données à d'autres parties, et les circonstances dans lesquelles peut ou doit s'opérer l'effacement ou la destruction des données interceptées.[20] Il est à noter que la chambre, rejetant l'argument des requérants selon lequel il était nécessaire d'actualiser les exigences susmentionnées, a confirmé sa jurisprudence établie selon laquelle l'autorisation d'un juge représente certes une garantie importante, voire une «bonne pratique», mais qu'elle ne peut en elle-même être nécessaire et suffisante pour garantir le respect de l'article 8 de la Convention.[21] Selon la chambre, ce qui est crucial c'est de prendre en compte le fonctionnement concret et effectif du système d'interception, notamment les garde-fous à l'exercice du pouvoir, et l'existence ou l'absence de toute indication relative à un abus

---

[17] Ibid., §§ 119-120, 124-125.

[18] En cause dans l'affaire *Big Brother Watch* est un système d'interception de masse («*bulk interception*») de communications externes, où une partie ne se trouve pas au Royaume-Uni, et de l'interception de masse des données de communication. En vertu d'un tel système, toutes les communications passant par certains câbles optiques sont interceptées par les autorités compétentes, mais la grande majorité est éliminée immédiatement par voie d'un traitement automatisé grâce à l'utilisation de filtres.

[19] L'arrêt de la chambre ayant fait l'objet d'un renvoi devant la Grande Chambre en vertu de l'article 43 de la Convention, ci-après les éléments principaux de l'arrêt de la Chambre sont décrits. Toutefois, cet arrêt n'est pas encore définitif.

[20] Arrêt de la chambre dans *Big Brother Watch*, précité, § 307. Il s'agit des exigences déjà signalées par la Grande Chambre dans l'arrêt *Zakharov*, précité, § 231 et dans d'autres affaires antérieures.

[21] Ibid., §§ 316-318. Voir, toutefois, l'opinion séparée du juge Koskelo, qui a considéré que la jurisprudence bien-établie de la CourEDH n'était pas à même de répondre aux défis posés par le «*technological 'sea change' which has taken place*» depuis que les exigences minimales de la jurisprudence ont été posées (§§ 11-15). Elle a considéré qu'une autorisation judiciaire préalable devait constituer une des exigences minimales requises (§ 20).

effectif.[22] Reste à savoir si la Grande Chambre confirmera une telle approche dans son arrêt à venir. S'agissant de l'interception massive de communications, la chambre a reconnu que la décision d'utiliser un tel système relève de l'ample marge d'appréciation dont bénéficie les États contractants.[23] Toutefois, en l'espèce, le système britannique ne satisfaisait pas à l'exigence relative à la qualité de la loi et n'était pas à même de limiter l'ingérence à ce qui est nécessaire dans une société démocratique. Or, d'une part, le processus de sélection, notamment en ce qui concerne le choix des porteurs pour l'interception, les sélecteurs et les critères de recherche utilisés pour filtrer les communications interceptées, et la sélection des éléments à faire examiner par un analyste posait problème. D'autre part, la chambre a conclu qu'il y avait une absence de véritables garanties applicables à la sélection des données de communication pertinentes à examiner.[24]

Dans l'affaire *Big Brother Watch* la chambre s'est également penchée pour la première fois sur la question de la compatibilité avec l'article 8 CEDH du régime de partage de renseignements.[25] Elle a confirmé que les exigences minimales susmentionnées relatives à la conservation, l'examen, l'utilisation, la diffusion, l'effacement et la destruction s'appliquent à un tel système. De même, elle a clarifié que, pour éviter les abus de pouvoir, il faut que le droit interne indique également les circonstances dans lesquelles des éléments interceptés peuvent être demandés auprès de services de renseignements étrangers. En jugeant que le droit interne en cause en l'espèce cadre avec les exigences résultant de l'article 8, la chambre a observé :

> « La Cour a toujours été pleinement consciente des difficultés rencontrées par les États pour protéger leur population contre la violence terroriste, laquelle constitue en elle-même une grave menace pour les droits de l'homme [...], et au cours des années passées elle a expressément reconnu – en réponse à des griefs fondés sur un large éventail d'articles de la Convention – la menace bien réelle à laquelle les États contractants sont actuellement confrontés en raison du terrorisme international [...]. Face à une telle menace, la Cour a considéré qu'il était légitime que les États contractants fassent preuve d'une grande fermeté à l'égard de ceux qui contribuent à des actes de terrorisme [...]. Du fait de la nature du terrorisme international, et en particulier de la complexité des réseaux terroristes internationaux, la Cour admet que l'adoption d'une telle position – et donc la prévention de la commission d'actes violents mettant en péril la vie de personnes innocentes – exige la circulation

---

22   Voir l'arrêt de la chambre dans *Big Brother Watch*, précité, §§ 316-320.
23   Ibid., §§ 317,
24   Ibid., §§ 387-388.
25   Selon la chambre, l'ingérence litigieuse ne réside pas dans l'interception elle-même, mais plutôt dans la réception des éléments interceptés puis dans leur conservation, examen et utilisation par les services de renseignements de l'État défendeur (*Big Brother Watch*, précité, §§ 419-420).

d'informations entre les services de sécurité de nombreux pays de toutes les régions du monde. Dès lors qu'en l'espèce cette «circulation d'informations» s'inscrivait dans un cadre législatif offrant de solides garanties contre les abus, la Cour admet que l'ingérence qui en est résultée était limitée à ce qui est «nécessaire dans une société démocratique».[26]

À ces trois arrêts s'ajoutent bien sûr les arrêts et décisions dans les affaires *Liberty, Kennedy, Zakharov et Szabó et Vissy* et de nombreuses autres affaires concernant la protection des données personnelles en général ou dans le contexte plus spécifique de la surveillance secrète ou de masse.

II. ARTICULATION ENTRE LE DROIT À LA VIE PRIVÉE ET LE DROIT À LA PROTECTION DES DONNÉES PERSONNELLES

À titre préliminaire, il faut souligner, comme il ressort très clairement et de manière répétée de la jurisprudence de la CourEDH, qu'il appartient à la CJUE et non pas à la Cour de Strasbourg d'interpréter le droit de l'Union.[27] Une comparaison, effectuée par un juge de cette dernière juridiction, entre la jurisprudence des deux Cours qui cherche à mettre en exergue les similarités tout en explorant certaines divergences entre les approches respectives ne devrait pas être considérée comme indiquant le contraire.

Il ressort également très clairement des arrêts de la CourEDH présentés ci-dessus que les droits au respect de la vie privée et à la protection des données personnelles protégés par la Convention se sont développés en parallèle et se chevauchent. Le *droit* à la protection des données personnelles fait incontestablement partie du droit au respect de la vie privée consacré par l'article 8 – voir déjà l'arrêt *Klass* en 1978 et l'arrêt *Malone* en 1984 sur des interceptions téléphoniques[28] – tout en ne figurant pas explicitement dans le libellé de l'article 8 de la Convention. Malgré l'adjonction à la Convention, de nombreux nouveaux droits, sous la forme de protocoles, aucune disposition spécifique dédiée à la protection des données personnelles n'a été ajouté. Que doit-on en déduire ? Vraisemblablement, pas

---

[26]   Ibid., §§ 445-446. En revanche, la Cour, s'agissant de l'obtention de données de communication auprès de fournisseurs de services de communications, a conclu à une violation de l'article 8 (§§ 463-468), le système britannique n'étant pas prévu par le droit interne, tel qu'interprété par les autorités nationales à la lumière de récents arrêts de la CJUE, tel *Digital Rights Ireland* et *Tele2*, précités. Quant à l'article 10, elle a jugé que l'absence d'exigences visibles dans la législation applicable limitant le pouvoir des services de renseignements de rechercher des éléments, journalistiques ou autres, confidentiels, ou qui imposent aux analystes une attention particulière à cet égard, conduit à une violation (§ 493).

[27]   Voir, par exemple, *Thimothawes*, précité, § 71.

[28]   *Malone c. Royaume-Uni*, 2 août 1984, Series A no. 82.

grand-chose. Dans un arrêt de juin 2017 – *Satakunnan et Satamedia* – la Grande Chambre de la CourEDH a rappelé sa jurisprudence constante selon laquelle la notion de « vie privée » figurant à l'article 8 est une notion large et non susceptible d'une définition exhaustive.[29] En outre, citant la Convention n° 108 du Conseil de l'Europe de 1981 et sa jurisprudence bien établie – *Amann, Leander, Uzun, Rotaru* entre autres[30] – elle a relevé :

> « L'article 8 de la Convention consacre [...] *le droit à une forme d'auto-détermination informationnelle*, qui autorise les personnes à invoquer leur droit à la vie privée en ce qui concerne des données qui, bien que neutres, sont collectées, traitées et diffusées à la collectivité, selon des formes ou modalités telles que leurs droits au titre de l'article 8 peuvent être mis en jeu ».[31]

Dans la jurisprudence de la Cour de Strasbourg donc, malgré l'absence de référence explicite à la protection des données personnelles, l'articulation entre le droit au respect de la vie privée et celui à la protection des données se fait de manière naturelle et de façon continue depuis des décennies.

Certes, la Charte consacre deux dispositions séparées à ces deux droits. La question de la relation ou de l'articulation entre eux donne donc lieu à un débat assez intense au niveau de la doctrine.[32] Le lecteur attentif peut d'ailleurs trouver dans la jurisprudence de la CJUE des formulations différentes dans différents arrêts et conclusions touchant à cette question d'articulation. Dans ses conclusions dans l'affaire *Digital Rights*[33], par exemple, l'avocat général Cruz Villalón a reconnu le lien étroit entre le « couple » de droits consacrés par les articles 7 et 8 de la Charte. Il a toutefois considéré que le lien qui les unit dépend essentiellement des données concernées. Pour lui, des données plus que personnelles (se rapportant essentiellement à la vie privée, au secret de la vie privée, y compris l'intimité) relèvent de l'article 7 de la Charte (vie privée) plutôt que de l'article 8 (données personnelles).[34] La CJUE, pour sa part, en jugeant la directive litigieuse invalide, s'est limitée à dire que la protection des données à caractère personnel, résultant de l'obligation explicite prévue à l'article 8 de

---

[29] Voir *Satakunnan Markkinapörssi Oy et Satamedia Oy c. Finlande* [GC], no. 931/13, § 129, CEDH 2017 (extraits) ; *S. et Marper*, précité, § 66, 4 décembre 2008, et *Vukota-Bojić c. Suisse*, no. 61838/10, § 52, 18 octobre 2016.

[30] Voir *Amann c. Suisse* [GC], no. 27798/95, CEDH 2000-II ; *Leander c. Suède*, no. 9248/81, 26 March 1987, Series A no. 116 ; *Uzun c. Allemagne*, no. 35623/05, CEDH 2010 (extraits), et *Rotaru c. Roumanie* [GC], no. 28341/95, CEDH 2000-V.

[31] Voir *Satakunnan*, précité, § 137.

[32] Voir, par exemple, le commentaire de I. Cameron sur l'arrêt *Tele2*, « Balancing data protection and law enforcement needs : *Tele2 Sverige and Watson* » (2017) 54 *CMLRev.* 1467-1496, 1492, ou celui de O. Lynskey sur *Google Spain*, « Control over personal data in a digital age : *Google Spain v. AEPD and Mario Costeja Gonzalez* » (2015) 78 *Modern Law Review* 522-534.

[33] *Digital Rights Ireland Ltd*, précité.

[34] *Ibid.*, §§ 61-67.

la Charte, revêt une importance particulière pour le droit au respect de la vie privée consacré à l'article 7. Pour la Cour de Luxembourg donc, la protection des données à caractère personnel joue un rôle important au regard de ce dernier droit.[35] Dans les arrêts *Digital Rights* et *Schrems*[36], le droit consacré à l'article 8 semble soutenir celui figurant à l'article 7 de la Charte ou, à tout le moins, en constitue une partie subsidiaire ou complémentaire.[37] Quant à l'arrêt *Tele2*[38], en réponse à la question de savoir si *Digital Rights* avait interprété les articles 7 et 8 de la Charte dans un sens allant au-delà de celui conféré à l'article 8 de la Convention par cette Cour, la CJUE a répondu que :

> « [L']'article 8 de la Charte concerne un droit fondamental distinct de celui consacré à l'article 7 de celle-ci et qui n'a pas d'équivalent dans la CEDH ».[39]

Le sens et la portée de cette dernière constatation seront sans doute précisés dans le cadre d'une question préjudicielle à venir. Si la question, telle que posée dans *Tele2*, a été jugée irrecevable, le fait qu'elle ait été posée montre d'ores et déjà pourquoi la question de l'articulation entre les deux droits n'est pas une question purement académique. Car l'existence ou l'absence d'équivalence ou plutôt de correspondance nous conduit sur le terrain de l'article 52 § 3 de la Charte et la règle d'interprétation ou de cohérence qu'il contient.[40]

Pour comprendre l'articulation entre les dispositions de la Convention et celles de la Charte dans ce domaine, plusieurs éléments pourraient mériter une réflexion. Il est incontestable que le droit de l'Union peut prévoir une protection plus favorable de droits correspondants (pour les appeler ainsi).[41] Autre chose

---

[35]   Ibid., §§ 48 et 53.
[36]   Arrêt *Schrems*, précité.
[37]   Ibid., § 78.
[38]   Arrêt *Tele2 Sverige*, précité.
[39]   Ibid., § 129. Voir également les conclusions de l'avocat général Saumandsgaard Øe dans cet arrêt, §§ 76-79, selon lequel : « l'arrêt DRI établit un droit qui ne correspond à aucun droit garanti par la CEDH, à savoir le droit à la protection des données à caractère personnel ». Voir, en revanche, les conclusions de l'avocat général Cruz Villalón dans l'affaire *Digital Rights Ireland*, précité, § 62, selon lesquelles le lien entre le droit au respect de la vie privée et celui à la protection des données « implique notamment que la jurisprudence de la CourEDH sur l'interprétation de l'article 8 de la CEDH, […], relative à la protection des données personnelles conserve, conformément à l'article 52 § 3 de la Charte, toute sa pertinence pour l'interprétation de l'article 8 de la Charte », ou les conclusions de l'avocat général Mengozzi dans l'avis 1/15, précité, § 171, qui observe que les articles 7 et 8 de la Charte sont fondés sur l'article 8 de la CEDH.
[40]   L'article 52, § 3, de la Charte dispose : « Dans la mesure où la présente Charte contient des droits correspondant à des droits garantis par la C[EDH], leur sens et leur portée sont les mêmes que ceux que leur confère ladite convention. Cette disposition ne fait pas obstacle à ce que le droit de l'Union accorde une protection plus étendue ».
[41]   Voir, par exemple, la proposition de l'avocat général Campos Sanchez-Bórdona d'aller dans ce sens s'agissant du principe de *ne bis in idem*, prévoyant une protection qu'il estimait aller au-delà du seuil minimum prévu par la Convention (*Luca Menci*, C-524/15, EU :C :2017 :667). Dans son arrêt, la CJUE n'a pas suivi son avocat général et a décidé que les

serait, semble-t-il, de ne voir aucune correspondance ou équivalence déjà en amont, de sorte que le seuil minimum de la Convention et l'article 52, § 3, de la Charte, ne joueraient aucun rôle. Certes, l'article 8 de la Charte n'apparaît pas sur la liste figurant dans les explications qui accompagnent la Charte, des *articles* de celle-ci dont le sens et la portée sont les mêmes que les articles correspondants de la CEDH.[42] Toutefois, il est à noter, d'une part, que cette partie des explications parle d'*articles,* tandis que l'article 52 § 3 parle de *droits.*[43] D'autre part, selon les explications, l'article 8 de la Charte est *fondé* sur l'article 8 de la CEDH et sur la Convention du Conseil de l'Europe de 1981.[44] Il appartient très certainement à la CJUE et non pas à la Cour de Strasbourg, d'interpréter le droit de l'Union. Mais la nature et le contenu de la réponse à cette question relative à l'articulation entre l'article 8 de la Convention et les articles 7 et 8 de la Charte influencent non seulement l'articulation entre la jurisprudence des deux Cours européennes sur la protection des données personnelles mais, surtout la réception, par les juridictions nationales, de la jurisprudence des deux Cours dans ce domaine et la facilité avec laquelle elles peuvent la comprendre, la suivre et l'appliquer.

Certes, le paragraphe 129 précité de *Tele2* pourrait simplement signifier que l'article 8 de la Convention ne prévoit pas *explicitement* un droit à la protection des données personnelles. Des passages d'autres arrêts relatifs à la protection des données à caractère personnel – tels *Volker et Schecke* – pointent dans cette direction.[45] Mais on pourrait espérer, dans ce cas, que les juridictions nationales le comprennent en ce sens.

---

exigences auxquelles l'article 50 de la Charte, en combinaison avec l'article 52, paragraphe 1er, de celle-ci, soumet un éventuel cumul de poursuites et de sanctions pénales ainsi que de poursuites et de sanctions administratives de nature pénale, assurent un niveau de protection du principe *ne bis in idem* qui ne méconnaît pas celui garanti à l'article 4 du Protocole no 7 à la CEDH, tel qu'interprété par la CourEDH (EU :C :2018 :197).

[42] L'importance des explications ressort de l'article 6 TEU, de l'article 52 § 7 de la Charte et de la jurisprudence de la CJUE. Voir, par exemple, *Åkerberg Fransson*, C-617/10, EU :C :2013 :105, § 20.

[43] Cette différence de langage ressort également de l'explication ad Article 7 : «Les droits garantis à l'article 7 correspondent à ceux qui sont garantis par l'article 8 de la CEDH». Voir également dans ce sens l'opinion séparée des juges Pardalos et Eicke dans l'affaire *Big Brother Watch*, précité, § 22, lorsqu'elle était devant une chambre de la première Section.

[44] Voir également les considérants 1, 2, 3, 10 et 11 de la directive 95/46.

[45] Voir *Volker et Schecke*, précité, § 52 :
«Dans ces conditions, il doit être considéré, d'une part, que le respect du droit à la vie privée à l'égard du traitement des données à caractère personnel, reconnu par les articles 7 et 8 de la charte, se rapporte à toute information concernant une personne physique identifiée ou identifiable […] et, d'autre part, que les limitations susceptibles d'être légitimement apportées au droit à la protection des données à caractère personnel, correspondent à celles tolérées dans le cadre de l'article 8 de la CEDH».
Il est à noter que dans son arrêt *Volker et Schecke* la CJUE se réfère à plusieurs reprises à la jurisprudence bien établie de la CourEDH relative à la protection des données et l'article 8 de la Convention.

III. MISSION ET MÉTHODOLOGIE DES DEUX COURS EUROPÉENNES DANS CE DOMAINE

Quant à la méthodologie applicable dans les affaires relevant de ce domaine, à première vue l'approche des deux juridictions est très similaire. L'analyse de la CourEDH suit, en général, un ordre bien précis – ingérence, légalité, buts légitimes et nécessité. Il est reconnu, dans le domaine de la surveillance de masse, que la question de la légalité de l'ingérence est étroitement liée à celle de savoir si le critère de la «nécessité» a été respecté.[46] Donc, des critères pouvant faire l'objet d'un examen dans le cadre de la légalité d'une ingérence litigieuse sont parfois rapportés à un examen conjoint de légalité et de proportionnalité.[47] Le raisonnement dans l'arrêt *Digital Rights*, à propos d'un renvoi préjudiciel soulevant des questions de validité, et dans l'arrêt *Tele-2*, au sujet d'un renvoi soulevant des questions d'interprétation, suit le cheminement similaire indiqué par l'article 52, § 1er, de la Charte[48] – existence d'une ingérence, respect ou non du contenu essentiel du droit, poursuite d'un objectif d'intérêt général et proportionnalité (dans le sens d'apte, approprié et nécessaire). Les similarités de méthode, de langage et d'inspiration jurisprudentielle se reflètent donc dans la jurisprudence des deux Cours et dans la «cross-fertilisation» qu'on y trouve.[49]

Malgré ces similitudes, il est peut-être utile de mentionner quelques points de divergence actuels ou potentiels, ou du moins quelques points sur lesquels les inflexions des deux juridictions semblent différentes, du moins en l'état actuel de la jurisprudence. Ces points se font ressentir tant au niveau de la mission que les deux juridictions sont appelées à remplir, que de celui du contenu des arrêts signalés. À ce dernier égard, on peut prendre comme exemple le contrôle judiciaire ou administratif préalable exigé par la CJUE dans *Digital Rights*.[50] Cela ne semble pas correspondre à l'approche de la CourEDH jusqu'à présent, confirmée récemment dans l'arrêt de la chambre dans *Big Brother Watch*,

---

46   Voir *Zakharov*, précité, § 236 et *Szabó et Vissy*, précité, § 54.
47   Comparez l'approche suivie dans *Liberty*, précité, §§ 59-69, où l'examen se concentre sur la légalité à celle dans les affaires *S. et Marper* ou *Zakharov*, précitées, où la Cour examine des critères similaires à l'aune de la nécessité.
48   La formule utilisée à l'article 52 § 1 de la Charte s'inspire bien évidemment de la jurisprudence de la CJUE relative aux droits fondamentaux en tant que principes généraux du droit de l'Union (voir, par exemple, *Karlsson*, C-292/97, EU :C :2000 :202, § 45).
49   On pourrait dire que les §§ 47 et 54 de l'arrêt *Digital Rights*, par exemple, se lisent comme un arrêt de la Cour de Strasbourg et, dans cette partie de l'arrêt, la Cour se réfère explicitement aux arrêts *S. et Marper*, précité ; *Liberty*, précité, et *Rotaru*, précité. Pour sa part, l'arrêt *Zakharov* inspire clairement à certains égards de l'arrêt *Digital Rights* et dans *Szabó et Vissy* une chambre de la quatrième section s'inspire de la CJUE de manière très explicite (même si sur l'exigence de la nécessité stricte elle n'a pas été suivie par d'autres chambres par la suite).
50   Voir *Digital Rights*, précité, § 62.

selon laquelle l'autorisation peut, selon le cas, intervenir à trois stades, à savoir avant, pendant ou après l'interception.[51] La Convention prévoyant un seuil minimum de droits garantis, cette divergence, dans la mesure où elle cherche une protection plus favorable, n'est pas problématique. Toutefois, il est à noter que là où il existait une jurisprudence assez abondante de la Cour de Strasbourg, l'arrêt *Digital Rights* opte, de manière sans doute légitime, pour une approche différente sans toutefois la mentionner et sans l'expliquer aux juridictions nationales.[52]

A. MISSION

La mission de chaque juridiction est également bien distincte et cela pourrait expliquer les différentes orientations jurisprudentielles susmentionnées. Les juges de Strasbourg opèrent un contrôle externe et *a posteriori*, en tant que juridiction internationale, jugeant concrètement, tous les éléments de fait sur table, la solution donnée par le juge national lorsqu'il a cherché à assurer le respect des droits fondamentaux dans une affaire devant lui. Leur rôle dans le domaine de la surveillance de masse est de veiller à ce que des garanties et procédures prévues soient capables de prévenir un abus de pouvoir. De même, dès lors que des intérêts concurrents (publics et privés) sont en jeu, la CourEDH veille à ce qu'un juste équilibre soit respecté entre eux. Elle ne refait pas le procès qui a eu lieu au niveau interne ; elle applique la doctrine de la « 4ème instance » qui signifie justement qu'elle refuse de s'ériger, en principe, en juge de 4ème instance, et laisse aux autorités nationales – principe de subsidiarité l'oblige – une marge d'appréciation large ou restreinte selon les circonstances.[53] De même, les éléments de preuve présentés devant eux ont déjà fait l'objet – si le principe d'épuisement a été respecté – d'un contrôle par les juridictions internes et ces dernières ont déjà examiné la mise en balance effectuée par les autorités nationales.[54]

---

51 Voir l'arrêt de chambre dans *Big Brother Watch*, précité, §§ 309, 316-320.

52 Voir D. Andersen, Report of the Independent Reviewer of Terrorism Legislation, « A Question of Trust », June 2015, para. 5.78 (a), p. 90.

53 Voir la comparaison entre le renvoi préjudiciel et la requête individuelle faite par mon collègue, G. Ravarani, « Les rapports entre les juridictions nationales et les cours européennes, Point de vue luxembourgeois » in *Liber Amicorum Rusen Ergec*, éd. Pasicrisie luxembourgeoise, 2017, p. 297.

54 Tant en ce qui concerne la subsidiarité qu'en ce qui concerne l'examen préalable par les juridictions internes, voir *A. et autres c. Royaume-Uni* [GC], no. 3455/05, § 154, CEDH 2009 : « La Cour est appelée à jouer un rôle subsidiaire par rapport aux systèmes nationaux de protection des droits de l'homme. [...] Si une requête est néanmoins introduite par la suite devant la Cour, celle-ci doit pouvoir tirer profit des avis de ces tribunaux, lesquels sont en contact direct et permanent avec les forces vives de leurs pays [...] ». Voir, à ce sujet, l'arrêt de chambre dans *Big Brother Watch*, § 256 : « The Court has repeatedly held that it is not its role to determine questions of fact or to interpret domestic law. This is especially so where

Le renvoi préjudiciel permet en revanche à la CJUE d'intervenir à un stade antérieur lorsque le juge national n'a pas encore statué définitivement. Les juges de Luxembourg fournissent l'interprétation officielle et contraignante du droit de l'Union – applicable au-delà de l'affaire de l'espèce. Le juge national de renvoi (lui-même transformé, par la procédure de renvoi et les principes de primauté et d'effet direct, en juge du droit de l'Union) doit appliquer cette interprétation dans une situation bien concrète. L'interprétation par la CJUE des textes législatifs est influencée, voire déterminée, par l'objectif qu'ils cherchent à atteindre, à savoir, dans le domaine de la surveillance de masse, le droit à la protection des données personnelles.[55] Si une telle procédure a de nombreux avantages, dans un domaine qui touche à sécurité nationale et dans lequel la question de preuves est extrêmement délicate, il s'agit d'une procédure avec, peut-être, certains désavantages. Selon l'Investigatory Powers Tribunal (IPT) britannique dans son renvoi préjudiciel dans l'affaire *Privacy International* :

« The [Security and Intelligence Agencies'] capabilities to use [Bulk Communications Data] supplied to them are essential to the protection of the national security of the United Kingdom, including in the fields of counter-terrorism, counter-espionage and counter-nuclear proliferation. [...] It is clear that the Grand Chamber in [Tele 2 Sverige and] Watson did not have the material to address any of the benefits of BCD in the context of national security in its judgment, not least because no evidence in that regard was put before the Court, and in any event, as discussed above, the focus [of the CJEU] was on criminal investigation. »[56]

B. MARGE D'APPRÉCIATION

Comment la différence entre les missions des deux Cours se traduit-elle dans le raisonnement adopté dans ce domaine ? S'agissant, par exemple, de la marge d'appréciation reconnue aux États membres dans ce domaine sensible, dans *Klass* et *Zakharov*, elle est caractérisée comme étant « un certain pouvoir discrétionnaire » ou comme leur laissant « une certaine marge d'appréciation ». Dans l'arrêt *Weber et Saravia* elle est « ample » ou « large », une qualification

---

domestic law is complex and, for reasons of national security, the State is not at liberty to disclose relevant information to it. [...] In such cases, therefore, it is particularly important that the domestic courts, which have access to the confidential documentation, first strike the 'complex and delicate balance' between the competing interests at stake ».

[55] Voir *Google Spain*, C-131/12, EU :C :2014 :317, § 53 : « au vu de l'objectif de la directive 95/46 d'assurer une protection efficace et complète des libertés et des droits fondamentaux des personnes physiques, notamment du droit à la vie privée, à l'égard du traitement des données à caractère personnel, cette dernière expression ne saurait recevoir une interprétation restrictive ».

[56] Voir §§ 42 et 59 de la décision de renvoi du IPT du 8 septembre 2017.

confirmée dans *Big Brother Watch*.[57] Dans l'affaire *Marper* la Cour a fourni les précisions suivantes concernant l'étendue de la marge d'appréciation :

« [Elle] est variable et dépend d'un certain nombre de facteurs, dont la nature du droit en cause [...], son importance pour la personne concernée, la nature de l'ingérence et la finalité de celle-ci ».[58]

Compte tenu de la nature des données en cause dans l'affaire *Marper* et donc de l'ampleur de l'ingérence – les données contenaient le patrimoine génétique des personnes concernées et étaient jugées comme étant particulièrement intrusives et intrinsèquement privées – la CourEDH a considéré que la marge était restreinte.

Il est donc intéressant de noter que dans l'arrêt *Digital Rights*, la CJUE, après avoir cité ce même extrait de l'arrêt *Marper*, a conclu que, compte tenu du rôle important que joue la protection des données à caractère personnel au regard du droit au respect de la vie privée et de l'ampleur et la gravité de l'ingérence dans ce droit que comportait la directive litigieuse, le pouvoir d'appréciation du législateur se révélait réduit et le contrôle par la CJUE devait être strict.[59] Pour le moment, s'agissant de données de communication et dans un domaine de surveillance où la sécurité nationale et la lutte contre le terrorisme sont en jeu, il semble qu'une marge si réduite accompagnée d'un contrôle si strict ne ressorte pas de manière si claire de la jurisprudence de Strasbourg. Certes, dans l'affaire *Szabó et Vissy*, la quatrième section a parlé d'un contrôle de « stricte nécessité ».[60] Toutefois, la Grande Chambre dans l'arrêt *Zakharov* n'a pas employé les mêmes termes, se référant à la stricte nécessité uniquement en relation avec la jurisprudence de la CJUE.[61] Dans l'affaire très récente *Centrum för rättvisa c. Suède*, relative à

---

[57] Voir *Klass*, précité, § 49 ; *Zakharov*, précité, § 232 ; *Weber et Saravia c. Allemagne*, précité, §§ 106 et 137, et l'arrêt de chambre dans *Big Brother Watch*, précité, §§ 314, 315 et 387. Dans *Kennedy*, précité, §§ 154, la Cour se réfère à « une certaine latitude » des États contractants pour apprécier la nécessité d'une mesure de surveillance et, dans *Liberty*, § 65, s'agissant de communications extérieures interceptées de manière systématique, à « une très large latitude pour capter les communications et les écouter ». Voir également *Leander*, précité, § 59, dans un contexte différent mais connexe : « les autorités nationales jouissent d'une marge d'appréciation dont l'ampleur dépend non seulement de la finalité, *mais encore du caractère propre de l'ingérence*. En l'occurrence, il échet de mettre en balance l'intérêt de l'État défendeur à protéger sa sécurité nationale avec la gravité de l'atteinte au droit du requérant au respect de sa vie privée ». Dans le contexte spécifique de la lutte contre le terrorisme, voir *A et autres c. Royaume-Uni*, précité, §§ 173-174.

[58] *S. et Marper*, précité, §§ 102-104.

[59] Voir *Digital Rights*, précité, §§ 47-48, et l'application par analogie de cet arrêt dans *Schrems*, précité, § 78 (pouvoir d'appréciation réduit de la Commission/contrôle strict par la CJEU).

[60] Voir *Szabó et Vissy*, précité, §§ 67, 71, 75-76 et 89.

[61] Voir *Zakharov*, précité, § 147. Dans l'affaire *Marper*, précité, § 104, la Cour s'est référée à la nécessité d'un « examen rigoureux » des mesures litigieuses, mais cela ressortait surtout du « caractère intrinsèquement privé » des données personnelles, voire intimes, en cause

l'interception massive de signaux électroniques, un arrêt de la troisième section de la Cour de Strasbourg a cherché à apporter quelques précisions additionnelles. Il a confirmé que les autorités nationales jouissent d'une large marge d'appréciation lorsqu'elles décident la meilleure manière de protéger la sécurité nationale et la décision d'opérer un certain type de système de surveillance tombe dans cette marge.[62] Toutefois, si les menaces actuelles confrontant les autorités nationales liées au terrorisme international et à la criminalité transfrontalière, ainsi qu'à la sophistication croissante des technologies de communication justifient une telle marge ample, la latitude accordée aux États quant à l'exploitation du dispositif choisi est en revanche plus étroite afin de minimiser le risque d'abus.[63] Dans *Big Brother Watch*, deux juges de chambre ont également attiré l'attention sur la différence entre l'approche de nécessité stricte adoptée par la CJUE et celle adoptée dans ce même domaine par la CourEDH.[64]

Dans ce contexte la jurisprudence strasbourgeoise dite «*Animal Defenders*» mérite également d'être mentionnée. Sans rentrer dans les détails de l'affaire, qui concernait l'article 10 de la Convention[65], on peut néanmoins rappeler ce que la CourEDH a énoncé au sujet du principe de proportionnalité :

> «[P]our déterminer la proportionnalité, d'une mesure générale, la Cour doit commencer par étudier les choix législatifs à l'origine de la mesure [...]. La qualité de l'examen parlementaire et judiciaire de la nécessité de la mesure réalisée au niveau national revêt une importance particulière à cet égard, y compris pour ce qui est de l'application de la marge d'appréciation pertinente [...]».[66]

---

dans ladite affaire. Dans l'arrêt *Kennedy*, précité, § 153, le caractère strictement nécessaire de mesures de surveillance était à juger à l'égard de la nécessité de préserver les institutions démocratiques. Voir également en ce sens *Drogojević c. Croatie*, no. 68955/11, § 84, 15 janvier 2015. En revanche, voir l'approche plus «fluide» dans *Weber et Saravia*, précité, §§ 105-107 ou *Kvasnica c. Slovaquie*, n° 72094/01, § 80, 9 juin 2009. Il convient en tout cas de rappeler que la plupart des affaires devant la CourEDH ont eu trait, jusqu'à présent, à l'interception des communications (contenu) et non à l'interception des données de communication.

62   Cette distinction a été confirmée par la chambre dans l'arrêt *Big Brother Watch*, précité, § 315.

63   *Centrum för rättvisa c. Suède* No. 35252/08, 19 juin 2018, §§ 112-113 et §§ 179-181. Cet arrêt de la troisième section a également fait l'objet d'un renvoi devant la Grande Chambre. Il n'est donc pas encore définitif.

64   Voir l'opinion séparée dans *Big Brother Watch* des juges Pardalos et Eicke, précitée, § 22 : « [the CJEU] indicated that access should be limited to what was strictly necessary for the objective pursued and, where that objective was fighting crime, it should be restricted to fighting serious crime. [...] Therefore, while there is some similarity in the language used by the two courts, the CJEU appears to have adopted a more prescriptive approach as regards the safeguards it considers necessary. »

65   *Animal Defenders c. Royaume-Uni* [GC], no. 48876/08, CEDH 2013 (extraits).

66   Ibid., § 108 et § 111, où la CourEDH a ajouté : «Il faut en conséquence reconnaître à l'État une certaine latitude pour procéder à pareille appréciation, complexe et tributaire des données propres à chaque pays, qui a joué un rôle crucial dans les choix législatifs examinés en l'espèce». En ce qui concerne la CJUE, le raisonnement au § 77 de l'arrêt *Volker et Schecke* semblait réfléchir un esprit similaire : «Il y a donc lieu de vérifier si le Conseil de l'Union

Si la Cour de Strasbourg ne raisonne pas en termes de présomption de légalité – notion présente dans *Schrems* mais non pas dans *Digital Rights* ou *Tele-2* – elle est respectueuse, en vertu de son rôle subsidiaire, des choix législatifs, tout en insistant sur un contrôle européen externe. Il ne s'agit pas d'un excès de «déférence» vis-à-vis des autorités nationales : le contrôle Strasbourgeois de la proportionnalité doit être réel et méticuleux, mais la CourEDH ne cherche pas à substituer son appréciation de questions de sécurité nationale à celle des autorités nationales si des garanties adéquates contre les abus sont en place. La question clé pour la CourEDH est si tel est le cas. Le prisme de contrôle de la Cour de Strasbourg apparaît donc comme différent de celui de Luxembourg. Ceci pourrait s'expliquer tout simplement par le fait que le type de mesure évalué n'est pas tout à fait le même (voire n'est pas évalué de la même façon), étant précisé que, en plus, le rôle des deux juridictions est différent.

C. NATURE DES DONNÉES INTERCEPTÉES ET AMPLEUR DE L'INGÉRENCE CONSTATÉE

Il se dégage de la jurisprudence des deux Cours qu'une ingérence dans le droit au respect de la vie privée peut être établie peu importe le caractère sensible des données personnelles qui font l'objet du traitement et en dépit de la question de savoir si les intéressés ont ou non subi d'éventuels inconvénients.[67]

Reste à savoir si l'évaluation de la *nature et de l'ampleur de l'ingérence* résultant de la simple interception de données de communication serait appréciée de la même façon par la Cour de Strasbourg qu'elle l'a été par la CJUE dans l'affaire *Digital Rights* et *Tele-2*. Dans cette dernière affaire, il est indiqué que les données de communication en cause :

> «[F]ournissent les moyens d'établir [...] le profil des personnes concernées, *information tout aussi sensible, au regard du droit au respect de la vie privée, que le contenu même des communications*».[68]

---

européenne et la Commission ont effectué une pondération équilibrée entre l'intérêt de l'Union à garantir la transparence de ses actions et une utilisation optimale des fonds publics, d'une part, et l'atteinte au droit des bénéficiaires concernés au respect de leur vie privée, en général, et à la protection de leurs données à caractère personnel, en particulier, d'autre part».

67   Il suffit de mentionner *Digital Rights*, précité ; *Österreichischer Rundfunk*, C-195/06, EU :C :2007 :613, ou *Google Spain*, précité, du côté de la CJUE et *Satakunnan*, précité, à l'égard de la Convention.

68   Voir *Tele2*, précité, § 99. Au § 65 de cet arrêt, la CJUE décrit l'ingérence constatée comme étant «d'une vaste ampleur et d'une gravité particulière dans l'ordre juridique de l'Union». Il est à noter que, dans l'avis 1/15, précité, la nature des données de passagers aériens en cause (données PNR) et donc de l'ampleur de l'ingérence aux articles 7 et 8 de la Charte ont été relativisées, voir § 150 : «même si les données PNR peuvent, le cas échéant, révéler des informations très précises sur la vie privée d'une personne, la nature de ces informations est

La même frontière n'a été franchie que partiellement par la Cour de Strasbourg jusqu'à présent. Si dans l'arrêt *Marper* la Cour a condamné de manière catégorique la conservation générale et indifférenciée de données personnelles, il s'agissait, il faut le souligner à nouveau, de données génétiques particulièrement intrusives et intrinsèquement privées faisant l'objet d'une conservation illimitée dans le temps.[69] Certes, dans l'affaire *Zakharov*, la Cour a reconnu que la simple existence d'un système de surveillance tel que celui qui était en cause constitue en soi une ingérence. Toutefois, il ne ressort pas encore clairement de la jurisprudence que tous les différents éléments caractérisant certains systèmes de surveillance de masse seraient jugés comme donnant lieu, dans chaque, cas à une ingérence d'une ampleur vaste (pour utiliser le langage de *Digital Rights*), comme exigeant des garanties procédurales identiques à celles en cause dans une affaire comme *Marper* ou comme exigeant un contrôle de nécessité stricte. Les différents éléments caractérisant ces systèmes – l'interception indifférenciée de données de communication, leur filtrage, la rétention des données filtrées aux fins d'une analyse ultérieure, l'accès uniquement à certaines données sélectionnées après un traitement automatisé et, le cas échéant, leur transfert vers d'autres autorités – pourraient exiger des approches différenciées.

Ces questions sont celles qui confrontent la CourEDH dans ce domaine actuellement. Dans l'affaire *Centrum för rättvisa*, susmentionnée, une chambre a examiné en détail les différents éléments du dispositif de surveillance suédois, mettant en exergue certains défauts, tout en penchant à la fin pour une constatation de non-violation dès lors que, selon la chambre, un examen global de la structure et du fonctionnement du dispositif a démontré que le cadre réglementaire a limité autant que possible le risque d'atteinte à la vie privée et compensé le manque de transparence du dispositif.[70] Un examen global similaire dans *Big Brother Watch* dans une autre chambre a conduit à une constatation partielle de violation de l'article 8 de la Convention. Dans cette dernière affaire, la chambre chargée de l'affaire a reconnu que l'acquisition de données de communication n'est pas nécessairement moins intrusive que l'acquisition du contenu des communications, reflétant ainsi en partie l'approche de la CJUE dans *Digital Rights*, *Tele2* et l'avis 1/15.[71] En revanche, selon cette chambre, la jurisprudence relative à la Convention : « distinguish[es] between different methods of investigation which result in different levels of intrusion

---

limitée à certains aspects de cette vie privée, relatifs en particulier aux voyages aériens entre le Canada et l'Union ». L'avocat général, pour sa part, § 176, a parlé d'une ingérence « d'une ampleur certaine et d'une gravité non-négligeable ».

69 Voir *S. et Marper*, précité, §§ 119 et 125.
70 Voir les conclusions aux §§ 179-181 de l'arrêt de la chambre dans *Centrum för rättvisa c. Suède*, précité.
71 Voir l'arrêt de la chambre dans l'affaire *Big Brother Watch*, précité, § 356.

into an individual's private life». Elle a relevé qu'on ne pourrait pas assumer sans plus qu'une interception de masse est plus intrusive qu'une interception ciblée.[72] Pour le moment, différentes formations de la CourEDH semble avoir accepté qu'il existe ce qu'on appellerait en anglais des « *gradations of intrusion* »[73] et il appartiendra à la Grande Chambre de trancher cette question de nouveau dans un proche avenir.

Dans un arrêt très récent de la CJUE, clarifiant un aspect de l'arrêt *Tele2* à la demande d'une juridiction de renvoi espagnol, on peut déceler un point d'inflexion dans la jurisprudence de cette Cour et peut-être la reconnaissance de ce même principe. Dans son arrêt *Ministerio Fiscal*, la CJUE a jugé que :

> «[C]onformément au principe de proportionnalité, une ingérence grave ne peut être justifiée, en matière de prévention, de recherche, de détection et de poursuite d'infractions pénales, que par un objectif de lutte contre la criminalité devant également être qualifiée de 'grave'. En revanche, lorsque l'ingérence que comporte un tel accès n'est pas grave, ledit accès est susceptible d'être justifié par un objectif de prévention, de recherche, de détection et de poursuite d''infractions pénales' en général. »[74]

Dans deux autres renvois préjudiciels pendants certaines juridictions nationales ont demandé à la CJUE de clarifier, voire de délimiter davantage, sa jurisprudence *Tele2*, de sorte qu'il convient d'attendre pour voir si cette récente inflexion de la part de la CJUE dans *Ministerio Fiscal* sera suivie par d'autres.[75]

---

[72]   Ibid., §§ 350 et 316 respectivement.

[73]   Voir, par exemple, *Malone*, précité, § 84 ; *Uzun*, précité, §§ 52 et 66 : « il y a lieu de distinguer, de par sa nature même, la surveillance par GPS d'autres méthodes de surveillance par des moyens visuels ou acoustiques qui, en règle générale, sont davantage susceptibles de porter atteinte au droit d'une personne au respect de sa vie privée car elles révèlent plus d'informations sur la conduite, les opinions ou les sentiments de la personne qui en fait l'objet. [...] ces critères relativement stricts, établis et suivis dans le contexte spécifique de la surveillance des télécommunications [...] ne sont pas applicables en tant que tels aux affaires comme le cas d'espèce qui a trait à la surveillance par GPS de déplacements en public et donc à une mesure qui, par rapport à l'interception de conversations téléphoniques, doit passer pour constituer une ingérence moins importante dans la vie privée de la personne concernée», ou, récemment, *Ben Faiza c. France*, no. 31446/12, § 74, 8 février 2018. La possibilité de distinguer entre différents types de données lors de la détermination du degré d'ingérence ressort, à première vue, de l'arrêt de la CJUE dans *Google Spain*, précité, § 81, (*c'est nous qui soulignons*) : « Si, certes, les droits de la personne concernée protégés par ces articles prévalent également, en règle générale, sur ledit intérêt des internautes, cet équilibre peut toutefois dépendre, dans des cas particuliers, *de la nature de l'information en question et de sa sensibilité pour la vie privée de la personne concernée* ainsi que de l'intérêt du public à disposer de cette information, lequel peut varier, notamment, en fonction du rôle joué par cette personne dans la vie publique. »

[74]   Voir l'arrêt dans *Ministerio Fiscal*, C-207/16, EU :C :2018 :788, §§ 56-57, et l'opinion de l'avocat général, EU :C :2018 :300, §§ 78-91.

[75]   Voir la demande de décision préjudicielle (DDP) dans l'affaire *Privacy International*, précitée, et celle plus récente de la Cour Constitutionnelle belge dans son arrêt n° 96/2018 du 19 juillet 2018 (C-520/18, *JO* 2018, C-408/39). Pour une analyse des questions soulevées par cette dernière demande voir F. Verbruggen, S. Royer et H. Severijns, «Reconsidering the blanket-data-retention-taboo, for human rights' sake ? », European Law Blog, 1 October 2018.

D. NATURE DES INFRACTIONS ET CATÉGORIES DE PERSONNES SUSCEPTIBLES D'ÊTRE VISÉES

La jurisprudence des deux Cours parle extensivement de la nature des infractions susceptibles de donner lieu à des mesures de surveillance et les catégories de personnes susceptibles d'être visées. Dans l'affaire *Zakharov*, la Cour de Strasbourg a relevé que « le critère de prévisibilité n'exige pas des États membres qu'ils énumèrent exhaustivement en les nommant les infractions qui peuvent donner lieu à une mesure d'interception ».[76] Il suffit de fournir des précisions suffisantes sur la nature des infractions en question. Jusqu'à présent, elle a également rejeté les arguments selon lesquels les termes « sécurité nationale » et « infractions graves » manquent de clarté, précisant dans l'arrêt *Kennedy* :

> « Par la force des choses, des menaces dirigées contre la sécurité nationale peuvent être de différentes natures et peuvent être imprévues et difficiles à définir à l'avance ».[77]

E. LIEN DE RATTACHEMENT ENTRE L'OBJET DE LA RÉTENTION ET LES DONNÉES CONSERVÉES

En examinant la méthodologie suivie par les deux juridictions, on découvre que des comparaisons sont à la fois nécessaires et risquées. Un effet trompe-l'œil peut résulter du fait que les deux juridictions examinent des pratiques de surveillance qui ne sont pas identiques et des ingérences qui, soit sont différentes, soit sont ou pourraient être évaluées différemment.

En ce qui concerne l'exigence d'un lien de rattachement entre l'objet de la rétention et les données conservées, on peut de nouveau réfléchir aux approches des deux Cours et se demander si une différence se dessine entre elles. La CJUE critique le fait que les mesures législatives de l'Union et les mesures nationales examinées n'aient pas été limitées à une conservation portant soit sur des données afférentes à une période temporelle ou une zone géographique ou sur un cercle de personnes susceptibles d'être mêlées d'une manière ou d'une autre à une infraction grave.[78] Ces catégories sont à la fois larges et étroites, de sorte qu'il est difficile de déterminer si la jurisprudence actuelle de la Cour de Strasbourg est plus souple ou non. Cette dernière juridiction parle d'un soupçon raisonnable à l'égard de la personne concernée et, de manière large, de la nécessité dans une société démocratique.[79] Dans l'arrêt *Zakharov*, la Cour rappelle que les mesures

---

[76]   Voir *Zakharov*, précité, § 244.
[77]   *Kennedy*, précité, § 159. Voir également l'arrêt de la chambre de la troisième section dans *Centrum för rättvisa c. Suède*, précité, § 119.
[78]   Voir *Digital Rights*, précité, § 59, et *Tele2*, précité, § 106.
[79]   Voir *Zakharov*, précité, § 260.

d'interception visant une personne non soupçonnée d'une infraction, mais susceptible de détenir des informations sur une telle infraction, pouvaient être justifiées au regard de l'article 8 de la CEDH.[80] C'est la précision de la loi qui compte lors de la désignation des catégories de personnes pouvant faire l'objet de la surveillance. Toutefois, là aussi une mise en balance entre précision, effectivité et capacité préventive s'impose. En ce qui concerne un système d'interception de masse, dans *Big Brother Watch* une chambre a considéré que le fait d'accepter la condition de preuve objective de soupçons raisonnables recherchée par les requérants serait incompatible avec la reconnaissance par la Cour que l'opération d'un tel système relève, en principe, de la marge d'appréciation de l'État :

> «Bulk interception is by definition untargeted, and to require 'reasonable suspicion' would render the operation of a such a scheme impossible. Similarly, the requirement of 'subsequent notification' assumes the existence of clearly defined surveillance targets, which is simply not the case in a bulk interception regime».[81]

Du point de vue de la CEDH, il faut peut-être observer qu'un profilage tel que celui avancé dans *Digital Rights* pourrait soulever des difficultés ; difficultés potentielles qui semblent avoir été reconnues par l'avocat général dans ses conclusions dans l'avis 1/15.[82]

F. PREUVES

Lorsqu'on examine des liens de rattachement, on s'engage sur le terrain des preuves que doivent apporter les États défendeurs pour justifier les mesures d'interception en cause. Comme indiqué précédemment, la CourEDH statue après les juridictions internes et après une analyse, par celles-ci, des preuves disponibles et de la mise en balance effectuée par les autorités compétentes.[83]

---

[80] *Zakharov*, précité, § 245. Dans *Weber et Saravia*, précité, § 115, la Cour rappelle qu'une série de conditions restrictives doivent être remplies pour qu'une mesure entraînant une surveillance stratégique puisse être imposée. Ce n'est que pour certains actes criminels graves – qui reflètent les menaces auxquelles la société se trouve confrontée et qui sont énumérés de manière détaillée – qu'il est possible de solliciter l'autorisation de procéder à une surveillance stratégique.

[81] Arrêt de la chambre de la première section dans *Big Brother Watch*, précité, § 317. Au § 329 la Cour a expliqué davantage la différence entre les systèmes d'intervention ciblés (stricte définition de communications interceptées, suivi par une analyse de toutes les communications ainsi interceptées) et de masse (interception plus vaste suivi par des contrôles plus stricts à l'étape de l'analyse où la plupart des communications est écartée).

[82] Voir les conclusions de l'avocat général Mengozzi, dans l'avis 1/15, précité, § 243. Voir également la DDP de la Cour Constitutionnelle belge, précitée, B.4.2. b).

[83] Voir, par exemple, l'arrêt *A et autres c. le Royaume-Uni*, précité, § 177, dans le contexte de l'article 15 CEDH : «Le ministre de l'Intérieur a soumis aux juridictions britanniques des éléments tendant à démontrer l'existence d'une menace réelle d'attentats terroristes dirigés contre le Royaume-Uni. La SIAC s'est vu communiquer d'autres informations, confidentielles.

La CJUE statue au cours de la procédure, tout en bénéficiant des interventions, parfois nombreuses, des États membres, notamment dans des affaires où des questions préjudicielles sont jugées sensibles.[84]

Les arrêts *Klass* et *Marper* avaient déjà mis le doigt, à mon sens, sur la difficulté à laquelle les juridictions européennes sont et seront confrontées à cet égard. Il ne leur appartient pas de substituer leur appréciation de ce que pourrait être la meilleure politique de surveillance à suivre à celle des autorités nationales. Toutefois, comme le dit la CourEDH dans l'arrêt *S. et Marper*, l'article 8 serait affaibli de manière inacceptable si l'usage des techniques scientifiques modernes était autorisé à n'importe quel prix et «sans une mise en balance attentive des avantages pouvant résulter d'un large recours à ces techniques, d'une part, et des intérêts essentiels s'attachant à la protection de la vie privée, d'autre part». Ces juridictions exigent des États qu'ils veillent à respecter le juste équilibre entre les intérêts publics et privés concurrents en jeu. En même temps, elles sont elles-mêmes confrontées à la nécessité de respecter l'équilibre entre ces deux constats – éviter un effet de substitution tout en demandant la preuve des avantages pouvant résulter des systèmes de surveillance en cause. L'avocat général Mengozzi, dans ses conclusions dans l'avis 1/15, souligne – à mon sens à juste titre – qu'il ne suffit pas d'imaginer, de manière abstraite, l'existence de mesures alternatives moins intrusives. Selon lui, il faut encore que ces mesures alternatives soient suffisamment efficaces.[85]

En réalité, s'agissant de preuves, la CourEDH pourrait se trouver face au scénario suivant. D'abord, il y aurait un examen des éléments de preuve d'efficacité par les

---

Tous les juges internes ayant connu de la présente affaire ont déclaré croire à la réalité du danger invoqué (sauf Lord Hoffmann, aux yeux duquel il ne représentait pas une menace de nature à «mettre en péril la vie de la nation», paragraphe 18 ci-dessus). La Cour estime quant à elle que, même si Al-Qaida n'avait pas encore commis d'attentat sur le sol britannique au moment où la dérogation fut établie, on ne saurait reprocher aux autorités nationales d'avoir cru à «l'imminence» d'un attentat au vu des éléments dont elles disposaient à l'époque pertinente, car une atrocité aurait pu se produire à tout instant, sans avertissement. L'exigence d'imminence ne doit pas recevoir une interprétation étroite au point d'obliger les États à attendre qu'un désastre survienne pour prendre des mesures propres à le conjurer».

[84]   On observe les interventions suivantes : affaire *Digital Rights* (8 États membres et 3 institutions de l'UE, y compris le Conseil) ; affaire *Schrems* (8 États membres, 2 institutions de l'UE et le Contrôleur européen de la protection des données) et affaire *Tele-2 Sverige* (15 États membres et 1 institution de l'UE). L'intervention devant la CourEDH par des États membres autres que l'État défendeur, même en formation de Grande Chambre, est beaucoup moins fréquente.

[85]   Conclusions de M. Mengozzi, avis 1/15, précité, § 208. Il a également mis en exergue, au § 216, la raison d'être des régimes tel le régime PNR : «l'intérêt même de (ces) régimes […] est précisément de garantir la transmission massive de données permettant aux autorités compétentes d'identifier, à l'aide d'outils de traitement automatisé et […] de critères d'évaluation préétablis, des individus, inconnus des services répressifs, mais qui paraissent présenter un 'intérêt' ou un risque pour la sécurité publique et qui sont, dès lors susceptibles d'être soumis ultérieurement à des contrôles individuels plus poussés. »

juridictions nationales avant qu'elles statuent définitivement. Il faut rappeler que tant les juridictions internes que la CourEDH ont un accès restreint aux pièces relatives à la sécurité nationale et à la menace terroriste. Ensuite, on pourrait imaginer la présentation, devant la Cour, par la partie requérante et par le gouvernement défendeur, d'élément de preuves allant dans des sens différents. Enfin, il y aurait sans doute des interventions de tiers intervenants apportant eux-mêmes d'autres preuves encore. Confrontée à des éléments de preuve et des analyses divergentes concernant l'efficacité des mesures de surveillance de masse en cause, une juridiction internationale se trouve bien évidemment dans une position difficile. Faudrait-il accepter, par exemple, des rapports qui mettent en cause, d'une manière générale, l'efficacité de mesures de surveillance de masse dans la lutte contre le terrorisme et la criminalité grave ou, en revanche, pencher pour des rapports comme celui du Independent Reviewer of Terrorism Legislation britannique de 2015/2016, qui a conclu :

> «[B]ulk interception power [...] has played an important part in the prevention of bomb attacks, the rescuing of hostages and the thwarting of numerous cyber attacks. [...] While alternative capabilities could sometimes be deployed, including targeted versions of the powers under review and the use of human agents, they were likely to produce less comprehensive intelligence and were often more dangerous [...], more resource intensive, more intrusive or – crucially – slower. In many cases, there was simply no realistic alternative to use of the bulk power».[86]

Dans le cadre du contentieux relatif à la menace terroriste et en relation avec l'application, par les autorités britanniques, de la dérogation prévue à l'article 15 de la Convention, la Grande Chambre de la Cour EDH a déjà relevé :

> «[L]a Cour n'en reconnaît pas moins que chaque gouvernement, garant de la sécurité de la population dont il a la charge, demeure libre d'apprécier par lui-même les faits à la lumière des informations qu'il détient. L'opinion de l'exécutif et du Parlement britannique importe donc en la matière, et il convient d'accorder un grand poids à celle des juridictions internes, qui sont mieux placées pour évaluer les éléments de preuve relatifs à l'existence d'un danger».[87]

IV. LA SURVEILLANCE DE MASSE EN CONTEXTE

Le contexte dans lequel s'insère cette jurisprudence relative à la surveillance de masse est reconnu et référencé par les deux Cours européennes.

---

[86] Voir D. Andersen, Independent Reviewer of Terrorism Legislation (UK), Report of the Bulk Powers Review, August 2016, § 9.14 (a) et (e). Voir également à cet égard §§ 353 et 386 de l'arrêt de chambre dans l'affaire *Big Brother Watch*.

[87] Voir *A et autres c. Royaume-Uni*, précité, § 180.

La lutte contre le terrorisme est un problème récurrent auquel la CourEDH est confrontée depuis le début de son existence.[88] Si dans l'arrêt *Klass* le terrorisme mentionné était surtout d'origine locale, dans l'affaire *Weber et Saravia,* on trouve une référence à «la lutte contre le terrorisme international» considéré comme une menace accrue pour les sociétés démocratiques.[89] Comme l'a souligné dans un autre contexte le juge Sicilianos, «la recrudescence et l'ampleur des attentats terroristes, ainsi que l'envergure des mesures antiterroristes de ces dernières années ont généré des requêtes qui ont nourri considérablement le contentieux 'terroriste' sous l'angle de nombreuses dispositions de la Convention».[90] Dans l'arrêt *Szabó et Vissy,* la Chambre a reconnu cette nouvelle réalité lorsqu'elle a relevé :

> «[I]t is a natural consequence of the forms taken by present-day terrorism that governments resort to cutting-edge technologies in pre-empting such attacks, including the massive monitoring of communications susceptible to containing indications of impending incidents».[91]

Dans l'arrêt *Klass* déjà, la Cour avait bien défini le défi auquel sont confrontées tant les autorités nationales compétentes que, implicitement, les juridictions internationales appelées à exercer un contrôle externe :

> «La latitude des États membres n'est pas illimitée compte tenu du danger, inhérent à pareille loi, de saper, voire de détruire, la démocratie au motif de la défendre».[92]

Vue dans son ensemble, la jurisprudence de la CourEDH liée au contentieux terroriste paraît à la fois prudente et équilibrée. Elle fait preuve de compréhension face aux difficultés, parfois extrêmes, de la lutte contre le terrorisme sans trahir les principes de sa mission et de sa jurisprudence. À ce dernier égard, il suffit de mentionner l'arrêt *Abu Qatada* rendu dans le cadre de l'article 6 (risque que des preuves obtenues par la torture soit admises dans le procès), les arrêts *Salduz* et

---

[88]   On rappelle la toute première affaire – *Lawless c. Irlande,* no. 332/57, 14 novembre 1960 – et la première affaire interétatique – *Irlande c. Royaume-Uni,* no. 5310/71, 18 janvier 1978

[89]   *Weber et Saravia,* précité, § 109. Voir également *Digital Rights,* précité, § 51 ; *Schrems,* précité, §§ 33 et 34, et *Tele-2,* précité, §§ 103 et 119. Il est à noter que, dans cette dernière affaire, la Cour se réfère principalement à la *criminalité grave* (11 références à «criminalité grave» aux §§ 102, 103, 108, 110, 111, 118 et 125 et dans le dispositif ; 2 références à terrorisme aux §§ 103 et 119). Dans l'affaire *Schrems* : 2 références à «criminalité» (§§ 33 et 34) ; pas de référence à «terrorisme».

[90]   Voir L.-A. Sicilianos, «La Cour européenne des droits de l'homme face à l'Europe en crise», Conférence SEDI/ESIL, CourEDH, 16 octobre 2015.

[91]   Voir *Szabó et Vissy,* précité, § 68.

[92]   Voir *Klass,* précité, § 49. Voir également *Szabó et Vissy,* § 68 : *« it would defy the purpose of government efforts to keep terrorism at bay, thus restoring citizens' trust in their abilities to maintain public security, if the terrorist threat were paradoxically substituted for by a perceived threat of unfettered executive power intruding into citizens' private spheres by virtue of uncontrolled yet far-reaching surveillance techniques and prerogatives ».*

Ibrahim relatifs également à l'article 6 (droit à l'accès à un avocat), l'arrêt *Ramirez Sanchez c. France* concernant l'article 3 (compatibilité du maintien à l'isolement de Carlos «le Chacal»), l'arrêt *del Rio Prada* relatif à l'article 7 § 1 (application rétroactive du droit pénal au détriment de la requérante) ou, plus récemment, l'arrêt *Tagayeva c. Russie* concernant l'article 2 (droit à la vie dans le contexte de la crise des otages de l'école de Beslan).[93]

Dans l'arrêt *Ibrahim* cette approche autant prudente qu'équilibrée ressort très clairement du passage suivant :

> «Il est hors de question que les droits tenant à l'équité du procès soient atténués pour la seule raison que les personnes concernées sont soupçonnées d'être mêlées à des actes de terrorisme. En ces temps difficiles, la Cour estime primordial que les Parties contractantes manifestent leur engagement pour les droits de l'homme et la prééminence du droit [...]. Il reste que, pour déterminer si la procédure dans son ensemble a été équitable, le poids de l'intérêt public à la poursuite de l'infraction particulière en question et à la sanction de son auteur peut être pris en considération [...]. De plus, il ne faut pas appliquer l'article 6 d'une manière qui causerait aux autorités de police des difficultés excessives pour combattre par des mesures effectives le terrorisme et d'autres crimes graves, comme elles doivent le faire pour honorer l'obligation, découlant pour elles des articles 2, 3 et 5 § 1 de la Convention, de protéger le droit à la vie et le droit à l'intégrité physique des membres de la population [...]».[94]

Si la jurisprudence examinée dans ce chapitre relève des articles 8 de la Convention et 7 et 8 de la Charte, le droit à la protection des données est loin d'être le seul droit fondamental en cause dans ce domaine. Il ne faut pas perdre de vue le droit à la liberté et à la sécurité, mentionné en passant par la CJUE dans l'arrêt *Digital Rights* et l'avis 1/15[95], voire les obligations positives incombant aux États membres en vertu de l'article 2 de la Convention relatif au droit à la vie ou en vertu d'autres dispositions telles l'article 3, voire même l'article 8. La nature et les effets de ces obligations positives ressortent de manière très claire des extraits suivants de l'arrêt récent *Tagayeva* relative à la crise des otages de Beslan :

> «[T]he Court confirms that it is acutely conscious of the difficulties faced by the modern States in the fight against terrorism and the dangers of hindsight analysis [...]. As the body tasked with supervision of the human rights obligations under

---

[93]   *Othman (Abu Qatada) c. Royaume-Uni*, no. 8139/09, CEDH 2012 (extraits) ; *Salduz c. Turquie* (GC), no. 36391/02, CEDH 2008 ; *Ibrahim et autres c. Royaume-Uni* [GC], nos. 50541/08 et 3 autres, CEDH 2016 ; *Ramirez Sanchez c. France* [GC], no. 59450/00, CEDH 2006-IX ; *Del Río Prada c. Espagne* (GC), no. 42750/09, CEDH 2013 ; *Tagayeva c. Russie*, no. 26562/07 et 6 autres, CEDH 2017 (extraits). Voir également l'aperçu de Sicilianos, précité.

[94]   Voir *Ibrahim*, précité, § 252.

[95]   Voir *Digital rights*, précité, § 42 ; avis 1/15, précité, § 149.

the Convention, the Court would need to differentiate between the political choices made in the course of fighting terrorism, that remain by their nature outside of such supervision, and other, more operational aspects of the authorities' actions that have a direct bearing on the protected rights. The absolute necessity test formulated in Article 2 is bound to be applied with different degrees of scrutiny, depending on whether and to what extent the authorities were in control of the situation and other relevant constraints inherent in operative decision-making in this sensitive sphere [...].

Turning to the question of positive obligation, the Court reiterates that Article 2 of the Convention may imply a positive obligation on the authorities to take preventive operational measures to protect an individual whose life is at risk from the criminal acts of another individual [...] Such a positive obligation may apply not only to situations concerning the requirement of personal protection of one or more individuals identifiable in advance as the potential target of a lethal act, but also in cases raising the obligation to afford general protection to society [...].

[O]perational decisions [...] are almost always complicated, and the police, who have access to information and intelligence not available to the general public, will usually be in the best position to make them [...]. This is especially so in respect of counter-terrorist activity, where the authorities often face organised and highly secretive networks, whose members are prepared to inflict maximum damage to civilians, even at the cost of their own lives. In the face of an urgent need to avert serious adverse consequences, whether the authorities choose to use a passive approach of ensuring security of the potential targets or more active intervention to disrupt the menace, is a question of tactical choice. However, such measures should be able, when judged reasonably, to prevent or minimise the known risk».[96]

Dans la jurisprudence relative à l'article 8, la mise en balance est généralement faite entre le droit à la vie privée, compris de manière large, et la sécurité nationale, comprise de manière abstraite. La citation des extraits de *Tagayeva* relatifs à l'article 2 ne doit pas être comprise comme voulant minimiser les risques tant pour l'individu que pour les sociétés démocratiques de systèmes de surveillance secrète et de masse. La CourEDH les avait déjà clairement identifiés en 1978 dans son arrêt *Klass*. Dans sa jurisprudence la CJUE les reconnaît également. La référence au contentieux terroriste et aux droits fondamentaux concernés cherche toutefois à placer la jurisprudence afférente dans son contexte plus large.[97] Un tel exercice contextuel semble essentiel afin d'éviter des positions absolutistes.

Si la CJUE a, jusqu'à présent, concentré son analyse sur la protection des droits à la vie privée et à la protection des données, mis en balance avec l'intérêt général de protection de la sécurité publique, la Cour Constitutionnelle belge, dans

---

[96] Voir *Tagayeva*, précité, extraits des §§ 481-93.
[97] C'est précisément ce que la chambre de la première Section semble vouloir faire aux §§ 445-446 de son arrêt *Big Brother Watch*, précité.

une demande de décision préjudicielle datant de juillet 2018, semble chercher une approche plus large et contextuelle, tenant en compte de manière plus concrète des droits fondamentaux autres que celles protégées par les articles 7 et 8 de la Charte. De même, la juridiction de renvoi belge, reprenant les travaux préparatoires belges relatifs à la législation nationale de surveillance en cause, souligne que l'obligation de conservation prévue par les lois nationales et mise en cause par la jurisprudence récente de la CJUE pourrait être dictée non seulement par la lutte contre le terrorisme ou la criminalité grave. Cette obligation pourrait ressortir également, selon les travaux préparatoires, de la recherche de la vérité dans de nombreuses formes de criminalité dans l'intérêt tant de la victime que de l'accusé. Mention expresse est faite de la sanction effective des abus sexuels à l'égard des mineurs et des obligations positives incombant aux États membres en vertu des articles 3 et 8 de la CEDH.[98]

CONCLUSION

Le sujet qui fait l'objet de ce chapitre nous confronte à des questions difficiles relatives à la marge d'appréciation dont jouissent les autorités compétentes ; la nature et l'ampleur des ingérences découlant de différents types ou étapes de surveillance ; l'étendue du contrôle judiciaire à effectuer et l'identification et la mise en balance des intérêts concurrents concrètement en jeu. Les deux juridictions européennes, mais surtout la CourEDH, étant donnée sa mission, sont appelées à sauvegarder la substance de différents droits fondamentaux en cause dans un contexte difficile et lorsque leur mission est souvent mal comprise. Dans de telles circonstances, et ainsi qu'on peut voir de l'exposé de la jurisprudence des deux Cours, chacune en pleine voie de développement, le dialogue entre elles et l'articulation claire des principes jurisprudentiels à appliquer par des juges nationaux est non seulement utile, il est indispensable.

---

[98] Voir la DDP belge, précitée, B.20.1-B.22.

FLOORS OR CEILINGS: EUROPEAN SUPRANATIONAL COURTS AND THEIR AUTHORITY IN HUMAN RIGHTS MATTERS

Eva BREMS
Senior Full Professor of Human Rights law, Ghent University

Jogchum VRIELINK
Associate Professor, Université Saint-Louis – Bruxelles,
Centre Interdisciplinaire de Recherches en droit
Constitutionnel et administratif (CIRC)

INTRODUCTION

In the field of human rights protection, two supranational courts operate in Europe, each with its distinctive mandate: the European Court of Human Rights (ECtHR) in Strasbourg, and the Court of Justice (ECJ) of the European Union in Luxemburg. Recently, the latter entered a thematic sphere that has long been on the table of the former, i.e. bans on the wearing of religious symbols or dress in specific contexts. Through a discussion of recent judgments of each of the two courts in this field (III. and IV.), this paper elucidates the differences in the respective courts' mandates, and explores the consequences thereof. We begin, however, by providing a brief outline of the role and place of the subsidiarity principle in both the ECHR and EU system (I. and II.).

I. THE BUZZWORD IN STRASBOURG IS SUBSIDIARITY

Of the two supranational human rights courts that operate in the sphere of human rights, the European Court of Human Rights – the Strasbourg Court – is undeniably identified most strongly with the topic. Indeed, the ECtHR has a specialized mandate to examine cases of alleged violations of the European Convention on Human Rights (ECHR) and its additional protocols. Yet despite the inherent importance of its mandate, the ECtHR leaves significant room for national authorities in the implementation of ECHR rights. On the one hand, this flows naturally from its exclusive focus on (civil and political) human rights, which are commonly interpreted as bottom-line rules. That is to say, the collective project of the States Parties to the ECHR is to guarantee a common bottom-line or floor of human rights protection, not to achieve uniformity in human rights protection standards or measures. In addition, the relationship between national authorities and the supranational court in the ECHR system, is explicitly based on the principle of subsidiarity[1], i.e. the fact that the role of the ECtHR in human rights protection is subsidiary to that of national authorities. In procedural terms, the central expression of the subsidiarity principle is the admissibility requirement at the ECtHR of exhaustion of domestic remedies.[2] In addition, the ECtHR developed since its early days a doctrine on the 'margin of appreciation of the national authorities'. This term indicates 'the measure of discretion allowed to the Member States in the manner in which they implement the Convention's standards, taking into account their own particular circumstances and conditions'.[3]

The 15th Protocol to the ECHR will, once it enters into force, insert a reference to both subsidiarity and the margin of appreciation in the Preamble of the ECHR: 'Affirming that the High Contracting Parties, in accordance with the principle of subsidiarity, have the primary responsibility to secure the rights and freedoms defined in this Convention and the Protocols thereto, and that in doing so they enjoy a margin of appreciation, subject to the supervisory jurisdiction of the European Court of Human Rights established by this Convention'.[4] As this formulation makes clear, the principle of subsidiarity is not only concerned with a degree of restraint by the ECtHR in light of the domestic margin of appreciation. Equally important is the national authorities' first-line responsibility for the protection of Convention rights. The margin of appreciation doctrine is the subject of intense academic debate. Some of the strongest criticism of the doctrine arises from contexts in which the impression exists that the effect of a wide margin of appreciation is to give authorities carte

---

[1]   On the subsidiarity principle in the ECHR, see amongst others, R. Spano, 'The Future of the European Court of Human Rights – Subsidiarity, Process-Based Review and the Rule of Law', *Human Rights Law Review*, 2018, https://doi.org/10.1093/hrlr/ngy015; M.I. Villa, 'Subsidiarity, margin of appreciation and international adjudication within a cooperative conception of human rights', *International Journal of Constitutional Law*, Volume 15, Issue 2, 1 April 2017, pp. 393–413.

[2]   Article 35(1) ECHR.

[3]   Y. Arai-Takahashi, *The Margin of Appreciation Doctrine and the Principle of Proportionality in the Jurisprudence of the ECHR*, Antwerp, Intersentia, 2002, p 2.

[4]   Protocol No. 15 amending the Convention on the Protection of Human Rights and Fundamental Freedoms, adopted 24 June 2013. It will enter into force as soon as all the States Parties to the Convention have signed and ratified it.

blanche for human rights restrictions in a particular field. That is to say that the margin of appreciation may sometimes seem to act as a disincentive for states to take seriously their first line responsibility of Conventionality control and human rights protection, thus undercutting one of the pillars of the subsidiarity principle. Such criticism is common amongst others in religious freedom cases, in which the Court holds that a wide margin of appreciation applies in principle, because it is a 'matter of general policy, on which opinions within a democratic society may reasonably differ widely.[5]

II. LUXEMBOURG: 'UNITY' WITH 'SUBSIDIARY SUBSIDIARITY'

The analogous debate concerning the EU and the European Court of Justice in particular, is somewhat more complicated. The EU's powers are defined by the various EU treaties. These treaties only grant the EU the authority to act within certain areas, collectively determined by the Member States. One means by which (a certain degree of) diversity in national approaches is made possible, under EU law, is the principle of subsidiarity. In some situations, at least. Under EU law, the traditional view – confirmed by the express language of the Treaty on European Union (TEU) (Article 5(3)) – holds that the principle of subsidiarity has no application whatsoever to the exercise of the Union's *exclusive* powers. This has also been confirmed by the ECJ: the principle of subsidiarity does not (directly) restrict the use of the exclusive powers of the Union.[6] The areas over which the EU holds exclusive competence are limited to the following six fields: common commercial policy; common agricultural policy; fisheries policy; transport policy; competition rules; and rules governing the free movement of goods, persons, services and capital.

Where the EU has *shared* competence the principle of subsidiarity does enter into play (and this is the case *a fortiori* where it concerns *supporting* competences), albeit still in a somewhat 'subsidiary' sense.[7] In those situations the principle serves to safeguard Member States' decision and policy making abilities, authorising EU intervention "only if and in so far as the objectives of the proposed action cannot be sufficiently achieved by the Member States", but can rather be better achieved at Union level "by reason of the scale or effects

---

5   ECtHR, Grand Chamber, *SAS v. France*, 1 July 2014, para. 129.
6   See e.g. Case T-420/05, *Vischim Srl. v. Comm'n*, 2009; Case C-288/11 P, *Mitteldeutsche Flughafen AG v. European Comm'n*; Case T-31/07, *Du Pont de Nemours (France) SAS v. European Comm'n*.
7   R. Schütze, "Subsidiarity after Lisbon: reinforcing the safeguards of federalism?", *Cambridge Law Journal* 2009, 68(3), 526.

of the proposed action" (Article 5(3) TEU). In other words, Article 5(3)[8] TEU posits three conditions for intervention by Union institutions in accordance with the principle of subsidiarity:

1. it must concern an area that does not fall within the Union's exclusive competence (non-exclusive or supporting competence)
2. the objectives of the proposed action cannot be sufficiently achieved by the Member States (necessity);
3. the action can, by reason of its scale or effects, be better achieved by the Union (added value).

Paul Craig discerns four (partly inter-related) rationales for subsidiarity in the context of EU law, in his seminal article on the issue.[9] Firstly, subsidiarity was to play a role as "a mechanism for alleviating disputes concerning the division of competence between the EC and the Member States".[10] Secondly, the principle was seen to have a normative dimension as well: "in areas where it was difficult to decide with exactitude the limits of federal power, subsidiarity would be used as part of the criterion". Thirdly, subsidiarity was meant to address (fears of) excessive centralization of the EU. Finally, subsidiarity was perceived "as a way of enhancing pluralism and the diversity of national values".

While the principle of subsidiarity has the most obvious significance for legislative procedures[11], it applies to all EU institutions (Amsterdam Protocol, Article 1). As such, this includes the judicial branch. In practice, however, it is rarely if ever (explicitly) applied to the EU courts; unjustly so, we would argue, since most of the reasons for which the principle of subsidiarity is levelled against the EU lawmaker are equally (and sometimes even *more*) relevant in the context of actions and interpretations by the ECJ (cf. *infra* IV.).

Closely related to the principle of subsidiarity is that of proportionality (Article 5(4) TEU): if and when EU institutions do decide to intervene, "the

---

[8]   The Charter of Fundamental Rights also includes a (brief) mention of subsidiarity. It stipulates that its provisions "are addressed to the institutions, bodies, offices and agencies of the Union with due regard for the principle of subsidiarity and to the Member States only when they are implementing Union law".

[9]   P. Craig, "Subsidiarity: a political and legal analysis", *Common Market Studies* 2012, 74.

[10]   Especially prior to the Lisbon Treaty, when there was an absence of Treaty provisions outlining the different types of Community competence.

[11]   Procedures vis-à-vis legislative action are also most specific. *Ex ante*, national parliaments monitor compliance with the principle of subsidiarity in accordance with the procedure set out in Protocol No 2 (Article 5(3) and Article 12(b) TEU). For *ex post* compliance with the principle, legal action can be brought before the Court of Justice, though case-law shows that Union institutions are granted a wide discretion in applying the principle. See, for a critique: G.A. Moens & J. Trone, "The principle of subsidiarity in EU judicial and legislative practice: panacea or placebo?", *Journal of Legislation* 2015, vol. 41, issue 1, 65–102.

content and form of that Union action shall not exceed what is necessary to achieve the objectives of the Treaties". To an important degree this proportionality element is contained within the subsidiarity principle already. To begin with, on the textual level since the TEU – concerning subsidiarity – provides that the EU "shall act only if *and in so far*" (Article 5(3) TEU) as the objectives of a measure cannot be sufficiently achieved by the Member States.[12] But on a conceptual level too, subsidiarity cannot be otherwise understood in the EU context than in terms of proportionality. This is because the subsidiarity question is never involved with 'whether' the EU may exercise powers in a general sense: the subsidiarity question is only ever posed in contexts where the EU enjoys a designated competence to begin with. The general question of whether Union action is permissible will thereby already be answered for that policy area.[13] Instead, the subsidiarity question will always be focused on a more specific act, policy or interpretation at issue. In other words: the principle serves to question whether a European institution (the legislator, the Commission or the EU judiciary) has *unnecessarily* and *disproportionately* restricted the autonomy of national authorities.[14]

Finally, apart from the subsidiarity and proportionality provisions, the EU's founding treaties explicitly accommodate national sensitivities and identities. These accommodations are sometimes highly specific, in that some of the Protocols exempt particular Member States from aspects of the integration programme or protect national specificities from challenges under EU law. More generally also, Article 4(2) TEU states that the Union shall respect Member States' "national identities, inherent in their fundamental structures, political and constitutional".[15] As such, the provision protects a Member State's national identity as expressed in its basic structures, most notably its political and constitutional ones. In the (relatively scarce) case-law pertaining to Article 4(2), the ECJ has ruled it to include, *inter alia*, "the status of the State as a Republic"[16] and "protection of a State's official national language".[17] Though the relationship between national identity and subsidiarity is a complicated one, for our present purposes it can suffice to point out that they are not unrelated to each other, and might serve to reinforce one another.

---

12   See in that sense the argument from the Swedish parliament: Reasoned opinion issued by the Swedish Riksdag on COM(2012) 0011.
13   R. Schütze, "Subsidiarity after Lisbon: reinforcing the safeguards of federalism?", *Cambridge Law Journal* 2009, 68(3), 532.
14   *Ibid.*, 533.
15   See extensively E. Cloots, *National identity in EU law*, Oxford, Oxford University Press, 2015.
16   ECJ, 22 December 2010, *Sayn-Wittgenstein*, C-208/09, ECLI:EU:C:2010:806, §92.
17   ECJ, 12 May 2011, *Runevič-Vardyn and Wardyn*, C-391/09, ECLI:EU:C:2011:291, §86.

Issues pertaining to religion are especially relevant from the perspective of subsidiarity and national identity, given the vast (historical, cultural and legal) differences that characterise EU Member States' dealings with religion (see *infra* III.D.). This also renders EU interference in religious matters highly sensitive.

III. *HAMIDOVIĆ v. BOSNIA AND HERZEGOVINA* (ECtHR): LITTLE GUIDANCE DESPITE A RARE VIOLATION FINDING

The present section will analyse a recent judgment of the ECtHR regarding a ban on religious symbols. It concerns a rare case in that the Court found a violation of Article 9 ECHR, despite the wide margin of appreciation for the national authorities. Nevertheless, as the analysis will show, the judgment offers little guidance for other states parties that may be confronted with similar, but slightly different, situations.

A. FACTS

The case of *Hamidović v. Bosnia and Herzegovina* concerns the punishment of a witness for wearing an Islamic skullcap in the courtroom. Islam is the majority religion in Bosnia and Herzegovina, with Muslims making up almost 51% of the population. The applicant, however, belongs to a community of Salafist Muslims, a minority practicing an orthodox interpretation of Islam. Their religious practice includes the wearing of a skullcap by men. In 2012, the applicant was summoned to appear as a witness in a criminal trial concerning a terrorist attack on the US Embassy in Sarajevo. The accused belonged to the same Salafist community as the applicant. In this trial, before the applicant was summoned, incidents had occurred with the accused refusing to stand up when the judges entered the courtroom, and refusing to take off their skullcaps in the courtroom. Asked to explain this behaviour, 'the accused stated that they only respected Allah's judgment and that they did not want to take part in rituals acknowledging man-made judgment'.[18] They were expelled from the courtroom for as long as they refused to obey the court's rules. When the applicant appeared as a witness, he stood up for the court as required, but when the President of the trial chamber ordered him to remove his skullcap, he refused to do so. He was then expelled from the courtroom, convicted for contempt of court and sentenced to a fine. The basis for the sanction was a

---

[18]   ECtHR, *Hamidović v. Bosnia and Herzegovina*, 5 December 2017, para. 6.

provision in the House Rules of the Judicial Institutions of Bosnia and Herzegovina, stating that 'Visitors must respect the dress code applicable to judicial institutions. Visitors shall not wear miniskirts, shorts, t-shirts with thin straps, open heel shoes and other garments that do not correspond to the dress code applicable to judicial institutions.' In addition to referring to this rule, the decision against the applicant also stated that 'in public institutions, it is not acceptable to display religious affiliation through clothing or religious symbols'.[19] Moreover, it found the witness refusal to accept the rules of the court and to show respect to the Court by accepting its warnings, to be a flagrant breach of order in the courtroom'.[20] The court decision explicitly linked the applicant's behaviour to that of the accused in the trial, stating that 'the frequency of such disrespectful behavior and contempt of court... undoubtedly presents a specific threat to society. ... A legitimate conclusion may be that it is essentially directed against the State and basic social values. Therefore, a severe and uncompromising reaction on the part of the State, staking all existing repressive measures, is crucial for dealing with such behavior.'[21]

An appeals chamber of the same court upheld the decision, but reduced the fine. As the applicant did not pay the fine, it was converted into 30 days of imprisonment. The applicant served this sentence. In 2015, the Constitutional Court of Bosnia and Herzegovina found no breach of Articles 9 and 14 ECHR. It did, however, find a violation of Article 6 ECHR on account of the automatic conversion of the fine into imprisonment.

In a broader perspective, the wearing of religious symbols in Bosnian courts has been the subject of a heated debate since at least 2015, when the High Judicial and Prosecutorial Council issued a circular stating that judges, prosecutors and court officers are forbidden to wear such symbols in the course of their duties. This affected 1 judge and approximately ten court officers who were wearing headscarves. The circular was condemned by several important domestic actors, notably the Islamic Community, the House of Representatives, two Cantonal Assemblies and the Agency for Gender Equality. Concerning other persons, such as parties or witnesses, who are present in the courtroom, the circular states that they may be ordered to remove a religious symbol 'if this is considered justified by a judge in a given case, taking into consideration the right to freedom of religion and equal access to justice, the organization of the proceedings and the need to maintain the authority of the judiciary'.[22]

---

[19]   Ibid., para. 7.
[20]   Ibid.
[21]   Ibid.
[22]   Ibid., para. 14.

B. JUDGMENT

With a six to one majority, the European Court of Human Rights found a violation of Article 9 ECHR (freedom of religion). The Court accepted that, despite the absence of an express statutory ban on skullcaps in the courtroom, there was a legal basis for the measure, in the provision that concerns the 'inherent power of the trial judge to regulate the conduct of proceedings in the State Court so as to ensure that no abuse of the court occurred and that the proceedings were fair to all parties, a provision that is inevitably couched in terms which are vague'.[23] As for the legitimate aim of the interference, the government had advanced two. One, 'to maintain the authority and impartiality of the judiciary', was rejected by the Court, with the argument that it is not expressly included in the second paragraph of Article 9 ECHR. In fact, this restriction ground is included only in Article 10 ECHR (freedom of expression). The Court did accept the legitimate aim of 'protecting the rights and freedoms of others', for which the government referred to 'the principle of secularism and the need to promote tolerance in a post-conflict society'.[24]

The Court found the violation in the proportionality assessment, despite its explicit recognition of 'the fundamentally subsidiary role of the Convention mechanism', and the wide margin of appreciation which should in principle be afforded in a case 'where questions concerning the relationship between State and religions are at stake, as rules in this sphere vary from one country to another according to national traditions and the requirements imposed by the need to protect the rights and freedoms of others and to maintain public order.'[25] The Court conducted a comparative study[26] of the legislation of 38 States Parties. It found that none of them regulate the wearing of religious symbols in the courtroom by private citizens. However, four states require private citizens to uncover their head in the courtroom. Only in one of these states, Belgium, this rule is applied to religious headgear (albeit by a minority of judges only).[27] Such comparative study suggests an intention to mobilize what is known as 'consensus reasoning'[28], i.e. a restriction of the margin of appreciation on the ground that the defendant state is an outlier in the face of a strong consensus among the States Parties of the Convention in favour of a more

---

[23]   Ibid., para. 33.
[24]   Ibid., par. 35.
[25]   Ibid., para. 38.
[26]   Ibid., para. 21.
[27]   On this issue, see E. Brems, C. Heri, S. Ouald Chaib, L. Verdonck, 'Head-Covering Bans in Belgian Courtrooms and Beyond: Headscarf Persecution and the Complicity of Supranational Courts', *Human Rights Quarterly*, vol 9, no. 4, November 2017, 882–909.
[28]   On this issue, see amongst others, K. Dzehtsiarou, *European Consensus and the Legitimacy of the European Court of Human Rights*, Cambridge, Cambridge University Press, 2015.

rights-protective approach. Yet the judgment makes no reference to consensus reasoning.[29]

The Court distinguishes the *Hamidović* case from cases that concern the wearing of religious symbols by public officials, 'who may be put under a duty of discretion, neutrality and impartiality, including a duty not to wear such symbols and clothing while exercising official authority'.[30] The Court adds that 'In democratic societies, private citizens, such as the applicant, are normally not under such a duty'.[31]

The Court grants that 'there may be cases when it is justified to order a witness to remove a religious symbol'[32], referring to the face veil. Yet in the central paragraph 41 of its brief motivation, the Court then makes a number of principled statements. First, 'the Court would emphasize that the authorities must not neglect the specific features of different religions'.[33] This is immediately followed by a statement about the importance of religious expression: 'Freedom to manifest one's religion is a fundamental right: not only because a healthy democratic society needs to tolerate and sustain pluralism and diversity, but also because of the importance to an individual who has made religion a central tenet of his or her life to be able to communicate that belief to others'.[34] The recital of principles concludes with the following: 'democracy does not simply mean that the views of a majority must always prevail. The role of the authorities is not to remove the cause of tension by eliminating pluralism, but to ensure that the competing groups tolerate each other'.[35]

In addition, the Court considers it relevant that the applicant had not shown a disrespectful attitude[36] and neither did he have 'any hidden agenda to make a mockery of the trial, incite others to reject secular and democratic values or cause a disturbance'.[37] Saïla Ouald Chaib accurately remarks that this argument seems out of place, given that it is unrelated to the 'legitimate aim' of protecting secularism, and seems instead to relate to the explicitly rejected aim

---

[29]   Still, in his dissenting opinion, Judge Ranzoni suggests that consensus reasoning may implicitly have led to a restriction of the margin of appreciation in this case (dissenting opinion of Judge Ranzoni, para. 23.

[30]   ECtHR, *Hamidović*, *o.c.*, para. 40.

[31]   Ibid., par. 40, *in fine*.

[32]   Ibid., para. 41.

[33]   Ibid.

[34]   Ibid. The same statement was made earlier in ECtHR, *Eweida and Others v. United Kingdom*, 15 January 2013, para. 81.

[35]   ECtHR, *Hamidović*, *o.c.*, para. 41. The same statement was made earlier in ECtHR, Grand Chamber, *SAS v France*, 1 July 2014, paras 127–28.

[36]   ECtHR, *Hamidović*, *o.c.*, para. 42.

[37]   Ibid., para. 41.

of maintaining the authority of the judiciary.[38] Judges De Gaetano and Bošnjak wrote concurring opinions, and judge Ranzoni dissented. The latter emphasized the subsidiary role of the Court. In his opinion, the Court should have adopted a more hands-off approach, restricting itself to a procedural control of the assessment made by the national courts.

C. THE BROADER SETTING: ECHR CASE LAW ON BANS OF RELIGIOUS SYMBOLS AND DRESS

As the comparative research conducted by the Court shows, the immediate impact of the *Hamidović* judgment, seems limited to Bosnia and Herzegovina, and Belgium[39], as no other Council of Europe state seems to expel people from courtrooms on the ground of wearing religious headgear. Yet it is useful to situate this case against the broader background of the Court's case law on bans of religious symbols and dress.

The European Court of Human Rights has addressed a significant number of cases in this field. In the addition to the Islamic skullcap featuring in *Hamidović*, these cases concerned bans applied to Islamic headscarves, Sikh turbans, Islamic face veils, a Christian cross, as well as in one case a complete religious costume. With the exception of the face veil cases, the bans were restricted to certain contexts. In the large majority of these cases, the Court found no violation, relying on a wide margin of appreciation of the States Parties. Several cases were so clear in the eyes of the Court, that it found the application inadmissible for being manifestly ill-founded.

In the context of public schools, the Court has validated headscarf bans for teachers[40] and students[41] alike, on grounds of neutrality, as well as – in the

---

[38] S. Ouald Chaib, case note under *Hamidović v Bosnia Herzegovina* (in Dutch), *European Human Rights Cases*, 2018/75 (5). Yet Judge Bošnjak, in his concurring opinion in *Hamidović*, states that 'the key arguments' for the finding of a violation of Article 9 'can be found in paragraph 42 of the judgment'.

[39] After submission of this paper, a judgment came out regarding a civil party in a criminal case who had to leave the courtroom on account of wearing a headscarf: ECtHR, *Lachiri v Belgium*, 18 September 2018.

[40] ECtHR, *Dahlab v. Switzerland*, (dec.), App. No. 42393/98, 15 Feb. 2001, ECtHR, *Kurtulmus v. Turkey* (dec.), App. No. 65500/01, 24 Jan. 2006 (university professor); ECtHR, *Karaduman v. Turkey* (dec.), App. No. 41296/04, 3 Apr. 2007; ECtHR, *Tandoğan v. Turkey* (dec.), App. No. 41298/04,3 Apr. 2007; ECtHR, *Çağlayan v. Turkey* (dec.), App. No. 1638/04,3 Apr. 2007; ECtHR, *Yilmaz v. Turkey* (dec.), App. No. 37829/05, 3 Apr. 2007.

[41] ECtHR, Grand Chamber, *Leyla Şahin v. Turkey*, 10 November 2005 (university student); ECtHR, *Bayrak v. France* (dec.), App. No. 14308/08, 30 June 2009; ECtHR, *Ghazal v. France* (dec.), App. No. 29134/08, 30 June 2009; ECtHR, *Aktas v. France* (dec.), App. No. 43563/08, 30 June 2009.

case of teachers – on grounds of the protection of the rights of students. In the case of *Ebrahimian v. France*[42], concerning the dismissal of a social assistant in a public hospital on account of her refusal to take off her headscarf at work, the Court legitimized, on grounds of neutrality, a ban on religious attire and symbols for employees in the entire public sector. When it comes to private sector employment, the Court has not yet addressed any case regarding Islamic religious attire. In the case of *Eweida v. UK*[43], however, the Court did find a violation of religious freedom on account of a ban on the wearing of a Christian cross worn by a British Airways employee, which the company justified with a reference to its corporate image. In the same case, the Court upheld a similar ban as applied to a nurse, on grounds of safety.[44] Referring to the safety argument, the Court has moreover accepted that religious clothing needs to be removed during safety checks[45] and during physical education classes[46], that a Sikh riding a motorcycle needed to replace his turban with a helmet[47], and that a photograph on a driver's license requires a bare head.[48] In an early case, a similar requirement concerning a photograph on a university diploma, was considered not even to interfere with religious freedom.[49]Furthermore, the Court rejected claims of niqab wearers against the French and Belgian bans on face covering in the public sphere.[50] In the eyes of the Court, the bans were justified in the light of the objective of 'living together'. In addition to the above-mentioned *Eweida* case concerning a Christian cross, the only other case in which a ban on individuals wearing religious symbols or dress was struck down before *Hamidović*, was *Arslan v. Turkey*.[51] This case concerned 127 members of the Islamic sect Aczimendi tarikatÿ. At the occasion of a religious ceremony, they toured the streets while wearing the distinctive dress of their group, which was made up of a turban, "salvar" (baggy "harem" trousers), a tunic and a stick. The Court found that the dress ban was not justified as there was no evidence of a threat for public order nor of inappropriate pressure on others.

When it was issued, the *Hamidović* judgment was thus one of only three cases in which the ECtHR found a ban on religious symbols in violation of article 9 ECHR. While *Eweida* concerns Christian women, *Hamidović* and *Arslan* concern claims

---

[42]   ECtHR, *Ebrahimian v. France*, 26 November 2015.
[43]   ECtHR, *Eweida and others v. UK*, 15 January 2013 (case of Ms Eweida).
[44]   Id., case of Ms Chaplin.
[45]   ECtHR, *Phull v. France* (dec.), App. No. 35753/03, 11 Jan. 2005; ECtHR, *El Morsli v. France* (dec.), App. No. 15585/06, 4 Mar. 2008.
[46]   ECtHR, *Dogru v. France*, App. No. 27058/05, 4 Dec. 2008.
[47]   ECtHR, *X v. UK*, App. No. 7215/75, 5 Nov. 1981.
[48]   ECtHR, *Mann Singh v. France* (dec.), App. No. 24479/07, 13 Nov. 2008.
[49]   ECmHR, *Karaduman v. Turkey* (dec.), App. No. 16278/90.
[50]   ECtHR, Grand Chamber, *SAS v. France*, 1 July 2014; ECtHR, *Belkacemi and Oussar v. Belgium*, 11 July 2017; ECtHR, *Dakir v. Belgium*, 11 July 2017.
[51]   ECtHR, *Ahmet Arslan and others v. Turkey*, 23 February 2010.

by Muslim men in contexts in which Islam is a majority religion.[52] The Court had until then rejected *all* article 9 accommodation claims of Muslims in states where Islam is a minority religion, including all such claims regarding Islamic dress. Needless to say, the Court had rejected all claims regarding accommodation of Islamic *women's* dress.[53] This line of case law is the subject of intense scholarly debate, which is predominantly very critical of the Court's approach.[54] In the context of this paper, we highlight a single line of critique, which is the claim that the Court's case law offers insufficient guidance to national authorities.

A judgment that relies on a wide margin of appreciation offers little guidance to domestic actors, as its central message is that it is for these domestic actors to make their own human rights assessment in their own context. Yet in practice, such judgments are often interpreted across the Council of Europe as a legitimation of the rights-restricting practice as such.[55] In Belgium for example, the headscarf case law of the European Court of Human Rights is used to legitimize headscarf bans, also in contexts (such as private employment and the delivery of goods and services) in which there is no ECtHR case law. The case law legitimizing headscarf bans in other fields, fuels the arguments and strengthens the positions of proponents of such bans, while discouraging the opponents.[56] Similarly, there can be little doubt that the Court's rulings on the face veil in Belgium and France, have encouraged other states, such as Denmark, to go ahead with a similar ban.[57] The Court's consistent findings of no violation in cases concerning bans on Muslim women's dress[58], sends the signal to domestic

---

52 Yet in both cases, the applicants belong to a specific Islamic sect that differs significantly from that which is adhered to by the majority population.

53 After submission of this paper, the Court issued the judgment of *Lachiri v. Belgium* (cf. *supra*), in which it found a violation on account of the banning of a headscarf wearer from a courtroom where she was a civil party in a criminal case.

54 See amongst others, S.E. Berry, 'Religious Freedom and the European Court of Human Rights' Two Margins of Appreciation', *Religion & Human Rights*, 2017, Volume 12, Issue 2–3, pp. 198–209; P. Cumper & T. Lewis, "Taking Religion Seriously"? Human Rights and Hijab in Europe – Some Problems of Adjudication', *Journal of Law and Religion*, Volume 24, Issue 2, 2008, pp. 599–627; J. Marshal, 'Conditions for Freedom? European Human Rights Law and the Islamic Headscarf Debate', *Human Rights Quarterly* Vol. 30, No. 3 (Aug., 2008), pp. 631–654.

55 Compare S. Sottiaux, & J. Vrielink, "Activism at the Admissibility Stage: A Threat to the Subsidiary Role of the ECtHR?", in Alen, A. (ed.), *Liber Amicorum Marc Bossuyt - Liberae Cogitationes*, Antwerp/Cambridge, Intersentia, 2013, 659–675.

56 On the wide range of headscarf restrictions in Belgium, see E. Brems, C. Heri, S. Ouald Chaib, L. Verdonck, 'Head-Covering Bans in Belgian Courtrooms and Beyond: Headscarf Persecution and the Complicity of Supranational Courts', *Human Rights Quarterly*, vol 9, no. 4, November 2017, 882–909.

57 The link is made in the press, see 'Danish government proposes ban on full-face veils', *The Guardian*, 6 February 2018.

58 The judgment in *Lachiri v. Belgium* (cf. *supra*), which was issued after submission of this paper, is the first finding of a violation regarding a headscarf ban. It is, however, very narrowly tailored to the facts of the case, thus not affecting the central argument in this paper.

actors that they have a free hand in this field. And yet, it may be assumed, for example on the basis of the judgments in *Eweida*, *Arslan* and *Hamidović*, that the Court will in fact not accept any and all restrictions of Muslim women's dress, that is to say that there are in fact limits to state discretion in this field, yet these have yet to be articulated by the Court.

We submit that it is desirable for the European Court of Human Rights to provide clear indications of the limits of state discretion, also in cases in which it finds no Convention violation on the grounds of a wide margin of appreciation. As the next section will show, the *Hamidović* judgment is unfortunately a missed opportunity in this regard.

D.   *HAMIDOVIĆ* AND THE CHALLENGE OF HUMAN RIGHTS GUIDANCE IN A SUBSIDIARITY CONTEXT

As explained *supra* (I.), the principle of subsidiarity entails that the national authorities have the primary responsibility for the protection of Convention rights. This is often used as a basis to claim that the subsidiary role of the Court entails a duty of restraint, and respect for the margin of appreciation of the national authorities. Yet in addition, the subsidiarity framework may also entail a role for the Court in enabling the national authorities in the exercise of their responsibility for the protection of Convention Rights. While respecting a domestic margin of appreciation, the Court should still set standards on *how* to secure Convention rights and freedoms, that function as binding guidelines to domestic authorities, and as limits to their margin of appreciation.

With regard to bans on religious symbols and other claims regarding religious accommodation and/or minority rights, it is particularly crucial for the Court to offer guidance that allows distinguishing legitimate restrictions of religious freedom from unjustifiable harassment of unpopular minorities. While it is possible and important for the Court to give guidance on limits to state discretion also in no-violation judgments, this task would seem easier in a judgment finding a violation. Also, that is the context in which it is most easily picked up by national authorities across Europe. Yet the guidance that can be derived from the *Hamidović* judgment is rather limited.

This starts with the first condition for a justifiable rights restriction, which is the legal basis of the measure. In this case, the Bosnian court has banned religious headgear on the basis of a general power to keep order in court. The ECtHR rather easily accepts this as a sufficient legal basis. Yet if the goal is to guide national authorities in distinguishing *bona fide* restrictions from minority harassment, that would not seem good enough. The requirement that human rights restrictions should be based on a general rule, is intended to bar *ad hoc* measures targeting specific individuals or groups. Applying a dress instruction (quoted *supra*) that manifestly seems intended to address issues of revealing or provocative dress styles, to religious headgear, is far from self-evident, and hence cannot automatically be considered foreseeable.[59] In our research, the present authors have encountered multiple examples of authorities using pre-existing generally worded rules to specifically restrict minority rights as soon as a new type of minority religious expression appears on the scene. These include the use of municipal carnival rules to ban face veils[60], and the use of generally worded dress rules for swimming pools to ban burkinis.[61] Such phenomena invite a more robust assessment of foreseeability as inherent in the legality requirement.

At least as important in cases in view of uncovering anti-minority bias, is critical scrutiny of the invoked legitimate aim. The Court in this case rejects one of the two legitimate aims proposed by the government, but accepts without much ado that 'protecting secularism' can fall under 'protecting the rights and freedoms of others'.[62] Its only argument is a reference to the judgments of *Sahin*[63] and *Arslan*.[64] In neither of these named cases, the link between secularism and the rights of others was explicitly made though. The categorical nature of the statement in *Hamidović* risks to be invoked in future case law as a broad umbrella for restrictions on religious expressions. Instead of assisting national authorities in developing fine instruments for distinguishing legitimate from illegitimate aims for the purpose of rights restrictions, the judgment thus seems content with a rather blunt criterion. It is interesting in this respect that De Gaetano in his concurring opinion objects that secularism falls within the ambit of 'protecting the rights and freedoms of others' 'only in exceptional cases, such as when the principle of secularism is embedded in the constitution of a country or where there is a long historical tradition of secularism'. As one commentator has argued, the impression is created that the Court places secularism on a higher level than religious beliefs, and equates pluralism with secularism, perspectives that many in Europe consider highly problematic.[65] In addition, there appears to be a tension

---

59 See also the concurring opinion of Judge De Gaetano on this point.
60 See J. Vrielink, S. Ouald Chaib and E. Brems, "The Belgian 'burqa ban'. Legal aspects of local and general prohibitions on covering and concealing one's face in Belgium", in A. Ferrari and S. Pastorelli (eds.), *The burqa affair across Europe; between public and private space*, Ashgate, 2013, 143–170.
61 See E. Brems, S. Ouald Chaib and K. Vanhees, "Burkini' Bans in Belgian Municipal Swimming Pools: Banning as a Default Option', forthcoming in *Netherlands Quarterly of Human Rights*, 2018.
62 ECtHR, *Hamidović, o.c.*, para. 35.
63 ECtHR, *Leyla Sahin, o.c.*, para. 99.
64 ECtHR, *Ahmet Arslan a.o., o.c.*, par. 43.
65 L. Graham, 'Skullcaps, courts and Article 9: Hamidović v Bosnia and Herzegovina', blogpost on @LewisGrahamLaw, 6 December 2017.

between the legal basis of the restriction, which is to be situated in a context of keeping order in the courtroom and preserving respect for the court, and the aim of protecting secularism. The impression is created that the secularism argument is mobilized as a *passe-partout*, in light of the fact that upholding the authority of the judiciary is not an acceptable aim for a restriction of an Article 9 right.[66] Finally, by ignoring instead of critically scrutinizing the government's argument that the ban is needed 'to promote tolerance in a post-conflict society', the Court foregoes an opportunity to unpack what *prima facie* is a harmful stereotype about Muslims and Islam as inherently intolerant. Saila Ouald Chaib rightly remarks that the contested measure itself seems hard to reconcile with an attitude of tolerance.[67]

Finally, the proportionality assessment in *Hamidović* is where most guidance might be expected, since this is where the violation is found. Yet the Court in this judgment seems to deliberately want to avoid ruling in a manner that might offer guidance for future cases with even slightly different configurations of facts. First of all, the Court distinguishes *Hamidović* from cases about religious symbols and clothing at the workplace, specifically including judicial officials, stating that this is 'a completely different issue'.[68] In the same movement, however, the judgment loses its power also with regard to attorneys. Attorneys wearing a headscarf have been banned from the bar in several Council of Europe states, including Belgium and Spain.[69] After *Hamidović*, hijab wearing law school graduates in these countries remain in the dark as to their career opportunities at the bar, until a courageous woman challenges a ban first domestically, and then – if needed – in Strasbourg. If only the Court had taken the trouble of addressing this matter in an obiter dictum, they would at least have legal certainty. In addition, a second distinction is made when the Court emphasizes, in the first line of its proportionality reasoning, that 'the applicant had no choice but to appear before the domestic court', as a witness who fails to appear risks being fined or arrested.[70] This line of reasoning casts doubt on the precedent value of *Hamidović* in all contexts in which the applicant voluntarily enters the context in which a ban applies. This includes all workplace contexts.[71] Yet it even casts doubt on the precedent value with regard to courtroom bans affecting members of the audience or civil parties, as is the case in Belgium.[72]

---

[66]   In the same vein, see S. Ouald Chaib, 'Hamidović c. Bosnie-Herzégovine: l'interdiction de couvre-chef religieux dans les prétoires viole l'article 9 de la Convention européenne des droits de l'homme', *Journal des Tribunaux*, 2018, no. 6731, 401–405, at 403.

[67]   S. Ouald Chaib, 'Hamidović c. Bosnie-Herzégovine: l'interdiction de couvre-chef religieux dans les prétoires viole l'article 9 de la Convention européenne des droits de l'homme', *Journal des Tribunaux*, 2018, no. 6731, 401–405, at 402.

[68]   ECtHR, *Hamidović*, *o.c.*, para. 26.

[69]   See ECtHR (dec.), *Barik Edidi v. Spain*, 26 April 2016 (the case was dismissed for failure to exhaust domestic remedies).

[70]   ECtHR, *Hamidović*, *o.c.*, par. 37.

[71]   L. Graham, *o.c.*

[72]   Brems, Heri, Ouald Chaib and Verdonck, *o.c.*

Neither is the succession of principled statements in paragraph 41 of the judgment particularly useful in terms of domestic guidance, without additional clarification of what such principles require, either in procedural or substantive terms.

IV. *ACHBITA/BOUGNAOUI* (ECJ): TOO MUCH GUIDANCE, DESPITE NOT FORCING A FINDING OF DISCRIMINATION

The present section analyses the first rulings by the European Court of Justice regarding a ban on religious (and other) symbols: the cases of *Achbita* and *Bougnaoui* (the most important of which is the former). Whereas the Court did not adjudicate these cases in the way in which the plaintiff would have wished, the analysis will show (or at least argue) that the ruling(s) nonetheless went too far in forcing states parties into a one size fits all solution, in similar situations.

A. FACTS

The case of *Achbita* and that of *Bougnaoui* both concern the issue of whether the prohibition of discrimination on the grounds of religion under the Employment Equality Directive 2000/78 makes it unlawful for a private-sector undertaking to dismiss a Muslim employee because she refuses to remove her veil at work. The case of *Achbita* originated in Belgium and that of *Bougnaoui* in France.

Much in the same way as French and (to a lesser extent) Belgian public authorities tend to do, two private firms invoked their own 'neutrality policy' before the Court of Justice in an attempt to justify the dismissal of employees on the ground that they insisted on wearing an Islamic headscarf at work. The central issue in both cases was a general ban on visible political, philosophical and religious symbols in the workplace.

We will limit ourselves to presenting the facts of the most relevant of the two cases, i.e. that of *Achbita*. Samira Achbita, a Muslim, worked at a firm that provided, inter alia, reception services for customers in both the public and private sectors. She started working at the company on 12 February 2003 as a receptionist. She was employed under an employment contract of indefinite duration. There was at that time an unwritten rule within the firm that workers could not wear visible signs of their political, philosophical or religious beliefs in the workplace. In April 2006, Ms Achbita informed her managers that she intended, in the future, to wear an Islamic headscarf during working hours.

Management informed her that such would not be tolerated because wearing visible political, philosophical or religious signs was contrary to the firm's policy of neutrality.

Ms Achbita did so nonetheless, as of 15 May 2006. On 29 May 2006, the firm's labour council approved an amendment to the workplace regulations, which came into force on 13 June 2006, according to which "employees are prohibited, in the workplace, from wearing any visible signs of their political, philosophical or religious beliefs and/or from engaging in any observance of such beliefs".

On 12 June 2006, Ms Achbita was dismissed on account of her continuing insistence that she wanted to wear the Islamic headscarf at work. She received a severance payment equivalent to three months' salary and benefits acquired under the terms of her employment contract.

Ms Achbita subsequently brought legal proceedings against her dismissal, which eventually wound up before the Belgian Supreme Court (the Court of Cassation). Said Court decided to stay the proceedings, in order to refer a question to the Court of Justice for a preliminary ruling. The question that the ECJ had to answer was, basically, whether a private employer is permitted – just like public authorities[73] – to prohibit employees from wearing religious and philosophical symbols, because he pursues 'neutrality'?[74] After all, such a neutrality policy comes within the ambit of European (and Belgian) discrimination legislation, which prohibits direct and indirect discrimination based on religion and other convictions.

B.   OPPOSING CONCLUSION(S)

A core question in the *Achbita* case was whether a ban on 'wearing any visible signs of their political, philosophical or religious beliefs' would amount to a

---

[73]   Although Directive 2000/78, in terms of the applicability of the prohibition of discrimination, does not make an explicit distinction between the public and private sector, it is usually assumed that the situation is nonetheless different, among others on the basis of Article 3 par. 1 Directive 2000/78 read together with the aforementioned duty of the EU to respect the national identity of its Member States (Article 4, 2 TEU). This does not imply that certain subjects or areas are entirely excluded from the scope of Directive 2000/78, but that nevertheless the *application* of this (and other) directive(s) should not detract from the national identity of Member States.

[74]   More specifically and literally, the question read: "Should Article 2(2)(a) of Directive 2000/78 be interpreted as meaning that the prohibition on wearing, as a female Muslim, a headscarf at the workplace does not constitute direct discrimination where the employer's rule prohibits all employees from wearing outward signs of political, philosophical and religious beliefs at the workplace?"

direct *or* to an indirect distinction (and potentially, therefore, to a forbidden direct or indirect discrimination). Direct discrimination – according to the relevant EU non-discrimination Directive (2000/78/EG) – shall be taken to occur where a person is 'treated less favourably than another is, has been or would be treated in a comparable situation on the grounds of religion or belief'. Indirect discrimination is somewhat more complicated. The relevant directive states that indirect discrimination 'shall be taken to occur where an apparently neutral provision, criterion or practice would put persons having a particular religion or belief (…) at a particular disadvantage compared with other persons'.

Whether the case involved direct or indirect discrimination was especially important as it heavily impacts the possible justifications. Direct discrimination can be justified only in exceptional circumstances. In the context of employment, the most important justification is that of the 'genuine and determining occupational requirement', which involves a functional proportionality test characterised by a high level of scrutiny.[75] It can serve as a justification only "where by reason of the nature of the particular occupational activities concerned or of the context in which they are carried out" a characteristic, related to a discrimination ground (including religion or belief) "constitutes a genuine and determining occupational requirement, provided that the objective is legitimate and the requirement is proportionate". Simply put: genuine and determining must be understood as 'almost indispensable'. Without having the personal characteristic that is related to a discrimination ground, it should be virtually impossible to do a certain job (e.g. allowing one to require black models for (black) skin coloured make-up). Indirect discrimination, on the other hand, allows for a so-called 'objective and reasonable justification', requiring that the indirectly distinguishing "provision, criterion or practice is objectively justified by a legitimate aim and the means of achieving that aim are appropriate and necessary". It again concerns a proportionality test, but of a more general nature and (in principle) with a significantly lower level of scrutiny.

Two advocates-general (AGs) reached seemingly opposing conclusions on this issue, in the cases of *Achbita* and *Bougnaoui*. The AG in the *Achbita* case was German Juliane Kokott. She argued, first of all, that the concept of religion in Directive 2000/78 should be understood in a broad sense: "It includes not only the faith of an individual as such (*forum internum*) but also the practice and manifestation of that religion, including in public spaces (*forum externum*)". She also felt that there was no reason to doubt (the sincerity of) the religious motivations, in the context of the case.

---

[75] Preceding consideration no. 23 of Directive 2000/78 underlines that the justification holds only "in very limited circumstances".

That being said, Kokott did not find there to be direct discrimination. After all, she reasoned, the neutrality requirement not only affects all religious believers in the same manner, but it also affects "a confirmed atheist who expresses his anti-religious stance in a clearly visible manner by the way he dresses, or a politically active employee who professes his allegiance to his preferred political party or particular policies through the clothes that he wears (such as symbols, pins or slogans on his shirt, T-shirt or headwear)", in exactly the same way.[76]

In the – on relevant points – similar case of *Bougnaoui*, the AG (British Eleanor Sharpston)[77] concluded that the neutrality policy *did* amount to a direct discrimination. In order to come to that conclusion, she looked at the way in which the ban was formulated, referring directly and explicitly to religion. That, in doing so, it allegedly disadvantaged all religions equally, made no difference, according to Sharpston: Bougnaoui was treated less favourably 'on the grounds of' her religion, as the directive requires, since someone "who had not chosen to manifest his or her religious belief by wearing particular apparel would not have been dismissed".[78] Sharpston also pointed out that the Court had, in previous case-law, always adhered to a broad definition of direct discrimination. For instance, in other case-law the 'neutral' requirement to be married – in countries that did not yet permit gay marriage – was seen by the court as direct and not as indirect discrimination.

Kokott's conclusion had conceded both points. She recognised that the ban, "on cursory examination", could be regarded as constituting direct discrimination within the meaning of the directive, since "the wording of that company rule is directly linked to religion". She also acknowledged that the Court "in its previous case-law concerning various EU-law prohibitions on discrimination" had "generally adopted a broad understanding of the concept of direct discrimination, and has, it is true, always assumed such discrimination to be present where a measure was inseparably linked to the relevant reason for the difference of treatment".[79] But she distinguished the present case from that earlier case-law in that the latter had always concerned "individuals' immutable physical characteristics", such as sex, age and sexual orientation, and not 'chosen' behaviour such as wearing religious headgear.[80] In the light of this, she

---

76 Conclusion Advocate-general J. Kokott, 31 May 2016, C-157/15, ECLI:EU:C:2017:203 (*Achbita*), §52. Hereinafter: 'Conclusion Kokott'.

77 Sharpston's conclusion was issued a few weeks after that of her colleague Kokott, so that the former could implicitly (albeit quite clearly) respond to the arguments and positions in the earlier conclusion. See also F. Dorssemont, "Vrijheid van religie op de werkplaats en het Hof van Justitie: terug naar *cuius region, illius religion?*", *Recht, religie en samenleving* 2017, no. 2, 36.

78 Conclusion Advocate-general E. Sharpston, 13 July 2016, C-188/15, ECLI:EU:C:2016:553 (*Bougnaoui*), §88. Hereinafter: 'Conclusion Sharpston'.

79 Conclusion Kokott, §43–44.

80 Conclusion Kokott, §45 (& 116).

considered "on closer examination" that a ban such as the one at issue in the case "cannot properly be classified as constituting direct discrimination".

To this Sharpston 'responded' that such a distinction does not follow from the legislation, since neither the directives nor their *travaux préparatoires* have anything to say in this regard (quite the contrary, both seem to suggest and encourage a similar approach across discrimination grounds). Sharpston further emphasized that she found Kokott's position on this issue to be misguided: "Here, I emphasise that, to someone who is an observant member of a faith, religious identity is an integral part of that person's very being. The requirements of one's faith – its discipline and the rules that it lays down for conducting one's life – are not elements that are to be applied when outside work (say, in the evenings and during weekends for those who are in an office job) but that can politely be discarded during working hours (...) [I]t would be entirely wrong to suppose that, whereas one's sex and skin colour accompany one everywhere, somehow one's religion does not".[81] Sharpston also failed to see how the direct discrimination that she found could be justified. There was, in any case, no genuine and determining occupational requirement, since nothing in the case suggested that, because Bougnaoui wore the Islamic headscarf, "she was in any way unable to perform her duties as a design engineer". Quite the contrary: the firm had even praised her abilities in this regard, and the dismissal letter expressly referred "to her professional competence".[82]

Kokott did accept that the ban led to an indirect discrimination, or rather: to an indirect distinction, "since such a rule is in practice capable of putting individuals of certain religions or beliefs – in this case, female employees of Muslim faith – at a particular disadvantage by comparison with other employees".[83] However, she argued, such a distinction could be justified by the company's policy of neutrality, in the pursuit of its business, the basis of which "ultimately [lies] in the fundamental right of freedom to conduct a business" (Article 16 of the Charter of Fundamental Rights). Kokott left the assessment *in concreto* to the national courts, but argued extensively that there was much to be said for the fact that the ban was legitimate (provided it was not internally contradictory, and provided it was applied and enforced consistently by the employer in relation to all of its employees)[84]: the AG considered it appropriate, necessary and proportionate for achieving the objective pursued, since less

---

[81] Conclusion Sharpston, §118. Neither does entering into an employment contract imply that one renounces the right to confess one's religious convictions, according to Sharpston: "When the employer concludes a contract of employment with an employee, he does not buy that person's soul. He does, however, buy his time" (§73).

[82] Conclusion Sharpston, §90–102.

[83] Conclusion Kokott, §57.

[84] *Ibid.*, §103.

intrusive means of achieving the same aim were not available (at least none that would avoid placing substantial additional organisational burdens on the employer).

Again Sharpston reached a contrary conclusion. In the hypothesis that the Court would consider the ban to (merely) result in indirect discrimination, the British AG still would not consider the prohibition to be justified as she believed it did not pass the necessity test. Sharpston, like Kokott, pays attention to the needs of the business community, but she concludes that the freedom to conduct a business (art. 16 Charter) does not automatically justify a derogation from the prohibition on discrimination: Sharpston pointed to previous case law that held that mere (alleged) financial loss is insufficient to justify discrimination, and she argued that due regard must be had to opposing rights and interests of others, including societal well-being. The British AG indicated that it *would* be possible for employers to impose a uniform and to stipulate that employees who wear an Islamic headscarf should adopt the colour of that uniform when selecting their headscarf (or that they propose or impose a uniform version of that headscarf). She also accepted that other forms of compromise could sometimes be considered necessary. But she did not see how a general prohibition of religious and philosophical signs could be proportionate, the legal situation being as it was.[85]

C.   RULING AND CRITICAL REFLECTION

How did the ECJ rule?[86] Like both AGs the Court accepts that Directive 2000/78 uses the term 'religion' in a broad sense – just as the ECHR and the

---

[85]   Conclusion Sharpston, §100. Sharpston more specifically points out that the Court has always held that direct discrimination cannot be justified on the ground of the financial loss that might be caused to the employer (ECJ, 3 February 2000, *Mahlburg*, C-207/98, EU:C:2000:64, §29). She also points out that the freedom to conduct a business – while one of the general principles of EU law, now enshrined in Article 16 of the Charter – is, according to the Court, "not an absolute principle but must be viewed in relation to its function in society (…) Accordingly, limitations may be imposed on the exercise of that freedom provided, in accordance with Article 52(1) of the Charter, that they are prescribed by law and that, in accordance with the principle of proportionality, they are necessary and genuinely meet objectives of general interest recognised by the European Union or the need to protect the rights and freedoms of others" (ECJ, 14 October 2014, *Giordano v Commission*, C-611/12 P, EU:C:2014:2282, §49). And the Court has found, in this regard, that the EU legislature was entitled, for instance, to adopt rules to limit that freedom in order to safeguard the freedom to receive information and the freedom and pluralism of the media guaranteed (Article 11 Charter) (ECJ, 22 January 2013, *Sky Österreich*, C-283/11, EU:C:2013:28, §66).

[86]   In the following, we focus (almost) exclusively on the ruling in the *Achbita* case. Although the conclusion of Sharpston and Kokott largely pertained to the same aspects, the *Bougnaoui* case concerned a different preliminary question from the one in *Achbita*. The former was concerned with whether a company could consider a customer's wish to not be confronted with a worker with an Islamic headscarf as a genuine and determining occupational

Charter of Fundamental Rights of the European Union do: therefore the concept of 'religion' in the directive "should be interpreted as covering both the *forum internum*, that is the fact of having a belief, and the *forum externum*, that is the manifestation of religious faith in public".[87] In other words, manifestations of a faith are part and parcel of the protected characteristic that is 'religion'.

Concerning the assessment of direct discrimination, the Court accepts that a specific ban on headscarves or applied to *Islamic headscarves only* would amount to direct discrimination.[88] More implicitly the rulings seem to suggest that a ban on *religious* signs only (and, as such, not including expressions of non-religious beliefs and philosophical convictions) would also be disallowed.[89] That too would, in principle, be direct discrimination. But the Court follows the core of Kokott's reasoning where it states that a prohibition of visible signs of *all* political, philosophical or religious beliefs does not constitute direct discrimination, because it "does not introduce a difference of treatment that is directly based on religion or belief" for the purposes of Directive 2000/78.[90] After all, such a rule "covers any manifestation of such beliefs without distinction", and therefore treats all employees the same.[91] In short, there is simply no one who is treated better or differently on the basis of the ban, as would be required for direct discrimination.

That may sound plausible, but it is debatable upon closer scrutiny. In a sense the question at issue is: (when) does a direct discrimination lose its direct character if you stack additional direct discriminations on top of it? A ban on visible signs and symbols of one specific religion would amount to discrimination. Likewise, the same would seem to go for a ban on visible signs and symbols of (all) religions (but of religions only). But by *simultaneously* making a direct distinction on the basis of (non-religious) beliefs and political convictions, the direct discrimination somehow disappears, according to the Court. That approach seems counter-intuitive and is contentious, for several reasons.

---

requirement. In the light of settled case law (most notably *Feryn*), the answer to this question was predictable and negative. See: ECJ, 14 March 2017, C-188/15, ECLI:EU:C:2017:204 (*Bougnaoui*), §41–42.

[87] ECJ 14 March 2017, C-157/15, ECLI:EU:C:2017:203 (*Achbita*), §28.

[88] ECJ, 14 March 2017, C-188/15, ECLI:EU:C:2017:204 (*Bougnaoui*), §34.

[89] At least *a contrario* as the Court concludes that there is no direct discrimination, because the ban applies to "political, philosophical and religious beliefs", "without distinction" and "to all expressions of such convictions". The suggestion seems that if only (all) religious beliefs would be banned (without philosophical and/or political convictions being included in the prohibition), this would still be direct discrimination. Incidentally, even Kokott's conclusion is explicit on the point that disadvantaging all religions, but *only* religions (without including non-religious beliefs), would amount to a form of direct discrimination: Conclusion Kokott, §50–52 and 55.

[90] ECJ 14 March 2017, C-157/15, ECLI:EU:C:2017:203 (*Achbita*), §32.

[91] *Ibid.*, §30.

Traditionally, the explicit use of a discrimination ground has tended to suffice for concluding to direct discrimination. That has generally been the case law of the court[92], in other contexts, as Sharpston rightly argued in her conclusion and as even Kokott accepted. In other words: in the traditional interpretation direct discrimination would not be considered to disappear by targeting visible expressions of *all* convictions (religious and otherwise).

In distinguishing religion from other grounds, the Court does not (explicitly) adopt Kokott's opposition between 'innate' grounds, on the one hand, and those that are the object of choice, on the other hand. That being said, there seem to be few other explanations for the Court's 'unequal treatment' of religion compared to other criteria.

The Court basically says: someone who would have expressed another religious or non-religious belief would also have been fired, and the rule at issue therefore does not introduce a difference in treatment. To begin with, it is not clear whether this is the case: while the first part of the ban prohibited the wearing of "political, philosophical or religious convictions", a second part prohibited "manifesting any ritual ensuing thereof".[93] That latter part of the ban is *de facto* almost exclusively aimed at religions, as the vast majority of non-religious philosophies and beliefs do not have any 'rituals', and the same goes for political convictions. Such convictions do have other forms of expression, which are

---

[92] See e.g. ECJ 8 November 1990, C-177/88, ECLI:EU:C:1990:383 (*Dekker*) §§12 en 17); ECJ 8 November 1990, C-179/88, ECLI:EU:C:1990:384 (*Handels- og Kontorfunktionærernes Forbund*) §13; ECJ 27 February 2003, C-320/01, ECLI:EU:C:2003:114 (*Busch*) §39); ECJ 20 September 2007, C-116/06, ECLI:EU:C:2007:536 (*Kiiski*) §55; ECJ 18 November 2010, C-356/09, ECLI:EU:C:2010:703 (*Kleist*) §31; ECJ 12 October 2010, C-499/08, ECLI:EU:C:2010:600 (*Ingeniørforeningen i Danmark*) §§23 en 24; ECJ 10 July 2008, C-54/07, ECLI:EU:C:2008:397 (*Feryn*); ECJ 12 December 2013, C-267/12, ECLI:EU:C:2013:823 (*Hay*) §§41 & 44. The person who is discriminated against does not even, according to the Court, need to be a 'bearer' of the characteristic on the grounds of which he was directly discriminated: for example, the Court ruled that the dismissal of a person due to his child's disability was nonetheless direct discrimination on the basis of disability, because the less favourable treatment took place 'on the grounds of' disability, even if it was not the disability of the person concerned. See: ECJ 17 July 2008, C-303/06, ECLI:EU:C:2008:415 (*Coleman*). Indeed, the direct use of a discrimination ground – although traditionally considered sufficient in other cases – sometimes is not even necessary, according to the Court's other case-law. For instance, the 'neutral' requirement to be married, in countries that did not (yet) provide for same sex marriage, was seen as direct and not as indirect discrimination, even though the criterion 'sexual orientation' itself was not employed. See: ECJ 1 April 2008, C-267–06, ECLI:EU:C:2008:179 (*Maruko*) and ECJ 10 May 2011, C-147/08, ECLI:EU:C:2011:286 (*Römer*).

[93] In the original Dutch: "het is aan de werknemers verboden om op de werkplaats zichtbare tekens te dragen van hun politieke, filosofische of religieuze overtuigingen en/of *elk ritueel dat daaruit voortvloeit te manifesteren*". Note, by the way way, that this was mistakenly (and overly 'constructively') translated in the English version of the ruling as "(...) and/or from engaging in any observance of such beliefs".

not, however, touched by the company's ban. As such, upon closer scrutiny, the formulation of the ban itself is far less neutral than the Court would suggest, regardless of its application (the latter will be addressed in discussing indirect discrimination: *infra*).

More important still is that the Court's choice of comparator is highly debatable. In case of direct discrimination, the reference person (comparator) with whom you compare – in order to determine whether a 'less favourable treatment' occurred – should be chosen while abstracting from the protected characteristic. Here it is useful to recall that the Court explicitly ruled (*supra*) that the term 'religion' in the Directive must be interpreted as also covering the public *manifestation* of a religious belief. In other words: the expression is an integral part of the ground of religion and belief. As such, 'abstracting' from that characteristic would seem to require that the Muslim woman, wearing a hijab, cannot be compared with an atheist with a 'God is dead' T-shirt. Rather, *both* of them ought to be compared with an employee who does not manifest any religion or belief (or even with someone who holds no religious, philosophical or political convictions at all). If you do that, it is difficult to conclude otherwise than that there was direct discrimination: employees in the first category are fired, the others are not.[94]

As far as indirect discrimination is concerned, the Court's analysis is more nuanced, (dis)agreeing with both of the advocates-general in part.

The Court considers an employer's wish to project an image of neutrality towards its customers to be a legitimate aim, in the light of the freedom to conduct a business, recognized in Article 16 of the Charter. Notably when the employer involves in its pursuit of that aim "only those workers who are required to come into contact with the employer's customers".[95] The judges are of the opinion that a ban on (all) visible political, philosophical and religious signs can also be a suitable or appropriate means to achieve this neutrality, provided "that that policy is genuinely pursued in a consistent and systematic manner"[96], and provided that it is included in the work regulations and applied without discrimination.

Concerning the measure's necessity, it must be ascertained whether the prohibition "covers only G4S workers who interact with customers"[97] so that it

---

[94] Compare: Conclusion Sharpston, §88. See also: F. Dorssemont, "Vrijheid van religie op de werkplaats en het Hof van Justitie: terug naar cuius region, illius religion?", *Recht, religie en samenleving* 2017, no. 2, 49.

[95] ECJ 14 March 2017, C-157/15, ECLI:EU:C:2017:203 (*Achbita*), §38.

[96] *Ibid.*, §40.

[97] *Ibid.*, §42.

does not unnecessarily affect others, for whom this is not the case. Furthermore, in this connection the Court demands that G4S should ascertain whether it would (have) be(en) possible to offer the employee "a post not involving any visual contact with those customers, instead of dismissing her", in order to "limit the restrictions on the freedoms concerned to what is strictly necessary".[98]

It remains to be seen, in practice, in how many cases the Court's ruling would render a ban possible. It also raises a new series of practical problems, for instance: which expressions must you ban as an employer if you want to be sufficiently 'coherent' in pursuing neutrality? Can you allow a hoody from a politically committed band? A rainbow pin? A T-shirt with 'proud to be a woman' (that might suggest feminist sympathies)? Must you forbid any garment that in any way betrays the individual conviction (or even the individuality)[99] of the wearer? These questions are important, since insufficient coherence would seem to imply the case would have to be analysed as direct discrimination after all.[100]

Finally, on a more principled level, it is not self-evident whether neutrality, in the private sector, can really serve as a legitimate aim to justify discrimination. Obviously, a company may decide to project a neutral image to its customers.[101] But unlike with public authorities no *duty* of neutrality rests upon companies. In the private sector the neutrality aim concerns a purely commercial objective. This would arguably imply that neutrality efforts of a private company cannot justify the same restrictions one individual rights as in the public context.[102]

The Court effaces that distinction entirely.[103] It simply accepts that the pursuit of the neutrality aim is legitimate, in that it relates to the freedom to conduct

---

[98]   *Ibid.*, §43. Albeit "taking into account the inherent constraints to which the undertaking is subject, and without G4S being required to take on an additional burden" (*ibid.*).

[99]   Sharpston is of the opinion that only such a ban could properly be seen as 'neutral': Conclusion Sharpston, §110.

[100]   X. Delgrange, 'Une nouvelle source du droit: le dress-code', in Y. Cartuyvels et al (eds.), *Le droit malgré tout, Liber amicorum François Ost*, Brussels, Presses de l'Université Saint-Louis, 2018.

[101]   See differently K. Lemmens, "Religie in de arbeidsrelaties: beroep of roeping?", in VRG alumni (ed.), *Recht in beweging*, Oud-Turnhout/Den Bosch, Gompels&Svacina, 2018, 401, who argues that the equality principle applies differently and potentially less strictly to private employers, especially since they can invoke (conflicting) human rights. However, that argument seems to ignore the lack of legal 'force' that the neutrality argument has (or rather: ought to have) in the private context.

[102]   Even if the neutrality duty in government context does not necessarily have to be interpreted as a 'strict' or 'exclusive' rather than a 'pluralistic' or 'inclusive' neutrality.

[103]   Something that is also evident from the fact that the Court seeks support in the ECtHR's case-law (pertaining to the public sector), stating that the fact that pursuit of the aim of neutrality can justify restrictions on the freedom of religion is already "borne out by the case-law of the European Court of Human Rights", referring more specifically to *Eweida and Others v. United Kingdom* (ECtHR, 15 January 2013, CE:ECHR:2013:0115JUD004842010, §94).

a business, recognised in Article 16 of the Charter, and that a prohibition on visible signs of religions and beliefs can also be considered 'strictly necessary' to achieve that aim, for employees who come in (visible) contact with customers. In this way, the prohibition of discrimination is completely subordinated to what are essentially commercial and financial considerations. Moreover, these considerations also strongly tend towards a 'client argument': what is at stake here exclusively concerns the image to the outside world (more specifically towards customers), with a view to conducting a business.[104] That seems at odds with the fact that, in *Bougnaoui*, the Court confirmed its earlier case law (developed in the context of race and ethnic origin)[105] that (subjective or discriminatory) wishes by clients cannot serve to justify discrimination. In *Bougnaoui* that meant that a customer's desire to have services provided by someone who did not wear a headscarf could not justify a ban on wearing such clothing.[106] However, if a company – 'pre-emptively' – decides to ban such signs and clothing in order to present customers with a 'neutral image', on the assumption that many customers are 'unfavourably disposed towards veiled employees' or to other visible signs of religion or belief, the legal problems are all of a sudden claimed to vanish.[107]

D. SUBSIDIARITY

Concerning the principle of subsidiarity the ECJ's decision seems to be characterised by the opposite problem from the one identified in the ECtHR's case-law. While the Strasbourg court fails to set adequate guidelines or limits to domestic authorities on *how* to secure Convention rights and freedoms, the court in Luxembourg arguably goes too far in this regard, leaving too little (and perhaps even no) space for national authorities in this context.

Besides, the support sought in *Eweida* is all the more puzzling since that case did not concern a general ban on visible signs of religion and belief for reasons of neutrality. Instead it concerned restrictions in light of the airline's brand and corporate image: British Airways required their staff to wear a uniform, but it accommodated religious symbols (e.g. turbans and headscarves in matching colours). While Ms. Eweida was not allowed to openly wear a cross on a chain, this was not for reasons of neutrality, but since the uniform code required that she not wear visible jewelry. Compare F. Dorssemont, "Vrijheid van religie op de werkplaats en het Hof van Justitie: terug naar cuius region, illius religion?", *Recht, religie en samenleving* 2017, no. 2, 55.

104 ECJ 14 March 2017, C-157/15, ECLI:EU:C:2017:203 (*Achbita*), §38.

105 ECJ 10 july 2008, C-54/07, ECLI:EU:C:2008:397 (*Centrum voor gelijkheid van kansen en voor racismebestrijding v. Firma Feryn NV*).

106 ECJ, 14 March 2017, C-188/15, ECLI:EU:C:2017:204 (*Bougnaoui*), §42. Stating earlier on that "subjective considerations, such as the willingness of the employer to take account of the particular wishes of the customer" cannot amount to a genuine and determining occupational requirement (§40).

107 E. Cloots, "Safe harbour or open sea for corporate headscarf bans? *Achbita and Bougnaoui*", *CMLRev* 2018, vol 55, 614.

That seems especially problematic, given the national diversity that characterises EU Member States' in religious matters. To begin with, there are marked differences among Member States in their *de facto* degree of religious diversity. In the words of Cloots: "Whereas countries such as Greece, Italy, and Poland are extremely homogeneous in terms of religious identity, things are quite different in, for instance, France, Belgium, the Netherlands or the United Kingdom".[108] More important still is the fact that there is not any single line to be distinguished in the way in which Member States deal with religion. The principles, structures and traditions vary widely in this regard, and they range from strict principles of (State) secularism in France, over systems with official State churches and (other) special positions for dominant religions, to active pluralism in countries like the Netherlands, the UK and Germany.

We have seen that the ECtHR's response to situations such as these is to afford a(n arguably overly) wide margin of appreciation to the States in deciding under what circumstances and to what extent a ban on the wearing of religious apparel is compatible with higher legal norms. The idea behind the Court's self-restraint is that national authorities have direct democratic legitimacy, and are in principle better placed than an international court to evaluate local needs and conditions.

Now, as explained above (*supra* II.) the ECJ's function and approach is a different one than that of the ECtHR, and the Court proceeded in this case as it usually tends to proceed, i.e. by clarifying the meaning of autonomous concepts of EU law in a general, uniform way. In this case that concerned direct and indirect discrimination on the basis of religion, under Directive 2000/78, and its relation to the freedom to conduct a business, with the Court ruling that a general (correctly and formally introduced) ban on visible signs of all religions, beliefs and political convictions does not amount to direct discrimination, and that the indirect discrimination that it might result in can be considered justified by the legitimate aim of wanting to project an image of neutrality towards customers, provided such a ban is pursued in a consistent, systematic and non-discriminatory manner, and if it is applied only to employees who come in (visible) contact with customers.

At a first glance, this outcome might seem like a Solomon's ruling. Moreover, for the cases' home countries – Belgium and France – it comes relatively close to the approach already adopted in the national case law.[109] However, the Court's one-

---

108   *Ibid.*, 589.
109   In Belgium, aside from the *Achbita* case, we can refer to the case concerning the retail chain store Hema. On 2 January 2013, the Labour Tribunal in Tongres concluded that Hema had discriminated by dismissing a Muslim woman, due to complaints from customers about her headscarf. The court saw the dismissal as a form of direct discrimination, as HEMA – despite

size-fits-all solution leaves several other countries – with a different tradition and a divergent (and often long-standing) interpretation of the relative weight of the rights and principles involved – forced to change their approach. Given what the Court decided and how it choose to decide it, countries with higher standards of protection against religious discrimination will be forced to 'level down' in light of the duty to respect the primacy of EU law.[110] This would imply that judges in the Netherlands, the United Kingdom and the Scandinavian (EU) countries cannot, for instance, decide that a general ('correctly introduced') ban on visible signs of religions, beliefs and political convictions amounts to direct discrimination. Nor can they decide to reject corporate neutrality as a legitimate aim for the indirect discrimination that such a ban may amount to. Likewise they are unable to rule that such a ban – respecting the Court's additional requirements – is not necessary or disproportionate for achieving that aim. The Court has decided all these issues for the whole of the EU.[111]

Some commentators have responded to this by saying that it remains entirely possible for Member States – that wish to do so – to introduce more specific legislation, granting a higher degree of protection, for instance by explicitly ruling out that neutrality can constitute a legitimate aim in the private sector to serve to justify indirect discrimination. However, things are not as simple. It seems unlikely to us that the ECJ would accept such an (legislative) approach, given that it grounded the very possibility of advancing neutrality as a legitimate aim, that can serve to restrict (religious and non-discrimination) rights, on the freedom to conduct a business, contained in the Charter. If that freedom – in the eyes of the Court – has sufficient weight to restrict the duties of non-discrimination flowing from Directive 2000/78, it is hard to see how additional national legislation could serve to achieve a different outcome. In other words, it

---

claims to this end – was unable to demonstrate that there was a clear neutrality policy at the moment of the facts. However, the court explicitly stated that the issue would be different if Hema *had* pursued a clear and consistent neutrality policy. The refusal or dismissal of workers wearing headscarves or other symbols of religion or belief would, according to the court, then have been justified.

In France, the best-known case concerns 'Baby Loup'. It concerned a French crèche that denied an employee (a vice director), as of a certain moment, to wear a headscarf, for reasons of neutrality and strict secularism (*laïcité*). Dismissal followed, since the employee did not accept the ban. A long legal battle ensued, the ultimate outcome of which was that the neutrality argument was accepted (as a genuine and determining occupational requirement). See: Conseil de prud'hommes de Mantes-la-Jolie, 13 December 2010, no. 10/00587, *Revue de droit du travail*, 2011, 182; Cour d'Appel de Versailles, 27 October 2011, no. 10/0562; Cour de Cassation française (Chambre sociale), 13 March 2013, no. 11. 28. 845, Cour d'Appel de Paris, 27 November 2013; No. 13/02981; Cour de Cassation française (association plénière), 25 June 2014, No. 13–28.368.

[110] See ECJ, 26 February 2013, *Melloni v. Ministerio Fiscal,* C-399/11, ECLI:EU:C:2013:107.

[111] See extensively, on this issue E. Cloots, "Safe harbour or open sea for corporate headscarf bans? *Achbita and Bougnaoui*", *CMLRev* 2018, vol 55, 621–624.

seems difficult – given the foundations of the Court's reasoning – to get around the issues that the rulings raise.

Would an alternative solution – more respectful of national traditions – have been possible? One might answer this question in the negative: after all, the Court was called upon to answer the questions raised by the national courts, and one might argue that it is hard to square with its role and task to defer the answers to those questions to the national courts.

Still, given that the EU (merely) has shared (and not exclusive) competence concerning non-discrimination, the principle of subsidiarity could, and arguably *should*, have entered into play *vis-à-vis* the national authorities. Recall that in situations of shared competence EU intervention is authorised "only if and in so far as the objectives of the proposed action cannot be sufficiently achieved by the Member States", but can rather be better achieved at Union level "by reason of the scale or effects of the proposed action" (Article 5(3) TEU). This principle holds as much for the Court as for the Commission, Parliament and other EU institutions, and it is hard to see what imperative 'objectives' had to be achieved here: if anything the Court is *undermining* the central objectives that the Council had in issuing Directive 2000/78, as the rulings amount to a levelling down of protection against discrimination, throughout the EU.[112] Moreover, the Court did so on the basis of debatable reasoning that appears to be out of line with its wider case-law concerning direct and indirect discrimination, on other grounds (*supra* IV.C.).

Of course one could argue that the Court's 'action' serves the 'objective' of guaranteeing the Charter's freedom to conduct a business (Article 16). But it is unclear why the determination of the exact weight of that right and the balance between that freedom and the right to non-discrimination on the grounds of religion could not have been left to Member states' national authorities, particularly in the light of the principle of proportionality (Article 5(4) TEU), and respect for national identity (Article 4(2) TEU) (*supra* II.). All the more, since matters related to fundamental rights – which both the non-discrimination directives and the Charter's freedom to conduct a business are – call less for a uniform application of EU law than do issues bearing a close link to the internal market.[113] The Charter itself even concedes as much in its Article 53.

Thus, an alternative manner in which the Court could have resolved the issue, was by deferring to national authorities, in a qualified way. More concretely, it would have seemed most defensible and coherent for the Court to have concluded to direct

---

[112] Compare Elke Cloots who argues that the Court's ruling ignores the intentions of the EU legislature: E. Cloots, "Safe harbour or open sea for corporate headscarf bans? *Achbita and Bougnaoui*", *CMLRev* 2018, vol 55, 591.

[113] *Ibid.*, 622–623.

discrimination in this case (*supra* IV.C.), however – given the close association of the neutrality issue with national traditions and identity of particular Member states – it would have been conceivable for the Court to have specified formalities and conditions under which such a direct discrimination might nonetheless be considered justified. Such a condition could, for instance, consist of sufficiently precise statutory authorisation, issued by the competent public authority, providing that 'neutrality' can be regarded as a genuine and determining occupational requirement, in certain circumstances (e.g. those circumstances under which the Court now finds the indirect discrimination to potentially be justified).

Such authorisation, moreover, already exists in France. As a result of a previous legal affair pertaining to the neutrality issue in the private context[114], a law was approved by the French Parliament in 2016 that explicitly enabled companies to invoke the principle of neutrality – in their labour regulations – in a way that limits the (religious) freedom of expression of employees. The core of the law reads as follows: "*Internal [company] regulations may contain provisions establishing the principle of neutrality and restricting the expression of employees' beliefs/convictions, provided these restrictions are justified by the exercise of other fundamental rights and freedoms or by requirements dictated by the proper functioning of the enterprise, and if such restrictions are proportionate to their aim*".[115]

The Court could have accepted this approach[116], and have required from other Member States wanting to provide the same possibility to do so in a similar(ly formalised) manner. That would have safeguarded the more extensive protection against religious discrimination that countries like the UK and the Netherlands wish to grant – arguably doing full justice to Directive 2000/78 – while at the same time being respectful of the national identity and autonomy of countries such as France.

CONCLUSION

The ECtHR and the CJEU operate in different institutional contexts. While the term 'subsidiarity' is used with regard to both EU law and ECHR law, it has a specific meaning in each of these contexts. Yet in both cases the principle of

---

[114] It concerned the '*Babyloup*' case: see *supra* footnote 109 for more information.
[115] Our transl. of: "*Le règlement intérieur peut contenir des dispositions inscrivant le principe de neutralité et restreignant la manifestation des convictions des salariés si ces restrictions sont justifiées par l'exercice d'autres libertés et droits fondamentaux ou par les nécessités du bon fonctionnement de l'entreprise et si elles sont proportionnées au but recherché*".
[116] Although arguably – for reasons *inter alia* of clarity and legal certainty – it would seem preferable that such specific statutory authorization (also) be included in the discrimination legislation implementing Directive 2000/78.

subsidiarity does perform similar functions. In this chapter, the focus has been on the function of regulating the respective room for the supranational (European) court and the national authorities in standard setting with regard to fundamental rights protection, and the freedom of religion in particular. The discussion of recent CJEU and ECtHR judgments in closely related settings – both regarding bans on religious headgear/dress, as applied to Muslims – unpacked the limits of each body's approach to that relationship of subsidiarity. In the ECHR context, subsidiarity is mobilized mostly to emphasize the need for restraint on behalf of the ECtHR, and for a margin of appreciation for domestic authorities in interpreting and implementing (including restricting) Convention rights. Religious freedom is one of several fields, in which the ECtHR has consistently applied a wide margin of appreciation, leading to scarcity of findings of violations of the Convention. Our analysis revealed that the ECtHR's case law, when it finds no Convention violation on the basis of a choice for a wide margin of appreciation for domestic authorities, offers little to no guidance for similar (but not completely identical) scenarios across Europe. Even when the Court *does* find a violation – as in the case that was discussed in this paper – narrow tailoring of the judgment to the facts of the case produces a similar result.

The opposite finding was made regarding the CJEU. In the EU law context, subsidiarity has had surprisingly little impact on the approach and reasoning of the CJEU. While subsidiarity is important in determining whether or not and especially to what extent EU law should come into play on a certain matter, it seems that, once a matter does come within the scope of EU law, it is expected that EU law is interpreted by the ECJ in a uniform manner across all EU Member States. The Luxemburg Court does not seem to fret much about any room for manoeuvre for the national authorities in the interpretation of EU law.

While these differences in approach may be explained by the different mandates and roles of these supranational courts, they are not necessarily justified or legitimate when both courts operate in the same sphere, i.e. human rights protection. What is more, it may be argued that the standard of proper interaction between the national and supranational legal spheres is not indifferent to the substance of the law that is at stake. Arguably, the fact that human rights are concerned, engenders some expectations or even requirements that both courts would be wise to heed. Far from a unique recipe for good practice, what the analyses in this paper bring out, is a concern for the undesirable effects of solutions that tend to either extreme of the spectrum expressing the respective position of the supranational court vis-à-vis the national authorities. To be clear, the national authorities concerned are all those that look to the supranational court for guidance on the matter – not only those of the country involved in the concrete case. Extreme concern for the national authorities' discretion, as in the

ECtHR example, minimizes the role of supranational human rights monitoring to the point of near-irrelevance, except in the one case in which the judgment is issued. On the other hand, complete disregard for national authorities' discretion, as in the CJEU example, seems incompatible with the reality of competing human rights, which are a feature of many of the most salient human rights debates.

In our reflections on potential solutions for these shortcomings, we have attempted to make abstraction of the outcomes of the cases. It is no secret that we hold critical opinions regarding the outcomes of the case law regarding the accommodation of minority religions of both the Strasbourg and Luxemburg courts. Yet, in order to focus on the point of the appropriate relationship between the national and supranational levels, we deliberately make abstraction of these points of view, and take the outcomes of the case law as they are. What we have tried to argue is that, even accepting the outcomes as they are, it is both necessary and possible for each of these courts to improve their approach so as to remedy the problems we identified. For both courts, this requires a more explicit awareness of the impact of their judgment beyond the case at hand, and a practice of carefully providing guidance for those other scenarios, while leaving room for a diversity of solutions.

CHILD ABDUCTION
IN THE CASE LAW OF THE COURT
OF JUSTICE OF THE EUROPEAN
UNION AND OF THE EUROPEAN
COURT OF HUMAN RIGHTS

Koen LENAERTS[*]

President of the Court of Justice of the European Union
Professor of European Union Law, KU Leuven

INTRODUCTION

In order to stress the importance placed on the welfare of children in the EU legal order, the authors of the Lisbon Treaty decided that the promotion of the rights of the child had to be added as one of the objectives pursued by the EU.[1] Those rights are enshrined in the Charter of Fundamental Rights of the European Union (the 'Charter'). In particular, Article 24 thereof provides that children have 'the right to such protection and care as is necessary for their well-being', 'the right to express their views freely' that must be 'taken into consideration on matters which concern them in accordance with their age and maturity'. Furthermore, according to the same provision, every child has 'the right to maintain on a regular basis a personal relationship and direct contact with both his or her parents, unless that is contrary to his or her interests'. Since the Charter enjoys constitutional status[2], the entire body of EU law – and more particularly all EU measures that affect children – must be consistent with the rights of the child.[3]

---

[*]   All opinions expressed herein are personal to the author.
[1]   See Article 3(3) TEU (stating that the EU 'shall promote [...] protection of the rights of the child'). See also Article 3(5) TEU (stating that '[i]n its relations with the wider world, the Union shall [...] contribute to [...] the protection of human rights, in particular the rights of the child'). See, generally, H. Stalford and E. Drywood, 'Coming of age? Children's rights in the European Union' (2009) 46 *Common Market Law Review* 143, at 144 (noting that 'the Lisbon Treaty which incorporates for the first time the "protection of the rights of the child" within the stated objectives of the [EU]').
[2]   Article 6(1) TEU.
[3]   See Article 24(2) of the Charter. See also CJEU, judgment of 26 April 2012, *Health Service Executive*, C-92/12 PPU, EU:C:2012:255, para. 127.

Since 'an unlawful removal of the child, following the taking of a unilateral decision by one of the child's parents, more often than not deprives the child of the possibility of maintaining on a regular basis a personal relationship and direct contact with the other parent'[4], child abduction is, in principle, contrary to the rights of the child as enshrined in Article 24 of the Charter.[5] That is all the more so where the parent left behind lives in a Member State other than that in which the child is present.

At international level, the 1980 Hague Convention protects children against the harmful effects of their wrongful removal or retention by establishing procedures to ensure their prompt return to the State of their habitual residence.[6] However, that Convention provides that under certain circumstances the courts of the Contracting Party where the child is present may adopt a decision ordering the non-return of the child (a 'non-return order'). In the light of Article 13(b) of that Convention, this may be the case where 'there is grave risk that his or her return would expose the child to physical or psychological harm or otherwise place the child in an intolerable situation'(e.g. domestic violence).

At EU level, the EU legislator adopted Regulation No 2201/2003 (the 'Brussels II a Regulation'[7]) that establishes a system of uniform jurisdiction rules for cross-border disputes relating to matrimonial matters and matters of parental responsibility.[8] The Brussels II a Regulation complements the rules laid down in the 1980 Hague Convention so as to 'form a unitary body of rules which applies to the procedures for returning children who have been wrongfully removed within the EU'.[9] Article 8(1) of the Brussels II a Regulation grants general jurisdiction in matters of parental responsibility to the courts of the Member State in which a child 'is habitually resident [...] at the time the court is seised'.[10] Accordingly, Article 10 of the Brussels II a Regulation provides that in the event of a wrongful removal or retention of a child, 'the courts of the Member State where the child was habitually resident immediately before the wrongful removal or retention shall retain their jurisdiction' (i.e. the courts

---

4 CJEU, judgments of 23 December 2009, *Detiček*, C-403/09 PPU, EU:C:2009:810, para. 56, and of 1 July 2010, *Povse*, C-211/10 PPU, EU:C:2010:400, para. 64.

5 See also Article 11 of the UN Convention on the Rights of the Child, adopted and opened for signature, ratification and accession by UN General Assembly resolution 44/25 of 20 November 1989. It entered into force on 2 September 1990.

6 Convention on the Civil Aspects of International Child Abduction, done at The Hague, on 25 October 1980. It entered into force 1 December 1983.

7 Council Regulation (EC) No 2201/2003 of 27 November 2003 concerning jurisdiction and the recognition and enforcement of judgments in matrimonial matters and the matters of parental responsibility, repealing Regulation (EC) No 1347/2000, [2003] OJ L 338/1.

8 See generally K. Lenaerts, 'The Best Interests of the Child Always Come First: the Brussels II *bis* Regulation and the European Court of Justice' (2013) 20 *Jurisprudencija* 1302.

9 Opinion 1/13 (Accession of third States to the Hague Convention) of 14 October 2014, EU:C:2014:2303, para. 78.

10 See Article 8(1) of the Brussels II a Regulation.

of the Member State of origin).[11] However, unlike the position under the 1980 Hague Convention, the courts of the Member State of origin have the final say as to whether the child should be returned or not, given that the Brussels II a Regulation confers on those courts the power to override a non-return order adopted pursuant to Article 13 of that Convention. Most importantly for present purposes, the exercise of that power is accompanied by the conferral of the primary responsibility for securing the rights of the child.

In the context of the European Convention on Human Rights (the 'ECHR'), the leading case in the European Court of Human Rights' (the 'ECtHR') case law, in respect of child abduction, is *X v. Latvia*.[12] In that case, the Grand Chamber sought to clarify its previous findings in *Neulinger and Shuruk v. Switzerland*[13], a judgment that had been heavily criticised for imposing on the courts of the State where the child is present the obligation to carry out an 'in-depth examination of the entire family situation', since that examination called into question the return mechanism set up by both the 1980 Hague Convention and the Brussels II a Regulation.[14] In *X v. Latvia*, the ECtHR laid down a series of principles that sought to strike a fair balance between preserving the effectiveness of the return mechanism and the achievement of effective protection of the rights guaranteed under Article 8 ECHR.[15] To that effect, it ruled that '[those] courts must not only consider arguable allegations of a "grave risk" for the child in the event of return [as provided for by Article 13(b) of the Hague Convention], but must also make a ruling giving specific reasons in the light of the circumstances of the case.'[16]

It follows from those observations that, where a child is wrongfully removed or retained within the EU, his or her rights are protected by a plurality of sources, i.e. the constitutions of both the Member State of origin and the Member State of enforcement, the Charter, the ECHR and international agreements that protect children, such as the 1980 Hague Convention and the 1989 UN Convention on the Rights of the Child.[17]

Whilst those sources all have in common the fact that they seek to strike the right balance between the rights of the child, those of the parents and public

---

[11]   Jurisdiction is retained until the child has acquired his or her habitual residence in another Member State and the conditions listed in Article 10(a) or (b) of the Brussels II a Regulation are met.

[12]   ECtHR, judgment of 26 November 2013, *X v. Latvia*, CE:ECHR:2013:1126JUD002785309.

[13]   This was also a judgment delivered by the Grand Chamber. See ECtHR, judgment of 6 July 2010, *Neulinger and Shuruk v. Switzerland*, CE:ECHR:2010:0706JUD004161507.

[14]   ECtHR, judgment of 26 November 2013, *X v. Latvia*, CE:ECHR:2013:1126JUD002785309, §§104–105.

[15]   *Ibid.*, §§92 et seq.

[16]   *Ibid.*, §107.

[17]   See above n 5.

policy objectives, the diversity that exists between them may, nevertheless, give rise not only to normative conflicts but also to conflicts of jurisdiction. That is because divergences in the rules laid down by those sources may lead to different outcomes in terms of identifying the court that has the responsibility for striking that balance in a particular case. Thus, the question that arises is how both the courts of the Member State of origin and those of the Member State of enforcement are to order that pluralism when confronted with the wrongful removal or retention of a child.[18]

By answering that complex question, this essay seeks to pay tribute to my dear friend and colleague at the KU Leuven, Paul Lemmens, for his outstanding contribution to the development of fundamental rights law, both as a legal scholar and as a judge at the ECtHR.[19] It is structured as follows. In Section II, it is argued that the rules set out in the Brussels II a Regulation establish a division of jurisdiction between the courts of the Member State of origin and those of the Member State of enforcement, according to which it is primarily for the former courts to determine whether the return of the child is in his or her best interests. Conversely, the courts of the Member State of enforcement may not second-guess that determination, as that would call into question not only the objectives of laying down clear rules pursued by both the 1980 Hague Convention and the Brussels II a Regulation, but also the principle of mutual trust between Member States' courts within the EU. Section III argues that the ECtHR is respectful of the way in which the principle of mutual trust – as given concrete expression in the Brussels II a Regulation – operates within the EU. This point is illustrated by the rulings of that court in cases such as *Šneersone and Kampanella v. Italy*[20], *Povse v. Austria*[21], *M.A. v. Austria*[22] and *Avotiņš v. Latvia*.[23] This is a positive development that facilitates the task of national courts in ordering pluralism, whilst providing for an effective level of fundamental rights protection. However, Section IV posits that the recent judgment of the ECtHR in *M.K. v. Greece* is a source of concern.[24] This is not only because it seems difficult to reconcile with the existing case law of the ECtHR, but also because it blurs the division of jurisdiction sought by the Brussels II a Regulation. Finally, a brief conclusion

---

[18]   The expression 'ordering pluralism' is borrowed from M. Delmas-Marty, *Ordering Pluralism: A Conceptual Framework for Understanding the Transnational Legal World* (Oxford, Hart Publishing, 2009).

[19]   See, e.g., P. Lemmens, 'The Relation between the Charter of Fundamental Rights of the European Union and the European Convention on Human Rights – Substantive Aspects' (2001) 8 *Maastricht Journal of European and Comparative Law* 49.

[20]   ECtHR, judgment of 12 July 2011, *Šneersone and Kampanella v. Italy*, CE:ECHR:2011:0712 JUD001473709.

[21]   ECtHR, decision of 18 June 2013, *Povse v. Austria*, CE:ECHR:2013:0618DEC000389011.

[22]   ECtHR, judgment of 15 January 2015, *M.A. v. Austria*, CE:ECHR:2015:0115JUD000409713.

[23]   ECtHR, judgment of 23 May 2016, *Avotiņš v. Latvia*, CE:ECHR:2016:0523JUD001750207.

[24]   ECtHR, judgment of 1 February 2018, *M.K. v. Greece*, CE:ECHR:2018:0201JUD005131216.

supports the contention that striving to achieve normative convergence between the Court of Justice of the European Union (the 'CJEU') and the ECtHR is the best way to strengthen the authority of both courts since such convergence provides clarity to national courts in the already complex field of child abduction.[25]

I. THE CASE LAW OF THE CJEU ON CHILD ABDUCTION

As interpreted by the CJEU, the Brussels II a Regulation 'is based on judicial cooperation and mutual trust which lead to mutual recognition of judicial decisions, the cornerstone for the creation of a genuine judicial area'.[26] In the context of child abduction, mutual trust means that the courts of the Member State of enforcement must trust the courts of the Member State of origin to provide an equivalent and effective level of judicial protection to the child that has been abducted.[27]

Unlike the 'general' procedure laid down in Section 2 of Chapter III of the Brussels II a Regulation, Articles 11(8), 40(1)(b) and 42(2) thereof set out a special procedure which seeks to guarantee the immediate return of the child wrongfully removed or retained, by excluding any appeal against the issuing of a certificate[28] and by precluding parties from opposing its recognition.[29] Indeed, the national public policy exception enshrined in Article 23 of the Brussels II a Regulation does not apply to proceedings concerning the non-return of a child.

In order for that special procedure to apply, the holder of rights of custody of the child unlawfully removed must first receive a negative answer from the courts of the Member State where that child is present. That negative answer takes the form of a non-return order adopted pursuant to Article 13 of the 1980 Hague Convention.[30] To this effect, in accordance with both Article 11 of the 1980 Hague Convention and Article 11(3) of the Brussels II a Regulation, the courts of the Member State where the child is present must act expeditiously. They

---

25 See, in this regard, K. Lenaerts, 'The ECHR and the CJEU: Creating Synergies in the Field of Fundamental Rights Protection', speech delivered at the ECtHR on the occasion of the solemn hearing for the opening of the Judicial Year, 26 January 2018, available at: <https://www.echr.coe.int/Documents/Speech_20180126_Lenaerts_JY_ENG.pdf>.
26 CJEU, judgment of 15 February 2017, *W and V*, C-499/15, EU:C:2017:118, para. 50.
27 CJEU, judgment of 22 December 2010, *Aguirre Zarraga*, C-491/10 PPU, EU:C:2010:828, paras 59 et seq.
28 CJEU, judgment of 11 July 2008, *Rinau*, C-195/08 PPU, EU:C:2008:406, para. 85.
29 *Ibid.*, para. 68.
30 *Ibid.*, para. 59.

are required to issue a judgment no later than six weeks after the application is lodged, unless exceptional circumstances make that impossible.

One of the main features of the system of recognition and enforcement established by the Brussels II a Regulation is that Article 11(8) thereof enhances the return mechanism set out in the 1980 Hague Convention in so far as it provides that the non-return order adopted pursuant to Article 13 of that Convention may be overridden by 'any subsequent judgment which requires the return of the child issued by a court having jurisdiction under the Regulation'.[31]

In addition, Article 42(1) of the Brussels II a Regulation eliminates the need for *exequatur* proceedings for the recognition and enforcement of a judgment ordering the return of a child that is issued pursuant to Article 11(8) thereof. Once a certificate pertaining to that judgment is delivered by the court of the Member State of origin in accordance with the requirements set out in Article 42(2) of the Brussels II a Regulation, any possibility for opposing the return of the child is, in principle, precluded. The party opposing recognition may only bring an action seeking rectification of the certificate before the courts of the Member State of origin and in accordance with the laws thereof.

When interpreting those provisions of the Brussels II a Regulation, the CJEU has sought to protect the effectiveness of the return mechanism set out in that Regulation whilst taking due account of the rights of the child. The underlying rationale of the CJEU's case law is that the wrongful removal or retention of a child is detrimental to his or her rights so that his or her return must be secured as soon as possible.[32] Three key judgments illustrate that point, i.e. *Rinau, Povse* and *Aguirre Zarraga*.

In *Rinau*, the CJEU stressed the importance of preserving the effectiveness of the return mechanism set out in the Brussels II a Regulation.[33] It held that the court of the Member State of origin may still issue a certificate based on Article 42(2) of the Brussels II a Regulation notwithstanding the fact that the non-return order adopted pursuant to Article 13 of the 1980 Hague Convention has been subsequently suspended, overturned, set aside or, in any event, has not become *res judicata* or has been replaced by a decision ordering the return of the child where such return has not effectively taken place. In that regard, the CJEU

---

[31]   See Article 11(8) of the Brussels II a Regulation.
[32]   This may explain why preliminary references concerning child abduction have been dealt with under the urgent preliminary reference procedure. See, in this regard, S. Bartolini, 'The Urgent Preliminary Ruling Procedure: Ten Years On' (2018) 24 *European Public Law* 213.
[33]   In that case, the Lithuanian Supreme Court was seized of an application for the non-recognition of a judgment of a German court awarding custody of a child to her father, who lived in Germany, and ordering her mother, who lived in Lithuania, to return the child to him.

reasoned that 'there would be a risk that the Regulation would be deprived of its useful effect, since the objective of the immediate return of the child would remain subject to the condition that the redress procedures allowed under the domestic law of the Member State in which the child is wrongfully retained have been exhausted'.[34]

Similarly, in *Povse*, a case involving the wrongful removal of a child by her mother from Italy to Austria, the CJEU was called upon to interpret the expression 'any subsequent judgment which requires the return of the child' contained in Article 11(8) of the Brussels II a Regulation. The question was whether that expression could be read as referring only to final judgments on rights of custody rendered by the court of the Member State of origin or whether it could also be construed so as to include provisional judgments of that court. In that regard, the CJEU recalled that the Brussels II a Regulation seeks the swift return of the child wrongfully removed or retained.[35] If the fact of obtaining a final judgment issued by the court enjoying jurisdiction by virtue of the Brussels II a Regulation were to operate as a prerequisite for the application of Article 11(8), then there would be a risk that such a court might rush to adopt a final decision on rights of custody, despite lacking either all the relevant information or the material needed for that purpose. Such a reading of Article 11(8) would be contrary to the best interests of the child. Last but not least, since the system set up by the EU legislator rests on the premise that the wrongful removal or retention of a child is detrimental to the best interests of that child[36], the longer the separation between the child and the father or the mother suffering from the wrongful removal or retention lasts, the greater the adverse effect on the fundamental rights of the child will be. Accordingly, in the light of Article 24 of the Charter, the court of the Member State of origin may, on the basis of Article 11(8) of the Brussels II a Regulation, issue a judgment ordering the return of the child, even if that judgment is not preceded by a final judgment of that court relating to rights of custody of the child.

In addition, the CJEU was called upon to determine whether a judgment ordering the return of the child issued by a court of the Member State of origin on the basis of Article 11(8) of the Brussels II a Regulation could be overridden by a subsequent judgment of a court of the Member State of enforcement. It held that there is, in principle, nothing the Member State of enforcement can do to oppose recognition and enforcement of a certified judgment issued on the basis of Article 11(8). The only recourse available to the party opposing recognition is to bring an action seeking the rectification of the certificate before the competent

---

34   CJEU, judgment of 11 July 2008, *Rinau*, C-195/08 PPU, EU:C:2008:406, para. 81.
35   CJEU, judgment of 1 July 2010, *Povse*, C-211/10 PPU, EU:C:2010:400, para. 62.
36   *Ibid.*, para. 64.

court of the Member State of origin and in accordance with the laws thereof.[37] However, such an action cannot amount to an appeal, such an appeal being ruled out by Article 43(2) of the Brussels II a Regulation. Rectification is thus limited to verifying that no material error has occurred, i.e. to ascertaining whether the certificate correctly reflects the judgment.[38] That is without prejudice to Article 47(2) which provides that a certified judgment is not enforceable if it is irreconcilable with a subsequent enforceable judgment of the competent court of the Member State of origin.[39] In concrete terms, this meant that the Italian courts had retained jurisdiction under the Brussels II a Regulation and could thus order the return of the child, the Austrian courts having no choice but to enforce that order.

In *Aguirre Zarraga*[40], a case concerning the non-return of a child from Germany to Spain, the German court asked, in essence, whether the certificate provided for by Article 42 of the Brussels II a Regulation ordering the return of a child could be disregarded by a court in the Member State of enforcement in circumstances where its issue amounted, in its view, to a serious violation of the child's fundamental rights, more particularly Article 24 of the Charter (the child concerned had not been heard)[41], or where that certificate contained a statement that was manifestly incorrect (it stated that the child had been heard when in actual fact, she had not).[42] In particular, the referring court asked whether it could decline to enforce a judgment ordering the return of a child where – contrary to what was, in its view, required by Article 42(2)(a) of the Brussels II a Regulation – that child had not been given the opportunity to be heard.

After recalling its previous findings in *Rinau* and *Povse*, the CJEU held that a court of the Member State of enforcement may not oppose the recognition of a judgment certified pursuant to the requirements laid down in Article 42(2). That being said, it pointed out that the fact that the court of the Member State of enforcement lacks the power to review a certified judgment adopted in accordance with Article 42(2) does not mean that the fundamental rights of

---

[37] *Ibid.*, para. 74.
[38] *Ibid.*, para. 71.
[39] AG Sharpston pointed out that, whilst it is not possible for an applicant to bring an appeal against the certificate, he or she may do so against the underlying return order adopted pursuant to Article 11(8) of the Brussels II a Regulation. Article 44 of that Regulation also supports the Advocate General's view as it provides that '[t]he certificate shall take effect only within the limits of the enforceability of the judgment'. This means that if the judgment adopted on the basis of Article 11(8) of the Regulation is quashed, the certificate produces no effects. See View of Advocate General Sharpston in *Povse*, C-211/10 PPU, EU:C:2010:344, point 125.
[40] CJEU, judgment of 22 December 2010, *Aguirre Zarraga*, C-491/10 PPU, EU:C:2010:828.
[41] *Ibid.*, para 35.
[42] *Ibid.*, para 36.

the child concerned, in particular his or her right to be heard, are deprived of judicial protection. First, the system set up by the Brussels II a Regulation rests on the principle of mutual trust. In the realm of fundamental rights, this means that it is presumed that all national courts provide an equivalent and effective level of judicial protection.[43] Second, when issuing a certificate on the basis of Article 42(2) of the Brussels II a Regulation, it is for the court of the Member State of origin to make sure that the child is able to express her views freely 'in accordance with [her] age and maturity'. In particular, that court must determine whether hearing the child is, in light of Article 24 of the Charter, in his or her best interests.[44] Third, it is 'within the legal system of the Member State of origin that the parties concerned must pursue legal remedies which allow the lawfulness of a judgment certified pursuant to Article 42 of [the Brussels II a Regulation] to be challenged'.[45] The CJEU observed that appeal proceedings had in fact been brought in Spain.[46]

II. SYNERGIES IN THE CASE LAW OF THE CJEU AND THE ECtHR

It follows from the case law of the CJEU that it is primarily for the court of the Member State of origin to determine whether the return of the child is in his or her best interests, and for the court of the Member State of enforcement to act with expediency so as to secure the prompt return of the child where the former court so requires. If the father or the mother of the child disagrees with the rulings made by the court of the Member State of origin, he or she must challenge those determinations before the courts of that Member State which must provide for an effective remedy. In this section, it is posited that this division of jurisdiction between the courts of the Member State of origin and those of the Member State of enforcement, provided for by the Brussels II a Regulation, is also the starting point of the case law of the ECtHR.

From the perspective of fundamental rights, the court of the Member State of origin may not issue a certificate ordering the return of the child automatically, disregarding compelling evidence showing that the return of the child is against his or her best interests. That court may not order the return of the child as a form of 'punishment' for the abducting parent, nor as a mechanism for ensuring the repatriation of its own nationals. As the CJEU held in *Povse*, 'before [ordering the return of the child], the court which has jurisdiction must take

---

43   *Ibid*, paras. 59 et seq.
44   *Ibid.*, para 64.
45   *Ibid.*, para 71.
46   *Ibid.*, para 72.

into consideration the reasons for and evidence underlying the decision of non–return. The consideration of those matters is one reason why such a judgment, once it is made, is enforceable, in accordance with the principle of mutual trust which underpins the [Brussels II a Regulation]'.[47] Failing to do so, the court of the Member State of origin would not only betray the trust placed on it by EU law, but would also run the risk of violating the abducting parent's and the child's right to respect for their family life as guaranteed by the ECHR. The judgment of the ECtHR in *Šneersone and Kampanella v. Italy* illustrates this point.[48]

In that case, the ECtHR was called upon, for the first time, to examine a case involving the application of the special procedure provided for by the Brussels II a Regulation that seeks to guarantee the immediate return of the child wrongfully removed or retained (e.g. Articles 11(7)–(8) and 42 of that Regulation). The facts of the case concerned the wrongful removal of a child by his mother from Italy to Latvia. The abducting mother and her son brought proceedings before the ECtHR against Italy, arguing that by ordering the child to be returned to his father, Italy had violated their right to respect for family life as guaranteed under Article 8 ECHR. The ECtHR sided with the applicants. It found that the Italian courts' reasoning was rather scant and did not address any of the risks associated with the return of the child that had been identified by the Latvian courts.[49] First, the Italian courts did not examine the two psychologist's reports drawn up in Latvia that advised against separating the child from his mother. Second, they made no reference to the fact that the child's father had not attempted to contact his son for more than four years. Third, the Italian courts had also failed to establish whether the father's home was suitable for young children. Fourth, the ECtHR found that limiting the child's contact with his mother to a month every second year after a short initial period together was 'a manifestly inappropriate response to the psychological trauma that would inevitably follow a sudden and irreversible severance of the close ties between [them]'.[50] Last but not least, those courts had not considered any alternative solutions for ensuring contact between the child and his father.

Šneersone and Kampanella v. Italy is, in my view, a positive development in that it obliges the courts of the Member State of origin to examine thoroughly whether the return of the child is warranted. It is also fully consistent with the *Bosphorus* presumption since in deciding whether the child should be returned to the Member State of origin, the court of that Member State is exercising a degree of discretion

---

[47] CJEU, judgment of 1 July 2010, *Povse*, C-211/10 PPU, EU:C:2010:400, para. 59.

[48] ECtHR, judgment of 12 July 2011, *Šneersone and Kampanella v. Italy*, CE:ECHR:2011:0712 JUD001473709.

[49] Ibid., §93.

[50] Ibid., §96.

that is circumscribed by the need to protect the rights of the child effectively.[51] From
an EU law perspective, the high-level of scrutiny carried out by the ECtHR operates
as a trust-building mechanism that gives impetus to the idea that mutual trust must
be earned by the courts having jurisdiction under the Brussels II a Regulation.[52]
In order to earn that trust, the ECtHR compels the courts of the Member State of
origin to demonstrate that the subsequent judgment ordering the return of the
child is the result of a balancing exercise between the competing interests at stake,
i.e. 'those of the child, of the two parents, and of public order'.[53] Thus, whilst the
recognition and enforcement of the subsequent judgment ordering the return of
the child is automatic, the decision-making process leading to such a judgment
must *not* be automatic. On the one hand, that decision must be adopted speedily
so as to secure, where appropriate, the swift return of the child. On the other hand,
the powers that the court of the Member State of origin enjoys under the Brussels
II a Regulation must be used with caution so as to guarantee compliance with
fundamental rights.[54] Most importantly, Šneersone and Kampanella v. Italy stresses
the fact that the primary responsibility for ensuring compliance with fundamental
rights lies with the courts of the Member State of origin, reinforcing the division of
jurisdiction sought by the Brussels II a Regulation.

On the contrary, once the court of the Member State of enforcement receives the
certificate providing for the return of the child, compliance with the principle of

---

51   ECtHR, judgment of 30 June 2005, *Bosphorus Hava Yolları Turizm ve Ticaret Anonim
      Şirketi v. Ireland*, CE:ECHR:2005:0630JUD004503698. According to the ECtHR, in order
      for the *Bosphorus* presumption to apply, the two following conditions must be fulfilled.
      First, the national authorities must not enjoy any margin of manoeuvre. Second, "the full
      potential of the relevant international machinery for supervising fundamental rights – in
      principle equivalent to that of the Convention – [has] been deployed". That full potential is
      not deployed where the national court against whose decisions there is no judicial remedy
      under national law, fails to make a reference to the CJEU, "even though [the latter court has]
      not had an opportunity to examine the question, either in a preliminary ruling delivered in
      the context of another case, or on the occasion of [a direct action]". See ECtHR, judgment
      of 6 December 2012, *Michaud v. France*, §§102–116. However, "this second condition should
      be applied without excessive formalism and taking into account the specific features of
      the supervisory mechanism in question … [It] would serve no useful purpose to make the
      implementation of the *Bosphorus* presumption subject to a requirement for the domestic
      court to request a ruling from the [CJEU] in all cases without exception, including those
      cases where no genuine and serious issue arises with regard to the protection of fundamental
      rights by EU law, or those in which the [CJEU] has already stated precisely how the applicable
      provisions of EU law should be interpreted in a manner compatible with fundamental rights".
      See ECtHR, judgment of 23 May 2016, *Avotiņš v. Latvia*, CE:ECHR:2016:0523JUD001750207,
      §109. See, in this regard, P. Beaumont and Others, 'Child abduction: recent jurisprudence of
      the European Court of Human Rights' (2015) 64 *International & Comparative Law Quarterly*
      39, at 54.
52   K. Lenaerts, '*La vie après l'avis*: Exploring the Principle of Mutual (yet not Blind) Trust'
      (2017) 54 *Common Market Law Review* 805, at 837.
53   ECtHR, judgment of 12 July 2011, *Šneersone and Kampanella v. Italy*, CE:ECHR:2011:
      0712JUD001473709, §91.
54   See P. Beaumont and Others, above 51, at 56.

mutual trust prevents that court from second-guessing the determinations made by the court of the Member State of origin as to whether the return of the child is in his or her best interests. It is true that in *X v. Latvia* the ECtHR held that when deciding whether to rely on Article 13(b) of the 1980 Hague Convention, the courts of the Member State of enforcement have the procedural obligation to examine whether allegations regarding a 'grave risk' for the child in the event of return are well-founded. They must carry out meaningful findings and state the reasons explaining why they consider that Article 13(b) applies (or does not apply) to the case at hand.

However, once the courts of the Member State of enforcement receive a subsequent judgment ordering the return of the child that is certified pursuant to Article 42 of the Brussels II a Regulation, those courts have no choice but to enforce such a certified judgment. That does not mean, however, that the rights of the child are left unprotected. It is simply that the responsibility for ensuring their effective judicial protection has been transferred to the courts of the Member State of origin. As *Šneersone and Kampanella v. Italy* shows, it is for the courts of the Member State of origin to explain why they have taken a different view from that of the courts of the Member State of enforcement.

Moreover, compliance with the fundamental rights of the parent left behind imposes on the courts of the Member State of enforcement the obligation to act swiftly. The longer those courts take to enforce the certified judgment, the more the relationship between the parent left behind and the child will deteriorate, and the greater the risk of violating their right to respect for family life will be. This approach, that underpins the philosophy of both the 1980 Hague Convention and the Brussels II a Regulation, is fully consistent with the rulings of the ECtHR in *Povse v. Austria*[55] and in *M.A. v. Austria*[56], two cases that were decided after the CJEU delivered its judgments in *Rinau*, *Povse* and *Aguirre Zarraga*.

The parental dispute in those two cases concerned the very same facts as those examined by the CJEU in *Povse*. In *Povse v. Austria*, it was the mother of the child who brought an action against Austria before the ECtHR arguing that, in deciding to enforce the Italian decision, Austria had violated her fundamental rights and those of her daughter. In *M.A. v Austria*, it was the father left behind who also brought an action against Austria on the ground that the Austrian courts had taken too long to enforce the subsequent judgment ordering the return of the child.

In *Povse v. Austria*, the ECtHR held that the *Bosphorus* presumption applied to the case at hand. Since the Austrian courts 'did not exercise any discretion in

---

55 ECtHR, decision of 18 June 2013, *Povse v. Austria*, CE:ECHR:2013:0618DEC000389011.
56 ECtHR, judgment of 15 January 2015, *M.A. v. Austria*, CE:ECHR:2015:0115JUD000409713.

ordering the enforcement of the return orders', the ECtHR ruled that 'Austria [had] therefore done no more than fulfil the strict obligations flowing from its membership of the European Union'[57], i.e. from the Brussels II a Regulation. Referring to the ruling of the CJEU in *Povse*, the ECtHR found that the Austrian courts had no choice but to enforce the judgment of the Italian courts ordering the return of the child, and concluded that Austria had violated neither the fundamental rights of the child nor those of her mother. It noted that 'it [was] open to the applicants to rely on their Convention rights before the Italian [c]ourts … Should any action before the Italian courts fail, the applicants would ultimately be in a position to lodge an application with the [ECtHR] against Italy'.[58]

Pursuing the same logic, in *M.A. v. Austria* which concerned the fundamental rights of the father of the same child, the ECtHR recalled its case law according to which Article 8 ECHR imposes positive obligations on the Member State of enforcement that require it to take appropriate measures ensuring that the parent left behind is reunited with his or her child. Accordingly, by failing to act expeditiously and to take sufficient steps to ensure the enforcement of his daughter's return to Italy, Austria had violated his rights under Article 8 ECHR.[59] Moreover, the rationale underpinning that judgment has been subsequently confirmed in cases such as *Sévère v. Austria*[60], *Mansour v. Slovakia*[61], and *Oller Kamínska v. Poland*[62], where the ECtHR also held that those Member States had violated the rights to respect for the family life of the parent left behind in so far as the enforcement of the judgment ordering the return of the child had not taken place expeditiously.

The rulings of the ECtHR in *Povse v. Austria* and *M.A. v. Austria* are both welcome developments that contribute to strengthening the principle of mutual trust in so far as they place the onus of securing compliance with fundamental rights on the courts of the Member State of origin.

More generally, the ruling of the ECtHR in *Avotiņš v. Latvia* appears to suggest that that court is willing to recognize the importance of the principle of mutual trust.[63] The Grand Chamber of the ECtHR held, after reaffirming that the

---

57   ECtHR, decision of 18 June 2013, *Povse v. Austria*, CE:ECHR:2013:0618DEC000389011, §82.
58   *Ibid.*, para. 86.
59   ECtHR, judgment of 15 January 2015, *M.A. v. Austria*, CE:ECHR:2015:0115JUD000409713, §137.
60   ECtHR, judgment of 21 September 2017, *Sévère v. Austria*, CE:ECHR:2017:0921JUD005366115, §116.
61   ECtHR, judgment of 21 November 2017, *Mansour v. Slovakia*, CE:ECHR:2017:1121 JUD006039915, §64.
62   ECtHR, judgment of 18 January 2018, *Oller Kamínska v. Poland*, CE:ECHR:2018:0118 JUD002848112, §97.
63   ECtHR, judgment of 23 May 2016, *Avotiņš v. Latvia*, CE:ECHR:2016:0523JUD001750207. See also ECtHR, judgment of 17 April 2018, *Pirozzi v. Belgium*, CE:ECHR:2018:0417JUD002105511

Bosphorus presumption – as further developed in *Michaud v. France*[64] – remains good law, that it 'is mindful of the importance of the mutual recognition mechanisms for the construction of the Area of Freedom, Security and Justice'.[65] Accordingly, the adoption of the means necessary to achieve such construction is, in principle, a wholly legitimate objective from the standpoint of the ECHR. As a matter of principle, the ECtHR endorsed the way in which EU law allocates responsibilities between the Member State which is competent for adopting the judicial decision in question and that responsible for enforcing it: the national court that adopts the contested decision has the primary responsibility for protecting the fundamental rights of the persons affected by that decision, rather than the court enforcing it. Nevertheless, '[the ECtHR] must verify that the principle of mutual recognition is not applied automatically and mechanically ... to the detriment of fundamental rights'.[66] As a result, where a serious and substantiated complaint is raised before the court of the executing Member State to the effect that the protection of an ECHR right has been manifestly deficient in the Member State of origin and this situation cannot be remedied by EU law, the *Bosphorus* presumption is set aside and the ECtHR no longer refrains from examining whether the execution of such decision entails a violation of the ECHR. In my view, the rationale underpinning *Avotiņš v. Latvia* is consistent with the interpretation of the principle of mutual trust endorsed by the CJEU in its Opinion 2/13.[67] It is, however, for future cases to clarify the 'exceptional circumstances' under which the Charter may impose limits on the operation of that principle in the context of child abduction.

III. BLURRING THE DIVISION OF JURISDICTION SOUGHT BY EU LAW

As mentioned in the introduction, whilst judgments such as *Šneersone and Kampanella v. Italy*, *Povse v. Austria*, and *M.A. v. Austria* strengthen the division of jurisdiction established by the Brussels II a Regulation, the same cannot be said of the recent ruling of the ECtHR in *M.K. v. Greece*.

That case concerned the wrongful retention of a child in Greece by his father. The mother of the child requested the return of the child to France in accordance

---

(where the ECtHR applied the *Bosphorus* presumption to Belgium's decision to execute a European arrest warrant).

64 See above n 51.

65 ECtHR, judgment of 23 May 2016, *Avotiņš v. Latvia*, CE:ECHR:2016:0523JUD001750207, §113.

66 *Ibid.*, §116.

67 Opinion 2/13 (Accession of the European Union to the ECHR) of 18 December 2014, EU:C:2014:2454, paras 191 and 192.

with the 1980 Hague Convention. However, unlike the situations at issue in *Rinau, Povse* and *Aguirre Zarraga*, this case did not involve questions pertaining to the enforcement of a subsequent judgment ordering the return of the child adopted pursuant to Article 11(8) of the Brussels II a Regulation and certified in accordance with Article 42 thereof.[68] This was because the Greek courts had not objected to the return of the child to France but had agreed to it.[69] The problem in this case arose from the fact that the Greek authorities had failed to enforce their own return order.[70]

Accordingly, the mother of the child brought proceedings before the ECtHR arguing that such a failure constituted a violation of her right to respect for family life as provided for in Article 8 ECHR. The key issue in the case was to determine whether Greece had fulfilled its positive obligations under that provision of the ECHR. The ECtHR found that it had, since the Greek authorities had acted with due diligence: they had examined the overall family situation, the way in which that situation had evolved and the best interests of the child in question as well as those of his brother.[71] Most importantly, in the light of his age and level of maturity (he was 13 at the time), the ECtHR found that the child's express wish to remain in Greece with his brother and father was a compelling argument that heavily influenced the choices made by the Greek authorities.[72]

In her dissenting Opinion, Judge Koskelo criticised the decision reached by the majority on the ground that it was at odds with basic principles of the rule of law. She posited that the best interests of the child may not be relied upon in order to 'creat[e] competences which an authority does not otherwise lawfully possess, or [to do] away with the limits of those competences'.[73] On the contrary, the best interests of the child must be reconciled with the principle of legality, given that those interests can only be taken into consideration in the appropriate procedural context. In concrete terms, this meant that the right of the child to be heard and the need for his or her views to be taken into account, important as they are, 'cannot be detached from the procedural context in which respect

---

68   ECtHR, judgment of 1 February 2018, *M.K. v. Greece*, CE:ECHR:2018:0201JUD005131216, §§22 and 89 (holding that Article 11(8) of the Brussels II a Regulation did not apply to the case at hand since the competent French court had not formally ordered the return of the child in a subsequent judgment ruling that parents were to share custody of the child; that domicile of the child was in France and that the father enjoyed a right of access and accommodation).
69   See Dissenting Opinion of Judge Koskelo in judgment of 1 February 2018, *M.K. v. Greece*, CE:ECHR:2018:0201JUD005131216, §39.
70   ECtHR, judgment of 1 February 2018, *M.K. v. Greece*, CE:ECHR:2018:0201JUD005131216, §§20, 21, 58 and 90.
71   *Ibid.*, §90. It is worth noting that the case only concerned the wrongful retention of one of the brothers, the oldest having expressed his wish to stay in Greece with his father.
72   *Ibid.*, §§86 to 88, 91 and 92.
73   See Dissenting Opinion of Judge Koskelo in judgment of 1 February 2018, *M.K. v. Greece*, CE:ECHR:2018:0201JUD005131216, §7.

for those rights must be ensured'.[74] It was for the competent courts under the Brussels II a Regulation, i.e. the French courts, to ensure the observance of those rights. In addition, she noted that the findings of the majority failed to deal with the fact that the Greek courts examined several applications brought by the father that involved matters of parental responsibility when, in fact, they should have dismissed them swiftly for lack of jurisdiction.[75] Last but not least, she observed that '[t]he majority's approach and conclusions in the present case are a cause for concern as regards a risk of circumvention arising in the event that the court of the Member State where the child is retained, instead of issuing a decision of non-return, issues an order for return which, however, is subsequently left unenforced'.[76]

In my view, Judge Koskelo has a point. The best interests of the child must be exercised in accordance with the principle of legality – which, in the context of child abduction, requires compliance with the division of jurisdiction established by the Brussels II a Regulation. As was pointed out by the majority in *M.K. v. Greece*, it is true that the second subparagraph of Article 13(b) of 1980 Hague Convention provides that the court of the Member State of enforcement 'may also refuse to order the return of the child if it finds that the child objects to being returned and has attained an age and degree of maturity at which it is appropriate to take account of its views'. However, the Greek courts did not object to the return of the child on the basis of the second subparagraph of Article 13(b). Instead, they adopted a decision ordering the return of the child without any indication that he had been heard. The child was only heard afterwards, i.e. in connection with criminal proceedings brought against his father for child abduction and, on the same day, by the Greek social services. In that regard, as pointed out by Judge Koskelo, doubts may arise regarding the quality and reliability of evidence that is obtained from the testimony of a child who knows that his father might be facing prison.[77]

A critical reading of the ruling of the ECtHR in *M.K. v Greece* reveals that compliance with the objectives pursued by Brussels II a Regulation excludes a 'third option' whereby the Member State of enforcement says 'yes in law' to the return of the child, but 'no in fact'. But, this *'tertium' non datur*: either the Member State of enforcement decides to return the child and does so in a timely manner, or it orders the non-return of the child pursuant to Article 13 of the 1980 Hague Convention (and in so doing, allows the Member State of origin to decide whether to override that non-return order by virtue of Article 11(8) of

---

[74]   *Ibid.*, §19.
[75]   *Ibid.*, §29.
[76]   *Ibid.*, §39.
[77]   *Ibid.*, §34.

the Brussels II a Regulation). A failure to return a child promptly after having decided that, as a matter of law, the child should be returned must constitute a violation of the rights to respect for family life of the parent left behind.

CONCLUDING REMARKS

The wrongful removal or retention of a child deprives him or her of the possibility of maintaining on a regular basis a personal relationship and direct contact with the parent left behind. Such deprivation is, in principle, contrary to the rights that the child enjoys under Article 24 of the Charter. On the basis of that premise, both the 1980 Hague Convention and the Brussels II a Regulation lay down procedures that seek to ensure the prompt return of the child to the Member State of his or her habitual residence. As Article 13 of the 1980 Hague Convention states, that premise is not absolute as there can be situations where the best interests of the child militate against his or her return, notably where 'there is grave risk that his or her return would expose the child to physical or psychological harm or otherwise place the child in an intolerable situation' or where 'the child objects to being returned and has attained an age and degree of maturity at which it is appropriate to take account of its views'.

The problem that arises is that both the courts of the Member State of origin and those of the Member State of enforcement may claim jurisdiction – or alternatively, none of those courts may do so – when assessing whether the child is to be returned or not. They may reach incompatible conclusions, leading to a situation where the courts make even worse a situation which already was really difficult for the child involved. That is why it is important to have clear and uniform rules of jurisdiction that establish which court is to have the final say on the return of the child and, consequently, the primary responsibility for protecting his or her fundamental rights. In the EU legal order, that court is the court of the Member State of origin as it enjoys, under Article 11(8) of the Brussels II a Regulation, the power to override a non-return order adopted by the courts of the Member State of enforcement pursuant to Article 13 of the 1980 Hague Convention.

Whilst the court of the Member State of origin must act expeditiously when deciding whether to override a non-return order, that court must treat that decision with caution. This is because compliance with Article 24 of the Charter prevents the court of the Member State of origin from using that power as a form of 'punishment' for the abducting parent or as a mechanism for ensuring the repatriation of its own nationals. As the CJEU held in *Povse*, and the ECtHR in *Šneersone and Kampanella v. Italy*, that court must take into consideration the reasons for and the evidence underlying the non–return order. If the court of the Member State of origin fails to do so and decides to override the non-return order in a subsequent judgment, that court runs the risk of violating both EU law and the ECHR. In my view, requiring the court of the Member State of origin to examine the findings that the court of the Member State of enforcement stated in the non-return order serves to reinforce mutual trust and comity between those courts, as it underscores the fact that the power to override the non-return order must be based on a balanced and properly-reasoned rationale.

However, it is not for the courts of the Member State of enforcement to second-guess whether the court of the Member State of origin took the right decision when it ordered the return of the child. Instead, as the CJEU held in *Aguirre Zarraga* and the ECtHR in *Povse v. Austria*, it is for the abducting parent to challenge the subsequent judgment ordering the return of the child before the courts of the Member State of origin. This is because the Member States must trust each other with regard to the ability of the judicial system of the Member State of origin to 'right its own wrongs'.

As to the powers of the courts of the Member State of enforcement, a distinction should be drawn between the application of Article 13 of the 1980 Hague Convention and the enforcement of a certified judgment pursuant to Article 42 of the Brussels II a Regulation. When the courts of the Member State of enforcement adopt a non-return order in application of Article 13 of the 1980 Hague Convention, those courts must, in the light of *X v. Latvia*, not only consider arguable allegations of a grave risk for the child in the event of return, but must also make a ruling giving specific reasons in the light of the circumstances of the case. This is consistent with EU law as the Brussels II a Regulation does not oppose such examination. By contrast, when the courts of the Member State of enforcement receive a certified judgment pursuant to Article 42 of the Brussels II a Regulation, they have no choice but to execute that judgment. As the ECtHR held in *Povse v. Austria*, that absence of discretion allows room for the application of the *Bosphorus* presumption. In addition, in the light of *M.A. v Austria*, delays in executing the judgment ordering the return of the child may constitute a violation of the right to respect for the family life of the parent left behind.

That said, the ruling of the ECtHR in *M.K. v. Greece* is a source of concern since it favours a situation where the Member State of enforcement says 'yes in law' but 'no in fact' to the return of the child, thereby undermining the principle of mutual trust, the effectiveness of the Brussels II a Regulation and the right to respect for the family life of the parent left behind.

However, this last judgment of the ECtHR is not sufficient in itself to call into question the converging trend that exists in the case law of both courts in respect of child abduction. Such normative convergence is important because it enables the CJEU and the ECtHR to create synergies in the field of fundamental rights protection that contribute to ordering pluralism, whilst avoiding conflicts of jurisdiction between national courts. This is of pivotal importance for those courts, given that they can best protect the rights of the child when their powers and responsibilities under both EU law and the ECHR are in harmony with each other.

THE RIGHT TO SAME SEX MARRIAGE

Manfred Nowak

Professor of International Law and Human Rights, University of Vienna
Secretary General of the Global Campus of Human Rights, Venice

INTRODUCTION

The right to same-sex marriage is one of the most controversial issues in modern human rights law and jurisprudence. The current article examines recent case-law of international, regional and domestic courts and human rights treaty bodies. A comparative analysis of this jurisprudence shows that domestic courts in a number of selected countries in all world regions seem to be more dynamic than regional courts and UN bodies. One of the main reasons for the reluctance of international bodies to accept a right of same-sex marriage is their traditional approach of applying a systematic interpretation of the right to privacy and non-discrimination in conjunction with the human right to marry, which seems to be restricted to heterosexual couples under international law. The author of the present article suggests a new look at this traditional type of interpretation and finds support for his approach in a recent dissenting opinion of his friend Paul Lemmens, to whom this article is dedicated.

I. SELECTED JURISPRUDENCE

A. EUROPEAN COURT OF HUMAN RIGHTS

1. Discrimination on the ground of sexual orientation

The European Court of Human Rights (ECtHR) has a long history of cases which had a major impact on reducing discrimination on the ground of sexual orientation in Europe, despite the fact that the European Convention on Human Rights (ECHR) does not contain a self-standing right to equality and non-discrimination. Some of these cases were dealt with under Article 8 alone, which grants to everybody the "right to respect for his private and family life, his home and his correspondence".[1] Already in 1981, the Court found that the prohibition of homosexual relations under criminal law in Northern Ireland violated Article 8.[2] In 1999, it held that Article 8 prohibits the discharge of homosexuals from the armed forces.[3] The leading case on same-sex marriage is *Schalk and Kopf v. Austria*.[4]

Other cases relied on the accessory discrimination clause of Article 14 ECHR (which does not contain an explicit ground of sexual orientation), taken in conjunction with Article 8. These cases include, inter alia, a different age of consent under criminal law for homosexual relations[5], the attribution of parental rights[6], permission to adopt a child[7], and the right to succeed to the deceased partner's tenancy.[8]

2. *Schalk and Kopf v. Austria (2010)*

The two male applicants, a same-sex couple, had requested the respective authorities in Vienna to proceed with the formalities to enable them to contract marriage. This request was refused on the basis of Article 44 of the Austrian Civil Code of 1811/12, which provided that marriage could only be contracted between two persons of opposite sex. In their application to the Austrian Constitutional Court, the applicants alleged discrimination in the exercise of their right to private life under the Austrian Constitution and under Articles 8 and 14 ECHR, which form part of the Austrian Constitution. They also complained about a violation of their right to marry under Article 12 ECHR, which reads as follows: "Men and women of marriageable age have the right to marry and to found a family, according to the national laws governing the exercise of this right". In a 2003 judgment, the Constitutional Court dismissed all claims by, *inter alia*, referring to the fact that Article 12 ECHR explicitly uses the term "men and women" in order to stress that the right to marry is restricted to persons of

---

[1] See, e.g. Christoph Grabenwarter, *European Convention on Human Rights – Commentary*, München 2014, 187 f; Francis Jacobs/Nigel White/Clare Ovey, *The European Convention on Human Rights*, 6th ed. by Bernadette Rainey/Elizabeth Wicks/Clare Ovey, Oxford 2014, 389 ff.

[2] *Dudgeon v. United Kingdom*, 22 October 1981, Series A no. 45; see also *Norris v. Ireland*, 26 October 1988, Series A no. 142; *Modinos v. Cyprus*, 22 April 1993, Series A no. 259.

[3] *Smith and Grady v. United Kingdom*, 27 September 1999, nos. 33985/96 and 33986/96, ECHR 1999-VI.

[4] See Pietro Pustorino, Same-Sex Couples Before the ECtHR: The Right to Marriage, in Daniele Gallo/Luca Paladini/Pietro Pustorino, *Same-Sex Couples before National, Supranational and International Jurisdictions*, Springer 2014, 400 ff.

[5] *L. and V. v. Austria*, 9 January 2003, nos. 39392/98 and 39829/98, ECHR 2003-I.

[6] *Salgueiro da Silva Mouta v. Portugal*, 21 December 1999, no. 33290/96, ECHR 1999-IX.

[7] *Fretté v. France*, 26 February 2002, no. 36515/97, ECHR 2002-I; *E.B. v. France* (Grand Chamber), 22 January 2008, no. 43546/02.

[8] *Karner v. Austria*, 24 July 2003, no. 40016/98, ECHR 2003-IX.

opposite sex.[9] At that time, Austrian law did not provide for any possibility to give legal effect to same-sex relations. However, in 2009, the Austrian Parliament passed the Registered Partnership Act, which provided same-sex couples with a formal mechanism for recognising their relationship and with rights that are fairly similar to those of married heterosexual couples.

When the ECtHR decided the case in 2010, the Registered Partnership Act was already in force. The Court examined the complaint both under Article 12 and under Article 14 in conjunction with Article 8. It observed that, "looked at in isolation, the wording of Article 12 might be interpreted so as not to exclude the marriage between two men or two women. However, in contrast, all other substantive Articles of the Convention grant rights and freedoms to "everyone" or state that "no one" is to be subjected to certain types of prohibited treatment. The choice of wording in Article 12 must thus be regarded as deliberate. Moreover, regard must be given to the historical context in which the Convention was adopted. In the 1950s, marriage was clearly understood in the traditional sense of being a union between partners of different sex."[10] The applicants had, however, relied on the Court's case-law according to which the Convention is a living instrument which is to be interpreted in the light of present-day conditions. On the basis of a comparative analysis of relevant legislation in the member States of the Council of Europe[11], the Court noted that, although the institution of marriage had undergone "major social changes since the adoption of the Convention", there was "no European consensus regarding same-sex marriage".[12]

With respect to Articles 8 and 14, the Court held that "the relationship of the applicants, a cohabiting same-sex couple living in a stable *de facto* partnership, falls within the notion of "family life", just as the relationship of a different-sex couple in the same situation would".[13] It also stressed, as in earlier cases, that "differences based on sexual orientation require particularly serious reasons by way of justification".[14] However, it finally denied a violation of Article 14, in conjunction

---

9   Judgment of the Austrian Constitutional Court of 12 December 2003, VfSlg 17098.
10   *Schalk and Kopf v. Austria*, 24 June 2010, no 30141/04, §55. In a concurring opinion, Judges Giorgio Malinverni and Anatoly Kovler strongly criticised this wording in the judgment and stressed that Article 12 ECHR "cannot be construed in any other way than as being applicable solely to persons of different sex".
11   Ibid, §§27 and 28. At the time of the judgment in 2010, six out of 47 member States had granted same-sex couples equal access to marriage (Belgium, the Netherlands, Norway, Portugal, Spain and Sweden), and 13 States had passed some kind of legislation permitting same-sex couples to register their relationships (Andorra, Austria, the Czech Republic, Denmark, Finland, France, Germany, Hungary, Iceland, Luxembourg, Slovenia, Switzerland and the United Kingdom).
12   Ibid, §58.
13   Ibid, §94.
14   Ibid, §97.

with Article 8, on the basis of a systematic interpretation which also takes Article 12 into account: The Court reiterated that "the Convention is to be read as a whole and its Articles should therefore be construed in harmony with one another ... Having regard to the conclusions reached above, namely that Article 12 does not impose an obligation on Contracting States to grant same-sex couples access to marriage, Article 14 taken in conjunction with Article 8, a provision of more general purpose and scope, cannot be interpreted as imposing such an obligation either".[15]

While the judgment of the ECtHR was unanimous with respect to not finding any violation of Article 12, the denial of a violation of Article 14 in conjunction with Article 8 was decided by four votes to three. In their dissenting opinion, judges Christos Rozakis, Dean Spielmann and Sverre Erik Jebens did, however, do not go as far as requiring States to provide for same-sex marriage. They congratulated the Court for having taken "a major step forward in its jurisprudence by extending the notion of "family life" to same-sex couples". But then they concentrated their dissent on the legal situation in Austria before the enactment of the Registered Partnership Act in 2009. In their view, any absence of a legal framework offering to same-sex couples "at least to a certain extent, the same rights or benefits attached to marriage ... would need robust justification".

3. Later case-law relating to same-sex marriage

The ECtHR has confirmed its jurisprudence that neither Article 12 nor Article 14 and 8 ECHR impose an obligation on the governments of the Contracting States to grant same-sex couples access to marriage in a number of more recent judgments. In the 2012 judgment of *Gas and Dubois v. France* it denied that the legal situation in France, which did not allow same-sex couples to have access to second-parent adoption, amounted to discrimination on the ground of sexual orientation.[16] The facts in the case of *Oliari and others v. Italy* are different from those in *Schalk and Kopf v. Austria* as the Italian legislation had neither provided for same-sex marriage nor for a registered partnership for same-sex couples. Although confirming its jurisprudence with respect to same-sex marriage, the Court in this 2015 judgment found a violation of Article 8 on the ground that "the Italian Government have overstepped their margin of appreciation and failed to fulfil their positive obligation to ensure that the applicants have available a specific legal framework providing for the recognition and protection of their same-sex unions."[17] With respect to Article 12, the Court noted the gradual evolution of States on the matter[18] but stressed that "it must not rush

---

15   Ibid, §101.
16   *Gas and Dubois v. France*, 15 March 2012, no 25951/07, §§66 ff.
17   *Oliari and others v. Italy*, 21 July 2015, nos 18766/11 and 36030/11, §185.
18   Ibid, §§53 ff and 192: In the meantime, a total of eleven member States of the Council of Europe (Belgium, Denmark, France, Iceland, Luxembourg, the Netherlands, Norway,

to substitute its own judgment in place of that of the national authorities, who are best placed to assess and respond to the needs of society".[19] In consequence the Court reiterated that "Article 12 of the Convention does not impose an obligation on the respondent Government to grant a same-sex couple like the applicants access to marriage."[20] This case-law was most recently confirmed in *Chapin and Charpentier v. France*.[21]

In the Grand Chamber judgment of *Hämäläinen v. Finland* of 2014, the Court had to decide whether a married transsexual person, who had undergone gender reassignment surgery from male to female while being married to a woman, has the right to remain married, now in a same-sex marriage. According to Finnish law, marriage was only permitted between persons of opposite sex, while same-sex couples had the right to enter into a registered partnership. When the applicant requested the local registry office to confirm her status as female and to change her male identity number to a female one, her request was refused on the ground that, in accordance with the Transsexuals Confirmation of Gender Act, she would have to transform her marriage into a registered partnership. As the applicant's wife had not given her consent to such transformation, the applicant's new gender could not be recorded in the population register. In a judgment of November 2012, the Camber noted that the applicant, therefore, had the "choice between remaining married and tolerating the inconvenience caused by the male identity number, or divorcing her spouse".[22] The Chamber reiterated the case-law that the ECHR does not impose an obligation on States parties to grant same-sex couples access to marriage and, since the registered partnership provided almost identical rights to same-sex couples, decided that there was no discrimination.[23] In July 2014 the Grand Chamber, by fourteen votes to three, confirmed that there has been no violation of Article 14 taken in conjunction with articles 8 and 12. It explicitly reiterated its earlier jurisprudence by referring to *Schalk and Kopf v. Austria*[24] and considered the case primarily under the aspect of positive obligations deriving from Article 8 and a lack of consensus among European States.[25] Since Finnish law offered the applicant three different options

---

Portugal, Spain, Sweden and the United Kingdom) had recognised same-sex marriage and 18 States (Andorra, Austria, Belgium, Croatia, the Czech Republic, Finland, France, Germany, Hungary, Ireland, Liechtenstein, Luxembourg, Malta, the Netherlands, Slovenia, Spain, Switzerland and the United Kingdom) had authorised some form of civil partnership for same-sex couples. The Court also referred to legal developments in the Council of Europe, the European Union and the United States.

19   Ibid, §191.
20   Ibid, §192.
21   *Chapin and Charpentier v. France*, 9 June 2016, no 40183/07, §§36–40 and 48.
22   *Hämäläinen v. Finland* (Grand Chamber), 16 July 2014, no 37359/09, §37.
23   Ibid, §§38–40.
24   Ibid, §§71 and 96.
25   Ibid, §§57 ff.

(remaining married and tolerating the inconvenience caused by the male identity number, converting the marriage into a registered partnership with the consent of the spouse, or divorce from her spouse), the Grand Chamber concluded that Finnish law had struck a fair balance between competing interests.[26]

Paul Lemmens, to whom this article is dedicated, together with his fellow judges András Sajó and Helen Keller, dissented from the majority opinion. They criticized the consensus and the positive obligations approach applied by the majority and, instead, applied the classical approach of examining the facts of the case in light of a possible justification under the limitation clause of Article 8(2) ECHR. They acknowledged that the "public interest in keeping the institution of marriage free of same-sex couples" might be protected by the ground of morals in Article 8(2). They argued, however, that Finland could not invoke a "pressing social need to refuse the applicant the right to remain married after the legal recognition of her acquired gender", because "the institution of marriage would not be endangered by a small number of couples who may wish to remain married in a situation such as that of the applicant".[27] With respect to Article 12, they argued that this provision "guarantees not only a right to marry, but also a right to remain married unless compelling reasons justify an interference with the civil status of the spouses".[28] In their opinion, gender reassignment is not such a compelling reason. Although Paul Lemmens and his two fellow judges did not go as far as to advocate a right to same-sex marriage, their dissenting opinion seems to have opened a door for a future change in the ECtHR's jurisprudence in this controversial matter.

B.   UNITED NATIONS HUMAN RIGHTS COMMITTEE

The International Covenant on Civil and Political Rights (CCPR) of 1966 is in this respect very similar to the ECHR. Article 17(1) provides that "No one shall be subjected to arbitrary or unlawful interference with his privacy, family, home or correspondence, nor to unlawful attacks on his honour and reputation", and Article 23(2) recognises the "right of men and women of marriageable age to marry and to found a family". In addition to the accessory prohibition of discrimination in Article 2(1), Article 26 also guarantees a stand-alone right to equality before the law without any discrimination and equal protection of the law. Sexual orientation is not explicitly mentioned as prohibited ground of discrimination.

---

[26]   Ibid, §88.
[27]   Ibid, Joint Dissenting Opinion of Judges Sajó, Keller and Lemmens, §12.
[28]   Ibid, §16.

In 1994, the Human Rights Committee decided the landmark case of *Toonen v. Australia*.[29] The case concerned the criminalisation of private sexual conduct between consenting adult homosexual men in the Criminal Code of Tasmania. The Committee found a violation of Article 17 in conjunction with Article 2 and did not further examine a violation of Article 26.

The question of same-sex marriage was addressed in the 2002 decision of *Joslin v. New Zealand*.[30] The applicants were two lesbian couples who had jointly assumed responsibility for children from earlier marriages. They applied under the Marriage Act 1955 to the local registry office for a marriage license which was refused. They claimed before the Committee that the failure of the Marriage Act to provide for homosexual marriage discriminated against them directly on the basis of sex and indirectly on the basis of sexual orientation. They alleged violations of Articles 16, 17, 23 and 26 CCPR. The Committee held that it could not find that by mere refusal to provide for marriage between homosexual couples, the State party had violated any of the Articles invoked.[31] It based this decision exclusively on its interpretation of Article 23(2)[32]: "Given the existence of a specific provision in the Covenant on the right to marriage, any claim that this right has been violated must be considered in the light of this provision. Article 23, paragraph 2, of the Covenant is the only substantive provision in the Covenant which defines a right by using the term "men and women", rather than "every human being", "everyone" and "all persons". Use of the term "men and women", rather than the general terms used elsewhere in Part III of the Covenant, has been consistently and uniformly understood as indicating that the treaty obligation of States parties stemming from article 23, paragraph 2, of the Covenant is to recognize as marriage only the union between a man and a woman wishing to marry each other."

In a concurring individual opinion, Committee members Rajsoomer Lallah and Martin Scheinin argued that "a denial of certain rights and benefits to same-sex couples that are available to married couples may amount to discrimination prohibited under article 26, unless otherwise justified on reasonable and objective criteria." Since the applicants had not made such claims, the Committee decision was unanimous in finding no violation.

---

29   *Toonen v. Australia*, 31 March 1994, no 488/1992. See Manfred Nowak, *U.N. Covenant on Civil and Political Rights, CCPR-Commentary*, 2nd ed, Kehl/Strasbourg/Arlington 2005, 391 f; Luca Paladini, Same-Sex Couples Before Quasi-Jurisdictional Bodies: The Case of the UN Human Rights Committee, in Daniele Gallo/Luca Paladini/Pietro Pustorino (*op cit*), 541 f.

30   *Joslin v. New Zealand*, 17 July 2002, no 902/1999. See Nowak (ibid), 525 f. See also Malcolm Langford, "Revisiting Joslin v. New Zealand: Same-Sex Marriage in Polarised Times (February 7, 2017); Luca Paladini, Same-Sex Couples Before Quasi-Jurisdictional Bodies: The Case of the UN Human Rights Committee, in Daniele Gallo/Luca Paladini/Pietro Pustorino (*op cit*), 544 ff; E. Brems and E. Desmet, *Integrated Human Rights in Practice: Rewriting Human Rights Decisions* (Edward Elgar, 2017).; University of Oslo Faculty of Law Research Paper No. 2017-12. Available at SSRN: https://ssrn.com/abstract=2912904.

31   Ibid, §8.3.

32   Ibid, §8.2.

C.   CONSTITUTIONAL COURT OF SOUTH AFRICA

1.   Discrimination on the ground of sexual orientation

South Africa became the first country in the world explicitly to include in its Interim Constitution 1993 and its final Constitution 1996 sexual orientation as one of the grounds of non-discrimination.[33] This was controversial but has to do with the fact that the Constitution of South Africa aimed at overcoming the Apartheid regime with a comprehensive Bill of Rights ensuring a fully inclusive society by combating not only racial discrimination, but also other forms of discrimination.[34] Racial and other forms of systematic discrimination were experienced as a violation of the right to human dignity, which explains the close relationship between these two human rights in the South African Constitution.[35]

The Constitutional Court of South Africa played from the very beginning a crucial role in applying and further developing the principle of non-discrimination on the ground of sexual orientation. In the so-called "Sodomy" judgment of 1999, the Court held that the common-law offence of sodomy was unconstitutional because it violated the rights to equality, dignity and privacy in Sections 9, 10 and 14 of the Constitution.[36] In a number of further judgments, the Court conferred spousal benefits on same-sex life partners.[37] The most important case is, however the Fourie judgment.

2.   The Fourie and Equality Project Judgment

In December 2005, the Constitutional Court of South Africa rendered a landmark judgment on same-sex marriage by combining two cases: the *Fourie* case[38] and the *Equality Project* case.[39] The applicants in the *Fourie* case, a lesbian

---

[33]   Section 8(2) of the Constitution of the Republic of South Africa Act 200 of 1993 and Section 9(3) of the South African Constitution 1996. See H de Ru, "A Historical Perspective on the Recognition of Same-Sex Unions in South Africa", in *Fundamina* 19(2) 2013, Unisa Press, 221 at 229 ff; Edmondo Mostacci, Different Approaches, Similar Outcomes: Same-Sex Marriage in Canada and South Africa, in Daniele Gallo/Luca Paladini/Pietro Pustorino (*op cit*), 85 f.
[34]   See, e.g., Jeremy Sarkin, "The Drafting of South Africa's Final Constitution From a Human-Rights Perspective", 47 *American Journal of Comparative Law* (1999), 67 at 68; Mary Patricia Byrn, "Same-Sex Marriage in South Africa: A Constitutional Possibility", 87 *Minnesota Law Review* (2002–2003), 511 at 514.
[35]   Sections 9 and 10 of the South African Constitution 1996.
[36]   *National Coalition for Gay and Lesbian Equality v. Minister of Justice*, 9 October 1998, 1999 (1) SA 6 (CC), §30.
[37]   See H de Ru (*op cit*), 236 ff.
[38]   *Minister of Home Affairs and Another v. Fourie and Another*, 1 December 2005, no CCT 60/04, 2006 (1) SA 524 (CC).
[39]   *Lesbian and Gay Equality Project and Eighteen Others v. Minister of Home Affairs and Others*, 1 December 2005, no CCT 10/05, 2006 (1) SA 524 (CC).

couple, contended that the common-law definition of marriage as a union of one man and one woman had excluded them from publicly celebrating their love and commitment to each other. The applicants in the *Equality Project* case challenged section 30(1) of the Marriage Act 25 of 1961, which referred exclusively to "husband" and "wife". The Court concluded unanimously that "the failure of the common law and the Marriage Act to provide the means whereby same-sex couples can enjoy the same status, entitlements and responsibilities accorded to heterosexual couples through marriage, constitutes an unjustifiable violation of their right to equal protection of the law under section 9(1), and not to be discriminated against unfairly in terms of section 9(3) of the Constitution. Furthermore, and for the reasons given in *Home Affairs*, such failure represents an unjustifiable violation of their right to dignity in terms of section 10 of the Constitution. As this Court said in that matter, the rights of dignity and equality are closely related. The exclusion to which same-sex couples are subjected, manifestly affects their dignity as members of society."[40]

Justice Albie Sachs delivered the carefully worded judgment. He referred to the historical development of South Africa and to the fact that the South African Constitution "represents a radical rupture with a past based on intolerance and exclusion".[41] "Equality means equal concern and respect across difference ... The acknowledgment and acceptance of difference is particularly important in our country where for centuries group membership based on supposed biological characteristics such as skin colour has been the express basis of advantage and disadvantage. South Africans come in all shapes and sizes. The development of an active rather than a purely formal sense of enjoying a common citizenship depends on recognising and accepting people with all their differences, as they are. The Constitution thus acknowledges the variability of human beings (genetic and socio-cultural), affirms the right to be different, and celebrates the diversity of the nation."[42] Then Justice Sachs explained in detail the significance of marriage in various fields of law, the impact of exclusion from it, and concludes[43]: "The exclusion of same-sex couples from the benefits and responsibilities of marriage, accordingly, is not a small and tangential inconvenience resulting from a few surviving relics of societal prejudice destined to evaporate like the morning dew. It represents a harsh if oblique statement by the law that same-sex couples are outsiders, and that their need for affirmation and protection of their intimate relations as human beings is somehow less than that of heterosexual couples." "By both drawing on and reinforcing discriminatory social practice,

---

40   Ibid, §114.
41   Ibid, §59.
42   Ibid, §60.
43   Ibid, §71.

the law in the past failed to secure for same-sex couples the dignity, status, benefits and responsibilities that it accords to heterosexual couples."[44]

Justice Sachs continued by responding to various religious arguments against same-sex marriage and concluded that in an open and democratic society contemplated by the Constitution, "there must be mutually respectful co-existence between the secular and the sacred".[45] He also dealt with the arguments derived from international law, which restricted the human right to marry to heterosexual couples, starting with Article 16(1) of the Universal Declaration of Human Rights 1948. He concluded "that while it is true that international law expressly protects heterosexual marriage it is not true that it does so in a way that necessarily excludes equal recognition being given now or in the future to the right of same-sex couples to enjoy the status, entitlements, and responsibilities accorded by marriage to heterosexual couples."[46]

With respect to a remedy, Justice Sachs arrived at a compromise. He ordered on the one hand that the "common law definition of marriage is declared to be inconsistent with the constitution and invalid to the extent that it does not permit same-sex couples to enjoy the status and the benefits coupled with responsibilities it accords to heterosexual couples". On the other hand he ruled that the "declaration of invalidity is suspended for twelve months from the date of this judgment to allow Parliament to correct the defeat."[47] Albie Sachs had offered this compromise in order to allow a broad public debate and to satisfy the concerns of religious groups and traditional leaders. However, Albie Sachs was criticised for having ignored the reality that public sentiment was predominantly against the legalisation of same-sex marriages.[48] In fact, after highly controversial discussions, Parliament in November 2006 adopted a Civil Union Act, which provided for same-sex couples and heterosexual couples to enter into a civil union, which is registered by way of either a marriage or a civil partnership with equal rights between marriage and civil partnership. However, the "superior marriage" under the Marriage Act 25 of 1961 continued to be reserved for heterosexual couples.[49] Nevertheless, South Africa, thanks to the judicial activism of the Constitutional Court, remained the first country in Africa to provide same-sex couples with some sort of same-sex marriage.

---

44   Ibid, §78.
45   Ibid, §94.
46   Ibid, §105.
47   Ibid, §162.
48   See H de Ru (op cit), 241 ff with further references.
49   See ibid, 245 ff. On the concept of the civil union, see also Mary Patricia Byrn (op cit), 539 ff;
      Pierre de Vos/Jaco Barnard, "Same-Sex Marriage, Civil Unions and Domestic Partnerships
      in South Africa: Critical Reflections on an Ongoing Saga", in 124 South African Law Journal
      (2007), 795 at 819 ff.

D. SUPREME COURT OF THE UNITED STATES

1. Discrimination on the ground of sexual orientation

While the ECtHR held already in 1981 that criminalization of private homosexual conduct between consenting adults violated the right to privacy in Article 8 ECHR[50], the US Supreme Court still upheld in 1986 the constitutionality of a Georgia law aimed at criminalizing certain homosexual acts.[51] Ten years later, the Court invalidated an amendment to Colorado's Constitution that sought to foreclose any branch or political subdivision of the State from protecting persons against discrimination based on sexual orientation.[52] It was only in 2003 that the Court overruled *Bowers*, holding that laws making same-sex intimacy a crime demean the lives of homosexual persons.[53] However, already in the same year the Supreme Judicial Court of Massachusetts held that the State's Constitution guaranteed same-sex couples the right to marry.[54] After that ruling, some additional States granted marriage rights to same-sex couples, either through judicial or legislative processes.[55]

2. Obergfell et al v. Hodges

On 26 June 2015, the Supreme Court, by a narrow majority of five to four votes, held that "the Fourteenth Amendment of the US Constitution of 1868[56] requires a State to license a marriage between two people of the same sex and to recognize a marriage between two people of the same sex when their marriage was lawfully licensed and performed out-of-State."[57] Justice Anthony

---

[50]   *Dudgeon v. United Kingdom*, 22 October 1981, Series A no 45: see above (A 1).

[51]   *Bowers v. Hardwick*, 478 U.S. 186 (1986).

[52]   *Romer v. Evans*, 517 U.S. 620 (1996).

[53]   *Lawrence v. Texas*, 539 U.S. 558 (2003). On the development of this jurisprudence of the US Supreme Court see, e.g., Kenji Hoshino, "A New Birth of Freedom?: Obergfell v. Hodges", in 129 *Harvard Law Review* (2015), 147; David E. Newton, *Same-Sex Marriage: A Reference Handbook*, 2nd ed., Santa Barbara, CA, 2016.

[54]   *Goodridge v. Department of Health*, 440 Mass. 309, 798 N.E. 2d 941 (2003); Antonio D'Aloia, From Gay Rights to Same-Sex Marriage: A Brief History Through the Jurisprudence of US Federal Courts, in Daniele Gallo/Luca Paladini/Pietro Pustorino (*op cit*), 33 ff.

[55]   See Appendix B (State Legislation and Judicial Decisions Legalizing Same-Sex Marriages), in *Obergfell v. Hodges*, 135 S.Ct. 2584 (2015), p 34.

[56]   The 14th Amendment to the US Constitution of 9 July 1868 granted citizenship to "all persons born or naturalized in the United States", which included former slaves recently freed. In addition, it forbids states from denying any person "life, liberty or property, without due process of the law" or to "deny to any person within its jurisdiction the equal protection of the laws". The 14th Amendment greatly expanded the protection of civil rights to all Americans and is cited in more litigation than any other amendment. However, it does not contain any explicit reference to the right to marry.

[57]   Ibid, 1.

Kennedy delivered the opinion of the majority. He based his opinion on both the Due Process Clause and the Equal Protection Clause of the Fourteenth Amendment, citing repeatedly the landmark judgment of *Loving v. Virginia*, which in 1967 had invalidated bans on interracial unions by stating that marriage is "one of the vital personal rights essential to the orderly pursuit of happiness by free men".[58] He also drew upon principles of liberty and equality developed for gays and lesbians in *Lawrence v. Texas*[59] and concluded that "the right to marry is a fundamental right inherent in the liberty of the person, and under the Due Process and Equal Protection Clauses of the Fourteenth Amendment couples of the same-sex may not be deprived of that right and that liberty."[60] Justice Kennedy concluded his opinion by stating as follows[61]: "No union is more profound than marriage, for it embodies the highest ideals of love, fidelity, devotion, sacrifice, and family. In forming a marital union, two people become something greater than once they were ... Their hope is not to be condemned to live in loneliness, excluded from one of civilization's oldest institutions. They ask for equal dignity in the eyes of the law. The Constitution grants them that right." There are many similarities with the judgment of the South African Constitutional Court delivered by Albie Sachs, such as the comparison between the prohibition of inter-racial and same-sex marriages in the recent past of both countries, and the emphasis on the human right to dignity.

All four conservative judges in the minority issued fairly strongly worded dissenting opinions. Chief Justice John Roberts called the majority's approach "deeply disheartening".[62] Justice Antonin Scalia drew attention to "this Court's threat to American democracy" and called the judgment a "judicial Putsch".[63] Justice Clarence Thomas stated that the majority "misapplies a clause focused on "due process" to afford substantive rights, disregards the most plausible understanding of the "liberty" protected by that clause, and distorts the principles on which this Nation was founded."[64] Finally, Justice Samuel Alito deplored "the deep and perhaps irremediable corruption of our legal culture's conception of constitutional interpretation."[65] President Barack Obama, on the other hand, called this historic judgment a "victory for America".[66]

---

[58]   *Loving v. Virginia*, 388 U.S. 1, 12 (1967).
[59]   *Lawrence v. Texas*, 539 U.S. 558 (2003), cited above.
[60]   *Obergefell v. Hodges*, 135 S.Ct. 2584 (2015), 22.
[61]   Ibid, 28.
[62]   Dissenting opinion of Chief Justice Roberts, joined by Justices Scalia and Thomas, 2.
[63]   Dissenting opinion of Justice Scalia, joined by Justice Thomas, 1 and 6.
[64]   Dissenting opinion of Justice Thomas, joined by Justice Scalia, 17.
[65]   Dissenting opinion of Justice Alito, joined by Justices Scalia and Thomas, 8.
[66]   See *The Guardian* of 26 June 2015.

E.   CONSTITUTIONAL COURT OF TAIWAN

On 24 May 2017, the Judicial Yuan of Taiwan, which acts as a constitutional court, declared in a binding Interpretation of the Taiwanese Constitution of 1949, as amended in 2005, that the provisions of Chapter 2 on Marriage of Part IV on Family of the Civil Code, which do not allow two persons of the same sex to create a permanent union of intimate and exclusive nature for the purpose of living a common life, "are in violation of constitution's guarantees of both the people's freedom of marriage under Article 22 and the people's right to equality under Article 7. The authorities concerned shall amend or enact the laws as appropriate, in accordance with the ruling of this Interpretation, within two years from the announcement of this Interpretation. It is within the discretion of the authorities concerned to determine the formality for achieving the equal protection of the freedom of marriage. If the authorities concerned fail to amend or enact the laws as appropriate within the said two years, two persons of the same sex who intend to create the said permanent union shall be allowed to have their marriage registration effectuated at the authorities in charge of household registration, by submitting a written document signed by two or more witnesses in accordance with the said Marriage Chapter."[67] With this important ruling, the Constitutional Court of Taiwan became the first court in Asia to recognize same-sex marriage.[68] This is remarkable as Article 22 of the Constitution of Taiwan does not contain any explicit right to marry, and the right to equality in Article 7 does not include sexual orientation as an explicit ground for impermissible discrimination.

Article 22 of the Constitution reads as follows: "All other freedoms and rights of the people that are not detrimental to social order or public welfare shall be guaranteed under the Constitution." However, the Court has ruled already earlier that the decisional autonomy to decide "whether to marry" and "whom to marry" is "vital to the sound development of personality and safeguarding of human dignity, and therefore is a fundamental right to be protected by Article 22 of the Constitution."[69] "The need, capability, willingness and longing, in both physical and psychological senses, for creating such permanent unions of intimate and excusive nature are equally essential to homosexuals and heterosexuals, given the importance of the freedom of marriage to the sound development of personality and safeguarding of human dignity. Both types of union shall be protected by the freedom of marriage under Article 22 of the Constitution."[70]

---

[67]   Judicial Yuan Interpretation, 24 May 2017, no 748, 1.

[68]   See, e.g., Chris Horton, "Court Ruling Could Make Taiwan First Place in Asia to Legalize Gay Marriage", *New York Times*, 24 May 2017; J.R WU, "Taiwan court rules in favour of same-sex marriage, first in Asia", Reuters 24 May 2017.

[69]   Judicial Yuan Interpretation, 24 May 2017, no 748, 10 with reference to Judicial Yuan Interpretation no 362.

[70]   Ibid, 10 f.

Article 7 of the Constitution reads as follows: "All citizens of the Republic of China, irrespective of sex, religion, ethnic origin, class or party affiliation, shall be equal before the law." Since these five classifications of impermissible discrimination are only illustrative, the Court ruled that "different treatment based on other classifications, such as disability or sexual orientation, shall also be governed by the right to equality under the said Article."[71] The Court then analysed some of the most common arguments against same-sex marriage and concluded[72]: "Disallowing the marriage of two persons of the same sex, because of their inability to reproduce, is a different treatment having no apparent rational basis ... Disallowing the marriage of two persons of the same sex, for the sake of safeguarding basic ethical orders, is a different treatment, also having no apparent rational basis. Such different treatment is incompatible with the spirit and meaning of the right to equality as protected by Article 7 of the Constitution."[73]

The group of international experts, which had examined the second periodic report of Taiwan under the International Covenant on Civil and Political Rights in early 2017, had encouraged the Government of Taiwan to allow for same-sex marriage.[74] The ruling Democratic Progressive Party, which had won the national elections in 2016, supported this change of attitude.[75] President Tsai Ing-wen had openly declared her support for same-sex marriage during her election campaign by saying: "In the face of love, everyone is equal."[76] One can therefore expect that the Executive and Legislative Yuan will prepare and enact a law within the two years authorized by the Judicial Yuan, which will go beyond the respective Civil Union Act of South Africa and introduce the unrestricted right to marry to both heterosexual and same-sex couples.

F.   CONSTITUTIONAL COURT OF AUSTRIA

On 4 December 2017, the Constitutional Court of Austria, which is the oldest constitutional court in the world, established by the Austrian Federal

---

[71]   Ibid, 11.
[72]   Ibid, 12.
[73]   Ibid, 13.
[74]   See Review of the Second Reports of the Government of Taiwan on the Implementation of the International Human Rights Covenants, Concluding Observations and Recommendations adopted by the International Review Committee, Taipei, 20 January 2017, para. 77: "*The Review Committee notes with appreciation the initiatives taken by the Government of Taiwan aimed at introducing same-sex marriage into Taiwanese law. The full realisation of these legislative changes would be a manifestation of Taiwan as a pioneer in the Asia-Pacific region, in combating discrimination on the basis of sexual orientation and gender identity.*" in Observations on the Review for the State Reports of Two International Human Rights Covenants in Taiwan: Written Interviews for International Experts, *Taiwan Human Rights Journal*, 2017, 124–129.
[75]   J.R Wu (*op cit*).
[76]   Chris Horton (*op cit*).

Constitution of 1920, recognized and authorized same-sex marriage as a human right in Austria. Although Western Europe was the world's pioneer in legalizing same-sex marriage, starting with the respective law in the Netherlands of 2001, these developments were all achieved by the legislative powers of the respective countries.[77] However, Austria is the first European country, which introduced same-sex marriage through a judicial decision.

The applicants in the original case leading to this judgment[78] were a lesbian couple living in a registered partnership since 2012 as well as their under-aged child. On 25 August 2015, the local authorities in Vienna rejected the request of the couple to register their marriage in accordance with §44 of the Austrian Civil Code of 1811/12, which provided that a marriage can only be contracted between two partners of the opposite sex.[79] Whereas the Austrian Constitutional Court in 2003 had still dismissed a similar claim in *Schalk and Kopf* on the basis of a systematic interpretation of the right to privacy, non-discrimination and the right to marry in Articles 8, 14 and 12 ECHR, it now decided to open *ex officio* a procedure to review the constitutionality of §44 of the Austrian Civil Code with respect to the right to equality and non-discrimination in Article 7 of the Austrian Federal Constitution 1920, as amended. Article 7 does not include sexual orientation as a specific ground for non-discrimination.[80] Interestingly enough, the Court avoided any reference to the right to marry in Article 12 ECHR. The ECHR, although being part of the Austrian Federal Constitution, is only mentioned once in the entire judgment, when the Court refers to the accessory discrimination clause in Article 14 ECHR as being similar to the discrimination grounds in Article 7 of the Constitution.[81]

With legal effect as of 31 December 2018, the Constitutional Court quashed the words "of opposite sex" in §44 of the Austrian Civil Code and the words "of the same sex" in the Registered Partnership Act of 2009, which had provided for registered partnership only for same-sex couples.[82] With this decision, it opened marriage to same-sex couples and at the same time registered partnership for

---

[77] As of today, the following 15 European countries have recognized same-sex marriage (in chronological order): the Netherlands (2001), Belgium (2003), Spain (2005), Norway and Sweden (2009), Iceland and Portugal (2010), United Kingdom (2012), France (2013), Luxembourg (2014), Denmark and Ireland (2015), Germany, Finland and Malta (2017): see *Der Standard* of 6 December 2017.

[78] Austrian Constitutional Court case no E 230–231/2016.

[79] See the case of *Schalk and Kopf* above under A 2.

[80] On the constitutional background and the registered partnership in Austria prior to the judgment of December 2017 see Giorgio Repetto, At the Crossroads Between Privacy and Community: The Legal Status of Same-Sex Couples in German, Austrian and Swiss Law, in Daniele Gallo/Luca Paladini/Pietro Pustorino (*op cit*), 277 f.

[81] Austrian Constitutional Court, 4 December 2017, no G 258/2017–9, 5.

[82] Ibid, 13.

heterosexual couples.[83] Compared to other judgments of a similar nature, such as the respective judgments of the Constitutional Court of South Africa or the Supreme Court of the United States, the reasoning of the Austrian Court is fairly laconic and lacks any deeper philosophical considerations and reflections. The Court stressed that same-sex couples continue to be exposed to discrimination in everyday life solely on the ground of their sexual orientation.[84] The legal differentiation between the institutions of marriage, which was only available for heterosexual couples, and registered partnership, which was only available for same-sex couples, resulted in different terminology ("being married" or "living in a registered partnership") in various official documents, which revealed the sexual orientation of the persons concerned even in situations, where the sexual orientation was totally irrelevant, but where this might have led to all forms of social exclusion and discrimination.[85] Despite the fact that the legal differences between marriage and registered partnership had been reduced in recent years to a considerable extent[86], this institutional differentiation, nevertheless, was no longer justified and, therefore, violated the right to equality and non-discrimination in Article 7 of the Austrian Constitution.[87]

G. INTER-AMERICAN COURT OF HUMAN RIGHTS

On 9 January 2018, the Inter-American Court of Human Rights (IACtHR) released a unanimous advisory opinion, requested by Costa Rica in 2016, to the effect that States parties to the American Convention on Human Rights (ACHR) of 1969 "must recognise and guarantee all rights stemming from a family bond made up by same-sex couples".[88] The ruling is based on Articles 11(2) (right to privacy), 18 (right to a name), and 24 (right to equality and non-discrimination) ACHR and established that couples in same-sex marriages have the same family and financial rights as heterosexual couples. The right to marry in Article 17(2), which as its counter-parts in Article 23(2) of the International Covenant on

---

[83] See, e.g., Helmut Graupner, "Ein historischer Tag – VfGH öffnet Ehe und EP für Alle", in *Jus Amandi* 04/2017.

[84] Austrian Constitutional Court, 4 December 2017, no G 258/2017–9, 11 with reference to VfSlg 19.492/2011.

[85] Ibid, 12.

[86] Ibid, 10.

[87] Ibid, 11 and 12.

[88] Inter-American Court of Human Rights, 24 November 2017, no OC-24/17. See Leiry Cornejo Chavez, "The Inter-American Court of Human Rights has spoken about gender identity and non-discrimination against same-sex couples. Would States listen?", in *PluriCourts Blog*, 15 January 2018, www.jus.uio.no/pluricourts/english/blog/leiry-cornejo-chavez/iacthr-same-sex-couples.html (last visited 23 January 2018). For an overview of the case law of the Court on human rights concerning same-sex couples see Laura Magi, Same-Sex Couples Before the Inter-American System of Human Rights, in Daniele Gallo/Luca Paladini/Pietro Pustorino (*op cit*), 441 ff.

Civil and Political Rights and Article 12 of the European Convention on Human Rights affords this right explicitly to "men and women", seems not to have played any significant role in this advisory opinion. Due to the difficulty in passing such laws in countries where there is strong opposition to same-sex marriage, the Court recommended that governments pass temporary decrees until new legislation will be enacted. The Court reasoned that opposition to same-sex marriage was generally based on religious or philosophical convictions and that these, while important, cannot supervene human dignity and autonomy.

II. COMPARATIVE ANALYSIS

In addition to the UN Human Rights Committee and the European and Inter-American Courts of Human Rights, this overview comprises some of the most important domestic judgments concerning same-sex marriage: The South African Constitutional Court was the first African court to recognize a right to same-sex marriage (in 2005), the Constitutional Court of Taiwan the first Asian court to do so (in 2017), and the Austrian Constitutional Court the first European court to open up marriage to same-sex couples (also in 2017). In between, the US Supreme Court in 2015 ruled that same-sex marriage shall be legalized in all federal states of the US. These four judgments in different world regions can all be considered as landmark decisions, which started a trend that certainly will be followed by high courts or parliaments in other countries. Usually, the opening up of the institution of marriage to same-sex couples has been achieved by the legislative power rather than by the courts.

It is interesting to note that the respective international courts and monitoring bodies seem to be more cautious than the domestic courts analysed above. By means of a systematic interpretation of the right to marry, the right to privacy and the right to equality and non-discrimination, the UN Human Rights Committee (in 2002) and the European Court of Human Rights (in 2010 and thereafter) concluded that the words "men and women" clearly indicate that the right to marry is reserved to heterosexual couples and that, consequently, the rights to privacy and non-discrimination cannot be interpreted as imposing on States parties an obligation to introduce same-sex marriage. In a recent advisory opinion of November 2017, the Inter-American Court of Human Rights held that States parties to the ACHR must guarantee all the rights that are derived from a family bond between people of the same sex. Whether this requires all States parties of the ACHR to establish the right to same-sex marriage remains to be seen. The experience with the legislative follow-up to the respective judgment of the South African Constitutional Court shows that such wording can also be interpreted as only requiring some sort of civil union or registered partnership under the condition that the rights and obligations deriving from such union are, in principle, equal to those of married heterosexual couples.[89]

The question arises whether the systematic interpretation applied by the UN Human Rights Committee and the European Court of Human Rights rules out interpretations which may lead to a different result. In *Joslin v. New Zealand,* two members of the UN Human Rights Committee (Rajsoomer Lallah and Martin Scheinin) had argued in a concurring opinion that "a denial of certain rights and benefits to same-sex couples that are available to married couples may amount to discrimination prohibited under article 26, unless otherwise justified on reasonable and objective criteria."[90] Both members agreed, however, with their colleagues that Article 23(2) CCPR can only be understood by means of both textual and historical interpretations as being restricted to persons of the opposite sex.

The European Court of Human Rights went a little further than the UN Human Rights Committee. In *Schalk and Kopf v. Austria*, the Court observed in 2010 that, "looking at it in isolation, the wording of Article 12 might be interpreted so as not to exclude the marriage between two men or two women." This *obiter dictum* was sharply criticized by judges Malinverni and Kovler in a concurring opinion, in which they stressed that Article 12 ECHR "cannot be construed in any other way than as being applicable solely to persons of different sex."[91] However, in view of a contextual interpretation of Article 12 as compared to other provisions of the Convention using the terms "everyone" or "no one", taking into account also the historical context, all judges agreed that Article 12 must be interpreted as applying to heterosexual couples only. Having found that, the Court applied a systematic interpretation and concluded that the right to privacy and the principle of non-discrimination must also be interpreted in line with Article 12, thus excluding a right to marry for same-sex couples to be derived from these provisions as well. In other words, the right to privacy and non-discrimination can also be satisfied by means of a registered partnership in which same-sex couples enjoy in principle the same rights as married heterosexual couples. This line of argumentation was confirmed in the more recent case-law, taking also into account that so far only a minority (albeit a rapidly growing minority) of European States had introduced the right to same-sex marriage and that there was, therefore, "no European consensus" in this respect.[92]

The strongest challenge to this jurisprudence was expressed in a joint dissenting opinion of Paul Lemmens and two fellow judges (András Sajó and Helen Keller)

---

[89]   See above (II C 2).
[90]   See above (II B).
[91]   See above (II A 2).
[92]   Ibid.

in the Grand Chamber judgment of *Hämäläinen v. Finland*.[93] Although they did not go as far as advocating a right to same-sex marriage, they criticized the consensus approach of the Court as a "potential instrument of retrogression and of allowing the "lowest common denominator" among the member States to prevail". With respect to the right to privacy in Article 8, they expressed the view that "the institution of marriage would not be endangered by a small number of couples who may wish to remain married in a situation such as that of the applicant".[94] Even though the facts of this case were very specific and the small number of couples mentioned only referred to transsexuals, this dissenting opinion acknowledged for the first time that, in the particular circumstances of this case, the recognition of a same-sex marriage by States parties for a limited amount of couples might be required by the right to privacy in Article 8 ECHR, despite the existence of Article 12.

Nevertheless, both the European Court of Human Rights and the UN Human Rights Committee, due to the application of a systematic interpretation of the rights to privacy and non-discrimination to be read together with the right to marry (which in their opinion only allows for heterosexual marriage) seem to have manoeuvred themselves into a situation where it will be fairly difficult to approve a human right to same-sex marriage – even when a clear majority of States in Europe or on a global level should have introduced same-sex marriages. In this respect it is interesting to note that the Austrian Constitutional Court, which traditionally has applied the ECHR and the same systematic interpretation as the ECtHR, finally ruled in favour of same-sex marriage solely on the basis of the right to equality and non-discrimination in the Austrian Constitution and, thereby, ignoring the ECHR.[95] It follows that international human rights bodies perhaps would have already accepted an obligation of States to allow same-sex marriage, if there was no right to marry included in the respective human rights treaties. The right to marry, therefore, functions as a stumbling block to fully overcome discrimination on the ground of sexual orientation.

Are there alternatives to this systematic interpretation? Paul Johnson and Silvia Falcetta from the University of York advocate that "Article 3 provides a powerful mechanism by which to challenge the Court's heteronormative interpretation of marriage and the "separate but equal" human rights regime that it has produced".[96] This is indeed an interesting approach, which is similar to the approaches taken by the Constitutional Court of South Africa, which

---

93   See above (II A 3).
94   Ibid.
95   See above (II F).
96   Paul Johnson/Silvia Falcetta, "Sexual Orientation Discrimination and Article 3 of the European Convention on Human Rights: Developing the Protection of Sexual Minorities", in *European Law Review* 2018 (in print), 34.

even found a violation to the right to dignity in section 10 of the South African Constitution[97], and the US Supreme Court which also argued strongly with the concept of dignity.[98] But even if the European Court applied Article 3, it might still feel obliged to use a systematic interpretation as we have seen by its reluctance to accept the death penalty as a violation of Article 3 ECHR.

This brings me to another solution, namely a fundamental criticism of this type of systematic interpretation of the ECHR.

CONCLUSION: NEED TO OVERCOME THE SYSTEMATIC INTERPRETATION OF THE ECHR AND CCPR

The European Commission and Court of Human Rights as well as the UN Human Rights Committee have applied this type of systematic interpretation in different situations, which finally turned out detrimental to the protection of human rights and which for a long time had blocked a dynamic interpretation of international human rights law in accordance with the principle that the ECHR and the CCPR are living instruments that need to be interpreted in the light of present day conditions.

One example is the evolving right to conscientious objection to compulsory military and alternative service. In the late 1960s and 1970s, conscientious objectors claimed that compulsory military and alternative service violated their right to freedom of conscience and religion in Article 9 ECHR and Article 18 CCPR. However, Articles 4(3)(b) ECHR and 8(3)(c)(ii) CCPR provided that the prohibition of forced or compulsory labour in Articles 4(2) ECHR and 8(2) CCPR shall not include any service of a military character or any national service required of conscientious objectors in countries where conscientious objection was recognized. This reference to "countries where conscientious objection is recognized" had been inserted in the 1950s and 1960s for the sole reason that at that time many countries had not yet recognised conscientious objection to military service. In the well-known case of *Grandrath v. Germany*, which was submitted by a minister of Jehovah's witnesses who had objected to both military and civilian service, the former European Commission of Human Rights in 1966 applied a systematic interpretation of the ECHR and concluded that there had been no violation of freedom of conscience and religion in Article 9 ECHR because Article 4(3) (b) had left it to the discretion of States whether to grant a right to conscientious

---

[97] See above (II C 2).
[98] See above (II D).

objection or not.[99] In the 1985 decision of *L.T.K. v. Finland*, the UN Human Rights Committee followed this case-law by applying the same systematic interpretation to Article 18 in conjunction with Article 8(3)(c)(ii) CCPR.[100] It took quite some time until both human rights bodies revised this systematic interpretation and recognised the right to conscientious objection to military service as part of freedom of conscience and religion. It was only in 2007 that the UN Human Rights Committee, in *Yoon and Choi v. South Korea*, "felt brave enough to declare that the right was actually recognised in the Covenant".[101] Finally, in 2011 the Grand Chamber of the ECtHR followed in *Bayatan v. Armenia* by explicitly rejecting the previous Commission case-law and instead taking a dynamic approach to Article 9 which would bring it in line with a trend among Council of Europe member States to recognise the right to conscientious objection.[102]

Another example is the death penalty. When the ECHR was adopted in 1950, most European countries still applied the death penalty. As a consequence, the right to life in Article 2(1) ECHR contains the following exception: "No one shall be deprived of his life intentionally save in the execution of a sentence of a court following his conviction of a crime for which this penalty is provided by law." A similar, though less comprehensive exception to the right to life had been inserted in 1966 into Article 6 CCPR. While the right to life was thus not an absolute right, Articles 3 ECHR and 7 CCPR contained from the very beginning an absolute prohibition of torture, inhuman or degrading treatment or punishment. Since both capital and corporal punishment were still widely practiced in Europe and other regions of the world during the 1950s and 1960s, these punishments were not considered as inhuman or degrading. However, public opinion slowly changed during the 1970s and 1980s. In 1978, the ECtHR held in the landmark judgment of *Tyrer v. UK* that the ECHR was a "living instrument" and that birching of a juvenile as a traditional punishment on the Isle of Man was no longer compatible with a modern understanding of human rights in Europe. Corporal punishment was thus considered as a degrading punishment in violation of Article 3 ECHR.[103] In *Osborne v. Jamaica*, the UN Human Rights Committee followed this dynamic interpretation and held that corporal punishment violated the prohibition of inhuman and degrading punishment in Article 7 CCPR.[104]

---

[99] European Commission of Human Rights, *Grandrath v. Germany*, 12 October 1966, no 2299/64.

[100] UN Human Rights Committee, *L.T.K. v. Finland*, 9 July 1985, no 185/1984: see critically Nowak, CCPR-Commentary (*op cit*), 421 f.

[101] Malcolm Langford (*op cit*), 16, referring to UN Human Rights Committee, *Yoon and Choi v. South Korea*, 23 January 2007, nos 1321 and 1322/2004.

[102] European Court of Human Rights, *Bayatan v. Armenia*, 7 July 2011 (GC), no 23459/03; see Jacobs/White/Ovey (*op cit*), 423 ff; Grabenwarter (*op cit*), 246.

[103] European Court of Human Rights, *Tyrer v. UK*, 25 April 1978, Series A 26.

[104] UN Human Rights Committee, *Osborne v. Jamaica*, 13 April 2000, no 759/1997: see Nowak, CCPR-Commentary (*op cit*), 167 f.

Although capital punishment can be considered as an aggravated form of corporal punishment, both the ECtHR and the UN Human Rights Committee applied a systematic interpretation between the right to life and the right to personal integrity and ruled that capital punishment could not be considered as inhuman or degrading punishment as it was explicitly exempted from the right to life in Articles 2 ECHR and 6 CCPR.[105] It was only in 2010 that the ECtHR for the first time overruled this systematic interpretation and found that the death penalty violated Article 3 ECHR.[106] However, the Court arrived at this conclusion only because most States parties had already ratified the 6th and 13th AP to the ECHR outlawing the death penalty and thereby in fact amending Article 2 ECHR.[107] The UN Human Rights Committee feels still bound by its systematic interpretation of Articles 6 and 7 CCPR and, therefore, has not yet found the death penalty to violate the right to personal integrity and dignity.

Both examples show that this type of systematic interpretation constitutes an obstacle to a more dynamic interpretation of international human rights law in light of present-day conditions. The same holds true for the right to same-sex marriage. Domestic courts in all world regions have found that traditional laws, which restrict the institution of marriage to heterosexual couples, constitutes discrimination on the ground of sexual orientation in the enjoyment of the right to privacy and dignity of same-sex couples. Since international human rights treaties contain an explicit human right to marry, which is worded in a traditional way of applying exclusively to heterosexual couples, international human rights treaty bodies, such as the ECtHR and the UN Human Rights Committee, feel bound by a systematic interpretation and, therefore, still hold that denying same-sex couples the right to marry does not amount to a discrimination on the ground of sexual orientation in the enjoyment of the right to privacy and family life. In my opinion, it is high time to change this restrictive understanding of a systematic interpretation and to replace it by a more dynamic interpretation. The dissenting opinion of Paul Lemmens and two of his fellow judges in *Hämäläinen v. Finland* might be a first step of changing this traditional and retrogressive systematic interpretation into a more dynamic one.

---

[105] See critically Nowak, CCPR-Commentary (*op cit*), 168 ff.

[106] European Court of Human Rights, *Al-Saadoon and Mufdhi v. UK*, 2 March 2010, no 61498/08.

[107] Ibid, §120: "Against this background, the Court does not consider that the wording of the second sentence of Article 2 §1 continues to act as a bar to its interpreting the words 'inhuman or degrading treatment or punishment' in Article 3 … as including the death penalty".

THE HUMAN RIGHTS ADVISORY PANEL'S OPINION IN THE *N.M. AND OTHERS v. UNMIK* CASE

Example of an Integrated Human Rights Approach

Marek NOWICKI
Former Member of the European Commission of Human Rights
International Ombudsperson in Kosovo
International Human Rights expert

Christine CHINKIN
Emerita Professor of International Law and Director of
the Centre on Women, Peace and Security
at the London School of Economics and Political Science (LSE)

Françoise TULKENS
Former Vice President of the European Court of Human Rights
Emerita Professor at the UCLouvain
Associate Member of the Belgian Royal Academy

As in all the places where he has been to, Paul Lemmens has left there an excellent memory. He was for 5 years (2007–2012) an outstanding member of the UNMIK Human Rights Advisory Panel (HRAP), very committed and creative. He was also a wonderful colleague and friend. When Paul Lemmens was elected in 2012 to succeed Françoise Tulkens as judge at the European Court of Human Rights, she succeeded him as a member of the Panel. We have shared in Kosovo a strong common experience which has marked all of us deeply.

We have chosen to contribute to this tribute by presenting one of the last cases decided by the Panel, concerning a dramatic situation experienced in Kosovo by the Roma population, namely the lead contamination in the internally displaced persons (IDPs) camps. It reveals the added value of an integrated human rights' approach covering almost all human rights instruments (II). The case has also been selected because it attracted the greatest attention of the United Nations, NGOs and the media. However, before analysing the case, we will present, briefly, the history of the Panel (I).

I. CREATION OF THE HUMAN RIGHTS ADVISORY PANEL

The 2016 Final Report of the HRAP offers an account of the Panel's history and evolution, its practice, caseload and contribution to human rights' jurisprudence.[1] This document, that we are partly taking up here, is a collective work of the members of the Panel in 2016, namely Marek Nowicki, presiding member, Christine Chinkin and Françoise Tulkens, members of the Panel. We were assisted by the lawyers of the Secretariat, Andrey Antonov, Anna Maria Cesano, Brandon Gardner and R. Dule Vicovac. An excellent team, highly professional and deeply committed.

A. THE SITUATION IN KOSOVO

The internal armed conflict during 1998 and 1999 between the Serbian forces and the Kosovo Liberation Army (KLA) is well documented. On 10 June 1999, acting under Chapter VII of the UN Charter, the UN Security Council (UNSC) adopted Resolution 1244 which decided upon the deployment of international security and civil presences in the territory of Kosovo, International Security Force (KFOR) and the United Nations Interim Administration in Kosovo (UNMIK) respectively. All legislative and executive authority, including control over the judiciary, was vested in the Special Representative of the Secretary-General (SRSG). UNMIK, as a surrogate state, had essentially the same powers as a state.

UNSC Resolution 1244 mandated UNMIK to "promote and protect human rights" in Kosovo in accordance with internationally recognized human rights standards. Indeed, the credibility and legitimacy of a UN mission mandated to carry out peace building tasks in a war-torn society is undermined without strict adherence to human rights. Therefore, after being established, UNMIK promulgated Regulation No. 1999/1 of 25 July 1999 "On the Authority of the Interim Administration in Kosovo", which stated that "all persons undertaking public duties or holding public office in Kosovo shall observe internationally

---

[1] See *The Human Rights Advisory Panel – History and Legacy – Kosovo, 2007–2016*, Final Report, Pristina, 30 June 2016; M. Nowicki, C. Chinkin and Fr. Tulkens, "Final Report of the Human Rights Advisory Panel", *Criminal Law Forum*, No. 28, 2017, pp. 77 et seq.

recognised human rights standards." UNMIK also promulgated Regulation No. 1999/24 of 12 December 1999 "On the Law Applicable in Kosovo", which listed the specific internationally recognised human rights instruments to be observed.

B.   FILLING A LACUNA IN HUMAN RIGHTS PROTECTION

By 2004, alleged human rights violations by UNMIK were attracting the attention of UN human rights treaty bodies, regional bodies such as the Organization for Security and Cooperation in Europe (OSCE) and Non-Governmental Organisations (NGOs) such as Amnesty International (AI) and Human Rights Watch (HRW). The major criticism of the situation regarding UNMIK's lack of adequate human rights accountability came from the Council of Europe (CoE). In its Opinion adopted in October 2004, the Venice Commission provided an overview of the human rights situation in Kosovo at that time: lack of security for non-Albanian communities; lack of freedom of movement for non-Albanian communities, which affected the possibility of having access to basic public services; insufficient protection of property rights; lack of investigation into abductions, killings and other serious crimes; lack of fairness and excessive length of judicial proceedings; difficult access to courts; detentions without independent review; corruption; human trafficking; lack of legal certainty, judicial review and right to an effective remedy for human rights violations.[2]

Against this background, it quickly became clear to the international community that it was not acceptable to leave, in the middle of Europe, a territory without human rights guarantees and protection. To fill this lacuna, three options have been considered: extending the jurisdiction of the European Court of Human Rights (ECtHR) to include the territory of Kosovo; establishing a Court of Human Rights in Kosovo, similar to the Human Rights Chamber established earlier in Bosnia and Herzegovina; creating an advisory committee which, however, would not have the power to issue binding decisions. By mutual agreement between the UNMIK's Office of the Legal Advisor and the UN Headquarters Office of Legal Affairs in New York, the last (minimal) option was chosen.[3]

---

[2]   European Commission for Democracy through Law ("Venice Commission"), *Opinion on Human Rights in Kosovo: Possible Establishment of Review Mechanism*, Opinion No. 280/2004, CDL-AD (2004)033, Strasbourg, 11 October 2004.

[3]   See B. Knoll and R.-J. Uhl, "Too little, too late: the Human Rights Advisory Panel in Kosovo", *European Human Rights Law Review*, Vol. 7, No. 5, 2007, pp. 534 et seq.

C. UNMIK REGULATION No. 2006/12

The HRAP was created by UNMIK Regulation No. 2006/12 "On the Establishment of the Human Rights Advisory Panel" to examine alleged violations of human rights by UNMIK.[4] Paul Lemmens was a member of the Panel between 2007 and 2012 and he played a very important role. The establishment of the Panel constitutes an unprecedented development in the context of United Nations missions. In this respect, the Panel is a pioneer mechanism concerning the imputability and the responsibility, with regard to human rights, for actions by international organisations.[5] In the Kosovo context, however, according to Regulation 2000/38, it should be recalled that there existed before, during almost five years (2000–2005), an international ombudsperson institution tasked to provide human rights oversight of the UN mission following international standard, including the European Convention on Human Rights (ECHR) and the International Covenant on Civil and Political Rights (ICCPR), within these parameters: "The ombudsperson should provide accessible and timely mechanisms for the review and redress of actions...by the interim civil administration".

What is remarkable – and unique – is that the Regulation 2006/12 vests the Panel with jurisdiction to hear a wide range of human rights complaints allegedly attributable to UNMIK under all the international instruments applicable in Kosovo: the Universal Declaration of Human Rights (UDHR), the European Convention for the Protection of Human Rights and Fundamental Freedoms of 4 November 1950 and the Protocols thereto (ECHR), the International Covenant on Civil and Political Rights of 16 December 1966 and the protocols thereto (ICCPR), the International Covenant on Economic Social and Cultural Rights of 16 December 1966 (ICESCR), the International Convention on the Elimination of All Forms of Racial Discrimination of 21 December 1965 (ICERD), the Convention on the Elimination of All Forms of Discrimination Against Women of 17 December 1979 (CEDAW), the Convention Against Torture and Other Cruel and Inhuman or Degrading Treatment or Punishment of 17 December 1984 (CAT) and the Convention on the Rights of the Child of 20 December 1989 (CRC).

---

[4] As UNMIK's responsibility with regard to justice and police in Kosovo was on 9 December 2008 transferred to the European Union (EU) which established the European Union Rule of Law Mission in Kosovo (EULEX), the Panel's competence was limited to facts occurring before that date.

[5] P. Klein, "Le Panel consultatif des droits de l'homme (*Human Rights Advisory Panel*) de la MINUK: une étape dans le processus de responsabilisation des Nations Unies?", in M. Kohen et al. (eds.), *Perspectives of International Law in the 21st century. Liber Amicorum Christian Dominicé*, Leiden-Boston, Martinus Nijhoff Publishers, 2012, pp. 225 et seq.; M. Beulay, "La responsabilisation des Nations Unies: perspectives d'améliorations d'un échec", *Observateur des Nations Unies*, Vol. 37, 2015, No. 2014–2, pp. 51 et seq.

As to the outcome of the proceedings before the Panel, Section 17 of the Regulation provided that the Panel "shall issue findings as to whether there has been a breach of human rights and, where necessary, make recommendations". Despite the inherent limitation of the action of the Panel, it intended to give a concrete meaning to the quasi-judicial nature of the mechanism set up by the Regulation, notably by formalizing the procedure, by stressing the fact that it was in control of the conduct of the proceedings, by emphasizing that the Panel's views would be based on legal norms, by providing for an adversary type of proceedings and by clarifying that its decisions (on admissibility) and opinions (on the merits) would be drafted in the way that court judgments are normally drafted.

D. THE PANEL'S LEGAL LEGACY

The number of cases received by the Panel increased when its existence became better known. Altogether 527 complaints were introduced. As to the identity of the complainants, most of them were Kosovo Serbs, only a few of them Kosovo Albanians. Some complainants belonged to minority groups, principally Roma, Ashkali and Egyptian. Many of the complaints concerned the death and disappearances of elderly relatives. As a matter of fact, as observed by C. Chinkin, the complaints paint "an extremely vivid picture of the human rights consequences of conflict where the conflict was based on ethnic divisions and also where it is coupled with transition from a socialist regime – two characteristics operating in the context of Kosovo".[6]

In light of the number of persons who fled Kosovo during and after the violence, abandoning their property in the process and leaving it vulnerable to being taken over, it is unsurprising that, from the beginning of 2008, a significant proportion of the complaints handled by the Panel were of a property nature. In order to create a legal mechanism to return these properties, UNMIK established quasi-judicial bodies that specialized in property cases. In the *Vučković* case, the Panel concluded that these bodies were judicial in function such that Article 6 of the ECHR applied to proceedings before it.[7]

From 2009 onwards, the majority of the complaints submitted in 2009 concerned the alleged lack of investigation by UNMIK police and judicial authorities into the events leading to abductions, disappearances and/or killings of complainants' close relatives in Kosovo. Inter-ethnic tensions and discrimination have remained

---

6   C. Chinkin, "The Kosovo Human Rights Advisory Panel" [PDF], *International Law Meeting Summary*, Chatham House, London, 26 January 2012, p. 11.
7   *Vučković v. UNMIK*, no. 03/07, opinion of 13 March 2010, §34.

pervasive in Kosovo in the aftermath of the conflict. Nonetheless, the Panel received only a limited number of complaints directly about discrimination, mostly from members of Kosovo non-majority communities in the context of the privatization of socially-owned enterprises.[8] However, the Panel was always alert to underlying direct and indirect discrimination.

Against this background, the main aspect of the Panel's legal legacy[9] is its contribution to the human rights jurisprudence.[10] The decision of the Panel to rely upon the ECHR and the jurisprudence of the ECtHR firmly planted the HRAP in Europe, in a context that was already well-known and established. Nevertheless, there are a number of cases where the Panel pushed the boundaries of the ECtHR jurisprudence, causing its cases to differ from (or extend) those of the ECtHR. They concerned, notably, the determination of legal standards applicable where the wrongdoings were committed by non-state actors; the applicability of the substantive protections of Article 2 of the ECHR to a UN body in the context of public protest as in the *Balaj and Others* case of 27 February 2015[11]; the extension of the Panel's competence *ratione temporis* through the procedural obligations of Article 2 of the ECHR, in particular the continuing nature of the obligation to investigate deaths in suspicious circumstances and disappearances as summarized in the *B.A.* case of 1 February 2013[12]; the applicability of Article 3 of the ECHR to a UN body involving violations with respect to the inhuman and degrading treatment of relatives of missing and/or murdered persons in the *Jocić* case of 24 April 2013[13]; the procedural aspect of Article 5 of the ECHR in the *Kostić and Others* case of 23 October 2015 and the failure to conduct gender-sensitive investigations into arbitrary detention of women.[14]

But the Panel was unique in that it was not only wedded to the ECtHR. The inclusion of a broad range of international human rights treaties in the Panel's constitutive instruments[15] allowed it a flexibility to be innovative and provided a unique

---

[8]   W. Benedek, "Kosovo – UNMIK accountability: Human Rights Advisory Panel finds discrimination in privatization cases", *Austrian Law Journal*, 2015, No. 2, pp. 276 et seq.

[9]   Another aspect of the Panel's legal legacy is related to the institutional and organisational conditions for a better functioning of this kind of panel in the future. See *The Human Rights Advisory Panel – History and Legacy – Kosovo, 2007–2016, op. cit.*, pp. 94–95.

[10]   C. Chinkin, "The Kosovo Human Rights Advisory Panel" [PDF], *International Law Meeting Summary*, Chatham House, London, 26 January 2012, p. 11.

[11]   *Balaj and Others v. UNMIK*, no. 04/07, opinion of 27 February 2015. See.

[12]   *B.A. v. UNMIK*, no. 52/09, opinion of 1 February 2013. See M. Beulay, "Human Rights Advisory Panel: La décision B.A. c. MINUK, illustration du sérieux d'une solution initialement cosmétique" [PDF], *Lettre "Actualités Droits-Libertés" du CREDOF*, 24 April 2013.

[13]   *Jocić v. UNMIK*, no. 34/09, opinion of 23 April 2013. See M. Beulay, "Human Rights Advisory Panel: Un approfondissement inédit de l'obligation des Nations Unies en matière d'enquête" [PDF], *Lettre "Actualités Droits-Libertés" du CREDOF*, 27 September 2013.

[14]   *Kostić and Others v. UNMIK*, nos. 111/09 et al., opinion of 23 October 2015.

[15]   *See supra*, paragraph 9.

opportunity to develop jurisprudence as a quasi-judicial body drawing on various sources. Thus, the Panel made use of the case-law also, of course, of the institutions of the Inter-American human rights system and the UN human rights treaties committees. This proved especially useful in the context of the Panel's cases concerning violence against women, where it made use of the CEDAW and its jurisprudence. This diversity of sources permitted the Panel to fit, where possible, the most relevant human rights jurisprudence to the context in Kosovo, including even looking at special rapporteurs' reports, for instance concerning the right to truth.[16]

II. THE *N.M. AND OTHERS v. UNMIK* CASE OF 26 FEBRUARY 2016

This case brought the historical marginalisation of the Roma in Europe to the attention of the Panel, along with the issue of multiple and intersectional discrimination suffered by the complainants as IDPs, as members of the Roma, Ashkali and Egyptian community in Kosovo and, for the female complainants, as women, placed in lead contaminated camps.

A. LEAD CONTAMINATION IN THE INTERNALLY DISPLACED PERSONS CAMPS

The complainants were 138 members of the Roma, Ashkali and Egyptian communities in Kosovo (men, women and children) who had been placed in the camps for IDPs set up in northern Mitrovicë/Mitrovica since 1999. All complainants claimed to have suffered lead poisoning on account of the soil contamination in the camps sites due to their proximity to the Trepca smelter and mining complex and also other health problems on account of the generally poor hygiene and living conditions in the camps. The *N.M. and Others* case raised very sensitive questions with regard to various human rights instruments and offers a perfect illustration of the cross-fertilization between them.[17]

B. RIGHT TO LIFE

As far as general principles are concerned, the Panel has relied on the relevant case-law of the various universal and regional instruments for the protection of human

---

[16] *D.L. v. UNMIK*, no. 88/09, opinion of 21 November 2013, §88.
[17] M. Beulay, "Le baroud d'honneur d'un organe malheureusement méconnu (obs. sous Panel consultatif des droits de l'homme, N. M. e.a. c. M.I.N.U.K., 26 février 2016)", *Rev. trim. dr. h.*, No. 109, 2017, pp. 201 et seq.

rights. Concerning the case-law of the ECtHR, the Panel recalled that the European Court has held that Article 2 not only imposes an obligation on authorities to refrain from taking life intentionally but also lays down a positive obligation to take appropriate steps to safeguard the lives of those within their jurisdiction. This obligation applies in the context of any activity, whether public or not, in which the right to life may be at stake, and *a fortiori* in the case of industrial activities which are by their nature dangerous, such as the operation of waste collection sites.[18] In particular, in the context of dangerous activities, the Court has found that special emphasis must be placed on regulations geared to the special features of the activity in question, particularly with regard to the level of the potential risk to human lives.

But the Panel also referred to the jurisprudence of the UN human rights treaty-bodies, finding that the right to life had been "too often narrowly interpreted". In this respect, the Human Rights Committee (HRC) has stated that the protection of this right requires that states adopt positive measures and, in this connection, has considered that "it would be desirable for States parties to take all possible measures to reduce infant mortality and to increase life expectancy, especially in adopting measures to eliminate malnutrition and epidemics".[19] The Committee has also stated that the duty to adopt positive measures in order to protect human life applies in principle to environmental matters, such as those involving the storage of radioactive waste in residential areas[20] or the exposure to radiation stemming from nuclear tests.[21]

The Panel further referred to the case-law developed by the Inter-American Court of Human Rights (IACtHR) concerning the alleged violation of the right to life of indigenous communities. The Inter-American Court has stated that the protection of the right to life entails the adoption of positive measures to ensure "access to conditions that may guarantee a decent life". The Court has determined that from this general obligation "special duties are derived that can be determined according to the particular needs of protection of the legal persons, whether due to their personal condition, or because of the specific situation they have to face, such as extreme poverty, exclusion or childhood".[22] The IACtHR has also clarified that "in order for this positive obligation to arise, it must be determined that at the moment of the occurrence of the events, the authorities knew or should have known about the existence of a situation posing an immediate and certain risk to the life of an individual or a group of individuals, and that the necessary

---

18 *N.M. and Others v. UNMIK*, no. 26/08, opinion of 26 February 2016, §194.
19 HRC, General Comment No. 6, U.N. Doc. HRI/GEN/1/Rev.1 (1994), §5.
20 HRC, *EHP v. Canada*, communication no. 67/1980, decision of 27 October 1982.
21 HRC, *Bordes and Temeharo v. France*, communication no. 167/1984, views of 22 July 1996.
22 IACtHR, *Sawhoyamaxa Indigenous Community v. Paraguay*, judgment of 29 March 2006, §§153–154; IACtHR, *Xákmok Kásek Indigenous Community v. Paraguay*, judgment of 24 August 2010.

measures were not adopted within the scope of their authority which could be reasonably expected to prevent or avoid such risk".[23]

In the present case, the Panel also took note of the reports of UN specialised agencies such as the World Health Organization (WHO) and human rights bodies (UN human rights treaty bodies and special rapporteurs), as well as those of other national and international human rights organisations (the Ombudsperson Institution in Kosovo, the Council of Europe Commissioner for Human Rights among others) covering the relevant period. The Panel noted that these bodies and organisations had inspected the camps and recorded the situation as posing a serious threat to the life and health of the Roma IDPs. In particular, the Panel recalled: the statements of WHO that half of the children tested were in a situation of "medical emergency" and that their "lives and development potentials are at risk"; the joint appeal from WHO and UNICEF calling on the IDPs to relocate them as an "emergency health requirement" and to pre-empt "serious health consequences"; the opinion of the Council of Europe Advisory Committee on the Framework Convention on the Protection of National Minorities stating that the situation of the IDPs "constitutes a serious health risk in particular for children and pregnant women"; the 2009 letter from the Council of Europe Commissioner for Human Rights to the SRSG stating that the children he had met in the camps were "clearly under-developed for their age" and defined the situation in the camps as a "humanitarian disaster".[24]

The Panel found that UNMIK's failure regarding the situation of the complainants was tainted by racial prejudice when, for instance, the health crises in the camps was blamed on the "unhealthy" life-style of the Roma, Ashkali and Egyptian IDPs. The Panel also highlighted UNMIK's failure to apply a gender-sensitive perspective to the situation, by omitting to consider how the lead contamination was differently and disproportionally affecting the health and well-being of women in the camps. Therefore, the Panel found that failing to take the required remedial actions – for example by not providing access to regular screening and adequate health care for pregnant women – resulted in additional direct and indirect discrimination, in violation of Article 12 of the CEDAW and of the CEDAW Committee General Recommendation No. 24.

---

[23] IACtHR, *Sawhoyamaxa Indigenous Community v. Paraguay*, §155.
[24] *N.M. and Others v. UNMIK*, no. 26/08, opinion of 26 February 2016, §206.

C. RIGHT TO BE FREE FROM INHUMAN OR DEGRADING TREATMENT

The Panel referred to the well-established case-law of the European Court of Rights establishing that Article 3, along with Article 2 of the ECHR, enshrines one of the most fundamental values of democratic society. It prohibits in absolute terms torture or inhuman or degrading treatment or punishment, irrespective of the circumstances and the victim's behaviour.[25] The panel also recalled that the ECtHR had held that special protection against torture, inhuman and degrading treatment shall be afforded to categories of persons, such as children and other "vulnerable persons"[26] and that, in this context, the Court had stated that the Roma have "become a specific type of disadvantaged and vulnerable minority", requiring "special protection" against ill-treatment.[27]

Therefore, the Panel attached great importance, in the present case, to the status of the complainants and their special situation of vulnerability as IDPs and as Roma. It noted that they had been displaced as a consequence of conflict and violence without, however, having access to refugee status and the rights attached to it. As members of a historically disadvantaged minority, they, along with other non-Serb minorities, found themselves in the aftermath of the conflict "caught between the two main ethnic communities in Kosovo". Within the complainants, the Panel noted the further vulnerability and the hardship faced by children and pregnant women, the most harmed by the absorption of lead when exposed to its harmful effects.[28]

Moreover, the Panel could not accept either the SRSG's argument that the Roma have historically lived in substandard living conditions, even prior to the conflict. The Panel found this comment discriminatory and debasing, since it suggests that the social and economic marginalisation of Roma is based on race and on their own actions and, as such, may be perpetuated without responsibility. To the contrary, the Panel considered that the historical marginalisation of the Roma and the traumatic experiences which had led them to their IDP status in Kosovo made the complainants especially vulnerable to degrading treatment and UNMIK additionally responsible for their well-being.[29]

---

[25]   *Ibid.*, §234.
[26]   *Ibid.*, §237.
[27]   *Ibid.*, §238.
[28]   *Ibid.*, §241.
[29]   *Ibid.*, §244.

D.   RIGHT TO HEALTH AND RIGHT TO AN ADEQUATE STANDARD OF LIVING

As observed by M. Beulay, the Panel's opinion in the case of *N.M. and Others* "illustrates the question of the accountability of the United Nations on a topical issue – the right to health and the right to an adequate standard of living – activity about which the Panel was one of the too rare players".[30]

Especially in this field, the Panel had the opportunity to rely and to use all UN Nations instruments, including, for the first time, Article 25 of the Universal Declaration. Furthermore, comprehensive definitions of both the right to health and the right to an adequate standard of living are found in the ICESCR, which also clarifies the scope of states' obligations to respect, protect and fulfil these rights.

The case-law of the ICESCR Committee provided the Panel with important and substantial guidelines to apply the provision of the Covenant to the situation at hand. For instance, right to health – which does not equate to the "right to be *healthy*" – shall be interpreted as an inclusive right extending "not only to timely and appropriate health care", but also to "underlying determinants of health", such as food and nutrition, housing, access to safe and potable water and adequate sanitation, safe and healthy working conditions, and a healthy environment, access to health related education and information.[31] For the right to health to be fulfilled, health facilities, goods, services and programmes shall be: available; accessible and affordable, which encompasses also the right to seek, receive and impart information concerning health issues; culturally acceptable and appropriate; of good quality.[32]

Concerning the core obligation to ensure minimum essential levels of the rights in question, the Committee has stated that, for example, "a state party in which any significant number of individuals is deprived of essential foodstuffs, of essential primary health care, of basic shelter and housing [...] is, *prima facie*, failing to discharge its obligations under the Covenant", unless it can demonstrate that "every effort has been made to use all resources that are at its disposition in an effort to satisfy, as a matter of priority, those minimum obligations".[33]

---

30   M. Beulay, "Le baroud d'honneur d'un organe malheureusement méconnu (obs. sous Panel consultatif des droits de l'homme, N. M. e.a. c. M.I.N.U.K., 26 février 2016)", *op. cit.*

31   UN ICESCR Committee, General Comment No. 14 *on the right to the highest attainable standard of health*, 11 August 2000, UN Doc. E/C.12/2000/4, §8 and §11 respectively.

32   *Ibid.*, §12.

33   ICESCR Committee, General Comment No. 3 *on the nature of State Parties' obligations*, 14 December 1990, UN Doc. E/1991/23, §10.

Moreover, the Committee has underlined that these minimum core obligations do apply "also in times of severe resource constraints", where authorities have obligations to protect "the vulnerable members of society".[34] Specifically concerning the right to adequate housing, the ICESCR Committee has also stated that, especially in times of economic crisis or other constraining situations, "due priority" and consideration should be given to "those social groups living in unfavourable conditions".[35]

Finally, the right to health and the right to an adequate standard of living, as envisaged in the ICESCR, apply to everyone "including non-nationals, such as refugees, asylum seekers, stateless persons, migrant workers …, regardless of their legal status", as well as to "internally displaced persons".[36] Further, these rights and principles are reflected in the UN Guiding Principles on Internal Displacement.[37]

Against this background, the Panel seized the opportunity to recall the principle that all human rights are universal, indivisible, interdependent and interrelated as they all emanate from the "dignity and worth inherent of the human person".[38] It noted the full applicability of the right to health and the right to an adequate standard of living, as well as of all other economic, social and cultural rights, to the complainants, regardless of their status as IDPs. In this respect, the Panel observed that the complainants were placed in makeshift shelters which did not have adequate access to water (running water as well as potable water), sanitation (adequate toilet and sewage system), electricity or heating. The Panel also referred to the findings that this housing, hygiene and nutrition situation in the camps created a situation whereby the complainants' exposure and vulnerability to lead poisoning, and consequently to a wide range of other diseases, was dramatically heightened.[39] In addition, in light of the obligation under Article 12.2 of the ICESCR to take steps to reduce child mortality and still-birth, prevent, treat and control diseases, the Panel recalled its findings under Article 2 of the ECHR that UNMIK had failed to provide systematic monitoring of the lead contamination in the camps, through regular blood testing.

The Panel was concerned that UNMIK's inadequate response to the crisis might have been driven by discriminatory stereotypes more than scientific evidence,

---

[34]　ICESCR Committee, General Comment No. 3, §12.

[35]　ICESCR Committee, General Comment No. 4, §11.

[36]　ICESCR Committee, General Comment No. 14, §§30 and 34 respectively.

[37]　United Nations, Guiding Principles on Internal Displacement, adopted by the Commission on Human Rights on 17 April 1998, doc. E/CN.4/1998/53/Add.2.

[38]　See preamble of the Vienna Declaration and Programme of Action, adopted by the World Conference on Human Rights, 25 June 1993, UN Doc. A/CONF.157/23.<

[39]　*N.M. and Others v. UNMIK*, no. 26/08, opinion of 26 February 2016, §275.

as the latter would have shown that proximity to the Trepca smelter and its tailing dams was the main source of lead contamination.[40] Taking note of the findings, among others, of the Council of Europe Commissioner for Human Rights stating that the life-threatening condition of approximately 600 Roma, for a decade in lead contaminated camps of northern Mitrovicë/Mitrovica has been "probably the most extreme case in Europe to safeguard Romas' right to health", the Panel considered shameful that such a record was attributable to the action and/or inaction of an entity of the United Nations – UNMIK – at the core of whose mandate was the protection of displaced persons from the conflict.[41]

E. PROHIBITION OF DISCRIMINATION

The complainants complained that, as members of the Roma community in Kosovo, they had been subject to general, direct and indirect, discrimination. They claimed that UNMIK's decision to place the Roma IDPs in the contaminated camps and its failure to move them to a safer environment was a further manifestation of discrimination against them, based on their Roma ethnicity. In support of their claim, the complainants argued that only the Roma IDPs, as compared to Kosovo IDPs of different ethnic origin, had been placed on a land known to be contaminated and that authorities had acted in a quicker manner to "return, rebuild and compensate" non-Roma inhabitants of Kosovo who had their property lost or destroyed during the conflict. The Panel deemed that his part of the complaint fell to be examined under the alleged violation Article 14 of the ECHR, taken in conjunction with Articles 2 (substantive obligation), 3 and 8 of the ECHR, as well as under the non-discrimination provisions of the ICCPR, ICESCR and ICERD.

It is well established that the prohibition of discrimination includes prohibition of indirect discrimination. The European Court states that "a general policy or measure that has disproportionately prejudicial effects on a particular group may be considered discriminatory notwithstanding that it is not specifically aimed at that group and that "discrimination potentially contrary to the Convention may result from a *de facto* situation". Likewise, under the ICERD Convention, the definition of discrimination shall be understood as extending "beyond measures which are explicitly discriminatory, to encompass measures which are not discriminatory at face value but are discriminatory in fact and effect". In assessing such indirect or *de facto* discrimination, the CERD Committee states that it must take full account of the particular context and circumstances of the

---

40   *Ibid.*, §280.
41   *Ibid.*, §282.

petition", since by definition indirect discrimination "can only be demonstrated circumstantially".[42]

In this respect, the ICESCR Committee has also stated that eliminating discrimination in the enjoyment of economic, social and cultural rights "requires paying sufficient attention to groups and individuals which suffer historical or persistent prejudice" and adopt measures "to prevent, diminish or eliminate the conditions and attitudes which cause or perpetuate" *de facto* discrimination". For example, "ensuring that all individuals have equal access to adequate housing, water and sanitation will help overcome discrimination against women and girl children and persons living in informal settlements and rural areas".[43]

As also noted above, the European Court, as well as the UN treaty bodies have recognised that, as a result of their turbulent history and uprooting, the Roma have become a specific type of disadvantaged and vulnerable minority, requiring special protection and consideration.[44]

F. DISCRIMINATION AGAINST WOMEN

The female complainants complained that the poor and hazardous living conditions in the camps had a particular negative impact on their life and health as women and that, therefore, they had been discriminated against on the ground of their ethnic origin as well as sex. The Panel recalled that the Panel's findings with respect to previous parts of the complaint were fully applicable to the female complainants. In addition, the Panel recalled that UNMIK had specific obligations towards the protection of women rights in the camps in accordance with the CEDAW Convention, applicable to UNMIK.[45]

In particular, the Panel deemed that the complainants' claim of discrimination based on sex fell to be examined under relevant provisions (Articles 1, 2 and 12) of the CEDAW which prohibits all forms of discrimination against women, defined in Article 1 of the Convention as: "any distinction, exclusion or restriction made on the basis of sex which has the effect or purpose of impairing or nullifying the recognition, enjoyment or exercise by women, irrespective of their marital status, on a basis of equality of men and women, of human rights and fundamental freedoms in the political, economic, cultural, civil or any other field".

---

[42]   *Ibid.*, §§288–289. See ICERD Committee, *L.R. et al. v. Slovak Republic*, decision of 7 March 2005, §10. 4.
[43]   *Ibid.*, §290.
[44]   *Ibid.*, §292.
[45]   *Ibid.*, §312.

Article 12 of the CEDAW establishes the legal obligation to eliminate discrimination against women in the access to health services throughout their life. In its General Recommendation No. 24, which clarifies the extent and scope of states' obligations under Article 12 of the Convention, the CEDAW Committee has stated the general obligation of authorities to "place a gender perspective" at the centre of all health programmes in order to address the distinctive features – such as biological (i.e. the reproductive function), socio-economic (i.e. unequal power relations) and psychological factors – that differ for women in comparison to men and which determine their respective health status. The CEDAW Committee has further highlighted specific measures that states parties have the obligation to take in fulfilment of the women's health rights. In this respect, the Committee has also stated that "while biological differences between women and men may lead to differences in health status, there are also societal factors that are determinative of the status of women and men and can vary among women themselves. For that reason, special attention should be given to the health needs and rights of women belonging to vulnerable and disadvantaged groups, such as migrant women, refugee and internally displaced women, the girl child and older women …".

The Panel further recalled that the obligations stated above did not cease to exist in periods of armed conflict or in states of emergency and they were due, without discrimination, to all those under the state's jurisdiction, that is citizens and non-citizens, such as refugees, asylum seekers, migrant workers and stateless persons.[46] In the regulatory and institutional vacuum within Kosovo in the aftermath of the conflict, the findings and recommendations of WHO experts, as well as other specialised bodies, should have guided UNMIK's actions in response to the health crisis in the camps. The Panel considered that there was little room for doubt that *de facto* the female complainants were additionally and disproportionately affected by the extremely unhealthy situation in the camps and that since its early days UNMIK had been aware of the high health risks posed by lead poisoning to pregnant women and children.

The Panel noted that, in these circumstances, UNMIK had the obligation under the CEDAW to recognise how the situation in the camps was affecting differently and disproportionately the female complainants and to adopt positive measures to adequately respond to their situation of particular disadvantage. These included: the obligation to ensure that the pregnant women could carry out their pregnancy in a safe environment, providing easy access to regular screening and adequate health care for pregnant women, access to adequate hygiene and nutrition, collection of data on still-births and miscarriages for the purpose of monitoring, provision of psychological and

---

46   *Ibid.*, §316.

support services to those women who had incurred miscarriage, abortion or still-birth.[47]

G.   CHILDREN'S RIGHTS

While recalling that the Panel's findings concerning other parts of the complaint are fully applicable to the children, the Panel noted that the CRC, directly applicable to UNMIK by virtue of UNMIK Regulation No. 1999/24 imposed specific obligations with respect to the protection of children's rights in the camps, which had not been fully considered in other parts of the complaint.[48] In particular, the Panel considered that this part of the complaint fell to be examined under Article 3 (right of the child to have his best interest taken as a primary consideration), Article 6 (child's inherent right to life), Article 24 (right of the child to the highest attainable standard of health), Article 27 (right of the child to a standard of living adequate for the her/his physical, mental, spiritual, moral and social development) and Article 37 (prohibition of inhuman and degrading treatment against children) of the CRC.[49]

In its General Comment No. 14, the CRC Committee has stated that Article 3 of the CRC, which states that the best interest of the child shall be a primary consideration in all actions concerning directly or indirectly children, places a "strong legal obligation" on the authorities. This means, that the authorities "may not exercise discretion as to whether children's best interests are to be assessed and described the proper weight as a primary consideration in any action undertaken".[50] The Committee has clarified that "primary consideration" means that "the child's best interests may not be considered at the same level as all other considerations". It states that "this strong position is justified by the special situation of the child: dependency, maturity, legal status and, often, voicelessness. Children have less possibility than adults to make a strong case for their own interests and those involved in decisions affecting them must be explicitly aware of their interests. If the interests of the children are not highlighted they tend to be overlooked".[51]

The child's right to have her/his best interest taken as a primary consideration is a substantive right but also a procedural rule: "whenever a decision is to be made that will affect a specific child, an identified group of children or children in general, the

---

[47]   *Ibid.*, §324.
[48]   *Ibid.*, §332.
[49]   *Ibid.*, §333.
[50]   CRC Committee, General Comment No. 14 *on the right of the child to have his or her best interest taken as primary consideration*, 20 May 2013, UN Doc. CRC/C/GC/14, §36.
[51]   CRC Committee, General Comment No. 14, §37.

decision-making process must include an evaluation of the possible impact (positive or negative) of the decision on the child or children concerned ...".[52]

Finally, the protection of the child's inherent right to life, survival and development, as well as the child's right to health and her/his health condition, are "central" when assessing and determining the child's best interest.[53] Further, the Committee has stated that an important element to consider in the process of assessing the best interest of the child in a specific situation is "the child's situation of vulnerability, such as disability, belonging to a minority group, being a refugee or an asylum seeker ... etc.".[54]

The Panel found it established that it was children who suffered the most, and in an irreversible manner, from the situation in the IDP camps, including the lead poisoning and the poor living and hygiene conditions. It considered that the lives and health of children should have been the overriding consideration guiding UNMIK's response to the situation. However, the Panel noted that UNMIK had not explained (nor provided any documentation in this respect) how the best interest of the children in the camps was considered, assessed and determined when deciding and enacting measures in response to the situation in the camps.[55] Consequently, the Panel found that, through its actions and omissions, UNMIK was responsible for compromising irreversibly the life, health and development potential of the complainants that were born and grew as children in the camps, in violation of Articles 3, 6, 24, 27 and 37 of the CRC.[56]

H.   RECOMMENDATIONS OF THE PANEL

The last part of the opinion is, as usual, devoted to the "Findings and recommendations". In the case of *N.M. and Others*, the Panel, urged UNMIK, *inter alia*, to publicly acknowledge its failure to comply with recognized international human rights standards and the effects of that failure on the complainants, to make a public apology to the families and to adequately compensate the victims for material and moral damages.[57]

---

[52]   CRC Committee, General Comment No. 14, §6 (c).
[53]   CRC Committee, General Comment No. 14, §§42 and 77.
[54]   CRC Committee, *ibid.*, §75.
[55]   *N.M. and Others v. UNMIK*, no. 26/08, opinion of 26 February 2016, §345.
[56]   *Ibid.*, §347.
[57]   L. Arimatsu, "Human Rights Advisory Panel urges the UN to compensate Roma, Ashkali and Egyptian families for lead poisoning in IDP camps", *OxHRH Blog*, 22 April 2016; R. Gladstone, "Roma poisoned at U.N. camps in Kosovo may get apology and compensation", *The New York Times*, 7 April 2016.

The HRAP being an advisory body and having only a consultative function, the main problem is the implementation by UNMIK and/or the United Nations of its recommendations which is close to non-existent.[58] In the Roma case, the situation is unfortunately almost the same, as observed by *The New York Times*.[59] In May 2017 the UN Secretary General A. Guterres confined himself to expressing the Organisation's profound regret for the suffering endured by all individuals living in the IDP camps. Because this kind of general statement is not going further than a personal/subjective feeling and implies nothing on a political level, it stays short of a public apology or of an acceptance of responsibility. "And, as far as compensation is concerned, the UN decided to merely launch a trust fund which will facilitate community-based initiatives to finance assistance projects. This proposal was heavily criticized by many human rights organisations arguing that creating an unfunded trust fund for charitable community projects instead of individual compensation for victims for its own failure is unacceptable.[60] "And in turn refusal to take responsibility for harm caused by the UN undermines the organization's ability to press governments and others to remedy their human rights abuses", L. Charbonneau, UN director at Human Rights Watch said.[61]

As the situation of evasion of responsibility and refusal of compensation is almost the same in Haiti concerning the cholera victims[62], it remains to be hoped that the United Nations will finally agree to adopt a new approach worthy of its role within the rule of law and a civilised world.

CONCLUSION

The last paragraphs of the Final Report's executive summary entail/express the main message of the Panel for the future.

"The importance of the HRAP was the very fact of its existence and its mandate to evaluate UNMIK's actions against international human rights instruments. When establishing such a quasi-judicial body, it seemed clear to the

---

58 See *The Human Rights Advisory Panel – History and Legacy – Kosovo, 2007–2016*, Final Report, *op. cit.*, pp. 86 et seq.

59 R. Gladstone, "Roma sickened in U.N. camps are still waiting for redress", *The New York Times*, 18 April 2017.

60 M. Ristic, "UN 'must compensate all Kosovo lead poison victims'", *Balkan Insight*, 7 September 2017.

61 L. Charbonneau and K. Rall, "UN should reconsider refusal to compensate Kosovo's victims", *Human Rights Watch*, 20 June 2017.

62 "Cholera victims' advocates denounce UN's evasion of responsibility in Kosovo", *Institute for Justice & Democracy in Haiti*, 26 May 2017; "Statement by Philip Alston, Special Rapporteur on Extreme Poverty and Human Rights", 71st session of the UN General Assembly, 3rd Committee, New York, 25 October 2016.

international human rights community that the UN's legitimacy and credibility is undermined where there is no such legal accountability. Further, the human rights system as a whole is weakened when states can observe the UN – one of the main guardians of the world's human rights system – itself failing to live up to the obligations it has promoted. So, the Panel was created mainly to be a contributing component to UN accountability – the first of its kind; secondarily, it was also hoped that the Panel would be able to provide some gains in ensuring the protection of human rights in Kosovo. ...

If we consider any future UN accountability mechanism and the optimum form such a mechanism should take, it has to be designed in a holistic way and crafted to the factual situation of the people on the ground and the political context of the mission. In particular, three main elements should be taken into account: (i) how it could operate effectively from the outset to take account of the human rights concerns of a vulnerable population in a post-conflict situation; (ii) how to ensure appropriate recommendations from the Panel with respect to complainants; and (iii) how to ensure an appropriate response from the UN mission in question.

The Panel identified some of the most important factors to be considered in any future institution set up for the same or similar purpose. Among them: a human rights Panel, not an 'advisory' Panel; set up by UN HQ, not by the mission (UN body, not UNMIK body); applicable to the whole international presence; established immediately after the mandating of the mission and included in its mandate; with procedures based on principles of fair, transparent adversarial processes; effective mechanisms for reparations, including payment of compensation, including for non-pecuniary damage.

Lastly, appropriate legal and policy planning would address ways to ensure independence from the UN mission but also its co-operation. It is also necessary to adopt measures to ensure public awareness right from the outset while also making sure that reality and expectation are compatible. At the end of the day, the UN must ensure not just compliance with recommendations in individual cases. It is hoped, more generally, the UN will adopt changes in practice and operations of its relevant missions to respect its promise to 'promote and protect human rights'".[63]

---

[63]   See *The Human Rights Advisory Panel – History and Legacy – Kosovo, 2007–2016*, Final Report, *op. cit.*, pp. 18–19, §§72, 75, 76 and 77.

THE UN GLOBAL COMPACT
FOR SAFE, ORDERLY AND REGULAR
MIGRATION: SOME REFLECTIONS

Jan WOUTERS

Full Professor of International Law and International Organisations
Jean Monnet Chair ad personam EU and Global Governance
Director of the Leuven Centre for Global Governance Studies –
Institute for International Law, KU Leuven

Evelien WAUTERS

PhD Candidate, Leuven Centre for Global Governance Studies –
Institute for International Law, KU Leuven

INTRODUCTION

This contribution, dedicated in friendship and esteem to Paul Lemmens, develops some reflections with regard to the United Nations (UN) Global Compact for Safe, Orderly and Regular Migration ('the Compact').[1] The Compact has been adopted by consensus on 10 December 2018 as the outcome document of the Intergovernmental Conference held in Marrakech.[2] It has been endorsed by the UN General Assembly ('UNGA') on 19 December of that same year, with a vote of 152 votes in favour to 5 against (Czech Republic, Hungary, Israel, Poland, United States) and 12 abstentions.[3]

---

[1]   UNGA, Intergovernmental Conference to Adopt the Global Compact for Safe, Orderly and Regular Migration, Draft Outcome Document of the Conference, A/CONF.231/3 ('the Compact'). The text of the Compact is laid down in A/CONF.231/3 and is the text of the agreed outcome reached on 13 July 2018.

[2]   A/CONF.231/L.1, item 10 of the provisional agenda.

[3]   Namely Algeria, Australia, Austria, Bulgaria, Chile, Italy, Latvia, Libya, Liechtenstein, Romania, Singapore, and Switzerland. 24 UN Member States were not present to take part in the vote (Afghanistan, Antigua and Barbuda, Belize, Benin, Botswana, Brunei Darussalam, Democratic People's Republic of Korea, Dominican Republic, Guinea, Kiribati, Kyrgyzstan, Micronesia, Panama, Paraguay, Sao Tome and Principe, Seychelles, Slovakia, Somalia, Timor-Leste, Tonga, Trinidad and Tobago, Turkmenistan, Ukraine, and Vanuatu). More than 50 States explained their position. From the viewpoint of the European Union (EU), it was a three-split vote and therefore a sign of great divisions: whereas 19 EU Member States voted in favour (including Belgium), three voted against (Czech Republic, Hungary, Poland), five

Paul will vividly remember how the Compact has become a hotly contested document in Belgium during the late autumn of 2018, how it even triggered a crisis, and, in the end, the collapse of the Belgian federal government in December 2018. To our knowledge, no other government in the world has ever collapsed over a non-binding UN document. So, what was all the fuss about?

In what follows, we will first discuss the genesis of the Compact and its content. We will then consider its legal and political status. Last but not least, we will look at the potential effects of the document for Belgium.

I. THE COMPACT: GENESIS AND CONTENT

A. GENESIS OF THE COMPACT

The governance of migration does not have a tradition of comprehensive discussions or decision-making in multilateral fora.[4] It has been, at best, the subject of bilateral agreements.[5] Although some cooperative efforts have emerged at a regional level[6], cooperation on migration and border control has taken place outside of formal international cooperation fora. Instead, most discussions on migration governance have taken place as part of rather technical processes or non-committal fora out of the public eye. In the European context, migration policy was developed first as part of the Schengen process, and only later formally became part of EU law.[7]

An example of these cooperative efforts on migration are the 'Regional Consultative Processes' (RCPs), such as the Budapest Process, and the Prague Process for Eurasia, the Colombo Process for Asia, and the Pacific and the Caribbean Migration Consultations (CMC) for the Americas.[8] Another example are the 'Interregional Forums on Migration' (IRFs), which include the Asia-EU Dialogue on Labour Migration, as well as the Abu Dhabi Dialogue. The latter are

---

abstained (Austria, Bulgaria, Italy, Latvia, Romania), and one (Slovakia) did not vote. All in all, 41 out of 193 UN Member States did not endorse the Compact.

[4]   Alexander Betts, 'Migration Governance: Alternative Futures' (2010) IOM Background Paper WMR 9.

[5]   Ibid.

[6]   The EU free movement regime, the Mercosur Residence Agreement (signed 6 December 2002), and the ECOWAS Protocol on the Free Movement of Persons (signed 28 May 1975) A/P.1/5/79.

[7]   The Amsterdam Treaty, in force since 1 May 1999, foresaw the transfer of asylum and migration issues from the so-called 'Third Pillar' to the 'First Pillar' of the Union within five years after the ratification and incorporation of the Schengen Agreement in the EU *acquis* (Art 2 (15)).

[8]   IOM, 'Regional Consultative Processes on Migration' www.iom.int/regional-consultative-processes-migration accessed 25 February 2019.

state-led, informal and non-binding dialogues on migration usually connecting two or more regions, *in casu* Asia and Europe, and Asia and the Middle East.[9] The axis with the largest variety of discussion fora is the Africa-Europe axis with the Tripoli Process, the Khartoum Process, the Africa-EU Partnership on Migration, Mobility and Employment (MME), the 5+5 Dialogue on Migration in the Western Mediterranean, the Rabat Process, and the Mediterranean Transit Migration (MTM) process.[10]

As mentioned above, these processes are of an intergovernmental nature, and are no paragons of public scrutiny. They have been characterised by a lack of public access, are rarely followed by final declarations or a press event accessible to the public, nor are they linked to a monitoring mechanism ensuring accountability for their decisions. In that manner, these processes risk being squandered as mere 'talk shops' or risk exacerbating international power imbalances. On the other hand, these RCPs and IRFS have been identified as great opportunities for inter-state dialogue, information sharing, and exploration of future cooperation opportunities on migration issues.[11]

For a long time, the UN has shied away from playing a noteworthy role in migration governance. The United Nations High Commissioner for Refugees (UNHCR), and the International Organization for Migration ('IOM') only address certain aspects of migration governance. UNHCR insists on a strict distinction between 'refugees' and 'migrants'[12], as its mandate stems from the 1951 Convention on the Status of Refugees.[13] As Betts put it: '[t]he refugee regime is unique in being an area of migration governance in which nearly all States have agreed to delegate authority to a formal, treaty-based governance framework'. In addition, IOM, which was until recently a non-UN agency, does not have a normative mandate, has weak protection responsibilities, and for now remains a mere service provider to States, relying on project-driven funding.[14] It should be noted, however, that this is not to say that migration remained entirely unaddressed as part of the UN. On 18 December 1990, the UNGA adopted

---

9   IOM, 'Inter-Regional Forums on Migration' www.iom.int/inter-regional-forums-migration accessed 25 February 2019.
10   Ibid.
11   Ibid. See also Amanda Klekowski Von Koppenfels, 'Informal but Effective: Regional Consultative Processes as a Tool in Managing Migration' (2001) 39 *International Migration* 61; Colleen Thouez and Frédérique Channac, 'Shaping International Migration Policy: The Role of Regional Consultative Processes' (2006) 29 *West European Politics* 370; Betts (n 4) 9.
12   See e.g., UNHCR, 'Asylum and Migration' www.unhcr.org/asylum-and-migration.html accessed 25 February 2019.
13   Convention relating to the Status of Refugees (28 July 1951) 189 UNTS 150 ('1951 Convention').
14   Betts (n 4) 15 ff; Joanna Apap, 'A Global Compact on Migration: Placing Human Rights at the Heart of Migration Management' (*European Parliamentary Research Service Blog*, January 2019) 5.

the International Convention on the Protection of the Rights of All Migrants Workers and Members of their Families (CRMW).[15] The Convention sets out minimum standards for the international protection of migrant workers and their families. It entered into force in 2003 but has only received 54 ratifications, among which none of the main international migration receiving countries.[16, 17] In addition, not a single EU Member State is a party to the Convention.

Another initiative was the 1994 UN Population and Development Conference held in Cairo, which produced the most comprehensive text on international migration ever adopted at the UN, up until the 2016 New York Declaration: the Cairo Programme of Action.[18] Its Chapter X considers the interactions between international migration and development, the rights of documented migrants, as well as possible actions to address undocumented migration. Furthermore, in 1999, the position of 'Special Rapporteur on the Human Rights of Migrants' was established by the UN Commission on Human Rights.[19] One of its main functions is to identify best practices, concrete areas and means for international cooperation on the rights of migrants.[20] Other initiatives, such as the 2005 Global Commission on International Migration (GCIM)[21], were criticised for the lack of a close follow-up.[22]

Nonetheless, the GCIM's call for greater consultation and cooperation at the regional and global level[23] amounted to the creation of new structures by UN Secretary-General Kofi Annan. The most important ones were the establishment of the Global Migration Group, an inter-agency group to coordinate work on migration among UN organs and other organisations linked to the UN, and the appointment of a Special Representative on Migration, Peter Sutherland. Annan also pushed for the calling of a High-Level Dialogue on International Migration

---

[15]   UNGA Resolution 45/158 (18 December 1990).

[16]   Betts (n 4) 9.

[17]   United States of America, Germany, Russian Federation, Saudi Arabia, United Kingdom, United Arab Emirates. See IOM, World Migration Report 2018, 32.

[18]   UN, 'Report of the International Conference on Population and Development' (18 October 1994) A/CONF.171/13.

[19]   UN Commission on Human Rights Res 1999/44 (27 April 1999).

[20]   UN Office of the High Commissioner on Human Rights (OHCHR), 'Special Rapporteur on the human rights of migrants' www.ohchr.org/en/issues/migration/srmigrants/pages/srmigrantsindex.aspx accessed 25 February 2019.

[21]   Kathleen Newland, 'Migration's Unrealized Potential: The Report of the Global Commission on International Migration' (*migrationpolicy.org*, 1 November 2005) www.migrationpolicy.org/article/migrations-unrealized-potential-report-global-commission-international-migration accessed 25 February 2019; Alexander Betts and Lena Kainz, 'The History of Global Migration Governance' Refugee Studies Centre Working Paper Series 2017, 122.

[22]   Betts and Kainz (n 20) 5.

[23]   Global Commission on International Migration (GCIM), 'Migration in an Interconnected World: New Directions for Action' (5 October 2005) www.refworld.org/docid/435f81814.html accessed 12 March 2019.

and Development to be held in New York on 14 and 15 September 2006.[24] Although the main outcome of the event was an overview of the discussions, which again highlighted the reluctance of States of the Global North to conduct migration governance discussions in a more formal, multilateral setting, Belgium agreed to hold a Global Forum on Migration and Development (GFMD) the next year, upon the proposal of the Secretary-General.[25]

Today, the GFMD and GMG are the two 'powerhouses' of the global migration governance architecture. While we have come a long way from having no set structures at all, the more recently developed 'architecture' has been criticised by, among others Special Rapporteur on the Human Rights of Migrants, François Crépeau, as too informal, ad-hoc, state-led, and forming an obvious retreat from the set UN structures under public scrutiny.[26] Nevertheless, it generated momentum, and Sutherland mobilised States to organise a new High-Level Dialogue in 2013.[27] This second High-Level Dialogue proved key in bringing a human rights dimension into discussions on migration, which were until then dominated by security considerations. In addition, migration was specifically included in the 2015 UN Sustainable Development Goals (SDGs).[28] For instance, SDG Target 10.7 reads as follows: '[f]acilitate orderly, safe, regular and responsible migration and mobility of people, including through the implementation of planned and well-managed migration policies'. Finally, in February 2017, a year before he died, Peter Sutherland published his legacy 'Sutherland Report', making recommendations to further enhance global migration governance. The Sutherland Report played a key role in the preparation of the New York Summit of September 2016, and served as a basis for the discussions on the Compact.

These initiatives in combination with the migration crisis in Europe, the Rohingya crisis in Myanmar, and the Central American crossings to the US, led governments to search for solutions at the global level. It was agreed that a High-Level Summit at the UN Addressing Large Movements of Refugees and Migrants would take place on 19 September 2016. At the Summit, the IOM was brought into the UN family, and was made a 'Related Organization' of the UN.[29] The main output of the Summit was the New York Declaration for Refugees and Migrants[30], adopted by all 193 UN Member States, establishing the

---

24   UNGA Res 58/208 (23 December 2003).
25   UNGA Res 65/170 (20 December 2010).
26   UNGA Res 68/283 (5 August 2013).
27   UNGA Res 68/L.5. (1 October 2013).
28   UNGA Res 70/1 (25 September 2015).
29   UNGA Res 70/976 (8 July 2016). It is unclear, however, what the 'adoption' of IOM will precisely entail as the expansion of its mandate did not go together which a change of its 'project-based funding model.
30   UNGA Res 71/1 (19 September 2016).

will of States to act collectively to protect refugees and migrants, and to address emerging challenges. The Declaration started off two diplomatic processes, which culminated in the drafting of two compacts, which were finalised in June[31], and July 2018[32] respectively. While the Migration Compact was a state-driven process, the Global Compact on Refugees was developed by UNHCR in consultation with UN Member States.

This brief overview shows that the adoption of the New York Declaration on Refugees and Migrants, and the subsequent Global Compact on Safe, Orderly and Regular Migration are the result of decades of international efforts to enhance the global migration governance architecture.

B.   CONTENT OF THE COMPACT

On 10 December 2018, the Compact was adopted by 164 UN Member States as an 'outcome document' of a two-day Intergovernmental Conference meeting in Marrakech on 10–11 December 2018. At the conference senior, government officials along with partners from civil society, the private sector and migrant communities gathered to discuss opportunities for partnership. The adoption of the Compact took place at the plenary opening session of the Conference on Monday 10 December 2018 – a symbolic moment, as it was the seventieth anniversary of the Universal Declaration of Human Rights. The Compact was subsequently endorsed by the UNGA by way of a concise resolution on 19 December 2018.[33] As indicated above, 152 UN Member States voted in favour of the Compact.[34] Interestingly, apart from the United States[35], all UN Member States took part until the end in the negotiating process leading up to

---

[31]   Global Compact on Refugees, Final Draft (26 June 2018) A/73/12.

[32]   Global Compact on Migration, Intergovernmentally Negotiated and Agreed Outcome (13 July 2018).

[33]   UNGA Res 73/L.66.

[34]   Five voted against it (Czech Republic, Hungary, Israel, Poland and US) and 12 abstained (Algeria, Australia, Austria, Bulgaria, Chile, Italy, Latvia, Libya, Liechtenstein, Romania, Singapore and Switzerland). In addition, 24 Member States were not present to take part in the vote.

[35]   The US pulled out from the negotiations on 2 December 2017. It did not participate in the Marrakech Conference and voted against in the UNGA. Nikki Haley, the US' Permanent Representative to the UN in New York, issued a statement indicating *inter alia*: 'America is proud of our immigrant heritage and our longstanding moral leadership in providing support to migrant and refugee populations across the globe ... But our decisions on immigration policies must always be made by Americans and Americans alone ... We will decide how best to control our borders and who will be allowed to enter our country. The global approach in the New York declaration is simply not compatible with US sovereignty.' See Patrick Wintour, 'Donald Trump pulls US out of UN global compact on migration' (*The Guardian*, 3 December 2017) www.theguardian.com/world/2017/dec/03/donald-trump-pulls-us-out-of-un-global-compact-on-migration accessed 12 March 2019.

the Compact. It was only after the final draft text was agreed that the political
context around the Compact became more toxic, and that first Hungary[36], and
later Austria (at the time President of the EU Council)[37], the Czech Republic[38],
and others announced they would not sign up to the Compact in Marrakech.
Although Belgium did support the Compact, its federal government lost its
majority over the prime minister's support of the document in Marrakech.

With the Compact, States aim to set out a cooperative framework ensuring that
migration happens in a safe, orderly, and regular manner. The Compact consists
of four parts, introduced by a preamble: a 'Vision and Guiding Principles', 23
objectives, a part on implementation, and the final 'Follow-up and Review' section.
The guiding principles are crosscutting and interdependent, and also include
human rights. The Compact's Vision and Guiding Principles provide in this respect:

> 'The Global Compact is based on international human rights law and upholds the
> principles of non-regression and non-discrimination. By implementing the Global
> Compact, we ensure effective respect, protection and fulfillment of the human rights
> of all migrants, regardless of their migration status, across all stages of the migration
> cycle. We also reaffirm the commitment to eliminate all forms of discrimination,
> including racism, xenophobia and intolerance against migrants and their families.'

Each of the objectives is followed by a set of actions for States to take in order
to achieve the objective (e.g., 'Objective 1: Collect and utilise accurate and
disaggregated data as a basis for evidence- based policies' and 'j) Develop and use
country-specific migration profiles'). The document has both broad (e.g., 'Objective
23: Strengthen international cooperation and global partnerships for safe, orderly
and regular migration') and more specific objectives (e.g., 'Objective 13: Use
migration detention only as a measure of last resort and work towards alternatives').

---

[36] Hungary pulled out on 18 July 2018, citing security concerns, just days after the finalisation
of the draft text and the conclusion of the last intergovernmental negotiation phase on 13 July
2018. However, already during the negotiations, it had distanced itself from the 'Group
of Member States of the European Union' on behalf of which Austria had consistently put
forward a common point of view.

[37] Austria announced its decision on 31 October 2018. Among the reasons for withdrawing
from the Compact, the Austrian government expressed its concern that the Compact could
eventually help 'making it a human right to find a new place around the globe' and lead to
the recognition of a 'human right to migration'. Freedom Party leader and Vice Chancellor,
Heinz-Christian Strache, told a news conference that they rejected any movement in that
direction. See Francois Murphy, 'Austria to shun global migration pact, fearing creep in
human rights' (*Reuters*, 31 October 2018), www.reuters.com/article/us-un-migrants-austria/
austria-to-shun-global-migration-pact-fearing-creep-in-human-rights-idUSKCN1N50JZ
accessed 12 March 2019.

[38] See Eline Schaart, 'Czech Republic latest EU country to reject UN migration treaty' (*Politico*,
14 November 2018), www.politico.eu/article/czech-republic-migration-refugees-latest-eu-
country-to-reject-united-nations-treaty/ accessed 12 March 2019.

At the same time, the Compact does not mention any 'new rights' or 'obligations', and largely refers to existing international instruments.[39] In addition, while the document is quick to emphasise that it is non-legally binding, and that it upholds the sovereignty of States[40], it does offer a few relatively novel ways forward, such as the Sustainable Development Goal[41] on reducing remittance costs.[42] On the other hand, strong language on an obligation for countries of origin to readmit nationals was included in the text[43], upon persistence of mainly the EU and its Member States, which view this as one of the greatest difficulties in migration management. They have greatly stressed the existence of such a duty in their own policies, including the European Commission's Migration Partnership Framework.[44] Up until the Compact, the EU and its Member States did not succeed in including this in a text adopted at the global level. It could therefore be submitted that the Compact negotiations culminated in a delicate balancing exercise between the protection of the rights of migrants from the Global South and strong calls for more effective returns, and addressing the drivers of migration, or, more or less, the interests of the Global South, on the one hand, and the Global North, on the other. Some have argued that the final version of the Compact clearly reflects practices for migration management which are typical for the EU, and that the Compact will carry the largest costs for the developing countries of the Global South.[45]

---

[39] The Compact's preamble explains that the Compact 'rests on the purposes and principles of the Charter of the United Nations' (para. 1) and 'also' on 'the Universal Declaration of Human Rights; the International Covenant on Civil and Political Rights; the International Covenant on Economic, Social and Cultural Rights; the other core international human rights treaties' (para. 2). Interestingly, in a footnote, among the 'core international human rights treaties' mention is made of the 1990 International Convention on the Protection of the Rights of All Migrant Workers and Members of their Families, which, as observed above, has only 54 Parties and has not been ratified by any EU Member State. See, for a critical comment, Jan Wouters, and Thomas Van Poecke, 'Puntjes op de i over het VN Migratiepact' (*De Tijd*, 22 November 2018), www.tijd.be/opinie/algemeen/puntjes-op-de-i-over-het-vn-migratiepact/10071751.html.

[40] Compact, para. 7.

[41] UNGA Res 70/1 (25 September 2015), Goal 10.c.

[42] Compact, Objective 20.

[43] Compact, Objective 21 and para. 37.

[44] European Commission, Communication From the Commission to the European Parliament, the European Council, the Council and the European Investment Bank on establishing a new Partnership Framework with third countries under the European Agenda on Migration (7 June 2016) COM(2016) 385 final, 7.

[45] Elspeth Guild and Katharine Weatherhead, 'Tensions as the EU Negotiates the Global Compact for Safe, Orderly and Regular Migration – EU Immigration and Asylum Law and Policy' (*EU Migration Law Blog*, 6 July 2018), eumigrationlawblog.eu/tensions-as-the-eu-negotiates-the-global-compact-for-safe-orderly-and-regular-migration/ accessed 12 March 2019; Narin Nadriz, 'Why EU Member States Should Not Hesitate to Vote for the Global Compact for Migration' (*Asser Institute Blog*, 29 November 2018), www.asser.nl/about-the-institute/asser-today/blog-why-eu-member-states-should-not-hesitate-to-vote-for-the-global-compact-for-migration accessed 12 March 2019.

But as with any international document, certainly those of the non-legally binding type, the strength of its language will mostly depend on the follow-up. The Compact's non-binding nature means that States may decide which parts to implement, or whether not to implement it at all. The Compact stipulates in this respect: 'We will review the progress made at the local, national, regional and global levels in implementing the Global Compact in the framework of the United Nations through a State-led approach and with the participation of all relevant stakeholders.[46] It also renamed the High-Level Dialogue on International Migration and Development into the 'International Migration Review Forum' ('IMRF'), which will take place every four years (from 2022), and will serve as the main platform to discuss progress.[47] The review at the global level should be complemented with reviews at the regional and national levels.[48] It is up to the President of the UNGA to organise consultations on the precise modalities of the IMRF and its link with the other review processes.[49] The Compact will also establish 'a capacity-building mechanism' whereby the UN, Member States, and private donors bring together technical, financial, and human resources to foster its implementation.[50]

Much of this implementation remains a void to this day. In particular, not much is known about how the Compact's implementation will be funded. On 2 January 2019, the President of the UNGA announced that the Permanent Representatives of Bangladesh and Spain will lead the intergovernmental consultations, to be finalised by 31 July 2019, in order to determine the modalities and organisational aspects of the International Migration Review Forum.[51] At the end of February 2019, some events were held at the UN in New York, among others – but not solely – focusing on the implementation of the Compact, including an international expert symposium[52], a one-day meeting on international migration and development[53], and a conference on youth and migration organised by the

---

46   Compact, para. 48.
47   Compact, para. 49.
48   Compact, paras 50 and 53, respectively.
49   Compact, para. 54.
50   Compact, para. 43.
51   President of the UNGA, 'Appointment of Co-Facilitators for the International Migration Review Forums' (21 December 2018) www.un.org/pga/73/2018/12/21/appointment-of-co-facilitators-for-the-international-migration-review-forums/ accessed 13 March 2019.
52   President of the UNGA, 'Opening Statement at the Expert Symposium On International Migration And Development' (26 February 2019) www.un.org/pga/73/2019/02/26/opening-statement-at-the-expert-symposium-on-international-migration-and-development/ accessed 13 March 2019.
53   High Level Debate on International Migration and Development, 'Statement by H.E. Mrs. María Fernanda Espinosa Garcés' (27 February 2019) www.un.org/pga/73/2019/02/27/high-level-debate-on-international-migration-and-development-4/ accessed 13 March 2019.

IOM.[54] Additionally, the UN Network on Migration[55], set up in December 2018, has scheduled consultations with NGOs on 4 April 2019 in Geneva.[56] One of the Network's tasks is also to establish the abovementioned capacity-building mechanism, which will, among others, consist of a start-up fund.[57] The fund will rely on voluntary contributions[58], and will be administered by the UN Multi-Partner Trust Fund Office[59], which also supported the Compact's intergovernmental conference and its preparatory process.[60]

Aside from its generally woolly and imprecise language, and its non-committal character, most experts agree that the Compact represents a milestone. After decades of slow development of the global migration governance architecture, the Compact offers a confirmation of the need to embed migration in formal, global (UN) cooperation structures, and sets out a direction for the future. It reaffirms the recognition of the importance of meeting human rights obligations – in total it counts 45 references to human rights – in the context of migration management. The Compact thus forms an important recognition that States cannot relieve themselves of the human rights commitments to which they have bound themselves, also with regard to migrants. At the same time, as stated above, the document does not contain any 'new rights': it merely further contributes to a human rights based approach to migration, an approach first inserted as part of the second High-Level Dialogue on Migration and Development in 2013. Dotted with human rights language and references to existing human rights instruments, the Compact endorses the principles of non-regression, *non-refoulement*[61], and non-discrimination.[62]

---

[54] See unofficeny.iom.int/international-dialogue-migration-youth-and-migration accessed 13 March 2019.

[55] Ana Maria Lebada, 'UN Launches Migration Network to Support Global Compact's Implementation' (*SDG Knowledge Hub*, 18 December 2018) sdg.iisd.org:443/news/un-launches-migration-network-to-support-global-compacts-implementation/ accessed 13 March 2019.

[56] European Council on Refugee and Exiles (ECRE), Platform for International Cooperation on Undocumented Migrants (PICUM), 'Implementing the Global Compact on Refugees and the Global Compact on Safe, Regular and Orderly Migration – What Role for the EU?' (6 February 2019) picum.org/wp-content/uploads/2019/02/GCR-and-GCM-joint-event-report-1.pdf accessed 13 March 2019.

[57] Compact, para. 43.

[58] Ibid.

[59] UN, 'Terms of Reference for the UN Network on Migration', 7 www.un.org/en/conf/migration/assets/pdf/UN-Network-on-Migration_TOR.pdf accessed 13 March 2019.

[60] UN, 'UN Multi-Partner Trust Fund to Support the Global Compact for Safe, Orderly and Regular Migration', Trust Fund Fact Sheet mptf.undp.org/factsheet/fund/MCS00 accessed 13 March 2019.

[61] As part of the fourth draft, a reference to *non-refoulement* was added, as well as a non-regression clause, in order to ensure that the Compact could never lead to break the *status quo* in human rights law.

[62] Compact, para. 15f.

II. LEGAL AND POLITICAL STATUS OF THE COMPACT

A. THE (NON-)BINDING NATURE OF THE COMPACT

Most convulsions centred around the legal and political consequences flowing from the Compact, including the binding or otherwise character of the document. Despite its somewhat confusing name, the Compact is not an international treaty, nor an international agreement. In addition, as stated above, it does not generate any new legal obligations for States. But as all international lawyers know, it is not the denomination that matters for establishing the legal nature of an international instrument. The Vienna Convention on the Law of Treaties defines a treaty as 'an international agreement concluded between States in written form and governed by international law, whether embodied in a single instrument or in two or more related instruments and *whatever its particular designation*'.[63] What truly matters to know whether States enter into a legally binding commitment, is their *intent* to create legal effects.[64] That is clearly not the case for the Compact. Although the Compact refers to its objectives as commitments[65], it also explicitly stipulates that it establishes a 'non-legally binding, cooperative framework'.[66] With the specific emphasis on its non-legally binding character, and the rather wide discretion as to the type of actions to be undertaken by the States, it is very clear that there is no intent at all to create legally binding obligations.

In fact, this was an explicit demand from the EU and its Member States during the negotiations.[67] In its 'fact sheet' on the Compact, the European Commission emphasised that 'no legal obligations arise under domestic or international law for participating States'.[68] In addition, the Compact also explicitly stipulates

---

[63] Vienna Convention on the Law of Treaties (adopted 23 May 1969, entered into force 27 January 1980) 1155 UNTS 331, Article 2(1)(a) (emphasis added by the authors).

[64] See Jan Wouters, Cedric Ryngaert, Tom Ruys and Geert De Baere, *International Law: a European Perspective* (Hart Publishing, 2018) 67.

[65] E.g., 'Objective 1: Collect and utilize accurate and disaggregated data as a basis for evidence-based policies (...)[t]o realize this commitment, we will draw from the following actions: a) Elaborate and implement a comprehensive strategy for improving migration data' (Compact, Objective 1).

[66] Compact, paras 7 and 15(b).

[67] 'EU input to the UN Secretary-General's report on the Global Compact on Migration' (18 September 2017) refugeesmigrants.un.org/sites/default/files/stocktaking_eu.pdf accessed 12 March 2019: 'The future Global Compact on Migration should be a non-legally binding document'. This contrasted with OAS, Migration in the Americas (21 June 2017) AG/RES. 2910 (XLVII-O/17); AU, Draft Common African Position (Cap) On The Global Compact For Safe, Orderly And Regular Migration (19 October 2017) AU/STC/MRIDP/4(II). See also Guild and Weatherhead (n44).

[68] European Commission, 'What is the Global Compact For Safe, Orderly And Regular Migration?' (14 November 2018) www.europa.eu/rapid/press-release_MEMO-18–6417_en.htm accessed 25 February 2019.

that it respects the national sovereignty of countries, as it reaffirms the 'sovereign right of States to impose their national migration policy and their prerogative in their jurisdiction, in conformity with international law'.[69] This led the German Ministry of Foreign Affairs to conclude that 'national sovereign rights will not be curtailed nor transferred. The Global Compact will not be an international agreement and will therefore have no legal effect on national legal systems.'[70]

Viewed as a whole, the Compact is a typical example of 'soft law', as often produced as part of UN initiatives: one may think in this respect, for instance, of the Universal Declaration of Human Rights (1948), the Charter for Economic Rights and Duties (1974), and the Rio Declaration on Environment and Development (1992). More recent examples include the UN Global Compact (2000), the Basic Principles and Guidelines on the Right to Remedy and Victims of Gross Violations of International Human Rights Law and Serious Violations of International Humanitarian Law (2006), the UN Global Counter-Terrorism Strategy (2006), the UN Declaration on the Rights of Indigenous Peoples (2007), the UN Global Plan of Action on Combat Trafficking in Persons (2010), and the UN Guiding Principles on Business and Human Rights (2011). In new domains of international law, 'soft law' has proven to be an important technique to build a consensus on certain principles between States in a way that is not yet legally binding.[71]

Apart from this practical consideration, soft law fulfils a number of important functions. It can indicate the potential direction in which new binding norms will develop.[72] Compliance with soft law instruments may lead to their inclusion in new binding instruments or may facilitate a crystallisation process, giving rise to customary international law.[73] The latter would of course require a certain density of State practice over time, and the recognition or acceptance of States that it reflects a legal norm (*opinio juris*).[74] This might prove rather difficult, again, due to the express mention of the non-binding nature of the Compact.

---

[69]   Compact, para. 15(c).

[70]   German Federal Foreign Office, 'A Global Compact for Safe, Orderly and Regular Migration' (3 November 2018) www.auswaertiges-amt.de/en/aussenpolitik/internationale-organisationen/vereintenationen/global-compact-for-migration-/2157720 accessed 12 March 2019.

[71]   See, for more examples, Marc Bossuyt and Jan Wouters, *Grondlijnen van internationaal recht* (Intersentia 2005) 139.

[72]   The Universal Declaration of Human Rights (UNGA Res 217 A (III) (10 December 1948)) is a soft law instrument which, although describing itself only as 'a common standard of achievement', opened the way to the two UN covenants that, together with the Declaration, are considered to constitute the 'international bill of human rights', namely the International Covenant on Civil and Political Rights, and the International Covenant on Economic, Social and Cultural Rights of 1966.

[73]   Anne Peters, 'The Global Compact for Migration: To Sign or Not to Sign?' (*EJIL: Talk!*, 21 November 2018) www.ejiltalk.org/the-global-compact-for-migration-to-sign-or-not-to-sign/ accessed 27 February 2019.

[74]   Wouters, Ryngaert, Ruys and De Baere (n 63) 134.

Alternatively, soft law may also serve as a tool for the interpretation of hard law, by domestic, regional, and international courts.[75]

Two additional elements deserve special attention when we consider the Compact's legal significance. First and foremost, the Compact is not a single document. It must be seen as part of a much broader global governance process of policy coordination. In that respect, the Compact can be considered a further elaboration on the basis of the 2030 Agenda for Sustainable Development[76] of September 2015[77], the 'Addis Ababa Action Agenda' (AAAA) on financing for development of July 2015[78], the Declaration of the 'High-Level Dialogue on International Migration and Development' of October 2013[79] and, last but not least, the New York Declaration for Refugees and Migrants of September 2016.[80] It may be interesting to note that, unlike the Compact itself, all of these aforementioned documents have been adopted by the UNGA by way of consensus.

Secondly, as indicated above, the Compact provides for arrangements on its joint implementation and a follow-up mechanism.[81] The Compact thus serves as a framework for future cooperation on migration, taking into account the existing architecture for development and migration, in the various forms that this may take: bilateral, multilateral, regional, or otherwise.

B.   STATUS OF A POTENTIAL JOINT STATEMENT OR EXPLANATION

A great number of countries, including Belgium, resorted to an explanation of position at the time of their endorsement by the UNGA, in order to address some of their concerns.[82] According to the UN's press release, the Belgian

---

[75]   See e.g., *Hirst v United Kingdom* App no 74025/01 (6 October 2005), para. 71 in which the European Court of Human Rights made reference to the Code of Good Practice in Electoral Matters of the Venice Commission, as one of its tools for interpretation, in order to determine the circumstances in which there may be a deprivation of the right to vote or to be elected.

[76]   In particular, Action Point 10.7 of the Sustainable Development Goals: 'facilitate orderly, safe, and responsible migration and mobility of people, including through implementation of planned and well-managed migration policies'.

[77]   UNGA Res 70/1 (25 September 2015).

[78]   Addis Ababa Action Agenda of Third International Conference on Financing for Development, endorsed by UNGA Res 69/313 (27 July 2015) ('Addis Ababa Action Agenda').

[79]   UNGA Res 68/4 (3 October 2013).

[80]   UNGA Res 71/1 (19 September 2016).

[81]   Compact, para. 15(b).

[82]   In total 49 countries: Fiji, Namibia, Canada, Chile, Ireland, Russian Federation, Singapore, Indonesia, Czech Republic, Poland, China, Comoros, Austria, Lebanon, Bangladesh, Australia, Italy, Slovenia, United Kingdom, Thailand, Nicaragua, Norway, Turkey, Iran, Belgium, Latvia, Ecuador, Estonia, Panama, Myanmar, Romania, Finland, Spain, Peru,

representative stated that 'the Global Compact is not legally binding and underscores the distinction between regular and irregular migration. For these and other reasons, his delegation supports the Global Compact'.[83]

Every State that participated in the Intergovernmental Conference of Marrakech or in the discussion that culminated in the UNGA's endorsement resolution, was free to produce such a statement. This could take the form of a position statement ('explanation of position') or an explanation of vote.[84] The procedural rules of the Intergovernmental Conference provided for the possibility of making a short explanation of vote before or after the vote[85], and this possibility is also provided for in the procedural rules of the UNGA.[86] As such, this is not the same as an 'interpretative declaration': that concept refers to a statement made by a State signing or ratifying a treaty, which reflects the view of that State on the interpretation of a specific treaty provision.[87]

Croatia, Georgia, Jordan, Switzerland, Libya, New Zealand, Republic of Korea, France, Liechtenstein, Egypt, Lithuania, Jamaica, Haiti, Albania and the Republic of Moldova.

[83] See UN, 'General Assembly Endorses First-Ever Global Compact on Migration, Urging Cooperation among Member States in Protecting Migrants' Meetings Coverage (19 December 2018) GA/12113 www.un.org/press/en/2018/ga12113.doc.htm. According to the same press release, the representative of Denmark spoke on behalf of Iceland, Lithuania, Malta and the Netherlands, stating that 'the Global Compact confirms the sovereign right of States to determine their migration policies in conformity with international law. The agreement creates no new legal obligations for States nor does it further international customary law or treaty commitments. States have the sole authority to distinguish between regular and irregular migrants and they will maintain the right to apply criminal law for migrants smuggled onto their territory. Further, issuing documents to migrants will not, unless specifically indicated, imply residency entitlements.'

[84] A position statement is made when a resolution has been adopted with consensus; an explanation of vote in case this has been done by vote. See Permanent Mission of Switzerland to the United Nations, 'The PGA Handbook. A Practical Guide to the United Nations General Assembly' (2011) 55 www.unitar.org/ny/sites/unitar.org.ny/files/UN_PGA_Handbook.pdf accessed 25 February 2019. For this distinction in the practice of the Human Rights Council, see Permanent Mission of Switzerland to the United Nations, 'Le Conseil des droits de l'homme: Guide pratique' (2015) 23 www.eda.admin.ch/dam/eda/fr/documents/publications/InternationaleOrganisationen/Uno/Human-rights-Council-practical-guide_fr accessed 25 February 2019. For examples of explanations of vote after the adoption of a resolution of the UNGA, including by Belgium, see the UN press release following the granting of the status of acting Non-Member Observer State to Palestine on 29 November 2012: UNGA, 'General Assembly Votes Overwhelmingly to Accord Palestine 'Non-Member Observer State' Status in United Nations' Press Release (29 November 2012) GA/11317 www.un.org/press/en/2012/ga11317.doc.htm accessed 25 February 2019.

[85] See UNGA, Provisional Rules of Procedure (22 August 2018) A/CONF.231/2, Rule 39: 'Representatives may make brief statements, consisting solely of explanations of vote, before the voting has commenced or after the voting has been completed. The presiding President may limit the time to be allowed for such explanations. The representative of a State sponsoring a proposal or motion shall not speak in explanation of vote thereon, except if it has been amended.'

[86] UNGA, 'Rules Of Procedure Of The General Assembly' (2008) A/520/Rev.17, Rule 88. See also Annex IV, paras 74–76, and Annex V, paras 6–7.

[87] UN, *Treaty Handbook* (United Nations, 2002) 16.

The following can be noted with regard to the status of the type of statements as made by Belgium in the UNGA. From an *international* legal perspective, such statements form a relevant element for the assessment of State practice and the *opinio juris* of States as part of the investigation into the existence of rules of customary international law.[88] However, an explanation of position or vote to a treaty would not lead to fewer obligations under that treaty for the State concerned, as it does not constitute (in principle) a reservation.[89] At the *domestic* level, such statements can be taken into account by national courts as relevant interpretative information that may help them to determine the extent of the international commitment entered into by their country.

Interestingly, a different approach has been followed by the German federal parliament. The German Bundestag approved the Compact in a vote on 29 November 2018[90], after it had adopted a resolution addressed to the German federal government, clarifying that the Pact does not generate any new legal obligations that may affect German migration legislation or that can be invoked before the German courts and tribunals.[91] In Switzerland, the country presiding the negotiations together with Mexico, the parliamentary involvement ended with a whimper when the parliament took control after a mere consultation, resulting in an abstention on the part of the Swiss government.[92]

III. EFFECTS FOR BELGIUM

The consequences of the Compact for Belgium, after its adoption on 10 December 2018, can be situated both at the international and domestic level.

---

[88] Sean D. Murphy, 'Identification of Customary International Law and Other Topics: The Sixty-Seventh Session of the International Law Commission' (2015) 109 *American Journal of International Law* 822, 825.

[89] Iain Cameron, 'Treaties, Declarations of Interpretation', *Max Planck Encyclopaedia of Public International Law* (2007) paras 3–4 opil.ouplaw.com.kuleuven.ezproxy.kuleuven. be/view/10.1093/law:epil/9780199231690/law-9780199231690-e1686 accessed 27 February 2019.

[90] 'German Bundestag Votes to Support UN Migration Pact' (*DW.COM*, 2018) www.dw.com/en/ german-bundestag-votes-to-support-un-migration-pact/a-46502244 accessed 27 February 2019.

[91] Deutscher Bundestag (27 November 2018) Document 19/6056: '*Der GCM begründet keine einklagbaren Rechte und Pflichten und entfaltet keinerlei rechtsändernde oder rechtssetzende Wirkung. Dazu gehört, das unsere Gesetze – zum Beispiel im Bereich des Ausländer-, des Sozial- und des Staatsbürgerschaftsrechts – sowie unseren behördlichen und gerichtlichen Entscheidungen uneingeschränkt gelten und durchgesetzt werden.*'

[92] Claudia Meier, 'What Now? An Implementation Proposal for the Global Compact for Migration' (*GPPI*, 10 December 2018) www.gppi.net/2018/12/10/what-now-an-implement ation-proposal-for-the-global-compact-for-migration accessed 12 March 2019.

Internationally, there is no legally binding effect, as was mentioned above. Only in so far as the Compact would give rise to the development of one or more international treaty texts at the international level, would there be legally binding consequences, and then obviously only insofar as Belgium would express its sovereign consent to be bound by such treaty/treaties. Another possibility would be the gradual establishment of customary international law in the field of migration. However, in light of the very polemic and politicised context of the debates, we currently seem rather far from this.[93]

Another possibility is that an international court would use the Compact to strengthen the existing international law obligations of Belgium. Reference is often made in this respect – and Paul will pay particular attention to this – to the European Court of Human Rights ('ECtHR'). Indeed, the ECtHR often cites non-binding instruments (besides treaties and national legislation) in its decisions. However, it does so mostly in the 'introductory part' of its decisions, and rarely uses them in the operative part of its decisions. For instance, in its judgment of 4 December 2007[94], the ECtHR referred to the 1957 UN Standard Minimum Rules for the Treatment of Prisoners. In its judgment of 27 September 1995, the ECtHR referred to the 1990 UN Basic Principles on the Enforcement and Enforcement Officials, and to the 1989 UN Principles on the Effective Protection and Investigation of Extra-Legal, Arbitrary and Summary Executions.[95] An example of a reference in the operative part is provided in the *Hirst v United Kingdom* judgment of 6 October 2005[96], in which the ECtHR made reference to the Code of Good Practice in Electoral Matters of the Venice Commission. It did, however, not employ such references as a stand-alone basis for deducing rights or obligations from them. Instead, the ECtHR used the code as one of its tools for interpretation[97], in order to determine the circumstances in which there may be a deprivation of the right to vote or to be elected; a right that has its own basis in Article 25 of the International Covenant on Civil and Political Rights.

As far as *domestic law* is concerned, the following may be noted. Belgium has a 'monist' tradition, in which international and national law are part of the same legal order.[98] This means that it is relatively easy for legal practitioners to invoke international standards, including soft law, before Belgium's courts and

---

93   With the exception of some basic principles such as *non-refoulement*.
94   *Dickson v UK App no 44362/04* (4 December 2007) para 30.
95   *McCann and Others v United Kingdom* App no 8984/91 27 September 1995, paras 138 and 140.
96   *Hirst v United Kingdom* App no 74025/01 (6 October 2005).
97   Ibid para. 71.
98   Bossuyt and Wouters (n 70) 148: [m]ost monistic systems assume that, in the event of incompatibility between national rules with international rules, the latter must be given priority and that in that case the national court must disregard the conflicting national rule' (authors' translation).

tribunals. This does happen quite frequently. However, it would be wrong to assume that Belgian judges would give an inappropriate scope to these standards. A sample from the case law of the Belgian Council of State[99] and the Council for Alien Litigation[100] seems to indicate that soft law is by no means considered binding or used as such. For instance, in its judgment of 18 September 2018 the Council for Alien Litigation again confirmed that resolutions of the UNGA are not legally binding in the Belgian legal order.[101]

What Belgian courts and tribunals do, is to use guidelines drawn up by UNHCR to interpret existing concepts; to the benefit of the (candidate) refugee, but also to the benefit of the government. To illustrate, in its judgment of 10 January 2017, the Council for Alien Litigation refers to the UNHCR's Guide to procedures and criteria for determining refugee status to clarify that 'prosecution or punishment for the purpose of refusing to perform conscription, in the context of a settlement to which all subjects are subject, cannot in principle be regarded as prosecution within the meaning of the Refugee Convention'.[102] In addition, in its judgment of 18 November 2014, the Council relies on the same guide to state that 'the burden of proof regarding the validity of an asylum application' lies in principle with the asylum seeker himself, and that the benefit of the doubt can only be allowed 'if all elements are examined and convinced of the credibility of the statements made'.[103] Besides, the Council for Alien Litigation[104] and the Office of the Commissioner General for Refugees and Stateless Persons ('CGRS')[105] also regularly rely on reports of NGOs such as Human Rights Watch or of international bodies such as UNHCR, to examine and sketch the situation in the country of origin.

CONCLUDING OBSERVATIONS

The UN Global Compact for Safe, Orderly and Regular Migration is definitely not a perfect instrument. The very nature of the intergovernmental process through which it came about has clearly affected it, both in terms of legal

---

[99] See e.g., RvS no 104.622 (13 March 2002); RvS no 126.922 (7 January 2003); RvS no 144.115 (4 May 2005); and, RvS no 155.998 (8 March 2006).
[100] See e.g., Case no 173.179 (4 July 2007); Case no 215 633 (24 January 2019); and, Case no 216 299 (31 January 2019).
[101] Case no 209.512 (18 September 2018).
[102] Case no 180.514 (10 January 2017) *Tijdschrift voor Vreemdelingenrecht* (427) 428.
[103] Case no 133.338 (18 November 2014) 10.
[104] See e.g. Case no 214 634 (28 December 2018) 6.
[105] The decisions on applications for international protection are not public. However, to illustrate, the country reports the CGRS relies on in taking its decisions, do so as well. See e.g., CGRS, 'Veiligheidssituatie In Mogadishu' (25 September 2018) www.cgrs.be/en/country-information/veiligheidssituatie-mogadishu-0 accessed 12 March 2019.

protection[106] and operational commitments.[107] A better communication on the international and national levels could have potentially prevented the late drop-outs of States which had the opportunity to fully influence its content. But, overall, the Compact is a considerable achievement, both politically and in terms of its content. In a field were common bases for discussion' were practically non-existent, the Compact constitutes a milestone, as it opened up opportunities for dialogue and cooperation and could act as a new standard of behaviour for the future.

However, the real litmus test will be the ability to transform these opportunities into action, for which more efforts will be needed. Given its woolly language, and non-elaborated implementation and review mechanisms, the Compact is a classic case of 'the proof of the pudding will be in the eating'. Despite its political importance, the Compact cannot be implemented in its current form. Therefore, NGOs and other observers have been active in facilitating discussions and formulating recommendations on the next steps to be taken.[108] One should, among others, define what each of the 'objectives' and 'actions' will mean in practice, in particular in view of the global (para. 49) and regional review (para. 50). What indicators will be used to measure progress? What are the priorities in reviewing progress? In addition, at what level should actions be implemented, as many of them mention several levels – and thus decision-makers – at once? Here, a crucial responsibility rests with the States, as the final text of the Compact stipulates: 'We will review the progress made at local, national, regional and global levels in implementing the Global Compact in the framework of the United Nations through *a State-led approach* and with the participation of all relevant stakeholders'.[109]

This is also where a lot is at stake for the EU. For quite some time, there was no clarity on the role of the EU during the negotiations of the Compact. Around the time of their beginning, it was held that the EU's public involvement in the

---

106   E.g., detention of children, and the concept of 'firewalls' (between enforcement authorities and entities providing services to irregular migrants).

107   The zero draft deferred until 2026 the discussion of specific measures to strengthen the global governance of international migration (New York Declaration, para. 49), but this paragraph did not make it to the final draft.

108   See e.g., Elspeth Guild and Tugba Basaran, 'The UN's Global Compact for Safe, Orderly and Regular Migration:
Analysis of the Final Draft and Monitoring Implementation' (*Refugee Law Initiative*, 17 September 2018) rli.blogs.sas.ac.uk/themed-content/global-compact-for-migration/; ECRE, and PICUM, 'Implementing the Global Compact on Refugees and the Global Compact on Safe, Regular and Orderly Migration – What Role for the EU?' (6 February 2019) picum.org/wp-content/uploads/2019/02/GCR-and-GCM-joint-event-report-1.pdf   accessed 13 March 2019.

109   Compact, para. 48 (emphasis added).

negotiations would be limited to an observer status.[110] But in the course of the Compact's genesis, the European Commission expressed its commitment to the implementation of the Compact.[111] Likewise, the European Parliament expressed its support with a resolution in April 2018.[112] By contrast, the Romanian Presidency of the Council has remained rather silent on the part envisaged for the EU in the implementation of the Compact. Crucially, Romania was among the twelve abstaining countries, together with four other EU Member States. The EU will have to do a good deal of critical introspection and soul-searching in light of the three-split vote of its membership at the UNGA in December 2018. All of this has the potential to complicate the implementation process and undermine cooperation within the EU.

Nevertheless, the coming months also offer opportunities. On 8 April 2019, a meeting of the High Level Working Group on Asylum and Migration and the EU's Working Group on UN matters (CONUN) is scheduled to take place. This offers an opportunity to discuss the implementation of both Global Compacts. In addition, the European Commission has carried out a 'fitness check' of existing legislation on legal migration of which the results are expected to be published soon. These results could be another trigger for discussions, including on the Compact.[113] Using the Compact as a guide for discussions and action on migration within the Union could move the EU and its Member States beyond the current impasse.[114] If, however, they would fail to do so, it could take a long time before another similar *momentum* will be found.

---

[110] EC, 'What Is The Global Compact For Safe, Orderly And Regular Migration?' Fact Sheet (14 November 2018) europa.eu/rapid/press-release_MEMO-18–6417_en.htm accessed 13 March 2019.

[111] EC, 'EU and IOM strengthen ties on global migration' (9 March 2017) ec.europa.eu/echo/news/eu-and-iom-strenghten-ties-global-migration_en accessed 13 March 2019; Apap (n14) 7: 'Under the European Commission's 2017 annual work programme, the Directorate-General for International Cooperation and Development (DG DEVCO) had earmarked €1.7 million in support of the migration compact process.'

[112] European Parliament, 'Addressing refugee and migrant movements: the role of EU external action' (5 April 2017) P8_TA(2017)0124.

[113] ECRE, and PICUM, 'Implementing the Global Compact on Refugees and the Global Compact on Safe, Regular and Orderly Migration – What Role for the EU?' (6 February 2019) 5 picum.org/wp-content/uploads/2019/02/GCR-and-GCM-joint-event-report-1.pdf accessed 13 March 2019.

[114] Sergio Carrera, Karel Lannoo, Marco Stefan and Lina Vosyliūtė, 'Some EU governments leaving the UN Global Compact on Migration: A contradiction in terms?' *CEPS Policy Insights* No 2018/15 (November 2018) 9 www.ceps.eu/system/files/PI2018_15_SCKLMSVL_UN%20Global%20Compact_0.pdf accessed 13 March 2019.

INTERNATIONAL HUMAN RIGHTS LAW VALUES AND THE FIGHT AGAINST TERRORISM

The *Abu Ghraib* Case and the European Vision of the U.S. *War on Terror*

Joaquín González Ibáñez*

*Professor of International Law and International Relations
at Alfonso X University, Madrid
Co-director of the Human Rights Berg Institute*

*Honoring the human and academic legacy of my professor and friend Paul Lemmens
for whom human rights, respect and a positive and constructive approach to life
have been his perennial and active legacy among us. Thank you Paul!*
Joaquín González Ibáñez

"Our Constitution and our philosophy of law have been characterized by a regard for the broadest possible liberty of the individual. But the dullest mind must now see that our national society cannot be so self-sufficient and so isolated that freedom, security, and opportunity of our own citizens can be assured by good domestic laws alone. Forces originating outside of our borders and not subject to our laws have twice in my lifetime disrupted our way of living, demoralized our economy, menaced the security of life, liberty, and property within our country. The assurance of our fundamental law that the citizen's life may not be taken without due process of law is of little avail against a foreign aggressor or against the necessities of war. Either submission or resistance will take life, liberty, and property without a semblance of due process of law [...]

*   I would like to state my gratitude to Professor Jamin B. Raskin who read the first draft of this essay and made important observations and comments about its content and form, as well as Guy Harpaz from Hebrew University of Jerusalem and Juan Carlos Sáinz Borgo from the United Nations Peace University of Costa Rica for their insight and constructive critiques to the ideas presented in this essay.

But we are at this moment at one of those infrequent occasions in history when convulsions have uprooted habit and tradition in a large part of the world and there exists not only opportunity, but necessity as well, to reshape some institutions and practices which sheer inertia would otherwise make invulnerable [...] But we can have nothing in common with the cynics who would have us avoid disillusionment by having no ideals, who think that because they do not believe in anything, they cannot be fooled. We must keep the faith roughly stated by Lord Chief Justice Coke that even the King is 'under God and the law [...]'

Any United Nations court that would try, say, Hitler or Goebbels would face the same choice. That is one of the risks that are taken whenever trials are commenced. The ultimate principle is that you must put no man on trial under the forms of judicial proceedings if you are not willing to see him freed if not proven guilty."

Robert H. Jackson, *The Rule of Law Among Nations*,
Conference at the American Society of International Law,
Washington, D.C. April 13, 1945

I. INTRODUCTION

More than a decade has passed since the events referred to in this text took place in the Abu Ghraib detention center in Iraq. Nevertheless, in 2019 perspective helps to ascertain in a more adequate way the different approaches of the American and European Union democracies that have fought against terrorism, after the terrorist attacks of September 11, 2001.

Two Presidential terms of Barack Obama and the current presidency of Donald Trump do not leave much room for a positive and realistic interpretation about the reinforcement of International Rule of Law and multilateralism. The lessons learnt about the shutdown of the detention center of Abu Ghraib and the impossibility of putting an end to Guantanamo as a prison for detainees seem today like an extraneous outcome, legal and ethical.

Nowadays the perspective of time prompts us to have a broader interpretation and leads us to the conclusion that democracies have not been imaginative or have interiorized the lessons of how best to protect its principles and strengthen their democratic institutions while fighting international terrorism.

II. A VISION OF HUMAN RIGHTS
AND THE RULE OF LAW AFTER ABU GHRAIB

A. ABU GHRAIB

One of Fernando Botero's paintings on the events that took place at Abu Ghraib prison portrays the image of a black-hooded figure standing on top of a box.[1] A person is naked beneath the black robe with outstretched arms from which wires run to some unseen source of electricity. This was one of the horrendous images that became public in April 2004 just hours after a U.S. government attorney had assured the Supreme Court that no detainee had endured torture at U.S. hands.[2] When the CBS news program *60 Minutes* ran the photograph of this scene, which served as the model for Botero's painting, the words that flashed up on the screen were: "Americans did this to an Iraqi prisoner."[3]

Botero walks in the path of other artists who have wanted to bear witness to the brutality of war. Francisco de Goya's "Disasters of War" (1812–1815) is one of the most graphic images to come out of the ruthless guerrilla war in the Iberian Peninsula. Goya's purpose was to keep faith with what happened through powerful black and white drawings that contain disturbing scenes of horror, brutality, torture and the savagery of war.[4] Pablo Picasso's famous 1937 painting "Guernica" was a silent but startling cry of pain at the pointless suffering inflicted on the civilian victims of wars.

Art and memory go hand in hand. The hooded face of Abu Ghraib, as the dark symbol of the American presence in Iraq, will certainly go down permanently in history. In future decades, the invasion of Iraq and all the specific accompanying fiascoes of the Bush Administration will dissolve from our memories. But still there will be a permanent memory inscribed in art, such as Fernando Botero's

---

[1] The Fernando Botero's Abu Ghraib series was presented for the first time to the American public, at American University, Washington, November 2007, available at www1.american. edu/cas/katzen/museum/2007nov_botero.cfm.

[2] Rumsfeld v. Padilla, 124 S. Ct. 2711 (2004); Rasul v. Bush, 124 S. Ct. 2686 (2004); Hamdi v. Rumsfeld, 124 S. Ct. 2633 (2004). Yaser Handi, an American citizen, was released after three years in custody. See. Diane Marie Amann, Abu Ghraib. *University of Pennsylvania Law Review*, Vol. 153, p. 2085, 2005, p. 2, available at SSRN: http://ssrn.com/abstract=951874.

[3] CBS News, *60 minutes*, April 28, 2004, available at www.cbsnews.com/stories/2004/04/27/60II/main614063.shtml.

[4] In one of the *Goya's Desastres* a wolf in *Goya's Desastre n. 74* you can read "¡Mísera humanidad. La culpa es tuya!" ("Miserable humanity. The fault is thine!") writes a wolf in Desastre n. 74. This comment, visible to the viewer, reflects quite accurately the artist's spirits during the Independence War, which entailed the material and moral ruin of Spain, as well as during the years that followed led by Ferdinand VII's absolutist reaction, which brought about the loss of a great part of the progress attained so arduously by the liberals in the Spanish 1812 Constitution.

paintings, that will prompt observers to ask themselves how it was possible that the oldest and greatest democracy on Earth betrayed its most important legacy to humankind: the rebellion against torture and cruelty in favor of human rights.

Prof. Diane Marie Amann reminds us that in the April 2004 argument in the *Hamdi case*, Justice John Paul Stevens asked Deputy Solicitor General Paul D. Clement:

> "But do you think there is anything in the law that curtails the method of interrogation that may be employed?" "I think that the United States is signatory to conventions that prohibit torture and that sort of thing,"

Clement firmly responded:

> "And the United States is going to honor its treaty obligations."

Afterwards, he pointed out that he could see no "basis for bringing a private cause of action against the United States".[5]

This contribution will *not* address the issue of which international or national laws – including the U.S. Constitution and several federal statutes, as well as judicial interpretations of statutes and the Constitution, military regulations, rules regarding detention found in customary international law and in treaties ratified by the United States, such as the Geneva Conventions on the laws of war, the Convention Against Torture, and the International Covenant on Civil and Political Rights – have been violated in the post-9/11 *War on Terror* conducted by the Bush Administration. Neither will we discuss what we believe to be wrongdoing and illegal policies in the international and domestic arena – Guantanamo, the Iraq War and Afghanistan secret detention facilities, Warrantless Surveillance programs, extraordinary rendition, torture memos and executive orders – beyond the constitutional limits. The goal is to understand if in the year 2019 the legal practice and the political and historical legacy after the 9/11 terrorist attacks and the 2003 invasion of Iraq really meant a new paradigm for the U.S. and the European democracies on how to fight terrorism, or on the contrary if it meant a weakening of international human rights standards and a "merger" of American and European visions.

---

5   See Diane Marie Amann, *Abu Ghraib* and note 15 *Id.* at 49. Clement mentioned only the Torture Victims Protection Act of 1991, Pub. L. No. 102–256, 106 Stat. 73 (codified at 28 U.S.C.A §1350 note) (allowing private lawsuit by person who suffers torture at hands of agent of a "foreign nation"), a statute that he correctly stated would provide no basis for relief. Transcript of Oral Argument at 49, *Hamdi* (No. 03–6696).

We assume that there are already clear international standards for addressing issues such as the treatment of "non-combatants" who commit atrocities, as Prof. Robert Goldman pointed out.

"Despite the fact that they call it terrorism, the law of war still applies. We didn't cease applying the law of war in World War II because the SS followed the German troops and committed terrorist acts… If we (Americans) can claim to justify this, our adversaries will say they can do this to us as well."[6] America undoubtedly has the most exposed military in the world because of its presence overseas of around 300.000 military personnel. It is irrelevant if prisoners under U.S. custody at Abu Ghraib or Guantanamo Bay are considered prisoners of war, civilians, or unprivileged combatants who may have engaged in terrorist violence; they are both legally responsible for their acts and protected by the law of war and human rights law. "It makes no difference how you classify them, (…) No one can be subjected to torture or inhumane treatment."[7]

---

[6]　See Sally Acharya, *Law professor defends human rights*, published at American Weekly, March 22, 2005.

[7]　See, *Protection of human rights and fundamental freedoms while countering terrorism*, Note by the United Nations High Commissioner for Human Rights, The High Commissioner for Human Rights 2004, Robert K. Goldman, p. 10 GE.05–10694 (E) 150205 E/CN.4/2005/103:
"C. The applicability and relevance of international humanitarian law when confronting terrorism involves armed conflict 16. A key issue affecting the protection of human rights in the struggle against terrorism concerns the divergent views of States about the nature of the struggle and, particularly, the measures they have employed in responding to it. Since 11 September 2001, some States, without disregarding the need for international cooperation, see this struggle as a new kind of war against a global terrorist network which essentially requires a military response. Other States, without discounting the use of military force in certain circumstances, view this struggle as not an entirely new phenomenon which requires enhanced international cooperation in law enforcement, intelligence gathering and sharing, extradition, and the like.
17. However States conceive of the struggle against terrorism, it is both legally and conceptually important that acts of terrorism not be invariably conflated with acts of war. For example, attacks against civilians, the taking of hostages, and the seizure and destruction of civilian aircraft are accepted by the international community to be forms of terrorism. But these acts can take place during peacetime, emergency situations or situations of armed conflict. If committed during an armed conflict, such acts may constitute war crimes. However, when such acts take place during peacetime or an emergency not involving hostilities, as is frequently the case, they simply do not constitute war crimes, and their perpetrators should not be labeled, tried or targeted as combatants. Such situations are governed not by international humanitarian law, but by international human rights law, domestic law and, perhaps, international criminal law […] Because denial of POW status to combatants potentially entails life or death consequences for the persons concerned, such status determinations should be made in strict conformity with applicable laws and procedures. In this regard, article 5 of the Geneva Convention relative to the Treatment of Prisoners of War (Third Geneva Convention) creates a presumption that a person who commits a hostile act is a POW unless a competent tribunal determines otherwise on an individualized basis.
23. Human rights law does not cease to apply when the struggle against terrorism involves armed conflict. Rather, it applies cumulatively with international humanitarian law…"

In the past, the Legal System in the U.S. and the Army manual of 1992 stated that International Conventions ratified by the U.S. and U.S. policy "expressly prohibit acts of violence or intimidation, including physical or mental torture, threats, insults, or exposure to inhumane treatment as a means of or aid in interrogation." The torture methods used by U.S. personnel "will bring discredit upon the U.S. and its armed forces while undermining domestic and international support for the war effort."[8]

In April 2009, Eric Holder, the U.S. Attorney General in the Obama Administration, speaking at the West Point Academy, stated that, "We will not sacrifice our values or trample on our Constitution under the false premise that it is the only way to protect our national security."[9] Months before, in the same respect, some leaders of the U.S. Army during the Bush Administration, like Major General Stone, who successfully shut down Abu Ghraib as a detention and torture facility in 2006, remained faithful to the law and transmitted the idea that America could only win the *War on Terror* – the hearts and minds of people around the world – with the respect and strength of American ideals. Even in detention facilities like Abu Ghraib, those ideals must prevail. Only policies inspired and guided by American values will ultimately legitimize the American effort in Iraq.

May 2007 saw one of the most violent periods, with indiscriminate attacks against the Iraqi population and the highest number of American soldiers killed (904 U.S. soldiers were killed in 2007).[10] During this time, the General that appointed Stone, General Petraeus, sent a reassuring message to the American troops, the American people and American allies from Bagdad.

> "Our values and the laws governing warfare teach us to respect human dignity, maintain our integrity, and do what is right. Adherence to our values distinguishes us from our enemy [...]
> What sets us apart from our enemies in this fight [...] is how we behave. In everything we do, we must observe the standards and values that dictate that we treat noncombatants and detainees with dignity and respect. While we are warriors, we are also human beings."[11]

---

8   See Louis Fisher, *The Constitution and 9/11. Recurring threat to America' s freedoms*, University Press of Kansas, Lawrence, 2008, p. 213, U.S. Department of the Army, FM34–52 Intelligence Interrogation, September 28, 1992, at 1–7.

9   See, *Eric Holder tells West Point: The law was not always followed in U.S. war against terror* by Jim Fitzgerald Associated Press, Wednesday April 15, 2009, at www.therightreasons.net/index.php?showtopic=14141.

10 See *Iraq Coaliation Casualty Count*, http://icasualties.org/Iraq/index.aspx, May 1, 2009.

11 Communication of Commander General Petraeus, Headquarter, Multi-National Force-Iraq, Baghdad, Iraq, APO AE 09342–1400. This paragraph was quoted in the *Senate Armed Services Committee Inquiry into the treatment of detainees in U.S. Custody, Executive Summary January,* 2008, p. XII of the report. This Senate Report underlined detailed evidence

International Law scholars, researchers, and observers of the violations of the Laws of the War in the last 40 years are poisoned by the Greek myth of Cassandra (Κασσάνδρα). Once the observer believes that he or she knows a catastrophic event will happen in the future, having already seen it repeated in prior conflicts in the last 40 years (or even experienced it first hand), the observer believes that there is nothing that can be done to stop the event from happening the same way again and, especially, that nobody will believe what he or she tries to tell others. One cinematic example of a Cassandra warning would be the powerful documentary on the Vietnam War, *Hearts and Minds*, directed by Peter Davis in 1974. This appalling subject of the work seems to be replicated in the documentary *Control Room* directed by Jehane Noujaim in 2004 focusing on the war in Iraq and the role played by Al Jazira. The script in some scenes is almost identical in the two films. In the two movies the characters have different names, are set in different time periods and different countries but the scenes are the same: weeping mothers and fathers clutching the corpses of their children and howling, "this is the freedom the U.S. is bringing us [...]". The two movies reveal a consistent lack of empathy and comprehension for other people, as in the scene where General Westmoreland states after a heartbreaking image of two children weeping at their father's grave: "The oriental does not put the same high price on life as those in the West. Life is cheap to the oriental as if the philosophy of the oriental expresses it, life is not important".

The Abu Ghraib torture episode has severely shocked the American public, which is in disbelief that it could be implicated in such horrors and that the nation could be so humiliated both internally and overseas.[12]

---

that the military's use of harsh interrogation methods on terrorism suspects was approved at the higher level of the Bush Administration. It discarded claims by former Defense Secretary Rumsfeld and others that Pentagon policies played no role in harsh treatment of prisoners at Abu Ghraib prison in Iraq or other military facilities.

The Senate report explained how some of the techniques used by the military at prisons in Afghanistan and at the naval base in Guantánamo Bay, Cuba, as well as in Iraq – stripping detainees, placing them in "stress positions" or depriving them of sleep – were originally conceived in a military program known as Survival Evasion Resistance and Escape, or SERE, intended to train American troops to resist abusive enemy interrogations.

This report showed that Mr. Rumsfeld's authorization was cited by a United States military special-operations lawyer in Afghanistan as "an analogy and basis for use of these techniques," See Brian Knowlton, *Report Gives New Detail on Approval of Brutal Techniques*, The New York Times, April 22, 2009.

12 See Erica Jong and her story titled *Botero Sees the World's True Heavies at Abu Ghraib*, published at Special to The Washington Post, Sunday, November 4, 2007; "But American torture is different from other tortures because of the high opinion we have of our country and ourselves. Torture is something others do. We are above that. We are reasonable people governed by a great Enlightenment document we call The Constitution. We help, not hurt people all over the world. It is the incongruity of our image of ourselves versus the reality of our behavior that stings most."

B. THE EUROPEAN VISION OF THE *WAR ON TERROR*. THE UNITED STATES AS GUARDIAN OR VIOLATOR OF RULE OF LAW: EUROPE'S PERSPECTIVE ON AMERICA IN THE POST-9/11 WORLD

1. Democratic values and European reasons

The post-9/11 era presents numerous challenges to the concept of law as a system that guarantees both liberty and security, and that provides an effective response to terrorism. In European eyes, Executive Orders from the President of the United States, George W. Bush, allowing U.S. officials to conduct "enhanced techniques of interrogation" – torture – have undermined the United States' reputation for respecting and following the law and has dramatically affected its political influence.[13] By using torture, the United States has wounded itself and helped its enemies in what is, in the final analysis, an inherently political conflict, a conflict where the critical target to be conquered is the allegiances and attitudes of young Muslims. By torturing prisoners, even no doubt with some of them implicated in committing serious crimes against Americans, the United States has made it impossible to render justice in their cases. Instead of providing due process within the rule of law, the U.S. sent them into an "endless limbo of injustice."[14] The reaction against this type of abuse of power is also reshaping an 'atlas of upset actors' in the international arena, as Dominique Moisi has defined in *The Geopolitics of Emotion: How Cultures of Fear, Humiliation, and Hope are Reshaping the World*.[15]

The foreign policy of the United States in the following decades after the terrorist attacks of September 11 has been defined and justified by America's role as protector of rule of law and democracy. On the other hand, in purporting to extend the rule of law and democratic principles throughout the world, the U.S. has in other respects severely compromised its commitment to these principles. Perception of the U.S. has become at best confused and at worst largely perverted as a result of its contradictory role *vis-à-vis* democratic norms and freedoms. Prof. Claudio Grossman[16] has for many years fostered the idea of law as a system that provides spheres of liberties and responsibilities, and one of the most important human tools for freedom and liberty. We share the same ideas around

---

[13] See A. Daugherty Miles, *Perspectives on Enhanced Interrogation Technique*, Congressional Research Services, January 8, 2016 available at https://fas.org/sgp/crs/intel/R43906.pdf.

[14] See Mark Danner, "The Red Cross Torture Report: What It Means," The New York Times Review of Books, Volume 56, Number 7, April 30, 2009.

[15] Dominique Moisi, *The Geopolitics of Emotion: How Cultures of Fear, Humiliation, and Hope are Reshaping the World*, Doubleday, New York, 2009.

[16] Claudio Grossman is Dean of American University-Washington College of Law and Chair of the United Nations Committee against torture.

the Rule of Law, and the pursuit of justice, and that is probably the reason of the uncomfortable and critical European vision that constantly checks the commitment of the U.S. as a leading nation and the most important partner for western allies.

The twenty-first century, born in the wake of the horrendous terrorist attacks in New York City, Washington, D.C. in 2001, London 2005 (the Underground and bus bombings), Madrid 2004 (train attacks) and Paris 2015 (Saint Dennis Stadium and Bataclan Theatre) epitomizes a new and complex period in history. Despite the inherent difficulties we face in ascertaining the direction of history, the principles of democracy and respect for human rights and market freedom will remain the main guidelines for the international community. The United States has historically taken the lead toward the promotion of democracy and market freedom. After September 11, that framework was re-designed as the U.S. appears to have traded some of its commitment to human rights and Rule of Law for the presumed safety and security of its citizens.

Primo Levi wrote in his book *La chiave a stella*[17] that "bridges are the opposite to frontiers." Bridges try to unify different realities, while frontiers may even destroy common and continuous realities. Bridges are needed nowadays in politics, international law, diplomacy, multilateralism and morality. As Levi noted, we need constantly to build up "bridges" among nations, cultures and civilizations and to avoid the construction of new frontiers that tend to separate and divide us. As Europeans, we observe the U.S. foreign action critically, but at the same time we respect and admire it for the functioning of the Rule of Law, its political institutions and the lack of authoritarian or undemocratic periods in its recent history. Those are "the active bridges" and the language used by any democratic regime to strengthen its leadership among democratic friends. Rule of law and respect for human rights form the common language and tradition of Western democratic States after the end World War II, even more pervasively after the fall of the Berlin Wall. One of the main goals of this contribution is to underline the common legal tradition and how the difference becomes alarming when there is not a thorough guarantee of Rule of Law, even in times of terrorism threat.

The aspiration of strengthening institutions and the Rule of Law has become part of the new goals of the United Nations, together with UN Charter articles 1 and 2 and the Sustainable Development Goals approved by the General Assembly in 2015.[18] In 2004, Kofi Annan, then UN Secretary-General, placed the international Rule of Law at the very heart of the organization's mission:

---

[17]   *La chiave a stella*, (The Wrench), Einaudi Editori, Torino, 1978.
[18]   A/RES/70/1, 18th September 2015, *Transforming our world: the 2030 Agenda for Sustainable Development*.

"(The Rule of Law) refers to principles of governance in which all persons, institutions and entities, public and private, including the State itself, are accountable to laws that are publicly promulgated, equally enforced and independently adjudicated, and which are consistent with international human rights norms and standards. It requires, as well, equality before the law, accountability to the law, fairness in the application of the law, separation of powers, participation in decision-making, legal certainty, avoidance of arbitrariness and procedural and legal transparency."[19]

In former times we understood the functioning of the *"Raison d'Etat,"* the *"National Interest"* and, during the Cold War, *"National security."* These concepts had a historical context and justification, but in 2019 *none* of the public policies of any Western State is sustainable without including an active respect for international human rights treaties and International Humanitarian Law. These principles are not to be considered "soft law" but as an integral part of law itself. Rule of law, accountability, and human rights are the heart, the mind, and the soul of democratic systems. Because the darkest episodes of humankind in the last century were created by Europeans – Colonialism, First and Second World Wars and the Holocaust – we believe deeply that the strengthening of the democratic system depends on the recognition of International Law as a binding limit for the respect of individual dignity. This is especially true in a global period with violent threats and a worldwide contest for power and legitimacy.

I frequently ask myself as a citizen and a Law professor if our responsibilities are always to improve human conditions and if law continues to be an effective and necessary means for that end. Progress means real enjoyment of rights, especially for the most vulnerable.

The year 1989 saw the fall of the Berlin Wall and the students' revolt in Tiananmen Square. About 3000 people were killed in one night, almost the same number as the people killed and *desaparecidos* (missing) during the *Coup d'Etat* of Augusto Pinochet and the years of his dictatorship. Apart from being a totalitarian regime, China's leaders did not respond in the domestic or international domain for the crimes committed as China was a superpower during the Cold War and at the beginning of the new period. Among other reasons argued by China were the UN Charter, Article 2.7 and the consideration of Human Rights violations as an "internal Affair." Human rights have never been *"internal affairs domain"* since the fall of the Berlin Wall and we have seen examples of the new legal philosophy, like the set-up of the International Criminal Court established in Rome in 1998, the detention of former dictator Augusto Pinochet by order of Spanish judicial authorities and the subsequent

---

[19] Secretary-General Kofi Annan's Report to the Security Council S/2004/16, 23 August 2004, para. 6.

ruling by *Audiencia Nacional* and *Tribunal Constitucional* in Spain claiming Universal Jurisdiction competence for gross violations of Human Rights.

I do not think that the legal and political reasoning offered by the Chinese government – that human rights are an "internal" affair – would ever be in the mind or on the tongue of a great power like America, which is the oldest and strongest democracy on Earth and was founded during the Enlightenment. But still, in these times of transition, international terrorism, and a *Manichean* approach to politics, a strong domestic and international system based in the Rule of Law and the respect of Human Rights is more necessary than ever.

The fight for liberties and dignity starts by the preservation of the culture, principles, rights, and duties that have made progress possible in Western life. Since the Enlightenment period and the American and French Revolutions, that system is based on the Rule of Law and the preservation of individual and public liberties. The very same challenge has been posed by the current international terrorism threat after September 11. If we deepen in our commitment to these values and principles, the democratic systems will be reassured and re-legitimized. Other courses of action put at risk the achievement of citizenship for all people and the very foundation of our political and legal systems.

American history, and the American legal system, contain formidable beacons of legal principles inspired in the Western democratic tradition, like the opening Statement by Justice Robert H. Jackson before the International Military Tribunal at Nuremberg on November 21, 1945. He pronounced these words in Court Room 600:

> "That four great nations, flushed with victory and stung with injury stay the hand of vengeance and voluntarily submit their captive enemies to the judgment of the law is one of the most significant tributes that Power has ever paid to Reason."[20]

But, regrettably, American legal history also includes abominable acts perpetrated by American public authorities like the abuses at Abu Ghraib, the illegal invasion of Iraq in 2003, the Guantanamo detention center and, during the Cold War, the support of another violent September 11, the bloody military coup of General Pinochet in Chile in 1973.

This being said, for European States the U.S. has remaines a guideline and reference point for liberty and security for the last 73 years, since the liberation of Europe. Nevertheless, we must acknowledge the radical turn of political events

---

[20] *Opening Statement Before the International Military Tribunal*, Nuremberg, Germany, November 21, 1945, available at www.roberthjackson.org/.

prompted by President Trump, specially the new attitude of the U.S. towards NATO and European States, the status of Jerusalem and the U.S. withdrawal of some relevant treaties: the 2013 UN Arms Treaty, the 1987 Intermediate-Range Nuclear Forces (INF) Treaty and the 2015 Paris Agreement on climate change mitigation.

After hearing for more than a decade of the shocking aspects of certain U.S. policies during the *War on Terror* like Abu Ghraib, Guantanamo, and extraordinary rendition programs, the U.S. remains to most Europeans a strong and admirable democratic system in 2019. Indeed, the response of the U.S. judicial system to claims of boundless executive authority had been particularly reassuring since *Hamdan v. Rumsfeld* in 2006. In this Supreme Court case through a habeas corpus petition – in which Salim Ahmed Hamdan challenged the authority and policy of military commissions at Guantánamo Bay – the Court required that in accordance with the conventions, Hamdan be tried by a "regularly constituted court affording all the judicial guarantees which are recognized as indispensable by civilized peoples."[21] The self-correcting feature of American judicial review was, if not necessarily speedy or fully effective, greatly comforting.

2. European cynicism

Undoubtedly, there is a lot of cynicism in Europe about U.S. policy after the September 11 attacks. There was complicity of European governments in the Extraordinary Rendition Program, where CIA planes carrying detainees from Guantanamo and other detention facilities landed in European airports for technical assistance with final destination in countries where the detainees would be returned and at risk of torture.[22] The Parliamentary Assembly of the Council of Europe published a definitive report on the cooperation of some European States with the "alleged" U.S. system of extraordinary renditions and secret detentions and unlawful inter-state transfers involving. Among the different conclusions the report declared that the system "resembles a 'spider's web' spun across the globe" and

> "the impression which some Governments tried to create at the beginning of this debate – that Europe was a victim of secret CIA plots – does not seem to correspond to reality. It is now clear – although we are still far from having established the whole truth – that authorities in several European countries actively participated with the

---

[21]   Hamdan v. Rumsfeld, 548 U.S. 557 (2006).
[22]   *European Parliament resolution on presumed use of European countries by the CIA for the transportation and illegal detention of prisoners.* Rapporteur: Giovanni Claudio Fava, Bulletin EU 12–2005.

CIA in these unlawful activities. Other countries ignored them knowingly, or did not want to know." (paragraph 285).[23]

European countries have also faced the scourge of terrorism during the last fifty years and have sometimes departed from democratic political principles and violated the Rule of Law. The fact that these were exceptions to a general respect for law cannot make them any more acceptable for Western European democracies. Some examples of breaches in the Rule of Law have been the British MI6 fight against the IRA terrorist group and the executions in combat of alleged terrorists; the systematic and indiscriminate use of torture during the Algerian War of Independence (1954–1962) by French Armed Forces; the "suicides" of three members of the Baader-Mainhof gang in Germany; the Italian extreme right lodges that were supported by the State against the communist threat and against the Red Brigades terrorist group (*Brigate Rosse*); and finally, the creation of the state-sponsored death squads GAL (Anti-Terrorist Liberation Group, GAL in its Spanish acronym) in Spain in 1983 to fight against ETA's terrorism in a paralegal structure of police officers financed by the Secret Service.

3. An example of democratic failure; the Spanish dirty war against terrorism

The case of Spanish departure from the rule of law was especially dramatic. It was Prime Minister Felipe Gonzalez – the same political leader who, after his

---

23 See, Parliamentary Assembly Report 7 June 2006, AS/Jur (2006) 16 Part II 7 June 2006, Committee on Legal Affairs and Human Rights, "Alleged secret detentions and unlawful inter-state transfers involving Council of Europe member states", Rapporteur: Mr. Dick Marty, Switzerland, ALDE. Specificly in the last paragraphs the *conclussión* of the report point to specific countries:
288. In this sense, it must be stated that to date, the following member States could be held responsible, at varying degrees, which are not always settled definitively, for violations of the rights of specific persons identified below (respecting the chronological order as far as possible):
– Sweden, in the cases of Ahmed Agiza and Mohamed Alzery;
– Bosnia-Herzegovina, in the cases of Lakhdar Boumediene, Mohamed Nechle, Hadj Boudella, Belkacem Bensayah, Mustafa Ait Idir and Saber Lahmar (the "Algerian six");
– The United Kingdom in the cases of Bisher Al-Rawi, Jamil El-Banna and Binyam Mohamed;
– Italy, in the cases of Abu Omar and Maher Arar;
– "The former Yugoslav Republic of Macedonia", in the case of Khaled El-Masri;
– Germany, in the cases of Abu Omar, of the "Algerian six", and Khaled El-Masri;
– Turkey, in the case of the "Algerian six".
289. Some of these above mentioned states, and others, could be held responsible for collusion – active or passive (in the sense of having tolerated or having been negligent in fulfilling the duty to supervise) – involving secret detention and unlawful inter-state transfers of a non specified number of persons whose identity so far remains unknown:
– Poland and Romania, concerning the running of secret detention centres;
– Germany, Turkey, Spain and Cyprus for being 'staging points' for flights involving the unlawful transfer of detainees;
– Ireland, the United Kingdom, Portugal.

rise to power in 1982, dragged Spain into modernity and helped to give Spain the global image of a dynamic and developed country with a model transition from dictatorship to democracy – who left the worst legacy of breach of the Rule of Law while trying to deter and fight terrorism.

The Spanish GAL – Anti-terrorist Liberation Group (*Grupo antiterrorista de liberación*) – death squads emerged in 1983 a year after the Socialist government of Felipe Gonzalez came to power, when killings by the Basque separatist group ETA (Basque Homeland and Freedom, in the Basque language *Euskadi ta Askatasuna*) were at their height (with approximately four people killed every month throughout the whole year). GAL's mission was to uproot ETA's "safe havens" across the border in France. Made up of members of the security forces and hired assassins, GAL was responsible for 28 murders between 1983 and 1987.[24] It is not difficult to understand the logic of the Spanish government going down this road. On average ETA was killing twenty times more people in the years following Franco's death than they did in the years before he died. Nevertheless, to understand the logic does not mean to justify it, at least in democratic countries that strive to uphold the Rule of Law.

Had this been done by the Franco regime during the dictatorship no one would have been surprised, but in fact it happened after Spain revived democracy long after the II Republic in 1936 after Franco's *Coup d'état* and the subsequent Spanish Civil War. For that same reason the international public protests and remains unhappy with the methods, for instance, of Russia fighting terrorism in Chechnya, with no accountability for public policies and individuals acting without respect to the Rule of Law and Human Rights. The core idea is that we citizens with democratic principles do not use the same means as terrorists and the ethical divergence lies in our commitment to democratic values whatever the scenario we might confront. We treasure the principles and system of laws that took a long time to achieve. Even alleged terrorists, of course, enjoy the same human rights, specifically due process.

The breach of Law by the Government was not just against the Spanish Constitution, but also failed the most basic obligations under international law, like the principle of sovereignty contained in the United Nations Charter, Article 2. Imagine what it means for one democratic state to carry out killings in the territory of a friendly democratic neighbor. It is almost difficult to imagine in the 80s what Italy's response would be if the French Government sent death squads over the Italic peninsula to execute Corsican nationalists who were living

---

24 Wayne Anderson, *The ETA (Inside the World's Most Infamous Terrorist Organizations Series): Spain's Basque Terrorists,* Rosen Publishing Group, 2003, and Paddy Woodworth, *Dirty War, Clean Hands*: ETA, the GAL and Spanish Democracy, Cork University Press, 2001.

in Italy or MI6 officers came to Spain to execute IRA supporters that spend their holiday vacation in the North of Spain.[25] The Spanish government's involvement in this shadowy armed group was the subject of a judicial inquiry and a Supreme Court trial which convicted two senior government officers, José Barrionuevo and Rafael Vera, who were sentenced by the Supreme Court to more than 10 years of imprisonment.

In the end the Rule of Law prevailed. Ironically, Judge Baltasar Garzón – a former member of the Socialist Government who renounced his seat as member of the Spanish Congress in 1993 – happened to be the magistrate that instructed the Criminal Proceeding against the Socialist Government. The outcome was the reinvigoration of the legal system and the strengthening of the Rule of Law because the responsible individuals were brought before justice and were held accountable for their deeds. The most important failure of European democracies when trying to overcome security threats posed by terrorism has been the appropriation of the same means used by terrorists themselves. By doing so, the governments have sent a message of no differentiation and no ethical difference among democrats and totalitarians; the delegitimization and debilitation of public institutions because of their lack of capacity to provide an effective lawful response; also in addition to the frequent absence of accountability, which means individual impunity for those who breached the law acting within the name of the State.

4.   Glimmers of the Cold War, victims, and empathy for the other

In 1985, the same year that Mikhail Gorbachev was elected Secretary General of the Soviet Communist Party, in the last hard hours of the Cold War, English singer Sting wrote *Russians,* a wonderful melody inspired by Russian composer Sergei Prokofiev's Romance Melody from the *Lieutenant Kije Suite.*[26] Sting wanted to outline the irrationality of the confrontation; at the bottom of the conflict sat individuals who were placed in the ruthless logic of the Cold War conflict. One of the dangers of the Cold War – an in any other war – is the failure and lack of empathy to understand the reasons of the other.

> "How can I save my little boy from Oppenheimer's deadly toy. There is no monopoly of common sense / On either side of the political fence / We share the same biology / Regardless of ideology / Believe me when I say to you / I hope the Russians love their children too."

Sting's argument was clear: empathy for the reasons of the other, which are mostly common to human beings: provide for your people and the constant

---

25   See also http://news.bbc.co.uk/2/hi/europe/141720.stm.
26   Sting, *Russians,* in "Dream Of The Blue Turtle", London, Universal, 1985.

human striving in the pursuit of better lives. After September 11, during the *War on Terror*, we have revived manners, habits, and visions from the Cold War rather than following the cultural and political values that arose out of the new freedom vision associated with the fall of the Berlin Wall on 9 November 1989. We should also remark that those "revived manners" seem to be now on stage in 2019 after Brexit, Russia meddling in the internal affairs of several states, including the presidential election won by Donald Trump in 2016 and the expansive commercial, military and foreign policies conducted by China.

At the same time, Europe has shown that a great deal of its inability to participate with efficacy in some current challenges comes directly from the Cold War. The conflicts in Iraq, Afghanistan, Syria and the Middle East remind us of European limitations. Shlomo Ben-Ami skillfully recalled *Europe's Dangerous Banalities*:

> "Europe's inability to help resolve the Arab-Israeli conflict (and others) does not stem from its positions on the core issues, which are only microscopically different from those held by the United States […]. Europe, as Denis de Rougemont put it in 1946, is *"la patrie de la mémoire,"* a tormenting and tormented memory, one must admit. […] To the Israelis, Europe became the essayist Mario Andrea Rigoni's "old lady, who after she had allowed herself all sorts of liberties […] and a great number of horrors, would like, once she has reached the age of society, fatigue, and weakness, to see the world adapt itself to her needs for moderation, equity, and peace […] It took Europe gruesome religious wars, two world wars, and more than one genocide to resolve its endemic disputes over borders and nationalism […] Its record in colonialism wrote monstrous pages in human history."[27]

It is perhaps true the assertion that we are still in 2019 in a transitional period from the Cold War, and we do not yet know how to characterize our time. That also helps us to understand why we still perceive continuous signs of the Cold War throughout America and Europe after half a century since the Cold War ended. The actions of individuals and the real accomplishment of policies prompt the changes in history. President Obama will most likely appear to us as the sign for all those significant, albeit slow, changes waiting to happen.

5.   Conflict casualties

Prof. Abdullahi Ahmed An-Na'im from Emory University has been speaking out about the common aspirations of human beings, regardless of their origin, culture, and citizenship. An-Na'im's efforts have been for in-depth recognition

---

[27]   Shlomo Ben-Ami, *Europe's Dangerous Banalities*, February 2009, available at www.project-syndicate.org.

of the "human vulnerability concept."[28] And it applies especially for victims of military conflicts.

According to a CNN count, as of April 2009, there were 4,597 coalition deaths in the war in Iraq – 4,280 Americans, two Australians, one Azerbaijani, 179 Britons, 13 Bulgarians, one Czech, seven Danes, two Dutch, two Estonians, one Fijian, five Georgians, one Hungarian, 33 Italians, one Kazakh, one Korean, three Latvians, 22 Poles, three Romanians, five Salvadoran, four Slovaks, 11 Spaniards, two Thai and 18 Ukrainians.[29] Nevertheless, we were unable to provide a thorough figure about Iraq's civilian victims. *Iraq Body Count* project (IBC)[30], is one of several efforts to record civilian deaths attributable to coalition and insurgent military action, sectarian violence, and criminal violence in Iraq since the U.S.-led 2003 invasion of Iraq. This refers to excess civilian deaths caused by criminal action resulting from the breakdown in law and order which followed the coalition invasion. Other efforts to provide an approximation to the number of civilians killed – like the research *A Mortality Study, The Human Cost of the War in Iraq 2002–2006*[31] performed by Johns Hopkins University, Al Mustansiriya University Baghdad, and Massachusetts Institute of Technology – were immediately rejected by President Bush.[32] The estimated death toll for Iraqi civilians since the invasion varies from the lowest figure, according to Iraq Body Count, of between 91,676 – 10,083 and the highest, from an *Opinion Research Business* survey conducted in August 2007, of between 733,158 and 1,446,063.[33]

In the fall of 2008 during the presidential debates between Senator McCain and Senator Obama, the war in Iraq was a presence and the candidates referred to the sacrifices of American Soldiers killed in the Iraq and Afghanistan campaigns. But we missed, especially from Senator Obama, any expression of empathy for, or even reference to, the thousands of innocent civilians killed as a result

---

[28] See interview with Professor An-Na'im, Atlanta, 10 October 2006, footnote 26 in Joaquin Gonzalez Ibanez, Jamin B. Raskin, Hisham Ramadan, The Arab Garden and Ground Zero, *Saberes Law Review*, Madrid, Alfonso X University, 2006, available at www.uax.es/publicaciones/saberes.htm.

[29] Source: 28th April, 2009, www.cnn.com/SPECIALS/2003/iraq/forces/casualties/.

[30] www.iraqbodycount.org/ On its database page the IBC states: "Gaps in recording and reporting suggest that even our highest totals to date may be missing many civilian deaths from violence." The group is staffed by volunteers consisting mainly of academics and activists based in the UK and the USA. The project was founded by John Sloboda and Hamit Dardagan.

[31] This report was published in the British medical journal *The Lancet*, Volume 368, Issue 9545, p. 1421–1428, 21 October 2006, available at www.thelancet.com/journals/lancet/article/PIIS0140-6736(06)69491-9/abstract.

[32] On the denial of the data see: *War blamed for 655,000 Iraqi deaths "President Bush says he does not consider report credible"* available at www.cnn.com/2006/WORLD/meast/10/11/iraq.deaths/.

[33] See www.opinion.co.uk/Newsroom_details.aspx?NewsId=78.

of an invasion that was illegal under international law. It was also an invasion orchestrated on false assumptions: Weapons of mass destruction, Al-Qaeda links to Iraq and 9/11, freedom for Iraqis, democracy for Iraq, nation building, etc. "The other," the victim, is part of the essence of a universal approach to human rights, and every single life must count equally. Paradoxically during the first three years of the Obama Administration 2009–2011, President Obama authorized 193 drone strikes in, more than four times the number of attacks that President George W. Bush authorized during his two terms.[34] Because of the pressure by public opinion to be more transparent, President Obama signed in 2016 an executive order requiring U.S. intelligence officials to publish the number of civilians killed in drone strikes outside of war zones.[35] This Obama Presidential Order was revoked by President Trump on March 6, 2019.[36]

At the end of his first term and analysis of data conducted by the British newspaper *The Guardian* and the human rights group *Reprieve* raised questions about accuracy of intelligence guiding 'precise' strikes (41 men targeted but 1,147 people killed by U.S. drone strikes). According to this death toll there was in tactical terms a dramatic increase of drones during the Obama Administration criticized under the expression 'kill for peace'. This strategy of the Obama Administration that eventually may backfire and represent a future blowback in

---

[34] See, *Covering Obama's Secret War. When drones strike, key questions go unasked and unanswered* by Tara McKelvey, *Columbia Journalism Review*, May/June 2011, available at https://archives.cjr.org/feature/covering_obamas_secret_war.php.

[35] Executive Order 13732 of July 1, 2016. "United States Policy on Pre- and Post-Strike Measures To Address Civilian Casualties in U.S. Operations Involving the Use of Force. The principles and goals are clearly defined in Section 1. Purpose: Section 1. Purpose. United States policy on civilian casualties resulting from U.S. operations involving the use of force in armed conflict or in the exercise of the Nation's inherent right of self-defense is based on our national interests, our values, and our legal obligations. As a Nation, we are steadfastly committed to complying with our obligations under the law of armed conflict, including those that address the protection of civilians, such as the fundamental principles of necessity, humanity, distinction, and proportionality.
The protection of civilians is fundamentally consistent with the effective, efficient, and decisive use of force in pursuit of U.S. national interests. Minimizing civilian casualties can further mission objectives; help maintain the support of partner governments and vulnerable populations, especially in the conduct of counterterrorism and counterinsurgency operations; and enhance the legitimacy and sustainability of U.S. operations critical to our national security. As a matter of policy, the United States therefore routinely imposes certain heightened policy standards that are more protective than the requirements of the law of armed conflict that relate to the protection of civilians.
Civilian casualties are a tragic and at times unavoidable consequence of the use of force in situations of armed conflict or in the exercise of a state's inherent right of self-defense. The U.S. Government shall maintain and promote best practices that reduce the likelihood of civilian casualties, take appropriate steps when such casualties occur, and draw lessons from our operations to further enhance the protection of civilians."

[36] See Executive Order on Revocation of Reporting Requirement, National Security & Defense, Issued on: March 6, 2019, available at https://www.whitehouse.gov/presidential-actions/executive-order-revocation-reporting-requirement/.

American Foreign policy.[37] Even in 2016 the death toll presented by the Obama Administration was contested for the inaccuracy and the claim of having had conducted 473 strikes Against Terrorist Targets Outside Areas of Active Hostilities, combatant death 2372–2581 and non-combatant deaths 64–116.[38]

6.   *Torture, accountability, and normal function of institutions*

General Carlo Alberto Dalla Chiesa, general of the Italian *carabinieri*, was a highly recognized public official well-known for campaigning against the Red Brigades terrorist group (*Brigate Rosse*) during the 1970s in Italy, and also as *prefect* for Palermo to stop the violence of the Second Mafia War in Italy. In 1982 Dalla Chiesa was killed along with his wife and their driver in Palermo just three months after taking command. When Aldo Moro, President of the Christian Democrat Party (*Democrazia Cristiana*) was kidnapped in 1978 by the Red Brigades, in a contested statement at the time, Dalla Chiesa declared in response to a suggestion that torture would be used in the investigation of a Red Brigade terrorist arrested a few days before: "Italy can survive the loss of Aldo Moro. It would not survive the introduction of torture."[39] His unswerving devotion to the Rule of Law was not in vain. In 1984 Ernesto Sabato in the foreword to the *Argentine National Commission on the Disappearance of Persons Report* during the *dirty war* of the Argentinean dictatorship, Dalla Chiesa was cited as an example of the principles and values that democracies must stand for.[40]

During an interview on January 11, 2009 elected President Obama said "while no one is "above the law"[…] my orientation's going to be to move forward."[41] On his second day as president, Obama issued orders banning torture and closing the Guantanamo Bay detention center; in the same act President Obama also scrapped every legal opinion and memo that justified harsh interrogations,

---

[37]   Seer the article *41 men targeted but 1,147 people killed: US drone strikes – the facts on the ground* by Spencer Ackerman, available at https://www.theguardian.com/us-news/2014/nov/24/-sp-us-drone-strikes-kill-1147. Regarding an analysis of different blowbacks of American Foreign policy see the 2005 documentary by Eugene Jarecki, *Why we fight*.

[38]   See Micah Zenko, Questioning Obama's Drone Deaths Data, Council on Foreign Relations, July 1, 2016, Washington. Available at https://www.cfr.org/blog/questioning-obamas-drone-deaths-data and of special interest the information released by The Washington Post Obama-led drone strikes kill innocents 90% of the time: report, October 15, 2015, by Andrew Blake, available at https://www.washingtontimes.com/news/2015/oct/15/90-of-people-killed-by-us-drone-strikes-in-afghani/.

[39]   See *Il generale nel suo laberinto*, published in La Repubblica, Roma, Sept. 4, 1982, www.repubblica.it/online/album/ottantadue/bocca/bocca.html.

[40]   See Report of CONADEP, National Commission on the Disappearance of Persons (*Comisión Nacional de Desaparecidos*), available at 1984<http://web.archive.org/web/20031013222809/http://nuncamas.org/english/library/images/linea350.gif> and www.desaparecidos.org.

[41]   See George Stephanopoulos, *Interview with President-Elect Barack Obama*, Jan. 11, 2009, available at http://abcnews.go.com/ThisWeek/Economy/story?id=6618199&page=1.

secret CIA prisons, and detentions of terror suspects outside the judicial system. In West Point Academy in April 2009, former Attorney General Eric Holder, looking back to the Bush Administration policies relating to torture of prisoners in Iraq, Afghanistan, and Guantanamo, affirmed that "The law was not always followed in U.S. war against terror." This statement implies, under any legal system and the regular functioning of the Rule of Law, the necessity to prosecute those who allegedly breach the law, under national or international obligations.[42]

Desmond Tutu has wisely identified the false dilemma, when it comes to human rights and accountability of perpetrators. Tutu was referring to the case of the arrest warrant issued for President Omar Hassan al-Bashir of Sudan last February by the International Criminal Court. The moment requires us to answer if we are "on the side of justice or on the side of injustice?" Tutu pointed out that the International Tribunal is based in Europe and prosecuting an African head of State, and so "the answer so far from many African leaders has been shameful. Because the victims in Sudan are African."[43] Bishop Tutu is arguing that questions of nationalism are irrelevant when it comes to human rights. What matters here is that the victims are human beings, African human beings, human beings killed because of the implementation of orders of an African leader. When it comes to torture, the perpetrator and his or her reasons are irrelevant; behind the reasons lies the destruction of human dignity and the violation of fundamental rights of the tortured.

The Constitutional system of *check and balances* involves a mutual control of the legislative, executive and judiciary in order to avoid any excess and misuse of powers of the competences assigned and limited by the Constitution. Under this idea, the U.S. Supreme Court Judge Ruth Bader Ginsburg, looking back to history and the effects of the lack of control of governmental decisions, stated "What happened in Europe was the Holocaust, and people came to see that popularly elected representatives could not always be trusted to preserve the system's most basic values."[44]

Prof. Richard J. Wilson, a human rights academic and former legal counsel of Guantanamo detainees like Omar Khadr, after several years defending the cause of human rights under American Law and international law, was able to explain

---

[42]   *Eric Holder tells West Point: The law was not always followed in U.S. war against terror* by Jim Fitzgerald / Associated Press, Wednesday April 15, 2009, available at www.cleveland.com/nation/index.ssf/2009/04/eric_holder_tells_west_point_t.html.

[43]   Desmond Tutu, *Will Africa Let Sudan Off the Hook?*, The New York Times, March 3, 2009.

[44]   Adam Liptak, *Ginsburg Shares Views on Influence of Foreign Law on Her Court, and Vice Versa*, The New York Times, April 12, 2009. These comments were pronounced by Ginsburg in a conference at Moritz College of Law at Ohio State University.

in a lucid way the weakness of international law norms in proceedings against Guantanamo detainees in the *War on Terror*.

> "As a teacher and practitioner of international human rights law, I have to admit that I have generally been disappointed with the response by the U.S. courts to issues put before them with international law dimensions. It is very clear that courts, particular the lower federal courts, are either ignorant of or hostile to international law norms, and this is reflected in their decisions. But for the decision by the Supreme Court in the *Hamdan* case in 2006, which gives some recognition of basic obligations under the law of war, the courts have generally shied away from grounding their decisions in international law concepts, even norms as basic as those protecting against torture. The generally exceptional nature of U.S. practice in international law is reflected in the court decisions dealing with Guantanamo, which are solidly based on domestic law, and thus skewed against protection of basic human rights norms recognized in international law."[45]

Following the same line of arguments, Mark J. Mc Keon, a former prosecutor at the International Criminal Tribunal for the former Yugoslavia from 2001 to 2006, made in April 2009 the sturdiest of the arguments "in favor of the application of the Rule of Law" in his statement *Why We must Prosecute*.[46]

> "In 2001 and the following few years, we at the international tribunal built a strong court case against Milosevic. We presented evidence that he had effective control over soldiers and paramilitaries who tortured prisoners and did worse. We brought into court reports of atrocities that had been delivered to Milosevic by international organizations to show his knowledge of what was happening under his command. And we watched as other heads of state were indicted for similar crimes, including Charles Taylor in Liberia and, of course, Saddam Hussein in Iraq.
> At the same time, I watched with horror the changes that were happening back home. The events are now well known: Abu Ghraib; Guantanamo; secret 'renditions' of prisoners to countries where interrogators were not afraid to get rough; secret CIA prisons where there appeared to be no rules [...] I hope that the United States has turned the page on those times and is returning to the values that sustained our country for so many years. But we cannot expect to regain our position of leadership in the world unless we hold ourselves to the same standards that we expect of others. That means punishing the most senior government officials responsible for these crimes. We have demanded this from other countries that have returned from walking on the dark side; we should expect no less from ourselves."

From a technical point of view, legal scholars like Stephen Vladeck, an American University constitutional law professor, say that bringing criminal charges against Bush, former vice president Dick Cheney, and other senior Bush

---

[45]   Joaquin Gonzalez Ibanez, interview with Prof. Richard J. Wilson, May 3, 2009, Washington DC.

[46]   Mark J. McKeon, *Why We Must Prosecute, The Washington Post, Torture Is a Breach Of International Law*, The New York Times, April 28, 2009.

Administration officials would be a "complex, highly-charged undertaking, and a conviction – even with strong evidence – would be an uncertainty at best." Based on what is in the public record thus far, the allegation that would have the most teeth is the one having to do with torture. Affirmed Vladeck: "There is a clear prohibition under both domestic and international law on torture. It clearly applied on the executive branch. And it's pretty clear that the executive branch disregarded it on several occasions."[47]

7. Spanish court Audiencia Nacional and impunity

In the meantime, Spanish Courts opened criminal proceedings to investigate high political figures in the Bush Administration's *War on Terror* in what might appear to be another paradoxical and Quixotic approach by Spanish Judicial Authorities.

In April 2009 the Spanish court *Audiencia Nacional* opened a criminal investigation into allegations of torture, made by four ex-detainees, over whose cases the *Audiencia Nacional* had jurisdiction for the reason that they once were charged in Spain with criminal activity in support of Al Qaeda.[48] The four claimed that they had suffered different acts of physical or psychological violence during the time of their detention in different countries while they were under the authority of U.S. officials.[49]

At the same time, Candido Conde Pumpido, Chief State Prosecutor, opposed pursuing the case. The future of the case depended on the decision of the Magistrate from *Audiencia Nacional*, magistrate Baltasar Garzon, who decided to let the case go forward.[50]

The former Bush officials – ex-Attorney General Alberto Gonzalez; David Addington, former Vice President Dick Cheney's chief of staff; ex-Pentagon general counsel William Haynes; former Defense Department undersecretary Douglas

---

[47] Joseph Williams, *Some call for Bush administration trials, Want ex-leader accountable on Iraq war*, published in *The Boston Globe*, February 3, 2009.

[48] See CNN Europe, April 23, 2009, *Spanish court sends Guantanamo case to new judge*, available at http://edition.cnn.com/2009/WORLD/europe/04/23/spain.court.guantanamo/.

[49] *Auto* April 27, 2009. Procedimiento: Diligencias Previas 150/09 – N, *Delito: Torturas y otros*. Juzgado central de instrucción, numero cinco, Audiencia Nacional, Madrid, available at www.rtve.es/contenidos/documentos/autoguantanamo.doc.

[50] Adriel Bettelheim, *Obama Tries to Chill Spanish Court's Guantánamo Bay Investigation*, April 16, 2009, at CQ Politic, available at http://blogs.cqpolitics.com/balance_of_power/2009/04/obama-tries-to-chill-spanish-c.html.
Nevertheless, the magistrate Baltasar Garzón career as a judge came to a dramatic end on February 2012 when the Spanish Supreme Court sentenced him to a 11-year suspension for illegally wiretapping conversations between remand prisoners and their lawyers in a corruption case involving the former prime minister, Mariano Rajoy's People's party.

Feith; Jay Bybee, a former assistant attorney general, and ex-Justice Department lawyer John Yoo – were accused of approving interrogation techniques that violate the 1984 United Nation Convention against Torture Spanish penal code, the Third Geneva Convention and the Spanish Criminal Code. Judge Garzón's brief underlines that "intellectual authors" as well as "material implementers" of abuse – those who "authorized" abuse as well as those who "practiced" it – are fair game for his investigation and a finding of criminal responsibility.

According to the *Auto* (Order) the four Guantanamo detainees are alleged to have suffered sleep deprivation and damage to their vision, both caused by cells lit all day and all night; constant broadcasting of "patriotic American songs" and other loud music; blows to the testicles and to the head; forced nudity; water boarding (the introduction of water into the nostrils to the point of a sensation of suffocation); subjection to extreme heat or extreme cold; prolonged confinement in a dark place underground; deprivation of food; death threats and sexual assault.

In 2014 the Spanish Congress initiated the reform of the Statute in where the Universal Jurisdiction was regulated (*Ley Orgánica del Poder Judicial*, 6/1985, July 1), and it prompted the closure of the Guantanamo investigation in January 2016 ordered by judge José de la Mata who stated in an *Audiencia Nacional Order* that with the new legal framework Spanish Judicial bodies did not enjoy jurisdiction to investigate the alleged torture system in Guantanamo.[51]

8.   The misuse of language and the War on Terror

In his book *LTI – Lingua Tertii Imperii*, Victor Kemplerer explains that one of the first victims of a war is the language and everything involving restrictions to freedom in the use and manipulation of language with political aims. Kemplerer was married to an "Aryan" woman, Eva Kemplerer, who unlike most German women during this period didn't want to leave her husband. Thus, he was not sent to an extermination camp (*Vernichtungslager*) but to work as a slave at a factory and to remove debris in his home town, Dresden.

Kemplerer was a professor of German Philology. But since, during the six years of war he had been prohibited from borrowing books from the library, owning books, and giving lessons, he devoted his time to observing the distortion of the language by the Third Reich.[52] It is surprising that all dictatorships have a

---

51   See also the appeal at Spanish Supreme Court Ruling on the end of the Guantanamo Investigation by the Audiencia Nacional, Tribunal Supremo, Sala de lo Penal, *Sentencia No: 869/2016, RECURSO CASACION (Spanish Supreme Court Appeal) No:* 308/2016.
52   Klemperer starts his argumentation of language as a powerful tool and weapon and repeatedly affirms "that language acts and thinks for us". He recounts the anecdote of a Jewish

lot of analogies: a common destiny for the whole community, the heroism, the abduction of the terms fatherland and flag, the final effort, the final destiny in common horizon, the criminalization of the dissident, the heroic death members of the group, the chosen, etc.

Of course, I am not suggesting that there was a totalitarian regime during the Bush Administration, but the systematic use of fear and constant misuse of language was a fact of daily life. It is sad to still hear echoes of the manipulation of qualms and suspicions that kept many Americans fearful and disoriented. During the Bush Administration, and under the terrorist threat, there were many new terms created and even a Homeland Security Department, a lot of heroes, constant alerts, the public discrediting of those who were skeptical of these policies, the labelling of political adversaries as unpatriotic, sacrifices for the freedom of the dead in Iraq and Afghanistan, and perhaps the most problematic new concept, the *War on Terror*. I find President Obama's statement that his government would never use that kind of terminology very judicious.[53] *War on Terror* is still, nowadays, an undefined non legal category: we know when it begins but not when it will finish, unless the power indicates its end.[54]

Peter Brooks, professor at Yale and responsible for the project *The Ethics of Reading*[55] states that in *The Torture Memo* written by Jay Bybee and John Yoo (the Legal Memorandum used by the Bush Administration to develop torture techniques for Guantanamo in February 2002) we can infer a lack of respect for the essence of the Rule of Law and public freedoms, as well as a modification of the semantics of democracy and the use of language for dubious political aims.

---

friend who took great consolation from reading the official German reports of the African battlefield in December 1941: "They are having a terrible time in Africa," he says. "They write: "Our troops who are fighting *heldenhaft* (heroically)" *Heldenhaft* sounds like an obituary, you can be sure of that." See at Victor Klemperer, *The Language of the Third Reich: LTI, Lingua Tertii Imperii – A Philologist's Notebook*, New York and London: Continuum Books, 2002.

[53]   Al Kamen, *The End of the Global War on Terror*, March 24, 2009, The Washington Post. Available at http://voices.washingtonpost.com/44/2009/03/23/the_end_of_the_global_war_on_t.html.

[54]   Probably the new terminology will be *"overseas contingency operations"*. The Guardian reported that Tony Blair was an avid supporter of Bush's terminology – "whatever the technical or legal issues about a declaration of war, the fact is we are at war with terrorism". Several experts reach the conclusion that the phrase was unhelpful. A *War on Terror* was too broad and vague ever to be won. These specialists of terrorism issues argued that not defining a group or ideology, but rather a type of violence as the enemy was incoherent. Even the Secretary of Defense Rumsfeld, one of the war's most active architects, tried unsuccessfully to persuade Bush to rename it the "global struggle against violent extremism". See Oliver Burkeman, *Obama administration says goodbye to 'war on terror.'* U.S. defense department seems to confirm use of the bureaucratic phrase 'overseas contingency operations', *The Guardian*, 25 March 2009. www.guardian.co.uk/world/2009/mar/25/obama-war-terror-overseas-contingency-operations.

[55]   See *The ethics of reading Project*, available at http://opa.yale.edu/news/article.aspx?id=2319.

It is simple and hideous "how language can be used, interpreted, manipulated to justify violence, and, perhaps, also to combat it".[56] Following the same line, Coetzee regrets in his work *Diary of a Bad Year*[57] how in the *War on Terror*, the Australian, Russian, British, and American governments have corrupted and distorted some of the words used in daily civic life.

Because of this cynical manipulation of language, Obama's plain-spoken presidential campaign was explosively effective. Clear words with solid and genuine meaning took center stage and refreshed American discourse without the threat of rhetorical manipulation like "if you are not with me, you are against me," which represents a mediocre and coarse discourse. There was a new language, new manners and new hopes. The reinvention of usual things and renovated values have reinvigorated the idea of democracy within the great American empire. Barack Obama, with his first campaign motto *"Believe in change, Yes we can"*, brought into the presidency of the United States a politician committed to human rights. As a member of a minority group who identifies closely with the movement to end racial segregation and who seeks to improve social welfare and respect for all individuals, Obama personified the nation's rejection of torture as an instrument of state policy. In respect to President Trump legacy we should wait untill the end of his first mandate, though we have already seen the prohibition of the use of some words in official documents and the use of language that is shaping American politics and institutional public life to a point that professor Karen J. Greenberg has declared that the Trump Administration is "assaulting the language of American Democracy".[58]

9. Common heritage of values and ideals

The United States shares with its Western allies the same ideas and core values based on a common history and the result of two centuries of interaction. There are also parallel paths and different manifestation on both sides of the Atlantic while trying to accomplish and put into practice the common ideas arising from the period of Enlightenment. The Rule of Law is central to the Enlightenment project. Rule of law is a system that provides certainty, legal enforcement, and feasibility of the application of international and domestic law. But that system

---

[56]   *How legal Rhetoric shapes the Law-The language of violence and torture*, Conference November 7, 2008, American University, Washington College of Law, available at www.wcl. american.edu/secle/fall/2008/081107.cfm.

[57]   See J. M. Coetzee, *Diary of a bad year*, Viking books, 2008.

[58]   Karen J. Greenberg, The Trump Administration's Dangerous Assault on Our Words, *The Nation*, May 17th, 2018. See also the Op-Ed by Jessica Winter, The Language of the Trump Administration Is the Language of Domestic Violence, *The New Yorker*, June 11, 2018; Dereck Thompson, Donald Trump's Language Is Reshaping American Politics, *The Atlantic*, February 15, 2019 and Lena H. Sun and Juliet Eilperin, CDC gets list of forbidden words: Fetus, transgender, diversity, *Washington Post*, December 15, 2017.

is "enlightened" by several elements that establish a radical difference between democratic and authoritarian regimes. The system is based in the pursuit of an ethical commitment around the idea of Justice. The Rule of Law contains a set of moral standards that are chosen by our conscience and reason, balancing what is right and what is considered wrong (good and evil). Because of these values and principles, one of the most important ideas is to remember that Law Schools in democratic countries hold an important responsibility, which is to transmit and "embed" into students the belief that the Rule of Law is one of the most important achievements of humankind. Progress in democracy means more freedom and the empowerment of individuals, especially those who are vulnerable and in weak situations.

No political and historical commitment in society is more important than the pursuit of Justice. Now after the fall of the Berlin Wall, "those wise restrains that make mankind free" prompt us to reaffirm the inherent value of Human rights, as it appears in the United Nations Preamble.

> "[…] to reaffirm faith in fundamental human rights, in the dignity and worth of the human person, in the equal rights of men and women and of nations large and small, and to establish conditions under which justice and respect for the obligations arising from treaties and other sources of international law can be maintained, and to promote social progress and better standards of life in larger freedom […] to employ international machinery for the promotion of the economic and social advancement of all peoples."

The failure to live up to these standards led to this misunderstanding on both sides of the Atlantic. The U.S. failed to comprehend the importance of how other nations perceive actions by the U.S., especially how U.S. Administrations take into consideration the common aspirations of human beings regardless of their origin, culture and citizenship, which prompt all of us to recognize in depth the value of the "human vulnerability concept".[59]

The message that Europeans have mostly taken from the new situation after September 11, 2001 was the U.S. choosing to behave according to unilateralism, preventive wars, and without respect for International Law, including International Humanitarian Law. There appeared to be a clear global agenda put into action, with specific political goals, to be reached by any means possible. It was a vision reminiscent of the ancient Spanish Proverb, "When politics steps into a room, justice escapes through the window".[60] After 9/11 Europeans

---

[59]   See foot note 36 included in *The Arab Garden and Ground Zero* published in Saberes 2006, Alfonso X University, interview with Professor An-Na'im, Atlanta, 10thth October 2006, available at www.uax.es/publicaciones/saberes.htm.

[60]   Spanish proverb from the Renaissance, *"Cuando la política entra por la puerta, la justicia escapa por la ventana"*.

understood the reasons and the legitimacy of American feeling, but still never agreed that there was a reason for the Bush Administration to downgrade the Rule of Law and democratic principle to second place. The same probably applies today in 2019 with President Trump policies on immigration and his decision to erect a wall in the Southern border and his implicit racist discourse. But especially, the unprecedented U.S. threat to arrest ICC judges if they pursue Americans for Afghan war crimes.

History shows that the absence of a system of Law that frames relations and provides security, accountability and a system of mutual rights and obligations means instead cycles of revenge, injustice, inequity and permanent unrest. Paradigmatically in the months and years leading up to the invasion of Iraq in 2003, there was "No shortage of international Law".[61]

The U.S. contributed to the marginalization of the United Nations "by undermining international humanitarian law, it squanders moral authority and the capacity to persuade and influence others."[62] If we add the policies of President Bush from 2001–2008 that fall under the coverage of *The War on Terror* it seems that international law was perceived as a dead weight hindering the pursuit of victory against the terrorists.

C. THE NEW VISION ON HUMAN RIGHTS AND INTERNATIONAL OBLIGATIONS

A decent respect for the opinions of other nations and international law was partially restored by the new diplomacy of the Obama Administration, specially in his second term. Rebuilding consensus and reassuring Americans and allies about the role of the U.S. were clear commitments in Obama's First Inauguration Speech in January 2009.

> "[…] As for our common defense, we reject as false the choice between our safety and our ideals. Our founding fathers faced with perils that we can scarcely imagine, drafted a charter to assure the rule of law and the rights of man, a charter expanded by the blood of generations.
> Those ideals still light the world, and we will not give them up for expedience's sake. […]"[63]

---

61   Michael Byers, *War Law*, Grove Press, New York, 2005, p. 142.
62   Ibid., Michael Byers, p. 154.
63   Robert H. Jackson Opening Statement before the International Military Tribunal *at Nuremberg*, November 21, 1945, available at www.roberthjackson.org/Man/theman2-7-8-1/.

That is the vision, that even before the elections, in Berlin in July 2008, and in Paris, Prague, Mexico, and other cities in the world, kept the public squares filled with thousands of citizens of other nations speaking out in favor of Obama's multilateral approach to common challenges. People perceived the idea that the President of the United States was changing the face of American politics and was willing to work *with* the rest of the allied nations.[64] The Obama First Inauguration speech was in many aspects brilliant and encouraging, but it affirmed his essential empathy in the international relations arena:

> "Our founding fathers faced with perils that we can scarcely imagine, drafted a charter to assure the Rule of Law and the rights of man, a charter expanded by the blood of generations.
>
> Those ideals still light the world, and we will not give them up for expedience's sake.
>
> And so, to all other peoples and governments who are watching today, from the grandest capitals to the small village where my father was born: know that America is a friend of each nation and every man, woman and child who seeks a future of peace and dignity, and we are ready to lead once more.
>
> Recall that earlier generations faced down fascism and communism not just with missiles and tanks, but with the sturdy alliances and enduring convictions.
>
> They understood that our power alone cannot protect us, nor does it entitle us to do as we please. Instead, they knew that our power grows through its prudent use. Our security emanates from the justness of our cause; the force of our example; the tempering qualities of humility and restraint.
>
> We are the keepers of this legacy, guided by these principles once more, we can meet those new threats that demand even greater effort, even greater cooperation and understanding between nations. We'll begin to responsibly leave Iraq to its people and forge a hard- earned peace in Afghanistan."

It is also important to acknowledge that some members of the new Obama Administration were appointed not only because of their political commitments, but also for their intellectual and professional capacity shown in their professional careers and their support for International Law. One important illustration of this was the nomination of Harold Koh as U.S. State Department's legal adviser.

---

[64]   Nelson Mandela highlighted the differences between to do *for* and to do *with*. The South African leader respected profoundly President Bill Clinton, since in the United States Clinton's policy had won over the confidence of black citizens, minorities, women, and the disabled, and it had meant a change in the traditional U.S. foreign policy in Africa. During the celebration of the Fiftieth Anniversary of the Universal Declaration of Human Rights, in December 10th, 1998, Nelson Mandela quoted Clinton's words during a conversation they had: "I admire Clinton; he has changed the face of American politics. [...] When he came here [South Africa] he set forth a very important question. He said: 'It used to be, when American policymakers thought of Africa at all, they would ask, what can we do *for* Africa, or whatever can we do *about* Africa? Those were the wrong questions. The right question today is, what can we do *with* Africa?'". See Carlin, John, *El gigante de la libertad, Mandela*, in Spanish weekly *El País Semanal*, published on December 6, 1998: 21–23.

John Kerry, Chair of the U.S. Senate's Committee on Foreign Relations, during the Nomination hearing for Harold Koh, stated that Dean Koh had been a fierce defender of the Rule of Law and human rights and he "understands that it is not a Rule of Law if it is invoked only when it is convenient, and it is not a Human Right if it applies only to some people. He knows that our nation is stronger and safer when our government adheres to fundamental American values."[65] Dean Koh represented an active "transnational" approach to international relations. He envisioned and America indelibly and unavoidably connected to the rest of the international community by a web of security, trade, diplomatic, commercial, historic, artistic, and familial relationships. In that society, international law represents the inner garment and all the nations should respect and adhere to the international obligations they have taken on. In his words, as he has been continually pointing out in any public meeting "this is not only the right thing to do, it is the smart thing to do."[66]

> "We limit our ability to lead internationally and to demand compliance by other states – including rogue states such as North Korea – when we are perceived as disobeying or disrespecting international law. [...] Our sovereign power and influence are magnified when we work with allies and international institutions. International law is a tool that can be used to advance U.S. interests in enhancing and disseminating the human and civil rights that are at the foundation of our constitutional framework."[67]

III. EPILOGUE

In 2019, Abu Ghraib is a detention facility almost forgotten. Few will likely recall that it was actually handed over to the Iraqi government in September 2006. It is certainly a place that is known by specific map coordinates. But Abu Ghraib is more than that: in the long run, it will be part of the same intellectual, cultural, political and emotional gallery as Goya's *Disasters War* and Picasso's *Guernica*. Abu Ghraib represents an extreme vision of the abuse of power, the threat to human dignity and military torture all by American hands.

---

[65] See, p. 1 of the U.S. Senate Committee on Foreign Relations, Chairman John F. Kerry. *Opening Statement for Harold Koh Nomination*, U.S. State Department's legal adviser hearing April 28, 2009 available at http://foreign.senate.gov/testimony/2009/KohTestimony090428p. pdf.

[66] For example, see comments during his keynote address: *The politics of implementation: The Role of Human Rights in Foreign Policy*, at the Conference Realizing the promise of the Universal Declaration of Human Rights: examining the first 60 years and beyond, December 2, 2008 American University Washington College of Law. See the web cast at www.wcl. american.edu/humright/center/webcast.cfm.

[67] See note 57, Statement from Koh's intervention before the Senate Committee on Foreign Relations.

The *War on Terror* is over, at least in the conceptualization and policies defined in the period 2001–2008. We have witnessed a comprehensive vision implemented during the Bush Administration which believed that "America was morally entitled to use untraditional weapons to combat an untraditional threat."[68] The Bush Administration believed that the terrorists forfeited any rights due to their atrocities and their will to annihilate and that the President's obligation to serve his country required him to do "whatever he and his advisers think helpful to that end".[69] Democracies often define themselves and strengthen or weaken the system depending on the response they deliver to security threats. As Ronald Dworkin put it in *Is democracy possible here?*[70] the response is of the utmost importance because "the implications of the step (are) not for your moral responsibilities but for your self-respect."

Governments that act in a way that deny the intrinsic importance of any human life can do that without an insult to their own dignity. So, it is crucial for you to decide when your actions do show contempt for the value of other people's lives as well. Some allegations of the Administration that should be checked are about the policies to preserve American freedom and if those policies abused human rights. If they violate human rights – regardless of who the President is – they are "indefensible" even if these are given a legal patina and, reportedly, make America safer. If America does not reconcile itself to this primacy of human rights, it will not be able to understand how reciprocity would be the natural response by the people offended. As Mark J. McKeon, former prosecutor at the International Criminal Tribunal for the former Yugoslavia, stated, the U.S. commission of crimes in the *War on Terror* is, certainly, different compared to crimes of other countries, and yet they are still violations that must be prosecuted under the Rule of Law.

> "To say that we should hold ourselves to the same standards of justice that we applied to Slobodan Milosevic and Saddam Hussein is not to say that the level of our leaders' crimes approached theirs. Thankfully, there is no evidence of that. And yet, torture and cruel treatment are as much violations of international humanitarian law as are murder and genocide. They demand a judicial response. We cannot expect the rest of humanity to live in a world that we ourselves are not willing to inhabit."[71]

President Obama's determination in his first days at Office to shut down Guantanamo, uphold the Rule of Law, and create zero tolerance for torture invited us to feel there were reasons for change and real signs of a return to the

---

[68]   Ronald Dworkin, *Is democracy possible here?*, Princeton University Press, 2006, p. 27.
[69]   Ibid., p. 27.
[70]   Ibid., p. 16.
[71]   Mark J. McKeon, *Why We Must Prosecute. Torture Is a Breach Of International*, The Washington Post, April 28, 2009.

democratic ideals, as well as a greater respect of Power towards fundamental rights and democracy. We were already able to see a representation of that "plausible" change in the last months of the Bush Presidency. Colonel Morris Davis appeared November 7, 2008 before the Inter-American Commission on Human Rights during the session devoted to the monitoring of the precautionary measures imposed by the Commission to the United States of America in relation to the case of Djamel Ameziani, who was at that moment under U.S. custody in Guantanamo. Since September 2005 Morris Davis was the Chief Prosecutor for the Military Commissions at Guantanamo and the person responsible for the proceedings against prisoners there. He appeared as a witness for the Human Rights Clinic Program of the Washington College of Law and CEJIL (The Center for Justice and International Law) against the United States. He started condemning the political proceedings at Guantanamo and comparing the trials there with the ones against the Nazis in 1942 in the *Ex parte Quirin* case.

He resigned on October 4, 2007 because of the impossibility he saw in conferring the minimum due process guarantees to the proceedings, objecting to the way the Prosecution Office hid evidence exonerating the arrested people and, in particular, because he found the Commission was simply a political court. Morris Davis resigned after being warned that he was expected to find all people in Guantanamo guilty, as explained by The New York Times in its article of August 2008, 7: *Guilty as ordered*. Listening to the words of Colonel Morris at an open session of the Inter-American Commission in favor of the principles and values of the Constitution of the United States and the value of international treaties is a very historic and educational experience. I personally witness his deposition in Washington at the Inter-American Commission of Human Rights; it reminded me of the words of Alonso Quijano (Don Quixote), who in a moment of surpassing lucidity, dignity and sorrow, says in the very moment he thought was about to dye: "I know who I am" (*"¡Yo sé quién soy!"*).[72]

Some months before the 1945 London Conference – where the Charter of Military Tribunals was adopted, creating the legal basis for the Nuremberg Trials – , within the Truman Administration the international legalism thesis

---

[72]   See October 28, 2009. *Hearings of the Regular Session of the IACHR: PM 259/02 – Detainees at the Guantánamo Naval Base/PM 211/08 – Djamel Ameziane, United States.* This session in the Inter American Commission of Human Rights was a piece of drama and emotions, with Morris Davis initially nervous and unsecured just before he presented his argument to the Commission. In January 2009, I contacted Morris Davis but he declined an interview. Morris had started to work at the Congressional Research Service (CRS) as the head of the Foreign affairs, defense, and trade division. Davis kindly responded that he regretted, but had to decline the interview under his new position that restricts him from commenting on issues likely to come before the Congress; Guantanamo Bay and the treatment of detainees are issues Congress was likely to consider this term.

of Henry Stimson prevailed over Morguenthau's "victors' justice" vision. That policy entitled Robert H. Jackson, American Chief Prosecutor at Nuremberg, to represent the best legacy of American Legal Principles and the threshold of her highest influence and appreciation from the rest of nations. His statement at Nuremberg, even still in the twenty-first century, marks a reference point for any country, culture and civilization that reveres Law as the most adequate system for the accomplishment of justice, peace and progress.

> "The privilege of opening the first trial in history for crimes against the peace of the world imposes a grave responsibility (...)" and spoke of the Allied "practical effort... to utilize International Law to meet the greatest menace of our times".[73] In the words of Jackson, the Nuremberg Tribunal represented the triumph of Law and "the best tribute that power has ever paid to Reason".

We agree with Henry Morgenthau's affirmation that "The respect which the people of the world have to international law is in direct proportion to its ability to meet their needs".[74] That also means that those nations that do not respect International Law and do not consider themselves accountable for their deeds will receive rejection and disapproval from those who voluntary submit to the limits and restrain of International Law, expecting justice and security from its application; certainly a system that is addressed to meet their needs: peace, security, human dignity, and justice.

Professor Jamin B. Raskin, since 2017 serving as the U.S. Representative for Maryland's 8th District, has wisely pointed out that the debate on what America performed during the *War on Terror* is certainly the "core issue" because it defines American morals and ethics, but also American aspirations to elaborate a system of liberty constructed around a genuine and true Rule of Law:

> "The horrors that took place at Abu Ghraib and Guantanamo are predictable within an ideology of perpetual war and military empire, but the official response has been one of mock surprise. The unfolding government response to these events has been: pretended shock, denial, a constant changing of the subject and continuing efforts to shift the public's attention away from criminal acts by government actors. But the Obama Administration seems far more serious about dealing with the reality of what happened and responding to the growing public outrage. As during other periods of war when laws were broken (the My Lai massacre during the Vietnam War, for example), the question of moral responsibility is being debated and dodged endlessly by our foreign policy establishment. But the key question for us as a democratic society is whether we will continue our commitment to the Rule of Law as a real

---

73   Gary J. Bass, *Stay the hand of vengeance,* Princeton University Press, 2000, p. 174.
74   Morgenthau to Truman, 29 May 1945, *Morgenthau Diary,* vol. 2 pp. 1544–45, cited in Gary J. Bass, *Stay the hand of vengeance.*

social practice and thus uphold it even against our own officers and commanders. In the final analysis, the question is whether our constitutional faith in the Rule of Law is going to be the organizing principle of our social life or mere window dressing and political rhetoric."[75]

From a European point of view, the leadership, the legal visions and leaderships of Robert H. Jackson and Telford Taylor, U.S. Chief Counsel at Nuremberg – and his unbiased vision in favor of the American democratic values presented in *Nuremberg and Vietnam. An American Tragedy*[76] – represent for American allies a legacy that have helped to solidify their reputation as one of the world's truly independent sources of moral authority. The American civil Society, civil servants in all different orders – military, judges, police, academia, school teachers, etc. – are again the main protagonists and principal characters of this process. As Prof. Louis Fisher put it in his work *The Constitution and 9/11. Recurring threat to America's freedoms*: "Free citizens cannot automatically defer to assertions and claims by those in authority, including the President".[77]

After World War I, Italian political scientist Guglielmo Ferrero defined political legitimacy as the "invisible genius of the city."[78] According to Ferrero, the main purpose of legitimacy is to provide explanations for the actions of government and to assure that these explanations will be accepted and recognized peacefully. Legitimacy permits governments to avoid dependence on coercion and violence to impose its will and command. The government relationship is founded on the

---

[75] Interview with Prof. Jamin B. Raskin, May 2009, Washington D.C. Jamin B. Raskin is professor of Constitutional Law and current U.S. Congressman.

[76] Telford Taylor, *Nuremberg and Vietnam. An American Tragedy,* The New York Times Books, 1971.

[77] Louis Fisher, *The Constitution and 9/11. Recurring threat to America's freedoms*, University Press of Kansas, Lawrence, 2008, p. 370.

[78] Guglielmo Ferrero was a disciple of Cesare Lombroso, the inventor of "criminal Anthropology," though Ferrero focused afterwards on historical studies and political theory, becoming one of the most prestigious intellectuals in Europe after World War I. President Theodore Roosevelt nominated Ferrero for a Nobel Prize in Literature for his study of the Roman Republic, a work that presents a radical change from Theodore Mommsen. After 1920, Ferrero became an ardent opponent of Mussolini and had to escape to exile in Switzerland. "The government will be far less frightened of its subjects and of their revolting, knowing that it can count on their voluntary and sincere consent. Being less frightened of its subjects, it will not have to terrorize them nearly as much; less terrorized, the subjects will obey willingly and cheerfully. The principles of legitimacy humanize and alleviate authority, because it is in accordance with their nature to be accepted sincerely, as just and reasonable, by everyone who rules and by the majority, at least, of those who obey. The acceptance of the principles is not always active, willed, and conscious of their deeper meanings. It can be – and frequently is in the masses – a habit more than a conviction, a slothful legacy from the past, a kind of resignation to the inevitable." See Guglielmo Ferrero, *The Principles of Power. The Great Political Crises of History*, translated by Theodore R. Jaeckel, New York: G.P. Putnam's Sons, 1941, p. 40. See, the "Introduction" to the Spanish version by Eloy García López, Guillermo Ferrero, *Los genios invisibles de la ciudad*, Tecnos, Madrid, 1998.

citizen's recognition that certain individuals have a moral right to their obedience, while they, in return, feel a duty to give that obedience. Where ruler and ruled agree on the principle, a government will not fear its subjects. Conversely, since illegitimate governments lack credibility, trust and consent, they are always forced to rely on violence and warfare. This unique relationship of public authority and citizens in democracy is characterized by a relative absence of fear and coercion.

There is no doubt that the soul of democracy lies in Rule of Law and respect for human rights, in other words they are the source of legitimacy of our political and legal system; inside and outside of national borders. Throughout history we have learnt that a clear sign and guarantee of the accomplishment of a process of democratization and recognition of the Rule of Law for democracies, as opposed to other forms of social organization, are found in the constant expansion and recognition of international human rights law and the progressive incorporation of the legal *acquis* contained in international treaties. Converging interests proclaimed in human rights treaties represent in practice the assumption by states of their acknowledgement of a common framework of reciprocal control, common goals, restraints, and principles.[79]

Certainly, the current scenario of 2019 of fake news, and the rise of populism in democracies on both sides of the Atlantic have left a short legacy under the leadership of President Trump and the policies fostered by the prime ministers of Poland, Hungary and Italy challenging the respect of human rights as well as the value of the rule of law within democratic life, plus their intention to criminalize migrants and minorities with public policies. All of this might indicate that should we face a future scenario as complex as the one described in the above analysis, the core issues in democratic societies like human rights, rule of law and active democratic citizenship will be left in a loathed place.

As we have stated on other occasions, the international rule of law with respect to human rights law represents an attempt on the part of the international community to realize an ethical and moral aspiration, reaffirming that the advancement of human rights symbolizes one of the most important forms of progress in the human condition. This is especially true because the progress of the human condition means access to the exercise of rights by vulnerable and excluded groups, generally women, children, indigenous peoples, poor and marginalized people, minorities, and, above all, victims. Human rights are *the rights of the other* and constitute a commitment to the cause of justice.[80]

---

[79] Villarroel, D., *El derecho convencional en los sistemas constitucionales de América latina*, México, Porrúa, 2005.

[80] J. Gonzalez Ibanez, "Legal Pedagogy, The Rule of Law and Human Rights: The Professor, The Magistrate's Robe and Miguel de Unamuno", *Journal of Human Rights Law*, Volume 6, Number 1, November 2012.

As Primo Levi put it, a country is considered the more civilised the more the wisdom and efficiency of its laws hinder a weak man from becoming too weak and a powerful one too powerful.[81]

As a result, in 2019, it is not difficult to have a distorted perception, or to be indifferent or ignorant to "the other" and have a lack of empathy, all represented by the executive order revocation signed by President Trump on March 6, 2019. The logic behind this order signed in 2016 by Obama was to minimize civilian casualties in order to further mission objectives; help maintain the support of partner governments and vulnerable populations, especially in the conduct of counterterrorism with the goal to maintain and promote best practices that reduce the likelihood of civilian casualties, take appropriate steps when such casualties occur, and draw lessons from operations to further enhance the protection of civilians.[82]

The dilemma about our legitimacy while fighting terrorism as democracies lies ahead. The achievement of justice for democratic states comes through the implementation of the international Rule of Law. The combination for this construction to achieve international justice – justice through the effective existence of the rule of law, which binds integrally Rule of Law and democracy – provides the philosophical and ethical aspiration of international law's machinery. In a way, democracy acts as a gateway to the Rule of Law. And there it is, the timeless question, precisely, where the core of the challenge is set: Might or right? It could be both, as long as democracies fight terrorism within democratic and rule of law principles their actions will be legitimized in the domestic and international domain. If this happens, it will mean that democracies have overcome the tensions and challenges that are part of the fight against terrorism and have been up to their legal, ethical and political commitments.[83]

---

81 P. Levi, *Se questo è un uomo*, Einaudi, Milan, 1997, p. 147. Translation by the author.
82 See Executive Order on Revocation of Reporting Requirement, National Security & Defense, Issued on: March 6, 2019. Available at https://www.whitehouse.gov/presidential-actions/executive-order-revocation-reporting-requirement/.
83 Part of references presented here were first presented in J.G. González Ibáñez, "International Rule of Law and Human Rights: The Aspiration of a Work in Progress", *The Journal Jurisprudence*, Volume 15, 2013. The author sees the Rule of Law as referring to a system that empowers individuals and other actors in the process of putting limits on power. Law is perceived as imperative and "It seems natural to think of laws as commands. In doing so, however, we have already begun to theorize about the nature of law [...]." D. Lyons, *Ethics and the Rule of Law*, Cambridge, Cambridge University Press, 1993, p. 37. We have set in law the community's aspirations in terms of what we perceive as the principles and values necessary to provide dignity, justice, respect and security to the members of a given community. As such, democracy is a system of rule by laws and not by individuals. In a democracy, the Rule of Law protects the rights of citizens, maintains order, and limits the power of government. As a consequence, all citizens are equal under the law and no one should be discriminated against on the basis of their race, religion, ethnic group, or gender. B.Z. Tamanaha, *On the Rule of Law*, Dambridge, Cambridge University Press, 2004, p. 141.

BIBLIOGRAPHY

Acharya, Sally, *Law professor defends human rights*, published at American Weekly, March 22, 2005.

Adam Liptak, *Ginsburg Shares Views on Influence of Foreign Law on Her Court, and Vice Versa*, The New York Times, April 12, 2009.

Amann, Diane Marie, *Abu Ghraib*, University of Pennsylvania Law Review, Vol. 153, p. 2085, 2005, p. 2, available at SSRN: http://ssrn.com/abstract=951874

Armstrong, Matt, *Major General Doug Stone and practicing the struggle for minds and wills*, July 1, 2008, available at http://mountainrunner.us/2008/07/major_general_doug_stone_pract.html

Anderson, Wayne, *The ETA (Inside the World's Most Infamous Terrorist Organizations Series): Spain's Basque Terrorists*, Rosen Publishing Group, 2003.

Ashraf Khalil, *Camp Bucca Turns 180 Degrees From Abu Ghraib*, January 19, 2005, available at http://articles.latimes.com/2005/jan/19/world/fg-bucca19

Audiencia Nacional of Spain, Auto April 27, 2009. Procedimiento: Diligencias Previas 150/09 – N, Delito: Torturas y otros. JUZGADO CENTRAL DE INSTRUCCIÓN, NUMERO CINCO, AUDIENCIA NACIONAL, MADRID, available at www.rtve.es/contenidos/documentos/autoguantanamo.doc

Bacevich, Andrew J., *The limits of power*, Herry Holt and Co., New York, 2008.

Bass, Gary J., *Stay the hand of vengeance*, Princeton University Press, 2000, p. 174.

Ben-Ami, Shlomo, *Europe's Dangerous Banalities*, February 2009 available at www.project-syndicate.org

Bettelheim, *Obama Tries to Chill Spanish Court's Guantánamo Bay Investigation*, April 16, 2009 at CQ Politic, available at http://blogs.cqpolitics.com/balance_of_power/2009/04/obama-tries-to-chill-spanish-c.html

Bonesana, Cesare, Marchese di Beccaria, *Of Crimes and Punishments*, Originally published in Italian in 1764, available at www.constitution.org/cb/crim_pun.htm.

Brooks, Robert, *The ethics of reading Project*, available at http://opa.yale.edu/news/article.aspx?id=2319.

Burkeman, Oliver, *Obama administration says goodbye to 'war on terror'*, The Guardian, March 25, 2009. available at www.guardian.co.uk/world/2009/mar/25/obama-war-terror-overseas-contingency-operations.

Byers, Michael, *War Law*, Grove Press, New York, 2005.

Carlin, John, *El gigante de la libertad, Mandela*, in Spanish weekly (*El País Semanal*), published on December 6th, 1998: 21–23.

CNN Europe, April 23, 2009, *Spanish court sends Guantanamo case to new judge*, available at http://edition.cnn.com/2009/WORLD/europe/04/23/spain.court.guantanamo/

Coetzee, J. M., *Diary of a bad year*, Viking books, 2008.

Cole, Davis, LOBEL, Jules, *Less safe, less free. Why America in losing the war on terror*, The new press, New York, 2007.

CONADEP, National Commission on the Disappearance of Persons *(Comisión Nacional de Desaparecidos)* available at 1984 <http://web.archive.org/web/20031013222809/http://nuncamas.org/english/library/images/linea350.gif> and www.desaparecidos.org

Danner, Mark, *The Red Cross Torture Report: What It Means*, The New York Review of Books, Volume 56, Number 7, April 30, 2009.

Daugherty Miles, A., *Perspectives on Enhanced Interrogation Technique, Congressional Research Services*, January 8, 2016 available at https://fas.org/sgp/crs/intel/R43906. pdf.

Dehghanpisheh, Babak, Scared Straight: Iraqi Style, *Newsweek, August 9, 2007, available at* MSNBC.COM. www.msnbc.msn.com/id/20200546/site/newsweek/page/0/.

Detwiler, Elizabeth, *Iraq: Positive Change in the Detention System,* July 2008, United States Institute of Peace, July 2008, available at www.ciaonet.org/pbei/ usip/0002185/f_0002185_1285.pdf

Dworkin, Ronald, *Is democracy possible here?* Princeton University Press, 2006.

European Parliament, *European Parliament resolution on presumed use of European countries by the CIA for the transportation and illegal detention of prisoners.* Rapporteur: Giovanni Claudio Fava, Bulletin EU 12–2005.

Financial Times, (no author mentioned)*Detainees chief sees Koran as key ally,* June 2, 2008, The Financial Times, July 16 2007, available at www.ft.com/cms/ s/0/24c2e12e-3334–11dc-a9e8–0000779fd2ac.html?nclick_check=1

Fisher, Louis, *The Constitution and 9/11. Recurring threat to America' s freedoms,* University Press of Kansas, Lawrence, 2008.

Fitzgerald, Jim, *Eric Holder tells West Point: The law was not always followed in U.S. war against terror* by The Associated Press, Wednesday April 15, 2009.

Ganivet, Angel, *Letters from Finland,* the Spanish version: *Cartas finlandesas, hombres del norte,* Nordica, Madrid, 2006.

Georgetown University, The Middle East & North Africa Forum, Major General Douglas Stone, *Reform in the US detention and detainee facilities post Abu Ghraib,* November 12, 2008.

Goldman, Robert K., *Protection of human rights and fundamental freedoms while countering terrorism,* United Nations High Commissioner for Human Rights, The High Commissioner for Human Rights 2004, page 10 GE.05–10694 (E) 150205 E/ CN.4/2005/103.

Gonzalez Ibanez, Joaquin, "International Rule of Law and Human Rights: The Aspiration of a Work in Progress", *The Journal Jurisprudence*, Volume 15, 2013

Gonzalez Ibanez, Joaquin, "Legal Pedagogy, The Rule of Law and Human Rights: The Professor, The Magistrate's Robe and Miguel de Unamuno", *Journal of Human Rights Law,* Volume 6, Number 1, November 2012.

Gonzalez Ibanez, Joaquin *interview with Jamin B. Raskin,* May 2009, Washington DC.

Gonzalez Ibanez, Joaquin, *interview with M. General Stone,* April 28, 2009, Pentagon, VA.

Gonzalez Ibanez, Joaquin, *interview with Egon Gutman,* February 2009, Washington D.C.

Gonzalez Ibanez, Joaquin, *interview with Prof. Richard J. Wilson,* May 3, 2009, Washington DC.

Greenberg, Karen J. *The Trump Administration's Dangerous Assault on Our Words,* The Nation, May 17th, 2018.

Hamdan v. Rumsfeld, 548 U.S. 557 (2006).

Hamdi v. Rumsfeld, 124 S. Ct. 2633 (2004).

Hassan, Muhammad Haniff, *Singapore's Muslim Community Based Initiatives against JI*, April 15, 2009, available at www.terrorismanalysts.com/pt/index. php?option=com_rokzine&view=article&id=19

Human Rights First, *Arbitrary Justice: Trial of Guantanamo and Bagram Detainees in Afghanistan*, HRF, 2008.

IACHR October 28, 2009, *Hearings of the Regular Session of the IACHR: PM 259/02 Detainees at the Guantánamo Naval Base/ PM 211/08, Djamel Ameziane.*

Inside Defense, (no author mentioned) *To understand insurgency in Iraq: read something old, something new*, December 2, 2004, available at www.defensenewsstand.com/ insider_books.asp

Iraq Coaliation Casualty Count, May 1, 2009, available at http://icasualties.org/Iraq/ index.aspx,.

Jackson, Robert H., *Opening Statement Before the International Military Tribunal*, Nuremberg, Germany, November 21, 1945, available at www.roberthjackson.org/

Jan. 11, 2009, http://abcnews.go.com/ThisWeek/Economy/story?id=6618199&page=1

Jim Fitzgerald, *Eric Holder tells West Point: The law was not always followed in U.S. war against terror*, Associated Press, Wednesday April 15, 2009, available at www. therightreasons.net/index.php?showtopic=14141

Jong, Erica, *Botero Sees the World's True Heavies at Abu Ghraib*, published at Special to The Washington Post, Sunday, November 4, 2007.

Kamen, Al, *The End of the Global War on Terror*, March 24, 2009, published at The Washington Post. Available at *http://voices.washingtonpost.com/44/2009/03/23/ the_end_of_the_global_war_on_t.html*

Karadsheh, Jomana, *War blamed for 655,000 Iraqi deaths "President Bush says he does not consider report credible"* available at www.cnn.com/2006/WORLD/meast/10/11/ iraq.deaths/

Kerry, John F, U.S. Senate Committee on Foreign Relations, Chairman John F. Kerry. *Opening Statement for Harold Koh* Nomination, U.S. State Department's legal adviser, April 2009.

Kersetz, Imre, *Fatelessness*, Random House, New York 2004.

Klemperer, Victor, *The Language of the Third Reich: LTI, Lingua Tertii Imperii--A Philologist's Notebook*, New York and London, Continuum Books, 2002.

Knowlton, Brian, *Report Gives New Detail on Approval of Brutal Techniques*, published in The New York Times, April 22, 2009.

Koh, Harold, Conference keynote address: *The politics of implementation: The Role of Human Rights in Foreign Policy*, at the Conference Realizing the promise of the Universal Declaration of Human Rights: examining the first 60 years and beyond, December 2, 2008 American University Washington College of Law. Available at www.wcl.american.edu/humright/center/webcast.cfm

Levi, Primo, *La chiave a stella*, (The Wrench), Einaudi Editori, Torino, 1978.

Liptak, Adam, *Ginsburg Shares Views on Influence of Foreign Law on Her Court, and Vice Versa*, The New York Times, April 12, 2009.

Mayer, Jane, *The dark side. The inside story on how the war on terror turned into a war on American ideals*, Doubleday, New York, 2008.

McKeon, Mark J., *Why We Must Prosecute, The Washington Post, Torture Is a Breach Of International Law*, The New York Times, April 28, 2009.

Mertus, A., *Julie, Bait and switch, Human Rights and U.S Foreign Policy*, Routledge, New York, 2007.

Miller, Judith, *Iraqi Militants Becoming Citizens*, published in Readers Digest, July 2008 Issue, available at www.judithmiller.com/512/iraqi-militants-becoming-citizens

Moisi, Dominique, *The Geopolitics of Emotion: How Cultures of Fear, Humiliation, and Hope are Reshaping the World*, Doubleday, New York, 2009.

Morgenthau, *Morgenthau to Truman*, May 29 1945, *Morgenthau Diary*, vol. 2 pp. 1544–45, cited in Gary J. Bass, *Stay the hand of vengeance*.

Naim, Moisés, *Hunger For America*, Washington Post, January 2, 2008, available at www.washingtonpost.com/wp-dyn/content/article/2008/01/01/AR2008010101298.html

Mottern, Nick and Rau, Bill, *Obama Faced With Iraq Detainee Human Rights, Debacle*, 3 December 2008 available at http://consumersforpeace.org/index.php?filename=archive-obama-iraq-human-rights.html

Nye, Joseph & Joseph Nye Jr. *Soft Power* 5–7, Public Affairs 2004.

Paust, J. Jordan, *Beyond the law, The Bush Administration unlawful responses in the "War" on Terror*, Cambridge UP, 2007.

Red Cross International Committee, *1948 Geneva Conventions* and additional Protocols available at The International Committee of the Red Cross, www.icrc.org/ihl.nsf/CONVPRES?OpenView

Repubblica, La, editorial, *Il generale nel suo laberinto*, published in La Repubblica, Roma, Sept. 4, 1982, www.repubblica.it/online/album/ottantadue/bocca/bocca.html

Scheuer, Michael, *Imperial Hubris*, Bresseys, INC, Washington DC, 2004.

Scheuer, Michael, *Marching toward hell. America and Islam after Iraq*, Free Press, New York, 2008.

Shlomo Ben-Ami, *Europe's Dangerous Banalities*, February 2009 available at www.project-syndicate.org

Stephanopoulos, George, Interview with President-Elect Barack Obama, January 11, 2009, available at http://abcnews.go.com/ThisWeek/Economy/story?id=6619291

Snyder, T., *Blood Lands*, Preface Europe, Vintage, London, 2010.

Sting, Russians, *Dream Of The Blue Turtle*, Universal, London, 1985.

Tamanaha, B.Z., *On the Rule of Law*, Cambridge University Press, 2004, p. 141.

Taylor, Telford, *Nuremberg and Vietnam. An American Tragedy*, The New York Times Books, 1970.

Tiger, Michael., *Thinking about terrorism*, (ABA)American Bar Association, Washington 2007.

Todorov, Tzvetan, Stanley Hoffmann (Preface), *The New World Disorder: Reflections of a European*, by, Politi Press, Malden, 2005.

Tutu, Desmond, *Will Africa Let Sudan Off the Hook?* The New York Times, March 3, 2009.

United Nations *Security Council Resolution 1483 (2003)*, Adopted by the Security Council at its 4761st meeting, on May 22 2003, available at www.uniraq.org/documents/Resolution1483.pdf

UNAMI *Report on Human Right (1 July-31 December 2008)*, available at http://uniraq.org/documents/UNAMI_Human_Rights_Report_July_December_2008_EN.pdf

Partlow, Joshua, *United Nations Report on Human Rights in Iraq*, Washington Post Foreign Service, Thursday, April 26, available at www.washingtonpost.com/wp

United Nations Office at Geneva, *Human Rights Council holds review, rationalization and improvement process for mandates on independence of judges and on torture*, June 4 2008, available at Www.Unog.Ch/Unog/Website/News_Media.Nsf/ (Httpnewsbyyear_En)/0A2BEE45EB2C22B0C125745E004D1CAB?Opendocument

WCL American University Conference, *How legal Rhetoric shapes the Law-The language of violence and torture*, Conference November 7, 2008, American University Washington College of Law, available at www.wcl.american.edu/secle/ fall/2008/081107.cfm

Williams, Joseph, *Some call for Bush administration trials, Want ex-leader accountable on Iraq war*, published in The Boston Globe, February 3, 2009.

Wilson, Richard, *War Stories: A reflection on defending an alleged enemy combatant Detained in Guantánamo Bay, Cuba en Derechos Humanos, relaciones internacionales y globalización*, Joaquin Gonzalez Ibanez editor, Gustavo Ibáñez Ediciones Jurídicas, Bogotá, 2007.

Wittes, B., *Law and the long war, The future on Justice in the age of terrorism*, Penguin, New York, 2008.

Woods, Andrew K. Woods, *The business ends*, Financial Times, June 27 2008, available at www.ft.com/cms/s/2/71c42ec0–40ca-11dd-bd48–0000779fd2ac.html?nclick_ check=1

Woodworth, Paddy, *Dirty War, Clean Hands*: ETA, the GAL and Spanish Democracy, Cork University Press, 2001.

Yoo, John, *War by other means*, Atlantic Monthly Press, New York, 2006.

Part III

Human Rights
in the Council of Europe
and the European Convention
on Human Rights

THE ABSENCE OF RUSSIAN PARLIAMENTARIANS IN PACE: A CLARIFICATION

Andrew Drzemczewski
Visiting Professor at Middlesex University School of Law, London
Former Head of the Parliamentary Assembly's Legal Affairs &
Human Rights Department, Council of Europe, Strasbourg

A SHORT INTRODUCTORY NOTE ADDRESSED TO PAUL

Being younger than I am, you may have a better memory, Paul, as to when we first met. I believe it was back in 1979 when you attended the Summer Session of the Strasbourg-based International Institute of Human Rights, after which you became my 'principal correspondent' who ensured, in effect, the accuracy of what I had written in my PhD with respect to the domestic status of the European Convention on Human Rights (ECHR) in Belgium, for which I owe you a huge debt of gratitude.[1] But our long and loyal friendship, including that of our respective spouses, Anne and Anne-Marie, was effectively 'sealed' when you hosted us in your home (as well as our new car purchased in Brussels) back in August 1984. So how could I not contribute to this *Liber Amicorum*? That said, my short contribution is somewhat tainted with political considerations. I trust that it will not cause too much discomfort to you as an outstanding 'black-letter' lawyer. But even if it does, our 40 years of friendship will, I'm sure, allow us and our spouses to discuss this thorny subject at our regular informal meetings in Strasbourg in the coming years… while you continue your distinguished career as a judge on the European Court of Human Rights in respect of Belgium, in the footsteps of Henri Rolin, Walter-Jean Ganshof Van Der Meersch, Jan De Mayer and Françoise Tulkens.

---

[1]   See A. Drzemczewski *European Human Rights Convention in Domestic Law. A Comparative Study*, Oxford University Press, 1983, esp.pp.63–70, 207–209 & 274–278. I still have in my possession your 6-page handwritten letter ('*Schepdaal, 11th January 1982*') in which you provided me with a significant number of last-minute corrections to my text, all of which I incorporated into the book!

I. THE CONTEXT

Why is there a need to provide a commentary on the participation, or rather the non-participation, of Russian parliamentarians in the work of the Parliamentary Assembly after the annexation of Crimea by Russia in March 2014? There are principally two inter-related reasons for so doing, both tied to the accuracy of (mis)information that has circulated in this respect.

The first concerns a misunderstanding of what 'sanctions' had actually been imposed by PACE in this respect. In an excellent book entitled *Russia and the European Court of Human Rights. The Strasbourg Effect* Petra Roter, when referring to the uneasy relationship between Russia and the Council of Europe which *"turned sour almost overnight due to Russia's foreign policy"* relating to the crisis in Ukraine and the annexation of Crimea, indicated erroneously that *"it was PACE that went the furthest in the form of non-recognizing the credentials of the Russian delegation to PACE."*[2]

The second point that needs clarification relates to the inappropriate suggestion that it is the Parliamentary Assembly's 'fault' that Russian parliamentarians have not been able to participate in, inter alia, the election of judges onto the European Court of Human Rights.[3] In a statement made by the Russian Foreign Minister, Sergey Lavrov, when he met the Council of Europe's Secretary General back in June 2018, Mr. Lavrov indicated that the Assembly was to blame for the fact that *"more than one-third of the judges at the ECHR have been elected without the participation of a delegation of Russian lawmakers,"* later specifying, in an interview in October 2018, that *"since our PMs were stripped of the right to vote, the Parliamentary Assembly has already elected, if I am not mistaken, 24 judges to the European Court of Human Rights. And the total number is 47. So, the majority of judges in the European Court are judges elected in the absence of the Russian votes. Similarly, a new Commissioner for Human Rights was elected without the Russian MPs. Next June, a new secretary general of the Council of Europe will be elected. So, due to the suspension of our right, which is granted to us by the Statute of the Council of Europe, to participate in these votes, the above functionaries of the Council of Europe (the judges, the commissioner for human*

---

2   P. Roter 'Russia in the Council of Europe: Participation à la carte' in L. Mälksoo & W. Benedek (Eds.), *Russian and the European Court of Human Rights. The Strasbourg Effect*, Cambridge University Press, 2018, pp.26–56, p.48 (although she subsequently – correctly – explains the PACE decision to deprive Russian parliamentarians of certain of their rights in the Assembly).

3   Article 22 of the ECHR, entitled 'Election of judges,' specifies *'The judges shall be elected by the Parliamentary Assembly with respect to each High Contracting Party by a majority of votes cast from a list of three candidates nominated by the High Contracting Party.'*

rights and soon, if this issue persists, the secretary general) will, in fact, not be legitimate for us."[4]

As will be explained, the Assembly has not deprived the Russian PACE delegation of its credentials and the absence of the Russian delegation in PACE is due to the Russian Parliament's own decision not to submit credentials for its delegation to sit therein; only members of the Assembly belonging to delegations whose credentials have been ratified by the Assembly may take part in the elections referred to by Mr. Lavrov.[5]

II. RUSSIAN PARLIAMENTARIANS IN PACE ... & THEIR ABSENCE

A. DECISIONS IN 2014 & 2015

For present purposes, it is not necessary to provide an overview of the procedure leading up to the Committee of Ministers' invitation for Russia to become a member State of the Council of Europe, specifying that the Russian PACE delegation be composed of 18 parliamentarians, and the latter's participation in the Assembly's work since 1996.[6] Suffice, to note, is that in April 2014 and again in January 2015 the Parliamentary Assembly decided to deprive Russian parliamentarians certain of their rights in the Assembly, including voting rights, in reaction to Russia's annexation of Crimea. But it did not take the drastic decision to divest the delegation from continuing to participate in its work.[7] In response, Russian parliamentarians initially decided not to engage themselves in

---

[4] International Affairs, video interview of 16 October 2018, available at http://en.interaffairs. ru/lavrov/733-foreign-minister-sergey-lavrovs-interview-with-euronews-moscow-october-16-2018.html (visited on 11 July 2019).

[5] For details consult Rules 6 to 12 of the Assembly's Rules of Procedure, accessible at www. assembly.coe.int/nw/xml/RoP/Rules.pdf, & an important clarification provided to the Assembly's Bureau by the Assembly's Committee on Rules of Procedure, Immunities & Institutional Affairs, document AS/Pro (2018) 20 def., available at http://website-pace.net/documents/19895/4457630/20181211-clarification-rightsofparticipationrepresentation-EN.pdf (both visited on 11 July 2019).

[6] Committee of Ministers Resolution (96)2 of 8 February 1996, available at https://rm.coe.int/CoERMPublicCommonSearchServices/DisplayDCTMContent?documentId=09000016806 2e4fa (visited on 11 April 2019). For commentaries consult, e.g., E. Klein 'Membership and Observer Status,' pp.40–92, esp. pp. 54–64, 70–73 & 85–92, and P. Leach 'The Parliamentary Assembly of the Council of Europe,' pp. 166–211, at pp. 186–195, in S. Schmahl & M. Breuer (Eds.) *The Council of Europe. Its Law & Politics,* Oxford University Press, 2017. See also footnote 32, below.

[7] See, in this connection Resolutions 1990 (2014) of 10 April 2014, & 2034 (2015) of 28 January 2015; for a fuller picture of PACE in-house initiatives related to this subject reference can also be made to PACE Resolution 2063 (2015) of 24 June 2015, as well as the aborted attempt to strengthen the Assembly's decision-making process concerning credentials and voting,

the Assembly's work and, as of 2016 the Russian Parliament has not submitted credentials of its delegation to the Assembly. Russia has also withheld its payments to the Organisation's budget.[8]

Of particular interest, in this connection, is the Assembly's approach to the use of 'sanctions' with respect to parliamentary delegations. When adopting the first of its Resolution's on this subject in April 2014, the Assembly stressed that *"political dialogue should remain the preferred way to find a compromise, and there should be no return to the pattern of the Cold War. Suspension of the credentials of the Russian delegation would make such a dialogue impossible, while the Assembly constitutes a good platform for keeping the Russian delegation accountable on the basis of Council of Europe's values and principles. The Parliamentary Assembly has the power and the opportunity in this veritable crisis to confront face-to-face one of its member States – the Russian Federation – with questions and facts and to demand answers and accountability."*[9]

B.   SINCE THEN…

Hence, formally as of January 2016 there has been no Russian delegation in PACE. Since that date, and unlike what is often erroneously indicated in the media, <u>no</u> 'sanctions' have been imposed by the Assembly with respect to Russian parliamentarians; the absence of the Russian delegation is the result of its own decision not to participate in the Assembly's work. In other words, the Russian Parliament has, of its own volition, decided not to participate in the work of the Parliamentary Assembly despite express invitations for it to do so prior to the Assembly sessions for the years 2016, 2017, 2018 and 2019.[10]

---

document 14621 of 21 September 2018. All these texts are available on the Assembly's portal: http://assembly.coe.int/nw/Home-EN.asp.

As concerns the specific issue of the annexation, by Russia, of Crimea, see Symposium 'The Incorporation of Crimea by the Russian Federation in the Light of International Law' in Vol.75 ZaöRV, C. Marxen, A. Peters & M. Hartwig (Eds.), 2015, pp.1–231 and S. SAYAPIN & E. TSYBULENKO (Eds.) *The Use of Force against Ukraine*, T.M.C. Asser Press, 2018, *passim*.

[8]   For a recent overview see K. Dzehtsiarou& D.K. Coffrey 'Suspension and expulsion of member States of the Council of Europe: difficult decisions in troubled times' in Vol.68 ICLQ 2019, pp.443–476, at pp.458–460.

[9]   Paragraph 14 of PACE Resolution 1990 (2014). 'Sanctions' imposed by the Assembly with respect to a national parliamentary delegation may remain in force (only) until the opening of the subsequent Ordinary Session, i.e., the following January.

[10]   Note can also be taken of the fact that the Cypriot parliamentary delegation was absent from the Assembly for a period of 18 years, from 1965 to 1983; see, in this connection, H. Klebes 'Human rights and parliamentary democracy in the Parliamentary Assembly' in F. Matscher & H. Petzold (Eds.), in *Protecting Human Rights: the European Dimension. Studies in honour of G.J. Wiarda*, Carl Heymanns Verlag, KG, 1988, pp.307–334, at p.313.

The Organisation's Statute of 1949 obliges all national parliaments to submit credentials of their delegations at the opening of each yearly ordinary session (Article 25[11]) and in line with current regulations credentials must be submitted every January. Non-submission of credentials automatically excludes a delegation from the Assembly's work for the whole year.

Based on provisions of its Rules of Procedure dating back to 1964, which have been modified and adapted over the years, the credentials of a parliamentary delegation, be it on procedural or substantive grounds, may be challenged or reconsidered by the Assembly if fundamental principles of the Organisation have not been respected by a member State, if there is a persistent failure to honour its obligations and commitments or if there is perceived a lack of cooperation in the Assembly's monitoring procedure.[12]

As explained by the Secretary General of the Assembly, over the last 70 years the Assembly has been extremely reluctant to turn down credentials.[13] Even if the credentials of delegations have been challenged in quite a number of instances[14], only twice – in respect of the parliamentary delegations of Greece in 1969 and Turkey in 1981 – has this actually occurred.[15] Hence, when serious infringements of Council of Europe norms are at issue, instead of turning-down or annulling credentials, the Assembly can instead restrict parliamentarians participation in certain activities (e.g., to vote, to be appointed a rapporteur, chair a committee), or to restrict their rights in representing the institution (e.g., within the Assembly itself or one of its bodies, external representation). The deprivation of a number of rights of members of a national delegation, on substantive grounds, has arisen only on three occasions in the history of the Assembly, each time with respect to the parliamentary delegation of Russia: in 2000 (suspension of the right to vote in plenary due to the second Chechen war); in 2014 (illegal annexation of Crimea/action with regard to Ukraine) and

---

[11] Text of Article 25 of the Statue of the Council of Europe: https://rm.coe.int/1680306052.

[12] See footnotes 6 & 8 above. As the credentials of parliamentarians from Bosnia-Herzegovina had not been submitted to PACE prior to the opening of the April 2019 part-session, this country's parliamentarians are not participating in the work of the PACE in 2019.

[13] W. Sawicki, on the Council of Europe's Intranet site, on 22 October 2018 available at http://assembly.coe.int/nw/xml/News/News-View-EN.asp?newsid=7257&cat=403 (visited on 11 July 2019). See also E. Klein 'Membership and Observer Status,' in *The Council of Europe*, footnote 7 above, pp.40–92 at p.72.

[14] Examples are provided by P. Evans & O. Silk in *The Parliamentary Assembly Practice and Procedure* (Council of Europe Publishing, 11th edition, 2012), at pp.109–116. There have, in effect, been over 40 instances in which such requests have been made!

[15] For details see, e.g., B. Haller *An Assembly for Europe. The Council of Europe's Parliamentary Assembly 1949–1989*, Council of Europe Publishing, 2006 at pp.106–110 & 115–122; H. Klebes, footnote 11 above, at pp. 313–314, and B. Wassenberg, *History of the Council of Europe*, Council of Europe Publishing, 2013, at pp.65–67 & pp.114–115.

in 2015 (continued illegal annexation of Crimea and the conflict in eastern Ukraine).[16]

III. RELATED ISSUES

A. THE COMMITTEE OF MINISTERS AND PACE

Whereas the Committee of Ministers can suspend or expel a State from the Organisation which violates Council of Europe standards (Article 8 of the Statute), which it has never done[17], the specific issue of penalties, or sanctions, that the Assembly can apply to parliamentarians is governed by its Rules of Procedure (see Article 28(a) of the Statute).[18] The expelling or suspension, by the Committee of Ministers, of a State which seriously violates the Organisation's norms is a politically complex exercise which necessitates a two-thirds majority of representatives casting a vote and a majority of representatives entitled to sit on the Committee. In so far as the Assembly is concerned, suspension of the right to representation therein is governed by its Rules of Procedure, which is a *modus operandi* distinct from that of the Committee of Ministers statutory right to suspend or expel a State from the Council of Europe (although its Resolution (51) 30 obliges it to consult the Assembly fist). The Assembly's procedure, as already indicated, has evolved and solidified, unopposed over a period of well over 50 years, and can be seen as a well-established self-regulating parliamentary variant, recourse to which the PACE can make independently of the statutory powers vested in the Committee of Ministers.[19]

---

[16] Consult, on the Assembly's portal, respectively, document 8949, §2, & document 8956, §1, of 2001, & Resolutions 1990 (2014), 2034 (2015) & 2063 (2015), available at: http://assembly.coe.int/nw/Home-EN.asp.
That said, the Assembly's Rules of Procedure insist that PACE delegations must include a percentage of members of the under-represented sex at least equal to that applying to their home parliament, and at least one member of each sex in all instances (Rule 6.2.a). Thus, if breach of this requirement is considered a substantive ground, then the Assembly's decision, in 2004, to ratify the Maltese and Irish delegations' credentials, suspending their voting rights for as long as these delegations contained no women, would need to be added to the list: see PACE Resolution 1360 (2004).

[17] Greece withdrew from the Organisation prior to the country's probable expulsion by the CM in 1969. Greece rejoined the Council of Europe in 1974.

[18] These issues, especially with respect to Russia, have been discussed in blogposts, in which can be found hyperlinks to primary sources, also available on the Assembly's portal: see A. Drzemczewski & K. Dzehtsarou 'Painful relations between the Council of Europe and Russia' in EJIL: *Talk!*, of 18 September 2018 https://www.ejiltalk.org/painful-relations-between-the-council-of-europe-and-russia/#comments and L.R. GLAS 'The Assembly's appeasement towards Russia' in Strasbourg Observers, of 27 September 2018 (including comments attached thereto) https://strasbourgobservers.com/2018/09/27/the-assemblys-appeasement-towards-russia/ (both visited on 11 July 2019).

[19] See, in this respect E. Klein, footnote 7 above, & F. Benoit-Rohmer & H. Klebes *Council of Europe Law. Towards a Pan-European Legal Order,* Council of Europe Publishing, 2005, esp.

In this connection, it has recently been suggested, erroneously, that the competence to exclude or sanction member States, including membership of parliamentary delegations, is the exclusive prerogative of the Committee of Ministers.[20] This suggestion must be forcefully rejected, simply because the Assembly rules on the questioning of credentials are based on a long-standing and unopposed (except by Russia recently) practice, accepted by all member States and the Committee of Ministers.[21]

Institutional rivalry between the two bodies is frequent, but their statutory relationship is premised on common purpose and effective cooperation, despite their fundamentally different composition and manner of functioning. The Committee of Ministers is composed, *de facto,* principally of diplomats and it is often unwilling or incapable, due to its propensity to seek consensus rather than to vote, to take a principled 'open stand' when confronted with major human rights violations in member States.[22] The Assembly exercises a degree of democratic control over the Committee of Ministers. Composed of national parliamentarians it can and often has strongly reacted to unacceptable infringements of Council of Europe standards.[23] An analysis of the manner in which the conflict in Chechnya was dealt with by both statutory organs, in the context of major human rights violations committed there by the Russian security forces, which resulted in the suspension of the voting rights of the Russian PACE delegation in April 2000, is instructive in this respect.[24]

The Assembly and the Committee of Ministers are both presently confronted with formidable challenges. How can, if at all, the Assembly and the Russian Parliament unravel 'the Gordian Knot' relating to the (obstinate) decision of

---

pp.40–44 & pp.65–71. At p. 66 the authors confirm that *'the Assembly's powers have never given rise to any dispute with the Committee of Ministers.'*

20 A. ALİ 'The Parliamentary Assembly of the Council of Europe and sanctions against the Russian Federation in response to the crisis in Ukraine,' Vol. 27 *Italian Yearbook of International Law* 2017, pp.78–91.

21 Discussed in blogposts referred to in footnote 19 above. See also, in this connection, paragraph 22 of the ICJ's 1971 Namibia Opinion https://www.icj-cij.org/files/case-related/53/053-19710621-ADV-01-00-EN.pdf & chapter 9 in N.M. Blokker's *International Institutional Law,* Brill, 6th revised ed, 2018, H.G. Schermers & N.M. Blokker, esp. paragraphs 1350–1350J.

22 See S. Palmer 'The Committee of Ministers' in *The Council of Europe. Its Law and Policies,* footnote 7 above, pp.137–165, esp. at pp. 160–163. Hence my doubts as to the likely efficacy of the recently proposed 'joint reaction procedure' proposed by the Assembly (see footnote 34, below).

23 See, e.g., comments by B. Wassenberg, footnote 16 above, at p.115, and P. Leach, footnote 7 above, at pp.192–193. In addition, and as indicated in footnote 15, recourse is often made by PACE members to the threat of 'sanctions,' including contesting of credentials, which more often than not, has given positive results.

24 See P.Leach 'The Parliamentary Assembly of the Council of Europe' in *The Council of Europe. Its Laws and Policies,* footnote 7, at pp.193–194.

the latter not to take part in the work of PACE, an issue which is inextricably linked with the Committee of Ministers duty to determine how to proceed if the Russian authorities maintain their decision not to pay their contribution into the Organisation's budget (see below)?[25]

B. BUDGETARY CONSIDERATIONS

As has been amply reported in the media, Russian parliamentarians, as well as high-ranking State officials, have made statements to the effect that their parliamentary delegation would return to the Assembly only after the latter removes from its Rules of Procedure all the above provisions which permit the challenge of credentials and the possible sanctioning of national delegations. Russia has also suspended its payments into the Organisation's budget.[26]

In June 2017 Russia suspended the payment of the remainder of its 2017 budgetary contribution to the Council of Europe until its demands are met. This decision must be seen in the wider context of the Committee of Ministers maintaining, for over a number of years, the policy of the Organisation's 'zero growth rate,' which in effect means no allowance for inflation (thereby actually reducing the budget), as well as the Turkish authorities' decision to withdraw Turkey's 'major contributor' status which it had assumed in 2016. The cumulative financial consequences of these decisions have resulted in an unprecedented short-fall in the Organisation's finances that will, if not overcome, result in the suspension of a number of (human rights) programmes, reduction of money made available to the European Court of Human Rights and a number of key monitoring bodies, as well as loss of jobs for staff members.[27]

The total contributions of all 47 member States to the Council of Europe's budget for 2019 are in the public domain and can be consulted online.[28] For present purposes, suffice it to refer to the situation concerning Russia's non-payment

---

[25]   See Report by the [Finnish] Chair of the Committee of Ministers to the Parliamentary Assembly (January-April 2019), document CM/AS (2019) 3, of 8 April 2019, paragraphs 25 & 26, available at https://search.coe.int/cm/Pages/result_details.aspx?ObjectId=090000168093d0dc (visited on 11 July 2019), & K. Dzehtsiarou & D.K. Coffey, footnote 9 above.

[26]   For comments on the stand taken by the Russian authorities – perceived as 'blackmail' in certain quarters – see footnotes 9 & 19, above; N.P. Engel 'Russland testet das Rückgrad des Europarates' ['Russian testing the backbone of the Council of Europe'], in Vol. 44 EuGRZ 2017, pp.720–722, as well as numerous comments on the Web, such as N. Tenzer 'Is Russia blackmailing the Council of Europe?,' EU Observer, 17 September 2018, available at https://euobserver.com/opinion/142849 (viewed on 11 July 2019).

[27]   See, K. Dzehtsiarou & D.K. Coffey, footnote 9 above, esp. pp.458–460, and Committee of Ministers document 'Council of Europe Programme & Budget 2018–2019, 2019 adjusted,' 18 December 2018, available at https://rm.coe.int/168090363f (visited on 11 July 2019).

[28]   See Committee of Ministers document, footnote 28 above, at p.20.

of its contributions (debt) to the Organisation since June 2017. Russia presently owes the Council of Europe about 54.7 million euro with respect to contributions for 2017 and 2018. And, if the debt + annual contribution of 32.6 million euro for 2019 (+ interest of 1% *per* month on sums due) are not paid by the end of June 2019, the total sum due would be in the region of 100 million euro (as all States' budgetary contributions for 2019 must be effectuated by that date).[29]

CONCLUDING REMARKS

The explanation as to why Russian parliamentarians are absent from PACE has been provided, but the 'Gordian Knot' still needs to be unravelled. How, if at all, can this be achieved? Without being able to provide an answer to this question, I allow myself a few concluding observations of a more general nature.

Obviously, some form of political 'arrangement' will need to be sought to (try to) resolve the present *impasse,* the seriousness of which cannot be underestimated. That said, the situation in which the Council of Europe finds itself today must be seen in the light of both the Committee of Ministers' and Assembly's 'accommodation,' not to say lowering, of the Organisation's accession requirements in respect of a number of States, including Russia which acceded to the Organisation in February 1996[30], and the undoubted beneficial aspects of the country's membership now stretching over a period of 23 years, despite many difficulties and shortcomings.[31] That said, membership of a 'democratic

---

[29] Article 9 of the Statute of the Council of Europe stipulates that *'The Committee of Ministers may suspend the right of representation on the Committee and the Consultative [Parliamentary] Assembly of a Member which has failed to fulfil its financial obligation during such period as the obligation remains unfulfilled.'* In November 1994 the Committee of Ministers agreed that, apart from exceptional circumstances having prevented a member State from fulfilling its obligation, Article 9 of the Council of Europe's Statute will be applied to any State which has failed to fulfil all or a substantial part of its financial obligation for a period of two years.

[30] See A. Drzemczewski 'Human Rights in Europe: An Insider's Views' in EHRLP 2017, pp.134–144, at pp.135–135. The Assembly *"believes that Russia – in the sense of Article 4 of the Statute – is clearly willing and will be able in the near future to fulfil the provisions of membership… as set forth in Article 3."* (Statutory Opinion No. 193 (1996) on Russia's request for membership. Emphasis added). For details see D. Chatzivassiliou 'L'adhésion de la Russie au Conseil de l'Europe,' in *Le Conseil de l'Europe acteur de la recomposition du territoire européen,'* Espace Europe, GRECER, n°10, mai 1997, Faculté de Droit, Grenoble, C. Schneider (Ed.), pp.27–60, *passim,* H. Klebes 'Le Conseil de l'Europe survivra-t-il à son élargissement?' in J.-F. Flauss & P. Wachsmann (Eds.), *Le Droit des Organisations Internationales. Recueil d'études à la mémoire de Jacques Schwob,* Bruylant Bruxelles, 1997, pp.175–202, & V. Dierić 'Admission to membership of the Council of Europe and legal significance of commitments entered into by new member States,' in Vol. 36 *ZaöRV* 2000, pp.605–629, at pp.619–620.

[31] See, e.g. the Assembly's (monitoring) reports relating to Russia, http://website-pace.net/en_GB/web/as-mon/main, those of its Legal Affairs & Human Rights Committee relating to, in particular, the North Caucasus www.assembly.coe.int/Committee/JUR/OverviewE.pdf, the Strasbourg Court's portal https://www.echr.coe.int/Documents/CP_Russia_ENG.

---

club' is undertaken voluntary, and it appears somewhat indecent to suggest that a relatively new member State which has clearly overstepped its commitments to the Organisation to unilaterally try to impose changes in the Assembly's long-established and accepted method of functioning.[32]

Were the Russian PACE delegation not to have excluded itself from the Assembly, and in the hope that credentials will be submitted as of 2020, its members would (and will) have the opportunity, from within the Assembly, to propose changes as to the manner in which the Assembly operates. And, more importantly, by reintegrating themselves into the parliamentary body they would secure for themselves the right to take part in the Assembly's key role of electing judges onto the Strasbourg Court, the Human Rights Commissioner and senior officials of the Council of Europe.[33]

Finally, the present situation must be seen in the wider political context in which the (continued) illegal annexation of Crimea, in particular, is closely tied to the Assembly's role as 'the conscience of Europe.' When a State seriously transgresses the Organisation's core values, and the Council of Europe's executive organ, the Committee of Ministers, reacts timidly, is reluctant to react and/or remains silent, the Assembly considers itself duty-bound to take a principled stand. Hence, even if the idea recently put forward by the Assembly, namely that of the setting-up of a 'joint Committee of Ministers/Assembly reaction procedure' with respect to States which seriously violate the Organisation's statutory obligations were to see the light of day (a 'paper tiger'?), this initiative does not help to resolve the present predicament facing the Council of Europe's two statutory organs.[34]

* * *

AN UPDATE (11 July 2019)

The Russian Parliament's decision not to submit credentials of its delegation prior to the opening of this year's PACE session in January 2019, the 'political agitation' at the Committee of Ministers meeting in Helsinki in May, tied to inappropriate pressure, not to say blackmail, by the Russian authorities' not to

---

pdf (updated in March 2019) and that of the CPT https://www.coe.int/en/web/cpt/russian-federation.

[32] As concerns the issue of prolonged unjustified non-payment of a State's contribution to the Organisation's budget, see article by K. Dzehtsiarou & D.K. Coffey, footnote 9, above, at pp.458–460 and footnote 30.

[33] See, in particular, PACE document AS/Pro (2018) 20 def. http://website-pace.net/documents/19895/4457630/20181211-clarification-rightsofparticipationrepresentation-EN.pdf/c254d449–3894–4aad-aab2–91b236dc1b42 (visited on 11 July 2019).

[34] See PACE Resolution 2277 (2019) & Recommendation 2153 (2019), both of 10 April 2019, available at http://assembly.coe.int/nw/xml/XRef/Xref-DocDetails-EN.asp?FileID=27663&lang=EN (viewed on 11 July 2019).

pay their budgetary contributions (as indicated above), led the Parliamentary Assembly to 'bend' its Rules of Procedure: see "Strengthening the decision-making of the Parliamentary Assembly concerning credentials and voting," Resolution 2287 (2019) of 25 June 2019.[35] This resulted in the return of the Russian PACE delegation into PACE whose members participated in the election of the Organisation's new Secretary General and two judges onto the Strasbourg Court during the June 2019 part-session.[36] Also, in the first week of July, the Russian authorities paid their financial dues to the Organisation for 2019; however, the debt owed for the years 2017 and 2018, plus interest payments thereon, remains unpaid (see B. BUDGETARY CONSIDERATIONS, above).

A pragmatic resolution of a difficult situation for the Council of Europe and its member States **or** a serious dent in the credibility of the Assembly for not having imposed 'internal sanctions' when ratifying the Russian delegation's credentials? Perhaps both. As concerns Resolution 2292 (2019) "Challenge, on substantive grounds, of the still unratified credentials of the parliamentary delegation of the Russian Federation,"[37] I can do no better than refer to the 'principled stand' taken and votes cast by, in particular, Lord (Donald) Anderson, Boriss Cilevičs and Sir Roger Gale in the debate leading up to the adoption of this Resolution on 26 June 2019.[38]

---

[35] Based on doc.14900, report of its Committee on Rules of Procedure, Immunities and Institutional Affairs, both available on the Assembly's portal (see footnote 8, above).

[36] See in this connection, in particular, blogpost by L.R.GLAS 'Russia left, threatened and won: Its return to the Assembly without sanctions' in Strasbourg Observers, of 2 July 2019, as well as my comment thereto, posted on 3 July 2019 https://strasbourgobservers.com/2019/07/02/russia-left-threatened-and-has-won-its-return-to-the-assembly-without-sanctions/ (visited on 11 July 2019).

[37] Based on doc.14992, report of the Monitoring Committee, both available on the Assembly's portal (see footnote 8 above).

[38] See Verbatim Records of PACE 3rd part-session, 26 June 2019, afternoon http://assembly.coe.int/nwbs/verbatim/?sessionid=201906&day=2019-06-26&afternoon=True&lang=EN&contentlang=EN For votes cast with respect to amendments proposed & the Resolution itself, see PACE portal: http://assembly.coe.int/nw/xml/Votes/DB-VotesResults-EN.asp?VoteID=37990&DocID=19023&selSession=201906 (both visited on 11 July).

THE RESEARCH DIVISION
OF THE EUROPEAN COURT OF
HUMAN RIGHTS AND ITS RELEVANCE
FOR THE COURT'S CASE-LAW

Mark E. Villiger

Prof. Dr. iur. University of Zurich, Switzerland
Former Judge and Section President at the European Court of Human Rights

INTRODUCTION

This contribution sets out to examine the relevance of the Research and Library Division of the European Court of Human Rights (henceforth: the 'Research Division'; and 'the Court') for its case-law on the European Convention on Human Rights (ECHR). The presentation aims at emphasising this author's great esteem for Paul Lemmens upon his 65th birthday as an eminent judge of the Court. In fact, the author was for several years a close colleague and friend of his and had the honour to serve as his Section President (2012–2015). As such, the author is well aware of Judge Lemmens's far-reaching knowledge of the Court's case-law. All these factors have inspired the following contribution.

Interestingly, the topic itself, namely the position and role of the Research Division within the Court, has been little, if at all, researched in European and international law. As such, this presentation appears to be a 'first'. Previous contributions failed to consider the workings of the Research Division in their entirety and their relevance for the Court's judgments. It is hoped herewith to shed some light on the Court's internal proceedings and to provide an up-to-date picture of what leads the Court to decide as it does. The contribution should interest all those who regularly undertake research on the Court's case-law.[1]

---

[1] My sincere thanks go to the Court's Research and Library Division which, during a most interesting interview on 18 December 2017 with its Head, Mr. St. Piedimonte, and the collaborators Mr. A. Raif-Meyer and Mrs. O. Andreotti, replied to my many questions and subsequently offered valuable comments on this text. I am also grateful to the Jurisconsult, Mr L. Early, for his helpful advice, and to Mrs. A. Brewer for her relevant linguistic proposals. See in respect of previous literature Bernhardt, R. (1999) 'Comparative Law in the Interpretation

I. STRUCTURE OF THE REGISTRY OF THE EUROPEAN COURT OF HUMAN RIGHTS

A. OVERVIEW

The Court's Registry, numbering some 650 staff members, consists of various Divisions, among them 28 *Legal Divisions* with case-lawyers preparing cases for the Sections / Chambers (a Section is an administrative entity of 9–10 judges within which a Chamber of 7 judges is constituted) and the Grand Chamber. Two further departments concern *Common Services* (Administration, Working Methods, Case Management, Press, Visitor, Public Relations, IT, Language, and Budget and Finances) and the *Jurisconsult's Directorate*. The latter consists of the *Case-Law, Information and Publications Division* (ensuring, *inter alia*, the publication of the Court's Reports of Judgments and Decisions and the Court's search machine in HUDOC) and the *Research and Library Division*.[2] Head of the Registry is the Court Registrar who in turn is placed under the authority of the Court President.

B. ROLE OF THE JURISCONSULT

The Jurisconsult's office was established in 2001, though his current role crystallised at the high level conference on the future of the Court at Interlaken in 2010 where the final declaration emphasized the "importance of ensuring the clarity and consistency of the Court's case-law".[3] In response, the Jurisconsult's functions were henceforth concentrated on these requirements.[4] The position

---

and Application of the European Convention on Human Rights' In S. Busu'ttil (ed.), *Mainly Human Rights. Studies in Honour of J.J.* CREMONA, La Valetta: Foundation Internationale Malta, 33–40; Ambrus, M. (2009) 'Comparative Law Method in the Jurisprudence of the European Court of Human Rights in the Light of the Rule of Law', *Erasmus Law Review*, 2 (3): 353–371; Dzehtsiarou, K., and Lukashevich, V. (2012) 'Informed Decision-Making: The Comparative Endeavours of the Strasbourg Court', *Netherlands Quarterly of Human Rights* 30 (3): 272–298; Berg, L. *et al.* (eds.) (2013) *Cohérence et impact de la jurisprudence de la Cour européenne des droits de l'homme. Liber amicorum* VINCENT BERGER. Oisterwijk: Wolf Legal Publishers. *N.B.*: All the judgments mentioned in this article concern the Court. Until 1996 they were published in 'Series A – Judgments and Decisions' (henceforth: Series A), since then, an annual selection is regularly published in Reports of Judgments and Decisions (henceforth: Reports). Where a judgment has not been published, it is referred to with the number of its application. For further research on the Court's judgments, see *infra*, n. 26.

2   See the Organigram at www.echr.coe.int/Documents/Organisation_Chart_ENG.pdf (visited on 01.01.18).

3   High Level Conference on the Future of the European Court of Human Rights, Interlaken Declaration (19 February 2010), p. 2.

4   See Fribergh, E., and Liddell, R. (2013) 'The Interlaken Process and the Jurisconsult, In L. Berg *et al.* (eds.), 177–187.

is also regulated in the Rules of Court.[5] One of the important tools at the Jurisconsult's disposal is the work undertaken by the Research Division.

II. STRUCTURE AND FUNCTIONS OF THE RESEARCH DIVISION

A. EVOLUTION

It does not appear that the former European Court of Human Rights (1959–1998) allocated staff specifically to research, though a publication service was responsible for its publications 'Series A – Judgments and Decisions' (1960–1996) and 'Series B – Pleadings, Oral Arguments and Documents' (1960–1987). Still, its long-time Registrar, M.-A. EISSEN (1968–1994) was renowned for his extensive personal compilations of the former Court's case-law.[6] It is striking, particularly if compared with today's judgments, how even the former Court's important judgments contained (other than the national legislation and practice at issue of the respondent Government) virtually no comparative legal analysis.[7] By 1998, however, the former Court in *Petrovic v. Austria* stated, though without referring to any comparative research, 'that at the material time, that is at the end of the 1980s, there was no common standard in this field, as *the majority of the Contracting States* did not provide for parental leave allowances to be paid to fathers'.[8]

The former European Commission of Human Rights (1954–1999) which as from 1985 was confronted with a growing number of cases, created in 1993 a new 'Division IV – Case Law and Research'. Apart from editing the Commission's publication 'Decisions and Reports', the Division's task was to analyse and prepare, *inter alia*, various compilations of the Commission's case-law. Again, this did not include any comparative legal research.

With the advent of the new Court in 1998, the first judgments appeared in which reference was made, for instance, to UN instruments. Thus, in *Selmouni*

---

5   See Article 18B (since 23.06.14) entitled 'Jurisconsult': 'For the purposes of ensuring the quality and consistency of its case-law, the Court shall be assisted by a Jurisconsult. He or she shall be a member of the Registry. The Jurisconsult shall provide opinions and information, in particular to the judicial formations and the members of the Court.'

6   See, e.g., Eissen, M.-A. (1996) *The Length of Civil and Criminal Proceedings in the Case-Law of the European Court of Human Rights*. Strasbourg: Council of Europe Publishing.

7   See for an illustration the following cases: *Handyside v. United Kingdom*, judgment of 07.12.76, Series A no. 24, concerning Article 10 ECHR; *De Cubber v. Belgium*, judgment of 26.10.84, Series A no. 86, on Article 6; *Rees v. United Kingdom*, judgment of 17.10.86, Series A no. 106, on Article 8; *Loizidou v. Turkey*, judgment of 18.12.96, Reports 1996-VI, on Article 1 of Protocol no. 1.

8   Judgment of 27.03.98, Reports 1998-II, §39 (*emphasis added*).

v. France, concerning a complaint under Article 3 about inhuman treatment and torture, the Court considered 'the increasingly high standard being required in the area of the protection of human rights and fundamental liberties correspondingly and inevitably requires greater firmness in assessing breaches of the fundamental values of democratic societies'; it thereby referred in passing to *one* instrument, namely the UN Convention against Torture and Other Cruel, Inhuman or Degrading Treatment or Punishment (1987).[9]

As from 2002, a new Research Division was created within the Court, at first with only one lawyer whose main role was to supervise the Court's library. The library soon became part of the newly created Research and Library Division, and two further lawyers from the Registry joined. Their first research report appeared in 2003.

B.   STAFF

Currently, the Research Division numbers 12 lawyers, 2 administrative assistants and 8 study visitors. As a rule, the 12 lawyers have practical case-law experience as they are mostly employed internally within the Registry's Case-Law Divisions, rarely are they recruited from other Services of the Council of Europe (e.g. the Secretariat of the European Social Charter). These lawyers have often terminated higher studies (at times with a PhD) in different countries; they are fluent in different languages and are able to undertake research concerning multiple legal orders. Of the 12 lawyers, 10 are established A-Grade lawyers, 2 are B-Grade lawyers who are at the beginning of their career and assist the A-Grades with research, and who, after some experience, obtain full responsibility.

The study visitors are usually integrated in a regular trainee program for three months or longer. Interestingly, a number of them hail from countries outside the Council of Europe. For instance, the Research Division regularly accommodates:
- two long-term study visitors from Yale University at New Haven / USA for 12 months (their stay being financed by that university); previously, a similar program existed with Columbia University in New York / USA;
- one study visitor from Renmin University / China for 6 months;
- one study visitor from the University of Hong Kong for six months;
- one study visitor from the Paris Institute of Political Studies (Sciences Po) for one year, dealing mainly with EU law;
- one study visitor from the Inter-American Court of Human Rights in San José / Costa Rica for six months, involving an exchange program with a lawyer from the Court's Registry;

---

[9]   Judgment of 28.07.99, Reports 1999-V, §§97, 101.

- one study visitor from the European Court of Justice in Luxembourg for six months;
- one study visitor from the French National School of Administration (ENA) for six months.

Clearly, this diverse list considerably enhances the Research Division's capacities and facilities to deal with comparative legal research.

C. FUNCTIONS

1. Research Reports

The Research Division exercises a number of functions which may be summarised as follows. At the centre of its work lie its Research Reports. These are prepared for a number of Chamber judgments and for virtually all Grand Chamber judgments. The parts reproduced in the judgments constitute the tip of the iceberg, the original report being far more extensive. By the time the Rapporteur has included it in the draft judgment, the Research Report will have been subject to much formal analysis, compression and arrangement.

These Research Reports may be divided into three categories:

a) Reports concerning the *Court's case-law* on a particular matter at issue in a pending case. Here, the Research Division will attempt to bring together all strands of the Court's previous case-law, occasionally also of the former Commission. This case-law is as a rule reflected in the judgment in The Law, often under the headline "The general principles applicable in this case".[10]
b) Reports concerning *European and international law*. The Research Division will compile all such materials which in any way relate to the matter at issue in the particular case. The results of this report will regularly feature in a summarised form in a separate section of the judgment under the title "Relevant international materials" or similar.
   This includes the many European and international organisations, such as the Council of Europe (with the resolutions of its Committee of Ministers and the Parliamentary Assembly) and its various instruments and bodies (Venice Commission, Social Charter, European Committee against Racism and Intolerance), the European Union (in particular the case-law of the European Court of Justice); the United Nations (including Resolutions of the General Assembly and the Security Council) and its various bodies, such as

---

10 See, e.g., *Salduz v. Turkey*, judgment of 27.11.08, Reports 2008-V, §§50–55, on legal representation under Article 6 ECHR.

the International Court of Justice or the various human rights institutions (Human Rights Committee), also specialised UN agencies such as UNESCO and the ILO.[11]

The Court has thereby justified its reference to these European and international legal materials with reference to Article 31 para. 3(c) of the Vienna Convention on the Law of Treaties.[12] It has stated that 'the Convention has to be interpreted in the light of any relevant rules and principles of international law applicable in relations between the Contracting Parties (Article 31 §3(c) of the Vienna Convention on the Law of Treaties'.[13] In fact, the Court thereby seems to overlook that, by referring to the Vienna Convention, it has already presupposed and considered 'rules and principles of international law' (Article 31 para. 3(c)).[14]

c) Reports concerning *comparative law* within the Member States of the ECHR. The Research Division will thereby examine how the particular issue is regulated in the domestic law of other Member States. Domestic law may include legislation, administrative practice and case-law of the judiciary. In a Chamber judgment, the Report may cover some 25–30 States, in a Grand Chamber judgment up to 46, i.e. all Member States except the respondent Government whose domestic law is summarised elsewhere in the judgment.[15] If the matter is novel and domestic law is scarce – for instance on the issue of full-face-veils as in *S.A.S. v. France* – the Report will cover those States and jurisdictions which have so far dealt with the matter.[16]

---

[11] See, for instance, *Bărbulescu v. Romania*, judgment of 05.09.17, *Reports* 2017, §§37–51, concerning the monitoring of an employee's use of the internet at his place of work under Article 8 ECHR, where the Court's judgment under the title 'International law and practice' had reference to: UN standards (including UN General Assembly Guidelines and the ILO); Council of Europe Standards (including the Council of Europe Convention for the Protection of Individuals with regard to Automatic Processing of Personal Data); and European Union law (including the Charter of Fundamental Rights and a Directive of the European Parliament and of the Council of the European Union).

[12] UNTS 1155, 23 May 1969, entry into force 27 January 1980. Article 31(3)(c) states: '3. There shall be taken into account, together with the context: ... (c) any relevant rules of international law applicable in the relations between the parties.'

[13] See *Bosphorus Hava Yolları Turizm ve Ticaret Anonim Şirketi v. Ireland*, judgment of 30.06.05, Reports 2005-VI, §150.

[14] See Villiger, M. E. (2005) 'Articles 31 and 32 of the Vienna Convention of Law of Treaties in the Case-Law of the European Court of Human Rights', In J. Bröhmer *et al.* (eds.), *Internationale Gemeinschaft und Menschenrechte – Festschrift für G Ress zum 70. Geburtstag.* Cologne: Carl Heymann, 317–330.

[15] This author found no judgment summarising comparative legal research of all 47 Member States. See *Dubská and Krejzová v. the Czech Republic*, judgment of 15.11.16, Reports 2016, §§67–68, concerning the role of midwives at home births under Article 8 ECHR, with research covering 43 Member States; *Lambert v. France*, judgment of 05.06.15, Reports 2015, §§72–76, on keeping a patient alive artificially under Article 2 ECHR, with research covering 39 States.

[16] Judgment of 01.07.14, Reports 2014-III (extracts), §§41–52, on domestic legislation and practice in Belgium, Netherlands, Spain and Switzerland.

Comparative law is the most complex of all the research functions, as the Research Division is called upon to compare many legal systems, often with disparate legal concepts and in different languages. The judgment will compress its research into a few paragraphs. When reading these summaries in the judgments (under the title, for instance, 'Law and Practice in Council of Europe member States'), one can only imagine how extensive and in-depth the actual research was.[17] Occasionally, the judgment reflects more directly the dimensions of the original Report.[18]

2. Ensuring consistency of case-law

In principle, the Court's five Sections are obliged to adhere to the Court's case-law; if a Section considers that a departure from precedent is necessary, it must relinquish the case to the Grand Chamber (Rule 72 §2 of the Rules of Court). The Grand Chamber, on the other hand, knows no *stare decisis* and may depart from earlier practice, for instance, in order to ensure that its interpretation of the ECHR reflects changes in society and remains in line with present-day conditions, though this is quite rare.[19] The difficulty for the Sections and the Grand Chamber lies therein that the borderline between a necessary adaptation of the case-law to new situations, on the one hand, and its outright change, on the other, is not always clear.

The potential lack of consistency of case-law has dogged the Court from its inception in 1998.[20] The Court was set up, together with the Grand Chamber, with four, later five (2006) Sections, and critique was omnipresent that each Section would resolve issues of interpretation of the ECHR on its own without any coordination with the other Sections. This prompted the Court in 2005

---

[17]   See, for instance, *S. and Marper v. United Kingdom*, judgment of 04.12.08, *Reports* 2008-V, §§45–49, on the taking and storage of fingerprints and DNA material under Article 8 ECHR. See on the subject Mahoney, P. and Kondak, R. (2015) 'Common Ground. A Starting Point or Destination for Comparative-Law Analysis by the European Court of Human Rights?' In A. Andenas and D. Fairgrieve, *Courts and Comparative Law*. Oxford: Oxford University Press, 119–140, in particular 127–136.

[18]   See the highly detailed 'Comparative law' report in the Chamber judgment in *Nait-Liman v. Switzerland*, judgment of 21.06.16, application no. 51357/07, §§48–76 (meanwhile referred to the Grand Chamber), on what issue or article of the ECHR? concerning the domestic law and practice of twenty-six Contracting States and also of two other countries (Canada and the United States) as regards the right under Article 6 ECHR to have torture claims (here: in Tunisia) heard by a domestic court.

[19]   See, e.g. *Cossey v. United Kingdom*, judgment of 27.09.90, Series A no. 184, §3; further examples mentioned in Chernichuk, V. 'L'objectif de coherence énoncé dans la jurisprudence de la Cour européenne des droits de l'homme', In L. Berg *et al.* (eds.) (*supra*, n. 1) 107–121, in particular 110–117.

[20]   See for instance, Tavernier, P., 'Cohérence de la jurisprudence de la cour européenne des droits de l'homme et l'incohérence dans la présentation de arrêts: quelques réflexions', In L. Berg *et al.* (eds.), (*supra*. n. 1) 403–429.

to introduce the so-called *Conflict Resolution Board*, which was to propose recommendations in order to avoid conflicting judgments. The Board consisted of the Court's so-called Bureau, i.e. the President, and the four, later five Section Presidents. The Jurisconsult would submit to the Board important questions of interpretation of the ECHR and any emerging divergences between the Sections. It was apparently overlooked that the ECHR does not envisage a role for such a Board (or even for the Bureau) to 'steer', let alone alter the Court's case-law; and that this decision falls alone to the judges of the Court. The Board's success was modest, holding some 14 meetings over five years, until at the Interlaken Conference in 2010 European States reacted and requested a more rigorous arrangement from the Court in this respect.[21]

It was thereupon decided to entrust solely the Jurisconsult with the task of examining the Court's draft judgments as to any inconsistencies with the case-law. As he was doing already in parallel with the work of the Conflict Resolution Board, the Jurisconsult would directly address all judges concerned in case of potential inconsistencies of case-law. Today, it is one of the Jurisconsult's most important functions to alert any of the five Sections if and when one of them in a proposed draft judgment appears likely to divert from previous case-law.

The procedure is as follows: on Wednesdays the Jurisconsult meets with his team of lawyers, including all A-lawyers of the Research Division and other experienced lawyers of the Registry, to discuss the proposed draft judgments on the agenda of the five Sections for the next week, in particular whether these judgments will diverge from established case-law. Where doubts transpire, these are transmitted to the Section judges before the Section meetings on the following Tuesday. Judges will then decide whether the case calls for a relinquishment to the Grand Chamber (*infra*, n. 22), whether the draft requires adaptations, or whether it can stand as it is. Incidentally, this review as part of the Jurisconsult's team of the Court's entire judicial output of each week offers the Research Division lawyers over time a virtually panoramic view of the entire case-law.

3. Assisting with referrals to the Grand Chamber

Where the Section has adopted a judgment, each party to the proceedings may, within three months following its delivery, request that the case be referred to the Grand Chamber. The case must raise a serious question of interpretation or application or a serious issue of general importance.[22] If no such request is made

---

21 As Fribergh and Liddell (*supra*, n. 4) 185, have put it, 'the lack of a formal basis ... meant that [the Board's] recommendations could not have the character of binding directives and this ... led to doubt as to whether it [was] able to fulfil its purpose'.

22 Article 43 ECHR.

within three months, the judgment becomes final. If such a request is made, a Panel of five judges will examine the request. Where it accepts the request, the case will be re-examined by the Grand Chamber. This Panel meets every few weeks.

The Research Division prepares for the five Panel judges a case-file for each Section judgment before it, containing a factual and legal overview of the judgment and a summary of the reasons given by the requesting party for its request for referral. Based thereupon the judges decide whether or not to refer the case to the Grand Chamber.

Importantly, as from 2018, the Research Division has changed its practice and will also, in addition to the above and where necessary, assist the Jurisconsult in indicating whether in the light of previous case-law there exists in respect of a case potentially to be referred to the Grand Chamber such a serious question of interpretation or application or a serious issue of general importance. This will also include such matters as the consistency of case-law and whether the particular case raises novel legal questions under the ECHR.

4. Case-law publications

The Research Division prepares in cooperation with the Case-Law, Information and Publications Division various publications on the Court's case-law, among which may be mentioned:

Any person undertaking research on the Court's case-law (including this author) will consider the Research Division's excellent *Case-Law Guides* on many ECHR articles (Articles 1, 4–9, 15 ECHR; Articles 2–3 of Protocol no. 1; Article 4 of Protocol no. 4; and Article 4 of Protocol no. 7) as well as the *Admissibility Guide*, often in different languages. It is envisaged to offer a Guide to every article of the ECHR by the end of 2018; and thereafter to bring these Case-Law Guides up-to-date every four months.[23]

Some of the Research Reports which are summarised in the Court's judgments are published in full in the Research Division's *Case-Law Research Reports*, e.g., on Bioethics, Cultural Rights, Freedom of Religion, Health Related Issues, Positive Obligations under Article 10 ECHR etc., often in different languages.[24] Whilst the summary in the respective judgment may appear short, these publications give an impression of the breadth and depth of the various reports.

---

[23]   See www.echr.coe.int/Pages/home.aspx?p=caselaw/analysis/researchreports&c= (visited on 01.01.18).

[24]   See www.echr.coe.int/Pages/home.aspx?p=caselaw/analysis/researchreports&c= (visited on 01.01.18).

5. Library division

The Research Division is in charge of the Court's Human Rights Library. This is an international court library specialising in the European human rights system. It provides a wealth of materials for research both in domestic and in international law enabling research work in calm and agreeable surroundings.[25]

6. Functions as case-lawyers

In order not to lose touch with the practical aspects of the Court's work, not least the dialogue with judges, lawyers of the Research Division are regularly encouraged to undertake functions as case-lawyers in assisting judges in the preparation of draft judgments, mainly in Grand Chamber cases and also as so-called non-judicial Rapporteurs in cases dealt with by Single Judges. These Judges decide on clearly inadmissible applications on the basis of a "Note" prepared by a Registry lawyer and supervised by the non-judicial Rapporteur.

D. WORKING METHODS AS REGARDS RESEARCH REPORTS

1. Sources

The main source of research is clearly the *internet*, in the case of the Court's case-law in particular *HUDOC*, which contains the Court's data base.[26] This quite extraordinary search engine enables everybody access to the Court's entire output, i.e. judgments and decisions, also communicated cases, advisory opinions and legal summaries from the Case-Law Information, the relevant resolutions of the Committee of Ministers of the Council of Europe, and the case-law of the former European Commission of Human Rights.

If the research request concerns comparative law, the *case-lawyers* in the Registry are as a rule requested to provide a summary of their respective national legislation and practice. This may provide an additional strain on case-lawyers (and their Heads of Division) who often work under pressure to achieve their own time-limits dealing with cases, in particular the so-called backlog. Research in comparative and international law is also extensively performed on a variety of national and international databases, whether available for free or

---

25   See Binder, N., 'The Library of the European Court of Human Rights – Still Necessary in our Google-Society?' In L. Berg *et al.* (eds.) (*supra.* n. 1) 177–187.
26   See https://hudoc.echr.coe.int/ (visited on 01.01.18).

on the basis of contracts concluded by the Court's Library which has a specific, though limited budget to this effect. The resulting replies are then transmitted to the national judge who may comment thereupon and also add further information.

The *Superior Courts Network* (SCN) is a further relevant source rapidly expanding and growing in importance. Currently the SCN numbers 65 Superior Courts in 37 countries. Its purpose is the shared responsibility of the Court and of national courts for the implementation of the ECHR. The SCN is managed by the Jurisconsult's Directorate. It was created by the Court to offer a forum of dialogue between the national and the European level and in particular to ensure the effective exchange of information on domestic and ECHR case-law and related information. It provides from each country and superior court a rapid and reliable compilation of national legislation and practice for the Court on a particular topic – and *vice versa* of the Court's case-law for the individual national courts. (Only the Court's case-law reports are circulated through the SCN, not reports on international and comparative law.) Any research requests or information which the Court transmits to the superior courts is always stripped of any references to the particular pending case at issue.

An important source of information is also the Court's *Human Rights Library* (*supra*, n. 25).

Occasionally, the Court has had recourse to research reports of *other institutions*. For example, in *Stübing v. Germany*, concerning consensual sexual acts between adult siblings under Article 8 ECHR, the judgment refers in addition to its own research to an expert report on various domestic legal systems prepared by the Max-Planck-Institute for Foreign and International Criminal Law.[27] In *X. et al. v. Austria*, concerning discrimination of same-sex couples under Article 8, the judgment relies on a study by the Council of Europe's Commissioner for Human Rights.[28]

2.   Workflow and productivity

As a rule, the Rapporteur in a pending case before the Grand Chamber or a Section and/or a case-lawyer will file a request with the Research Division for *research* on a particular point in that case. At the outset, the procedure is

---

[27]   Judgment of 12.04.12, application no. 43547/08, §30; see also *Oleksandr Volkov v. Ukraine*, judgment of 09.01.13, Reports 2013-I, §§81–82, with reference to a comparative law research of the Max-Planck-Institute for Comparative Public Law and International Law on 'Judicial Independence in Transition'.

[28]   Judgment of 19.02.13, Reports 2013-II, §55.

informal: the Research Division will provisionally discuss scope and aim of the request with the Rapporteur and the case-lawyer, also in the light of its previous reports. Once the framework of the research has been established, an official request is filed. This goes to all lawyers of the Research Division. Depending on individual lawyers' current tasks, their working schedules for the next weeks and their specialisation (some Research Division lawyers have considerable experience, e.g., in the right to a fair trial according to Article 6 ECHR, or in the right to freedom of information according to Article 10 ECHR), a particular lawyer is selected who will then become responsible for the research. He or she will thereby remain in close contact with the requesting judge and case-lawyer.

Once the research report is ready, there is often a language check, thereafter a so-called Quality Check by the Head of Division in Chamber Cases, by the Deputy Jurisconsult in Grand Chamber Cases. This Quality Check, omnipresent in today's Court to ensure high standards, goes back to the former Commission when concrete drafting difficulties arose in the early 1990s. (Note that the Jurisconsult himself has no formal role to play in the control of these Research Reports). Finally, the Research Report is sent to the requesting judge and case-lawyer to be included in the case-file for judges in the Grand Chamber or Section case. The Report remains confidential. A summary is further contained in the Rapporteur's confidential preparatory note on the case which is equally distributed to judges. Eventually, parts of the Research Report will appear in the final judgment available to all.

The main challenge for the research lawyer is to sift through the mass of raw materials, to bring together different strands of research, to analyse and appreciate the materials and provide a synthesis on some 20 to 30 pages. This task is at the same time scientific, academic and practical. The timeframe for the lawyer to prepare such a report is between 4 and 12 weeks, depending on the nature and scope of the report (a comparative law report will typically require no less than 12 weeks). According to informal statistics, in 2016, the Research Division prepared 52 Research Reports of which 19 were on the Court's case-law, 16 on comparative law, and 17 on international law and the European Union.[29] In view of this it would seem that the Research Division is a most productive, maybe even *the* most productive, centre of comparative research on an international scale. This is certainly a fact unknown to many.

---

[29] See the comparable figures in Mahoney and Kondak (*supra*, n. 17) 125: in 2013 the Research Division prepared 59 reports, 29 of which concerned the Court's case-law, 16 comparative law, and 14 reports international law and the European Union.

III. THE RESEARCH DIVISION'S RELEVANCE FOR THE COURT'S CASE-LAW

A. INDIRECT RELEVANCE

One may distinguish between the direct and indirect relevance of the Research Division's work for the Court's case-law. To begin with, there are various ways in which the Research Division *indirectly*, or 'softly', influences the Court's work.

For instance, the Research Division contributes as part of the Jurisconsult's team to the *consistency of case-law* by informing judges weekly of any draft judgments before one of the five Sections which might contradict previous case-law (*supra*, n. 19). It is impossible to quantify this influence, not least as all the Section documents are confidential and no 'inconsistency warnings' are tangible. Neither does it transpire from a Grand Chamber judgment whether the Chamber relinquished the case, or its judgment was referred to the Grand Chamber due to lack of consistency of case-law or for any other reason. It can be assumed, however, that the Jurisconsult's weekly intervention plays an important, indeed central role in a matter which is indeed of considerable significance for Member States, since it offers judges on a broad basis information as to the consistency of case-law of which they would otherwise not necessarily be aware.

Furthermore, it can be assumed that the Research Division will play an important role as from 2018 when assisting the Jurisconsult in informing the *Panel of Five Judges* about the case-law behind a particular case which in turn enables the Panel to decide whether or not to refer a case to the Grand Chamber. Again, these documents will be confidential (*supra*, n. 22).

The Research Division's various *case-law publications* (*supra*, n. 23) influence equally though indirectly the Court's case-law. For instance, the Case-Law Guides will considerably assist applicants and their legal representatives in preparing an application before the Court (or indeed, by convincing them *not* to submit such an application) which in turn facilitates the Court's task in dealing with the application in its judgment or in its inadmissibility decision.

B. DIRECT IMPACT

Then, there are the means which influence the Court's case-law more or less *directly*, though again, these cannot be quantified in any manner. It cannot be the purpose of this contribution to provide a complete quantitative overview of what would be many hundreds, if not thousands of judgments. However, there follow some recent examples which illustrate the manner in which the Research Division influences the court's judgments – and also permit some more general conclusions.

1) Mention must first be made of the Research Division's Reports direct impact on the *Court's case-law* relating to a particular matter before the Grand Chamber or a Section. The Court's judgments in principle follow a *syllogistic approach*: the Court will examine the facts complained of in the light of the ECHR's relevant provisions and of its pertinent case-law, before drawing conclusions as to whether or not there has been a violation of the ECHR. It goes without saying that the basis of the pertinent case-law is of overriding importance when reaching the particular conclusion. Thus, as in countless other cases, in its judgment in *Salduz v. Turkey*, concerning the right of being assisted by a lawyer as from the moment of an accused's arrest, the Court first established 'the general principles applicable in this case' and then applied these 'principles to the present case' (though upon closer reading it rather superimposed the facts upon its previous case-law, which is actually how it should be done).[30]

2) Next, reference may be made to the Research Division's *comparative and international case-research* summarised in the Court's judgments enabling it to draw conclusions as to a particular issue in the case and more generally as to public interest, consensus, the margin of appreciation, trends in domestic legislation, etc. The conclusions are often (though not always) striking.

Thus, in *Khamtokhu and Aksenchik v. Russia,* the applicants complained that upon their criminal conviction, they had been given life sentences, whereas a female or juvenile offender or an offender aged 65 or over convicted of the same or comparable offences would not have been given a sentence of life (Article 14 taken together with Article 5 ECHR). The Court found no violation of these provisions. The judgment contains an extensive survey on comparative law of 37 Member States. As a result thereof, the Court concluded, *inter alia*, that 'the available data, as well as the above elements, provide a sufficient basis for the Court to conclude that there exists a public interest underlying the exemption of female offenders from life imprisonment by way of a general rule and that 'beyond the consensus not to impose life imprisonment on juvenile offenders and to provide for a subsequent review in those jurisdictions which do so for adult offenders ... there is little common ground between the domestic legal systems of the Contracting States in this area. ...The disparity in approach to other groups of offenders which Contracting States have chosen to exempt from life imprisonment is even more salient.'[31]

---

30 *Supra*, n. 10; see also *Buzadij v. Moldova*, judgment of 05.07.16, Reports 2016, §104, on the notion of house arrest in the Court's case-law; *Al Khawaja v. United Kingdom*, judgment of 15.12.11, Reports 2011-VI, §124, on the Court's case-law on the fear of witnesses in criminal proceedings to testify.

31 Judgment of 09.02.16, Reports 2017, §§19–22, §§82–84.

In *Meier v. Switzerland* the issue concerned the requirement for prisoners to continue working after having reached retirement age. The Court saw no violation of Article 4 ECHR. It presented in its judgment an impressive comparative survey of the legislation adopted by 28 Member States in this respect – clearly relying on a report of the Research Division – on the basis of which it concluded that the research 'shows that, in sixteen of those countries, sentenced prisoners are not required to work after reaching retirement age. In the remaining twelve member States surveyed, the issue is not explicitly addressed in domestic law. However, these countries usually provide for exemptions from the requirement for prisoners to work, notably on account of their capacities and their age. Consequently, the arrangements put in place by these countries resemble the approach taken in Switzerland. The Court therefore concludes that, in the absence of sufficient consensus among the Council of Europe member States on the requirement for prisoners to work after they have reached retirement age, the Swiss authorities enjoyed a considerable margin of appreciation'.

In *Armani da Silva v. United Kingdom* the applicant complained that the decision of the British authorities not to prosecute any individuals following the fatal shooting of her cousin by police officers was in breach of Article 2 ECHR, which required the authorities to conduct an effective investigation. The Court found no breach of this provision. It relied in its comparative law survey on the legislation of some 27 Member States as well as notably on four Common Law countries (Australia, New Zealand, Canada, USA).[32]

Bedat v. Switzerland concerned the complaint of a journalist under Article 10 ECHR about the 'chilling effect' of a fine in criminal proceedings for having published information covered by the secrecy of criminal violations. The Court disputed this, noting in particular 'that the disclosure of information covered by the secrecy of judicial investigations is punishable in all thirty Council of Europe member States whose legislation was studied in the present case [and that] in those circumstances, it cannot be maintained that such a penalty was liable to have a deterrent effect on the exercise of freedom of expression by the applicant or any other journalist wishing to inform the public about ongoing criminal proceedings.'[33]

The case of *Biao v. Denmark* concerned family reunification under Article 8 ECHR and in particular distinctions obtaining in this respect between Danish nationals themselves. The Court's judgment summarises research covering a total of 29 Member States as to the conditions for applying for such reunification and in particular for granting or refusing it. The Court also examined the European Convention on Nationality with its Explanatory Report, EU-law and statements of the European Committee against Racism

---

[32]   Judgment of 30.03.16, Reports 2016, §§229–239, §269.
[33]   Judgment of 29.03.16, Reports 2016, §§80–81, with reference to §§22–23.

and Intolerance and the Human Rights Commissioner of the Council of Europe – often critical of the Danish situation. After reviewing these different texts, the Court found a violation of Article 8 ECHR: 'having regard to the very narrow margin of appreciation in the present case, the Court finds that the Government have failed to show that there were compelling or very weighty reasons unrelated to ethnic origin to justify the indirect discriminatory effect … That rule favours Danish nationals of Danish ethnic origin, and places at a disadvantage, or has a disproportionately prejudicial effect on persons who acquired Danish nationality later in life and who were of ethnic origins other than Danish.'[34]

A quite extensive exercise in comparative law can be found in *Nait Liman v. Switzerland*.[35] This applicant complained that the Swiss courts had declined jurisdiction to deal with his claims for damages as a result of having been tortured in Tunisia. The Court saw no breach of Article 6 para. 1 ECHR. In respect of the comparative legal research it noted: 'the survey showed that none of the 26 European States covered by the present survey currently recognise universal civil jurisdiction in respect of acts of torture; such a jurisdiction existed only in the United States and, to a more limited extent, in Canada'.[36]

In *Stanev v. Bulgaria*, one of the issues was the direct access to court of persons with mental disorders wishing to have their status judicially reviewed. With reference to various compilations in the judgment, in particular of the situations in altogether 20 Member States, the Court saw in 18 of these States 'trends emerging in national legislation and the relevant international instruments' enabling it to draw the conclusion that Article 6 para. 1 'must be interpreted as guaranteeing in principle that someone who has been declared partially incapable, as is the applicant's case, has direct access to a court to seek restoration for his or her legal capacity.' As a result, it found a violation of Article 6.[37]

Interestingly and conversely, there are examples where the Court was not convinced by its own extensive comparative research in the judgment. For instance, the case of *İzzettin Doğan and Others v. Turkey* concerned the issue under Article 14 in conjunction with Article 9 ECHR that followers of the Alevi faith were discriminated against as compared with those citizens who adhered to the Sunni branch of Islam. In its judgment the Court found a breach of these provisions. It lengthily examined the situation in 34 of 47 Member States as to the organisation of relations between the State and religious communities. A wide array of possible situations is depicted, and indeed, the Court noted that 'the comparative-law materials … show that the relationship between the State

---

34   Judgment of 24.05.16, Reports 2016, §§47–61, §§132–139.
35   *Supra*, n. 18.
36   Judgment of 02.06.16, application no. 51357/07 (meanwhile referred to the Grand Chamber), §§48–76, §118.
37   Judgment of 17.01.12, Reports 2012-I, §§72–95, §§243–248.

and religions may take a variety of forms depending on the context.' Whilst this could have easily led the Court to conclude that the State had a wide margin of appreciation in this respect, the Court then rather concentrated, *inter alia*, on the fact that the Alevi faith lacked legal protection and that there was a glaring discrimination against its believers.[38]

Similarly, in *Karácsony and Others v. Hungary*, concerning parliamentarians who had been fined for disorderly conduct in Parliament, the Court carried out a comparative-law survey of the disciplinary measures applicable to members of parliament for disorderly conduct within Parliament. Again, the research summarised in the judgment is impressive, covering legislation and practice of 44 out of 47 Member States. The Court noted that 'despite differences related to the nature and extent of the disciplinary measures, the member States generally accept the need for regulations sanctioning abusive speech or conduct in parliaments.' Again, the Court could have inferred therefrom that national discretion in such matters would be large. However and to the contrary, it referred to the danger of parliamentary autonomy being employed to suppress the freedom of expression as in Article 10 ECHR and found a breach of this provision.[39]

Finally, mention may be made of the Court's judgments in two cases – *Schatschaschwili v. Germany* and *Kafkaris v. Cyprus* – where it refers to comparative legal research without the judgment actually containing a summary in this respect.[40]

3) On the whole, these few cases suffice to demonstrate that the Research Division exercises a *considerable influence on the Court's judgments* and hence its case-law. It does so by compiling the Court's previous case-law which enables the Court to decide, given a set of facts in a particular case, whether to apply this case-law, to adapt it or to change it. The Research Division does so further by collecting International and European Materials as well as comparative case-law research among the Member States, thereby enabling the Court to gauge the European and international 'acceptance' and the

---

[38] Judgment of 26.04.16, Reports 2016, §§60–64, §175, §§176–185. See for another well-known example *A, B and C v. Ireland*, judgment of 16.10.2010, *Reports 2010-VI*, §112, §§235–236, concerning the prohibition of abortion in Ireland, where the joint partly dissenting opinion voiced the criticism that despite a virtual uniformity in legislations of Member States, 'this will be one of the rare times in the Court's case-law that Strasbourg considers that such consensus does not narrow the broad margin of appreciation of the State concerned'.

[39] Judgment of 17.05.16, Reports 2016, §§42–61, §145, §§147–162.

[40] See *Schatschaschwili v. Germany*, judgment of 15.12.15, Reports 2015, §108, on the applicant's complaints under Article 6 ECHR that in criminal proceedings he had not been able to examine certain witnesses; here the Court referred to 'the diverse legal systems in the Contracting States, and in particular in the context of both common-law and continental-law systems'. In *Kafkaris v. Cyprus*, judgment of 12.02.08, Reports 2008-I, §104, concerning life imprisonment, the Court observed 'that at the present time there is not yet a clear and commonly accepted standard amongst the member States of the Council of Europe concerning life sentences and, in particular, their review and method of adjustment'.

'consensus' of any of its conclusions. All these compilations, which are more or less summarised in the judgments, appear essential for judges when deciding on a case. It is interesting to note that occasionally the Court, while listing the comparative legal research, will nevertheless go against this research in its conclusion. This would appear a very transparent and enlightened way of adapting or even changing the case-law. It also demonstrates the important independent position of the Research Division within the Court.

CONCLUSION

FRIBERGH and LIDDELL remind us that 'the only real guarantee of the Court's authority and the long-term effectiveness of the ECHR is the quality of its jurisprudence'[41] In the context of this article, it is proposed that the Court's authority will depend on the consistency of its case-law; on reliable research on its position in a particular case in European and international law; and how the judgment will relate to the legislation and practice of the Member States.

This short survey of the Research Division's role and functions reveals how highly professional the comparatively small number of persons in the Division deal with these matters, particularly if one compares its modest staff numbers (12 lawyers, 2 administrative assistants and 8 study visitors) with the enormous resources which, for example, international university institutions have at their disposal for comparative law research. Indeed, the outsider marvels at how so few people are able to assist the Court in so many ways and to provide one of the most productive centers of comparative legal research.

It is hoped that the earlier, not entirely unjustified criticism that both the former Court and the new Court in its early years undertook only rudimentary research which was 'underdeveloped, ad hoc, and inconsistent'[42], has been shown in this contribution to be meanwhile largely unfounded. Indeed, the past critics have no longer deemed it necessary to reiterate their previous views. It is true that the Research Division remains something of an *éminence grise* within the Court's Registry, not least as its (presumably) often extensive reports find only summary reflection in the judgments. It remains difficult to quantify its impact which, without any doubt, is considerable. One would only wish that the Division continues to be duly staffed in order to undertake this enormous and most valuable work which serves the Court in producing consistent and high-quality jurisprudence. On the whole, it is hoped that this contribution has shed more light on the Research Division's many endeavours and its relevance for the Court.

---

41   *Supra* n. 4, p. 177.
42   Mahoney and Kondak (*supra* n. 17) 126, with further reference.

À PROPOS DES MOYENS ALTERNATIFS DE RÈGLEMENT DES REQUÊTES AU SEIN DE LA COUR EUROPÉENNE DES DROITS DE L'HOMME

Françoise Elens-Passos[*]

Greffière adjointe (2015-2019) à la Cour européenne des droits de l'homme

INTRODUCTION

Je suis très heureuse de pouvoir offrir ces quelques réflexions pour rendre hommage à Paul Lemmens que je connais depuis 1983. À cette époque, alors que j'étais membre du secrétariat de feu la Commission européenne des droits de l'homme et Paul, avocat au barreau de Bruxelles, nous échangions déjà des informations relatives à la Convention, un sujet de prédilection en commun. C'est donc avec beaucoup de joie que j'ai appris son élection comme juge à la Cour européenne des droits de l'homme. Il avait la lourde tâche de prendre le relais de la talentueuse Françoise Tulkens.

La Cour européenne des droits de l'homme («*la Cour*») est connue surtout pour ses arrêts qui influencent le droit des quarante-sept pays membres du Conseil de l'Europe, tout en façonnant un ordre public européen des droits de l'homme. Il est donc tout à fait normal que cette partie de l'activité de la Cour soit la plus visible, compte tenu de son impact. Néanmoins, il est aussi de notoriété publique que la Cour souffre d'une charge de travail beaucoup trop lourde comparativement aux ressources dont elle dispose. En dépit de résultats significatifs obtenus dans le cadre du processus de réforme, la charge de travail reste une cause de préoccupation sérieuse. Un défi essentiel vise à réduire l'arriéré sans porter préjudice au droit de recours individuel pour permettre à la Cour de se concentrer sur les affaires soulevant les questions les plus importantes et ainsi de statuer, dans des délais raisonnables, sur des affaires nouvelles relatives à des allégations graves de violation des droits de l'homme.

---

[*]   L'auteur s'exprime ici à titre personnel, sans engager la responsabilité de la Cour.

Face à l'afflux des requêtes, lors de la Conférence ministérielle sur les droits de l'homme des 3 et 4 novembre 2000, la question s'est posée de savoir comment la Cour pouvait faire face à cette charge tout en ne perdant pas de sa légitimité. La Cour s'est efforcée de moderniser et d'améliorer ses méthodes de travail afin de réduire son arriéré.[1] Divers audits ont été réalisés et rapports rédigés, dans lesquels on retrouve à plusieurs reprises Lord Woolf, connu au Royaume-Uni comme un défenseur des modes alternatifs de règlement des différends. L'expansion des règlements amiables et le développement de la déclaration unilatérale fait partie de son héritage.[2] De leur côté, les États parties à la Convention se sont réunis à cinq reprises dans le cadre de conférences de haut niveau. La première s'est tenue à Interlaken en février 2010[3], la deuxième à Izmir en 2011, ensuite Brighton en 2012, Bruxelles en 2015 et enfin Copenhague en 2018.[4] À Interlaken, l'objectif était d'établir un plan d'action, destiné à trouver des solutions indispensables pour sauver une Cour qui se trouvait alors au bord de l'asphyxie. Il s'agissait d'assurer l'efficacité à long terme du mécanisme de contrôle de la Convention. Dans le cadre du processus d'Interlaken, de très nombreuses réformes ont été entreprises par la Cour qui ne pourront pas être abordées dans la présente contribution.[5]

Les cinq conférences de haut niveau ont chacune, à leur tour, réitéré leur attachement au droit de recours individuel, une pierre angulaire du système de la Convention. Le droit individuel de pétition est néanmoins parfois considéré comme la cause principale de l'augmentation de la charge de travail du tribunal et de l'arriéré actuel des affaires pendantes. A l'occasion de ces conférences, a également été mis en exergue le principe de subsidiarité, lequel implique une responsabilité partagée entre les États parties et la Cour, à savoir la responsabilité qui incombe, au premier chef, aux États de mettre en œuvre et de faire appliquer la Convention au niveau national sous le contrôle ultime de la Cour.

---

[1] Voir E. Lambert Abdelgawad, *Measuring the judicial performance of the European Court of human rights*, International Journal for Court Administration, Vol. 8, 2 May 2017, p. 22. L'auteure décrit ce changement comme une révolution managériale en plusieurs étapes et affirme que, si elle a permis de réduire le nombre de requêtes, elle a progressivement érodé le droit de recours individuel.

[2] Étude des méthodes de travail de la Cour, rapport de ‹The Right Honorable The Lord Woolf›, Décembre 2005 (Site Internet de la Cour), pp. 39-43 ; Rapport du groupe des sages au Comité des Ministres du Conseil de l'Europe, novembre 2006, CM(2006)203, §§ 106-108.

[3] Conférence de haut niveau sur l'avenir de la Cour européenne des droits de l'homme, déclaration d'Interlaken du 19 février 2010, adoptée à l'issue de la conférence des 18 et 19 février 2010.

[4] Déclaration d'Izmir du 27 avril 2011, de Brighton du 20 avril 2012, de Bruxelles du 27 mars 2015 et de Copenhague du 13 avril 2018.

[5] Voir sur le site Internet de la Cour, les notes sur les mesures de réforme qui ont pour objet de présenter la situation de la Cour en ce qui concerne, en particulier, celles mises en œuvre après la déclaration et le plan d'action d'Interlaken et des conférences subséquentes.

Ce principe de subsidiarité a conduit le greffe à renforcer la coopération avec les États Parties à la Convention, en vue de promouvoir l'objectif commun de rendre le système plus efficace. Ce principe implique notamment que les États aient une possibilité réelle et effective, aux différents stades de la procédure, d'accorder eux-mêmes un redressement aux requérants au moyen notamment du règlement amiable et de la déclaration unilatérale, solutions alternatives aux procédures contentieuses auxquelles les différentes conférences ont encouragé les États à donner priorité, en particulier pour les affaires répétitives.

I. LES ORIGINES DU RECOURS AUX MOYENS ALTERNATIFS ET LEUR GENÈSE

Le recours aux moyens alternatifs, du moins au règlement amiable, trouve son origine dans les travaux préparatoires de la Convention européenne des droits de l'homme (« *La Convention* »). Dans le cadre de ceux-ci, l'Assemblée consultative du Conseil de l'Europe s'est interrogée sur la nécessité de donner à la « Commission d'enquête », devenue la Commission européenne des droits de l'homme, le pouvoir de chercher la conciliation des parties en cause.[6] Une telle phase de conciliation avait l'avantage d'offrir aux États un moyen d'échapper à la publication d'un rapport constatant les faits et, a fortiori, à un recours devant la Cour pour le règlement judiciaire de l'affaire. Répondant à l'un de ses collègues s'étonnant de l'idée de vouloir accorder une place à la conciliation en matière de droits fondamentaux, un membre de cette Assemblée releva qu'il fallait se situer dans le champ du droit international où « entrent en jeu non seulement les intérêts des citoyens, mais aussi les intérêts des États et donc des susceptibilités des gouvernements et des peuples. Il était donc nécessaire, dans ce domaine, de laisser la porte largement ouverte à la conciliation pour éviter le risque de conséquences très graves et dangereuses pour tous ».[7] Pierre-Henri Teitgen, alors rapporteur de la Commission des affaires juridiques et administratives, ajoutait à titre d'explication qu'il fallait distinguer deux hypothèses différentes. « Dans une première série de cas, l'État incriminé a édicté une règle légale ou règlementaire qui viole les obligations de la Convention. Dans une autre série d'hypothèses, il a accompli un acte qui viole les mêmes obligations. Il est évident que s'il s'agit d'un acte, la conciliation est possible. L'État incriminé peut dire : je reconnais mes torts et offre réparation. La victime peut dire à son tour : dans ces conditions, je suis satisfait. Lorsqu'il y a une règle que l'État a édictée et qui méconnaît les obligations de la Convention, l'État peut consentir lui-même à la retirer. S'il retire la règle, la victime a légalement satisfaction. Par conséquent, je

---

6   Conseil de l'Europe, *Recueil des travaux préparatoires de la Convention européenne des Droits de l'Homme*, Volume 1, pp. 185, 225 et 233.
7   *Ibidem*, Volume 2, p. 207.

crois que la conciliation n'est pas une notion qui est fondamentalement contraire aux préoccupations qui animent nos travaux. ».[8] L'institution du règlement amiable appartient ainsi à la famille des règles contenues dans la Convention qui servent le droit souverain des États parties à réparer par eux-mêmes le tort causé à un individu en particulier.[9]

Les mots « règlement amiable », et non le vocable « conciliation », ont finalement été retenu à l'article 28 du texte original de la Convention, adopté en 1950, qui stipulait : « Dans le cas où la Commission retient la requête, (…) elle se met à la disposition des intéressés en vue de parvenir à un règlement amiable de l'affaire qui s'inspire du respect des Droits de l'homme, tel que les reconnaît la Convention. ».

Depuis l'entrée en vigueur de la Convention en 1953, la procédure de règlement amiable a évolué. Elle a joué un rôle mineur jusqu'à l'entrée en vigueur du Protocole n° 11, le 1er novembre 1998, établissant une Cour unique et permanente puisque seules 422 requêtes ont été réglées à l'amiable durant cette période. À la suite de l'entrée en vigueur du Protocole n° 11, entre 1998 et 2006, le nombre a un peu augmenté vacillant entre 167 et 297 pour prendre son envol en 2007 avec 432 règlements amiables. L'adoption d'une politique proactive en 2006 et l'entrée en vigueur du Protocole n° 14, le 1er juin 2010, ont amplifié le phénomène.[10] Cette politique consiste à l'identification précoce, par le greffe des affaires propices à un règlement amiable et à la prise d'initiative rapide pour régler ces affaires. Cette politique a été facilitée par l'application de la procédure d'examen conjoint de la recevabilité et du fond d'une requête (article 29 § 3 du règlement de la Cour (« *le Règlement* »).

S'intéresser aux modes alternatifs de résolution des requêtes, tout particulièrement au règlement amiable et au développement à partir de 2007 d'une nouvelle pratique qui découle de l'échec du règlement amiable, la déclaration unilatérale, signifie aborder la question de leur base légale, de leur mise en œuvre et procédure ainsi que de leur rôle, difficultés et avantages.

---

[8]   *Ibidem*, pp. 207-208.

[9]   Voir C.L. Rozakis, *Unilateral declarations as a means of settling human rights disputes : a new tool for the resolution of disputes in the ECHR's procedure*, Liber amicorum Lucius Caflish, Martinus Nijhoof, 2007, p. 1004.

[10]   Depuis 2010, le nombre des règlements amiables a continué à augmenter avec toutefois une diminution en 2015 et 2017. Ainsi, en 2010, on en dénombre 670 ; en 2011 : 829 ; en 2012 : 1 303 ; en 2013 : 1 481 ; en 2014 : 1 696 ; en 2015 : 1 660 ; en 2016 : 2 006 ; en 2017 : 1 529 et en 2018 : 2 184. Pour des détails sur la situation antérieure au Protocole n° 14, H. Keller, M. Forowicz et L. Engi, *Friendly settlements before the European Court of Human Rights*, Oxford, Oxford University Press, 2010, pp. 14-58, ainsi que, pour une analyse de la jurisprudence postérieure au Protocole n° 14, H. Keller et D. Suter, *Friendly settlements and unilateral declarations : an analysis of the ECtHR's case law after the entry into force of Protocole No.14*. in Samantha Besson (Ed.), The European Court of Human Rights after Protocol 14 – Preliminary Assessment and Perspectives, Zürich : Schulthess 2011, pp. 55-92.

II. LES RÈGLEMENTS AMIABLES

A. LA BASE LÉGALE

Les règlements amiables sont régis actuellement par les articles 37 et 39 de la Convention, ainsi que par les articles 43 et 62 du règlement. L'article 39 § 1 de la Convention stipule qu' «à tout moment de la procédure, la Cour peut se mettre à la disposition des intéressés en vue de parvenir à un règlement amiable de l'affaire s'inspirant du respect des droits de l'homme tels que les reconnaissent la Convention et ses Protocoles».

B. LA MISE EN ŒUVRE ET LA PROCÉDURE DU RÈGLEMENT AMIABLE

1. L'initiative et le moment de la procédure auquel peut intervenir un règlement amiable

L'article 39 § 1 de la Convention prévoit qu' «à tout moment de la procédure», la Cour peut se mettre à la disposition des parties en vue de parvenir à un règlement amiable. Les règlements amiables peuvent ainsi être conclus à tous les stades de la procédure, mais la procédure diffère selon l'état de la procédure et l'organe de jugement auquel a été attribuée la requête.

Les parties peuvent être à l'origine d'une proposition de règlement amiable, à tout stade de la procédure et sans y avoir été invitées par le greffe. Rien n'empêche en effet un Gouvernement ou un requérant d'entrer en contact une fois la Cour saisie et de conclure, même avant que la requête ne soit examinée par un organe de décision (juge unique, comité ou chambre), un arrangement entre eux sans l'intermédiaire de la Cour. Le cas échéant, le requérant informe la Cour qu'il n'entend plus maintenir sa requête et l'affaire sera rayée du rôle sur la base de l'article 37 § 1 a) du règlement, sous réserve néanmoins de l'article 37 § 1 *in fine*.[11] La Cour a souligné l'importance de reconnaître aux États le droit de contacter directement un requérant dans le but de régler une affaire pendante devant elle.[12]

---

[11] Si les parties sont parvenues à un accord sans l'intervention du greffe dans les négociations, le litige est considéré comme résolu et radié sur une autre base légale que celle du règlement amiable. À ce jour, vu la multiplicité des situations pouvant donner lieu à radiation, le système informatique de la Cour ne permet pas de dégager le nombre de ce type d'arrangements. Voir les articles 27 § 1 de la Convention et 52 A § 1 du règlement pour le juge unique, les articles 28 § 1 a) de la Convention et 53 § 1 du règlement pour le comité et l'article 54 du règlement concernant la compétence de la chambre.

[12] *Yevgeniy Alekseyenko c. Russie*, n° 41833/04, § 173, arrêt du 27 janvier 2011.

L'initiative émane toutefois en général du greffe. Dans ce dernier contexte, il est utile de rappeler que la « mise à disposition » de la Cour, en vue de la conclusion des affaires par règlement amiable, relève d'une obligation résultant du texte de l'article 62 du règlement et se traduit, dans toute communication d'une affaire au Gouvernement, soit par l'envoi de déclarations chiffrées et/ou qualifiées, soit par l'invitation plus générale adressée aux parties d'indiquer leur position à cet égard.

Les règlements amiables peuvent aussi porter uniquement sur l'application de l'article 41 de la Convention. Ainsi lors de l'adoption d'un arrêt sur le bien-fondé, la Cour, au cas où la question de la satisfaction équitable n'est pas en état pour être décidée, peut réserver la question et se mettre à la disposition des parties afin de parvenir à un règlement amiable au niveau d'une Chambre[13] ou de la Grande Chambre.[14]

2. Les types des affaires et les conditions du règlement amiable

Le règlement amiable concerne tous les types d'affaires. Néanmoins, statistiquement, la majorité des règlements amiables portent sur les affaires répétitives dans lesquelles il existe une jurisprudence bien établie concluant à la violation d'une disposition de la Convention (par exemple, durée de procédure, durée de la détention provisoire et de non-exécution) ou un arrêt pilote adopté après la mise en œuvre de la procédure pilote prévue à l'article 61 du règlement. C'est ce type de règlement qui est visé par le Protocole n° 14 et qui a été identifié comme un moyen de réduire la charge de travail de la Cour. Il continue à être encouragé dans le cadre des conférences de haut niveau.

Les règlements amiables, à l'instar des déclarations unilatérales, comme nous le verrons ci-dessous constituent effectivement une composante essentielle du suivi de la procédure de jugement pilote. Une grande chambre de la Cour a suivi cette approche pour la première fois dans les affaires *Broniowski*[15] et *Hutten-Czapska*[16] en adoptant deux arrêts de *règlement amiable pilote*. La même approche a été suivie dans une autre affaire pilote récente au niveau d'une chambre, dans le cadre de l'arrêt pilote *Rutkowski et autres*[17] concernant la durée excessive de procédure. L'arrêt pilote a donné lieu à une décision de suivi du 20 juin 2017 entérinant des règlements amiable et acceptant des déclarations unilatérales.[18]

---

[13] Par exemple, *Wolfer et Sarfert c. Allemagne* (satisfaction équitable-radiation), nos 59752/13 et 66277/13, 14 décembre 2017.

[14] Par exemple, *S.J. c. Belgique* (radiation)[GC], n° 70055/10, arrêt du 19 mars 2015.

[15] *Broniowski c. Pologne* (règlement amiable) [GC], n° 31443/96, §§ 38-42, arrêt du 28 septembre 2005.

[16] *Hutten-Czapska c. Pologne* (règlement amiable) [GC], n° 35014/97, §§ 36-43, arrêt du 28 avril 2008.

[17] *Rutkowski et autres c. Pologne*, nos 72287/10 et 2 autres, arrêt du 7 juillet 2015.

[18] *Jan Zaluksla, n° 53491/10, et Rogalka et 398 autres c. Pologne*, (déc.), 20 juin 2017 qui contient de très nombreuses références à d'autres procédures pilotes.

Dans les affaires plus délicates concernant, par exemple, les droits consacrés par les articles 2 et 3 de la Convention ainsi que 8 à 11, la Cour a un rôle pédagogique à jouer en la matière mais lorsque la jurisprudence est établie, un règlement amiable peut être tenté. Dans ce cas, il peut être fait recours à des déclarations qualifiées dans lesquelles le Gouvernement regrette la survenance des faits, offre un dédommagement et parfois s'engage à prendre des mesures individuelles ou générales. Comme mesure individuelle, s'agissant d'un défaut d'enquête dans le cadre d'un décès, l'État peut s'engager à mener de nouvelles investigations[19] ou se déclarer prêt à adopter des mesures de caractère général, telle une modification législative, propres à éviter les répétitions.[20] Néanmoins, les déclarations qualifiées de règlement amiable restent rares.[21]

3. La procédure

Dans les négociations de règlement amiable, un rôle actif a toujours été confié aux greffiers, agissant sur les instructions de la chambre ou du président de celle-ci ou à l'initiative du juge rapporteur.[22] Les juges rapporteurs sont impliqués d'une certaine manière dans la procédure du règlement amiable mais de façon limitée, dans la mesure où ils restent juges dans l'affaire. Dans la pratique, les juges rapporteurs sont consultés si une question de principe se pose, de façon à augmenter les chances d'entérinement du règlement amiable. Ils doivent aussi être informés des tentatives de règlement amiable dans des affaires difficiles mais pas nécessairement dans les affaires répétitives. Dans ce dernier cas de figure, il est précisé dans la lettre de communication que l'affaire dont il s'agit se prête particulièrement bien à un règlement amiable et le greffe joint à la lettre une proposition chiffrée basée sur les barèmes, tels que développés par la jurisprudence dans des affaires similaires et utilisés dans le cadre de l'application de l'article 41 concernant la satisfaction équitable. Dans les affaires moins évidentes, dites normales et prioritaires, dans lesquelles, vu la jurisprudence, un règlement amiable est envisageable, le greffe, dans la lettre de communication de l'affaire, ne communique pas directement de propositions concrètes de règlement amiable mais informe les parties de la possibilité de régler l'affaire à l'amiable et de la possibilité de demander au greffe de les aider. Les parties sont libres de faire des propositions ou de demander au greffier d'en faire.

---

[19]   *Memis c. Turquie* (règlement amiable), n° 42593/98, § 18, arrêt du 21 février 2006.

[20]   *Cahide Orak (Hazar) et autres c. Turquie* (déc.), n° 10248/04, 6 janvier 2009, *Seyfettin Ozdemir* et *Emine Ozdemir c. Turquie* (déc.), n° 64733/01, 14 septembre 2006.

[21]   Voir sur l'article 10, *Altan c. Turquie* (*règlement* amiable), n° 32985/96, arrêt du 14 mai 2002 ; sur l'usage de la force excessive ayant entraîné la mort ou des blessures, *Boztas et autres c. Turquie* (règlement amiable), n° 40299/98, arrêt du 9 mars 2004, *Güler et autres c. Turquie* (règlement amiable), n° 46649/99, arrêt du 22 avril 2003.

[22]   *Capsky et Jeschkeova c. la République Tchèque* (satisfaction équitable), n°s 25784/09 et 36002/09, § 22, arrêt du 9 février 2017).

Avec l'idée de promouvoir ce mode alternatif de règlement des requêtes, la Cour a récemment modifié sa pratique. Jusqu'au 31 décembre 2018, la phase de règlement amiable (non contentieuse) était conduite parallèlement à la phase d'observations (contentieuse), les gouvernements disposant, après communication d'une requête, d'un délai de seize semaines pour produire leurs observations. Pendant les huit premières semaines, ils étaient également tenus de dire à la Cour s'ils étaient disposés à conclure un règlement amiable. Depuis le 1er janvier 2019, à titre d'expérience et sauf exception, une phase non contentieuse spécifique a été mise en place afin de faciliter les règlements amiables. La nouvelle procédure se caractérise par deux éléments. Premièrement, le greffe de la Cour fait en principe une proposition de règlement amiable dès la communication de la requête au gouvernement défendeur. Deuxièmement, la procédure se scinde en deux phases distinctes : une phase non contentieuse spécifique d'une durée de douze semaines suivie d'une phase contentieuse d'une durée de douze semaines aussi. A l'issue de la phase d'expérimentation, la Cour décidera si elle poursuit ou non cette pratique.

Aux termes des articles 39 de la Convention et 62 § 2 du règlement de la Cour, les négociations en vue de parvenir à un règlement amiable sont confidentielles. Dans l'arrêt *Mirolubovs*[23], la Cour a rappelé que l'obligation de «confidentialité», telle qu'elle est comprise par la Convention et le règlement, doit être interprétée à la lumière de l'objectif général, à savoir celui de faciliter le règlement amiable en protégeant les parties et la Cour contre d'éventuelles pressions. Dès lors, si le fait de communiquer à un tiers le contenu des documents relatifs au règlement amiable peut en principe constituer un «abus» au sens de l'article 35 § 3 de la Convention, l'on ne saurait pour autant en tirer une interdiction totale et inconditionnelle de montrer ces documents à un tiers quelconque ou de lui en parler. En effet, une interprétation aussi large et rigoureuse risquerait de porter atteinte à la défense des intérêts légitimes du requérant – par exemple, lorsqu'il s'agit pour lui de se renseigner ponctuellement auprès d'un conseil éclairé dans une affaire où il est autorisé à se représenter lui-même devant la Cour. Au demeurant, il serait trop difficile, sinon impossible, pour la Cour de contrôler le respect d'une telle interdiction. Ce que les articles 39 § 2 de la Convention et 62 § 2 du règlement interdisent aux parties, c'est d'accorder une publicité aux informations litigieuses, que ce soit par le biais des médias, dans une correspondance susceptible d'être lue par un grand nombre de personnes, ou de toute autre manière. Les affaires dans lesquelles la Cour a constaté qu'une partie requérante avait porté atteinte au principe de confidentialité et qu'un tel comportement constituait un abus du droit de recours individuel au sens de l'article 35 § 3 a) de la Convention, sont peu nombreuses.[24] Le caractère confidentiel de la procédure relative au règlement

---

23   *Miroļubovs et autres c. Lettonie*, n° 798/05, § 68, arrêt du 15 septembre 2009.
24   Pour un exemple d'application, *Abbasov et autres c. Azerbaijan* (déc), n° 36609/08, §§ 30-35, 28 mai 2013.

amiable persiste jusqu'à l'issue de la procédure, y compris sur la question de l'application de l'article 41 de la Convention, au cas où la question a été réservée au stade du jugement sur le bien-fondé.[25]

Au cas où les parties s'accordent sur les termes du règlement amiable, la Cour raye la requête par une décision sur la base de l'article 39 de la Convention, après s'être assurée que le respect des droits de l'homme garantis par la Convention et ses Protocoles n'exige pas la poursuite de l'examen de l'affaire. Cette décision se limite à un bref exposé des faits et reproduit généralement les termes de la solution adoptée. Lorsque la requête a été déclarée recevable, la Cour raye la requête du rôle par un arrêt.[26]

L'accord final, acté dans la décision ou le jugement, est public. La décision de radiation sur la base d'un règlement amiable peut concerner toute la requête ou certains griefs seulement.

Il faut se féliciter du changement opéré par le Protocole n° 14 qui a confié l'exécution des radiations faisant suite à un règlement amiable au Comité des Ministres. Une mise en œuvre effective des règlements amiables est essentielle si l'on veut que la procédure inspire confiance aux requérants et à leurs conseils. En pratique, l'exécution des règlements amiables ne pose pas de problème.

C. LE RÔLE, DIFFICULTÉS ET AVANTAGES DE LA PROCÉDURE DE RÈGLEMENT AMIABLE

Le rôle du règlement amiable, comme moyen alternatif de règlement des requêtes visant à gagner en efficacité, a été attaqué Des critiques ont ainsi été formulées à l'encontre des compromis que la conclusion d'un règlement amiable pouvait entraîner contre l'intérêt d'un particulier – qui, en tant que partenaire faible, pouvait parfois succomber aux pressions de l'État défendeur – et aux intérêts de la protection des droits de l'homme de manière plus générale, notamment dans les situations où l'obtention d'un règlement amiable prive le système européen de la capacité d'ordonner des mesures générales contre un État par un jugement.[27]

---

[25] *Heldenburg c. la République Tchèque* (satisfaction équitable), n° 65546/09, § 22, arrêt du 9 février 2017 et *Capsky et Jeschkeova c. la République Tchèque* (satisfaction équitable), n°s 25784/09 et 36002/09, §§ 13-23, arrêt du 9 février 2017.

[26] Pour plus de détails sur la procédure, voir P.Dourneau-Josette, *Les modes de règlement alternatifs des requêtes devant la Cour européenne des droits de l'homme : les règlements amiables et déclarations unilatérales*, R.A.E-L.E.A.2014/3, pp. 565-580 ; C. Dubois et E. Penninckx, *La procédure devant la Cour européenne et le Comité des Ministres*, Wolters Kluwer, 2016, pp. 261-293.

[27] Voir parmi d'autres, O. de Schutter, *Le règlement amiable dans la convention européenne des droits de l'homme : entre théorie de la fonction de juger et théorie de la négociation, in Les*

La réponse à cette critique peut être simple : la Convention offre deux soupapes de sûreté dans son texte qui peuvent servir à garantir la bonne administration de la justice, même dans ce processus extrajudiciaire. La première est que le consentement du demandeur est toujours requis ; la seconde est que le consentement ne suffit pas. La Cour a le devoir, en vertu de la Convention, non seulement de suivre la conduite des négociations, mais aussi d'examiner leurs résultats. Après la communication, il appartient à la Cour d'accepter ou non la solution proposée par les parties et de décider en conséquence. La Cour est en mesure de la rejeter, en particulier lorsqu'elle n'est pas convaincue que le règlement amiable a respecté les droits de l'homme. Quant au risque de pressions, la jurisprudence de la Cour est très claire sur le fait que les mesures prises par l'État dans le cadre de négociations ne peuvent comporter aucune forme de pression, d'intimidation ou de coercition, directe ou indirecte, au risque de poser problème sur le terrain de l'article 34 *in fine* qui interdit toute entrave à l'exercice efficace du droit de recours individuel.[28]

Il convient de souligner que la notion de règlement amiable est peu connue de certains États, où ni le Gouvernement ni les représentants des requérants ou ceux-ci ne sont familiers avec cette procédure. La Cour doit donc faire œuvre pédagogique auprès d'eux. En revanche, là où elle est connue, il faut relever un effet boomerang du traitement des requêtes selon une procédure simplifiée. Ainsi, en certaines matières, dont les conditions de détention et la durée de procédure, dans lesquelles les États tardaient à prendre des mesures pour remédier à la situation, des afflux de requêtes similaires ont été introduites par des avocats qui, en quelque sorte, se spécialisaient.

Le nombre de règlements amiables reste néanmoins modeste par rapport au grand nombre d'affaires pendantes. La Cour cherche toujours aujourd'hui à les augmenter non seulement par une modification de sa pratique mais également dans le cadre de nouvelles formes de coopération fondées sur la responsabilité partagée du système de la Convention. Cela implique pour le sujet qui nous occupe de collaborer avec les agents gouvernementaux pour identifier les catégories de cas qui peuvent être traitées de manière non contentieuse et d'expliquer aux requérants que la procédure de règlement amiable dans laquelle il est un acteur, est entourée de garanties suffisantes. Cette procédure a l'avantage d'offrir aux parties une plus grande flexibilité ; elle est plus rapide et dès lors moins chère qu'une procédure ordinaire.[29] Elle permet aussi d'épargner des

---

droits de l'homme au seuil du troisième millénaire : *Mélanges en hommage à Pierre Lambert* (Bruxelles, Bruylant, 2000), p. 225.

28   *Yevgeniy Alekseyenko c. Russie, op.cit.*, § 173.
29   Voir H. Keller, m. Forowicz et L. Engi, *op.cit.*, pp. 91-103 ainsi que L.R. Glas, *The theory, potential and practice of procedural dialogue in the European Convention of human rights system*, Intersentia, 2016, pp. 276-278.

ressources au niveau des agents du Gouvernement, qui rencontrent des difficultés pour faire face au travail engendré par le traitement rapide et en nombre des requêtes dirigées contre leur État.

III. LES DÉCLARATIONS UNILATÉRALES

A. LA BASE LÉGALE

Acte discrétionnaire, la déclaration unilatérale est un instrument créant des obligations, qui se situe à la frontière entre la responsabilité de l'État et le règlement amiable : l'État redresse le tort fait à un individu par ses propres moyens.

Contrairement au règlement amiable qui a toujours fait partie du processus judiciaire, la déclaration unilatérale n'est pas mentionnée dans la Convention mais est le résultat d'une pratique jurisprudentielle, fondée sur l'article 37 § 1 c) de la Convention, consistant pour la Cour a accepté des déclarations unilatérales d'États, en tant que motif valable de radiation d'une requête du rôle de la Cour, malgré le refus d'un demandeur de consentir aux termes proposés par un défendeur. Ce développement trouve son origine dans un jugement du 26 juin 2001 dans l'affaire *Akman c. Turquie*[30] portant sur le décès d'un individu résultant de l'usage d'une force excessive par les forces de l'ordre de l'Etat défendeur. La même approche a été suivie dans trois affaires turques, *Haran, Togcu* et *T(ashin). A(car).*[31] dans lesquelles l'article 2 de la Convention était aussi en cause. Cette dernière affaire, suite à son renvoi, a donné l'occasion à la Grande Chambre dans un arrêt du 6 mai 2003 de dresser une liste non exhaustive de facteurs à prendre en considération pour évaluer si une déclaration unilatérale constitue une base suffisante pour rayer une requête.[32]

En 2012, sur la base des critères jurisprudentiels, le recours à la déclaration unilatérale a été codifié dans l'article 62A du règlement. Conformément à cette disposition, une déclaration unilatérale doit reconnaître clairement qu'il y a eu violation de la Convention à l'encontre du requérant, contenir un engagement de l'État de fournir un redressement adéquat et, le cas échéant, de prendre les mesures correctives nécessaires.

---

[30]   *Akman c. Turquie* (radiation), n° 37453/97, CEDH 2001-VI.

[31]   *Haran c. Turquie*, n° 25754/94, 26 mars 2002, *Togcu c. Turquie*, n° 27601/95, 9 avril 2002 et *T.A. c. Turquie*, n° 26307/95, 9 avril 2002.

[32]   *Tashin Acar c. Turquie* (exception préliminaire)[GC], n° 26307/95, §§ 74-86, voy. pour une analyse de l'évolution de jurisprudence, E. Myjer, *It is never too late for the State : friendly settlements and unilateral declarations*, Liber amicorum Luzius Wildhaber, Engel, 2007, pp. 318-323 et C.L. Rozakis, *op.cit.*, pp. 1005-1010.

Les statistiques montrent qu'entre juin 2001 et fin 2006, les déclarations unilatérales sont restées exceptionnelles. On en dénombre une grosse dizaine. À partir de 2007, leur nombre, une trentaine, progresse et concerne surtout les affaires répétitives. Depuis lors, il n'a cessé d'évoluer. Des pics ont été connus en 2015 avec 2 970 déclarations unilatérales, principalement dans des affaires italiennes, en 2016 avec 1 766 dans le cadre de requêtes répétitives italiennes, roumaines et russes pour en 2017, retomber à 753.[33]

B. LA MISE EN ŒUVRE ET LA PROCÉDURE DE LA DÉCLARATION UNILATÉRALE

1. L'initiative et le moment de la procédure auquel peut intervenir une déclaration unilatérale

L'initiative appartient au Gouvernement. Il peut demander l'aide du greffe pour formuler la déclaration. Priorité étant donnée au règlement amiable, la Cour n'examine en principe une déclaration unilatérale qu'après communication pour observations d'une affaire et l'échec du règlement amiable[34] et elle peut le faire à tout stade de la procédure, y compris lorsqu'il s'agit de statuer sur la question de la satisfaction équitable, réservée au stade de l'arrêt sur le bien-fondé.[35] Les prétentions disproportionnées des requérants dans les affaires répétitives expliquent souvent l'échec des règlements amiables et la présentation d'une déclaration unilatérale. A ce stade, la question peut se poser de savoir si, au cas où un État présente une déclaration unilatérale avant le début de la procédure de règlement amiable, la Cour peut-elle se soustraire à son obligation en vertu de l'article 39 de la Convention de se mettre à la disposition des parties en vue de garantir un règlement et passer directement à la procédure de déclaration unilatérale. Lors des premières radiations sur la base d'une déclaration unilatérale, certains ont émis des réserves sur cette question.[36] Pour eux, dans cette situation, un effort sérieux doit être fait pour obtenir le consentement du requérant sur le contenu de la déclaration. C'est uniquement au cas où ce consentement s'avèrerait pratiquement impossible à obtenir que la Cour pourrait prendre acte des termes de la déclaration et décider de rayer la requête du rôle. D'autres ont manifesté leur appui pour une utilisation plus courante de la déclaration unilatérale et estiment

---

[33] Depuis l'introduction de la politique proactive en 2006, les chiffres ont tendance à croître : en 2007 : 30 ; en 2008 : 93, en 2009 : 167 ; en 2010 : 553 ; en 2011 : 703 ; en 2012 : 606 ; en 2013 : 409 ; en 2014 : 502 ; en 2014 : 502 ; en 2015 : 2 970 ; en 2016 : 1 756 ; en 2017 : 753 et en 2018 : 866.

[34] *Bazhenhov c. Russie*, n° 37930/02, § 39, 20 octobre 2005.

[35] Voir par exemple *Racu c. Moldavie* (satisfaction équitable-radiation), n° 13136/07, arrêt du 20 avril 2010.

[36] En ce sens, C.L. Rozakis, *op.cit.*, p. 1011 et opinion séparée des juges Bratza, Tulkens et Vajic dans l'arrêt *Tashin Acar* précité note 32.

que le principe de subsidiarité trouve à s'appliquer en matière de déclaration unilatérale, en particulier pour les affaires répétitives.[37] La pratique a résolu cette question car, en règle générale, une déclaration unilatérale n'est acceptée par la Cour qu'après une tentative de règlement amiable. Néanmoins, dans les affaires répétitives suivant ou non un arrêt pilote ou un arrêt de référence, dit *leading*, elle a admis que le Gouvernement peut soumettre une déclaration unilatérale sans qu'une tentative de règlement amiable ne soit engagée.[38]

2. Les types des affaires et les conditions de la déclaration unilatérale

Tous les types d'affaires sont susceptibles d'être visés. Néanmoins, les conditions d'acceptation d'une déclaration unilatérale par la Cour ne sont pas les mêmes pour toutes les affaires. Après l'arrêt *Tashin Acar* précité, la Grande Chambre, dans l'arrêt *Jeronovičs*[39], a eu l'occasion de rappeler les facteurs à prendre en considération lors de l'examen d'une déclaration unilatérale. Parmi ceux-ci figurent la nature des concessions formulées dans la déclaration unilatérale, en particulier la reconnaissance d'une violation de la Convention[40] et l'engagement de verser une réparation adéquate pour une telle violation, l'existence d'une jurisprudence pertinente claire et complète à cet égard – en d'autres termes, le point de savoir si les questions soulevées sont analogues à celles déjà tranchées par la Cour dans les affaires précédentes -, les modalités du redressement que le gouvernement entend offrir au requérant et la question de savoir si ces modalités permettent ou non d'effacer les conséquences de la violation alléguée.

Pour ce qui est des affaires répétitives, la Cour se limite en général à prendre acte de la reconnaissance claire de violation à l'encontre du requérant et ensuite examine la nature des engagements pris par le gouvernement défendeur et les concessions consenties. Le paiement d'un somme d'argent couvrant le préjudice (matériel, moral) et éventuellement les frais est en principe toujours présent. La somme proposée doit être quantifiée, y compris quant aux frais, et le montant doit être en lien étroit avec les barèmes utilisés dans le cadre de la satisfaction équitable, avec la possibilité pour la Cour d'accepter une légère diminution. Dans des catégories spécifiques d'affaires faisant suite à un jugement de principe, la Cour a accepté que les déclarations unilatérales se limitent à une reconnaissance de violation.[41]

---

[37] E. Myjer, *op.cit.*, p. 324.

[38] Voir, par exemple, *Union of Jehova's Witnesses and Others v. Georgia* (déc.), n° 72874/01, §§ 23-25, 21 avril 2015.

[39] *Jeronovičs c. Lettonie* [GC], n° 44898/10, § 64, arrêt du 5 juillet 2016.

[40] Par exemple, *P.F. c. Belgique*, n° 70759/12, décision du 23 août 2016 ; *Guido Jacobs* (n° 4956/12) et *Emiel Haesbrouck* (n° 55802/12) *c. Belgique*, décision de comité du 13 décembre 2018. Pour une reconnaissance peu claire, *Ahmad Basra c. Belgique*, n° 47232/17, § 10, décision du 10 juillet 2018.

[41] Voir *Henryk Urban et Ryszard Urban c. Pologne*, n° 23614/08, arrêt du 30 novembre 2010 et les décisions ultérieures de radiation prises par un comité dont *Mecha c. Pologne*, n° 29680/09 (déc), 20 novembre 2012 et *Stobik c. Pologne*, n° 23352/09 (déc), 19 novembre 2013.

En revanche, les déclarations unilatérales soumises dans les affaires délicates ou complexes, où sont en cause des allégations sérieuses de violation concernant des droits ne souffrant aucune dérogation, font l'objet d'un examen particulièrement approfondi et attentif. Dans le cadre des affaires soulevant des griefs sous l'angle des articles 2 et 3 et où les faits sont imputables à des agents de l'État, la portée des obligations d'un État, plus particulièrement la question de savoir si celui-ci, lors du dépôt d'une déclaration unilatérale, doit s'engager à rouvrir une enquête lorsqu'est en cause l'obligation procédurale de mener une enquête conforme aux exigences de la Convention, a été abordée par la Cour dans plusieurs affaires.

Dans l'arrêt précité *Jeronovics*, la Cour a réaffirmé sa compétence pour scruter avec soin les engagements auxquels se réfère un gouvernement dans sa déclaration unilatérale et à interpréter l'étendue de ces engagements à la lumière de sa jurisprudence. Elle s'est référée à une décision récente rendue dans le cadre d'une requête concernant les obligations de l'État au titre de l'article 2, à savoir *Zarkovics et autres c. Croatie*.[42] La Cour y a déclaré que sa décision de rayer du rôle sur la base de la déclaration unilatérale les griefs tirés des articles 2 et 14 de la Convention, lesquels avaient trait au défaut d'enquête effective sur un homicide, ne préjugeait pas de «l'obligation continue du Gouvernement de mener une enquête conforme aux exigences de la Convention». Il s'ensuit que le Gouvernement devra, en principe, entreprendre une enquête qui soit pleinement conforme aux exigences de la Convention, s'agissant d'une obligation continue. Dans *Jeronovics*, la Cour a expliqué que «le paiement d'une indemnité, qu'il résulte de la déclaration unilatérale ou d'une procédure interne en dommage-intérêts ne saurait suffire, eu égard à l'obligation qui incombe à l'État, en vertu de l'article 3, de mener une enquête effective dans les affaires de mauvais traitements délibérés par des agents de l'État». Elle a ajouté qu' «on ne saurait dire qu'en versant l'indemnité indiquée dans sa déclaration unilatérale et en reconnaissant une violation des diverses dispositions de la Convention, l'État défendeur s'est acquitté de l'obligation procédurale continue qui lui incombe, au titre de l'article 3 de la Convention».

Cette dernière condition pose parfois problème car, pour différents motifs, certains pays ont des difficultés à introduire une telle clause dans les déclarations unilatérales.[43] Ainsi l'affaire *Mishina c. Russie*[44], a donné lieu à une discussion intéressante sur l'acceptation ou non de la déclaration unilatérale, dans un cas où un Gouvernement alléguait l'impossibilité de conduire une enquête effective après un long délai. La Cour a estimé que les conditions permettant de procéder à la radiation sur la base de la déclaration unilatérale ne se trouvaient

---

[42] N° 75187/12, § 23, décision du 9 juin 2015.
[43] Voir *Jeronovičs*, *op.cit.*, note 40, §§ 116 et 118.
[44] N° 30204/08, arrêt du 3 octobre 2017, § 28.

pas remplies, en rappelant l'importance de l'obligation de mener une enquête efficace. Consciente des difficultés que peuvent rencontrer les autorités internes dans la conduite d'une enquête plusieurs années après les faits, elle a rappelé que ces difficultés ne pouvaient permettre au Gouvernement d'échapper à ses obligations découlant de l'article 2 de la Convention. Elle a également rappelé que «la procédure de déclaration unilatérale revêt un caractère exceptionnel et que lorsqu'il s'agit de violations des droits les plus fondamentaux garantis par la Convention, cette procédure n'a pas vocation d'éluder l'opposition du requérant à un règlement amiable ou de permettre au Gouvernement d'échapper à sa responsabilité pour de telles violations ».

Le 20 mars 2018, la Cour a adopté un jugement intéressant[45] dans une affaire relative à l'article 6 de la Convention, interprétant l'absence de réponse d'un requérant à la déclaration unilatérale d'un gouvernement comme présumant du fait que celui-ci avait pris connaissance des termes de ladite déclaration et n'avait pas d'objections à leur égard en dépit du fait que d'autres requérants de la même affaire avaient objecté que la radiation sur la base d'une telle déclaration les empêcherait de demander le réexamen de l'affaire, objection retenue par la Cour. La question ne se pose néanmoins pas dans les mêmes termes dans une affaire relative aux articles 2 et 3 de la Convention où il existe une obligation, de la part du Gouvernement, à offrir un recours sous la forme d'une procédure permettant d'enquêter sur les causes d'un décès ou de mauvais traitements. En principe, dans ce type d'affaires, sauf circonstances particulières[46], la Cour ne déduit pas du silence du requérant qu'il n'a pas d'objections à l'encontre de la déclaration.

3. La procédure

Suite à l'échec d'un règlement amiable ou dans les autres cas autorisés, l'État soumet, dans le cadre d'une procédure publique et contradictoire, une déclaration et demande à la Cour de rayer l'affaire sur cette base. La déclaration unilatérale est alors adressée au requérant afin d'obtenir ses commentaires. Le fait pour un requérant de l'accepter équivaut pour la Cour à un règlement amiable

---

[45]   *Igranov et autres c. Russie*, n° 42399/13 et 8 autres, §§ 22-27, dans laquelle les requérants se plaignaient d'une violation procès équitable compte tenu du rejet de leur demande de comparaître devant une juridiction civile.

[46]   *Ahkim c. Belgique* (déc.), n° 27399/17, § 14,10 juillet 2018 où la Cour a accepté une déclaration unilatérale dans une affaire concernant l'article 3 en l'absence d'une clause de réouverture de la procédure interne dans la mesure où le requérant ne se plaignait pas d'une quelconque ineffectivité de l'instruction préalable de l'affaire(*a contrario*, *Tashin Acar c. Turquie*, § 84) et ne contestait pas les faits tels qu'établis par les juridictions internes s'appuyant sur les éléments mis en lumière au cours de l'enquête pénale (*ibid.*, § 78). Voir aussi *Ihsan Seker et autres c. Turquie*, n° 58175/10, décision de comité du 18 décembre 2018.

et l'affaire est alors rayée du rôle sur la base de l'article 39 de la Convention.[47] En cas d'objections du requérant, la Cour les examine minutieusement mais peut estimer néanmoins qu'elle peut accepter la déclaration unilatérale après avoir contrôlé que les conditions étaient réunies. Quelle que soit la teneur d'une déclaration unilatérale, la Cour n'a aucune obligation de l'accepter car le respect des droits de l'homme peut exiger la poursuite de la requête. Ainsi, la Cour n'accepte pas une déclaration unilatérale lorsque la détention provisoire, dont la durée fait l'objet de la requête, se poursuit ou qu'il n'a pas été mis fin aux conditions dégradantes de détention, dont se plaint un requérant.

En cas d'acceptation par la Cour de la déclaration unilatérale, l'affaire est rayée du rôle en vertu de l'article 37 § 1 c) de la Convention. La radiation peut ne concerner qu'une partie de la requête et le surplus fait l'objet d'un examen séparé[48] et parfois uniquement la question de la satisfaction équitable.[49]

Lorsque l'une des conditions ci-dessus n'est pas remplie, le juriste prépare une note de procédure proposant le rejet de la déclaration unilatérale ou alors la déclaration unilatérale est rejetée succinctement dans le cadre de l'arrêt qui statuera sur le bien-fondé de l'affaire.[50] En cas de refus, la Cour ne publie généralement pas le texte de la déclaration unilatérale. Elle se borne à indiquer que le texte de la déclaration n'offre pas une base suffisante pour conclure que le respect des droits de l'homme n'exige pas la poursuite de l'examen de la requête. Dans plusieurs affaires, la Cour a refusé d'entériner une déclaration unilatérale en raison de l'impact incertain de celle-ci sur la possibilité d'obtenir une réouverture judiciaire.[51]

Le Comité des Ministres n'est pas en charge de l'exécution d'une déclaration unilatérale. Néanmoins, lorsque la déclaration unilatérale est entérinée dans le cadre d'un arrêt, un certain contrôle par le Comité des Ministre est permis. Celui-ci, en revanche, ne contrôle pas, à ce jour, leur exécution. En cas de non respect des engagements, la requête peut être réinscrite à l'ordre du jour en

---

[47]   Voir, par exemple, *L. c. Pays-Bas*, n° 68613/13, décision du 2 mai 2017.

[48]   Par exemple, *François Marc-Antoine c. France*, n° 37377/06, décision du 20 avril 2010 ; *Waltraud Stork c. Allemagne*, n° 486/14, décision du 26 juin 2018.

[49]   Par exemple, *Werra Naturstein GmbH & Co KG c. Allemagne* (satisfaction équitable-radiation), n° 23377/12, arrêt du 19 avril 2018.

[50]   Par exemple, *De Tommaso c. Italie* [GC], n° 43395/09, §§ 133-140, arrêt du 23 février 2017.

[51]   *Aviakompaniya A.T.I., ZAT c. Ukraine*, n° 1006/07, § 33, arrêt du 5 octobre 2017 et *Dridi c. Allemagne*, n° 35778/11, arrêt du 26 juillet 2018 qui font référence à l'affaire belge *Hakimi c. Belgique*, n° 665/08, § 29, arrêt du 29 juin 2010. Dans une décision de comité du 13 mars 2018 relative aux requêtes *Catherine Willems et Yvan Gorjon c. Belgique*, n°ˢ 74209/16 et 75662/16, la Cour, à la lumière de l'article 442 *bis* CIC modifié, a pris une position différente et a accepté la déclaration unilatérale. Voir aussi *Viviane Goyens et Paul Robben c. Belgique*, n° 47739/08, décision de comité du 13 mars 2018.

vertu de l'article 37 § 2 de la Convention.[52] En outre, en cas de non-respect récurrent des engagements généraux pris par un État, la Cour peut toujours ne plus accepter des déclarations unilatérales dans la matière couverte par ces engagements généraux.[53]

C. LE RÔLE, DIFFICULTÉS ET AVANTAGES DE LA PROCÉDURE DE DÉCLARATION UNILATÉRALE

La procédure lancée en 2017 garantit le règlement rapide des litiges dans une situation où la déclaration unilatérale donne une satisfaction objective à un requérant qui lui-même n'est pas opposé au contenu de la déclaration. A l'instar du règlement amiable, elle permet aussi de faire face à la charge de travail de la Cour, particulièrement concernant les affaires répétitives.[54] Les montants octroyés sont similaires à ceux qui seraient obtenus dans le cadre d'une procédure contentieuse car basés sur le barème utilisé tant dans le cadre de la satisfaction équitable que dans celui du règlement amiable. Dès lors le risque pour un requérant de recevoir une indemnisation moindre est peu important.

Certains estiment que cette procédure heurte l'esprit de la Convention et sa philosophie protectrice des droits individuels. À cela, il suffit de rétorquer que les critères fixés par la Cour et leur interprétation donnent aux requérants un gage que celle-ci veille à leurs droits. L'élément manquant, à savoir l'accord, a rendu la Cour extrêmement prudente, comme le prouve sa jurisprudence, lorsqu'elle décide d'entériner une déclaration unilatérale.

CONCLUSION

Rien dans la politique proactive de la Cour ne vient contrarier l'objectif de la Cour qui est de maintenir et renforcer le système de protection des droits individuels mis en place en 1950. Les deux procédures étudiées ci-dessus, menées dans le respect de leurs caractères respectifs, ont la même finalité, à savoir mettre fin à l'examen d'une requête. Leur fil conducteur est de libérer des ressources et du temps judiciaire pour se concentrer sur le nombre relativement restreint des cas qui méritent une attention particulière. Cependant, afin d'endiguer le flot de nouvelles affaires répétitives et de permettre à la Cour de maîtriser leur volume, il faut espérer qu'un règlement amiable ou une déclaration unilatérale, comme

---

[52] Voir *Jeronovičs, op.cit.,* note 39, §§ 67-68.
[53] Voir *Burmych et autres c. Ukraine* (radiation) [GC], nos 46852/13 et autres, arrêt du 12 octobre 2017.
[54] Voir H. Keller, M. Forowicz et L. Engi, *op.cit.,* pp. 103-106.

c'est le cas du règlement amiable pilote, comprenne un engagement d'éliminer la cause de la violation pour éviter des violations similaires futures.

La maturité plus grande du système de la Convention et l'existence d'une jurisprudence abondante dans de nombreux domaines tant au niveau des principes qu'à celui du dédommagement accordé permet aujourd'hui d'encourager le recours aux moyens alternatifs de règlement des requêtes. La Cour veille en tout état de cause à que l'acceptation des règlements amiables et des déclarations unilatérales ne fasse pas obstacle à l'interprétation progressive du contenu et de l'ampleur des droits garantis. Dans des domaines délicats, le recours à des déclarations qualifiées de règlement amiable ou de déclaration unilatérale est une bonne solution.

Il ne faut pas oublier que dans le cadre de la procédure de règlement amiable et de déclaration unilatérale, un rôle important revient non seulement aux États mais aussi aux requérants et à leurs représentants, appelés à rechercher, avec les autorités nationales, une solution non contentieuse fondée sur la jurisprudence de la Cour et susceptible de les satisfaire. Cela s'accompagne aujourd'hui d'un renforcement de la coopération et de la communication, laquelle a fait d'énormes progrès ces dernières années. Une relation de synergie entre les systèmes nationaux et celui de la Cour et entre tous les acteurs de la Convention est vitale pour une protection effective et dans des délais raisonnables des droits de l'homme.

LES « DROITS CIVILS »
DE L'ARTICLE 6 : À LA RECHERCHE
DE LA FORMULE MAGIQUE

Georges RAVARANI

Juge à la Cour européenne des droits de l'homme

L'alerte est lancée : la Cour européenne des droits de l'homme (« la Cour ») serait-elle en train de gaspiller ses énergies et de jouer sa crédibilité en s'enfonçant toujours davantage dans les méandres de la définition des droits civils[1] relevant de l'article 6, § 1er[2], de la Convention européenne de sauvegarde des droits de l'homme et des libertés fondamentales (« la Convention ») ? Côté énergies, il est étonnant de constater combien d'arrêts de Chambre, voire de Grande Chambre, traitent, non pas du procès équitable en matière de contestations sur des droits civils, mais du préalable, à savoir de la définition d'un « droit civil », dont seule la présence peut déclencher l'applicabilité de l'article 6, § 1er, dans son volet civil. Côté crédibilité, la jurisprudence de la Cour en la matière est fortement critiquée pour être illisible. Dernier avatar, la Cour suprême du Royaume-Uni, dans un jugement très critique du 10 mai 2017[3], a refusé d'appliquer la jurisprudence de la Cour en la matière en attendant une clarification par la Grande Chambre.

---

[1] Il est vrai que l'article 6 parle de droits et obligations, mais il ne paraît pas nécessaire, dans cette incursion essentiellement brève dans la matière, d'envisager de manière séparée l'aspect « obligations » : on considère qu'à chaque droit correspond une obligation corrélative.

[2] En principe, dans l'ensemble de la présente contribution, c'est le § 1er de l'article 6 qui est visé mais pour alléger le texte, il sera le plus souvent fait référence au seul article 6.

[3] *Poshteh v Royal Borough of Kensington and Chelsea*, [2017] UKSC 36. L'arrêt que la Cour suprême refuse de suivre est l'arrêt *Fazia Ali c. Royaume-Uni* du 20 octobre 2015, 40378/10. L'arrêt s'inscrit dans une certaine lignée d'arrêts de la juridiction suprême du Royaume-Uni qui tentent de scruter le fil rouge dans la jurisprudence de la Cour en matière de droits civils de l'article 6. V., p. ex., les observations de Lord Collins dans *Tomlinson et al [incl Ali] v Birmingham City Council* [2010] UKSC 8 : « 60.The Strasbourg Court has said that it is not necessary to give what it has called an « abstract definition » of the concept of civil rights and obligations : *Benthem v Netherlands* (1985) 8 EHRR 1 at [35] ; *Feldbrugge v Netherlands* (1986) 8 EHRR 425 at [27] ; and *Deumeland v Germany* (1986) 8 EHRR 448 at [61]. It is understandable that the Court has been reluctant to provide abstract definitions. What is not so comprehensible is its apparent reluctance to enunciate principles which will enable a line to be drawn between those rights in public law which are to be regarded as 'civil rights' and those which are not to be so regarded. »

L'affaire dont avait à connaître la Cour suprême du Royaume-Uni était la suivante : une ressortissante iranienne s'étant vu reconnaître le statut de réfugiée demandait la mise à disposition d'un logement en application du « Housing Act 1996 » en vertu duquel les autorités municipales sont obligées de trouver un logement pour certaines personnes. Si les autorités locales ont une obligation en la matière, elles disposent en revanche d'une grande latitude dans le choix de ce qui est convenable. En cas de désaccord de l'intéressé, elles peuvent lui faire une « offre ultime » et la décision afférente peut être attaquée en justice. La question était de savoir si le droit que l'intéressé peut faire valoir constitue un droit civil au sens de l'article 6. La Cour suprême n'a pas apprécié l'arrêt *Fazia Ali c. Royaume-Uni* qui a retenu que la prétention en question à être logé constitue un droit civil au sens de l'article 6 et elle a déclaré préférer que la Grande Chambre se prononce à cet égard avant d'envisager de changer sa position.[4]

Le résultat est là : une cour suprême refuse de se plier à la jurisprudence de la Cour en matière d'applicabilité de l'article 6, § 1er. Qu'on estime qu'elle le fasse à bon ou à mauvais escient, c'est un fait : il n'y a donc aucune exagération à estimer qu'il y a urgence en la matière.

Les difficultés qu'éprouve la Cour à trouver sa voie seraient-elles insurmontables ? cinquante ans d'hésitations et de casuistique tendent à accréditer cette idée. Faut-il dès lors, fataliste, continuer à se contenter d'expédients à propos de chaque nouveau « droit civil » invoqué d'une part et récusé de l'autre, fort des nombreuses issues proposées par la doctrine qui n'ont pas, en général, trouvé d'écho dans la jurisprudence de la Cour ? Peut-être…

J'ai eu, avec mon collègue et ami Paul Lemmens, éminent spécialiste en la matière à qui je dédie les présentes lignes, d'innombrables discussions vraiment passionnantes sur le domaine d'application de l'article 6 en matière civile. S'il paraît que nous n'ayons pas réussi, jusqu'à présent, à nous mettre entièrement d'accord, il semble que nos analyses respectives se rejoignent sur un constat : la Cour a – contrainte et forcée – pris quelques libertés avec le concept de « droits » au sens de l'article 6.

Quoi qu'il en soit et au-delà de notre débat peut-être, un modeste état des lieux destiné à identifier les causes des blocages (I.) pourrait, avec une sérieuse dose d'optimisme, ouvrir des perspectives de sortie de l'impasse (II.).

---

4   « *…we should await a full consideration by a Grand Chamber before considering whether (and if so how) to modify our own position* » (par. 37).

I. ÉTAT DES LIEUX

Si l'on veut identifier la racine des errements de la notion, il faut naturellement revenir à sa genèse, c'est-à-dire aux les travaux préparatoires de l'article 6. On verra cependant que pour identifier la notion de droits civils, les travaux préparatoires constituent un faux-problème (A.) et que les réelles difficultés proviennent de l'attitude de la Cour qui a d'autres préoccupations que celle de s'en tenir à l'originaire sens du concept (B.).

A. UN FAUX-PROBLÈME : LES TRAVAUX PRÉPARATOIRES

Il est impossible de faire ici le récit exhaustif de la genèse de l'article 6, encore que la lecture des travaux préparatoires et de leurs nombreux rebondissements soit très instructive. Quelques éléments méritent d'être relevés :

- les travaux préparatoires de l'article 6 lui-même sont extrêmement lapidaires et ne fournissent pas d'explication au sujet de la notion de «droits civils»[5] ;
- en réalité, l'origine de la notion est à rechercher dans les négociations qui ont abouti à la Déclaration universelle des droits de l'homme proclamée le 10 décembre 1948 par l'Assemblée générale des Nations-Unies[6] et au projet de Pacte international relatif aux droits de l'homme adopté par la Commission des droits de l'homme du Conseil économique et social lors de la cinquième session tenue du 9 mai au 20 juin 1949[7] ;

---

[5] On y lit seulement que *«une discussion a eu lieu (...) à propos des mots 'du caractère civil...'. Les pays dits de 'Common law' avaient fait observer que les 'civil rights and obligations', tels qu'ils sont reconnus par les organes administratifs, ne sont pas l'objet d'une garantie devant une juridiction administrative. A cet égard, la différence est importante avec les pays dits 'de droit civil'. Aussi, les mots 'in a suit of law' (contestation dans le texte français) permettraient d'écarter du champ d'application de la Convention les procès administratifs.»*

[6] V. pour un récit exhaustif des travaux préparatoires de ces deux textes, Jacques Velu, Le problème de l'application aux juridictions administratives, des règles de la Convention européenne des droits de l'homme relatives à la publicité des audiences et des jugements, Revue de droit international et de droit comparé, 1961, p. 129 et s. ; Pieter Van Dijk, The interpretation of «civil rights and obligations» by the European Court of Human Rights – one more step to take, *in* Protecting Human Rights : The European Dimension, Studies in honour of Gérard J. Wiarda, Carl Heymans Verlag 1990, p. 131 et s. – Dans le texte initial du projet, la version française parlait de droits et obligations en matière civile, tandis que la version anglaise ne mentionnait que les *«rights and obligations»*. Sur proposition de la délégation égyptienne, qui craignait une interprétation restrictive de la notion, les mots «en matière civile» furent supprimés (v. Jacques Velu, *op. cit.*, p. 145).

[7] Le texte de l'article 6 § 1 est la reproduction textuelle de la version française de l'article 13 dudit texte («contestations sur des droits et obligations de caractère civil»). La version anglaise se présente comme suit : *«in the determination of his rights and obligations in a suit at law»*. Ce sont ces deux versions qui forment l'actuel article 14 du Pacte international relatif aux droits civils et politiques, adopté par l'Assemblée générale des Nations Unies le 16 décembre 1966 et entré en vigueur le 23 mars 1976.

- lors de l'élaboration du Pacte, la version anglaise ne parlait que de « *rights and obligations* » tandis que la version française parlait de « droits et obligations civils ». Les délégations étaient d'accord pour considérer les deux versions linguistiques comme synonymes, le mot « civil » ne devant pas être lu dans une conception étroite, mais comme incluant les droits privés, publics, administratifs et politiques[8] ;

- dans l'esprit des auteurs, la *summa divisio* était à établir entre la matière pénale et la matière civile, avec la précision qu'on n'admettait pas de droits qui ne relevaient ni de l'une, ni de l'autre catégorie ;

- la délégation américaine s'étant inquiétée de ce que la formule « *rights and obligations* » puisse être comprise comme très large et aboutisse à judiciariser toutes sortes de litiges se déroulant devant des fonctionnaires et n'étant pas susceptibles d'être portés devant un tribunal[9], elle proposa alors d'utiliser la formule des droits et obligations invoqués « *in a suit of law* », pour éviter de conférer aux individus un recours contentieux dans pratiquement toutes matières dans lesquelles il s'agissait de « déterminer » les droits et obligations des individus et non seulement un recours administratif ou non contentieux.[10] D'où la proposition de placer l'article surtout sur un plan procédural : les garanties de procédure envisagées n'existeraient que lorsqu'il s'agira de déterminer les droits et obligations des individus au cours d'une action pénale ou d'une action civile, étant souligné que le mot civil était toujours entendu dans un sens large[11] ;

- lors de l'élaboration de la Convention européenne des droits de l'homme, le premier projet reproduisait à l'identique l'article 10 de la Déclaration universelle des droits de l'homme. Les mots « de caractère civil » ne se trouvaient donc pas dans ce texte. Le deuxième projet s'inspirait du projet de pacte international des droits de l'homme, la version française comportant les mots « de caractère civil », tandis que la version anglaise rendait ces

---

[8] Jacques Velu, *op. et loc. cit.* – Les termes « droits civils » ont un domaine beaucoup plus vaste en anglais, où ils correspondent *grosso modo* au concept français de « libertés publiques », tandis que dans les systèmes romano-germaniques, ils peuvent recouvrir, de manière large, le sens de « droit privé » par opposition au « droit public », et de manière plus étroite, servir à distinguer ce qui est purement civil de ce qui est commercial, rural, industriel, etc. (Jacques Velu et Rusen Ergec, Convention européenne des droits de l'homme, 2ᵉ éd. Bruylant 2014, n° 420, p. 452).

[9] « …beaucoup de droits et d'obligations civiles, comme par exemple, celles qui se rapportent au service militaire et aux impositions, sont généralement déterminées par des fonctionnaires plutôt que par des tribunaux ; d'autre part, le texte initial semble suggérer que tous les droits et toutes les obligations de ce genre doivent nécessairement être déterminées par un tribunal indépendant et impartial… ». Il a été fait remarquer que ces explications montraient que la délégation américaine également comprenait dans un sens large l'expression « *civil rights and obligations* » puisqu'aussi bien, selon cette délégation, ladite expression recouvrait notamment les droits et obligations en matière militaire ou fiscale. V. Jacques Velu, *op. cit.*, p. 151.

[10] Jacques Velu, *op. cit.*, p. 152.

[11] Jacques Velu, *op. cit.*, p. 153.

derniers par « *in a suit of law* ». La veille de la signature de la Convention, ces mots furent remplacés dans la version anglaise par « *civil* », et cela sans explication[12] ;

– on ne saurait enfin négliger le contexte historique dans lequel ces textes ont été élaborés : il y a 70 ans, la frontière entre les sphères civile et publique, c'est-à-dire celle des relations entre les individus et celle des relations entre l'individu et l'Etat était beaucoup plus tranchée qu'aujourd'hui. Mais à l'heure actuelle, dès lors que l'Etat-providence donne naissance, dans le chef des citoyens, à de nombreux droits économiques et sociaux à l'égard de l'Etat, la frontière entre les sphères d'action publique et privée de l'Etat tend à s'estomper.[13]

Quoi qu'il en soit, il ne découle pas des travaux préparatoires de la Convention que les mots « droits civils » utilisés dans l'article 6, § 1er, s'opposent forcément aux droits politiques qui seraient exclus de son champ d'application. Les auteurs n'opposaient pas droits privés et droits publics.

Cette opposition procède de la jurisprudence de la Cour.

B. LE VRAI PROBLÈME : LA JURISPRUDENCE DE LA COUR

La jurisprudence de la Cour est problématique tant en ce qui concerne les droits existant dans les législations internes des Etats (1.) que ceux reconnus par la Convention elle-même (2.).

1. Les droits existant dans les législations internes

Très tôt, la Cour s'est écartée de la division entre contestations relevant du droit pénal et, *à défaut*, du droit civil, division pourtant présente dans les travaux préparatoires. Elle dit très clairement dans l'arrêt *Le Compte* : « …l'article 6 ne vaut que pour l'examen des 'contestations sur [des] droits et obligations de caractère civil' et du 'bien-fondé de toute accusation en matière pénale'. Certaines 'causes' échappent à son empire faute de se ranger dans l'une de ces catégories ».[14]

Depuis une cinquantaine d'années, la Cour essaie, d'affaire en affaire et en se gardant de formuler une règle générale, de déterminer ce qui est à entendre par

---

[12] Jacques Velu, *op. cit.*, p. 159.

[13] V. l'opinion dissidente du juge Peer Lorenzen dans l'affaire *Ferrazini c. Italie* [GC], n° 44759/98, 12 juillet 2001.

[14] *Le Compte, Van Leuven et De Meyere c. Belgique*, n° 6878/75, 23 juin 1981, § 41.

« contestation sur un droit civil » au sens de l'article 6 et ce qui ne répond pas à ce qualificatif. Si on peut affirmer qu'elle a, en fin de compte, rangé un assez grand nombre de droits, ou du moins de contestations, sous le concept des droits civils, elle a toujours eu à cœur de ne pas faire bénéficier de la protection du procès équitable ce qu'elle considère comme des contestations portant sur des droits politiques.[15]

On pouvait peut-être tenir pour acquis qu'une contestation portée en justice et pouvant, en cas de gain du procès, être reconnue – en d'autres mots, une prétention *a priori* défendable – constitue un droit au sens de l'article 6, c'est-à-dire qu'au stade de la décision de l'applicabilité de l'article 6, la Cour n'avait pas à juger si le droit revendiqué est reconnu en droit national avec une certitude quasiment absolue. Mais un arrêt au moins jette le trouble : dans l'arrêt de Grande Chambre *Karoly Nagy c. Hongrie,* la Cour s'est livrée à un examen approfondi de l'existence du droit revendiqué pour finalement en nier l'existence et refuser l'applicabilité de l'article 6.[16] A s'en tenir à cet arrêt, il semblerait qu'on ne puisse plus se contenter d'une simple contestation rendant plausible ou du moins possible le succès d'une demande en droit national, mais qu'il faille examiner l'existence même du droit plutôt que le sérieux de la contestation. Mais dans l'arrêt *Regner c. République tchèque*, rendu cinq jours plus tard, la Grande Chambre a conclu à l'applicabilité de l'article 6 à propos de contestations où le demandeur ne peut faire valoir aucun droit subjectif, à la seule condition que l'avantage ou le privilège revendiqué, une fois accordé, crée un droit (civil).[17]

Selon la jurisprudence de la Cour, le point de départ est constitué par le droit national pertinent et l'interprétation qu'en font les juridictions internes. L'article 6 n'attache aux « droits et obligations » aucun contenu matériel déterminé dans l'ordre juridique des États contractants : la Cour ne saurait créer, par voie d'interprétation de l'article 6, un droit matériel n'ayant aucune base légale dans l'État concerné.[18] L'exemple peut-être le plus éclatant est celui de la responsabilité civile : celle-ci ne fait pas partie des droits fondamentaux reconnus par la Convention. Si un Etat excluait, p. ex., toute responsabilité civile des pouvoirs publics, il n'appartiendrait pas à la Cour de « lire » l'existence d'une telle responsabilité dans le droit national concerné.[19]

---

15 Toutes les démarches de la Cour ne vont certainement pas dans le sens d'une restriction de l'applicabilité de l'article 6. V. p. ex. l'important arrêt *Golder c. Royaume-Uni,* n° 4451/70, 21 février 1975, qui a lu dans l'article 6 le droit d'accès à un tribunal.

16 *Karoly Nagy c. Hongrie* [GC], n° 56665/09, 14 septembre 2017. V. en particulier, à cet égard, l'opinion dissidente du juge Linos-Alexandre Sicilianos.

17 *Regner c. République tchèque* [GC], n° 35289/11, 19 septembre 2017, § 105. Le terme « civil » est mis entre parenthèses parce que, dans la comparaison avec l'arrêt *Karoly Nagy,* c'est l'aspect « droit » qui importe.

18 *Al-Dulimi and Montana Management Inc. v. Suisse* [GC], no. 5809/08, § 97, 21 juin 2016.

19 *Markovic c. Italie* [GC] n° 1398/03, 14 décembre 2006.

Cependant, autonomie des notions oblige, la Cour ne saurait être liée par les qualifications le cas échéant arbitraires des législations ou jurisprudences nationales et il est alors de son devoir de requalifier certaines notions.

Le propos de la présente contribution n'est certainement pas de faire un inventaire des droits qui ont été respectivement qualifiés de civils et de ceux qui se sont vu refuser cette qualification, puisqu'il s'agit de rechercher un critère général. On peut juste retenir que certains droits, intimement liés à la personnalité et à la vie familiale des individus, à leurs biens, sont reconnus comme civils. Si les droits régissant la vie entre les individus peuvent être qualifiés sans hésitation comme droits civils, ce sont les droits invoqués à l'encontre des pouvoirs publics qui posent problème.[20] Ainsi certains droits, relevant de la sphère publique, de la relation de l'individu avec la puissance publique, ont été considérés comme constituant des droits politiques. Il s'agit p. ex. de la police des étrangers, du contentieux des élections, du service militaire.

Mais le tableau se brouille très vite à propos de droits difficiles à classer dans une seule catégorie. Certains droits sont tellement à cheval sur l'aspect public et l'aspect privé qu'il faut être devin pour s'aventurer à prédire dans quel sens la balance va pencher. Ainsi des licences d'exportation ou d'exploitation d'une ligne de taxi[21] ou d'une station GPL[22] ont été considérées comme mettant en cause des droits civils.

Le plus grand pas vers l'inclusion dans le champ des droits civils, en dépit d'une forte intervention de l'administration, a été accompli à propos de droits dérivant de la sécurité sociale.[23]

Il en est encore ainsi de la fonction publique. L'arrêt *Pellegrin* excluait encore de manière péremptoire les litiges entre l'administration et certains de ses agents, à savoir ceux qui participent à l'exercice de la puissance publique[24], mais impliquait déjà que la fonction publique n'était plus exclue systématiquement de l'article 6. Huit ans plus tard l'arrêt *Vilho Eskelinen* va beaucoup plus loin en y incluant en principe le contentieux de la fonction publique, quitte à laisser aux Etats la possibilité d'établir que le fonctionnaire en question y échappe.[25]

---

[20]   Arrêt *Ringeisen*, n° 2614/65, 16 juillet 1971, § 94 ; *König c. Allemagne*, n° 6232/73, 29 juin 1978.

[21]   *Pudas c. Suède* n° 10426/83, 27 octobre 1987.

[22]   *Benthem c. Pays-Bas*, n° 8848/80, 23 octobre 1985.

[23]   *Feldbrugge c. Pays-Bas*, n° 8562/79, 25 mai 1986, § 27 s.

[24]   *Pellegrin c. France*, n° 28541/95, 8 décembre 1999, § 66.

[25]   *Vilho Eskelinen c. Finlande*, n° 63235/00, 19 avril 2007. Pour échapper à la présomption d'applicabilité de l'article 6, « il appartiendra à l'Etat défendeur de démontrer, premièrement, que d'après le droit national un requérant fonctionnaire n'a pas le droit d'accéder à un tribunal, et, deuxièmement, que l'exclusion des droits garantis à l'article 6 est fondée s'agissant de ce fonctionnaire » (§ 41 *in fine*).

Il est intéressant de noter que la Cour identifie, dans l'arrêt *Vilho Eskelinen*, comme un des indices de la soumission d'un litige à l'article 6, sa judiciarisation volontaire par l'Etat. Le critère est dangereux parce qu'on voit mal pourquoi il ne serait pas appliqué à d'autres domaines, très sensibles il est vrai, comme avant tout les domaines fiscal, électoral et d'immigration et d'asile où il existe en général des procédures judiciaires très complètes. L'arrêt en question prend cependant le soin, dans un *obiter dictum*, d'exclure expressément ces trois domaines.[26] Il ne livre pourtant aucune explication et on peut sincèrement se demander s'il en existe une qui soit rationnelle. Justement, alors même qu'il touche de très près le patrimoine des citoyens et peut le cas échéant les ruiner, le contentieux fiscal demeure exclu de l'applicabilité de l'article 6.[27]

Toujours est-il, on vient de le voir, qu'alors que les travaux préparatoires ne l'y obligeaient point, la Cour utilise le concept «civil» pour exclure les droits et obligations qui relèvent des prérogatives de souveraineté de l'Etat.

Or, la Cour n'a elle-même pas respecté, par la suite, le vœu exprimé au cours de l'élaboration de la Convention, de ne pas faire rentrer les procès administratifs dans les prévisions de l'article 6, en y incluant bien des actions relevant manifestement de la sphère administrative, comme des procès portant sur des permis de construire, pour ne nommer que le cas le plus emblématique.[28]

Le critère pour dénier à des droits la qualification «civile» serait-il à rechercher dans le pouvoir discrétionnaire accordé à celui qui est appelé à conférer un droit ? Il y a d'extrêmes réticences à considérer des contestations portant sur de tels «privilèges» comme portant sur des «droits». En effet, en principe, dès lors que, p. ex., une autorité de nomination jouit d'un pouvoir d'appréciation très large pour nommer un prétendant à un poste déterminé et que celui qui attaque en justice le refus de nomination obtient gain de cause, on ne peut que difficilement affirmer qu'une fois la décision de refus annulée, le postulant aurait un *droit* à être nommé.[29] Pourtant, les choses ne semblent pas très limpides. La Cour

---

[26] Arrêt précité, § 61.

[27] *Ferrazini c. Italie*, précité.

[28] V., p. ex., l'affaire *Kyrtatos c. Grèce*, no. 41666/98, du 22 mai 2003 ; *MIF sud c. France*, no. 57220/00 du 11 septembre 2002 ; *McGonnell c. Royaume-Uni*, no. 28488/98, du 8 février 2000.

[29] Il serait en effet excessif voire inadmissible de considérer la nomination – possible après la décision d'annulation – comme une suite directe de la contestation du refus de nomination en justice. Pour raisonner dans les catégories de la causalité, l'annulation est, dans ces circonstances, une condition parmi d'autres à une nomination subséquente, mais certainement pas la cause adéquate. Une fois l'annulation obtenue, les pendules sont remises à zéro. Le prétendant au poste peut poser sa candidature à nouveau, mais sans aucune certitude d'être choisi. Or, une jurisprudence bien établie de la Cour exige que l'issue de la procédure soit «directement déterminante pour le droit en question, un lien ténu ou des répercussions lointaines ne suffisant pas à faire entrer en jeu l'article 6 § 1» (voir, parmi de nombreux autres précédents, *Le Compte, Van Leuven et De Meyere*, précité, § 47 ; *Boulois c. Luxembourg*

---

affirme de manière constante que la seule présence d'un élément discrétionnaire dans le libellé d'une disposition légale n'exclut pas, en soi, l'existence d'un droit et que l'article 6 s'applique alors même que la procédure judiciaire porte sur une décision discrétionnaire heurtant les droits du requérant.[30] C'est d'ailleurs précisément ce point qui a suscité l'hostilité de la Cour suprême du Royaume-Uni à suivre la Cour dans son arrêt du 10 mai 2017. Elle distingue entre deux catégories de droits : «...*a distinction could be drawn between the class of social security and welfare benefits whose substance was defined precisely, and which could therefore amount to an individual right of which the applicant could consider herself the holder, and those benefits which were, in their essence, dependent on the exercise of judgment by the relevant authority*»[31] et elle exclut cette dernière catégorie de celle des droits civils. Il n'est pas facile de suivre le raisonnement de la Cour suprême et la Cour de Strasbourg, dans l'arrêt que celle-ci refuse de suivre, avait clairement envisagé la nature particulière de l'obligation des autorités locales et répondu que même si l'obligation de celles-ci se limitait à procurer à l'intéressé «*a benefit in kind*», la discrétion afférente «*had clearly limits : once the initial qualifying conditions (…) had been met (…) the Council was required to secure that accommodation was provided by one of three means... *».[32]

Pourquoi alors tant de réticences ? L'origine serait-elle à chercher dans le souci formulé en 1948 par la délégation américaine, lors de l'élaboration de la notion de «droits civils», à savoir celui d'éviter que trop de litiges avec l'administration donnent naissance à des «droits» pouvant être portés devant les tribunaux ? L'arrêt prémentionné de la Cour suprême du Royaume-Uni est éloquent à ce sujet puisqu'il formule exactement la même préoccupation : la juridiction suprême n'est pas près d'accepter, sauf décision de la Grande Chambre, que des décisions des autorités administratives chargées de procurer des logements à des personnes qui en ont besoin, puissent donner lieu à un procès en bonne et due forme, sous

---

    [GC], no 37575/04, 14 décembre 2010, § 90, *Bochan c. Ukraine (no. 2)* [GC], no. 22251/08, 5 février 2015, § 42, *Paroisse gréco-catholique Lupeni et autres c. Roumanie* [GC], no 76943/11, 29 novembre 2016, § 71, et *Regner*, précité, § 99).

30   V. les arrêts et décisions citées au § 102 de l'arrêt *Regner*, précité.

31   Arrêt précité, § 20, référence à son arrêt *Ali v. Birmingham City Council*.

32   Arrêt précité, § 59. Dans l'arrêt *Tomlinson*, précité, Lord Kerr a déclaré : «*78.Where the decision involves an evaluative judgment one can quite see that a judicial review challenge would be appropriate but where a conclusion on a simple factual issue is at stake, judicial review does not commend itself as an obviously suitable means by which to rid the original decision of its appearance of bias. In particular, judicial review might be said to be a singularly inapt means of examining issues of credibility which lie at the heart of the present appeals. Judicial review is suitable to deal with issues such as the rationality of the judgment reached ; whether relevant factors have been taken into account ; whether sufficient opportunity has been given to the affected party to make representations etc. All of these take place on – if not an agreed factual matrix – at least one in which the areas of factual controversy are confined. It is quite different when one comes to decide a sharply conflicting factual issue.*»

peine de réduire indûment leur pouvoir d'appréciation. Elle s'est déclarée «déçue» de l'absence de prise en considération de ses *«concerns over 'judicialisation' of the welfare services and the implication for local authority resources.* »[33]

2. *Les droits fondamentaux reconnus par la Convention*

Autre réel problème, la Cour exclut souvent de la catégorie des droits civils des droits reconnus comme fondamentaux par la Convention elle-même. C'est ainsi qu'en matière de contentieux relatifs à l'entrée, au séjour et à l'éloignement des étrangers, la Cour a retenu que le fait qu'une mesure d'interdiction du territoire ait pu entraîner «accessoirement» des conséquences importantes sur la vie privée et familiale de l'intéressé ne saurait suffire à faire entrer la procédure afférente dans le domaine des droits civils protégés par l'article 6.[34] Même son de cloche en matière fiscale : même si le contentieux fiscal met clairement en jeu les droits garantis par l'article 1er du Protocole additionnel, il ne relève pas de l'article 6.[35]

Seulement, ces affirmations ne sont pas toujours appliquées avec la cohérence souhaitable.[36] C'est ainsi que dans une affaire où il s'agissait du droit à l'instruction – protégé par l'article 2 du Protocole additionnel – la Cour a conclu à l'applicabilité de l'article 6. Il est vrai que le droit interne avait déjà conféré des droits qui pouvaient faire l'objet d'une action en justice.[37] En matière de droit à la liberté, à propos d'un régime pénitentiaire emportant certaines restrictions à une série de droits communément reconnus aux détenus, la Cour a conclu à l'application de l'article 6 en soulignant que «certaines au moins des limitations sérieuses établies (…) – comme celles visant ses contacts avec sa famille et celles ayant une retombée patrimoniale – relèvent assurément des droits de la personne et, partant, revêtent un caractère civil» au sens conventionnel du terme.[38] Plus

---

33   Arrêt précité, § 33. – Il semble qu'ainsi, la notion de «droit civil» serve de substitut à la distinction entre droit subjectif reconnu en droit interne – ou que la Cour requalifie comme tel malgré les réticences voire l'opposition des instances nationales – et certaines prétentions qui ne se voient pas reconnaître le statut de droit subjectif pouvant être invoqué en justice. On peut discuter du remplacement de la notion de «contestation sur un droit» par celle de «droit subjectif reconnu en droit interne», mais de fait la Cour a elle-même déjà diligenté la notion de droit subjectif (l'arrêt *Salesi c. Italie*, n° 13023/87, 26 février 1993, § 19, parle, à propos d'allocations d'aide sociale, «d'un droit subjectif de caractère patrimonial, résultant des règles précises d'une loi»). Quoi qu'il en soit, en réalité cela n'a pas grand-chose à voir avec la notion de droit civil.

34   *Maaouia c. France*, n° 39652/98, 5 octobre 2000, § 36 s.

35   *Ferrazini c. Italie*, précité.

36   Pour un tableau plus vaste des incohérences en la matière, v. Sébastien Van Drooghenbroeck, Vint-cinq ans après Benthem : sens et non-sens d'une applicabilité limitée de l'article 6 de la Convention européenne des droits de l'homme dans le contentieux de droit public, Liège, Strasbourg, Bruxelles, parcours des droits de l'homme, *Liber amicorum* Michel Melchior, Anthemis 2010, p. 704 s.

37   *Emine Araç c. Turquie*, n° 9907/02, 23 septembre 2008 ; dans le même sens *Orsus c. Croatie*, n° 15766/03, 16 mars 2010.

38   *Ganci c. Italie*, n° 41576/98, 30 octobre 2003, § 25 ; v. aussi *Enea c. Italie* [GC], n° 74912/01, 17 septembre 2009.

notable encore, alors que la Cour avait clairement affirmé dans l'arrêt *Pierre-Bloch*[39] que l'article 6 ne s'applique pas en matière de contentieux électoral, cette affirmation s'est vue émoussée dans la suite de ce qu'on a appelé un mouvement de procéduralisation.[40] C'est ainsi que la Cour a retenu dans un arrêt subséquent que « le principe d'effectivité des droits exige que les décisions constatant le non-respect des [conditions d'éligibilité] dans le cas de tel ou tel candidat soient conformes à un certain nombre de critères permettant d'éviter l'arbitraire. En particulier, ces décisions doivent être prises par un organe présentant un minimum de garanties d'impartialité » et « la procédure du constat d'inéligibilité doit être de nature à garantir une décision équitable et objective ».[41] Elle alla même, par la suite, dans le cadre d'une affaire de contestation d'attribution d'un siège de député au Parlement, jusqu'à exiger que cette contestation pût être jugée dans le cadre d'une procédure judiciaire et non être soumise à un contrôle seulement politique.[42]

Face à tant de tergiversations, faut-il continuer dans cette voie, rendre la jurisprudence de la Cour toujours plus illisible, voire provoquer la résistance des juridictions nationales ?

II. ALLER PLUS LOIN : TROIS PROPOSITIONS

A bien soupeser les préoccupations des auteurs de la Convention et les tentatives de la Cour d'y déférer, ainsi que l'insatisfaction que la méthode casuistique adoptée jusqu'à présent a engendrée, il semble qu'il faille chercher des critères plus sûrs donnant lieu à des résultats plus prévisibles.

Peut-on définir positivement, par voie générale, les droits civils ? Certains s'y sont essayés, mais la notion de droit civil semble répondre à tant d'acceptions différentes qu'il paraît impossible de trouver une formule faisant l'unanimité.[43]

---

[39] *Pierre-Bloch c. France*, n° 24194/94, 21 octobre 1997.
[40] Sébastien Van Drooghenbroeck, *op. cit.*, n° 29, p. 709.
[41] *Podkolzina c. Lettonie*, n° 46726/99, 9 avril 2002, § 35.
[42] *Grosnaru c. Roumanie*, n° 78039/01, 2 mars 2010, § 54.
[43] V. p. ex. l'opinion dissidente des commissaires Melchior et Frowein dans l'affaire *Benthem* qui considèrent qu'il « *faut considérer comme droits de caractère civil tous les droits qui sont des droits individuels dans l'ordre juridique interne et qui ressortissent du domaine de la liberté générale de l'individu, dans son activité professionnelle ou toute autre activité autorisée par la loi. Il en est et demeure ainsi même lorsque, pour des raisons d'utilité publique et de protection de l'intérêt général, l'Etat a reçu des pouvoirs de surveillance quant à l'exercice de ces droits. Ces pouvoirs peuvent se déployer selon des techniques très différentes : l'agrément donné à des actes privés, octroi ou retrait de licences ou d'autorisations, notamment en liaison avec l'usage d'un bien ou l'exercice d'une activité professionnelle* » (*Benthem c. Pays-Bas*, n° 8848/80, rapport de la Commission, p. 41, § 9). Les plages d'incertitude demeurent. Quid, p. ex. du droit fiscal qui met l'individu face à l'Etat mais porte sur le patrimoine de l'individu ? Et l'immigration ? La définition en cause permet-elle de l'inclure ou de l'exclure avec certitude ?

Quid de l'inverse, consistant à définir les droits politiques[44] et à affirmer qu'*a contrario*, tous les autres droits sont des droits civils ? Le procédé est plus prometteur, mais il semble douteux qu'il puisse trouver l'adhésion générale.

Une troisième voie, plus modeste dans la démarche, pas forcément dans les résultats, mérite à tout le moins d'être esquissée. Celle-ci pourrait se réaliser par trois procédés indépendants, mais pouvant être cumulés, les deux premiers se rapportant aux droits reconnus dans les législations nationales (A.), et le troisième aux droits reconnus par la Convention (B.).

A. LES DROITS RECONNUS PAR LA LÉGISLATION NATIONALE

PREMIERE PROPOSITION : Dès que pour un droit ou un intérêt, la loi nationale prévoit un recours devant un tribunal établi par la loi, les garanties de l'article 6, § 1ᵉʳ, s'appliquent.

L'arrêt *Regner c. République tchèque*[45] identifie une situation où, sans reconnaissance d'un droit matériel, il y a quand-même possibilité d'agir en justice.

(v. pour une critique du système proposé par les commissaires Melchior et Frowein, Pieter Van Dijk, *op. cit.*, p. 143). – V. encore la position plus radicale du juge De Meyer prise dans son opinion séparée jointe à l'arrêt *H c. Belgique*, n° 8950/80, 30 novembre 1987 : ont un caractère civil « tous les droits et obligations qui ne se rapportent pas, plus particulièrement, à la détermination du 'bien-fondé' d'une accusation en matière pénale ».

[44] A quoi opposer les droits civils : aux droits publics ? politiques ? Il serait peut-être plus facile pour la Cour de définir ou d'énumérer les droits qu'elle considère comme ne constituant *pas* des droits civils. Il pourrait s'agir des droits attachés à la qualité de citoyen et des droits et obligations qui concourent à l'exercice de la souveraineté dans l'Etat : élections, service militaire, nationalité, statut des étrangers pour n'énumérer que ceux-ci. V., dans ce sens Paul Lemmens, Geschillen over burgerlijke rechten en verplichtingen. Het toepassingsgebied van den artikelen 6, lid 1, van het Europees verdrag over de rechten van de mens en 14, lid 1, van het international verdrag inzake burgerrechten en politieke rechten, thèse, Louvain 1987, p. 212, n° 172, cité *in* Jacques Velu et Rusen Ergec, *op. cit.*, n° 421, p. 454.

[45] *Regner c. République tchèque* [GC], précité. Sans proposer de critère pour déterminer ce qui constitue un droit ou une obligation au sens de l'article 6, l'arrêt tente de classer les différents arrêts de la Cour, très variés et à première vue très épars, dans quatre catégories. Il procède du constat que quelquefois la Cour reconnaît des droits matériels, quelquefois des droits procéduraux, et de celui que ces droits peuvent parfois se combiner. Il arrive ainsi au constat suivant (§§ 101 à 105) :
« 101. (...) les droits (...) conférés par les législations nationales peuvent être soit matériels, soit procéduraux, soit encore une combinaison des deux.
102. Aucun doute ne saurait exister sur le fait qu'il y a droit au sens de l'article 6 § 1 lorsqu'un droit matériel reconnu en droit national est assorti du droit procédural permettant d'en faire sanctionner le respect en justice. La seule présence d'un élément discrétionnaire dans le libellé d'une disposition légale n'exclut pas, en soi, l'existence d'un droit (*Camps c. France* (déc.), n° 42401/98, 23 novembre 1999, *Ellès et autres c. Suisse*, n° 12573/06, 16 décembre 2010, § 16, *Boulois*, précité, *a contrario*, § 99, et *Miessen c. Belgique*, n° 31517/12, § 48, 18 octobre 2016). En effet, l'article 6 s'applique lorsque la procédure judiciaire porte sur une décision discrétionnaire heurtant les droits du requérant (*Pudas c. Suède*, 27 octobre 1987, § 34, série A

Il y a en effet des cas, dans certaines législations, où la loi confère à des personnes le droit d'agir en justice pour réclamer le respect de certaines obligations légales alors même que ces personnes ne peuvent pas faire valoir de droit matériel.[46] L'arrêt précise que dans de tels cas, l'article 6, § 1er, est applicable, à condition que l'avantage ou le privilège, une fois accordé, crée un droit civil. Dans un arrêt de chambre subséquent, *Mirovni Inštitut c. Slovénie*[47], la Cour a appliqué le principe énoncé dans l'arrêt *Regner* à une procédure d'appel de candidatures à l'obtention d'une subvention publique de recherches. Tout en relevant que le candidat évincé n'avait aucun droit à l'octroi d'un financement et que l'examen au fond des différentes candidatures relevait du pouvoir discrétionnaire des autorités nationales, elle a conclu à l'applicabilité de l'article 6, notant au passage qu'il y a eu «une évolution de la jurisprudence de la Cour vers l'application du volet civil de l'article 6 à des affaires ne portant pas à première vue sur un droit civil mais pouvant avoir des répercussions directes et importantes sur un droit de caractère privé d'un individu (*De Tommaso c. Italie* [GC], n° 43395/09, § 151, CEDH 2017 (extraits)).»[48]

---

n° 25-A, *Obermeier c. Autriche*, 28 juin 1990, § 69, série A n° 179, et *Mats Jacobsson c. Suède*, 28 juin 1990, § 32, série A n° 180-A).

103. En revanche, l'article 6 n'est pas applicable là où la législation nationale, sans conférer un droit, accorde un certain avantage qu'il n'est pas possible de faire reconnaître en justice (*Boulois*, précité, § 90, affaire qui concernait le refus par une commission pénitentiaire d'accorder une autorisation de sortie à un détenu, sans recours possible devant une juridiction administrative). La même situation se présente lorsqu'une personne ne se voit reconnaître par la législation nationale qu'un espoir de se faire accorder un droit, l'octroi de celui-ci dépendant d'une décision entièrement discrétionnaire et non motivée des autorités (*Masson et Van Zon*, précité, §§ 49-51, *Roche*, précité, §§ 122-125 et *Ankarcrona c. Suède* (déc.), n° 35178/97, 27 juin 2000).

104. Il existe par ailleurs des cas où la législation nationale reconnaît à une personne un droit matériel sans pour autant que, pour une raison quelconque, il existe le moindre recours juridictionnel pour le faire reconnaître ou sanctionner en justice. Tel est le cas, par exemple, des immunités juridictionnelles prévues par la loi nationale. L'immunité apparaît ici non pas comme un tempérament à un droit matériel, mais comme un obstacle procédural à la compétence des cours et tribunaux nationaux pour statuer sur ce droit (*Čudak c. Lituanie* [GC], n° 15869/02, CEDH 2010).

105. Dans certaines hypothèses, enfin, le droit national, sans reconnaître forcément de droit subjectif à un individu, lui confère en revanche le droit à une procédure d'examen régulière de sa demande, appelant le juge compétent à statuer sur des moyens tels que l'arbitraire, le détournement de pouvoir ou encore les vices de procédure (*Van Marle et autres c. Pays-Bas*, 26 juin 1986, série A n° 101, pp. 11-12, § 35, ainsi que, *mutatis mutandis*, *Kök c. Turquie*, n° 1855/02, § 36, 19 octobre 2006). Tel est le cas de certaines décisions pour lesquelles l'administration dispose d'un pouvoir purement discrétionnaire d'octroyer ou de refuser un avantage ou un privilège, la loi conférant à l'administré le droit de saisir la justice qui, au cas où celle-ci constaterait le caractère illégal de la décision, peut en prononcer l'annulation. En pareil cas, l'article 6 § 1 de la Convention est applicable, à condition que l'avantage ou le privilège, une fois accordé, crée un droit civil».

[46] ...même pas de manière défendable, à moins de considérer que l'espoir, dépendant d'une multitude d'autres facteurs, de se voir accorder un avantage après le succès de l'action en justice, constitue un «droit» qu'on peut prétendre de manière défendable comme reconnu en droit interne, ce qui paraît excessif, voire inadmissible. V. aussi *supra*, note de bas de page 29.

[47] *Mirovni Inštitut c. Slovénie* 13 mars 2018, n° 32303/13.

[48] La formule employée au § 105 de l'arrêt *Regner* a une forte potentialité dès lors que les exigences du procès équitable jouent non seulement en cas de privation d'un droit, mais également en cas de recours contre le refus d'octroyer un privilège, comme p. ex. de nommer quelqu'un

Mais l'arrêt *Regner* est loin d'avoir résolu tous les problèmes. Qu'en est-il du droit d'agir contre une autorisation de construire illégale délivrée à un tiers où il faut et il suffit, du moins dans certaines législations, justifier d'un intérêt, ce qui signifie que celui qui introduit l'action doit être concrètement et individuellement touché par la mesure ? Le requérant se fait en quelque sorte l'avocat de la légalité objective que le juge administratif est appelé à rétablir moyennant l'annulation de la décision administrative irrégulière. Il a le droit d'agir mais son action, à condition d'être couronnée de succès, ne créera pas dans son chef un droit subjectif, condition posée par l'arrêt en question pour qu'une action relève de l'article 6.

Pour en rester au jugement précité de la Cour suprême britannique: la ressortissante iranienne qui sollicitait un logement (indépendamment de la question de savoir si sa contestation portait sur un droit civil ou si son action tendait à voir reconnaître dans son chef un droit subjectif ou encore, si le juge disposait d'un large pouvoir d'appréciation), n'avait-elle pas droit à ce que sa cause fût jugée dans le cadre d'un procès équitable ? Ne serait-il pas étrange que dans un tel cas, où la loi prévoit un recours juridictionnel devant une juridiction ordinaire, l'on se dispense de l'équité d'un procès ? Pour le dire avec les mots de J.-P. Costa : «Y aurait-il, pour les Etats contractants, un droit au procès inéquitable ? ».[49]

D'ailleurs, la Cour n'a-t-elle pas elle-même déjà déclaré que «lorsqu'un Etat confère des droits qui se prêtent à un recours judiciaire[50], ceux-ci peuvent en principe passer pour des droits de caractère civil au sens de l'article 6 § 1 » ?[51]

à un poste, que ce soit pour des causes objectives (minimum d'âge, possession de certains diplômes, etc.) ou subjectives (personnalité à évaluer au cours d'un entretien). Bien entendu, le recours a plus de chances d'être couronné de succès si la décision de refus procède d'une erreur objective patente, p. ex. de l'affirmation que le candidat n'a pas l'âge requis alors que cela n'est manifestement pas vrai. Mais même des raisons subjectives avancées peuvent faire l'objet d'un contrôle juridictionnel. Bien entendu, le prétendant ou occupant d'un poste politiquement sensible aura des difficultés à attaquer une décision prise au motif d'un manque ou de perte de confiance du pouvoir politique. Mais si on le refuse ou on le démet de ses fonctions parce que la couleur de sa peau ne plaît pas… Il a le droit de faire constater que la décision a été prise, non pas discrétionnairement, mais arbitrairement.

[49] Jean-Paul Costa, les droits et obligations de caractère civil selon la jurisprudence de la Cour européenne des droits de l'homme, *in* La justice civile au vingt-et-unième siècle, Mélanges Pierre Julien, Edilaix 2003, p. 105.

[50] De quel recours judiciaire parle-t-on ? Se contentera-t-on d'un recours en pure légalité voire limité à la régularité formelle de la décision attaquée, sans contrôle, au fond, de la réalité des faits à la base de la décision, ou exigera-t-on que le juge auquel on appliquera les exigences de l'article 6 exerce un contrôle de «pleine juridiction» au sens où l'entend la Cour ? C'est essentiellement cet aspect de l'extension du champ d'application de l'article 6 qui inquiète les juridictions britanniques, v. *supra, sub* I. B., 1.

[51] *Emine Araç c. Turquie*, précité, § 21, citant comme allant dans le même sens, *Tinnelly & Sons Ltd et autres et McElduff et autres c. Royaume-Uni*, 10 juillet 1998, § 61, Recueil des arrêts et décisions 1998-IV.

Les conséquences de l'acceptation par la Cour de cette première proposition seraient loin d'être négligeables, mais elles seraient dans la lignée des travaux préparatoires qui tendaient à soumettre à l'article 6 les droits et obligations invoqués « *in a suit of law* ».[52]

Il est vrai que, dans la plupart des pays, les contentieux des étrangers et le contentieux fiscal, pour ne nommer que ceux-ci, passeraient sous l'égide de l'article 6 dès lors que les contentieux y afférents peuvent être portés devant d'authentiques juridictions, répondant aux critères établis par la Cour en la matière.

On objectera que l'effet pervers de l'applicabilité de l'article 6 sera peut-être que certains Etats éviteront de judiciariser certaines procédures administratives, de peur de voir les critères du procès équitable appliqués extensivement. Doit-on vraiment s'attendre à tant de cynisme de la part des États?[53]

Plus grave, la Cour pourrait et voudrait-elle renverser cinquante ans de jurisprudence et, ce qui plus est, prendre à bord de gros contentieux comme le contentieux fiscal et le contentieux des étrangers ? La proposition faisant passer tout recours juridictionnel sous l'égide de l'article 6 l'impliquerait.

DEUXIEME PROPOSITION : Toute contestation sur un droit que l'on peut prétendre, au moins de manière défendable, reconnu en droit interne, est présumée être de nature civile.

Cette proposition est indépendante de la précedente : il y a des matières où justement, la loi nationale prévoit un droit, mais sans recours juridictionnel, et où la Cour identifie l'existence d'une contestation qui, à condition d'être couronnée de succès en justice, donnerait lieu à la reconnaissance du droit.

Il s'agit là de l'application de la jurisprudence *Golder* – droit à un tribunal – et de l'extension de la présomption *Vilho Eskelinen* à toutes les matières. Eu égard au fait que les arrêts de la Cour ont eu les pires difficultés à limiter la présomption à la matière de la fonction publique et que les arguments avancés sont loin d'être convaincants, au lieu d'imposer au requérant de prouver le caractère civil de la contestation dans les cas douteux, on conclurait au caractère en principe civil de la contestation, ce qui contribuerait à faciliter notablement les choses. Les Etats pourraient toujours combattre la présomption en prouvant qu'un recours juridictionnel a été expressément exclu et que cela est justifié par les intérêts de l'Etat.

---

[52] V. *supra, sub* I., A.

[53] La solution pourrait se réclamer de la jurisprudence de la Cour qui exige que des procédures nationales non requises par la Convention, comme l'appel en matière civile, doivent néanmoins respecter les exigences de l'article 6, v. p. ex. *Levages Prestations Services c. France*, n° 21930/93, 23 octobre 1996, § 44 ; *Poitrimol c. France*, n° 14032/88, 23 novembre 1993, §§ 13-15.

B. LES DROITS RECONNUS PAR LA CONVENTION

TROISIEME PROPOSITION : Tous les droits fondamentaux reconnus par la Convention constituent des droits civils au sens de l'article 6, § 1ᵉʳ.

De par leur nature, la presqu'intégralité des droits fondamentaux reconnus par la Convention s'attachent de manière tellement étroite à la personne humaine et à sa sphère privée qu'ils peuvent sans problème être qualifiés de civils.[54]

Du point de vue des conséquences découlant de la soustraction de ces droits à la sphère civile et donc à la protection par l'article 6, il apparaît comme parfaitement illogique de faire bénéficier de cette protection des droits par définition «non fondamentaux», tandis que ceux qui se voient reconnaître ce statut n'en bénéficient pas.[55]

D'aucuns répondront que les droits fondamentaux reconnus par la Convention ne sont pas, *per se,* des droits pouvant être invoqués en justice et que pour qu'il en soit ainsi, ils doivent encore être reconnus en droit interne pour relever de

---

[54] Dans l'arrêt *Hirst c. Royaume-Uni (n° 2)* [GC], du 6 octobre 2005, n° 74025/01, la Cour a reconnu même au droit de vote un caractère subjectif :
« 56. L'article 3 du Protocole no 1 paraît à première vue différent des autres dispositions de la Convention et de ses Protocoles garantissant des droits car il énonce l'obligation pour les Hautes Parties contractantes d'organiser des élections dans des conditions qui assurent la libre expression de l'opinion du peuple et non un droit ou une liberté en particulier.
57. Toutefois, eu égard aux travaux préparatoires de l'article 3 du Protocole no 1 et à l'interprétation qui est donnée de cette clause dans le cadre de la Convention dans son ensemble, la Cour a établi que cet article garantit des droits subjectifs, dont le droit de vote et celui de se porter candidat à des élections (*Mathieu-Mohin et Clerfayt c. Belgique*, arrêt du 2 mars 1987, série A no 113, pp. 22-23, §§ 46-51) (…).»

[55] Pis, quelquefois, soumettre une situation à l'article 6 ou non dépend plus d'un point de vue adopté que d'une distinction rationnelle. Le droit des étrangers en est un bon exemple. Un étranger se fait rayer des registres de la population et ne peut dès lors plus revenir dans le pays qu'il a habité pendant longtemps. Son recours est rejeté par les tribunaux. Il s'adresse à la Cour. Est-il correct, comme cela semble pourtant être la jurisprudence constante de la Cour, de dire qu'il n'a pas de droit civil au respect de l'article 6 puisqu'il s'agit d'une affaire d'entrée et de séjour des étrangers (*Makuc et al. c. Slovénie*, n° 26828/07, 31 mai 2007, § 186 : «…
Article 6 § 1 of the Convention does not apply to proceedings regulating a person's citizenship and/or the entry, stay and deportation of aliens, as such proceedings do not involve either the 'determination of his civil rights and obligations or of any criminal charge against him' within the meaning of 6 § 1 of the Convention…». Dans le jugement sur le fond rendu le 26 juin 2012, la Grande Chambre examina l'affaire sur la base de l'article 8 et constata une violation) et de dire en même temps qu'il peut se prévaloir de l'article 8 puisqu'il a résidé longtemps au pays et y a établi une vie familiale ? N'y a-t-il pas quelque contradiction : n'y a-t-il pas eu, tout simplement, violation d'un droit civil consistant dans le droit du requérant à une vie familiale et n'a-t-il pas droit – *à ce titre* – sous l'article 6, à un procès équitable ? La distinction (il s'agit d'une espèce de détour) entre police des étrangers et vie familiale ayant une influence sur la législation sur les étrangers (la tenant en fait en échec) semble artificielle. Il serait plus réaliste d'affirmer que la police des étrangers met en jeu les droits privés et familiaux.

l'article 6. Sinon ils ne relèvent que de l'article 13 qui assure une protection moindre que l'article 6 (recours effectif par opposition à procès équitable).[56]

Ceci est certainement vrai des systèmes dualistes et la Cour a expressément reconnu que l'article 13 n'implique pas une obligation des Etats parties « d'intégrer la Convention aux systèmes nationaux. »[57] Pour les systèmes monistes, la situation paraît plus simple en ce que l'approbation de l'instrument international intègre les dispositions de celui-ci directement dans le droit national et elles font dès lors partie du droit national où, à condition d'être suffisamment précises, elles peuvent conférer des droits subjectifs et être directement invoquées en justice. Mais même pour les systèmes dualistes, la Cour a précisé que les Etats concernés doivent assurer à quiconque relève de leur juridiction la substance des droits et libertés reconnus par la Convention.[58] Ces Etats doivent donc prévoir des dispositions nationales correspondant aux droits de la Convention et on pourra, pareillement, reconnaître à ces dispositions le caractère de droits civils.

Ainsi, si un Etat refuse à un de ses ressortissants de rentrer dans son pays pour voir sa famille, celui-ci ne peut-il pas tout simplement invoquer l'article 8 pour réclamer le *droit civil* de les rejoindre ? Et si des personnes veulent organiser une manifestation et qu'elles se voient opposer un refus par l'administration sans possibilité d'attaquer ce refus devant un tribunal (p. ex. seulement devant une administration hiérarchiquement supérieure), ne peuvent-ils pas attaquer ce refus en invoquant l'article 10 ? Et si, dans un système dualiste, la loi nationale

---

[56] Il ne s'agit pas *ipso facto* de droits civils qu'on pourrait, en tant que tels, faire sanctionner en droit interne et l'article 6 ne s'applique pas au cas où on se plaint de la violation d'un droit fondamental reconnu par la Convention (seule). Il ne s'agit que d'une obligation de l'Etat de les reconnaître ou, plus précisément, de ne pas y interférer de manière indue et non pas d'un droit opposable. La formule suivante contenue dans un récent arrêt de la Grande Chambre accréditerait cette idée : « La Cour rappelle que, pour que l'article 6 § 1 sous son volet « civil » trouve à s'appliquer, il faut qu'il y ait 'contestation' sur un 'droit' que l'on peut prétendre, au moins de manière défendable, reconnu en droit interne, *et ce, qu'il soit protégé par la Convention ou non* » (*Paroisse gréco-catholique de Lupeni et autres c. Roumanie* [GC], n° 76943/11, 29 novembre 2016, § 71). – A noter que l'article 47 de la Charte des droits fondamentaux de l'Union européenne consolide, dans une seule et même disposition, le droit à un recours effectif (par. 1er) et à un tribunal impartial (par. 2).

[57] *James et al. C. Royaume-Uni* [plén.], n° 8793/79, 21 février 1986, § 84 : « '... ni l'article 13 (art. 13) ni la Convention en général ne prescrivent aux États contractants une [façon] déterminée d'assurer dans leur droit interne l'application effective de toutes les dispositions de cet instrument' (arrêt *Syndicat suédois des conducteurs de locomotives*, du 6 février 1976, série A no 20, p. 18, par. 50). (...) ».

[58] *James et al. C. Royaume-Uni*, loc. cit. : « Bien que donc non tenus d'incorporer la Convention à leur système juridique national, ils n'en doivent pas moins, aux termes de l'article 1 (art. 1) et sous une forme ou une autre, y assurer à quiconque relève de leur juridiction la substance des droits et libertés reconnus (arrêt *Irlande c. Royaume-Uni* du 18 janvier 1978, série A no 25, p. 91, par. 239). Sous réserve de ce qui suit, l'article 13 (art. 13) garantit l'existence en droit interne d'un recours effectif permettant de s'y prévaloir des droits et libertés de la Convention tels qu'ils peuvent s'y trouver consacrés. ».

---

ne prévoit pas de recours juridictionnel, on dirait – arrêt *Golder* oblige – qu'il y a manquement à prévoir l'accès à un tribunal.

Il est vrai que cette démarche risque *a priori* d'enlever à l'article 13 une grande partie de son utilité et de le faire supplanter par l'article 6.

Même si cela était vrai, réduire la portée de l'article 13 à une peau de chagrin serait bien moins illogique que la solution consistant à faire bénéficier les droits découlant de la Convention d'une protection moindre que les autres droits reconnus par les législations nationales.

Mais il y a plus : en réalité, à partir de leur libellé et de leur genèse, les articles 6 et 13 peuvent s'appliquer cumulativement sans que l'un n'éclipse l'autre : il a en effet été montré, et là les textes français et anglais divergent encore (le texte français parlant de «recours effectif» tandis que le texte anglais vise un «*effective remedy*»), que les finalités respectives des deux textes sont différentes, voire complémentaires. L'article 13 vise la protection efficace des droits garantis par la Convention et la réparation en cas de violation, tandis que l'article 6 vise de manière autonome le procès équitable pour y parvenir.[59] L'article 13 énoncerait un droit matériel et l'article 6 un droit procédural.

* * *

Application de l'article 6 dès qu'un droit national instaure une procédure juridictionnelle en faveur des particuliers ou dès qu'une garantie prévue par la Convention est en jeu, extension de la jurisprudence *Vilho Eskelinen* à tous les contentieux : la ou les formules magiques ont-elles été trouvées ? Certainement pas. Tout au plus quelques pistes beaucoup plus modestes. La démarche telle qu'elle vient d'être esquissée serait-elle encore trop ambitieuse ou hasardeuse ? Rassurons ceux qui craignent une extension constante du champ d'application matériel de la Convention, le champion étant l'article 8. Si telle était la motivation de leur réticence, elle procéderait pourtant d'une méconnaissance fondamentale de la nature et de la finalité de l'article 6. A la différence de la plupart des autres dispositions, l'article 6 ne consacre aucun droit matériel digne de protection au nom des droits de l'homme. Il ne fait «que» garantir les standards du procès équitable. Appliquer l'article 6 de manière généreuse ne revient donc pas à étendre le champ d'application matériel de la Convention. L'appliquer de manière restrictive conduit en revanche à des résultats décevants et, osons le dire, anachroniques : n'y a-t-il pas quelque chose de totalement insatisfaisant à ce que les gardiens des droits fondamentaux se désintéressent, p. ex. de la manière dont on peut faire valoir ses droits lorsqu'on s'estime injustement imposé ?

---

[59]   V., dans ce sens, G. Sperduti, présentation orale dans l'affaire *König*, 16 novembre 1977, Publ. Cour, série B, vol. 25, p. 194 et s.

Il est vrai que l'adoption de l'une, voire des trois des voies esquissées, engendrerait un nombre plus grand de litiges soumis au contrôle de la Cour. Puisque les procès fiscaux et ceux portant sur les demandes d'asile tomberaient très probablement sous l'article 6, on pourrait même parler d'avalanche et d'extension de la juridiction de la Cour difficile à accepter par les Etats membres, surtout par les temps qui courent. Ceci est indéniable. Mais il s'agit d'un argument politique, de politique juridictionnelle, qui ne remet pas forcément en question les arguments juridiques en faveur d'une réorientation de la jurisprudence de la Cour en matière de procès équitable. Il s'agira en dernière analyse d'un choix à opérer et dans celui-ci, il ne faut pas oublier que la situation actuelle donne lieu, aussi, à des mécontentements.

Et n'oublions pas que les propositions faites apparaissent comme pâles par rapport à l'article 47 de la Charte des droits fondamentaux de l'Union européenne relatif au recours effectif et à un procès équitable. Non seulement le droit de l'Union a-t-il pris l'option délibérée de soumettre aux exigences du procès équitable les contestations relatives à des droits civils (avec la limitation, il est vrai, qu'il faut qu'il s'agisse de la mise en œuvre du droit de l'Union)[60], mais de plus, le recours n'est considéré comme effectif que s'il peut être exercé devant un tribunal indépendant préétabli par la loi[61] et tous les droits, ceux découlant des traités européens comme ceux découlant du droit national[62], sont visés.[63]

Strasbourg, avril 2018

---

[60] Charte, art. 51, paragraphe 1er. V. aussi les Explications relatives aux dispositions du projet de Charte des droits fondamentaux de l'Union européenne, Texte des explications relatives au texte complet de la Charte, tel que repris au doc. CHARTE 4422/00 CONVENT 45, *sub* art. 45. – Puisque, conformément à l'article 52, paragraphe 3, 1e phrase de la Charte, dans la mesure où celle-ci contient des droits correspondant à des droits garantis par la Convention, leur sens et leur portée sont les mêmes que ceux que leur confère ladite convention, les exigences du procès équitable telles qu'élaborées par la Cour s'appliquent en droit de l'Union même dans des domaines où, selon la jurisprudence de cette même Cour, l'article 6 n'est pas applicable, p. ex. dans les matières fiscale et d'asile.

[61] A noter les réticences de la délégation britannique qui craignait que le texte – tel qu'il a été adopté – ouvre un droit d'accès à un tribunal pour des contestations sur des droits économiques et sociaux, v. Norbert Bernsdorff, Martin Borowsky, Die Charta der Grundrechte der Europäischen Union, Handreichungen und Sitzungsprotokolle, Nomos Verlagsges. 2002, p. 276.

[62] … pour autant qu'ils appliquent le droit de l'Union, v. Norbert Bernsdorff, Martin Borowsky, *op. cit.*, p. 176.

[63] Un exemple saisissant du fossé existant entre la jurisprudence de la Cour de justice de l'Union européenne et celle de la Cour de Strasbourg est constitué par les arrêts ZZ c. *Secretary of State for the Home Department* du 4 juin 2013 (n° C-300/11) de la première et l'arrêt *Regner c. République tchèque*, précité, de la seconde.

LA COUR EUROPÉENNE DES DROITS DE L'HOMME ET LE DÉNI DE JUSTICE[*]

Dean Spielmann

Ancien Président de la Cour européenne des droits de l'homme
Juge au Tribunal de l'Union européenne

L'on prête au juriste allemand Rudolf von Jhering la phrase célèbre : «*Ennemie jurée de l'arbitraire, la forme est la sœur jumelle de la liberté*»[1] et le juge Paul Lemmens y souscrirait certainement. Au service de la liberté, les questions de procédure occupent une place prépondérante dans la jurisprudence de la Cour européenne des droits de l'homme. Ces questions se déclinent à travers les très nombreux arrêts relatifs à l'article 6 de la Convention, et la contribution du juge Paul Lemmens à l'œuvre jurisprudentielle, dans ce domaine comme dans d'autres, est exceptionnelle.[2]

---

[*] L'auteur tient à remercier M. Panayotis Voyatzis et Mme Camille Truttmann, respectivement référendaire et ancienne stagiaire au Tribunal de l'Union européenne, pour l'aide apportée à l'occasion de l'élaboration de la présente contribution.

[1] R. von Jhering, *L'esprit du droit romain dans les diverses phases de son développement*, (2ᵉ éd.), trad. (sur la 3ᵉ éd.) par O. de Meulenaere, Paris, Marescq, Gand, F. Clemm, 1877, t. III, § 50, pp. 157 et 158 (note de bas de page omise) :
«Mais bien mieux encore l'époque des empereurs byzantins, l'oraison funèbre dont ils accompagnèrent la disparition de la forme, l'aversion et le mépris qu'ils lui témoignèrent, nous feront toucher du doigt le rapport qui existe entre la liberté et la forme. *Ennemie jurée de l'arbitraire, la forme est la sœur jumelle de la liberté*. La forme est en effet le frein qui arrête les tentatives de ceux que la liberté entraîne vers la licence : elle dirige la liberté, elle la contient et la protège. Les formes fixes sont l'école de la discipline et de l'ordre et par conséquent de la liberté, elles sont un boulevard contre les attaques extérieures : – elles savent rompre ; plier, jamais. Le peuple qui professe le vrai culte de la liberté comprend d'instinct la valeur de la forme, il sent qu'elle n'est pas un joug extérieur, mais *le palladium de sa liberté*».

[2] Voy. parmi de nombreux exemples, la remarquable opinion partiellement dissidente du juge Paul Lemmens, jointe aux arrêts de chambre *Radomilja et autres c. Croatie* (n° 37685/10, 28 juin 2016) et *Jakeljić c. Croatie*, (n° 22768/12, 28 juin 2016) concernant la technique de la «requalification d'un grief» par la Cour européenne des droits de l'homme. Cette opinion a été suivie dans l'arrêt de Grande Chambre *Radomilja et autres c. Croatie* ([GC], n° 37685/10, §§ 110-127, 20 mars 2018). Ou encore, l'opinion concordante du juge Paul Lemmens et de la juge Helena Jäderblom, jointe à l'arrêt *Ostendorf c. Allemagne* (n° 15598/08, 7 mars 2013) concernant l'interprétation de l'article 5 de la Convention, suivie par un arrêt de la Cour Suprême du Royaume Uni du 15 février 2017 (*R v. The Commissioner of Police for the Metropolis*, [38], per Lord Toulson, (rejoint par Lord Mance, Lord Dyson, Lord Reed et Lord Carnwath), d'abord, et par un l'arrêt de Grande Chambre de la Cour européenne des droits de l'homme (*S., V. et A. c. Danemark* [GC], n°s 35553/12, 36678/12 et 36711/12, § 102, 22 octobre 2018), ensuite. Et plus récemment, le juge Paul Lemmens a joint, ensemble avec le juge Valeriu Grițco, une opinion

Constituant sans doute une forme extrême de la violation du droit à un procès équitable, le déni de justice « simple », par opposition à sa version « flagrante », n'a été appréhendé que récemment par la Cour européenne des droits de l'homme.[3] Cela peut surprendre. En effet, le droit international a relativement tôt classé, sous une forme très restrictive d'ailleurs intimement liée au principe de non-discrimination, le déni de justice comme une violation caractérisée des droits fondamentaux.

Dans les lignes qui suivent, nous essayons de démontrer que la notion de déni de justice a évolué en s'émancipant de sa conception traditionnelle du droit des gens. Notre contribution s'articulera donc en deux étapes. Après avoir rappelé la conception traditionnelle du déni de justice en droit international, nous esquisserons l'évolution de la jurisprudence de la Cour européenne des droits de l'homme en la matière.

I. LE DÉNI DE JUSTICE ET LE DROIT INTERNATIONAL CLASSIQUE

La Cour européenne des droits de l'homme n'a jamais appréhendé le déni de justice d'après l'approche traditionnelle du droit des gens, même si cette approche reste d'actualité. Celle-ci a d'ailleurs fait l'objet d'un nombre impressionnant d'études.[4] Dans le cadre limité de la présente contribution, il ne nous est pas possible de rappeler les nombreuses controverses discutées dans la doctrine du

---

dissidente commune à l'arrêt *Guðmundur Andri Ástráðsson c. Islande* (n° 26374/18) du 12 mars 2019. Dans cet arrêt, la Cour a jugé que la procédure par laquelle une juge avait été nommée à la cour d'appel s'analyse en une violation flagrante des règles qui étaient alors applicables. Aux points 7 et 8 de leur opinion dissidente commune, les juges Lemmens et Griţco présentent une belle synthèse de la jurisprudence en matière de « déni de justice flagrant ».

3   Concernant la version « flagrante », voy. déjà dès 1989, l'arrêt *Soering c. Royaume Uni*, (7 juillet 1989, § 113, série A n° 161) concernant l'extradition et dès 1992, l'arrêt *Drozd et Janousek c. France et Espagne*, (26 juin 1992, § 110, série A, n° 240), concernant l'exécution de décisions judiciaires étrangères. Sur ce point, voy. *infra*, sub. II, 1.

4   Voy. à titre exemplatif : E.M. Borchard, *The Diplomatic Protection of Citizens Abroad*, New York, Banks Law Publ. Co, 1916 ; C. Eagleton, « Denial of Justice in International Law », *A.J.I.L.*, 1928, pp. 538-559 ; J.W. Garner, « International Responsibility of States for Judgments of Courts and Verdicts of Juries amounting to Denial of Justice », *B.Y.I.L.*, 1929, pp. 181-189 ; C. Durand, « La responsabilité internationale des États pour déni de justice », *R.G.D.I.P.*, 1931, pp. 694-748 ; G.G. Fitzmaurice, « The meaning of the term "Denial of Justice" », *B.Y.I.L.*, 1932, pp. 93-114 ; C. De Visscher, « Le déni de justice en droit international », *R.C.A.D.I.*, vol. 52, (1935-II), pp. 363-442 ; C. Eagleton, « Local redress and Denial of Justice in recent cases », Manuscrit typographié (réalisé après 1934), en notre possession et ayant appartenu à Charles de Visscher. Nous ignorons si cette étude a été publiée. Parmi les études récentes, voy., J. Paulsson, *Denial of Justice in International Law*, Cambridge, Cambridge University Press, 2005, 279 pp. ; F. Francioni, « Access to Justice, Denial of Justice and International Investment Law », *E.J.I.L.*, 2009, pp. 729-747 ; L.-M. Hong-Rocca, *Le déni de justice substantiel en droit international public*, Paris, Éd. Univ. Panthéon-Assas, 2012, 722 pp. ; Z. Douglas, « International Responsibility for domestic adjudication : Denial of Justice deconstructed », *I.C.L.Q.*, 2014, pp. 867-900 ; L. Savadogo, « Déni de justice et responsabilité de l'État pour les actes de ses juridictions », *J.D.I.*, 2016, pp. 826-876 ; en droit public interne, L. Favoreu, *Du déni de justice en droit public français*, (Préface de Jean Waline), Paris, L.G.D.J., 1965, 582 pp. ;

droit international.[5] Toutefois, pour bien comprendre la position «originale» de la Cour de Strasbourg, une présentation de synthèse de la notion classique du déni de justice nous paraît indispensable. On l'a déjà mentionné, dans sa conception traditionnelle, le déni de justice reste intimement lié au principe de «non-discrimination» des étrangers.[6] «*L'État se doit d'accorder aux ressortissants étrangers une certaine protection juridictionnelle [et] [t]out manquement à cette obligation coutumière – et de plus en plus souvent conventionnelle – constitue un déni de justice*».[7] Cette conception du déni de justice, qui semble toujours être valable dans le droit international des investissements[8], ne cadre plus guère avec la philosophie moderne des droits de l'homme, détachée de la «nationalité» du bénéficiaire. En témoigne la jurisprudence de la Cour européenne des droits de l'homme qui sera présentée dans la deuxième partie de notre contribution.

Situons cette jurisprudence résolument moderne dans la perspective historique. Comme il a été relevé, «*le droit d'avant-guerre, s'il ignore encore les droits de l'homme, les abord[ait] parfois et les annon[çait]*».[9] Une telle annonce s'est notamment manifestée dès l'entre-deux guerres dans la «Déclaration des droits internationaux de l'homme» de l'Institut de droit international, qui, dans sa session de New-York du 12 octobre 1929[10], a insisté sur le fait «*qu'il importe d'étendre au monde entier la reconnaissance internationale des droits de l'homme*». Ainsi, certains de ces droits étaient solennellement proclamés. Le droit à la vie, la liberté et à la propriété (article 1er), à la liberté religieuse (article 2), à la liberté du choix de langue et à l'enseignement de celle-ci (article 3). Etaient également prévus, le principe de non-discrimination (article 4) et d'égalité (article 5), ainsi qu'une disposition consacrée à l'interdiction de retrait de nationalité (article 6).[11]

---

du même auteur, «Résurgence de la notion de déni de justice et droit au juge», in *Gouverner, administrer, juger – Liber Amicorum Jean Waline*, Paris, Dalloz, 2002, pp. 513-521.

5   Même terminologiques. E. Jiménez de Aréchaga dit p.ex. ceci : «This is one of these "magic formulas" like that of "natural law", which adds strength and prestige to a claim», tout en acceptant que l'expression «déni de justice» a fait l'objet d'une signification précise et limitée par une série de sentences arbitrales et par les États à l'occasion de la Conférence de codification [du droit international] de 1930. Voy., E. Jiménez de Aréchaga, «General Course in Public International Law», *R.C.A.D.I.*, vol. 159, (1978-I), pp. 280-281. L'une des difficultés concerne aussi les liens subtilement tissés entre l'obligation de l'épuisement des voies des recours internes et le délit international du *déni de justice*. Sur cette question, A.A. Cançado Trindade, *The application of the rule of exhaustion of local remedies in international law*, Cambridge, Cambridge University Press, 1983, spéc. pp. 126 (avec notes aux pp. 348 et 349), 283 et 284 (avec notes aux pages 411 et 412) ; Bin Cheng, *General Principles of Law as Applied by International Courts and Tribunals*, London, Stevens and Sons, 1953, pp. 177-180 ; Voy. également L. Savadogo, *op. cit.*, pp. 860-873 et C. Eagleton, «Local redress ..., *op. cit.*

6   A.-C. Kiss, ««La condition des étrangers en droit international et les droits de l'homme», in *Miscellanea W.J. Ganshof van der Meersch*, Bruxelles, Bruylant, 1972, I, pp. 499-511.

7   Nguyen Quoc Dinh, *Droit international public*, (8e éd. par P. Daillier, M. Forteau et A. Pellet), Paris, L.G.D.J., 2009, p. 866, n° 474.

8   Voy. à ce sujet notamment les exemples cités par L. Savadogo, *op. cit.*, pp. 827-876.

9   R. Goy, «La Cour permanente de Justice internationale et les droits de l'homme», *Liber Amicorum Marc-André Eissen*, Bruxelles, Bruylant, 1995, pp. 199-232, pp. 199-200.

10   *Ann. I.D.I.*, 1929, vol. 35-II, pp. 110-138 et pp. 298-300.

11   D. Spielmann, «Une internationalisation avant la lettre des droits de l'homme ? / À propos de l'avis consultatif de la Cour permanente du Justice internationale du 4 décembre 1935»,

Le caractère limité de la liste est certes surprenant. Texte embryonnaire, formulé de manière vague, celle-ci n'en constitue pas moins l'une des premières manifestations d'une internationalisation des droits fondamentaux.[12]

Mais qu'en est-il du droit à un procès équitable, de l'interdiction du déni de justice, absents de la déclaration ?

On l'a déjà dit, ce n'est qu'implicitement, et tout au plus à travers le principe de non-discrimination et d'égalité, que le droit (de l'étranger) de voir sa cause examinée par la Justice de l'État dont il n'est pas le ressortissant, trouvait sa place dans le contexte du développement de la protection diplomatique classique en droit des gens.[13] En réalité, le même Institut avait déjà précisé, dès 1927 (session de Lausanne), mais sans la lier expressément à la protection des droits de l'homme, la responsabilité de l'État pour déni de justice. Dans sa résolution du 1er septembre 1927 sur « *la responsabilité internationale des États à raison des dommages causés sur leur territoire à la personne et aux biens des étrangers* »[14], on lit ce qui suit :

---

in L. Caflisch, J. Callewaert, R. Liddell, P. Mahoney et M. Villiger (éd.), *Liber Amicorum Luzius Wildhaber. Droits de l'homme – Regards de Strasbourg*, Kehl-am-Rhein, Strasbourg, Arlington, 2007, pp. 403-422, spéc. p. 415.

[12] D. Spielmann, « Une internationalisation... », *op. cit.*, p. 415.

[13] Le standard minimal du traitement des étrangers remonterait à la pratique diplomatique depuis le 18e siècle. R. Kolb, « The Protection of the Individual in Times of War and Peace », in B. Fassbender & A. Peters, *The Oxford Handbook of the History of International Law*, Oxford, Oxford University Press, 2012, pp. 317-333, aux pp. 332 et 333 :

« The concept of a 'minimum standard of treatment of aliens' was developed in the diplomatic practice of States since the 18th century. It grew out of the old practice of reprisals for the torts committed on the subjects of a king abroad, initially often merchants. If *lettres de représailles* could he meted out in order to recover the losses illegally suffered by a citizen abroad, it was implicit that a ruler could first complain to the other that a tort had been committed and require that the matter be investigated and eventually the tort repaired. Hence, diplomatic protection developed under the umbrella of restrictive necessity : reprisals were not lawful if there had not been an attempt to obtain peaceful reparation from the wrongdoing collectivity. The claim brought forward in such cases was, from the point of view of substantive law, that some rights of the foreigner under international law (that is, due to his State of origin) had been violated.

This, in turn, progressively produced a catalogue of substantive rights, which has been progressively claimed in diplomatic protection. Roughly speaking, these rights concentrated around the following four spheres : (i) life, liberty and honour (for example, habeas corpus) ; (ii) property ; (iii) freedom of religion and creed ; (iv) denial of justice (fair trial : access to a local tribunal and also a substantively due process of law). The minimum standard of treatment was thus the international legal institution coming closest to modern human rights law. It differed structurally from human rights law only in the restricted entitlement to the granted rights : these were rights only of the foreigners. International law thus in that time uphold the rule that the treatment of its own nationals by a State was a domestic affair which it could not regulate. Conversely, the treatment of foreigners was not simply domestic affair since the rights of other States (through their nationals) were at stake. Hence, international law could deal with these aspects. After 1945, it has been claimed that the minimum standard was abandoned. It discriminatory edge (foreigners/nationals) was henceforth resented. Thus, the minimum standard has been held to have merged into the more general human right law movement and indeed it has been progressively retreating in State practice. However, diplomatic protection for violation of granted rights (be they minimum standard rights or human rights) has remained frequent ». (notes de bas de pages omises).

[14] *Ann. I.D.I.*, 1927, vol. 33-III, p. 331.

« Article 5. L'État est responsable du chef de déni de justice :

1° Lorsque les tribunaux nécessaires pour assurer la protection des étrangers n'existent ou ne fonctionnent pas ;

2° Lorsque les tribunaux ne sont pas accessibles aux étrangers ;

3° Lorsque les tribunaux n'offrent pas les garanties indispensables pour assurer une bonne justice ».

D'après cette approche classique, détachée de la protection des droits de l'homme, le déni de justice peut donc être défini, selon l'une des trois définitions du *Dictionnaire Salmon*, comme « *[f]ait illicite d'un État à la suite de la violation d'une norme relative à l'exercice de la fonction juridictionnelle à l'égard des étrangers* ».[15]

Trois formes y sont distinguées :

a) Le déni de justice par le refus de l'accès aux tribunaux ;

b) Le déni de justice procédural ou formel : à la suite de graves irrégularités de procédure ;

c) Le déni de justice substantiel ou matériel : lorsque les décisions sont manifestement injustes au fond.[16]

Mais, précise le *Dictionnaire Salmon* en se fondant sur la jurisprudence de la Cour internationale de Justice, « *[l]e déni de justice peut, sous les formes appropriées, passer du droit des étrangers aux droits de l'homme* ».[17] C'est ainsi que la Cour de La Haye, dans son arrêt du 5 février 1970 a énoncé qu' « *[e]n ce qui concerne plus particulièrement les droits de l'homme (…), on doit noter qu'ils comportent aussi une protection contre le déni de justice* ».[18]

La notion du déni de justice devient par conséquent détachable du standard minimum de protection des étrangers pour s'inviter dans le cadre plus général du

---

[15] J. Salmon, (dir.), *Dictionnaire de droit international public*, (Préface de G. Guillaume), Bruylant, AUF, 2001, v° « Déni de justice », pp. 320 et 321. Les deux autres définitions proposées sont les suivantes : « A. Dans le sens le plus général, « tout refus d'accorder à quelqu'un ce qui lui est dû » (Calvo, *Dictionnaire*, t. I, p. 237) » et « B. Fait d'un organe juridictionnel refusant d'exercer sa fonction à l'égard d'un justiciable ». Commentant les articles 5 et 6 du projet CDI « sur la responsabilité des États », et plus particulièrement la difficulté de l'indépendance constitutionnelle des juridictions dans le contexte de l'imputabilité des actes des « organes » de l'État, Joe Verhoeven relève à juste titre qu'« [i]l paraît abusif (…) d'imposer à l'État l'obligation de réparer les conséquences dommageables de toute « erreur » commise par un juge. Seule la violation systématique par ses tribunaux d'une règle de droit international impose raisonnablement à l'État d'en assumer la responsabilité. Cette difficulté propre au pouvoir judiciaire n'épuise pas la question du *déni de justice*, qui vise plus largement le refus d'un État d'accorder aux étrangers un accès « convenable » à ses tribunaux ». J. Verhoeven, *Droit international public*, Bruxelles, Larcier, 2000, p. 622. Sur le principe d'attribution et de l'unité de l'État, voy. aussi, L. Savadogo, pp. 830 et 831 et la nombreuse jurisprudence citée.

[16] *Ibid.*

[17] *Ibid.*

[18] C.I.J., *Barcelona Traction, Light and Power Company, Limited*, arrêt du 5 février 1970, Rec. 1970, p. 47, § 91. Voy. aussi R. Jennings et A. Watts, *Oppenheim's International Law*, 9e éd. Vol. I, Peace, Londres et New York, Longman, 1996, p. 543.

droit à un procès équitable, garanti notamment par l'article 6 de la Convention européenne des droits de l'homme.

La jurisprudence de la Cour de Strasbourg a ainsi permis de donner un relief particulier à cette notion par l'absence de référence réductrice au traitement minimal des étrangers.

II. LE DÉNI DE JUSTICE ET LA PROTECTION EUROPÉENNE DES DROITS DE L'HOMME

A. LE DÉNI DE JUSTICE EXTERNE

Conformément à l'article 1er de la Convention européenne des droits de l'homme, des violations perpétrées en dehors de l'espace européen de protection des droits de l'homme ne relèvent pas de la juridiction des Hautes Parties contractantes. Par ailleurs, la Cour a été instituée « *[a]fin d'assurer le respect des engagements résultant pour les Hautes Parties contractantes de la (…) Convention et de ses Protocoles*» (article 19). Constater une violation du droit à un procès équitable commise dans un État non membre du Conseil de l'Europe ne relève par conséquent pas de la compétence de la Cour.

Celle-ci s'est toutefois appropriée le pouvoir de constater une violation de l'article 6 de la Convention si une Partie contractante prête son concours en reconnaissant ou en exécutant une décision, rendue dans un État tiers et constitutive d'un «déni de justice flagrant». Ainsi, la reconnaissance et l'exécution de décisions judiciaires étrangères peuvent dans une telle hypothèse, certes extrême, se heurter aux exigences de la Convention européenne des droits de l'homme.[19] Cette problématique a donné lieu à beaucoup de commentaires.[20] L'on n'y reviendra pas.

De même, une Haute Partie contractante peut contrevenir à l'article 6 de la Convention en cas d'expulsion ou d'extradition réalisée ou projetée si dans le pays requérant les procédures à intervenir contreviennent manifestement et

---

[19]   *Drozd et Janousek c. France et Espagne*, 26 juin 1992, série A, n° 240.

[20]   Surtout dans les travaux de Patrick Kinsch. Voy. à titre d'exemple, P. Kinsch, «Droits de l'homme, droits fondamentaux et droit international privé», *R.C.A.D.I.*, vol. 318, (2005), pp. 291-292, du même auteur, «Le droit international privé au risque de la hiérarchie des normes : l'exemple de la jurisprudence de la CEDH en matière de reconnaissance des jugements», *Ann. dr. eur.*, 2007, pp. 957-973 et «La non-conformité du jugement étranger à l'ordre public international mise au diapason de la Convention européenne des droits de l'homme», *Rev. crit. D.I.P.*, 2011, pp. 817-823. Voy. aussi pour des cas d'application jurisprudentiels. D. Spielmann, «La reconnaissance et l'exécution des décisions judiciaires étrangères et les exigences de la Convention européenne des droits de l'homme. Un essai de synthèse», *R.T.D.H.*, 2011, pp. 761-786 et aussi la contribution dans J.-F. Akandji-Kombé, *L'homme dans la société internationale. Mélanges en hommage au Professeur Paul Tavernier*, Bruxelles, Bruylant, 2013, pp. 973-992. *Adde* S. Menétrey, «Le contrôle de l'incidence indirecte par la Cour européenne des droits de l'homme à l'épreuve du droit de l'Union», in I. Riassetto, L. Heuschling et G. Ravarani (coord.), *Liber Amicorum Rusen Ergeç*, Luxembourg, 2017, pp. 229-237.

de façon massive aux règles du procès équitable. Inauguré par l'arrêt *Soering c. Royaume Uni* du 7 juillet 1989[21], cette ligne jurisprudentielle a été appliquée à de nombreuses reprises. Les principes ont été résumés dans l'arrêt *Othman* du 17 janvier 2012[22] et d'autres arrêts.[23] Ils ont été rappelés récemment dans l'arrêt

---

[21]   *Soering c. Royaume Uni*, 7 juillet 1989, série A n° 161, p. 45, § 113.

[22]   *Othman (Abu Quatada) c. Royaume Uni*, n° 8139/09, CEDH 2012-I (extraits) :
«258. Il est établi dans la jurisprudence de la Cour qu'une décision d'expulsion ou d'extradition peut exceptionnellement soulever une question sous l'angle de l'article 6 lorsque le fugitif a subi ou risque de subir un déni de justice flagrant dans l'Etat requérant. Ce principe a été énoncé pour la première fois dans l'arrêt *Soering c. Royaume-Uni* (7 juillet 1989, § 113, série A n° 161) puis confirmé dans plusieurs autres affaires (voir par exemple *Mamatkoulov et Askarov* [[GC] n°s 46827/99 et 46951/99, CEDH 2005-I], §§ 90-91, et *Al-Saadoon et Mufdhi c. Royaume-Uni*, n° 61498/08, § 149, CEDH 2010).
259. Dans la jurisprudence de la Cour, l'expression «déni de justice flagrant» s'applique aux procès manifestement contraires aux dispositions de l'article 6 ou aux principes consacrés par cet article (*Sejdovic c. Italie* [GC], n° 56581/00, § 84, CEDH 2006-II, *Stoichkov* [*c. Bulgarie*, n° 9808/02, 24 mars 2005], § 56, et *Drozd et Janousek* [*c. France et Espagne*, 26 juin 1992, série A, n° 240], § 110). Même si elle n'a pas encore eu à définir cette expression en termes plus précis, la Cour a néanmoins eu l'occasion de dire de certaines formes d'injustice qu'elles pouvaient être constitutives d'un déni de justice flagrant. Ce fut le cas des situations suivantes :
–   condamnation in absentia sans possibilité d'obtenir un réexamen au fond de l'accusation (*Einhorn*, [*c. France* (déc.), n° 71555/01, CEDH 2001-XI], § 33, *Sejdovic*, précité, § 84, et *Stoichkov*, précité, § 56),
–   procès sommaire par sa nature et mené dans le mépris total des droits de la défense (*Bader et Kanbor c. Suède*, n° 13284/04, § 47, CEDH 2005-XI),
–   détention dont il n'était pas possible de faire examiner la régularité par un tribunal indépendant et impartial (*Al-Moayad* [*c. Allemagne* (déc.), n° 35865/03, 20 février 2007], § 101),
–   refus délibéré et systématique de laisser un individu, en particulier un individu détenu dans un pays étranger, communiquer avec un avocat (*ibidem*).
260. (…) pour qu'il y ait «déni de justice flagrant», il faut que soient réalisés certains critères stricts d'injustice. Le déni de justice flagrant va au-delà de simples irrégularités ou défauts de garantie au procès qui seraient de nature à emporter violation de l'article 6 s'ils avaient lieu dans l'Etat contractant lui-même. Il faut qu'il y ait une violation du principe d'équité du procès garanti par l'article 6 qui soit tellement grave qu'elle entraîne l'annulation, voire la destruction de l'essence même du droit protégé par cet article.
261. Pour déterminer si tel est le cas, la Cour applique le même degré et la même charge de la preuve que lorsqu'elle examine les affaires d'expulsion au regard de l'article 3. C'est donc au requérant qu'il incombe de produire des éléments aptes à prouver qu'il existe des motifs sérieux de croire que, s'il était expulsé de l'Etat contractant, il serait exposé à un risque réel de faire l'objet d'un déni de justice flagrant. S'il le fait, il appartient ensuite au Gouvernement de dissiper tout doute à ce sujet (voir, mutatis mutandis, Saadi [[GC] n° 37201/06, CEDH 2008], § 129) (…)
267. (…) l'admission d'éléments de preuve obtenus par la torture est manifestement contraire non seulement aux dispositions de l'article 6, mais aussi aux normes internationales les plus fondamentales en matière d'équité de la procédure. Non seulement pareille admission rendrait l'ensemble du procès immoral et irrégulier, mais encore elle le ferait aboutir à une issue totalement dépourvue de fiabilité. Il y aurait donc déni de justice flagrant si pareils éléments étaient admis dans un procès pénal. La Cour n'exclut pas que des considérations analogues puissent s'appliquer à l'égard d'éléments de preuve obtenus par des mauvais traitements non constitutifs de torture (…)».
Concernant le résumé des principes, voy. aussi, l'arrêt *Philip Harkins c. Royaume-Uni*, n° 71537/14, 15 juin 2017, §§ 61-67.

[23]   Récemment, dans l'arrêt *Al Nashiri c. Roumanie*, n° 33234/12, §§ 716-718, 31 mai 2018 et les références à la jurisprudence.

Pirozzi contre Belgique[24] dans le contexte du mandat d'arrêt européen (ici, une remise du requérant par les autorités belges aux autorités italiennes) :

> « 57. Il est établi dans la jurisprudence de la Cour qu'une décision d'expulsion ou d'extradition peut exceptionnellement soulever une question sous l'angle de l'article 6 lorsque le fugitif a subi ou risque de subir un déni de justice flagrant dans l'État requérant. Ce principe a été énoncé pour la première fois dans l'arrêt *Soering c. Royaume-Uni* (7 juillet 1989, § 113, série A n° 161) puis confirmé dans plusieurs autres affaires (voir par exemple *Mamatkoulov et Askarov c. Turquie* [GC], n°s 46827/99 et 46951/99, §§ 90-91, CEDH 2005-I, *Al-Saadoon et Mufdhi c. Royaume-Uni*, n° 61498/08, § 149, CEDH 2010, et *Othman (Abu Qatada) c. Royaume-Uni*, n° 8139/09, § 258, CEDH 2012 (extraits)). En l'espèce, ce principe doit être appliqué dans le contexte particulier de l'exécution par un État membre de l'UE d'un MAE délivré par les autorités d'un autre État membre de l'UE ».

La Cour n'a pas constaté de manquement à l'article 6 § 1 de la Convention.[25] Mais l'affaire est évidemment intéressante en ce qu'elle a donné l'occasion à la Cour d'appliquer la notion de « déni de justice flagrant » à un cas de figure mettant en cause deux Hautes Parties contractantes mais concernant la réglementation de l'ordre juridique intégré de l'Union européenne. Par ailleurs, il semble que dorénavant, le « déni de justice flagrant » devient synonyme du critère de l'»insuffisance manifeste » au sens de la jurisprudence *Bosphorus*[26] et développé dans les arrêts *Michaud*[27] et *Avotiņš*[28] :

> « 63. Dans cet esprit, lorsque les juridictions des États qui sont à la fois parties à la Convention et membres de l'UE sont appelées à appliquer un mécanisme de reconnaissance mutuelle établi par le droit de l'UE, telle que celui prévu pour l'exécution d'un MAE décerné par un autre État européen, c'est en l'absence de toute insuffisance manifeste des droits protégés par la Convention qu'elles donnent à ce mécanisme son plein effet ([*Avotiņš c. Lettonie* [GC], n° 17502/07, CEDH 2016,] § 116).

> 64. En revanche, s'il leur est soumis un grief sérieux et étayé dans le cadre duquel il est allégué que l'on se trouve en présence d'une insuffisance manifeste de protection d'un droit garanti par la Convention et que le droit de l'UE ne permet pas de remédier à cette insuffisance, elles ne peuvent renoncer à examiner ce grief au seul motif qu'elles appliquent le droit de l'UE (*idem*, § 116). Il leur appartient dans ce cas de lire et d'appliquer les règles du droit de l'UE en conformité avec la Convention ».[29]

---

[24]   *Pirozzi c. Belgique*, n° 21055/11, 17 avril 2018.
[25]   §§ 67-72.
[26]   *Bosphorus Hava Yolları Turizm ve Ticaret Anonim Şirketi c. Irlande* [GC], n° 45036/98, CEDH 2005-VI.
[27]   *Michaud c. France*, n° 12323/11, CEDH 2012.
[28]   *Avotiņš c. Lettonie* [GC], n° 17502/07, CEDH 2016.
[29]   Comp. cet arrêt avec les conclusions de l'avocat général E. Tanchev, rendues le 28 juin 2018 dans l'affaire C-216/18 PPU, *Minister for Justice and Equality contre LM (Défaillances du système judiciaire)* et l'arrêt rendu dans la même affaire en date du 25 juillet 2018. Cette affaire concerne trois mandats d'arrêt européen dans le contexte de l'évolution et des réformes

Dans sa version externe, le déni de justice «flagrant» est donc dorénavant appréhendé par la Cour européenne des droits de l'homme dans deux hypothèses qu'il faut soigneusement distinguer.

Le premier cas de figure concerne les situations présentant un élément d'extranéité par rapport à la Haute Partie contractante. L'extradition ou l'expulsion vers un État tiers, la reconnaissance et/ou l'exécution de décisions émanant de juridictions étrangères à l'espace européen des droits de l'homme en constituent les exemples classiques.

Le deuxième cas de figure est celui du contrôle dilué opéré par la Cour en raison du respect du système du droit de l'Union. Le déni de justice doit être manifeste pour que la présomption de protection équivalente en faveur du droit de l'Union soit mise en veilleuse.

Ces deux hypothèses présentent cependant une caractéristique commune : Prenant leur source dans un ordre juridique différent de celui de la Convention, – qui reste «l'instrument constitutionnel de l'ordre public européen»[30] –, les violations du procès équitable, réalisées ou potentielles, ne seront appréhendées par la Cour que si le déni de justice «saute aux yeux» ou, en d'autres termes, est «flagrant». La Cour reste donc très prudente. Notons aussi, comme nous le verrons, que le caractère «flagrant» du déni réapparaît même dans des situations purement internes. Mais d'abord, explorons les cas de figure où la Cour arrive à la conclusion qu'un procès qui a été mené devant les juridictions nationales, a été tellement vicié, qu'il ne peut résulter que dans un déni de justice.

B. LE DÉNI DE JUSTICE INTERNE

La violation du droit de l'accès à la justice, l'examen d'une cause dans un délai déraisonnable ou l'inexécution d'une décision judiciaire interne sont assurément constitutifs d'une méconnaissance de l'article 6 de la Convention. En témoigne la riche jurisprudence de la Cour européenne des droits de l'homme, qui n'hésite pas, dans certains cas du moins, à lier le constat de violation au principe de la prééminence du droit dans une société démocratique.[31]

---

du système judiciaire polonais qui ont conduit la Commission européenne à adopter une proposition motivée invitant le Conseil de l'UE à constater l'existence d'un risque clair de violation grave, par la République de Pologne, de l'une de valeurs communes aux États membres, à savoir l'État de droit. La demande de décision préjudicielle a été introduite par la High Court d'Irlande.

[30] *Loizidou c. Turquie (exceptions préliminaires)*, 23 mars 1995, série A, n° 310, § 75.

[31] Voy. D. Spielmann, «La jurisprudence de la Cour européenne des droits de l'homme sur l'État de droit», *in L'État de droit en droit* international, Société française pour le droit international, Colloque de Bruxelles, Paris, Pedone, 2009, pp. 179-188. Concernant la non-exécution d'un jugement définitif, voy. l'arrêt *Timofeyev c. Russie* du 23 octobre 2003, n° 58263/00, CEDH-2002-II, (cité par J. Paulsson, *op. cit.*, pp. 168-169) :

«40. The Court reiterates that Article 6 § 1 secures to everyone the right to have any claim relating to his civil rights and obligations brought before a court or tribunal ; in this way

Si la violation du droit à un procès équitable peut ainsi revêtir des formes très variées, il n'en demeure pas moins que de telles violations n'en constituent pas nécessairement un déni de justice stigmatisant[32] et encore moins un «déni de justice flagrant».[33]

---

it embodies the «right to a court», of which the right of access, that is the right to institute proceedings before courts in civil matters, constitutes one aspect. However, that right would be illusory if a Contracting State's domestic legal system allowed a final, binding judicial decision to remain inoperative to the detriment of one party. It would be inconceivable that Article 6 § 1 should describe in detail procedural guarantees afforded to litigants – proceedings that are fair, public and expeditious – without protecting the implementation of judicial decisions ; to construe Article 6 as being concerned exclusively with access to a court and the conduct of proceedings would be likely to lead to situations incompatible with *the principle of the rule of law* which the Contracting States undertook to respect when they ratified the Convention. Execution of a judgment given by any court must therefore be regarded as an integral part of the «trial» for the purposes of Article 6 (see *Burdov* [n° 59498/00, CEDH 2002-III], § 34)». Nous soulignons.

[32] Une décision d'irrecevabilité du 27 juin 2017 (*J.P. Nau et Bakona S.àr.l. c. le Luxembourg* (25426/15) mentionne toutefois un jugement interne – rare – du tribunal d'arrondissement de Luxembourg du 22 mai 2013 (n° 127/2013 XVII) [*Société de droit des Iles Vierges Britanniques Farnell Holdings Ltd. c. État luxembourgeois*] par lequel l'absence d'une décision de justice rendue en première instance dans une affaire civile après onze ans de procédure constituait un déni de justice engageant la responsabilité de l'État. Dans cette affaire, le tribunal a accordé à la demanderesse, à la lumière des éléments du dossier, la somme de 1000 EUR *ex æquo et bono* en réparation de son dommage moral résultant du déni de justice. (Voy. *J.P. Nau et Bakona S.àr.l. c. le Luxembourg*, n° 25426/15, § 33). Dans le jugement du 22 mai 2013, le tribunal d'arrondissement de Luxembourg s'est exprimé comme suit :
«L'article 4 du code civil prévoit que le juge qui refusera de juger, sous prétexte du silence, de l'obscurité ou de l'insuffisance de la loi, pourra être poursuivi comme coupable du déni de justice. Il est admis que cette disposition prohibe non seulement le refus de répondre aux requêtes ou le fait de négliger de juger les affaires en état, mais aussi plus largement, tout manquement de l'État à son devoir de protection juridictionnelle de l'individu. Ainsi le déni de justice peut être invoqué quand le justiciable ne parvient pas, pour des raisons de fait ou de droit, à trouver un juge, de même que dans le cas où l'accès au juge est possible, mais que cet accès ne permet pas d'assurer le respect du droit à un jugement effectif, notamment le droit d'obtenir dans un délai raisonnable une décision susceptible d'exécution. La notion de déni de justice prend un caractère objectif dans la mesure où on l'entend non seulement comme le refus de répondre aux requêtes ou le fait de négliger de juger les affaires en état de l'être, mais aussi, plus largement, comme «tout manquement de l'État à son devoir de protection juridictionnelle de l'individu» (*Jurisclasseur*, droit civil, article 4, fasc. unique, n° 53 et n° 60 et s.).
C'est partant à bon droit que la demanderesse a invoqué les règles relatives au déni de justice pour fonder sa demande et c'est à bon droit que cette partie a fait valoir que les arguments du défendeur relatifs au déroulement concret de l'affaire ne sont pas pertinents dans ce contexte. En effet, dans le cadre du déni de justice tel que défini plus haut, la faute n'est plus subjectivement définie par rapport au comportement du magistrat mais objectivement appréhendée au travers des actes ou faits traduisant l'inaptitude du service public de la justice à remplir sa mission. Le déni de justice ne résulte pas obligatoirement d'un acte volontaire du juge. Le régime de la responsabilité évolue vers une mise en œuvre plus facile de la réparation allant jusqu'à l'effacement de la faute au profit d'une prise en compte objective de l'atteinte à une obligation professionnelle majeure (*Jurisclasseur*, droit civil, article 4, fasc. unique, n° 53). Au vu de ces principes, l'absence d'une décision de justice de première instance dans une affaire civile, après écoulement d'un délai de onze années, constituent un déni de justice engageant la responsabilité de l'État sur base de l'article 1er alinéa 1er de la loi du 1er septembre 1988. C'est partant à bon droit que la demanderesse a requis à être indemnisée du préjudice qui en est résulté pour elle».

[33] Voy. toutefois les arrêts *Sejdovic c. Italie* ([GC], n° 56581/00, § 84, CEDH 2006-II) et *M.T.B c. Turkey*, n° 47081/06, 12 juin 2018, § 62, retenant le «déni de justice flagrant» concernant

---

Mais la mauvaise appréciation des faits et des preuves peut atteindre, – exceptionnellement -, des dimensions telles que l'on se trouve en présence d'un déni de justice. Certes, la Cour européenne des droits de l'homme est assez réticente pour réexaminer les faits qui ont été appréciés par les juridictions nationales.[34] Toutefois, et on a déjà eu l'occasion de le signaler[35], l'examen

---

la condamnation par défaut sans avoir l'opportunité de présenter des moyens de défense. *Adde*, pour d'autres références jurisprudentielles, W.A. Schabas, *The European Convention on Human Rights, A Commentary*, Oxford, Oxford University Press, 2015, p. 316.

[34] Les principes ont été rappelés et résumés dans l'arrêt *Moreira Ferreira c. Portugal (n° 2)*, ([GC], no 19867/12, CEDH 2017) :

«83. La Cour rappelle que, dans l'arrêt *Bochan (n° 2)*, [[GC], n° 22251/08, CEDH 2015] elle a examiné, sous l'angle du volet civil de l'article 6 de la Convention, la question d'un manque d'équité résultant du raisonnement suivi par les juridictions internes. Les principes posés par la Cour dans cet arrêt peuvent se résumer comme suit :

a) Il n'appartient pas à la Cour de connaître des erreurs de fait ou de droit éventuellement commises par une juridiction interne, sauf si et dans la mesure où elles peuvent avoir porté atteinte aux droits et libertés sauvegardés par la Convention, par exemple si elles peuvent exceptionnellement s'analyser en un «manque d'équité» incompatible avec l'article 6 de la Convention (*ibidem*, § 61).

b) L'article 6 § 1 de la Convention ne réglemente pas l'admissibilité des preuves ou leur appréciation, matière qui relève au premier chef du droit interne et des juridictions nationales. En principe, des questions telles que le poids attaché par les tribunaux nationaux à tel ou tel élément de preuve ou à telle ou telle conclusion ou appréciation dont ils ont eu à connaître échappent au contrôle de la Cour. Celle-ci n'a pas à tenir lieu de juge de quatrième instance et elle ne remet pas en cause sous l'angle de l'article 6 § 1 l'appréciation des tribunaux nationaux, sauf si leurs conclusions peuvent passer pour arbitraires ou manifestement déraisonnables (*ibidem*, § 61, voir également les affaires qui y sont citées : *Dulaurans c. France*, n° 34553/97, §§ 33-34 et 38, 21 mars 2000, *Khamidov c. Russie*, n° 72118/01, § 170, 15 novembre 2007, et *Andelković c. Serbie*, n° 1401/08, § 24, 9 avril 2013 ; ainsi que l'application de cette jurisprudence dans des arrêts plus récents : *Pavlović et autres c. Croatie*, n° 13274/11, § 49, 2 avril 2015, *Yaremenko (n° 2)* [n° 66338/09, 30 avril 2015], §§ 64-67, et *Tsanova-Gecheva c. Bulgarie*, n° 43800/12, § 91, 15 septembre 2015).

84. La Cour rappelle également que, selon sa jurisprudence constante reflétant un principe lié à la bonne administration de la justice, les décisions judiciaires doivent indiquer de manière suffisante les motifs sur lesquels elles se fondent. L'étendue de ce devoir peut varier selon la nature de la décision et doit s'analyser à la lumière des circonstances de chaque espèce (*García Ruiz c. Espagne* [GC], n° 30544/96, § 26, CEDH 1999-I). Sans exiger une réponse détaillée à chaque argument du plaignant, cette obligation présuppose que la partie à une procédure judiciaire puisse s'attendre à une réponse spécifique et explicite aux moyens décisifs pour l'issue de la procédure en cause (voir, parmi d'autres exemples, *Ruiz Torija c. Espagne*, 9 décembre 1994, §§ 29-30, série A no 303-A, et *Higgins et autres c. France*, 19 février 1998, §§ 42-43, *Recueil des arrêts et décisions* 1998-I). De plus, dans les affaires concernant les ingérences dans les droits protégés par la Convention, la Cour vérifie si la motivation des décisions rendues par les juridictions nationales n'est pas automatique ou stéréotypée (*mutatis mutandis, Paradiso et Campanelli c. Italie* [GC], n° 25358/12, § 210, CEDH 2017). Par ailleurs, la Convention ne requiert pas que les jurés donnent les raisons de leur décision et l'article 6 ne s'oppose pas à ce qu'un accusé soit jugé par un jury populaire même dans le cas où son verdict n'est pas motivé. Il n'en demeure pas moins que pour que les exigences d'un procès équitable soient respectées, le public, et au premier chef l'accusé, doit être à même de comprendre le verdict qui a été rendu (*Lhermitte c. Belgique* [GC], n° 34238/09, §§ 66 et 67, CEDH 2016)».

[35] Voy. D. Spielmann, «La Cour européenne des droits de l'homme et l'erreur de fait», in I. Riassetto, L. Heuschling et G. Ravarani (coord.), *Liber Amicorum Rusen Ergeç*, Luxembourg,

défaillant des faits par les juridictions nationales peut être constitutif d'un déni de justice. L'arrêt *Anđelković* du 9 avril 2013[36] constitue un exemple rare où la Cour est allée jusqu'à constater un tel déni. Elle a estimé que le caractère arbitraire de la décision de justice interne, qui essentiellement ne reposait sur aucune base légale et n'avait établi aucun lien entre les faits constatés, le droit applicable et l'issue du procès, était constitutif d'un déni de justice.[37]

Qu'en est-il d'un simple examen insatisfaisant d'une cause ? Le cas de figure est prévu par l'article 35 § 3 (b) de la Convention, qui permet de déclarer irrecevable une requête pour absence de préjudice important. *De minimis non curat praetor.*[38] Or, l'une des conditions pour appliquer ce critère d'irrecevabilité est que l'affaire ait été « dûment examinée par un tribunal interne ».[39] D'après la jurisprudence, cette condition de l'examen judiciaire approprié viserait à éviter le « déni de justice ».[40] L'utilisation des termes « déni de justice » peut paraître quelque peu malheureuse. En effet, tout d'abord et fondamentalement, il est permis de se poser la question si la conclusion de l'absence d'un examen judiciaire approprié équivaut *dans tous les cas* à un « déni de justice » au sens exceptionnel de la jurisprudence. Nous ne le pensons

---

2017, pp. 353-363 et « Le fait, le juge et la connaissance : Aux confins de la compétence interprétative de la Cour européenne des droits de l'homme », in P. d'Argent, B. Bonafé et J. Combacau (coord.), *Les limites du droit international. Essais en l'honneur de Joe Verhoeven*, Bruxelles, Bruylant, 2015, pp. 519-535.

[36] *Anđelković c. Serbie*, n° 1401/08, 9 avril 2013.

[37] § 27. Comp. avec l'arrêt *Pavlović c. Serbie*, (n° 13274/11, 2 avril 2015). La Cour a constaté une « erreur manifeste » concernant le remboursement des frais et dépens, sans que la Cour mentionne le « déni de justice ». *Idem*, dans l'arrêt *Okan Güven et autres c. Turquie* (n° 13476/05, 14 novembre 2017) par lequel la Cour a conclu qu'une décision définitive et défaillante au niveau de sa motivation, devait, dans les circonstances de l'espèce être considérée comme étant arbitraire, ou à tout le moins, manifestement déraisonnable (§ 94). Dans l'arrêt *Sukhanov et autres c. Russie*, (n°s 56251/12 et 2 autres, 7 novembre 2017), concernant un prétendu désistement des instances, la Cour a décidé que l'application d'une disposition du code de procédure civile paraissait manifestement arbitraire, puisqu'elle ne faisait pas de lien entre les faits établis, la disposition applicable et l'issue du procès (§ 51) en concluant que les décisions de justice revêtaient un caractère arbitraire et s'analysaient donc en un « déni de justice ». § 54.

[38] W. Schabas, *The European Convention on Human Rights. A Commentary*, Oxford, Oxford University Press, 2015, p. 781.

[39] Voy. D. Spielmann et O. Chernishova, « Examiner à la loupe le dérisoire ? Examining futilities under the magnifying glass ? "No Significant Disadvantage" : Overview of the first years of application » in, O. Chernishova & M. Lobov (éds.), *Essays in honour of Anatoly Kovler. Judge of the European Court of Human Rights in 1999-2012*, Oisterwijk, Wolf Legal Publishers, 2013, pp. 143-157, spéc. pp. 154-156.

[40] En effet, dans sa décision d'irrecevabilité *Korolev c. Russie*, (n° 25551/05, 1 juillet 2010, CEDH-2010), la Cour s'est exprimée comme suit : « Article 35 § 3 (b) does not allow the rejection of an application on the ground of the new admissibility requirement if the case has not been duly considered by a domestic tribunal. Qualified by the drafters as a second safeguard clause (see Explanatory Report, § 82), its purpose is to ensure that every case receives a judicial examination whether at the national level or at the European level, in other words, to avoid a *denial of justice*. » (mise en exergue ajoutée).

pas.[41] Ensuite, se pose la question du lien entre la recevabilité et le fond. Est-ce que la recevabilité de la requête concernant une affaire qui n'a pas été « dûment examinée par un tribunal » implique inévitablement une violation de l'article 6 de la Convention, du moins si le requérant a présenté un grief séparé dans ce sens ? C'est probablement la raison pour laquelle la Cour, en cas de doute, joint souvent cette question de recevabilité (examen approprié par un tribunal interne) au fond (violation éventuelle de l'article 6) pour conclure le cas échéant à la violation de l'article 6 en ce que l'affaire n'a pas été « dûment examiné par un tribunal » sans pour autant nécessairement faire grand cas d'un « déni de justice ».[42] Quoi qu'il en soit, nous n'approfondissons pas cette question étant donné que la condition de l'examen approprié par un tribunal interne a vocation à disparaître avec l'entrée en vigueur prochaine du Protocole n° 15.[43]

La dénaturation des constats précédemment opérés par la Cour européenne des droits de l'homme constitue un problème à part. Elle peut entraîner un constat de violation de l'article 6 de la Convention, comme nous le montre l'arrêt *Bochan c. Ukraine (n° 2)*.[44] Cette affaire concernait l'inexécution du premier arrêt *Bochan* du 3 mai 2007.[45] La Cour a noté que, dans sa décision du 14 mars 2008, la Cour suprême a grossièrement dénaturé les constats opérés par elle dans son arrêt du 3 mai 2007. La Cour suprême a notamment expliqué que la Cour avait conclu que les décisions rendues en l'espèce par les tribunaux nationaux étaient licites et fondées et que la requérante avait obtenu une satisfaction équitable pour le manquement à la garantie de « délai raisonnable », ce qui est totalement erroné.[46] La Cour a observé que le raisonnement de la Cour suprême ne se réduisait pas simplement à une lecture différente d'un texte juridique. Il ne peut être regardé que comme étant « manifestement arbitraire » ou comme

---

41 Toutefois, en 2004, dans un cas très exceptionnel, la Cour a conclu au « déni de justice » dans une affaire à l'occasion de laquelle plusieurs juridictions avaient, tour à tour, décliné leur compétence en portant ainsi atteinte à la substance même du droit à un tribunal. Voy. *Beneficio Cappella Paolini c. Saint-Marin*, n° 40786/98, 13 juillet 2004, cité par M.-A. Beernaert et F. Krenc, *Le droit à un procès équitable dans la jurisprucence de la Cour européenne des droits de l'homme*, Limal, Anthemis, 2019, p. 85.

42 Voy. *Selmani et autres c. l'ex-République yougoslave de Macédoine*, n° 67259/14, §§ 30 et 40 à 42, 9 février 2017. Néanmoins, parfois, la Cour examine au stade de la recevabilité la question de savoir si l'affaire a été dûment examinée par un tribunal, sans la joindre au fond du grief tiré de l'article 6 de la Convention. Voy, en ce sens, *Živić c. Serbie*, §§ 40 et 46, n° 37204/08, 13 septembre 2011. Voy. également, en ce qui concerne l'article 5 § 3 de la Convention, *Bannikov c. Lettonie*, n° 19279/03, § 59, 11 juin 2013. Sur l'article 5 de la Convention et le déni de justice, voy. aussi *infra*.

43 Art. 5 du Protocole d'amendement. Cet amendement est destineé à donner un plus grand effet à la maxime *de minimis no curat praetor* (Commentaire des articles du Rapport explicatif, § 23).

44 *Bochan c. Ukraine (n° 2)* [GC], n° 22251/08, CEDH 2015. Sur cette affaire, voy. D. Spielmann, « La Cour européenne des droits de l'homme et l'erreur de fait », *op. cit.*, p. 357.

45 *Bochan c. Ukraine*, n° 7577/02, 3 mai 2007.

46 § 63.

emportant un «déni de justice», la dénaturation de l'arrêt rendu en 2007 dans la première affaire *Bochan* précitée ayant eu pour effet de faire échouer la démarche de la requérante tendant à voir examiner sa demande à la lumière de cet arrêt dans le cadre de la procédure de type cassation prévue par le droit interne. À cet égard, il y a lieu de noter que dans son arrêt de 2007 la Cour avait conclu que, au vu des circonstances de la réattribution de l'affaire aux tribunaux inférieurs par la Cour suprême, les doutes nourris par la requérante quant à l'impartialité des magistrats ayant connu de l'affaire, y compris ceux de la haute juridiction, étaient objectivement justifiés.[47] La Cour a donc conclu, à partir de ses constats sur la nature et les répercussions du vice dont était entachée la décision de la Cour suprême du 14 mars 2008, que la procédure dénoncée n'a pas satisfait aux exigences d'équité du procès énoncées à l'article 6 § 1 de la Convention et qu'il y a donc eu violation de cette disposition.[48]

En revanche, dans un arrêt du 11 juillet 2017, rendu dans l'affaire *Moreira Ferreira c. Portugal (n° 2)*[49], la Cour est arrivée à la conclusion que le refus de la réouverture d'une procédure pénale après le constat par la Cour d'une violation de la Convention[50] n'emportait pas une violation de l'article 6 de la Convention. La Cour a rappelé sa jurisprudence constante selon laquelle la Convention ne garantit pas le droit à la réouverture d'une procédure, ainsi que l'absence d'approche uniforme parmi les Etats membres quant aux modalités de fonctionnement des mécanismes de réouverture existants.[51] En particulier, elle a souligné que dans son arrêt du 5 juillet 2011, la chambre avait indiqué qu'un nouveau procès ou une réouverture de la procédure représentait «en principe un moyen approprié de redresser la violation constatée». Un nouveau procès ou une réouverture de la procédure étaient ainsi qualifiés de moyens appropriés mais non pas nécessaires et uniques. La Cour s'était donc abstenue de donner des indications contraignantes quant aux modalités d'exécution de son arrêt.[52] Partant, la Cour n'a pas conclu que la lecture par la Cour suprême de l'arrêt rendu par la Cour en 2011 était dans son ensemble le résultat d'une erreur de fait ou de droit manifeste aboutissant à un déni de justice.[53] Eu égard au principe de subsidiarité sur lequel se fonde la Convention et aux formules employées par la Cour dans son arrêt de chambre du 5 juillet 2011, celle-ci a estimé que le refus par la Cour suprême d'octroyer à Mme Moreira Ferreira la réouverture de la procédure n'a pas dénaturé les constats de cet arrêt et que les motifs invoqués relèvent de la marge d'appréciation des autorités nationales.[54]

---

[47]   § 64.
[48]   § 65.
[49]   *Moreira Ferreira c. Portugal (n° 2)* [GC], no 19867/12, CEDH 2017.
[50]   *Moreira Ferreira c. Portugal*, no 19808/08, 5 juillet 2011.
[51]   § 91.
[52]   § 92.
[53]   § 97.
[54]   § 98.

La question du déni de justice s'est également posée en termes d'accès à la justice.

Ainsi, dans une affaire introduite par deux requérants contre la Russie, ceux-ci se plaignaient du refus des juridictions internes d'examiner leurs recours en l'absence de preuves présentées à l'appui de leurs demandes. Dans son arrêt du 13 mars 2018[55], la Cour a estimé, concernant le deuxième requérant, que les décisions de justice contestées s'analysent en un déni de justice et qu'elles ont emporté violation de l'article 6 § 1 de le Convention.[56]

Dans l'affaire *Naït-Liman contre Suisse*, la Cour a examiné si le refus des tribunaux suisses d'examiner une action en réparation portant sur des actes allégués de torture commis en Tunisie était constitutif d'une violation de l'article 6 de la Convention.

Dans son arrêt du 15 mars 2018[57], la Cour a considéré au terme d'une étude de droit comparé que le droit international ne faisait pas peser d'obligation sur les autorités suisses d'ouvrir leur for en vue de faire statuer sur le fond de la demande de réparation de M. Naït-Liman, ni au titre d'une compétence universelle civile pour acte de torture, ni au titre du for de nécessité.[58] Il en résulte que les autorités suisses jouissaient d'une large marge d'appréciation en la matière.[59] S'agissant des conditions fixées par le législateur, la Cour a conclu qu'en instituant un for de nécessité aux conditions fixées à l'article 3 de la loi fédérale sur le droit international privé (LDIP), le législateur suisse n'a pas outrepassé sa marge d'appréciation. S'agissant de la marge d'appréciation des juridictions nationales, la Cour n'a discerné aucun élément manifestement déraisonnable ou arbitraire dans l'interprétation faite par le Tribunal fédéral en son arrêt du 22 mai 2007, par lequel Tribunal fédéral rejeta le recours de M. Naït-Liman, considérant que les tribunaux suisses n'étaient pas compétents à raison du lieu.[60] La Cour a rappelé cependant que cette conclusion ne met pas en cause le large consensus dans la communauté internationale sur l'existence d'un droit des victimes d'actes de torture à une réparation appropriée et effective, ni le fait que les États sont encouragés à donner effet à ce droit.[61] Dans son opinion dissidente, le juge Georgios A. Serghides a toutefois conclu que le requérant s'est heurté à un déni de justice, au mépris de l'article 6 § 1 de la Convention. Selon

---

[55]   *Adianko et Basov-Grinev c. Russie*, nᵒs 2872/09 et 20454/12, 13 mars 2018.
[56]   Les questions en cause concernaient des informations fournies mais dont l'absence fut reprochée au requérant, l'exigence de présenter des preuves écrites de la conclusion d'un contrat de travail, l'espérance légitime, mais frustrée du requérant de se prévaloir de l'assistance judiciaire, le manquement du juge d'assurer un contrôle préliminaire des demandes en vue des débats contradictoires et le rejet d'une seconde demande, pourtant corrigée. §§ 47-55.
[57]   *Naït-Liman c. Suisse* [GC], nᵒ 51357/07, 15 mars 2018.
[58]   §§ 182-202.
[59]   §§ 203-204.
[60]   §§ 205-216.
[61]   § 218.

lui, « *l'interprétation et l'application faites par le Tribunal fédéral de l'article 3 de la LDIP étaient arbitraires et manifestement déraisonnables, ce qui a entraîné un déni de justice et, partant une violation du droit d'accès à un tribunal, au mépris de l'article 6 de la Convention* ».[62]

Une dernière question mérite d'être posée. C'est celle concernant le déni de justice qui se répercute par ricochet sur le respect (ou non) d'une autre disposition de la Convention, par exemple, l'article 5 qui garantit le droit à la liberté et à la sûreté. Dans son arrêt *Ilaşcu et autres* du 8 juillet 2004[63], la Cour a donné la réponse suivante :

> « 461. L'exigence de régularité posée par l'article 5 § 1 a) (« détention régulière » ordonnée « selon les voies légales ») n'est pas satisfaite par un simple respect du droit interne pertinent ; il faut que le droit interne se conforme lui-même à la Convention, y compris aux principes généraux énoncés ou impliqués par elle, notamment celui de la prééminence du droit expressément mentionné dans le préambule de la Convention. A l'origine de l'expression « selon les voies légales » se trouve la notion de procédure équitable et adéquate, l'idée que toute mesure privative de liberté doit émaner d'une autorité qualifiée, être exécutée par une telle autorité et ne pas revêtir un caractère arbitraire (voir notamment l'arrêt *Winterwerp c. Pays-Bas* du 24 octobre 1979, série A no 33, pp. 19-20, § 45).
>
> En outre, le but de l'article 5 étant de protéger l'individu contre l'arbitraire (voir, entre autres, l'arrêt *Stafford c. Royaume-Uni* [GC], n° 46295/99, § 63, CEDH 2002-IV), la « condamnation » ne saurait être le résultat d'un déni de justice flagrant (voir, *mutatis mutandis*, l'arrêt *Drozd et Janousek c. France et Espagne* du 26 juin 1992, série A no 240, pp. 34-35, § 110) ».

Insistant ainsi sur la différence entre des violations simples de l'article 6 de la Convention et la violation caractérisée *et manifeste* de cette disposition, le « déni de justice *flagrant* », la Cour applique un critère particulièrement sévère. Ceci a été confirmé dans un arrêt du 17 mars 2016[64] :

> « 99. The « flagrant denial of justice » test is a stringent one. A flagrant denial of justice goes beyond mere irregularities or lack of safeguards in the trial procedures that result in a breach of Article 6 of the Convention. What is required is a breach of the principles of fair trial that is so fundamental as to amount to a nullification, or destruction of the very essence, of the right guaranteed by that Article (see *Othman (Abu Qatada) v. the United Kingdom*, no. 8139/09, § 260, 17 January 2012 and *Tsonyo Tsonev v. Bulgaria (no. 3)*, no. 21124/04, § 59, 16 October 2012). Under Article 5 § 1 (a), it is the detention of the person concerned, and not the person's conviction, which has to be lawful. Only if the violation of Article 6 could be said to amount to a « flagrant denial of justice », would Article 5 § 1 (a) be violated (see *Radu v. Germany*,

---

62   Points 8 à 42 de l'opinion.
63   *Ilaşcu et autres c. Moldova et Russie* [GC], n° 48787/99, CEDH 2004-VII.
64   *Hammerton c. Royaume Uni*, n° 6287/10, 17 mars 2016.

no. 20084/07, § 88, 16 May 2013). As the purpose of Article 5 is to protect the individual from arbitrariness, a conviction cannot be the result of a flagrant denial of justice (*Ilaşcu and Others* [*v. Moldova and Russia* [GC], no. 48787/99, ECHR 2004-VII], § 461) ».

La différence entre la violation simple de l'article 6 et sa variante *caractérisée* et *manifeste* a d'ailleurs été particulièrement mise en exergue dans cet arrêt. Concluant à l'absence de violation de l'article 5 § 1 de la Convention, la Cour a retenu ce qui suit :

« 119. While the Court of Appeal rightly accepted that the failure to ensure that the applicant had access to a lawyer was a violation of Article 6, the Court does not consider that such a violation is comparable to any of the situations listed at *Tsonyo Tsonev*, [*v. Bulgaria (no. 3)*, no. 21124/04, § 59, 16 October 2012], § 59. To find otherwise would come close to removing the distinction between a violation of Article 6 and a flagrant denial of justice, if it did not actually do so. The Court also observes that the applicant in *Tsonyo Tsonev* complained about a lack of representation and that, although the Court found that there had been a violation of Article 6, it did not accept that there had been a flagrant denial of justice. It cannot therefore be said that the violation of Article 6 in the present case went beyond a mere irregularity or lack of safeguards in the trial process and amounted to « a nullification, or destruction of the very essence, of the right guaranteed by that Article » (see paragraph 99 above). Accordingly, the Court finds that the violation of Article 6 in the present case did not amount to a flagrant denial of justice ».[65]

Qu'il soit simple ou flagrant, le déni de justice n'est donc retenu par la Cour européenne des droits de l'homme comme étant constitutif d'une violation de la Convention que dans des cas exceptionnels.

CONCLUSION

Que pouvons-nous retenir de ce qui précède ? Tout d'abord, que la notion « classique » de déni de justice, si elle conserve quelque pertinence en droit international public, n'en est pas moins dénuée d'une grande utilité dans l'espace européen des droits de l'homme. Des violations du droit à un procès équitable, ne constituant pas nécessairement des cas extrêmes de déni de justice sont efficacement appréhendées par la Cour européenne des droits de l'homme et par les juridictions nationales à travers le prisme de l'article 6 de la Convention. Ensuite, la Cour européenne des droits de l'homme s'est dotée, à travers la notion de déni de justice flagrant, d'une part de la faculté de

---

65   Comp. cependant pour un cas de détention après une condamnation, qui a été rendue à la suite d'un « déni de justice flagrant », l'arrêt *Gumeniuc c. Moldova* (n° 48829/06, 16 mai 2017).

protéger le justiciable contre l'injustice commise à l'extérieur de la juridiction des Hautes Parties contractantes et d'autre part, d'appréhender des situations très exceptionnelles de nature, notamment à se répercuter sur le respect d'autres droits de la Convention, dont celui de la liberté et de la sûreté. Enfin, la stigmatisation du déni de justice lui permet, dans des cas exceptionnels, de réexaminer des questions de fait et de droit traditionnellement réservées à l'analyse des juridictions nationales. En un mot, la notion du déni de justice a subi une véritable métamorphose sous l'influence de la protection internationale des droits de l'homme.

Luxembourg, le 28 mars 2019

'ARBITRARY OR MANIFESTLY UNREASONABLE'

The Arbitrariness Exception to the Fourth Instance Doctrine under Article 6 of the European Convention on Human Rights

Robert SPANO[*]

INTRODUCTION

The European Convention on Human Rights does not exist in isolation from the domestic laws of the Member States. In fact, national laws, as interpreted and applied by the domestic judiciary, may influence Convention protections. For example, Article 5 § 1 of the Convention requires that detention only be imposed in accordance with a 'procedure prescribed by law'. This lawfulness requirement refers back directly to national detention rules, both substantive and procedural.[1] In addition, the 'qualified provisions', Articles 8 to 11 of the Convention, require that an interference with the rights protected by paragraph 1 of these provisions be 'in accordance with' or 'prescribed by' law which, again, refer back to the legal basis for the interference in national law. Moreover, in cases that implicate procedural rights under Article 6 of the Convention, the European Court of Human Rights (hereinafter 'the Strasbourg Court' or 'the Court') is often asked to examine the way in which national courts have interpreted and applied their domestic procedural rules.

Unsurprisingly, national judges, in particular those at the top levels of the domestic judiciary, may not show particular enthusiasm for the Strasbourg Court directing them as to how to interpret the domestic laws in their respective

---

[*]   Judge and Vice President, European Court of Human Rights, elected in respect of Iceland. The views expressed herein are personal.

[1]   See, e.g., *Mooren v Germany* [GC], no. 11364/03, 9 July 2009, §72: 'Where the "lawfulness" of detention is in issue, including the question whether "a procedure prescribed by law" has been followed, the Convention refers essentially to national law and lays down the obligation to conform to the substantive and procedural rules thereof'.

Member States. They justifiably consider it to be their task to determine what the national law is, although it is clear that when it comes to the Convention it is the Strasbourg Court that is the ultimate arbiter of its content.

To regulate this delicate relationship between itself and national courts, and also to police its own jurisdictional boundaries under Articles 19 and 32 of the Convention, the Court[2] has developed a principle that requires it to restrict its review powers when assessing the interpretations given to domestic laws by national judges or their findings of fact. This principle is most commonly termed the *fourth instance doctrine* in academic writings.[3] As the Court has repeatedly held, it is a 'fundamental principle' that it is 'for the national authorities, notably the courts, to interpret and apply domestic law'.[4] Hence, it is not the function of the Court to 'deal with errors of fact or law allegedly committed by the national court unless and insofar as they may have infringed rights and freedoms protected by the Convention'.[5] The Court has also stated that the doctrine applies 'even in those fields where the Convention 'incorporates' the rules of that law, since the national authorities are, in the nature of things, particularly qualified to settle the issues arising in this connection. ... This is particularly true when ... the case turns upon difficult questions of interpretation of domestic law'.[6] Lastly, the Court has further formulated these general principles by stating that it should not 'act as a fourth instance body'[7] ('quatrième instance').

---

2   Maija Dahlberg has briefly recounted the history of the fourth instance doctrine in the case-law of the Commission and the old Court, see her article, ' ... It is Not Its Task to Act As a Court of Fourth Instance: The Case of the European Court of Human Rights', *European Journal of Legal Studies*, 2014, Vol. 7, No. 2, 94–95.

3   R. Goss, *Criminal Fair Trial Rights – Article 6 of the European Convention on Human Rights*, Hart Publishing, 2014, 42–58; G. Lautenbach, *The Concept of the Rule of Law and the European Convention on Human Rights*, Oxford University Press, 2013, 80–83; Harris, O'Boyle & Warbrick, *Law of the European Convention on Human Rights*, (third edition) Oxford University Press, 2014, 17–18. See also, M. Dahlberg, *supra*, n 2, 84–118. In the Inter-American human rights system, the Commission developed the so-called 'fourth instance formula' in the late 1980s on the basis of Article 47(b) of the American Convention on Human Rights, see, D.R. Pinzón, 'The "Victim Requirement, The Fourth Instance Formula and the Notion of "Person" in the Individual Complaint Procedure of the Inter-American Human Rights System', *ILSA Journal of International & Comparative Law*, 2000–2001, Vol. 7, 369–383, at 376.

4   This principle applies in general also to domestic legal rules that originate in other norms of international law or the law of the European Union, see especially *Avotiņš v Latvia* [GC], no. 17502/07, 23 May 2016, §100: 'The Court reiterates that it is not competent to rule formally on compliance with domestic law, other international treaties or European Union law ...' I will not discuss this strand of Convention case-law in this article.

5   See, e.g., one of the most recent Grand Chamber judgments of the Court referring to the fourth instance doctrine, *Naït-Liman v Switzerland* [GC], no. 51357/07, 15 March 2018, §116–117.

6   *Radomilja and Others v Croatia* [GC], nos. 37685/10 and 22768/12, 20 March 2018, §149, and *Winterwerp v Netherlands*, no. 6301/73, Series A no. 33, 24 October 1979, §46.

7   *De Tommaso v Italy* [GC], no. 43395/09, 23 February 2017, §170. See also, *Zubac v Croatia* [GC], no. 40160/12, 5 April 2018, §79; *Lupeni Greek Catholic Parish and Others v. Romania*

Importantly, the fourth instance doctrine is not absolute. The Court has prudently kept the door open by qualifying the scope of the doctrine by making it clear that the Court will not rely upon interpretations or applications of domestic laws by national judges if they are 'arbitrary or manifestly unreasonable'.[8] This exception to the fourth instance doctrine will be termed the *arbitrariness exception* for the purposes of this piece. I will explore this particular limitation on the fourth instance doctrine by analysing first the theoretical elements of the doctrine itself (Part I) and then explore the Court's relative intensity of review when applying the doctrine and the conceptual components of the arbitrariness exception (Part II). Finally, I will briefly examine recent judgments of the Court in which it has been called upon to apply the arbitrariness exception to the fourth instance doctrine in cases examined primarily under the civil limb of Article 6 § 1 of the Convention (Part III) before concluding (final Part IV).

It is not without reason that I have chosen this topic for the *Liber Amicorum* published in honour of my dear colleague and friend, Judge and Professor Paul Lemmens. Having had the great pleasure of working closely with Paul for over five years in the Strasbourg Court, including approximately three years together in the same Section of the Court, it has become clear to me that Paul and I share a particular interest in the intricacies and complexities of Article 6 cases. His knowledge of this field of Strasbourg jurisprudence is vast and goes back to the days when he wrote his doctoral thesis on the scope of the application of Article 6 §1 of the Convention and Article 14 § 1 of the International Covenant on Civil and Political Rights.[9] We have debated these issues amongst ourselves and with our colleagues in many cases that have come before us which has always been enlightening. I hope that my reflections in this article will prove useful for our continuing debates in the years to come.

[GC], no. 76942/11, 29 November 2016, §90 and *Bochan v Ukraine (no. 2)* [GC], no. 22251/08, 5 February 2015, §61.

8   *Naït-Liman v Switzerland, supra* n 5, §116: '... It follows that the Court cannot call into question the findings of the domestic authorities on alleged errors of domestic law unless they are arbitrary or manifestly unreasonable.' See also, for example, *Anheuser-Busch Inc. v Portugal* [GC], no. 73049/01, 11 January 2007, §85. The Court has sometimes worded the arbitrariness exception in more elaborate terms, see e.g., *Anđelković v Serbia*, no. 1401/08, 9 April 2013, §24: '... the Court will not question the interpretation of domestic law by the national courts, save in the event of evident arbitrariness ..., in other words, when it observes that the domestic courts have applied the law in a particular case manifestly erroneously or so as to reach arbitrary conclusions and/or a denial of justice ...'

9   P. Lemmens, *Geschillen over burgerlijke rechten en verplichtingen. Over het toepassingsgebied van de artikelen 6, lid 1, van het Europees Vedrag over de rechten van de mens en 14, lid 1, van het Internationaal Verdrag inzake burgerrechten en politieke rechten*, Publikaties Interuniversitair Centrum voor Staatsrecht – Proefschriften en verhandelingen, XIII, Kluwer, Antwerp, 1989.

I. THE THEORETICAL FOUNDATIONS OF THE FOURTH INSTANCE DOCTRINE

The use of the fourth instance doctrine in the Court's case-law is not a novel phenomenon. Indeed, as commentators have noted, early in its work the Commission was 'fond of saying' that the Convention organs were not a court of appeal for domestic courts and could not intervene on the basis that a domestic court had come to the 'wrong' decision or made a mistake. Their role was to ensure compliance with the provisions of the Convention by the Contracting States.[10]

Historically, the Court has not laid detailed theoretical groundwork for the doctrine, but rather applied it pragmatically on a case-by-case basis. The Court has thus, prudently in my view, refrained from opining in an abstract manner on the foundations of the fourth instance doctrine.[11] Yet it is one of the cornerstones of the institutional balance that underpins the Convention system, in particular the relationship between the Strasbourg Court and national courts. Therefore, before proceeding further, it might be useful to reflect briefly on its theoretical foundations as they may shed light on the scope and substance of the doctrine, as enshrined within a legal principle in the Court's case-law which can influence the outcome of Convention disputes.

Here, I would mention the following five elements:

First, the fourth instance doctrine is an institutional norm directed at the distribution of competences between the Court and the national judiciary. It directs the Strasbourg judge to be cautious, circumspect and prudent when it comes to analysing the substantive findings of national judges, both as to the content of domestic laws and the facts adduced. As the Court reiterated in the recent Grand Chamber judgment in the case of *Károly Nagy v Hungary*, an Article 6 access to court case, 'where the superior national courts have analysed in a comprehensive and convincing manner the precise nature of the impugned restriction of access to court, on the basis of the relevant Convention case-law and the principles drawn therefrom, [the] Court would need strong reasons to differ from the conclusion reached by those courts by substituting its own views from those of the national courts on a question of interpretation of domestic

---

[10]   K. Reid, *A Practitioner's Guide to The European Convention on Human Rights*, (fifth edition), Sweet & Maxwell, 2015, 64.

[11]   M. Dahlberg, *supra* n 3, 88: '... the fourth instance nature of the case is evaluated in a rather rough and brief manner'. Other scholars have gone further and considered it justified to criticise the Court for its 'lack of explanation for the fourth instance doctrine, and of the way in which that doctrine works', arguing that it is 'compounded by the lack of any jurisprudential or case authority for the doctrine', see R. Goss, *supra*, n 4, 46, n 50.

law'.[12] In other words, on such issues, the Court will afford the national judges a wide margin of deference. This is, in and of itself, a very important starting point when an application is examined in Strasbourg. For the purposes of the Convention, national law will, as a departing point of principle, be interpreted and applied by the judges in the Contracting States, not by the Court.

Second, as a norm that influences the interplay and differing roles of the Strasbourg Court and the national judiciary, the fourth instance doctrine is premised on good faith collaboration between the international and national judges in the enforcement of Convention guarantees.[13] In this sense, the doctrine is closely related to another pillar of the Convention system, the principle of subsidiarity.[14] This nexus manifests itself in at least two ways. Firstly, when national courts apply the Convention in national proceedings, and are called upon to interpret domestic laws, the application of the Convention by national courts becomes 'consistent with the principle of subsidiarity' as noted by some prominent commentators.[15] Secondly, the close relationship between the fourth instance doctrine and the principle of subsidiarity is particularly apparent when it comes to findings of fact by national judges. As the Court explained in *F.G v Sweden*, '[by] virtue of Article 1 of the Convention the primary responsibility for implementing and enforcing the guaranteed rights and freedoms is laid on the national authorities. The machinery of complaint to the Court is thus subsidiary to national systems safeguarding human rights. This subsidiary character is articulated in Articles 13 and 35 § 1 of the Convention. … [Where] domestic proceedings have taken place, it is not the Court's task to substitute its own assessment of the facts for that of the domestic courts and, as a general rule, it is for those courts to assess the evidence before them'.[16] On this basis, I have argued elsewhere that in this sense 'the fourth instance doctrine may, to some extent, merge with the principle of subsidiarity'.[17]

---

12 *Károly Nagy v Hungary* [GC], no. 56665/09, 14 September 2017, §62.
13 This element has a basis in old Commission case-law, see *X v Netherlands*, no. 2621/65, Recueil 19, 1 May 1966, §§100–105, where the Commission found that it should only adjudicate on matters of national law where the authorities had misapplied the law in *bad faith*, see also, G. Lautenbach, *supra* n 4, 80.
14 It should be noted that Protocol 15 to the Convention, which will come into force when all 47 Member States have ratified it (see Article 7 of the Protocol), will add a new recital to the Preamble to the Convention with explicit references to the principle of subsidiarity and the margin of appreciation. This addition to the Preamble will also reinforce to some extent the textual foundations of the fourth instance doctrine.
15 Harris, O'Boyle & Warbrick, *supra* n 4, 26.
16 *F.G. v Sweden* [GC], no. 43611/11, 23 March 2016, §§117–118. See also, *Radomilja and Others v Croatia*, *supra* n 7, §150.
17 R. Spano, 'The Future of the European Court of Human Rights – Subsidiarity, Process-Based Review and the Rule of Law', 2018, *Human Rights Law Review* 2018, 19, 473-494; 485. Some scholars have gone further and stated that the 'fourth instance doctrine constitutes the principle of subsidiarity and adheres to it on the basis that the Contracting States are the main actors under the Convention'. See, M. Dahlberg, *supra* n 2, 85. Still others claim that there is

Third, the fourth instance doctrine takes account of the need to entrust national judges with enforcing Convention guarantees at domestic level in cases where, as the Court has stated, the Convention itself 'incorporates' the rules of national law, 'since the national authorities are, in the nature of things, particularly qualified to settle the issues arising in this connection', especially when difficult interpretations of national law are required.[18] The doctrine is therefore conceptually based not only on a functional distribution of power between the international and national judges, as described above, but is also sensitive to the fact that the latter are in principle more knowledgeable and have more expertise on matters of domestic law, which may influence the scope of Convention guarantees.

Fourth, it has been argued by scholars that the fourth instance doctrine finds support at the theoretical level in principles of general international law, in particular that of national sovereignty. Dahlberg has argued that the doctrine must be viewed through the lens of theories of institutional legitimacy in which an international forum, like the Strasbourg Court, is called upon to review national decision-making. In the exercise of this task, the international forum must, she argues, retain its legitimacy through justificatory argumentation that respects the limits of its competences vis-à-vis the domestic authorities.[19] A different, although related, lens through which this element of institutional legitimacy can perhaps be viewed is one which emphasises the importance of retaining and preserving mutual trust and confidence in the administration of international justice.

Fifth, the arbitrariness exception to the fourth instance doctrine, as elaborated in the Court's case-law, might finally be considered as shedding light on the theoretical foundations of the doctrine itself and its relationship with the rule of law, a principle that permeates the whole of the Convention.[20] By limiting the scope of the doctrine to interpretations and applications of domestic law that are not 'arbitrary or manifestly unreasonable', the Court accentuates the rule of law foundations of the principle.[21] In other words, by conditioning its deference

---

no substantive difference between the fourth instance doctrine, the margin of appreciation and the principle of subsidiarity, see J. Christoffersen, *Fair Balance: Proportionality, Subsidiarity and Primarity in the European Convention on Human Rights*, Martinus Nijhoff Publishers, 2009, 239–240.

[18] *Radomilja and Others v Croatia, supra* n 6, §149.

[19] M. Dahlberg, *supra* n 2, 86 and 88–92. Dahlberg concludes, in an abstract manner, that at the level of institutional legitimacy, 'it is recognised that democratically non-accountable judges in Strasbourg should not use their jurisdiction to override national authorities', see M. Dahlberg, *supra* n 3, 95. She also notes, at 95–96, that in 'addition to upholding national sovereignty, the fourth instance doctrine also respects the principle of democracy. Respecting the choices and evaluations made by the national authorities reflects respect for the democratically elected members of the parliament and the people who have democratically voted for their representatives'.

[20] See, generally, G. Lautenbach, *supra* n 3, and R. Spano, *supra* n 17, at 493.

[21] Conversely, Lautenbach questions 'whether legality and the rule of law do not demand that the ECtHR should actively and strictly review whether national law is complied with', *supra* n 3, 80.

towards national judges acting in a manner that is not arbitrary or manifestly unreasonable when interpreting or applying domestic laws, the Strasbourg Court assists in the development of a legal culture at national level, in particular in the judiciary, that respects the inherent values of a democratic system based on the rule of law and not the capricious rule of men.

II. INTENSITY OF REVIEW UNDER THE FOURTH INSTANCE DOCTRINE AND THE DUAL ELEMENTS OF THE ARBITRARINESS EXCEPTION

The relative intensity of review under the Fourth Instance Doctrine

In principle, the fourth instance doctrine applies in all cases under the Convention so long as the Court is called upon to review the legal and factual findings of national courts. However, the intensity of the Court's review may, importantly, differ depending on the nature and substance of the Convention right in question. In particular, the Court's review is stricter when the Convention right is itself formulated as a requirement that an adequate legal basis exists in domestic law, as is the case under Articles 5[22] and 7 of the Convention.[23] Furthermore, as I will explain in Part IV, the Court has recently reformulated the arbitrariness exception to the fourth instance doctrine in cases examined under Article 6 § 1 of the Convention, in particular when these require a procedural fairness review under paragraph 1 of the provision.

The dual elements of the arbitrariness exception

Before proceeding further, it is necessary to examine the conceptual formulation of the arbitrariness exception in the Court's case-law. As previously noted, the formula for the exception adopted by the Court comprises two elements.

---

[22]   *Mooren v Germany, supra*, n 2, §73: 'Although it is in the first place for the national authorities, notably the courts, to interpret and apply domestic law, under Article 5 § 1 failure to comply with domestic law entails a breach of the Convention and the Court can and should therefore review whether this law has been complied with'.

[23]   As the Grand Chamber held in *Kononov v Latvia* ([GC], no. 36376/04, 17 May 2010, §198) 'the Court's powers of review must be greater when the Convention right itself, Article 7 in the present case, requires that there was a legal basis for a conviction and sentence. Article 7 § 1 requires the Court to examine whether there was a contemporaneous legal basis for the applicant's conviction and, in particular, it must satisfy itself that the result reached by the relevant domestic courts (a conviction for war crimes pursuant to section 68-3 of the former Criminal Code) was compatible with Article 7 of the Convention, even if there were differences between the legal approach and reasoning of this Court and the relevant domestic decisions. To accord a lesser power of review to this Court would render Article 7 devoid of purpose'.

An interpretation of domestic law must neither be 'arbitrary' nor 'manifestly unreasonable'.[24] The references by the Court to these two elements of the exception, which are not expressed cumulatively, but presented in the alternative ('or'), begs the question whether there is a meaningful distinction to be made between the two. The Court has never to my knowledge addressed that question in an abstract manner and I should tread carefully in attempting to provide an answer.[25]

It might, however, be useful to note that at least at the semantic level there are some differences between the two elements. On the one hand, 'arbitrariness' often, although not always, encompasses a subjective element. In a decision-making process, the decision-maker, by acting arbitrarily, has acted in bad faith or in clear contravention of existing rules, often, but not necessarily, for an ulterior (illegal) motive. An arbitrary decision can also be based on random choice or personal whim. That is why the arbitrary use of public power is anathema to the rule of law. Furthermore, arbitrariness may manifest itself in the decision-maker deviating without reason or any clear justification from reaching a result that he or she has reached in other analogous cases.[26] 'Manifest unreasonableness' seems, on the other hand and at first glance, to direct the analysis more to the nature and scope of the result or outcome itself. It thus asks whether the result is, as such, just or fair. It may therefore include a type of proportionality assessment. In sum, it seems that an 'arbitrary' interpretation of domestic law can never be considered 'reasonable', whereas the opposite does not necessarily follow; a manifestly unreasonable result does not, by definition, have to flow from arbitrary decision-making.

Applying this analysis to the exception to the fourth instance doctrine, one may perhaps justifiably conclude that by relying on the two elements of 'arbitrariness' and 'manifest unreasonableness' as the test for its assessment, the Court aims to retain some flexibility in its review of the 'Conventionality' of interpretations

---

24   See *supra* n 9.

25   However, as I explain in Part IV, in a recent Grand Chamber judgment, *Moreira Ferreira v Portugal (no. 2)*, the Court clarified somewhat the concept of 'arbitrariness' in the context of the exception to the fourth instance doctrine as applied in Article 6 fair trial cases.

26   It should, however, be noted that in the Court's case-law, alleged arbitrariness in national judicial practice, creating legal uncertainty due to the delivery of conflicting decisions on a particular topic, is the subject of an independent, although related, strand of case-law under Article 6 § 1 of the Convention which is traditionally assessed on the basis of the criteria set forth in the Grand Chamber judgment in the case of *Nejdet Şahin and Perihan Şahin v Turkey* [GC], no. 13279/05, 20 October 2011. There the Court held that in examining such an allegation, the criteria that guides its assessment consists in establishing 'whether "profound and long-standing differences" exist in the case-law of a supreme court, whether the domestic law provides for machinery for overcoming these inconsistencies, whether that machinery has been applied and, if appropriate, to what effect', see §53. A recent judgment at the level of the Grand Chamber applying the *Nejdet Şahin* criteria is *Lupeni Greek Catholic Parish and Others v Romania*, *supra*, n 7, see §§116–135.

of domestic law. Thus, were the Court to limit its review to arbitrariness, and exclude the latter component, it might create the risk that the threshold, already high under the current test, would be overly deferential towards national judges and thus not commensurate to the overall aims of the system, namely, to make Convention rights practical and effective.[27] However, inversely, by requiring the unreasonableness to be 'manifest', the Court seeks to limit its ability to second-guess (and thus possibly overrule) substantive outcomes or results of interpretations of national laws that the Strasbourg judge merely disagrees with or considers to be wrong in the sense that he or she would have opted for a different, more applicant-friendly, interpretation had he or she sat in the national court.

III. APPLICATION OF THE ARBITRARINESS EXCEPTION IN CASES UNDER THE CIVIL LIMB OF ARTICLE 6 § 1 OF THE CONVENTION

In this part, I will before concluding explore some recent case-law of the Strasbourg Court, in particular Grand Chamber judgments, in which the applicants invited the Court to disregard interpretations and applications of domestic law in the course of examining their complaints under the civil limb[28] of Article 6 § 1 of the Convention, in particular in cases in which the applicant, or applicants, alleged a violation of their right of access to court.[29] Along the way I will attempt to develop some elements that may be of use in analysing the Court's case-law in this area.

A very high threshold – A restrictive approach by the Strasbourg Court

At the outset it is important to note, as emphasised by some commentators, that 'it is very exceptional for the Court to disagree with any decision by a national court on its interpretation and application of its own national law'.[30] The

---

27   *Airey v. Ireland*, App. no. 6289/73, 9 October 1979, §24.

28   I will thus not discuss the case-law of the Court on the application of the fourth instance doctrine in cases examined under the criminal limb of Article 6 § 1 of the Convention. For a critical appraisal of this strand of the Court's case-law, see R. Goss, *supra* n 3, 42–58.

29   As noted above, I do not intend to deal in particular with cases in which the Court has been called upon to re-evaluate the *facts*, as adduced by the domestic courts, which is, however, also an essential aspect of the fourth instance doctrine as outlined in Part I of this article. On this issue, see M. Dahlberg, *supra* n 3, 98–115, which presents a case study of 44 Article 6 cases and categorises the role of the fourth instance doctrine in these cases into the following four categories: 1) clear fourth instance nature, 2) length of proceedings, 3) balancing approach, and 4) disregard of the fourth instance approach.

30   Harris, O'Boyle and Warbrick, *supra* n 3, 18. Of course, this applies primarily in cases not implicating the strict review of national laws required under Articles 5 and 7 of the Convention, see Part III of this article.

arbitrariness exception sets a very high threshold for intervention, as discussed above in conformity with the elements underpinning the theoretical foundations of the doctrine elaborated in Part II.

Two recent examples of this restrictive approach to its review in dealing with important Article 6 § 1 issues are the Court's Grand Chamber judgments in *Naït-Liman v Switzerland* and *Károly Nagy v Hungary*.

In the first judgment, the Court rejected the applicant's invitation to find that the Swiss Federal Supreme Court had interpreted a domestic '*forum necessitatis*' rule in a civil case in a manner that was arbitrary or manifestly unreasonable for the purposes of the right of access to court.[31] In the second case, the Court was called upon to examine whether the refusal of the domestic courts to decide upon the applicant's pecuniary claim, which stemmed from his service as a pastor for the Reformed Church of Hungary, had violated his right of access to court. Finding in the negative, the Court held that given the overall legal and jurisprudential framework existing in Hungary at the material time when the applicant lodged his claim, the domestic courts' conclusion that his pastoral service had been governed by ecclesiastical law and their decision to discontinue the proceedings could not be deemed arbitrary or manifestly unreasonable.[32]

Although the threshold is thus set high, it must, however, be emphasised that the arbitrariness exception is not an empty vessel. In its case-law, the Court has in some rare cases disregarded the findings of domestic courts in their interpretation or application of national law. An example[33], which is directly on point for the purposes of this discussion, is the Court's judgment in *Anđelković v Serbia*. The applicant complained that the court of final instance had rejected his claim for outstanding holiday pay for reasons which had not been correct in law, in breach of Article 6 of the Convention. The Court observed that the Serbian labour law governing holiday pay was 'not vague and ambiguous', but clearly provided for the instances in which employees were entitled to such additional payments. The first-instance court had established certain facts and found that the applicant had had a legal entitlement to the holiday pay claimed. The District Court had overturned that judgment on appeal and rejected the applicant's claim 'without even making reference to the facts and the labour law as presented by the first-instance court'. Nor had it referred 'to what the law was, how it should have been applied to the applicant's case or whether the conditions stipulated

---

[31] *Naït-Liman v Switzerland, supra* n 5, §214.
[32] *Károly Nagy v Hungary, supra* n 12, §76.
[33] See, also, *Dulaurans v France*, no. 34553/97, 21 March 2000, §38, in which the Court found a violation of Article 6 § 1 because of a 'manifest error of assessment' by the Court of Cassation ('une erreur manifeste d'appréciation'), although the Court's finding was primarily based on the national court's inadequate reasoning on appeal in a civil case.

in the applicable collective and enterprise bargaining agreements had been met in the applicant's case. The District Court, while disregarding applicable employment law, [had] rejected the applicant's claim on the sole ground that "to accept the applicant's claim would mean that the applicant would be treated more favourably than his colleagues, who had not received payment of outstanding holiday pay from their employer either'". The Court found that this 'reasoning had no legal foundation' and was based on what appears to be an 'abstract assertion quite outside of any reasonable judicial discretion. Furthermore, a connection between the established facts, the applicable law and the outcome of the proceedings [had been] wholly absent from the impugned judgment'. The Court therefore found that such an 'arbitrary District Court's ruling [had] amounted to a denial of justice in the applicant's case'.[34]

Prima facie indicia of arbitrariness or manifest unreasonableness

Although the fourth instance doctrine is premised on the idea that the Strasbourg Court will respect the national judges' interpretations of domestic law that are not arbitrary or manifestly unreasonable, that does not mean that the Court can exclude its own independent verification of whether there are indicia of such elements in the domestic courts' reasoning.[35] By definition that may require the Strasbourg judge to examine, at least at the *prima facie* level, whether the interpretation given to a legal provision by the national judiciary has a basis, *inter alia,* in (1) the text of the provision in question, (2) its *travaux préparatoires* and/or (3) in domestic judicial practice.[36]

For example, in the Grand Chamber judgment in *Regner v the Czech Republic,* the applicant complained of the unfairness of the proceedings in which he had sought to challenge a decision revoking his security clearance. In his view, the administrative courts had refused him access to decisive evidence, classified as confidential, which had been made available to them by the defendant party. The applicant alleged, *inter alia,* that the intelligence report that had served as the basis for the decision to revoke his security clearance had been classified in the lowest category of confidentiality. Therefore, he claimed, domestic law did not give the authorities the right to refuse to disclose the report's contents. The Court rejected this submission noting that, as could be seen from the Supreme Administrative Court's case-law,

---

34   *Andelković v Serbia, supra* n 8, §27.
35   Of course, as I will discuss below, scant or non-existent reasoning in a domestic judicial decision can, in and of itself, be a sufficient indicator of arbitrariness under the Court's case-law, see, e.g., *Dulaurans v France, supra* n 33, §38.
36   As to cases examined under the criminal limb of Article 6 § 1 of the Convention, the Court has been criticised by some scholars for failing to 'provide guidance as to how it determines which cases demand that the European Court itself engages with the national court's factual and legal analysis in order to determine whether a breach of the Convention has occurred', see R. Goss, *supra,* n 4, 46.

domestic law (Law no. 412/2005) was applicable to 'any information classified as confidential' and thus not limited to 'data of a higher degree of confidentiality'. The Court concluded that 'accordingly, the application of section 133(3) of Law no. 412/2005 by the domestic courts [did] not appear to be arbitrary or manifestly unreasonable'.[37] It goes without saying that the Court's finding is to some extent based on its own independent examination of the *text of the domestic law*, as seen against the background of the interpretation given to it by the national courts.[38]

In other cases, *judicial practice* at domestic level may be the decisive element in the Court's determination, as was the case in the above-mentioned Grand Chamber judgment in *Naït-Liman v Switzerland*. In rejecting the applicant's invitation to find that the Swiss Federal Supreme Court had interpreted a domestic '*forum necessitatis*' rule in a civil case in a manner which was arbitrary or manifestly unreasonable for the purposes of the right of access to court, the Court referred in particular to the 'relevant practice of the Swiss courts' and also to the fact that 'domestic case-law on this issue [was] relatively limited and [concerned] diverse cases', including situations that could not be compared with the applicant's case.[39]

In my experience serving in the Strasbourg Court, there can be a very 'fine line' between an international judge examining at the *prima facie* level whether there are indicia of arbitrariness or manifest unreasonableness in the interpretations of domestic laws, and the Strasbourg judge going further than the fourth instance doctrine allows and vicariously 'taking a seat' in the judicial panel at national level. Indeed, the narrow majorities in the above-mentioned Grand Chamber judgments demonstrate the challenges facing the Court in this regard. However, ensuring that the line is not crossed is key so the Court can effectively navigate the boundaries of its role under the Convention in its dialogue with national courts. The judgments discussed above demonstrate in my view the Court adopting a prudent and cautious approach along the lines mandated by the theoretical foundations of the fourth instance doctrine discussed in Part II above. Hence, these Grand Chamber judgments provide in my view helpful guidance on the preferred approach to be taken in this area.

---

[37] *Regner v the Czech Republic* [GC], no. 35289/11, 19 September 2017, §159.

[38] See here also, *Gestur Jónsson and Ragnar Halldór Hall*, nos. 68273/14 and 68271/14, 30 October 2018 (pending before the Grand Chamber), §72: 'Therefore, taking account of the reasoning of the Supreme Court, which is the highest court in the Icelandic judicial system interpreting domestic law, and viewing the wording of the provisions in question in the light of the particular facts of the present case ..., the Court finds that the Supreme Court's interpretation and application of the provisions of the [Code of Criminal Procedure] to the applicants' case cannot be considered arbitrary or manifestly unreasonable within the meaning of the Court's case-law ... '.

[39] *Naït-Liman v Switzerland, supra* n 5, §214.

The arbitrariness exception as an element of procedural fairness

The assessment required by the arbitrariness exception under the fourth instance doctrine is, in Article 6 § 1, cases often closely related to the question whether the national proceedings were, viewed globally, procedurally fair. As the Court held in its Grand Chamber judgment in *Moreira Ferreira v Portugal (no. 2)* 'in exceptional cases ... errors [of law or fact committed by the national courts] may be said to constitute "unfairness" incompatible with Article 6 of the Convention'.[40] This means that the nature and scope of the error of interpretation or application of domestic law, alleged by the applicant, must in Article 6 cases implicating procedural rights, such as the right of access to court, be such as to influence directly elements of procedural fairness.

In this case, the applicant complained that the national Supreme Court had dismissed her application for review of a criminal judgment delivered against her which had been the subject of a previous application to the Strasbourg Court in which the Court had found a violation of Article 6 of the Convention.[41] She submitted that the Supreme Court's judgment amounted to a 'denial of justice' because that court had incorrectly interpreted and applied the relevant provisions of the Code of Criminal Procedure and the conclusions of the previous judgment by the Strasbourg Court, thus depriving her of the right to have her conviction reviewed.[42] Having reviewed its previous case-law, the Court stated the following:[43]

> '85. It transpires from the above-mentioned case-law that a domestic judicial decision cannot be qualified as arbitrary to the point of prejudicing the fairness of proceedings unless no reasons are provided for it or if the reasons given are based on a manifest factual or legal error committed by the domestic court, resulting in a "denial of justice" ...
>
> 86. The question in the instant case is whether the reasons provided for the judicial decision given by the Supreme Court complied with the standards of the Convention.'

---

40 *Moreira Ferreira v Portugal (no. 2)* [GC], no. 19867/12, 11 July 2017, §83. See also, *Bochan v Ukraine* (no. 2), *supra* n 7, §61.

41 *Moreira Ferreira v Portugal*, no. 19808/08, 5 July 2011.

42 It should be made clear that although the discussion in this Part is primarily directed at cases in which the Court examined the civil limb of Article 6 of the Convention, the Court in *Moreira Ferreira (no. 2)* in fact applied the criminal limb of that provision. It found that the Supreme Court's scrutiny was to be viewed as an extension of the proceedings concluded by the initial judgment in the applicant's case at domestic level, which was the subject of a previous judgment of the Court from 5 July 2011, see, *supra* n 41. Therefore, in the Court's view, the 'Supreme Court once again focused on the determination, within the meaning of Article 6 § 1 of the Convention, of the criminal charge against the applicant', *Moreira Ferreira v Portugal (no. 2)*, *supra*, n 40, §72. However, as will be explained, the principles enunciated in *Moreira Ferreira (no. 2)*, §85, which are the subject of the discussion here, were directly applied subsequently in an Article 6 § 1 civil limb case, *Tibet Menteş and Others v Turkey*, nos. 57818/10, 57822/10, 57825/10, 57827/10 and 57829/10, 24 October 2017.

43 *Moreira Ferreira v Portugal (no. 2)*, *supra*, n 40, §§85–86.

A narrow majority of the Court (9 votes to 8) found that it could not conclude that the 'Supreme Court's reading of the Court's 2011 judgment was, viewed as whole, the result of a manifest factual or legal error leading to a "denial of justice"'. It held that 'having regard to the principle of subsidiarity and to the wording of the Court's 2011 judgment' the 'Supreme Court's refusal to reopen the proceedings as requested by the applicant was not arbitrary'.[44]

The Court's novel formulation of the arbitrariness exception in paragraph 85 of *Moreira Ferreira (no. 2)* was subsequently applied in the judgment in *Tibet Menteş and Others v Turkey*, examined under the civil limb of Article 6 §1 of the Convention.[45] The applicants complained that their right to payment for overtime work, as established during the proceedings before the national first instance court, had been denied to them as a result of a presumption that had been unjustifiably applied by the Turkish Court of Cassation. By a majority (4 votes to 3), the Second Section of the Court rejected the applicants' allegations. Referring to the formulation of the arbitrariness exception in paragraph 85 of *Moreira Ferreira (no. 2) v Portugal* it found that the Court did not have 'sufficient grounds to conclude that the Court of Cassation's interpretation of domestic law was based on a manifest factual or legal error, resulting in a "denial of justice"'.[46]

From the above discussion of recent Convention case-law, it can be inferred that the issue of whether the high threshold of applicability for the arbitrariness exception in Article 6 cases has been reached, taking account of the formulation in *Moreira Ferreira (no. 2)*, is one that can often be very delicate and difficult on the available facts, as the closely divided Court in the above-mentioned cases demonstrates. Furthermore, by making clear that the arbitrariness standard requires a showing of a 'manifest legal or factual error, resulting in a 'denial of justice', a very strict standard indeed, the Court has given even more prominence to the fourth instance doctrine in the area of procedural rights under Article 6 of the Convention.[47] When one takes account of the explicit reference by the Grand Chamber in its conclusion in *Moreira Ferreira (no. 2)* to

---

[44] *Moreira Ferreira v Portugal (no. 2), supra,* n 39, §§97–98. It should be emphasised here that the Court's examination was not directed at the Supreme Court's interpretation of domestic law, but rather at the domestic court's interpretation of the Strasbourg Court's case-law, see also, *Bochan v Ukraine* (no 2), *supra* n 7, §64, in which the Court, in a similar case, came to a contrary conclusion, finding that the 'Supreme Court's reasoning [did] not amount merely to a different reading of a legal text. it [could] only be construed as being "grossly arbitrary" or as entailing a "denial of justice"', in the sense of distorting the presentation of the 2007 judgment in the first Bochan case.

[45] *Tibet Menteş and Others v Turkey, supra* n 42.

[46] *Tibet Menteş and Others v Turkey, supra,* n 42, §49.

[47] It remains to be seen whether the Court will in the future apply a similar standard in cases implicating the fourth instance doctrine under other Convention provisions.

the 'principle of subsidiarity'[48], it might perhaps be argued that this development is commensurate with the recent shift in the Court's case-law which, as I have discussed elsewhere, seeks to incentivise national judges to examine cases implicating Convention rights in good faith, in accordance with Convention standards and the principle of the rule of law. If these conditions are fulfilled, the Court may defer to the views of the national judiciary.[49]

CONCLUSION

In this article, I have attempted to explore the fourth instance doctrine in the case-law of the European Court of Human rights and its theoretical foundations and to analyse the conceptual elements of the arbitrariness exception to the doctrine. Lastly, I have discussed recent case-law, in particular at Grand Chamber level, relating to the application of the exception in cases examined under the civil limb of Article 6 § 1 of the Convention.

As argued above, the fourth instance doctrine is a fundamental norm of Convention law that regulates the role of the Court when called upon to examine the interpretation and application of domestic laws by national courts in cases implicating Convention rights. It has been a perennial feature of the Convention system for decades, applied on a case-by-case basis in a pragmatic manner, first by the old Court and the Commission and, after 1998, by the current Court.

Through the years, the Convention's legal space has become more complex. Currently, the international judge and the national judiciary are constantly called upon to navigate ever more diverse and novel fields of law; these are often unclear, or manifest an attempt by legislators to take account of the multitude of factors and policies that percolate at the domestic level on the basis of the principle of national sovereignty, also taking account of existing international law obligations. Therefore, it is imperative that good faith collaboration between the Strasbourg Court and the national judges in the Member States of the Council of Europe be adequately reflected in a prudent, but principled, application of the fourth instance doctrine. In that way both types of actors can respect and enforce their respective fields of competences under the rule of law, so as to fulfil, under European supervision, the ultimate aim of the Convention system, to secure to every person within the jurisdiction of the Member States the rights and freedoms provided for by the Convention.

---

[48] *Moreira Ferreira v Portugal (no. 2), supra,* n 40, §98.
[49] R. Spano, *supra,* n 17, at 15.

WRESTLING WITH THE 'HIDDEN AGENDA'

Toward a Coherent Methodology for Article 18 Cases

Egidijus Kūris

*Judge of the European Court of Human Rights (2013–)**
Judge (1999–2008) and President (2002–2008)
of the Constitutional Court of Lithuania
Professor at the Faculty of Law, Vilnius University

INTRODUCTION: OF ARTICLE 18 IN GENERAL

Most rights[1] enshrined in the European Convention on Human Rights are not absolute; States can restrict them on the condition that a legitimate aim is pursued and a proper balance is struck between that aim and the restriction imposed. Another condition is set out in Article 18 of the Convention "Limitations on use of restrictions on rights". It reads:

> "The restrictions permitted under this Convention to the said rights and freedoms shall not be applied for any purpose other than those for which they have been prescribed."

"Said rights" denote substantive rights, enshrined in the Convention (and its Protocols). Article 18 itself does not enshrine any particular substantive right, only, figuratively speaking, the "umbrella right" not to have one's rights violated by the authorities pursuing purposes ulterior to those warranted by various Articles of the Convention. In this sense Article 18 has no independent role. Unlike Rudyard Kipling's cat, Article 18 does not "walk by himself": it is an escort. Being of an accessory nature, it can be invoked and applied not "as of its own", but only in conjunction with some other Article. That other Article can be breached either without or together with Article 18; but Article 18 cannot be invoked not in conjunction with another Article.

---

[*] The views expressed are of the author and do not represent those of the Court.
[1] For the sake of convenience, I omit "and freedoms" (except in quotations).

In view of the fact that various Articles define what restrictions can be imposed on respective rights, a legitimate question may be asked, why at all there was needed a separate Article, setting limitations on these restrictions. This directs us to the philosophy underlying the Convention. The entire philosophy ("the whole structure"[2]) of the Convention rests on the general assumption that authorities act in good faith; the European Court of Human Rights (ECtHR) has called this statement "foundational".[3] The drafters of the Convention did not deem political persecution to be a matter of course in Europe, but they did not wholly exclude it. They realistically and self-critically conceded that even democratically elected (or appointed) and controlled authorities can at times resort to such restrictions of individuals' rights which are triggered by motives alien to law. Article 18 bans the use of restrictions, triggered by purposes, ulterior to, but, as a rule, camouflaged as falling under, those specified in various restriction-warranting Articles of the Convention. Authorities tend to disavow such improper and illegal purposes, which are therefore aptly called "hidden agenda". Though Article 18 does not mention politics, and "ulterior purposes" or "hidden agenda" also are euphemisms, let us call a spade a spade: Article 18 is primarily about (or rather against) political persecution. From *travaux préparatoires* to the Convention it can be inferred that it was designed to counter not any misuse of power, but only that which is brought about by improper purposes, thus constituting the breach of the authorities' good faith. The presumption of good faith should preclude the invocation of Article 18 in each and every case where a restriction was imposed on a right because the authorities had erred. For tackling such situations, invocation of other Articles should suffice. In order to find a violation of Article 18, the authorities' bad faith should be proven. What is decisive for proving the bad faith is the ulterior (improper) nature of the motives behind the act.

The early ECtHR's case-law encompasses a couple of cases where Article 18 claims had no political dimension; but in the course of time, expectancy grew that the alleged ulterior motives are somehow related to politics or policy. In theory, invocation of Article 18 in an outside-of-politics context is not precluded. But so far the general tendency was that Article 18 case-law[4] developed in the direction of the most restrictive invocation of that Article. It has resulted in the

---

2   *Khodorkovskiy v. Russia* (no. 5829/04, 31 May 2011).
3   *Khodorkovskiy and Lebedev v. Russia* (no. 11082/06, 25 July 2013).
4   It should go without saying that not all relevant case-law can be dealt with here in detail. For a more detailed presentation of the relevant judgments and decisions see: *Guide on Article 18 of the European Convention on Human Rights* on the ECtHR webpage (https://www.echr.coe.int/ Documents/Guide_Art_18_ENG.pdf; visited on 15/12/2018). *Update-note after the submission of the article*: The case-law of the ECtHR cited in this article encompasses judgments and decisions adopted before 1 January 2019. Accordingly, a later case, in which a violation of Article 18 was found (in conjunction with Article 5), *Navalnyy v. Russia (no. 2)* (no. 43734/14, 9 April 2019) is not examined (that judgment is not final at the time of adding of this update-note).

scope of invocation of Article 18 being constricted to such an extent, that its significance has been unduly diminished.

In 2017, the ECtHR's Grand Chamber (GC) in its judgment in *Merabishvili v. Georgia*[5] attempted at clarifying its approach to Article 18 (which, as it was widely recognised, lacked consistency and coherence), *inter alia*, the relation between that Article and its counterparts, many of which permit certain restrictions on respective rights. It developed a new doctrine in which, however, one important point had not received enough spotlight: that Article 18 is, first and foremost, politics- or policy-related. It was not meant to be just "one more" Article: it reinforces the limits of restrictions permitted under other Articles (*ex abundante cautela*). At the same time it has its own *raison d'être*: to provide legal basis for the response to the political foul play, in particular the use of administrative and legal levers for politically motivated victimisation of individuals, and thus to protect democratic governance and the rule of law. Article 18 is called to provide security and certainty to individuals that authorities will not come after them, if they profess greater independence in their thoughts, expression or actions than that with which the reigning political class would be comfortable. Its significance thus should not be underestimated.

It follows from the wording of Article 18 ("restrictions permitted") that it can be invoked in conjunction with only those Articles, which enshrine a right, subject to restrictions permitted under the Convention, i.e. a qualified rather than absolute right.[6] In the ECtHR's case-law it is undisputed that Article 18 cannot be invoked with Articles 3 or 4, because the rights enshrined therein are not limitable. On the other hand, rights not necessarily have to be made limitable by explicit wording; the ECtHR has accepted yet in *Golder v. the United Kingdom*[7] that implied limitations are also present in the Convention. Still, it has been stipulated in one part of the ECtHR's recent case-law that the application of Article 18 is excluded in conjunction with Articles 6 and 7, because they allegedly do not contain any express or implied restrictions that may form the subject of examination under Article 18; some complaints under that conjunction were rejected.

Regrets have been expressed that the potential of Article 18 remains largely unused.[8] Article 18 case-law is scarce. This scarcity is not overly surprising. From the

---

5   *Merabishvili v. Georgia* ([GC], no. 72528/13, 28 November 2017).
6   Cf., e.g., *Timurtaş v. Turkey* (no. 23531/94, Report of the Commission, 29 October 1998). But some analysts argue that an application of Article 18 should be considered also with rights which are absolute under the Convention (see, e.g., Helmut Satzger, Frank Zimmerman, Martin Eibach. "Does Art. 18 ECHR Grant Protection against Politically Motivated Criminal Proceedings?" in 4(2) *European Criminal Law Review* (2014), 91–113; 4(3) *European Criminal Law Review* (2014), 248–264.
7   *Golder v. the United Kingdom* ([Plenary], no. 4451/70, 21 February 1975).
8   See, e.g., Helen Keller and Corina Heri, "Selective Criminal Proceedings and Article 18 of the European Convention on Human Rights' Untapped Potential to Protect Democracy", in 36 (2016) (1–6) *Human Rights Law Journal*, 1–10; Başak Çalı. *Merabishvili v. Georgia: Has the*

outset, Article 18 was not expected to be applied often. The drafters and the High Contracting Parties believed that such level of democratic maturity had been already achieved, where instances of political persecution could be but singular (though not unthinkable). Otherwise, supranational judicial review of the observance of the Convention would have not come into being. With the advent of polities whose liberal declarations and commitments (even if sincere) to part with inveterate authoritarian inclinations outpaced their actual advancement towards democratic consolidation, the use of power machinery against political opponents has become representative of some quarters of the expanded Council of Europe. At the same time, illiberal tilts have grown rife and bigoted intolerance has ploughed its way up to decision-making circles in some member States, which were believed (perhaps prematurely, if not altogether wantonly) to have had long ago developed sustainable democracies. Nowadays, politically motivated abuse of power is not (any longer) limited to isolated episodes. The creeping decomposition of sometime "progressive stability" and the augmenting numbers of those (not only opposition activists) whose well-being has been adversely affected by the degeneration of politics render Europe's reliance on its relative immunity to undemocratic tendencies short-sighted and call for an understanding approach to the plaints of victims.

The ECtHR has a role to play in countering undemocratic tendencies. Article 18 was meant to be a tool for that. Still, though the need of its application has grown visibly, its breaches were found only in a handful of cases. The ECtHR's approach to Article 18 complaints has been predominantly one of reluctance: they were routinely dismissed, the dismissal being accompanied by a parsimonious one- or-two-sentence incantation about the ECtHR not finding it necessary to examine them, thus spreading two regrettable messages: that the alleged political persecution merited no judicial inspection, and that the alleged victims did not deserve even an explanation.

After *Merabishvili*, the whole Article 18 case-law framework is undergoing change. Further I discuss the somewhat zigzagged evolution of that case-law. I focus not (so much) on the meritorious aspects of the resolved issues, but on the structural ones. Then I come to the landmark case of *Merabishvili*, which introduced important (even if ambiguous) doctrinal changes. I, however, do not purport to arrive at any categorical conclusions as to the future of Article 18 case-law – for the reasons which will become clear in due course.[9]

Mountain Given Birth to a Mouse? <https://verfassungsblog.de/merabishvili-v-georgia-has-the-mountain-given-birth-to-a-mouse/> (visited on 5/10/2018); Corina Heri. *Merabishvili, Mammadov and Targeted Criminal Proceedings: Recent Developments under Article 18 ECHR.* <https://strasbourgobservers.com/2017/12/15/merabishvili-mammadov-and-targeted-criminal-proceedings-recent-developments-under-article-18-echr/> (visited on 5/10/2018).

[9] This article is a story, a narrative. I did my best to be accurate in discussing the legal points, but I made use of the editors' advice not to overload the text with references. I thus do not indicate

I. THE FIRST STEPS

When reflecting on how to present a mazy, labyrinthine topic (which is in fact what Article 18 case-law is), I have not come across a sounder advice than this:

> "'Begin at the beginning,' the King said, very gravely, 'and go on till you come to the end: then stop.'"[10]

I shall try to follow this wisdom.

A. PRE-HISTORY

The following of the King's advice sends me back to the 1950s and 1960s – only to ascertain that there was nothing there on the issue, save few occasional mentions of Article 18 in the Commission's[11] reports. Article 18 was not invoked until the 1974 case of *Kamma v. The Netherlands.*[12] The applicant claimed that though his detention on remand for alleged extortion was allowed under Article 5 §1 (c), this time was also used to investigate murder; his right to liberty was thus limited for the purpose other than explicitly prescribed. Notably, this complaint contained not even a hint as to the political nature of the persecution. The Commission opined that the suspicion of murder would have been enough to detain the applicant on remand anyway. The use of the allegedly wrong procedure had thus not amounted to a restriction on his right to liberty being applied for a purpose other than those for which it had been prescribed (investigation of a crime). No breach of Article 18 was found in conjunction with Article 5.

In the 1970s, 1980s and 1990s the ECtHR examined several cases, in which Article 18 was directly or indirectly invoked, but found no violation of this Article (often dismissing the complaints summarily). In *Bozano v. France*[13] the applicant, sentenced *in absentia* in Italy, took refuge in France and was deported from there. The ECtHR found a breach of Article 5 §1 on account of the abuse of the deportation procedure, but deemed it unnecessary to examine the same issue under Article 18.

"Politicisation" of Article 18 complaints began with *Oates v. Poland.*[14] The applicant, an Australian national, alleged that he had been detained in Poland

---

throughout the text the concrete paragraphs of the judgments cited, and the references to the cases mentioned will appear in the footnotes only once, at the first mention (with few exceptions).

10 Lewis Carrol, *Alice's Adventures in Wonderland. Through the Looking Glass.* Harmondsworth: Puffin Books, 1976, p. 154.

11 European Commission of Human Rights, in place until the establishment of the permanent Court in 1998.

12 *Kamma v. The Netherlands* (no. 4771/71, Report of the Commission, 17 July 1974).

13 *Bozano v. France* (no. 9990/82, 18 December 1986).

14 *Oates v. Poland* (dec., no. 35036/97, 11 May 2000).

"for political reasons". The ECtHR held that the applicant had not submitted any *prima facie* evidence pointing towards the violation of Article 18 and found that that complaint (and also the one under Article 5 §1) was manifestly ill-founded.

In *Lukanov v. Bulgaria* the applicant was arrested and detained for taking part in collective governmental decisions in his capacity of Deputy Prime Minister. He claimed that his persecution was politically motivated. The Commission declared the application under Articles 5 §1 and 18 admissible[15], but, having examined the case on the merits and having found a breach of Article 5 §1, held that it was not necessary to examine the same issue under Article 18.[16] The ECtHR took the same stance, holding that no separate issue arose under Article 18.[17] In the same vein, in *United Communist Party of Turkey and Others v. Turkey*[18] the ECtHR held that it was unnecessary to determine whether there has been a violation of Article 18 in view that

> "the applicants [...] [i]n their memorial to the Court [...] accepted the Commission's conclusion that it was unnecessary to decide whether those provisions had been complied with in view of the finding of a violation of Article 11 [and] did not pursue those complaints in the proceedings before the Court, which sees no reason to consider them of its own motion".

In other cases Article 18 complaints were not rejected as inadmissible, but no breaches were found. In *Akdivar v. Turkey*[19] the applicants alleged that their homes were burnt and that they were forcibly and summarily expelled from their village by State security forces; that they were discriminated because of their Kurdish origin; and that their experiences represented an authorised practice by the State. The ECtHR found violations of Article 8 of the Convention and Article 1 of Protocol no. 1, but not of Articles 14 or 18. On this issue, the Court limited itself to merely stating that these complaints were examined by the Commission, which found that, "in the light of the evidence submitted to it, they were unsubstantiated". This announcement referred to the Commission's statement, which was not less minimalist and too frugal to be called "reasoning":

> "The Commission has examined the applicant's allegations in the light of the evidence submitted to it, but considers them unsubstantiated."[20]

---

15 *Lukanov v. Bulgaria* (dec., no. 21915/93, 12 January 1995).
16 *Lukanov v. Bulgaria* (no. 21915/93, Report of the Commission, 16 January 1996).
17 *Lukanov v. Bulgaria* (no. 21915/93, 20 March 1997). The applicant had not lived to that judgment, because the Court began deliberating on his case two months after he had been shot dead by perpetrators, unknown to this day.
18 *United Communist Party of Turkey and Others v. Turkey* ([GC], no. 19392/92, 30 January 1998).
19 *Akdivar and Others v. Turkey* ([GC], no. 21893/93, 16 September 1996).
20 *Akdivar and Others v. Turkey* (no. 21893/93, Report of the Commission, 26 October 1995).

B.   *GUSINSKIY* AND BEYOND

A violation of Article 18 (in conjunction with Article 5) was first found in *Gusinskiy v. Russia*.[21] The applicant, who was the head and the majority shareholder of a media company, had been arrested, but later released. During the detention, a Russian Minister had offered to drop the criminal charges against him if he would sell his company to State-controlled gas monopoly at a price to be determined by the latter. Upon signing the agreement the criminal proceedings were discontinued. The ECtHR held that the criminal proceedings and the detention on remand had been used as commercial bargaining strategies, which was not their purpose. The applicant's liberty thus had been restricted not only for the purpose of bringing him before the competent legal authority on reasonable suspicion of having committed an offence, but also for reasons alien to those permitted under Article 5 §1 (c).

Then followed *Cebotari v. Moldova*.[22] Criminal charges had been brought not only against the applicant, but also against the company, which was an applicant in another ECtHR case, *Oferta Plus S.R.L. v. Moldova*.[23] The criminal proceedings against the applicant had been discontinued, but they had been reopened, following the communication, by the ECtHR, of the company's complaints to the Government. As a result of the reopening, the applicant was arrested and remanded in custody. His *habeas corpus* requests were rejected. The ECtHR held that there had been no reasonable suspicion that the applicant had committed an offence and that in fact his arrest and detention aimed at nothing else than putting pressure on him with a view to hindering the company, *Oferta Plus*, from pursuing its application before the ECtHR. The applicant's arrest was visibly linked not to the allegedly illegal actions which he might have committed, but to the company's application pending before the ECtHR. The fact of pressure was established already in the company's case, *Oferta Plus S.R.L.*, in which a violation of, *inter alia*, Article 34 with regard to the company was found. The finding of a violation of Article 18 in *Cebotari* therefore was predetermined.

It took almost a half of a decade for the Court to find yet another violation of Article 18. This happened in *Lutsenko v. Ukraine*[24] and, a year later, in *Tymoshenko v. Ukraine*.[25] Whereas in *Cebotari* the political dimension was not so visible, in the two cases against Ukraine it was no less salient than in *Gusinskiy*. Both applicants were opposition politicians (Mr Lutsenko a former government minister, and Ms Tymoshenko a former Prime Minister and a

---

21   *Gusinskiy v. Russia* (no. 70276/01, 19 May 2004).
22   *Cebotari v. Moldova* (no. 35615/06, 13 November 2007).
23   *Oferta Plus S.R.L. v. Moldova* (no. 14385/04, 19 December 2006).
24   *Lutsenko v. Ukraine* (no. 6492/12, 7 March 2012).
25   *Tymoshenko v. Ukraine* (no. 49872/11, 30 April 2013).

leader of opposition). In neither of these cases the Court, quite cautiously, did explicitly accept the allegations that the whole criminal proceedings against the applicants had pursued political purposes; it focused instead on specific aspects of the proceedings. However, in both these cases the authorities' motives for the applicants' detention demonstrated an undisguised abuse of power and thus served as a direct proof of the "hidden agenda". In *Lutsenko* the investigator had requested to place the applicant in pre-trial detention on the ground that, by communicating with the media, the latter was trying to distort public opinion, discredit the prosecuting authorities and influence his upcoming trial. It was thus clearly demonstrated that the applicant's arrest was an attempt to punish him for publicly disagreeing with the charges against him, which alone showed that the detention had pursued a reason not envisaged by Article 5 §1 (c). In *Tymoshenko* the prosecution's request to place the applicant in pre-trial detention and the corresponding court order showed that the real purpose of her detention had been to punish her for disrespect towards the court and perceived obstructive conduct during hearings. Being handled this direct proof, the ECtHR could absolve itself from looking into the broader political context of the applicants' situation (although the applicants requested this). In the first of these cases, the Court found as many as six violations of various provisions of Article 5, and in the second three violations of that Article. In addition, in both cases a violation of Article 18 was found in conjunction with Article 5. However, the Court, by four votes to three, dismissed Ms Tymoshenko's allegations that with respect to her there has been also a violation of Article 3.

Altogether, by the end of 2018, breaches of Article 18 were found in twelve cases against six States: Azerbaijan (*Ilgar Mammadov v. Azerbaijan*[26]; *Rasul Jafarov v. Azerbaijan*[27]; *Mammadli v. Azerbaijan*[28]; *Rashad Hasanov and Others v. Azerbaijan*[29]; *Aliyev v. Azerbaijan*[30]); Georgia (*Merabishvili*); Moldova (*Cebotari*); Russia (*Gusinskiy; Navalnyy v. Russia*[31]); Turkey (*Selahattin Demirtaş v. Turkey (no. 2)*[32]); Ukraine (*Lutsenko; Tymoshenko*). The figure is modest, when

---

[26] *Ilgar Mammadov v. Azerbaijan* (no. 15172/13, 22 May 2014).
[27] *Rasul Jafarov v. Azerbaijan* (no. 69981/14, 17 March 2016).
[28] *Mammadli v. Azerbaijan* (no. 47145/14, 19 April 2018).
[29] *Rashad Hasanov and Others v. Azerbaijan* (nos. 48653/13, 52464/13, 65597/13 and 70019/13, 7 June 2018).
[30] *Aliyev v. Azerbaijan* (no. 71200/14, 20 September 2018); not (yet) final at the time of writing of this article. *Update-note after the submission of the article*: This judgment became final on 4 February 2019. The period of more than three months between the delivery of the judgment and its becoming final reveals that there had been a request for relinquishment of the case to the Grand Chamber, but it was not granted.
[31] *Navalnyy v. Russia* ([GC], nos. 29580/12, 36847/12, 11252/13, 12317/13 and 43746/14, 15 November 2018).
[32] *Selahattin Demirtaş v. Turkey (no. 2)* (no. 14305/17, 20 November 2018). At the time of writing of this article, the judgment was not (yet) final, and the Turkish authorities had made it clear that they were considering a request for the referral of the case to the GC. *Update-note after*

juxtaposed to 33 cases, in which the ECtHR found no violation of Article 18, or close to three hundred cases, in which an Article 18 issue was raised, but the complaints were rejected as not meriting examination and thus inadmissible[33] (in some of these cases breaches of conjoined Articles were found). Though seven of the above-mentioned cases, in which the ECtHR found violations of Article 18, were decided in 2012–2018, the overall low figure of the breaches found does not reflect today's reality of "political justice" in a number of countries in such its manifestations as seizures of property, arrests, prosecutions, detentions, trials, convictions, suppression of expression, assembly and movement, and ingenuine restrictions of civic action, all triggered by ulterior motives.

II. THE HIGHEST STANDARD

The above-provided low figure can be partly explained by the "very exacting standard of proof", which the ECtHR employed in Article 18 cases until *Merabishvili*.

A. THE BURDEN OF PROOF

The "very exacting standard of proof" took its roots in the presumption of good faith. In *Khodorkovskiy*[34] (no violation of Article 18), the Court stated that

> "any public policy or an individual measure may have a 'hidden agenda', and the presumption of good faith is rebuttable. However, an applicant alleging that his rights and freedoms were limited for an improper reason must convincingly show that the real aim of the authorities was not the same as that proclaimed (or as can be reasonably inferred from the context). A mere suspicion that the authorities used their powers for some other purpose than those defined in the Convention is not sufficient to prove that Article 18 was breached."

Onus probandi thus was on the applicant. In order to refute the presumption of good faith, he had to provide "incontrovertible and direct proof" to the contrary. This was an extremely heavy burden on him. The burden of proof might shift to the Government only regarding the Article conjoined with Article 18, but not Article 18 itself; the burden of proof regarding the latter

---

the submission of the article: They indeed requested the referral, and the request was granted. The case is pending before the GC (a hearing being scheduled for September 2019).

33   Excluding applications declared inadmissible under Article 27 by the "Court sitting in a single-judge formation", the number of which is unknown.

34   Note 2 *supra*.

rested with the applicant, even where a *prima facie* case of improper motive was established.

This methodology made a certain amount of sense – but it lacked sensibility. It was explainable and thus good "library law". But, after all, most people are not lawyers. They are concerned with the law as it affects them in real life. For them, this methodology hardly could seem fair, because it effectually determined that the party which alone benefited from the "incontrovertible and direct proof" requirement was the abusive authority, if it had been skilful enough to leave no traces of impropriety of its activities. It was unrealistic to believe that the applicants always were able to furnish the requisite evidence, in particular that which was in the exclusive possession of the adversary, while the applicants could be even not at liberty (quite often they were in detention). This discouraged potential applicants from raising Article 18 claims.

B.   NO RULE WITHOUT A RESERVATION?

The "incontrovertible and direct proof" doctrine contained an important reservation that the finding of a violation of Article 18 could be "reasonably inferred from the context", i.e. from contextual evidence. Even being so, this reservation was mentioned, as only if by the way, in but a few judgments. The practice of admission of contextual evidence was even scantier. In *Khodorkovskiy and Lebedev*[35] the ECtHR admitted that the assumption of good faith was rebuttable in theory, but difficult to overcome in practice. This statement, however, not eased, but reinforced the *onus* put on the applicant: the Court "was satisfied that such standard was met only in few cases" (three by that time, which was mid-2013).

The ECtHR's case-law is replete with instances where the applicants were unable to satisfy the Court's rigidity and thus to benefit from the above-mentioned reservation, rendering this reservation a mere theoretical tool, practically devoid of applicability. In *Khodorkovskiy* Article 18 complaint focused not on the specific purposes of the authorities' pressure (as in *Gusinskiy* or *Cebotari*), but on the assertion that the criminal proceedings against the applicant had been based solely on political motives and had aimed at his exclusion from Russia's social and political life. The ECtHR accepted that the applicant, a major shareholder of the *Yukos* oil company and one of the richest persons in Russia, had "political ambitions which admittedly went counter to the mainstream line of the administration" (he was supporting opposition parties); that he "could become a serious political player"; and that "it was a State-owned company

---

[35]   Note 3 *supra*.

which benefited most from the dismantlement of the applicant's industrial empire." Still, the ECtHR held that "any person in the applicant's position would be able to make similar allegations" and that "it would have been impossible to prosecute a suspect with the applicant's profile without far-reaching political consequences". In the Court's words, the "high political status does not grant immunity", consequently, the fact that the suspect's political opponents or business competitors might benefit from him being put in jail "should not prevent the authorities from prosecuting such a person if there are serious charges against him". The ECtHR was persuaded that the charges against the applicant amounted to a "reasonable suspicion" within the meaning of Article 5 §1 (c) and dismissed the prevailing opinion that the "applicant's prosecution was driven by the desire to remove him from the political scene and, at the same time, to appropriate his wealth", because "the judge must base his decision only on evidence in the legal sense". Having stated that, it instantly dismissed "the findings of several European courts in the proceedings involving former *Yukos* managers and *Yukos* assets" (which it called "probably the strongest argument in favour of the applicant's complaint under Article 18"), because "the evidence and legal arguments before those courts might have been different from those in the case under examination" and even "assuming, that all courts had the same evidence and arguments before them", the Strasbourg Court's "own standard of proof applied in Article 18 cases is very high and may be different from those applied domestically". Even if the "applicant's case may raise a certain suspicion as to the real intent of the authorities" (with far-reaching legal implications), this was not sufficient for concluding that

> "the whole legal machinery of the respondent State in the present case was *ab initio* misused, that from the beginning to the end the authorities were acting with bad faith and in blatant disregard of the Convention. This is a very serious claim which requires an incontrovertible and direct proof. Such proof [as in *Gusinskiy*] is absent from the case under examination."

It is the *Khodorkovskiy* judgment of 2011 in which the contextual evidence reservation was introduced. Despite that, in this very case the ECtHR dismissed all contextual evidence, including "the findings of several European courts" (no matter how strong), as allegedly not fitting its very high standard of proof.

C. OF APPEARANCES: NOT BELIEVING WHAT (EVERY)ONE SEES

Two years after *Khodorkovskiy*, in *Khodorkovskiy and Lebedev* (the case which involved the same applicant), the ECtHR stated that, where allegations of improper motives were made, it had to show particular diligence. Then it expounded:

> "Even where the appearances speak in favour of the applicant's claim of improper motives, the burden of proof must remain with him or her. [...] [T]he standard of proof in such cases is high. Otherwise the Court would have to find violations in every high-profile case where the applicant's status, wealth, reputation, etc. gives rise to a suspicion that the driving force behind his or her prosecution was improper."

This argument contains a logical error. "May" does not preordain "must". No bridge can be unconditionally spanned between a mere "suspicion" and the finding of a violation of Article 18 "in every [?!] high-profile case". What is more, is the ECtHR's negative approach to "appearances" as such. But there is a vast difference between speculative "appearances" based on the applicant's "status, wealth [or] reputation" and "appearances", which are facts known to every schoolboy. An outright rejection of admissibility of "appearances" as a reliable proof is at odds with the fact that often there are "appearances" available (sometimes measured in library stacks), which corroborate each other to such an extent that, on the balance of probabilities, they are as reliable as "incontrovertible and direct proof". No single "appearance" can in and of itself be as firm as a "direct" proof, but their combinations can – and often are.

But it appears that, for the Court, appearances did not matter at all, if the Government was able to provide a minimum of Convention-friendly substantiation of the restriction of a right. In *Handyside v. the United Kingdom*[36], the ECtHR admitted that there had been a political element in the decision to ban the distribution of the applicant's book, but it was not decisive, and that the "fundamental aim" of the applicant's conviction was the same as proclaimed by the authorities and "legitimate" under Article 10. In *Khodorkovskiy and Lebedev* the Court went further. It admitted, albeit in a roundabout way, that the applicants fell victims of political persecution, but conceded that there might have been some purposes (even if not predominant) for which the authorities might legitimately persecute them:

> "The Court is prepared to admit that some political groups or government officials had their own reasons to push for the applicants' prosecution. However, it is insufficient to conclude that the applicants would not have been convicted otherwise. Elements of 'improper motivation' which may exist in the present case do not make the applicants' prosecution illegitimate 'from the beginning to the end': the fact remains that the accusations against the applicants were serious, that the case against them had a 'healthy core', and that even if there was a mixed intent behind their prosecution, this did not grant them immunity from answering the accusations."

---

[36]   *Handyside v. the United Kingdom* (no. 5493/72, 7 December 1976).

The ECtHR then went to conclude:

"In sum, and in so far as the criminal proceedings at the heart of the present case are concerned, the Court cannot find that Article 18 was breached."

By holding on to its own standard of proof in Article 18 cases which "is very high and may be different from those applied domestically", the ECtHR in fact made that standard the highest possible. Still, it was not completely impossible to meet. In *Gusinskiy, Cebotari, Lutsenko* or *Tymoshenko* "incontrovertible and direct proof" was available. Be that as it may, the methodology employed in setting the "height" of that standard makes eyebrows raise. The ECtHR aligned its standard to instances where the authorities have left irrefragable traces of their "real aim" which was not only "not the same as that proclaimed", but also Convention-unfriendly. To compare, in criminal investigation the requirement that only such proof can be admitted in order for the crime to be uncovered would amount to requiring that only those burglaries are considered to be proven, where the perpetrator had left his fingerprints all over the strongbox, doors and other items, including, the crowbar obligingly abandoned at the crime scene, as well as his ID and cell phone; other proof does not reach the yardstick, so these crimes are written off. A typical perpetrator, however, attempts not to leave traces but to hide them. Hardly a typical authority, which politically persecutes its adversary, should do otherwise.

The ECtHR, by stating that its own standard "may be different from those applied domestically" (an incontestable truth), rejected such analogies as a matter of principle. This raises other questions. Does the fact that the Strasbourg Court's standard may differ from "those applied domestically" is a guideline that they must differ? And is the highest standard necessarily the most appropriate for the ECtHR? After all, the ECtHR is a human rights court, but it was inclined to apply this standard to the proof presented by those claiming that their rights had been violated, and not to the respondent Governments, who enjoyed every benefit of doubt. Given the ratio of findings and not-findings of breaches of Article 18, it is obvious (with hindsight) that some abusers eluded responsibility in a number of cases of prominent victims of "political justice", where the ECtHR was respondent-friendly.

The inordinate rigidity of the ECtHR's standard of proof has been a target of pointed criticism in the Judges' separate opinions in a number of cases. For instance, in *Tymoshenko* Judges Karel Jungwiert, Angelika Nußberger and André Potocki contended that although

"the Court rightly applies a very exacting standard of proof [...] [t]his requirement must not [...] be such as to render it impossible for the applicant to prove a violation of Article 18.
[...]

[…] [T]he wording of Article 18 contains the word 'purpose', which necessarily refers to a subjective intention which can be revealed only by the person or persons holding it, unless it is – accidentally – documented in some way … Generally, knowledge about what the Court calls a 'hidden agenda' is within the sphere of the authorities and is thus not accessible to an applicant. It is therefore necessary to accept evidence of the authorities' improper motives which relies on inferences drawn from the concrete circumstances and the context of the case. Otherwise the protection granted by Article 18 would be ineffective in practice."[37]

D. MISSION POSSIBLE? THE CAMEL GOES THROUGH THE EYE OF A NEEDLE

There was no sign of trusting contextual evidence in Article 18 case-law until mid-2014, when the ground-breaking judgment in *Ilgar Mammadov* legitimised it as the proof allowing for the establishment of facts "to a sufficient degree".

In that case the applicant was remanded in custody for suggesting, in his blog post, that the official version of riots in one of the Azerbaijani towns may have been untrue and attempted at a cover-up. He was accused in the official press statement by the Prosecutor General's Office and the Ministry of Interior, issued a day after the post, of having illegally aimed at inflammation of the situation. It was not rebutted by the Government that there had existed no information or evidence giving rise to a "reasonable" suspicion that the applicant had committed any of the criminal offences he was charged with. Accordingly, a breach of Article 5 was found. It also was not rebutted that the applicant's arrest had been linked to his specific blog entries (although the prosecution had not made any references to them), which shed light on the "true causes" of the protests, which the Government had reportedly attempted to withhold from the public and which had been picked up by the press. The actual purpose of the applicant's remand thus had been to silence or punish him for criticising the Government and attempting to disseminate what he believed to be the true information the Government were trying to hide. His liberty thus was restricted for ulterior purposes. A violation of Article 18 taken together with Article 5 was found. The ECtHR, having stated that it had to base its decision on "evidence in the legal sense" and its own assessment of the specific relevant facts, for the first time in an Article 18 case based its judgment not on some not-possible-to-obtain "direct" evidence of improper motives of the applicant's persecution, but on the proof that "followed from the combination of the relevant case-specific facts".

---

[37] See also concurring opinion of Judges András Sajó, Nona Tsotsoria and Paulo Pinto de Albuquerque (as well as one of mine) in *Tchankotadze v. Georgia* (no. 15259/02, 21 June 2016), urging the ECtHR to reconsider its standard of proof in Article 18 cases.

This approach was crystallised two years later in *Rasul Jafarov v. Azerbaijan*, where the ECtHR stated:

> "[D]epending on the circumstances of the case, improper reasons cannot always be proven by pointing to a particularly inculpatory piece of evidence which clearly reveals an actual reason [...] or a specific isolated incident. In this case [...] it can be established to a sufficient degree that proof of improper reasons follows the combination of relevant case-specific facts."

This looks like the bringing of the "highest standard" of proof down to earth, closer to the reality of life, and bridging the gap between the legal reasoning and the common sense. This issue was profoundly addressed in *Merabishvili*. But let us first look at the cases in which the ECtHR avoided the examination of Article 18 complaints. So far they constitute the bulk of Article 18 case-law.

III. PATTERNS OF AVOIDANCE

Through the years, the ECtHR's practice of dismissal of Article 18 complaints has become increasingly divergent. The Court has manufactured at least five methodologies of not upholding Article 18 complaints, or structural patterns of avoidance of going into their examination. After *Merabishvili*, some of them should not survive. Yet some do revive.

A. A MERE ESCORT, NOT KIPLING'S CAT

The first pattern is structurally not problematic. Having found no violation of the conjoined Article, the ECtHR also finds no breach of Article 18. This was so in *Handyside v. the United Kingdom* or *Gündem v. Turkey*.[38] Usually, in such cases the ECtHR briefly states that Article 18 complaints need not to be examined. In *Handyside* the formal declaration of no violation of Article 18 (in the operative part of the judgment) was preceded by a one-sentence "reasoning" that the complaint under Article 18 together with two other Articles "did not support examination since the Court ha[d] already concluded that the said restrictions concerned aims that were legitimate under these two last-mentioned Articles" (i.e. Article 10 and Article 1 of Protocol no. 1). In *Engel and Others v. The Netherlands*[39] the Court found Article 6 to be inapplicable in its criminal

---

[38]   *Gündem v. Turkey* (no. 22275/93, 25 May 1998).
[39]   *Engel and Others v. The Netherlands* ([Plenary], nos. 5100/71, 5101/71, 5102/71, 5354/72 and 5370/72, 6 June 1976).

limb and no violation of that Article in its civil limb with regard to two of the applicants, which enabled it to state that

> "[t]he [...] conclusions on the applicability and observance of Article 6 [...] in the case of [the] two applicants [...] [made] it unnecessary for it to rule on [the] complaint [under Article 18 together with Article 6] "[40]

Such brevity does not demonstrate a contempt of the applicants: as Article 18 is a mere escort to the conjoined Article, and not Kipling's cat that "walks by himself", a longer explanation of why no separate examination of the complaints under it had to be undertaken would have no added value.

B.   NO ULTERIOR MOTIVES BEHIND THE VIOLATION

The second pattern is where the finding of a breach of the Article with which Article 18 is conjoined does not suffice for finding a breach of Article 18. In *Akdivar and Others* violations of two conjoined Articles were found, but not that of Article 18. This pattern was employed in a series of cases against Russia, including *Khodorkovskiy, OAO Neftyanaya Kompaniya Yukos v. Russia*[41], and *Khodorkovskiy and Lebedev*, and Turkey, including *Tahsin Acar v. Turkey*[42] (the last GC Article 18 case before *Merabishvili*). The allegations under Article 18 in relation to the conjoined Articles were dealt with extremely succinctly and then dismissed. The ECtHR used different wording to substantiate the dismissal. In *Lukanov* it was satisfied that no breach of Article 18 had been established by the Commission and agreed with them.[43] In *İpek v. Turkey*[44] it merely stated that "no violation [of Article 18 could] be established on the basis of the evidence before [the ECtHR]". Eventually a template took shape: "[t]he Court [...] has already examined this allegation in the light of the evidence submitted to it, and found that it was unsubstantiated", accordingly, "no violation of [the] provision [of Article 18] has been established".[45] In *Khodorkovskiy, OAO Neftyanaya Kompaniya Yukos*, and *Khodorkovskiy and Lebedev* the reasoning is a bit more extensive and the concluding formula more cautious: the Court "is satisfied" that it "cannot find that Article 18 was breached". Such formula fits better where the applicants are too well-known as victims of political persecution to be arrogantly repulsed for the failure to present "incontrovertible and direct proof", although the contextual evidence is

---

[40]   The ECtHR examined complaints under Article 6 in conjunction with Article 14, but found no breach.

[41]   *OAO Neftyanaya Kompaniya Yukos v. Russia* (no. 149, 2/95, 20 September 2011).

[42]   *Tahsin Acar v. Turkey* ([GC], no. 26327/05, 8 April 2004).

[43]   Also see, e.g., *Selçuk and Asker v. Turkey* (no. 23184/94, 24 April 1998).

[44]   *İpek v. Turkey* (no. 25760/94, 17 February 2004).

[45]   E.g. *Tepe v. Turkey* (no. 27244/95, 9 May 2003).

abundant. This, however, is not always the case. In *Kasparov and Others v. Russia*[46] the ECtHR, having found breaches of Articles 6 and 11, dismissed the applicants' complaints under Article 18 in conjunction with Article 7 as "manifestly ill-founded", i.e. "not disclos[ing] any appearance of a violation of the rights and freedoms set out in the Convention or its Protocols" (presumably the *prima facie* evidence presented did not meet the Court's high standard of proof).

One may disagree (as I do) with the merits of some of the judgments falling under this pattern, but the latter is coherent from a structural perspective. Even if the "very exacting standard of proof" was too demanding on the applicants, it was namely that standard which had to be met: if the required proof was not presented, "blame the messenger", which, alas, was the applicant himself.

C. UNDESERVING COMPLAINTS

The third pattern includes the cases where violations of the conjoined Article are found, but Article 18 complaint is not examined at all. The ECtHR simply declares that it is "not necessary" to examine it. That's it. The Court has accumulated a rich practice of "no necessity" pronouncements. Why a separate examination of Article 18 complaints is held to be not necessary, however, remains unknown to the outside world (unless a stingy hint is dropped).

For instance, in *Nemtsov v. Russia*[47] the ECtHR found breaches of Articles 3, 5 §1, 6 §1, 11 and 13 in conjunction with Article 3, but refused to enter into the examination of the alleged breach of Article 18. Still and all, the refusal itself was less perplexing than its "reasoning":

"[The Court] has found above that the applicant had been arrested, detained and convicted of an administrative offence arbitrarily and unlawfully and that this had had an effect of preventing or discouraging [the applicant] and others from participating in protest rallies and engaging actively in opposition politics [...]."

And then:

"Having regard to those findings, the Court considers that the complaint under Article 18 of the Convention raises no separate issue and it is not necessary to examine whether, in this case, there has been a violation of that provision."

The readership is left in bewilderment as to what standards of logic or justice this simulacrum of reasoning purported to satisfy. From a structural perspective,

---

46 *Kasparov and Others v. Russia* (no. 21613/07, 3 October 2013).
47 *Nemtsov v. Russia* (no. 1774/11, 31 July 2014).

once a violation of the conjoining Article is found, the complaints under Article 18, which does not enshrine any substantive right, necessarily raise a separate issue, because they cannot be subsumed by the complaints under other Articles. Of course, it happens that Article 18 complaints are wholly unsubstantiated and therefore can be legitimately dismissed by employing some laconic formula (as in *Oates*). But the finding of a violation of, say, Article 5 or 6, or 11, or 13 – all the more so of all of them, and all the more so if the violations had been arbitrary – is in and of itself a deadly imperative for the Court to examine the complaints under Article 18 and to look into whether there has been no violation of Article 18. This imperative is self-evident where the victim of the authorities' arbitrariness is a political opposition activist.

In *Nemtsov*, the "no separate issue" formula is preceded with the statement that the applicant's arrest, detention and conviction were arbitrary and unlawful. As numerous arbitrary breaches of the Convention rights were established, Article 18 complaint perforce demanded no less than judicial scrutiny allowing for a formal finding. Truth to say, that finding was obvious to any reasonable person. Arrests, detentions, convictions – they all are acts of the authorities. When authorities act arbitrarily, all the more so when they are consequential in their arbitrariness, they implement a policy. They have an agenda. They have motives and purposes. Article 18 is all about the authorities' "purposes" and "motives" and "agenda". The agenda of the authorities merited being looked into, so it could be ascertained whether it had not been a "hidden agenda", and being named what it was – bad faith. No other court, except the ECtHR, could do this in a legally authoritative form. It, however, declined to name the extent and the nature of the authorities' abuse. The gist of the case was thus leached out, and the examination of its merits resulted in a semi-manufacture. It is unimaginable that the Court cut off the examination of the applicant's complaints at a stage where it did not know yet, what would have been its finding under Article 18, had it dared to duly address the issue, because it itself explicitly affirmed that the applicant's arbitrary (that is to say, not incidental, but discretionary, wilful, capricious) and unlawful arrest, detention and conviction (that is to say, not an isolated act, but the whole set of masterful decisions) "had the effect of preventing and discouraging him and others from participating in protest rallies and engaging actively in opposition politics". The arbitrariness of the applicant's arrest, detention and conviction effectively glued these actions together into one chain of systematic political persecution, which resulted not so much in ("had the effect of") preventing and discouraging the applicant and the "others" from opposition politics (regarding the applicant, it did not, as he continued to be active in opposition politics), but first and foremost was deliberately aimed at that prevention and discouragement. The authorities had suppressed the democratic rights of their political opponent. They acted in bad faith. The real purpose of their actions thus ran against the very heart of democracy and the rule of law, which Article 18 was meant to protect. Alas, the ECtHR lacked the will to decree this. In such cases the "no separate issue" formula amounts to no less than the *laissez-faire* to the authorities' arbitrariness.

The *Nemtsov* template migrated almost verbatim to *Navalnyy and Yashin v. Russia*[48] and *Frumkin v. Russia*.[49] In yet another case, *Kasparov v. Russia*[50], which involved another well-known political activist, the ECtHR found the violations of Articles 5 §1 and 11, but again held that it was "not necessary" to examine the complaint under Article 18 (together with Article 7) in the "light" of its own finding that the "applicant had been arrested and detained arbitrarily and unlawfully and that this prevented him from participating in an opposition rally". The word "light" used in this context denotes blackness.

Article 45 requires that reasons be "given for judgments, as well as for decisions declaring applications admissible or inadmissible". The judgments of the *Nemtsov* type overtly circumvent this requirement. They neither declare Article 18 applications admissible, nor inadmissible – only undeserving of examination. Still, there are reasons behind any decision, and even such holding should be reasoned. This is the standard which the ECtHR applies to the judgments of domestic courts: not providing reasons for a judicial decision amounts to a denial of justice.[51] Reasons not disclosed are reasons concealed. By concealing the reasons behind its own decisions the Court, alas, opens itself to criticism that in refusing to examine "hidden agenda" allegations it itself is guided by some agenda which it does not disclose.

Judge Helen Keller observed in her dissenting opinion in *Kasparov* that in the past the ECtHR had held that "in view of the scarcity of the case-law under that Convention provision, in each new case where allegations of improper motives are made the Court must show particular diligence", but "[t]hat diligence [was] missing here", thus "fail[ing] to do justice to the victims of targeted criminal proceedings" and "reinforc[ing] the relegation of Article 18 to an insignificant role in which it is not being used for its intended purpose".

---

48   *Navalnyy and Yashin v. Russia* (no. 76204/11, 4 December 2014).
49   *Frumkin v. Russia* (no. 74568/12, 5 January 2016).
50   *Kasparov v. Russia* (no. 53659/07, 11 October 2016).
51   In a recent GC case, the Court, having recapitulated its case-law pertaining to the reasoning of court judgments, generalised that "a domestic judicial decision cannot be described as arbitrary to the point of prejudicing the fairness of proceedings unless no reasons are provided for it or the reasons given are based on a manifest factual or legal error committed by the domestic court, resulting in a 'denial of justice'. See *Moreira Ferreira v. Portugal (no. 2)* ([GC], no. 19867/12, §85, 11 July 2017); see also *Tibet Menteş and Others v. Turkey* (nos. 57818/10, 57822/10, 57825/10, 57827/10 and 57829/10, 24 October 2017).

To no avail. The same pattern was followed in yet another case involving the same applicant, *Kasparov and Others v. Russia* (no. 2).[52] In this case, violations of Articles 5 §1, 6 §1 and 11 were found, but Article 18 complaints were left unexamined. The reasoning which was meant to substantiate the lack of necessity of examination was even more jaw-dropping than in *Nemtsov* (as it did not employ even the camouflaging "no separate issue" formula). It consisted of few sentences, laid out in the following sequence:

(1) "The applicants complained that their arrest and detention on administrative charges had pursued the aim of undermining their rights to freedom of assembly and freedom of expression, and had been for political revenge. They complained of a violation of Article 18 [...]."

(2) "[T]his complaint is linked to the complaints examined above under Articles 5 and 11 of the Convention and must therefore likewise be declared admissible."

(3) "The Court has found above that the applicants' arrest and administrative detention had the effect of preventing and discouraging them and others from participating in protest rallies and actively engaging in opposition politics [...] and has found a violation of Articles 5 and 11 [...]."

(4) "In view of this, the Court considers that it is not necessary to examine whether, in the present case, there has been a violation of Article 18 [...]."

And the resolution:

"[T]here is no need to examine the complaint under Article 18 [...]."

This reasoning amounted to nothing less than the avoidance *par excellence* of the examination of politically motivated abuse, because by all imaginable standards of logic and goodwill the fourth thesis had to contain not the words "not necessary", but "absolutely necessary". *Kasparov and Others (no. 2)* is even more striking, as it is in stark contrast with an earlier case, which involved the same applicant, *Kasparov and Others* (discussed above in the context of the second pattern: violations of Articles 6 and 11). In that case, the applicant's (and his co-applicants') complaints under Article 18 in conjunction with Article 7 were rejected, because the ECtHR ostensibly was not presented with requisite *prima facie* evidence meeting its threshold. As the judgment in *Kasparov and Others (no. 2)* does not contain a standard reproach that the respective complaints "do not disclose any appearance of a violation", one can assume that in that case such evidence was presented. Still, it appeared to be "not necessary". Ifs and buts, salvos or whims are more difficult to satisfy than even the highest standards of proof.

---

[52] *Kasparov and Others v. Russia (no. 2)* (no. 51988/07, 13 December 2016). The applicants waited nine years for their case to be decided, which alone should have induced requisite diligence on the ECtHR's part.

D. CRIPPLING OF ARTICLE 18

Under the fourth pattern of avoidance, Article 18 complaints are found to be incompatible *ratione materiae* with the provisions of the Convention. In *Navalnyy and Ofitserov v. Russia*[53], having found a breach of Article 6 §1, the ECtHR rejected the related Article 18 complaint as incompatible *ratione materiae* with the provisions of the Convention, because

> "the provisions of [...] Articles [6 and 7], in so far as relevant to the present case, do not contain any express or implied restrictions that may form the subject of the Court's examination under Article 18 of the Convention."

This was by far the biggest novelty in narrowing the scope of invocation of Article 18 and reducing its potential (and arguably one of the biggest confusions in the ECtHR's case-law). As mentioned, Article 18 can be invoked in conjunction with only those Articles, which enshrine a qualified but not absolute right, such as Articles 3 or 4. The impossibility of the conjunction of Article 18 with Articles 3 and 4 stems from the text of the Convention, *travaux préparatoires* and logic. The inhibition of its conjunction with Articles 6 and 7 stems from one single judgment, *Navalnyy and Ofitserov*, adopted by four votes to three. Until then such conjunction was a matter of routine. In *Kasparov and Others* the complaints under Article 18 in conjunction with Article 7 were rejected not on *ratione materiae* grounds, but as "manifestly ill-founded" (whatever the dubious merits of that rejection), which means that they could have been examined on the merits, had they met the ECtHR's threshold (unless the Court decided that that was "not necessary"). In *Khodorkovskiy and Lebedev* the ECtHR examined the alleged violation of Article 18 together with, *inter alia*, Articles 6 and 7, but found no breach.

Navalnyy and Ofitserov thus ran counter to the established case-law. It brushed aside *Engel and Others*. It cold-shouldered *Golder* where it was explicitly stated that the "right of access to the courts is not absolute". It disregarded the recent *Nemtsov* judgment where the ECtHR explicated that

> "[the] complaint [under Article 18 in conjunction with, inter alia, Article 6] is linked to the complaints examined above under Articles 5, 6, and 11 [...] and must therefore likewise be declared admissible."

Leaving aside the flimsiness of non-examination, in *Nemtsov*, of Article 18 complaint as ostensibly raising no separate issue, it is baffling how the elements, habitually perceived as interlinked, virtually overnight could have become unconjoinable. And yet they did. The complaints that earlier could be left unexamined, if the Court saw

---

53   *Navalnyy and Ofitserov v. Russia* (nos. 46632/13 and 28671/14, 23 February 2016).

no necessity in their examination, now – as if by a whisk of a wand – have become impossible to examine. The wonder-monger pulled a rabbit out of the hat and introduced it to the audience as "Article 18 in its new scope of applicability". Few were excited, as the rabbit appeared to be a genetically engineered cripple.

Navalnyy and Ofitserov extraordinarily badly sat in the already existing helter-skelter of Article 18 case-law. Three dissenting Judges, George Nicolau, Helen Keller and Dmitry Dedov, observed that the limiting of scope of application of Article 18 was done "without necessity or justification"; moreover, the right enshrined in Article 6 was not absolute and undeniably permitted limitations. They underlined that the relevance of Article 18 was particularly significant in the context of the first applicant's complaints, as he had an arguable claim to the effect that the criminal proceedings against him (which were unfair and thus in violation of Article 6 §1) contained an abusive element.

For some time it was not clear whether the *Navalnyy and Ofitserov* novelty was a one-off restriction (which the obscure formula "in so far as relevant to the present case" might imply), or a precedent to be followed. Quite soon it was used as a precedent in *Navalnyye v. Russia*[54], decided by partly the same judicial formation.

The Chamber of a different Section, however, took a more cautious approach in *Ilgar Mammadov v. Azerbaijan (no. 2)*.[55] It noted that the applicant did not specify with which other complaint(s) he intended to link his Article 18 complaint; but given that the complaint under Article 6 was the "main [one] in the present case", Article 18 was invoked presumably in conjunction with Article 6. The ECtHR then recalled both *Navalnyy and Ofitserov* and some competing precedents. Having given some prominence to the fact that the complaint under Article 18 was rejected in *Navalnyy and Ofitserov* "in the circumstances relevant to that case", it held that the question whether Article 6 contained any express or implied restrictions relevant for the examination under Article 18 "remain[ed] open". Having had regard to its findings under Article 6 §1 (violation), it opted for a *Nemtsov*-type resolution that "there [was] no need to give a separate ruling on the complaint under Article 18 in the present case". Four judges (Angelika Nußberger, Nona Tsotsoria, Síofra O'Leary and Mārtiņš Mits) in their joint concurring opinion related the case under consideration with *Ilgar Mammadov*, an earlier case of 2014, which involved the same applicant and where a violation of Article 18 in conjunction with Article 5 was found. They asked:

> "If pre-trial detention is found to be abusive as it has been used for another purpose than the one for which it has been allowed by the Convention – how then can the trial

---

54   *Navalnyye v. Russia* (no. 101/15, 17 October 2017).
55   *Ilgar Mammadov v. Azerbaijan (no. 2)* (no. 919/15, 16 November 2017).

concerning the same criminal proceedings involving the same charges stemming from the same events be regarded differently? How can it be seen just as a violation of Article 6 of the Convention and not also as an abuse of power?"

The co-authors constituted a majority which, if they opted to, could have decided on the admissibility of Article 18 complaints in defiance of *Navalnyy and Ofitserov*, bringing about an even greater inconsistency of Article 18 case-law. *Ilgar Mammadov (no. 2)* was a compromise: the four supported the *Nemtsov*-type resolution, while the fundamental question was left "open". Frankly, it was not even close to being "open" before the *Navalnyy and Ofitserov* upturn. The co-authors urged that the "applicability of Article 6 in conjunction with Article 18 [...] [had] to be clarified in the near future". This could be read as a hint to the then forthcoming GC judgment in *Merabishvili*, already adopted, but not yet delivered at the time of examination of *Ilgar Mammadov (no. 2)* (three of the judges in *Ilgar Mammadov (no. 2)* were in the composition in *Merabishvili*, and two of them co-authored the opinion cited above).

E. THE TRIUMPH OF THE HIGHEST STANDARD

To join the fray, the fifth pattern of avoidance was invented. It took its roots in *Kasparov and Others* (second pattern), but was consolidated in *Tchankotadze*.[56] The applicant claimed that the initiation of criminal proceedings against him and the imposition of pre-trial detention had been a direct outcome of a clear, specific public threat to "jail" him by Mr Mikheil Saakashvili, then a presidential candidate and later elected, during the latter's election campaign; as soon as Mr Saakashvili had been elected President, the threat materialised. The ECtHR found violations of Articles 5 §1 and 6 §1. As to the complaint under Article 18 (in conjunction with Article 5), it relied on its position of principle on the presumption of good faith and the "very exacting standard of proof", and rejected this complaint as manifestly ill-founded. It held that

> "by limiting the evidence to substantiate his joined complaint under Articles 5 and 18 of the Convention to the reference to the threat against him by the then candidate for the Presidency of the country, the applicant failed to discharge the requisite burden of proof. It cannot therefore be said that a *prima facie* case has been established that there were improper motives behind the applicant's criminal prosecution and detention [...]."

Despite some similarity, *Tchakontadze* differs from *Kasparov and Others* in one essential respect. In *Kasparov and Others* the ECtHR resorted to mere

---

56   Note 37 *supra*.

statement that it examined the Article 18 complaint and found no "appearance" of a violation, whereas in *Tchankotadze* it indeed examined that complaint (in conjunction with Article 5): the reasoning is proof-oriented and lengthy, not a template-based mantra.

F. FIVE IS NOT THE LIMIT

There are no clear watersheds between the five patterns presented above; they both overlap and contradict each other. This is too rich a plurality. In fact, the diversity is greater. There are judgments which do not fall neatly into any of them. In *Sisojeva v. Latvia*[57] the request to find a breach of Article 18 was rejected because it came not from the applicant, but from the third party intervener, the Russian Government. In *Denisov v. Ukraine*[58] Article 18 complaint was rejected as lodged outside the six-month time-limit. And so on.

The law of the Convention is constantly evolving. Still, it should not evolve in all possible directions. A new GC judgment where the growing, both in volume and diversity, Article 18 case-law could be clarified, was much expected. After all, there still was no leading judgment on the matter. Now there is one, *Merabishvili*.[59] As the earlier Article 18 case-law, it also displays consistency in inconsistency.

IV. ADDRESSING (OR NOT) THE CASE-LAW'S HANDICAPS

The GC judgment in *Merabishvili* was delivered on 28 November 2017, less than two weeks after *Ilgar Mammadov (no. 2)*, which declared that the question of conjunction of Article 18 with Article 6 (and, by extension, several others, including Article 7) was "open". If there was a hope that *Merabishvili* might shed some light on this obscurity, this hope was set aside for the future, as *Merabishvili* did not address that issue. But, besides that, there were other issues in need of clarification, most notably the concept of ulterior purpose and the standard of proof for Article 18 purposes. I shall deal with these three issues consecutively.

---

[57] *Sisojeva v. Latvia* ([GC], no. 60654/00, 15 January 2007).

[58] *Denisov v. Ukraine* ([GC], no. 76639/11, 25 September 2018).

[59] Note 5 *supra*. For an insightful analysis of that judgment see Floris Tan, "The Dawn of Article 18: A Safeguard against European Rule of Law Backsliding?", in 9 (2018) 1, *Goettingen Journal of International Law*, 109-141.

A. A TELLING SILENCE

Merabishvili concerned the former Prime Minister of Georgia, against whom criminal proceedings were opened. He argued that his pre-trial detention aimed at removing him from political life. The Chief Prosecutor at night covertly removed him from his cell, questioned him and threatened him with a worsening of his situation if he did not provide information about proceedings not related to his case (on the foreign bank accounts of the former President Mikheil Saakashvili and the death of the former Prime Minister Zurab Zhvania). The applicant was convicted. The GC, by nine votes against eight, found that there had been a violation of Article 18 in conjunction with Article 5 §1. There was less disagreement on the reasoning leading to this finding. The GC's minority endorsed it, while four majority Judges (Ganna Yudkivska, Nona Tsotsoria and Faris Vehabović; and Georgios A. Serghides) in their concurring opinions disagreed with one important part of it which, paradoxically, substantiated the finding with which they agreed.

The judgment is moderately self-critical. It largely admits inconsistencies and even contradictions in Article 18 case-law and attempts at reassessing it. Parts of *Merabishvili* can be read as the Court's tacit concession that justice was denied in some previous cases. Those judgments most likely will never be reviewed, but the applicants can have moral satisfaction that they were right in raising their issues, which were dismissed, as is now obvious, without due justification.[60]

The judgment contains an overview of Article 18 case-law, which is divided into periods prior to and after *Gusinskiy*. It aims at setting guidance for the future Article 18 cases. It endeavours to provide a general concept of ulterior purposes (not using the term "hidden agenda") and guidelines for deciding which Article 18 complaints should fall under the ECtHR's examination and under what conditions breaches of this Article (in conjunction with another Article) are to be found.

The basics have not changed in essence. As before, Article 18 is perceived as having no "independent existence" and being applicable only in conjunction with another Article, which sets out or qualifies the rights under the Convention. Its wording complements that of the restriction-warranting Articles. At the same time, it is "autonomous", as it expressly prohibits the States from restricting the rights guaranteed by the Convention for the purposes not prescribed by it. A breach of Article 18 therefore may be found, even if there was no breach of the Article, in conjunction with which it is applied.[61]

---

[60] Mr Nemtsov, unfortunately, cannot. He was killed not long after the delivery of the ECtHR judgment in his case; the reasons for this killing remain murky.

[61] The finding of a breach of Article 18 alone, however, seems to be only a theoretical possibility, because "the case law always analyses [the] application [of Article 18] separately and after first examining the substantive right at stake and whether the Court finds the right has been

The judgment passes around in silence the issue of the possibility for Article 18 to be conjoined with Article 6 (or Article 7), effectively suppressing any allusion to even the very existence of the problem (there is not a single reference to *Navalnyy and Ofitserov*). Although that issue was in no direct relation to Mr Merabishvili's situation, the omission is regrettable (especially given the fact that the judgment contains other dicta). The issue seems to have been intentionally left obscure. Still, some resemblance of a clarification can be deducted from distantly related doctrinal provisions read together. For instance, the combination of the thesis that Article 18 is "no[t] independent" in that sense that its wording complements that of the restriction-warranting clauses and the thesis that it is "autonomous" to that extent that it "does not [...] serve merely to clarify the scope of those restriction clauses", but "expressly prohibits the [restriction of] the rights [...] for purposes not prescribed by the Convention itself", may be read, even if inconclusively, as an indirect and tacit rehabilitation of Articles 6 and 7 as potential "partners" of Article 18. More importantly, the GC stated that the rule that Article 18

> "can only be applied in conjunction with an Article [...] which sets out or qualifies the rights and freedoms [...] derives both from its wording, which complements that of clauses such as, for example, the second sentence of Article 5 §1 and the second paragraphs of Articles 8 to 11, which permit restrictions to those rights and freedoms, and from its place in the Convention at the end of Section I, which contains the Articles that define and qualify those rights and freedoms."

On the surface, this may look like commonplace litany. It is not that trite though. The omission of Articles 6 and 7 in the listing of the restriction-warranting Articles (as well as the use of the word "clauses") betrays the GC's reluctance to directly address the issue of Articles 6 and 7 and thus unavoidably, even if not explicitly, to admit that *Navalnyy and Ofitserov* was a gaffe, if not something worse. But diction is a two-timing helper. Even the most careful precaution may not prevent unwanted guests ousted through the door from intruding through the chimney. The choice of words in the above-cited fragment unearths what the GC wanted to elide. The listing of the restriction-warranting Articles is preceded by the caveat "for example". This implies that Section I of the Convention contains also other Articles that allow for restrictions of rights. But that Section (not the Protocols, which are subsequent to the Convention) contains no other explicit restriction-warranting clauses. Accordingly, the "remaining"

---

breached or not, it does not reiterate its reasoning from the perspective of art. 18 because it has already been done in the test of proportionality of the material limits applied internally to the right itself" (Pablo Santolaya, "Limiting Restrictions on Rights. Art. 18 ECHR (A Generic Limit on Limits according to Purpose)", in Javier Garcia Roca, Pablo Santolaya (2012), *Europe of Rights: A Compendium on the European Convention of Human Rights*, 535–536).

warrantings of restrictions are implicit.[62] Such interpretation would be in line with the ECtHR's fundamental stance in *Golder* and its structural approach in *Engel, Kasparov and Others, Khodorkovskiy and Lebedev,* or *Nemtsov.* Be that as it may, the opportunity to clarify the issue of Articles 6 and 7 was missed.[63]

B.   A HEALTHY CORE IN A SICK MANTLE

As to when Article 18 is brought into play, *Merabishvili* was innovative. The GC started by stating (descriptively) that rights could be restricted: either solely for a purpose which was not prescribed by the Convention; or both for an ulterior purpose and that prescribed by the Convention, i.e. the plurality of purposes (a notion by then unknown in the ECtHR's case-law). The question arises

> "whether the prescribed purpose invariably expunges the ulterior one, whether the mere presence of an ulterior purpose contravenes Article 18, or whether there is some intermediary answer."

The GC seized the third option. Where a right was restricted for a plurality of purposes, the presence of an ulterior purpose cannot of itself give rise to a breach of Article 18; but a finding that the restriction pursued a Convention-friendly purpose does not necessarily rule out a breach of Article 18. A restriction could be compatible with the substantive Convention provision authorising it but still be in breach of Article 18 because it was "chiefly" meant for an ulterior purpose. What is decisive is whether the ulterior purpose was predominant (in continuing situations the assessment of which purpose was predominant may vary over time). This may look like an entirely new standard.[64]

It is not new though, at least not entirely. It is a resurrection of *Khodorkovskiy and Lebedev*'s "healthy core" approach, with that – progressive to a certain extent – clarification, that for dismissing an Article 18 complaint the "healthy core" must dominate over what perhaps could be called the "sick mantle", but in assessing which of the two dominates, not only direct evidence was to be admitted. In *Khodorkovskiy and Lebedev* the finding of no violation of

---

[62]   The dubious appropriateness of the use of the word "clauses" (and not "Articles" or "provisions") in this context would be another matter.

[63]   Neither it was seized in a later GC case, *Denisov,* because the issue raised there was that of Article 18 in conjunction with Article 1 of Protocol no. 1 (which appeared to have been lodged outside the six-month time-limit). Nor was this issue addressed in *Navalnyy v. Russia,* adopted a couple of months later, where the applicant had not raised the issue of conjunction of Article 18 with specifically Articles 6 or 7. In the latter case, however, the GC copy-pasted long passages from *Merabishvili,* including the confusing "exemplary" listing of restriction-warranting Articles of Section I of the Convention.

[64]   See, e.g., Corina Heri. *Op. cit.,* note 8 *supra.*

Article 18 relied on its "very exacting", Government-indulging standard of proof, which scorned "appearances", while accepting as non-determinative and even permissible political groups' and government officials' "push[ing] for the applicants' prosecution" for "their own reasons". *Merabishvili* rejected that standard (I deal with this issue below).

Merabishvili does not call for invocation of Article 18 in each and every case where restrictions do not meet all the requirements of respective restriction-warranting Articles (and thus are "ulterior" to the permitted purposes in the broad sense). On the contrary: separate examination of Article 18 complaint is only warranted if the claim that a restriction had been applied for an ulterior purpose "appears to be a fundamental aspect of the case", in other words, that whatever (if anything) was "healthy" in the motives behind a restriction was not the "core" of the case against the applicant. For establishing that, some test should be applied: the so-called predominant purpose test.

Mention (yes, mention; not elaboration) of the "fundamental aspect" in the judgment looks like an euphemistic pointing to politics, which leaves, at the same time, some space for lodging politics- or policy-unrelated Article 18 complaints. If a restriction overstepped the limits set out a respective restriction-warranting Article, but the ulterior purpose was not a "fundamental aspect of the case", the ECtHR should find a violation of that Article, but not of Article 18. The "fundamental aspect" thus is the determining criterion: if the ulterior motive constituted a "fundamental aspect" of the case against the applicant, Article 18 is applicable; if not, then not; but then the other Article is applicable (although not necessarily has been violated).

The reading that the authorities' abuses will not go unnoticed by the ECtHR, if Article 18 complaint does not satisfy the "fundamental aspect" criterion, because they would be assessed under some other Article, can be sequential if only "fundamental aspect" denotes politics or policy. Such reading would correspond to the original intent of the drafters and to the *raison d'être* of Article 18 as a barrier against undemocratic tendencies, as well as to the notion of "autonomy" of Article 18, as employed in *Merabishvili*. But this is only my wishful guess.

It is unfortunate that it is not explained anywhere in the judgment what is exactly meant by the "fundamental aspect of the case", in particular whether it has anything to do with what is outside the domain of politics or policy. This key notion is used only once throughout the whole text of the judgment. References to the earlier cases, provided in order to elucidate this notion, are misleading. Six cases referred to are all Article 14 and not Article 18 cases; they deal with a "clear inequality of treatment in the enjoyment of the right in question [which] is a fundamental aspect of the case". But it is obvious that what is fundamental in a discrimination context is not (so necessarily) fundamental in an abuse of power context. What is more, the case-law referred to is nothing more than self-referring: the five subsequent judgments only provide references to a single earlier judgment, *Airey v. Ireland*.[65] Still, quantitatively abundant citation hardly can cloak the lack of arguments on the substance. It is not explained in *Airey* what is meant by the "fundamental aspect of the case" as a general notion: there it was not at all intended as a general concept. No less disconcerting is that that judgment from 1979 concerned separation proceedings in Ireland in the era of prohibition of divorce. There the notion of "fundamental aspect" was employed – in no relation to Article 18 – in order to substantiate the ECtHR's refusal to look into the merits of the discrimination complaint as undeserving of examination under Article 14 in conjunction with Article 6 §1. That point, so unfriendly to the woman applicant, was adopted by four votes to three; unsurprisingly, all the members of the Chamber were men. So much for progress.

However, the "fundamental aspect" of *Merabishvili*'s own fallacy is that it commands not to assess under Article 18 the abuses triggered by ulterior motives, if they belong to the "sick mantle", when the latter is smaller than the "healthy core". The three co-authors of the concurring opinion point to that the ECtHR was criticised for overlooking the "fundamental aspects" in politically sensitive cases. The GC did not provide any clarification as to how that "fundamental aspect" (nowhere explained) could be distinguished from those which are not "fundamental". There cannot be any quantifiers – and there are none. And had they been available, they would not have helped anyway, because even a relatively minor ulterior purpose contaminates their whole plurality.[66] The "healthy core" is unable to heal the "sickness" of the "mantle". On the contrary: if *mens sana in corpore sano*, then *corpore sano*, no matter big or small in relation to *mens*, is a *conditio sine qua non* for *mens sana*. The GC's approach suggests that the law of the Convention allows – or even requires – not to take into account some ulterior purposes behind the restrictions on rights, unless they were dominating over the "healthy core": they are deemed as legally immaterial, insignificant. Such neutralisation of part of the ulterior purposes amounts to their trivialisation, toleration or, as one author put it, normalisation of bad faith.[67] The tolerance for rights' limitations based on improper purposes, as long as there is a predominant "healthy core", is the main criticism of the *Merabishvili* doctrine by the authors of the concurring opinions.

---

[65]   *Airey v. Ireland* (no. 6289/73, 9 October 1979).
[66]   A joke has a circulation that if you mix a kilo of manure with three kilos of jam, what you get is not four kilos of jam: it's four kilos of manure.
[67]   Başak Çalı. *Op. cit.*, note 8 *supra*.

If there are no quantifiers for weighing the "core" *vis-à-vis* the "mantle", the only measure to be used in their juxtaposition stems from axiology. The value approach is incompatible with whitewashing of the "sick mantle": whenever there was an ulterior (politics- or policy-related) purpose behind a restriction of individual's rights, Article 18 must come into play. Most restrictions of rights are not politics- or policy-related. The ECtHR should look attentively into each allegation under Article 18 and sort them out thus rendering "unto Caesar the things that are Caesar's, and unto God the things that are God's" (Mk 12:17). Once there is an arguable claim that there had been an ulterior purpose behind a restriction, this is the domain of Article 18. If that claim appears to be true, Article 18 has been breached *de facto*, even if – often contrary to what every schoolboy knows – the Strasbourg Court dodges the legal assessment and pronouncement of what is obvious. To the extent *Merabishvili* might be conducive to such self-restraint, it would constitute but one more pattern of avoidance of examination of Article 18 complaints.

C. DOWN TO EARTH, BACK TO COMMON SENSE – AT LEAST IN THEORY

On the issue of the standard of proof the GC, having humbly admitted that the ECtHR's approach to proof in Article 18 cases "has not been entirely consistent", backed away from the overly restrictive, applicant-unfriendly "highest standard" stance which reigned that case-law. The GC saw no reason to restrict the ECtHR to "incontrovertible and direct" proof, neither to apply a "special standard of proof" to Article 18 complaints. Instead, it endorsed adherence to the "usual approach to proof". The proof has to be beyond reasonable doubt, but it can follow also from the "coexistence of sufficiently strong, clear and concordant inferences". The circumstantial (i.e. contextual) evidence is defined as

> "information about the primary facts, or contextual facts or sequences of events which can form the basis for inferences about the primary facts."

In addition,

> "[r]eports or statements by international observers, non-governmental organisations or the media, or the decisions of other national or international courts are often taken into account to, in particular, shed light on the facts, or to corroborate findings made by the Court."

The first kudos go, of course, to *Rasul Jafarov*, a Chamber case of 2016. The endorsement – at last – of contextual evidence two years later in *Merabishvili*, a GC case, amounts to an overhaul of the ECtHR's proof practice in Article 18 cases. It is a promise that the Strasbourg Court will no longer demand that the applicants present proof beyond their capabilities, or that the Strasbourg Court will haughtily dismiss the findings of European (or other international) courts.

This turnaround may be helpful in neutralising, at least to some extent, one negative ramification of the "healthy core" approach. The Governments usually are not at pains in proving the presence of some seemingly, or ostensibly, legitimate reason behind the impugned restriction, while it is difficult to prove ulterior motives (on the whole, establishing motives is more demanding than establishing observable acts). Rehabilitation of contextual evidence makes invocation of Article 18 somewhat easier, especially if the "usual approach to proof" includes (as it should do) also the ECtHR's usual approach to the shift of the burden of proof. If that is so, *Merabishvili* has something very healthy of its own: if not the core of the doctrine, then at least its mantle.

IN LIEU OF CONCLUSION: BEYOND *MERABISHVILI*

I pledged to follow the advice of *Alice's* King – but I cannot "come to the end". So far there has been no "end" in this Article 18 case-law saga. *Merabishvili* marked a new beginning. The old case-law remains valid, even if parts of it have lost legitimacy. To quote William Faulkner's *Requiem for a Nun*, "the past is never dead; it's not even the past". The ECtHR tends to routinely, often mechanically cite its earlier judgments without looking into their context. In *Merabishvili*, the GC, while turning away from the methodology underlying some unsustainable judgments, nevertheless prolonged their breathing, be it *Khodorkhovskiy and Lebedev* or *Airey*. Be that as it may, *Merabishvili* was a promise. But the proof is in the pudding. Promises kept are laudable; promises not kept are compromised. Future will show, whether the prospective case-law will employ less or no less citations from *Nemtsov* or *Navalnyy and Ofitserov* or *Kasparov and Others (no. 2)*. Better less.

When *Merabishvili* was delivered, it could be expected that this imperfect (and in some sense even deficient) tool could prove to be instrumental in practice and, if need be, could be improved in the course of its usage. The first two post-*Merabishvili* judgments in cases against Azerbaijan, *Mammadli* and *Rashad Hasanov and Others*, which concerned the politically motivated persecution of civil society activists and human rights defenders, relied on the fairer, more realistic standard of proof, as re-defined in *Merabishvili*. The ECtHR found for the applicants (violation of Article 18 in conjunction with Article 5), holding that

> "proof of an ulterior purpose derive[d] from a juxtaposition of the lack of suspicion with contextual factors."

In the end of 2018 the contextual evidence was conducive for finding a violation of Article 18 in *Selahattin Demirtaş v. Turkey (no. 2)*[68], where the applicant was an opposition MP, arrested and held in police custody (violation of Article 18 in conjunction with Article 5 §3).

But the most important post-*Merabishvili* case was *Navalnyy*, examined first by the Chamber, and then by the GC. In early 2017, the Chamber held[69] that in view of the fact that "the applicant's arrest and administrative detention had the effect of preventing and discouraging him and others from participating in protest rallies and actively engaging in opposition politics", owing to which it has found a violation of Articles 5 and 11, it was

> "not necessary to examine whether, in the present case, there has been a violation of Article 18 [...] in conjunction with Articles 5 or 11 [...] or of Article 14."

The Chamber's faithfulness, in *Navalnyy*, to the escapist pattern designed in *Nemtsov* and *Kasparov and Others (no. 2)*, however, encountered one difficulty: while the Chamber's judgment was not yet final, the GC had already held (on 8 March 2017) the hearing and the first deliberations in *Merabishvili*, which presumably heralded (at least for the insiders) that that embarrassing pattern was to be reviewed. Little wonder was that Mr Navalnyy's request for the referral of his case to the GC was granted. On 15 November 2018 the GC found for the applicant:[70] in two episodes of the applicant's arrest there has been a violation of Article 18 in conjunction with Articles 5 and 11 (the first victory of a Russian opposition activist after *Gusinskiy* in an Article 18 case). In particular, the GC stated that the applicant

> "was specifically and personally targeted as a known activist, even in the most innocuous situation remotely resembling a public gathering [...]."

In substantiating its findings, the Court noted that

> "there [was] converging contextual evidence corroborating the view that the authorities were becoming increasingly severe in their response to the conduct of the applicant, in the light of the opposition leader, and of other political activists and, more generally, in their approach to public assemblies of political nature."

---

68 Note 32 *supra*. In this context, an earlier case, which involved the same applicant, could be mentioned. In *Selahattin Demirtaş v. Turkey* (no. 15028/09, 23 September 2015) the Court found no violation of Article 2, where there had been a public, clear and undisguised incitement to kill the applicant, which was not duly investigated by the domestic authorities.

69 *Navalnyy v. Russia* (nos. 29580/12, 36847/12, 11252/13, 12317/13 and 43746/14, 2 February 2017).

70 Note 31 *supra*.

The GC relied on various sources presenting the corroborating contextual evidence, including the changes in Russian legislation, documents of various Council of Europe bodies raising concern about the restrictions of freedom of assembly in Russia, but (this must not be overlooked) also on the ECtHR's own findings in the earlier cases involving the same applicant, in particular *Navalnyy and Ofitserov* and *Navalnyye*, where the Court found that the applicant's earlier criminal sentences were arbitrary and manifestly unreasonable, although in these cases it did not find a violation of Article 18. This was an indirect admission (even if a reluctant one) that in the earlier cases, which involved the same applicant, to the extent that he complained under Article 18, he had not received the justice which he had asked for (this, by extension, applies to some of the earlier cases involving other Russian opposition activists). For, with hindsight, if the earlier conclusions that the applicant was convicted arbitrarily, even if not couched as formal findings of a violation of Article 18, can serve as a contextual evidence for finding of a violation of Article 18 in a later case, which is the last link in the chain of the applicant's political persecution, there hardly can be a reason for not endowing that later finding with the status of corroborating evidence when assessing his Article 18 complaints in these earlier cases, that is to say, other links in the same chain. Ah yes, according to the reasoning employed in *Navalnyy and Ofitserov* and *Navalnyye*, in these cases justice was not denied to the applicant (and his co-applicants), but was not possible to be delivered, because his (their) Article 18 complaints were found incompatible *ratione materiae* with the provisions of the Convention. Future will show when and how this "open" question will be clarified. Sooner or later (better sooner) it will have to be answered; for "there is nothing covered, that shall not be revealed; and hid, that shall not be known" (Mt 10:26).

It is too early to rejoice at the change of course.[71] Even in *Navalnyy*, the ECtHR found a violation of Article 18 in only two episodes out of seven complained of. It stated that it would

---

[71] The temptation is high though, and this is understandable. An expert on Article 18 case-law writes: "[T]he Grand Chamber sends a powerful message and addresses the crux of the matter: the interferences with Navalnyy's Convention rights are not mere incidents, they are part of a broader ulterior aim, which is to suppress the opposition and which strikes at the heart of democracy and the rule of law. Especially considered in tandem with the judgment in *Selahattin Demirtaş v. Turkey (no. 2)* of just a few days later, this clearly illustrates the Court is willing to take up a role in safeguarding democracy from oppressive governmental interference, and in countering rule of law backsliding." Floris Tan, *The European Court's Role as Warden of Democracy and the Rule of Law: Navalnyy v Russia* (http://echrblog.blogspot. com/2018/11/guest-blog-on-grand-chamber-judgment-in.html; visited on 15/12/2018). The issue of "striking at the heart of democracy and the rule of law" is addressed, in its own right, in the partly concurring, partly dissenting opinion of Judges Aleš Pejchal, Dmitry Dedov, Georges Ravarani, Tim Eicke and Péter Paczolay, where they argue that Article 18 was not the most appropriate tool to assess whether the authorities' actions against the applicant were an abuse of their powers; in their view, it would have been more appropriately and more effectively examined under Article 17.

"concentrate its examination on the fifth and sixth episodes, in respect of which it [had] concluded that the interference with the applicant's right to a peaceful assembly did not pursue a legitimate aim, in violation of Article 11, and [had] found that his arrest and detention were arbitrary and unlawful, in violation of Article 5 §1."

As to the other episodes, the Court stated that it

"seriously doubt[ed] that any legitimate aim provided for in Article 11 §2 was pursued, but [saw] no need to reach a firm conclusion on this point, considering that the interference was in any event not 'necessary' [...]."

What does this structure of reasoning imply? The ECtHR examined Article 18 complaints only where it found that there had not been a legitimate aim for an interference into the applicant's right under the Convention. Where it did not establish the absence of the legitimate aim, it brushed these complaints off. This is a totally new criterion for addressing Article 18 complaints: the latter now can be addressed only where the Court concludes that there was no legitimate aim for an interference into one's right. This approach mirrors the "healthy core" methodology. In that methodology, if it has not been conclusively established that a restriction had been applied for an ulterior purpose which "appears to be a fundamental aspect of the case", Article 18 complaint is not warranted. In the "absence of legitimate aim" methodology, Article 18 complaints are examined only if it has been conclusively established that the interference had not pursued a legitimate aim. Here's the rub: the absence of the legitimate aim may be not established either because: the examination of the complaints was undertaken but resulted in a finding that there had been such an aim (however meagre); or the Court has declined from undertaking such examination, having held that there is "no need" to establish this determinative circumstance. In *Navalnyy*, the GC did not conclusively establish the absence of the legitimate aim solely because it saw "no need" to reach a "firm conclusion on this point", notwithstanding that it itself "seriously doubt[ed]" that a legitimate aim had been pursued and, moreover, that it found a violation of Article 11 in all seven episodes.

In addition to this new pattern of avoidance of examination of Article 18 complaints, the discredited third pattern has not been abandoned. In *Mehmet Hasan Altan v. Turkey*[72] and *Şahin Alpay v. Turkey*[73] (both judgments were delivered on the same day), the ECtHR resorted to the old "not necessary to examine" pattern of avoidance. In both cases violations of Article 5 §1 and

---

[72]   *Mehmet Hasan Altan v. Turkey* (no. 13237/17, 20 March 2018).
[73]   *Şahin Alpay v. Turkey* (no. 16538/17, 20 March 2018).

Article 10 were found. Both judgments then contain the following substitute for reasoning:

> "Having regard to the conclusions reached above under Article 5 §1 and Article 10 of the Convention, the Court does not consider it necessary to examine this complaint separately."

Above I have hinted that future will show, whether the prospective case-law will employ less or no less citations from *Nemtsov* or *Navalnyy and Ofitserov* or *Kasparov and Others (no. 2)*, and I added: better less. Now I have to correct myself. There was a third option: in addition to no reasoning, no references too. Apparently, this method will not be used for long. In *Haziyev v. Azerbaijan*[74], where the applicant was a journalist and political activist and in which a violation of Article 5 was found, the ECtHR used the language, so painfully familiar to those applicants, whose Article 18 complaints were found undeserving of examination (please note the references):

> "[H]aving regard to the conclusions reached above under Article 5 […] in the circumstances of the present case the Court does not consider it necessary to examine this complaint [i.e. under Article 18] separately (see *Mehmet Hasan Altan v. Turkey*, no. 13237/17, §216, 20 March 2018, and *Şahin Alpay v. Turkey*, no. 13568/17, §186, 20 March 2018)."

If this approach persists, may *Merabishvili* rest in peace. *Haziyev* has returned things back to where they were – on a new referential basis. Old wine in a new bottle.

Future will show, to what extent the Court will want to remain in blissful innocence that its overt forgetfulness of the imperative of Article 45 to give "reasons […] for judgments, as well as for decisions", especially with regard to the member States, which have an increasingly upsetting human rights record (such as Turkey, Russia or Azerbaijan) is not noticed.

Future will also show how the ECtHR will tackle those borderline situations where the balance between the ostensibly "healthy" "core" and the "sick mantle" is foggy, in particular with regard to the big players on the European arena. As things stand one year after *Merabishvili*, it may go both ways[75]: either the doctrine

---

[74] *Haziyev v. Azerbaijan* (no. 19842/15, 6 December 2018); not (yet) final at the time of writing of this article. *Update-note after the submission of the article*: This judgment became final on 6 March 2019.

[75] In fact, as we have seen, *Merabishvili* itself went both ways. One analyst characterised the doctrinal elements of *Merabishvili* as steps forward or back; his balance was that there were made two steps forward and one back. See Floris Tan. *The Dawn of Article 18*, cited above, note 59 *supra*.

(and the practice of its application) will be reshaped and adjusted so that it is brought in line with the inherent purpose of Article 18 and challenges of today; or – *plus ça change, plus c'est la même chose* – Article 18 case-law reverts back to its restrictive, applicant-unfriendly, regime-pandering mode.

"The future's uncertain and the end is always near."[76]

UNIFORMITY AND THE EUROPEAN COURT OF HUMAN RIGHTS

Janneke GERARDS

Professor of Fundamental Rights law, Utrecht University,
Montaigne Centre for Rule of Law and Administration of Justice

INTRODUCTION

For the Court of Justice of the EU (CJEU) it is obvious: providing for a uniform interpretation of EU law belongs to its very core business.[1] Uniformity thereby has a particular meaning, in that the rights and duties of EU citizens, companies and government authorities should be the same in all member states of the EU.[2] Such uniformity is of immense importance for the EU legal order, since it lies at the basis of the freedom of movement between the member states as well as of the mutual recognition of judgments, arrest warrants, expulsion decisions and the like. Surely, there is continuous debate on the objective of uniformity in the EU. To the extent uniformity implies mutual trust and mutual recognition, for example, this is not always accepted. Sometimes exceptions to the principles of mutual trust and mutual recognition are allowed if it turns out that the rule of law and fundamental rights are not sufficiently respected in a certain member state.[3] Nevertheless, the CJEU has never stopped to emphasise the primary

---

[1]   This core task is mainly expressed by the preliminary reference procedure of Article 267 TFEU. See e.g. M. Broberg and N. Fenger, *Preliminary references to the European Court of Justice* (Oxford, Oxford University Press, 2010) 2; A. Arnull, *The European Union and its Court of Justice* (Oxford, Oxford University Press, 2006) 97.

[2]   Another aim of striving for legal unity or uniformity may be to bring about legal certainty, for example by avoiding that several highest national courts provide for diverging definitions of similar notions or legal rules. For the EU legal order, legal certainty is an important rationale for accepting the principles of mutual trust and mutual recognition; see e.g. *Donnellan*, CJEU 26 April 2018, Case C-34/17, ECLI:EU:C:2018:282, para. 45. For the ECHR legal order, the ECtHR has equally recognised the importance of legal certainty in relation to diverging case-law in the light of Article 6 ECHR; on this, see e.g. *Nejdet Şahin and Perihan Şahin v. Turkey*, ECtHR (GC) 20 October 2011, no. 13279/05, ECLI:CE:ECHR:2011:1020JUD001327905. Nevertheless, the aim of creating legal certainty will not be specifically addressed in this contribution.

[3]   See most famously e.g. *Aranyosi and Căldăraru*, CJEU 5 April 2016, Case C-404/15, ECLI:EU:C:2016:198. More recently, this has also been recognised for the right to a fair trial

importance of these principles for the EU, and also the ECtHR has recognised this.[4] In the same vein, the CJEU has allowed some leeway to the member states where moral issues are concerned, such as the definition of the notion of an 'embryo'[5] or the meaning of 'human dignity'[6], but such leeway remains exceptional. Rather than breaking the rule of uniformity, these exceptions emphasise its importance.

This story of the importance of uniformity and mutual trust is almost overly well-known for the EU legal order. The interesting question is whether and to what extent it can also be told for that other European legal order; the one that is constituted by the European Convention of Human Rights (ECHR or Convention). To a certain degree, it could be expected that uniformity is important also to this legal order. After all, fundamental rights are claimed to be universal, and if anything, this means that it should not matter for their validity and meaning whether they are claimed in Armenia, Belgium, Iceland or Russia.[7] From this perspective, the Convention rights should be uniformly guaranteed in all Convention States, just like the EU member states should guarantee EU law in a uniform manner. Moreover, according to Article 32 of the ECHR, the jurisdiction of the European Court of Human Rights (ECtHR or Court) 'shall extend to all matters concerning the interpretation and application of the Convention', which certainly could be read to mean that the Court can provide for a final and uniform interpretation. Combined, these factors would seem to imply that the ECtHR has just as important a task as the CJEU has to strive for uniformity, albeit that its task is limited to the remit of fundamental rights protection. In particular, the expectation could be that ECHR rights are

---

by an independent and impartial court; see LM, CJEU 25 July 2018, Case C-216/18 PPU, ECLI:EU:2018:586.

[4] See e.g. *Donnellan*, CJEU 26 April 2018, Case C-34/17, ECLI:EU:C:2018:282, para. 40; for the recognition by the ECtHR, see e.g. *Pirozzi v. Belgium*, ECtHR 17 April 2018, no. 21055/11, ECLI:CE:ECHR:2018:0417JUD002105511, para. 59.

[5] See e.g. *International Stem Cell Corporation*, CJEU 18 December 2014, Case C-364/13, ECLI:EU:C:2014:2451.

[6] See classically *Omega Spielhallen*, CJEU 14 October 2004, Case C-36/02, ECLI:EU:C:2004:614. See further e.g. G.T. Petursson, *The Proportionality Principle as Tool for Disintegration in EU Law – of Balancing and Coherence in the Light of the Fundamental Freedoms* (diss. Lund University, 2014) and J.H. Gerards, 'Pluralism, Deference and the Margin of Appreciation Doctrine', 17(1) *European Law Journal* (2011) 80–120.

[7] Of course, however, of old there is much debate on the meaning of the claim of universality; see e.g. R.D. Sloane, 'Outrelativizing Relativism: A Liberal Defense of the Universality of International Human Rights', 34 *Vanderbilt Journal of Transnational Law* (2001) 527–596 and E. Brems, *Human Rights: Universality and Diversity* (Leiden/Boston, Martinus Nijhoff Publishers, 2001). More specifically for the ECHR context, see Greer, S. (2017), 'Universalism and Relativism in the Protection of Human Rights in Europe: Politics, Law and Culture', in P Agha (ed), *Human Rights between Law and Politics: The Margin of Appreciation Doctrine in Post-National Contexts* (London: Bloomsbury/Hart, 2017) 17–26.

uniformly defined and delineated in the Court's case-law to ensure that the Convention rights mean the same thing in all European States.

Yet, whilst most lawyers will easily associate the CJEU's jurisprudence with such notions as 'uniform interpretation', 'harmonisation', 'mutual trust', 'mutual recognition' or 'convergence', such connections are far less likely to be made in relation to the ECtHR. Instead, the Convention system is usually associated with quite contrary notions, such as 'subsidiarity', 'margin of appreciation' and 'respect for diversity', which allow for differentiation rather than enhance uniform protection. Indeed, these notions have great political impact. They have been stressed time and again in the various High Level Declarations adopted over the past eight years, most recently in the Copenhagen Declaration.[8] The States have even decided that these notions warrant a codification in the Convention's Preamble, which will be effected if Protocol 15 enters into force.[9] Hence, a uniform level of protection would seem to be far less important for the ECHR system than it is for the EU legal order.

Consequently, the value of uniformity as an objective for the ECHR legal system is debatable. There may be arguments in favour of recognising such an objective, but there are also clear arguments against it. The intriguing question is how the ECtHR relates to this topic. Does it expressly and consciously strive for uniformity, and, if so, how does this show in the Court's reasoning? And which explanations could be given for the particular role of uniformity in the ECHR system? These are the questions that are central to this contribution. It will turn out that the Court usually does *not* act as a highest national court and it clearly does not aim for a uniform reading of the Convention in the same way as the CJEU does for the EU. At the same time, the findings of this study also show that uniformity can be an important, though usually unintended effect of the Court's argumentative approach.

To show all this, this chapter will first briefly discuss some contextual points that are of relevance to the Court's *modus operandi*. Those well-acquainted with the system may want to skip this and continue reading the two main sections, which focus on the role of uniformity in the interpretation of the terms and notions contained in the Convention and the assessment of interferences with

---

8   For the Copenhagen Declaration, see www.justitsministeriet.dk/sites/default/files/media/ Forsidebilleder_2018/copenhagen_declaration.pdf, in particular paras. 6 et seq. For references to earlier High Level Declarations and a brief analysis of the role of the various notions of subsidiarity, margin of appreciation and deference, see J.H. Gerards and S. Lambrecht, 'The Draft Copenhagen Declaration: Food for Thought', *Strasbourg Observers Blog*, 25 February 2018 and J.H. Gerards, 'The draft Copenhagen Declaration and the Court's dual role – the need for a different definition of subsidiarity and the margin of appreciation', *Strasbourg Observers Blog*, 28 February 2018.

9   Protocol No. 15, ETS-no. 213, via www.coe.int/conventions.

Convention rights. This contribution is concluded by providing a tentative explanation for the found effects of uniformity for the ECtHR's case-law in the light of the characteristics of the Convention system.

I. CHARACTERISTICS OF THE ECHR SYSTEM

A. FUNCTIONS OF THE ECtHR

The ECtHR has different functions within the Convention system[10], two of which are of particular importance to the assessing the role of uniformity in its case-law.[11] First, there is the function of legal protection and access to justice, which is based on Articles 19 and 34 ECHR. The Court serves as a safety net if national protection of Convention rights has proved to be insufficient and if it has appeared impossible for the individual to obtain redress for this on the national level.[12] Second, the Court's function is one of interpretation, which is a rather more constitutional function.[13] This function is closely connected to the question who has the final say in Europe as to which rights and obligations follow from the Convention and how they should be guaranteed. On the one hand, Article 1 ECHR clarifies that the States Parties must guarantee the rights laid down in the Convention. Indeed, this principle of 'primarity' is often emphasised in the various High Level Declarations, including the most recent Copenhagen Declaration.[14] On the other hand, it is not fully to the States to decide on the contents of these rights and obligations. The preamble to the Convention makes very clear that the Convention's objective is to establish a 'greater unity' between the members of the Council of Europe and the Convention is meant to be a first step towards the 'collective enforcement' of fundamental rights.[15] These objectives

---

[10] See more elaborately e.g. B. Çalı, 'The purposes of the European Human Rights System: one or many?', *European Human Rights Law Review* (2008) 299–306 and J.H. Gerards, 'The prism of fundamental rights', 8(2) *European Constitutional Law Review* (2012) 173–202.

[11] See also De Londras, who speaks of the Court's 'dual functionality': F. De Londras, 'Dual functionality and the persistent frailty of the European Court of Human Rights', *European Human Rights Law Review* (2013) 38–46.

[12] De Londras, *supra* n. 11; see further J.H. Gerards and L.R. Glas, 'Access to justice in the European Convention on Human Rights system', 35(1) *Netherlands Quarterly of Human Rights* (2017) 11–30.

[13] Hence, this function is also sometimes characterised as the Court's constitutional role; see already E.A. Alkema, 'The European Convention as a Constitution and its Court as a Constitutional Court', in P. Mahoney et al. (eds.), *Protecting Human Rights: The European Perspective – Studies in Memory of Rolv Ryssdal* (Cologne, Carl Heymans, 2000) 41–63.

[14] For this term, see J. Christoffersen, *Fair Balance: Proportionality, Subsidiarity and Primarity in the European Convention on Human Rights* (Leiden/Boston, Martinus Nijhoff Publishers, 2009); for the High Level Declarations, see *supra* n. 8.

[15] The Committee of Ministers also forms part of this collective enforcement mechanism; see Article 46 ECHR. On the functioning of this mechanism, see elaborately L.R. Glas, *The*

are sought to be realised by means of establishing a supranational mechanism of supervision. As part of this collective supervisory system, the ECtHR has been entrusted with the task of dealing with 'all matters concerning the interpretation and application of the Convention'.[16] This also means that the Court has an important task in explaining what the various Convention rights mean.[17]

Of these two functions, that of interpretation most clearly reflects the Court's task to provide for a certain degree of uniformity. At the same time, it is clear that both tasks are closely related. Only if the Court would read a uniform minimum level of protection into the Convention, the collective enforcement mechanism can live up to the expectations. Such uniform interpretation would provide for clear norms and standards that would be equally valid and important in all the European States. In turn, such clarity allows the States to be held accountable for violations of these norms within the collective system, and individuals can benefit from this because they have direct access to redress and just satisfaction on the European level.

B.   INDETERMINACY OF THE TERMS AND NOTIONS OF THE CONVENTION

The uniform determination of a minimum level of protection in the ECHR system is complicated by the very fact that the Convention contains fundamental rights norms. Regardless of the powerful rhetoric of the universality of human rights, there is relatively little consensus on their exact meaning.[18] Perhaps such consensus may exist where the core of fundamental rights is concerned, and on a relatively high level of abstraction. (Almost) everyone will agree, for example, that the prohibition of torture means that the police may not use iron bars to hurt a suspect so as to make him confess a crime he has not committed, or that the right to family life means that a child may not be removed from its parents without good reason.[19] On this level, it is also relatively easy to provide for a uniform definition of fundamental rights. Matters become rather more complicated where the periphery of fundamental rights is concerned, or, in some cases, where a more concrete level of abstraction is chosen. For example, there

---

[   ] *Theory, Potential and Practice of Procedural Dialogue in the European Convention on Human Rights System* (Antwerp, Intersentia, 2016).

[16]   Article 32 ECHR.

[17]   See in more detail e.g. J.H. Gerards, 'The European Court of Human Rights', in A. Jákab, A. Dyevre and G. Itzcovich (eds.), *Comparative Constitutional Reasoning* (Cambridge, Cambridge University Press, 2017) 237–276.

[18]   See further e.g. Sloane, *supra* n. 7, Brems, *supra* n. 7 and Greer, *supra* n. 7.

[19]   Cf. B. Baade, 'The ECtHR's Role as a Guardian of Discourse: Safeguarding a Decision-Making Process Based on Well-Established Standards, Practical Rationality, and Facts', 31 *Leiden Journal of International Law* (2018)(2) 335–361 at 339.

will be considerable controversy over the question of whether the right to remain free from degrading treatment implies that everyone (including undocumented aliens) have a right to food and shelter.[20] Similarly, there may be little consensus on the question if the right to family life encompasses a right to have more than two registered parents, for example where a child is raised by a male same-sex couple which has been given birth to by a female friend.[21]

The text of the Convention offers very few clues to solving such controversies on the meaning of the rights contained in it.[22] The formulation of the Convention rights is open and indeterminate. For example, the Convention may clearly say that protection should be offered against inhuman and degrading treatment, but it does not explain what this means, and it may stipulate that family life should be respected, but it does not describe what, then, constitutes a 'family'. To answer such questions, the Convention's *travaux préparatoires* are not of much help either.[23] It has been well-documented that societal views on what fundamental rights have significantly changed over time, and the many technological developments also make it difficult to interpret the Convention exactly in line with the intention of its drafters as expressed in the preparatory documents.[24]

The indeterminacy of the Convention thus makes it very difficult to give a uniform interpretation. In particular, if the text and the *travaux* do not offer any guidance, it is not self-evident what should be the basis for such a uniform interpretation. Perhaps the Court could find such guidance in the minimum level of protection on which all the European States agree.[25] It is not so easy

---

[20] There is much to do about this in the Netherlands, which has given rise to an (unsuccessful) application to the ECtHR in *Hunde v. the Netherlands*, ECtHR 5 July 2016 (dec.), no. 17931/16, ECLI:CE:ECHR:2016:0705DEC001793116. In Dutch, see e.g. D. Mohammadi, 'Opvang van uitgeprocedeerde vreemdelingen: waarom we het voorbeeld van de gemeenten moeten opvolgen' [Shelter for undocumented aliens: why we would have to follow the municipalities' lead], *Ars Aequi* (2015) 749–761.

[21] Again, this is an issue on which there is considerable controversy in the Netherlands; see e.g. the recent report by the State Committee on Recalibration of Parenthood: *Child and Parents in the 21st Century* (The Hague 2016). See more generally on these issues and the differences between the European States: N.R. Koffeman, *Morally Sensitive Issues and Cross-Border Movement in the EU. The Cases of Reproductive Matters and Legal Recognition of Same-Sex Relationships* (Cambridge, Intersentia, 2015).

[22] See elaborately e.g. H.C.K. Senden, *Interpretation of Fundamental Rights in a Multilevel Legal System. An analysis of the European Court of Human Rights and the Court of Justice of the European Union* (Antwerp, Intersentia, 2011); also: Baade, *supra* n. 19, at 341.

[23] *Id.*; see also A. Mowbray, 'Between the will of the Contracting Parties and the needs of today: extending the scope of Convention rights and freedoms beyond what could have been foreseen by the drafters of the ECHR', in E. Brems and J.H. Gerards (eds.), *Shaping Rights in the ECHR. The Role of the European Convention of Human Rights in Determining the Scope of Human Rights* (Cambridge, Cambridge University Press, 2013) 17–36.

[24] *Id.*

[25] The risks of this approach have mainly been discussed in relation to EU law; see the principled debate between J. Coppel and O'Neill, 'The European Court of Justice: Taking Rights

to tell, however, what it means to say that there is a 'European consensus' on a certain interpretation, nor how such a consensus can be determined.[26] In addition to this, it is questionable why *State* consensus should be guiding the Court. Suppose that in Malta, many people object to abortion and Maltese legislation on this matter is very restrictive.[27] Now suppose Malta would be the last State in Europe where such objections are held so strongly. Should that be in the way of an interpretation of the right to respect for one's private life of Article 8 of the Convention as including a right to abortion? This question is even more difficult to answer if it is added to it what it really means to say that 'in Malta, strong objections exist against abortion'. To all probability, also in Malta, there will be people who are in favour of permitting abortion. Indeed, there may be people who feel that they are the victims of the majority's views and their reflection in legislation. Since the Convention rights should be about the needs, autonomy and dignity of individuals, rather than about majority views in certain States, many scholars have held that State-based consensus reasoning is deeply problematic.[28] Consequently, consensus will be a shaky basis for the determination of a uniform definition of fundamental rights.

Rather more moral foundations for interpretation of Convention also can be found, but these are often essentially contested.[29] For example, in relation to the right to abortion and the question as to its protection under the Convention, it is possible to find support for reading such a right into the Convention in fundamental values such as personal autonomy. However, such values will unavoidably conflict with equally fundamental values of human dignity and the sanctity of life. There are hardly any ways for a Court to make a rational, legitimate and well-founded choice between such conflicting values.

Seriously?', 29 *Common Market Law Review* (1992) 669–692 and J.H.H. Weiler, 'Fundamental Rights and Fundamental Boundaries: On Standards and Values in the Protection of Human Rights', in N.A. Neuwahl and A. Rosas (eds.), *The European Union and Human Rights* (Boston/The Hague, Kluwer Law International, 1995) 51–76.

[26]   In addition, there is a risk that this approach leads to a 'race to the bottom', as explained (again for the EU framework) by M.P. Beijer, *The Limits of Fundamental Rights Protection by the EU. The Scope for the Development of Positive Obligations* (Cambridge, Intersentia, 2017) 214. It is also shown by empirical studies that the minimum level of protection of fundamental rights may be reduced if the Court opts for a consensus-based approach; see A.T. Guzman and K. Linos, 'Human Rights Backsliding', 102 *California Law Review* (2014) 603–654.

[27]   Cf. the 2017 report by the Council of Europe's Human Rights Commissioner; www.coe.int/en/web/commissioner/-/malta-should-step-up-efforts-to-enhance-protection-of-women-s-and-migrants-rights.

[28]   See in particular G. Letsas, *A Theory of Interpretation of the European Convention on Human Rights* (Oxford, Oxford University Press, 2007) 123. More positive on this is S. Dothan, 'Judicial Deference Allows European Consensus to Emerge', 18 *Chicago Journal of International Law* (2018)(2) 393–419.

[29]   Cf. L. Zucca, *Constitutional Dilemma's. Conflicts of Fundamental Legal Rights in Europe and the USA* (Oxford, Oxford University Press, 2007).

If this is accepted, it is clear that it will be extremely difficult to find an appropriate and uncontested basis for a uniform definition of Convention rights. Consequently, in some cases it may be easier and more appropriate to avoid a uniform interpretation of such notions than to accept one.

C.   INSTITUTIONAL POSITION OF THE ECtHR

Finally, the role of uniformity in the case-law of the ECtHR is determined by the Court's institutional position. In doing its work, the Court is confronted with a double constitutional dilemma.[30] First, as is true for each court that has to review legislation or policy measures for their compatibility with higher law, the Court faces the 'countermajoritarian difficulty'.[31] Inevitably, it may have to choose between declaring a legislative measure or an administrative decision to be incompatible with a Convention fundamental right, and accepting it because of its (direct or indirect) democratic legitimacy. The second constitutional dilemma is caused by the position of the ECtHR as a supranational court. As has been emphasised above, the Convention gives the primary responsibility to the State for protecting the Convention rights, and the Court's own role is one of supervising the way they have discharged their obligations under the Convention.[32] In determining what these Convention obligations entail, the Court needs to pay heed to the States' sovereignty and to the specificities of their legal systems. Consequently, the Court constantly has to compromise between its role as the ultimate guarantor of the Convention rights and the freedom of the States to protect these rights as they think fit.

D.   CONCLUSION

The three characteristics of the Convention system described in this section make that the Court faces particularly complex questions on a daily basis. It is its task to guarantee an effective minimum level of protection that is the same for all the States and their residents. Hence, there is an invitation to strive for uniformity. At the same time, it is very difficult for the Court to achieve such uniformity because of the indeterminacy of the Convention rights and the obligations following from them and because of the double constitutional

---

[30]   See J.H. Gerards, '"Hard Cases" in the Law', in A. in 't Groen et al. (eds.), *Ferment of Knowledge. Dilemmas in Science, Scholarship and Society* (Leiden, Leiden University Press, 2007).

[31]   Much has been written on this. For a useful review, see K. Roosevelt III, *The Myth of Judicial Activism* (New Haven/London, Yale University Press, 2006).

[32]   In essence, this is what subsidiarity comes down to. Between many other authorities, see R. Spano, 'Universality or Diversity of Human Rights? Strasbourg in the Age of Subsidiarity', 14 *Human Rights Law Review* (2014) 487–502.

dilemma. It is this field of tension which sets the stage for how, in practice, the Court deals with uniformity in its case-law.

II. UNIFORMITY AND CONVENTION INTERPRETATION

In the light of the notion of universality and in the light of the Court's interpretative function, it may be expected that the Court would mainly strive to offer uniformity through its definition of the various terms and notions of the Convention. Indeed, from a very early stage in the development of its argumentative approach, the Court has consistently held that it would not be desirable to base its Convention interpretations on the national definitions of notions such as 'court' or 'association'.[33] If one State, for example, would decide not to regard a motor club as an association, such an interpretative approach would mean that motor clubs in that particular State would not be protected by the freedom of association of Article 11 ECHR.[34] An autonomous and independent definition clearly avoids such differences in the level of protection to be offered by the Convention.

Thus, it would seem that uniformity plays an important role in the Court's interpretation. A closer study of the Court's reasoning reveals, however, that the Court never expressly refers to notions of uniformity or legal unity as an argument for choosing an autonomous interpretation. Instead, it generally points to the importance of avoiding unequal treatment of applicants in different States (admittedly a closely related point)[35], and especially to the risk that States try to evade the protection offered by the Convention by settling on a very restrictive national definition of fundamental rights notions.[36] Hence, although equivalent protection may be an effect of the Court's approach of autonomous interpretation, it seems that creating uniformity is not as such an objective for the Court, at least not according to its reasoning.

In addition to this, there are several exceptions to the rule of autonomous interpretation. In the first place, there are a few cases in which there is such a

---

[33] See further Senden, *supra* n. 22, at 178ff.
[34] Cf. *Chassagnou and Others v. France*, ECtHR (GC) 29 April 1999, nos. 25088/94, 28331/95 and 28443/95, ECLI:CE:ECHR:1999:0429JUD002508894, para. 100.
[35] See the examples mentioned by Senden, *supra* n. 22, at 294–295.
[36] *Chassagnou and Others v. France*, ECtHR (GC) 29 April 1999, nos. 25088/94, 28331/95 and 28443/95, ECLI:CE:ECHR:1999:0429JUD002508894, para. 100; see more recently e.g. *M. v. Germany*, ECtHR 17 December 2009, no. 19359/04, ECLI:CE:ECHR:2009:121 7JUD001935904, para. 120 and *Tatár and Fáber v. Hungary*, ECtHR 12 June 2012, nos. 26005/08 and 26160/08, ECLI:CE:ECHR:2012:0612JUD002600508, para. 38.

degree of controversy on the correct definition of a human rights between and within the States Parties that the Court does not want to provide for a uniform interpretation. A classic example is the definition of the right to life of Article 2 ECHR, which raises the question as to when life can be held to begin. If the Court would autonomously answer this question by accepting that life starts at conception, or soon afterwards, the text of Article 2 ECHR would imply that this life should be protected to an almost absolute degree.[37] In that case, it would be incompatible with the Convention if a State would legally permit abortion, regardless of the grounds and circumstances the State would advance in justification. By contrast, if the Court would accept that life begins at birth, abortion legislation would completely fall outside the scope of protection of Article 2 and no protection would be offered against abortion legislation at all, however faulty or ill-considered.[38] Clearly, thus, providing for a uniform, autonomous interpretation of Article 2 presented the Court with a difficult and controversial choice. As is well-known, in the famous *Vo* case, the Court decided to dodge this choice by refusing to provide for an autonomous interpretation.[39] It considered the lack of consensus in Europe regarding the beginning of life to be so significant that any effort to provide a uniform interpretation would be uncalled-for. The Court has adopted a similar approach in a handful of other cases, such as a case on whether a self-purported religious community really can be regarded as such[40], and the case-law on when civil servants are so closely related to primary state functions that their claims can no longer be considered 'civil' in nature for the purposes of the right to access to court and a fair trial.[41] In these cases, the respect for constitutional identity and for national or moral differences prevail over the objective of providing for uniformity or – in the Court's terminology – equality.

---

[37] Clearly, Article 2(2) ECHR clearly describes in which exceptional circumstances the State may legitimately allow that someone's life is taken; abortion is not one of these circumstances.

[38] This solution was advocated by some commentators; see A. Plomer, 'A Foetal Right to Life? The Case of *Vo v. France*', 5 *Human Rights Law Review* (2005) 311–338 and T. Goldman, '*Vo v. France* and Fetal Rights: The Decision Not To Decide', 18 *Harvard Human Rights Law Journal* (2005) 277.

[39] *Vo v. France*, ECtHR (GC) 8 July 2004, no. 53924/00, ECLI:CE:ECHR:2004:0708 JUD005392400, paras. 82–85.

[40] *Kimlya and Others v. Russia*, ECtHR 1 October 2009, no. 76836/01, ECLI:CE:ECHR:2009:100 1JUD007683601; conspicuously, the Court has never repeated this reasoning in its later case-law on this matter, so it may be suspected that this has been a one-off exception.

[41] On the issue of which functions are 'really' public functions, opinions in Europe strongly diverge; the Court has tried to find a solution to this by leaving it primarily to the States to provide their own definitions. See *Vilho Eskelinen and Others v. Finland*, ECtHR (GC) 19 April 2007, 63235/00, ECLI:CE:ECHR:2007:0419JUD006323500, para. 62. The Court is less absolute in this case than it was in *Vo*, however, since it is still prepared to review the strength of the arguments adduced by the States in support of their view that civil servants in certain public functions should be excluded from the right to access to a court and to a fair trial; see para. 62.

Admittedly, the number of cases in which the Court deliberately decides not to embark on an autonomous approach are few and far between. In many more cases, however, the Court opts for a closely related approach which can be dubbed the 'in for a penny, in for a pound' approach.[42] This approach entails that the Court does not provide a uniform and autonomous interpretation of a Convention provision, but connects the applicability of Convention provisions to the national recognition of a certain individual right. A classic illustration is the case of *E.B. v. France*, in which the Court explained that the right to respect for one's family life as such does not cover the right to constitute a family.[43] For the circumstances of the case, this implied that the prohibition of adoption of a child by a single lesbian woman would remain outside the scope of protection of the Convention, and hence outside the Court's jurisdiction. The Court prevented this consequence by explaining that in France, single parent adoption as such is legally permitted, even without there being a Convention obligation to offer access to such adoption.[44] The Court also acknowledged that there is a certain connection between adoption (and founding a family) and the right to respect for existing family life under the Convention.[45] Combining these two arguments, the Court reasoned that the right to single parent adoption, which the French State had voluntarily provided for, should be granted and regulated in accordance with the minimum guarantees of the Convention. In particular, the enjoyment of this right should be granted without discrimination in the sense of Article 14 ECHR, which included discrimination based on sexual orientation.[46] Other case-law shows a similar line of reasoning, for example giving access to the procedural rights guaranteed by the Convention, such as the right to a fair trial or access to court (Article 6 ECHR) if a State has voluntarily provided for a right to appeal (which Article 6 does not guarantee as such).[47] Hence, if the State is 'in for the penny' of providing access to a certain right or benefit, it also should be 'in for the pound' of accepting that minimum human rights guarantees should be offered in providing this right or benefit. At the same time, this means that an equivalent level of protection of Convention rights cannot be invoked in those States where the right concerned has not been provided in the first place.

---

[42] For this terminology and for a further analysis, see J.H. Gerards, 'The European Court of Human Rights and the national courts – giving shape to the notion of 'shared responsibility', in J.H. Gerards and J.W.A. Fleuren (eds.), *Implementation of the European Convention on Human Rights and of the judgments of the ECtHR in national case law. A comparative analysis* (Antwerp, Intersentia, 2014) 13–94, section 4.5.3.

[43] *E.B. v. France*, ECtHR (GC) 22 January 2008, 43546/02, ECLI:CE:ECHR:2008:0122 JUD004354602, para. 41.

[44] *Id.*, para. 49.

[45] *Id.*

[46] *Id.*; more recently, see also e.g. *Pajić v. Croatia*, ECtHR 23 February 2016, no. 68453/13, ECLI: CE:ECHR:2016:0223JUD006845313.

[47] See recently, with many references, *Zubac v. Croatia*, ECtHR 5 April 2018, no. 40160/12, ECLI:CE:ECHR:2018:0405JUD004016012, para. 80.

In States where the possibility for single parent adoption is not recognised, for example, single lesbian mothers cannot successfully invoke the Convention if they are discriminated against, nor do individuals have access to the Court to complain about a difference in treatment or a lack of access to procedural rights before an appeal court if the right to appeal is not recognised in certain cases at all. Hence, the 'in for a penny, in for a pound' approach far from guarantees a uniform level of Convention rights protection. Quite to the contrary, it makes the degree to which non-discrimination and procedural rights are guaranteed dependent on the rights that States decide to recognise.[48]

In defining the terms and notions of the Convention, thus, uniformity may be an important value in theory, and in practice, the Court indeed pays attention to its equality aspect in some cases in which it provides for an autonomous interpretation. At the same time, in most cases, uniformity or equality are not expressly mentioned as a ground for adopting autonomous interpretations, and there are many cases in which the Court decides to refrain from a uniform approach.

III. UNIFORMITY AND THE APPLICATION OF CONVENTION RIGHTS

A. INTRODUCTION

Evidently, even if someone may generally claim the enjoyment of a Convention right in a certain situation, it still may be that the exercise of that right is subject to reasonable limitations. Just like the Convention rights themselves, the conditions for justifiable restrictions contain rather open wording. The permissibility of a certain limitation or restriction usually can be assessed only by very carefully studying the context in which it is made. In addition to this, the Court has accepted that the States Parties are often better placed than the Court is to decide which restrictions to the exercise of Convention rights are needed to pursue certain legitimate aims.[49] The Court therefore often leaves considerable leeway to the States to make their own choices, in particular by applying its famous margin of appreciation doctrine or by applying lenient tests such as the 'excessive and individual burden' test in cases on Article 1 of Protocol 1.[50] The consequence of the application of this type of doctrines and

---

[48]   See further Gerards, *supra* n. 42.

[49]   For some recent examples, see *Garib v. the Netherlands*, ECtHR (GC) 6 November 2017, no. 43494/09, ECLI:CE:ECHR:2017:1106JUD004349409, para. 137 and *Hamidović v. Bosnia and Herzegovina* ECtHR 5 December 2017, no. 57792/15, ECLI:CE:ECHR:2017:1205 JUD005779215, para. 38.

[50]   Much has been written on this; for a recent contribution, with many references to sources, see J.H. Gerards, 'Dealing with Divergence. Margin of Appreciation and Incrementalism in the

tests is that the concrete application of the Convention may be rather diverse, just like the final level of protection offered in particular individual cases. To all expectation, therefore, uniformity is not easy to achieve in relation to the review of restrictions of fundamental rights. At the same time, the Court has always stressed that, in the end, and regardless of any margin of appreciation to be granted to the States, it will retain its supervisory role. Only then can it do justice to its task of offering individual justice and redress and of formulating a clear minimum level of protection. This section will show that in many cases the exercise of this supervisory role may lead to a certain convergence on the national level, and thereby, even if unintentionally, to a certain degree of uniformity.

B. LESS LEEWAY, MORE UNIFORMITY

The Court's case-law firstly discloses a rather uniform level of protection in cases concerning core aspects of Convention rights. Examples of such core aspects are the obligation to respect peaceful protests[51], the fairness of criminal procedure[52], or the respect for freedom of association in relation to political parties.[53] In relation to these aspects the Court allows for hardly any exceptions or limitations, it leaves a very narrow margin of appreciation, and it maintains a high level of protection. The Court in these cases usually accepts justifications only if they meet very clear, precise and detailed conditions and requirements. In the case-law on demonstrations and political parties, such well-defined and high standards can clearly be seen, just as in the case-law setting standards on the use of hearsay evidence in criminal procedure.[54] The Court will usually closely and strictly review if the respondent State has met these standards and if not, it will easily find a violation. It is hardly surprising that the Court leaves little room for diversity in these cases, since they concern central aspects of the Convention and the collective enforcement mechanism has been designed precisely so as to enable the protection of these rights by the Court.[55] If national levels of

---

Case-Law of the European Court of Human Rights', *Human Rights Law Review* (2018), 495-515.

51 E.g. *Lashmankin and Others v. Russia*, ECtHR 7 February 2017, nos. 57818/09 and 14 other cases, ECLI:CE:ECHR:2017:0207JUD005781809, para. 412.

52 E.g. *Al-Khawaja and Tahery v. the United Kingdom*, ECtHR (GC) 15 December 2011, nos. 26766/05 and 22228/06, ECLI:CE:ECHR:2011:1215JUD002676605; *Schatschaschwili v. Germany*, ECtHR (GC) 15 December 2015, no. 9154/10, ECLI:CE:ECHR:2015:1215JUD000915410

53 E.g. *Vona v. Hungary*, ECtHR 9 July 2013, 35943/10, ECLI:CE:ECHR:2013:0709JUD003594310, para. 53.

54 See the cases mentioned *supra*, n. 51, 52 and 53.

55 Cf. R. Spano, 'The Future of the European Court of Human Rights – Subsidiarity, Process-Based Review and the Rule of Law', *Human Rights Law Review* (2018).

protection of these rights were to diverge in relation to these core aspects, the very objectives of the ECHR would be undermined.

Since the Court consistently defines these tests in relatively general terms for specific situation types, they have a strong precedential value. Over time, national authorities learn to expect which standards the Court applies, and they may anticipate on this by applying these standards in their own decision-making. Eventually this may bring about a certain harmonisation of national law and policy. However, the reasoning in cases where the Court applies strict review demonstrates that the Court does not intentionally or consciously strive towards legal unity or uniformity.[56] The Court explains its strictness mainly by emphasising the importance of the need to protect the values underlying the Convention, such as the value of being able to freely express one's views, of protecting the fairness and openness of criminal procedures, or of protecting pluralism and democracy.[57] Uniformity thus is a by-product of the Court's work in protecting core rights, rather than an aim in itself.

C. PROCEDURAL OBLIGATIONS

Another example of the Court's indirect contribution to uniformity can be found in the case-law on procedural positive obligations. In relation to nearly all substantive provisions of the Convention, the Court has defined a significant number of positive obligations that help to guarantee the fairness and quality of national decision-making procedures.[58] These obligations complement those which already follow from the requirements of access to court and to an effective remedy protected by Articles 6 and 13 ECHR. For example, in relation to cases concerning separation of children from their parents and taking them into care, the Court has set specific requirements for the quality of the national legislation and national procedures to ensure that the best interests of the child are respected.[59] In cases about severe environmental damage the Court has required under Article 8 ECHR that prompt and effective investigations are conducted and interested parties are sufficiently involved in decision-making

---

[56] This is demonstrated by a case-law analysis of about 350 cases for a different research project; for the outcomes of this study, see Gerards, *supra* n. 50.

[57] See the cases mentioned *supra*, n. 51, 52 and 53.

[58] For a recent and comprehensive overview, see (in Dutch) T. de Jong, *Procedurele waarborgen in materiële EVRM-rechten* [Procedural guarantees in substantive ECHR rights] (Deventer, Kluwer, 2017); see also e.g. E. Brems and L. Lavrysen, 'Procedural Justice in Human Rights Adjudication: The European Court of Human Rights', 35 *Human Rights Quarterly* (2013) 176–200 and Spano, *supra* n. 55.

[59] E.g. *Barnea and Caldararu v. Italy*, ECtHR 22 June 2017, no. 37931/15, ECLI:CE:ECHR:2017:0 622JUD003793115.

procedures.[60] In cases concerning expulsion of aliens under Article 3 ECHR, the Court requires that it is sufficiently examined which risks the alien will face in the receiving country[61]; and so on. In some of these cases, the Court will grant a wide margin of appreciation to the State in discharging its substantive obligations because of the sensitive nature of the case or because of the better placed argument. By contrast, in relation to the procedural obligations the Court may still minutely review if sufficient guarantees have been offered to reduce the risk of arbitrariness in the use of a widely drafted competence.[62] In relation to Articles 2 and 3, moreover, non-compliance with a procedural obligation can lead to an independent finding of a violation, even if it has not been established that the State is responsible for a violation of the right to life or the prohibition of inhuman and degrading treatment.[63]

As a result of these developments, procedural positive obligations have started to lead a life of their own and a 'feedback loop' is created by finding a violation of the Convention if a State does not comply with its procedural positive obligations.[64] The consistent enforcement of these positive obligations may induce States to actually abide by them. Especially since these positive procedural obligations are defined with increasing precision and detail, this may eventually bring about some degree of uniformity in the organisation of their systems of decision-making and legal protection, even if there are many different ways of guaranteeing the outcomes the Court is looking for.[65] At the same time, the Court has never expressly mentioned legal unity, convergence or uniformity as arguments in formulating its procedural positive obligations.[66]

---

60 E.g. *Jugheli and Others v. Georgia*, 13 July 2017, no. 38342/05, ECLI:CE:ECHR:2017:0713 JUD003834205.

61 E.g. *Ndidi v. the United Kingdom*, ECtHR 14 September 2017, no. 41215/14, ECLI:CE:ECHR:2 017:0914JUD004121514.

62 See e.g. *Bărbulescu v. Romania*, ECtHR (GC) 5 September 2017, no. 61496/08, ECLI:CE:ECH R:2017:0905JUD006149608, in particular paras. 113 and 121. On this, see also e.g. P. Popelier and C. Van de Heyning, 'Subsidiarity Post-Brighton: Procedural Rationality as Answer?', 30 *Leiden Journal of International Law* (2017) 5–23.

63 See already *Šilih v. Slovenia*, ECtHR (GC) 9 April 2009, no. 71463/01, ECLI:CE:ECHR:200 9:0409JUD007146301 and, for an example of the consequences of this approach, *Vasylchuk v. Ukraine*, ECtHR 13 June 2013, no. 24402/07, ECLI:CE:ECHR:2013:0613JUD002440207, paras. 53 and 63 et seq.

64 See in more detail J.H. Gerards, 'Procedural review by the ECtHR – a typology', in J.H. Gerards and E. Brems, *Procedural review in European fundamental rights cases* (Cambridge, Cambridge University Press, 2017) 127–160 and see Spano, *supra* n. 55 and O.M. Arnardóttir, 'The "procedural turn" under the European Convention on Human Rights and presumptions of Convention compliance', 15 *International Journal of Constitutional Law* (2017)(1) 9–35 at 14.

65 See D. Kosař, 'Nudging Domestic Judicial Reforms from Strasbourg: How the European Court of Human Rights shapes domestic judicial design', 13 *Utrecht Law Review* (2017)(1) 112–123 and (in Dutch) L.M. Huijbers, 'Procedurele toetsing, het EHRM en rechtseenheid en diversiteit' [Procedural review, the ECtHR and legal unity and diversity), *Ars Aequi* (2018)(1).

66 As is clear from the case-law analysis made for Gerards, *supra* n. 64.

Indeed, to the extent that there is a degree of uniformity, it mainly seems to be a chance result of the Court's search for a balance between maintaining a high level of protection of Convention rights, interpreting the Convention in such a way individual redress can reasonably be offered, and respect for the primary role of the States.

D. GENERAL PRINCIPLES, STANDARDS AND FACTORS

Uniformity also does not appear to be the express objective of the third unifying approach the Court employs. In exercising its interpretative function, the Court often formulates general principles, standards or factors which are relevant to its assessment of the reasonableness of an interference.[67] Well-known examples are the lists of factors it takes into account in deciding on conflicts between the freedom of expression and the right to someone's reputation[68], or between the freedom of the State to decide on the access and status of migrants and an aliens' right to respect for his private and family life.[69] The Court usually is not very strict in applying these lists of factors, which makes them different from the standards discussed above in relation to the core aspects of Convention rights. The Court does not clarify, for example, how much weight should be given to factors such as the degree to which someone's reputation has been affected or the way a newspaper article has been worded. Moreover, the factors are usually defined rather loosely and openly so as to allow for application in other cases as well as for application by national authorities.[70]

Nevertheless, the consistent use of these general principles can have a somewhat unifying effect. This is true in particular because of another development in the Court's case-law, which is that it will more easily find a violation if the general principles and standards have not or insufficiently been taken into account by the national authorities.[71] By contrast, it may expressly commend national courts for using the factors correctly or it may leave a wider margin of appreciation in such cases.[72] Just as for the procedural positive obligations, the formulation

---

[67] On this approach, see further e.g. Gerards, *supra* n. 17 and see elaborately S. Smet, *Resolving Conflicts between Humn Rights. The Judge's Dilemma* (Routledge, 2017).

[68] See classically *Von Hannover v. Germany*, ECtHR 24 June 2004, no. 59320/00, ECLI:CE:ECH R:2004:0624JUD005932000.

[69] See classically *Üner v. the Netherlands*, ECtHR (GC) 18 October 2006, no. 46410/99, ECLI: CE:ECHR:2006:1018JUD004641099 and *Maslov v. Austria*, ECtHR (GC) 23 June 2008, no. 1638/03, ECLI:CE:ECHR:2008:0623JUD000163803.

[70] On this, see more in-depth Gerards, *supra* n. 50.

[71] See in-depth Gerards, *supra* n. 64; for an example of the Court's approach, see e.g. *Novaya Gazeta and Milashina v. Russia*, ECtHR 3 October 2017, no. 45083/06, ECLI:CE:ECHR:2017:1 003JUD004508306.

[72] See e.g. *Ndidi v. the United Kingdom*, ECtHR 14 September 2017, no. 41215/14, ECLI:CE:ECH R:2017:0914JUD004121514. See further Arnardóttir, *supra*, n. 64 and Gerards, *supra* n. 64.

of these standards and their use by the Court and national authorities may have the effect that national authorities start embedding them in their own legislation, decisions and case-law.[73] In turn, eventually, this may bring about a certain convergence of national law and practice, at least in certain situation types (such as conflicts between the freedom of expression and the right to protection of one's reputation, or conflicts between the right to family life and the public interest of national security). Again, however, the Court has never expressly invoked any notions of uniformity or unity as an argument to justify its development of general principles, standards and factors. Here, this seems to be the coincidental result of the combined aims of guaranteeing an appropriate level of protection of fundamental rights on the national level and enhancing the efficiency, consistency and legal certainty of the Court's own reasoning.

CONCLUSION

In the introduction to this contribution, the question was raised what role uniformity plays in the ECtHR's reasoning and the requirements the Court sets for the States Parties. The answer to that question is that the Court does not expressly aim for uniformity, but it does use methods that may contribute to a certain convergence of national law and practice. Another finding is that there is little truth in the common assumption that the Court mainly effects uniformity through the definition of Convention rights. Surely the Court often provides for an autonomous interpretation of the terms and notions of the Convention and it thereby sets a standard for all the States Parties to meet. The considerations informing this autonomous interpretation are not, however, the values of uniformity or legal unity as such, as would be the case for the CJEU. Instead, autonomous definitions are mainly intended to prevent States from hiding behind their own definitions to escape the effects of the Convention, and to avoid unwarranted differences in treatment between individuals living in different States. In addition, it has been shown that there are several notable exceptions to the rule of autonomous interpretation, especially where the Court applies the 'in for a penny, in for a pound' approach. The Court then still exercises some supervision, but the States can avoid this by simply not recognising a certain right or benefit in their national laws.

---

[73]   This effect on national law is well-documented; see already L.R. Helfer, 'Redesigning the European Court of Human Rights: Embeddedness as a Deep Structural Principle of the European Human Rights Regime', 19 *European Journal of International Law* (2008) 125–159; for an in-depth case-study of the impact of certain tests on national case-law, J.H. Gerards and J.W.A. Fleuren (eds.), *Implementation of the European Convention on Human Rights and of the judgments of the ECtHR in national case law. A comparative analysis* (Antwerp, Intersentia, 2014).

Appearances are even more deceptive where the review of reasonableness of Convention rights is concerned. The Court employs many principles and doctrines to pay deference to the States, such as the better placed argument or the margin of appreciation doctrine. Indeed, the effect of this is that the precise degree and level of Convention rights protection may differ for each individual case. In cases concerning core issues of Convention law, however, the Court requires compelling interests as justification. It thereby sets clear and specific standards the national measures and decisions should meet, which bring about a certain degree of uniformity in these specific fields. Some convergence of national law also can be the result of the procedural positive obligations the Court has defined in its case-law as well as of the Court's definition of lists of general principles, standards and factors. Uniformity in national standards and national procedures is enhanced even further as a result of the Court's tendency to enforce national compliance with its standards, either positively or negatively. As was mentioned above, uniformity is never expressly mentioned as the objective of these approaches. Instead, they are a by-product of pursuing objectives of effective protection of fundamental rights, and, perhaps surprisingly, of the Court's efforts to respect the principle of subsidiarity. Even if it is therefore beyond question that the Court effects a certain degree of uniformity, it appears to do so in a different way and with different objectives than the CJEU does, and also in a different way from what is often thought.

The main explanation for the typicality of the ECtHR's approach is likely to be found in the typical characteristics of the Convention system: the double role of the Court (offering individual justice while setting general standards), the inherent indeterminacy of fundamental rights provisions, and the Court's complex institutional setting. Whereas the functions of legal protection and interpretation clearly imply a desire for uniformity, the controversies surrounding their interpretation and the indeterminacy of the Convention provisions stand in the way of seeing uniformity as a major Convention objective. Moreover, institutionally it is almost impossible to expressly define and maintain a uniform level of legal protection in a system that is so strongly based on subsidiarity of the collective enforcement system, even if the Court also has a significant interpretative function. Thus, it is understandable that the Court acts very prudently and very differently from the CJEU, and that it produces uniformity not by design, but only as a side-effect of its main aim of supervising the compliance with Convention obligations by the States.

LA COUR EUROPÉENNE
DES DROITS DE L'HOMME :
REGARDS CRITIQUES ÉTATIQUES

Isabelle Niedlispacher

Agente du Gouvernement belge devant la Cour

INTRODUCTION

L'originalité du système européen tient principalement au fait qu'il constitue le modèle le plus abouti dans le domaine de la protection internationale des droits de l'Homme.

La Convention européenne garantit en effet non seulement des droits et libertés mais elle instaure aussi un contrôle juridictionnel spécifique pour garantir leur application.

Instrument constitutionnel de l'ordre public européen[1], la Convention européenne est un « instrument vivant » qui doit se lire à la lumière des conditions de vie actuelles[2] et crée des obligations subjectives qui bénéficient d'une garantie collective de surveillance de leur mise en œuvre. Tout individu peut s'en prévaloir devant les tribunaux internes de l'Etat dont il relève de la juridiction[3] après avoir épuisé les voies de recours internes. Le mécanisme de sauvegarde instauré par la Convention est en effet subsidiaire par rapport aux systèmes nationaux de garantie des droits de l'Homme. D'une part, les Etats doivent être les premiers garants du respect de la Convention, d'autre part, ils n'ont pas à répondre de leurs actes devant un organisme international avant d'avoir eu la possibilité de redresser la situation dans leur ordre juridique interne.[4]

Comme l'a encore rappelé la Déclaration de Bruxelles du 27 mars 2015, actuellement, le système de contrôle de la Convention repose sur le droit

---

[1]   CEDH, 23 mars 1995, *Loizidou c. Turquie*, § 70.
[2]   CEDH, 9 octobre 1979, *Airey c. Irlande*, § 26.
[3]   CEDH, 12 décembre 2001, *Bankovic et autres c. Belgique et autres*, § 80.
[4]   CEDH, 1er mars 2010, *Demopoulos et autres c. Turquie*, §§ 69 et 97.

de recours individuel, consacré à l'article 34. Ce droit de recours individuel constitue la spécificité du système de contrôle de la Convention, sa «pierre angulaire».[5]

Ainsi, toute personne se voit-elle reconnaître un droit d'accès direct à la Cour européenne des droits de l'Homme, qu'elle soit personne physique ou morale, ressortissante d'un Etat partie ou apatride, humble ou fortunée.[6] Depuis l'entrée en vigueur du Protocole 11 à la Convention, l'individu s'est vu reconnaître au plan international un véritable droit d'action pour faire valoir des droits et libertés qu'il tient directement de la Convention.[7]

Bien évidemment, la Cour a été amenée à statuer sur des thématiques qui n'étaient pas prévisibles lors de la signature de la Convention en 1950. Depuis plus de 50 ans, elle s'est prononcée sur de nombreux sujets de société : des questions liées à l'avortement, le suicide assisté, les fouilles à corps, l'esclavage domestique, le droit pour une personne née sous X de connaître ses origines, l'adoption par des homosexuels, le port du foulard islamique dans les établissements d'enseignement, la protection des sources journalistiques, la discrimination à l'égard des Roms ou encore des questions touchant à l'environnement.

Le 25 janvier 2012, le Premier Ministre britannique David Cameron déclarait cependant devant l'Assemblée parlementaire du Conseil de l'Europe que la Cour européenne ne devait pas être une «Cour des petits litiges» mais au contraire se concentrer sur «les plus sérieuses violations des droits de l'Homme» et «ne pas compromettre sa propre réputation en contrôlant des décisions nationales qui n'ont pas besoin de l'être».[8]

Exerçant la présidence semestrielle du Comité des Ministres du Conseil de l'Europe, il convoquait en avril 2012 à Brighton une conférence de haut niveau sur l'avenir de la Cour destinée à examiner une série de mesures propres à diminuer le nombre d'affaires devant elle. Nombreux sont ceux qui s'étaient

---

5   La Déclaration de Bruxelles du 27 mars 2015 débute par ces mots : «La Conférence […] réaffirme l'attachement profond et constant des Etats parties à la Convention […] et leur engagement fort à l'égard du droit de recours individuel devant la Cour européenne des droits de l'Homme en tant que pierre angulaire du système de protection des droits et libertés énoncés dans la Convention».

6   F. Krenc, *Dire le droit, rendre la justice. Quelle Cour européenne des droits de l'Homme ?*, Anthémis, 114/2018.

7   CEDH, Gde Ch., *Mamatkulov c. Turquie*, 4 févr. 2005, § 122. Dans le système en vigueur jusqu'au 1er novembre 1998, la compétence de la Commission en matière de droit de recours individuel était subordonnée à une déclaration formelle d'acceptation des Hautes Parties Contractantes pour une durée déterminée.

8   La Cour européenne des droits de l'Homme à la recherche d'un second souffle, Rapport d'information de MM. J-P Michel et P. Gélard fait au nom de la commission des lois n° 705 (2011-2012), 25 juillet 2012, www.senat.fr.

alors inquiétés de ces propositions tendant à encadrer par divers moyens le travail de la Cour de Strasbourg.

Si la nécessité du système conventionnel n'était en principe que très rarement remise en doute, l'institution elle-même de la Cour et son degré d'intervention dans les affaires tranchées par le juge national était l'objet constant de débats qui allaient d'une supposée intrusion du juge européen dans des matières où devait prévaloir la sensibilité et les spécificités nationales, à une critique des méthodes d'interprétation de la Cour ainsi que du manque d'uniformité de sa jurisprudence.

De mon analyse en tant qu'Agente, ces critiques ont sans doute toujours existé mais elles sont devenues plus visibles et audibles dans certains Etats à l'occasion de certaines affaires sensibles politiquement sans jamais contribuer pour autant à une augmentation préoccupante de la méfiance des Etats à l'égard de la Cour.

La critique par certains politiques est d'autant plus aisée qu'il existe, au sein du public européen, une grande méconnaissance du système de la Convention et une confusion de ce système avec celui de l'Union européenne, ce qui leur permet de rejeter sur la Cour la difficulté qu'il existe dans de nombreux domaines à trouver le juste équilibre entre les intérêts de la collectivité et ceux de l'individu.

Les Conférences ministérielles sont une occasion pour les Etats de s'exprimer et, s'ils ne le font pas dans une homogénéité parfaite, beaucoup de leurs préoccupations convergent.

En effet, les controverses qu'ont pu susciter, à juste titre ou non, certaines décisions de la Cour ne doivent pas occulter le fait qu'elle a été confrontée pendant plus d'une quinzaine d'années à une situation importante d'engorgement menant à des délais de jugement confinant parfois au déni de justice.

Pour continuer à jouer efficacement son rôle essentiel de mécanisme européen de protection des droits de l'Homme, des réformes tant internes qu'institutionnelles devaient être mises en œuvre pour permettre à la Cour de faire face à l'afflux de requêtes dont 50 pour cent proviennent de 10 Etats sur les 47 que compte le Conseil de l'Europe.

L'étendue des réformes à mettre en œuvre n'était cependant pas perçue uniformément au sein des Etats membres. A la menace liée à son engorgement depuis les années 2010 s'ajoutaient les défis migratoires, sécuritaires, économiques et identitaires qui frappaient toute l'Europe.

Asseoir son autorité, réaffirmer son utilité et assurer l'application rapide de ses arrêts, voilà quelques défis auxquels est confrontée la Cour au moment où la Belgique prend, à la mi-novembre 2014, la présidence tournante semestrielle du Conseil de l'Europe.

La présidence belge, qui a fait de l'exécution des arrêts de la Cour un des axes prioritaires de son programme, examinera également la responsabilité des Etats dans l'efficacité du fonctionnement de la Cour.

Organe judiciaire du Conseil de l'Europe, composée d'un juge par Etat membre, elle est chargée «d'interpréter la Convention pour que les droits de l'Homme ne soient pas théoriques et illusoires mais pratiques et effectifs» explique le juge belge, Paul Lemmens. Elle peut être saisie par tout particulier ayant épuisé les voies de recours internes et a rendu des arrêts aussi importants que l'arrêt *Salduz* qui prévoit qu'un suspect doit bénéficier de l'assistance d'un avocat ou l'arrêt *Taxquet* qui a obligé la Belgique à motiver ses arrêts de cour d'assises.[9]

Si les condamnations prononcées par la Cour sont souvent «acceptées», quelques thèmes plus sensibles, comme l'asile et l'immigration et la politique sociale ou culturelle suscitent parfois des critiques des gouvernements. Ainsi, après que la Cour a condamné le Royaume-Uni pour son refus d'accorder le droit de vote à certains détenus, David Cameron avait-il estimé que «les interprétations du texte de la Convention ont conduit à un ensemble de choses qui sont franchement mauvaises», laissant entendre que son pays pourrait choisir d'appliquer la jurisprudence de la Cour «autant qu'il est possible».[10]

Les débats sur la légitimité de la Cour ne sont ainsi ouverts généralement que par un petit nombre de jugements, pas par la masse de la jurisprudence. Preuve en est, comme le constate Koen Lemmens[11], qu'il n'existe d'ailleurs pas de corrélation entre «l'attitude hostile ou amicale générale » des Etats membres et le pourcentage de violations constatées à leur égard par la Cour. En France, les questions du voile islamique, de l'euthanasie ou de la gestation pour autrui sont des questions fort sensibles, en Italie, la question de la présence de crucifix dans les classes a été sensible et en Turquie, celle des relations avec le Nord de Chypre.

La Cour est également confrontée à «une érosion des droits fondamentaux», constate Paul Lemmens. Dans les pays où le droit à la vie et les principales libertés fondamentales sont garantis, la Convention et la Cour protègent souvent les droits des minorités moins défendues, comme les détenus ou les Roms.[12]

---

[9] Les défis de la Cour européenne des droits de l'Homme, Belga News, 10 novembre 2014, www. rtbf.be.
[10] Ibid.
[11] K. Lemmens, Présentation Midi du droit au SPF Justice, 15 décembre 2017.
[12] Ibid.

Il faut néanmoins constater que, partout, le statut de la Convention s'est significativement développé au fil du temps de sorte que rares sont ceux qui, aujourd'hui, contestent son rôle d'instrument constitutionnel vivant de l'ordre public européen qui doit se lire à la lumière des conditions de vie actuelles.[13] Ce statut l'a d'ailleurs souvent protégée des rares critiques touchant son essence. Comme l'écrit Frédéric Krenc[14], la Convention est bien davantage qu'un accord multilatéral entre Etats, elle place véritablement l'individu au cœur de son projet démocratique !

Faut-il rappeler l'apport énorme – et pourtant assez évident dirait-on aujourd'hui – de l'arrêt *Marckx c. Belgique* de la Cour du 13 juin 1979.[15] Différents ministres de la Justice avaient bien déposé des projets de loi tendant à mettre fin au traitement inégal des enfants « naturels », nés hors mariage par rapport aux enfants légitimes mais les Chambres législatives n'avaient pas encore trouvé le temps d'adapter la législation à l'évolution de la société.

D'ailleurs, comme le souligne très justement Paul Lemmens dans son exposé du Dialogue entre juges lors de la rentrée solennelle de la Cour en 2015, les juridictions nationales et la Cour ont fondamentalement les mêmes objectifs.

Chacune a une responsabilité non seulement en ce qui concerne la protection des droits fondamentaux – garantis par les constitutions nationales, la Charte des droits fondamentaux de l'Union européenne et par la Convention – mais aussi, plus généralement, en ce qui concerne la défense de l'Etat de droit et de la démocratie.

La critique ouverte de la jurisprudence de la Cour est d'ailleurs assez limitée dans la sphère judiciaire et, malgré les réticences de certaines hautes juridictions en Belgique ou ailleurs, la majorité s'inscrit résolument dans le dialogue institutionnel institué par la Cour par le biais du Réseau des Cours supérieures ainsi que le Protocole 16 instaurant un mécanisme de demande d'avis consultatifs des hautes juridictions nationales à la Cour sur des questions de principe relatives à l'interprétation ou à l'application des droits et libertés définis par la Convention ou ses protocoles (voir *infra*).

La prédominance du dialogue entre les juges nationaux et strasbourgeois est en effet essentielle car tout en favorisant la compréhension mutuelle et la coopération loyale entre les institutions, le dialogue institutionnel peut aller jusqu'à donner la possibilité exceptionnelle d'influencer la jurisprudence européenne et le futur développement du système de la Convention.

---

13   CEDH, 9 octobre 1979, *Airey c. Irlande*, § 26.
14   F. Krenc, op.cit.
15   CEDH, 13 juin 1979, *Marckx c. Belgique*.

Le présent article s'efforce de retracer brièvement la dernière tempête qu'a essuyé la Cour et de brosser le tableau des perspectives auxquelles elle pourrait faire face dans les années à venir.

I. LA CONFÉRENCE MINISTÉRIELLE D'AVRIL 2018

La déclaration de Copenhague fut adoptée lors de la Conférence de haut niveau d'avril 2018 sous présidence danoise du Comité des Ministres du Conseil de l'Europe.

Le projet de déclaration du 5 février 2018 du Gouvernement danois avait été largement critiqué par le monde académique, les ONG, les institutions nationales des droits de l'homme et des membres de parlements nationaux à l'Assemblée parlementaire du Conseil de l'Europe pour le préjudice qu'il pouvait porter à l'indépendance et à l'autorité de la Cour.

Nombreux étaient celles et ceux qui déploraient la confusion relative à la juridiction de la Cour et à son rôle, spécialement dans la définition de la nature subsidiaire du système de la Convention, le dommage potentiel à l'universalité des droits de l'homme ainsi que l'objectif d'installer de nouveaux canaux de «dialogue» pouvant avoir pour effet d'exposer la Cour à une pression politique injustifiée des gouvernements nationaux.[16]

Nombreuses de ces craintes étaient partagées par les Etats qui, au cours d'intenses négociations sur le projet de déclaration, sont parvenus à améliorer sensiblement, supprimer ou atténuer les caractéristiques critiquables du projet initial et à en changer le ton général.

Comme le relèvent Janneke Gerards et Sarah Lambrecht[17], le projet initial présentait ainsi le rôle de la Cour exclusivement sous un angle tronqué de la subsidiarité et non celui que l'on entend communément sous les notions doctrinales de subsidiarité et de marge d'appréciation, indiquant en réalité à la Cour comment elle devrait appliquer la marge d'appréciation et quand elle devrait éviter d'intervenir. La déclaration finale rappelle au contraire la jurisprudence de la Cour sur ces principes.

Les paragraphes controversés relatifs à la manière selon laquelle la Cour devrait aborder les questions d'asile et d'immigration ont été supprimés. Le texte final rappelle fort justement que le renforcement du principe de subsidiarité ne vise pas à limiter ou à diminuer la protection des droits de l'homme mais à souligner

---

16   Https ://strasbourgobservers.com/2018/04/18/the-final-copenhagen-declaration-fundamentally-improved-with-a-few-remaining-caveats.

17   Ibid.

la responsabilité des autorités nationales de garantir les droits et libertés consacrés dans la Convention.

De même, le texte final de la Déclaration de Copenhague n'encourage plus les Etats Parties à discuter le développement général de domaines de la jurisprudence de la Cour présentant un intérêt particulier pour eux et, le cas échéant, à adopter des textes exprimant leurs points de vues généraux. Ne sont plus non plus prévues des séries de rencontres informelles des Etats Parties avant la fin 2019 pour débattre des développements significatifs de la jurisprudence de la Cour. En lieu et place, la Présidence danoise organise à la fin 2018, en guise de suivi de la Conférence d'experts de haut-niveau de 2017 de Kokkedal, une réunion informelle des Etats Parties et autres intervenants au cours de laquelle peuvent être discutées les évolutions générales de la jurisprudence dans le respect de l'indépendance de la Cour et du caractère contraignant de ses arrêts et décisions.

Comme le projet initial par contre, le texte final de la Déclaration souligne que l'exécution des arrêts constitue une obligation primordiale et encourage l'implication de la société civile dans le dialogue relatif à la mise en œuvre de la Convention.

Il encourage aussi à juste titre la Cour à soutenir des tierces interventions accrues et les Etats parties à développer la capacité nécessaire à accroître la coordination et la coopération en cette matière encore sous-exploitée.

On le voit, le texte final de la Déclaration ministérielle est très différent du texte initial, démontrant ainsi que la critique de la Cour qui animait une part du monde politique danois n'a pas été largement partagée au sein des gouvernements des autres Etats Parties.

Il en avait été de même lors de la Déclaration de Brighton en 2012 à l'issue de laquelle le système de la Convention avait été renforcé après avoir été sérieusement remis en question.

Mon expérience d'Agente du Gouvernement est que les Conférences ministérielles qui se sont succédées depuis la Conférence d'Interlaken en 2010 ont finalement toujours été l'occasion pour les Etats de réaffirmer leur attachement au droit de recours individuel, à l'indépendance de la Cour et à la force obligatoire de ses arrêts.

II. LES GRANDES TENDANCES ET L'ÉVOLUTION PROBABLE

Le 24 janvier 2019, à la conférence de presse annuelle de la Cour[18], le Président Raimondi a présenté le bilan 2018 et indiqué qu'à la fin de l'année, le nombre de

---

[18] Communiqué de presse du Greffier de la Cour, CEDH 034 (2019), 24 janvier 2019.

requêtes pendantes devant la Cour s'élevait à 56 350 soit un chiffre pratiquement identique à celui de la fin de l'année 2017.

Cette stabilité est due au fait que le nombre de requêtes attribuées à une formation judiciaire en 2018 était de 43 100 tandis que pratiquement le même nombre d'affaires avait fait l'objet d'une décision ou d'un arrêt.

La Cour a rendu 1014 arrêts (14 par la Grande Chambre, 463 par les Chambres à 7 juges et 537 par les Comités à 3 juges) au cours de l'année 2018.

Les principales violations constatées concernent le droit à la liberté et à la sûreté (art. 5), l'application de traitements inhumains ou dégradants (art. 3) ainsi que le droit à un procès équitable (art. 6).

Un problème systémique demeure : le traitement d'un noyau dur de quelques 22.000 affaires de Chambre qui, en général, soulèvent des questions prioritaires répétitives comme celle de la surpopulation carcérale. Le risque potentiel d'engorgement de la Cour avec de nombreux cas de fonctionnaires turcs limogés à la suite de la tentative de coup d'Etat de l'été 2016, plane toujours par ailleurs.

En 2018, 58.000 requêtes sont pendantes devant la Cour, soit une régression de 30% par rapport à l'année précédente.[19] 80% des requêtes proviennent de 6 pays : la Fédération de Russie, la Roumanie, l'Ukraine, la Turquie, l'Italie et l'Azerbaïdjan. Ce sont essentiellement des situations structurelles dans ces pays qui donnent lieu à un volume de requêtes considérable. Il est dès lors essentiel que les juridictions des Etats membres appliquent correctement le principe de la subsidiarité.

La question de la subsidiarité et de la responsabilité partagée demeure centrale : la Cour est et doit rester l'instance de dernier recours, après l'épuisement des voies de recours internes.

C'est donc en amont du processus, au niveau des juridictions nationales, à travers un fonctionnement fluide de la justice et une bonne application de la Convention que viendra la réduction du nombre des affaires pendantes à Strasbourg.

A cet égard, en 2017, la Cour a rejeté plus de 27.000 requêtes turques directement liées à la tentative de coup d'Etat de 2016 et 6.000 affaires hongroises pour non-épuisement des voies de recours internes.

Pour endiguer le problème du nombre d'affaires pendantes qui relèvent des dysfonctionnement structurels des systèmes judiciaires dans certains pays tels la Roumanie, la Bulgarie et l'Ukraine, la Cour a développé encore le recours aux arrêts pilotes, technique désormais bien éprouvée. Une fois le principe de l'arrêt

---

[19] Rapport 2018, Représentation permanente de la Belgique auprès du Conseil de l'Europe.

pilote posé, l'examen des affaires similaires est reporté et il appartient à l'Etat concerné d'adopter les mesures générales nécessaires indiquées par la Cour. Cette technique a permis de radier du rôle de la Cour plus de 12.000 affaires ukrainiennes mais avec le risque que, sur le terrain, la protection des droits humains n'en soit pas nécessairement renforcée à court terme.

L'une des grandes nouveautés de l'année 2017 avait été la motivation des décisions de juges uniques, cheval de bataille de la présidence belge du Conseil de l'Europe en 2015. Pourquoi ?

Parce que, même brève, la motivation joue un rôle didactique essentiel permettant à terme d'endiguer de nouvelles requêtes en plus d'être nécessaire au maintien de la confiance des justiciables en la justice.

L'une des grandes nouveautés de l'année 2019[20] sera l'instauration d'une phase non contentieuse obligatoire au moment de la communication d'une requête, inspirée par la Déclaration de Copenhague de février 2018 afin de permettre aux requérants d'obtenir une réponse plus rapidement. Les Etats sont ainsi invités à jouer un rôle plus actif en ayant recours plus fréquemment aux règlements amiables et aux déclarations unilatérales dans les affaires dans lesquelles ils n'ont pas besoin d'un arrêt de la Cour pour adapter les droits fondamentaux aux réalités actuelles.

L'exécution des arrêts par les Etats – déjà au cœur des défis relevés par la Conférence de Bruxelles – demeure un enjeu majeur en termes de crédibilité et d'effectivité du système de la Convention et aussi de moyen de lutter efficacement contre l'engorgement de la Cour par des affaires similaires à celles dans lesquelles elle s'est prononcée.

La surveillance de l'exécution relève de la compétence du Comité des Ministres, organe collégial qui s'inscrit dans le principe de la responsabilité partagée de la mise en œuvre de la Convention aux côtés de la Cour et des Etats.

En 2018, 2.705 affaires en attente d'exécution ont été closes, soit une augmentation régulière depuis cinq ans.

Plusieurs affaires sensibles concernant la Russie n'ont cependant pas progressé : *Youkos* (affaire relative à l'indemnisation des actionnaires de cette entreprise pétrolière dans laquelle la Cour constitutionnelle russe a conclu que le paiement d'une indemnisation de quasi 2 milliards d'euros aux plaignants contrevenait à la Constitution) ; *Navalny* (l'opposant politique, par rapport à qui la Cour a constaté à nouveau que, malgré une nouvelle procédure, le droit pénal avait été

---

[20]   Ibid.

interprété de manière arbitraire et imprévisible à son détriment) et *Catan* (affaire relative au droit à l'instruction des enfants en langue moldave, en Transnistrie, dans une zone contrôlée par la Russie).

Aucun progrès non plus concernant les groupes d'affaires turco-chypriotes *Xenides-Arestis* (dédommagements à la suite de mises sous séquestre ou de spoliation de biens immobiliers à la suite de l'occupation de Chypre Nord il y a quarante ans).

Concernant l'Azerbaïdjan, la Cour reste saisie de l'affaire *Mammadov* sous l'angle de la procédure en manquement prévue à l'article 46-4 de la Convention car l'opposant politique est sorti de prison en 2018 mais n'a pas été libéré inconditionnellement comme l'impliquait l'arrêt de la Cour de 2014.

Bonne nouvelle en ce qui concerne le Royaume-Uni par contre : l'affaire Hirst relative à l'interdiction générale de voter pour les détenus a pu être clôturée.

Concernant la Belgique, 20 affaires sont en cours de surveillance dont 9 en procédure soutenue. Le 13 mars 2018, le Ministre de la Justice, Koen Geens, avait pris part à un débat thématique sur l'exécution des arrêts et le problème systémique des conditions de détention.

Lors de son intervention, le Ministre a fait le point sur la mise en œuvre du « Plan Prisons » et informé le Comité des progrès en cours concernant la réduction de la surpopulation carcérale, en baisse de près de 20% et l'aménagement de peines alternatives pour les peines courtes.

La question de l'internement et de l'encadrement psycho-médial des détenus souffrant de troubles psychiatriques est également en progression.

L'enfermement des étrangers illégaux est réduit au strict minimum.

La surveillance de l'exécution de l'arrêt *Trabelsi* a pris fin en décembre 2018 par résolution finale du Comité des Ministres prenant note des garanties obtenues auprès du Parquet et à obtenir auprès des magistrats américains du siège quant à l'absence de peine de réclusion à perpétuité incompressible par principe.

L'exécution des arrêts est et restera sans doute toujours un défi quotidien pour les Etats.

Avec l'élaboration du Protocole 15, un nouveau considérant avait été ajouté à la fin du préambule de la Convention contenant une référence au principe de subsidiarité et à la doctrine de la marge d'appréciation. Il est destiné à renforcer la transparence et l'accessibilité de ces caractéristiques du système de la Convention et à rester cohérent avec la doctrine de la marge d'appréciation telle que développée par la Cour dans sa jurisprudence.

En formulant cette proposition, la Déclaration de Brighton avait également rappelé l'engagement des Hautes Parties contractantes à donner plein effet à leur obligation de garantir les droits et libertés définis dans la Convention, en amont – comme premières garantes du respect de la Convention au niveau national –, comme en aval, par une prompte exécution des arrêts et décisions définitifs de la Cour, comme le rappelle encore la Déclaration de Bruxelles.

Un autre protocole vient parfaire le système : le Protocole n° 16 à la Convention, entré en vigueur le 1er août 2018. Il prévoit la possibilité pour les hautes juridictions des États parties d'adresser des demandes d'avis consultatifs à la Cour sur des questions de principe relatives à l'interprétation ou à l'application des droits et libertés définis par la Convention ou ses protocoles. Les hautes juridictions des 10 États ayant ratifié le Protocole (l'Albanie, l'Arménie, l'Estonie, la Finlande, la France, la Géorgie, la Lituanie, Saint-Marin, la Slovénie et l'Ukraine) peuvent désormais s'adresser à la Cour pour des demandes d'avis non contraignants dans le cadre d'affaires pendantes devant elles. La Belgique les rejoindra dans quelques mois à l'issue de la procédure de ratification en cours faisant suite à sa signature du Protocole dit « du dialogue » le 8 novembre 2018. Il lui permettra, comme à tous les Etats l'ayant ratifié, de faire jouer à plein régime le principe de subsidiarité en s'adressant en amont au juge européen en cas de doute sur l'interprétation ou l'application des droits et libertés définis par la Convention ou ses protocoles dont il est le premier garant dans les affaires qui lui sont soumises évitant peut-être ainsi des recours à la Cour sur des questions complexes.

Pas de système harmonieux sans dialogue continu entre ses protagonistes. L'objectif global du Réseau des cours supérieures (SCN : Superior Courts Network) est d'enrichir le dialogue et la mise en œuvre de la Convention. Son objectif opérationnel plus concret est de créer des moyens pratiques et utiles d'échanger les informations pertinentes portant sur la jurisprudence relative à la Convention et sur des questions connexes. Le président de la Cour en a confié la gestion au jurisconsulte de la Cour et d'après nos informations, on peut parler d'un processus couronné de succès d'échanges réguliers entre la Cour et les juridictions supérieures des Etats faisant l'objet du projet pilote. Comme l'a rappelé le Président Raimondi, la mise en place du Réseau en octobre 2015 a constitué une étape importante du dialogue avec les juridictions nationales. Avant tout, elle a répondu à un besoin de coopération concrète et d'échanges d'information entre les juridictions nationales et la Cour. Le Réseau fait désormais partie du paysage de la Convention. Le fait qu'il se soit développé si rapidement montre que juridictions nationales et Cour comprennent que la voie à suivre passe par un dialogue plus approfondi. L'entrée en vigueur récente du Protocole N° 16 constitue un autre indicateur fort à cet égard.

Oui, mais, parallèlement au dialogue, s'il y a constat de violation, jusqu'où la Cour doit-elle aller pour ordonner réparation ? Les arrêts doivent-ils avoir un caractère prescriptif ?

La Cour de Strasbourg peut-elle ou devrait-elle pouvoir recommander, ou même imposer, aux Etats de prendre certaines mesures ?

Cette question fait l'objet de de plus en plus de débats dans la mesure où, encouragée par le défaut pour les Etats de mettre en œuvre tous les arrêts, la Cour s'est départie de son approche déclaratoire originaire strictement limitée à l'indication de mesures réparatrices pour spécifier parfois des mesures individuelles ou générales non pécuniaires.

Pour le Juge à la Cour élu au titre de l'Islande Robert Spano[21], la pratique en matière de mesures réparatrices de la Cour est importante pour l'efficacité et la légitimité renforcées du système de la Convention.

Preuve en est que la division du travail entre la Cour et le Comité des Ministres a – particulièrement dans le contexte des affaires susceptibles de faire l'objet d'arrêts pilotes et d'autres affaires incluant des violations structurelles ou systémiques de la Convention – évolué d'une attitude passive de la Cour à une attitude plus proactive dans l'indication de mesures individuelles ou générales non-pécuniaires.

Toutefois, il n'est pas sûr que la Cour ait déjà adopté une approche cohérente en la matière, spécialement dans les affaires ordinaires, que ce soit au niveau d'une chambre ou de la Grande Chambre.

En tant qu'Agent du Gouvernement, j'ai pu observer que la Cour indique à cet égard plus fréquemment des mesures générales que des mesures individuelles non-pécuniaires, aussi bien dans ses arrêts « ordinaires » que pilotes. Si la pratique grandissante de la Cour d'indiquer les mesures réparatrices générales pour éviter que le problème ne se réitère dans les mêmes termes est parfois perçue par les Etats comme entachant le principe de subsidiarité, cette pratique est toutefois majoritairement acceptée. Même les arrêts qui n'emporteraient pas une adhésion immédiate ou complète sont d'ailleurs exécutés dans leur intégralité. Mais, surtout, la plupart des Agents et des acteurs nationaux estiment qu'il est souvent utile d'avoir des indications spécifiques quant à l'interprétation et à l'exécution visées de l'arrêt. D'une part, cela peut aider la Cour à penser à la faisabilité de ses décisions. D'autre part, cela dote l'Agent du Gouvernement de moyens pour encourager l'exécution et les autorités visées, de possibilités de demander davantage de moyens en vue de l'exécution.[22]

---

21   Seminar The Evolving Remedial Practice of the European Court of Human Rights, 8 novembre 2017, Dr Alice Donald, School of Law, Middelsex University London (UK).

22   Ibid.

Je me dirige vers la conclusion de mon bref survol que je souhaite précéder d'une esquisse des perspectives pour le développement de la protection des droits humains en Belgique.

La note de politique générale Justice approuvée par la Chambre des représentants de Belgique le 24 octobre 2018 reprend au volet « Droits de l'Homme », le souhait, conformément à la Déclaration de Bruxelles, de maintenir le dialogue avec le Parlement fédéral en matière de suivi des arrêts de la Cour.

C'est ainsi que le 22 février 2019, le bureau de l'Agente du Gouvernement a accompagné le Ministre de la Justice au Parlement pour présenter son rapport annuel relatif au contentieux devant la Cour en ce compris l'exécution des arrêts qui continuera bien entendu à bénéficier de la priorité nécessaire, tant sur le plan des mesures individuelles que sur le plan des mesures générales. Les questions des parlementaires démontraient à la fois leur connaissance du système de la Convention et leur vif intérêt pour le développement des droits fondamentaux en Belgique et la surveillance de leur protection par des organes indépendants.

Ainsi fut évoqué le projet de loi portant assentiment au Protocole facultatif à la Convention des Nations Unies contre la torture voté par le Parlement le 18 juillet 2018. Parallèlement, le Conseil central de surveillance pénitentiaire était renforcé et la meilleure solution, recherchée pour parvenir à un mécanisme de prévention national de la torture et des traitements inhumains ou dégradants pour les lieux où les personnes sont privées de leur liberté.

Furent également évoqués les travaux en vue de la mise en place d'un mécanisme national des droits de l'Homme poursuivis en collaboration avec le Ministre de tutelle pour l'Egalité des chances. La loi créant l'Institut fédéral de protection et de promotion des droits humains a été adoptée ce 25 avril 2019. L'IFDH veille à une action concertée avec les organismes sectoriels de protection et de promotion des droits fondamentaux de compétence fédérale. Il facilite le dialogue et coopère avec les organisations chargées de protection et de promotion des droits humains au niveau fédéral et des entités fédérées ainsi qu'avec les organisations de la société civile.

Par ailleurs, dans le cadre du suivi de la Déclaration de Bruxelles de mars 2015, le bureau de l'Agente du Gouvernement, à l'instar d'autres Etats, échange des informations avec les organes exerçant déjà partiellement en Belgique le mandat d'une institution nationale des droits de l'homme par la transmission des arrêts définitifs et des plans et bilans d'action prêts à être diffusés par le Conseil de l'Europe.

La transmission des décisions et arrêts définitifs peut ainsi donner lieu à un échange de vues en amont de la soumission de nos plans et bilans d'action au

Conseil de l'Europe, celle de nos plans et bilans d'action peut, elle, donner lieu à des réactions en aval du processus.

Nous informons également les organes exerçant le mandat d'une INDH de la possibilité qu'ils ont de recevoir de la Cour une notification des affaires communiquées, ce qui leur permet, le cas échéant, de faire tierce intervention pour éclairer la Cour sur les enjeux du litige.

Sur le plan de la politique criminelle[23], la lutte contre le racisme, l'antisémitisme, l'islamophobie ainsi que les autres crimes de haine et la discrimination sera poursuivie en 2019.

En outre, dans le nouveau Code pénal, on utilisera davantage le mobile discriminatoire comme circonstance aggravante ou comme élément d'infractions violentes ou d'autres infractions pertinentes et cela pourra entraîner une peine plus sévère.

Les travaux de la Commission d'évaluation concernant la législation anti-discrimination contribueront à optimiser encore la législation. La proposition de la Commission interministérielle de droit humanitaire, accompagnée de l'avis d'Unia, visant à incriminer plus largement le négationnisme devrait prochainement être discutée au Parlement.

Le monde académique se sent, quant à lui, pousser des ailes. Une ébauche de grande réforme de la Constitution voit le jour. Une soixantaine de professeurs et chercheurs en droit constitutionnel et sciences politiques ont décidé au Nord comme au Sud du pays de se pencher sur le texte fondamental approuvé il y a 188 ans et réformé maintes fois.[24]

Les lacunes sont de taille : il n'y a pas, dans la Constitution, d'interdiction de la torture et de l'esclavage, de droit à un procès équitable ni de protection de la liberté de circulation.

Ces principes se trouvent bien entendu dans la Convention mais pour les académiques, cela ne suffit pas. Il suffirait d'une décision du gouvernement, sans vote au Parlement, pour que la Belgique se retire de traités internationaux et que ces droits disparaissent. « Si l'on intègre ces droits dans la Constitution, il est beaucoup plus difficile de les modifier parce que la Constitution se révise difficilement » précise Céline Romainville de l'UCLouvain.[25] Et l'air du temps rend ce renforcement plus important qu'il y a quelques années. « Avant, on disait que jamais un gouvernement ne se retirerait de la Convention, mais dans

---

23   Note de politique générale Justice, Doc. Chambre 54 3296/015, 24 octobre 2018.
24   Ibid.
25   Bernard Demonty, Article Au secours, la Constitution prend la poussière !, *Le Soir*, mis en ligne le 14 février 2019 à 06 :00.

une série de gouvernements européens, le retrait de la Convention n'est plus un tabou. Rien que pour cela, il y a une nécessité d'intégrer ces droits dans la Constitution ».[26]

Les scientifiques qui ont analysé la Constitution proposent même d'y ancrer le principe d'une politique climatique effective. Un article prévoit déjà que le développement durable est un objectif des différentes entités du pays. L'idée serait d'y ajouter la nécessité d'une politique climatique efficace et coordonnée menée en étroite collaboration par le fédéral et les entités fédérées.

Les académiques relèvent aussi en matière d'élections et de gouvernance que les élus se contrôlent eux-mêmes, les parlements concernés étant aujourd'hui compétents en Belgique pour vérifier la régularité de leur élection. Il faudrait sans doute prévoir un recours à la Cour constitutionnelle ou au Conseil d'Etat pour la personne qui dénonce une irrégularité et à qui on refuse de recompter les votes.[27]

Les soixante professeurs et chercheurs sont unanimes : la refonte du Sénat suite à la sixième réforme de l'Etat est un échec. Alors, soit on le renforce comme un vrai Sénat fédéral soit on abandonne cette logique fédérale et on en fait une assemblée de citoyens tirés au sort. Si on n'arrive à réaliser aucun de ces scénarios, certains envisagent même sa suppression.[28]

Parmi les défauts de la Constitution actuelle, il y aurait aussi l'absence d'exigence de parité réelle entre hommes et femmes. On ne peut pas avoir un gouvernement où il n'y a que des hommes ou que des femmes, il faut une femme au moins ou un homme au moins. Mais cela ne va pas au-delà, dit Céline Romainville. L'idée serait de prendre la même mesure pour les gouvernements que pour les collèges, la démocratie locale prévoyant un tiers de représentants de l'autre sexe.[29]

CONCLUSION

Que conclure de tout cela ?

Je pense pouvoir conclure que la Cour exerce une part de responsabilité très importante dans la progression des droits fondamentaux sur notre continent et au-delà.

---

[26]   Ibid.
[27]   Ibid.
[28]   Ibid.
[29]   Ibid.

Elle doit alterner prudence et audace afin de ne pas menacer le consensus européen sur les questions politiques et sociales délicates, telles les questions migratoires, sécuritaires et identitaires. La Cour doit aussi comprendre le formalisme imposé par les juridictions nationales sans être complaisante avec l'imposition de formes qui rompraient un juste équilibre entre accessibilité réelle et réaliste.

Elle doit bien entendu répondre au requérant en lui rendant justice mais ne pas se laisser saturer en succombant à la tentation de se répéter à l'envi pour pouvoir continuer à exercer son autre mission de dire le droit de la Convention.

Selon moi, comme nulle autre juridiction internationale, notre Cour européenne sait garder le cap entre petits désamours et grosses tempêtes, plaintes et contestations, incrédulités et désarroi des autorités nationales administratives, politiques ou judiciaires.

Non seulement elle alterne résilience et audace dans ses arrêts en fonction de sa prise de pouls de l'évolution sociale nationale mais encore elle sait se montrer créative et pragmatique pour maîtriser son succès et ne pas se laisser engloutir par sa mission de rendre la justice à l'égard de chaque requérant au mépris de sa mission de dire le droit de la Convention pour permettre que les violations ne se perpétuent pas inutilement.

Si le continent européen est éprouvé par des tensions qui affectent la protection des droits de l'Homme et que les principes de subsidiarité et de la marge d'appréciation des Etats dans l'application de la Convention se voient plus que jamais sacralisés, il y a toutefois des volontés, de véritables élans même, et à tous niveaux, gouvernemental comme académique, en faveur de la progression constante des droits et libertés fondamentaux pour les adapter aux réalités et défis de la société actuelle.

Je crois sincèrement que la préservation et même l'évolution des droits humains est l'affaire de tous, au quotidien, dans la vie privée ou professionnelle, comme électeur ou comme élu. Quel que soit son parcours de vie ou sa vision du monde, chacun d'entre nous détient une petite parcelle de responsabilité dans la préservation de la démocratie, de la paix et de la douceur de vivre ensemble sur le continent européen et au-delà.

Les Agents des Gouvernements devant la Cour ont vocation à exercer, eux aussi, leur part de responsabilité dans le système de la Convention au moment de leur analyse de la requête et de la détermination de la stratégie la plus même de répondre honnêtement et adéquatement à la problématique qu'elle soulève comme lors de l'exécution prompte et complète d'un arrêt.

Je relève à cet égard que la Cour a encore, en ce début 2019, développé une stratégie habile et pragmatique en invitant les Etats à faire le meilleur usage possible du principe de subsidiarité.

En prévoyant deux phases procédurales obligatoires sous la forme d'une réflexion non-contentieuse préalable à la poursuite éventuelle de la phase contentieuse, la Cour permet à l'Etat de ne pas succomber à la facilité de la laisser se prononcer dans les cas où cela ne s'avèrerait pas nécessaire parce qu'il a déjà l'intention ou la possibilité d'initier une réforme en s'y engageant formellement dans le cadre d'un règlement amiable ou d'une déclaration unilatérale sans attendre un arrêt.

Dans ce cas, pareil engagement de l'Etat est déjà un commencement d'exécution puisque l'Etat s'engage à prendre des mesures individuelles ou collectives pour remédier à la situation contraire à sa lecture de la Convention sans attendre que la Cour en porte une responsabilité superflue et en choisissant lui-même l'étendue de son engagement et les moyens de le mettre en œuvre, sous la surveillance du Comité des Ministres pour les règlements amiables et la menace d'une réinscription au rôle en cas d'inexécution pour les déclarations unilatérales.

Au travers de mon humble exposé, j'ai tenté de rendre hommage à notre juge belge à la Cour qui, jour après jour, exerce sa part de responsabilité dans le développement des droits fondamentaux. Je lui souhaite encore beaucoup d'aventures passionnantes sur cette très belle route.

THE IMPLEMENTATION OF THE CRPD IN THE ECHR: CHALLENGES AND OPPORTUNITIES

Jenny E. GOLDSCHMIDT[*]

Emeritus Professor in Human Rights Law, Utrecht University

INTRODUCTION

The European Convention of Human Rights (ECHR) does not exist in 'splendid isolation' but is part of a broader regional and international human rights system. Interactions between these systems occur in various ways. Some harmonisation is usually seen as desirable to increase the impact of the system as a whole. On the other hand, a certain amount of pluralism (not relativism!) can be defended too, to increase application of the instruments in the specific context (regional or topical). Pluralism may also promote a 'pushing-up' effect in the implementation of human rights when the various monitoring institutions are in a position to develop more solid interpretations using the frames of other instruments.

The United Nations Convention on the Rights of Persons with Disabilities of 2006 (CRPD) is one of the most recent instruments, which does not add new rights to the existing UN Bill of Rights, but is a further elaboration of these. The CRPD is thus an important frame for the interpretation of human rights of people with disabilities. Therefore, it is most relevant to consider its relevance in practice of the case law of the European Court of Human Rights (ECtHR) in the development of the ECHR as a 'living instrument'.

The explicit reference to basic principles in the CRPD itself (Article 3) urges the ECtHR to take these into account in its interpretation of the rights of people with disabilities (and this can be also the case when other groups are involved but that goes beyond the scope of this contribution).

---

[*] This contribution was finalised in the Summer of 2018. More recent developments on this subject were therefore not included.

Inclusion can be seen as the underlying concept of the CRPD. The Committee on the Rights of Persons with Disabilities gives a description of 'inclusion' in paragraph 9 of its General Comment on the Right to inclusive education (Article 24 CRPD)[1], which can adapted for other areas as follows: 'inclusion encompasses a transformation in culture, policy and practice in all formal and informal ... environments to accommodate the different requirements and identities of individual persons, together with a commitment to remove the barriers that impede that possibility'. Inclusion aims at the incorporation of differences in the legal, social and cultural systems, instead of making exceptions or exclusions to the general rules and norms which do not take their specific characteristics into account.

In this contribution I will investigate the implications of such an inclusive approach under the ECHR, examining the (possible) interpretation of the rights of people with disabilities by the ECtHR from the perspective of the CRPD.

I.   THE INCLUSIVE APPROACH OF HUMAN RIGHTS

Essential of human rights is the principle of inclusion: all people are born free and equal in dignity and rights, as stated first article of the Universal Declaration of Human Rights. Human rights thus imply the ambition of an inclusive society, where everybody can participate in his or her own way, within the limits of the law and with respect for the rights of others.

This ambition of inclusion demands an open mind of all. We all have our own perceptions of what is 'normal' and what is 'deviant', our own perspectives and our prejudices, even when we are not aware of these. These personal characteristics are not good or wrong per se. However, for human rights practitioners it is relevant to unveil these attitudes and opinions when they hinder others to enjoy their human rights, to be equal in dignity and rights. Therefore, we may expect human rights scholars and practitioners to have this open mind, and to be aware of their own limitations and to be willing to listen to others. Unfortunately, not all possess these qualities. In the years I worked with Paul Lemmens, mostly in the context of the European Master Program of Human Rights and Democratization (Venice), I admired him exactly because of this open attitude. Being an eminent scholar, an highly estimated expert in human rights combining a rich academic and practical experience, Paul always listened to all arguments and was open to other perspectives, even when it was not always easy to convince him to change his opinion.

---

[1]   General Comment No. 4 (2016), 2 September 2016.

For that reason in my contribution to Paul Lemmens I will reflect on the possible impact of the UN Convention on the Rights of People with Disabilities (CRPD or Convention) on the interpretation of the European Convention of Human Rights (ECHR).

As O'Cinneide reaffirms, the CRPD 'in its detail, range and precision goes further than …other instruments' and considering the extent to which the other instruments as the ECHR provide protection for persons with disabilities can be seen as 'an acid test of the functioning of rights instruments…'.[2]

The development of the concept of inclusiveness in human rights thus reached a new stage with the adoption of this convention, which has implications that go far beyond the rights of disabled people.[3] This impact is caused by the incorporation of principles that have been developed in the application of the various international, regional and national human rights law. As a recent convention, the CRPD was able to profit from the outcomes of these. As a Judge in the European Court of Human Rights, Paul Lemmens is at the core of this development and, as we will see below, participates actively in the development of the Court's argument.

II. PURPOSE AND PRINCIPLES OF THE CRPD

The starting point of the concept of inclusion the Convention lies in the Preamble under (a) and (e) which are reflected in the Purpose of the Convention in Article 1:

> 'The Purpose of the Convention is to promote, protect and ensure the full and equal enjoyment of all fundamental rights and freedoms by all persons with disabilities, and to promote respect for their inherent dignity.
> Persons with disabilities include those who have long-term physical, mental, intellectual or sensory impairments which in interaction with various barriers may hinder their full and effective participation in society on an equal basis with others.'

Essential is the reference to the interaction between the impairment of a person and the barriers in society. In the Preamble under the (e) the barriers are further defined as 'attitudinal and environmental'. This is exactly what inclusion means: removing the barriers that prevent people to enjoy their rights. It is not only

---

2   Com O'Cinneide, Extracting Protection for the Rights of Persons with Disabilities from Human Rights Frameworks: Established Limits and New Possibilities, in: Oddny Mojoll Anardotti, G. Quinn a.o., *The UN Convention on the Rights of Persons with Disabilities*, Brill, 2009, pp. 163–198, at p. 167.
3   Heiner Bielefeldt, *Zum Innovationzpotenzial der UN-Behindertenrechtskonvention*, Essay, Deutsches Institut für Menschenrechte, 3. aktualisierte und erweiterte Auflage, Juni 2009, https://www.institut-fuer-menschenrechte.de/uploads/tx_commerce/essay_no_5_zum_inno vationspotenzial_der_un_behindertenrechtskonvention_aufl3.pdf.

the difference that is relevant: it is the combination of the impairment and the barriers that excludes people. And the barriers are not only physical barriers but also, and perhaps more importantly, the invisible, often unconscious prejudices and stereotypes in the minds of others. This aspect is also recognized in the Convention on the Elimination of all Forms of Discrimination against Women (CEDAW), which obliges in Article 5(a) the State Parties to take all appropriate measures 'to (m)odify the social and cultural patterns of conduct of men and women, with a view to achieving the elimination of prejudices and customary and all other practices which are based on the idea of the inferiority or the superiority of either of the sexes or on stereotyped roles for men and women'.

The CRPD further enumerates in Article 3 the principles of the Convention, which can be considered as elements or conditions of the general purpose of inclusion:
(a) Respect for inherent dignity, individual autonomy including the freedom to make one's own choices, and independence of persons;
(b) Non-discrimination;
(c) Full and effective participation and inclusion in society;
(d) Respect for difference and acceptance for persons with disabilities as part of human diversity and humanity;
(e) Equality of opportunity
(f) Accessibility
(g) Equality between men and women;
(h) Respect for the evolving capacities of children with disabilities and respect for the rights of children with disabilities to preserve their identities.

These principles are relevant for the interpretation of rights of all people who are considered as 'different', and are treated less favourably than others, and therefor they are also relevant for the European Court of Human Rights (ECtHR) as interpretative tools.

In the context of the case law of the ECtHR I want to illuminate some concepts related to these principles: admissibility, autonomy, participation and equality. As mentioned, I will focus on the relevance of the CRPD in the implementation of the ECHR and more specific on a selection of the cases dealing with disability.[4] I am aware of the relevance of other instruments than the CRPD in this context, both of the Council of Europe (such as Recommendation No. R (99) 4 of the Committee of Ministers of the Council of Europe on principles concerning the legal protection of incapable adults (adopted on 23 February 1999) and others, but the interaction with these goes beyond the scope of this article. I think this approach can be justified by the fact that the CRPD does not add any new rights

---

[4] The Factsheet of the Court on Persons with Disabilities is most helpful in this context: see https://www.echr.coe.int/Documents/FS_Disabled_ENG.pdf.

or entitlements but 'covers a number of existing rights in a manner that addresses the needs and situation for persons with disabilities'[5]: all other relevant instruments remain relevant but have to be applied in accordance with the CRPD.

III. ACCESSIBILITY

Accessibility as a principle is further guaranteed in Article 9 of the CRPD. In 2014 the Committee on the Rights of Persons with Disabilities (the Committee) elaborated more precisely in a General Comment which are the contents and obligations emanating from this provision.[6]

The General Comment starts with emphasizing the 'conditio sine qua non' character of the accessibility: 'Without access to the physical environment, to transportation, to information and communication, including information and communications technologies and systems, and to other facilities and services open to the public, persons with disabilities would not have equal opportunities for participation in their respective societies'.[7] The Committee refers to the other UN Conventions which contain provisions related to or guaranteeing accessibility, such as Article 25(c) of the International Covenant on Civil and Political Rights, on equal access to public service, Article 5(f) of the International Convention on the Elimination of all Forms of Racial Discrimination, on general access to places intended for use by the general public. This reaffirms that the CRPD does not add new rights to the core body of human rights instruments, but is a further elaboration of these rights to guarantee the enjoyment thereof by all people with disabilities. It includes a more detailed description of the duties of the state to respect, protect and fulfil these.

Accessibility is closely related to the idea of universal design, in particular to new goods and services, meaning that in the creation thereof accessibility is taken into account. The Committee holds that '…application of universal design makes society accessible for all human beings, not only persons with disabilities'.[8] A distinction is made between new buildings etcetera and the accessibility of existing ones. Also, the group-based duty of accessibility will always be complemented by the obligation to provide a reasonable accommodation for individuals whose impairments are not (yet) taken into account by accessibility

---

5   Nandine Devi, Jerome Birkenbach, Gerold Stucki, Research Paper. Moving towards substituted or supported decision-making? Article 12 of the Convention on the Rights of Persons with Disabilities, ALTER, *European Journal of Disability Research* 5 (2011), p. 251.
6   Committee on the Rights of Persons with Disabilities, General Comment No, 2 (2014), CRPD/C/GC/2.
7   GC 2, Par 1.
8   GC 2, Par. 16.

standards. Whereas the obligation to provide accessibility is unconditional, the duty of reasonable accommodation is restricted by the condition that it should not impose an undue burden.[9]

When dealing with the relationship with other articles of the Convention under IV of the General Comment, the Committee refers briefly to access to justice: law-enforcement agencies and the judiciary have to be accessible too.[10] Accessibility in court proceedings is not restricted to physical accessibility: it implies also that adequate accommodations such as sign language for deaf people must be made available, as the Court ruled in the case of *Z.H. v. Hungary*.[11] Although this case dealt with the circumstances of detention, it is also relevant with regard to court procedures. The specific conditions of disabled asylum seekers for example, demand also more specific attention. A report on deaf asylum seekers in the Netherlands showed that they face practical (no adequate sign or other interpretation) and emotional barriers which in practice prevent them to use the procedure in an effective way.[12]

Access to court is also important for people with mental disabilities: accessibility in general 'should be provided to all persons with disabilities, regardless of the type of impairment....'.[13] The access to justice of people with disabilities is closely related to the equal recognition before the law, as guaranteed in Article 12 of the CRPD. Article 12 has been interpreted by the Committee in its first General Comment of 2014.[14] Below more attention will be paid to this article, but here it is important to note that the Committee emphasizes the universal value of legal capacity and in the paragraphs 8 and 39 of the General Comment the recognition of this right is applied to Article 13 of the CRPD, guaranteeing access to justice.

IV. ACCESSIBILITY IN THE ECtHR CASE LAW

The ECtHR's decision in the case of *Stanev v. Bulgaria* in 2012[15] can be seen as a landmark case in the application of the right to a fair trial (Article 6 paragraph 1 ECHR) in case of mental disabilities. The case is about a person under partial guardianship who is placed in an institution with a very bad reputation and who seeks a review of his guardianship and of his placement in this institution.

---

9   GC 2, Par. 26.
10   GC 2, Par. 37.
11   See ECtHR 8 November 201, No. 28973/11.
12   Https://www.dovenschap.nl/wp-content/uploads/2015/09/Rapport-dove-asielzoekers.pdf.
13   CRPD General Comment No. 2 (2014), par. 13.
14   General Comment No. 1 (2014) Article 12, CRPD/G/GC/1.
15   17 January 2012, No. 36760/06.

Under the Bulgarian Law he could not challenge these independently. The Court held under paragraph 241 that

> 'the right of access to the courts is not absolute and requires by its very nature that the State should enjoy a certain margin of appreciation in regulating the sphere under examination ... In addition, the Court acknowledges that restrictions on a person's procedural rights, even where the person has been only partially deprived of legal capacity, may be justified for the person's own protection, the protection of the interests of others and the proper administration of justice. However, the importance of exercising these rights will vary according to the purpose of the action which the person concerned intends to bring before the courts. In particular, the right to ask a court to review a declaration of incapacity is one of the most important rights for the person concerned since such a procedure, once initiated, will be decisive for the exercise of all the rights and freedoms affected by the declaration of incapacity, not least in relation to any restrictions that may be placed on the person's liberty .... The Court therefore considers that this right is one of the fundamental procedural rights for the protection of those who have been partially deprived of legal capacity. It follows that such persons should in principle enjoy direct access to the courts in this sphere'.

The Court concluded that there was a violation of Article 6 paragraph 1, and ordered that mr. Stanev should decide whether he would stay in this home, and awarded him damages.

As a consequence, Stanev could move to a home of his own choice, closer to his familiar environment. Moreover, a reform of the Bulgarian guardianship law started.[16]

The CRPD was one of the references used by the Court in the application of the ECHR.

Even though the most substantive aspect of the decision was related to the right to liberty and security of the person guaranteed in Article 5 of the ECHR, the recognition of the right of access to court of people with mental disabilities seems to me an essential aspect too: without this, the enforcement of the rights of the CRPD becomes actually impossible for those entitled.

Therefore I use this example to illustrate the scope of accessibility of the CRPD for the work of the ECtHR.

An earlier case dealing with direct physical admissibility of the court and law offices was declared inadmissible by the court.[17] The Court reaffirms 'that

---

[16]   See: https://www.escr-net.org/caselaw/2016/stanev-v-bulgaria-app-no-3676006-european-court-human-rights.

[17]   ECHR 27 April 2010, *Farças v. Romania*, nr. 32596/04 (in French only).

hindrance in fact could contravene the Convention just like a legal impediment and that limitation of access to a court could not go as far as interfering with an individual's entitlement to a fair hearing. It took the view that the impossibility for a person to bring legal proceedings on account of a lack of special access to courthouses for persons with reduced mobility could be regarded as a hindrance in fact capable of impeding access to a court in the absence of any alternative means to remedy the situation'[18]

In this case the facts were contested, and the applicant could not convince the Court that the relevant buildings and institutions were completely inaccessible for him. As explained in the press release: 'The Court also had doubts about the pertinence of the applicant's argument that he could not have brought any judicial proceedings without a lawyer because, firstly, the assistance of a lawyer was not necessary to initiate the proceedings in question, and secondly, the applicant had been able, on his own, to lodge his application with the European Court of Human Rights.'

In the context of the CRPD it can be discussed whether the Court's interpretation of Article 6 paragraph 1 is strict enough: the Court allows the state a margin of appreciation how to realise the right of access to court and access to an effective remedy (Article 34 ECHR), and seems to accept that claimants may have no other choice than being represented by others. In the context of the CRPD the independent access to justice has to be the starting point.

The starting point has to be the accessibility equal to others. This has been reaffirmed by the Court recently in two cases on higher education. Paul Lemmens was one of the judges sitting in both cases. The first case of *Çam v. Turkey*[19] a blind applicant has passed both the selection test for the Turkish Music Academy and the medical examination (which concluded that she could be admitted to the courses 'where a sight was not required'). Subsequently, she was refused because the Director held that none of the sections of the Academy could be considered as not requiring eyesight.

The Court applies Article 14 of the ECHR (non-discrimination) in combination with the right to education (Article 2 of Protocol no. 1), stating that the candidate's blindness had been the sole reason for refusal. The Court refers to the right to education as defined in the CRPD and reaffirms the interpretation of equal treatment and non-discrimination as given in earlier case law: discrimination occurs not only when there is a different treatment of similar

---

[18] See press release: https://hudoc.echr.coe.int/eng-press#{%22itemid%22:[%22003-3270987-3667739%22]}.

[19] ECHR 23 May 2016, No. 51500/08 (French only).

cases but also in case of denial of different treatment in order to reach equality without objective and reasonable justification.

The Court explains under paragraph 65 that this implies that the music academy had the duty to provide a reasonable accommodation: 'À cet égard, la Cour considère que l'article 14 de la Convention doit être lu à la lumière des exigences de ces textes au regard des aménagements raisonnables – entendus comme "les modifications et ajustements nécessaires et appropriés n'imposant pas de charge disproportionnée ou indue apportée, en fonction des besoins dans une situation donnée" – que les personnes en situation de handicap sont en droit d'attendre, aux fins de se voir assurer "la jouissance ou l'exercice, sur la base de l'égalité avec les autres, de tous les droits de l'homme et de toutes les libertés fondamentales" (article 2 de la Convention relative aux droits des personnes handicapées, paragraphe 38 ci-dessus). De tels aménagements raisonnables permettent de corriger des inégalités factuelles qui, ne pouvant être justifiées, constituent une discrimination... '. The Court incorporates the positive duty to provide a reasonable accommodation in Article 14 of the ECHR referring to definition in Article 2 of the CRPD: "Reasonable accommodation" means a necessary and appropriate modification and adjustments not imposing a disproportionate or undue burden, where needed in a particular case to ensure persons with disabilities the enjoyment or exercise on an equal basis with others of all human rights and fundamental freedoms'. Thus, in this case the Court has no problem to interpret the ECHR in line with the CRPD, even when at the time of the national procedure the CRPD was not yet ratified by Turkey.[20]

In 2018 another case on the accessibility of an institution for higher education was decided, also against Turkey. This case of *Enver Sahin vs. Turkey*[21] is very interesting because it reflects a thorough understanding of the different aspects of accessibility. At the same time the Court can also with very good reasons be criticized for giving a too restrictive interpretation of this concept, as explained in very clear terms by Paul Lemmens in his dissenting opinion.

The claimant in this case was already a student at the University when he became disabled as a consequence of an accident. When he wants to continue his studies after recovery, he is faced with the fact that the premises are not accessible for him. The University admits this, and because the necessary reconstructions cannot be realised in a short term, offers a personal assistant and the possibility to be carried to the class room on the third floor by way of 'reasonable

---

[20] See the thought of Jan-Peter Loof on the possible reluctance if the Court to apply international law too actively published under the Strasbourg Observers' blog on the *Stanev* case: https://strasbourgobservers.com/2012/02/29/stanev-v-bulgaria-the-grand-chambers-cautionary-approach-to-expanding-protection-of-the-rights-of-persons-with-psycho-social-disabilities/.

[21] ECHR 30 January 2018, no. 23065/12.

accommodation'. This is refused by the claimant, who holds that: "l'offre faite par l'administration de lui fournir l'assistance d'un accompagnant illustrait la méconnaissance par celle-ci de sa situation personnelle et des implications de cette dernière. Il ajoutait qu'il serait dégradant pour lui d'être placé, du fait de son handicap, dans une situation de dépendance par rapport à un tiers, et il donnait notamment l'exemple de l'atteinte à son intimité que constitueraient la présence et l'assistance constantes d'un tiers. Il affirmait en outre que le fait d'être porté par un individu dans les escaliers du bâtiment présentait assurément un risque de chute ..." (see par. 13): it is both degrading and risky to be carried up and down the stairs.

The Court again applies Article 14 of the ECHR in conjunction with the Article 2 of Protocol 1 and also with Article 8, the right to private life and family life, referring to the relevant provisions of the CRPD, including the respect for human dignity as individual autonomy (Article 3(a) and the obligation to ensure accessibility as guaranteed in Article 9 (par. 70). Here too, as in the *Çam* case, the Court focusses on the question whether the offer to provide assistance could be seen as a reasonable accommodation in this case. The Court gives a very fundamental reasoning, and refers to earlier case law holding that the possibility for persons with a disability to live independently and fully develop their sense of dignity and self-worth was of paramount importance, and that the very essence of the Convention was respect for human dignity and human freedom, including the freedom to make one's own choices.[22] Subsequently, the Court rules that in this case the assistance offered cannot be seen as acceptable.

Paul Lemmens is dissenting because in his opinion the case should have been decided primarily under Article 2 of the 2nd Protocol: the right to education and not under the prohibition of discrimination (Article 14 ECHR). He gives a very solid argument that the admissibility of (higher) education itself is at stake. This goes beyond the provision of a reasonable accommodation: referring to the general Comment no. 2 of the Committee, Lemmens analyses this difference between the general obligation to guarantee admissibility and the less substantive duty to provide a reasonable accommodation. In paragraph 25 of his dissenting opinion he explains that the obligation to ensure admissibility is an obligation *ex ante*, which is related to groups, whereas the duty to provide a reasonable accommodation is an obligation *ex nunc* and related to individuals (see also: paragraph 25 of the General Comment no. 2). In Lemmens's view Turkey has violated the right to education because it has not been sufficiently been explained that the necessary measures to guarantee accessibility could not have been taken in the course of time. For that reason, in his opinion, there is

---

22   See Press release of the Court: ECHR 037 (2018) 30.01.2018.

no room to pose the question on the provision of a reasonable accommodation under Article 14.

This extensive analysis of the substance of admissibility makes the dissenting opinion of Lemmens essential reading for all involved in disability law: it can only be hoped that it will be an incentive for the court to further scrutinize its interpretation of accessibility when applying the ECHR in relation to the CRPD.

V. AUTONOMY

Above some attention has already been paid to the relevance of independent decision-making, legal capacity and other aspects of the autonomy of persons with disabilities. Autonomy reflects one of the principles of the CRPD, described in Article 3(a): 'Respect for inherent dignity, individual autonomy including the freedom to make one's own choices, and independence of persons'.

Thus autonomy includes independent decision-making. This entails the right to exercise legal capacity, as laid down in Article 12, which was one of the most controversial issues during the drafting process.[23] The Committee wrote its very first General Comment on this article.[24] Legal capacity is described as 'a universal attribute inherent in all persons by virtue of their humanity.' (par. 8). Crucial is the distinction made between legal capacity and mental capacity. 'Legal capacity is the ability to hold rights and duties (legal standing) and to exercise these rights (legal agency)... Mental capacity refers to the decision-making skills of a person, which naturally vary from one person to another...' (par. 13).

Legal capacity is 'an inherent right according to all people' (GC par. 14) laid down in paragraph 2 of Article 12). Mental capacity is a more complex concept and not easily to establish, depending not only from the skills of a person but also from environmental and social factors (par. 13 GC). The absolute nature of legal capacity implies that it can never be substituted. Par. 3 of Article 12 obliges the Stares to take appropriate measures to provide access by persons with disabilities to the support they may require in exercising their legal capacity. Supported decision-making is fundamental different from substituted decision-making as explained by N. Devi et al.[25] Supported decision making is considered to be the basic principle in the interpretation of legal capacity and can be developed in different ways. In their paper Devi et al. clarify the differences and consequences. They also analyse the risks and complications of this model, but

---

[23] See N. Devi et al, 2011, p. 249–264.
[24] CRPD General Comment No. 1 (2014), CRPD/C/CG/1.
[25] See above, footnote 2.

still the States are obliged to implement a supported decision- making frame. This is also the challenge for the ECtHR: how to safeguard the legal capacity of people with mental disabilities?

VI. AUTONOMY IN THE ECtHR CASE LAW

Guardianship has often been an aspect of cases based on Article 5 ECHR, the right to liberty and security, when persons with mental disabilities challenge their placement in an institution, often in combination with a complaint on the guardianship. In the case of *D.D. v. Lithuania*[26] the court upheld a minimal legal capacity by saying that: '(i)n such cases, when the conflict potential has a major impact on the person's legal situation, such as when there is a proposed change of guardian, it is essential that the person concerned should have access to court and the opportunity to be heard either in person or, where necessary, through some form of representation. Mental illness may entail restricting or modifying the manner of exercise of such a right, but it cannot justify impairing the very essence of the right, except in very exceptional circumstances.' (par. 118)

In the case of *Stanev v. Bulgaria* (see above, footnote 12), the replacement of the guardian appointed was one of the measures asked for by the plaintiff. This is a rather fundamental aspect of legal capacity: it can be hold that a person who is dependent on supported decision making has the right to be supported by a person he can trust or at least does not refuse altogether. That seems to be the bottom line. In the case of *Stanev* the guardian, an officer appointed by the Municipal Council (no family member being available) had never met the applicant. Mr Stanev was dependent on the consent of this guardian to be placed in another home or institution than the home he was forced to stay (which the Committee for the Prevention of Torture (CPT) ordered to close because of the inhuman and degrading treatment of the inhabitants). Stanev had unsuccessfully tried to be released from this partial guardianship and to restore his legal capacity.

The Court refers to Article 12 CRPD as relevant law. But in the decision itself the focus is on the access to Court and the right to have an effective remedy only, and the Court does not really examine the preliminary complaint that Stanev had no other option than accepting this guardian. The obligation to provide adequate support in decision-making might have had more fundamental consequences, also in relation to the violations of Article 8 ECHR, as explained by Lycette Nelson in the blog on the case.[27]

---

[26] 14 February 2012, No. 13469/06.
[27] Https://strasbourgobservers.com/2012/02/29/stanev-v-bulgaria-the-grand-chambers-cautionary-approach-to-expanding-protection-of-the-rights-of-persons-with-psycho-social-disabilities/.

Later, in the *Ivinovic v. Croatia* case the Court seized the opportunity to clarify its position on this aspect.[28] In this case the legal capacity itself was at the core of the case. Ms Ivinovic had been partially deprived of her legal capacity divesting her of the power to dispose of her money and other assets and to make independent decisions concerning her medical treatment. The complaint was based on Article 8 ECHR because deprivation of legal capacity may amount to an interference with the private life of the person concerned.

The Court gave a clear view on the procedural requirements related to guardianship:

'44. Even when the national authorities establish with the required degree of certainty that a person has been experiencing difficulties in paying his or her bills, deprivation, even partial, of legal capacity should be a measure of last resort, applied only where the national authorities, after carrying out a careful consideration of possible alternatives, have concluded that no other, less restrictive, measure would serve the purpose or where other, less restrictive measure, have been unsuccessfully attempted. However, there is no indication that any such option was contemplated in the present case.

45. As regards the representation of the applicant in the proceedings at issue, the Court notes that an employee of the Centre was appointed as the applicant's legal guardian (see paragraph 10 above). However, given that it was the Centre itself that had instituted the proceedings for deprivation of the applicant's legal capacity, her appointment as the applicant's legal guardian put her into a conflict of loyalty between her employer and the applicant as her ward. In the present case the guardian gave her full consent to the application for partial deprivation of the applicant's legal capacity, and made no submissions as regards the evidence to be presented. Notwithstanding the fact that the applicant engaged the services of a lawyer at her own expense (see paragraph 10 above), it cannot but be noted that national law does not provide for obligatory representation of the person concerned by an independent lawyer, despite the very serious nature of the issues concerned and the possible consequences of such proceedings.'

This leads the Court to the conclusion that there is a violation of Article 8. In her interesting blog Valeska David explains that this case is a step forward because the Court 'suggests that mental and legal capacity cannot be equated', but nevertheless does not entirely 'unpack the consequences of distinguishing between them'.[29] A more substantive approach would also have required a substantial review, going beyond the procedural approach of the Court in this case, which could have been helpful for the states to implement the international obligations.

---

[28]   EctHR 18 September 2014, No. 13006/13.
[29]   Https://strasbourgobservers.com/2014/10/23/ivinovic-v-croatia-legal-capacity-and-the-missing-call-for-supportive-decision-making/.

This case was based on Article 8 ECHR, which often is used to claim autonomy. Independent decision-making is closely related to private life. An example is the case of *McDonald v. the United Kingdom*.[30]

Ms McDonald, being disabled after a stroke, receives an allowance for care, including night care as she is not able to go to the toilet without assistance. When her allowance is reduced, based a.o. on the argument that she might use incontinence pads and sheets, the plaintiff brings the case to the Court because the decision to reduce her care constituted an unjustified interference with her right to respect for her private life. In particular, she argued that it was difficult to conceive of a factual situation which established more of a "direct and immediate link" to the rights protected under Article 8 than a disabled person's need or assistance to reach a toilet or commode where they could urinate and defecate in dignity.

The Court mentions the CRPD, Article 3 and the Right to Independent Living of Article 19. The Court, however, cannot agree with the assumed violation of Article 8 for the entire period, but, referring to earlier case law, reaffirms that 'the very essence of the Convention was respect for human dignity and human freedom; indeed, it was under Article 8 that notions of the quality of life took on significance because, in an era of growing medical sophistication combined with longer life expectancies, many people were concerned that they should not be forced to linger on in old age or in states of advanced physical or mental decrepitude which conflicted with their strongly held ideas of self and personal identity' (under 47). This is a most relevant recognition of the right to autonomy and the positive obligations the State has to provide persons with a disability with assistance.[31]

Thus there is still a way to go but the Strasbourg court is providing very valuable support in the clarification and implementation of the principle of autonomy as enacted in the CRPD.

VII. PARTICIPATION

The principles of the CRPD are interrelated. Accessibility is a precondition for almost all other rights, equality a substantive element of all and also the principle of participation is closely related to other principles such as accessibility and legal capacity.

---

[30] ECtHR 20 May 2014, No. 4241/12.
[31] See also: https://strasbourgobservers.com/2014/06/04/mcdonald-v-the-united-kingdom-a-step-forward-in-addressing-the-needs-of-persons-with-disabilities-through-article-8-echr/.

'Nothing about us without us' is an important slogan in the promotion of rights for persons with disabilities. The CRPD itself was the result of a process where the disability movement was closely involved. The principle of participation and involvement is Article 5(3) of the CRPD obliging the States to involve persons with disabilities in all decision-making processes. Recently, the Committee published a Draft General Comment on Articles 4.3 and 33.3 of the CRPD.[32]

The implementation of this principle is one of the most challenging exercises for the States, which is most relevant also for other parts of public life, where the debate on new forms of democracy is going on.[33]

VIII. PARTICIPATION IN THE ECtHR CASE LAW

As far as the relation with the ECHR concerns, the link with the right to vote (Article 3 of Protocol No. 1 ECHR) is obvious, but also many cases related to the right to private life (art. 8 ECHR) de facto concern the impossibility of persons with disabilities to participate not only in private, but also in public life, because of inaccessibility of premises for example.

In practice the exercise of the right to vote often is problematic for persons with disabilities. Polling stations are not always accessible for them. Moreover, the vote forms are mostly not accessible for visually impaired or persons with learning disabilities, whereas it is not always permitted to be supported when casting the vote. Finally, the information on elections both from the State as from the participants in the debates, such as the programs and propaganda from the parties, are not accessible to all (no subtitles on TV etcetera). In its General Comment on Article 12, the Committee refers to the right to vote in relation to the deprivation of legal capacity (par. 8). In the Draft Comment on participation the Committee also mentions the relation with Article 29 of the CRPD, the right to participate in public life.

In the decision of the Court in *Ajalos Kiss v. Hungary*[34] the Court refers to the CRPD (Articles 1, 12 and 29) as relevant for the case. Mr Kiss had been omitted from the electoral register, and held that this measure, imposed on him because he was under partial guardianship for manic depression, constituted an unjustified deprivation of his right to vote, which was not susceptible to any remedy since it was prescribed by the Constitution, and which was

---

32   16 March 2018, https://www.ohchr.org/en/hrbodies/crpd/pages/gc.aspx.
33   See also: Jenny E. Goldschmidt, New Perspectives on Equality: Towards Transformative Justice through the Disability Convention? *Nordic Journal of Human Rights*, 35 (2017) 1, 1–14.
34   20 May 2010, no. 38832/06.

discriminatory in nature. He relied on Article 3 of Protocol No. 1, read alone or in conjunction with Articles 13 and 14 of the Convention.

The Court refers to earlier case-law reaffirming the fundamental character of the right to vote, and although it leaves the State a rather wide margin of appreciation in general, determining whether restrictions on the right to vote can be justified in modern times and, if so, how a fair balance is to be struck.' (par. 41). However, in this case the Court 'cannot accept, that an absolute bar on voting by any person under partial guardianship, irrespective of his or her actual faculties, falls within an acceptable margin of appreciation. Indeed, while the Court reiterates that this margin of appreciation is wide, it is not all-embracing (*Hirst v. the United Kingdom (no. 2)* [GC], op. cit., §82). In addition, if a restriction on fundamental rights applies to a particularly vulnerable group in society, who have suffered considerable discrimination in the past, such as the mentally disabled, then the State's margin of appreciation is substantially narrower and it must have very weighty reasons for the restrictions in question (cf. also the example of those suffering different treatment on the ground of their gender – *Abdulaziz, Cabales and Balkandali v. the United Kingdom*, 28 May 1985, §78, Series A no. 94, race – *D.H. and Others v. the Czech Republic* [GC], no. 57325/00, §182, ECHR 2007-..., or sexual orientation – *E.B. v. France* [GC], no. 43546/02, §94, ECHR 2008-...). The reason for this approach, which questions certain classifications per se, is that such groups were historically subject to prejudice with lasting consequences, resulting in their social exclusion. Such prejudice may entail legislative stereotyping ...' (par. 42). The Court held that there had been a violation of Article 3 of Protocol 1.

In the wording of the Court in the previous argument make a clear connection with the last principle of the CRPD to be considered here: equality and non-discrimination.

IX. EQUALITY AND NON-DISCRIMINATION

Sandra Fredman concludes in her article on Article 14 of the ECHR that the Court has been 'receptive to the importance of framing an equality guarantee that is responsive to the complex ways in which equalities manifest' but also holds that '(i)n relation to disability, it is still far beyond other jurisdictions which have made significant commitment to reasonable accommodation'.[35] We have seen already above that there are also more positive examples of a fundamental

---

[35] Sandra Fredman, Emerging from the Shadows: Substantive Equality and Article 14 of the European Convention on Human Rights, *Human Rights Law Review* 16 (2016), 273–301, pp. 300–301.

approach to equality, including the obligation to provide a reasonable accommodation, which is part of a substantive equality frame. The Court has developed different aspects of this approach in its case law, by recognizing the obligation to address differences and disadvantage by positive measures, the obligation to combat stereotypes and to give additional attention and protection to vulnerable groups, such as disabled persons.

In its General Comment no. 6 on Equality and non-discrimination[36] the Committee has extensively clarified the meaning of the principle. It introduces in paragraph 11 the concept of inclusive equality which resembles Fredman's substantive model, adding the participatory aspect: 'It embraces a substantive model of equality and extends and elaborates on the content of equality in: (a) a fair redistributive dimension to address socioeconomic disadvantages; (b) a recognition dimension to combat stigma, stereotyping, prejudice and violence and to recognize the dignity of human beings and their intersectionality; (c) a participative dimension to reaffirm the social nature of people as members of social groups and the full recognition of humanity through inclusion in society; and (d) an accommodating dimension to make space for difference as a matter of human dignity. The Convention is based on inclusive equality.'

The first case were Article 14 ECHR was applied on the ground of disability was the case of *Glor v. Switzerland*.[37] In this case the imposition of an exemption tax for people who were unwilling to perform military service was held to be discriminatory when it was applied to persons who are not unwilling, but unfit for public service.

The payment of taxes has been at stake also in a more recent case which also contains some other interesting aspects on the scope of non-discrimination and reasonable accommodation. In the case of *Guberina v. Croatia*[38], the Court (Paul Lemmens sitting) had to consider the imposition of a real property tax on parents who purchased a new property because the place they had (flat on third floor without lift) was no longer suitable since they had a severely disabled child (in a wheelchair). The plaintiffs held that the imposition of this tax was discriminatory and a violation of Article 14 and a violation of the right to property, Article1 of Protocol 1. This is a case of 'discrimination by association': the plaintiffs themselves are not disabled but they are victim of discrimination based on the disability of someone they are closely related to. The Court here clarifies that 'Article 14 of the Convention also covers instances in which an individual is treated less favourably on the basis of another person's status or

---

[36] CRPD/G/GC/6.
[37] ECHR 30 April 2009, no. 13444/04.
[38] ECHR 22 March 2016, no. 23682/13.

protected characteristics.' (paragraph 78) which is entirely in line with the CRPD, as explained in paragraph 20 of the general Comment on equality. This definition of discrimination by association has also been adopted by other courts.

Apart from this clarification the *Guberina* case could also have been a more substantive step forward in the clarification of the obligation to provide reasonable accommodations, because the Court states that 'the issue in the instant case is not the fact that the relevant domestic legislation left no room for an individual evaluation of the tax exemption requests of persons in the applicant's situation. The issue in the present case is rather that the manner in which the legislation was applied in practice failed to sufficiently accommodate the requirements of the specific aspects of the applicant's case related to the disability of his child and, in particular, to the interpretation of the term "basic infrastructure requirements" for the housing of a disabled person'. (paragraph 93). The obligation to provide a reasonable accommodation is thus implied implicitly, when the Court investigates whether there was an objective and reasonable justification for treating this case in the same way as others, but is not used explicitly in the Court's conclusion that the authorities had no 'objective and reasonable justification for their failure to take into account the inequality inherent in the applicant's situation when making an assessment of his tax obligation.' (paragraph 98). Thus there has been a violation of Article 14 of the Convention in conjunction with Article 1 of Protocol No. 1.

X. STEREOTYPES AND PREJUDICES

One of the most persistent obstacles to the realisation of equality is the existence of stereotypes and prejudices. The Court shows an increasing awareness of this.[39] In relation to disability the case of *Kacper Nowakowski v. Poland*[40] is relevant: a deaf father was denied the required contact arrangements with his (also hearing impaired) son after divorce a.o. on the basis of complications in the communication. The father lodged a complaint on violation of Articles 8 and 14 ECHR. The Court concludes that there is a violation of Article 8. Attention is paid to the specific needs of the father and also the fact that it cannot too easily be assumed that alleged barriers are real: ' 93... the domestic courts should have envisaged additional measures, more adapted to the specific circumstances of the case (see, *mutatis mutandis*, Gluhaković, cited above, where in regulating contact the authorities failed to take into account the father's work schedule). Having

---

[39] See also: Alexandra Timmer, Towards an Anti-Stereotyping Approach for the European Court of Human Rights, *Human Rights Law Review*, 11 (2011), 707–738.
[40] ECHR 10 January 2017, No. 32407/13.

regard to the specifics of the applicant's situation and the nature of his disability, the authorities were required to implement particular measures that took due account of the applicant's situation. The Court refers here to the second sentence of Article 23 §2 of the Convention on the Rights of Persons with Disabilities, which provides that "State Parties shall render appropriate assistance to persons with disabilities in the performance of their child-rearing responsibilities." (see paragraph 49 above).

The Court further notes that the domestic courts failed to obtain expert evidence from specialists familiar with the problems faced by persons suffering from a hearing impairment. The experts stressed their limited competence in respect of persons suffering from a hearing impairment. Furthermore, the expert report relied on by the courts did not address possible means of overcoming the barriers resulting from the disability in question. The experts focused on the existence of barriers instead of reflecting on possible means of overcoming them.'

These considerations are as such in line with the CRPD's principle of inclusive equality, but the Court could, here too, have been more explicit in the identification of prejudices and stereotypes. That would also imply that there might have been good reasons to establish not only a violation of Article 8, but also of Article 14. In general the Court seems to be reluctant to accept arguments of authorities on the (lack of) capacities of disabled persons, which are given to restrict their rights when these arguments are not based on due examination and investigation: this can be seen as a way to combat stereotypes.

The Court took a very clear stands on stereotypes in a case that dealt with discrimination on the basis of age and gender, the case of *Carvalho Pinto de Sousa Morais v. Portugal*.[41] In this case the Portuguese court held in appeal that the damages for medical liability for the plaintiff could be reduced, as 'at the time of the operation the plaintiff was already 50 years old and had two children, that is, an age when sex is not as important as in younger years, its significance diminishing with age'. (Paragraph 16).

The Court pays attention to scope of gender equality: the advancement of gender equality is today a major goal for the member States of the Council of Europe and very weighty reasons would have to be put forward before such a difference of treatment could be regarded as compatible with the Convention ... In particular, references to traditions, general assumptions or prevailing social attitudes in a particular country are insufficient justification for a difference in treatment on the grounds of sex' (paragraph 46). Because of the assumption on sexuality of women of 50 years old, the age and sex of the women seem to have been decisive

---

[41]   ECHR 25 July 2017, No. 17484/15.

in this case. These considerations show the prejudices prevailing in the judiciary in Portugal, the Court says, concluding that Article 14 in conjunction with Article 8 has been violated. It will be clear that a similar situation may occur in a case of a disabled person. This approach of stereotype attitudes thus is most relevant for the rights of persons with disabilities too. It is also a sensitive approach for the Court, as in many cases stereotypes and prejudices still prevail in the legal cultures of the State parties, which may be used by some to put into question whether it is within the competence of the Court has to challenge these. I am not convinced by these arguments, as the obligation to combat stereotypes and prejudices is part of international conventions, such as the CRPD, but also the CEDAW (see art.5), which are ratified by the State parties themselves.

The above mentioned *de Sousa Morais* case is also important as an example of intersectionality, i.e. the combination of two (or more) grounds of discrimination, and for that reason it can regretted that the Court focusses only on the gender aspect, and not equally on age.

Intersectionality is an important aspect of the equality doctrine: individuals should be protected against discrimination on all grounds (see paragraph 2 of Article 5 CRPD) and this implies that intersections between disability and other grounds are included. The CRPD is the first convention that explicitly contains provisions on intersectionality in the Articles 6 (women with disabilities) and 7 (children with disabilities). Forced contraception or forced sterilisation of women with mental disabilities is an example of an intersectional violation of their rights. Thus far, there is no clear decision of the ECtHR on this issue.[42]

XI. TOWARDS INCLUSIVE HUMAN RIGHTS

Much more can be said about the value of the CRPD principles for the interpretation of the ECHR. What has become clear, hopefully, is that the CRPD, as one of the youngest human rights instruments, provides the Court with a frame that can be applied to proceed on the road the Court is already taken to improve the protection of human rights of specific groups. The term vulnerable groups is often used in this context and can be seen as a promising one, but it also entails risks of reaffirmation of the vulnerability, as Peroni and Timmer argue.[43] The addition and incorporation of the principles of autonomy, accessibility, participation and inclusive equality can help to contribute to an empowering interpretation.

---

[42]　See A.S. v. Hungary (CEDAW).
[43]　Lourdes Peroni and Alexandra Timmer, Vulnerable Groups: The promise of an emerging concept in European Human Rights Convention Law, *CON* (2013) Vol. 11, No. 4, 1056–1085.

As Sandra Fredman explains, courts have a crucial role to in the promotion of equality and accessibility: it is only by giving an opportunity to those who cannot participate fully in the democratic process that litigation supplements democracy.[44] This holds also for the ECtHR. In that way the Court can contribute to the inclusion of the rights and perspectives of the underrepresented and less advantaged groups in society.

The CRPD challenges the ECtHR to reconsider its own jurisprudence, as can be required to incorporate differences instead of reaffirming inequality by allowing exceptions or accommodations, which leave the excluding normative frames untouched.

The progressive realisation of the rights of the ECHR demands a more fundamental re-thinking of the cases and laws that are considered and an unveiling of the neutrality of the underlying perspectives.

In some cases the ECtHR seems aware of this, but as explained above, it seems often reluctant to take a more substantive approach, as it could have done in cases like *Ivinovic v. Croatia* and *Sahin v. Turkey* for example. This seems in line with Paul Lemmens's open personal attitude towards others. We can only hope that he continues to contribute to the development of human rights law in other capacities after his retirement from Leuven.

---

[44] Sandra Fredman, *Human Rights Transformed, Positive Rights and Positive Duties*, Oxford University Press 2008, p. 107.

THE EUROPEAN COURT OF HUMAN RIGHTS AND INTERNATIONAL INVESTMENT ARBITRATION

Existence of a Judicial Dialogue?

Charline DAELMAN

Human Rights Consultant
Voluntary Scientific Researcher KU Leuven

INTRODUCTION

The recent success and overall increase of international investments, has consequences on the complexity of its legal framework. Where international investment law strode forward independently for many years, its interaction with other areas of international law, and more specifically human rights, intensified. It is expected that with the expansion of international investments, an inevitable cross-fertilisation occurs between international investment law and other international law disciplines, such as human rights law. The question arises whether this is actually the case and whether there is a relationship between international investment law and human rights law. More specifically, this article focuses on the potential existence of a judicial dialogue between the European Court of Human Rights (ECtHR) and international investment arbitration and the characterisation of such a relationship. The article will first address the relationship between international investment law and human rights law by looking at its origin and basic foundations, but also the characteristics that they share content wise. In Part II, we will look at the specific ECtHR case law references in international investment arbitration cases and more specifically, their function and whether they are readily accepted by investment arbitration tribunals. Part III addresses the investor protection that is provided by the ECtHR. The final part touches upon the particular situation in which an investment conflict is ruled upon by both an investment arbitration tribunal and the ECtHR.

I. RELATIONSHIP BETWEEN INTERNATIONAL INVESTMENT LAW AND HUMAN RIGHTS LAW

A. ORIGIN AND BASIC FOUNDATIONS

The sources of international investment law are fragmentised and although there were attempts to create a multilateral instrument[1], international investment law remains primarily bilaterally constructed, i.e. between a private party and a state or between two states. The focus lies on the promotion of foreign investment and the protection of the foreign investor and its property against arbitrary interference of the host state. Human rights law developed primarily multilaterally between states after the atrocities of the two World Wars, almost simultaneously at the international and regional level. It is a system created by states to offer protection to the individual against the unlawful interference of the state.

The recent increase of concluded BITs might give the impression that from a historical point of view, international investment law is more recent than human rights law, which can be dated back to the 1945 United Nations Charter and the 1948 Universal Declaration of Human Rights. Nonetheless, the protection of foreign investment clearly existed before the recognition at the international level of fundamental human rights. Because of the industrial revolution, investments by foreigners took place as from the mid-1800s. These investors originated from industrialised countries and sought opportunities in less or not yet developed countries. As a result hereof, rules were constructed relating to the access to and exercise of diplomatic protection. They included state obligations towards aliens and a set of minimum protection standards which expanded in substance and authority later on, in the context of *acquired rights.*[2] So although the protection of foreign investment was not yet imbedded in a multilateral or bilateral instrument, customary international law already provided protection for investors under the general principles relating to the protection of citizens abroad.[3] Thus, the concept of the *alien* might actually chronologically precede the concept of the *individual,* i.e. the human being that is considered the bearer of human rights.

The legal status of aliens is established on the direct link between the alien and the state of origin from which it bears the nationality. In contrast,

---

1   Havana Charter (1948); Guidelines on the Treatment of Foreign Investment (1992); and the Multilateral Agreement on Investment (1998).

2   R. Lillich, *The International Law of State Responsibility for Injuries to Aliens* (1983), at 412.

3   P.M. Dupuy, 'Unification Rather then Fragmentation of International Law? The Case of International Investment Law and Human Rights Law' in Dupuy, Francioni, Petersmann (2009), 47.

human rights are enjoyed by all individuals regardless of their nationality or any other link with a specific country. They are derived from the inherent nature as a human being which results in their inalienable character.[4] At the same time, the protection of human rights has an objective character as it does not depend on the reciprocity of inter-state relations, which is the case in the protection of the alien. In modern times the foreign private investor transformed to private corporations with legal personality, but their nationality still determines their identification as foreign or alien. The current protection provided by international investment law still greatly depends on the nationality of the investor. The majority of investment treaties, typically bilateral, are constructed to favour the nationals of the respective state parties to the agreement.[5] Implicitly and through the use of non-discriminatory treatment clauses, such as the most-favoured-nation clause, the protection of certain BITs can also overflow to non-nationals, but the basic premise remains that the provided protection is determined by the nationality of the investor. The nationality of the investor is thus primordial for the application of substantial protection standards and establishes the jurisdiction of and access to an arbitral tribunal. In contrast, human rights are not conferred upon a human being based on nationality. The nationality could however, determine the access and competence to a regional human rights court. The nationality test thus remains a fundament of international investment law, although it is not necessarily a decisive element in human rights law.

When looking at the origins and basic foundation, there is a significant difference between the protective system of aliens, on which international investment law is based, and the security regime provided by human rights. Because of the nationality principle, international investment law provides a narrower basis for protection in comparison to human rights law. Although investor rights and human rights have a different origin and focus and are built on different normative concepts, there is also a parallel between them. Both focus on the individual or private actor (investor) that is challenged by the exercise of public power by the (host) state. In comparison to the classic concept of public international law, non-state actors are provided with direct rights and claims against a sovereign state in both international investment law and human rights law. Both fields are thus characterised by an asymmetrical relationship, in which the individual is protected against the unlawful interference of the state.[6]

---

4   Ibid.
5   Ibid., at 48–49.
6   M. Hirsch, 'Investment Tribunals and Human Rights: Divergent Paths', in Dupuy, Francioni, Petersmann (2009), 107; A. Kulick, *Global Public Interest in International Investment Law*, Cambridge University Press (2012), at 272.

B. CONTENT

Since the legal status of the alien chronologically precedes that of the individual as a human being, it is interesting to see whether this results in similarities in content between international investment law and human rights law.

A first common denominator is the principle of non-discrimination. The presence of this principle in human rights law is apparent, but also in international investment law it has an embedded place via the use of fair and equitable treatment clauses, most-favoured-nation clauses and national treatment clauses. Although these clauses are not necessarily assigned a similar definition in all investment treaties and agreements, there is a common basis to the totality of their different legal perceptions.[7] Therefore, it is also important for the uniformity of international investment law that international investment arbitrators refer to international standards in interpreting the different non-discrimination clauses provided for in investment treaties and agreements. These international standards are often proven to be leading interpretations in the human rights system (see below).

The concept of access to justice also plays a central role in both international investment law and human rights law. In international investment law it is considered a breach of the host state's obligation if a non-discriminatory access to justice is not guaranteed. A positive duty is put on the host state 'to provide a fair trial of a case to which a foreigner is a party'.[8] Several international and regional human rights treaties also include the principle of access to justice.[9] When interpreting access to justice, international investment tribunals refer to general international law to define what a 'denial of justice' actually entails. Hereby, tribunals adhere to the case-law of the International Court of Justice, but also to the human rights standards provided for by the ECtHR.[10] Not only substantially, but also procedurally there are resemblances between international investment law and human rights law when it comes to access to justice. When an international investment or human rights dispute arises, it will typically be adjudicated to a specialised body in the form of an international investment tribunal, human rights Committee or a regional human rights court. The judge

---

[7]   I. Tudor, *The Fair and Equitable Treatment Standards in the International Law of Foreign Investment* (2008), at 315.

[8]   *Loewen Group Inc and Raymond Loewen v United State of America*, ICSID Case No ARB(AF) 98/3, Final Award, 26 June 2003, at para 132.

[9]   Articles 8, 10 and 11 UDHR; Article 14 ICCPR; Articles 6 and 13 ECHR; Article XVIII American Declaration of the Rights and Duties of Man (1948) (ADRDM); Articles 8 and 25 IACHR.

[10]   *Mondev International Ltd v United States of America*, ICSID Case No ARB(AF)/99/2, Award, 11 October 2002.

or arbitrator will be able to decide upon a case based on the special jurisdiction that is provided for in a specific legal instrument.[11] A characteristic that is common to international investment law and human rights law. Nonetheless, in international investment law, the prior exhaustion of local remedies or the invocation of diplomatic protection is no longer a precondition for access to an international investment tribunal. For example, according to Article 26.1 of the ICSID Convention and depending on a number of other conditions, the investor possesses the right of direct access to international arbitration.[12] In human rights law and especially in the regional human rights protection systems, there remains a strong adherence to the *local remedies rule* to have access to the competent human rights court.[13] Although in essence, there is a direct access to justice in the sense that the individual can file its complaint directly to the human rights court, it will first have to exhaust all local remedies. In the case that the local remedies do not qualify as effective, adequate or sufficient, the injured individual will be able to file the complaint directly without having to exhaust the local remedies.[14] So although this creates a procedural difference between international investment law and human rights law, it might be of a more superficial nature.

A final possible similarity in content between international investment law and human rights law is the protection against expropriation. Investment treaties and agreements protect the international investor against direct and indirect expropriation without fair compensation. This does not mean that any confiscation of investors' property is illegitimate as there is the possibility of regulatory takings. Expropriation can be justified and lawful if: (i) there is a public purpose; (ii) is it is carried out in a non-discriminatory manner; (iii) it is carried out under due process of law; and (iv) compensated by a prompt, adequate and effective compensation. Although the right to property is contested as a general human right, it is included in the Inter-American and European regional human rights system.[15] Article 1, Protocol 1 to the European Convention on Human Rights (ECHR) provides for the peaceful enjoyment of his or hers possessions and thus for the protection of property.[16] When interpreting whether an expropriation was lawful, investment arbitrators fall back on the case-law of the European Court of Justice (ECJ) and of regional human rights courts such as the ECtHR.[17]

---

[11] M. Sornarajah, *The International Law on Foreign Investment*, Cambridge University Press (2011), at 55.
[12] R. Dolzer and C. Schreuer, *Principles of International Investment Law* (2008).
[13] *Supra* n 11, at 48.
[14] Article 13 ECHR.
[15] *Supra* n 11, at 52.
[16] Article 1, Protocol 1 ECHR.
[17] *Supra* n 11, at 53.

The influence of the legal status of an alien on that of the individual as a human being becomes apparent through the substantial content similarities between international investment law and human rights law. Although their foundation is very distinct from one another, they share several concepts and principles. The chronological precedence of the alien before the individual as a human being, insinuates that certain general principles that first belonged to the specific protection of investors have been transformed and generalised to the protection of human rights. As a result, international investment law and human rights law are not as distinct and there is more overlap than traditionally assumed.

II. REFERENCES TO THE ECtHR CASE LAW IN INTERNATIONAL INVESTMENT ARBITRATION

An empirical study by Steininger confirms that more than 80% of all human rights references, included in a sample of 46 investment arbitration cases, refer specifically to the ECHR and the case law of the ECtHR. This confirms that there is a considerable connection between investment arbitration tribunals and the ECtHR. This could be explained by geographical factors such as the nationality of the investors and the membership of the respondent states. From the 46 investment arbitration cases, 34 foreign investors originated from Europe. However, from the sample of investment arbitration cases, only a third includes respondent states that are a party to the ECHR. This shows that the immediate membership of respondent states does not justify the prominence of the ECHR and the ECtHR's case law and insinuates that it has a special status within international investment arbitration, especially considering the highly developed case law of the ECtHR.[18] In this part, we will further address the functionality of the references to the ECHR and ECtHR's case law and the manner in which investment tribunals address these references.

A. THE FUNCTION OF THE REFERENCES TO THE ECHR AND ECtHR'S CASE LAW

The author's analysis of the relation between international investment law and human rights law shows that the different actors involved in an investment dispute refer to human rights law and case law for a variety of reasons. Four main categories of reference can be established: (i) human rights as a source of inspiration for the interpretation of investment agreement clauses; (ii) human rights as part of the context of the investment dispute; and (iii) conflicts, in

---

[18] S. Steininger, "What's Human Rights Got To do With It? An Empirical Analysis of Human Rights References in Investment Arbitration", *Leiden Journal of International Law* (2018), 31, at 40.

respect of the host state, between obligations under human rights law and obligations under investment law.

1. The interpretation of investment clauses

Investment tribunals explicitly acknowledge the value of human rights and human rights case law for the interpretation of investment clauses. In the *Thunderbird* case[19], arbitrator Wälde stated that the relevance follows from the similarity between the litigation frameworks of investment law and regional human rights law in the sense that both frameworks protect the individual against state actions and provide it with direct legal recourse against the state. More specifically, the judicial recourse of individuals against states under the ECHR is the most comparable to treaty-based investor-state arbitration.[20] Therefore, he proposes to draw analogies with the case law of regional human rights courts, such as the ECtHR, to inform the interpretation of the NAFTA safeguards. The *Mondev* tribunal also referred to human rights jurisprudence on several occasions and mentioned that the ECtHR's case-law erupts from a different region and does not specifically deal with investment protection. As a result, it could, at most, provide guidance when interpreting the potential scope of NAFTA's guarantee of "treatment in accordance with international, including fair and equitable treatment and full protection and security".[21] The tribunal's dismissive argument, i.e. the human rights jurisprudence is developed in a different region and does not deal with investment protection specifically, is not convincing. Firstly, the 'right to a court' is, as the tribunal recognised, established in major human rights conventions, both regionally and internationally. Secondly, considering human rights as not dealing with investment protection is incorrect as investors, both in the capacity of an individual and as a company, have submitted claims to the ECtHR for violations of their human right to property.[22]

Besides the general acknowledgement, investment tribunals refer to the ECHR and ECtHR's case law to interpret specific investment clauses. Firstly, the *Loewen* tribunal made use of human rights to determine the content of the FET standard.[23] Secondly, to interpret the vaguely formulated expropriation clause in

---

[19] *International Thunderbird Gaming Corporation v The United Mexican States*, UNCITRAL, Award, 26 January 2006.

[20] *International Thunderbird Gaming Corporation v The United Mexican States*, UNCITRAL, Separate Opinion T. Wälde, 1 December 2005, at para 141.

[21] *Mondev International Ltd v United States of America*, ICSID Case No ARB(AF)/99/2, at para. 144.

[22] *Rosenzweig and Bonded Warehouses v Poland*, ECtHR, Judgement, 28 July 2005; *Zlinsat v Bulgaria*, ECtHR, Judgement, 15 June 2006; *Anheuser-Busch Inc v Portugal*, ECtHR (GC), Judgement, 11 January 2007.

[23] *Loewen Group, Inc and Raymond L Loewen v United States of America*, ICSID Case No ARB(AF)/98/3, Award on Merits, 26 June 2003, at para 167.

investment agreements, the parties in investment disputes fall back on ECtHR's case law to: (i) define the difference between direct and indirect expropriation[24]; (ii) to establish what constitutes property[25]; (iii) to explain which measures amount to expropriation[26]; and (iv) to adopt the 'proportionality' test as a device to evaluate interferences with the right to property.[27] Thirdly, third parties base their claim to be admitted as a party or amicus curiae in the proceedings and other requests on the ECHR and ECtHR's case law.[28] Finally, parties in the investment disputes refer to human rights case law to determine the standard for the calculation of the damages. For example, in the *Siemens* case, the host state disputed the use of the 'fair market value' standard to determine the damages and referred to ECtHR's case law confirming that the right to property does not guarantee a right to full compensation in all circumstances.[29]

2. Providing context to the investment dispute

Besides calling upon human rights law and case law to interpret investment clauses, parties in investment arbitration cases also refer to the ECHR and ECtHR's case-law in a direct and indirect manner to provide context to an investment dispute. In the *Glamis Gold* case for example, the respondent state drew analogies between the investment case at hand and the *Taskin* case decided by the ECtHR.[30]

3. Conflict situation between human rights and investment law obligations

Host states have referred to the human rights in general, and the ECHR more specifically, to argue that 'obligations under investment treaties do not undermine obligations under human rights treaties, and thus, the [Investment] Treaty should be construed and interpreted consistently with international canons aimed at fostering respect for human rights'.[31] Although the investment

---

24 *Ronald S Lauder v The Czech Republic*, UNCITRAL, Final Award, 3 September 2001, at para 200.

25 *Saipem SpA v the People's Republic of Bangladesh*, ICSID Case No ARB/05/07, Decision on Jurisdiction and Recommendation on Provisional Measures, 21 March 2007, at para 130.

26 *Revere Copper and Brass Inc v Overseas Private Investment Corporation*, American Arbitration Association Case No 1610013776 (24 August 1978), at para 113.

27 *Técnicas Medioambientaled Tecmed SA v The United Mexican States*, ICSID Case No ARB(AF)/00/2, at para 122.

28 *Piero Foresti, Laura de Carli & Others v The Republic of South Africa*, ICSID Case No ARB(AF)/07/01, Petition for Limited Participation as non-Disputing Parties in term of Articles 41(3), 27, 39, and 35 of the Additional Facility Rules, 17 July 2009, at para 6.8.

29 *Siemens A.G. v. The Argentine Republic*, ICSID Case No. ARB/02/8, Award, 6 February 2007, at para 346.

30 *Glamis Gold Ltd v The United States of America*, UNCITRAL, Counter-Memorial of the USA, 19 September 2006.

31 *EDF International SA, SAUR International SA and Leon Participaciones Argentina SA v Argentine Republic*, ICSID Case No ARB/03/23, Award, 11 June 2012, at para 192.

tribunal did not question the potential significance or relevance of human rights in connection to international investment law as such, it decided that the required actions by Argentina were not in violation of its human rights obligations.[32]

B. ACCEPTANCE OF THE ECHR AND ECtHR'S CASE LAW REFERENCES

Host states use human rights references in many different situations, except for as an independent claim. For the interpretation of investment clauses, the human rights references by host states are often dismissed by the tribunal as not relevant or raised by the host state in bad faith. Rarely, the investment tribunal will accept the relevance of human rights case-law to interpret international investment law but will not apply it to or distinguish it from the case at hand. When investment tribunals make reference to human rights, they primarily do so to interpret investment clauses. They make use of ECtHR and IACtHR case law as a source of inspiration to interpret vaguely formulated investment standards but always in such a manner that confirms the protective status of the investor.

The author's analysis demonstrates that investment tribunals readily accept human rights references when they confirm the protective status of the investor. When the host states or third parties call upon human rights law or case-law, the investment tribunals are more hesitant to accept them. Steininger's study also showed that human rights arguments introduced by the investor have a stronger impact than those introduced by the respondent.[33] Investment tribunals thus do accept the relevance of international human rights law, primarily for the interpretation of investment law, but adopt it in such an inconsistent manner that it only benefits the investor and not the other parties involved.

III. INVESTOR PROTECTION PROVIDED BY THE ECtHR

Under the ECHR, companies can call upon certain specific human rights, such as the right to property and the right to a fair trial. As a consequence, investors also enjoy the protection provided by the ECHR and can file an application to protect their interests with the ECtHR.

---

[32] *EDF International SA, SAUR International SA and Leon Participaciones Argentina SA v Argentine Republic*, ICSID Case No ARB/03/23, Award, 11 June 2012, at paras 909–914.

[33] *Supra* 18, at 43.

In the *Bimer v Moldova* case[34], the applicant company was owned by foreign investors and thus benefitted from special incentives and guarantees under the Law on Foreign Investments.[35] In 1994 the president adopted a decree allowing the creation and operation of duty free shops at land, water and air-border crossings.[36] In July and December 1998, the applicant company received two licenses to operate a duty free shop and a duty free bar within the shop.[37] Four years later, the Moldovan Parliament amended the Customs Code restricting duty free sales outlets to international airports and on board aircraft flying international routes.[38] As a result, all duty free outlets that were not located on such premises, needed to be closed.[39] Shortly hereafter, the applicant company lodged a court action against the amendment with the Court of Appeal. Amongst others, the applicant argued that the amendment conflicted with the Law of Foreign Investments which stated that the activity of a foreign company could only be terminated by a governmental decision or a court order, and only if the company seriously breached Moldovan law and its articles of incorporation.[40] Also, the same law provided that if new, less favourable legislation would be adopted, companies owned by foreign investors were entitled to fall back on the old legislation for a period of ten years.[41] The Court of Appeal ruled in favour of the applicant company.[42] The Customs Department appealed and the Supreme Court of Justice (SCJ) annulled the judgment of the Court of Appeal and dismissed the applicant's action. According to the SCJ, the decision of the first-instance court was wrong because the amendment did not result in a total termination of the activity of duty free shops but just the termination of their activity in certain places.[43] Before the ECtHR, the applicant company argued that the closure of its duty free shop and bar violated its right under Article 1, Protocol 1 ECHR.[44]

According to the ECtHR, the applicant company's license to operate the duty free shop and bar, constituted a possession under Article 1, Protocol 1 ECHR (right to property).[45] The ECtHR stated that the order had the immediate and intended effect of discontinuing the applicant's duty-free business and of terminating its license and therefore interfered with its right to property.[46]

---

34   *Bimer v Moldova*, ECtHR, Judgement, 10 July 2007.
35   Ibid., para 7.
36   Ibid., para 8.
37   Ibid., para 10.
38   Ibid., para 11.
39   Ibid., para 12.
40   Ibid., para 16.
41   Ibid., para 17.
42   Ibid., para 18.
43   Ibid., para 20.
44   Ibid., para 31.
45   Ibid., para 49.
46   Ibid., para 51.

When discussing the lawfulness of the interference, it reiterated that it is in the first place for the domestic authorities, notably the courts, to interpret and apply domestic law. The ECtHR did not find grounds in the present case to question the view of the Court of Appeal establishing that the immediate closure of the applicant's duty-free business was not lawful under domestic law.[47] As a result, the ECtHR decided that there was an unlawful interference with the applicant's right to the peaceful enjoyment of its possessions[48] constituting a violation of Article 1, Protocol No. 1 ECHR.[49]

The *Regent Company v Ukraine* case[50] specifically dealt with the enforcement of an award by the International Commercial Arbitration Court. The applicant was a privately owned commercial company that was registered in the Seychelles but its address was in London.[51] In December 1998, a limited liability company (COM) started up proceedings before the International Commercial Arbitration Court at the Chamber of Commerce and Industry of Ukraine against a state-owned company, Oriana, seeking an award for breach of contract. The arbitration tribunal accepted COM's claim and ordered the Oriana Company to pay compensation. In February 2003, the applicant company concluded a contract with COM taking over the latter's right to claim the awarded debt by the arbitration tribunal. However, the Ukrainian authorities consistently refused to enforce the arbitration award.[52] The applicant was of the opinion that the non-enforcement of the arbitration award resulted in a violation of Article 6 §1 ECHR and Article 1, Protocol No. 1 ECHR.[53]

The ECtHR confirmed the applicability of Article 6 to the proceedings in this case.[54] According to the ECtHR, one of the main reasons why the authorities failed to enforce the final arbitration award was the insolvency of the Oriana state-owned company. Although the ECtHR accepted that the appropriations for the payment of state debts could cause delays in the enforcement of judgements, they could not be accepted as an excuse for failure to comply with its obligations under Article 6 §1 ECHR.[55] Moreover, the facts showed that the state authorities did not take any measures to remedy the situation. Therefore, the ECtHR decided that the continued non-enforcement of the arbitration tribunal judgement amounted to a violation of Article 6 §1 ECHR.[56] In relation to Article 1, Protocol

---

[47] Ibid., para 58.
[48] Ibid., para 59.
[49] Ibid., para 60.
[50] *Regent Company v Ukraine*, ECtHR, Judgement, 3 April 2008.
[51] Ibid., para 6.
[52] Ibid., paras 19–32.
[53] Ibid., para 51.
[54] Ibid., para 56.
[55] Ibid., para 59.
[56] Ibid., para 60.

1 ECHR, the ECtHR acknowledged that a judicial claim could only constitute a possession if it was sufficiently enforceable.[57] It recognised that an assignment of a debt could amount to such a 'possession'. According to the ECtHR, the domestic court's judicial decisions acknowledging the applicant as a creditor in the domestic proceedings, proved that the applicant had an enforceable claim that constituted a 'possession'.[58] The ECtHR decided that the lack of enforcing the arbitration award amounted to a violation of Article 1, Protocol No. 1 ECHR.[59]

In the *Shesti Mai Engineering OOD and Others v Bulgaria* case[60], the applicants owned almost 50% of the shares in a limited liability company called MTFU.[61] In 1999, a city court of one judge granted a request by the representative of a third-party company to enter the names of five members of a new board of directors in the register of companies.[62] The newly appointed management took control of MTFU's premises evicting by force the former management.[63] It organised two general meetings of MTFU's shareholders but denied access to the applicants. During these meetings, it was decided to cancel all existing shares and to issue a new share register from which the applicants' names were left out.[64] The applicants decided to instigate court proceedings in order to repeal the city court's decision and all the corresponding entries in the register of companies.[65] Their application was ultimately granted.[66] In the meantime, the new MTFU management increased the company's share capital by more than twenty times without allowing the applicants to enlist for any of the newly created shares.[67] The applicants found that the city court acted in an arbitrary fashion and allowed third parties to take over the company, which resulted in a violation of Article 1, Protocol No. 1 ECHR.[68]

The ECtHR underlined the positive obligation that rested upon states to ensure the effective enjoyment of property rights, even in cases dealing with litigation between private parties. Bulgaria was thus obliged to provide judicial recourse by offering procedural guarantees and enabling the domestic courts to decide effectively and fairly on any dispute between private parties.[69] In this specific case,

---

[57] See *Burdov v Russia*, ECtHR, Judgment, 7 May 2002, at para 40; *Poltorachenko v Ukraine*, ECtHR, Judgment, 18 January 2005, para 45.
[58] *Supra*, at para 61.
[59] *Supra*, at para 62.
[60] *Shesti Mai Engineering OOD and Others v Bulgaria*, ECtHR, Judgement, 20 September 2011.
[61] Ibid., at para 9.
[62] Ibid., at paras 16–17.
[63] Ibid., at para 19.
[64] Ibid., at para 20.
[65] Ibid., at para 24.
[66] Ibid., at para 27.
[67] Ibid., at para 47.
[68] Ibid., at para 63.
[69] Ibid., at para 79.

the events were triggered by the city court's decision to enter new members on the board of directors in the register of companies. The court decided at its own discretion without any resolution of the company's bodies and hereby grossly disregarded the rules of procedure.[70] The ECtHR found that the actions of the state had such severe consequences for the applicants that there was an interference with their property rights. Although the applicants immediately sought the annulment of that decision, their claim was examined under the normal court procedures which lasted for over four years. During this time, the applicants had no effective means to resist the new management's actions. The blatant unlawfulness of the situation demanded urgent measures to prevent further harm to the applicant's interests.[71] However, the procedures available under Bulgarian law did not succeed in providing effective redress or in giving adequate protection to the applicants against the consequences of the registration decision resulting in third parties fraudulently taking over the company.[72] Therefore, the ECtHR held that Bulgaria unlawfully interfered with the applicants' possessions and that the failure to undo this interference resulted in a violation of Article 1, Protocol 1 ECHR.[73]

The *Mamatas and Others v Greece* case[74] occurred in 2011 when the Greek debt crisis was at its peak.[75] The international institutional investors acknowledged their responsibility in the problem because they had lent great sums of money well beyond Greece's reimbursement capabilities. Therefore, they decided to waive their right to full reimbursement and negotiated a consensual reduction of their claims against Greece. It was assured by the authorities that this renegotiation procedure would not include individual bondholders.[76] However, new legislation was adopted and the individual bondholders, including the applicants, were subjected to a procedure which included the exchange of their bonds for other less valuable securities issued by the state with a view to reduce the Greek public debt.[77] The applicants were of the opinion that the forced exchange resulted in the expropriation of their property violating Article 1, Protocol 1 ECHR.[78]

According to Greek law, the bondholders had a pecuniary claim against the state for an amount equivalent to the nominal value of their bonds upon expiry of their securities. Therefore the ECtHR accepted that there was a 'legitimate expectation' that their claim would be met and therefore they possessed 'property'

---

70 Ibid., at para 81.
71 Ibid., at para 87.
72 Ibid., at para 91.
73 Ibid., at para 92.
74 *Mamatas and Others v Greece*, ECHR, Judgement, 21 July 2016.
75 Ibid., at para 9.
76 Ibid., at para 12.
77 Ibid., at paras 14–25.
78 Ibid., at para 56.

protected under Article 1, Protocol 1 ECHR.[79] The new legislation adopted by the Greek state resulted in a new agreement altering the conditions governing the bonds, including a cut in their nominal value, which was also applicable to the applicants.[80] According to the ECtHR, the mandatory participation of the applicants in the procedure and the modification of the selected securities amounted to an interference with the applicants' right to property.[81] This procedure was clearly prescribed by law which was accessible and whose consequences were foreseeable.[82] Also, the ECtHR acknowledged that the serious political economic and social crisis in Greece forced the state to adopt measures to maintain economic stability and restructure the debt which was in the best interests of the community. Since the adopted legislation resulted in a reduction of the Greek debt, the acclaimed measures pursued an aim in the public interest.[83] The ECtHR further stated that the amount that the applicants expected to receive when their bonds matured, could not serve as the reference point to assess the loss they suffered. The nominal value of the bonds already diminished by the declining state solvency and Greece would not been able to honour its obligations under the contractual clauses of the old bonds.[84] Also, it was necessary that all bondholders would agree to the restructuring of the Greek debt because otherwise the whole project would collapse.[85] Therefore, the ECtHR accepted that the Collective Action Clauses were appropriate and necessary to reduce the Greek public debt and save Greece from bankruptcy.[86] It stressed that investing in bonds could never be considered as completely risk-free.[87] Since the impugned measures did not upset the fair balance between the public interest and the protection of the applicants' property nor inflict any excessive burden on them, the ECtHR decided that the reasons were not disproportionate to their legitimate aim and thus did not result in a violation of Article 1, Protocol 1 ECHR.[88]

The case-law of the ECtHR confirms that companies, and more specifically investors, also fall back on the protection provided by the ECHR. The ECtHR rarely refers to international investment law when assessing the investors' claims. It may consider a specific investment contract to inform the background of the claim, but it will not for example refer to international investment law to interpret human rights law.

---

[79]   Ibid., at para 87.
[80]   Ibid., at para 92.
[81]   Ibid., at paras 93–94.
[82]   Ibid., at paras 99–100.
[83]   Ibid., at paras 103–105.
[84]   Ibid., at para 112.
[85]   Ibid., at para 115.
[86]   Ibid., at para 116.
[87]   Ibid., at para 117.
[88]   Ibid., at paras 119–120.

IV. THE ADJUDICATION OF AN INVESTMENT CONFLICT BY BOTH INVESTMENT ARBITRATION TRIBUNALS AND THE ECtHR

A. ROMPETROL v. ROMANIA

The case of *Rompetrol v. Romania*[89] is of particular relevance, as Rompetrol's investors already sued Romania before the ECtHR.[90] The applicants were former employees of Rompetrol who invested in the foreign operations of the company. Shortly after investing, the payment of interest and the restitution of capital was ceased before the applicants recovered their investments. The applicants filed several criminal complaints for which final judgment was only ruled almost 10 years later. As a result, they alleged that there was a breach of Article 6 ECHR (right to a fair hearing) because, amongst other things, their right to obtain a decision on their claims within reasonable time was violated. The ECtHR confirmed a violation of Article 6 ECHR in respect of one applicant and struck out or declared the other applications inadmissible. In the investment arbitration case, Rompetrol argued that Romania violated its obligations under the Netherlands and Romania BIT.[91] These claims arose from measures taken by Romanian anti-corruption and criminal prosecution authorities against two company officers that directed the affairs of the company. According to Rompetrol, the actions consisting out of arrest, detention, travel-ban and wire-tapping, were politically and economically motivated and therefore violated the fair and equitable treatment, full protection and security and non-impairment standard. Although the applicants were different actors in both cases, the facts at hand were similar and therefore this case sheds an interesting light on the potential judicial dialogue between international investment tribunals and the ECtHR.

The arbitration tribunal summarised that although there was no dispute on the relevance of the ECHR as a relevant source for the interpretation of the BIT, there was no agreement on the relevance of the ECHR and its case law for the specific issues at stake. According to Romania, the ECHR provides a bench-mark standard for the protection of the individual and therefore, any system or practice that would meet the ECHR standards would *a fortiori* satisfy the requirements of the BIT for the treatment of investments.[92] However,

---

[89] *The Rompetrol Group NV v Romania*, ICSID Case No ARB/06/3, Award, 6 May 2013.

[90] *Affaire Association des Personnes Victimes du Systeme SC Rompetrol et SC Geomin SA et Autres v Roumaine*, Judgment, 25 September 2013.

[91] Agreement on encouragement and reciprocal protection of Investments between the Government of the Kingdom of the Netherlands and the Government of Romania, 19 April 1994.

[92] *Supra* n 89, at para 169.

Rompetrol was of the opinion that the BIT needed to be acknowledged as a *lex specialis*, both in time and in substance, so that the ECHR standards could not be seen as a mere incidental or secondary interest.[93] The reliance on ECHR jurisprudence was misplaced as the human rights standards set a 'floor', but not a 'ceiling' that would limit the level of protection that might be granted under the BIT.[94]

The investment tribunal concluded that: (i) it was not competent to decide on issues regarding the application of the ECHR within Romania, either to natural persons or to corporate entities; (ii) the governing law for the issues to decide upon would be the BIT; and (iii) the category of materials for the assessment of the BIT provisions is not a closed one and may include the consideration of other common standards under the international regime, including those in the area of human rights.[95]

B.   YUKOS v. RUSSIA

A similar scenario took place in the *Yukos v Russia* case, in which both the ECtHR[96] and an international investment tribunal[97] ruled upon similar facts. In the ECtHR proceedings, Yukos argued that there were irregularities in its tax liability proceedings and that its tax assessments and their subsequent enforcement were unlawful and lacked proportionality.[98] It claimed that the Russian courts' interpretation of the relevant tax laws were selective and unique, since many other Russian companies had also used domestic tax havens.[99] Therefore, according to Yukos, the Russian conduct resulted in a violation of several ECHR standards such as Article 6 (right to a fair trial), Article 1 of Protocol No 1 (right to property) and Article 13 (right to an effective remedy). Also in the international investment proceedings, the claimants argued that the measures taken by the Russian governments resulted in the bankruptcy of Yukos, after which its assets were acquired by Russian state-owned companies. Besides the harassment of Yukos' executives, the measures amounted to a violation of the fair and equitable treatment (FET) standard (Article 10(1) Energy Charter Treaty (ECT)) and to an indirect expropriation (Article 13(1) ECT). In the end, both legal proceedings resulted in Russia being convicted of having violated the ECHR and the ECT.

---

93   Ibid., at para 169.
94   Ibid., at para 60(d).
95   Ibid., at para 172.
96   *OAO Neftyanaya Kompaniya Yukos v Russia*, ECtHR, Judgment, 20 September 2011.
97   *Yukos Universal Limited (Isle of Man) v The Russian Federation*, PCA Case No AA 227, Award, 18 July 2014.
98   *Supra* n. 96, at paras 619–624.
99   Ibid., at paras 608–609.

Both instances addressed the simultaneous character of the proceedings when discussing their jurisdiction. According to Article 35 §2 ECHR, the ECtHR cannot deal with applications that are substantially the same as a matter that was already submitted to another international body and which does not include any relevant new information. Nonetheless, according to the ECtHR the international investment proceedings that were brought by the shareholders of Yukos, were not substantially the same as the ECtHR's case because the claimants in both cases were different. The claimants in the arbitration proceedings were Yukos's shareholders acting as investors, where it was Yukos itself that acted as a claimant in the ECtHR proceedings. As a result, the ECtHR decided that it could consider the merits of the case, even though it was also being considered under international investment proceedings.[100]

In the investment proceedings, the Russian government argued that the ECtHR claims shared the same fundamental basis and therefore the claims made in the investment proceedings should be dismissed.[101] This followed from the fork-in-the-road provision (Article 26(3)(b)(i) ECT) which provides that consent to international arbitration cannot be given if the investor previously submitted the dispute under other listed means. However, the claimants specified that to be in line with the fork-in-the-road provisions in general, the other proceedings must withstand the 'triple identity' test: (i) identity of parties; (ii) cause of action; and (iii) object of the dispute.[102] The investment arbitration tribunal followed the claimants' position and established that the proceedings before the ECtHR did not pass the 'triple identity' test and therefore did not trigger the fork-in-the-road provision confirming its jurisdiction.[103] Also in the merits phase, Russia raised the fork-in-the-road objection, alleging that the damages sought by the claimants were the same as before the ECtHR which would lead to a potential double recovery.[104] However, the investment tribunal stood its ground and saw no reason to change its view on the objection.[105] Both the ECtHR and the investment tribunal followed a similar reasoning when establishing their jurisdiction but neither discussed their relationship in depth.

Also in the merits phase, neither judicial organ addressed how their judgements would relate to one another. Although the proceedings took place simultaneously at one point, the judgement of the ECtHR preceded the decision of the investment tribunal. As a result, both the claimant as Russia referred to

---

100   Ibid., at paras 519–526.
101   *Supra* n. 97, at para 71.
102   Ibid., at para 593.
103   Ibid., at paras 598 and 601.
104   Ibid., at para 1258.
105   Ibid., at para 1271.

the ECtHR judgement at several points to strengthen their arguments, but they were never explicitly addressed by the investment tribunal. This could be seen as a missed opportunity to shed some light on how the ECtHR's judgement could relate to and impact the decision of the investment tribunal.

CONCLUSION

The discussion of the foundations and basic notions of international investment law and human rights law challenged the traditional viewpoint that these are two very distinct branches of public international law. The provided overview emphasised that they have more in common than expected at first glance. The shared foundations and characteristics reveal a clear interconnectedness between international investment law and human rights law without denying their differences. When looking at this relationship between international investment law and human rights law, one questions their sphere of influence and impact, and the existence of a balanced character.

The analysis of the ECHR and ECtHR case law references in international investment arbitration cases, demonstrated that investment tribunals readily accept ECHR and ECtHR case law references when they confirm the protective status of the investor. When the host states or third parties call upon human rights law or case-law, the investment tribunals are more hesitant to accept them. Investment tribunals thus do accept the relevance of international human rights law, primarily for the interpretation of investment law, but adopt it in such an inconsistent manner that it only benefits the investor and not the other parties involved. The adoption of the ECHR and ECtHR case law by international investment tribunals thus primarily results in enforcing the protective status of investors, where the adequate use of the ECHR and ECtHR case law would result in a more balanced protection of all involved parties and would not just benefit the status of the investor.

The discussion of the relevant case-law of the ECtHR confirmed the one-sided character of the relationship between international human rights law and international investment law with human rights law influencing international investment law, but international investment law not impacting human rights law nor being a source of inspiration for its adoption at all. As a result, the ECtHR is primarily used by investors as an additional judicial recourse to call upon to enforce their protective status.

When tackling the specific situations in which the ECtHR and investment arbitration tribunals touched upon the same investment conflicts, it became clear that there is no clear acknowledgement of a potential judicial dialogue between the two instances, let alone a clarification of the nature of such a judicial dialogue and how they relate to one another. Considering the existence of an unbalanced relationship between international investment law and human rights law and the fact that this is at present resulting in an unbalanced and unwanted confirmation of the protective status of the investor, there lies great potential in the acknowledgement and characterisation of the judicial dialogue between international investment tribunals and the ECtHR.

Part IV

Human Rights
and Societal Transformations

TERRORISM AND HUMAN RIGHTS

Jos SILVIS

Procurator General at the Supreme Court of the Netherlands
Former Judge of the European Court of Human Rights

TRIBUTE

As a Judge elected in respect of Belgium in 2012, Paul Lemmens is one among the 47 Judges of the European Court of Human Rights responsible for further clarifying the proper meaning of the norms of the European Convention on Human Rights in Cases lodged by applicants. His impressive wisdom and balanced judgment do not simply spring from formidable character traits which he certainly possesses. A strong academic background, years of intensive interaction with colleagues and students in the university, combined with a professional career that brought him in the Council of State were the building blocks of his profile before he entered the Court. There I was privileged to learn to know him as colleague and friend. He is probably the most prudent man I have ever met. The kind of man to whom you would patiently entrust to judge the most difficult of all cases, like those concerning countering terrorism. In fact he took part in the composition of the Court judging some of the well-known cases addressed in the following.

I.   THE CONCEPT OF TERRORISM

Terrorism is commonly understood to refer to acts of violence that target civilians in the pursuit of political or ideological aims. In legal terms, although the international community has yet to adopt a comprehensive definition of terrorism, existing declarations, resolutions and universal "sectoral" treaties relating to specific aspects of it define certain acts and core elements.[1] In the refugee case Lounani v. Belgium before the Court of Justice of the European Union Advocate-General Sharpston observes that whilst UN Security Council Resolutions identify a range of activities that are to be considered to be contrary

---

[1]   Human Rights, Terrorism and Counter-terrorism. Factsheet no. 32, Office of the United Nations High Commissioner for Human Rights, Terrorism and Counter-terrorism (2008).

to the aims and purposes of the United Nations, there is no general definition in international law of terrorism or terrorist.[2] In Saadi v. Italy, an expulsion case of a terrorist suspect to Tunisia, terrorists are described as persons who channel their fundamentalist faith into violent action.[3] In the same judgment of the European Court of Human Rights (ECtHR) there is a referral to a report of Human Rights Watch on Tunisia, noting that the 2003 anti-terrorism law gave a very broad definition of "terrorism", which could be used to prosecute persons merely for exercising their right to political dissent.

The European Court of Human Rights holds no definition of its own of terrorism; it can operate with different concepts in relation to the domestic context from which an issue may be brought to the Court. The reality behind the concepts is very relevant. Obviously, labelling a situation as terrorism not automatically establishes the State's intervention as legitimate.

II. NEGATIVE AND POSITIVE OBLIGATIONS

There is an abundancy of judgments of het European Court of Human Rights dealing with terrorism.[4] Terrorism in its current posture in western society manifests non-governmental violence and threats of violence. And so the question arises as to what *positive obligations* there may be for the state to protect its citizens against the threats of terrorism.

The ECtHR has long accepted that Articles 2 and 3 of the Convention entail positive obligations for States to protect the life and to prevent ill-treatment of the persons within their jurisdiction. As far back as the judgment in Osman v. the United Kingdom, a tragic shooting which led to the death of Mr Osman and the wounding of his son, the Court held as follows[5]:

> "The Court notes that the first sentence of Article 2 §1 enjoins the State not only to refrain from the intentional and unlawful taking of life, but also to take appropriate steps to safeguard the lives of those within its jurisdiction."

For the Court, and bearing in mind the difficulties involved in policing modern societies, the unpredictability of human conduct and the operational choices

---

2   Opinion of 31 May 2016, C-573/14, no. 7 (A-G Sharpston).
3   *Saadi v. Italy* (GC), 3720/06, 28 February 2008.
4   See HUDOC: *European Court of Human Rights Factsheet on Terrorism and on Secret Detention Sites.* These sheets were particularly helpful in preparing this contribution.
5   *Osman v. the United Kingdom*, 28 October 1998, §115, Reports of Judgments and Decisions 1998 VIII; see also *Opuz v. Turkey* (no. 33401/02, ECHR 2009); *Mastromatteo v. Italy* [GC], 37703/97, ECHR 2002 VIII); and *Maiorano and Others v. Italy*, 28634/06, 15 December 2009.

which must be made in terms of priorities and resources, such an obligation must be interpreted in a way which does not impose an impossible or disproportionate burden on the authorities.

In the opinion of the Court where there is an allegation that the authorities have violated their positive obligation to protect the right to life in the context of their duty to prevent and suppress offences against the person, it must be established to its satisfaction that the authorities knew or ought to have known at the time of the existence of a real and immediate risk to the life of an identified individual or individuals from the criminal acts of a third party and that they failed to take measures within the scope of their powers which, judged reasonably, might have been expected to avoid that risk.

The Court has recently clarified the scope of States' positive obligations when it comes to preventing terrorist attacks.[6] This case concerns a hostage-taking in a school. One of the issues raised by the applicants concerns the absence of preventive measures despite the fact that the intelligence services had been informed of the risk of terrorist attacks and of the presence of terrorists in the area. Unanimously, the Court held that there had been a violation of Article 2 (right to life) of the European Convention on Human Rights, arising from a failure to take preventive measures. The authorities had been in possession of sufficiently specific information of a planned terrorist attack in the area, linked to an educational institution. Nevertheless, not enough had been done to disrupt the terrorists meeting and preparing; insufficient steps had been taken to prevent them travelling on the day of the attack; security at the school had not been increased; and neither the school nor the public had been warned of the threat.

III. COUNTER-TERRORISM AND THE DEROGATION CLAUSE

Posing the question whether counter-terrorism is compatible with human rights makes it relevant to note first that the Convention on Human Rights has a derogation clause in Article 15, applicable in time of emergency in respect of relative rights (like liberty, privacy, fair trial requirements). This clause affords to the governments of the States parties, in exceptional circumstances, the possibility of derogating, in a temporary, limited and supervised manner, from their obligation to secure certain rights and freedoms under the Convention. The use of that provision is governed by the following procedural and substantive conditions:

---

6   *Tagayeva and Others v. Russia*, 26562/07, 13 April 2017.

- the right to derogate can be invoked only in time of war or other public emergency threatening the life of the nation;
- a State may take measures derogating from its obligations under the Convention only to the extent strictly required by the exigencies of the situation;
- any derogations may not be inconsistent with the State's other obligations under international law.

This clause has been applied recently several times.[7] In the wake of the terrorist attacks in Paris on 13 November 2015 France declared a state of emergency ('état d'urgence') for the whole nation.[8] President Hollande publicly announced this state of emergency already on the same evening the attacks took place. This French state of emergency is based on an Act from 1955, which was originally intended to deal with the Algerian war of independence. The state of emergency can be declared in the event of an imminent danger to the public order, or in relation to events which amount, by their nature and severity, to a public disaster.

The French 'état d'urgence' gives exceptional powers to the Minister of the Interior and to prefects (state representatives at the local level). They can pronounce house arrests for any person whose actions prove dangerous for security and public order, without prior judicial authorisation. Moreover, such an allegedly dangerous person can be obliged to surrender his or her passport or ID card. The prefects can regulate or forbid circulation and gathering in some areas. The Minister and the prefects can order places of gathering to be closed. Also, house searches can be executed without prior authorisation by a judge. The powers of house arrest and house searches without prior judicial authorisation are difficult to reconcile with the peacetime standards of the European Convention on Human Rights (ECHR) and the case law of the European Court of Human Rights.

Prolongation of the state of emergency beyond twelve days can only be decided in France by Act of Parliament. And this is exactly what happened: an Act to prolong the state of emergency for another three months entered into force on 20 November 2015 and was prolonged afterwards. President Macron ended the state of emergency on the first of November 2017 while introducing a new anti-terror law.

---

[7] Recent examples: on 5 June 2015 Ukraine notified the Secretary General of the Council of Europe that given the emergency situation in the country, the authorities of Ukraine had decided to use Article 15 of the European Convention on Human Rights to derogate from certain rights enshrined in the Convention. On 21 July 2016, following an attempted coup. The Secretary General of the Council of Europe has been informed by the Turkish authorities that Turkey will notify a derogation.

[8] The French government notified the Secretary General of the Council of Europe on 25 November 2015, in accordance with Article 15(3) ECHR, that the measures taken during the state of emergency may derogate from the obligations under the Convention.

The derogation clause in the Convention offers a wider discretion for States to restrict rights when emergency is threatening the life of the nation. But there is a category of rights which are excluded from being affected by this clause, these rights continue to apply during such states of emergency. Most prominent non-derogable rights, often labelled absolute rights, are the right to life, except in respect of deaths resulting from lawful acts of war, and the right not to be subjected to ill-treatment. Furthermore the prohibition of slavery and the principle of legality are non-derogable, according to Article 15 §2 of the Convention. Non-derogability of the legality principle is subject to Article 7 §2, namely that the article shall not prejudice the trial and punishment of acts at the time of its committal criminal according to the general principles of law recognized by civilized nations (the Nuremberg clause). The Court extended the scope of the legality principle to protect convicted persons, including convicted terrorists, against modifications of sentences in the course of the execution of imprisonment.[9]

I will go into some of the Court's case-law concerning the absolute right to life and the right not to be ill-treated, as well as case-law concerning relative rights, but before doing so I should indicate that there are more non-derogable rights than those mentioned in Article 15 §2. Additional protocols to the Convention also hold prohibitions of derogation, like the one concerning the 'ne bis in idem' principle as laid down in Article 4 of Protocol No. 7. According to that principle no one should be punished twice for the same (idem) crime. This does not stand in the way of convicting a terrorist twice in subsequent trials, unless the same crimes are being tried. In Ramda v. France, §§81–84, the Court recalled the principle of a facts-based assessment of the idem element and applied it to the prosecution of terrorist offences.[10] The applicant, an Algerian national, was extradited from the United Kingdom to France on charges related to a series of terrorist attacks in 1995 in France. He was first tried and convicted by a criminal court (tribunal correctionnel) on charges concerning his participation in a group aimed at preparing terrorist attacks. And he was subsequently tried and convicted by an assize court (cour d'assises) on charges of complicity to commit a series of particular crimes such as murder and attempted murder. After carrying out a comparative examination of the numerous facts set out in the decisions rendered in both procedures (§§87–93), the Court noted that those decisions had been based on a large number of detailed and distinct facts (§94). It

---

[9] See *Del Rio Prada v. Spain*, no. 42750/09, 21 October 2013, §77–80. Judge Lemmens opposed awarding non-pecuniary or moral damage to the applicant (see his joint partly dissenting opinion). In *Arrozpide Sarasola and Others v. Spain*, 65101/16, 23 October 2018 (not final) concerning ETA members that had served pre-trial detention in France, Spain's refusal to reduce the penalty on account of that pre-trial detention did not run counter Article 7, according to the Court, since the penalty had not thereby been modified.

[10] *Ramda v. France*, no. 78477/11, 17 December 2017.

concluded that the applicant had not been prosecuted or convicted in the second proceedings for facts which were substantially the same as those of which he had been convicted under the first proceedings (§95). Finally, the Court drew on the obligation on the State to prosecute grave breaches of Article 2 developed in Marguš v. Croatia [GC], §§127–128, and applied it to the terrorism context (§96).[11]

IV. ABSOLUTE RIGHTS

A. COUNTER-TERRORISM IN DIRECT ACTION AND THE RIGHT TO LIFE, THREE EXAMPLES IN THE COURT'S CASE-LAW

1. McCann: "Death on the Rock"[12]

A classic case on the positive obligations to respect the right to life in counter-terrorism action, is McCann v. the United Kingdom.[13] The facts may be sketched as follows. Early in 1988 the United Kingdom, Spanish and Gibraltar authorities concluded that the Provisional IRA (Irish Republican Army – "IRA") were planning a terrorist attack on Gibraltar. To prevent this attack the Commissioner of Police of Gibraltar was assisted by specialized military and security officers. According to the Commissioner the terrorist target was highly probably the band and guard of the First Battalion of the Royal Anglian Regiment during a ceremonial changing of the guard at Ince's Hall on 8 March 1988. There were indications that the method of the terrorist attack would be to strike with a car bomb. An IRA unit of three persons was assumed to carry out the attack, among them an expert bomb-maker. The Commissioners plan was for an arrest to be carried out once all the members of the terrorist unit were present and identified and they had parked a car which they intended to leave before having it detonated.

Four soldiers were to arrest the IRA suspects; however their instructions included the possible need to shoot. The three suspects were closely followed by soldiers. Just before the intended arrest soldiers thought the suspects were about to detonate bombs by pressing a button and therefore the suspects were gunned down. It appeared afterwards that there had been no risk of detonating bombs, because there were no explosives in the car. The applicants, representatives of the estates of the deceased, brought the case to Strasbourg.

---

11   *Marguš v. Croatia* [GC], no. 4455/10), 27 May 2014.
12   The gunning down of the suspects in Gibraltar was reconstructed in a documentary entitled "Death on the Rock" Thames Television 28 April 1988.
13   *McCann and Others v. The United Kingdom*, 18984/91, 27 September 1995.

The authorities were faced with a fundamental dilemma. On the one hand, they were required to have regard to their duty to protect the lives of the people in Gibraltar including their own military personnel and, on the other, to have minimum resort to the use of lethal force against those suspected of posing this threat in the light of the obligations flowing from both domestic and international law. The Court's case-law concerning terrorism cases has been constructed around the balancing of the different interests at stake: on the one hand, the protection of the fundamental rights of the terrorists or suspected terrorists, and on the other hand the interests of national security, the preservation of public order and the protection of the rights of others. In this case the Court is not persuaded that the killing of the three terrorists constituted the use of force which was no more than absolutely necessary in defence of persons from unlawful violence within the meaning of Article 2–2-a of the Convention.

2. The siege at the Dubrovka Theatre

In the evening of 23 October 2002 a group of armed terrorists belonging to the Chechen separatist movement took some 900 people hostage in the Moscow "Dubrovka" theatre. The applicants in Finogenov and others v. Russia that brought their case to the Court in Strasbourg were either hostages or relatives of those hostages who died in the course of the subsequent rescue operation.[14] The hostages were held at gunpoint and the theatre building was booby-trapped. The terrorists demanded the immediate withdrawal of Russian troops from the Chechen Republic. Negotiations were conducted and several hostages were shot dead. Meanwhile, the authorities created a "crisis cell" under the command of the Federal Security Service, which was in charge of planning a rescue operation. In the morning of 26 October 2002 Russian security forces pumped an unknown narcotic gas into the main auditorium through the building's ventilation system. A few minutes later, when almost all the terrorists had lost consciousness under the influence of the gas, the special squad stormed the building and killed most of them. The hostages were then evacuated from the building and transported to hospitals in ambulances or city buses. However, some 125 hostages died either on the spot, during transportation or in hospital. The rescue plan had been flawed in many respects: there appeared to have been no centralised coordination of the various services involved; there were no instructions on how information about the victims and their condition should be exchanged (one result of this was that some victims received multiple doses of the antidote); it was unclear what order of priorities had been set for the medics; no medical assistance was provided during the mass transportation of victims on city buses; and there was no clear plan for the distribution of victims to the various hospitals, with significant numbers arriving at the same hospital at the same time. The Court concluded

---

14   *Finogenov and Others v. Russia*, 18200/03, 27311/03, 20 December 2011.

that the rescue operation had not been sufficiently prepared and that the State had therefore failed to fulfil its positive obligations under Article 2.

3. Responsibility for use of lethal force in the London subway

The third example on the right to life in a counterterrorism context concerns a tragic event in the London subway.[15] The applicant's cousin, Jean Charles de Menezes, was shot dead, in error, by Special Firearms Officers (special firearms officers, SFO's) while on the underground in London in the wake of a series of bombs on the city's transport network in July 2005. After his death extensive investigation was conducted and detailed investigation reports were published. Whilst no individual officer was disciplined or prosecuted, the Office of the Commissioner of the Police of the Metropolis (OCPM) was found guilty of criminal charges under health and safety legislation. The applicant complained under Article 2 of the Convention about the failure to prosecute any individuals for her cousin's death. The case having been referred in December 2014, the Grand Chamber found no violation of the procedural limb of Article 2 of the Convention. The judgment contains a comprehensive outline of the procedural investigative requirements in cases concerning the use of lethal force by State agents.

The judgment clarifies what the Court meant in McCann v. the United Kingdom [GC], §200, by an "honest belief [that the use of force was justified] which is perceived, for good reasons, to be valid at the time but which subsequently turns out to be mistaken". The Court did not adopt the stance of a detached observer (objectively reasonable) but rather considered it should put itself in the position of the officer, in determining both whether force was necessary and the degree needed. The Grand Chamber found that the principal question was whether the person had an "honest and genuine" belief and, in this regard, the Court will consider whether the belief was "subjectively reasonable" (the existence of subjective good reasons for it). One of the more novel aspects of the case concerns the prosecutorial decision not to prosecute any individual police officer but to prosecute the police force (the OCPM), a decision made on the basis of the "threshold evidential test". The test is "whether there was sufficient evidence to provide a realistic prospect of conviction". The Court accepted this test to be adequate.

B. THE RIGHT NOT TO BE ILL-TREATED (ARTICLE 3)

It's a well-documented fact that ill-treatment of persons is at risk to occur in the course of counter-terrorist activities. This may be so when security officers or military men are in hot pursuit of suspected terrorists. Another example

---

[15] *Armani Da Silva v. the United Kingdom*, 5878/08, 30 March 2016.

concerns the widely debated methods of interrogation in a situation of a ticking bomb. What methods are allowed when it is likely that the individual being interrogated is supposed to have knowledge about an upcoming event of terrorism? In Brussels (2016) one of the arrested suspects was said to deny giving information about a rucksack with explosives somewhere in that city. At the time there might have been an acute risk for citizens. From the perspective of the Convention the answer as to what method of interrogation would be acceptable, is relatively simple. Torture or Inhuman and degrading treatment are absolutely forbidden, also in situations of emergency.

Article 3 of the Convention, as the Court has observed on many occasions, enshrines one of the fundamental values of democratic society.[16] Even in the most difficult of circumstances, such as the fight against organised terrorism and crime, the Convention prohibits in absolute terms torture or inhuman or degrading treatment or punishment.[17]

Establishing that there is a state of emergency therefore cannot legitimize ill-treatment. This may illustrated by cases the Court dealt with concerning a. the United Kingdom and IRA terrorist suspects, b. Turkey in relation to the PKK, and c. Spain dealing with separatist terrorists.

a. In the early seventies terrorist campaign by the IRA and others in Northern Ireland led to a situation of public emergency threatening the life of the nation. This however could not legitimize inhuman or degrading treatment torture. In the inter-state case of Ireland v. the United Kingdom (known as the hooded men case) the Court concluded in 1978 that five techniques of interrogation (sensory dissociation), as applied in combination in relation to IRA suspects, undoubtedly amounted to inhuman and degrading treatment, although their object was the extraction of confessions, the naming of others and/or information and although they were used systematically, they did not, according to the Court, occasion suffering of the particular intensity and cruelty implied by the word torture as so understood. Here the Court differed from the Commission that unanimously had expressed the opinion that the combined use of the five techniques in the cases before it not only constituted a practice of inhuman treatment but also of torture in breach of Article 3. That opinion had not been contested by the United Kingdom before the

---

16   Article 3 covers a wide range of activities: from the police officer slapping in the face of a protesting arrested young offender in *Bouyid v. Belgium*, 23380/09, 28 September 2015 to torture in its most extreme form.

17   See the *Ireland v. the United Kingdom* Judgment of 18 January 1978, Series A no. 25, p. 65, para. 163, the *Soering v. the United Kingdom* Judgment of 7 July 1989, Series A no. 161, p. 34, para. 88, and the *Chahal v. the United Kingdom* Judgment of 15 November 1996, Reports 1996-V, p. 1855, para. 79.

Court. A request to revise the classic judgment was concluded inadmissible in 2018 since the newly discovered facts concerning the level of knowledge of high ranking British officials, after the opening of the British archives, about the detrimental effects of the five techniques would presumably at the time of its judgment not have led the Court to another appreciation of the qualification of inhuman treatment and not torture under Article 3 of the Convention.[18]

b. Some Turkish cases spring from the armed conflict between the Republic of Turkey and various Kurdish insurgent groups which have demanded separation from Turkey to create an independent Kurdistan. The main militant group is the Kurdistan Workers' Party or PKK. The PKK was founded on 27 November 1978 and it has since then been involved in armed clashes with Turkish security forces. The full-scale insurgency, however, did not begin until 15 August 1984, when the PKK announced a Kurdish uprising. The first insurgency lasted until 1 September 1999, when the PKK declared a unilateral cease-fire. In a Turkish case the Court considered, in the light of all the material before it, that the particular extent and impact of PKK terrorist activity in South-East Turkey in 1992 had undoubtedly created, in the region concerned, a "public emergency threatening the life of the nation". The Court found in its judgment Aksoy v. Turkey (Application no. 21987/93), 18 December 1996, that in this context the applicant had been subjected to torture. It appeared that Mr Aksoy was arrested and taken into custody on 26 November 1992 together with thirteen others, on suspicion of aiding and abetting PKK (Workers' Party of Kurdistan), being a member of the Kiziltepe branch of the PKK and distributing PKK tracts. Turkey had thereby violated Article 3 of the Convention. In another Turkish case, Ilhan v. Turkey, the applicant, suspected of PKK activities, was severely beaten at the time of his arrest.[19] The beatings, including to the head, were carried out with rifle butts when the security forces "captured" the applicant who was in hiding. A significant period of time then lapsed before the applicant had access to medical treatment. In the Court's view this treatment also amounted to torture.

c. In the abovementioned British and Turkish cases the Court found substantive violations of Article 3 of the Convention in cases of counter-terrorism. The Court could not find such substantive violation in cases concerning Spain, published in French only. The context of these cases is as follows. After the dictatorship of Francisco Franco in Spain that lasted from 1939 until his death in 1975, the new Spanish democracy has not been free from tensions with

---

18   ECtHR 20 March 2018, 5310/71 (Decision).
19   *Ilhan v. Turkey*, 22277/93, [GC], 7 June 2000.

separatist militant or terrorist groups, like the Terra Lliure (TL) in Catalonia and the Basque Euskadi ta Askatasuna (ETA). In fighting terrorism Spain has made use of dedicated legislation in which the incommunicado detention, a form a secret detention, of persons is a central element. The incommunicado detention can be used against persons presumed to be member of an armed band or having links with armed bands or persons who are terrorists or rebels. Persons subjected to this regime are very much restricted in communication) (like to have the fact of his detention and the place in which he is being held at any given time made known to the relative or other person of his choice); he is not entitled to the interview with his lawyer. There are many claims of persons stating to have undergone forms of torture in such incommunicado detention in Spain. Although many applications claiming Article 3 violations of the Convention by Spain in its fight against separatist movements, the Court could not establish substantive violations in that regard. A number of persons claiming to have been tortured while in Spanish incommunicado detention came to the European Court of Human Rights. In cases like these the Court is faced with problems of establishing facts. Therefore it has shown painstakingly difficult to find substantial violations of Article 3 of the Convention following these complaints. It is important that the Court interprets Article 3 of the Convention in view of the States' obligation under Article 1 of the Convention such that it implies a procedural obligation. In many cases the Court held that where an individual raises an arguable claim that he has been seriously ill-treated by the police or other agents of the state unlawfully and in breach of Article 3, that provision, read in conjunction with the state's general duty under Article 1 of the Convention to "secure to everyone within their jurisdiction the rights and freedoms defined in … [the] Convention", requires that there should be an effective official investigation. The investigation should be capable of leading to the identification and punishment of those responsible. Otherwise, despite its fundamental importance, the general legal prohibition of torture and inhuman or degrading treatment or punishment would be ineffective in practice and it would be possible in some cases to state officials trample on, enjoying virtual impunity, the rights of those within their control. In the case of Martinez Sala and Others v. Spain, the applicants complained of torture and other ill-treatment during custody in Catalonia.[20] The arrests took place in a context of fear of the Spanish authorities that terrorist attacks would take place before or during the Olympic Games in Barcelona in 1992. The Court was not convinced that the investigations were sufficiently thorough and effective to meet the aforementioned requirements of Article 3. Thus the Court did not find any substantial violation of Article 3, but found only a procedural violation. This pattern is repeated in other Spanish torture cases, most of which concern applicants with an ETA background, like the case of Otamendi

---

[20]   *Martinez Sala and Others v. Spain*, 58438/00, 2 November 2004.

Egiguren v. Spain.[21] Mr Martxelo Otamendi Egiguren, is a Spanish journalist who was born in 1957 and lived in Tolosa (Spain). At the material time he was the publication director of the Basque daily newspaper Euskaldunon Egunkaria. On the subject of the alleged ill-treatment, the European Court of Human Rights found that "the judicial review of the conditions of the [applicant's] incommunicado detention in police custody [had been] neither sufficient nor effective". In more recent cases of Etxebarria Caballero v. Spain (application no. 74016/12) and Ataun Rojo v. Spain (no. 3344/13) again the focus had to be on the investigation by the Spanish authorities into ill-treatment allegedly sustained by the applicants while they were held incommunicado in police custody. They were arrested by the police and placed in secret police custody in the context of judicial investigations concerning, in particular, their alleged membership of the terrorist organisation ETA. In these two cases, the Court held again, unanimously, that there had been a violation of Article 3 (prohibition of inhuman or degrading treatment) of the European Convention on Human Rights on account of the lack of an effective investigation into the applicants' allegations of ill-treatment.

C. INTERNATIONAL COOPERATION: EXTRADITION AND RENDITION

Requests to extradite suspects of terrorism give rise to a number of questions.[22] In extradition matters interim measures play an important role. Applying Rule 39 the Court may prevent that extradition would occur before the Court is satisfied that the requested extradition would not cause an irreparable and serious violation of the human rights of the applicant, mostly concerning Article 2 or 3. Neglecting that Rule 39 is applied normally results in the Courts' finding of a violation of Article 34 by the respondent State. Ever since Soering v. United Kingdom it is clear that the State's responsibility could be engaged if it decided to extradite a person who risked being subjected to ill-treatment in the requesting country.[23] In Saadi v. Italy the Court finds a violation of Article 3 if the applicant were to be deported to Tunisia where he claimed to have been sentenced in absentia in 2005 to 20 years' imprisonment for membership of a terrorist organisation.[24] In Babar Ahmad and Others v. the United Kingdom – the Court concludes that conditions of detention in super-max US prison would not constitute a violation in case of

---

21   *Otamendi Egiguren v. Spain*, 47303/08; *Etxebarria Caballero v. Spain*, 74016/12 and *Ataun Rojo v. Spain* 3344/13.
22   Extradition and Human Rights Diplomatic assurances and Human Rights in the Extradition Context, Presentation J. Silvis, 20 May 2014, PC-OC meeting in Strasbourg/F.
23   *Soering v. United Kingdom*, 038/88, 7 July 1989.
24   *Saadi v. Italy* [GC], no. 37201/06, 28 February 2008.

extradition.[25] The applicants were indicted on various charges of terrorism in the United States, which requested their extradition. In the Trabelsi v. Belgium case[26] extradition had been effected of a Tunisian national from Belgium to the United States, where he is being prosecuted on charges of terrorist offences and is liable to life imprisonment. The Court held that the applicant's extradition to the United States entailed a violation of Article 3 (prohibition of inhuman or degrading treatment) of the Convention. It considered that the life sentence to which the applicant was liable in the United States was irreducible inasmuch as US law provided for no adequate mechanism for reviewing this type of sentence, and that it was therefore contrary to the provisions of Article 3.[27]

While extradition is a regulated and transparent cooperation between States, at least some European states have entered with the United States in covert operations and more specifically with the CIA in capturing terrorist suspects and secretly rendering them into CIA detention. This is extensively set out in the so-called secret rendition cases before the European Court of Human Rights, of which the El Masri is the first.[28] The case concerned the complaints of a German national of Lebanese origin, Khaleid El Masri, that he had been a victim of a secret "rendition" operation during which he was arrested, held in isolation, questioned and ill-treated in a Skopje hotel for 23 days, allegedly by Macedonian State agents, then transferred to CIA (Central Intelligence Agency) agents who brought him to a secret detention facility in Afghanistan, a CIA-run facility which media reports have identified as the "Salt Pit", a brick factory north of the Kabul business district that was used by the CIA for detention and interrogation of some high-level terror suspects, where he was further ill-treated for over four months. On 28 May 2004, he was taken, blindfolded and handcuffed, by plane to Albania and subsequently to Germany. Mr El-Masri then weighed about 18 kilos less than a few months earlier when he had left Germany. Immediately after his return to Germany, he contacted a lawyer and has brought several legal actions since before he lodged his application with the European Court of Human Rights on 20 July 2009. The European Court of Human Rights found the applicant's account to be established beyond reasonable doubt and held that "The former Yugoslav Republic of Macedonia" had been responsible for his torture and ill-treatment both in the country itself and after his transfer to the United States authorities in the context of an extra-judicial "rendition".[29]

---

25   *Babar Ahmad v. United Kingdom*, 24027/07, 10 April 2012.

26   *Trabelsi v. Belgium*, 140/10, 4 September 2014.

27   Also a violation was found of Article 34 for not obeying the Interim measure under Rule 39.

28   *El Masri v. the former Yugoslav Republic of Macedonia*, 13 December 2012 [GC].

29   See also *Al Nashiri v. Poland*, 24 July 2014, 28761/11, and the case of *Husayn (Abu Zubaydah) v. Poland*, 7511/13, 24 July 2014. Further *Abu Zubaydah v. Lithuania*, 31 May 2018, 46454/11 and *Al Nashiri v. Romania*, 33234/12, 31 May 2018.

In December 2014 the US Senate Intelligence Committee report on CIA torture[30] was published, following a declassification of secrecy. In this report the rendition, detention and interrogation of El Masri, Al Nashiri and Abu Zubaydah are also described. It is acknowledged by the CIA that it "lacked sufficient basis to render and detain al-Masri," and that the judgment by operations officers that al-Masri was associated with terrorists who posed a threat to U.S. interests "was not supported by available intelligence."

V. RELATIVE RIGHTS

A. DETENTION

The right not be deprived of one's liberty unlawfully is a relative right. The first case ever dealt with by the Court was the *Lawless v. Ireland* about preventive detention of suspects in an alleged state of emergency following terrorist threats.[31] G.R. Lawless was first arrested with three other men on 21st September 1956 in a disused barn. The police discovered in the barn a Thompson machine-gun, six army rifles, six sporting guns, a revolver, an automatic pistol and 400 magazines. Lawless admitted that he was a member of the IRA and that he had taken part in an armed raid when guns and revolvers had been stolen. The Court accepted that the detention of G.R. Lawless from 13th July to 11th December 1957 when there had been no intention to bring him to trial was founded on the right of derogation duly exercised by the Irish Government in pursuance of Article 15 of the Convention. In the case of *Hassan v. the United Kingdom* [GC] the Court has accepted derogation from convention rights in an analogous manner to Article 15 despite the fact that no notification of derogation from its Convention obligations had taken place by the State.[32] This case concerned an arrest of an individual named Hassan in an anti-terrorist action in Iraq. As regards procedural safeguards, the Court considered that, in relation to detention taking place during an international armed conflict, Article 5 §§2 and 4 must also be interpreted in a manner which took into account the context and the applicable rules of international humanitarian law.

A. and Others v. the United Kingdom [GC] concerns the detention of individuals with a view to expel them, while deportation was prohibited at the time because of risk of ill-treatment (Article 5–1-f).[33]

---

[30] Officially: Report of the Senate Select Committee on Intelligence Committee Study of the Central Intelligence Agency's Detention and Interrogation Program, December 2014.
[31] *Lawless v. Ireland* (No. 3), 332/57, 1 July 1961.
[32] *Hassan v. The United Kingdom*, 29750/09, 19 September 2014.
[33] *A. and Others v. The United Kingdom*, 3455/05, 19 February 2009.

Following the terrorist attacks of 11 September 2001 on the United States of America, the British Government considered the United Kingdom to be under threat from a number of foreign nationals present in the country who were providing a support network for extremist Islamist terrorist operations linked to al-Qaeda. Since certain of these individuals could not be deported because they risked ill-treatment in their country of origin, the Government considered it necessary to create an extended power permitting their detention where the Secretary of State reasonably believed that their presence in the United Kingdom was a risk to national security and reasonably suspected that they were an "international terrorist". Since the Government considered that this detention scheme might not be consistent with Article 5 §1 of the Convention, they issued a derogation notice under Article 15, in which they referred to the provisions of Part 4 of the Anti-Terrorism, Crime and Security Act 2001 ("the 2001 Act"), including the power to detain foreign nationals certified as "suspected international terrorists" who could not "for the time being" be removed from the United Kingdom. The Court observed that the highest domestic court had concluded that, though there had been a public emergency threatening the life of the nation the measures taken in response had not been strictly required by the exigencies of the situation. The Court did not reach a contrary conclusion. The derogating measures were disproportionate in that they discriminated unjustifiably between nationals and non-nationals.

In *Sher and Others v. the United Kingdom*[34] the Court was faced with arrests and detention of Pakistani nationals in connection with an anti-terrorism operation. Their homes were searched over a period of some 10 days pursuant to warrants covering a lengthy list of items, including correspondence, books and electronic equipment. The applicants remained in custody for a total of 13 days after a District Judge authorised their further detention at two successive hearings. The applicants were legally represented at the open hearings but did not have a special advocate to represent them during the closed session. They were ultimately released without charge. In the Convention proceedings, the applicants complained under Article 5 §4 of the Convention that they had been denied an adversarial procedure during the hearings of the applications to prolong their detention. The Court was satisfied that the threat of an imminent terrorist attack had provided ample justification for the imposition of some restrictions on the adversarial nature of the proceedings concerning the warrants for further detention, for reasons of national security. Terrorism thus falls into a special category. Article 5 §4 does not preclude the use of a closed hearing wherein confidential sources of information supporting the authorities' line of investigation are submitted to a court in the absence of the detainee or his lawyer. In the context of terrorism, though Contracting States cannot be required to establish the reasonableness of the suspicion grounding the arrest of a suspected

---

34   *Sher and Others v. The United Kingdom*, 5201/11, 20 October 2015.

terrorist by disclosing confidential sources of information, the Court has held that
the exigencies of dealing with terrorist crime cannot justify stretching the notion
of "reasonableness" to the point where the safeguard secured by Article 5 §1(c)
is impaired (O'Hara v. the United Kingdom, §35).[35] What is essential is that the
authorities disclose adequate information to enable a detainee to know the nature
of the allegations against him and to have the opportunity to refute them, and to
participate effectively in proceedings concerning his continued detention. While
the derogation clause may widen the legitimate possibilities for the State to detain
suspects, quite another matter is using restrictions of fundamental freedoms
intentionally to muzzle political opponents. Such action would run counter the
essence of political democracy. Therefore Article 18 of the Convention holds a
limitation use of restrictions on rights. The restrictions permitted to the rights
and freedoms shall not be applied for any purpose other than those for which
they have been prescribed. In the case of Navalny v. Russia the Grand Chamber
of the Court addressed this fundamental issue additional to the absence of proper
reasons explaining why the arrests and detention were necessary in the light of
the circumstances that had amounted to arbitrary deprivation of liberty.[36] This
arbitrary use of pre-trial detention concerning the applicant Navalny, violating
Article 5 of the Convention, was of greater significance than that of an ordinary
private individual. Detention and other restrictive measures were clearly
designated to set aside an opposition politician and his fellow travellers who
were committed to playing an important public function through democratic
discourse. Here the very essence is at stake of democracy as a means of organising
society, in which individual freedom could only be limited in the general interest,
that is, in the name of the "higher freedom". In the light of those elements, the
Court found it established beyond reasonable doubt that the restrictions imposed
on the applicant Navalny pursued an ulterior purpose (which was of significant
gravity), namely to suppress political pluralism, a hallmark of "effective political
democracy" governed by "the rule of law", both concepts referred to in the
Preamble to the Convention. There had therefore been a violation of Article 18
in conjunction with both Article 5 (detention) and Article 11 of the Convention
(freedom of peaceful assembly). The case of Navalny v. Russia did not directly
concern counter-terrorism but abuse of restrictions may easily occur in contexts
of alleged counter-terrorism while the predominant ulterior purpose being that
of stifling pluralism and limiting freedom of political debate.[37]

---

[35] *O'Hara v. the United Kingdom*, 37555/97, 16 October 2001.
[36] *Navalny v. Russia*, [GC], 29580/12, 36847/12, 11252/13 et al., 15 November 2018. See
      Merabishvili v. Georgia [GC], 72508/13, 28 November 2017, Information Note 212; *Navalnyy
      and Yashin v. Russia*, 76204/11, 4 December 2014, Information Note 180; *Navalnyy and
      Ofitserov v. Russia*, 46632/13 and 28671/14, 23 February 2016, Information Note 193;
      and *Navalnyye v. Russia*, 101/15, 17 October 2017. See also the Guide on Article 18 of the
      Convention.
[37] *Selahattin Demirtaş v. Turkey* (no. 2), 14305/17, 20 November 2018 (not final).

B. FAIR TRIAL: ACCESS TO A LAWYER

On 21 July 2005, two weeks after 52 people were killed as the result of suicide bombings in London, further bombs were detonated on the London public transport system but, on this occasion, failed to explode. The perpetrators fled the scene. The first three applicants were arrested but were refused legal assistance for periods of between four and eight hours to enable the police to conduct "safety interviews". The fourth applicant was not suspected of having detonated a bomb and was initially interviewed by the police as a witness. However, he started to incriminate himself by explaining his encounter with one of the suspected bombers shortly after the attacks and the assistance he had provided to that suspect. The police did not, at that stage, arrest and advise him of his right to silence and to legal assistance, but continued to question him as a witness and took a written statement. He was subsequently arrested and offered legal advice.[38] The Grand Chamber considered it necessary to clarify the two stages of the Salduz test for assessing whether a restriction on access to a lawyer was compatible with the right to a fair trial and the relationship between those two stages. It recalled that the first stage of the Salduz test required the Court to assess whether there were compelling reasons for the restriction, while the second stage required it to evaluate the prejudice caused to the rights of the defence by the restriction, in other words, to examine the impact of the restriction on the overall fairness of the proceedings and decide whether the proceedings as a whole were fair.

The criterion of compelling reasons was a stringent one: having regard to the fundamental nature and importance of early access to legal advice, in particular at the first interrogation of the suspect, restrictions on access to legal advice were permitted only in exceptional circumstances, and had to be of a temporary nature and be based on an individual assessment of the particular circumstances of the case. Relevant considerations when assessing whether compelling reasons had been demonstrated was whether the decision to restrict legal advice had a basis in domestic law and whether the scope and content of any restrictions on legal advice were sufficiently circumscribed by law so as to guide operational decision-making by those responsible for applying them.

Where a respondent Government convincingly demonstrated the existence of an urgent need to avert serious adverse consequences for life, liberty or physical integrity in a given case, this could amount to compelling reasons to restrict access to legal advice for the purposes of Article 6. However, a non-specific claim of a risk of leaks could not. As to whether a lack of compelling reasons for restricting access to legal advice was, in itself, sufficient to found a violation of Article 6, the Court reiterated that in assessing whether there has been a breach

---

[38]   *Ibrahim and Others v. the United Kingdom* [GC] – 50541/08, 50571/08, 50573/08 et al. 2016, 13 September 2016.

of the right to a fair trial it is necessary to view the proceedings as a whole, and the Article 6 §3 rights as specific aspects of the overall right to a fair trial rather than ends in themselves. The absence of compelling reasons does not, therefore, lead in itself to a finding of a violation of Article 6.

However, the outcome of the "compelling reasons" test was nevertheless relevant to the assessment of overall fairness. Where compelling reasons were found to have been established, a holistic assessment of the entirety of the proceedings had to be conducted to determine whether they were "fair" for the purposes of Article 6 §1. Where there were no compelling reasons, the Court had to apply a very strict scrutiny to its fairness assessment. The failure of the respondent Government to show compelling reasons weighed heavily in the balance when assessing the overall fairness of the trial and could tip the balance in favour of finding a breach of Article 6 §§1 and 3 (c). The onus would be on the Government to demonstrate convincingly why, exceptionally and in the specific circumstances of the case, the overall fairness of the trial was not irretrievably prejudiced by the restriction on access to legal advice.

As with the first three applicants, the Grand Chamber accepted that there had been an urgent need to avert serious adverse consequences for life, liberty or physical integrity. However, it found that the Government had not convincingly demonstrated that those exceptional circumstances were sufficient to constitute compelling reasons for continuing with the fourth applicant's interview after he began to incriminate himself without cautioning him or informing him of his right to legal advice. In so finding, it took into account the complete absence of any legal framework enabling the police to act as they did, the lack of an individual and recorded determination on the basis of the applicable provisions of domestic law of whether to restrict his access to legal advice and, importantly, the deliberate decision by the police not to inform the fourth applicant of his right to remain silent. In the absence of compelling reasons for the restriction of the fourth applicant's right to legal advice, the burden of proof shifted to the Government to demonstrate convincingly why, exceptionally and in the specific circumstances of the case, the overall fairness of the trial was not irretrievably prejudiced by the restriction on access to legal advice. The Grand Chamber found that the Government had not discharged that burden, for the following reasons: (a) the decision, without any basis in domestic law and contrary to the guidance given in the applicable code of practice, to continue to question the fourth applicant as a witness meant that he was not notified of his procedural rights; this constituted a particularly significant defect in the case; (b) although the fourth applicant had been able to challenge the admissibility of his statement in a 'voir dire' procedure at the trial, the trial court did not appear to have heard evidence from the senior police officer who had authorised the continuation of the witness interview and so, along with the court of appeal, was denied the opportunity of scrutinising the reasons for the decision and determining whether an appropriate assessment of all relevant factors had been carried out; (c) the statement formed an integral and significant part of the probative evidence upon which the conviction was based, having provided the police with the framework around which they subsequently built their case and the focus for their search for other corroborating evidence; and (d) the trial judge's directions left the jury with excessive discretion as to the manner in which the statement, and its probative value, were to be taken into account, irrespective of the fact that it had been obtained without access to legal advice and without the fourth applicant having being informed of his right to remain silent.

C. PRIVACY AND SECURITY

1. UN sanctions

Terrorism even more than crime in general gives rise to restrictions of personal freedom by the State and to secret intrusions of privacy. This may happen in various ways. Very serious restrictions may flow from UN sanctions. Under Articles 25 and 103 of the Charter, States are required to comply with binding decisions of the Security Council adopted under Chapter VII, even where this would entail violating their obligations under another international treaty. The issue of sanctions ordered by the UNSC was dealt with by the ECtHR in the case of Nada v. Switzerland [GC], which concerned a ban on the applicant transiting through Swiss territory, which was the only way out of the small Italian enclave where he lived. That restriction had been imposed by the Swiss authorities in pursuance of a number of UNSC resolutions relating to the fight against terrorism (particularly the Taliban and al-Qaeda). The Court first of all acknowledged the admissibility of the application *ratione personae*: even though the case concerned the application of a UNSC resolution, the impugned decisions had not been taken by the Swiss authorities. On the merits of the case, the Court observed that the terms of the resolution had been clear and explicit, imposing on Switzerland an obligation to take measures capable of breaching human rights. The Court deduced that there had been a rebuttal of the presumption that a UNSC resolution could not be interpreted as imposing on member States an obligation contravening the fundamental principles relating to human rights protection. Furthermore, the Court did not contest the binding force of the UNSC resolution, although it did note that Switzerland had some limited, but nonetheless real, discretion in the application of such resolutions (see, in particular, §179). Under those circumstances, the State could no longer hide behind the binding nature of the resolutions; on the contrary, it should have persuaded the Court that it had taken – or at least had attempted to take – "all possible measures to adapt the sanctions regime to the applicant's individual situation" (§96).[39]

---

[39] *Nada v. Switzerland*, 10593/08, 12 September 2012. See: Guide on Article 1 of the Convention, Council of Europe/ European Court of Human Rights 2018, p.24. A. similar conclusion was

2. Accessing personal information

With regard to accessing personal information held by security services, the ECtHR has held that obstacles to access may constitute violations of Article 8 (Haralambie v. Romania, §96; Joanna Szulc v. Poland, §87). However, in cases concerning suspected terrorists, the Court has also held that the interests of national security and the fight against terrorism prevail over the applicants' interest in having access to information about them in the Security Police files (Segerstedt-Wiberg and Others v. Sweden, §91). Particularly in proceedings related to operations of State security agencies, there may be legitimate grounds to limit access to certain documents and other materials (Turek v. Slovakia, §115).[40]

3. Secret intrusion

Secret intrusion interferes with privacy of persons. One of the key problems for the victim of secret surveillance is to substantiate such a status. In Roman Zakharov v. Russia the Court has clarified the scope of the safeguards which must accompany surveillance of communications from the standpoint of Article 8 of the Convention.[41] The applicant Zakharov is an editor who is actively involved to promote the independence of the regional mass media, freedom of speech and respect for journalists' rights, and provides legal support, including through litigation, to journalists. He brought judicial proceedings against three mobile network operators, complaining of interference with his right to privacy of his telephone communications. The Court accepted that an applicant can claim to be the victim of a violation occasioned by the mere existence of secret surveillance measures or of legislation permitting such measures. Having established the admissibility the question whether a violation has occurred is established by the Court along the lines of general principles developed in its case-law concerning secret surveillance. Any interference can only be justified under Article 8 §2 if it is in accordance with the law, pursues one or more of the legitimate aims to which paragraph 2 of Article 8 refers and is necessary in a democratic society in order to achieve any such aim (see Kennedy, cited above, §130).

4. In accordance with the law

The wording "in accordance with the law" requires the impugned measure both to have some basis in domestic law and to be compatible with the rule

---

reached in *Al-Dulimi and Montana Management Inc. v Switzerland* [GC], 5809/08, 21 June 2016.

40   *Haralambie v. Romania*, no. 21737/03, 27 October 2009; *Joanna Szulc v. Poland*, no. 43932/08, 13 November 2012; *Segerstedt-Wiberg and Others v. Sweden*, no. 62332/00, ECHR 2006-VII; *Turek v. Slovakia*, no. 57986/00, ECHR 2006-II (extracts). See: Guide on Article 8 of the European Convention on Human Rights, Council of Europe/ European Court of Human Rights, 2018, p. 35.

41   *Roman Zakharov v. Russia* [GC], 47143/06, 4 December 2015.

of law, which is expressly mentioned in the Preamble to the Convention and inherent in the object and purpose of Article 8. The law must thus meet quality requirements: it must be accessible to the person concerned and foreseeable as to its effects (see, among many other authorities, Rotaru v. Romania [GC], no. 28341/95, §52, ECHR 2000 V; S. and Marper v. the United Kingdom [GC], nos. 30562/04 and 30566/04, §95, ECHR 2008; and Kennedy, cited above, §151).

5. Foreseeability in the context of secrecy

Foreseeability in the special context of secret measures of surveillance, such as the interception of communications, cannot mean that an individual should be able to foresee when the authorities are likely to intercept his communications so that he can adapt his conduct accordingly. However, especially where a power vested in the executive is exercised in secret, the risks of arbitrariness are evident. It is therefore essential to have clear, detailed rules on interception of telephone conversations, especially as the technology available for use is continually becoming more sophisticated. The domestic law must be sufficiently clear to give citizens an adequate indication as to the circumstances in which and the conditions on which public authorities are empowered to resort to any such measures. Moreover, since the implementation in practice of measures of secret surveillance of communications is not open to scrutiny by the individuals concerned or the public at large, it would be contrary to the rule of law for the discretion granted to the executive or to a judge to be expressed in terms of an unfettered power. Consequently, the law must indicate the scope of any such discretion conferred on the competent authorities and the manner of its exercise with sufficient clarity to give the individual adequate protection against arbitrary interference. In its case-law on secret measures of surveillance, the Court has developed the following minimum safeguards that should be set out in law in order to avoid abuses of power: the nature of offences which may give rise to an interception order; a definition of the categories of people liable to have their telephones tapped; a limit on the duration of telephone tapping; the procedure to be followed for examining, using and storing the data obtained; the precautions to be taken when communicating the data to other parties; and the circumstances in which recordings may or must be erased or destroyed.

6. Necessary in a democratic society

As to the question whether an interference was necessary in a democratic society in pursuit of a legitimate aim, the Court has acknowledged that, when balancing the interest of the respondent State in protecting its national security through secret surveillance measures against the seriousness of the interference with an applicant's right to respect for his or her private life, the national authorities enjoy a certain margin of appreciation in choosing the means for achieving the legitimate aim of protecting national security. However, this margin is subject to European supervision embracing both legislation and decisions applying it. In view of the risk that a system of secret surveillance set up to protect national security may undermine or even destroy democracy under the cloak of defending it, the Court must be satisfied that there are adequate and effective guarantees against abuse. The assessment depends on all the circumstances of the case, such as the nature, scope and duration of the possible measures, the grounds required for ordering them, the authorities competent to authorise, carry out and supervise them, and the kind of remedy provided by the national law. The Court has to determine whether the procedures for supervising the ordering and implementation of the restrictive measures are such as to keep the interference to what is necessary in a democratic society.

While in the case of Roman Zakharov a legal framework provided for some supervision by prosecutors, it was not capable in practice of providing adequate and effective guarantees against abuse. The "interference" was therefore not in keeping with the level "necessary in a democratic society".

CONCLUDING REMARK

The above sketch of case-law on countering terrorism gives an impression of the dilemmas the ECtHR faces. Obviously States need to counter acts of violence that target civilians in the pursuit of political or ideological aims. Citizen's protection is a positive obligation for the State, itself a prime matter of human rights. Respecting the right to life of suspected terrorists, abstaining from ill-treatment and being dedicated to careful preparation of interventions when use of force is inevitable, do not hamper effective counter-terrorism. Gathering information secretly is not in violation with human rights, when this is foreseeable, in accordance with the law and necessary in a democratic society for the combat of terrorism. But the aim of counter-terrorism cannot dismiss a proper assessments of proportionality in advance and a sound evaluation afterwards. Case-law of the European Court of Human Rights shows examples of States well-balanced reactions to terrorism, but also of cases where rights were violated. Counter-terrorism holds a double threat, that of not erasing terrorism effectively and that of lacking restraint and wisdom. Keeping in touch with fundamental values is always important, it may be crucial when these values are under attack by terrorism. Where terrorists seek to destroy democratic values and fundamental rights and freedoms it is evident that States should not proactively do that job for them.

EMBED PRIVACY BY LEGALITY AND A STRONG HUMAN RIGHTS COMMISSION

Nathalie Van Leuven

Researcher CIRC, Université Saint-Louis – Bruxelles
Honorary Auditor Council of State
Director Vormingplus Midden- en Zuid-West-Vlaanderen

In the first years of my academic research my promotor prof. Paul Lemmens encouraged me to write an article about the right to private life.[1] This topic seemed to be of particular interest to him.

Even in those days my supervising professor would prefer to pay cash in the supermarket in order to avoid profiling by supermarket chains. Today, as we all depend on several social media for personal or social purposes, I very often ponder over this supermarket incident. In the daily implementation of the demands of General Data Protection Regulation (GDPR), I think about... my promotor and his visionary crusade for the sacred right to privacy.

This research of 2005 demonstrated that the right to private life was developing: from a right to be let alone to a right to development and personal choices: for example a right to be legally recognised as transgender[2], a right to be protected in the professional sphere[3], a right to develop one's personality (for example to live as a gipsy)[4], a right not to be forced to linger in old age.[5] The research reflected our assumption and we both warmly welcomed this case-law. In a belief in a more democratic society with more free choices of citizens, the

---

[1]   N. Van Leuven, "Privacy: een onrustig begrip in volle ontplooiing", in P. Lemmens, *Uitdagingen door en voor het EVRM*, Mechelen, Wolters Kluwer België, 2005, 3–20; The author would like to thank Frédéric Vanneste and Anneleen Princen, who provided helpful review efforts.
[2]   ECtHR, 11 July 2002, *Christine Goodwin / United Kingdom*.
[3]   ECtHR, 16 December 1992, *Niemietz / Germany*; ECtHR, 16 April 2002, *Stes Colas Est / France*.
[4]   ECtHR, 18 January 2001, *Chapman / United Kingdom*.
[5]   ECtHR, 29 April 2002, *Pretty / United Kingdom*.

European Court of Human Rights would lead us to a better and deeper form of democracy…

Many years and (in my case) many invisible grey hairs later, we will analyse the further development of the scope of the right to private life in the case-law of the European Court of Human Rights, in which professor Paul Lemmens seated and is still seating.

Moreover, this article attempts to contribute to the organisation of human rights and privacy protection in elaborating on some privacy questions of vulnerable groups in the Flemish and Belgian society. In the past years I had the opportunity to meet social organisations and to look at real life issues with my academic and Council of State glasses. This switch in perspective was often an eye-opener.

I. RIGHT TO PRIVATE LIFE: FURTHER DEVELOP-MENT OF THE SCOPE OF THE RIGHT TO PRIVATE LIFE

A. THE RIGHT TO BE LET ALONE IN AN ERA OF MOBILE PHONES AND MESSENGER

The fear of my promotor not to be able to be let alone has come true: the possibility to trace all persons by mobile phones, internet and financial behaviour has become a reality. Anno 2017 dismissed employers due to using the firm's messenger account for personal purposes can argue that the dismissal by a private employer has to be examined under the positive obligation of the State to protect private life.[6]

The Court observes nowadays that there can be an interference with the right to private life as a result of the mere existence of legislation permitting secret surveillance measures and a risk of being subjected to such measures, rather than as a result of any specific surveillance measures applied. Secret surveillance legislation under which any person using the mobile-telephone services of Russian providers can have his mobile-telephone communications intercepted – without ever being notified of the surveillance – affects all users of these mobile-telephone services. The no provision for effective remedies for persons who suspect that they were subjected to secret surveillance, makes the Court conclude to an interference of Article 8 of the Convention.[7]

---

6   ECtHR, Gr. Ch., 5 September 2017, *Bărbulescu / Romania*, §§108–109.
7   ECtHR, Gr. Ch., 4 December 2015, *Roman Zakharov / Russia*, §§174–175.

B.   GIVING BIRTH, BECOMING A PARENT (OR NOT) AND ABORTION

The Court accepts that the impossibility for women to be assisted when giving birth in their private home comes within the scope of their right to private life. The Court considers giving birth as a unique and delicate moment in a woman's life. It encompasses issues of physical and moral integrity, medical care, reproductive health and the protection of health-related information. These issues, including the choice of the place of birth, are therefore fundamentally linked to the woman's private life and fall within the scope of that concept for the purposes of Article 8 of the Convention.[8]

In the Grand Chamber judgment Paradiso and Campanelli / Italy the Court finds an interference in the right to private life, in the case of removal of a baby from a couple, wrongly believing that their seminal fluid had been used for the embryo implanted in the surrogate mother's womb. In fact there was no DNA tie between the couple and the baby. Due to a procedure conforming Italian legislation the baby was removed and placed in a home.[9] Some dissenters, among whom Paul Lemmens, correctly argued that there was moreover an interference in the right to family life of the couple whereas the applicants and child lived together for six months and had forged closed bonds with the child in the first stages of his life.[10]

In the Grand Chamber judgment Evans / United Kingdom the Court deals with the question whether there exists a positive obligation on the State to ensure that a woman who has embarked on treatment for the specific purpose of giving birth to a genetically related child and subsequently becomes infertile, should be permitted to proceed to implantation of the embryo notwithstanding the withdrawal of consent by her former partner, the male gamete provider. The Grand Chamber agrees with the Chamber that "private life", which is a broad term encompassing, inter alia, aspects of an individual's physical and social identity including the right to personal autonomy, personal development and to establish and develop relationships with other human beings and the outside world incorporates the right to respect for both decisions to become and not to become a parent.[11] In the same line of thought the Court considers in S.H. a.o. /Austria that the right of a couple to conceive a child and to make use of medically assisted procreation for that purpose is also protected by Article 8, as

---

[8]   ECtHR, Gr. Ch., 15 November 2016, *Dubská and Krejzová /the Czech Republic*, §163; See also ECtHR, 14 December 2010, *Ternovsky / Hungary*, §22.

[9]   ECtHR, Gr. Ch., 24 January 2017, *Paradiso and Campanelli / Italy*, §163.

[10]   *Ibid.*, joint dissenting opinion of judges Lazarova, Trajkovska, Bianku, Laffranque, Lemmens and Grozev.

[11]   ECtHR, Gr. Ch., 10 April 2007, *Evans / United Kingdom*, §71.

such a choice is an expression of private and family life.[12] The Court enlarges the scope of Article 8 due to fast-moving medical and scientific developments. Nevertheless in the earlier decisions the Court judged that there was no right to become a parent or to adopt a child[13], but more and more the Court uses a broader scope of Article 8 towards the individual wish to become a parent in a genetic sense.

With respect to the issue of abortion the Court underlines that both to have and not to have a child or to become genetic parents are protected within the scope of Article 8 of the Convention. The Court has also stated, that legislation regulating the interruption of pregnancy touches upon the sphere of the private life of the woman. The Court emphasizes that Article 8 cannot be interpreted as meaning that pregnancy and its termination pertain uniquely to the woman's private life as whenever a woman is pregnant, her private life becomes closely connected with the developing foetus. The woman's right to private life thus must be weighed against other competing rights and freedoms invoked including those of the unborn child. As to the protection of the unborn life, the Court refers – as it did in the past – to the missing consensus of the countries of the Council of Europe and offers the States a broad margin of appreciation.[14]

C.   SEXUAL IDENTITY

The scope of protection of sexual identity is further enlarged by the European Court. "The Court's judgments in this sphere had hitherto concerned legal recognition of the gender identity of transgender persons who had undergone reassignment surgery"[15] and "the conditions of access to such surgery".[16] In 2017 the Court brought the legal recognition of the gender identity of a transgender person who has not undergone gender reassignment treatment approved by the authorities, or who do not wish to undergo such treatment, within the scope of application of Article 8 of the Convention.[17]

---

[12]   ECtHR, Gr. Ch., 3 November 2011, *S.H. e.o. / Austria*, §82.
[13]   E. Comm. HR, 10 July 1997, *Di Lazzaro / Italy*, DR 90-B, 134; E. Comm. H.R., 10 July 1975, *X / Belgium and the Netherlands*, D.R. 7, 75; ECtHR, 26 May 2002, *Fretté / France*, §32.
[14]   ECtHR, Gr. Ch., 16 December 2010, *A, B and C / Ireland*; ECtHR 20 March 2007, *Tysiąc / Poland*, §106; ECtHR, Gr. Ch., 8 July 2004, *Vo / France*, §§76, 80 and 82.
[15]   ECtHR, 17 October 1986, *Rees / the United Kingdom*; ECtHR, 27 September 1990, *Cossey / the United Kingdom*; ECtHR, 25 March 1992, *B. / France*; ECtHR, Gr. Ch., 11 July 2002, *Christine Goodwin / the United Kingdom*; ECtHR, Gr. Ch., 11 July 2002, *I. v. the United Kingdom*; ECtHR, 23 May 2006, *Grant / the United Kingdom*; ECtHR, Gr. Ch., 16 July 2014, *Hämäläinen / Finland*.
[16]   ECtHR, 12 June 2003, *Van Kück*.
[17]   ECtHR, 6 April 2017, *A.P., Garçon and Nicot / France A.P.*, §§93–94.

The scope of protection of people with a homosexual orientation under Article 8 is widened indirectly by Article 14 of the Convention. The private life of homosexuals has gained protection through Article 14 of the Convention. In the Fretté case in 2002 the Grand Chamber did not accept a violation of Articles 14 and 8 of the Convention in the refusal of a State to grant an adoption to a single homosexual man. The French States' argument that this man was not equipped to offer a child a suitable home from a psychological, child-rearing and family perspective convinced the Court who could not find a violation in the States' decision. The Court took into account a broad margin of appreciation of the State.[18] The case-law changed in the E.B. / France judgment of 2008. The Court found a violation of Articles 14 and 8 of the Convention in the French refusal of authorisation to a person to gain a possibility to adopt due to his sexual orientation.[19]

D. PARTICIPATION OF VULNERABLE GROUPS TO SOCIETY

In the A.-M.V. / Finland case, the European Court stresses the right to develop one's personality and to make one's own choices. In this case a mentor of an intellectually disabled person decided to relocate him against his will, from his foster family to his home town. He was placed in his home town in a special living unit for intellectually disabled adults. The refusal of the authorities to change the decisions of the mentor is judged as an interference in the applicant's right to respect for his private life.[20] In this case, the Court does not find a violation of Article 8, but "recalls its findings to the effect that where a restriction on fundamental rights applies to a particularly vulnerable group in society that has suffered considerable discrimination in the past, then the State's margin of appreciation is substantially narrower and it must have very weighty reasons for the restrictions in question. The reason for this approach, which questions certain classifications per se, is that such groups were historically subject to prejudice with lasting consequences, resulting in their social exclusion. Such prejudice could entail legislative stereotyping which prohibits the individualised evaluation of their capacities and needs. In the past, the Court has identified several vulnerable groups who suffered different treatment on account of their sex, sexual orientation, race or ethnicity, mental faculties or disability".[21]

In the same line of thought, the Court clearly accepts that negative stereotyping of a group, when it reaches a certain level, can impact on the group's sense of

---

18   ECtHR, 26 May 2002, *Fretté / France*, §42.
19   ECtHR, 22 January 2008, *E.B. / France*, §96; see also ECtHR, 15 March 2012, *Gas and Dubois / France*.
20   ECtHR, 23 June 2017, *A.-M.V. / Finland*, §§76–77.
21   Ibid., §73.

identity and the feelings of self-worth and self-confidence of members of the group. It is in this sense that it is affecting the private life of members of the group. Racist verbal abuse and attempted assault in the presence of a child is judged as an interference in the right to private life.[22]

E.   CHOICES IN PROFESSIONAL LIFE

Whereas in the past, private lawyers were surprised at first that the office of an employer or employee was protected under Article 8, the Court goes all the way nowadays and emphasizes the importance of a developed professional life as a pillar to the right to private life. As a result the refusal from inscription to the Greek Bar of a third country national who studied in Greece was seen as an interference in Article 8 of the Convention.[23]

In the Fernandez Martinez case a priest worked for seven years as a teacher of religious instruction. During this period he decides to resign from priesthood and to marry a woman. Due to his married status his contract is not renewed. According to the European Court of Human Rights this non-renewal of the contract comes within the ambit of Article 8 of the Convention. While the Court judges that no general right to employment or to the renewal of a fixed-term contract can be derived from Article 8, the Court reaffirms that it would be too restrictive to limit the notion of "private life" to an "inner circle" in which the individual may live his own personal life as he chooses and to exclude therefrom entirely the outside world not encompassed within that circle.[24]

F.   SELF-EXPRESSION

Finally there is no doubt that self-expression falls within the ambit of Article 8: the refusal of a prison to let a prisoner grow his beard, is a clear interference in the right to privacy.[25]

G.   CONCLUSION

We devoted the first part of the article to the scope of Article 8 of the Convention and the answers on the question whether there is or is not an interference

---

[22]   ECtHR, 12 April 2016, *R.B. / Hungary*, §§78–80.
[23]   ECtHR, 28 May 2009, *Bigaeva / Greece*, §§23–24.
[24]   ECtHR, Gr. Ch., 12 June 2014, *Fernandez Martinez / Spain*, §§109–113.
[25]   ECtHR, 14 June 2016, *Biržietis / Lithuania*, §45.

of Article 8 of the Convention. It is obvious that the Court – more than ever – chooses the path of a broad interpretation of privacy in its judgment on interferences of the right to privacy. A first remark is that new scientific possibilities and questions are enlarging the scope of this right. Secondly, we can distinguish an indirect enlargement of the scope of the right to privacy of homosexuals and transgenders, often by means of Article 14 of the Convention. Finally, it strikes us that the Court is increasingly attentive to vulnerable groups: for groups that have suffered discrimination in the past, the margin of appreciation of the State is narrower and the State needs weighty reasons to restrict the right to privacy. Assaulting these groups is also seen as an interference.

II. VULNERABLE HUMAN BEINGS AND UNVEILED PRIVACY-RELATED ISSUES

We noticed that the Court is receptive to consider an interference of Article 8 when vulnerable groups are concerned and narrows the margin of appreciation of the State in these particular cases.

In this second part of the contribution we do want to take a closer look at the privacy protection of two vulnerable groups in Belgium. This part is based on input gathered from practice. Firstly, we study the right to privacy of a person with psycho-social problems searching for a job in the framework of social enterprises. Secondly, the text discusses the above mentioned right to privacy versus right to life of an unborn person exhibiting signs of Down or other future diseases.

In this part we do not assess whether there is an interference of the right or not. Rather, we focus on the protection of legality (the question whether the interference is foreseeable by law) and the organisation of human rights and privacy protection in Belgium.

A. RIGHT TO PRIVACY OF JOB SEEKERS WITH PSYCHO-SOCIAL PROBLEMS

Conform the Flemish federate law called "maatwerkdecreet"[26], a person with serious psycho-social problems that make him/her unable to work in the regular labour market can get a ticket to work in social enterprises (the

---

26   Decree of 12 July 2013 betreffende maatwerk bij collectieve inschakeling, *BS* 2 September 2013.

so-called "maatwerkbedrijven", in the past known as the "beschutte en sociale werkplaatsen"). In older legislations this group of people was defined by three objective standards: 5 years of unemployment and low education. The third criterion of psycho-social problems was seen as inherent if the first two criteria were fulfilled.[27]

Artikel 7 of this maatwerkdecreet states: "The Public employment service of Flanders (VDAB) determines the individual need for support from the job seeker for the job support measures based on a list of indications." This seems a very helpful service to vulnerable persons. However, the Flemish government delegates the composition of the list of indications to the Minister.[28]

In the ministerial decree to execution of the Articles 13 and 51 of the Flemish Government decree, we can read that a ticket to work in social enterprises is obtained by a person who has at least 5 problems in the field of labour self-sufficiency (arbeidsmatige zelfredzaamheid): to solve problems (1), to take decisions (2), cognitive flexibility (3), time management (4), development of capabilities (5), confidence (6), to cope with stress (7), psychologic stability (8), coping style (9), labour tempo (10), attention (11). I hope that all the amici of prof. Paul Lemmens have less than 5 problems… Nevertheless, this list is so wide-ranging that any self-critical human could see him(her)self meet the criteria.

In the annex of this ministerial decree we do find indications used by the Public employment service of Flanders (VDAB) of their 'International classification of functions (ICF) instrument' to confer job support measures. The instrument investigates leniency, accuracy, psychologic stability, confidence, reliability, motivation, yearning, rage control, attention, time management, cognitive flexibility, insight, stamina and pain sense.

As to activities and participation the Public Employment service is testing the following elements: to develop skills, to apply knowledge, to count, to solve problems, to take decisions, to cope with stress, mobility, a good body care, a good health care, acquisition of housing, establishment of relationships, economic independency and social activities.

In this personality disorder test the Public Employment service researches environmental and external factors such as: support and relation with close relatives, friends, colleagues, hierarchy, and other service providers, social attitude and products and technology. Personal factors are considered: labour

---

27   Decree of 14 July 1998 inzake sociale werkplaatsen, *BS* 2 September 1998.
28   Article 13 and 51 of the decision of the Flemish Government of 17 February 2017 in execution of the decree of 12 July 2013, *BS* 18 April 2017.

experience, education, family, coping style, knowledge of the Dutch language and medical factors. Other labour competences on the verification list are fine and gross motor skills and labour rhythm.[29]

In our opinion, this is a serious violation of the Belgian legality principle guaranteed by Article 22 of the Constitution. According to Article 22 of the Belgian Constitution everyone has the right to privacy, except in those cases and under the circumstances determined by "law". "Law" is interpreted as a formal legislation, contrary to the ECHR definition of legality for human rights interferences. Essential elements have to be determined by formal law, adopted in Parliament and delegations are only possible for the domains determined by Parliament. The Constitutional Court acknowledges this stronger higher standard of national protection in comparison to Article 8 of the Convention which cannot be limited conforming Article 53 of the European Convention of Human Rights.[30] A delegation to a Flemish Government's decree is not contrary to the principle of legality provided that the delegation is described with sufficient precision and concerns the execution of measures of which the essential elements have been determined by law.[31] The federate law has to offer the basic guarantees against privacy violations.[32] In casu the federate law does not offer any guarantees, but the guarantee of vagueness and camouflage.

In reading Article 7 of the Maatwerkdecreet "The Public employment service of Flanders (VDAB) determines the individual need for support from the job seeker for the job support measures based on a list of indications.", there is no precise delegation to the Flemish Government. Without reading the decrees of Government and Minister no one would ever think of intrusive privacy related questions to the most vulnerable jobseekers. It felt rather uncomfortable to hear the Public Employment Service of Flanders declaring that this ICF instrument operates as 'a black box': "No one executing the survey and posing the questions to the job seeker knows which need for support will come out of this instrument and questions…". None of these legal norms determine how long this research may take (in practice it takes sometimes more than a year between the question to be analysed and the obtainment of the ticket to enter a social enterprise), whether the job seeker has the right to remain silent on certain sensitive

---

29 Ministerial decree of 20 February 2018 tot uitvoering van artikel 13 en 51 van het besluit van de Vlaamse Regering van 17 februari 2017 tot uitvoering van het decreet van 12 juli 2013 betreffende maatwerk bij collectieve inschakeling, BS 12 maart 2018.

30 Constit. Court no. 151/2006, 18 October 2006, B.5.6.

31 Constit. Court no. 94 /2006, 14 June 2006, B.19; Adv. Op. Council of State no. 53.953/1 of 29 October 2013 on "een voorontwerp van decreet 'betreffende de landinrichting'."

32 Adv. Op. Council of State no. 53.683/3 of 4 October 2013 on "een ontwerp van besluit van de Vlaamse Regering 'houdende de vergunningsvoorwaarden en het kwaliteitsbeleid voor gezinsopvang en groepsopvang van baby's en peuters'. "

questions, whether the job seeker has the right to be accompanied by a lawyer or a person (s)he trusts, whether he has the right to appeal. This personality research is not only executed by VDAB, but also by other associations such as gtb (geïntegreerde trajectbegeleiding).[33] The cooperation and tender model of governments are often based on a market philosophy and on financial concerns. Doubts may arise in relation to the attribution of this personality researches to external organisations. How does the Public Employment service of Flanders guarantee the privacy protection of the vulnerable job seeker when no privacy guarantee is mentioned in the basic legislation?

Delegating these drastic interferences in the private life of the most vulnerable on the Flemish labour market to a minister is without any doubt unconstitutional.

In earlier advices the Council of State argued that allowing state officers to interfere in the right to privacy, should be described by formal law.[34] The Constitutional Court also demands a precise formal law. A delegation to another power is possible on two conditions: the delegation should be described clearly enough and concern the execution of measures of which the legislator has preliminarily determined the essential elements.[35] This did not happen.

Thereby, the Council of State, Legislative section, has advised many times that the Government has legislative powers. The government can only delegate this legislative competence to the Minister in accordance to the Constitution as to executive measures of secondary or minor character.[36]The above mentioned personality research is not an executive measure of secondary or minor character.

In fact today no one is securing the right to privacy of the vulnerable job seeker in his or her personality investigation and procedure towards a ticket to a protected labour market or not. Firstly, due to lots of misfortunes and misery

---

[33] Https://www.gtb-vlaanderen.be/over-gtb/historiek.

[34] Adv. Op. Council of State no. 45.112/3 of 23 September 2008 on "een ontwerp van besluit van de Vlaamse Regering "betreffende het erkennen van centra voor landbouweducatie en het subsidiëren van landbouweducatieve activiteiten."

[35] Cons. Court no. 94/2006, B.19; Cons. Court no. 148/2015, B.5.3; J. Van Nieuwenhove, "Delegatie van regelgevende bevoegdheid in België", TvW 2017, 202.

[36] Adv. Op. Council of State no. 28678/1 of 12 July 2005 on "een ontwerp van koninklijk besluit "tot wijziging van artikel 35ter van de wet betreffende de verplichte verzekering voor geneeskundige verzorging en uitkeringen, gecoördineerd op 14 juli 1994""; Adv. Op. Council of State no. 39002/1/V of 18 August 2006 on "een ontwerp van koninklijk besluit "tot wijziging van het koninklijk besluit van 12 december 2001 betreffende de dienstencheques""; A. Alen en Muylle, Handboek van het Belgisch Staatsrecht, 127129; H. Coremans, M. Van Damme, J. Dujardin, B. Seutin en G. Vermeylen, Beginselen van wetgevingstechniek en behoorlijke regelgeving, 195; J. Velaers, De Grondwet en de Raad van State, 379380; M. Van Damme, Elementen van legisprudentie, 157158.

most of our poorest citizens do see the system of justice as one big wall, as a part of society to which they do not belong. Secondly, they are afraid of the authority that is screening them in order to obtain a labour place. Those who live from unemployment benefits, risk reduced benefits in case of a negative screening. Thirdly, they are not properly protected by labour unions as they are not working yet. On a federal scale there is a federal Charter of the social secured[37], guaranteeing a reasonable time, appeal procedures and information duties as to services of federal social security institutions. None of these guarantees is applicable here...

One could argue that in a particracy where political parties dominate the political process rather than the elected Members of Parliament, the formal legality principle is a vain principle. The Members of Parliament of the majority are considered as followers of their party's instructions.

Nevertheless, this case made me doubt...imagine that interferences of human rights are always mentioned in the preamble of a formal law and elaborated in its essential elements in the text itself. In that case the Members of Parliament of opposition (and majority) could play the role of the first public watchdog of human rights protection and at least question human rights interferences.

The Council of State, Legislative section, could be the second human rights defender. The institution should therefore be given the responsibility it deserves to advice upon the most important Parliamentary Bills. This system could only work properly if we had a good human rights commission playing the role of a pitbull and helped by the indications of Parliament, Council of State and of federations and NGOs in the field. The establishment of a human rights commission to investigate human rights interferences based on legal texts and on empirical field experience would be a step in the right direction towards a strengthened human rights protection.[38] Links between the human rights commission and civil society are indispensable for its success. The human rights commission could teach the civil society on human rights protection.[39] Civil society could help this commission to identify human rights interferences and to raise awareness on certain issues.[40] This human rights commission should be very accessible to every citizen.[41]

---

37   Law of 11 April 1995 tot invoering van het Handvest van de sociaal verzekerde, *BS* 6 september 1995.
38   P.B.C.D.F. van Sasse van Ysselt, "Een nationaal mensenrechteninstituut: door de bomen het bos weer zien?", *Justitiële verkenningen* 2012, 33.
39   *Ibid.*, 37.
40   G. de Beco, "National human rights institutions in Europe", *Hum. Rts. Law Rev.* 2007, 341.
41   P.B.C.D.F. van Sasse van Ysselt, "Een nationaal mensenrechteninstituut: door de bomen het bos weer zien?", *Justitiële verkenningen* 2012, 32. On 25 April 2019 the law on the

B. INADEQUACY OF THE LEGALITY PRINCIPLE AND VAGUENESS BY THE ECtHR: THE QUESTION OF NONINVASIVE PRENATAL TESTING (NIPT) AND THE FOLLOWING TESTS

The Belgian Constitution demands a formal law for criminal convictions, to impose punishments (Articles 12 and 14 of the Constitution), to introduce taxes, exemptions and reductions of taxes (Articles 170 and 172 of the Constitution), the recruitment of the army (Article 182 of the Constitution), the assignment of a judge (Article 13 of the Constitution), house searches (Article 15 of the Constitution), expropriation (Article 16 of the Constitution), the organisation, recognition and subsidising of education (Article 24, §5), the organisation of the freedom of reunion (Article 26 of the Constitution), the free use of languages (Article 30 of the Constitution), the consultation of official documents (Article 27 of the Constitution) and interferences in the right to privacy (Article 22 of the Constitution).

The Belgian Constitution does not mention the right to life. In a formal reading the Belgian Constitution does not demand that restrictions on the right to life are regulated by a formal law.[42]

A governmental act of 15 October 2017 that modifies Article 33*bis* of the governmental act of 14 September 1984 on the nomenclature of medical treatments and their mandatory assurance regulates the reimbursement of the non-invasive prenatal test.[43] This test is a search for a.o. trisomy 21 in the blood of the pregnant mother from the 12th week of pregnancy. In a way this test is the democratisation of the non-invasive prenatal testing (NIPT). Since the first of July 2017, women pay 8.68 euro for this test. Before this decision women could have this test and were informed about the possibility by their gynaecologist, but had to pay 290 euro.

The High Council of Health (Hoge Gezondheidsraad) advised on NIPT in advice 8912.[44] The Council recommends Belgium to ratify the Convention of Oviedo and the Protocols on Prenatal Testing. The High Council states that

---

establishment of the national human rights institute was adopted by the Belgian Parliament; see also *Parl.St.* Kamer 2018-2019, nr. 54-3670/001.

[42] J. Van Nieuwenhove, "Delegatie van regelgevende bevoegdheid in België", *TvW* 2017, 202–203.

[43] Koninklijk besluit tot wijziging van het artikel 33*bis* van de bijlage bij het koninklijk besluit van 14 september 1984 tot vaststelling van de nomenclatuur van de geneeskundige verstrekkingen inzake verplichte verzekering voor geneeskundige verzorging en uitkeringen, *BS* 25 October 2017.

[44] Advice 8912 of 7 May 2014 of the High Council of Health, ?https://www.health.belgium.be/sites/default/files/uploads/fields/fpshealth_theme_file/19095725/Implementatie%20van%20niet-invasieve%20prenatale%20genetische%20screening%20van%20trisomie%2021%20%28Syn

tests on Trisomy 21 were executed before, but in more invasive tests, namely by a amniocentesis with risk for the life of the foetus.

Arguments against this new prenatal testing come mainly from families or care institutions for persons with disability. They fear that this test, which is organised as a test that any pregnant woman could have immediately, will lead to further stigmatising disabled people and to fierce discussions on the economic and social burden of the disabled.[45] Other critics on early obligatory or highly recommended NIP tests are the possibility that the children are unaffected (false positives) and that even if the children have the syndrome, they may lead to a good life.[46] Finally the tests and the ensuing abortions (carried out in about 90% of the positive cases) send the message to persons with DS and their families that these children are an unnecessary burden to society (Gordon 2015). In addition to these three concerns, one should mention that standard prenatal scanning for DS and other genetic disorders or diseases could lead to a less tolerant view in general on persons who are different from the healthy norm in our society in the future (Parens 2015).[47]

Administration data indicate that in 2015 45 children with Down were born. In 2016 31 children with Down were born. The Report of the administration suggests that the decrease was due to the new prenatal screening test, which was not even democratised at that time.[48] Surprisingly, in 2017 42 children with Down were born. A further decrease of children with Down is expected... only as from 2018 we can observe the effects of the democratised NIPT in the number of children with Down.[49]

Nowadays laboratories are researching new diseases that will be tested on the foetus in the future. Some hospitals take the lead in executing tests on diseases which are not yet tested in other hospitals. Some are already testing the disease of Turner, a chromosomal condition that affects development in females. The most common feature of Turner syndrome is short stature, which becomes

---

droom%20van%20Down%29%20in%20de%20Belgische%20zorgpraktijk%20%28mei%202014%29%20%28HGR%208912%29.pdf.

[45] Ibid.

[46] F. Svenaeus, "Phenomenology of pregnancy and the ethics of abortion", Med. Health Care and Philos 2018, 21, 84.

[47] Advice 8912 of 7 May 2014 of the High Council of Health,?https://www.health.belgium.be/sites/default/files/uploads/fields/fpshealth_theme_file/19095725/Implementatie%20van%20niet-invasieve%20prenatale%20genetische%20screening%20van%20trisomie%2021%20%28Syndroom%20van%20Down%29%20in%20de%20Belgische%20zorgpraktijk%20%28mei%202014%29%20%28HGR%208912%29.pdf.

[48] Het kind in Vlaanderen 2017, p. 142, see https://www.kindengezin.be/img/KIV2017.pdf.

[49] "De nip-test en waarom journalistieke kwaliteit een beetje nipt was", see https://www.vrt.be/vrtnws/nl/2018/11/08/de-nip-test-het-geboortecijfer-en-een-rekensom.

evident by about age 5. An early loss of ovarian function (ovarian hypofunction or premature ovarian failure) is also very common. The ovaries develop normally at first, but egg cells (oocytes) usually die prematurely and most ovarian tissue degenerates before birth. Many affected girls do not undergo puberty unless they receive hormone therapy, and most are unable to conceive (infertile).

A lot of research and prenatal tests are in the pipeline. Research creates endless possibilities. The law must predict possible future problems and try to form a new liveable legal framework. It is essential that legal frameworks are introduced on prenatal counselling. Some gynaecologists and hospitals are executing this task as good as they can, but there are often no clear guidelines on the information that the doctor must give about these tests at the level of the hospital.

In a privacy and human rights context, these prenatal tests opened my eyes at several levels.

The decision to have the foetus tested could be judged as an indirect interference in its right to life. C. Stevens puts it this way: "The use of prenatal testing thus becomes an indicator of a society's view of what it means to be a fully-fledged human being."[50]

Firstly, we encourage the European Court of Human Rights to be more daring on this point. There will always be different opinions and absence of consensus on delicate issues such as abortion. The question of the start of life remains fascinating and unresponded. Nevertheless, we wish the European Court of Human Rights the courage to adapt its vague fiction in the case-law on the right to life.

The European Court is very clear on the one hand. In R.R. / Poland the Court emphasises the relevance of the information which the applicant sought to obtain by way of genetic testing to the decision concerning continuation of her pregnancy. The timely access of information in the framework of a Polish Act was at stake here. In this case a mother was denied prenatal tests after first indications of deformation of the foetus due to the disease of Turner. The Court concludes correctly to an interference in and violation of the right to private life and the prohibition of torture, inhuman and degrading treatment of the pregnant mother.[51]

On the other hand, the Court remains vague on the unborn life. It states in its case-law "that the unborn child is not regarded as a "person" directly protected

---

50   See C. Stevens, "Debating human rights and prenatal testing in Japan", *Asian Studies Association of Australia* 2013, 319.
51   ECtHR, 26 May 2011, *R.R./ Poland*, §199.

by Article 2 of the Convention and that if the unborn do have a "right" to "life", it is implicitly limited by the mother's rights and interests. The Convention institutions have not, however, ruled out the possibility that in certain circumstances safeguards may be extended to the unborn child."[52]

As the possibilities of medical science are growing, a certain selection of mankind before birth has started and is out of the scope of the European Court of Human Rights as the Court does not clearly acknowledges a right to life to the unborn life. As a result the Court's attention is focussed on the protection of the (born) individual against arbitrary interference by public authorities.[53] This position will be insufficient in the future. In our opinion "the unborn" will in certain circumstances need a right to life that can be balanced against other interests.

A courageous European Court of Human Rights would be the first step to help Belgian constitutionalists to impose proper Parliamentary debates on life-changing issues.

If one accepts that the reimbursement of prenatal tests has an impact on the life of the foetus we have to rewrite the very formal legality principle in the Belgian Constitution. We cannot allow constitutionalists to lose their time in reducing the formal legality test to rights formally included in the list (of chapter II of) the Belgian Constitution which is too restricted.

It is incomprehensible that Parliament is obliged to decide on issues concerning privacy intrusion such as for example house searches around pig stables[54], but that decisions to reimburse tests that are affecting judgments on the value of unborn life and the life of the foetus can be taken without a law adopted by the Parliament. In a broader sense of democratic decision making processes it is staggering that tests to give the possibility to abortion for reasons of 'disease' or 'disability' are reimbursed without hearing the people that are suffering the disease of disability that is the subject of the tests. More tests are coming. It is time to create a proper framework. We simply cannot allow to regulate all questions of bio- and eugenetics in a High Commission of Health and by Royal decrees without including Parliament and people and families involved.

...

---

[52]   ECtHR, 8 July 2004, *Vo v. France*, §80; ECtHR, 5 September 2002, *Bosso / Italy*.
[53]   ECtHR, 20 March 2007, *Tysiąc / Poland*, §109.
[54]   See a.o. Adv. Op. Council of State no. 45.112/3 of 23 September 2008 on "een ontwerp van besluit van de Vlaamse Regering "betreffende het erkennen van centra voor landbouweducatie en het subsidiëren van landbouweducatieve activiteiten."

All these difficult issues remind me of a Summer Course in Strasbourg where my promotor sent me a year after the Cassin competition on bio-ethics and human rights. In a discussion about the European foetuses in the freezer in the framework of in vitro fertilization and the destruction of these foetuses I was overwhelmed by the bewilderment of my African colleagues. Our European individualistic view on the individual right to privacy and right to life was sickening to them. Their subsequent description of the African views on the concept of life was deeply inspirational to me: life does not only belong to ourselves, life is a river coming from our predecessors and belonging to our successors...This philosophy is encouraging to oblige us Europeans to balance the right to life of the foetus against the right to privacy of the mother.

CONCLUSION

The scope of the right to private life is widening due to scientific and societal changes. In practice, the contribution puts some question marks on the legality principle.

It is sometimes not implemented by legislators in cases of interferences of the right to (private) life of the most vulnerable in our society, such as job seekers in social enterprises. This should be monitored properly by Parliament, Council of State, legislative section and the future Human Rights Commission.

The case of prenatal tests and the reimbursement of these blood tests are taken as an example to question the list of human rights that could only be restricted by a formal law in Belgium (the right to life is not listed) and to question whether the vagueness on the right to life of the unborn has to remain in Strasbourg if laboratories will be able to test anything the further decades and centuries.

CLAIMING THE CONVENTION'S 'DUTIES AND RESPONSIBILITIES' IN THE FACE OF ILLIBERALISM

Michaël MERRIGAN

Affiliated Junior Researcher KU Leuven
Lawyer at the Brussels Bar

INTRODUCTION

Those who have had the honour to know and work with Paul Lemmens, are well aware of his dedication to the protection of human rights. His approach is not that of the single-cause activist, whose role he certainly acknowledges, but that of the thoughtful and conscientious examiner. Individuals have rights, but they do not live in isolation from one another. They live in a community which, in turn, has certain interests of its own. These interests, if recognised and adequately protected, benefit everyone in the community, and strengthen overall rights protection. By choice or fate, and probably both, Paul Lemmens has always found himself in the middle of this tension between individual and community. As a judge at the Belgian Council of State, as a member of the UNMIK Human Rights Advisory Panel in Kosovo and, later, as a judge at the European Court of Human Rights, the main task of the offices he held, which he regarded as a fundamental duty and responsibility, was to balance the rightful claims of the individual against the necessities of community life. His constant interest, and goal, was, therefore, to seek to reconcile the never fully reconcilable, namely, the free individual, and the community in which she or he lives, and, if all goes well, is able to thrive. While the circle can never be completely squared, Paul's good temper never failed.

This perhaps explains Paul's interest in the question of individual rights and responsibilities in human rights law. When I proposed to him to work precisely on this topic for my PhD research, he was immediately enthusiastic. In this article, I will raise a point which, in my view, has been underexposed and which can be invoked to argue for a greater focus on individual duties and responsibilities at this moment in time. This point is that, in view of the crisis affecting human rights and liberal democracy today, the way in which 'duties and responsibilities' have been invoked by the European Court of Human Rights, within the framework of Article 10 ECHR, not only indicates the limits of freedom of expression, but also points at the role individuals can play in resisting illiberal tendencies in society.

I. DUTIES AND RESPONSIBILITIES AS TABOO

Human rights naturally presuppose human duties. At their most basic level, universal rights require equally universal correlative duties to respect those rights. There can, for instance, be no universal right to life, if there is no universal duty to respect other people's right to life. Although human rights, both in the way in which they are invoked colloquially, and within the human rights legal framework, are more complicated than this[1], it is clear that individual duties and responsibilities have an essential role to play in the human rights framework.[2]

Nevertheless, the focus in human rights law has always been mostly on the legal obligations of States. Attempts to emphasise the underlying duties and responsibilities of individuals have been met with great reservations among human rights scholars and activists alike. This was most obvious in the case of several attempts to draft lists and declarations listing individual duties and responsibilities. One of the best-known projects was the Inter-Action Council's *Universal Declaration of Human Responsibilities*[3], which was met with important reservations and even outright criticism.[4] While individual duties and responsibilities form a natural part of the human rights order, there has been a persistent fear that emphasising them would lead to a weakening of the human rights acquis, as it would, *inter alia*, open the door to an unjustified

---

[1] The direct correlation between rights and duties only applies to the negative aspects of liberty rights and not, for instance, to socio-economic rights, which require the intervention of an intermediary actor like the State to connect antecedently unspecified obligation-bearers and right-holders. For instance, the rights to housing or education require social housing to be built and primary schools to be established. See e.g. Onora O'Neill (2005), "The dark side of human rights", *International Affairs* 81(2), (427-439) 431.

[2] See, for instance, Asbjørn Eide (1999), "Human rights require responsibilities and duties" in Karel Vasak, *Karel Vasak amicorum liber: Les droits de l'homme à l'aube du XXIe siècle*, Brussels: Bruylant, 581-598; see also the recent study by Eric Robert Boot (2017), *Human duties and the limits of human rights discourse*, Cham: Springer.

[3] InterAction Council, *A Universal Declaration of Human Responsibilities*, 1 September 1997, http://www.interactioncouncil.org/universal-declaration-human-responsibilities.

[4] See, for instance, Ben Saul (2001), "In the shadow of human rights: Human duties, obligations, and responsibilities", *Colum. Hum. Rts. L. Rev.* 32(3), (565-624) 566, and Amnesty International (1998), *Muddying the waters. The Draft 'Universal Declaration of Human Responsibilities': no complement to human rights*, 31 March 1998, IOR 40/002/1998, available at https://www.amnesty.org/en/documents/ior40/002/1998/en.

curtailment of rights by authoritarian rulers, lead to the legal rights framework being compromised by legally elusive moral and ethical considerations, and lead to rights being made conditional upon the fulfilment of vague and ill-defined duties and responsibilities to the State.

The case law of the European Court of Human Rights nevertheless regularly invokes individual duties and responsibilities explicitly, especially in the framework of Article 10 ECHR, which deals with freedom of expression and whose text includes an explicit reference to 'duties and responsibilities'.[5] It can be argued that this reference to 'duties and responsibilities' in the Convention seems to transcend the mere regulation of expression, and that it, in fact, serves as a reminder of the fundamental role each and every individual can play in safeguarding and upholding the democratic society we live in. This realisation would seem to be especially urgent in our day since we are, at this moment in time, confronted with a rise in illiberalism, both through the establishment of 'illiberal democracies', and through illiberal populist tendencies within established liberal democracies. These developments are challenging the liberal-democratic framework of which the European Convention of Human Rights forms the bedrock. In what follows, in section II, I will first have a closer look at the idea of illiberalism, and its rise in recent years. I will show how recent illiberal tendencies entail an attack especially on liberal-democratic offices and functions within society. Subsequently, in section III, I will show how this observation offers an interesting perspective on the potential role of the reference to duties and responsibilities in the European Convention on Human Rights.

II. THE RISE OF ILLIBERAL DEMOCRACY

A. LIBERAL DEMOCRACY, ILLIBERALISM AND POPULISM

Liberal democracy can be understood as a democratic form of government in which political power is constrained by the rule of law, and which has at its centre the respect for, and protection of, fundamental rights and freedoms. It thus brings together democracy and constitutional liberalism or, in other words, the ideas of democracy, on the one hand, and liberty (rights) and the rule of law, on the other. In Europe, and among the proponents of liberal democracy in general, the term 'democracy' is mostly understood to refer to its liberal

---

[5] Article 10 § 2 ECHR: "The exercise of these freedoms, *since it carries with it duties and responsibilities*, may be subject to such formalities, conditions, restrictions or penalties as are prescribed by law and are necessary in a democratic society [...]".

variant.[6] The 'democratic society', which figures prominently in the case law of the European Court of Human Rights, is of course not 'merely' democratic[7]; it is, necessarily, the liberal variant of democratic[8]; otherwise, the Convention itself would be superfluous.

There is no inevitability in the marriage between democracy and liberalism; it is, as we are re-discovering once again in Europe, quite possible to have some form of democracy without liberalism. We then speak of 'illiberal democracy', a term coined by Fareed Zakaria.[9] The term is not without controversy. After all, a regime in which liberty rights are generally not respected, cannot be a fully functioning substantive democracy, in spite of formally organised elections.[10]

While the term 'illiberal democracy' was first used to refer more to the traditional autocracies experimenting with electoral democracy in the '90s, it can now be linked to the threat to liberalism posed by 'populism', in some

---

[6] Michael Freeden (2008), "European liberalisms: An essay in comparative political thought", *European Journal of Political Theory* 7(1), (9–30) 22.

[7] Although democracy *per se* is a minimum requirement: *United Communist Party of Turkey and Others v. Turkey*, judgment of 30 January 1998, *Reports of Judgments and Decisions* 1998-I, § 45: "Democracy thus appears to be the only political model contemplated by the Convention and, accordingly, the only one compatible with it". Moreover, the preamble of the European Convention on Human Rights holds that the fundamental freedoms mentioned in it "are best maintained on the one hand by an effective political democracy and on the other by a common understanding and observance of the human rights upon which they depend".

[8] Democracy "constitutes a fundamental element of the "European public order", which entails an "effective and meaningful democracy governed by the rule of law", *Karácsony and Others v. Hungary* [GC], judgment of 17 May 2016, nos. 42461/13 and 44357/13, § 141.

[9] Fareed Zakaria (1997), "The rise of illiberal democracy", *Foreign Aff.* 76(6), 22-43. This type of regime is sometimes also referred to as a '*democradura*', from the Spanish '*democracia*' and '*dictadura*'. For the sake of completeness, it must be added that the reverse of illiberal democracy is also possible: liberalism without democracy. In this case the regime is a dictatorship (i.e. it lacks democracy) in which civil liberties are mostly respected. This type of regime is called a 'liberal autocracy' or '*dictablanda*', a word that is derived from the Spanish '*dictadura*' (dictatorship) and '*blanda*' (soft). Examples include the Austro-Hungarian Empire or, more recently, Hong Kong before it was handed over to China.

[10] Müller therefore decries the fact that by labeling a regime an illiberal democracy, it still receives the "most coveted political prize" in today's world, and this undeservedly, namely the label 'democracy'. As he wrote in an op-ed in the build-up to the recent 2018 elections in Hungary, "Yet 'illiberal democracy' fails to capture what is wrong with these regimes. It also gives leaders like Mr. Orban a major rhetorical advantage: He is still left with the designation 'democrat,' even as it is democracy itself — and not just liberalism — that is under attack in his country." He continues: "In Hungary, it is not just the rule of law that has been under threat. Rights essential for democracy itself — especially rights to free speech, free assembly and free association — have been systematically attacked. As media pluralism disappears, citizens cannot get critical information to make up their minds about their government's record. Unless one wants to say that a democracy remains a democracy as long as the government does not stuff the ballot boxes on Election Day, it is crucial to insist that democracy itself is being damaged." Jan-Werner Müller (2018), "Democracy still matters", 5 April 2018, *nytimes. com*, https://www.nytimes.com/2018/04/05/opinion/hungary-viktor-orban-populism.html.

cases mixed with nativism, i.e., when the interests of 'native' inhabitants are pitted specifically against those of newcomers.[11] A fully agreed definition of populism is lacking.[12] However, it is generally agreed that populism, in modern democratic societies, centres around an appeal to 'the people', who are regarded as a monolithic group, and distinguished from the so-called 'elite'.[13] As such, populism also comes with its own rhetorical style, typified by simplicity and directness[14], and with a 'revivalist' mood[15] which often centres on a charismatic leader.[16] Because of its fundamental structure, i.e., 'the people' versus 'the elite', populism is exclusionary on two fronts: internally, since it pits one part of the people ('the people') against another ('the elite'); and externally, since it pits 'the people', usually described along ethnic or national lines, against those who are not 'the people', i.e., those of a different ethnicity, nationality or culture.

---

[11]   Takis S. Pappas (2018), "Dealing with modern illiberal democracies: from vintage electoral autocracy to today's jumble of populism with nativism", in Arne Muis and Lars van Troost (eds.), *Will human rights survive illiberal democracy?*, Amsterdam: Amnesty International Netherlands, 25-30, https://www.amnesty.nl/content/uploads/2015/10/illiberal-democracy-PDF-20mrt.pdf.

[12]   For an overview of definitions, see Pappas, who lists a number of definitions of populism as movement, style, ideology, discourse, strategy, political culture and 'omnibus concept': Takis S. Pappas (2016), "Modern populism: research advances, conceptual and methodological pitfalls, and the minimal definition" in W.R. Thompson (ed.), *Oxford research encyclopedia of politics*, http://oxfordre.com/politics/view/10.1093/acrefore/9780190228637.001.0001/acrefore-9780190228637-e-17, appendix.

[13]   See Margaret Canovan (1999), "Trust the people! Populism and the two faces of democracy", *Political Studies* 47(1), (2-16) 3; Jan Jagers and Stefaan Walgrave (2007), "Populism as political communication style: An empirical study of political parties' discourse in Belgium", *European Journal of Political Research* 46(3), (319-345) 322. See also Team Populism (2018), *Policy brief on populism in Europe and the Americas: what, when, who and so what?*, June 2018, http://populism.byu.edu/App_Data/Publications/SegoviaMemo%20_final.pdf, 2.

[14]   Margaret Canovan (1999), "Trust the people! Populism and the two faces of democracy", *Political Studies* 47(1), (2-16) 5. See also Block and Negrine who, with regard to the communication style of Venezuela's Hugo Chavez and the UK's Nigel Farrage, conclude that both "used elements associated with identity, rhetoric, and the media effectively (a) to use and reinvent cultural symbols to construct collective identity; (b) to lead by communication through brutally antagonizing the elite and connecting with their publics (the disenfranchised or discontented with middle-ground politics) by skillfully using abrasive but also colloquial, relatable, patriotic rhetoric; and (c) to create ongoing controversy and to become media events themselves via a strategic use of all forms of media." The authors conclude that "[p]opulist leaders use abrasive, belligerent, direct, and simple language to connect with disenchanted publics and to present themselves as those with a solution to existing and continuing problems. Indeed they accuse others of exacerbating the problems. Other political actors (the center-ground elite), by and large, work with a pluralist conversation, seeking consensus rather than confrontation and keeping distant and protected by walls of political correctness." Elena Block and Ralph Negrine (2017), "The populist communication style: Toward a critical framework", *International Journal of Communication* 11, (178-197) 189-190.

[15]   Margaret Canovan (1999), "Trust the people! Populism and the two faces of democracy", *Political Studies* 47(1), (2-16) 6.

[16]   Margaret Canovan (1999), "Trust the people! Populism and the two faces of democracy", *Political Studies* 47(1), (2-16) 6.

There is some debate about whether populism is democratic or not[17], although one could argue that, in substance, it cannot be. It is true that, as representatives of 'the people', populists present themselves, in one sense, as arch-democrats. However, in reality they only represent a faction of the people, to the exclusion, internally, of 'the elite' and, externally, of 'the Other', often people of another ethnic or cultural descent. Hence, while they therefore present themselves as democrats, openly subscribe to electoral democracy, and can therefore be elected into power, they do not support the fundamental premises of substantive democracy, which, among other things, presupposes a level of equality and equal rights for all people, including minorities.[18] Although there is less discussion as regards the illiberal character of populists, it is generally agreed that populism invariably proves to be illiberal. Populists ultimately deny rights (freedom of expression, of assembly, etc.) to groups of people, and end up interpreting the rule of law to serve the will of 'the people', while 'the people' is interpreted restrictively to exclude swaths of individuals. The exclusion, internally and externally, goes against the basic tenets of liberalism. Pappas therefore argues that contemporary populism is essentially democratic illiberalism.[19]

From a liberal perspective, the fundamental problem with populists is their choice to exclude certain people from the enjoyment of rights. This happens in discourse, first, and through a weakening of the rule of law, second. Populism eventually undermines central institutions of liberal democracy, including civil rights, electoral quality, and the separation of powers, and can eventually lead to "long-term erosion of democratic norms and social cohesion".[20] Hence, while populist parties and politicians make use of the liberal-democratic tools available to them, their approach and ideas ultimately lead to the undermining of liberal democracy.

---

[17] See in general terms Benjamin Moffitt (2017), "Liberal illiberalism? The reshaping of the contemporary populist radical right in Northern Europe", *Politics and Governance* 5(4), (112-122) 113. Krasev, for instance, believes populism is antiliberal but not antidemocratic: Ivan Krasev (2007), "Is East-Central Europe backsliding? The strange death of the liberal consensus", *Journal of Democracy* 18(4), (56-64) 60.

[18] Margaret Canovan (1999), "Trust the people! Populism and the two faces of democracy", *Political Studies* 47(1), (2-16) 7.

[19] Takis S. Pappas (2016), "Modern populism: Research advances, conceptual and methodological pitfalls, and the minimal definition" in W.R. Thompson (ed.), *Oxford research encyclopedia of politics*, available at http://oxfordre.com/politics/view/10.1093/acrefore/9780190228637.001.0001/acrefore-9780190228637-e-17, 15. Pappas even goes as far as saying that "the terms 'populism' and 'democratic illiberalism' are in this view perfectly substitutable and can be used interchangeably in our efforts to study modern populism, as carrying exactly the same meaning and denoting exactly similar things."

[20] Team Populism (2018), *Policy brief on populism in Europe and the Americas: what, when, who and so what?*, June 2018, http://populism.byu.edu/App_Data/Publications/SegoviaMemo%20_final.pdf, 4.

The precise delineations between a healthy liberal democracy, a liberal democracy with significant illiberal tendencies, and an illiberal democracy, or between an illiberal democracy and an autocracy, are by no means clear-cut. The most typical example of what is currently often regarded as an illiberal democracy, in Europe, is Hungary, whose prime minister even explicitly described his country as an illiberal democracy.[21] However, some would argue that Hungary is no longer even an illiberal democracy. It is, instead, at least in the eyes of some of its critics, an authoritarian State.[22] Even in solid liberal democracies, there can be both incidental and systemic problems with the protection of certain rights and the rule of law[23], without these States losing the label of 'liberal democracies'. In other cases, notably in Central and Eastern Europe, there is a feeling that once-liberal democracies are 'backsliding' into illiberal democracies. It is, therefore, necessary to see all countries on a continuum between fully liberal and fully illiberal, with virtually all countries somewhere in between these two extremes.

B.   THE RISE OF ILLIBERALISM

Generally speaking, there seems to be a strong consensus that illiberalism, in its populist manifestation and otherwise, worldwide and in Europe, is on the rise. The number of countries where liberal democracy has significantly backslidden, as well as the number of people affected by this backsliding, has sharply increased in recent years.[24] In 2017, the population living in the countries backsliding on liberal democracy outnumbered the population living in the countries

---

21 Prime Minister Orbán held the following: "[…] the Hungarian nation is not simply a group of individuals but a community that must be organised, reinforced and in fact constructed. *And so in this sense the new state that we are constructing in Hungary is an illiberal state, a non-liberal state.* It does not reject the fundamental principles of liberalism such as freedom, and I could list a few more, but it does not make this ideology the central element of state organisation, but instead includes a different, special, national approach." (stress added) For the full text of the speech, see The Hungarian Government, *Prime Minister Viktor Orbán's speech at the 25th Bálványos Summer Free University and Summer Camp,* 26 July 2014, Tusnádfürdő (Băile Tuşnad), Romania, http://www.kormany.hu/en/the-prime-minister/ the-prime-minister-s-speeches/prime-minister-viktor-orban-s-speech-at-the-25th-balvanyos-summer-free-university-and-student-camp.

22 See for instance Daniel Hegedüs (2018), "Responding to illiberal democracies' shrinking space for human rights in the EU", in Arne Muis and Lars van Troost (eds.), *Will human rights survive illiberal democracy?*, Amsterdam: Amnesty International Netherlands, (57-65) 60, https://www.amnesty.nl/content/uploads/2015/10/illiberal-democracy-PDF-20mrt.pdf. Hegedüs argues the only truly illiberal democracy in Europe at this moment is Poland.

23 One just has to think of problems with the excessive length of trials and the many cases from, e.g., Italy that ended up at the European Court of Human Rights in this regard.

24 V-Dem Institute (2018), *Democracy for all? Annual democracy report 2018,* https://www.v-dem.net/media/filer_public/3f/19/3f19efc9-e25f-4356-b159-b5c0ec894115/v-dem_democracy _report_2018.pdf, 18.

advancing in this regard.[25] Moreover, the number of countries whose leaders can be considered 'somewhat populist' doubled from 7 in 2004 to 14 in recent years, while 15 countries "experienced a significant overall increase in populist discourse" in the past two decades.[26] Across the world, important challengers have arisen to contest the liberal-democratic status quo. It suffices to give just a few examples from among the Council of Europe's member States. Diverse as they are in their historical origins, the causes at work, the factors influencing the particular context, and the scope and consequences of developments on the ground, these examples all reflect a climate of uncertainty with regard to the liberal-democratic project.

In the **Netherlands**, the right-wing populist party PVV under the leadership of Geert Wilders – recently convicted for hate speech –[27] has gained much ground in the past few years, though falling short of becoming the largest party in the parliamentary elections of 2017. In **France**, the extreme-right and populist Front National of Marine Le Pen became a serious contender for the 2017 presidential elections, after winning a large share of the votes in the regional elections. In spite of its eventual defeat at the polls, the fact that it won the first round of the elections, and that the party appealed to such a significant segment of the voting public, indicate that the Front National is still a force to be reckoned with.[28] In the **United Kingdom**, a majority of voters chose by referendum to leave the European Union after a campaign fraught with anti-immigrant sentiment, in which calls were also made to withdraw from the European Convention on Human Rights, and the incumbent prime minister vowed to 'rip up human rights laws that impede new terror legislation'.[29] In **Germany**, the populist

---

[25] V-Dem Institute (2018), *Democracy for all? Annual democracy report 2018*, https://www.v-dem. net/media/filer_public/3f/19/3f19efc9-e25f-4356-b159-b5c0ec894115/v-dem_democracy_repo rt_2018.pdf, 19. As V-Dem explains in its report (p. 16), its 'Liberal democracy index' "reflects both the liberal and electoral principles of democracy, each of which constitutes one half of the scores for the Liberal Democracy Index". The report contains more information on the exact methodology used.

[26] See Paul Lewis, Caelainn Barr, Seán Clarke, Antonio Voce, Cath Levett, Pablo Gutiérrez (2019), "Revealed: the rise and rise of populist rhetoric", 6 March 2019, *theguardian.com*, https://www.theguardian.com/world/ng-interactive/2019/mar/06/revealed-the-rise-and-rise-of-populist-rhetoric. The research was funded by the US-based non-profit organization theguardian.org and led by Kirk Hawkins, an associate professor at Brigham Young University.

[27] Rechtbank Den Haag, 9 December 2016, ECLI:NL:RBDHA:2016:15014, https://uitspraken. rechtspraak.nl/inziendocument?id=ECLI:NL:RBDHA:2016:15014. The judgment is subject to appeal.

[28] Angelique Chrisafis (2017), "Marine Le Pen defeated but France's far right is far from finished", 7 May 2017, *theguardian.com*, https://www.theguardian.com/world/2017/may/07/ marine-le-pen-defeated-front-national-far-from-finished.

[29] Rowena Mason and Vikram Dodd (2017), "May: I'll rip up human rights laws that impede new terror legislation", 6 June 2017, *theguardian.com*, https://www.theguardian.com/ politics/2017/jun/06/theresa-may-rip-up-human-rights-laws-impede-new-terror-legislation.

anti-EU and anti-immigration AfD scored more than 12% of the votes and more than 13% of the seats in the 2017 federal elections, leading Cass Mudde to call it the country's *schwarzer Sonntag*.[30] In **Hungary**, as already mentioned above, a regime with outspoken authoritarian tendencies, under the leadership of prime minister Viktor Orban and his party Fidesz, has further expanded its reach, explicitly rejecting liberal democracy and, instead, openly calling its goal the establishment of an 'illiberal democracy'. In **Poland**, the Law and Justice Party (PiS) has also sailed an increasingly illiberal course, undermining, among other things, the independence of the Constitutional Tribunal and attempting to impose severe media restrictions.[31] In **Greece**, still in dire straits after the debt crisis crippled its economy, the antidemocratic Golden Dawn movement rose to prominence, gaining 18 of the 300 seats in parliament.[32] In **Turkey**, freedom of expression and association, among other rights, have been severely curtailed, especially since the attempted coup against president Erdogan.[33] **Russia** has openly rejected the idea of 'Western' liberal democracy, and has increasingly and openly started propagating illiberal change across the world.[34]

Although the examples are diverse, together they point (at least) to a shift in mood when it comes to the central pillars of liberal democracy, i.e. human rights protection through the rule of law, across the Council of Europe area. It is perhaps not so much the existence of each of these developments in themselves which is surprising[35], but rather the brazenness with which disregard for established human rights standards has been propagated, the fact that these developments are taking place more or less simultaneously within Europe,

---

[30] Cas Mudde (2017), "What the stunning success of AfD means for Germany and Europe", 24 September 2017, *theguardian.com*, https://www.theguardian.com/commentisfree/2017/sep/24/germany-elections-afd-europe-immigration-merkel-radical-right.

[31] This proposal, however, didn't make it: Associated Press (2016), "Poland scraps proposed media restrictions in wake of street protests", 20 December 2016, *theguardian.com*, https://www.theguardian.com/world/2016/dec/20/poland-scraps-proposed-media-restrictions-in-wake-of-street-protests; see also Anne Applebaum (2016), "Illiberal democracy comes to Poland", 22 December 2016, *washingtonpost.com*, https://www.washingtonpost.com/news/global-opinions/wp/2016/12/22/illiberal-democracy-comes-to-poland. For more on the situation in Poland, see also Wojciech Przybylski (2018), "Poland: illiberalism in the making", in Edit Zgut (ed.), *Illiberalism in the V4: Pressure points and bright spots*, Budapest: Political Capital and Friedrich Naumann Stiftung, 24-36, http://www.politicalcapital.hu/pc-admin/source/documents/pc_fnf_v4illiberalism_pressurepoints_20180605.pdf.

[32] Election of September 2015. In the elections of May 2012 it even obtained 21 seats.

[33] Agence France-Presse (2017), "Turkey arrests 1,000 and suspends 9,100 police in new crackdown", 27 April 2017, *theguardian.com*, https://www.theguardian.com/world/2017/apr/27/turkey-arrests-1000-suspends-9100-police-new-crackdown.

[34] Emily Tamkin (2017), "The real Russian threat to Central Eastern Europe", *foreignpolicy.com*, 30 March 2017, http://foreignpolicy.com/2017/03/30/the-real-russian-threat-to-central-eastern-europe-2.

[35] After all, they all have their own precursors and are hardly wholly unique from a historical perspective.

including in established liberal democracies, and the confusion with which defenders of the liberal-democratic model have struggled in their attempts to find convincing responses to these illiberal movements.

C. THE THREAT OF ILLIBERAL POLITICS

The threat posed by illiberalism in the context of (nominally) liberal-democratic societies seems to be at least threefold. First of all, and most obviously, the people living in an illiberal society suffer from a deficit in rights protection. Although such an illiberal society may still nominally be a democracy (at least from a procedural point of view), rights protection is reduced or abolished, and minorities, in particular, but essentially all individuals, are left vulnerable both to unqualified majority rule and the abuse of State power.

Second, illiberal tendencies in established democracies tend to provoke knee-jerk reactions from proponents of liberalism, who struggle with the conundrum of how to contain illiberalism within a liberal democratic logic. This leads to what is sometimes called 'illiberal liberalism', which aims at outlawing behaviour which is perceived to be in conflict with liberal values. While even the European Convention on Human Rights, *inter alia* in its Article 17, foresees the possibility of outlawing claims aimed at destroying the liberal framework, the question, of course, is when, and to what extent, certain (rights) claims are contrary to the rights listed in the Convention, or to what extent limitations of individual rights are really strictly necessary in a democratic society. How far can liberal democracy go in outlawing illiberal behaviour, without itself becoming illiberal? Illiberal overreach, in the name of liberalism, is certainly possible. Discussions on the limits of liberalism have arisen especially in relation to perceived threats to 'Western civilisation' by non-European immigrants who are thought to hold non-liberal convictions. For instance, questions have arisen about the need to 'integrate' immigrants into society and the extent to which this can be done. The 'civic integrationism' that has developed in certain countries is often characterised by punitive measures for those immigrants who do not comply with the integration standards set out.[36] While liberal democracy must defend itself, the way in which it needs to do this without acting in a self-defeating way, is less clear.

Third, there is a wider threat emanating from illiberal regimes, which extends to the very core of the liberal-democratic project. The evident initial success of

---

[36] See, in this regard, Triadafilos Triadafilopoulos (2011), "Illiberal means to liberal ends? Understanding recent immigrant integration policies in Europe", *Journal of Ethnic and Migration Studies*, 37(6), 861–880, in particular 875, fn. 1.

illiberal democracies can undermine trust in liberal democracy as a concept, thereby further spreading the appeal of illiberal democracy. As Zakaria explains:

> "Illiberal democracies gain legitimacy, and thus strength, from the fact that they are reasonably democratic. Conversely, the greatest danger that illiberal democracy poses – other than to its own people – is that it will discredit liberal democracy itself, casting a shadow on democratic governance."[37]

The threat stemming from the very existence of illiberal democracies is thus that they are corrosive to support for, and appreciation of, liberal democracy elsewhere.

D.   ILLIBERALISM AS AN ATTACK ON LIBERAL-DEMOCRATIC OFFICES AND FUNCTIONS

Societies do not generally become illiberal overnight, but as a result of a long and, by times subtle, process of 'illiberalisation', often couched in the language and customs of liberalism and the law. As Dobson notes,

> "Today's dictators understand that in a globalized world the more brutal forms of intimidation – mass arrests, firing squads, and violent crackdowns – are best replaced with more subtle forms of coercion. Rather than forcibly arrest members of a human rights group, today's most effective despots deploy tax collectors or health inspectors to shut down dissident groups. Laws are written broadly, then used like a scalpel to target the groups the government deems a threat."[38]

More specifically, this process of 'illiberalisation' takes root by attacking the functions and institutions elementary to the liberal-democratic framework. For instance, in a liberal democracy, parliamentarians have the elementary duty and responsibility to study and discuss proposed legislation. However, when fundamental constitutional reforms are introduced to Parliament in an untimely manner, so that no time is left for effective study or discussion, the fulfilment of this burden is made impossible and, simply put, parliamentarians cannot fulfil their essential task. This is precisely what happened with the new Hungarian constitution in 2011.[39] Similarly, judges also have an essential task in society.

---

[37]   Fareed Zakaria (1997), "The rise of illiberal democracy", *Foreign Aff.* 76(6), (22-43) 42.

[38]   William J. Dobson (2013), *The dictator's learning curve: Inside the global battle for democracy*, New York: Anchor, 5.

[39]   Eszter Zalan (2018), "A warning from Hungary: Building an illiberal zombie in the EU threatens political rights and democratic freedoms", in Arne Muis and Lars van Troost (eds.), *Will human rights survive illiberal democracy?*, Amsterdam: Amnesty International Netherlands, (39-45) 41, https://www.amnesty.nl/content/uploads/2015/10/illiberal-democr acy-PDF-20mrt.pdf.

In Hungary, however, the government limited the powers of the constitutional court, limited the number of ombudspersons, and forced judges into retirement in violation of EU law.[40] Moreover, journalists were banned from parliament[41], rendering their task of reporting on parliamentary topics more difficult, if not impossible, and newspapers were closed[42], further hampering journalists from carrying out their fundamental task of serving as a watchdog in a democratic society. Similarly, in Turkey, purges, which included the sacking of many university deans[43], as well as of police, members of the military, academics, media personalities and members of the civil service[44], made it impossible for these people to fulfil their elementary tasks, and constituted a strong warning to those remaining in function to fulfil their tasks in accordance with government views. These purges therefore not only constituted a limitation of academic freedom, freedom of expression, and freedom of belief and other rights, they also constituted a clear and brutally enforced *de facto* obligation to those not yet arrested to conform to the regime, and to exercise their professions in function of the regime's interests. In the same vein, the obligation for NGOs that receive foreign funding to register as foreign agents, as applicable in Russia[45], "creates the illusion in society that these groups work for foreign interests,"[46] depriving them of their necessary reputation for independence and, thereby, creating a reality in which independent work is made much more difficult, and pro-government behaviour is encouraged. The tax raids systematically carried out against NGOs

---

[40] Eszter Zalan (2018), "A warning from Hungary: Building an illiberal zombie in the EU threatens political rights and democratic freedom", in Arne Muis and Lars van Troost (eds.), *Will human rights survive illiberal democracy?*, Amsterdam: Amnesty International Netherlands, (39-45) 41, https://www.amnesty.nl/content/uploads/2015/10/illiberal-democra cy-PDF-20mrt.pdf. See also *Commission v. Hungary*, Judgment of 6 November 2012, C-286/12, http://curia.europa.eu/juris/liste.jsf?num=C-286/12.

[41] Eszter Zalan (2017), "Hungary's media deconstructed into Orban's echo chamber", 10 July 2017, *euobserver.com*, https://euobserver.com/beyond-brussels/138466.

[42] Eszter Zalan (2018), "Journalists furious as Hungary's largest newspaper closes", 10 October 2016, *euobserver.com*, https://euobserver.com/political/135416.

[43] Patrick Kingsley (2016), "Turkey sacks 15,000 education workers in purge after failed coup", 20 July 2016, *theguardian.com*, https://www.theguardian.com/world/2016/jul/19/turkey-sacks-15000-education-workers-in-purge.

[44] Kareem Shaheen (2018), "'Suffocating climate of fear' in Turkey despite end of state of emergency", *theguardian.com*, 19 July 2018, https://www.theguardian.com/world/2018/jul/18/turkeys-state-of-emergency-ends-but-crackdown-continues.

[45] Eszter Zalan (2018), "A warning from Hungary: Building an illiberal zombie in the EU threatens political rights and democratic freedoms", in Arne Muis and Lars van Troost (eds.), *Will human rights survive illiberal democracy?*, Amsterdam: Amnesty International Netherlands, (39-45) 43, https://www.amnesty.nl/content/uploads/2015/10/illiberal-democra cy-PDF-20mrt.pdf.

[46] Eszter Zalan (2018), "A warning from Hungary: Building an illiberal zombie in the EU threatens political rights and democratic freedoms", in Arne Muis and Lars van Troost (eds.), *Will human rights survive illiberal democracy?*, Amsterdam: Amnesty International Netherlands, (39-45) 43, https://www.amnesty.nl/content/uploads/2015/10/illiberal-democra cy-PDF-20mrt.pdf.

in Russia[47] serve as an extra form of intimidation. When, also in Hungary, the names of 200 academics, journalists, human rights advocates and others were published, labeling them as "mercenaries" of George Soros[48], this constituted a clear threat to the individuals involved, as well as an impediment to the fulfilment of the essential tasks these individuals ought to fulfil in, and to the benefit of, a liberal-democratic society. Moreover, again in Hungary, the Central European University, founded by George Soros, who also founded the Open Society Foundations, was forced to leave the country[49], in a blow not only to academic freedom but, more generally, to an important remaining liberal-democratic voice in Hungary.

The realisation that 'illiberalisation' of society constitutes, *inter alia*, an attack on, and erosion of, fundamental tasks and functions within society, opens an interesting link to the Court's case law with regard to Article 10 ECHR.

III. DUTIES AND RESPONSIBILITIES IN THE FACE OF ILLIBERALISM

A. ARTICLE 10 ECHR

Article 10 ECHR[50], in its second paragraph, which deals with the limitations of freedom of expression, explicitly mentions 'duties and responsibilities'. Interestingly enough, it does this in a way which seems to pre-suppose their existence quite apart from any legal translation and, in fact, as a background

---

[47] Miriam Elder (2013), "Russia raids human rights groups in crackdown on 'foreign agents'", 27 March 2013, *theguardian.com*, https://www.theguardian.com/world/2013/mar/27/russia-raids-human-rights-crackdown.

[48] Griff Witte (2018), "Two hundred names appeared on an enemies list in Hungary. Thousands more asked to join", *washingtonpost.com*, 15 May 2018 https://www.washingtonpost.com/news/worldviews/wp/2018/05/15/two-hundred-names-appeared-on-an-enemies-list-in-hungary-thousands-more-asked-to-join.

[49] Shaun Walker (2018), "'Dark day for freedom': Soros-affiliated university quits Hungary", *theguardian.com*, 3 December 2018, https://www.theguardian.com/world/2018/dec/03/dark-day-freedom-george-soros-affiliated-central-european-university-quits-hungary.

[50] "1. Everyone has the right to freedom of expression. This right shall include freedom to hold opinions and to receive and impart information and ideas without interference by public authority and regardless of frontiers. This Article shall not prevent States from requiring the licensing of broadcasting, television or cinema enterprises.
2. The exercise of these freedoms, *since it carries with it duties and responsibilities*, may be subject to such formalities, conditions, restrictions or penalties as are prescribed by law and are necessary in a democratic society, in the interests of national security, territorial integrity or public safety, for the prevention of disorder or crime, for the protection of health or morals, for the protection of the reputation or rights of others, for preventing the disclosure of information received in confidence, or for maintaining the authority and impartiality of the judiciary." (stress added)

to, and justification of, legal limitations on individuals' freedom of expression. Such legal limitations must ultimately still fulfil the 'classic' three conditions: They must be prescribed by law, fulfil a legitimate aim, and be proportional to the aim pursued, i.e., they must be necessary in a democratic society. The reference to 'duties and responsibilities', therefore, does not allow for implied limitations.[51]

The aims, due to their wide formulation, rarely provide a problem for States aiming to justify a particular restriction (rather, the problem with the imposed obligations is usually to be found in their necessity in a democratic society). They all envisage, in very broad lines, areas in which the democratic society has legitimate interests. While the 'duties and responsibilities' mentioned in Article 10 ECHR therefore undoubtedly also include correlative duties (i.e., horizontal duties by the duty-bearer to respect a right directly held by another individual), this category of duties constitutes only one of the legitimate aims enabling the State to impose restrictions on individuals' freedom of expression. The other categories, in fact, constitute duties and responsibilities which more commonly benefit individuals via mediation by the liberal-democratic State, i.e., in fact, the *democratic society* so often referred to in the Court's case law. It is the community as a whole which expects the individual to contribute to 'national security', 'territorial integrity', 'public safety' and the 'authority and impartiality of the judiciary', but also to pay attention to the reputation, health and morals of others, *following which* individuals benefit individually.

The duties and responsibilities in art. 10 ECHR therefore are not 'human rights duties' *per se*, i.e., they are not merely those which correlate to existing individual human rights. They are, in the first place, *liberal-democratic* duties and responsibilities, i.e., duties and responsibilities which the liberal-democratic *society* has a justified expectation that the individual will indeed fulfil. While it is the State that will ultimately enforce these duties and responsibilities, these duties and responsibilities do not simply serve the State, regardless of the aims pursued by the State. Instead, they serve the liberal-democratic society, and, consequently, the State cannot impose obligations which are not strictly necessary in such a society. This is, after all, the very reason why the Court acts as the ultimate supervisor and verifies whether the imposed obligations are, in fact, necessary in a democratic society.

---

51   D.J. Harris, M. O'Boyle, E.P. Bates and C.M. Buckley (2014), *Law of the European Convention on Human Rights*, Oxford: Oxford University Press, 683.

B. THE COURT AND THE IMPORTANCE OF OFFICES AND FUNCTIONS

How then is this reference to 'duties and responsibilities' invoked by the Court? It seems the Court refers to 'duties and responsibilities' in its necessity test, when it evaluates the proportionality of restrictions placed by a State on an individual's freedom of expression. While all individuals have duties and responsibilities when exercising their freedom of expression[52], the Court hereby regularly links the notion to the institutionalised roles people fulfil in society, and especially to their professional functions, in order to identify the specific duties and responsibilities these professionals hold. Logically, the pre-legal duties and responsibilities may go further than what is strictly necessary in a democratic society. What is strictly necessary only indicates the limits of the legal obligation imposed on the individual, i.e. the legal restriction of the right. In other words, when judges are legally expected to be impartial[53], that legal obligation is clearly rooted in a duty that goes beyond what can be legally established and sanctioned. We, as a society, count on our judges to be *truly* impartial, and expect them to strive for the greatest possible impartiality.

The case law of the Court is rife with examples where the Court identifies duties and responsibilities in function of the institutional role people fulfil in the liberal-democratic society – i.e. the functions society counts on them to perform – as well as the specific impact they may have because of their specific function. In what follows, we provide a few examples.

Civil servants, for instance, have been held to have a duty of loyalty and discretion.[54] As the Court explained, "[s]ince the mission of civil servants in a democratic society is to assist the government in discharging its functions, and since the public has a right to expect that they will help and not hinder the democratically elected government, the duty of loyalty and reserve assumes special significance for them. In addition, in view of the very nature of their position, civil servants often have access to information which the government, for various legitimate reasons, may have an interest in keeping confidential or secret. Therefore, the duty of discretion owed by civil servants will also generally be a strong one."[55]

---

52   See, for instance, *Stoll v. Switzerland* [GC], judgment of 10 December 2007, no. 69698/01, ECHR 2007-V, § 102; *Lindon, Otchakovsky-Laurens and July v. France* [GC], judgment of 22 October 2007, nos. 21279/02 and 36448/02, ECHR 2007-IV, § 51.

53   *Baka v. Hungary* [GC], judgment of 23 June 2016, no. 20261/12, § 164.

54   See, a.o., *Baka v. Hungary* [GC], judgment of 23 June 2016, no. 20261/12, § 162; *Guja v. Moldova* [GC], judgment of 12 February 2008, no. 14277/04, ECHR 2008, § 70; *Rekvényi v. Hungary* [GC], judgment of 20 May 1999, no. 25390/94, ECHR 1999-III, § 43; *Vogt v. Germany* [GC], judgment of 26 September 1995, Series A no. 323, § 59.

55   *Guja v. Moldova* [GC], judgment of 12 February 2008, no. 14277/04, ECHR 2008, § 71.

Public officials in the judiciary, for their part, should show restraint, and protect the authority and impartiality of the judiciary.[56] Even the dissemination of information that is fully accurate, must occur "with moderation and propriety."[57] In the exercise of their adjudicatory function, judges are required to exercise maximum discretion regarding the cases they are dealing with so as to "preserve their image as impartial judge."[58] The Court stressed that "each judge is responsible for promoting and protecting judicial independence."[59]

As regards **lawyers,** the Court has held that, "[i]n their capacity as officers of the court, they are subject to restrictions on their conduct, which must be discreet, honest and dignified", in return for which "they also benefit from exclusive rights and privileges that may vary from one jurisdiction to another – among them, usually, a certain latitude regarding arguments used in court."[60] The Court explained that their "special status [...] gives them a central position in the administration of justice as intermediaries between the public and the courts,"[61] and that this "explains the usual restrictions on the conduct of members of the Bar."[62] It added that, "[m]oreover, the courts – the guarantors of justice, whose role is fundamental in a State based on the rule of law – must enjoy public confidence. Regard being had to the key role of lawyers in this field, it is legitimate to expect them to contribute to the proper administration of justice, and thus to maintain public confidence therein."[63]

Police officers, too, are held to have special duties and responsibilities[64], the Court maintaining that they "play a primordial role in ensuring internal order and security and fighting crime." Therefore, "[t]he duty of loyalty and reserve

---

[56] *Baka v. Hungary* [GC], judgment of 23 June 2016, no. 20261/12, § 164; *Wille v. Liechtenstein* [GC], judgment of 28 October 1999, no. 28396/95, ECHR 1999-VII, § 64.

[57] *Baka v. Hungary* [GC], judgment of 23 June 2016, no. 20261/12, § 164.

[58] *Baka v. Hungary* [GC], judgment of 23 June 2016, no. 20261/12, § 164.

[59] *Baka v. Hungary* [GC], judgment of 23 June 2016, no. 20261/12, § 168; see, in general also *Poyraz v. Turkey*, judgment of 7 December 2010, no. 15966/06, § 55 et seq.; see also *Harabin v. Slovakia*, decision as to the admissibility of 29 June 2004, no. 62584/00.

[60] *Steur v. the Netherlands*, judgment of 28 October 2003, no. 39657/98, ECHR 2003-XI, § 38; see also *Veraart v. the Netherlands*, judgment of 30 November 2006, no. 10807/04, § 51.

[61] *Nikula v. Finland*, judgment of 21 March 2002, no. 31611/96, ECHR 2002-II, § 45. see also *Schöpfer v. Switzerland*, judgment of 20 May 1998, *Reports of Judgments and Decisions* 1998-III, § 29; and Casado Coca v. Spain, judgment of 24 February 1994, Series A no. 285-A, § 54.

[62] *Nikula v. Finland*, judgment of 21 March 2002, no. 31611/96, ECHR 2002-II, § 45. see also *Schöpfer v. Switzerland*, judgment of 20 May 1998, *Reports of Judgments and Decisions* 1998-III, § 29; and *Casado Coca v. Spain*, judgment of 24 February 1994, Series A no. 285-A, § 54.

[63] *Nikula v. Finland*, judgment of 21 March 2002, no. 31611/96, ECHR 2002-II, § 45; see also *Schöpfer v. Switzerland*, judgment of 20 May 1998, *Reports of Judgments and Decisions* 1998-III, § 29.

[64] See *Trade Union of the Police in the Slovak Republic and Others v. Slovakia*, judgment of 25 September 2012, no. 11828/08, § 67.

assumes special significance for them, similarly as in the case of civil servants."[65] They also face a requirement of discipline.[66] The Court agreed "that police officers should act in an impartial manner when expressing their views so that their reliability and trustworthiness in the eyes of the public be maintained."[67] The neutrality of the police force is also important, and can require special restrictions, especially in view of a country's particular history.[68]

Military personnel, too, are faced with special duties and responsibilities, as "the proper functioning of an army is hardly imaginable without legal rules designed to prevent servicemen from undermining military discipline."[69] The Court held that there exists a "legitimate interest of a democratic State in ensuring that its army properly furthers the purposes enumerated in Article 10 § 2".[70] Soldiers thus have to remain discreet when it comes to the performance of their duties and the exercises they conduct[71], and must make sure their force retains credibility and enjoys public confidence.[72] As it also held with regard to police officers[73], the Court noted that, [b]earing in mind the role of the army in society, [...] it is a legitimate aim in any democratic society to have a politically neutral army".[74]

Secret agents were also regarded as having special duties and responsibilities, since they must "ensure that their conduct does not undermine the confidence active members may have in their present and future security".[75]

The Court also identified **teachers** as having special duties and responsibilities, which seem to include at least not "tak[ing] advantage of [their] position to indoctrinate or exert improper influence in another way on [...] pupils during lessons."[76]

---

[65] *Trade Union of the Police in the Slovak Republic and Others v. Slovakia*, judgment of 25 September 2012, no. 11828/08, § 69.

[66] *Szima v. Hungary*, judgment of 9 October 2012, no. 29723/11, § 32.

[67] *Trade Union of the Police in the Slovak Republic and Others v. Slovakia*, judgment of 25 September 2012, no. 11828/08, § 70.

[68] *Rekvényi v. Hungary* [GC], judgment of 20 May 1999, no. 25390/94, ECHR 1999-III.

[69] *Engel and Others v. the Netherlands*, 8 June 1976, Series A no. 22, § 100; see in general also *Hadjianastassiou v. Greece*, 16 December 1992, Series A no. 252, § 46; and *Rekvényi v. Hungary* [GC], judgment of 20 May 1999, no. 25390/94, ECHR 1999-III, § 43; see also *Vereinigung demokratischer Soldaten Österreichs and Gubi v. Austria*, judgment of 19 December 1994, Series A no. 302, §§ 35-36.

[70] *Lahr v. Germany*, decision as to the admissibility of 1 July 2008, no. 16912/05.

[71] *Pasko v. Russia*, judgment of 22 October 2009, no. 69519/01, § 86.

[72] *Matelly v. France*, decision as to the admissibility of 15 September 2009, 30330/04. The case concerned the '*gendarmerie*' as branch of the military.

[73] *Rekvényi v. Hungary* [GC], judgment of 20 May 1999, no. 25390/94, ECHR 1999-III, § 42.

[74] *Erdel v. Germany*, decision as to the admissibility of 13 February 2007, no. 30067/04.

[75] *Blake v. the United Kingdom*, decision as to the admissibility of 25 October 2005, no. 68890/01, § 159.

[76] *Vogt v. Germany* [GC], judgment of 26 September 1995, Series A no. 323, § 60.

The Court went on to expand on the special duties and responsibilities of **politicians**, by positing that it is crucial that politicians refrain from discourse which promotes intolerance[77] and do not spend public funds in a discriminatory way.[78] Politicians, moreover, 'should be especially attentive to the protection of democracy and its principles, as their ultimate goal is to get into a position of power'.[79]

Considerable attention has been afforded to the duties and responsibilities of members of the **press**, whose main task is 'to impart information and ideas on all matters of public interest'.[80] The press, it is often said, fulfils a 'vital role' in liberal-democratic society, serving as "public watchdog."[81] Journalists are expected to "[act] in good faith and on an accurate factual basis and provide 'reliable and precise' information in accordance with the ethics of journalism."[82] The Court added that "[t]hese considerations play a particularly important role nowadays, given the influence wielded by the media in contemporary society: not only do they inform, they can also suggest by the way in which they present the information how it is to be assessed. In a world in which the individual is confronted with vast quantities of information circulated via traditional and electronic media and involving an ever-growing number of players, monitoring compliance with journalistic ethics takes on added importance."[83]

Finally, to conclude the list of examples, **publishers**, too, are accorded duties and responsibilities, and "are vicariously subject to the 'duties and responsibilities' which authors take on when they disseminate their writing".[84]

---

77 *Féret v. Belgium*, judgment of 16 July 2009, no. 15615/07, § 75; *Erbakan v. Turkey*, judgment of 6 July 2006, no. 59405/00, § 64.

78 *Willem v. France*, Judgment of 16 July 2009, no. 10883/05, § 37.

79 *Féret v. Belgium*, judgment of 16 July 2009, no. 15615/07, § 75.

80 See, for instance, *Satakunnan Markkinapörssi Oy and Satamedia Oy v. Finland* [GC], judgment of 27 June 2017, no. 931/13, 27 June 2017, § 125.

81 See, for instance, *Satakunnan Markkinapörssi Oy and Satamedia Oy v. Finland* [GC], judgment of 27 June 2017, no. 931/13, 27 June 2017, § 126; *Leempoel & S.A. ED. Ciné Revue v. Belgium*, judgment of 9 November 2006, no. 64772/01, § 65; *Chauvy and Others v. France*, judgment of 29 June 2004, no. 64915/01, ECHR 2004-VI, § 67; *Éditions Plon v. France*, judgment of 18 May 2004, no. 58148/00, ECHR 2004-IV, § 43; *Bladet Tromsø and Stensaas v. Norway* [GC], judgment of 20 May 1999, no. 21980/93, ECHR 1999-III, § 68.

82 *Stoll v. Switzerland* [GC], judgment of 10 December 2007, no. 69698/01, ECHR 2007-V, § 103; *Magyar Helsinki Bizottság v. Hungary* [GC], judgment of 8 November 2016, no. 18030/11, § 159; *Leempoel & S.A. ED. Ciné Revue v. Belgium*, judgment of 9 November 2006, no. 64772/01, § 66.

83 *Stoll v. Switzerland* [GC], judgment of 10 December 2007, no. 69698/01, ECHR 2007-V, § 104.

84 *Éditions Plon v. France*, judgment of 18 May 2004, no. 58148/00, ECHR 2004-IV, § 50; *Öztürk v. Turkey* [GC], judgment of 28 September 1999, no. 22479/93, ECHR 1999-VI, § 49.

C.   DUTIES AND RESPONSIBILITIES AS A CATALOGUE OF RIGHTS

It is clear that the journalist who exposes corruption by a politician, does not in the first place have a duty correlating to another individual's primary right (although other individuals do have a right to receive information). Rather, the liberal-democratic society has a legitimate interest in such behaviour being exposed and halted, and therefore counts on the journalist as the 'public watchdog'.

Similarly, the judge has a duty to be impartial and independent. Surely, in doing so, he is fulfilling the right to a fair trial of the defendant. However, as an organ of the State, the judge's duty can hardly be regarded as a horizontal correlative duty to the defendant's human right. The judge, in the first place, owes it to society to take seriously the role assigned to him, since society relies on the judge to guarantee justice to all.

It seems, then, that the duties and responsibilities in Article 10 ECHR betray a much broader logic than is apparent at first sight. Liberal democracy, the only ideology compatible with the European Convention, entails its own set of behavioural expectations. What emerges from the Court's case law is therefore a set of liberal-democratic duties and responsibilities which, *inter alia* (but not exclusively) connects to offices and functions in a democratic society, and which can be held to be pre-supposed by the Convention.

While these duties and responsibilities are often associated with what limits an individual, allowing States to use them as a basis when imposing necessary legal obligations, the result can also be seen as a call for action at the individual level. In times of rising illiberalism, most notably in the form of populism, which entails *par excellence* an attack on the institutionalised roles and functions essential for a democratic society, Article 10 § 2 ECHR provides a glimpse of a rallying cry of decentralised action – liberal resistance, if you want – in favour of liberal democracy. In the logic of the European Convention on Human Rights, judges, lawyers, civil servants, teachers, publishers and journalists all have duties and responsibilities. However, they owe these duties and responsibilities to liberal-democratic society, and not in the first place to the State. The State can only impose obligations on individuals based on these duties and responsibilities, in as far as these obligations involve a legitimate aim and are *necessary in a democratic society*. The individual who seeks to preserve the freedom of his society, can, therefore, invoke his duties and responsibilities as rights against the illiberal(ising) State, when the imposed obligations are contrary to what a democratic society requires. The journalist who exposes governmental corruption, the magistrate who calls on his colleagues to resist regime pressure and remain independent, the civil servant who refuses to release confidential personal information, the teacher who takes a stand against State propaganda: they all have the Convention on their side. A few remarks are in order here.

First of all, there are more examples in the Court's case-law of duties and responsibilities, connected to functions, which the space of this contribution does not allow me to elaborate upon. However, there is no reason why the logic of the connection of special duties and responsibilities to professional functions should be limited to the cases explicitly mentioned in the Court's case law. In the logic of the Convention, everyone has duties and responsibilities, although the nature and scope of these duties and responsibilities will differ in function of, *inter alia*, one's specific role and impact on society, the ways in which society relies on this particular role, and the individual's role in a particular time and place.

Second, duties and responsibilities connected specifically to functions are not absolute. They function as essential priorities which are to be heeded in function of liberal democracy, as it is conceived of here and now, and they may need to be balanced by other duties and responsibilities. Moreover, their scope and content depend on the division of labour within a given liberal-democratic society, and they are, therefore, the consequence of an explicit as well as implicit societal negotiation. What is necessary in one society at a given time, may not be necessary in another society, or at another time. Town criers and street lighters used to be essential to the functioning of society, but their functions are redundant today. Ethical codes may have different details in different jurisdictions. However, the broad lines are nevertheless clear, and the case law can, therefore, reveal general rules to live by. Judges must be impartial and independent, journalists must provide precise and reliable information, civil servants must be discreet with the information they process, and politicians must refrain from sparking intolerance. Guidelines and rules which are not compatible with these principles have no place in twenty-first century, European liberal-democracy, and the onus is on those governments who think otherwise to make a case for deviating from them.

Third, invoking duties and responsibilities as rights, does not, from a legal perspective, give them an autonomous meaning. The applicable legal test for determining whether a restriction on an individual's right – *in casu* the right to comply with one's liberal-democratic duties and responsibilities – is compatible with the Convention, must still follow the rules set out in the Convention, e.g., in the case of Article 10 ECHR, the threefold consideration of legality, legitimate aim, and necessity in a democratic society. Nevertheless, the awareness of one's individual power, by regarding duties and responsibilities as rights, can contribute to sustaining the Convention's liberal-democratic framework, in the face of a creeping (and sometimes outright) illiberalisation of society.

CONCLUSION

The American president, John F. Kennedy, once famously declared, "And so, my fellow Americans: ask not what your country can do for you – ask what you can do for your country. My fellow citizens of the world: ask not what America will do for you, but what together we can do for the freedom of man."[85]

As it turns out, part of the response to the questions Kennedy proposed for humankind's consideration can be found in the case law of Article 10 ECHR. In this contribution I have focused on the duties and responsibilities connected to one's function in a democratic society, that is to say, through one's profession. One thing that individuals can do for their country, and for the 'freedom of man', is to be aware of the critical role each plays in upholding the liberal-democratic framework. While this may sound abstract at first, the case law of the European Court of Human Rights has been steadily providing a catalogue of principles which each 'individual', in their own way, with respect to their own function in society, and in view of their capacities, can use as a guide, thereby claiming duties and responsibilities as tools to promote freedom.

---

[85] J.F. Kennedy, *Inaugural address*, Washington DC, 20 January 1961, https://www.jfklibrary. org/Research/Research-Aids/Ready-Reference/JFK-Quotations/Inaugural-Address.aspx.

DEBATING RITUAL SLAUGHTER IN BELGIUM: A MULTILEVEL FUNDAMENTAL RIGHTS PERSPECTIVE[*]

Gerhard VAN DER SCHYFF
Associate Professor, Department of Public Law and Governance
Law School, Tilburg University, The Netherlands

Stefan SOTTIAUX
Professor, Leuven Centre for Public Law, KU Leuven, Belgium
Attorney Bar of Antwerp

INTRODUCTION

A topic that has attracted popular and scholarly attention for many years is that of ritual slaughter.[1] Or rather, legislation requiring that animals be stunned before slaughter without exceptions for ritual slaughter practices. Switzerland was one of the first countries to ban the slaughter of animals without prior stunning in 1893.[2] Other countries followed suit, such as Norway in 1930

---

[*]   This contribution was completed before the Constitutional Court of Belgium on 4 April 2019 (case 2019-053) requested preliminary rulings from the European Court of Justice on the topic of ritual slaughter.

[1]   J.W. Sap, C.M. Zoethout and G. van der Schyff, *Ritual Slaughter, Animal Welfare and the Freedom of Religion*, VU University Press, Amsterdam, 2017; G. van der Schyff, "Ritual slaughter and religious freedom in a multilevel Europe: the wider importance of the Dutch case", *Oxford Journal of Law and Religion* 2014, (76); C.M. Zoethout, "Ritual slaughter and the freedom of religion: some reflections on a stunning matter", *Human Rights Quarterly* 2013, (651); M.-C. Foblets and J. Velaers, "Godsdienstvrijheid en het onbedwelmd slachten van dieren" in D. De ruysscher, P. De Hert and M. De Metsenaere (eds.), *Een leven van inzet. Liber amicorum Michel Magits*, Kluwer, Mechelen, 2013, (375) 379–381; P. Lerner and A.M. Rabello, "The prohibition of ritual slaughtering (kosher schehita and halal) and freedom of religion of minorities", *Journal of Law and Religion* 2006/2007, (9); W.A.R. Shadid and P.S. van Koningsveld, "Legal adjustments for religious minorities: the case for the ritual slaughtering of animals" in W.A.R. Shadid and P.S. van Koningsveld (eds.), *Islam in Dutch Society: Current Developments and Future Prospects*, Kok Pharos, Kampen, 1992, (2).

[2]   See Zoethout, 2013, note 1, 660.

and Sweden in 1938, with Denmark being one of the most recent additions to the list in 2014.[3] The issue is also one of debate in other countries, such as the Netherlands where a second legislative attempt is currently underway to introduce blanket stunning, after a previous attempt was defeated in the Senate in 2012.[4] In 2018, the vice-chancellor of Austria called for all animals to be stunned prior to slaughter, thereby scrapping religious exemptions.[5] The trend to require the stunning of all animals has not been repeated in Germany, where in 2002 the country's Constitutional Court upheld the right of a Muslim butcher to slaughter animals without prior stunning.[6]

A blanket requirement to stun animals leads to questions about the extent to which freedom of religion may be limited in the process. This is because followers of Islam and Judaism often reject the stunning of an animal when it is slaughtered as not being in accordance with their religious precepts. The issue of allowing ritual slaughter raises various questions about the exercise of freedom of religion in relation to animal welfare, which is the usual reason advanced for requiring the stunning of animals.

The case of Belgium presents a current-day example of where prohibiting ritual slaughter by requiring the blanket stunning of animals questions the right to freedom of religion.[7] Belgium is particularly of interest as the country's federal structure means that each of the three regions is free to legislate on the topic. While the regions of Wallonia and Flanders have recently insisted on blanket stunning irrespective of religious objections, the capital region of Brussels has not followed suit. This state of affairs raises interesting questions from a national perspective, but also from a supranational angle. The multilevel architecture of the European constitutional space means that the question is no longer a purely national one, as it might have been a number of decades ago. National jurisdictions, including political institutions and courts, have to consider supranational requirements in deciding the question of ritual slaughter. In this regard, the right to freedom of religion as protected in Article 9 of the European Convention on Human Rights (ECHR) has come to play an important role in debating the issue. While this provision is of central importance, European Union (EU) law is increasingly becoming important to the topic of ritual slaughter too.

---

3   *Ibid.* See also the report *Legal Restrictions on Religious Slaughter in Europe* of March 2018 drafted by the Staff of the Global Legal Research Center, especially 4–6 for Denmark. The Report can be accessed at: https://www.loc.gov/law/help/religious-slaughter/religious-slaughter-europe.pdf.
4   See Van der Schyff, 2014, 83 regarding the first attempt. For the second bill, see Dutch House of Representatives, 2017–2018, II, 34 908, Nos. 1–3.
5   As reported in *The Jerusalem Post*, see https://www.jpost.com/Diaspora/Far-right-Austrian-leader-calls-for-ban-on-ritual-slaughter-563287.
6   BVerfG, Judgment of the First Senate of 15 January 2002 – 1 BvR 1783/99.
7   See C. De Coster, "Hoe koosjer is onverdoofd slachten?", *Rechtskundig Weekblad* 2017, (1563).

This contribution will consider the question of whether prohibiting ritual slaughter by requiring the blanket stunning of animals infringes the right to freedom of religion as it applies in Belgium. In what follows the notion of ritual slaughter will be explained more closely, after which the attention will be turned to the state of play in the Belgian context, as measured against that country's Constitution and applicable ECHR and EU law.

I. RITUAL SLAUGHTER EXPLAINED

Ritual slaughter can be defined as an act motivated by religious belief whereby an animal is slaughtered following the precepts of the religion concerned. Ritual slaughter is sometimes also referred to as religious slaughter. The terms can be used interchangeably. This contribution will use the term ritual slaughter seeing the prevalence of its use in academic literature and in the popular and legislative debate in Belgium.

Islam and Judaism come to the fore when ritual slaughter is discussed. In Islam the practice is known as *dhabihah* and *schechita* in Judaism. Both these religions require special procedures to be followed in slaughtering qualifying warm vertebrates for human consumption.[8] Meat not prepared according to each religion's dictates is considered unfit for human consumption. Although different in some respects, both religions prohibit their followers from ingesting blood. As a consequence, the slaughterer is required to cut an animal's throat allowing its blood to drain. In Islam the slaughterer may also be Christian or Jewish if they are not a Muslim, whereas Jewish law requires a follower of that faith to perform the act. Meat not so prepared is considered *haram* or forbidden in Islam, and *kosher* in Judaism if prepared properly.

The issue from a legal angle, and especially a human rights perspective, concerns the stunning of animals that are slaughtered combined with a religion's rejection of such stunning. Proponents of stunning advance that it reduces the animal's suffering when it is killed.[9] Stunning can take various forms such as gassing an animal, applying electrical current or shooting a bolt through its head.[10]

---

8   Zoethout, 2013, note 1, 652–657.
9   Federation of Veterinarians of Europe, *Slaughter of Animals without Prior Stunning* (FVE/02/104) (2002), (www.fve.org/news/position_papers/animal_welfare/fve_02_104_slaughter_prior_stunning.pdf, accessed 16 May 2018); Zoethout, 2013, note 1, 657–659.
10   See the Final Report of 25 June 2007 entitled *Study on the Stunning/Killing Practices in Slaughterhouses and Their Economic, Social and Environmental Consequences. Part I Red Meat*, 11ff prepared for the Directorate General for Health and Consumer Protection of the European Commission http://ec.europa.eu/food/animal/welfare/slaughter/report_parti_en.pdf.

The effect of stunning can be reversible, where an animal can be revived, or permanent, depending on the chosen method. As to the moment of stunning it can be "pre-cut", before the act of slaughter takes place, or immediately after the act, known as "post-cut" stunning. Given that the practice of stunning is not prescribed by Islam or Judaism, many adherents of these religions do not accept that stunning is compatible with their religious convictions. While some religious authority in Islam allows the stunning of an animal, not everyone agrees that stunning is compatible with ritual slaughter.[11] In the case of Judaism, stunning is often rejected as incompatible with religious slaughter.

The tension inherent between those calling for the stunning of all animals and those rejecting it on religious grounds calls for closer inspection. As explained in the introduction, the Belgian context will be used to discuss this tension.

II. FEDERATING THE KINGDOM OF BELGIUM AND ANIMAL WELFARE

While federations are often the product of centrifugal forces that forge a new state out of existing territories, Belgium is an example of where a once model unitary state has been the topic of decentralisation to such an extent that a federation was born. The constitutional revision of 1993 acknowledged that the country was a federation, although it could probably have been called a federation long before that.

As a consequence of the country's far-reaching federalisation, various topics were entrusted to the cultural and linguistic communities and territorial regions that together form the sub-entities of the federal kingdom. For present purposes the regions are more important than the three communities. This is because each region is now competent to legislate on the topic of animal welfare. Prior to federalisation the welfare of animals was a topic regulated by national and federal legislation. For instance, the law of 22 March 1929 made cruelty to animals a crime, thereby augmenting the Penal Code that criminalised the killing of animals in some instances.[12] Other legislation was to follow, such as the law of 2 July 1975 regarding the protection of animals and the law of 14 August 1986 regarding the protection and welfare of animals.[13] The purpose of this latter law includes the general welfare of animals in addition to protecting them from cruelty. Chapter Six of the 1986 law regulates the killing of animals. The point of

---

[11]   See Zoethout, 2013, note 1, 666.
[12]   Articles 538–542 of the Penal Code; *BS* 29 March 1929.
[13]   *BS* 18 July 1975; *BS* 3 December 1986.

departure is that vertebrates are only to be killed and slaughtered after stunning.[14] However, Article 16(1)(2) exempted ritual slaughter from the injunction to stun animals.

Although discussed in adopting the law of 1986, it was felt that extending the injunction to stun to also include ritual slaughter would restrict the right to freedom of religion too much.[15] The exemption was challenged in 2004 by a bill tabled by Jean-Marie De Decker in the Senate wanting to cancel the religious exemption from stunning animals.[16] The Council of State, however, was critical of the bill. The Council has a double function, it is the Administrative Supreme Court but also comprises a section that acts as an advisory body in legislative and statutory matters. It is in this latter capacity that the Council advised that:

> "In the final instance, with the abolition, in the interest of animal welfare, of the exception from the requirement of prior stunning in the event of ritual slaughter, freedom of religion as guaranteed in Article 9 of the Convention is disproportionately affected. As a consequence, some believers would no longer have the possibility to purchase and eat meat that they consider to be in accordance with religious rules."[17]

The bill was not taken further as parliament was disbanded for new elections. While the 1986 law was amended to regulate the location of slaughter and the qualifications of the slaughterer, the religious exemption stayed intact.[18]

The status quo came to be challenged after the federalisation of animal welfare as a consequence of the Sixth Constitutional Reform of Belgium. The Reform meant that as of 1 July 2014 the three Belgian regions became responsible for animal welfare. To date bills have been tabled in all three regional parliaments

---

[14] Articles 15, 16 of the 1986 law.

[15] Additional reports (commissions of justice and agriculture/small business), *Parl.St.* Senate 1982–1983, No. 469/11, 16–20; Report (joint commissions of justice and agriculture/small business), *Parl.St.* Chamber 1985–1986, No. 264/10, 20–23.

[16] Amendment bill of the law of 5 September 1952 on meat inspection and trade and the law of 14 August 1986 on the protection and welfare of animals, regarding ritual slaughter, *Parl.St.* Senate 2003–2004, No. 3-808/1, 36 and 38 (Article 7).

[17] Council of State, Legislative Division, Opinion No. 40.350/AV of 16 May 2006, *Parl.St.* Senate 2005–2006, No. 3-808/6, 6. Authors' translation of: "*Ten slotte wordt met de afschaffing van de afwijking van het vereiste van voorafgaande verdoving in geval van rituele slachting, teneinde het dierenwelzijn te bevorderen, op een onevenredige wijze afbreuk gedaan aan de vrijheid van godsdienst die is vastgelegd bij artikel 9 van het Verdrag. Hierdoor zouden sommige gelovigen geen enkele mogelijkheid meer hebben vlees aan te schaffen en te eten dat door hen conform met de religieuze voorschriften wordt geacht.*"

[18] Law of 7 February 2014 regarding animal welfare, international trade in wildlife and plants and animal health, *BS* 28 February 2014, which added a third paragraph to Article 16 of the 1986 law.

aiming to scrap the religious exemption for ritual slaughter in the 1986 law. In what follows the position in the Brussels Capital Region is outlined briefly before the discussion turns to the position in Flanders and Wallonia.

A.   BRUSSELS CAPITAL REGION

A few attempts have been made to scrap the religious exemption from the 1986 law on animal welfare in the Brussels parliament. The first bill was tabled by Dominiek Lootens-Stael on 1 October 2014.[19] The proposal was rejected by a majority. On 3 February 2017 and 6 March 2018, further bills were tabled by other members, again aimed at scrapping the exemption.[20] For the time being though, the religious exemption from stunning still applies in Brussels.

B.   FLEMISH REGION

After the Flemish Parliament became responsible for animal welfare two bills were tabled intending to extend the requirement to stun to all animals selected for slaughter. The first bill was tabled in October 2014 by Hermes Sanctorum, then of the Greens, and the second by a group of parliamentarians from the *Vlaams Belang* party in May of 2015.[21]

As it did regarding De Decker's earlier bill in the Senate, the Council of State was critical of these attempts at scrapping the religious exemption. In its opinion, delivered on 29 June 2016, the Council explained that:

> "As already explained in opinion 40.350/AV, the introduction of the obligation of prior stunning in the event of ritual slaughter, in order to promote animal welfare, is a disproportionate infringement of religious freedom. The proposed measures make

---

[19]   Amendment bill of the law of 14 August 1986 on the protection and welfare of animals and the law of 5 September 1952 on meat inspection and trade, in order to prohibit ritual slaughter without stunning, *Parl.St.* Brussels Parliament 2014, No. A-25/1.

[20]   Amendment bill of the law of 14 August 1986 on the protection and welfare of animals, in order to prohibit the ritual slaughter of animals without prior stunning, *Parl.St.* Brussels Parliament 2016–2017, No. A-480/1; Amendment bill of the law of 14 August 1986 on the protection and welfare of animals, on the methods allowed for slaughtering animals, *Parl.St.* Brussels Parliament 2017-2018, No. A-648/1.

[21]   Amendment bill of the law of 14 August 1986 on the protection and welfare of animals, regarding painless slaughter, *Parl.St.* Flemish Parliament 2014–2015, No. 111/1; Amendment bill of the law of 14 August 1986 on the protection and welfare of animals and the law of 5 September 1952 on meat inspection and trade, in order to prohibit ritual slaughter without stunning, *Parl.St.* Flemish Parliament 2014–2015, No. 351/1.

it disproportionately difficult for a number of religious believers to purchase and eat meat considered by them in accordance with their religious rules."[22]

The Council of State arrived at this opinion by reference to comparative law. The Council referred to a similar opinion drafted by its neighbour the Council of State of the Netherlands and a judgment by the German Federal Constitutional Court.[23] Both these bodies were critical of requiring the stunning of animals without allowing religious exemptions. The Council of State drew on the opinion of its Dutch neighbour in pointing out that animals did not possess a legal status comparable to that of humans.[24] This meant that the question of limiting ritual slaughter was not the same as deciding a case of conflicting human rights. A similar reliance was put on the German decision in explaining that animal welfare does not trump religious freedom as a matter of course.[25]

The Council of State in Belgium did not leave the matter at advising against the bills' adoption, as it suggested an alternative route. The Council suggested that an approach be taken that respects both the right to freedom of religion and the need to minimise animal suffering in a balanced way.[26] To this end it proposed (i) that animals be slaughtered in a manner that causes them death in the fastest and least painful manner, (ii) that ritual slaughter takes place solely in abattoirs provided there is enough capacity, and that (iii) the process be checked. The Council further suggested that a dialogue be started with the religious communities concerned in developing the measures.

On 7 July 2016, Ben Weyts, the Flemish minister responsible for animal welfare appointed Piet Vanthemsche as an independent party in leading the dialogue suggested by the Council of State.[27] A consultation with various stakeholders took place after which Vanthemsche presented his report on 29 March 2017. The report recommended a blanket ban on stunning, explaining that the effects of stunning had to be reversible or that post-cut stunning be practiced.[28] In his report, he

---

22   Council of State, Legislative Division, Opinions Nos. 59.484/3 and 59.485/3 of 29 June 2016, *Parl.St.* Flemish Parliament 2014–2015, No. 111/2, 15. Authors' translation of: *"Zoals reeds is uiteengezet in advies 40.350/AV wordt met de invoering van de verplichting van voorafgaande verdoving in geval van rituele slachting met het oog op de bevordering van het dierenwelzijn, op een onevenredige wijze afbreuk gedaan aan de godsdienstvrijheid. De voorgestelde maatregelen maken het immers voor een aantal gelovigen onevenredig moeilijk om vlees aan te schaffen en te consumeren dat door hen in overeenstemming met hun religieuze voorschriften wordt geacht."*
23   *Ibid.,* 13, 15, 16.
24   *Ibid.,* 15.
25   *Ibid.,* 16.
26   *Ibid.,* 16–17.
27   Amendment bill of the law of 14 August 1986 on the protection and welfare of animals, regarding permissible methods of animal slaughter, *Parl.St.* Flemish Parliament 2016–2017, No. 1213/1, 2–3.
28   Report of the exchange of views on behalf of the Committee on the Environment, Nature, Spatial Planning, Energy and Animal Welfare published by Gwenny De Vroe and Els Robeyns

acknowledged that the proposals would be acceptable for a part of the Islamic community, but would probably not be accepted by the Jewish community.[29]

The Flemish Parliament copied the proposals in the Vanthemsche Report. In this regard a law was adopted on 7 July 2017 that removed the religious exemptions when stunning animals, thereby amending the law of 1986 that applied hitherto.[30] Interestingly, the Flemish Parliament did not request an opinion from the Council of State before the adoption of the legislation.

In translating the proposals in the Vanthemsche Report, the Flemish Parliament decreed in Article 3(2) that:

> "If animals are slaughtered using methods in accordance with religious rites, the stunning must be reversible and may not result in the death of the animal."[31]

This would mean that stunning takes place by means of electric current in ensuring that it is reversible. As the technique of stunning by means of electric current is not as advanced in the case of bovine animals, a temporary exemption was allowed for such animals. Bovine animals can be subjected to post-cut stunning until such time as the Flemish Government warrants that such animals too be subjected to electric current based on technological advances.

The decree, effective from 1 January 2019, is the subject of cases brought before the Constitutional Court for its nullification for violating the right to freedom of religion.

C. WALLOON REGION

In Wallonia events took a similar course to those in Flanders after animal welfare became a regional competence. In January 2015 and October 2016 private bills were tabled aimed at ending the religious exemption from stunning animals.[32]

---

on the report regarding ritual slaughter without stunning, *Parl.St.* Flemish Parliament 2016–2017, No. 1134/1, 57–58.

[29] *Ibid.*, 58.

[30] Articles 3 and 4 of the Flemish decree of 7 July 2017 amending the law of 14 August 1986 on the protection and welfare of animals, regarding permissible methods of animal slaughter, *BS* 18 July 2017.

[31] Authors' translation of: *"Als dieren worden geslacht volgens speciale methoden die vereist zijn voor religieuze riten, is de bedwelming omkeerbaar en is de dood van het dier niet het gevolg van de bedwelming."*

[32] Amendment bill of the Act of 14 August 1986 on the protection and welfare of animals, regarding prohibiting the ritual slaughter of animals without prior stunning, *Parl.St.* Walloon Parliament 2014–2015, No. 110/1; Bill to ban slaughter without stunning in Wallonia, *Parl.St.* Walloon Parliament 2016–2017, No. 604/1.

These proposals were submitted to the Council of State for its advice, which was given on 20 February 2017.[33] In the Council's opinion, the bills would have resulted in an unjustifiable interference with the right to freedom of religion. In arriving at this view, the Council referred to previous federal and Flemish attempts at introducing similar legislation. In addition, the Council considered the bills in the light of the EU Regulation on the protection of animals at the time of killing of 2009.[34] At this juncture it becomes necessary to pay closer attention to this Regulation in following the Council's reasoning.

The Regulation on the protection of animals at the time of killing provides in Article 4(1) that animals must be stunned when slaughtered:

> "Animals shall only be killed after stunning in accordance with the methods and specific requirements related to the application of those methods set out in Annex I. The loss of consciousness and sensibility shall be maintained until the death of the animal."

However, sub-Article 4 of the same provision reads as follows:

> "In the case of animals subject to particular methods of slaughter prescribed by religious rites, the requirements of paragraph 1 shall not apply provided that the slaughter takes place in a slaughterhouse."

The matter is not left at that, as Article 26(1) of the Regulation provides that Member States are not prevented from "maintaining any national rules aimed at ensuring more extensive protection of animals" when they are slaughtered. Apart from allowing existing rules to continue carrying force, Article 26(2) allows the following:

> "Member States may adopt national rules aimed at ensuring more extensive protection of animals at the time of killing than those contained in this Regulation in relation to the following fields: (…) (c) the slaughtering and related operations of animals in accordance with Article 4(4)."

The Council of State recognised that the bills were in pursuit of a legitimate aim, especially when measured against Article 13 TFEU, which reads as follows:

> "In formulating and implementing the Union's agriculture, fisheries, transport, internal market, research and technological development and space policies, the Union and the Member States shall, since animals are sentient beings, pay full regard to the welfare requirements of animals, while respecting the legislative or

---

[33] Council of State, Legislative Division, Opinions Nos. 60.870/4 and 60.871/4 of 20 February 2017, *Parl.St.* Walloon Parliament 2016–2017, No. 604/2.

[34] Council Regulation (EC) No. 1099/2009 of 24 September 2009 on the protection of animals at the time of killing.

administrative provisions and customs of the Member States relating in particular to religious rites, cultural traditions and regional heritage."

The Council of State opined that scrapping the exemption for ritual slaughter would amount to a disproportional limitation of religious freedom, adding that it had not seen how the bills sought to achieve the correct balance between such freedom on the one hand and animal welfare on the other in the context of Article 26(2) of the Regulation.[35] This led the Council to advise that the bills be re-evaluated with respect to their derogation from the exemption from blanket stunning in the Regulation. It seems as if the Council's view stresses the second part of Article 13 TFEU, requiring of Member States to pay attention to "religious rites" in pursuing animal welfare over the opportunity to increase the standard of animal welfare set out in the Regulation.

A third bill was tabled in the Walloon Parliament on 19 April 2017 by various of its members aimed at the scrapping the exemption, in the mean time the parliamentary discussion continued of the two bills on which the Council of State had advised. A dialogue with the various stakeholders was not initiated, as it had been the case in Flanders, although interested parties were eventually heard by the relevant parliamentary commission. The Walloon Parliament adopted a decree on 18 May 2018 removing the religious exemptions from stunning from the 1986 law on animal welfare. Similar to the Flemish decree, the Walloon decree provides that ritual slaughter must entail reversible stunning and may not result in the death of the animal.[36] The decree is effective from 31 August 2019, this later date was chosen to allow for improvement in effecting reversible stunning. In studying the debates on ritual slaughter in the Walloon Parliament, it becomes clear that the Vanthemsche Report was referred to in shaping its views, given this the Flemish decree is discussed first in this contribution although the Walloon decree was adopted first.

III. RITUAL SLAUGHTER AND HIGHER LAW

The pertinent question, having discussed the Flemish and Walloon decrees, relates to their treatment in terms of higher law. Can the decrees, which remove the religious exemptions from stunning in their respective regions be justified? In addressing this question, the decrees will be discussed together given their near simultaneous adoption and scope. Attention will first be paid to the Constitution of Belgium, after which ECHR and EU law will each feature respectively.

---

[35] Council of State, Legislative Division, Opinions Nos. 60.870/4 and 60.871/4 of 20 February 2017, *Parl.St.* Walloon Parliament 2016–2017, No. 604/2, 8–9.

[36] Articles 2 and 3 of the Walloon decree of 18 May 2017 amending Articles 3, 15 and 16 and including Article 45*ter* in the law of 14 August 1986 regarding the protection and welfare of animals, *BS* 1 June 2017.

A. CONSTITUTION OF BELGIUM

In evaluating the decrees the most striking issue that arises under the Constitution pertains to the separation between state and religion. Belgium is known for having a close relationship with officially recognised religions, in that such religions enjoy state funding. To this end, Article 181(1) of the Constitution provides that the state pays the salaries and pensions of ministers of religion. The "nearness" between the state and religion, to use Winfried Brugger's classification, is offset by various other Articles.[37] For instance, Article 21 of the Constitution outlines a few important examples of the separation between the state and religion:

> "The State does not have the right to intervene either in the appointment or in the installation of ministers of any religion whatsoever or to forbid these ministers from corresponding with their superiors, from publishing the acts of these superiors, but, in this latter case, normal responsibilities as regards the press and publishing apply. A civil wedding should always precede the blessing of the marriage, apart from the exceptions to be established by the law if needed."[38]

The quoted provision is clearly designed to prevent the state from interfering with the governance of religions, including those benefitting from state finance. The second part of the provision emphasises the separation between the state and religion by distinguishing religious marriages from civil marriages and determining the order in which they are to be solemnised. The state is not to interfere with religion, nor may a religious practice such as marriage be sanctioned by the state. Religion enjoys freedom of action, while the state enjoys independence from religion. This conclusion is accentuated by the fact that Article 19 of the Constitution guarantees everyone the right to freedom of religion, while Article 20 reads as follows:

> "No one can be obliged to contribute in any way whatsoever to the acts and ceremonies of a religion or to observe its days of rest."[39]

The effect of the latter provision is to prohibit individuals and other parties, including the state, from requiring the observance of religion. The effect of this

---

[37] W. Brugger, "Separation, equality, nearness: three church-state models", *International Journal for the Semiotics of Law* 2012, (263).

[38] The original text reads: *"L'État n'a le droit d'intervenir ni dans la nomination ni dans l'installation des ministres d'un culte quelconque, ni de défendre à ceux-ci de correspondre avec leurs supérieurs, et de publier leurs actes, sauf, en ce dernier cas, la responsabilité ordinaire en matière de presse et de publication. Le mariage civil devra toujours précéder la bénédiction nuptiale, sauf les exceptions à établir par la loi, s'il y a lieu."*

[39] The original text reads: *"Nul ne peut être contraint de concourir d'une manière quelconque aux actes et aux cérémonies d'un culte, ni d'en observer les jours de repos."*

is to emphasise religious freedom and the separation between the state and religion.

It is in light of these interpretations of the Constitution that both the Flemish and Walloon decrees are to be evaluated. In doing so it becomes apparent that both legislatures, probably inadvertently, overstepped the separation between the state and religion.[40] By requiring that stunning has to be reversible when ritual slaughter takes place, and that the animal may not die from such stunning, a religious practice is in effect codified in law. As the legislature may not prescribe religious doctrine and practice, or force anyone to observe such doctrine or practice, it may not define a religious practice such as ritual slaughter. The effect of the legislation is to make the doctrinal development of ritual slaughter dependent on legislative approval, as legislation now codifies the practice. By overstepping the separation between the state and religion the bearers of the right to freedom of religion are now prevented from deciding for themselves how to practice their religion.

In achieving its aim of promoting animal welfare by removing religious exemptions to stunning, both legislatures should have described the acts of slaughter and stunning without reference to religion. This would have codified the practices of slaughter and stunning without also codifying a religious practice at the same time. Although a fundamental constitutional principle has been violated, the transgression can easily be rectified by reformulating the legislation while still achieving blanket stunning.

The next question concerns whether the Flemish and Walloon legislation can be said to be compatible with religious freedom.

B. EUROPEAN CONVENTION ON HUMAN RIGHTS

To date the European Court of Human Rights (ECtHR) has decided one case dealing with ritual slaughter and the right to freedom of religion in Article 9 ECHR. The case being *Cha'are Shalom Ve Tsedek v. France*, decided in 2000.[41] In this matter, the French state recognised one organisation in order for it to conduct Jewish ritual slaughter without stunning animals, but denied a second organisation similar recognition. The second organisation took issue with the thoroughness employed by the first organisation in carrying out ritual slaughter,

---

[40]   G. van der Schyff, "Recent legislation on ritual slaughter in Flanders evaluated: perspectives from the separation of state and religion and freedom of religion", *Recht, Religie en Samenleving/Droit, Religion et Société/Law, Religion and Society* 2017 (5), 10–11.

[41]   ECtHR, Application No. 27417/95, *Cha'are Shalom Ve Tsedek v. France*, judgment 27 June 2000.

hence its desire to conduct such slaughter in a stricter fashion.[42] The second, or applicant, organisation complained of France violating the right to freedom of religion by refusing it recognition and therefore making it impossible for the organisation to slaughter animals in accordance with its religious precepts.[43]

Importantly, the ECtHR recognised that ritual slaughter is protected under Article 9(1) ECHR, which not act every act motivated by religion or belief can lay claim to under the Convention. The ECtHR held that:

> "It follows that the applicant association can rely on Article 9 of the Convention with regard to the French authorities' refusal to approve it, since ritual slaughter must be considered to be covered by a right guaranteed by the Convention, namely the right to manifest one's religion in observance, within the meaning of Article 9."[44]

The next stage of the inquiry, namely whether there was an interference by the state with this right, became the deciding factor in the case. Finding an interference with the protection a right offers is usually a straightforward matter in ECtHR case law. However in *Cha'are Shalom Ve Tsedek* the ECtHR explained that there would be an interference with the right "only if the illegality of performing ritual slaughter made it impossible for" the bearers of the right to consume meat from animals "slaughtered in accordance with the religious prescriptions they considered applicable".[45] As the people concerned could import qualifying meat, incidentally from Belgium at the time, the ECtHR found that the right to ritual slaughter had not been interfered with by France.[46] The ECtHR continued that even if there had been an interference, it would have been justifiable in terms of the limitation requirements in Article 9(2) ECHR given the state's margin of appreciation.[47]

In applying *Cha'are Shalom Ve Tsedek* to the Flemish and Walloon legislation it quickly becomes clear that if people affected in the two regions could obtain qualifying meat from elsewhere, Article 9(1) ECHR would not be interfered with. Qualifying meat could probably be imported from abroad, if not accessed from Brussels where legislation still allows for religious exemptions from stunning. Although obtaining meat in this manner may be possible, some critical remarks can be made about the compatibility of the ritual slaughter legislation with the ECHR.

An important remark concerns the fact that the ECtHR set a high threshold in the case of ritual slaughter before an interference with Article 9(1) ECHR could be

---

[42]   *Ibid.*, para. 60.
[43]   *Ibid.*, paras. 58, 61. A violation of Article 14 ECHR was also pleaded.
[44]   *Ibid.*, para. 74.
[45]   *Ibid.*, para. 80.
[46]   *Ibid.*, para. 81.
[47]   *Ibid.*, para. 84.

found. The consequence of this is that although a wide and generous interpretation was given by the Court to the scope of the right by protecting ritual slaughter as such, the effectiveness of such protection was quickly put in doubt given the high threshold for establishing an interference with it.[48] Finding an interference with a right should amount to identifying a *factual* disturbance with its protection, and not to narrowing down the range of possible disturbances as the ECtHR did in *Cha'are Shalom Ve Tsedek*.[49] Setting a high threshold limits the effective protection that a bearer of the right can lay claim to as a matter of course. This places a heavy onus on the bearer to prove that their right had been interfered with, instead of shifting the onus to the state in having to justify its factual interference with religious freedom. The state is so allowed to pursue a wide range of measures regarding the right to ritual slaughter without engaging the guarantees of Article 9 ECHR. It is because of this criticism that the minority opinion in *Cha'are Shalom Ve Tsedek*, which rejected the high threshold for finding an interference, deserves support over that of the majority.[50] The consequence of adopting the minority's view would be to find that the Flemish and Walloon legislation interferes with the right to ritual slaughter in Article 9(1) ECHR.

A finding of an interference necessitates the application of the limitation provision in Article 9(2) ECHR to determine if the interference was justified, or amounted to a violation of the right in Article 9(1) ECHR. In this regard, the margin of appreciation that would have been left to France had there been an interference needs to be put in a critical perspective. The ECtHR noted that such a margin was the consequence of the "delicate relations between the Churches and the State".[51] This view is probably too wide as a general rule. In respect of the Flemish and Walloon legislation it can be argued that a number of factors necessitate the ECtHR having closer regard to the proportionality of the interference than a margin would otherwise allow. For instance, while in *Cha'are Shalom Ve Tsedek* the question was whether a second organisation had to be recognised in order to perform ritual slaughter, the Flemish and Walloon legislation makes the practice as such impossible. The interference with Article 9(1) ECHR is therefore deeper than had been the case in *Cha'are Shalom Ve Tsedek*. Also, the legislation concerns ordinary people, as opposed to for example civil servants who are bound more closely to the state and its goals in discharging their duties. This is comparable to *Arslan v. Turkey* where laws restricting ordinary

---

[48]   Advocating a wide or generous interpretation of ECHR rights that are subject to limitation, see G. van der Schyff, "Interpreting the protection guaranteed by two-stage rights in the European Convention on human rights: the case for wide interpretation", in E. Brems and J. Gerards (eds.), *Shaping Rights in the ECHR: The Role of the European Court of Human Rights in Determining the Scope of Human Rights*, Cambridge University Press, Cambridge, 2013 (65).

[49]   Van der Schyff, 2014, note 1, 91.

[50]   *Cha'are Shalom Ve Tsedek v. France*, note 41, para. 1 of the joint dissenting opinion of judges Bratza, Fischbach, Thomassen, Tsatsa-Nikolovska, Panţiru, Levits and Traja.

[51]   *Ibid.*, para. 84.

people from wearing religious attire in public were found to have been unnecessary, thereby violating Article 9(1) ECHR.[52] These points, as well as the fact that various Member States of the Council of Europe allow religious exemptions from stunning, should caution the ECtHR against adopting a (wide) margin. Instead, the bench should be encouraged to investigate whether reasonable alternatives could have been pursued by the Belgian regions in advancing animal welfare, while not overly restricting the right to freedom of religion. An example of such a reasonable alternative might be the 2012 covenant signed by various stakeholders in the Netherlands, ranging from religious representatives to the government.[53] The covenant was an attempt to increase animal welfare, while still allowing for animals not to be stunned when slaughtered according to religious rites.

A situation could also arise whereby the evidence presented to the ECtHR, or another court, leads to reasonable doubt whether animals do indeed suffer more when they are not stunned in comparison to animals that are stunned. In other words, doubts may arise about the core of the argument for allowing animal welfare concerns to prevail over the exercise of religious freedom. It is submitted than the absence of a (wide) margin would also have an effect in such cases by giving the benefit of the doubt to the bearer of the right to ritual slaughter, instead of the legislative or executive view that blanket stunning should be practised.[54] This would be a way of recognising the value of religious freedom in cases requiring stricter judicial scrutiny in the absence or reduction of a Member State's discretion in limiting ritual slaughter.

This discussion has shown that *Cha'are Shalom Ve Tsedek* may be of limited value in the case of the Flemish and Walloon legislation. As a consequence, closer scrutiny may be called for in deciding if the regional legislation is indeed necessary in a democratic society, as required by Article 9(2) ECHR.

C. CHARTER OF FUNDAMENTAL RIGHTS OF THE EUROPEAN UNION

The ECHR, as protected by the ECtHR, is an indelible fixture of human rights protection across most of the European continent. To this level of protection another layer has been added in the shape of EU law, and in particular by the Charter of Fundamental Rights (CFREU) in those Council of Europe states also

---

[52] ECtHR, App. No. 41135/98, *Arslan v. Turkey,* judgment 23 February 2010.

[53] Dutch House of Representatives, 2011–2012, 31 571, No. 22. In 2018 a private bill, critical of the covenant, was tabled. The bill wants to introduce blanket stunning in the interest of animal welfare. See Dutch House of Representatives, 2017–2018, 34 908, No. 3 (explanatory memorandum). An earlier bill was defeated in parliament after the adoption of the covenant.

[54] Van der Schyff, 2014, note 1, 99–100.

belonging to the EU. After becoming binding in 2009 with the coming into force of the Treaty of Lisbon, the CFREU has increasingly featured in the case law of the European Court of Justice (ECJ). This also holds for freedom of religion.[55] An overview of the Charter reveals the right to freedom of religion in Article 10(1):

"Everyone has the right to freedom of thought, conscience and religion. This right includes freedom to change religion or belief and freedom, either alone or in community with others and in public or in private, to manifest religion or belief, in worship, teaching, practice and observance."

In reading the provision it quickly becomes apparent that its wording is copied from Article 9(1) ECHR. This is no co-incidence, as Article 52(3) CFREU provides as follows:

"In so far as this Charter contains rights which correspond to rights guaranteed by the Convention for the Protection of Human Rights and Fundamental Freedoms, the meaning and scope of those rights shall be the same as those laid down by the said Convention. This provision shall not prevent Union law providing more extensive protection."

The law as it applies to Article 9 ECHR is therefore the point of departure in applying Article 10(1) CFREU. The level of protection guaranteed by the ECHR can be increased as the provision explains, and acts a minimum level of protection as can be deduced from Article 53 CFREU. To the extent that the Flemish and Walloon legislation implements EU law in the meaning of Article 51(1) CFREU, Article 10(1) CFREU would need to be respected. It becomes clear that by derogating from the rule that religions be exempted from stunning in Article 4(4) of the earlier mentioned Regulation on the protection of animals at the time of killing, the regional legislation indeed implements EU law and therefore attracts the protection of the right to freedom of religion in Article 10(1) CFREU.

The preceding discussion of Article 9 ECHR consequently applies to ritual slaughter in EU law as well. This means that following the ECtHR judgment in *Cha'are Shalom Ve Tsedek v. France*, Article 10(1) CFREU will not be interfered with by the Flemish and Walloon legislation, provided that qualifying meat can be obtained from elsewhere. Additionally, had the right been interfered with, a margin of appreciation might be granted that leaves the decision whether to derogate from Article 4(4) of the Regulation to the discretion of the Flemish and Walloon legislatures. However, were the doubts expressed above about a margin of appreciation to be accepted and copied to EU law, Article 10(1) CFREU would

---

[55] ECJ, C-157/15, *Achbita, Centrum voor gelijkheid van kansen en voor racismebestrijding v. G4S Secure Solutions NV*, judgment 14 March 2017; ECJ, C-188/15, *Bougnaoui, Association de défense des droits de l'homme (ADDH) v. Micropole SA*, judgment 14 March 2017.

lead to an inquiry into whether reasonable alternatives for the current legislation can be sought that lessen the interference with the right to ritual slaughter.

The argument could also be considered that EU law lends itself to a higher level of protection of freedom of religion than that foreseen by the ECHR. In this regard, the fact that Article 13 TFEU draws attention to the need to respect "religious rites" in Member States when paying "full regard" to animal welfare requirements could be read as an internal qualifier intended to highlight the importance of the right to freedom of religion, in addition to Article 10(1) CFREU. Also, the question arises whether any derogation from Article 4(4) of the Regulation may abolish its exemption from stunning for ritual slaughter altogether, or simply modify it. On a different set of facts, the ECJ held that an exception to not having to disclose certain documents could not be interpreted in such a manner as to "deprive of any practical effect" the possibility not to disclose those type of documents.[56] By analogy it could be argued that the religious exemption from stunning in Article 4(4) of the Regulation cannot be nullified through derogation on the basis of Article 26(2) of the same Regulation. In addition, the opinion of Advocate General Wahl in *Liga van Moskeeën en Islamitische Organisaties Provincie Antwerpen, VZW and Others v. Vlaams Gewest* can be mentioned as an example of where EU law might lend itself to a high level of fundamental rights protection without a clear or direct recourse to the ECHR.[57] Although the latter case concerned ritual slaughter, the facts again differ from the Flemish and Walloon legislation at issue in this contribution. In *Liga van Moskeeën en Islamitische Organisaties* the question related to whether the rule in Article 4(4) of the mentioned Regulation, requiring that ritual slaughter without stunning must *always* be conducted in approved slaughterhouses, was valid in light of the right to freedom of religion in Article 10(1) CFREU.[58] According to the Advocate General there had been no interference with the right to freedom of religion, but had there been an interference it would not have been justifiable.[59] In deciding the case, the ECJ followed the Advocate General's Opinion by holding that the contested provision of the Regulation had indeed not interfered with the right to freedom of religion, or rather caused a "restriction" of the right in the words of the bench.[60] However, leaving aside the ECJ's conclusion that there had been no interference

---

[56]   ECJ, C-673/13 P, *Commission v. Stichting Greenpeace Nederland and PAN Europe*, judgment 23 November 2016, para. 81.

[57]   ECJ, C-426/16, *Liga van Moskeeën en Islamitische Organisaties Provincie Antwerpen, VZW and Others v. Vlaams Gewest*, Opinion 30 November 2017.

[58]   Article 4(4) of the Regulation was read together with Article 2(k) of the same regulation, which provides as follows: "For the purposes of this Regulation, the following definitions shall apply: (...) (k) 'slaughterhouse' means any establishment used for slaughtering terrestrial animals which falls within the scope of Regulation EC No 853/2004".

[59]   *Ibid.*, paras. 89, 95.

[60]   ECJ, C-426/16, *Liga van Moskeeën en Islamitische Organisaties Provincie Antwerpen, VZW and Others v. Vlaams Gewest*, judgment 29 May 2018, paras. 59, 68, 79, 83–84.

with the right, the Advocate General's analysis of the merits if there had been an interference speaks of a very high level of protection of freedom of religion. This high level of protection, evidenced by the Opinion taking into account less onerous means of achieving the aim of the contested rule, is based on general EU law on how to conduct a proportionality exercise.[61] While reference is made to the ECtHR and the value of its interpretation of Article 9 ECHR, the Advocate General merely explains that such an interpretation "may (...) have some relevance for, or at least be a source of inspiration for the interpretation of Article 10 of the Charter."[62] Applied to the Flemish and Walloon legislation on ritual slaughter, the level of protection proposed by the Advocate General in *Liga van Moskeeën en Islamitische Organisaties* would require a very exacting justification in order to limit religious freedom as it does. This is because the latter case did not depart from a margin of appreciation for the state, the absence of which would have meant a rather strict proportionality exercise had Article 10(1) CFREU indeed been interfered with according to the Advocate General.

IV. ON FUNDAMENTAL RIGHTS, LAWYERS, ACADEMICS AND JUDGES

The case of ritual slaughter illustrates well the multilevel architecture in Europe when it comes to fundamental rights protection. As explained, not only do the Constitution of Belgium and the ECHR play an important role in deciding whether blanket stunning may be required in Flanders and Wallonia, but EU law is increasingly important too. Whereas lawyers, academics and judges had to master a single jurisdiction in the past, while taking some note of other jurisdictions, the current state of play is very different. Today they have to know not only one jurisdiction intimately, but a number in order to negotiate a set of facts in a meaningful and relevant way when it comes to applying higher law, and in particular fundamental rights law. It is only when the combined impact of the Constitution, the ECHR and EU law (in particular the CFREU) is understood, that the question of blanket stunning in Belgium can be considered properly. The case of ritual slaughter also shows that all may not be equal, as each jurisdiction brings with it its own questions and levels of protection. Whether the Flemish and Walloon legislation complies with fundamental rights may ultimately be a question of which jurisdiction applies. For example, whereas a margin of appreciation in the context of the ECHR might not lead to a violation of the right to freedom of religion by the two regions, the same does not follow automatically for the EU context where the concept of a margin is not (yet) as

---

61 ECJ, C-426/16, *Liga van Moskeeën en Islamitische Organisaties Provincie Antwerpen, VZW and Others v. Vlaams Gewest*, Opinion 30 November 2017, paras. 123, 128.

62 *Ibid.*, para. 48.

common, and where a higher level of protection may be provided than that set by the ECtHR. The latter seems quite plausible if the Opinion in *Liga van Moskeeën en Islamitische Organisaties* is anything to go by in determining the appropriate level for protecting the right to freedom of religion in Article 10(1) CFREU.

There is obviously a lot work still to be done in the field of fundamental rights protection in Europe, given the host of specific and general questions that a case such as ritual slaughter occasions. In this regard, the varied career of Paul Lemmens as a lawyer, a member of the Council of State of Belgium, an academic at the KU Leuven and as a judge in the ECtHR can serve as an example of how to address the overlapping and at times competing jurisdictions at play in deciding fundamental rights issues.

LIVING A LIFE IN HUMAN DIGNITY: A CONCRETE, NOT AN ABSTRACT LEGAL QUESTION

Frédéric VANNESTE

First Auditor in the Belgian Council of State
Assistant Professor University of Antwerp
Voluntary Scientific Collaborator KU Leuven

INTRODUCTION

The Grand Chamber of the ECtHR emphasized in 2015 in *Bouyid v. Belgium* that "respect for human dignity forms part of the very essence of the European Convention of Human Rights, alongside human freedom".[1] That remains a quite intriguing statement. If human dignity forms part of the very essence of human rights treaties, one may wonder what its legal implications are. That is not easy to say. Human dignity is a complex, controversial and polysemic concept.[2] Paul Lemmens is aware of that. His former human rights students probably remember he started his human rights course with a discussion on the famous "dwarf tossing" case (see also *infra*). And long before the partly dissenting opinion of judges De Gaetano, Lemmens and Mahoney in the *Bouyid* case (see *infra*), it must have been around the year 2006 when I was his teaching assistant, he also wrote a complete moot court case for students about slapping in the face, probably with the idea of discussing the concept of human dignity. These examples make me hope that Paul Lemmens might like an article on the subject.

Another reason for dealing with this concept in this *liber amicorum* is that it allows me to invite Paul Lemmens to express and develop his viewpoint on human dignity in future cases of the European Court of Human Rights, be it in a concurring or dissenting opinion, and by so doing foster more discussion which hopefully will help to refine the current approach of human rights courts.

---

[1]   ECtHR (GC), *Bouyid v. Belgium*, judgment of 28 September 2015, *Reports* 2015-V, §89.
[2]   See for instance, C.-A. Chassin, "La notion de dignité de la personne humaine dans la jurisprudence de la Cour de justice" in A. Biad and V. Parisot (ed.), *La Charte des droits fondamentaux de l'Union européenne*, Anthemis, 2018, (137) 260.

As human dignity forms part of the "very essence of the European Convention of Human Rights", a better understanding of it may appear to be crucial for a variety of (future) cases about, for instance, biogenetics, reality television, asylum cases, terrorism, prisoners treatment, prohibition of racism etc. Human dignity aims to be an overarching term, a general principle of law that gives guidance to the interpretation of all other human treaty norms.[3] Therefore, it is important to contribute to a better understanding of the legal implications of the concept.

Of course, it is all too easy to friendly invite Paul Lemmens to express his viewpoint, without giving my own. This contribution will therefore explore the concept of human dignity, first briefly through a philosophical lens and then through a legal one, essentially relying on the already mentioned "dwarf-tossing case" and case law from institutions that were crucial in Paul Lemmens's career: the ECtHR and the (Belgian) Council of State. It does not claim to be a complete analysis of the concept of human dignity and the case law on the subject – that would require a book or PhD. I rather refer to selected cases to explore the legal boundaries of the concept of human dignity. These reflections do not close the discussion but are – so I hope – the starting point of further debates. Because if there is something that PAUL likes, it is a good, honest and intelligent discussion: "C'est du choc des idées que jaillit la lumière".

I. PHILOSOPHICAL CONCEPT

Human dignity has two components.

"Human" refers to our genus: *homo*, which not only refers to *homo sapiens*, but which also includes references to other extinct species as *homo erectus* or *homo neanderthalensis*. The very use of this component suggests that there are other dignities, like animal dignity or vegetal dignity. Otherwise it would be redundant to add "human" to the word "dignity". There must therefore be something specific to humans that qualifies their dignity. Some argue that it is their intelligence, the use of language or the use of reason, others refer to the ability of humans to be self-conscious or to express compassion.

Another current argues that we should overcome the dichotomy between humans and animals. Singer, for instance, maintains that sentience[4] is the basis of all

---

3   ECJ, *Netherlands v. European Parliament and Council*, judgment of 9 October 2001, C3–77/98, §70 in which the fundamental right to human dignity and integrity is considered to be a general principle of Community law. For the idea that general principles of law underlie the ECHR see F. Vanneste, *General International Law before Human Rights Courts*, Intersentia, Antwerp-Oxford, 2009, 385–405.

4   Sentience is the capacity to feel, perceive or experience subjectively.

rights, implying that not only humans but all animals are right-bearers.[5] Harari in turn argues that we are all living organisms, based on algorithms.[6] Perhaps one day we will consider it obsolete to refer to "human dignity" instead of "dignity".[7]

"Dignity" is the second component and comes from the Latin word "dignitas", that refers to the ancient Greek "axa", which means "first principle of reason".[8] The Greek emphasis on rationality and self-consciousness is echoed by Blaise Pascal: a human being is self conscious, which differentiates him from the animal.[9] One century later, Immanuel Kant writes about dignity as "the condition under which something can alone be an end in itself".[10] All rational beings stand under the law that each of them is to treat himself and all others, never merely as means, but always at the same time as an end in themselves. Kant seems[11] to define dignity as an "absolute internal value", grounded in the autonomy of human beings, that enables them to treat one another with respect. Dignity is grounded in *autonomy*[12] and requires *respect*[13]:

---

5   P. Singer, *Animal Liberation* (2nd ed.), London: Jonathan Cape, 1990.

6   Y. Harari, *Homo Sapiens: A brief history of Humankind*, London: Harvill Secker, 2014, 253–54: "Yet if we take the really grand view of life, all other problems and developments are overshadowed by three interlinked processes: 1. Science is converging on an all-encompassing dogma, which says that organisms are algorithms and life is data processing. 2. Intelligence is decoupling from consciousness. 3. Non-conscious but highly intelligent algorithms may soon know us better than we know ourselves. These three processes raise three key questions, which I hope will stick in your mind long after you have finished this book: 1. Are organisms really just algorithms, and is life really just data processing? 2. What's more valuable – intelligence or consciousness? 3. What will happen to society, politics and daily life when non-conscious but highly intelligent algorithms know us better than we know ourselves?". See also Y. Harari, *Homo Deus: A Brief History of Tomorrow*, London: Harvill Secker, 2016.

7   For Nussbaum's position on animal dignity see i.a. M. Nussbaum, *Creating capabilities*, Harvard University Press, 2011, 157 *et seq.*

8   J. Fierens, "La dignité humaine comme concept juridique", *J.T.* 2002, 577–582.

9   J. Fierens, "La dignité humaine comme concept juridique", *J.T.* 2002, 577–582.

10   In Kant's own famous words in *Groundwork of the Metaphysics of Morals* (1785): "In the kingdom of ends everything has either a price or a dignity. What has a price can be replaced by something else as its equivalent; what on the other hand is raised above all price and therefore admits of no equivalent has a dignity. What refers to general human inclinations and needs has a market price; that, which even without presupposing a need, conforms with a certain taste, that is, with a delight, satisfaction in the mere purposeless play of our mental powers, has a fancy price; but what which constitutes the condition under which alone something can be an end in itself, has no merely a relative worth, that is, a price, an inner worth value, that is, dignity." Cited in A. Pele, "Kant On Human Dignity: A Critical Approach -- Kant E A Dignidade Humana: Uma Interpretação crítica", *EJJL* 2016, 493–512.

11   A. Pele, for instance, argues that this reading is incorrect and that Kant was less concerned with the intrinsic worthiness of the human beings, than with establishing the authority of morality. A. Pele, "Kant On Human Dignity: A Critical Approach -- Kant E A Dignidade Humana: Uma Interpretação crítica", *EJJL* 2016, 493–512.

12   Kant defines autonomy of the will as "... the property of the will by which it is a law to itself" and even describes it as the "... ground of the dignity of human nature and of every rational nature" (cited by Pele, *l.c.*, 504).

13   Regarding the notion of respect, Kant emphasizes that the rational human being, as an end in himself, has a dignity, an "absolute inner worth", through which it instills respect" (Pele, *l.c.*, 504).

slavery, for instance, cannot take away the dignity of an individual, it is a power that it does not have, but it denies or fails to respect it.[14] Whatever, the exact meaning of Kant's theory was, his expressions have construed our modern common understanding of human dignity. Indeed, today, most agree to define human dignity as an inherent and absolute worthiness of the human person.[15] Pele explains this definition as follows: "In relation with the first aspect *(inherent value)*, an intrinsic (or internal) worth is acknowledged in all human beings in order to justify not only their autonomy, but also the equality of all individuals *(equal dignity)*. [...] The second characteristic *(absolute value)* refers explicitly to the invulnerability (or inviolability) of the human being, or to put it in other words, to the protection of the vulnerability and integrity of the human person."[16]

If we turn to contemporary thinkers, one cannot leave Martha Nussbaum aside, who does not exclusively ground dignity in rationality.[17] Basing herself on "an intuitive notion of human dignity" she identifies a list of central human capabilities that are implicit in the idea of life worth of human dignity.[18] She is continuously updating a list of ten central capabilities that "can be convincingly argued to be of central importance in any human life, whatever else the person pursues or chooses. They are held to have value in themselves, in making a life fully human. [...] They support our powers of practical reason and choice, and have a special importance in making any choice of a way of life possible."[19] It is important to stress that she is talking about "capabilities". This means that citizens must be left free to determine their course after they have the capabilities.[20] She argues that "capabilities, not *functionings*, are the appropriate political goals, because room is thereby left for the exercise of human freedom."[21] A person who has normal

---

14   A. Compte-Sponville, *Dictionnaire philosophique*, PUf, 2001, 174.
15   A. Pele, "Kant On Human Dignity: A Critical Approach -- Kant E A Dignidade Humana: Uma Interpretação crítica", *EJJL* 2016, 497.
16   Ibidem.
17   See M. Nussbaum, *Frontiers of Justice*, Cambridge, Harvard University Press, 2007, 159: "Kant contrasts the humanity of human being with their animality. Although Rawls does not do so explicitly, he does make personhood reside in (moral and prudential) rationality, not in the needs that human beings share with other animals. The capabilities approach, by contrast, sees rationality and animality as thoroughly unified. Taking its cue from Aristotle's notion of the human being as a political animal, and from Marx's idea that the human being is a creature 'in need of a plurality of life-activities', it sees the rational as simply one aspect of the animal, and at that, not the only that is pertinent to a notion of truly human functioning."
18   M. Nussbaum, *Frontiers of Justice*, Harvard University Press, Cambridge 2007, 70: "what people actually are able to do and to be, in a way informed by an intuitive idea of a life that is worthy of the dignity of the human being. I identify a list of central human capabilities, arguing that all of them are implicit in the idea of a life worthy of human dignity."
19   M. Nussbaum, "Capabilities and Human Rights", 66 *Fordham L. Rev.* 1997, (273), 286; M. Nussbaum, *Frontiers of Justice*, Cambridge, Harvard University Press, 2007, 70.
20   M. Nussbaum, "Capabilities and Human Rights", 66 *Fordham L. Rev.* 1997, (273) 289, M. Nussbaum, *Frontiers of Justice*, Cambridge, Harvard University Press, 2007, 75–81.
21   M. Nussbaum, *Creating capabilities*, Cambridge, Harvard University Press, 2011, 25.

opportunities for sexual satisfaction can always choose a life of celibacy. A person who has opportunities for play can always choose a workaholic life. What is interesting in this approach is that it emphasizes that respect for human dignity does not entail the same "functions" for every human being.[22/23] Her approach also stresses that the "capabilities in question should be pursued for each and every person"[24] and "that there is a threshold level of each capability, beneath which it is held that truly human functioning is not available to citizens".[25] However, she also specifies that "within certain parameters it is perfectly appropriate that different nations should [specify the capabilities] somewhat differently, taking their histories and special circumstances into account."[26]

II. LEGAL CONCEPT

As already stated, the ECtHR argues that "respect for human dignity forms part of the very essence of the European Convention of Human Rights".[27] Many references to human dignity can be found in the Preamble of international texts[28] and in the context of other specific fundamental rights like the right to equality[29] and the prohibition of torture, inhuman or degrading treatment. The concept of human dignity seems also to have an autonomous meaning in positive law. For instance, article 1 of the Charter of Fundamental Rights of the European Union

---

[22]   It also looks "at people one by one, insisting on locating empowerment in *this* life and in *that* life, rather than in the nation as a whole." M. Nussbaum, "Capabilities and Human Rights", 66 *Fordham L. Rev.* 1997, (273) 285.

[23]   M. Nussbaum, *Frontiers of Justice*, Cambridge, Harvard University Press, 2007, 75: "The capabilities to which all citizens are entitled are many and not one, and are opportunities for activity, not simply quantities of resources. Resources are inadequate as index of well-being, because human beings have varying need for resources, and also varying abilities to convert resources into functioning. Thus two people with similar quantities of resources may actually differ greatly in the ways that matter most for social justice. This issue will become especially salient when we confront the theory with issues of impairment and disability."

[24]   M. Nussbaum, *Creating capabilities*, Cambridge, Harvard University Press, 2011, 24: "So the attitude toward people's basic capabilities is not a meritocratic one – more innately skilled people get better treatment – but, if anything, the opposite: those who need more help to get above the threshold get more help. In the case of people with cognitive disabilities, the goals should be for them to have the same capabilities as 'normal' people, even though some of those opportunities may have to be exercised through a surrogate, and the surrogate may in some cases supply part of the internal capability if the person is unable to develop sufficient choice capability on her own, for example, by voting on that person's behalf even if the person is unable to make a choice."

[25]   M. Nussbaum, *Frontiers of Justice*, Cambridge, Harvard University Press, 2007, 70–71.

[26]   M. Nussbaum, *Frontiers of Justice*, Cambridge, Harvard University Press, 2007, 78–79.

[27]   ECtHR (GC), *Bouyid v. Belgium*, judgment of 28 September 2015, *Reports* 2015-V, §89.

[28]   See i.a. the Preamble to the Universal Declaration of Human Rights (UDHR) which states that "recognition of the inherent dignity and of the equal and inalienable rights of all members of the human family is the foundation of freedom, justice and peace in the world".

[29]   Article 1 UDHR provides that "all human beings are born free and equal in dignity and rights".

(December 7, 2000) states that "human dignity is inviolable. It must be respected and protected".[30] At domestic level, the Belgian Constitution was amended in 1994, to introduce the right of everyone to lead a life in conformity with human dignity (actual Article 23 of the Belgian constitution). All these examples confirm that human dignity is a legal concept, recognized in positive law. This recognition in positive law begs the question what legal consequences are to be attached to human dignity. Case law on the subject matter shows that human dignity is referred to in essentially three different legal contexts: 1° the obligation to *respect* human dignity 2° the obligation to *protect* human dignity 3° human dignity as a legitimate aim *to limit other* fundamental rights and freedoms. In each of these contexts human rights courts seem to adopt an essentially objective or abstract approach towards human dignity. It is not the impact of the contested measure on the individual that matters so much, it is the impact on our – all of us – humanity. I argue, however, that another, more concrete approach towards human dignity is possible.

A. RESPECTING HUMAN DIGNITY

Human dignity entails a negative obligation for the State to respect every human.[31] Because he or she is a human being he or she must be treated with respect and in the same way as all other human beings. In a legal context the concept of human dignity has until today essentially been used to answer the question whether or not specific rights, like equality or the right to integrity, are respected. In a way it is used as an interpretative tool, to support the argumentation. It is, however, as I will further explain, often used in a far too abstract way, almost as if a simple reference to it, makes it unnecessary to develop the reasoning and analyse the concrete facts of the case. Human dignity can be relied upon, but it is necessary to explain its scope and relevance for the concrete case.

This can be illustrated by an analysis of the Grand Chamber judgment *Bouyid v. Belgium* in which both the majority and the minority fail to adequately develop their conception of human dignity.

In that landmark case the Grand Chamber of the ECtHR rules that even an isolated slap, without serious or long-term effects, inflicted thoughtlessly by a police officer who was exasperated by the applicants' disrespectful or provocative conduct, in a context of tension between the members of the applicants' family

---

[30] For an overview of other international human rights texts and instruments referring to this concept, see ECtHR (GC), *Bouyid v. Belgium*, judgment of 28 September 2015, *Reports* 2015-V, §§45–46.

[31] The obligation to respect means that the State should not interfere in the rights of the individual. The obligation to protect is related to the positive obligations of the State, this means that the State should guarantee human dignity (see *infra*).

and police officers in their neighbourhood, is a "serious attack on the individual's dignity" and therefore amounts to a degrading treatment in the sense of Article 3 ECHR. Referring to previous case law the Grand Chamber considers "it particularly important to point out that, in respect of a person who is deprived of his liberty, or, more generally, is confronted with law-enforcement officers, any recourse to physical force which has not been made strictly necessary by his own conduct diminishes human dignity and is, in principle, an infringement of the right set forth in Article 3".[32]

The Grand Chamber does not explain what the words "in principle" mean. In the following paragraphs the ECtHR seems to suggest that any violation of human dignity by the police is a violation of Article 3 ECHR. In fact, it seems the Grand Chamber is essentially referring to human dignity to downplay the importance of the concrete impact of the slap of the face on the applicants. It argues that a slap has a considerable impact on the person receiving it, without feeling the need to demonstrate that this was the case for the applicant.[33] Moreover, the Court reiterates that it may well suffice that the victim is "humiliated in his own eyes" for there to be degrading treatment within the meaning of Article 3 of the Convention. Indeed, it "does not doubt that even one unpremeditated slap devoid of any serious or long-term effect on the person receiving it *may* be perceived as humiliating by that person".[34] But again it does not explain whether it *was* effectively perceived as humiliating by the applicant. It rather states in general terms that the slap inflicted by law-enforcement officers on persons under their control, highlights the superiority and inferiority which by definition characterises the relationship between the former and the latter in such circumstances. The fact that the victims know that such an act is unlawful, constituting a breach of moral and professional ethics by those officers, "*may* furthermore arouse in them a feeling of arbitrary treatment, injustice and powerlessness".[35] For the majority it suffices that the victim, who was in a vulnerable position, is humiliated in his own

---

32   ECtHR (GC), *Bouyid v. Belgium*, judgment of 28 September 2015, *Reports* 2015-V, §88 and §100.
33   ECtHR (GC), *Bouyid v. Belgium*, judgment of 28 September 2015, *Reports* 2015-V, §104:"A slap has a considerable impact on the person receiving it. A slap to the face affects the part of the person's body which expresses his individuality, manifests his social identity and constitutes the centre of his senses – sight, speech and hearing – which are used for communication with others. Indeed, the Court has already had occasion to note the role played by the face in social interaction (see S.A.S. v. France [GC], concerning the ban on wearing clothing intended to conceal the face in public places; no. 43835/11, §§122 and 141, ECHR 2014 (extracts)). It has also had regard to the specificity of that part of the body in the context of Article 3 of the Convention, holding that "particularly because of its location", a blow to an individual's head during his arrest, which had caused a swelling and a bruise of 2 cm on his forehead, was sufficiently serious to raise an issue under Article 3 (see Samüt Karabulut v. Turkey, no. 16999/04, §§41 and 58, 27 January 2009)."
34   Emphasis added.
35   Emphasis added.

eyes, whatever the psychological or physical impact of the slapping on the person in question. The standard of "humiliation in his own eyes" is already a criterion used by the ECtHR to assess the level of severity of State action in the context of Article 3. In this case the ECtHR, however, seems to invoke human dignity to argue that "in his eyes" does not mean that the ECtHR must establish that the applicants effectively felt humiliated, but that it suffices to refer to the facts themselves because any human being in that situation would have felt humiliated.

The dissenting judges De Gaetano, Lemmens and Mahoney do not agree. It is interesting to quote their reasoning at length (and not only because by doing so Paul Lemmens is actually himself contributing to his own *liber amicorum*, but above all because the dissenters rightly emphasize the importance of assessing all the circumstances of the case):

> "4. We are prepared to accept, as the majority did, that where a person is under the control of the police, any recourse to physical force which has not been made strictly necessary by the person's conduct diminishes human dignity (see paragraphs 88 and 100 of the judgment).
>
> We are able to reach that conclusion without resorting to the detailed observations on human dignity set out both in the part of the judgment dealing with international texts, instruments and documents (paragraphs 45–47) and in the "Law" part (paragraphs 89–90). Indeed, we wonder what practical purpose is served by these observations, given that the majority provide no indication of how the notion of human dignity is to be understood. The observations are presented as though they intend to establish a doctrine, but in reality they do not offer the reader much by way of enlightenment.
>
> 5. That said, should it be accepted that any interference with human dignity constitutes degrading treatment and hence a violation of Article 3? Without going that far, the majority appear to be suggesting that any interference with human dignity resulting from the use of force by the police will necessarily breach Article 3. We consider that in so finding, the majority have departed from the well-established case-law to the effect that where recourse to physical force diminishes human dignity, it will "in principle" constitute a violation of Article 3. The relevant case-law is in fact referred to twice in the judgment (in paragraph 88, with references to Ribitsch v. Austria, 4 December 1995, §38, Series A no 336; Mete and Others v. Turkey, no. 294/08, §38, 4 October 2011; and El-Masri v. "the former Yugoslav Republic of Macedonia" [GC], no. 39630/09, §207, ECHR 2012, and in paragraph 100). In our view, the use of the term "in principle" implies that there are exceptions, that is to say instances of interference with human dignity that nevertheless do not breach Article 3. On this point we would refer to the Ireland v. the United Kingdom judgment, in which the Court found that there could be "violence which is to be condemned both on moral grounds and also in most cases under the domestic law of the Contracting States but which does not fall within Article 3 of the Convention" (see Ireland v. the United Kingdom, 18 January 1978, §167, Series A no. 25).

This is because there are forms of treatment which, while interfering with human dignity, do not attain the minimum level of severity required to fall within the scope of Article 3 (see, for example, Ireland v. the United Kingdom, cited above, §162, and, among recent judgments, El-Masri, cited above, §196; Svinarenko and Slyadnev v. Russia [GC], nos. 32541/08 and 43441/08, §114, ECHR 2014 (extracts); and Tarakhel v. Switzerland [GC], no. 29217/12, §94, ECHR 2014 (extracts)).

6. The main question arising in the present case is whether this minimum level was attained in respect of the applicants.

The majority begin by pointing out that the assessment of this minimum depends on all the circumstances of the case (see paragraph 86 of the judgment). Subsequently, however, they show no further concern for the specific circumstances, instead simply adopting an eminently dogmatic position: any conduct by law-enforcement officers which diminishes human dignity constitutes a violation of Article 3, irrespective of its impact on the person concerned (see paragraph 101).

For our part, we consider that the specific circumstances are of fundamental importance. It is not for the Court to impose general rules of conduct on law-enforcement officers; instead, its task is limited to examining the applicants' individual situation to the extent that they allege that they were personally affected by the treatment complained of (see, mutatis mutandis, Lorsé and Others v. the Netherlands, no. 52750/99, §62, 4 February 2003; Van der Ven v. the Netherlands, no. 50901/99, §50, ECHR 2003-II; and Lindström and Mässeli v. Finland, no. 24630/10, §41, 14 January 2014). Certain factors dictate that the seriousness of the violence inflicted on the applicants should be put in perspective. These concern in particular the duration of the treatment, its physical or psychological effects, the intention or motivation behind it, and the context in which it was inflicted (see the aspects held to be relevant in the Court's case-law, as recapitulated in paragraph 86 of the judgment). As the Chamber noted, both the incidents in the present case involved an isolated slap inflicted thoughtlessly by a police officer who was exasperated by the applicants' disrespectful or provocative conduct, in a context of tension between the members of the applicants' family and police officers in their neighbourhood, and there were no serious or long-term effects (Chamber judgment of 21 November 2013, §51). Although the treatment complained of was unacceptable (see paragraph 3 above), we are unable to find that it attained the minimum level of severity to be classified as "degrading treatment" within the meaning of Article 3 of the Convention.

7. [...]"

In the dissenters' approach it is not necessary to clarify the notion of human dignity because "there are forms of treatment which, while interfering with human dignity, do not attain the minimum level of severity required to fall within the scope of Article 3". In the light of the reasoning of the Grand Chamber the dissenting judges should in my opinion at least have tried to explain their conception of human dignity, albeit to simply explain why certain treatments which interfere with human dignity are no degrading treatment. More importantly, if they had adopted another approach to human dignity this could have allowed them to explain how the established notion of "humiliation in his own eyes" should be interpreted and applied. In doing so, they could have reinforced their main argument that the majority should have shown more concern for the specific circumstances, instead of "simply adopting an eminently dogmatic position", to use the dissenters' words.

The "eminently dogmatic position" of the majority seems grounded in a dogmatic reading of human dignity as "an inherent and absolute worthiness of the human person" (see *supra*). Slapping in the face by the police, is then always unacceptable because it reduces a person to a means and not an end in itself. The majority does not dare to go as far as to state that any slapping by any person is an affront to human dignity. This would, however, be the logical conclusion of its approach to human dignity.[36] There seems to be little room for an assessment of the concrete facts.

Instead, we argue that there is no abstract human dignity, there is the human dignity of *this* concrete person in *this* concrete situation. One should assess whether State action affects the basic capabilities of a concrete person to live a life in dignity. Of course, respect for psychological and physical integrity is essential and minimum standards have to be met.[37] But if we want to rely on human dignity, the main question in the present case should be whether the person in question was impeded at a certain moment in time, when slapped in the face or later because of this slapping, from the capability to live a worthy and dignified life (or put differently: did State acts attain a minimum level of severity as to impede the individual, albeit temporarily, to live a life in dignity). Or to rephrase it in even more simple words: did the person in question feel humiliated by the particular slapping in the face. This is in my opinion the right question to assess whether he "was humiliated in his own eyes", which is a recognized standard to assess the level of severity under article 3 ECHR. To answer that question it remains crucial to "examine the applicant's individual situation". Given the concrete context of tension, the attitude of the applicant and the absence of any serious or long-term effects it is quite possible to argue that the slapping in the face had no impact at all on his capability to live a worthy

---

[36]   With this approach to human dignity it is hard to understand why, for instance, slapping in the face by parents, even if it is inadvertently and because of the tireless and exasperating behaviour of their children, would not be an affront to human dignity and, therefore a violation of Article 3. Parents are no state agents, but it could be said that there is a positive obligation for States to penalize this violation of human dignity.

[37]   In Nussbaums' approach "bodily integrity" is the third central capability, M. Nussbaum, "Capabilities and Human Rights", 66 *Fordham L. Rev.* 1997, (273) 287; M. Nussbaum, *Frontiers of Justice*, Cambridge, Harvard University Press, 2007, 76.

and dignified life. The isolated slap, which according to the majority *may* have aroused feelings of powerlessness, did not necessarily really arouse such feelings. One could equally argue that given the facts the slap rather disclosed a feeling of powerlessness by the police rather than an intention to humiliate, and that the applicant immediately understood this. The slap might only have enforced his contempt for the police. Given his attitude and history with the police it can be advanced that he was not even humiliated in his own eyes; he might as well just have been surprised, immediately understanding that this slapping would mean trouble for the police and an asset, a strengthening of his (legal) position vis-à-vis the police. The concrete circumstances of the case, and especially the ensuing reaction of the victim, which should be closely analysed, may lead to the conclusion that he was not 'humiliated in his own eyes', that his capability to live a dignified life is at no point affected. The difficulty of analysing this can be solved by shifting the burden of proof: if the applicant can credibly argue that the particular conduct "humiliated him in his own eyes", it will be up to the State to demonstrate that this was not the case as the particular circumstances of the case demonstrate.[38]

However, the fact that the second applicant was a minor in a repressive context at the material time is for me –contrary to the dissenting judges- an indication of vulnerability that should nevertheless lead to the conclusion of a violation of human dignity and Article 3 in respect of the second applicant. Because of his young age, even a single slap by the police is likely to have decisive long-term effects on his future, his trust in the police and his approach of violence. One cannot expect that a minor understands that a slapping in the face by the police is not intended to humiliate but rather an expression of powerlessness that he can exploit.

What this case illustrates is that even in the context of negative obligations of the State it is advisable to clarify the notion of human dignity (something neither the majority nor the minority really do). Indeed, a better understanding of human dignity might contribute to a better understanding of the specific rights, like for instance the scope of Article 3 ECHR. Human dignity should not be used as a

---

[38] This is merely using the same logic of ECtHR (GC), *Bouyid v. Belgium*, judgment of 28 September 2015, *Reports* 2015-V, §83 and 84: "82. Allegations of ill-treatment contrary to Article 3 must be supported by appropriate evidence. To assess this evidence, the Court adopts the standard of proof "beyond reasonable doubt" but adds that such proof may follow from the coexistence of sufficiently strong, clear and concordant inferences or of similar unrebutted presumptions of fact [...].83. On this latter point the Court has explained that where the events in issue lie wholly, or in large part, within the exclusive knowledge of the authorities, as in the case of persons within their control in custody, strong presumptions of fact will arise in respect of injuries occurring during such detention. The burden of proof is then on the Government to provide a satisfactory and convincing explanation by producing evidence establishing facts which cast doubt on the account of events given by the victim."

rationalization of an abstract assessment of facts (like the majority in *Bouyid* is essentially doing). On the contrary, respecting human dignity is respecting the idea that individuals must be capable to live a dignified life and make their own reasoned choices. Assessing their capability to do so depends on all the concrete circumstances of the case and the concrete vulnerability of each individual. Arguing that respect for human dignity is an absolute right means that we should respect everyone's dignity, in all places, at all time, without exceptions or the possibility to limit the right.[39] It does not mean that the concrete circumstances play no role at all to assess whether the requisite level of severity is reached.[40] Because we are all vulnerable in different ways at different places and in different moments of life.

B.   PROTECTING HUMAN DIGNITY

Article 1 of the Charter of Fundamental Rights of the European Union states that "human dignity must be respected and protected". This particular recognition of human dignity in positive law reminds us that human dignity contains a negative ánd a positive obligation. Human dignity does not only entail an obligation to respect other human beings. It also requires State action. Article 23 of the Belgian constitution offers a good starting point to illustrate how the right to human dignity is not about protecting an abstract idea of humanity, but is about concrete steps by the authorities to guarantee the possibility of individuals to live a life in dignity.[41]

Article 23 of the Belgian constitution states that everyone has the right to lead a life in keeping with human dignity.[42] To this end the laws must guarantee economic, social and cultural rights, taking into account corresponding

---

[39]   Article 3 ECHR does not have any limitation clause. See also ECtHR (GC), *Gäfgen v. Germany*, judgment of 1 June 2010, §107: the absolute nature of the right 'does not allow for any exceptions or justifying factors or balancing of interests' or ECtHR (GC), *Ireland v. United Kingdom*, judgment of 18 January 1978, §163.

[40]   The dissenters also point out that "the prohibition of torture and inhuman or degrading treatment or punishment is absolute, regardless of the conduct of the person concerned (see paragraph 108 of the judgment). We too subscribe to the absolute nature of this prohibition. However, it only applies once it has been established that a particular instance of treatment has attained the requisite level of severity."

[41]   ECJ, *Jobcenter Berlin Neukölln v. Alimanovic*, judgment of 15 September 2015, C-67/14, 45: "However, in the present case it must be found that [...] the predominant function of the benefits at issue in the main proceedings is in fact to cover the minimum subsistence costs necessary to lead a life in keeping with human dignity". For a recent overview of ECJ case law on human dignity see C.-A. Chassin, "La notion de dignité de la personne humaine dans la jurisprudence de la Cour de justice" in A. Biad and V. Parisot (ed.), *La Charte des droits fondamentaux de l'Union européenne*, Anthemis, 2018, 137–260.

[42]   Article 23 Belgian Constitution.

obligations, and determine the condition for exercising them. It is therefore clearly an obligation for the legislator to draft laws in order to protect human dignity. It is, however, not clear what happens if the legislator does not act at all. It is also debated whether or not individuals could draw concrete subjective rights from Article 23, requiring concrete State action.[43] Be it as it may, the three highest courts in Belgium, the Constitutional Court, the Cour de Cassation and the Council of State, do certainly recognize that there is a *standstill* obligation for all the economic, social and cultural rights covered by Article 23 of the Constitution.[44] This means that "the legislator cannot substantially reduce the level of protection offered by the existing applicable legislation, without any reason of general interest".[45] The Constitutional Court has, for instance, ruled that "the substantial reduction of the social help offered to foreigners who are authorized to live on the territory because they have a work permit cannot be justified by a motive of general interest".[46] In a recent judgment the Constitutional Court ruled that the obligation to pay a fee of 50 euro for every procedure launched by a *pro bono* lawyer was a considerable reduction of the protection offered by the right to judicial aid as protected by Article 23 of the Constitution. This reduction could not be justified by a reason of general interest and was contrary to the *standstill*-obligation enshrined in that article.[47] These examples show that courts derive concrete legal obligations from the obligation to protect human dignity. In Belgium, however, as in many other countries, those obligations, especially when they relate to social and economic rights, are still more easily accepted in an objective contentieux, where the constitutionality of laws is at stake, than in a subjective one, in which subjective rights are invoked. And even in the former there is no full proportionality test, but only the more specific standstill obligation.

The *detour* via the standstill (for social and economic rights) impedes in my opinion to ask the right question: it is not the reduction in itself that is potentially a violation of human dignity, it is rather the lack of adequate protection insofar as it does not allow to live a dignified life that is problematic. As long as social help, for instance, is adequate and sufficient, there is no need to argue that a reduction is problematic. Relying on standstill, which is in fact merely another way to make a proportionality test[48], amounts to the bizarre

---

[43]   See, F. Vanneste, *Rechtswaarborgen in een herijkte welvaartsstaat. Over de cruciale rol van (sociale) grondrechten in België*, in: Preadviezen van de Vereniging voor het Vergelijkend Recht tussen België en Nederland 2012, Den Haag: Boom Juridische Uitgevers, 11–60.

[44]   See i.a. Belgian Cour de Cassation, judgment of 18 May 2015, S.14.0042.F: "Comme l'a encore récemment rappelé le Conseil d'Etat, cette définition [du standstill] vaut indistinctement pour toutes les matières couvertes par l'article 23 de la Constition."

[45]   Own translation.

[46]   Belgian Constitutional Court, judgment of 1 October 2015, 133/2015 (own translation).

[47]   Belgian Constitutional Court, judgment of 21 June 2018, 77/2018, B.17.3.

[48]   Belgian Council of State, *Coomans*, judgment of 17 November 2008, n° 187998.

construction that courts can determine whether human dignity is protected by the State when there is already some protection, but cannot do so when there is none. As I already developed elsewhere, basing myself on *Coomans*, a landmark judgment of the Belgian Council of State, the rights enshrined in Article 23 of the Belgian constitution should be interpreted as other (civil and political) human rights.[49] The fact that they all pursue the same common aim of protecting human dignity underscores this view. To determine the scope of the State's positive obligations, be it economic or social or civil rights, a fair balance or adequate proportionality test suffices: all circumstances should be taken into account, whereby not only the emergency of the case[50] but also the duties of the individual[51] and the specific context of the country should be of paramount importance. This is no plea for a *gouvernement des juges*. Courts already grant a wide margin of appreciation to the legislator when establishing the existence of positive obligations, and they should keep doing so. It is only when human dignity is in danger in a concrete situation that courts can establish a violation of a positive obligation. Courts can accept a significant reduction in the level of protection of social, economic and cultural rights, even without having to rely on the general interest, as long as an adequate and sufficient protection of fundamental rights remains guaranteed in order for the individual to be able to live a dignified life. I'm not sure that this approach would necessarily be more expensive for States…Although I have to admit that it makes it more difficult for judges: balancing various interests in a concrete situation is more difficult than assessing whether or not there is a significant reduction of protection. That is, however, true for the interpretation and application of all human rights.

Emphasizing the importance of a right to human dignity amounts to recognizing the interdependence of human rights and the need for a minimal protection of *all* those rights. This reminds of Nussbaums's approach to human dignity: a minimal protection of civil, political, social and economic rights is required to be able to live a dignified life.

---

[49] Belgian Council of State, *Coomans*, judgment of 17 November 2008, n° 187998. F. Vanneste, *Rechtswaarborgen in een herijkte welvaartsstaat. Over de cruciale rol van (sociale) grondrechten in België*, in: Preadviezen van de Vereniging voor het Vergelijkend Recht tussen België en Nederland 2012, Den Haag: Boom Juridische Uitgevers, 37.

[50] Belgian courts have often relied on human dignity in emergency cases to grant certain subjective rights. For an overview see F. Vanneste, *Rechtswaarborgen in een herijkte welvaartsstaat. Over de cruciale rol van (sociale) grondrechten in België*, in: Preadviezen van de Vereniging voor het Vergelijkend Recht tussen België en Nederland 2012, Den Haag: Boom Juridische Uitgevers, 45–47 and H. Funck, 'L'article 23 de la constitution à travers la jurisprudence des cours et tribunaux (1994–2008): un droit en arrière fond ou l'ultime recours du juge?', in: W. Rauws en M. Stroobant (ed.), *Sociale en economische grondrechten*, Antwerpen/Louvain-la-Neuve, Intersentia/Anthemis, 69–111.

[51] Article 23 of the Belgian constitution also refers to the "corresponding obligations".

C. HUMAN DIGNITY AS A LEGITIMATE AIM TO LIMIT OTHER FUNDAMENTAL RIGHTS AND FREEDOMS?

Human dignity has also been used to limit other fundamental rights and freedoms. The most famous case in that respect is probably the so-called "dwarf-tossing" case.[52] In that case the French Council of State[53] and, subsequently, the Human Rights Committee upheld a ban on dwarf tossing[54], which the applicant considered to be a violation of his right to work, right to privacy and dignity[55], on grounds of ... human dignity. The Human Rights Committee's reasoning was not very elaborated[56]:

> "7.4 The ban on throwing ordered by the State party in the present case applies only to dwarves (as described in paragraph 2.1). However, if these persons are covered to the exclusion of others, the reason is that they are the only persons capable of being thrown. Thus, the differentiation between the persons covered by the ban, namely dwarves, and those to whom it does not apply, namely persons not suffering from dwarfism, is based on an objective reason and is not discriminatory in its purpose. The Committee considers that the State party has demonstrated, in the present case, that the ban on dwarf tossing as practised by the author did not constitute an abusive measure but was necessary in order to protect public order, which brings into play considerations of human dignity that are compatible with the objectives of the

---

[52]   For another famous case with an objective approach towards human dignity see ECJ, *Omega Spielhallen- und Automatenaufstellungs-GmbH v. Oberbürgermeisterin der Bundesstadt Bonn*, judgment of 14 October 2004, C-36/02, §39: "the prohibition on the commercial exploitation of games involving the simulation of acts of violence against persons, in particular the representation of acts of homicide, corresponds to the level of protection of human dignity which the national constitution seeks to guarantee in the territory of the Federal Republic of Germany. It should also be noted that, by prohibiting only the variant of the laser game the object of which is to fire on human targets and thus 'playing at killing' people, the contested order did not go beyond what is necessary in order to attain the objective pursued by the competent national authorities".

[53]   By an order dated 27 October 1995 the Council of State argued that dwarf tossing was an attraction that affronted human dignity, respect for human dignity being part of public order and the authority vested in the municipal police being the means of ensuring it, and second, that respect for the principle of freedom of employment and trade was no impediment to the banning of an activity, licit or otherwise, in exercise of that authority if the activity was of a nature to disrupt public order. The Council of State went on to say that the attraction could be banned even in the absence of particular local circumstances.

[54]   Wearing suitable protective gear, the applicant, who suffered from dwarfism, would allow himself to be thrown short distances onto an air bed by clients of the establishment staging the event (a discotheque).

[55]   HRC, *Wackenheim v. France*, 15 July 2002, U.N. Doc. CCPR/C/75/D/854/1999: "3. The applicant affirms that banning him from working has had an adverse effect on his life and represents an affront to his dignity. He claims to be the victim of a violation by France of his right to freedom, employment, respect for private life and an adequate standard of living, and of an act of discrimination. He further states that there is no work for dwarves in France and that his job does not constitute an affront to human dignity since dignity consists in having a job."

[56]   HRC, *Wackenheim v. France*, 15 July 2002, U.N. Doc. CCPR/C/75/D/854/1999, 7.4.

Covenant. The Committee accordingly concludes that the differentiation between the author and the persons to whom the ban ordered by the State party does not apply was based on objective and reasonable grounds."

It is striking that the applicant and the Human Rights Committee rely on dignity to come to opposite conclusions. Once more it seems that different conceptions of human dignity lead to different outcomes: either you consider, like the Human Rights Committee, human dignity to be an abstract concept, arguing that even in the absence of local circumstances that threaten public order, respect for human dignity requires a ban because allowing dwarf-tossing amounts to opening the floodgates to exploitation of vulnerable persons; or you take a more concrete approach, like Wackenheim, arguing that human dignity requires central human capabilities in order to be able to live a life worth of human dignity. In his view his capability to work is unjustly curtailed. Like all human beings, he is endowed with reason and conscience, which is of course not affected by being a dwarf. Therefore, he is able to make the decision of whether he would like to take part in the activity of dwarf tossing at his own will. The ban on dwarf tossing diminishes his autonomy and deprives him of the right to choose for himself. As there are no particular local circumstances that show that he or other dwarfs are exploited or are at risk of being so, the ban should in his opinion be annulled.

Again, I argue that human dignity should not be used as a rationalization of an abstract assessment of facts. In this case the HRC is relying on human dignity to legitimize an interference by the State in the rights of Wackenheim. Without much explanations the HRC states that the State may consider it necessary to interfere in the rights of Wackenheim because of public order. It does not explain how human dignity can be an aspect of a (moral) public order. Neither does it explain how public order or human dignity is affected by this concrete ban and if its conclusion amounts to recognizing that respect for human dignity can be different from state to state.[57] It even fails to make any proportionality test. It is not because a ban can legitimately aim to protect public order that it automatically means that this ban is proportionate. By referring to human dignity, the HRC seems to argue that it is not any longer necessary to balance the rights of Wackenheim and the rights of others.

This case begs the question whether human dignity is an appropriate concept to limit certain rights, like in this context the right to privacy, the right to equality

---

[57] The HRC considered that States may prohibit dwarf tossing because of human dignity, but on the other hand it did not state that there is a positive obligation on states to prohibit dwarf tossing because of human dignity. See also ECJ, *Omega Spielhallen- und Automatenaufstellungs-GmbH v; Oberbürgermeisterin der Bundestadt Bonn*, judgment of 14 October 2004, C-36/02.

or the right to work. Limitation clauses in human rights treaties do not refer to this concept as a legitimate aim to interfere with specific rights.[58] Moreover, limitations of rights and freedoms must be strictly interpreted. It is, therefore, advisable to avoid referring to human dignity to legitimize interferences. It is better to rely on concepts like "public order" or "rights of others" to assess whether an interference pursues a legitimate aim and is necessary in a democratic society. And if courts still wish to refer to "human dignity as being part of public order"[59] they should at least develop this reasoning and explain why their conception of human dignity allows them to avoid any balancing of rights and make abstraction of the concrete impact of the contested acts on individuals and society. The Human Rights Committee failed to do so in *Wackenheim v. France.*[60]

In our view, respecting human dignity is respecting the idea that individuals must be capable to live a dignified life and make their own reasoned choices. We therefore agree with *Wackenheim* that if anything, it was his dignity, his possibility to live the dignified life that he wants that was primarily affected.

---

[58] The catalogue of legitimate aims in the ECHR includes interests of national security, territorial integrity or public safety, the prevention of disorder or crime, the protection of health or morals, the interest of well-being of the country, the protection of public order, the maintenance of *ordre public*, the protection of the reputation, the protection of rights and freedoms of others, the prevention of the disclosure of information received in confidence and the maintenance of the authority and impartiality of the judiciary. This list of legitimate aims enumerated under the second paragraphs of Articles 8–11 ECHR and the third paragraph of Article 2 of Protocol No. 4 is exhaustive, although the Strasbourg organs have very rarely found a violation of convention rights by reference to the legitimate aim standard. (P. Van Dijk, F. Van Hoof a.o., *Theory and Practice of the European Convention on Human Rights*, Antwerp-Oxford, Intersentia, 2006,340). The limitation clauses under Articles 8–11 ECHR and Article 2 of the Fourth Protocol do not mention "human dignity" as a legitimate aim.

[59] For another approach linking the protection of human dignity to the protection of *public order* see, for instance, the French Council of State in the Dieudonné case, French Council of State *ass. Ministre de l'intérieur c. Société Les Productions de la Plume et M. Dieudonné M'Bala M'Bala*, n° 374508, 9 January 2014, or ECJ, *Omega Spielhallen- und Automatenaufstellungs-GmbH v; Oberbürgermeisterin der Bundesstadt Bonn*, judgment of 14 October 2004, C-36/02. Compare with the more restrictive approach of the Dutch Council of State where they interpret public order as "the orderly course of community life in the physical public space" ("het ordelijk verloop van het gemeenschapsleven in de fysieke openbare ruimte"). In so doing the Dutch Council of State upholds a permit for an event with "Sinterklaas" and Black Pete (Dutch Council of State, judgment of 12 November 2014, 201406757/1/A3). The applicants argued that the character of Black Pete reflected negative stereotypes of people of African descent and that the event would, therefore attain human dignity and disrupt public order.

[60] Compare the position of the Dutch Council of State (see previous fn.) with the position of Committee on the Elimination of Racial Discrimination (CERD) on Black Pete. The latter "recommends that the State party finds a reasonable balance, such as a different portrayal of Black Pete and ensure respect of human dignity and human rights of all inhabitants of the State Party". CERD, *Concluding observations on the nineteenth to twenty-first periodic reports of the Netherlands*, 28 August 2015, CERD/C/NLD/CO/19–21.

As already stated, we argue that we should look at the impact of the acts on the individual's dignity, rather than referring to human dignity in general. In the particular circumstance there were no reasons to adduce that Wackenheim's right to integrity or that of others was in danger or that he was at risk of being exploited. In the light of this, we fail to see how the ban was necessary to protect "public order".[61] The only reason to uphold the ban could be the fact that other dwarfs would face the risk of being exploited or feel humiliated (and therefore be affected in their dignity). Protection of the rights of others is indeed a legitimate aim to interfere with the rights of Wackenheim. However, no concrete indications of such risk are mentioned by the HRC. The HRC prefers to refer to an abstract notion of human dignity, and by doing so it does not have to compare and weigh the impact of the ban on WACKENHEIM's capability to live a dignified life on the one side and on other human beings' capability to live a dignified life on the other side.

CONCLUSION

To end this contribution I'd like to quote PAUL MARTENS: "Nous ne savons plus très bien où situer la dignité humaine, ni prévoir ce qu'elle nous réserve depuis qu'elle est devenue juridique, mais nous avons à notre disposition tous les éléments utiles pour participer au débat, la solution ne pouvant plus désormais nous être imposée par les sujets supposés savoir."[62] Confronted with the ambivalence of the concept of human dignity, it is quite understandable that judges, like the dissenters in the Bouyid case, might try to avoid the concept of human dignity. But perhaps MARTENS is right: the concept does exist in legal texts, we should have the courage to understand and debate it.[63] At a time when some argue that there is no free will[64], this debate seems even more important.

---

61   In our opinion it is better and less controversial to limit "public order" in principle to the physical public space (like the Dutch Council of State). Relying on moral public order should only be possible when there is a clear and unequivocal consensus in society.

62   P. Martens, "Encore la dignité humaine: réflexions d'un juge sur la promotion par les juges d'une norme suspecte", in *Les droits de l'homme au seuil du troisième millénaire – Mélanges en hommage à Pierre Lambert*, Bruxelles, Bruylant, 2000, 561–579.

63   J. Fierens, "La dignité humaine comme concept juridique", *J.T.* 2002, 579.

64   Y. Harari, *Homo Sapiens: A brief history of Humankind*, London: Harvill Secker, 2014, 263: "At the same time, a huge gulf is opening between the tenets of liberal humanism and the latest findings of the life sciences, a gulf we cannot ignore much longer. Our liberal political and judicial systems are founded on the belief that every individual has a sacred inner nature, indivisible and immutable, which gives meaning to the world, and which is the source of all ethical and political authority. This is a reincarnation of the traditional Christian belief in a free and eternal soul that resides within each individual. Yet over the last 200 years, the life sciences have thoroughly undermined this belief. Scientists studying the inner workings of the human organism have found no soul there. They increasingly argue that human behaviour is determined by hormones, genes and synapses, rather than by free will – the

Because if there is no free will, how should we then understand human dignity? Are (quasi)-judicial bodies, like the ECJ, the ECtHR and the HRC in their various landmark cases on the subject, right to adopt an abstract and objective approach?[65] This contribution essentially argues that human dignity is especially important to recognize the interdependence of human rights and the claim that economic, social and cultural rights should not be treated differently. It should not be used to defend an abstract analysis of concrete cases. It remains crucial to take the concrete circumstances and vulnerability of the individual into account, analysing the concrete impact of State action on the individual and society. Given its ambiguity one may even argue that it would be better to avoid using the concept. But it is perhaps this ambiguity that also makes its strength: it invites us, judges, law-makers and citizens, to determine every day again what is necessary in our democratic society to allow everyone to live a dignified life. It is not just a philosophical question, it is a question which is the essence of human rights law.

---

same forces that determine the behaviour of chimpanzees, wolves and ants. Our judicial and political systems largely try to sweep such inconvenient discoveries under the carpet. But in all frankness, how long can we maintain the wall separating the department of biology from the departments of law and political science?".

[65] C.-A. Chassin, "La notion de dignité de la personne humaine dans la jurisprudence de la Cour de justice" in A. Biad and V. Parisot (red.), *La Charte des droits fondamentaux de l'Union européenne*, Anthemis, 2018, (137) 158: "Dans l'acceptation retenue par la Cour de justice à l'occasion de l'affaire Omega, on retrouve indéniablement cette même 'exigence morale collective de la sauvegarde de la dignité, le cas échéant, aux dépens du libre-arbitre de la personne'. La dignité est alors une forme de 'paternalisme d'Etat', imposé à l'individu contre ses propres choix."

RELIGIOUS DIVERSITY IN EUROPE: A SHARED RESPONSIBILITY OF COURTS, PARLIAMENT AND SOCIETY

Marie-Claire FOBLETS

Max Planck Director of the Institute for Social Anthropology, Halle, Germany
Professor KU Leuven and Maarten Luther University Halle

Jan VELAERS

Professor University of Antwerp
Assessor in the Council of State of Belgium
Member of the Venice Commission

INTRODUCTION

The inspiration for this paper comes from a contribution by Paul Lemmens, in December 2013, to the closing conference of a European research project that focused on the governance of religious diversity in a number of European countries. In his argument, Paul Lemmens speaking in his capacity of a judge at the European Court of Human Rights (hereinafter ECtHR) warned against exaggerated expectations of the role that the ECtHR can play in the protection of freedom of religion. The fact that in many areas the ECtHR allows a considerable margin of appreciation to the Contracting States has its reasons.[1] European

---

[1]   See, for example, ECtHR 5 December 2017, *Hamidovic v. Bosnia*, §129. "It is also important to emphasise the fundamentally subsidiary role of the Convention mechanism. The national authorities have direct democratic legitimacy and are, as the Court has held on many occasions, in principle better placed than an international court to evaluate local needs and conditions. In matters of general policy, on which opinions within a democratic society may reasonably differ widely, the role of the domestic policy-maker should be given special weight (see, for example, *Maurice v. France* [GC], no. 11810/3, §117, ECHR 2005-IX). This is the case, in particular, where questions concerning the relationship between State and religions are at stake (see, *mutatis mutandis*, ECtHR 27 June 2000, *Cha'are Shalom Ve Tsedek v. France*, §84, and ECtHR 25 November 1996 *Wingrove v. the United Kingdom*, §58, *Reports* 1996-V; see also ECtHR 10 November 2005, *Leyla Şahin v. Turkey*, §109). As 25 November 1996 regards Article 9 of the European Convention on Human Rights (ECHR), the State should thus, in principle, be afforded a wide margin of appreciation in deciding whether and to what extent a limitation of the right to manifest one's religion or beliefs is 'necessary'. That being said, in delimiting the extent of the margin of appreciation in a given case, the Court must also have

history has been marked by religious diversity, and each of the Contracting States has developed its own position regarding the relationship of church and state and the way that public authorities deal with religious and philosophical pluralism, in the light of their own history and their own constitutional, political, social and cultural context. If the ECtHR wishes over the long term to remain the protector of the freedom of religion under the terms of a Convention that today links no fewer than 47 Contracting States, this will only be possible by taking into account the different histories and contexts. This reality explains why the ECtHR often seems to take a rather reticent position when it comes to the protection of freedom of religion, even at the risk of disappointing certain people.[2]

Lemmens's position implies that the primary responsibility for the protection of the freedom of religious lies with the national authorities. In this paper we will address the question which authority specifically within the domestic legal order of a state should take this responsibility: the legislature or the judiciary? The ECtHR's reticence does not mean, however, that national judges must likewise be reticent, but the national judicial authorities ought not to be overburdened either. The latter situation is all too frequent today, or at any rate that is how many judges see it, as suggested by the results of a survey of judges on which we will draw extensively in this paper. When it comes to a matter as important as the freedom to manifest religious belief and the ability to protect that freedom adequately and transparently, legislators cannot avoid their responsibilities. As we can see in the daily news, the topic of religious freedom is an extremely sensitive one today, and legislative initiatives themselves often give rise to heated social debates at the national level.[3] Legislators have to deal carefully with the various opinions and expectations of their constituents regarding this matter. In a context of growing pluralism, with new cultures and religions coexisting in each State, this is anything but an easy exercise.

---

regard to what is at stake therein (see among other authorities, ECtHR 26 September 1996 *Manoussakis and Others v. Greece*, §44, and *Leyla Şahin*, cited above, §110). It may also, if appropriate, have regard to any consensus and common values emerging from the practices of the States Parties to the Convention (see, for example, ECtHR (GC) 7 July 2011 *Bayatyan v. Armenia*, §122).

2   See S.C. Prebersen, "Evolutive Interpretation of the European Convention on Human Rights", in: P. Mahoney & R. Rysdal (eds), *Protecting Human Rights: the European Perspective*, Heymans, 2000, 1127–1137; A. Nieuwenhuis, "European Court of Human Rights: State and Religion, Schools and Scarves. An Analysis of the Margin of Appreciation as Used in the Case of Leyla Sahin v. Turkey", *Eur.Const. L.Rev.*, 2005, 495; G. Pitt, "Religion or Belief: Aiming at the Right Target?", in: H. Meenan (ed.), *Equality Law in an Enlarged European Union: Understanding the Article 13 Directives*, CUP, 2007, 209ff.

3   See esp. R. Bottoni, R. Cristofori and S. Ferrari (eds), *Religious Rules, State Law and Normative Pluralism – A Comparative Overview*, Springer (Ius Comparatum, vol. 18), 2016.

I. RELIGIOUS DIVERSITY AND SECULAR MODELS IN EUROPE: A COMPARATIVE ANALYSIS

We first need to situate, if only briefly, the above-mentioned research project. RELIGARE – an acronym for 'Religious Diversity and Secular Models in Europe: Innovative Approaches to Law and Policy' – was a project which ran from February 2010 to January 2013 and was funded under Framework Programme 7 (Socio-economic Sciences and Humanities – Area 8.3. 'Major trends in society and their implications'). Ten countries (9 EU Member States – Belgium, Bulgaria, Denmark, Germany, Great Britain, France, Italy, the Netherlands, Spain – and Turkey)[4] and 13 research teams from these countries were involved. In the context of Europe's growing religious diversity, RELIGARE focused on the challenges faced by State law in four areas of social life: the family, the labour market, public space and state support to religions. The project investigated and analysed which constitutional frameworks and accompanying instruments are best suited to guaranteeing respect for the rights of all individuals to freedom of thought, conscience and religion and to non-discrimination on the grounds of religion or belief. The project mapped the often divergent approaches to these four areas taken by the countries covered in the study. More specifically, drawing on the various national experiences, the goal was to identify responses – whether legislative, judicial, or elaborated through best practices – that allow for an adequate balance of the principles of equality and non-discrimination with the protected fundamental rights of freedom of thought, conscience and religion.

Two findings in particular that come from the RELIGARE project will be highlighted, as they are directly linked with the issue of governance of religious diversity in contemporary Europe. The *first* finding concerns the stronger protection granted in many domestic legal orders in Europe to mainstream/majority religions, i.e., the belief systems that are perceived as 'home-grown'.[5] The problem is not the protection in itself, but its potential discriminatory effects against other minority religions and belief systems. The *second* finding revolves around some of the difficulties that accompany the application in very different situations and contexts and on a case-by-case basis of human rights standards of protection to issues of freedom of religion and belief, and where the role of courts is at stake. The concerns Paul Lemmens expressed on the occasion of the

---

[4] M.-Cl. Foblets and K. Alidadi, Summary Report on the RELIGARE Project, Summer 2013, 60 pp; reprinted in M.-Cl. Foblets, K. Alidadi, J.S. Nielsen and Z. Yanasmayan (eds), *Belief, Law and Politics. What Future for a Secular Europe?*, Farnham, Ashgate, 2014, 11–54.

[5] In the same sense: L. Zucca, *A Secular Europe. Law and Religion in the European Constitutional Landscape*, Oxford, Oxford University Press, 2012; S. Mancini, "The Power of Symbols and Symbols as Power: Secularism and Religion as Guarantors of Cultural Convergence", *Cardozo Law Review*, 2008–2009, p. 2631.

final RELIGARE conference in December 2013 focused on this role of courts in particular, thereby expressing some reservations regarding what can be expected from the judiciary, and from the ECtHR in particular, when it comes to the governance of religious diversity in contemporary Europe.

A. FIRST FINDING: STRONGER CONSTITUTIONAL PROTECTION GRANTED TO MAJORITY RELIGIONS AND TRADITIONAL FAITH COMMUNITIES

The RELIGARE project took as its starting point the secular nature of the State in European countries, which means that the governance of religious diversity is historically grounded in the reasoning that secularising the State and its institutions ultimately disconnects them from any specific religion and, by the same token, makes the democratic legal (State) order more inclusive of minorities, both religious and, more generally, philosophical. With a view to regulating the relationships between State institutions and religions, national legislatures in the vast majority of the countries in Europe thus made the historic choice to secularise State law.[6] In practice, one can distinguish three different models of secular States.[7] The *first* involves countries where there is, in principle, a strict separation between religion and the State. In such systems, such as those of France and until recently Turkey as well, State policy can be implemented only by means of secular laws and is, therefore, to be kept strictly separate from religious beliefs. Such States relegate religion, in theory at least, to the private sphere and oppose its legal, administrative and political incorporation into State structures (although in reality the State does take account of religion and belief). A *second* model, by contrast, accepts institutional – albeit symbolic – links between the State and religion, such as the arrangement between the Church of

---

[6] See esp. A. Dierkens and J.-P. Schreiber (eds), *Laïcité et sécularisation dans l'Union européenne*, Bruxelles, Ed. de l'Université de Bruxelles ("Problèmes d'Histoire des religions"), Tome XVI, 2006; Y. Lambert, "Le rôle dévolu à la religion par les européens", *Sociétés contemporaines* 37 (2000), 11–33; R. Torfs, "Models of freedom of religion in the European Union and in the United States", in: *Between Caesar and the Lord – Relation between Religion and the State in the Countries of Asia and Europe*, Beijing, Kungcki Cultural Group, 2004, 225–252; 155; G. D'Costa *et al.* (eds), *Religion in a Liberal State*, Cambridge, Cambridge University Press, 2013; V. Bader, *Secularism or Democracy?: Associational governance of religious identity*, Amsterdam University Press, 2007; A. Berg-Sørensen (ed.), *Contesting Secularism: comparative perspectives*, Farnham, Ashgate, 2013.

[7] See esp. G. Robbers (ed.), *State and Church in the European Union*, Baden-Baden, Nomos, 2005; European Consortium for Church-State Research, *Church and State in Europe. State Financial Support. Religion and the School*, Milano, Giuffrè, 1992; S. Knights, *Freedom of Religion, Minorities and the Law*, Oxford, Oxford U.P., 2007, 14; J. Martinez-Torron *et al.* (eds), *Religion and the Secular State: national reports/La religion et l'Etat laïque: rapports nationaux*, Madrid, Servicio de Publicaciones de la Facultad de Derecho de la Universidad Complutense de Madrid, 2015.

England and the State in the United Kingdom. The *third* category combines non-establishment with conditional (limited) legal, administrative and/or political pluralism. The latter arrangement usually takes the form of the requirement that the State be neutral towards religion(s), i.e., by placing all religions and denominations on a non-discriminatory footing. A neutral State may support religions, but should it decide to do so, it should be careful not to favour one religion over another.[8] Countries like Belgium and the Netherlands fall into this third category.

Strikingly, one of the findings of the cross-country comparative analysis carried out within the RELIGARE project is that, *in practice*, the historical majority religions in the ten countries under scrutiny are generally[9] granted some kind of preferential treatment.[10] In some cases these treatments are constitutionally guaranteed; in other cases they are based on legislation, for example the laws on Sunday rest and public holidays.[11] These laws have for the most part developed over the course of the country's history, and that is in a sense to be expected, since history unavoidably leaves the marks of its own logic and rules.[12] The laws in question are therefore not considered to be in breach of the principle of neutrality of the State. Yet, with the arrival of new religious groups and communities across Europe, some of the historically developed forms of protection of traditional religions have come under criticism, giving rise in some cases to the question why similar benefits are not (yet) granted to minority religions and belief systems, and whether or not this constitutes outright discrimination[13] that would make it necessary to reshape the legal frameworks in place in order to accommodate these new groups.[14]

---

[8] See ECtHR 31 July 2008, *Religionsgemeinschaft der Zeugen Jehovas and others v. Austria*, §92; ECtHR 8 April 2014, *Magyar Keresztény Mennonita Egyház and others v. Hungary*; ECtHR (GC) 26 April 2016, *Izzettin Dogan and others v. Turkey*.

[9] In some States, e.g. in Belgium, minority religions such as Islam also have the status of a "recognised church", which involves preferential treatment.

[10] Some authors, for that matter, have raised the question whether there is a need to revise the meaning of secular(ity) and secularism. See, for example: S. Mancini and M. Rosenfeld (eds), *Constitutional Secularism in an Age of Religious Revival*, Oxford, Oxford University Press, 2014.

[11] See esp. Stéphanie Hennette Vauchez, "Religious Holidays in Employment – Austria, France and Spain", *European Equality Law Review*, 2018, no. 2, 263–77.

[12] N. Bhuta (ed.), *Freedom of Religion, Secularism and Human Rights*, Oxford, Oxford University Press, 2019. For a comparative analysis that is not limited to Europe, see: J. Fox, *Political Secularism, Religion and the State. A Time Series Analysis of Worldwide Data*, Cambridge, Cambridge University Press, 2015.

[13] *Ibid.*, 104–135; see also: J.T.S. Madeley and Z. Enyedi (eds), *Church and State in Contemporary Europe. The Chimera of Neutrality*, London/Portland, Fr. Cass, 2003; L. Zucca and C. Ungureanu (eds), *Law, State and Religion in the New Europe; Debates and Dilemmas*, Cambridge University Press, 2012.

[14] This is true beyond European countries as well: M.K. Bhamra, *The Challenges of Justice in Diverse Societies? Constitutionalism and Pluralism*, Farnham, Ashgate, 2011.

One would expect that with the growing awareness of increasing religious diversity, legislatures in secular democracies throughout Europe would have started revising these frameworks where necessary in their respective domestic legal orders. Issues revolving around religion and the risks of discriminatory treatment of some people, especially when it comes to structural discrimination, should be addressed primarily through legislation and a deliberative democratic process. However, a closer look at what has been done thus far shows that, to date, legislatures throughout Europe are not particularly keen to revise the laws in place. We will return to this point below. As a consequence, it is often up to the judiciary to offer provisional responses and ad hoc solutions to litigants who claim more robust recognition of the plurality of religions and beliefs in concrete cases. The question of whether the courtroom is the right place to develop more appropriate and sustainable forms of governance of religious diversity relates directly to the concerns Paul Lemmens was addressing at the final RELIGARE conference, and leads us here to the second finding.

B. SECOND FINDING: JUDICIAL PRACTICE AND RELIGIOUS DIVERSITY

In his monograph *Law and Religion*, Russell Sandberg speaks of a 'juridification of religion' being at play in contemporary societies. It takes different forms, one of them being the growing tendency for conflicts to be resolved by or with reference to law; another is a process of 'legal framing' by which people increasingly think of themselves and others as legal subjects and holders of rights.[15] The RELIGARE findings confirm this observation by providing evidence of the fact that, throughout Europe, judges are ever more frequently called upon to handle individual situations that are often highly sensitive. National courts, as well as the European Court of Human Rights and, more recently, also the Court of Justice of the European Union (CJEU) for issues concerning the interpretation and the application of European Union law, are tasked with the often far from easy exercise of balancing individuals' claims for protection of their freedom of religion against other interests, such as law and order, public health, gender equality, human dignity, children's rights, etc.[16]

Some of these courts' judgments are analysed extensively both in legal commentaries and in the media, in particular when they touch on highly

---

[15] R. Sandberg, *Law and Religion*, Cambridge, Cambridge University Press, 2011, 193.
[16] See for a number of number of case studies drawing on the case law of the ECtHR, esp. S. Smet and E. Brems (eds), *When Human Rights Clash at the European Court of Human Rights: conflict or harmony?* Oxford/New York, Oxford University Press, 2017.

political issues such as the display of religious symbols in the public space[17], the construction of places of worship[18], religious dress codes[19], ritual slaughter[20], male and female circumcision, etc., and on how to accommodate certain claims related to these issues.

Judges, all over Europe, deserve to be praised for their commitment to the search for fair solutions in even the most intricate cases that often involve burning issues. Yet at the same time, one should probably be concerned not to entertain excessively high expectations regarding what the role of the judiciary can and should be in governing religious diversity: judges should not be tasked too frequently with the responsibility of having to fill in the gaps of a legislative framework which fails to provide for adequate protection of freedom of religion, particularly of new religious minorities. To do so effectively, judges need to take into account, as far as possible, the specific needs and claims of such minorities, all the more so since the scope of a court's ruling is by definition limited.

We see at least three reasons to avoid excessively burdening the judiciary with the search for new(er) forms of protection of freedom of religion that would more adequately take into account the needs and claims of minorities (particularly, but not exclusively, new minorities). A *first* reason is that litigation is and should remain a rare *ultimum remedium*. A *second* reason is that, in a secular State's legal order, judges have no competence to get involved in purely religious issues. A

---

[17]　See for an illustration of such extensive comment, esp. J. Temperman (ed.), *The Lautsi Papers: Multidisciplinary Reflections on Religious Symbols in the Public Classroom*, Leiden/Boston, Martinus Nijhoff Publishers, 2012.

[18]　See esp. F. Fregosi, "Issue of the Funding of Worship in Islam: worship, imams and mosques, as viewed through texts and practice", in F. Messner (ed.), *Public Funding of Religions in Europe*, Farnham, Ashgate, 2015.

[19]　See esp. S. Ferrari *et al.* (eds), *The Burqa Affair across Europe: between public and private space*, Farnham, Ashgate, 2013; D. McGoldrick, *Human Rights and Religion: the Islamic Headscarf Debate in Europe*, Oxford, Hart, 2006; C. Longmans and G. Coene, "Harmful Cultural Practices and Minority Women in Europe: from headscarf bans to forced marriages and honour related violence", in C. Longman and T. Bradley (eds), *Interrogating Harmful Cultural Practices: Gender, Culture and Coercion*, Farnham, Ashgate, 2015, 51–66; W.C. Durham *et al.* (eds), *Islam, Europe and Emerging Legal Issues* (Part II: European Approaches to the Islamic Headscarf Controversy), Farnham, Ashgate, 2012, 89–208.

[20]　See esp. C.M. Zoethout, "Ritual Slaughter and the Freedom of Religion: Some Reflections on a Stunning Matter", *Human Rights Quarterly*, 35(2013), p. 651–672; F. Zuolo, "Equality among Animals and Religious Slaughter", *Historical Social Research/Historische Socialforschung*, 2015, no. 4, p. 110–127; F. Bergeaud-Blackler, "New Challenges for Islamic Ritual Slaughter: An European Perspective", *Journal of Ethnic and Migration Studies*, 33 (2007), n° 6, p. 965–980; M.-C. Foblets and J. Velaers, "In Search of the Right Balance. Recent Discussions in Belgium and The Netherlands on Religious Freedom and the Slaughter of Animals without Prior Stunning", in: B. Schinkele, R. Kuppe, E.M. Synek, J. Wallner and W. Weishaider (eds), *Religion, Recht Kultur: Festschrift für Richard potz Zum 70. Geburtstag*, Wien Universitätsverlag, 2014, p. 67–85; M. Schreuer, "Belgium Bans Religious Slaughtering Practices, Drawing Praise and Protest", *The New York Times*, 7 January 2019.

third reason has to do with the way, in judicial practice, that human rights serve as the standard of measurement when it comes to assessing claims for protection of freedom of religion. In reality, it turns out that human rights allow for divergent reactions and too often make the decision of the court unpredictable.

All three reasons would require further clarification, but we will limit ourselves here to the third reason, which gives us the opportunity to go deeper into the oral remarks made by Paul Lemmens at the above-mentioned closing conference in December 2013. Those remarks have not lost any of their relevance since 2013, quite the contrary, it seems to us. He gave three reasons for avoiding exaggerated expectations from what the judiciary can do with its powers when it comes to protecting the freedom of religion.

As regards the first reason, Paul Lemmens drew attention to the fact that judges must, when hearing cases involving human rights protection, build on the factual material and especially on the arguments that the parties to the case put forward. Judges are bound to engage with those arguments and limit themselves to the information provided by the parties. That can in some cases represent a serious limitation.

Moreover, in cases adjudicated by the European Court of Human Rights, the Court must in its investigation take into account the specific legislation in force in the Contracting State concerned. That means that some reasonings cannot simply be extrapolated to situations in other Contracting States, even if at first glance they appear to have much in common.

Some situations, moreover, are so closely linked to the specific historical, political, social and cultural context in which the dispute arose, that the Court takes the view that the solution would best be found within that context, namely, at national level. Whenever the Court is convinced that this is the case, it invokes the principle of the 'margin of appreciation', which means that the Court holds that the competent authorities in the Contracting State concerned are best placed to determine the appropriate balance of the interests at issue in the given case.[21] Some critics see an overly frequent invocation of the 'margin of appreciation' as posing a risk that the Court avoids its responsibility to define that balance itself, and that the parties that have turned to the Court to seek redress in a situation in which they felt themselves to be victims, will be denied the protection they hoped

---

[21] See esp. S. Greer, *The Margin of Appreciation: Interpretation and Discretion under the European Convention on Human Rights*, Council of Europe Publishing (Human Rights files, n° 17) 2000; Y. Arai, *The Margin of Appreciation Doctrine and the Principle of Proportionality in the Jurisprudence of the ECHR*, Mortsel, Intersentia, 2002; M. Iglesias Vila, "Subsidiarity, Margin of Appreciation and International Adjudication within a Cooperative Conception of Human Rights", *International Journal of Constitutional Law*, 2017, 393–413.

for[22]: the solution will in such cases have to be found within the legal order of the State concerned, and will not come from the ECtHR. However, an invocation of the 'margin of appreciation' can, according to Paul Lemmens, also be understood in a different, less critical way: a certain reticence on the part of the Court is necessary if the Court wishes to safeguard its legitimacy over the long term. Three reasons, in other words, according to Paul Lemmens, that challenge us to take a realistic view of the role that the European Court of Human Rights may or may not play when it comes to protecting religious freedom in Europe.

The reticence shown by the Strasbourg Court, and for which Paul Lemmens gave reasons, does not mean, however, that the national judge must take an equally reticent position.[23] The latter can hand down justice in the light of his or her own national political, cultural and social context and in the light of the constitutional values and norms regarding the relationship between church and state and on the coexistence of various religions and philosophies.[24] In practice, however, we see that national courts also take divergent views as regards the protection of freedom of religion, with some judges taking a more prudent approach than others.

In what follows, we examine a notion that has, in cases of protection of freedom of religion, caused much debate in several European countries in recent years, and in which the judicial authorities have been called upon repeatedly to find a solution. The issue is the freedom to express one's religion or belief in the workplace, and its role in the relationship between employer and employee. The differences of opinion in case law are great, at both national and European levels.[25]

---

[22] Along these lines, see K. Henrard, "Beyond Lautsi: an alternative approach to limiting the government's ability to display religious symbols in the public workplace", in K. Alidadi, M.-C. Foblets and J. Vrielink (eds), *A Test of Faith. Religion and Diversity in the European Workplace*, Farnham, Ashgate, 2012.

[23] In the same vein: ECtHR (GC) 29 September 2009, *A. v. UK* (regarding Art. 15 ECHR): "*the doctrine of the margin of appreciation has always been meant as a tool to define relations between the domestic authorities and the Court; it could not have the same application to relations between the different organs of the State at the domestic level.*"

[24] The Belgian Council of State stated: "*Er dient te worden benadrukt dat de beoordelingsmarge die het Europees Hof voor de Rechten van de Mens aan de staten lijkt te laten inzake de relatie tussen de Staat en de godsdiensten en de levensbeschouwelijke opvattingen, moet worden gezien binnen het bestek van de subsidiaire toetsing die dit Europees Hof verricht ten aanzien van de interne praktijken en dat ze in het interne recht dus niet noodzakelijkerwijs betekent dat, in het kader van de preventieve toetsing verricht door de afdeling wetgeving van de Raad van State en van de toetsing die eventueel a posteriori verricht wordt door het Grondwettelijk Hof, geen striktere eis wordt gesteld wat betreft naleving van de grondwettelijke beginselen verbonden aan de vrijheid van denken, meningsuiting en godsdienst.*" Opinion 44.521/AV, 20 May 2008, on a draft law 'applying to the separation of the State and religious or non-confessional philosophical organisations or communities'. See J. Velaers, *De Grondwet. Een artikelsgewijze commentaar. Deel I*, Brugge, Die Keure, 2019, p. 331.

[25] The case law on this issue was collected and analysed in the framework of the RELIGARE project. More recently, see P. Joassart, "Les convictions religieuses dans les relations de travail", *Orientations*, 2016, 8, 49–61.

II. RELIGIOUS CONVICTION
AND THE WORKPLACE

This illustration draws from the area of employment law and is based on data collected within the framework of the RELIGARE research project concerning the protection of the freedom of religious conviction in the workplace.[26]

The workplace is a key area in debates about the governance of religious diversity in contemporary society.[27] In Europe, very generally speaking, two legal frameworks permit the courts to assess the claims for protection of the freedom of religion in issues of employment, and the two are intertwined: the non-discrimination framework and the freedom of religion framework. In the European Union, an important legal framework for non-discrimination on the grounds of religion and belief in the employment area was established in Directive 2000/78 (the Employment Equality Directive).[28] This Directive, which aims to implement the principle of equal treatment in EU member states as regards employment and occupation, prohibits direct discrimination, indirect discrimination[29], harassment and incitement to discriminate on the grounds of religion or belief, disability, age or sexual orientation. The Directive also protects against victimisation on the basis of the same grounds. Freedom of thought, conscience and religion is guaranteed by Article 9 of the European Convention on Human Rights and Article 10 of the EU Charter of Fundamental Rights, as well as by national (constitutional) provisions. The Employment Equality Directive does not explicitly include a right for employees to ask their employers or labour unions for reasonable accommodation in the workplace on the basis of religion or belief. The concept (which comes from the US religious discrimination context) was introduced into the Directive, but was limited to the grounds of disability. Some EU member states have included in their national legislation (limited) rights to reasonable accommodation for religious beliefs or practices or similar measures.[30]

---

[26]   See esp. L. Vickers, *Religious Freedom, Religious Discrimination and the Workplace*, Oxford/ Portland, Hart, 2008; K. Alidadi et al. (eds), *op.cit.*, Farnham, Ashgate, 2012 and, more recently, F. Hendrickx (ed.), *Reasonable Accommodation in the Modern Workplace. Potential and Limits of the Integrative Logics of Labour Law*, Alphen a/d Rijn, Wolters Kluwer (Bulletin for Comparative Labour Relations – 93), 2016.

[27]   See also: Interim report A/69/261 (2014) of the Special UN Rapporteur on freedom of religion or belief (Focus: *Tackling religious intolerance and discrimination in the workplace*).

[28]   Council *Directive 2000/78/EC* of 27 November 2000 establishing a general framework for equal treatment in employment and occupation.

[29]   The Directive defines indirect discrimination as 'an apparently neutral provision, criterion or practice [which] would put persons having a particular religion or belief ... at a particular disadvantage compared with other persons'. Such a provision, criterion or practice can be justified if there is a legitimate aim and the means of achieving that aim are appropriate and necessary. Many member states have adopted this definition, sometimes verbatim.

[30]   See esp. L. Vickers, "Religious Interests in the European Workplace: Different Perspectives", in K. Alidadi et al. (eds), *op.cit.*, 2012, 13–32.

RELIGARE data show, however, that, in practice, employers and other stakeholders such as labour union leaders are not necessarily keen to make the right to express one's religion in the workplace a priority, arguing that religion or belief should remain confined to the private lives of individuals. From this point of view, people are free to have a religion, but should keep it to themselves when outside the comfort of their own home (or in any case when at work). What is to be done, then, when there is a conflict between workplace rules and obligations that are felt to be of a religious nature, potentially leading to significant employment exclusion, and thus social exclusion? The question is all the more urgent in the case of individuals who not only identify with minority religions but also wish to practise those religions publicly? Should those people make a claim? What has arisen thus far in case law is but the tip of the iceberg.[31] In a labour market where rules and expectations are not designed with the needs of religious minorities in mind, empirical evidence shows that individuals only very rarely call upon a judge; instead, people experiment with a variety of 'coping' mechanisms to deal with exclusion.[32] Litigation is indeed a rare *ultimum remedium*. What occurs instead is self-exclusion, which is a widespread and under-investigated phenomenon. Some forms of expressing one's religion or belief, such as when a Muslim wears a headscarf or objects to certain types of tasks at work, are self-handicapping.[33] That is, a person thereby excludes him- or herself from certain opportunities so as to avoid having to compromise their religious convictions.[34] RELIGARE data run counter to the general perception that religious minorities are very demanding, and show on the contrary a prevalent attitude of acceptance of their minority situation, as well as a refusal to see themselves as victims.

Yet, exclusion from employment may push minorities into unemployment or poverty. Therefore, it should be the concern of legislators primarily, and not of the courts, to combat this reality.[35] This is all the more true since the two above-

---

[31]   For instance, on the issue of objection to physical contact (e.g., in the form of shaking hands) with members of the opposite sex there is only minimal case law, and only in some countries, such as the Netherlands.

[32]   For instance, in France the Bureau de Chabbath allows Jewish employees to search for and match up with job openings where accommodation for the Sabbath will not be a problem (see www.50ansbdc.org/EMPLOI/).

[33]   S. Ghumman and L. Jackson, "The downside of religious attire: the Muslim headscarf and expectations of obtaining employment" *Journal of Organizational Behavior*, 2010, 4.

[34]   Such a decision can at times be very rational. To give just one example: when a company has a 'neutrality policy', it may appear futile for a woman, even if highly educated, to apply for a job if she wishes to wear a headscarf on the job. For a critique of such company neutrality policies, see K. Alidadi, "The 'Integrative Function' of Labour Law in Ebb? Reasonable Accommodation for Religion or Belief and Company 'Neutrality Policies' in Belgium", in F. Hendrickx (ed.), *o.c.*, 2016, 119–143.

[35]   This was also the view of the Special UN Rapporteur on freedom of religion or belief, Heiner Bielefeldt, in his 2014 report on religious discrimination in the workplace (see above note 28).

mentioned legal frameworks – the non-discrimination framework and the human rights framework – leave ample leeway for the courts to adopt divergent approaches to assessing claims based on religion. And indeed, in practice, national courts interpret the existing protections against religious or belief-related discrimination, including indirect discrimination, very differently.[36] The case law offers no unequivocal answer. Especially in cases involving indirect discrimination, courts are rather hesitant to provide protection under the given frameworks.

One illustration of this point relates to the adoption by private companies of so-called neutrality policies that invoke the criterion of 'neutrality' as a ground for banning all religious, philosophical, and often even political expressions in the workplace. Do such policies, which in effect exclude employees who wear religious attire, amount to discrimination, whether direct or indirect?[37] On 14 March 2017, the European Court of Justice handed down two judgments regarding a ban on wearing religious symbols in the workplace.[38] An internal rule by a (private) company that bans the wearing of visible signs of political, philosophical or religious beliefs was found, according to the CJEU, not to be a case of direct discrimination. With such an internal measure, everyone is, after all, required to dress and behave in a neutral way, so that there is no difference in treatment that could be based directly on religion or belief within the meaning of the above-mentioned Directive 2000/78/EC.[39] In a case involving a Belgian company (the G4S Secure Solutions case), the Court left it to the national judge to determine whether or not there was a difference in treatment based indirectly on religion or belief. That would be the case if it were determined that the apparently neutral provision in fact led to persons having a particular religion or belief being put at a particular disadvantage. Such indirect discrimination can in turn be justified, according to the Court, by the legitimate aim of the employer to project an image of neutrality towards its customers, provided the means of achieving that aim are appropriate and necessary. From that perspective, the Court held that it must therefore be determined whether the ban applies to all employees or only to those interacting with customers. In the latter instance, the company must see if it can offer the employee a post that does not involve visual contact with customers and where the employee would therefore be permitted

---

[36] See esp. F. Hendrickx, *o.c.*, 2016.

[37] Two referrals for preliminary rulings by the CJEU had been made, one by the French Cour de Cassation and one by the Belgian Cour de Cassation, relating to the question of wearing a Muslim headscarf in the workplace and involving the issue of 'general neutrality bans' on religious dress. See (BE) Cass. 9 March 2015, AR S.12.0062.N; (FR) Cass. (Chambre sociale), no. 630 of 9 April 2015 (13–19.855), ECLI:FR:CCASS:2015:SO00630.

[38] CJEU 14 March 2017, no. 157/15, *G4S Secure Solutions*; CJEU 14 March 2017, no. C-188/15, *Bougnaoui & ADDH* (http://curia.europa.eu).

[39] See footnote 29.

to wear clothing that expresses political, philosophical or religious beliefs, as long as this does not place any additional burden on the company. The judgment thus allowed freedom of enterprise and the associated economic and monetary interests of the employer to serve as a decisive factor in determining whether or not discrimination was involved.[40]

This approach – placing the freedom of enterprise above freedom of religion – has been viewed critically by many authors.[41] In the two cases in which the Court of Justice of the European Union handed down a decision on 14 March 2017, the positions of the advocates general on the question of (direct) discrimination were diametrically opposed to each other. Advocate General Sharpston, in the case involving a French company, considered that such an undifferentiated ban amounted to direct discrimination[42], whereas in the Belgian case, Advocate General Kokott took the view that this was not the case as long as the ban was not based on *"(...) stereotypes or prejudice against one or more particular religions or against religious beliefs in general"*. The Court ultimately found in favour of the freedom of enterprise. Undoubtedly, that is not the last word on the question of measures that limit freedom in the workplace. It is to be expected that the ECtHR will take a position on such measures, and so it remains to be seen what considerations it will make. In the *Eweida v. UK* decision, the ECtHR, after a thorough investigation of the specific circumstances, had held that the "corporate image" of a company did *not* outweigh respect for the employee's freedom of religion.[43]

Assessing national traditions and practices throughout Europe and taking into account the reminder by Paul Lemmens of the very raison d'être of the principle of the margin of appreciation, one cannot but conclude that for the time being – and no doubt for some time to come – the implementation of the provisions

---

[40] Even if the last word rests with the national judge, who has to determine the legitimacy and proportionality of the neutrality policy within the company.

[41] See esp. L. Vickers, "Achbita and Bougnaoui: One Step Forward and Two Steps Back for Religious Diversity in the Workplace", *European Labour Law Journal*, 2017, 232–257; R.E. Howard, "Islamic Headscarves and the CJEU: Achbita and Bougnaoui", *Maastricht Journal of European and Comparative Law*, 2017, p.

[42] She underpinned her position with, among other things, the following example *(...) un ingénieur d'études travaillant chez Micropole qui n'aurait pas choisi de manifester ses croyances religieuses en portant une tenue vestimentaire particulière n'aurait pas été licencié"* (§88).

[43] ECtHR, 15 January 2013, *Eweida and others v. The United Kingdom*, 48420/10, 59842/10, 51671/10 & 36516/10; M. Hill, "Religious Symbolism and Conscientious Objection in the Workplace: An Evaluation of Strasbourg's Judgment in *Eweida and others v. United Kingdom*", *Ecclesiastical Law Journal*, 2013, 191–203; J. Maher, "Eweida and Others: a new era for article 9?", *International and Comparative Law Quarterly*, 2014, 213–233; M. Pearson, "Article 9 at the Crossroads: Interferences before and after Eweida", *Human Rights Law Review*, 2013, 580–602.

of the European Convention on Human Rights, and more recently also of the principles enshrined in the European Charter, concerning the protection of the freedom of religion will vary widely from State to State, from jurisdiction to jurisdiction, and even from court to court, not to mention from judge to judge. The sharply divided nature of the case law is evidenced by daily practice at all levels of jurisdiction, an observation that applies to the vast majority of the European countries that were studied in the RELIGARE project. And what is true for the workplace also applies to other instances of protection of freedom of religion.[44]

III. JUDGES SPEAK: CASE LAW IS THE WORK OF HUMAN BEINGS

The observation that the standard reference for judges throughout Europe when it comes to assessing claims to protection of freedom of religion are human rights, and that human rights allow for divergent interpretations, is corroborated by the findings of a survey we conducted in the period January to November 2014 among some 100 judges from 14 European countries in cooperation with the European Network of the Councils of the Judiciary (hereafter ENCJ).[45] The survey reveals some of the difficulties that come with the application of standards of protection grounded in human rights. A large majority of judges who participated to the survey adopt a pragmatic approach to the sharply divided case law on freedom of religion: they see religious diversity in its new form as a societal issue in need of more appropriate legislative solutions and overarching policies, but with no expectation that 'ideal' solutions will become available in the short run, as the issue is simply too complex and sensitive.[46] Hence they seek to acknowledge religious and cultural diversity within the existing normative framework (domestic/State), using the legal techniques at their disposal and of course taking account of the specific circumstances of the case at hand. This includes knowing the relevant case law, avoiding overturning precedent, being familiar with ECtHR decisions, and making the best use of general principles. They treat matters concerning religion or cultural diversity as questions of contextualization in each individual case: in addition to religion, other factors such as cultural diversity, socio-economic status, gender, age and knowledge of language are also mentioned as influencing the outcome of cases. Judges also emphasise the

---

44 See esp. W.C. Durham and D. Thayer (eds), *Religion and Equality: law in conflict*, London/New York, Routledge, 2016.

45 Findings published in: L. Vetters and M.-Cl. Foblets, "Culture all Around? Contextualizing anthropological expertise in European courtroom settings", *International Journal of Law in Context*, 2016, no. 3, 272–292.

46 See also A. Scolnicov, *The Right to Religious Freedom in International Law: Between Group Rights and Individual Rights*, London, Routledge, 2012.

importance of procedural factors such as the availability of extra time, the use of specially trained translators or other mediators, and a basic attitude of respect towards parties with different religious and cultural backgrounds.

All in all, the majority of the judges who responded to the survey show a high degree of motivation to better understand the impact of some religious factors in particular, even if they have no competence to intervene in religious affairs. In assessing individual claims they consider, among other things, "(...) *how important a religious practice is to the claimant, and if important and there are no compelling public interests against it, whether it can be accommodated or, on the contrary, whether there is some norm against it; if so, the question to answer will be whether the interference with the practice is justified and proportionate"*.[47] A German judge notes that in the field of labour law, 'reasonable accommodation' has gained prominence. He offers two illustrations of this: "*When an employee in a warehouse refuses to handle beer crates on grounds that it conflicts with his religious beliefs, he is no longer fit for the job and his contract may therefore be terminated. But if it is possible to reorganise the distribution of tasks in such a way that he no longer has to handle beer crates but can be entrusted with another task, it is not reasonable and therefore not justifiable to terminate his contract. In another case, a judge ruled that an employer cannot terminate the contract of a female sales clerk who converted to Islam and decided to wear a headscarf simply on the unsubstantiated grounds that this would have a negative impact on sales. The employer was required to wait and prove the expected negative impact on sales before making his decision"*. These are just two testimonies, of course, but they are illustrative of an approach on the part of the courts that is dictated by the requirements for consideration of the specificities of each case individually, and the practical consequences of the decision. It may induce differences in emphasis.

In the end however, pragmatism is not without risks. One such risk is unpredictability, particularly when the existing legal standards are open to interpretation or when the number of existing legal solutions (either through *supra-* and international regulation or through case law) is small. The hallmarks of a trustworthy and well-functioning judicial system are consistency, transparency and accountability. Somewhat paradoxically, however, even as these three hallmarks become ever more important as European society diversifies, they also become ever harder to achieve.

When asked whether they would welcome clearer legislation, several lower court judges who participated in the ENCJ survey were unambiguous: they would indeed welcome more clarity in the law, even if some legislative initiatives

---

[47] Drawing here on the testimony of an English judge.

would place new constraints on individual freedom of religion and belief and considerably reduce one's personal autonomy in deciding how to give concrete expression to it. In a sense, restrictive laws release the judge from having to determine where to draw the boundaries of claims for protection.[48] Although the ENCJ survey is not representative, involving some 100 judges, it nevertheless gives voice to the judiciary in a way that stimulates further reflection: for some practitioners, what matters is clarity in the law. Whether clarity means, in effect, less protection of religion and of some religions in particular, is a question they feel falls outside the scope of their professional responsibility.

IV. THE WAY FORWARD: IS THERE NEED FOR LEGISLATIVE INTERVENTION?

With respect to the highly divided nature of the case law in addressing issues of protection of protection of religious conviction, one can adopt basically two positions. Either one perceives no serious problem with placing high (possibly even excessive) expectations on what the judiciary can effectively do when it comes to addressing claims involving freedom of religion, and hence satisfies oneself with the pragmatic approach of judges as evidenced in the case law. One sees no problem with unpredictability and inconsistency, or chooses not to worry about them.

Or one argues in favour of legislative intervention. This is easier said than done, however. While the results of the RELIGARE project suggest that some legal frameworks still in force are at least partly outdated, they also show that where in recent years amendments have been adopted, they often tend to show greater restrictiveness towards practices inspired by religion and hence are often received with mixed feelings by the members of the communities concerned, who regard the new restrictions as discriminatory.

Many examples of such much-debated legislative interventions can be cited: the prohibition against women wearing full-face veils in the public space, the so-called 'burqa bans'[49], the ban on ritual slaughtering[50], the

---

48   Along a similar line of thinking: S. Conly, *Against Autonomy: Justifying Coercive Paternalism*, Cambridge, Cambridge University Press, 2013.

49   R. McCrea, "The Ban on the Veil and European Law", *Human Rights Law Review*, 2013, 57–97; S. Nanwani, "The Burqa Ban: an unreasonable limitation on religious freedom or a justifiable freedom?", *The Emory International Law Journal*, 2011, 1432–1474; P. Chesler, "Ban the Burqa? The Argument in Favor", *Middle East Quarterly*, 2010, 33–45; P. Fournier, "Headscarf and Burqa Controversies at the Crossroad of Politics, Society and Law", *Journal for the Study of Race, Nation and Culture* (introduction to Special Issue: "Illegal Covering: Comparative Perspectives on Legal and Social Discourses on Religious Diversity"), 2013, 689–703.

50   F. Bergeaud-Blackler, "Animal Rights Movements and Ritual Slaughtering: autopsy of a moribund campaign", in N. Gülifer (ed.), *Islam and Public Controversy in Europe*, Farnham,

criminalisation of unregistered religious marriages[51], the parliamentary debates in several countries concerning the physical integrity of infant boys (i.e., circumcision)[52], to mention but a few recent examples. In each of these cases, the discussions have at times been extremely emotional, nourished by arguments grounded in antagonistic views on the role of legislation when it comes to granting fundamental rights in Europe to Jewish and Muslim minorities in particular. Many of these legislative initiatives and the debates on them have driven a wedge between proponents of the opposing sides and have split public opinion, often with the support of the media, thereby hampering the development of a culture of inclusive tolerance and respect towards religious minorities.

The challenge for legislators in Europe today is to develop a consistent set of rules that reconcile differences and can deal in a consistent, transparent and accountable way with the requirements of fair regulation of increasing social, cultural, religious and philosophical diversity in secular (democratic) contexts, including the blending of groups and communities. That task falls to the legislature, or as Frank Schorkopf recently put it: *"In funktional differenzierten Gesellschaften, wie sie in modernen Industriestaaten vorzufinden sind, können kollektive Verbindlichkeiten nicht dem Lauf der Dinge überlassen bleiben. Es bedarf gerade wegen der pluralen Gesellschaft, mit ihrer Meinungsvielfalt und ihren Meinungsschwankungen, mit ihrer zwangsläufigen Neigung zur Dissoziation, einen Modus, kollektiv verbindlichen Regeln anzunehmen und durchzusetzen. Die Politik liefert Regeln und Verfarhen dafür, entsprechende Verbindlichkeit herzustellen, die in der Verfassung gewährleistet werden".*[53]

In order to bring about an inclusive society in which various religious and philosophical communities can enjoy their rights in mutual respect, legislators must show empathy and engage in dialogue with those communities: the quest for balance between protecting the freedom of religion on the one hand, and limiting it for the benefit of other legitimate interests equally worthy of protection, must take

---

Ashgate, 2013, 187–200.

[51] R.C. Akhtar, "Unregistered Muslim Marriages: an emerging culture of celebrating rites and conceding rights", in J. Miles *et al.* (eds), *Marriage Rites and Rights*, Oxford, Hart, 2015, 167–192; A. Moors, "Unregistered Muslim Marriages: anxieties about sexuality and Islam in the Netherlands", in M. Berger (ed.), *Applying Shari'a in the West: Facts, Fears and the Future of Islamic Rules on Family Relations in the West*, Leiden, Leiden University Press, 2013, 141–164.

[52] G.C. Denniston *et al.* (eds), *Circumcision and Human Rights*, Berlin, Springer 2009; S. Janson, "Circumcision of Young Boys: a conflict between parental and child rights. The Swedish experience from a medical point", in M. Jänterä-Jareborg (ed.), *The Child's Interests in Conflict: the Intersections between Society, Family, Faith and Culture*, Antwerp, Intersentia, 2016, 111–124; M.-C. Foblets, "The Body as Identity Marker: circumcision of boys caught between contrasting views on the best interest of the child", *ibid.*, 125–162.

[53] F. Schorkopf, *Staat und Diversität. Agonaler Pluralismus für die liberale Demokratie*, Paderborn, F. Schöningh, 2017, p. 44.

place in a spirit of openness, pluralism and tolerance, the distinguishing features of a democratic society.[54] That spirit should also permeate society as a whole.

V. THE GOVERNANCE OF RELIGIOUS DIVERSITY: A RESPONSIBILITY FOR SOCIETY AS A WHOLE

Religious diversity presents many challenges, not only to the relationship between mainstream society and minorities or between individuals who need to find ways to get along with one another despite differences, stereotypes and biases. Some years ago Paul Bramadat observed, *"[A]n effective model of State governance must now, in addition to pursuing other supposedly secular objectives, seek to create the context in which members of ethno-religious minority communities can negotiate identities for themselves in relation to the dominant national cultures. Such integration is easier said than done, and in each of the jurisdictions … quite distinct challenges emerge".*[55] For Bramadat, the endeavour should be a multi-faceted approach, rooted in long-term thinking about how to include religious minorities in all areas of social life, including education (e.g., the issue of religious symbols worn by teachers or students at school), housing and law enforcement. Paul Bramadat is no doubt right: issues of religious diversity need to be addressed not only through legislation or adjudication by the judiciary but must also, if not primarily, be supplemented by a much broader spectrum of policy initiatives in a number of fields, including education, social services, legal aid provision, etc., whenever these can facilitate the search for balanced solutions compatible with a democratic understanding of the functioning of pluralist democracies.

In the realm of employment, for instance (the example we have examined above), one such initiative is accommodation in cases of conflict between workplace standards, rules or practices and an employee's religious practice(s), i.e., via adjustments to the workplace rules or practices that can smooth over existing tensions. Certain accommodations may be without cost, while others may involve a high cost, so it is important to develop standards that balance the interests of the different stakeholders.[56] A shared workplace, a shared public space, education, various experiences of deliberative democracy, etc., each in its own way may

---

[54]   C. Sterkens and H.-G. Ziebertz (eds), *Political and Judicial Rights through the Prism of Religious Belief*, Cham, Springer, 2018.

[55]   P. Bramadat and M. Koenig (eds.) *International Migration and the Governance of Religious Diversity*, Montreal/Kingston, McGill-Queen's University Press, 2009, 6.

[56]   RELIGARE developed a comparative case law database with religious discrimination/ religious freedom cases and commentaries, as well as a comparative sociological study, including of good practices, with a view to prove helpful for decision makers such as employers, religious leaders, judges, lawyers, academics, politicians, NGOs, or labour union representatives.

offer the opportunity to overcome differences, stereotypes and biases along the path towards a sustainable 'living together', but it requires work to achieve such outcome. It may be a daunting task, and what works or does not work is of course highly dependent upon the immediate context. But when it does indeed work, accommodation offers a major advantage, namely by allowing for resolution of tensions and management of workplace conflicts without recourse to litigation or disciplinary proceedings wherever possible. Accommodation is also in line with Bramadat's suggestion, quoted above, that members of minority communities be given the opportunity to negotiate their identities with(in) the majority society.

CONCLUSION

Governance of religious diversity is very likely one of the questions, if not *the* question, that will determine the future of European societies. The models of governance inherited from the past – even if regularly and carefully re-examined in the light of the criteria for protection as defined in human rights instruments – suffer from not having been conceived for the needs of today's increasingly plural and secular society. Since the majority religions for which numerous arrangements were put in place have diminished considerably in importance, this disjunction between a past that is now well and truly over, and a future that has yet to be built with the consent of new, often very dynamic religious communities, represents a major challenge.

In this contribution we have identified two observations, borrowed from research recently completed or still under way, each of which is symptomatic of the current situation in Europe: on the one hand, the hesitation on the part of legislators to call into question the legal privileges granted to the religions that historically constituted a majority and that are seen as still predominant, even if actual practice among their members is declining. On the other hand, there is the increasing recourse to the judicial authorities whose role can, by their very nature, only be fragmentary and ad hoc.

The reticence of the ECtHR to which Paul Lemmens referred in December 2013, and for which he gave well founded reasons, can also be seen as an indirect incentive, first and foremost for legislators, to work out sustainable solutions in their own countries (under the supervision of a Constitutional Court, where necessary) that allow religious and philosophical diversity to continue to be a feature of European democratic societies without certain groups or communities having to feel excluded or targeted as a result. That would lighten the burden on the judiciary considerably. An appropriate regulatory framework can calm the debate about religious and philosophical diversity.

EPILOGUE

Anne DEWAELE
Written with the great support of Martine, Eric and Vincent

'*Pour vivre il faut aimer*'
Madeleine Delbrêl

"Ensemble"

"*Ensemble*"[1] is the short and powerful word that came to symbolise the wedding of one of Paul's assistants – a dear friend and co-author of this book. It was written on the invitations, mentioned during the service, and later appeared again on the birth announcement cards of each of this joyful "ensemble's" children. It is a whole life program in one single word, and therefore touched my mind and heart forever.

This is perhaps why I was taken aback when two of Paul's colleagues asked me to join their efforts in compiling this *Festschrift*, arguing: "When we see Paul, we see you. You two are together, always. You should be part of this initiative as well." I would like to thank, from the bottom of my heart, both Stephan Parmentier and Koen Lemmens, as well as Louise Reyntjens, for their diligence and hard work, despite their busy schedules.

This epilogue is first and foremost meant to be a sincere word of thanks to the initiators and to the kind contributors of this work, but also to all the people who, in one way or another, have had a profound influence on Paul's professional life. For every human being is largely shaped by the encounters, collaborations, and exchanges of ideas with his fellow man. For various reasons some of these persons are not mentioned in this book, or they are no longer among us. It is impossible to recite all these people by name. I will, however, give some examples of such encounters in the following paragraphs. They will make my message clearer: Paul has become the person that he is, thanks to the input of the many people he has met along the way.

---

[1] Meaning 'together' in French.

Because Paul and I are each other's sounding boards and mirrors, this epilogue will inevitably shed some light on important parts of our journey together.

Heart

If a child – or an adult who still has the heart of a child – draws the shape of a heart, it will spontaneously start at the top, and make graceful swirls to the left and the right, all the way down, where both ends will meet again. Let's consider this pen stroke as the road Paul and I are travelling. The central part symbolically holds all the names of the people that play a vital role in Paul's constellation, for after all: a beating heart keeps a person alive. *'Pour vivre il faut aimer'*: one has to be passionate about people and work in order to live.

Starting point

UFSIA (Antwerp University) 1972–1973: We met during our first years as law students in Antwerp. Teachers of great character and authenticity would leave a lasting impression. I remember the delicate Philosophy classes by Libert Van der Kerken, the critical History lessons of Karel van Isacker, the meticulous study of Roman Law with Raymond Derine, Econom(etr)y by Emiel Van Broekhoven, Jacques Claes' intriguing views on Psychology. Jean Van Houtte made us never forget that human beings are meant to live together and interact in a well-organised society. Robert Janssens and Fernand Van Neste bestowed upon us a passion for the inextricable link between law, morality and fundamental human values.

That solid – Jesuit – formation provided us with the same strong foundation. Paul's passage through "St. Ignatius" did not go unnoticed, as he acted as student representative in all sorts of academic bodies. In those early days we struck up precious, lifelong friendships. After a few years Paul and I got married in Antwerp. Our traditional wedding pictures were taken in UFSIA's enclosed garden in the Prinsstraat. It was pouring with rain that day. We knew each other as students, but we barely knew each other 'to the core'. However, we started off "ensemble". I was somehow wholly and completely convinced that Paul was the one and only.

America

1977. The lure of the United States was always present in Paul's family. Chicago is imprinted in his genes. Paul turned down scholarships for a Master's degree in Law at prestigious universities so that we could attend *Northwestern University School of Law* in Chicago together. From the outset it would seem, our starting point was characterised by a broad horizon. We got acquainted with the case law system, in another language and – quite surprisingly for us, European students – in very progressive, interactive classes. The open yet competitive 'melting pot' society in the States requires one to brazenly express one's own opinion, and to do so clearly. A willingness to listen to one another and to seek harmony were equally important prerequisites to participate in the debates. The courage to speak openly as well as listening to differing opinions have since invariably become an essential part of Paul's social attitude.

Professor Victor Rosenblum's Administrative Law classes, as well as his and his large family's warm hospitality and lifelong friendship have greatly influenced Paul: Rosenblum possessed a great creative wit, humour and humility. When professor Rosenblum passed away in 2006, Paul immediately left for the funeral, which, oddly enough, was an eye-opener for him: there was nothing sad about the funeral, rather did it celebrate the reunion of those who had known and loved Victor Rosenblum, with vivid, grateful and humorous testimonies in his honour.

Lawyer

Paul's internship at the Brussels Bar, starting in 1976, was the result of an unexpected phone call from Mr. Ludovic De Gryse. Pure luck, or was it providence? It turned out to be an immense gift for Paul. Not only because of the thorough and kind guidance offered by Mr. De Gryse: "He taught me that a lawyer's main strength is to be honest to the judge. No tricks, but rather an open discussion about the strengths and weaknesses of one's position in the case."[2] Mr. De Gryse's proposition above all offered Paul the opportunity to practice law, and experience the application of the law as an added value to mere theoretical legal knowledge, an insight that would stay with Paul forever. Moreover, Mr. De Gryse introduced Paul to the very specific written procedure before the Court of Cassation, a technique which he continued to apply with great joy and satisfaction in all the years to come as a lawyer.

Working at the Brussels Bar, in a mainly French-speaking firm, allowed him to learn and appreciate a different legal style and language in close cooperation with Mr. Lucien Simont, Etienne Gutt, and Paul Alain Foriers among others. In 1982, Paul had the chance, at the end of his internship, to defend before a jury – under the watchful eye of Mr. Pascal Van der Veren – a young offender of a crime of passion. Even though Paul ardently requested that his client be acquitted, the jury found the defendant guilty, resulting in a 20-year prison sentence. This

---

[2]   Thus Paul in 'Klaar en fier om jurist te zijn' in Sébastien De Rey and Bernard Tilleman (Eds.), *Brieven aan jonge juristen*, Hannibal/die Keure, 2018, 142.

experience did not, however, dampen Paul's enthusiasm as a lawyer. Long-lasting friendships were formed at this firm with young confrères Ludo Cornelis, Brigitte Dauwe, Kristien Van Lint, Sylviane Velu, Luc De Coninck …

Children

Meanwhile our family expanded in the eighties with the birth of three children: Martine, Eric and Vincent. They embody the other half of our drawing of a heart, representing the private part of the journey, making our *"ensemble"* richer. I believe that children are born with an intuitive intelligence, that they can see and hear with their heart and can sense the way their parents – notwithstanding their defaults and weaknesses – want to offer them safety and love, support and confidence, roots and wings.

As with all his students and assistants, Paul strongly believes in the individual character and independence of each of his children. He respects the person, their strengths and opinions, and won't needlessly intervene. This reserve and respect of everyone's autonomy and highly individual privacy is fundamental to Paul.

'Home' has always been Paul's favourite workplace: it is where he can concentrate best, despite the sometimes noisy buzz of children and now even grandchildren running around.

University

Academics and the practice of law are not separate in Paul's mind. Both are intertwined, and keep him balanced as a jurist.

"De Valk" becomes his familiar office, first as an assistant to Procedural Law professor Guido van Dievoet, later in the department of Constitutional Law, with human rights increasingly becoming his main focus. His doctoral thesis, relating to Article 6 ECHR – fair trial – combines these two fields of interest.

In hindsight I can safely say that Paul always felt at home at Leuven's faculty of law, to a large extent because of his easy-going relationship and collaboration with so many dear colleagues. Louis-Paul Suetens and Jan De Meyer in particular proved instrumental in Paul's development. His undeniable ability to see things in their proper perspective, as well as his freedom of thought and his sense of humour should be attributed to these two academic teachers. Furthermore, Paul enjoys himself most as an inquisitive scholar, a jurist *'pur sang'*, a conscientious researcher, and especially as a teacher. I believe that teaching in a well-structured, educational and inspiring way, meanwhile passing on his passion for human rights to his students, brings Paul great joy. In dealing with his students and assistants, Paul would always display a great deal of commitment.

Judiciary

In addition to his academic tasks, the practice of law – first as a lawyer and later as a judge – constitutes the other, equally significant component of Paul's vocation as a jurist. As an auditor, and later councillor in the Council of State, and now as a judge in the European Court of Human Rights (ECtHR), Paul recognises the importance of taking into consideration the various conflicting interests between an individual and the state. His function as a judge has made him even more aware of the importance of a competent and independent judiciary, in which citizens can put their trust. It is an essential pillar – today regrettably often considered an obstacle – of our democracy and rule of law. To investigate the factual conflict situation, to analyse and balance the conflicting interests, to interpret and apply the legal rules "to do justice to the law, not to one's own view of the law"[3], is a demanding task, which Paul very much takes to heart.

In Strasbourg, following Protocol No. 15 and the Court's case law, Paul has a clear perception of what the role of the ECtHR and its relation to the national courts should be, believing firmly in the richness of a true '*dialogue des juges*'.

Saying yes

Paul has a hard time saying no. To decline a guest speaker request, or any extraprofessional invitation, deeply affects Paul, who would rather say yes than to be conscience-smitten. This extraordinary sense of responsibility is what drives Paul. He is always motivated and eager to work. Sometimes even in spite of his physical limits. This attitude is characteristic of his upbringing. Paul's father, a physician, was at least as hard-working and selfless as he is. Above the fireplace in Paul's family home was a wooden sign on the wall that said: "*Aspera non fugiam*", which can be translated as: "*I will not shy away from difficulty*". Paul has taken this to heart. It put him into contact with a wide array of fascinating people, who we – his wife and children – have come to know and cherish as well.

Since it is impossible to be exhaustive, I can only give some examples of the tasks and assignments Paul truly liked. There is, for starters, the *A.P.R.* – *Algemene Praktische Rechtsverzameling* – which forms a warm circle of committed friends and fellow lawyers and their spouses: Jules Dhaenens, Marcel Storme, Jan Ronse,

---

[3]   Thus Paul in 'Klaar en fier om een jurist te zijn', *supra* n. 2, p. 145.

Ward Forrier, Willy Van Eeckhoutte, amongst many others. There is the UNMIK panel in Kosovo, where Paul enthusiastically spent several days a month to screen alleged human rights violations by U.N. officials in the aftermath of the Balkan Wars. Both professionally and on a personal level, the names of Marek Nowitzki, Christine Schinkin, Andrzej, Anna Cesano will forever evoke fond memories.

There was the *Transatlantic Dialogue* between the law faculties of KU Leuven and Chicago's Northwestern University, spearheaded by Doug Cassel, Stephan Sawyer and David Scheffer, always bringing about lively summer courses, exchanges and conferences.

The foundation in 1997 of the E.M.A. (later E.I.U.C. and now Global Campus of Human Rights) saw Paul often traveling to San Nicoló in Venice, which gradually became, for both of us, a very special place. Teaching human rights to master students coming from all over Europe, the traditional moot court on Saturday, the graduation ceremonies, the brainstorming sessions on the future of the program: it was all on his mind for many years. Antonio Papisca, the visionary founder of the program, will forever hold a special place in Paul's heart, as well as Daniela Napoli, Horst Fischer, Manfred Nowak, and many other colleagues and staff members.

There have been many human rights conferences, both domestically and abroad, where Paul accepted to participate and lecture, each and every one of them adding valuable professional and personal exchanges.

Paul's readiness to participate in and contribute to these events demonstrates just how much he loves doing what he does, or as he would put it himself: "Use your legal talent for the benefit of others".[4]

Just law?

No, not just law. Paul loves his family, his children, his son-in-law Marcelo and grandchildren Lisandro and Malena, and everyone in the large Lemmens family, for who he tries to be a reliable anchor figure. To gather and spend time with his beloved friends, no matter the distance, is one of Paul's most precious pastime activities. He particularly enjoys going to the theatre – he occasionally acts himself – and is mad about wild sixties rock 'n' roll. When Bruce Springsteen or The Rolling Stones embark on a new tour, he will be the first to buy tickets. All these passions, combined with his insatiable appetite for newspapers and books, make for excellent diversions, and almost make Paul forget about law.

---

[4]   *Supra* n. 2, p. 146.

Together in Strasbourg: fundamental values and principles

Gradually we are reaching the point where both halves of the heart – as laid out by the converging pen strokes – meet again. The heart is now filled with hundreds of names of people that helped drawing Paul's very image. In a few years Paul's professional career is coming to an end. This emeritus status can be considered as a first step in the process of his retirement. Our children have all flown the nest. Two grandchildren joyfully put up their arms whenever they see their grandfather.

Whereas at the very beginning of the drawing of the heart I didn't know Paul too well, in the real sense of the word, I must acknowledge that after all those years of wandering together and meeting many people along the way, the very essence of Paul's personality has become clear. The extent of our similarity in values and fundamental beliefs has become especially apparent here in Strasbourg, adding to the solid basis on which we are eager to continue our path together.

This struck me several times listening to the pleadings during Grand Chamber public hearings of the Court and later upon reading important judgments of the Court on complaints of an individual citizen that touch on fundamental values and principles. In this limited context I would like to refer to two such complaints.

I think of the case of *Vinter*[5], where the Court again stated that respect for human dignity is the very essence of the Convention system, and therefore no life sentenced prisoner, whatever the nature of his crime, can be lawfully deprived of his freedom without at least a chance to someday regain his freedom. A life sentence in order to be lawful under art. 3 of the Convention should therefore not be irreducible, but provide at least a possibility of review, a prospect of rehabilitation and of conditional release. To deprive a person of any glimmer of hope of a 'new' life is considered incompatible with human dignity.

I further recall several complaints against the Belgian state based on the deplorable fate of persons suffering from mental disorders detained without any appropriate psychiatric treatment.[6] In a series of leading judgments since 2012[7] the Court held the Belgian state liable of violation of Articles 3 and/or 5 §1(e) of the Convention, bringing forth in Belgium new legislation and an improvement of the conditions of compulsory confinement of mentally ill detainees. To detain mentally ill subjects without appropriate individual psychiatric care not

---

5   ECtHR, GC, 9 July 2013, *Vinter and Others v. the United Kingdom* (nos. 66069/09, 130/10 and 3896/10) §§104–122, especially §113.

6   See '*Geïnterneerd: cel of zorg?*', a publication by the Belgian Human Rights League, 2012. See also the documentary '9999' by Ellen Vermeulen (2014)- www.9999themovie.com/.

7   ECtHR, GC, 31 January 2019, *Rooman v. Belgium* (no. 18052/11) refers in §201 to this recent case law. ECtHR, *W.D. v. Belgium*, 6 September 2016, pilot judgment no. 73548/13.

only constitutes an 'inhuman and degrading treatment' under Article 3 of the Convention, but renders the compulsory confinement and deprivation of liberty *in se* unlawful under Article 5 §1 (e) of the Convention. The Court in its case law thus gradually clarified and refined its principles to hold that: 'it should now be considered that there exists a close link between the "lawfulness" of the detention of persons suffering from mental disorders and the appropriateness of the treatment provided for their mental condition.' It is for the state authorities to prove *in concreto* that such individualised appropriate treatment is offered.[8] This gradual development, over time, of an interpretation of the meaning to be given to the obligations in Article 5 §1 (e) can be seen as an example of the Court applying the Convention as a 'living instrument', to provide a more effective protection, based on human dignity.

Based on an analysis of the case law of the Court, it appears that several fundamental values and principles emerge that can be identified as underlying the Convention.[9] Under the headings of *'Freedom, Equality and Fraternity'* Paul identifies several such fundamental values that are common to different European states. This practice of *common values* may refer to a *consensus* in a certain area, which the Court may take into account when interpreting the provisions of the Convention or delimiting the extent of the margin of appreciation for national authorities. Human dignity, personal autonomy or right to self-determination, respect for each person's individuality (non-discrimination), respect for minorities (pluralism, diversity), freedom of expression and dialogue in an open (democratic) society, solidarity between individuals and community (fair balance/principle of proportionality), solidarity with vulnerable persons, democracy and rule of law are common values and principles underlying the Convention as they emerge from the case law of the Court. They constitute a European public order.

Respect for these values and principles enhance tolerance, a more human society and hope of sustainable peace. Witnessing his unremitting devotion to human rights over the years, I am convinced that Paul wholeheartedly embraces these values and principles as ideals emerging from the Convention provisions and applied in the case law of the Court. They are what make him *'the lawyer with the human touch'* whom I love. They constitute the common ground that supports

---

8 ECtHR, GC, *Rooman v. Belgium, supra* nr. 7, §§205–211, especially §§207 and 208.

9 Paul Lemmens, 'The European Convention on Human Rights as an instrument of European public order, based on common values', in *Les droits humains comparés – à la recherche de l'universalité des droits humains*, Publications de l'Institut International des Droits de l'Homme n° 40, éd. A. Pedone, Paris, 2019, p. 11–28. See also art. 2 of the Treaty on European Union. See also the contribution of Wouter Vandenhole, 'Of Principles and Values: an Explorative Reading of Separate Opinions of Judge Paul Lemmens', in this *Liber Amicorum*.

our "ensemble" as an entity of intertwined and shared beliefs, shaping our life choices – past, present and future.

Es muß das Herz bei jedem Lebensrufe
Bereit zum Abschied sein und Neubeginne,
Um sich in Tapferkeit und ohne Trauern
In andre, neue Bindungen zu geben.
Und jedem Anfang wohnt ein Zauber inne,
Der uns beschützt und der uns hilft zu leben.

From *Stufen*
Hermann Hesse

PRE-REGISTRATION LIST

A

Benoît ALLEMEERSCH, Advocaat Quinz, KU Leuven

Prof. em. dr. André ALEN, President of the Belgian Constitutional Court, KU Leuven

Argo, Antwerpen

B

Balie Provincie Antwerpen, Gerechtsgebouw, Antwerpen

Bibliothèque Leon Graulich, Université de Liège

Bibliothèque Universitaire Moretus Plantin, Namur

Prof. em. dr. Marc BOES, KU Leuven

Prof. dr. Ingrid BOONE, KU Leuven

Prof. em. dr. Marc BOSSUYT, Honorary Commissioner General for Refugees and
    Stateless Persons, Emeritus President of the Constitutional Court, UAntwerpen

Jan BOUCKAERT, Stibbe

Sven BOULLART, Sven Boullart Advocaten, Gent

Eva BREMS, Ghent University

C

Prof. em. Douglass CASSEL, Notre Dame Law School, Counsel, King & Spalding,
    New York

Prof. em. Christine CHINKIN, Director of the Centre on Women, Peace and Security,
    London School of Economics and Political Science

Stefanie COOL, Chevron Phillips Chemicals, Diegem

Paul COOREMAN, VOF Cooreman-Mertens, Zele

Laura CORRADO, European Commission – Head of the Legal Migration and
    Integration Unit (DG HOME)

Prof. em. Herman COUSY, KU Leuven

D

David D'HOOGHE, Heverlee

Charline DAELMAN, Human Rights Consultant, KU Leuven

Prof. em. Ludovic DE GRYSE, Avocat à la Cour de Cassation honoraire, UAntwerpen
    (UFSIA)

Alain DE NAUW, Brussel

Jan DE VLEESCHOUWER, Welle

Carlos DE WOLF, D&V Advocatenkantoor, Maarkedal

Beatrijs DECONINCK, Eerste Voorzitter Hof van Cassatie

Anne DEWAELE

Ererector Roger DILLEMANS, KU Leuven

Prof. em. Eric DIRIX, Hof van Cassatie, KU Leuven

Andrew DRZEMCZEWSKI, Middlesex University School of Law – London, Former
Head of the Parliamentary Assembly's Legal Affairs & Human Rights Department,
Council of Europe, Strasbourg

E

Françoise ELENS-PASSOS, Greffière adjointe (2015-2019) à la Cour européenne des
droits de l'homme

Luc ELIAERTS, Wilrijk

F

FLAMEY Advocaten, Antwerpen

Marie-Claire FOBLETS, Max Planck Director of the Institute for Social Anthropology,
KU Leuven, Maarten Luther University Halle

G

Prof. dr. Janneke GERARDS, Utrecht University

Jan GHYSELS, Janson Baugniet, Brussel

Prof. em. Jenny E. GOLDSCHMIDT, Utrecht University

Prof. dr. Joaquín GONZÁLEZ IBÁÑEZ, Alfonso X University, Madrid, Co-director of
the Human Rights Berg Institute

GSJ-advocaten, Antwerpen

H

Magda HANSSENS, Allen & Overy (Belgium) LLP, Brussel

Tony HEEREN, Erevoorzitter Rechtbank van Eerste Aanleg Limburg, en Pia DEWAELE

Prof. em. Frank HUTSEBAUT, KU Leuven

J

Emmanuel JACUBOWITZ, BVBA Advocatenkantoor Jacubowitz Emmanuel, Oudergem

Prof. dr. Geert JOCQUÉ, Hof van Cassatie, KU Leuven

K

Peter KEMPEES, Head of Division, Registry of the European Court of Human Rights

Hans KLUWER, Intersentia

Egidijus KŪRIS, Judge of the European Court of Human Rights, Professor at the Faculty
of Law, Vilnius University

L

Eric LEMMENS

Koen LEMMENS, KU Leuven

Vincent LEMMENS

Koen LENAERTS, President of the Court of Justice of the European Union, KU Leuven

Prof. Steven LIERMAN, KU Leuven

Johan LIEVENS, KU Leuven – Faculteit Rechtsgeleerdheid

M

Marcelo en Martine MARAFUSCHI-LEMMENS

Michaël MERRIGAN, KU Leuven, Lawyer at the Brussels Bar

Egbert MYJER, Former Judge, European Court of Human Rights

Kris MOEREMANS, uitgever Intersentia

N

Isabelle NIEDLISPACHER, Agente du Gouvernement belge devant la Cour

Manfred NOWAK, University of Vienna, Secretary General of the Global Campus of
Human Rights, Venice

Marek NOWICKI, Former Member of the European Commission of Human Rights,
International Ombudsperson in Kosovo

O

Síofra O'LEARY, Juge à la Cour européenne des droits de l'homme, Collège d'Europe,
Bruges

P

Stephan PARMENTIER, KU Leuven

Jan PEETERS, Advocaat-vennoot, Stibbe, Brussel

R

Georges RAVARANI, Juge à la Cour européenne des droits de l'homme

Louise REYNTJENS, KU Leuven

Rieder & Verdonck advocaten, Brugge

S

Prof. dr. Ilse SAMOY, KU Leuven, advocaat

Tom SCHEIRS, Intersentia

Jos SILVIS, Procurator General at the Supreme Court of the Netherlands, Former Judge
of the European Court of Human Rights

Prof. dr. Stefan SOTTIAUX, KU Leuven, advocaat

Robert SPANO, Judge and Vice President of the European Court of Human Rights

Dean SPIELMANN, Ancien Président de la Cour européenne des droits de l'homme,
Juge au Tribunal de l'Union européenne

Prof. em. Jean SPREUTELS, Président honoraire de la Cour constitutionnelle de
Belgique, ULB

Prof. dr. Sophie STIJNS, Gewoon Hoogleraar Instituut voor Verbintenissenrecht KU
Leuven

Eddy STORMS, Eerste Voorzitter DBRC (Dienst van de (Vlaamse)
Bestuursrechtscolleges), KU Leuven

Greta SUETENS-BOURGEOIS, Holsbeek

T

Prof. em. Françoise TULKENS, Former Vice President of the European Court of Human
Rights, UCLouvain

V

Prof. em. dr. Dirk VAN DEN AUWEELE, KU Leuven

Gerhard VAN DER SCHYFF, Tilburg University

Jachin VAN DONINCK, Advocaat, Praktijkassistent UGent, Vrijwillig wetenschappelijk medewerker VUB

Prof. dr. Sébastien VAN DROOGHENBROECK, Université Saint-Louis – Bruxelles, Assesseur à la Section de législation du Conseil d'État de Belgique

Prof. em. Jean VAN HOUTTE, Ererector UAntwerpen (UFSIA)

Pascale VAN HOUTTE, uitgever Intersentia

Jef VAN LANGENDONCK, KU Leuven

Nathalie VAN LEUVEN, Researcher CIRC, Université Saint-Louis – Bruxelles, Director Vormingplus Midden- en Zuid-West-Vlaanderen

Jacques VAN MALLEGHEM, Advocaat

Jeroen VAN NIEUWENHOVE, Raad van State

Prof. Piet VAN NUFFEL, KU Leuven, Legal Service, European Commission

Prof. Caroline VAN SCHOUBROECK, KU Leuven

Filip VAN VOLSEM, Raadsheer in het Hof van Cassatie

Philippe VANDE CASTEELE, Advocaat

Prof. em. mr. Hugo VANDENBERGHE, Ereondervoorzitter van de Senaat

Prof. dr. Wouter VANDENHOLE, Chair in Human Rights, University of Antwerp

Monique VANDYCK, Administratief directeur, KU Leuven – Faculteit Rechtsgeleerdheid

Prof. Beatrix VANLERBERGHE, Advocaat, UAntwerpen

Frédéric VANNESTE, Council of State, UAntwerpen, KU Leuven

Jan VELAERS, UAntwerpen, Council of State, Member of the Venice Commission

Sylviane VELU, Conseiller honoraire à la Cour de cassation de Belgique

Prof. Frank VERBRUGGEN, KU Leuven

An VERMAERCKE, Intersentia

Willem VERRIJDT, Law clerk in the Belgian Constitutional Court, KU Leuven

Prof. dr. Mark E. VILLIGER, University of Zurich, Switzerland, Former Judge and Section President at the European Court of Human Rights

Jogchum VRIELINK, Université Saint-Louis – Bruxelles

W

Evelien WAUTERS, Leuven Centre for Global Governance Studies – Institute for International Law, KU Leuven

Kristof WINDEY, Lige Advocaten, Antwerpen

Jan WOUTERS, Jean Monnet Chair ad personam EU, Director of the Leuven Centre for Global Governance Studies, KU Leuven

Marieke WYCKAERT, KU Leuven